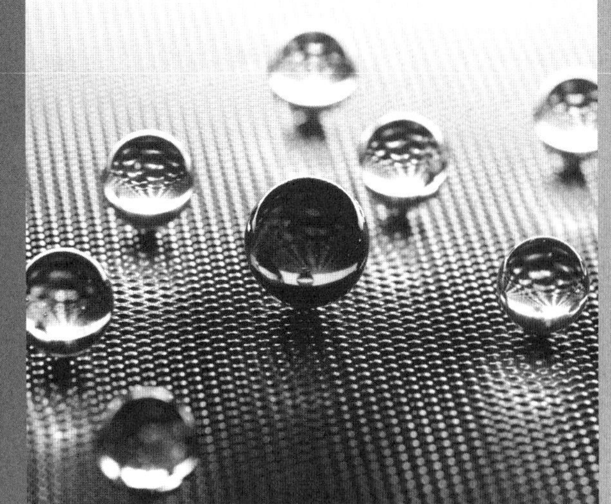

KT-225-340

THE AUDIT PROCESS

PRINCIPLES, PRACTICE AND CASES

FIFTH EDITION

Iain Gray
Former Chair of the Auditing Special Interest Group of the British Accounting and Finance Association

Stuart Manson
Essex Business School, University of Essex

University of the Highlands and Islands Perth College
LIBRARY
Barcode No: 007109631
Supplier: Dawson
Classmark: 657.45 GRA
Cost: £40.44
Location: 1 Week Loan
Date Received: 5/15

SOUTH-WESTERN CENGAGE Learning™

Australia • Brazil • Japan • Korea • Mexico • Singapore • Spain • United Kingdom • United States

The Audit Process, 5th Edition

Iain Gray and Stuart Manson

Publishing Director: Linden Harris

Publisher: Brendan George

Development Editor: Annabel Ainscow

Content Project Editor: Alison Cooke

Production Controller: Eyvett Davis

Marketing Manager: Amanda Cheung

Typesetter: KnowledgeWorks Global, India

Cover design: Adam Renvoize

© 2011, Cengage Learning EMEA

ALL RIGHTS RESERVED. No part of this work covered by the copyright herein may be reproduced, transmitted, stored or used in any form or by any means graphic, electronic, or mechanical, including but not limited to photocopying, recording, scanning, digitizing, taping, Web distribution, information networks, or information storage and retrieval systems, except as permitted under Section 107 or 108 of the 1976 United States Copyright Act, or applicable copyright law of another jurisdiction, without the prior written permission of the publisher.

While the publisher has taken all reasonable care in the preparation of this book, the publisher makes no representation, express or implied, with regard to the accuracy of the information contained in this book and cannot accept any legal responsibility or liability for any errors or omissions from the book or the consequences thereof.

Products and services that are referred to in this book may be either trademarks and/or registered trademarks of their respective owners. The publishers and author/s make no claim to these trademarks.

The Author has asserted the right under the Copyright, Designs and Patents Act 1988 to be identified as Author of this Work. This work is adapted from *The Audit Process,* 4th edition, published by South-Western, a division of Cengage Learning, Inc. © 2008.

For product information and technology assistance, contact **emea.info@cengage.com**.

For permission to use material from this text or product, and for permission queries, email **emea.permissions@cengage.com**.

British Library Cataloguing-in-Publication Data
A catalogue record for this book is available from the British Library.

ISBN: 978-1-4080-3049-3

Cengage Learning EMEA
Cheriton House, North Way, Andover, Hampshire, SP10 5BE
United Kingdom

Cengage Learning products are represented in Canada by Nelson Education Ltd.

For your lifelong learning solutions, visit **www.cengage.co.uk**

Purchase your next print book, e-book or e-chapter at **www.cengagebrain.com**

Printed in China by RR Donnelley
3 4 5 6 7 8 9 10 – 15 14 13

BRIEF CONTENTS

Contents vi
Acknowledgements xvi
Index of Legal Cases xviii
Preface xix

1 **Why are auditors needed?** 1
2 **An overview of the postulates and concepts of auditing** 29
3 **The meaning and importance of auditor independence: factors affecting independence and measures to attain it** 60
4 **Audit regulation** 108
5 **The risk-based approach to audit: audit judgement** 153
6 **The search for evidence explained** 212
7 **Systems work: basic ideas 1** 240
8 **Systems work: basic ideas 2** 285
9 **Testing and evaluation of systems** 329
10 **Substantive testing, computer-assisted audit techniques and audit programmes** 358
11 **Sampling and materiality** 395
12 **Final work: general principles, analytical review of financial statements, non-current assets and trade receivables** 423
13 **Final work: specific problems related to inventories, construction contracts and trade payables** 485
14 **Final review: post-balance sheet period, provisions, contingencies, letter of representation** 530
15 **Assurance engagements and internal audit** 564
16 **The auditors' report** 609
17 **Fraud and going concern** 654
18 **The audit expectations gap and corporate governance** 690
19 **The auditor and liability under the law** 730
20 **Criticisms and developments in auditing** 762
21 **Examination hints and final remarks** 815

Index 821

CONTENTS

Acknowledgements xvi
Index of Legal Cases xviii
Preface xix
Walk through tour xxvi
About the website xxix

1 Why are auditors needed? 1

Learning objectives 1
Opening remarks 2
Introduction to basic principles through a simple case 3
Case study 1.1: Andrew and James, Part 1 4
Case study 1.1: Andrew and James, Part 2 5
Case study 1.1: Andrew and James, Part 3 6
Case study 1.1: Andrew and James, Part 4 8
Justification of audit 9
Introduction to truth and fairness in accounting 12
Basic audit framework 15
Some initial ideas on an extended role for audit 15
Assurance services 20
Summary of principles 21
Definition of an audit of financial and other information 23
The auditors' code: the fundamental principles of independent auditing 23
Summary 25
Key points of the chapter 26
References 26
Further reading 27
Self-assessment questions (solutions available to students) 27
Self-assessment questions (solutions available to tutors) 28
Topics for class discussion without solutions 28

2 An overview of the postulates and concepts of auditing 29

Learning objectives 29
The importance of theory and concepts in underpinning auditing practice 30
The postulates of auditing 32
The concepts of auditing: credibility, process, communication, performance 33
Audit quality 48
Introduction to the audit expectations gap 50
The layers of regulation and control 52
Summary 57

Key points of the chapter 57
References 58
Further reading 58
Self-assessment questions (solutions available to students) 58
Self-assessment questions (solutions available to tutors) 58
Topics for class discussion without solutions 59

3 The meaning and importance of auditor independence: factors affecting independence and measures to attain it 60

Learning objectives 60
Introduction 61
Independence and the role of audit 61
Definitions of independence 64
Practitioner and profession independence 65
Conflict, power of auditor and client and effect on perceived independence 70
Published codes of ethics 77
General principles of the IFAC code 78
Audit firm's control environment 80
Safeguards to counter threats to integrity, objectivity and independence 86
Small entities 101
Other pronouncements on auditor independence 101
Summary 104
Key points of the chapter 104
References 106
Further reading 106
Self-assessment questions (solutions available to students) 106
Self-assessment questions (solutions available to tutors) 107
Topics for class discussion without solutions 107

4 Audit regulation 108

Learning objectives 108
The need for regulation 109
Company law regulation 112
Historical overview of the UK regulatory system in force until 2003 113
Monitoring audit firms' standards 116
Present regulatory system 116
Financial Reporting Council (FRC) 118
The Professional Oversight Board (POB) 119
Accountancy and Actuarial Discipline Board (AADB) 121
Auditing Practices Board (APB) 121
Accounting Standards Board (ASB) 126
Financial Reporting Review Panel (FRRP) 126
Audit monitoring 126
Report of the Coordinating Group on Audit and Accounting issues (CGAA) 127

Further regulation of auditing by the law and accounting profession 130
The statutory and practical relationships 130
Rules on appointment, removal and resignation of the auditor 133
Case study 4.1: Rosedale Cosmetics plc, Part 1 134
Case study 4.1: Rosedale Cosmetics plc, Part 2 136
Case study 4.1: Rosedale Cosmetics plc, Part 3 138
Case study 4.1: Rosedale Cosmetics plc, Part 4 141
Case study 4.1: Rosedale Cosmetics plc, Part 5 142
Private companies 145
Case study 4.1: Rosedale Cosmetics plc, Part 6 145
Summary 146
Key points of the chapter 146
References 147
Further reading 148
Suggested solutions to tasks 148
Self-assessment questions (solutions available to students) 150
Self-assessment questions (solutions available to tutors) 151
Topics for class discussion without solutions 152

5 The risk-based approach to audit: audit judgement 153

Learning objectives 153
Why is a risk-based approach to audit an aid to the auditor? 154
Broad approach to minimize audit risk 156
A practical example 167
Case study 5.1: Edengrove Limited 167
Other practical matters 169
Case study 5.2: Kemback Limited, Part 1 173
Case study 5.2: Kemback Limited, Part 2 176
Business risk approach to audit 178
Business risk and inherent risk approaches: similarities and dissimilarities 181
The business risk approach and smaller clients and smaller audit firms 184
Analytical review as a risk analysis tool 185
Judgement in accounting and auditing and its relationship to risk 186
Management of the audit process 189
The terms of reference provide the audit framework 190
Case study 5.3: Hughes Electronics Limited 191
Planning the assignment 194
Case study 5.4: County Hotel Limited, Part 1 195
Case study 5.4: County Hotel Limited, Part 2 196
Summary 202
Key points of the chapter 203
References 204
Further reading 204
Suggested solutions to tasks 205
Self-assessment questions (solutions available to students) 207
Self assessment questions (solutions available to tutors) 210
Topics for class discussion without solutions 211

6 The search for evidence explained 212

Learning objectives 212
The audit defined as a search for evidence to enable an opinion to be formed 213
Forming conclusions on the basis of evidence: the exercise of judgement 216
Reliability of audit evidence (grades of audit evidence) 220
Case study 6.1: Ridgewalk plc 224
The business risk approach to gathering audit evidence 228
The stages of the audit process and the evidential requirements at each stage 229
Limited assurance and compilation engagements and agreed upon procedures 232
Conclusion 234
Summary 234
Key points of the chapter 235
References 236
Further reading 236
Self-assessment questions (solutions available to students) 236
Self-assessment questions (solutions available to tutors) 237
Topics for class discussion without solutions 239

7 Systems work: basic ideas 1 240

Learning objectives 240
Introduction 241
Layers of regulation and control expanded 243
Case study 7.1: High Quality Limited (small independent supermarket) 255
Case study 7.2: Entity in the financial services sector: Caiplie Financial Services 258
Accounting and quality assurance/control systems 258
General controls 260
Case study 7.3: Cash received system: Horton Limited 265
Summary 281
Key points of the chapter 281
References 283
Further reading 283
Self-assessment questions (solutions available to students) 283
Self-assessment questions (solutions available to tutors) 283
Topics for class discussion without solutions 284

8 Systems work: basic ideas 2 285

Learning objectives 285
Introduction 286
Application controls 286
Data capture/input controls 287
Processing controls 294
Output controls 296
Database systems 297

E-commerce 299
Audit approaches to systems and controls 305
Summary 326
Key points of the chapter 326
Further reading 327
Self-assessment questions (solutions available to students) 327
Self-assessment questions (solutions available to tutors) 328
Topics for class discussion without solutions 328

9 **Testing and evaluation of systems** 329

Learning objectives 329
Introduction 330
Sales and debtors system 330
Case study 9.1: Broomfield plc: sales and debtors system 330
Payroll system 333
Case study 9.2: Wages payroll: Troston plc 333
Purchases and creditors system 335
Case study 9.3: Broomfield plc: part of purchases and trade creditors system 337
General and application controls in a sales system 338
Case study 9.4: Burbage Limited 338
Tests of control 341
Evaluation of systems and audit conclusions 353
Summary 355
Key points of the chapter 355
Reference 355
Further reading 355
Self-assessment questions (solutions available to students) 355
Self-assessment questions (solutions available to tutors) 356
Topics for class discussion without solutions 357

10 **Substantive testing, computer-assisted audit techniques and audit programmes** 358

Learning objectives 358
Introduction 359
Substantive testing of transactions, account balances and disclosures 359
Case study 10.1: Powerbase plc: the substantive audit programme for purchases 361
The use of audit software 364
Directional testing 373
Substantive audit programmes for wages 375
Substantive audit programmes for cash and bank balances 377
Communication of audit matters to those charged with governance (management letter) 378
Audit management with the computer 383
Summary 385
Key points of the chapter 385

Reference 386
Further reading 386
Self-assessment questions (solutions available to students) 386
Self-assessment questions (solutions available to tutors) 387
Topics for class discussion without solutions 388
Appendix 10.1: Substantive audit programme for production wages: Troston plc 389
Appendix 10.2: Substantive audit programme for cash/bank: County Hotel Limited 392

11 Sampling and materiality 395

Learning objectives 395
Introduction 396
What is sampling? 396
Designing and selecting the sample for testing 397
Case study 11.1: An example of judgemental sampling: Broomfield plc 398
Sample selection methodology 400
Evaluation of test results 404
Monetary unit sampling (MUS) 405
Comparative advantages of statistical and non-statistical sampling 407
Alternative statistical sampling methods 407
Materiality 408
Summary 419
Key points of the chapter 419
References 420
Further reading 421
Self-assessment questions (solutions available to students) 421
Self-assessment questions (solutions available to tutors) 422
Topics for class discussion without solutions 422

12 Final work: general principles, analytical review of financial statements, non-current assets and trade receivables 423

Learning objectives 423
Introduction 424
Pre-final work 424
Balance sheet date work 425
Bridging work between conclusion of interim work and the balance sheet date 427
Analytical procedures 428
Case study 12.1: Kothari Limited: analytical review 431
Case study 12.2: Art Aid Limited: analytical review 437
Detailed final audit work: general matters 441
Tangible non-current assets and depreciation 448
Case study 12.3: Pykestone plc: non-current assets 448
Trade receivables and sales 464
Case study 12.4: Sterndale plc: ageing statement 467

Case study 12.5: Sterndale plc: analytical review of sales and trade receivables 469
Summary 480
Key points of the chapter 480
Further reading 482
Self-assessment questions (solutions available to students) 483
Self-assessment questions (solutions available to tutors) 483
Topics for class discussion without solutions 484

13 **Final work: Specific problems related to inventories, construction contracts and trade payables** 485

Learning objectives 485
Introduction 486
Inventories 486
Analytical procedures 491
Case study 13.1: Billbrook Limited: analysis of inventory, Part 1 491
Case study 13.1: Billbrook Limited: analysis of inventory, Part 2 492
Case study 13.2: Greenburn Limited: stocktaking instructions 498
Valuation of construction contracts 509
Case study 13.3: Graves Limited: construction contracts 510
Trade payables and purchases 515
Analytical procedures 518
Summary 526
Key points of the chapter 526
Further reading 527
Self-assessment questions (solutions available to students) 527
Self-assessment questions (solutions available to tutors) 529
Topics for class discussion without solutions 529

14 **Final review: post-balance sheet period, provisions, contingencies, letter of representation** 530

Learning objectives 530
Introduction 531
Post-balance sheet events 531
Provisions, contingent liabilities and contingent assets 537
Going concern 546
Audit work to detect post-balance sheet events and contingencies 547
Management letter of representation 549
Audit documentation 554
Role of the final review 558
Summary 559
Key points of the chapter 559
Further reading 561
Self-assessment questions (solutions available to students) 561
Self-assessment questions (solutions available to tutors) 562
Topics for class discussion without solutions 563

15 Assurance engagements and internal audit 564
Learning objectives 564
Introduction 565
Assurance engagements 565
Case study 15.1: Protecting the environment in an area of scenic beauty 577
Case study 15.2: Gilling Limited 580
Internal audit 584
Case study 15.3: Greenburn Limited: fleet of vans 585
Case study 15.4: Photocopy costs in an educational institution 587
Case study 15.5: Barnton plc 588
How to make the internal audit function effective 591
Reliance on internal audit by the external auditor 594
Outsourcing of internal audit work 596
Case study 15.6: Internal audit at Troston plc 597
Auditing in the public sector 599
Summary 603
Key points of the chapter 603
Further reading 605
Self-assessment questions (solutions available to students) 605
Self-assessment questions (solutions available to tutors) 607
Topics for class discussion without solutions 608

16 The auditors' report 609
Learning objectives 609
Introduction 610
The unmodified opinion 611
The modified audit opinion 626
Disclaimer of responsibility 637
Reporting on corporate governance issues 638
Electronic publication of auditors' reports 646
Summary 648
Key points of the chapter 648
Further reading 649
Self-assessment questions (solutions available to students) 650
Self-assessment questions (solutions available to tutors) 651
Topics for class discussion without solutions 653

17 Fraud and going concern 654
Learning objectives 654
Introduction to fraud 655
Responsibility for fraud detection 656
Recent debates relating to fraud 667
Case law relating to fraud 670
Auditing scandals 672
Consideration of law and regulations 674
Introduction to going concern 676
Directors' and auditors' responsibilities for going concern 677
Reporting on going concern 683

Summary 684
Key points of the chapter 684
References 686
Further reading 686
Appendix 17.1 687
Self-assessment questions (solutions available to students) 687
Self-assessment questions (solutions available to tutors) 688
Topics for class discussion without solutions 689

18 The audit expectations gap and corporate governance 690

Learning objectives 690
The audit expectations gap 691
The causes of the audit expectations gap, possible developments and solutions 692
Corporate governance 705
Summary 719
Key points of the chapter 719
References 720
Further reading 721
Self-assessment questions (solutions available to students) 721
Self-assessment questions (solutions available to tutors) 722
Topics for class discussion without solutions 723
Appendix 18.1 724

19 The auditor and liability under the law 730

Learning objectives 730
Introduction 731
Criminal liability 731
Civil liability 732
Case law 733
Auditing standards 749
Professional conduct 750
Potential ways of reducing auditor liability 750
Summary 756
Key points of the chapter 757
References 758
Further reading 758
Self-assessment questions (solutions available to students) 759
Self-assessment questions (solutions available to tutors) 760
Topics for class discussion without solutions 761

20 Criticisms and developments in auditing 762

Learning objectives 762
Introduction 763
Regulation of auditing 763
Independence 771
The critics' view of the way forward 776
Response to criticisms 779
Audit quality 781

The audit society 795
Summary 809
Key points of the chapter 809
References 810
Further reading 813
Self-assessment questions (solutions available to students) 814
Self-assessment questions (solutions available to tutors) 814
Topics for class discussion without solutions 814

21 Examination hints and final remarks 815

Learning objectives 815
Introduction 816
General examination hints 816
Auditing as an examination subject 819
Final remarks 819

Index 821

ACKNOWLEDGEMENTS

The authors and publishers wish to thank the following professional bodies who have kindly given permission for the use of their past examination questions in this book:

Association of Chartered Certified Accountants
The Institute of Chartered Accountants in England and Wales
The Institute of Chartered Accountants in Ireland
The Institute of Chartered Accountants of Scotland

The authors and publishers would also like to thank the following who have kindly given permission for short verbatim extracts of material for which they hold copyright, to be reproduced in this book:

The International Federation of Accountants (IFAC)
The Auditing Practices Board (APB)
CCH, A Wolters Kluwer business
International Accounting Standards Board (IASB)

The authors and publishers would also like to thank Vodafone Group Services Limited who has given the publisher permission to reproduce the extract from Vodafone Group Plc's 2009 Annual Report which appears in Chapter 18. However, Vodafone in no way endorses the content of this book.

In preparing this book the authors benefited from discussions on auditing with the following individuals: Tony Berry, the late Mary Bowerman, Alex Dunlop, Pik Liew, Sean McCartney, Michael Sherer, Joanna Stevenson, Mahbub Zaman, Jamil Ampomah, Emad Awadallah and Ursula Lucas. Although we would like to blame these individuals for any errors or inadequacies of expression remaining in the book we will follow custom and practice and accept the blame for any such deficiencies. We received many useful comments and feedback from students we have taught at the Universities of Essex, Sheffield Hallam and Stirling. Support of a more general variety was provided by the following colleagues: Jo Brewis, Paul Klumpes, Prem Sikka and Andrew Wood. We also acknowledge the insights we have gained by discussing the subject of auditing with Magda Abou-Seada, Ilias Basioudis, Vivien Beattie, Jerry Coakley, Emer Curtis, Stella Fearnley, Ian Fraser, Catherine Gowthorpe, David Gwilliam, David Hatherly, Emmanual Haven, Christopher Humphrey, Lisa Jack, Marjana Johansson, Phil Johnson, Steve Leonard, Helena Liu, Bill McInnes, Yuval Millo, Pat Mould, Ian Percy, Nikola Petrovic, Brenda Porter, Michael Power, Kat Riach, Liya Shen, the late Jayne Smith, Kim Smith, Stuart Turley, Shahzad Uddin and participants at the annual National Auditing Conference now the Audit and Assurance Conference. Particular thanks go to Laurie Orgee for his helpful comments on some aspects of computer systems and to Martyn Jones of Deloitte for insights into modern audit approaches. We also had useful discussions with Christine Helliar, Louise Crawford and Susan Whittaker on problems faced by students of auditing and how these can be resolved. We also owe a debt of gratitude for the forbearance of Loraine,

Simon, Josslin and Dorothea. Finally, we are grateful to the publishers for their encouragement and patience.

The author and publishers would like to thank the following reviewers who provided invaluable commentary for this new edition: Ilias Basioudis (Senior Lecturer Aston University), Roy Chandler (Professor, Cardiff University), John Craner (Teaching Fellow, University of Birmingham), Louise Crawford (Lecturer, Dundee University), Ian Dennis (Senior Lecturer, Oxford Brookes University), Ian Dewing (Senior Lecturer, University of East Anglia), Julie Drake (Principal Lecturer, University of Huddersfield), Astero Michael (Lecturer, Intercollege Limassol) and Susan Whittaker (Senior Lecturer, University of West of England).

INDEX OF LEGAL CASES

ADT Ltd vs *BDO Binder Hamlyn* [1996] B.C.C. 808 732
Andrew and others vs Kounnis Freeman [1999] 2 B.C.L.C. 641 746
Anns vs Merton London Borough Council [1978] A.C. 728 737
AWA Ltd vs Daniels t/a Deloitte Haskins & Sells [1992] 7 A.C.S.R. 759, [1992] 9 A.C.S.R. 383 753
Bank of Credit and Commerce International (Overseas) Ltd (In Liquidation) vs Price Waterhouse [No.2], [1998] B.C.C. 617, [1998] E.C.C. 410 759
Barings plc (In Liquidation) and Another vs Coopers & Lybrand and Others (No. 8) [2000] All ER [D] 616 753
Candler vs *Crane Christmas & Co.* [1951] C.A. [1951] 2K.B. 164 [1951] 1 All E.R. 426, [1951] 1 T.L.R. 371 733
Caparo Industries plc vs *Dickman and Others* [1989] Q.B. 653, [1989] 2 W.L.R. 316, [1989] 1 All E.R. 798, [1989] 5 B.C.C. 105, B.C.L.C. 154, [1990] 2 A.C. 605, [1990] 2 W.L.R. 358, 1 All E.R. 568, [1990] B.C.C. 164, [1990] B.C.L.C. 273. 758
Coulthard & Orrs vs *Neville Russell* [1998] 1 B.C.L.C. 143, [1998] B.C.C. 359 759
Donaghue vs *Stevenson* [1932] S.C. [H.L.] 31. 733
Electra Private Equity Partners vs KPMG Peat Marwick [2001] B.C.L.C. 589 759
Galoo Ltd and Others vs *Bright Grahame Murray (A Firm)* [1994] B.C.L.C. 492, [1994] 1 W.L.R. 1360, [1995] 1 All E.R. 16, [1994] B.C.C. 319. 743
Hedley Byrne & Co. vs *Heller and Partners Ltd* [1963] A.C. 465, [1963] 2 All E.R. 575, [1963] 3 W.L.R. 101. 734
Irish Woollen Co. Ltd vs *Tyson and Others* [1900] 26 Acct. L. R. 13. 671
James McNaughton Paper Group Ltd. vs *Hicks Anderson & Co.* [1991] 2 W.L.R. 641, [1991] 2 Q.B. 113, [1991] 1 All E.R. 134, [1991] B.C.L.C. 163, [1990] B.C.C. 891 741
Jarvis plc vs *PricewaterhouseCoopers* [2000] 2 B.C.L.C. 368. 144
JEB Fasteners Ltd vs *Marks Bloom & Co.* [1981] 3 All E.R. 289. 735
Man Nutzfahrzeuge AG v Freightliner Ltd and Ernst & Young [2007] EWCA Civ 910 759
Morgan Crucible Co. vs *Hill Samuel Bank Ltd. And Others* [1991] Ch 295, [1991] 1 All E.R. 148, [1991] 2 W.L.R. 655, [1991] B.C.L.C. 178, [1991] B.C.C. 82. 743
Re Kingston Cotton Mill Co (No. 2) [1896] 2 Ch 279. 670
Re Thomas Gerrard & Son Ltd [1967] 2 All E.R. 525, [1967] 3 W.L.R. 84, [1968] Ch 455. 671
Royal Bank of Scotland vs *Bannerman Johnstone Maclay and Others* [2002] S.L.T. 181 637
Sasea Finance Limited [in liquidation] vs *KPMG* [2000] 1 B.C.L.C. 236, [2000] 1 All E.R. 676. 667
Twomax Ltd and Goode vs *Dickson, McFarlane and Robinson* [1983] S.L.T. 98. 735

PREFACE

Members of the following accounting bodies are permitted by company law to act as auditors of limited companies in the British Isles, so it is appropriate that auditing should occupy an important place in their examination schemes:

Association of Chartered Certified Accountants (ACCA)
The Institute of Chartered Accountants in England and Wales (ICAEW)
The Institute of Chartered Accountants in Ireland (ICAI)
The Institute of Chartered Accountants of Scotland (ICAS)

This book provides a sound basis for the study of auditing for the above bodies' examinations and also for the examinations of the Institute of Internal Auditors (IIA) and of the Chartered Institute of Public Finance and Accountancy (CIPFA).

The book will be suitable for studies of auditing at degree level.

Since the fourth edition of this book was published, the International Auditing and Assurance Standards Board (IAASB) has redrafted the International Standards on Auditing (ISAs) and the International Standard on Quality Control (ISQC1). These were redrafted to improve their clarity under the terms of the Clarity project. IAASB has also issued a Glossary of Terms and the Preface to the International Standards on Quality Control, Auditing, Review, Other Assurance and Related Services. IAASB is one of the independent standard-setting boards of the International Federation of Accountants (IFAC). This fifth edition contains references to the newly clarified standards and also, where appropriate, to the clarified ISAs (UK and Ireland) published by the Auditing Practices Board (APB). The ISAs are designed to support the auditor in obtaining reasonable assurance in forming their opinions. They are structured as follows:

1 The first section contains:
   - an introduction
   - overall objectives of the auditor
   - definitions
   - requirements.
2 The second section contains:
   - application and other explanatory material supporting the requirements (in some cases explanatory material is contained in appendices).

The paragraph numbers in the second section are prefixed by 'A'. We quote from the first and second sections and the appendices when we believe it is appropriate to support our discussion of the audit process. Regarding the ISAs (UK and Ireland) it is important to note that the paragraph numbers are identical to the ISAs published by IAASB, but that the ISAs (UK and Ireland) are supplemented by sub-paragraphs.

As far as accounting standards are concerned, International Financial Reporting Standards (IFRSs), including International Accounting Standards (IASs), affecting the work of the auditor have also been adopted in the UK and Ireland. Currently, standards issued by the Accounting Standards Board bear two basic titles – Statements of Standard Accounting Practice (SSAPs) and Financial Reporting Standards (FRSs). SSAPs and FRSs contain paragraphs stating the extent of compliance with IFRSs and IASs. In this book we shall quote, where necessary, from IFRSs and IASs, but shall inform you where there is a divergence from those standards in the UK and Ireland. We would mention at this point that we do not consider all the detailed requirements of accounting standards in this book (in other words this book is not about accounting (or indeed auditing standards)). We are concerned primarily with principles and where these principles have been reflected in official standards, we quote from those standards.

Since writing the fourth edition a new companies act, Companies Act 2006, came into force in Great Britain and we have redrafted Chapter 4 to take account of this. Students outside of Great Britain should refer to company legislation in their own jurisdiction. Various other chapters have been amended to take account of the new Companies Act and of other recent documents and pronouncements issued by the FRC, APB and the ICAEW.

As in previous editions we have adopted the framework of the audit year of a firm of auditors auditing the financial statements of a variety of organizations. Care has been taken to ensure that the practical work of the auditor is presented as clearly and logically as possible so that the student will have a good appreciation of what the audit process is about. Students are recommended to take note of any important developments relating to international accounting and auditing standards.

One of the strengths of this book, in our view, is the carefully paced tutorial approach that has been adopted throughout, which means that it can be used as a tool in the classroom as well as for private study. We have attempted to make the book as readable and interesting as possible.

Regrettably, auditing is often seen as being deadly boring. This is not our view and we would go so far as to say that those who believe it to be boring will tend to be unimaginative and bad auditors in consequence. Auditing affects most people in society, either directly or indirectly, and its current role is changing, and in some important areas, is being extended. Our hope is that this book will prove to be a useful vehicle for providing an understanding of what auditing is about and that it will be a valuable contribution to the auditing debate.

THE FRAMEWORK OF THE BOOK

The chapters contain detailed study material illustrated by many examples, case studies and questions. Some of the questions – called tasks or activities – are within the body of the text and they involve the student in a self-learning process; they expect students to advance the argument themselves either using principles discussed in the text or by using their common sense and imagination. In each case, you should make sure that you try to answer these questions before proceeding to the next part of the text. In the case of tasks, the suggested solutions are provided at the end of each chapter, whereas for the activities the solution is provided immediately following the question.

At the end of each chapter there is a comprehensive range of self-assessment questions designed to help you decide if the material in the text has been understood. Auditing in practice requires the exercise of considerable judgement in the context of a particular set of circumstances and some of the questions are mini-case studies aimed at giving you experience in analysing and interpreting information and forming reasoned conclusions. Suggested solutions to some of these questions have been provided for students on the website at **www.cengage.co.uk/graymanson5**. Other solutions are only available to recognized tutors on the same website, for which they need to register.

Figure 0.1 shows how the audit process flows through the contents of the study chapters. You will find it useful to look back at this diagram occasionally

FIGURE 0.1 Stages in the auditing process and how they are covered in the chapters.

Setting the scene	Chapter 1 Why are auditors needed?
	Chapter 2 An overview of the postulates and concepts of auditing
	Chapter 3 The meaning and importance of auditor independence: factors affecting independence and measures to attain it
	Chapter 4 Audit regulation
	Chapter 5 The risk-based approach to audit: audit judgement
	Chapter 6 The search for evidence explained
Starting the audit process	Chapter 5 The risk-based approach to audit: audit judgement
	Chapter 12 Analytical review of financial statements
Systems work and transactions testing	Chapter 7 Systems work: basic ideas 1
	Chapter 8 Systems work: basic ideas 2
	Chapter 15 Assurance engagements and internal audit
	Chapter 9 Testing and evaluation of systems
	Chapter 10 Substantive testing, computer-assisted audit techniques and audit programmes
	Chapter 11 Sampling and materiality
Pre-final and balance sheet date work and final work	Chapter 10 Substantive testing, computer-assisted audit techniques and audit programmes
	Chapter 12 Final work: general principles, analytical review of financial statements, non-current assets and trade receivables
	Chapter 13 Final work: specific problems related to inventories, construction contracts and trade payables
	Chapter 14 Final review: post-balance sheet period, provisions, contingencies, letter of representation
Analytical review of accounts	Chapter 12 Final work: general principles, analytical review of financial statements, non-current assets and trade receivables
Audit reporting	Chapter 16 The auditor's report
	Chapter 17 Fraud and going concern
	Chapter 15 Assurance engagements and internal audit
The auditor's liability under law	Chapter 19 The auditor and liability under the law
Critical examination of auditing and new developments	Chapter 18 The audit expectations gap and corporate governance
	Chapter 20 Criticisms and developments in auditing

when studying individual chapters (right-hand column) to locate the subject you are studying within a particular stage of the auditing process (left-hand column).

Note that the chapters are not set out in strict numerical sequence. This is because some chapters are relevant to more than one stage. Some of the chapters do not fit into the process itself but are useful in that they throw light onto how auditing is viewed and on possible directions that auditing will take in the future.

Please note that official Examination Questions, together with suggested solutions, can be found on the website for the book at www.cengage.co.uk/graymanson5

These contain two sets of questions, both sets taken from recent papers of the accounting bodies in Great Britain and Ireland. The first set has been presented in the form of two examination papers, each containing six questions. Suggested solutions have been provided for the questions on these papers but of course you should first attempt to answer them by yourself. The second set contains selected questions which you can use as additional exercises to test your knowledge and understanding for yourself. Your tutors may wish to set some of these questions as a formal exercise, so check with them before attempting any. Suggested solutions to the second set of questions are available on the website mentioned above.

HOW TO USE THIS BOOK

NOTE FOR TUTORS

The authors have prepared Guidance Notes for tutors to accompany this book. This guidance is available in the lecturers' section of the Cengage Learning website at **www.cengage.co.uk/graymanson5**.

To use the book intelligently you need to plan your work and set aside regular time each week for study. If you have no prior knowledge of auditing, you will probably need about 150 hours of study to cover the material in this book to examination standard – say about 4.5 hours per week of concentrated study over a period of eight to nine months. Time for additional reading and for practice questions is included in this total and it is *absolutely essential* for you to devote time to these. Auditing as a subject requires both literacy and to some extent numeracy – particularly the former in the examination context – and it is vital that you gain experience in expressing yourself and writing up your solutions to the selected questions. You should not look at the suggested solutions until you have worked the questions yourself. Don't forget that frequently there may be no single 'correct' solution. If this is the case our suggested solution will make it clear.

Your approach to using the book should be something like this:

- Read the **learning objectives** at the beginning of the chapter then briefly skim through the chapter page by page to get a feel for the length and complexity of the subjects it covers. It might also be useful at this stage to have a brief look through the **summary** at the end of the chapter.
- Begin reading the chapter, following up where necessary the occasional suggestions for further reading, references to source material or cross-references to other parts of the text, and make sure you understand each section before moving on. The **marginal notes** are usually brief explanatory notes that have been devised to carry information or advice which is *not* essential to your understanding of the subject or your mastery of your own particular syllabus. Make notes in the remaining marginal space as you go along, especially on those topics featured in the learning objectives.
- When you come to each **task** or **activity** you should attempt to answer it before moving on. Check your own answers against the **suggested solutions** at the end of each chapter (in the case of tasks) and against our comments following each activity. If your answers are incorrect, make sure you understand where and why you went wrong before moving on to the next subject. Sometimes tasks will require you to think of answers which have not been specifically covered in the preceding text, but by using a combination of common sense and imagination you should still be able to answer them. These questions are designed to involve you actively in the learning process, not simply to test your knowledge; they ask you to engage in critical thought at strategic points throughout the text and this will ultimately deepen your understanding of the subject. Don't be tempted to skip them. Indeed, you may lose out if you do, since later topics often require an understanding of the areas covered by them.

At the end of each chapter you will find a series of **self-assessment questions**. These have been designed to test your understanding of the main points in each chapter so you should attempt them whenever they appear. Suggested solutions to some of these questions have been provided on the website in the student/lecturer section at **www.cengage.co.uk/graymanson5**. Other solutions are only available to recognized tutors on the same website. If you answer any of the questions incorrectly, make sure you check back in the text to find out why. Often the commentary on the answers will give you a good idea of where and why you went wrong. Make sure you follow up these leads.

Occasionally it may be advisable for you to tackle one of the full examination questions. Remember that it is good practice to ask yourself, before you start the question, what area of knowledge it is designed to test. Once you have completed your answer, study the answer provided in the answers section on the student side of the companion website, noting the main points of principle and checking back if any of your answers are wrong.

At intervals in your study you will need to build in revision sessions. It may be helpful to rework the self-assessment questions in earlier chapters to identify areas needing priority revision attention.

You should aim to have completed your main studies at least one month before the examination. The final month should be the time for revision, not for initial learning. Work and rework the practice questions, noting the points of principle and remembering the vital importance of speed in examination work.

COMPANION WEBSITE

The companion website can be found at **www.cengage.co.uk/graymanson5**.

For students

- Answers to self-assessment questions (student questions)
- Additional Appendix material for chapters in the book
- Related links

For tutors

- Guidance notes for tutors
- PowerPoint lecture slides
- Additional Appendix material for chapters in the book
- Answers to self-assessment questions (tutor questions)
- Official examination questions with suggested solutions

RECOMMENDED FURTHER READING

This book is intended to be a good friend and counsellor as you progress towards your accountancy qualification or towards satisfying the auditing component of degree and similar courses. As such, not only will it provide a framework for your study, it will give you guidance on the background information you need. It is essential that you keep yourself informed about developments in the accounting profession and in the wider world. We shall recommend additional reading both in and at the end of each chapter, as we believe that wide reading is essential to success.

The authors wish to emphasize *two* matters here:

- We will not reproduce whole auditing guidelines, accounting standards, other professional statements and so on in this book. We assume that you have in your possession at least the professional material listed below and we shall be discussing and commenting on it in the text. The reason for this is that you should, even at this early stage, see yourself as a potential qualified accountant and should get used to referring to the material in the same way that a professional accountant would in practice:
  (a) International Financial Reporting Standards (IFRSs) including International Accounting Standards (IASs) and their UK and Ireland equivalents (if you are based in the UK or Ireland) – Financial Reporting Standards (FRSs) and Statements of Standard Accounting Practice (SSAPSs).

(b) International Standards on Auditing (ISAs) and the International Standard on Quality Control (ISQC) and (if you are based in the UK and Ireland) equivalent ISAs and ISQC (UK and Ireland) issued by the Auditing Practices Board (APB).

(c) Code of Ethics for Professional Accountants issued by the International Federation of Accountants (IFAC) or, if you are based in the UK and Ireland, the APB Ethical Standards – ES1 to ES5 and ES Provisions Available for Small Entities (PASE).

What this book does is to comment on these standards and guidelines so that you will be able to appreciate their meaning and select important extracts for your own use. We have included reference to standards in the **Further reading** section of chapters where they are of general interest to the matters discussed in the chapter concerned.
We have departed from this principle only to the extent that we have provided (in the Appendix material to Chapter 4 on the Cengage website) relevant sections from the Companies Act 2006, and discussed these sections in Chapter 4. It is our intention that students should think of themselves at an early stage as professional people and that professional material should be read in the original.

- Additional reading is a vital feature of understanding the world in which accountants live and work. The authors recommend the following:

(a) *Accountancy* (published by ICAEW), *The Accountants' Magazine* (published by ICAS), *The Certified Accountant* (published by ACCA)

(b) *Accountancy Age*

(c) *(Certified) Student Accountant*

(d) A good daily and Sunday newspaper.

WALK THROUGH TOUR

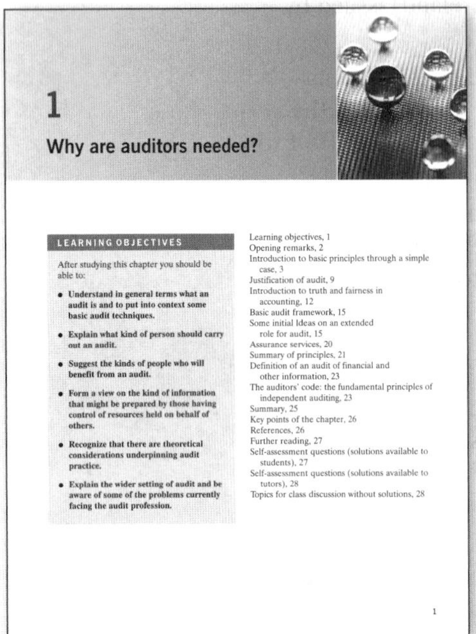

1

Why are auditors needed?

LEARNING OBJECTIVES

After studying this chapter you should be able to:

- **Understand in general terms what an audit is and to put into context some basic audit techniques.**
- **Explain what kind of person should carry out an audit.**
- **Suggest the kinds of people who will benefit from an audit.**
- **Form a view on the kind of information that might be prepared by those having control of resources held on behalf of others.**
- **Recognize that there are theoretical considerations underpinning audit practice.**
- **Explain the wider setting of audit and be aware of some of the problems currently facing the audit profession.**

Learning objectives, 1
Opening remarks, 2
Introduction to basic principles through a simple case, 3
Justification of audit, 9
Introduction to truth and fairness in accounting, 12
Basic audit framework, 15
Some initial Ideas on an extended role for audit, 15
Assurance services, 20
Summary of principles, 21
Definition of an audit of financial and other information, 23
The auditors' code: the fundamental principles of independent auditing, 23
Summary, 25
Key points of the chapter, 26
References, 26
Further reading, 27
Self-assessment questions (solutions available to students), 27
Self-assessment questions (solutions available to tutors), 28
Topics for class discussion without solutions, 28

1

Learning objectives Appear at the start of every chapter to help you monitor your understanding and progress through the chapter.

2 Why are auditors needed?

OPENING REMARKS

When the authors of this book first joined the accounting and auditing profession we never imagined that auditing would become the subject of such debate about the independence and competence of auditors and even about the detailed procedures that auditors use. Auditors have of course always discussed audit matters among themselves, but since corporate scandals involving very large companies such as Enron and WorldCom started to come to light in 2000, governments and the public have begun to get involved, particularly as there have been later examples of major corporate fraud such as Parmalat in Italy and Satyam in India. The recent and continuing credit crunch has also made people query the morals and competence of top management and ask why the auditors had not taken earlier action with regards to the exposure of financial institutions as a result of poor lending decisions. Auditing has become headline news not just in the business pages of newspapers but on front pages and in editorials, and in television news bulletins and discussion programmes. Even the President of the United States mentioned auditing in his State of The Union Address in 2002. Auditing has become an exciting subject. There may have been corporate scandals in the past, such as Maxwell and Polly Peck in the United Kingdom and Ultramares Corp in the United States and Cambridge Credit in Australia, but never on the scale of those in the early years of the twenty-first century and never before resulting in the collapse of a major accounting firm. The result of these events is that big question marks have been placed over the competence and independence of auditors and over the apparent failure of corporate governance.

We do not wish you to place all the blame for the debacles on the shoulders of auditors. We shall see that other reasons for the scandals include inadequate accounting standards, and boardroom cultures that encourage the manipulation of figures for company or personal gain.

In this book we will introduce you to these important issues and explain the steps taken to remedy what are seen as lapses from the conduct expected of auditors and, indeed, of company managements. Much of this book will be about how a competent audit should be carried out. We shall focus, among other things, on the role of audit and explain why it is important that the audit function is seen to be carried out by competent and independent people on behalf of a number of groups interested in the performance and position of a variety of entities. In the process, we will meet up with organizations engaged in manufacture and sale of goods, in trading of various kinds and in the provision of services.

Before moving on to discuss basic principles, we give brief details of the Enron, WorldCom, Parmalat and Satyam scandals to give you a flavour of the problems faced by the accounting and auditing profession:

- Enron, USA: This company hid its real level of debt by putting £8.5 billion of group liabilities into special purpose vehicles whose financial statements were not consolidated with those of the company. The company became bankrupt and the audit firm, Arthur Andersen, went out of business as a result of obstructing justice by, among other things, shredding documents relating to the audit.
- WorldCom, USA: This company, in an attempt to maintain stated profit levels, treated revenue costs (over $3.8 billion) as capital expenditure. There was also understatement of loans amounting to some $2.5 billion. Arthur Andersen were the company auditors.

Marginal notes Appear throughout, brief explanatory notes.

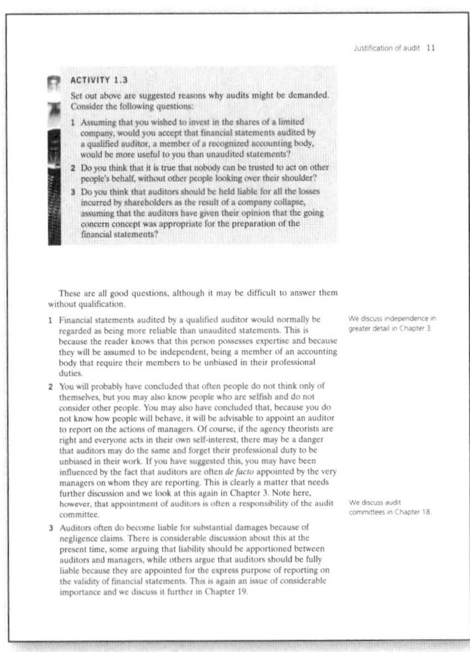

Justification of audit 11

ACTIVITY 1.3

Set out above are suggested reasons why audits might be demanded. Consider the following questions:

1 Assuming that you wished to invest in the shares of a limited company, would you accept that financial statements audited by a qualified auditor, a member of a recognized accounting body, would be more useful to you than unaudited statements?
2 Do you think that it is true that nobody can be trusted to act on other people's behalf, without other people looking over their shoulder?
3 Do you think that auditors should be held liable for all the losses incurred by shareholders as the result of a company collapse, assuming that the auditors have given their opinion that the going concern concept was appropriate for the preparation of the financial statements?

These are all good questions, although it may be difficult to answer them without qualification.

1 Financial statements audited by a qualified auditor would normally be regarded as being more reliable than unaudited statements. This is because the reader knows that this person possesses expertise and because they will be assumed to be independent, being a member of an accounting body that require their members to be unbiased in their professional duties.

We discuss independence in greater detail in Chapter 3.

2 You will probably have concluded that often people do not think only of themselves, but you may also know people who are selfish and do not consider other people. You may also have concluded that, because you do not know how people will behave, it will be advisable to appoint an auditor to report on the actions of managers. Of course, if the agency theorists are right and everyone acts in their own self-interest, there may be a danger that auditors may do the same and forget their professional duty to be unbiased in their work. If you have suggested this, you may have been influenced by the fact that auditors are often *de facto* appointed by the very managers on whom they are reporting. This is clearly a matter that needs further discussion and we look at this again in Chapter 3. Note here, however, that appointment of auditors is often a responsibility of the audit committee.

We discuss audit committees in Chapter 18.

3 Auditors often do become liable for substantial damages because of negligence claims. There is considerable discussion about this at the present time, some arguing that liability should be apportioned between auditors and managers, while others argue that auditors should be fully liable because they are appointed for the express purpose of reporting on the validity of financial statements. This is again an issue of considerable importance and we discuss it further in Chapter 19.

Activities Appear throughout, involving you actively in the learning process.

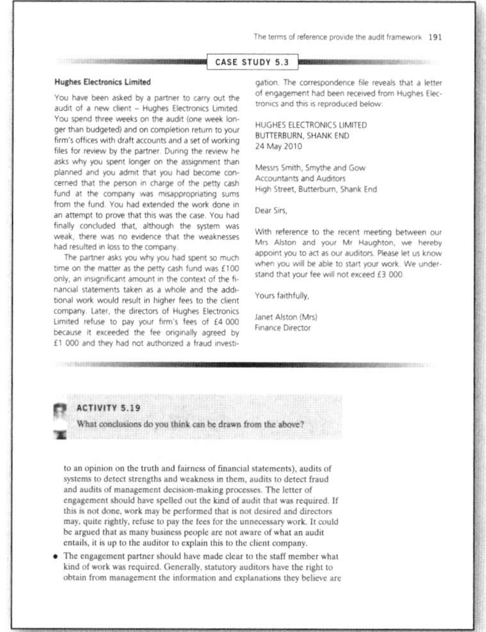

The terms of reference provide the audit framework 191

CASE STUDY 5.3

Hughes Electronics Limited

You have been asked by a partner to carry out the audit of a new client – Hughes Electronics Limited. You spend three weeks on the audit (one week longer than budgeted) and on completion return to your firm's offices with draft accounts and a set of working files for review by the partner. During the review he asks why you spent longer on the assignment than planned and you admit that you had become concerned that the person in charge of the petty cash fund at the company was misappropriating sums from the fund. You had extended the work done in an attempt to prove that this was the case. You had finally concluded that, although the system was weak, there was no evidence that the weaknesses had resulted in loss to the company.

The partner asks you why you had spent so much time on the matter as the petty cash fund was £100 only, an insignificant amount in the context of the financial statements taken as a whole and the additional work would result in higher fees to the client company. Later, the directors of Hughes Electronics Limited refuse to pay your firm's fees of £4 000 because it exceeded the fee originally agreed by £1 000 and they had not authorized a fraud investigation. The correspondence file reveals that a letter of engagement had been received from Hughes Electronics and this is reproduced below:

HUGHES ELECTRONICS LIMITED
BUTTERBURN, SHANK END
24 May 2010

Messrs Smith, Smythe and Gow
Accountants and Auditors
High Street, Butterburn, Shank End

Dear Sirs,

With reference to the recent meeting between our Mrs Alston and your Mr Haughton, we hereby appoint you to act as our auditors. Please let us know when you will be able to start your work. We understand that your fee will not exceed £3 000.

Yours faithfully,

Janet Alston (Mrs)
Finance Director

ACTIVITY 5.19

What conclusions do you think can be drawn from the above?

to an opinion on the truth and fairness of financial statements), audits of systems to detect strengths and weakness in them, audits to detect fraud and audits of management decision-making processes. The letter of engagement should have spelled out the kind of audit that was required. If this is not done, work may be performed that is not desired and directors may, quite rightly, refuse to pay the fees for the unnecessary work. It could be argued that as many business people are not aware of what an audit entails, it is up to the auditor to explain this to the client company.

- The engagement partner should have made clear to the staff member what kind of work was required. Generally, statutory auditors have the right to obtain from management the information and explanations they believe are

Case studies Appear throughout, help bring all learning points to life in a very accessible manner.

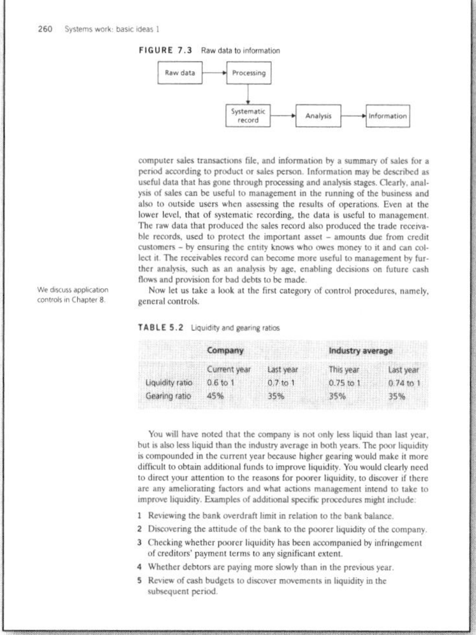

260 Systems work: basic ideas 1

FIGURE 7.3 Raw data to information

computer sales transactions file, and information by a summary of sales for a period according to product or sales person. Information may be described as useful data that has gone through processing and analysis stages. Clearly, analysis of sales can be useful to management in the running of the business and also to outside users when assessing the results of operations. Even at the lower level, that of systematic recording, the data is useful to management. The raw data that produced the sales record also produced the trade receivable records, used to protect the important asset – amounts due from credit customers – by ensuring the entity knows who owes money to it and can collect it. The receivables record can become more useful to management by further analysis, such as an analysis by age, enabling decisions on future cash flows and provision for bad debts to be made.

We discuss application controls in Chapter 8.

Now let us take a look at the first category of control procedures, namely, general controls.

TABLE 5.2 Liquidity and gearing ratios

	Company		Industry average	
	Current year	Last year	This year	Last year
Liquidity ratio	0.6 to 1	0.7 to 1	0.75 to 1	0.74 to 1
Gearing ratio	45%	35%	35%	35%

You will have noted that the company is not only less liquid than last year, but is also less liquid than the industry average in both years. The poor liquidity is compounded in the current year because higher gearing would make it more difficult to obtain additional funds to improve liquidity. You would clearly need to direct your attention to the reasons for poorer liquidity, to discover if there are any ameliorating factors and what actions management intend to take to improve liquidity. Examples of additional specific procedures might include:

1 Reviewing the bank overdraft limit in relation to the bank balance.
2 Discovering the attitude of the bank to the poorer liquidity of the company.
3 Checking whether poorer liquidity has been accompanied by infringement of creditors' payment terms to any significant extent.
4 Whether debtors are paying more slowly than in the previous year.
5 Review of cash budgets to discover movements in liquidity in the subsequent period.

Figures and tables Appear throughout, as a visual aid to help the reader to grasp key concepts.

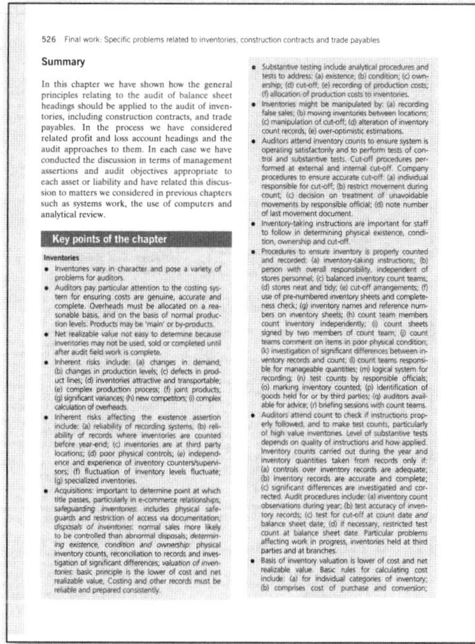

526 Final work: Specific problems related to inventories, construction contracts and trade payables

Summary

In this chapter we have shown how the general principles relating to the audit of balance sheet headings should be applied to the audit of inventories, including construction contracts, and trade payables. In the process we have considered related profit and loss account headings and the audit approaches to them. In each case we have conducted the discussion in terms of management assertions and audit objectives appropriate to each asset or liability and have related this discussion to matters we considered in previous chapters such as systems work, the use of computers and analytical review.

Key points of the chapter

Inventories

- Inventories vary in character and pose a variety of problems for auditors.
- Auditors pay particular attention to the costing system for ensuring costs are genuine, accurate and complete. Overheads must be allocated on a reasonable basis, and on the basis of normal production levels. Products may be 'main' or by-products.
- Net realizable value not easy to determine because inventories may not be used, sold or completed until after audit field work is complete.
- Inherent risks include: (a) changes in demand; (b) changes in production levels; (c) defects in product lines; (d) inventories attractive and transportable; (e) complex production process; (f) joint products; (g) significant variances; (h) new competitors; (i) complex calculation of overheads.
- Inherent risks affecting the existence assertion include: (a) reliability of recording systems; (b) reliability of records where inventories are counted before year-end; (c) inventories are at third party locations; (d) poor physical controls; (e) independence and experience of inventory counters/supervisors; (f) fluctuation of inventory levels fluctuate; (g) specialized inventories.
- Acquisitions: important to determine point at which title passes, particularly in e-commerce relationships; *safeguarding inventories*: includes physical safeguards and restriction of access via documentation; *disposals of inventories*: normal sales more likely to be controlled than abnormal disposals; *determining existence, condition and ownership*: physical inventory counts, reconciliation to records and investigation of significant differences; *valuation of inventories*: basic principle is the lower of cost and net realizable value. Costing and other records must be reliable and prepared consistently.
- Substantive testing include analytical procedures and tests to address: (a) existence; (b) condition; (c) ownership; (d) cut-off; (e) recording of production costs; (f) allocation of production costs to inventories.
- Inventories might be manipulated by: (a) recording false sales; (b) moving inventories between locations; (c) manipulation of cut-off; (d) alteration of inventory count records; (e) over-optimistic estimations.
- Auditors attend inventory counts to ensure system is operating satisfactorily and to perform tests of control and substantive tests. Cut-off procedures performed at external and internal cut-off. Company procedures to ensure accurate cut-off: (a) individual responsible for cut-off; (b) restrict movement during count; (c) decision on treatment of unavoidable movements by responsible official; (d) note number of last movement document.
- Inventory-taking instructions are important for staff to follow in determining physical existence, condition, ownership and cut-off.
- Procedures to ensure inventory is properly counted and recorded: (a) inventory-taking instructions; (b) person with overall responsibility, independent of stores personnel; (c) balanced inventory count teams; (d) stores neat and tidy; (e) cut-off arrangements; (f) use of pre-numbered inventory sheets and completeness check; (g) inventory names and reference numbers on inventory sheets; (h) count team members count inventory independently; (i) count sheets signed by two members of count team; (j) count teams comment on items in poor physical condition; (k) investigation of significant differences between inventory records and count; (l) count teams responsible for manageable quantities; (m) logical system for recording; (n) test counts by responsible officials; (o) marking inventory counted; (p) identification of goods held for or by third parties; (q) auditors available for advice; (r) briefing sessions with count teams.
- Auditors attend count to check if instructions properly followed, and to make test counts, particularly of high value inventories. Level of substantive tests depends on quality of instructions and how applied. Inventory counts carried out during the year and inventory quantities taken from records only if: (a) controls over inventory records are adequate; (b) inventory records are accurate and complete; (c) significant differences are investigated and corrected. Audit procedures include: (a) inventory count observations during year; (b) test accuracy of inventory records; (c) test for cut-off at count date *and* balance sheet date; (d) if necessary, restricted test count at balance sheet date. Particular problems affecting work in progress, inventories held at third parties and at branches.
- Basis of inventory valuation is lower of cost and net realizable value. Basic rules for calculating cost include: (a) for individual categories of inventory; (b) comprises cost of purchase and conversion;

Key points of the chapter Key points conclude the chapter and highlight the core learning points covered.

58 An overview of the postulates and concepts of auditing

References

American Accounting Association (1973) *A Statement of Basic Auditing Concepts*, Sarasota, FL: American Accounting Association, 1973.
Bell, B.B., Marrs, F.O., Solomon, I. and Thomas, H. (1997) *Auditing Organizations Through a Strategic-Systems Lens*, KPMG Peat Marwick LLP.
Briloff, A.J. (1986) 'Corporate Governance and Accountability: Whose Responsibility?', unpublished paper presented at the University of Connecticut, Storrs, Connecticut , April.
Flint, D. (1988) *Philosophy and Principles of Auditing: An Introduction*, Basingstoke: Macmillan Education Ltd.
Gowthorpe, C. and Porter, B. (2004) *Audit Expectation–Performance Gap in the United Kingdom in 1999 and Comparison with the Gap in New Zealand in 1989 and in 1999*, ICAS.
Mautz, H.A. and Sharaf, R. (1961) *The Philosophy of Auditing*, Sarasota, FL: American Accounting Association.
Normanton, E.L. (1966) *The Accountability and Audit of Governments: A Comparative Study*, Manchester: Manchester University Press.
Porter, B. (1993) 'An Empirical Study of the Audit Expectation–Performance Gap', *Accounting and Business Research*, 24 (93): 49–68.

Further reading

We would recommend the following:

Bell, B.B., Marrs, F.O., Solomon, I. and Thomas, H. (1997) *Auditing Organizations Through a Strategic-Systems Lens*, KPMG Peat Marwick LLP.
Bell, T.B., Peecher, M.E. and Solomon, I. (2005) *The 21st Century Public Company Audit, Conceptual Elements of KPMG's Global Audit Methodology*, KPMG International.
Cadbury, A. (1990) 'The Corporate Governance Agenda', *Corporate Governance*, 8(1): 7–15. Institute of Chartered Accountants of Scotland (1993) *Auditing into the Twenty-First Century*, ICAS.
Moizer, P. (1991) 'Independence', in M. Sherer and S. Turley (eds), *Current Issues in Auditing*, 3rd edn, London: Paul Chapman Publishing Ch. 3. This chapter also discusses ethical approaches.

Although published quite a time ago the books by Mautz and Sharaf and Flint in the references above contain good discussion of the postulates and concepts underpinning auditing.

Self-assessment questions (solutions available to students)

2.1 Identification of management assertions in respect of figures in the financial statements is a vital part of the audit process. State whether you agree with this statement, giving practical examples.

2.2 Explain what is meant by the principle of auditor integrity. How do you think we should ensure that the principle is adhered to?

2.3 Auditors are expected to approach their work with thoroughness and with an attitude of professional scepticism. What do you think that professional scepticism means in practice?

2.4 You are auditing a company that shows a loss for the year of £700 000. This figure is after charging impairment of property, plant and equipment of £1 500 000. As a part of your work you note that in the Directors' Report a profit of £800 000 is quoted as profit for the year. What are your responsibilities in respect of this matter?

Self-assessment questions (solutions available to tutors)

2.5 Explain how auditing theory might give useful insights into the practice of auditing. Your answer should make reference to the postulates and concepts of auditing.

2.6 Why do you think that the collapse of Enron and other scandals affecting large companies may have resulted in a widening of the audit expectations gap?

2.7 Explain why the general public is just as interested in the way that large companies, including banks, behave as are the shareholders of those companies. What do you think is meant by the public interest?

2.8 The trade payables figure in most companies is normally material in the context of the financial statements taken as a whole. What assertions do you think that management is

References and further reading These provide helpful directions to further sources of information.

150 Audit regulation

another person as auditor other than the retiring auditor.

> Special notice is at least 21 days.

(d) s.511(2) (s.515(3), (failure to re-appoint auditor) indicates that the auditor proposed to be removed; and the auditor proposed to replace such a person must be sent copies of the relevant resolutions (s.515(3)).

(e) Note from s.511(3) to (6) that the removed auditor can make representations (not exceeding a reasonable length) to be sent to members or in certain circumstances to be read at the meeting but they must not be defamatory. Similar provisions apply to auditors not being reappointed (s.515(4)to (7)).

(f) When you come to read further in the Case study note that:

- (i) The Companies Acts requirements are supplemented by professional requirements. In many ways the latter are more stringent than the former.
- (ii) James was certain that he and his staff had acted correctly. If he were not so, it would have been difficult for him to have made representations.
- (iii) Note also that the decision to make representations was taken despite James's belief that he would be lucky to persuade the shareholders to allow him to stay in office.
- (iv) Interestingly, Andrew McOwan saw fit to tell James Thomson of the outcome of the medical complaint.

You should remember two professional people are trying to resolve a difficult professional situation. Both would be required to treat the information that they had given to each other in strict professional confidence.

Task 4.3

The text answers all the questions posed. You should, however, note the following:

(a) John Dewar accepted the appointment when he knew that Sir Frederick had resigned. You must understand that the relationship between auditor and management is very important. Great care must be taken to ensure there is mutual respect on both sides.

(b) John Dewar's audit work confirmed the conclusions of Andrew McOwan. The remaining directors' decision to cooperate with John Dewar is an indication of awareness of their responsibilities following Sir Frederick's departure.

Self-assessment questions (solutions available to students)

4.1 Consider the following statements and explain why they might be true or false:

- (a) The directors may not appoint the first auditor, neither may they appoint an auditor to fill a vacancy caused by the death of the incumbent auditor.
- (b) The remuneration of auditors is not always fixed by the company in general meeting.
- (c) When auditors are dismissed during their term of office, remuneration may nevertheless be claimed.
- (d) Auditors who are dismissed have the right to make such representations to shareholders as they wish.

4.2 Janet Helmsley is auditor of Skiplam Ltd for the year ended 30 September 2010. She and her staff are examining the inventory figure in the accounts and have become concerned that the inventory count sheets are inaccurate because the test counts they had made at the year-end did not agree with the quantities on the inventory sheets prepared by the company. Also, as the inventory sheets had not been numbered, there was no way that they or the company officials could be certain that all sheets had been accounted for.

Required:

(a) State whether you think that this would be a reason for believing that the company had not kept proper accounting records (refer to CA 2006 s.386).

Apart from the above matter, Janet also concluded that the valuation of inventories could not be

Self-assessment questions (solutions available to students) At the end of all chapters, these are designed to test your understanding of the main points in each chapter, and attempt them wherever they appear. Suggested solutions have been provided on the student side of the website www.cengage.co.uk/graymanson5.

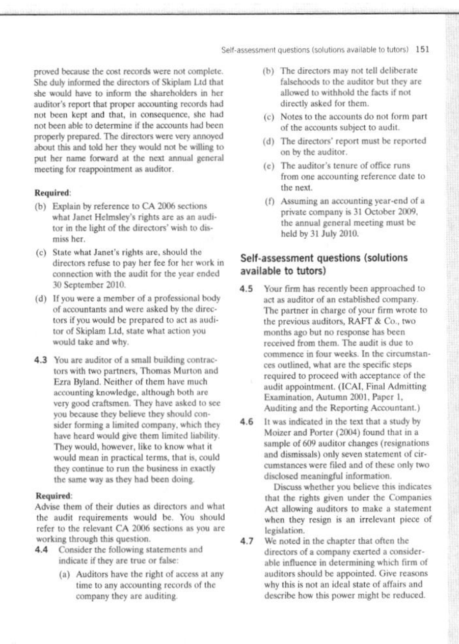
Self-assessment questions (solutions available to tutors) 151

proved because the cost records were not complete. She duly informed the directors of Skiplam Ltd that she would have to inform the shareholders in her auditor's report that proper accounting records had not been kept and that, in consequence, she had not been able to determine if the accounts had been properly prepared. The directors were very annoyed about this and told her they would not be willing to put her name forward at the next annual general meeting for reappointment as auditor.

Required:

- (b) Explain by reference to CA 2006 sections what Janet Helmsley's rights are as an auditor in the light of the directors' wish to dismiss her.
- (c) State what Janet's rights are, should the directors refuse to pay her fee for her work in connection with the audit for the year ended 30 September 2010.
- (d) If you were a member of a professional body of accountants and were asked by the directors if you would be prepared to act as auditor of Skiplam Ltd, state what action you would take and why.

4.3 You are auditor of a small building contractors with two partners, Thomas Murton and Ezra Byland. Neither of them have much accounting knowledge, although both are very good craftsmen. They have asked to see you because they believe they should consider forming a limited company, which they have heard would give them limited liability. They would, however, like to know what it would mean in practical terms, that is, could they continue to run the business in exactly the same way as they had been doing.

Required:
Advise them of their duties as directors and what the audit requirements would be. You should refer to the relevant CA 2006 sections as you are working through this question.

4.4 Consider the following statements and indicate if they are true or false:

- (a) Auditors have the right of access at any time to any accounting records of the company they are auditing.
- (b) The directors may not tell deliberate falsehoods to the auditor but they are allowed to withhold the facts if not directly asked for them.
- (c) Notes to the accounts do not form part of the accounts subject to audit.
- (d) The directors' report must be reported on by the auditor.
- (e) The auditor's tenure of office runs from one accounting reference date to the next.
- (f) Assuming an accounting year-end of a private company is 31 October 2009, the annual general meeting must be held by 31 July 2010.

Self-assessment questions (solutions available to tutors)

4.5 Your firm has recently been approached to act as auditor of an established company. The partner in charge of your firm wrote to the previous auditors, RAFT & Co., two months ago but no response has been received from them. The audit is due to commence in four weeks. In the circumstances outlined, what are the specific steps required to proceed with acceptance of the audit appointment. (ICAI, Final Admitting Examination, Autumn 2001, Paper 1, Auditing and the Reporting Accountant.)

4.6 It was indicated in the text that a study by Moizer and Porter (2004) found that in a sample of 609 auditor changes (resignations and dismissals) only seven statement of circumstances were filed and of these only two disclosed meaningful information.

Discuss whether you believe this indicates that the rights given under the Companies Act allowing auditors to make a statement when they resign is an irrelevant piece of legislation.

4.7 We noted in the chapter that often the directors of a company exerted a considerable influence in determining which firm of auditors should be appointed. Give reasons why this is not an ideal state of affairs and describe how this power might be reduced.

Self-assessment questions (solutions available to lecturers) As previous, but solutions are only available to lecturers, on **www.cengage.co.uk/graymanson5**.

About the website

The mission of Cengage Learning EMEA is to shape the future of global learning by delivering high quality education, reference and research materials for our world wide users.

All of our Higher Education textbooks are supported by comprehensive website resources. The website resources are carefully tailored to the specific needs of the students and instructors.

Visit the dedicated companion website for *The Audit Process: Principles, Practice and Cases* at **www.cengage.co.uk/graymanson5** to find valuable teaching and learning material including:

For students

- Answers to self-assessment questions (student questions)
- Additional Appendix material for chapters in the book
- Related links

For lecturers

- Guidance notes for tutors
- PowerPoint lecture slides
- Additional Appendix material for chapters in the book
- Answers to self-assessment questions (tutor questions)
- Official examination questions with suggested solutions

1 Why are auditors needed?

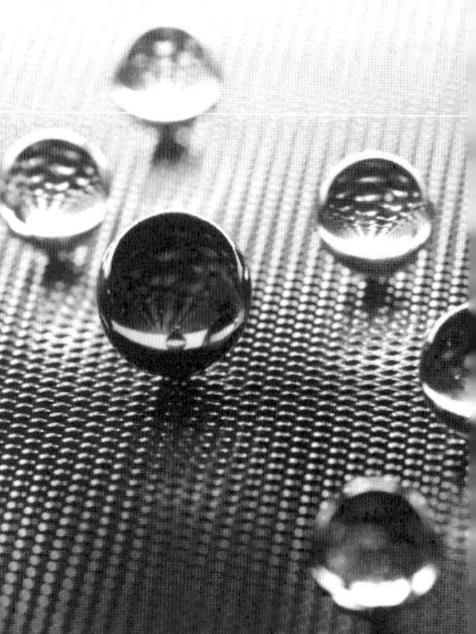

LEARNING OBJECTIVES

After studying this chapter you should be able to:

- **Understand in general terms what an audit is and to put into context some basic audit techniques.**
- **Explain what kind of person should carry out an audit.**
- **Suggest the kinds of people who will benefit from an audit.**
- **Form a view on the kind of information that might be prepared by those having control of resources held on behalf of others.**
- **Recognize that there are theoretical considerations underpinning audit practice.**
- **Explain the wider setting of audit and be aware of some of the problems currently facing the audit profession.**

Learning objectives, 1
Opening remarks, 2
Introduction to basic principles through a simple case, 3
Justification of audit, 9
Introduction to truth and fairness in accounting, 12
Basic audit framework, 15
Some initial ideas on an extended role for audit, 15
Assurance services, 20
Summary of principles, 21
Definition of an audit of financial and other information, 23
The auditors' code: the fundamental principles of independent auditing, 23
Summary, 25
Key points of the chapter, 26
References, 26
Further reading, 27
Self-assessment questions (solutions available to students), 27
Self-assessment questions (solutions available to tutors), 28
Topics for class discussion without solutions, 28

OPENING REMARKS

When the authors of this book first joined the accounting and auditing profession we never imagined that auditing would become the subject of such debate about the independence and competence of auditors and even about the detailed procedures that auditors use. Auditors have of course always discussed audit matters among themselves, but since corporate scandals involving very large companies such as Enron and WorldCom started to come to light in 2000, governments and the public have begun to get involved, particularly as there have been later examples of major corporate fraud such as Parmalat in Italy and Satyam in India. The recent and continuing credit crunch has also made people query the morals and competence of top management and ask why the auditors had not taken earlier action with regards to the exposure of financial institutions as a result of poor lending decisions. Auditing has become headline news not just in the business pages of newspapers but on front pages and in editorials, and in television news bulletins and discussion programmes. Even the President of the United States mentioned auditing in his State of The Union Address in 2002. Auditing has become an exciting subject. There may have been corporate scandals in the past, such as Maxwell and Polly Peck in the United Kingdom and Ultramares Corp in the United States and Cambridge Credit in Australia, but never on the scale of those in the early years of the twenty-first century and never before resulting in the collapse of a major accounting firm. The result of these events is that big question marks have been placed over the competence and independence of auditors and over the apparent failure of corporate governance.

We do not wish you to place all the blame for the debacles on the shoulders of auditors. We shall see that other reasons for the scandals include inadequate accounting standards, and boardroom cultures that encourage the manipulation of figures for company or personal gain.

In this book we will introduce you to these important issues and explain the steps taken to remedy what are seen as lapses from the conduct expected of auditors and, indeed, of company managements. Much of this book will be about how a competent audit should be carried out. We shall focus, among other things, on the role of audit and explain why it is important that the audit function is seen to be carried out by competent and independent people on behalf of a number of groups interested in the performance and position of a variety of entities. In the process, we will meet up with organizations engaged in manufacture and sale of goods, in trading of various kinds and in the provision of services.

Before moving on to discuss basic principles, we give brief details of the Enron, WorldCom, Parmalat and Satyam scandals to give you a flavour of the problems faced by the accounting and auditing profession:

- Enron, USA: This company hid its real level of debt by putting £8.5 billion of group liabilities into special purpose vehicles whose financial statements were not consolidated with those of the company. The company became bankrupt and the audit firm, Arthur Andersen, went out of business as a result of obstructing justice by, among other things, shredding documents relating to the audit.
- WorldCom, USA: This company, in an attempt to maintain stated profit levels, treated revenue costs (over \$3.8 billion) as capital expenditure. There was also understatement of loans amounting to some \$2.5 billion. Arthur Andersen were the company auditors.

- Parmalat, Italy: This company was a multinational dairy and food corporation which collapsed in 2003 following revelations that its total liabilities were fraudulently understated and assets overstated. It is difficult to quantify the total misstatements which may be as much as 14 billion Euros. Like Enron, the company structure was very complex, many of its subsidiaries being registered in tax havens. The corporation had hidden the fact that significant subsidiaries were loss-making and it is claimed that one of its subsidiaries overstated its assets by as much as 38 per cent of Parmalat's total stated assets. The corporation was audited by Grant Thornton
- Satyam, India: This is a very recent (2009) case which has been described as India's Enron. It seems that over many years the Satyam corporation, which specializes in computer services, inflated its reported cash and bank balances, while overstating revenues and profits, and understating liabilities. The amount of the fraud is said to exceed $1 billion. The company was audited by PricewaterhouseCoopers

There are other large companies that manipulated their accounting figures in recent years but these four are significant and representative.

These cases show that it is not only in the United States that major scandals affecting companies and auditors have taken place. However, some leading accountants in the British Isles have claimed that the various accounting and auditing disasters could not happen here for a variety of reasons. The authors are not so sanguine and, later in the book, we discuss the background to some of the problems encountered and discuss further what steps might be appropriate to, at least, reduce the likelihood that they will not recur.

See Chapter 20.

So when you are reading about the audit process in this and later chapters, please do not assume that auditors always get the right answer, nor that companies are always assiduous in applying accounting standards in the desired manner. Bear in mind, too, that it seems that Enron had been applying the strict letter of the US accounting rules concerning the special purpose vehicles.

In addition, you should note that the spate of accounting and auditing scandals has focused attention on the purpose of audit. What is the value of audit? Why are auditors employed at great cost to society? Should there be fundamental changes to the way that companies are managed – that is, how should they govern themselves to the greater benefit of society as a whole? We are likely to see greater emphasis on the function of audit and how the independence of the auditor can best be achieved. We discuss independence and professional ethics generally in Chapter 3. The Arthur Andersen example should be in the forefront of all our minds. As students you should be aware of the major issues affecting the accounting and auditing professions. We shall cover these issues in this book, including the impact that the scandals have had on the way that auditors plan their work, the techniques they use in the performance of their duties and the relationship between the auditor and management of client companies. We want you to be fully aware of what is happening in the auditing world today.

It is worth mentioning that after Andersen's collapse the Supreme Court in the United States overturned the 2002 criminal conviction of Anderson for obstruction of justice. Note too that it is extremely difficult for auditors to discover carefully hidden fraud carried out by senior managers. We discuss this matter further in Chapter 17.

INTRODUCTION TO BASIC PRINCIPLES THROUGH A SIMPLE CASE

Clearly, the cases referred to above involve very large companies but at this stage we are introducing you to the circumstances of a very small business, but a business nevertheless, that will, we think, help you to understand what an

We shall see in Chapter 4 – see page 145 – that small businesses that meet certain criteria relating to size are not legally required to have an audit, even where such businesses have the benefit of limited liability.

audit is, how it might be carried out and some of the principles that apply to all audits. Later in the chapter we suggest a brief formal framework of an average audit that will show how an audit is planned and conducted. The scene for the small business is set in Case study 1.1 (Andrew and James, Part 1), which you should now read.

CASE STUDY 1.1

Andrew and James, Part 1

On 1 March 2010 Andrew and James, two old friends in their early thirties, had recently been declared redundant, each having received £10 000 in redundancy pay. James said that he felt like using the money on travel to see the world, but Andrew had seen a notice in the local newspaper, advertising the sale of bankrupt stock and suggested that the two of them go into business together. His further suggestion was that they should buy an old lorry he had seen for sale for £8000 by a second-hand motor vehicle-dealer and to travel from place to place in the North of England selling the bankrupt stock at a good mark-up. Andrew thought that they might be able to sell for £2.50 what had cost them £1.00.

An accountant would say that the estimated gross margin was 60 per cent, calculated as:

Gross profit × 100 / Sales = 1.50 × 100 / 2.50 = 60%

James allowed himself to be convinced that this was a marvellous idea; they bought the lorry for £8000 and on 1 April 2010 spent £12 000 on bankrupt stock. On 2 April, James fell off the back of the lorry, breaking an arm and a leg. Andrew visited him in hospital, told him not to worry; he would look after their joint venture and would only take 10 per cent of the profits for his trouble before sharing the proceeds of the venture equally between them. On 1 October, having spent the whole summer touring from place to place in the North of England, Andrew appeared on James' doorstep, James in the meantime having recovered the use of his limbs. Andrew took a wad of banknotes from his bag, informing James that this represented his share of the joint venture, which had just been wound up, and that James' share amounted to £12 960.

ACTIVITY 1.1

Try to answer the following two questions before reading on:

1 What was James' position in relation to that of Andrew in the summer of 2010?

2 If you were James, what would you now do?

Regarding the first question, James is clearly a provider of capital, as indeed is Andrew. The difference between them is that Andrew is an owner/manager, whereas James has been forced to take a passive role. Andrew is similar to a director of a limited company (holding shares therein) and James is similar to a shareholder that had entrusted his funds to the directors of such a company.

Regarding question 2, James finds himself in a curiously uninformed position. It looks as if the return in six months is £2960 on an initial investment of £10 000. The return looks very good – some 59 per cent per annum – much better than he could have got from a building society, particularly in the aftermath of the credit crisis; nevertheless, how does he know that Andrew has calculated his share properly or even whether he has deliberately cheated him? Let us assume that he now asks you for your advice on how Andrew has calculated the £12 960, mentioning that businesses usually prepare financial statements. (James has not been wasting his six months enforced rest. He has bought a book on accounting.)

Andrew is somewhat surprised when you appear on the scene with James, but after a lot of prevarication he produces a somewhat dog-eared piece of paper from his bag and shows you the financial statements that he has prepared. The financial statements are in the form of a simple receipts and payments account and contain the information in Case study 1.1, Part 2, which you should now review.

CASE STUDY 1.1

Andrew and James, Part 2

Andrew and James Joint Venture: 1 April to 30 September 2010

	£	£
Cash introduced	20 000	
Purchase of lorry		8 000
Purchase of bankrupt stock		12 000
Motor expenses		5 000
Other purchases		26 000
Sales	54 000	
Interest to John		200
Sale of lorry to Andrew	6 000	
	80 000	51 200
Balance		28 800
	80 000	80 000
Balance	28 800	
Less: 10% wage	2 880	
	25 920	
Half to Andrew	12 960	
Half to James	12 960	

ACTIVITY 1.2

On the basis of your review, make a list of the matters you would like to raise with Andrew on James' behalf.

The following are the principal points we believe you should raise with Andrew on James' behalf:

- Andrew has purchased the lorry from the business himself. How was the price calculated and what is he going to do with it anyway?
- What is the payment of interest of £200 to John for?
- Andrew has not calculated his wage on the profit but on the total cash on hand in the business.

  Assuming the other figures are all right the profit is calculated as follows:

	£	£
SALES		54 000
Purchase of bankrupt stock	12 000	
Other purchases	26 000	
COST OF SALES		38 000
GROSS PROFIT	(29.63%)	16 000
Motor expenses	5 000	
Interest to John	200	
Depreciation of lorry	2 000	
		7 200
Net profit		8 800

  On this basis Andrew's 'wage' should only be £880.

Doing calculations for yourself before you talk to managers (in this case – Andrew) gives you information that will enable you to get more information. You could ask Andrew why the profit is less than expected and this would force him to give a precise answer. We would say that 'information breeds information'.

- Remember that Andrew had said in March that they could expect a gross return of 60 per cent of sales. However, the gross profit percentage shown in the above statement is only 29.63 per cent, less than half of that expected (£32 400, 60 per cent of £54 000).
- The payments of £8000 for the lorry and £12 000 for the bankrupt stock are in order as James was present when the payments were made and he would therefore be prepared to accept them.
- You may wonder – as no doubt James would also – if there were any inventories at the end of the period and, in particular, if Andrew intends to sell the remaining inventories (if any), using the lorry he has purchased from the business.

Let us assume that you have discussed the above points with James in your capacity as professional adviser and that, armed with this information, you manage to elicit the further information from Andrew, shown in Part 3 of the Case study.

CASE STUDY 1.1

Andrew and James, Part 3

- The lorry had been used for six months and a reduction of £2000 seemed reasonable. ('Yes, but second-hand prices for that make and age of lorry are currently £7000, according to published information used by the motor vehicle trade; also has Andrew adjusted for vehicle licence fee and insurance paid in advance?') 'No', says Andrew, 'but they only amount to £800'.

Getting information about lorry prices in this way is a good example of obtaining reliable evidence from an independent source. Questioning whether the road tax and insurance has been adjusted is a good example of the professional accountant at work.

- Payment of interest to John was in respect of a loan of £4000 that John had made to the business because, after buying the lorry and bankrupt stock, there was no money left to pay the other expenses. The loan had been repaid on 30 September 2010. (You may decide to accept this, although at 10 per cent per annum in current circumstances this is somewhat high.)
- Andrew admits that the calculation of the wage at the end of the venture was a mistake. At this stage, of course, you may be somewhat concerned that Andrew may have made more unwitting mistakes.

Note that anyone who is interested in finding out if accounting and other information has been properly prepared, will wish to know if the person preparing it is competent.

- Andrew agrees that he had originally said that they could make a bigger profit but this was because the profit on the other purchases had been much lower. Also, the lorry had not been secure and he thinks there had been some theft of stock. 'Yes, but can you make an estimate of inventory losses?', asks James. 'Perhaps £4000', suggests Andrew. 'And what kind of margin did you get on the other purchases?', James persists. 'Well, I thought I could get about 50 per cent on cost, the way you are doing it, it would be 33 per cent on sales. The inventory losses were all of items bought after the bankrupt inventory had been sold.'

Andrew implies that gross margins have not met expectation because of differing sales mix (in that there have been sales at two differing rates of gross profit) and because of loss of assets. It would be normal for business people to take precautions to safeguard the assets of their organization and this we discuss in Chapters 7 and 8.

- Andrew says there was no inventory on hand at the end of the period, apart from some insignificant items which he disposed of in a closing-down sale. He says that he purchased the lorry so that he could calculate the amount due to each partner.

Following your discussions with Andrew and James, you decide to compare the revised expected gross profits with those obtained by Andrew. This calculation is done on the basis of what Andrew has told you so far:

There is an important matter of principle, regarding the belief in the honesty or integrity of management. It is not really possible to carry out an audit where there are serious doubts about management integrity and auditors will in practice take steps to form views about the honesty of people from whom they are obtaining information. ISA 200 – *overall objectives of the independent auditor and the conduct of an audit in accordance with international standards on auditing* suggests in paragraph A43 that auditors should adopt an attitude of professional scepticism in their work. This means being wary about assuming honesty and integrity of management and those charged with governance. We discuss this further in Chapter 2.

	£	£	£ Revised expected gross profit
Sales		54 000	
Purchases: bankrupt inventory	12 000		18 000 (150% of £12 000, 60% of £30 000)
Other	26 000		13 000 (50% of £26 000, 33% of £39 000)
Less: Inventory losses at cost	–4 000		–2 000 (50% of £4000, 33% of £6000)
Cost of sales		34 000	
Gross profit		20 000	29 000

At this stage you might suggest that £9000 seems to be unaccounted for. 'Well, I had to live', says Andrew, who clearly does not appreciate the difference between drawings and charges against profits. You explain that anything he had withdrawn for his own personal expenditure could not be regarded as a legitimate expense of the business he was running on behalf of Andrew and himself. You then ask him two related questions that are both good auditors' questions: 'How did you run the business?' and 'What kind of system did you have?' Andrew then says that he had a bag on the lorry and any takings went

CASE STUDY 1.1

Andrew and James, Part 4

Andrew and James Joint Venture: 1 April to 30 September 2010 (amended statement)

Sales		63 000	(£54 000 (Cash banked) + 9000)
Purchases			
Bankrupt stock	(12 000)		
Other (including stock losses)	(26 000)		
		(38 000)	
Gross profit (39.68%)		25 000	
Running expenses	4 200		(£5 000 – 800)
Depreciation of lorry	1 000		(£8 000 – £7 000)
Interest	200		
		5 400	
Net profit		19 600	
Shared as follows:			
Andrew: 10% of £19 600	1 960		
50% of (£19 600 – 1960)	8 820		
		10 780	
James:50% of (£19 600 – 1960)		8 820	
		19 600	
On this basis Andrew and James would be entitled to share in the £28 800 cash on hand as follows			
James: Original capital	10 000		
Share of the profit	8 820		
		18 820	
Andrew: Original capital	10 000		
Share of profit	10 780		
	20 780		
Drawings: – Cash	(9 000)		
Lorry under-valued	(1 000)		
Motor expenses	(800)		
		9 980	
		28 800	

into the bag; he took out of the bag anything he needed for meals and other personal expenditure and banked the rest from time to time. The £54 000 was what he had banked.

At this stage you believe you can prepare financial statements that better reflect what has really occurred. You would be unwise to suggest that the financial statements will be accurate, as much of the evidence you have collected is very subjective with a large element of estimation. In any event, your knowledge of accounting suggests that it is by nature judgemental and that the most that can be expected is a reasonable picture. The financial statements are set out in the final part of the Case study (Part 4).

This is a system, however bad it seems to be. It would have been better if Andrew had used a pre-numbered cash receipts book and had given receipts for all money received. A professional accountant might have made such a recommendation, coupled with the proposal that all sales proceeds be banked intact.

JUSTIFICATION OF AUDIT

In our discussion, you acted as professional advisor to James, a party interested in the way in which a business was being run on his behalf. You may have wondered if you were preparing financial statements or acting as independent auditor of them, as the skills needed for accounting and auditing are similar. The major distinction is that the auditor is expected to remain unbiased in relation to the financial statements, whereas an accountant becomes involved in the preparation of the figures, making it difficult to maintain a distance from them. You will see later in this book that many auditors do provide accounting services to companies and later we shall ask you to consider whether auditors should perform this dual function. At this stage, we shall merely ask you if you believe you had provided a valuable service to Andrew and James.

It is fairly obvious that you provided a valuable service to James, the interested party providing funds but not engaged in day-to-day management. Equally, we suggest that you have provided a valuable service to Andrew, the manager, as you have added value to the financial statements, making them more believable and providing a basis for decision making by Andrew and James and others. If you were to add your signature to the financial statements together with a brief opinion as to their validity, they might become even more valuable. Andrew and James might be able to use your opinion to persuade third parties to help them finance their business, or the Inspector of Taxes might be willing to accept them as the basis of determining taxable income.

If you have compiled the financial statements using information given to you and have not looked for evidence to prove its reliability, you might not wish to give an opinion, but merely state what you have done. We discuss this kind of engagement in Chapters 6 and 15.

One justification of audit must be, therefore, that, by your intervention, you have improved the value of the information in the financial statements. This so-called 'information hypothesis' suggests that auditors are required because the information subject to audit becomes more reliable as the result of audit and, because it is more reliable, it is more useful to decision makers.

Another reason put forward to justify audit is that the providers of resources cannot trust the managers to use the resources on their behalf and may suspect that they are diverted to the benefit of the managers. This is one of the basic ideas of *agency theory*, the main features and assumptions of which are summarized below.

We have illustrated the basic ideas in relation to the Andrew and James case.

Basic ideas of agency theory

- Both the owners (principals) of the organization and the managers (agents) employed to manage it on their behalf are regarded as people who try to maximize their own wealth. We saw in the case of Andrew and James that Andrew (who was both a principal in his own right and an agent as far as the other principal (James) was concerned) was not entirely open about how well the joint venture had performed.

- As a result James (the owner not involved in running the joint venture) clearly needed a monitoring mechanism in the form of a financial report. This is another assumption of agency theory, but the theory suggests too that agents are likely to favour the preparation of a financial report as the principals will otherwise be unwilling to believe that they are telling the truth. (Andrew did produce a report, albeit a somewhat inadequate one.)
- Different groups of rational individuals (we can regard both Andrew and James as being rational) have different information and this allows informed individuals to profit at other people's expense. Clearly, Andrew was well informed about the business and James (initially) was not.
- A further assumption of agency theory (and one of particular interest to us) is that agents will recognize that, for the owners to believe the report on their performance, which they (the managers) provide, the owners will wish to have the information verified by an independent party. (This was where you stepped in to advise James.) According to agency theory you would have to be independent of both Andrew and James if you were to perform the monitoring in a manner acceptable to third parties.
- Agency theory also suggests that the appointment of professional external auditors will be preferred as this is the most cost-effective of monitoring devices. (Audits are, of course, not cost-free and the assumption is that a professional auditor would be more efficient than anyone else.) When limited companies were first formed, it was common practice for shareholders or directors to act as auditors, but by the end of the nineteenth century professional auditors were being increasingly asked to perform the audit role, even before there was a legal requirement for audit.

An interesting article by Mills (1990) suggests that audits were effectively required by common law in medieval times in England.

Thus, under strict agency theory, external financial reports are regarded as reports to owners (partners or shareholders) and the external auditor is seen to act for and on their behalf. One of the major perceived beneficiaries of the audit, however, is the manager group itself.

A useful discussion of the three justifications discussed here is to be found in Wallace (1980).

We would mention at this stage a further justification for audit – that auditors can provide a degree of insurance to people relying upon the information subjected to audit. This is known as the *insurance hypothesis* because people who have lost as the result of reliance on the opinion given by the auditor may be able to recover damages from auditors, assuming negligence on their part. Bad management cannot normally be insured against (and a large number of failed companies get into difficulties because of bad management), but a successful damages claim against the auditor is effectively the equivalent of a successful claim against an insurance company. This may be seen as a further justification for the existence of the audit function.

ACTIVITY 1.3

Set out above are suggested reasons why audits might be demanded. Consider the following questions:

1 Assuming that you wished to invest in the shares of a limited company, would you accept that financial statements audited by a qualified auditor, a member of a recognized accounting body, would be more useful to you than unaudited statements?
2 Do you think that it is true that nobody can be trusted to act on other people's behalf, without other people looking over their shoulder?
3 Do you think that auditors should be held liable for all the losses incurred by shareholders as the result of a company collapse, assuming that the auditors have given their opinion that the going concern concept was appropriate for the preparation of the financial statements?

These are all good questions, although it may be difficult to answer them without qualification.

1 Financial statements audited by a qualified auditor would normally be regarded as being more reliable than unaudited statements. This is because the reader knows that this person possesses expertise and because they will be assumed to be independent, being a member of an accounting body that require their members to be unbiased in their professional duties.

We discuss independence in greater detail in Chapter 3.

2 You will probably have concluded that often people do not think only of themselves, but you may also know people who are selfish and do not consider other people. You may also have concluded that, because you do not know how people will behave, it will be advisable to appoint an auditor to report on the actions of managers. Of course, if the agency theorists are right and everyone acts in their own self-interest, there may be a danger that auditors may do the same and forget their professional duty to be unbiased in their work. If you have suggested this, you may have been influenced by the fact that auditors are often *de facto* appointed by the very managers on whom they are reporting. This is clearly a matter that needs further discussion and we look at this again in Chapter 3. Note here, however, that appointment of auditors is often a responsibility of the audit committee.

We discuss audit committees in Chapter 18.

3 Auditors often do become liable for substantial damages because of negligence claims. There is considerable discussion about this at the present time, some arguing that liability should be apportioned between auditors and managers, while others argue that auditors should be fully liable because they are appointed for the express purpose of reporting on the validity of financial statements. This is again an issue of considerable importance and we discuss it further in Chapter 19.

INTRODUCTION TO TRUTH AND FAIRNESS IN ACCOUNTING

Before you prepared the financial statements for the partnership, you did have some doubts as to whether you could prepare a set of financial statements that were accurate. What were the two basic reasons for this?

In the first place, you were concerned that there was not enough evidence to prove what Andrew was saying. In the second place, you knew from your reading that accounting cannot produce an 'accurate' answer because of the amount of judgement involved in the preparation of them and that the most that can be expected is a reasonable picture. Auditors would say that James had insufficient evidence to prove the assertions that Andrew was making about the financial statements.

You, of course, have prepared the financial statements, but on the basis of assertions made by Andrew.

ACTIVITY 1.4

Now identify three areas where judgement has been exercised in the preparation of the financial statements.

We suggest the following three areas:

1 The estimate of the drawings that Andrew had taken out of the business before banking the takings.
2 The 'value' of the lorry taken over by Andrew.
3 The estimate of inventory losses.

The estimates of drawings and inventory losses were only necessary, of course, because of the inadequacy of the system that Andrew used in running the business, but it is none the less true that estimates are often necessary in the preparation of financial statements. The accountant (who for many companies will be a professional accountant) engaged in the preparation of financial statements, often has to exercise judgement in determining whether estimates are valid. The auditor is similarly interested in forming views about accounting estimates, although we will find later in this book that the evidence to support the estimates will be persuasive rather than absolutely certain.

There is an International Standard on Auditing in the area, ISA 540 – *auditing accounting estimates, including fair value accounting estimates, and related disclosures*, and you should refer to this. We discuss audit evidence in greater depth in Chapter 6.

ACTIVITY 1.5

Suggest five instances where estimates are necessary in accounting and where judgement will have to be exercised.

Five instances (there are many others) are:

1 Useful lives of fixed assets in determining the depreciation charge.
2 Saleability or usability of inventories (in determining whether net realizable value is less than cost).

3 Collectability of trade receivables (in determining the size of the bad and doubtful debts provision).
4 The amount of profit to be taken up on construction contracts.
5 The estimates of fair values in accounting (These represent a particularly difficult area for auditors).

The consequence of this is that the most that can be expected from financial statements is that they give a reasonable picture of what they are designed to show. The question that we must ask ourselves is whether there are areas where we would expect accuracy in financial statements. What do you think? You may use Andrew and James or give any other examples in your reply.

The answer, of course, is that we would always strive to be as accurate as possible. Companies will be very keen to ensure that trade receivables are properly recorded, that inventories have been accurately counted, that all trade payables and non-current assets owned have been completely and accurately determined. In the case of Andrew and James, the lorry purchase (£8000) should be recorded at that amount and not at £7500. You will recognize that these examples are all bookkeeping examples and you will know by now that, although accurate records are a prerequisite of proper financial statements, accounting is much more than bookkeeping and is the means to provide the reasonable or true and fair view in the financial statements.

We used the term 'reasonable' in relation to the financial statements prepared above, but we wish to add the words 'in the circumstances', reflecting the fact that the evidential matter available to prove the figures was very flimsy in this particular case. However, the case is an extreme example and one could argue that any set of financial statements are 'reasonable (or fair) in the circumstances of the organization', with the added proviso that it depends on viewpoint. You have, no doubt, heard the story of the three blind men who were led up to an elephant and asked to say what it was. The first, who was standing by its side felt the broad expanse of its hide and suggested that it was a wall. The second, standing by its tail, said that it was a piece of rope. The third, who was standing by the trunk, suggested that it was a hose-pipe.

Each of the blind men gave a truthful account of their perceptions of the elephant from their own particular standpoints. They collected the facts they had at their disposal, interpreted them and gave an honestly held opinion as to the nature of the elephant. You might well argue that they would have given a different answer if they had been better informed (that is, had more facts at their disposal) but that is a feature of life of many fields of human activity, including that of business and accounting. The story can, perhaps, help you to recognize that your perception of the truth, that is your opinion or belief about a set of circumstances, may depend:

- upon viewpoint; and
- upon the amount of information that is made available to you.

This book is not, of course, about elephants (despite our hope that you will show an elephantine ability not to forget its contents); it is about auditing and about the auditor's duty in relation to financial and other information used by others. But the story of the blind men's reports on the elephant is intended to help you to understand the important accounting and auditing concept of the *true and fair view*. The words 'true and fair view' have never been defined in law, but we would like you to explain the concept in simple terms.

ACTIVITY 1.6

Imagine that a young relative has picked up a textbook of yours, has come across the term 'true and fair view' and has asked you what it means in practical terms.

Do not imagine that truth and fairness in accounting is an easy matter. In Chapter 14 we introduce you to some procedures that auditors carry out at the end of the audit process. We shall see that those final procedures are vital to forming an opinion on truth and fairness.

If you have managed to define the 'true and fair view' you have succeeded where many have failed. We did not, of course, expect you to come up with a definition, but we do think you might have mentioned the following points:

- Financial statements should not mislead the reader. If the company is experiencing liquidity problems, we would expect the financial statements to show this. If the company finances its non-current assets by leasing rather than buying we would expect the reader to be informed. If the company is expanding or declining we would expect the financial statements to reflect the circumstances.
- Financial statements need to have a degree of accuracy built into them. The reader has a right to expect that the sales are genuine and have been completely and accurately recorded. Even here, however, there are degrees of accuracy. If the total sales figure recorded in the financial statements is £10 000 000, it is unlikely that an omitted sale of £1000 would cause the reader to be misled.
- In many instances the profit and loss account, balance sheet and cash flow statements cannot give a true and fair view on their own and must be supplemented by notes. For instance, financial statements that were not accompanied by a statement of accounting policies adopted in their preparation would not normally be deemed to give a true and fair view. The reader needs to know, for instance, whether the financial statements contain an element of profit on construction contracts not yet complete and on what basis profit has been taken up. Likewise the true and fair view will only be obtained if the date of repayment of a long-term borrowing is stated in the financial statements. Clearly, if a loan is repayable in two years' time rather than ten years, knowledge of this fact gives you a different view of the liquidity of the organization.
- One important aspect of financial statements that give a true and fair view, particularly if they bear an opinion of an independent and competent auditor, is that they can be relied upon because they give a reasonable view of the financial affairs and results of the business.

One final point is that auditors try to collect sufficient appropriate evidence to prove that the financial statements are true and fair before giving their own opinion. A major risk for auditors is that they may give an inappropriate opinion because they have failed to identify business risks and to collect the evidence to reduce the risk of giving an opinion. We adopt a risk-based approach to audit in this book and we want you to think about risk at the outset.

BASIC AUDIT FRAMEWORK

In our description and discussion of the Andrew and James case, we did not try to establish a framework for conducting an audit. The protagonists tended to act in a piecemeal sort of way and had obviously not planned their work at all. We are still at an early stage of explaining the audit process but we do think that a basic framework of audit will be useful to you. Here is a company, Gilsland Electronics Limited, that wishes to change its auditors. Its name suggests that it is engaged in the electronics industry but initially the auditor will not know much about how the company operates or about its management. Table 1.1 shows the various stages, together with a brief explanation of each.

In Chapter 4 we shall find that certain procedures have to be performed *before* the appointment is accepted, including contacting the previous auditor to see if there are any professional reasons why we should not accept the appointment.

The first thing that you will notice perhaps is that the auditor splits the audit year into four stages. Sometimes these stages will all be merged but in larger companies they will take place at particular times in the year. We assume that Gilsland is large enough for the auditor to plan work at different times of the year.

We discuss all these matters in greater detail in the following chapters, but we have given you this basic framework here to give you a feel for the way that auditors approach the audit process.

SOME INITIAL IDEAS ON AN EXTENDED ROLE FOR AUDIT

When we use the words 'role of audit' we mean what the task or function of audit is supposed to be. The basic question is: 'Why do people think that auditors should be appointed?' Now you may feel that we have already answered this question to some extent in this chapter, but so far we have concentrated on audit as a means to prove that information prepared by organizations can be relied upon. Now we want to consider whether an audit would be seen to be necessary in proving that organizations are behaving in a way desired by people who are affected by them. We set out below a number of different organizations, all of which have an important impact on people. In each case, explain why an audit might be desired and suggest broad objectives of the auditor. To show you what we mean we set out a few ideas concerning the local authority case.

- A local authority providing services to people living in the area. The principal sources of funds used by local authorities in the provision of their services are local taxpayers, central government and borrowing. Because local authorities use public funds there is a general belief that these funds should be used carefully, that is, not wastefully but efficiently and effectively in such a way that value for money expended is obtained. Central governments often impose a duty upon auditors to ensure that local authorities do obtain value for money. Similarly, there may be requirements that auditors should ensure, among other things, that the activities of local authorities are within the law.

TABLE 1.1 The auditor's year Gilsland Electronics Limited

Date	Event	Comments
Preliminary stages		
30 March 2010	Firm asked to carry out work.	Sometimes a company will choose an audit firm because of recommendation from business contacts, sometimes as a result of a selection process involving a number of firms. Whatever the process, reputation of the firm will be important.
3 April 2010	Preliminary meeting to discuss terms of reference, forming the basis for the letter of engagement sent by auditor firm to Gilsland.	Assuming that the audit firm accepts the audit assignment, it is important that both the company and auditors are aware of their respective responsibilities. This is the role of the letter of engagement, which explains, among other things, the responsibilities of the directors for preparing financial statements and the duties of the auditors.
24 to 28 April 2010	Visit to company to familiarize with industry and company. Meet management. Prepare first (global) plan and fee estimate. Make initial assessment of areas of potential risk.	We suggested above that, initially, the auditors would know little more than the apparent fact that the company is in the electronics industry. At this stage the auditors will talk to management, form a view on their integrity and competence and find out the nature of the business and the manner in which it is managed. This stage might come prior to the agreement to act as auditors as normally they would be interested in determining the integrity and competence of management before formal acceptance. The electronics industry is one where technology changes quickly and this might give rise to certain inherent risks.
2 May 2010	Write to company confirming fee estimate and proposed dates for carrying out interim and final examinations. If necessary, issue memorandum assessing the first matters that need to be brought to the attention of management.	Having found out more about the company the auditors would be aware of potential problems (for instance, whether it is difficult to value inventories accurately) and the amount of work that they would feel to be necessary. If there are problems (for instance, standard costs used to value inventories are out of date) the auditors will often raise the matter in a formal letter to management.
Systems work and transactions testing		
3 weeks from 9 October 2010	Interim examination of Gilsland's accounting and internal control systems. Work directed towards systems and transactions processed by systems.	Management is responsible for putting in accounting and internal control systems to enable them to manage the company properly and to ensure within reason that the accounting records are accurate. You will remember that Andrew's system for controlling the business was far from satisfactory. Clearly, the auditors will be very interested in how well the accounting and control systems work. The interim examination

TABLE 1.1 *(Continued)*

Date	Event	Comments
		will be devoted to ensuring that the systems are satisfactory and that the transactions processed and the balances held by them are accurate. If they are adequate then the auditors will be able to rely on those systems and may in consequence be able to reduce the amount of detailed work they do on transactions and balances.
15 November 2010	Issue memorandum on internal control and other matters of interest to management and those charged with governance (Management Letter). This memorandum may be delayed until after the final audit, although if there are serious weaknesses in internal control, it would be wise to send a memorandum to the client without delay.	We noted above a preliminary letter to management and those charged with governance might be desirable if there were immediate problems causing concern. Similarly, after the auditors have spent some time looking at systems, transactions and balances in some detail, they may well find more matters requiring client attention. If, for instance, the auditors found that not all sales were being recorded, this would be a matter not only of concern to them as auditors but also to management and those charged with governance
	Those charged with governance are 'The person(s) . . . with responsibility for overseeing the strategic direction of the entity and obligations related to the accountability of the entity.' See Glossary of Terms. They include independent directors forming the audit committee. We discuss the role of 'those charged with governance' and of the audit committee in various parts of this book, but principally in Chapter 18.	
Preparation for final work		
4 and 5 December 2010	Review of company arrangements for year-end inventory counts and preparation of financial statements; discuss known problems and new financial reporting standards.	At this stage the auditors may be aware that there are some things that could go wrong (for instance, how far advanced is management in calculating the new standard costs). They would want to find out if the company systems for counting inventories are satisfactory (May we see your inventory count instructions please?) and inform management of new accounting standards that they should apply.
31 December 2010	Attend count of inventories, observe company procedures, make test counts and write inventory count memorandum for working papers.	This is a useful bit of evidence gathering to satisfy yourself that an important figure in the financial statements is properly stated. The auditors will keep details of test counts made for comparing later with the company inventory records. The memorandum is written evidence for the audit files to show the count of inventories has been properly performed.

TABLE 1.1 *(Continued)*

Date	Event	Comments
Final work		
3 weeks from 12 March 2011	Perform analytical review of draft financial statements and verification procedures on assets and liabilities, including post balance sheet events work.	At this stage the auditors will try to prove that the various balance sheet and profit and loss account figures have been properly calculated. Are, for instance, the inventories and trade receivables and purchases and sales genuine and accurate and complete? We saw too in the Andrew and James case that analytical reviews can be very useful in proving whether the figures make sense in the light of what the auditors know about the company. The reference to post-balance sheet work is because many events can occur after the balance sheet date that help to prove the validity of the financial statements. For instance, the fact that a trade receivable has been paid after the balance sheet date will help to prove the collectability of trade receivables. We discuss the meaning of 'genuine, accurate and complete in Chapter 6. See Table 6.2 on page 219.
2 April 2011	Review working papers, discuss results of audit with management, including suggested amendments to the financial statements, obtain a management representations letter, check that the accounting records are in agreement with the financial statements. Directors sign financial statements. Finally, issue audit report.	At this stage the auditors bring together the results of all the work they have done. The big question at this stage is: Do the financial statements taken together give a true and fair view of the results and position of the company? There are two important steps taken by management at this stage: 1 They confirm to the auditors in writing that representations made by them to the auditors on important matters are still valid, for instance, that they have made available to the auditors all the books and records of the company and that in their view the company will continue as a going concern in the foreseeable future. 2 They sign the financial statements, thus giving their formal approval to them. You will remember that Andrew made many representations or assertions to James about the business and its financial statements. James might have got Andrew to sign the amended financial statements to signify his agreement. Finally, the auditors issue their formal report on the truth and fairness of the financial statements

TABLE 1.1 *(Continued)*

Date	Event	Comments
2 May 2011	Send note of charges for audit and other professional work to the company	Often the auditors will ask for payments on account of fees as the work progresses, but this is the point where the final fee note is rendered. The fees will, of course, be discussed with management before the formal note is issued.

ACTIVITY 1.7

Now consider a possible role for audit in these cases:

- A university providing educational services to students.
- Water companies supplying water to private customers.
- A hospital serving people in the surrounding area.
- A nuclear power station feeding electricity into the national grid.
- A charity collecting from the public to provide funds to specified good causes.

There is considerable debate about the groups to whom organizations should be accountable. Some take the narrow view that the market should be supreme, whereas at the other end of the spectrum are those who believe that organizations are accountable to many disparate groups, including society nationally and internationally. (Briloff (1986) calls these disparate groups 'publics'.)

In answering a question like this, you need to consider the objectives of each organization named and to think about the needs of the people affected by its activities.

- Most universities use public funds for the provision of educational services, and a very important 'public' in their case is the student body, particularly as students or their parents are often asked to contribute towards their fees. Students have a very real interest in ensuring that the standards of the educational services provided are of good quality. Auditors might be asked to carry out teaching quality audits, both on behalf of their providers of funds and their main customer, the student. Bodies such as the Quality Assurance Agency in the UK, which is concerned with the quality of education, will also be an important public.
- Water companies are required by law in many countries to supply water of a defined quality. The main reason for this is to ensure that the health of consumers of water is not endangered. One possible way of ensuring quality of water would be to require a quality audit by a person or persons independent of the water company.
- A hospital is another example of an organization using public funds and for this reason value for money (VFM) audits are a feature of auditing in the National Health Service in the UK. Apart from this, however, standards of health care are a real concern to doctors who send their patients to hospitals for treatment and, of course, to the patients themselves. It is not

uncommon for medical audits to be carried out to ensure that medical treatments are or have been appropriate.

In April 1986, a nuclear reactor at Chernobyl in the Ukraine exploded, causing widespread fallout over many countries.

- The safety of a nuclear power station is of considerable concern to those living in the immediate vicinity and, as Chernobyl showed, to a wide number of people further afield. One response to a major threat of this nature is the requirement for a safety audit to be carried out to ensure that the community is protected. In this case we might also use the term 'environment audit'.
- Charities have considerable tax advantages in many countries, but only when their activities are for charitable purposes as defined by law. In addition, the public making donations to the charity will have an interest in ensuring that the money collected goes to the intended good cause and that a disproportionate amount is not absorbed by administration expenses. In the UK there are provisions in the Charities Act 2006 that allow charities to be subject to audit to ensure that funds are not wasted and that they are used for intended purposes.

These examples show that audit is being used for purposes far removed from merely confirming that financial statements give a true and fair view. We shall refer to this again when we discuss the Audit Society in Chapter 20, but a useful critical text that discusses the increasingly wide arena in which audit plays a role is *The Audit Explosion* by Michael Power, published in 1994. We might mention at this point that the definition of special audits would need to be drafted in different terms from the definition of an audit of financial and other information set out on page 23.

ASSURANCE SERVICES

This is a good point to introduce you to the term 'assurance services' as applied to the many different kinds of work performed by auditors, culminating in the expression of an opinion. The audit of financial statements is an assurance service, as the opinion on their truth and fairness is itself an assurance regarding the quality of the statements. The auditor carrying out work on any of the special organizations discussed in the above section will provide an assurance for the benefit of their users, although the assurance may not necessarily be couched in true and fair view terms.

Assurance services are usually held to mean a broad set of services designed to improve the quality of information. The kinds of services that auditors are increasingly providing for companies are business risk assessments, measuring business performance against predetermined criteria, assessments of the reliability of information and other systems and assessments of the viability of e-commerce and the particular risks facing companies engaged in this new activity. The auditor is in a particularly good position to provide such services, but we shall also take a look at the potential threats to independence when auditors are engaged in activities for the particular benefit of management. In Chapter 15 we discuss assurance services in some detail and, in particular draw your attention to the opinions or assurances that auditors can give in respect of different kinds of assurance services. We shall also discuss, among other things, International Standards on Assurance Engagements (ISAEs)

As you are no doubt aware, assurance services are now being examined in auditing examination papers. For instance, Paper P7 of the Chartered Association of Certified Accountants, which is sat by students worldwide, is named 'Advanced Audit and Assurance', and the auditing paper at the professional stage of the Institute of Chartered Accountants in England and Wales is titled: 'Audit and Assurance'.

SUMMARY OF PRINCIPLES

The simple example of Andrew and James reveals that the following matters seem to be important:

- For Andrew and James (two users of accounting information), the preparation of reliable financial statements was a matter of great importance. 'Reliable' means, of course, being able to rely on the financial statements and in our discussion above we suggested that this is one of the aspects of truth and fairness in financial statements.
- You carried out an investigation of the business as reflected in the financial statements on behalf of James (and perhaps to the benefit of Andrew also). In fact, you carried out an *audit*, using a number of useful techniques:
  1. The review of financial statements to see if they made sense in the light of things you knew about – in the process we made simple use of the accounting technique of ratio analysis (expected and actual gross profit percentage).
  2. Enquiry as to the system that Andrew used in running the business – not a good system but, nevertheless, a system.
  3. Calculation of figures before discussing the financial statements with Andrew so you could talk as an informed person to him. Andrew was initially much better informed than James himself.
  4. The use of information from a source, independent of the person running the business, to arrive at a better picture of the 'value' of the lorry.
  5. The use of actual personal experience in relation to the purchase of lorry and bankrupt inventory – James knew this had happened as he had seen it with his own eyes and he was able to tell you about this.

  There are *two* important matters that should be emphasized at this point:

  (i) It would seem that the auditor has to behave in a competent manner if a successful audit is to be carried out.

  (ii) An audit is clearly a *search for evidence* to arrive at what the auditor perceives to be the truth.
- In carrying out this investigation we have suggested that an attitude of professional scepticism should be adopted, rather than assuming that management running the organization possess integrity. You will

remember, however, from our brief discussion of agency theory that it is an open question as to whether people always act in their own self-interest.

- Generally speaking, it is not possible for the provider of funds to a business to carry out an audit of the type that you carried out. Normally, shareholders and other users are not competent to do this or would not be allowed to do so, even though, as we have seen, in the early history of limited companies, shareholders and directors did carry out audits. Imagine, however, how impossible it would be for an ordinary shareholder of a large corporation to investigate (that is, audit) the financial statements.

Do not assume that business people are engaged in fraudulent activity (a common student misapprehension in the experience of the authors). There are probably far more incompetent people in the business world than swindlers.

- However, it does seem that there may be doubts as to whether it is wise to rely on financial statements that have not been audited. We say that unaudited financial statements lack sufficient credibility to form a reliable basis for decision making. We noted that Andrew had made a number of false assumptions and errors when drawing up the original receipts and payments account. We introduced you to the information hypothesis which supports the view that audit is required because audited information is more useful to the reader. In this connection it is worth mentioning that sole traders and partnerships are not required to have an audit in most parts of the world, but their financial statements may nevertheless be audited because such bodies as the tax authorities and banks may ask for an audit to take place. Banks, of course, often ask for personal guarantees from proprietors and directors as well.
- A person who can add credibility to the financial statements is clearly not someone like Andrew, who was too closely involved in the management process. Perhaps, it is not even James, who, although not involved in management, does have a close interest. An inspector of taxes, for instance, would probably not be happy to accept James as a person independent of the business and would prefer financial statements that had received the seal of approval from a properly qualified and independent person. Only a person entirely independent of the management of an organization and not financially involved with it can add the desired credibility to the financial statements. We noted in this respect that this was one of the prime ideas of agency theory, although we did query whether auditors might be influenced by self-interest, thus reducing their independence.
- One matter to note here is that we felt we lacked enough evidence to prove that the financial statements of Andrew and James gave a true and fair view. It seems that uncertainty may be, on occasion, an important matter, but clearly lack of evidence makes it more risky for those (managers and auditors) who are required to state whether financial statements give a true and fair view. On this question of risk we did note that auditors are often faced with considerable damages as the result of negligent work and that users of financial statements can use the auditor as an insurer of an otherwise uninsurable risk.

We shall be discussing the above principles in greater depth in later chapters in the book, but we are now in a position to suggest a definition of auditing, which will prove useful in our subsequent discussions.

DEFINITION OF AN AUDIT OF FINANCIAL AND OTHER INFORMATION

> An audit is an investigation or a search for evidence to enable reasonable assurance to be given on the truth and fairness of financial and other information by a person or persons independent of the preparer and persons likely to gain directly from the use of the information, and the issue of a report on that information with the intention of increasing its credibility and therefore its usefulness.

We have referred to reasonable assurance in the above definition, because it is not normally possible for the auditor to give absolute assurance because of the uncertainties associated with accounting. When we come to discuss assurance engagements in Chapter 15 we shall see that in many engagements it is not possible to give reasonable assurance but only a limited form of assurance. It is important for you to recognize that auditors do not give guarantees that the financial information is true and fair, nor do they give assurance as to future viability of the organization nor the efficiency or effectiveness with which management has conducted its affairs.

We have already seen that truth and fairness has never been defined, but International Financial Reporting Standards, including International Accounting Standards (IFRs and IASs), are being developed by the International Accounting Standards Board (IASB) to achieve:

> high quality, transparent and comparable information in financial statements and other financial reporting to help participants in the various capital markets of the world and other users of the information to make economic decisions

(see paragraph 6 of the Preface to IFRSs). In other words they are designed to achieve truth and fairness in financial reporting and to encourage comparable standards throughout the world.

THE AUDITORS' CODE: THE FUNDAMENTAL PRINCIPLES OF INDEPENDENT AUDITING

We set out in Table 1.2 the Nine Fundamental Principles of Independent Auditing developed by the Auditing Practices Board (APB) and published in February 1996, in its publication: *The Audit Agenda: Next Steps*. These are now in Appendix 2 to Scope and Authority of Pronouncements (revised) issued by APB in 2009. We shall place these principles into the context of auditing postulates and concepts in Chapter 2 and refer to them from time to time throughout this book.

We discuss the role of APB in detail in Chapters 4 and 20.

TABLE 1.2 The Auditors' Code

Principle	APB comment	Author comment
1. Accountability	Auditors act in the interests of primary stakeholders, whilst having regard to the wider public interest. The identity of primary stakeholders is determined by reference to the statute or agreement requiring an audit: in the case of companies the primary stakeholder is the general body of shareholders.	Note the reference to the wider public interest and also to 'stakeholders', implying that there are interested parties other than shareholders. We shall discuss this matter in greater detail when we consider Auditor Liability in Chapter 19.
2. Integrity	Auditors act with integrity, fulfilling their responsibilities with honesty, fairness, candour, courage and confidentiality. Confidential information obtained in the course of the audit is disclosed only when required in the public interest, or by operation of law.	This provides an ethical dimension. Later we shall discuss specific areas where auditors are required by law to report to regulators.
3. Objectivity and Independence	Auditors are objective and provide impartial opinions unaffected by bias, prejudice, compromise and conflicts of interest. Auditors are also independent; this requires them to be free from situations and relationships which would make it probable that a reasonable and informed third party would conclude that the auditors' objectivity either is impaired or could be impaired.	We discuss independence principally in Chapter 3.
4. Competence	Auditors act with professional skill, derived from their qualification, training and practical experience. This demands an understanding of financial reporting and business issues, together with expertise in accumulating and assessing the evidence necessary to form an opinion.	Note the emphasis on financial reporting and business issues and on the accumulation and assessment of evidence. We shall discuss audit evidence in Chapter 6.
5. Rigour	Auditors approach their work with thoroughness and with an attitude of professional scepticism. They assess critically the information and explanations obtained in the course of their work and such additional evidence as they consider necessary for the purposes of their audit.	The idea of 'professional scepticism' is an interesting one and one that we will find repeated in the ISAs. It means adopting a questioning attitude at all times during the audit.
6. Judgement	Auditors apply professional judgment taking account of materiality in the context of the matters on which they are reporting.	The ability to exercise judgment is a very intangible quality and we shall discuss it in relation to risk assessment at greater length in Chapter 5.

TABLE 1.2 *(Continued)*

Principle	APB comment	Author comment
7. Clear, complete and effective communication	Auditors' reports contain clear expressions of opinion and set out information necessary for a proper understanding of that opinion. Auditors communicate audit matters of governance interest arising from the audit of financial statements with those charged with governance of an entity.	We shall discuss audit reporting in Chapter 16 and the question of reporting in the public interest when we introduce you to fraud and illegal acts in Chapter 17. We discuss corporate governance in Chapter 18.
8. Association	Auditors allow their reports to be included in documents containing other information only if they consider that the additional information is not in conflict with the matters covered by their report and they have no cause to believe it to be misleading.	This refers to the fact that most company reporting packages contain elements to which the audit report is not specifically directed. Two examples in the UK and Ireland are the Directors' Report and the Chairman' s Report. The auditor does have a duty to ensure that there is no conflict between the information contained in reports such as those mentioned and the financial statements. ISA 720 – *The auditor's responsibilities relating to other information in documents containing audited financial statements*, deals with this matter. We discuss audit reporting in Chapter 16.
9. Providing value	Auditors add to the reliability and quality of financial reporting; they provide to directors and officers constructive observations arising from the audit process; and thereby contribute to the effective operation of business, capital markets and the public sector.	A basic principle of auditing is that it enables external user groups to place greater reliance on the financial statements and that auditors are in an excellent position to give advice to internal users, thereby increasing management effectiveness.

Summary

This chapter has introduced you to a simple audit situation and has suggested a number of important ideas about auditing, including possible extensions of auditing. We have also drawn the recent scandals affecting the accounting and auditing profession to your attention. The principles highlighted in the chapter, including those listed in the Auditors' Code, will be discussed more formally later. Similarly we discuss later the potential impact of the recent scandals on the way that auditors conduct their work and on the way in which the profession may be regulated.

You should now try to answer the self-examination questions at the end of the chapter. When you are doing this try to imagine what a sensible and logical thinking person would suggest. Auditing often needs more than the exercise of simple common sense; it requires the exercise of reason and, in many cases, specialized knowledge, but common sense does help. It is not sufficient merely to make a guess; in each case you should justify your answer. When you have made a note of your own answers, check them against the suggested solutions on the website: www.cengage.co.uk/graymanson5. If any of your answers are different, make careful note of the explanation given and re-read the appropriate part of the chapter to make sure that you understand where you went wrong.

As we indicated in the Preface, some of the solutions are only available to tutors.

Key points of the chapter

- Auditing has become headline news after recent corporate scandals and the competence and independence of auditors have been questioned and focused attention on the purpose of audit and the way in which companies are managed.
- Important auditing issues are considered through the Andrew and James case: (a) distinction between the position of manager and of owner not involved in management; (b) audit as a search for evidence; (c) the use of simple procedures to test management assertions; (d) idea that information breeds information; (e) importance of management integrity; (f) professional scepticism; (g) importance of accurate bookkeeping; (h) use of information from independent sources; and (i) personal experience as a source of evidence.
- Three justifications of audit : (a) the information hypothesis; (b) agency theory; (c) the insurance hypothesis.
- Difficulties in proving the accuracy of financial statements include: (a) insufficient evidence; (b) judgement in the preparation of financial statements.
- Truth and fairness is not easily defined but we expect financial statements: (a) not to mislead the reader; (b) to have a degree of accuracy built into them; (c) to be supplemented by explanatory notes; (d) to give a reasonable view of financial affairs and results; (e) to be proved to be true and fair (or not) on the basis of sufficient appropriate audit evidence.
- Audit is an assurance engagement, but some assurance engagements can only support limited assurance.
- The typical basic framework for a larger audit assignment: (a) preliminary stages; (b) systems work and transactions testing; (c) preparation for final work; (d) final work.
- Audit may have specific roles in relation to many different organizations.
- 'Assurance services' are usually held to mean a broad set of services designed to improve the quality of information. Auditors are in a good position to provide these services, but there may be a threat to independence.
- Important issues are: (a) users value reliable financial statements; (b) auditors must be competent and independent; (c) audit is a search for evidence; (d) auditors should adopt an attitude of professional scepticism.
- An audit is an investigation or a search for evidence to enable reasonable assurance to be given on the truth and fairness of financial and other information by a person or persons independent of the preparer and persons likely to gain directly from the use of the information, and the issue of a report on that information with the intention of increasing its credibility and therefore its usefulness.
- The Auditors' Code comprises principles of Accountability, Integrity, Objectivity and Independence, Competence, Rigour, Judgement, Clear, complete and effective communication, Association, and Providing value.

References

Auditing Practices Board (1996) *The Audit Agenda: Next Steps*, APB, February.

Auditing Practices Board (2009) 'Scope and Authority of Pronouncements (revised)', APB, October.

Briloff, A.J. (1986) 'Corporate Governance and Accountability: Whose Responsibility', Unpublished paper presented at the University of Connecticut, Storrs, Connecticut, April.

Mills, P.A. (1990) 'Agency, Auditing and the Unregulated Environment: Some Further Historical Evidence', *Accounting, Auditing, & Accountability Journal*, 3(1): 54–66.

Power, M. (1994) *The Audit Explosion*, London: Demos.

Wallace, W. (1980) 'The Economic Role of the Audit in Free and Regulated Markets', teaching tool developed through the support of Touche Ross and Co.

Further reading

Some useful introductory articles on auditing which you may read to support your studies in this chapter are:

Beattie, V., Fearnley, S. and Brandt, R. (2001) *Behind Closed Doors: What Company Audit is Really About*, Basingstoke and New York: Palgrave.

Benston, G.J. (1985) 'The Market for Public Accounting Services: Demand, Supply and Regulation', *Journal of Accounting and Public Policy*, 4: 33–79.

Flint, D. (1971) 'The Role of the Auditor in Modern Society: An Exploratory Essay', *Accounting and Business Research*, Autumn: 287–93.

Flint, D. (1988) *Philosophy and Principles of Auditing: An Introduction*, Basingstoke: Macmillan Education Ltd.

Sikka, P. (2004) 'Some Questions About the Governance of Auditing Firms', *International Journal of Disclosure and Governance*, Vol. 1(2): March, 186–200.

Hatherly, D.J. (1999) 'The Future of Auditing: The Debate in the UK', *European Accounting Review*, 8, 1: 51–65.

Maltby, J. (1999) 'A Sort of Guide, Philosopher and Friend: The Rise of the Professional Auditor in Britain', *Accounting, Business & Financial History*, Vol. 9, No.1, pp.29–50.

You may also find the following publications of some interest:

Power, M. (1994), *The Audit Explosion*, Demos, London

Wallace, W.A. (2004), The Economic Role of the Audit in Free and Regulated Markets: A Look Back and a Look Forward, *Research in Accounting Regulation*, Vol.17, pp.267–298.

Relevant ISAs are:

- ISA 200 – Overall objectives of the independent auditor and the conduct of an audit in accordance with international standards on auditing.
- ISA 540 – Auditing accounting estimates, including fair value accounting estimates, and related disclosures.
- ISA 720 – The auditor's responsibilities relating to other information in documents containing audited financial statements.

Self-assessment questions (solutions available to students)

1.1 Which of the following people do you think would be suitable to be the auditor of a limited company in your local town?

(a) The chief accountant of the company, a member of ACCA.

(b) A shareholder owning 10 per cent of the ordinary shares.

(c) A shareholder owning 1 per cent of the ordinary shares.

(d) A member of ICAS, who is employed by a local Building Society.

(e) A member of ICAEW, a partner in a firm of Chartered Accountants.

(f) The sales director of the company.

(g) A German Wirtschaftsprüfer (a Wirtschaftsprüfer is empowered by German law to audit, among other things, public limited companies in Germany).

1.2 Which of the following people do you think would wish to be certain that the financial statements of a major public company had been properly prepared?

(a) The ordinary shareholders.

(b) The employees.

(c) People thinking of buying shares in the company.

(d) The Inspector of Taxes responsible for the tax affairs of the company.

(e) A member of the public.

(f) A supplier of goods to the company.

(g) The government

(h) The council of the local Stock Exchange.

1.3 If Andrew and James in our simple case had said that motor expenses amounted to £4000, suggest:

(a) What kinds of expenditure would probably be included in the heading 'motor expenses'.

(b) How you would satisfy yourself that the amount of each expenditure heading was reasonably accurate.

1.4 Why do you consider that audit might be seen to be necessary in the case of an engineering company whose employees operate dangerous machinery? Suggest appropriate audit objectives, but do not restrict yourself just to financial audit.

Self-assessment questions (solutions available to tutors)

1.5 Why do you think that the auditors will need a letter from management saying that they have provided them with all the books and records of the company? Try to think of a scenario where management might try to understate cash receipts for their own benefit.

1.6 We have not discussed this at length yet but can you at this stage suggest what benefits society should derive from a competent, independent and effective audit function?

1.7 Suggest why auditors might be in a good position to provide a service giving assurance on the effectiveness of the company's information and control system. Take a look at Table 1.1 while you are considering this matter.

1.8 WorldCom tried to maintain profit levels by treating revenue costs (over $3.8 billion) as capital expenditure. Explain what the impact would be if revenue costs (such as repairs to plant and machinery) were to be treated as capital assets. What do you think the auditor should have done to discover such malpractice?

Solutions available to students and Solutions available to tutors

These can be found on the website in the student/lecturer section at: www.cengage.co.uk/graymanson5.

Topics for class discussion without solutions

1.9 The Andrew and James case study is a good introduction to the principles of auditing. Discuss.

1.10 The Auditors' Code shows that auditing is a complex activity. Discuss.

2

An overview of the postulates and concepts of auditing

LEARNING OBJECTIVES

After studying this chapter you should be able to:

- **Explain how auditing theory, concepts and principles underpin auditing practice.**
- **Identify the basic postulates of auditing and explain why they are important.**
- **Define the auditing concepts under the general headings of credibility of the auditor, process of audit, communication by the auditor and performance of the auditor's work.**
- **Explain the implications of truth and fairness in relation to financial statements and the work of the auditor.**
- **Define the audit expectations gap and identify its components.**
- **Understand that the regulatory framework of auditing provides the criteria by which audits are conducted and encompasses the concepts of auditing.**
- **Recognize how organizations attempt to control their internal environment in the context of external influences.**

Learning objectives, 29
The importance of theory and concepts in underpinning auditing practice, 30
The postulates of auditing, 32
The concepts of auditing: credibility, process, communication, performance, 33
Audit quality, 48
Introduction to the audit expectations gap, 50
The layers of regulation and control, 52
Summary, 57
Key points of the chapter, 57
References, 58
Further reading, 58
Self-assessment questions (solutions available to students), 58
Self-assessment questions (solutions available to tutors), 58
Topics for class discussion without solutions, 59

THE IMPORTANCE OF THEORY AND CONCEPTS IN UNDERPINNING AUDITING PRACTICE

Auditors are on the whole very practical people and those members of the auditing profession, engaged in independent public accountancy, even go so far as to call themselves practitioners. There is, of course, a danger that some practitioners will believe that they do not need a philosophy or set of unifying theories that explain what they do or should do, and that they are problem solvers seeking practical solutions to practical problems. We intend to show you that theories play a vital role in underpinning practice and start with a brief explanation by Mautz and Sharaf who wrote a seminal book on auditing in 1961: 'One reason ... for a serious and substantial investigation into the philosophy and nature of auditing theory is the hope that it will provide us with solutions, or at least clues to solutions, to problems that we now find difficult.' They then go on to say that a philosophy (or set of unifying theories) has three aspects of value to us:

The Philosophy of Auditing, published by the American Accounting Association. See page 4.

1 It gets back to first principles, to the rationale behind the actions and thought which tend to be taken for granted.

2 It is concerned with the systematic organization of knowledge in such a way that it becomes at once more useful and less likely to be self-contradictory.

3 It provides a basis whereby social relationships may be moulded and understood.

We shall examine the above rationale for a philosophy by asking you to consider two postulates (or basic ideas) of auditing. Many of the matters in this chapter were suggested by Mautz and Sharaf and by Flint (1988) and you are encouraged to refer to these texts if you wish to examine the subject in greater detail.

ACTIVITY 2.1

One of the postulates formulated by Flint reads as follows: 'The subject matter of audit ... is susceptible to verification by evidence.' In other words, it is possible to find evidence to prove what you want to prove. Now try answering these questions:

1 As a starting point, do you believe that this postulate is important in the context of audit?

2 Do you believe that the postulate will by and large hold true?

3 Are there any circumstances where it might not hold true and, if so, what conclusions might you draw as a consequence?

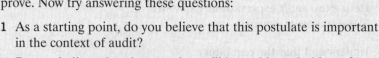

To consider the first question, the postulate is clearly an important starting point. If it is *not* possible to find evidence to prove that a statement is true or false or reasonable or unreasonable, there would be no point in auditors examining information and reporting on its validity.

This leads to the second question and one more difficult to answer. Most auditors would argue that most of the time they can form conclusions on whether, for instance, systems are working properly or whether inventories exist or have been valued at the lower of cost and net realizable value. There have, however, been many recent cases that would lead us to believe that auditors have, in fact, failed to find the evidence needed to prove the existence of underlying problems affecting organizations. Polly Peck, for instance, collapsed only a short time after the company's financial statements had been given an audit opinion that cast no doubt on its continued existence. This leads to the important question: Was the evidence not available or did the auditors fail, for whatever reason, to find it? We shall see in Chapter 6 that evidence is often hard to come by (for instance, evidence to prove that inventories will be sold above cost, that trade receivables be realized, that a legal case will go in the company's favour, that the bank will continue to offer an overdraft facility). In the first two examples above (inventories and trade receivables), the auditor may obtain enough evidence from such matters as sales of inventory items since the year-end or the trade receivable's past payment record. The latter two examples (legal case and bank overdraft) are, however, likely to be more problematic because no one can tell with certainty what the outcomes will be. Even in these cases some form of evidence may be available, albeit about an uncertain outcome, for instance, an opinion by a solicitor.

Polly Peck, Robert Maxwell, BCCI, SSL International and Equitable Life are examples in the UK.

As far as the third question is concerned, there may well be circumstances where the postulate might appear not to hold true, although that does not necessarily mean that it is not useful to us. For instance, the auditor might be unable to form an opinion because evidence is not available, because accounting records were destroyed by fire before being examined. In circumstances such as this the company and the auditor would have to find ways of reporting what has happened. In other words the postulate, proven to be invalid, may help us to decide on the action to be taken as a result.

We discuss audit reporting in Chapter 16.

ACTIVITY 2.2

Another postulate of auditing formulated by Flint reads as follows:

'Essential distinguishing characteristics of audit are the independence of status and freedom from investigatory and reporting constraints.' In other words, the auditor has to be free from any relationships with the company, its management and its user groups that would threaten the credibility of the auditor's report. Auditors are allowed freedom in their search for evidence and the way in which they report. Now consider the following questions:

1. What do you think is meant by 'independence of status' in practical terms?
2. Why do you think that it is important?
3. Do you think that the above postulate is a helpful starting point for recognizing that auditor independence is a vital element in making the audit report believable?

You will have noted that independence (and objectivity) represent one of the nine principles of independent auditing, included in the Auditors' Code (see Chapter 1, page 23).

We discuss independence in greater detail in Chapter 3, but you will recognize that the postulate suggests that the auditor should do nothing that would lead people to doubt that the opinion of the auditor is unbiased. Just think what conclusions you might draw if you found out that the auditor of a company in the travel industry had taken advantage of a free (but normally expensive) holiday offered by the client. Quite likely you would be very cynical about the professionalism of the auditor and would question the value of an audit if the auditor was thought to be 'in the pocket' of company management.

Adherence to the postulate would be a good starting point for ensuring that the auditor's report is believable. It is, however, only a starting point and the next question, discussed further in Chapter 3, is: 'What steps should be taken to ensure that the auditor is not only independent but is perceived to be independent?' You might suggest that auditors should not own shares in the company subject to audit, as this might influence their opinion. This is indeed one of the requirements of the profession's current code of ethics, although we did note in Chapter 1 that in the nineteenth century it was common for auditors to be shareholders of the company they were auditing, a circumstance that we would see as unacceptable today. This shows us that the conduct expected of auditors and the approach to independence may change over time.

However, the proximity of shareholders to management in the nineteenth century might mean that independence was not an issue.

It is perhaps too early in this book for you to appreciate all the implications of theory underpinning audit practice and the way the auditor behaves and we shall return to this question from time to time. Nevertheless, we hope that this brief discussion has persuaded you that some theoretical basis for the auditor's work is both helpful and necessary.

THE POSTULATES OF AUDITING

We have already looked at two postulates of auditing above, and you know by now that they are basic assumptions or guiding principles that set the scene for the practice of auditing.

1961, p. 37.

Let us now formalize our understanding of what a postulate is. Mautz and Sharaf suggested that postulates are essential to the development of an intellectual discipline and are the foundation for the erection of any theoretical structure. Thus, they suggested that postulates are not themselves theories but are the necessary basis for theory. They also said that postulates are assumptions that do not lend themselves to direct verification, but are a basis for inference, even though they may be susceptible to challenge in the light of later advancement of knowledge.

Here is one of the original postulates as formulated by Mautz and Sharaf:

> There is no necessary conflict of interest between the auditor and the management of the enterprise under audit. (p. 42)

ACTIVITY 2.3

Consider the above postulate, remember that it was formulated some 50 years ago, and suggest why you think that Mautz and Sharaf included it in their list of tentative postulates. Decide whether it is a valid postulate today.

The reason that we asked you to remember that it was formulated some 50 years ago, is that society is likely to have changed substantially over that period and the attitudes of both management and auditors are likely to have changed as well. Mautz and Sharaf may well have put the notion of no necessary conflict into the postulate because pressures on management to strive for a good picture of their organization were less than they are today. Managers then were probably much more secure in their employment than they are today and may, therefore, have been more relaxed regarding the financial statements, which to the outside world were a measure of their success. A further point is that Mautz and Sharaf accepted at the time that financial statements were objective statements of reality. There are few, we would argue, who would accept this today. Further, auditors in the early 1960s were not subject to the degree of litigation and potential litigation with which they are faced today. Increasingly, too, some of the benefits accruing to senior executives are tied to the performance of the company's shares on stock exchanges with resultant pressure to keep published profits at a high level, whether justified or not.

In addition, there are pressures within society today to extend the role of audit to encompass a wider range of stakeholders with the result that the financial statements upon which the auditor is reporting are becoming increasingly complex. At the same time, potential liability may increase if rights are extended to groups of people that had few rights in 1961. We discuss auditor's liability in Chapter 19, but at this stage you should note that there is considerable debate about the groups of people to whom the auditor owes responsibility and the amount of damages that might be claimed in the event of negligence being proven. Later in this chapter we shall introduce you to the audit expectations gap, but note now that auditing is very much more in the public eye than it was 1961 and the expectations of society are high.

We discuss the audit expectations gap in greater length in Chapter 18. See pages 691 to 705.

For these reasons we may doubt whether this particular postulate would be valid today. However – and this is a big however – many modern auditors appear to be placing considerable trust in management where they have decided to adopt the business risk approach to auditing, which involves a measure of participation between auditor and management. We discuss the business risk approach to auditing in Chapter 5, but note here that before this approach is adopted, the auditors would have to be certain that management is of high integrity.

We set out in Table 2.1 a list of the postulates formulated by Flint.

THE CONCEPTS OF AUDITING: CREDIBILITY, PROCESS, COMMUNICATION, PERFORMANCE

The dictionary definition of a concept includes the following: 'a thing conceived, a general notion; an idea'. Mautz and Sharaf: p. 54 suggested that 'Concepts provide a basis for advancement in the field of knowledge by facilitating communication about it and its problems'. We shall return to auditing concepts in greater detail later in the book, but this section will give you an overview of the ideas of auditing that help us to talk sensibly about it. We have

TABLE 2.1 Audit postulates

Postulate	Comment
1. The primary condition for an audit is that there is a relationship of accountability or a situation of public accountability.	The argument is that audit exists because of a need to prove the validity of statements produced by those who are accountable. Figure 2.1 on page 37 shows the relationship between accountability and audit and we comment on this figure before reviewing audit concepts. 'Accountability' is one of the nine principles of independent auditing in the Auditors' Code, which makes reference to the wider public interest and also to 'stakeholders', implying that there are interested parties other than shareholders. We discuss this matter in greater detail when we consider Auditor Liability in Chapter 19.
2. The subject matter of accountability is too remote, too complex and/or of too great a significance for the discharge of the duty to be demonstrated without the process of audit.	This postulate follows from the previous one, suggesting that major corporations are so huge and complex, accountability cannot be achieved unless an auditor examines the accountability statements, produced by management. In other words accountability without audit is not possible.
3. Essential distinguishing characteristics of audit are the independence of its status and its freedom from investigatory and reporting constraints.	We have discussed this postulate in response to Activity 2.2, but we look at the question of independence in greater detail in Chapter 3.
4. The subject matter of audit, for example, conduct, performance or achievement or record of events or state of affairs or a statement of fact relating to any of these, is susceptible to verification by evidence.	We discussed this postulate in response to Activity 2.1, but look at audit evidence in Chapter 6 and throughout this book
5. Standards of accountability, for example, conduct, performance, achievement and quality of information, can be set for those who are accountable: actual conduct, etc can be measured and compared with these standards by reference to	This postulate requires agreement on how accountability can be discharged. The first step has been the requirement for published financial statements, but this has been strengthened by generally accepted accounting standards such as International Financial Reporting Standards (IFRSs) including International

TABLE 2.1 *(Continued)*

Postulate	Comment
known criteria and the process of measurement and comparison requires special skill and judgement.	Accounting Standards (IASs), compliance with which are designed to assist in achieving accountability. We believe that the postulate is necessary, but have to recognize that the achievement of acceptable standards of accountability is fraught with difficulty. It is worth noting that published financial statements are only one form of account used to achieve accountability. In some cases the problems associated with achieving accountability are even more severe, environmental accounting, for instance.
6. The meaning, significance and intention of financial and other statements and data, which are audited, are sufficiently clear that the credibility given thereto as a result of audit can be clearly expressed and communicated.	This postulate suggests there is a clear relationship between what is being audited and the ability to report on it. In other words it would be difficult if not impossible to report on information if there was no agreement on how the information was prepared or what the information represented.
7. An audit produces an economic or social benefit.	We saw in Chapter 1 that an audit adds credibility to financial and other information and noted that 'Providing value' is one of the nine principles of independent auditing. If it can be shown that such information produces an economic or social benefit, audit can also be shown to do the same because credible information is more useful than information not having that quality. An example of an economic benefit might be the redistribution of scarce resources to organizations shown by published information to be using them more effectively. Such redistribution of resources may bring social benefits as well by, for instance, improving employment prospects. We shall see later that some auditors are now using a business risk approach to audit, which they believe will increase the value of audit to management and implicitly also to the shareholders.

TABLE 2.2 Concepts of auditing

Group	Concept
CREDIBILITY	Competence Independence Integrity and ethics
PROCESS	Risk Evidence Audit judgement Materiality
COMMUNICATION	Reporting Truth and fairness Association
PERFORMANCE	Due care Standards Control of audit quality Rigour

drawn on the framework of concepts formulated by Mautz and Sharaf and Flint, but have modified the framework to take account of the fundamental principles of auditing contained in the Auditors' Code (Table 1.2). The important point is that the postulates, concepts and fundamental principles, whatever you like to call them, provide a rationale and framework for auditing. No doubt they are not the last word on what auditing is about.

You will note that the concepts of auditing shown in Table 2.2 have been grouped under the main headings of credibility, process, communication and performance, to help us to consider the concepts in a systematic way.

We shall review the concepts in greater detail below, but before we do so, it will be useful to introduce you to the relationship between accountability and audit in a more formal way and at the same time set the scene for understanding what the audit process is about. We set out in Figure 2.1 a diagram adapted from *A Statement of Basic Auditing Concepts* published by The American Accounting Association (AAA) in 1973. This figure suggests that there are four parties to the accountability/audit process:

1 *The preparer/source.* This heading encompasses those individuals who control resources provided by others and who have the responsibility for preparing the accounting reports that show the position and results of the activities controlled by them. In the agency literature this party would be recognized as the manager-agent. If accounting reports are to aid the achievement of accountability they will have to reflect the actual economic events and actions that affected the organization for which the accounting reports are prepared.

You will remember that in the Auditors' Code these users are known as stakeholders.

2 *Users of accounting information.* As the name 'users' implies, these are the individuals that have an interest in the organization preparing the accounting reports. Some of them, such as shareholders, may perhaps be

FIGURE 2.1 Communication of accounting information

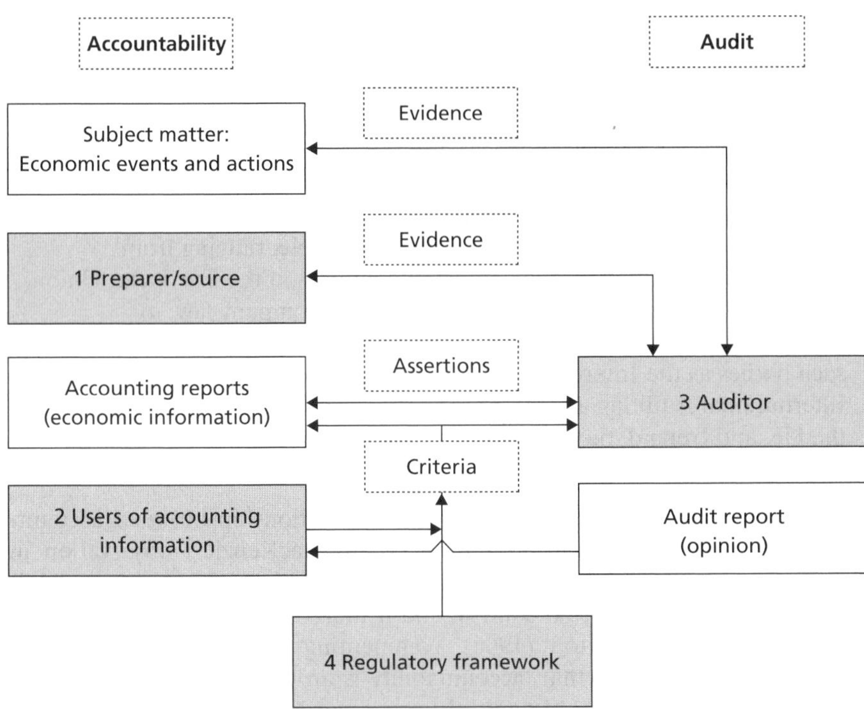

identified with the principals of agency theory. Others are not recognized as having direct ownership interests, such as customers, suppliers and employees, and there is considerable debate about the extent to which they are entitled to accounting information to inform their actions. Briloff (1986) has commented on the wide groups, using the term 'publics' instead of 'users', to whom accountability is owed in the following terms:

> When we consider the total environment in which these corporate entities exist, and to which they relate, we see them as having compelling responsibilities to a broad spectrum of 'publics'. This nexus of publics includes: management, shareholders, labour, government, customers, and consumers, as well as neighbours in the communities in which the corporation operates. Further, as concern for ecology and the well-being of consumers and posterity intensifies, this responsibility will extend to the total society and environment. And because of the multinational character of our major corporate entities, this responsibility and related accountability must be viewed on a universal canvas.

3 *The auditor.* This party, of course, is the one that examines the accounting reports prepared by the preparer/source and issues an audit report to the users following the examination. We shall see that the auditor of limited companies in many countries is appointed by shareholders, one of the publics identified by Briloff above, although we shall also see that more often than not management has considerable influence over who will be auditor. Note that the auditor reports to the shareholders, one of the user

groups. However, the report, being in the public domain, may be used by users other than shareholders.

4 *The regulatory framework.* AAA, in the original diagram published in 1973, showed the criteria governing the actions of the auditor as emanating from the users. This may still be so in certain cases, as, for instance, where a bank may ask for a special purpose audit. For this reason we have retained the line from the users through 'criteria' to the auditor in Figure 2.1. However, the more important source of the criteria today are a range of individuals or bodies who exercise a regulatory role, ranging from parliament that (often, in the context of countries in the European Union as the result of directives of the Union) creates company law, to professional bodies who monitor the performance of their members and to such bodies as the International Accounting Standards Board (IASB), the International Auditing and Assurance Standards Board (IAASB), and, in the UK and Ireland, the Accounting Standards Board (ASB) and the Auditing Practices Board (APB).

Figure 2.1 suggests that there is a very close relationship between accountability and audit, a relationship reinforced by MacKenzie's observation in 1964 (in relation to audit in the public sector): 'Without audit, no accountability; without accountability, no control; and if there is no control, where is the seat of power?' Normanton (1966), commenting on this observation, reenforced it by suggesting that 'accountability is an abstraction, which is only given reality by the process of audit'. In other words, the financial statements prepared by management cannot become a tool of accountability until an independent auditor has examined and reported on them.

See Normanton, 1966.

There are two elements in Figure 2.1, which will be very useful when we come to look at the audit process – 'assertions' and 'evidence'. By assertions are meant the statements, explicit or otherwise, made by management, that are embodied in the financial statements. The overriding assertion made by management about financial statements prepared in accordance with company law in the European Union is that they give a true and fair view. This overriding assertion provides the main objective of the external auditor – to form an opinion on the truth and fairness of financial statements. This is not very helpful to auditors in practice and they break down this overriding assertion into a series of assertions to give specific objectives for their work. Thus, for instance, in the case of trade receivables stated at £15 million, managers are implicitly asserting that they are genuine, are accurately calculated and complete, giving the auditor a clear objective, that of proving that management assertions are valid.

ACTIVITY 2.4

Consider the figure of inventories appearing in the balance sheet of a company. Identify the assertions that management might implicitly make about inventories by including them in the financial statements. Suggest how such identification may aid the audit process.

You doubtless identified the following assertions, implicit or otherwise:

1 The inventories exist.
2 The inventories are in good condition, that is, they are saleable above cost or are useable in the production process.
3 The inventories belong to the company.
4 The inventories have been valued at the lower of cost and net realizable value.
5 Cost has been determined in accordance with IAS 2: 'Inventories', taking into account present condition and location and an appropriate allocation of overheads.
6 Where applicable, net realizable value has been properly calculated taking into account selling prices and costs still to be incurred in the following period.

SSAP 9 – Stocks and long-term contracts – is still valid in the UK and Ireland for non-listed companies, the requirements of which accord closely with IAS 2, and also IAS 11 'Construction contracts'. Listed companies are required to apply international accounting standards.

You may well have identified other implicit assertions in addition to these, but the point we wish to emphasize is that analysis of assertions is an aid to the auditor because it sets the scene for the evidence search and, indeed, influences the audit search process.

The problem for the auditor is that there is risk attached to each of these assertions; for instance, management may assert that inventories exist, when in fact, they do not. ISA 315 – *Identifying and assessing the risks of material misstatement through understanding the entity and its environment* is one of the ISAs which considers the risks facing the auditor. It has a section titled 'Identifying and Assessing the Risks of Material Misstatement' in which risk of material misstatement at the financial statement level and at the assertion level are discussed. We shall look at assertions in a more formal way later, but note at this stage that risk at the financial statement level means risks that relate pervasively to the financial statements as a whole and potentially affect many assertions (see paragraph A105). Risk at the assertion level are the risks affecting specific classes of transactions, account balances and disclosures (see paragraph A109).

ACTIVITY 2.5

Taking the assertion: 'The inventories exist', what evidence would you seek to prove this assertion?

The obvious evidence search would be for the auditor to observe a physical count of inventories held by the company and to make a comparison between inventories actually on hand and the inventory records. A further test would be to compare the count sheets with the inventory valuation sheets to ensure the quantities are identical on both. Sometimes inventories may be held by other parties and the auditor would obtain the necessary evidence by confirmation from them. In this respect, Figure 2.1 shows that evidence may be obtained from both internal and external sources.

Now let us return to the concepts identified above, and the headings under which they are organized:

- *Credibility* is clearly about whether people will believe the auditors when they issue their reports. The implication is that the auditors must ensure that they are seen to be competent, independent and behaving with integrity and in an ethical way.
- *Process*, on the other hand, is concerned with *how* audits are performed. We saw in Chapter 1 and above that auditors seek evidence to prove statements or assertions made by management in respect of the whole financial statements and items in them. During the audit process, they also evaluate the risk that they will fail to find matters that affect the view given by the financial statements. They make judgements and continually assess if things they find are material (significant) enough to alter what they think about the organization and the statements that reflect its position and activities.
- *Communication.* You might regard reporting as being part of the process of audit – and indeed it is – but as it is that part of the process which results in auditors communicating their views to other parties, including those charged with governance, it is useful to highlight the idea of communication. Auditors do not just communicate in a formal report at the end of the process, however, but also when they come across matters that will be useful to management, or when they find matters that are relevant to those charged with governance, including members of the audit committee of a company client. We have put 'truth and fairness' under the heading of communication, as this concept is an important element in the statements upon which auditors are reporting. Truth and fairness is clearly an accounting as well as an auditing concept and is closely linked to materiality and judgement. You should note that the financial statements and accompanying notes, upon which the auditors report, normally form only part of the reporting package that companies present to the shareholders. This means that auditors have to ensure that the parts on which they are *not* reporting are not in conflict with those parts subject to the audit report.

We shall discuss the relevance of communicating with those charged with governance, including members of the audit committee, later in this book, but principally in Chapters 16 and 18.

- *Performance.* The final heading highlights the fact that auditors are expected to perform their work with due care, in accordance with accepted standards and that auditors should have their own quality control procedures to ensure that audit work is properly carried out. Clearly, the concepts are interrelated; for instance, a legitimate expectation is that the audit evidence search will be carried out with due care, so the concept of audit evidence is related to that of due care. The process also has to be conducted thoroughly and in a critical and questioning manner, that is, with rigour.

We comment as follows on the individual concepts.

Credibility concepts

The following credibility concepts concern the personal qualities of the auditor.

Competence

This is one of the nine fundamental principles of independent auditing in the Auditors' Code. We ask the question: Are the auditors competent? Are they capable of carrying out the audit task to an expected standard? We discuss this question in Chapter 4 and, in particular, consider the steps that have been or could be taken to ensure that auditors are properly performing the audit task. Later in the present chapter and in Chapter 18, we shall see that competence is also an important element of the audit expectations gap.

See Chapter 1, page 23.

Independence

We have already seen that independence (a further fundamental principle of auditing) is expected of the auditor. We discuss independence in some depth in Chapters 3 and 20, what it means, the problems associated with it, and again steps that have been or could be taken to ensure that auditors are unbiased in their work, particularly in the light of the revelations concerning the conduct of auditors after the collapse of Enron and other large corporations.

See Chapter 1, page 23.

Integrity and ethics

Auditors are expected to behave with integrity by fulfilling their responsibilities with honesty, fairness and truthfulness, and in an ethical manner. This basically means that the auditor has standards of personal conduct expected of a professional person. Professional people are faced very often with ethical dilemmas in their work and it is vital that they are aware of the kinds of response expected of them. This is again one of the nine fundamental principles of independent auditing. The Auditors' Code refers to confidentiality as one aspect of integrity, but in some cases (discussed in Chapter 17) auditors may be required by law to report to regulators, thus breaking the absolute principle of confidentiality. Mark Twain, the American author once said, 'If in doubt, do the right thing.' This sounds like a very worthy statement, but what is 'right' is not always so clear, and often needs careful examination of all the issues.

We discuss official pronouncements on integrity and ethics in Chapter 3.

ACTIVITY 2.6

Assume that you are auditing the transfers from the main cash fund of a client to the petty cash fund. To your surprise you find an entry for £500 in the cash book, described as 'Transfer to petty cash', has no corresponding 'receipts' entry in the petty cash book. You find that the £500 appears in the bank statement on the day the entry was made in the cash book. You suspect that the cashier may have pocketed the amount in question and you discuss this with your immediate superior. However, he tells you to ignore it as the cashier is a long-term employee of the client and is, moreover, a personal friend. What would you do? Does this case help you to understand what an ethical dilemma is?

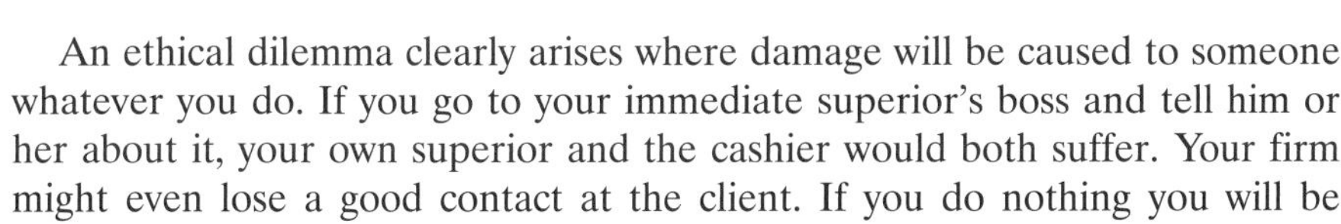

An ethical dilemma clearly arises where damage will be caused to someone whatever you do. If you go to your immediate superior's boss and tell him or her about it, your own superior and the cashier would both suffer. Your firm might even lose a good contact at the client. If you do nothing you will be placed in a position of 'moral hazard', because you have behaved in a way (even doing nothing is 'behaviour') that you know is wrong and you will in future think less of yourself as a professional. Furthermore, if you have taken no action this time, the cashier may decide that you are an incompetent auditor and be encouraged to misappropriate funds of the company in future. Apart from this, if management subsequently find the fraud, they may conclude that your firm is not doing the job properly and seek to replace it with a more 'competent' firm.

Solutions to ethical dilemmas require first an analysis of the situation, consideration of possible actions and the consequences of each, and then making a firm decision on the basis of your deliberations. Making ethical decisions may be quite difficult for personal reasons, even where it is quite clear what an ethical professional person should do.

It is, of course, very easy to say that we should always behave in an ethical way. Looking at particular cases, however, does help us to identify the ethical dilemmas and can help you to decide what you should do, once you have decided what the consequences are of particular courses of action.

ISA 200 – *Overall objectives of the independent auditor and the conduct of an audit in accordance with international standards on auditing.*

We should mention at this point that ISA 200 states in paragraph 14: 'The auditor shall comply with relevant ethical requirements, including those pertaining to independence, relating to financial statement audit engagements.' It then goes on to say in paragraph A14 that 'relevant ethical requirements ordinarily comprise Parts A and B of the International Federation of Accountants' Code of Ethics for Professional Accountants (the IFAC Code) related to an audit of financial statements together with national requirements that are more restrictive.' In the case of the UK and Ireland the relevant national requirements are issued by APB. We discuss the IFAC and APB requirements in Chapter 3.

Process concepts

Risk

We discuss the concept of audit risk and business risk and distinguish between them in greater detail in Chapter 5, and intend to make risk a central feature when analysing the audit process. Business risk is the risk that an entity will fail to meet its objectives, whereas audit risk is the risk that the auditors will fail to reach proper conclusions about accounting information on which they are reporting. All companies are faced with a variety of business risks, such as risks that a rival company will put a competitive product on the market or that the company may suffer a loss in reputation because its activities have caused adverse impacts on the environment.

Some business risks *may* form part of audit risk; for instance the new product might make an existing product unsaleable. If the auditors do not become aware of this, they may risk giving an opinion that the accounting information gives a true and fair view when it does not. For this reason auditors spend much time before and after the audit commences, analysing risk and planning to spend more time on the crucial areas (where risk is highest), and less where it is lower. We shall see in Chapter 5 that over-auditing (doing too much in some areas) can be just as dangerous for the auditor as under-auditing (doing too little), as it uses resources that could be more profitably used in the risky areas. The International Standard of Auditing in the area is ISA 315 and paragraph 11 explains that the auditor shall obtain an understanding of the entity and its environment and goes on to say in 11 (d) that this understanding should encompass the entity's objectives and strategies, and those related business risks that may result in risks of material misstatement. The important point here is that auditors have to know the client company well, including the external and internal environment. Audit approaches have changed considerably as a result in recent years and auditors have been put into an excellent position to advise management and to add value. Those firms that adopt a business risk approach to audit claim that they have a much better chance of adding value if this broader approach is adopted. As we have seen above, adding value is one of the fundamental principles of auditing.

ISA 315 – *identifying and assessing the risks of material misstatement through understanding the entity and its environment.*

ISA 200 describes audit risk in its definitions paragraph 13 as:

> The risk that the auditor expresses an inappropriate audit opinion when the financial statements are materially misstated. Audit risk is a function of the risks of material misstatement and detection risk.

We discuss materiality in Chapter 11 and detection risk in Chapter 5, where we also discuss the other components of audit risk – inherent risk and control risk. At this stage we shall just give you the definitions of the three components of audit risk, taken again from paragraph 13 of ISA 200, together with brief examples:

> Inherent risk – The susceptibility of an assertion about a class of transaction, account balance or disclosure to a misstatement that could be material, either individually or when aggregated with other misstatements, before consideration of any related controls.

For instance, management might have made an assertion, stated or implied, that all cash received in respect of trade receivables has been completely and accurately recorded. The inherent risk is that the cash will not be recorded, or will be recorded incorrectly, in the company's records. Non-recording of cash would clearly make it easy to misappropriate it, while incorrect recording might help to hide a teeming and lading fraud.

Think of 'teeming and lading' as 'emptying and filling'. It is the term given to a procedure for hiding misappropriation of cash received – which would mean that the trade receivables account will be overstated. Management might investigate when items become seriously overdue, but to prevent this, the person who has misappropriated the cash, will post subsequent monies received not to the correct account but to (or partly to) the account which is overstated.

> Control risk – The risk that a misstatement that could occur in an assertion about a class of transaction, account balance or disclosure and that could be material, either individually or when aggregated with other misstatements, will not be prevented, or detected and corrected, on a timely basis by the entity's internal control.

To take the cash receipts case again, if the control of these receipts were to be in the hands of the person holding the trade receivables ledger, a control weakness would exist and control risk would be high. Clearly if the person keeping the ledger was also responsible for receiving cash the possibility of creating a teeming and lading fraud would be much increased.

Neither inherent risk nor control risk can be altered by the auditor, as they reside in the audited entity. However the auditor can carry out procedures to reduce their impact, which leads us to a further component of audit risk:

> Detection risk – The risk that the procedures performed by the auditor to reduce audit risk to an acceptably low level will not detect a misstatement that exists and that could be material, either individually or when aggregated with other misstatements.

An example of detection risk might be where the auditor failed to request confirmation of trade receivables from third parties that the amounts stated in the records were accurate thus failing to detect that cash payments had been misappropriated. You should note that detection risk is under the control of the auditors, whereas the other two are entity risks, existing independently of the audit of the financial statements.

Evidence

We saw in Figure 2.1 that evidence is central to the audit process and we discuss many aspects of evidence in a number of chapters of this book. You already know that auditors gather evidence to test that management assertions are valid and in Activity 2.5 you were given the opportunity to think about the evidence needed to prove the existence of inventories. We shall see that some kinds of evidence are stronger or more convincing than others and in Chapter 6 consider the various kinds of evidence available to the auditor and how reliable they may be. There is an international standard of auditing in the area (ISA 500 – *Audit evidence*) and we shall ask you to refer to this later.

Audit judgement

The auditor uses professional judgement in assessing risk and there are many other areas where audit judgement will be exercised, not least in forming conclusions about the validity of figures appearing in the financial statements. The concept highlights the fact that often there is no certainty about whether an accounting figure is right or wrong. We can perhaps help you to understand this concept by giving you an activity to perform.

ACTIVITY 2.7

Assume that an engineering company is replacing a lathe. The previous lathe had a useful economic life of ten years and the company wrote it off in ten equal instalments. The new lathe has a number of new features, including electronic guidance, and operates much more efficiently and quickly than the previous lathe. The company wishes to write it off over ten years, as was the case for the previous lathe. You have to make a judgement as to whether the company's policy is appropriate. What evidence would you seek? Do you think you would be able to conclude that the assertion of a ten-year life is valid on the basis of available evidence? What do you think would be the critical factor in making a judgement about this matter?

The management assertion is that the new lathe will have a ten-year life. You would need to find out if the new lathe was similar enough to the old one to persuade you that this was likely. The problem is that the new lathe is clearly different, and perhaps of most concern is the fact that it has sophisticated electronic devices that may be more or less robust than a manually controlled lathe.

Useful evidence might be the documentation put forward by the production unit to justify the purchase of the new lathe and minutes of meetings at which the tangible non-current assets budgets were considered – to discover management's view at the time the purchase was made. This would include technical assessments (will the lathe last for ten years?), economic assessments (will demand for the products produced by the lathe last for ten years?) and management policy decisions (do we need the lathe to keep our costs competitive with those of other manufacturers?). It may be possible to find critical reviews in the trade press of the lathe. The auditors would have to be review manufacturer's specifications and to hold discussions with production personnel. When we consider audit evidence in Chapter 6, we shall see that much evidence is persuasive rather than certain. If the evidence all points in the same direction (that is each piece of evidence corroborates the other evidence) you may be able to form a view with some certainty. Thus, if the trade press comments on the robustness of the lathe, if directors' minutes show that directors have made decisions based on costs and expected outputs over a ten-year period, if production personnel confirm this and if the manufacturer's specifications emphasize the expected length of useful life of ten years, you might find the evidence very persuasive. You would also have to form views on the competence of management and other officials and, based on the available evidence, you will probably be able to form a view on the likelihood of a ten-year useful life.

The ability to exercise judgement is a very intangible quality and we shall discuss it in relation to risk assessment at greater length in Chapter 5.

Materiality

We consider materiality in Chapter 11, but at this stage we show you what the International Standard on Auditing, ISA 320 – *Materiality in planning and performing an audit* has to say in paragraph 2:

> Financial reporting frameworks often discuss the concept of materiality in the context of the preparation and presentation of financial statements. Although financial reporting frameworks may discuss materiality in different terms, they generally explain that:
>
> - Misstatements, including omissions, are considered to be material if they, individually or in the aggregate, could reasonably be expected to influence the economic decisions of users taken on the basis of the financial statements;
> - Judgments about materiality are made in light of surrounding circumstances, and are affected by the size or nature of a misstatement, or a combination of both; and
> - Judgments about matters that are material to users of the financial statements are based on a consideration of the common financial information needs of users as a group. The possible effect of misstatements on specific individual users, whose needs may vary widely, is not considered.

You can see that we are back to judgement again, so it is likely that materiality will be a difficult concept for the auditor to handle in practice.

Unfortunately, you cannot normally go to users and ask if their judgement has been affected so you have to make up your own mind. The answer is probably: 'It depends'. If the company had had a profit of £1 000 000 last year, you might decide that the amount of £75 000 was material because the profit had

See Activity 2.8 on the following page.

ACTIVITY 2.8

Assume that a company has a profit in its draft financial statements of £1 000 000. During your audit you find an error that reveals that inventories are overstated by £75 000. Do you think that the misstatement would reasonably influence the decisions of an addressee of the auditors' report? In other words, would addressees think differently about the company if its profit were restated to £925 000?

gone down significantly enough to make people worry about future profitability. You might also decide that the amount was material because it caused the key gross margin ratio to drop below the industry average. We clearly need more information in this case to form a view about materiality.

There is a lot more to materiality than is suggested above, but what is certain is that auditors have to plan their work in such a way as to make it likely that they will find errors or misstatements that are material in their impact on the financial statements. We will see that auditors may take a more conservative view about what is material, so that they plan to find errors and misstatements of (say) £50 000, rather than those of (say) £75 000. If they do not find matters of material significance, they will be plainly at risk and ISA 320 notes (in paragraph 6):

> In planning the audit, the auditor makes judgments about the size of misstatements that will be considered material. These judgments provide a basis for:
>
> (a) Determining the nature, timing and extent of risk assessment procedures;
> (b) Identifying and assessing the risks of material misstatement.
> (c) Determining the nature, timing and extent of further audit procedures.
>
> Risk and materiality are clearly central to the auditor's work.

Communication concepts

Reporting

You will remember that the fundamental principle of 'clear, complete and effective communication', contained in the Auditors' Code reads, among other things, as follows: 'Auditors' reports contain clear expressions of opinion and set out information necessary for a proper understanding of that opinion.'

We discuss reporting in Chapter 10 (where we introduce you to the management letters issued by the auditor, often at interim dates before the year-end), Chapter 16 (where we consider the auditors' report on financial statements) and in Chapter 17 (when we introduce you to fraud and going concern).

Truth and fairness

We have already introduced you to the concept of truth and fairness in Chapter 1, where we saw that the 'true and fair view' has never been defined and in some ways it is easier to say what it is not, and, in particular, that it is not 'correctness'. It is to do with the validity of the message given by the financial statements. If, for instance, the company has suffered significant losses on disposal of fixed assets, the financial statements should reveal this. If the company has changed the basis of measuring profits (perhaps as a result of a new accounting standard, we would expect this fact to be disclosed, together with the effect on the profit for the year.

Association

We have placed 'association' under this heading because it is a fundamental auditing principle of relevance to reporting. It refers to the fact that most company reporting packages contain elements to which the audit report is not specifically directed. ISA 720 gives examples of such elements in paragraph A3: 'A report by management or those charged with governance on operations, Financial summaries or highlights, Employment data, Planned capital expenditures, Financial ratios, Names of officers and directors, Selected quarterly data.' Other examples relevant in the UK and Ireland include the Directors' Report and the Chairman's Report, the auditors having a duty to ensure that there is no conflict between the information contained in reports such as those mentioned and the financial statements. We discuss the action that should be taken by auditors in Chapter 16 where we consider audit reporting.

ISA 720 – *The auditor's responsibilities relating to other information in documents containing audited financial statements.*

Performance concepts

The main point to be emphasized here is that auditors are professional people, and there is an expectation therefore that they will carry out their work in accordance with the standards of their profession and with the care expected by those relying on their work. Due care and standards are clearly related, but there is much discussion at the present time as to whom the auditor owes a duty of care. Is it to all the publics identified by Briloff above, or is it only some of them? In Chapter 19 we shall consider this question in some depth, when we look at auditors' liability under the law. It is the courts that decide legal matters, but they might well look to the International Standards of Auditing when deciding if an auditor has been negligent in the performance of his or her duty. Some countries may extend the requirements of ISAs in their own countries as APB has done for the UK and Ireland.

Quality control is commonly used to describe the procedures used to ensure that the outputs from a process are of the desired standard. A car manufacturer uses quality control procedures such as inspection and test driving when deciding whether a motor vehicle is fit to be delivered to a customer. Firms of auditors also use the term to describe the procedures used to ensure that their product – the audit opinion – is fit to be made public, and used by the public. An example of a quality control procedure used by a firm of auditors would be the provision of training courses to give people in the firm the skills necessary to perform the audit task properly. We will meet up with the topic and the concept of quality control again in Chapter 4 and elsewhere. There is an important international standard on quality control in the area, ISQC1 – *Quality control for firms that perform audits and reviews of historical financial statements, and other assurance and related services engagements.* One important feature of ISQC1 is that it highlights the need for an engagement quality control review, and that engagement quality control reviewers should be appointed to perform such reviews. Audit quality is a very hot topic at the present time and we discuss it in a separate heading immediately below.

We have put the auditing principle of 'rigour' into this section, although it could be equally well placed under the heading 'process'. The idea of 'professional scepticism' as an aspect of 'rigour' is an interesting one and it is referred to in the ISAs. It means, among other things, adopting a questioning attitude at all times during the audit.

AUDIT QUALITY

As we mentioned above the question of audit quality is currently a hot topic. We shall discuss the topic in greater detail in Chapters 4 and 20, but you should note here that professional accounting firms have started to publish so-called transparency reports prepared in accordance with the provisions of the Statutory Auditors (Transparency) Instrument 2008 issued by the Professional Oversight Board (POB). The POB had previously issued the 'Audit Quality Framework' and had indicated that Transparency Reports might represent a useful opportunity for audit firms to set out the steps that they are taking to achieve audit quality by reference to the Framework. We shall take a brief look at a recent report issued by Deloitte and titled 'An Open Book' to show you how firms have approached the requirement of the framework.

The POB is an operating body of the Financial Reporting Council (FRC), the UK's independent regulator responsible for promoting confidence in corporate governance and reporting. POB is responsible, among other things, for monitoring the quality of the auditing function in relation to economically significant entities. It was established as a response to the European Union's 8th Company Law directive.

Deloitte introduces the section titled 'Quality' as follows:

> Our delivery of quality is achieved through effective internal quality control systems and a focus on leadership, communication, infrastructure and performance management. We have rigorous processes, systems and tools supported by a consultative culture. These processes are in place not only where required by regulation, but across our business.

The firm addresses audit quality under a number of different headings: Quality and risk management framework, Audit process, Partner-led approach, People development, Quality control, Audit quality and risk management, Accounting and auditing expertise, Reporting, A fair fee, Practice protection group and Business risk appraisal. We realize that we have not yet introduced you to many of these matters, but we shall ask you to perform an activity in respect of three selected headings.

ACTIVITY 2.9

Consider the three headings, Partner-led approach, People development and Accounting and auditing expertise, and say what you think the firm is suggesting under the three headings. Think about quality as you formulate your answer and consider the role of partners and other staff within the firm.

When conducting an engagement, whether auditing, or other activities, a firm will appoint a partner (known as the engagement partner) to take responsibility for the assignment. In this case, Deloitte is basically stating that the engagement partner oversees the engagement, including helping staff to plan the activity, consider risk, search for evidence, and in fact ensure that high quality is maintained throughout. The firm is also suggesting that partners are very experienced and are fit persons to supervise audit and other engagements.

Furthermore the firm makes the point that the other staff employed by the firm are also personally of high quality and that it has continuous development programmes in force to ensure that partners and staff are kept up-to-date and that their quality is maintained.

There are, of course, many areas of expertise that the firm would wish to maintain, but accounting and auditing expertise is of particular relevance to the audit process and the firm has therefore highlighted this particular area of expertise.

Basically, what the firm is saying is that audit quality is a function of various factors and that the existence of a control framework in the firm and well-paid and good staff, properly supervised, will ensure that quality is maintained.

It has to be said that there has been some criticism of the transparency reports issued by professional firms. For instance, a recent lead story of *Accountancy Age* was titled 'Clients blind on audit quality' and the leader suggested that firms should reveal more about how they maintain and enhance audit quality, so that clients and potential clients have a better basis for comparing different audit firms when they are choosing their auditors.

Accountancy Age, 3 December 2009, pages 1 and 2.

POB itself has suggested that the audit industry should produce more quantitative data to better equip investors and companies with the tools needed to scrutinize their auditors. POB clearly believes that the reports are too bland and do not give enough hard facts to back up claims of audit quality, sufficient to enable clients and potential clients to compare the firms with each other, hence the Accountancy Age headline 'Clients blind on audit quality'. The Association of British Insurers (ABI), which represents 20 per cent of investments in the London stock market, has also suggested there was little information in the public domain to compare auditors.

One of the problems is that it is very difficult to define audit quality and to decide on the specific factors that would give insights into how well firms are addressing the issue. For instance, should firms give more detailed information about time devoted to planning audit assignments? Or statistics on the average mix of partner and other staff time on the average audit, if there is such a thing? Students should keep an eye open for future pronouncements of the POB on how audit quality might be measured.

Of interest in this connection is that some firms use Key Performance Indicators (KPIs) to aid review of audit quality. PricewaterhouseCoopers (PwC), for instance, performs reviews of selected audits on a quarterly basis. PwC also carries out an Assurance Quality Review (AQR) annually of a sample of audits by personnel independent of the offices responsible for the audits, and gives a grading to each audit selected from 'satisfactory' through 'needs improvement' to 'unsatisfactory'. PwC is regulated in the UK by the ICAEW and an annual Audit Compliance Review (ACR) monitors compliance with the ICAEW's Audit Regulations. The ACR includes a review of procedures performed by the compliance department. The compliance department is

We discuss the role of the ethics partner in Chapter 3. See page 80. We discuss the POB and AIU in greater detail in Chapters 4 and 20.

headed by the ethics partner, and is responsible for independence training and consultation. We have taken this information from the 2009 report of the Audit Inspection Unit (AIU) of the POB. The report regarded the KPI and ACR processes to be particular strengths within the quality monitoring procedures. AIU reporting is at a very early stage, but it is likely in our view that it may turn out to be a vehicle for ensuring best practice. If the KPIs were to be published they might add greater transparency to methods used to enhance audit quality.

INTRODUCTION TO THE AUDIT EXPECTATIONS GAP

This term is used to describe the difference between the expectations of those who rely upon audit reports about what auditors should do and what they are perceived to do. We shall discuss the audit expectations gap in some depth in Chapter 18 but as it is a topic of much current interest, we believe we should introduce it as this point.

The 1993 study was subsequently updated by a study carried out in 1999/2000 by Porter and Gowthorpe in the United Kingdom (Gowthorpe and Porter 2004).

The gap is not a simple gap between two sets of views about the role and performance of audit. To help us explain the gap we have drawn on work by Porter (1993) in New Zealand, which is particularly useful because of the structure she uses to identify the different elements of the gap. The structure developed by her is set out in Figure 2.2, but it has been slightly adapted to give examples of the components identified.

The components are as follows:

1 *A reasonableness gap* that arises because people expect more of audit than it can give in practical terms, such as detecting all instances of fraud, however small. The above studies by Porter and by Porter and Gowthorpe have shown that there is a belief in some quarters that the auditor examines every single transaction and balance, whereas in practice auditors examine samples of transactions and balances from a population, when forming conclusions about the whole population. It would clearly be unreasonable to examine all transactions and balances of a large company.

2 *A performance gap* between what can reasonably be expected of auditors and what they are perceived to do. This gap is itself split in two:

- *A deficient standards gap*, which is the gap between what auditors can be reasonably expected to do and what the profession and the law asks them to do. Thus, a user might reasonably expect auditors to report cases of misappropriation of assets of a company by directors or senior employees to a regulator. If the law and profession do not require this, a deficient standards gap would exist. It is interesting to note that in the UK the auditor has a duty to report this and other matters to regulators of organizations engaged in the provision of financial services, including banks and building societies, although it is not presently a general requirement.
- *A deficient performance gap* (which might be described as a 'rotten auditing' gap). Thus, if the auditing profession has issued a standard that says that auditors should observe the client company's inventory-count procedures,

FIGURE 2.2 Structure of the audit expectation performance gap

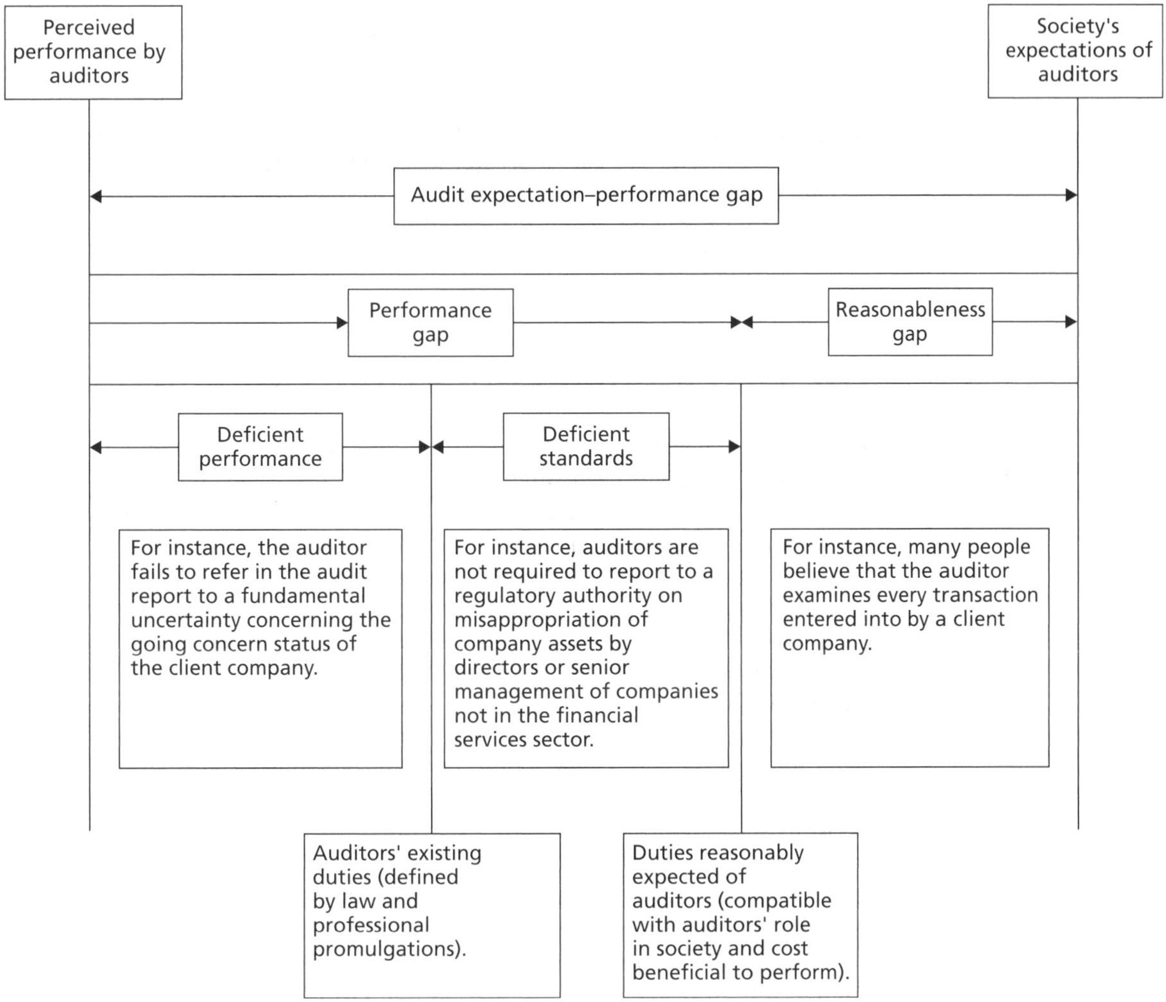

but the auditors fail to do so, their performance would be said to be deficient because they have not behaved in a manner consistent with professional auditing standards.

It is clear from the above brief discussion that the expectations gap has arisen for different reasons. Once one has seen that the gap consists of different components, then one can seek solutions to close the component gap. Thus, if there is evidence that many auditors are failing to perform adequately, one might introduce post-qualification experience measures, or even, at the extreme, withdraw their practising certificate. You might note that there are those who suggest that adopting the broader business risk approach to audit rather than the narrower audit risk approach, may cause expectations to rise, which, if not met, will cause the gap to widen.

Some commentators argue that the gap can never be closed. At the National Auditing Conference in Spring 2001, Porter herself suggested that the gap had become a 'chasm' and Enron and other cases may subsequently have caused even further widening. However, in a more recent study published in a 2008 report to AICPA and IAASB Porter suggests that the gap has closed to a fair extent in the UK (though not in New Zealand) because of (a) better monitoring of auditors' performance and (b) more widespread discussion about corporate governance and financial affairs in general amongst the UK populace. We discuss the expectations gap at greater length in Chapter 18.

This has been a very brief introduction to the audit expectations gap, but we think that it will be useful for you to learn something of current problems as we proceed through the book, rather than just confronting you with them in Chapters 18 and 20.

THE LAYERS OF REGULATION AND CONTROL

This heading suggests that there are disparate kinds of regulation and control which exist alongside each other, seemingly independent, but in fact closely related and impacting on each other. The main layers of regulation and control are first, the external environment and second, the internal environment.

There are many external influences on companies that we can usefully describe in general terms as 'the external environment'. This external environment includes all commercial relationships the company has with its competitors, customers and suppliers of all kinds, whether suppliers of goods, of services and of labour. It also includes other companies with which it cooperates on projects and providers of funds. Sometimes competitors cooperate as when mineral oil companies jointly fund oil pipelines. The relationships are just not one-to-one. All the people and groups we have mentioned above are likely to have relationships with each other. It is important that auditors are aware of all these relationships as, otherwise, it will be difficult to understand how companies operate and the pressures on them. For instance, if a competitor introduces a new product to the market, the company may not only lose customers, but may lose profitability and liquidity, thereby affecting its relationship with suppliers through slower payment and its ability to raise funds from banks or the capital markets. Auditors clearly have an interest in these matters as they are likely to affect the view given by the financial statements. We discuss how companies manage these relationships when we look at the internal environment in Chapter 7.

Useful further reading in the area is a KPMG text *Auditing Organizations Through a Strategic-Systems Lens* (*Bell et al.* 1997).

Apart from commercial and financial relationships, further important influences on companies, particularly large companies, include the framework of regulations imposed on companies from various sources, but, just as importantly, the expectations of society about the way that companies should behave. We have used the term 'expectations of corporate governance' to describe the way that companies behave or should behave to meet the expectations of society. Of course, the external regulatory framework and expectations about corporate governance impinge on the way that companies manage and control themselves internally. These ideas we have set out in Figure 2.3. We expand this figure and discuss it in greater depth in subsequent chapters but an introduction in this early chapter to the matters appearing in Figure 2.3 is appropriate. We have chosen the term 'layers of regulation and control' to indicate that regulation and control operate at different levels both outwith a

FIGURE 2.3 Layers of regulation and control

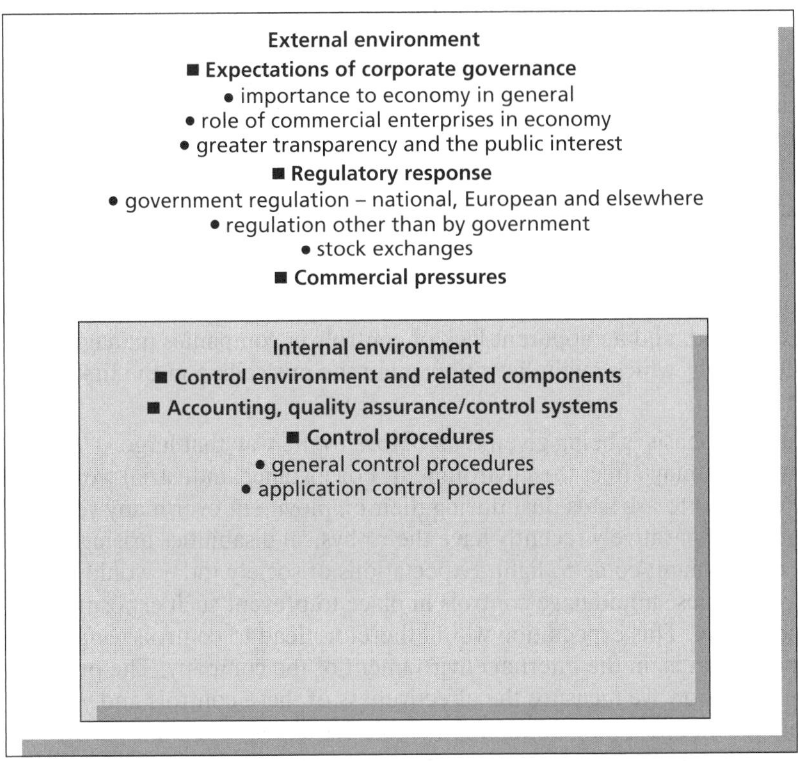
External environment
■ Expectations of corporate governance
• importance to economy in general
• role of commercial enterprises in economy
• greater transparency and the public interest
■ Regulatory response
• government regulation – national, European and elsewhere
• regulation other than by government
• stock exchanges
■ Commercial pressures
Internal environment
■ Control environment and related components
■ Accounting, quality assurance/control systems
■ Control procedures
• general control procedures
• application control procedures

company and within it. As we have mentioned before we want to keep you informed of important matters affecting accountants and auditors as we proceed through this book, although we shall discuss them in depth later on.

Expectations of corporate governance

Corporate governance is the name given to the structures in place within a company or imposed by society to control how companies are governed. Large listed companies play a very important role in society and their success or failure has an effect on all of us, whether we live in the country where those companies are located or not. In the 1980s there was an increasing lack of confidence among many sections of society on the way that companies were governed, including internal controls within companies, how they reported and the way in which auditors conducted their work and reported their findings. There was a complete lack of understanding, for instance, as to how Robert Maxwell could raid the pension funds of the Mirror Group without intervention from within or outwith the group.

This was very similar to the disbelief that a huge company like Enron could collapse in 2001 when an international firm of auditors with a good reputation (Arthur Andersen) was supposedly looking after the stakeholders' interests.

We discuss the development of corporate governance rules in greater detail in Chapters 16 and 18, but note the following matters here:

1 The fact that large companies are so important that society has to find a way of controlling them in the public interest. There is an increasing awareness that the shareholder group is not the only group requiring

protection from the management group. For instance, it seems that Railtrack, owning the railway infrastructure in Great Britain until 2002, was putting the interests of shareholders before the safety of passengers, a most important stakeholder group of that company. It is clear that the banking sector which provoked the credit crisis world-wide in 2008 has responsibilities to much wider groups, including the general public, than its fund managers and shareholders.

2. In view of the above it is clear that there has to be greater transparency as regards how companies organize themselves and attempt to satisfy their user groups. For instance, much publicity was given to mis-selling of personal pension schemes, which left many people with pensions lower than expected, and an apparent lack of controls in companies managing pension funds, which might have prevented the mis-selling in the first place.
3. Greater emphasis is being given than before to the way that large corporations may affect the environment. For instance, industrial workers were exposed to asbestos dust during their employment over many years, but only comparatively recently have their physical disabilities arising from their employment come to light. Expectations of society today would be that companies should have controls in place to prevent such exposure in the first place. This expectation would therefore lead to controls *within* the company, that is, in the internal environment of the company. The problem of course is how we measure the effectiveness of these controls and you will remember that postulate number 5 in Table 2.1 did assume the existence of appropriate measures, perhaps an unwarranted assumption in some fields of human activity.

At the time of writing, there are basically two opposing views on the role of accounting standards – whether they should set out very tight rules to cover every eventuality or whether they should set forth principles that should be followed if a true and fair view is to be obtained.

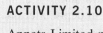

ACTIVITY 2.10

Annets Limited produces toxic waste as a by-product of a production process and stores it in a special warehouse about one mile from a small town. The people living in the town have recently expressed doubt about the safety of the storage facility but the company claims that the risks are lower than those that government regulations permit.

What are the issues you would wish to consider in this case? What questions would you ask?

There is clearly a public interest issue, in that toxic waste escaping from the storage facility might affect public health, particularly among the young. The company clearly has a duty to reveal the nature of the toxic waste, the nature of the storage and what they mean when they say that risks are lower than government regulations permit. What are these government regulations, when were they drafted and are they subject to regular governmental review? What controls does the company have in place to ensure that no losses of waste are occurring? It would be well to remember, in a case like this, that there have been cases of losses of radioactive material from nuclear power plants. Do they carry out regular tests of the local environment to ensure that there are no problems? What is the nature of the tests that they perform? How reliable are they? Who carries out the tests? Clearly, if they were carried out by local independent health and safety inspectors they would be more reliable as far as the community was concerned than they were performed by the company's own staff.

It may be difficult to answer some of these questions, but they are typical of the sort of questions that companies are now being faced with, especially as public expectations are becoming more and more demanding.

We ask you to note here that the corporate governance controls will need to be put in place within companies and that it is individual companies that will be reporting on the existence of appropriate controls and appropriate corporate governance measures, such as competent and independent non-executive directors. However, it is perhaps the need to be seen to protect the public interest that is the driving force behind the greater concern for effective corporate governance.

The Combined Code on Corporate Governance recommends that listed companies have non-executive directors on their board (see Chapter 18).

Regulatory framework

We have mentioned regulation several times earlier in this chapter. Some believe that regulation is necessary but others believe that the market will automatically result in good audits being performed, that the pressure to preserve reputation will force auditors to carry out their work competently, independently and ethically. The conclusion that they draw is that regulation by the state and profession is unnecessary, or if it is, that it should be kept to a minimum.

We take a closer look at regulation in Chapter 4.

The state has intervened in the form of a series of Companies Acts, requiring, among other things, that annual audits be performed for limited companies above a certain size. Much company law in the UK and Ireland is now being affected by directives and regulations coming from the European Union, to aid the smooth running of the European market, but some regulations of governments from outside the European Union are now affecting auditors in the UK and Ireland. This is state regulation, but regulation can take other forms. Thus, when the profession issues guidance on the behaviour of auditors; when accounting standards and auditing standards are issued by the appropriate bodies, they are regulating the accounting and auditing profession. We might observe that regulations are rarely introduced unless they are perceived to be necessary to address existing problems. You might ask yourself why traffic is required to drive on one side of the road only or why, in the audit context, auditors are required to have obtained certain qualifications before they are allowed to audit limited companies, or why, the profession has thought fit to introduce monitoring of professional firms, or why the Sarbanes-Oxley Act introduced legislation to enhance the quality of auditors' work in 2002, shortly after the collapse of Enron.

The Sarbanes-Oxley Act on Corporate Reporting and Responsibility adopted by Congress in the United States in 2002 contains rules on review of audit working papers and files of accounting firms and their quality control procedures, applying these rules to non-US firms who issue an audit opinion on US companies and when non-US firms issue an opinion upon which US firms rely when issuing their own audit opinion.

The importance of the regulatory framework is that it provides not only rules as to whom should be allowed to perform audits but also sets the criteria by which the audit is conducted. For instance, the Companies Act 2006 in Great Britain sets the scope of the audit by requiring financial statements to give a true and fair view and further requiring that the auditor form an opinion on whether the financial statements do indeed give such a view. Similarly, the IAASB and APB set standards by which the audit is conducted by requiring, for instance, that the auditor should obtain sufficient appropriate audit evidence to be able to draw reasonable conclusions on which to base the auditor's opinion (paragraph 4 of ISA 500 – *Audit evidence*). We have seen that there are many similar standards – on audit risk, on materiality, on audit reporting, on quality control, as well as others concerned with such practical matters as the preparation of engagement letters and of working papers. Apart from state regulation and regulation coming from such bodies as IASB, IAASB, ASB and APB, the Stock Exchange (and exchanges in other parts of the world) also issue rules that are applicable to any company seeking a listing on the exchanges.

Commercial pressures

You can see that we have included commercial pressures in the external environment; this is because the way that the market behaves will have a big impact on the way that companies perform and the manner in which they control themselves. For instance, an economic downturn might reduce demand for the company's products or services and the company would need to have a strategy to deal with this. We have already mentioned above that companies may be faced with pressures from competitors, such as the introduction of a new and improved product. The company should have internal systems to report such new developments and would need to respond. If the directors had already anticipated such an event they might have been able to improve their own product lines in time. Thus, the internal environment of the company has to be adapted constantly as a result of pressures in its external environment.

What Figure 2.3 tells us is that the external environment is a vitally important factor influencing the kinds of controls and management's approaches within the internal environment of companies. The needs of society may well force a company to create a control environment that includes the adoption of a management philosophy or operating style that takes into account not only the need for efficient management and the maximization of shareholder wealth, but also the needs of customers, employees and other interested user groups. In Activity 1.7 we introduced you to the idea of maintenance of water quality by a water company as being an issue of prime importance. In such a company, we would expect the management philosophy to include a statement on water quality as well as (say) quantity of water supplied. We would expect to find control measures to prevent pollution of drinking supplies and public beaches by proper control of sewage disposal. These measures would be internal to the company, but proper corporate governance would require the measure not only to be in force, but seen to be in force through corporate governance reports. The same applies to the scenario we envisaged in Activity 2.10. Basically, the company procedures would be those required to provide answers to the many questions we suggested above.

We shall return to Figure 2.3 when we discuss internal controls in Chapter 7. At this stage we ask you to note that company managements and auditors play a societal role, however much they are operating in the internal environment of their companies and clients respectively.

Summary

In this chapter we have introduced you to a structure for understanding the audit process, placing it very firmly in an accountability context. We have suggested that an understanding of the assumptions and ideas underpinning auditing is necessary if the practical discipline of auditing is to be successfully pursued. For this reason we gave you an overview of auditing postulates and of auditing concepts. We looked particularly closely at one of the credibility concepts of auditing – independence. We introduced you to the audit expectations gap and regulation, and highlighted the question of audit quality. Finally, we set the scene for discussion of corporate governance, regulation and controls in companies, all of which will be discussed in greater depth later in the book. Now, you should attempt the self-assessment questions that follow, referring where necessary to the text.

Key points of the chapter

- Theories underpin practice. A philosophy has three aspects: (1) gets back to first principles; (2) systematic organization of knowledge; (3) provides a basis for moulding and understanding social relationships. Postulates are essential to development of an intellectual discipline and are the foundation for any theoretical structure, but they may not hold good for ever, as attitudes in society and the commercial and professional world may change.
- The text discusses 7 postulates of auditing.
- Concepts provide a basis for advancement in the field of knowledge by facilitating communication about it and its problems. They are grouped under four headings: (1) credibility; (2) process; (3) communication; (4) performance.
- Credibility concepts concern the personal qualities of auditors: (a) competence; (b) independence; (c) integrity and ethics. Ethical dilemmas arise where damage will be caused to someone whatever you do, but require analysis, consideration of possible actions and consequences, and a firm decision. Ethical guidance is issued by the professional bodies.
- Process is concerned with how audits are performed – seeking evidence, evaluating risk; making judgements and assessments. There are two types of risk: audit risk that the auditor will fail to reach proper conclusions about accounting information; and business risk that an entity will fail to meet its objectives. Auditors analyse risk and address areas where risk is highest. Business risk approaches may have a much better chance of adding value. Audit risk comprises three components: (i) inherent risk; (ii) control risk; (iii) detection risk. Evidence and audit judgement are both central to the audit. process. Auditors plan their work to make it likely that they will find material errors or misstatements.
- Communication concerns audit reporting. Truth and fairness is about the validity of the message given by the financial statements. Association is of relevance to reporting as company reporting packages contain elements to which the audit report is not specifically directed.
- Performance concerns several issues – that auditors are expected to perform their work with due care and with rigour (encompassing 'professional scepticism'). Quality control comprises procedures to ensure the audit opinion is fit to be made public. Users need to be able to assess audit quality of individual firms.
- There are four parties to the accountability/audit process: (1) preparer/source; (2) users of accounting information; (3) auditor; (4) regulatory framework. The text explains the relationship to agency theory, which assumes that all parties attempt to maximize their wealth.
- There is a close relationship between accountability and audit. Two important elements in the accountability and audit process are 'management assertions' and 'evidence' required to form audit conclusions.
- The 'audit expectations gap' is used to describe the difference between expectations of what auditors should do and what they are perceived to do. The components are: (1) reasonableness gap; (2) performance gap, comprising (a) a deficient standards gap and (b) a deficient performance gap. Solutions can be sought to close each component, but the gaps may also expand as circumstances change.
- Layers of regulation and control are described under two headings: (a) external environment; (b) internal environment; and indicate that regulation and control operate at different levels outwith and within a company.
- The external environment includes all commercial relationships, other companies with which it cooperates, and providers of funds. Auditors must be aware of these relationships to understand how companies operate and the pressures on them.
- Corporate governance refers to structures within companies imposed by society to control how companies, particularly large ones, operate.
- The regulatory framework comprises controls imposed by a wide range of bodies. Commercial and other pressures in the external environment are important because they have an impact on company performance and the way they control themselves.

References

American Accounting Association (1973) *A Statement of Basic Auditing Concepts*, Sarasota, FL: American Accounting Association, 1973.

Bell, B.B., Marrs, F.O., Solomon, I. and Thomas, H. (1997) *Auditing Organizations Through a Strategic-Systems Lens*, KPMG Peat Marwick LLP.

Briloff, A.J. (1986) 'Corporate Governance and Accountability: Whose Responsibility?', unpublished paper presented at the University of Connecticut, Storrs, Connecticut , April.

Flint, D. (1988) *Philosophy and Principles of Auditing: An Introduction,* Basingstoke: Macmillan Education Ltd.

Gowthorpe, C. and Porter, B. (2004) *Audit Expectation–Performance Gap in the United Kingdom in 1999 and Comparison with the Gap in New Zealand in 1989 and in 1999*, ICAS.

Mautz, H.A. and Sharaf, R. (1961) *The Philosophy of Auditing*, Sarasota, FL: American Accounting Association.

Normanton, E.L. (1966) *The Accountability and Audit of Governments: A Comparative Study*, Manchester: Manchester University Press.

Porter, B. (1993) 'An Empirical Study of the Audit Expectation–Performance Gap', *Accounting and Business Research*, 24 (93): 49–68.

Further reading

We would recommend the following:

Bell, B.B., Marrs, F.O., Solomon, I. and Thomas, H. (1997) *Auditing Organizations Through a Strategic-Systems Lens*, KPMG Peat Marwick LLP.

Bell, T.B., Peecher, M.E. and Solomon, I. (2005) *The 21st Century Public Company Audit, Conceptual Elements of KPMG's Global Audit Methodology*, KPMG International.

Cadbury, A. (1990) 'The Corporate Governance Agenda', *Corporate Governance*, 8(1): 7–15. Institute of Chartered Accountants of Scotland (1993) *Auditing into the Twenty-First Century*, ICAS.

Moizer, P. (1991) 'Independence', in M. Sherer and S. Turley (eds), *Current Issues in Auditing*, 3rd edn, London: Paul Chapman Publishing Ch. 3. This chapter also discusses ethical approaches.

Although published quite a time ago the books by Mautz and Sharaf and Flint in the references above contain good discussion of the postulates and concepts underpinning auditing.

Self-assessment questions (solutions available to students)

2.1 Identification of management assertions in respect of figures in the financial statements is a vital part of the audit process. State whether you agree with this statement, giving practical examples.

2.2 Explain what is meant by the principle of auditor integrity. How do you think we should ensure that the principle is adhered to?

2.3 Auditors are expected to approach their work with thoroughness and with an attitude of professional scepticism. What do you think that professional scepticism means in practice?

2.4 You are auditing a company that shows a loss for the year of £700 000. This figure is after charging impairment of property, plant and equipment of £1 500 000. As a part of your work you note that in the Directors' Report a profit of £800 000 is quoted as profit for the year. What are your responsibilities in respect of this matter?

Self-assessment questions (solutions available to tutors)

2.5 Explain how auditing theory might give useful insights into the practice of auditing. Your answer should make reference to the postulates and concepts of auditing.

2.6 Why do you think that the collapse of Enron and other scandals affecting large companies may have resulted in a widening of the audit expectations gap?

2.7 Explain why the general public is just as interested in the way that large companies, including banks, behave as are the shareholders of those companies. What do you think is meant by the public interest?

2.8 The trade payables figure in most companies is normally material in the context of the financial statements taken as a whole. What assertions do you think that management is implicitly making about the trade payables figure? Suggest one audit step for each assertion, which you might take to prove that the assertion is valid.

2.9 What is meant by audit quality and why is it important?

Solutions available to students and Solutions available to tutors

These can be found on the website in the student/lecturer section at: www.cengage.co.uk/graymanson5.

Topics for class discussion without solutions

2.10 The audit function is vital to society. Discuss.

2.11 Do you think that most auditors are interested in a philosophical approach to their work. If not, why not?

3

The meaning and importance of auditor independence: factors affecting independence and measures to attain it

LEARNING OBJECTIVES

After studying this chapter you should be able to:

- **Explain the importance of auditor independence and the practical implications for the auditor in meeting the demands of the audit role.**
- **Define auditor independence.**
- **Understand the difference between practitioner and profession independence.**
- **Explain how various kinds of conflict and risk can affect the independence of the auditor.**
- **Identify factors that can affect the respective power of auditor and client and perceptions of auditor independence.**
- **Recognize that previous academic studies have influenced the profession in the preparation of its ethical guidance.**
- **Critically evaluate Codes of Ethics issued by IFAC and APB and suggest further ways in which auditor independence could be strengthened.**
- **Discuss the role of the engagement partner, the ethics partner and the engagement quality control reviewer.**
- **Discuss recent changes in the rules relating to independence introduced in the European Union and the United States.**
- **Evaluate the arguments for and against mandatory auditor rotation.**

Learning objectives, 60
Introduction, 61
Independence and the role of audit, 61
Definitions of independence, 64
Practitioner and profession independence, 65
Conflict, power of auditor and client and effect on perceived independence, 70
Published codes of ethics, 77
General principles of the IFAC code, 78
Audit firm's control environment, 80
Safeguards to counter threats to integrity, objectivity and independence, 86
Small entities, 101
Other pronouncements on auditor independence, 101
Summary, 104
Key points of the chapter, 104
References, 106
Further reading, 106
Self-assessment questions (solutions available to students), 106
Self-assessment questions (solutions available to tutors), 107
Topics for class discussion without solutions, 107

INTRODUCTION

In Chapter 2, we discussed briefly the public expectation that auditors should be independent of those whose work they are auditing and to whom they are reporting. In Chapter 1 we set out the fundamental principles of independent auditing, of which the one on objectivity and independence reads as follows:

> Auditors are objective and provide impartial opinions unaffected by bias, prejudice, compromise and conflicts of interest. Auditors are also independent, this requires them to be free from situations and relationships which would make it probable that a reasonable and informed third party would conclude that the auditors' objectivity either is impaired or could be impaired.

See page 24.

In this chapter we discuss the nature and role of independence in greater detail. We consider a number of elements, which may inhibit the auditor from being independent of the subject matter of the audit. Definitions of audit invariably include the notion of 'independence'. Thus, Flint (1988), defining audit in broad terms, sees independence as an essential element:

> The social concept of audit is a special kind of examination by a person other than the parties involved which compares performance with expectation and reports the result; it is part of the public and private control mechanism of monitoring and securing accountability.

The quality of independence is perceived to be relevant to many different kinds of auditing and assurance services. Because of the Enron Corporation and other scandals, the importance of auditor independence has received unwelcome media exposure. In particular we consider briefly some of the provisions contained in the US Sarbanes-Oxley Act of 2002, which is one of the direct responses to the Enron scandal.

INDEPENDENCE AND THE ROLE OF AUDIT

We shall see later that there is uncertainty about the role of audit, but one of the more important roles is contained in Flint's definition of audit referred to above, that of 'monitoring and securing accountability'. Flint suggests that:

> The character of accountability does not wholly lend itself to precise definition and is of an evolving nature adjusting to changes in social, political and economic thought and in the ethics and standards of society.

While it may be true that accountability cannot be defined precisely, we can give you some ideas about the concept that will aid understanding. Stewart (1984) suggested that two elements had to be present if a true *bond* of accountability is to exist:

- An *account*. A set of published financial statements is an example of an account.
- A *holding to account*. This means that action can be taken to make the preparers of the account liable for the matter of their account. Thus, the directors preparing the financial statements can be held to account by the shareholders, who, if they wish, can sack them.

Thus, a set of financial statements is an important accountability document, but – and this is of interest for students of auditing – only if it can be shown to be a document that paints a valid picture. This is why audit is so important; it is a vital element in achieving accountability. We have seen that Mackenzie (1964) suggested that, without audit, there can be no accountability, the argument being that credibility can only be given by persons seen to be independent of the subject of the audit and of any interested stakeholders.

There are a number of different classification systems but we feel that these will give you some insight into the nature of accountability. A useful discussion of accountability in the public sector is to be found in Sinclair (1995).

We may also gain more insight into accountability by looking at broad classifications of accountability. The classifications are as follows:

- *Political accountability*. This kind of accountability is often used to describe the direct chain of accountability between public servant, elected representatives and the electors. In practice, it may result in a clear division between accountability for policy decisions by elected representatives to electors and accountability for administration by public servants to the elected representatives. It could be argued that directors of a company have political accountability to the shareholders who elect them, although the electorate in this case is more restricted than that for central or local government.
- *Public accountability*. This kind of accountability is wider than political accountability and is used to describe the accountability of those controlling resources to the public at large. In some cases accountability to the public is clear as, for instance, of a company in the financial services industry giving advice to members of the public. In other cases such accountability may not be so clear. For instance, to what extent could the directors of a mineral oil company be held accountable to the public for their pricing policy?
- *Managerial accountability*. Accountability of this type arises because of the position that a person occupies within a hierarchy, as where subordinates are held to account by their superiors. Questions might be asked such as: 'You were set this target; why did you not achieve it?' 'Our policy is to provide clean water to members of the public; why did you allow contamination to take place?'
- *Professional accountability*. This kind of accountability is that which exists in a professional or expert group, where members of the group have a sense of duty to other members of the group or profession. Thus members of an accounting body might have a sense of accountability in respect of the professional standards of that body and towards their fellow members. Professional accountability might also be seen in a group of experts within a company, as where a group of engineers might have a sense of duty towards maintaining high technical standards.
- *Personnel accountability*. This sort of accountability is individual in nature and is about being accountable to yourself for maintaining your personal set of values. We argue that we all have a set of personal values that we try to maintain, even though we may infringe them from time to time. It can, however, be a very powerful kind of accountability, particularly if it is supported by the culture of the organization within which you work.

The different kinds of accountability can clearly co-exist in organizations. For instance, individual directors might have a managerial accountability to the full board, with the whole board and individual directors having political accountability to shareholders. It can be argued that agency theory is concerned primarily with political and managerial accountability, as contract is an important element of it. If this is the case, the existence of the other kinds of accountability (public, professional and personal) may reduce the force of political (and managerial) accountability and therefore of agency theory because they introduce considerations other than the well-being of the managers and principals. For instance, engineers may insist on higher degrees of safety as a professional requirement than wished by managers and principals.

The important question for us is whether the auditor is responsible for helping to achieve *all* classes of accountability. In particular, is the auditor there to secure public accountability (a wide view of accountability) or political accountability (a restricted accountability in the sense that it is due to a restricted group of individuals)? We have suggested that directors and the board are politically accountable to shareholders. As auditors address their reports to shareholders, one might think that they are only responsible for securing political accountability. If this view were to prevail, the role of audit would be a restricted one, but there are many who argue that the role should be extended and that accountability by directors of companies should be to wider groups in society. We discuss this matter at greater length later in this book when we consider in Chapter 20 various criticisms of the auditing profession and the response of the profession to those criticisms.

ACTIVITY 3.1

Now consider the following situations and ask yourself if the independent auditor could aid accountability:

1 A manager is contracted to set up an effective computerized payables system.
2 A newspaper publishes figures of circulation for the previous six months.
3 A local authority lays down written rules that the streets should be cleaned once every two weeks.

Ask who is accountable to whom. What form might the accountability statement take, and could an auditor audit the statement?

In case one, the manager would seem to be accountable to the person who asked for the task to be performed. The accountability document might be a simple assertion, contained in the report from the manager, saying that the system was up and running. Auditors could test the operation of the system and report on its effectiveness. If they were seen to be independent, competent and ethical, the manager's report would become credible and accountability would be achieved.

In case two, the same applies. The accountability document is the statement by the newspaper that its average daily sales were (say) 500 000 over a period of time. The newspaper is accountable to its readers and advertisers. An

FIGURE 3.1 The role of audit

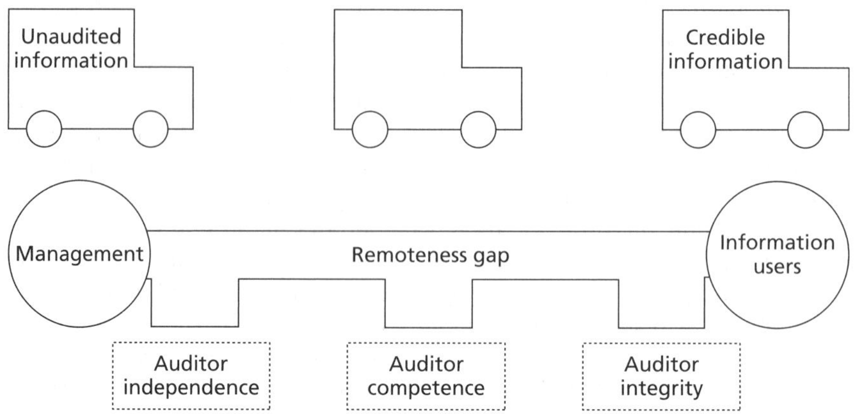

auditor might seek evidence to support it by checking print runs, usage of newsprint, recorded sales, returns from newsagents and so on.

In case three, the local authority's written statement that streets were cleaned at two-weekly intervals would be an accountability document, and the authority would be accountable to residents and local taxpayers, to name but two groups. The statement is auditable and the auditor could examine cleansing department records, and correspondence from residents, and might even visually inspect the streets to see how clean they were. This latter step would be one measuring effectiveness of the cleaning programme rather than whether cleaning took place on a two-weekly basis. To prove the accuracy of the local authority's records, the auditor might observe the cleaning of selected streets and check that the cleansing department's records were accurate.

Independence is not the only quality of the auditor which adds to the credibility of audit reports. Competence and the integrity of the auditor are, as we saw in Chapter 2, just as important.

We turn now to the concept of independence, which is of some importance in relation to accountability. Lee (1986) suggests that the need for independence is derived from the 'remoteness gap' between managers running the organization and stakeholders having an interest in it. His basic argument is that in those cases where the stakeholders do not have the opportunity to question or even know the managers who are accountable to them, the independent auditor, with adequate powers to obtain the information needed, must stand in their place. The role of audit can be seen in Figure 3.1.

DEFINITIONS OF INDEPENDENCE

In looking for a definition of auditor independence one has to say that the words that are used to describe it all tend to have an indefinable quality about them. Flint (1988), for instance, uses the following expressions to describe independence: 'completely objective', 'unprejudiced by previous involvement in the subject of audit', 'uncompromised by vested interest in the outcome or its consequences', 'unbiased and uninfluenced by considerations extraneous to the matter at issue'. You will observe that many of the words used by Flint are in respect of intangible qualities that are not easily observable – objective, unprejudiced, uncompromised, unbiased, uninfluenced.

In the discussion that follows we intend to trace the development of work done in analysing auditor independence and to identify factors that may have an impact upon it. We then take a look at what the profession and others think should be done to ensure that the intangible qualities referred to above do exist and are seen to exist in auditors.

PRACTITIONER AND PROFESSION INDEPENDENCE

Mautz and Sharaf identified two types of independence: practitioner-independence and profession-independence. These two types are clearly related as all audit practitioners are members of a profession, but Mautz and Sharaf distinguished between the two because people often distinguish between individuals and the profession to which they belong.

Philosophy of Auditing (1961).

Practitioner independence

Mautz and Sharaf noted that 'practitioner-independence … is basically a state of mind' and analysed the pressures and factors 'which may colour or influence his disinterestedness'. They identified three dimensions of practitioner independence and suggested a number of guides or clues to help the auditor to determine whether independence may have been infringed. These we set out in Table 3.1 and include:

- Programming independence, requiring that auditors have freedom to develop their own programme, both as steps to be included and the amount of work to be performed, within the overall bounds of the engagement.
- Investigative independence, requiring that no legitimate source of information is closed to the auditors. This requires that the auditors have freedom to examine information that the auditors themselves deem to be relevant. Thus, if the auditors wish to examine budgets and forecast accounts of the following period, they should be allowed to do so.
- Reporting independence, meaning that the contents of the report are determined by the scope of examination. They suggest that the following neatly expresses this requirement: 'You tell us what to do and we'll tell you what we can write in our report; you tell us what you want us to say in our report and we'll tell you what we have to do.'

ACTIVITY 3.2

A friend of yours is a partner in charge of an office of her firm. You are aware that one of the matters that will affect her income and her progress through the firm is the additional income she brings into the firm from existing and potential clients. Do you think that this will affect her independence in relation to your clients? What do you think should be included in ethical standards or codes for professional accountants and auditors in respect of this matter?

We discuss ethical standards and codes later in this chapter.

TABLE 3.1 Three dimensions of practitioner independence and guides or clues as to areas of infringement

Programming independence	Investigative independence	Reporting independence
1a Freedom from managerial interference or friction intended to eliminate, specify or modify any portion of the audit. This requires that the auditor has freedom to develop his or her own programme and the amount of work to be performed, within the overall bounds of the engagement.	**1b** Direct and free access to all company books, records, officers and employees, and other sources of information with respect to business activities, obligations and resources.	**1c** Freedom from any feeling of loyalty or any obligation to modify the impact of reported facts on any party.
2a Freedom from interference with or an uncooperative attitude respecting the application of selected procedures.	**2b** Active cooperation from managerial personnel during the course of the auditor's examination.	**2c** Avoidance of the practice of excluding significant matters from the formal report in favour of their inclusion in an informal report of any kind.
3a Freedom from any outside attempts to subject the audit to review other than that provided for in the audit process.	**3b** Freedom from any managerial attempt to assign or specify the activities to be examined or to establish the acceptability of evidential matter.	**3c** Avoidance of intentional or unintentional use of ambiguous language in the statement of facts, opinions and recommendations, and in their interpretation
	4b Freedom from personal interests or relationships leading to exclusion from or limitation of the examination of any activity record or person that otherwise would have been included in the audit.	**4c** Freedom from any attempt to overrule the auditor's judgement as to appropriate content of the audit report, either factual or in his or her opinion.

3a means that once the terms of the audit engagement have been agreed (for instance, an opinion to be given on the truth and fairness of information), the auditor must have the freedom to set the programme to meet those terms.

This is not an easy matter for the profession. Looked at objectively, the partner's independence would seem to be affected. One way to generate additional income from existing clients is to be friendly with their managers, so that the auditors will be the first to be considered if additional services are required. These services might include consultancy advice on accounting systems or advice on filling personnel vacancies within the client organization. This is fraught with danger as managers with the power to ask you to provide those services, may also be those who wish a certain view to be shown by the financial statements. For instance, there might be doubt about the ability of a subsidiary company to stay afloat in current adverse economic conditions, but being a matter of judgement about a future event, the partner might be unconsciously swayed towards management's view that the company will survive. Mautz and Sharaf point out that often 'the greatest threat to independence is a slow, gradual, almost casual erosion of his "honest disinterestedness"' and that 'this possibility requires constant attention to the maintenance of independence by all concerned'. You might have suggested that the ethical standards and codes should highlight more clearly the pressures on individuals and the ways that firms might alleviate them. One suggestion might be to ensure that any request by managers for additional services should be passed to other individuals within the audit firm not associated with the client. Whether this would be enough to reduce the adverse effect on apparent independence is a matter of conjecture. You might also have suggested that the statement should advise firms providing audit services to refrain from providing consultancy services.

Profession independence

Mautz and Sharaf suggested that: 'like the individual practitioner, the profession as a whole must avoid any appearance of lacking independence'. They suggest, however, that 'Auditing, unfortunately, does not have any "built-in" characteristics that assure the sceptic of its integrity and independence.'

They give the example of the judiciary 'giving the impression of as nearly complete independence as can be obtained', with a hierarchy of courts so that the decisions of lower judges are scrutinized by higher and more experienced judges and note that 'nothing like this exists in auditing'. In a telling addition to these comments Mautz and Sharaf refer to the fact that: 'auditing suffers from what may be described as "built-in anti-independence factors"', and list the features which they believe lead the public to doubt the independence of the auditor as a member of the auditing profession. These features are presented in Table 3.2. Mautz and Sharaf sum up this section as follows:

We shall see later in this chapter that published ethical standards do not allow success in selling non-audit services to influence staff remuneration and promotion prospects in an audit firm. In practice it might be difficult to determine if these requirements are being adhered to. Even the courts have been accused of bias in recent years.

> It seems clear that there are forces at work within the profession presenting some challenges to the image of profession-independence. Accounting appears to be intimately associated with business-like characteristics in its structure and operation. There is little about public accounting that would encourage the uninformed person … to see auditors as possessing the ultimate in independence.

Later writers have introduced intellectual rigour into the analysis of independence issues, often by reference to agency theory, and analysed the basic independence factors in the context of self-interest. Watts and Zimmerman (1986)

TABLE 3.2 Reasons to question auditor independence

Reason	Examples	Comments
A The close relationship which the profession of public accounting has with business	1 Apparent financial dependence	The apparent financial dependence derives from the fact that the audit of business companies represent the bulk of audit work and that auditors are directly reliant on business companies for the bulk of their income.
	2 Existence of a confidential relationship	One of the ethical requirements of the auditing profession is that the relationship between auditor and client should be a confidential one. The problem is that shared secrets imply a degree of intimacy and outsiders may feel that this results in a threat to objectivity.
	3 Strong emphasis on service to management	Regarding the strong emphasis on service to management, you should note that the publicity material of many firms stress ability to serve management's interests in many different ways. Again it is likely that this tendency in the profession will give an appearance of dependence to outsiders.
B The organization of the profession	1 Tendency towards the emergence of a limited number of large firms	The tendency towards the emergence of a limited number of large firms observed by Mautz and Sharaf in 1961, has become even more apparent in recent years with the emergence of the Big Four audit firms. There may be valid reasons for this to happen as small or even medium-sized firms may lack resources to service their larger clients. However, the problem is that firms, particularly the large ones, can look more like a business venture than a professional type of service. The fact that the firms have to be well organized and businesslike gives this impression, but there has also been a conscious move away from the provision of a service *per se* to a business/profit-oriented view of their activities. The firms have made great play recently of the profit that they

Note, however, in the case of client companies operating in a regulated industry the auditor may have a duty to report direct to regulators, thus breaking the confidentiality rule.

TABLE 3.2 *(Continued)*

Reason	Examples	Comments
		make from their various activities, including audit. In practice they give the impression of being more like large corporations than professional partnerships.
	2 Lack of professional solidarity	The lack of professional solidarity derives from the fact of strong competition between audit firms. There are rules in existence requiring contact with outgoing auditors when taking over an engagement from a competing firm, but the impression is gained that firms are fighting hard to gain and retain clients. You should ask yourself if the appearance of lack of objectivity might be present because of competitive pressures.
	3 Tendency to introduce 'salesmanship'	Regarding the 'salesmanship' question, large firms are very conscious of the need for practice development. Mautz and Sharaf did accept that seeking to provide a service is not in itself unprofessional, but suggested that there is more to a profession than merely rendering a service.

This does not just apply to large firms. Small and medium-sized firms are also in a very competitive market.

discuss the question of the auditors' monitoring activities, taking the view that such monitoring will not be valuable to people interested in the activity of organizations unless they consider that the likelihood is high that auditors will report significant matters of concern. These writers believe in the ability of markets to influence human behaviour and recognize that the auditor is important in making believable what managers report to owners and others. Watts and Zimmerman consider, however, that the probability of them reporting matters of concern is likely to be high because of the adverse effects on their reputation if their failure to report comes to light. They note that 'the very existence of a demand for the auditor's services depends on that probability's level being high'.

We shall see later that published ethical standards state that a hot review by an independent person within the firm would be performed where it is expected that the fees regularly exceed a certain percentage of a firm's annual fee income.

Nine per cent of total fees may be significant enough to suggest that the auditor might not be unbiased in relation to the client. On the other hand, the circumstances of the overstatement do strongly suggest that incompetence is likely. Any investigation of the case would consider the existence of both factors – incompetence and lack of independence.

See Activity 3.3 on page 70

ACTIVITY 3.3

You own some shares in an unlisted company in the building industry at a time when the industry faces considerable problems because of lack of orders, but when you read the audit report, you find that the auditors have stated that, in their opinion, the financial statements of the previous year give a true and fair view. The company collapses shortly afterwards and it comes to light that the value of long-term contract work in progress has been significantly overstated, because total fixed costs of all contracts had been allocated to each contract instead of its proportion of total costs. It also becomes known that the fees from the assignment represented 9 per cent of the total fees of the auditing firm. How would you prove that the auditor lacked independence in this case or was merely incompetent?

CONFLICT, POWER OF AUDITOR AND CLIENT AND EFFECT ON PERCEIVED INDEPENDENCE

We now wish to introduce you to some interesting ideas on independence, those of Goldman and Barlev, writing in 1974, and Shockley in 1982. We know that these writings lie some time in the past, but this makes them no less valid. Goldman and Barlev first identified possible areas of conflict between different groups of people associated with organizations and suggested that, where conflict existed, pressures affecting independence might arise:

- Conflicts of interest between the auditor and the client organization (management and shareholders) because the (truthful) audit report may not be seen as in the interests of either management or shareholders or both groups.
- Conflict between the auditor's professional duty and self-interest. A typical scenario might be compliance with management's wishes even if not professionally acceptable in order to retain the assignment.
- Conflict between managers and shareholders. The managers may wish to mislead the shareholders for their own reasons, even if only on a short-term basis.
- Conflict between the client organization and third parties. The organization may, for instance, wish to mislead outside providers of finance (such as lenders) about its position to enhance the likelihood that further finance is forthcoming, even though this may not be in the best interests of the third party.

This notion of self-interest has been reflected in published ethical standards.

An important element in Goldman and Barlev's work was emphasis on matters that increase or decrease the respective power of the client organization (effectively the managers) and the auditor. Other writers built on their ideas and work by Shockley (1982) we believe is particularly useful for students wanting to understand the various factors that may affect the perception of independence.

Shockley produced a conceptual model (see Figure 3.2) based on previous studies that had identified certain factors as having an impact on the auditor's ability to withstand pressure. He emphasized that the various independence factors may have both positive and negative effects on the power of firms (managers) and auditors, and that a great deal of work is still required to determine the 'value' of the pluses and minuses of each. The factors identified are as follows:

IMPORTANT NOTE

When we come to look at the IFAC and APB ethical standards later in this chapter we shall see that the work of Goldman and Barlev, and Shockley, particularly the latter, has had a huge impact on the development of these standards.

This suggests that the work of academics can have considerable influence on the way that professional accountants and auditors behave.

1 Provision of non-audit or non-assurance services, termed management advisory services (MAS).
2 Competition in the auditing profession (competition).
3 The period for which the auditor has held the position (tenure).
4 Size of the audit firm (size).
5 The flexibility of accounting standards (accounting flexibility).
6 The degree of severity of professional sanctions and their application (professional sanctions).
7 The extent of the auditor's legal liability to third parties (legal liability).
8 The fear the auditor might have of losing clientele and of losing his or her reputation (fear of losing clientele, reputation).

The emphasis of Figure 3.2 is on perceived independence because being seen to be independent is just as important from the point of view of adding credibility to the subject of the audit as actual independence.

In reading the above diagram you should note that, as in algebra, a plus (+) multiplied by a plus (+) gives a plus (+), that a minus (−) turns a plus into a negative (−), but a minus (−) turns a minus (−) into a plus (+). Thus, two plus factors (+ and +) results in a plus (+); a plus factor and a minus factor (+ and −) results in a minus (−); whereas two minus factors (− and −) result in a plus (+). You may find Figure 3.2 difficult to read at first, but if you follow the logic of the lines from the factor to perceived independence, you should find it quite easy to understand.

We illustrate Shockley's argument, using his notation, by reference to the eight factors listed above. In the process we summarize the arguments that suggest that each factor may have a positive or negative effect on perceived independence.

FIGURE 3.2 Shockley's (1982) conceptual model of perceived independence

Tenure
n+
p+
q+
o−
d+
Value of auditor to client
e+
h−
Competition
MAS
Z
Perceived independence
c+
Dependence of client on auditor
a+
m+
i+
Auditor's ability to withstand pressure
t+
b−
X
Dependence of auditor on client
s+
Y
g−
r+
Legal liability
j−
f+
X
Accounting flexibility
Size of audit firm
k−
Y
i+
Z
Professional sanctions
Fear of losing clientele

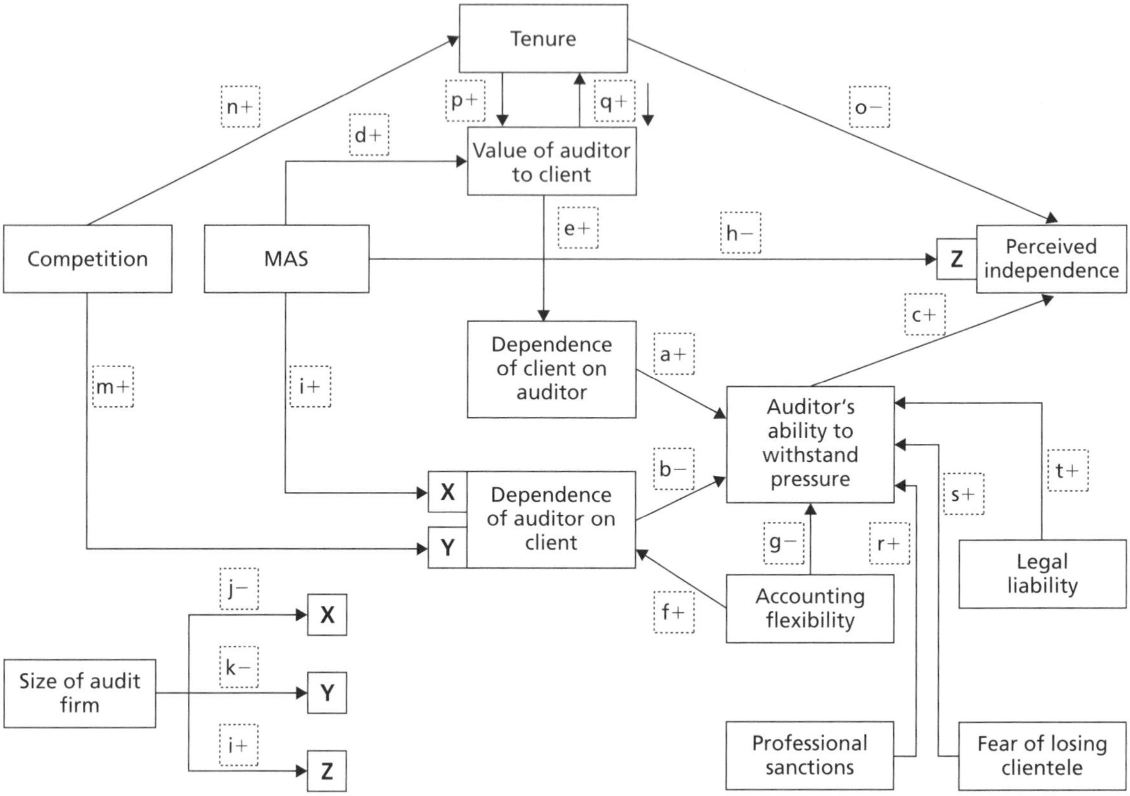

1 Provision of MAS services by the auditor

Line 'deac': taking this line, the MAS may be said to increase positively (through operator 'd') the value of the auditor to the client and that there will be increased dependence of the client on the auditor (shown by operator 'e'). The argument then runs that this makes it easier to withstand pressure by the client (operator 'a') and that through operator 'c', this results in a perception (by users) of greater independence of the auditor.

Line 'ibc'; taking the counter (non-independence) argument, the greater the provision of MAS services the greater (through line operator 'i') the dependence of the auditor on the client (because of the value of the fees to the auditor), thus reducing (through operator 'b') the auditor's ability to withstand pressure – with a consequent negative effect (through operator 'c') on perceived independence.

In this case, however, Shockley introduces (through what he calls a 'detached variable') consideration of the size of the audit firm. Thus operator 'i', indicating increased dependence of the auditor, may be affected by the detached variable 'X' (operator 'j') which indicates that a large firm may be less dependent on a particular client (and therefore more able to withstand pressure). Thus, a small firm 'ibc' will result in a detrimental effect on perceived independence, whereas, the argument runs, the large firm 'ibc' will not have an adverse effect or not such a great negative effect.

Operator 'h' suggests that there is a direct negative relationship between MAS and perceived independence because of concerns that the auditor may become a quasi-employee or an advocate of the client, may have a financial interest in the success of the business or be placed in the position of auditing his or her own decisions.

In this case, however, Shockley notes that size of the audit firm may be of relevance through detached variable 'Z'. He notes that in small professional firms the auditor and the consultant are frequently the same person, whereas in large professional firms audit and consultancy arms are usually in separate departments.

Line 'dqo' suggests that MAS increases ('d') the value of the auditor to the client and that there will be increased likelihood of long tenure (operator 'q') with a consequent negative impact on perceived independence through that long tenure (operator 'o').

Before discussing other elements in Shockley's diagram, note that Shockley did not form firm conclusions as to how much of the appearance of independence was affected by the various lines. What he did say was that there may be an effect and it is up to researchers, regulators and the profession to make policy on the basis of careful investigation, basically to determine how strong the various pluses and minuses are. He notes in relation to MAS (as we have seen above) that his model shows four paths that have potential impacts on the perception of independence, but three are negative and one is positive so that net effect of MAS restrictions are indeterminate.

2 Competition in the auditing profession (competition)

There are possible negative effects on perceived independence, arising from competition within the profession. The Cohen Committee in the United States, among others, had reservations about the impact of competition on the effectiveness of audit. Cohen in particular was concerned that competition might have an adverse effect on audit quality. In Shockley's view, poor audit quality might arise in this case because of lack of independence.

Figure 3.2 (through operator 'm') suggests that competition for audit clients increases audit dependency on the client because increased competition makes it more likely that an auditor will be replaced by one prepared to agree with management. Variable 'Y' shows the belief in a potentially greater risk for smaller firms.

There is a possible positive effect on perceived independence in that competition may cause tenure (see below) to reduce, thus improving perceptions of independence through path 'no'.

3 The period of time the auditor has been in office (tenure)

The concern about tenure arises because if a company and an auditing firm have been in close association for a long time this may lead to auditors identifying with their client's management with a consequent detrimental effect on independence. This view has led to suggestions that audit firms should be rotated with the added benefit that this would: (i) result in automatic checks of the work of the previous auditor; (ii) encourage audit innovation; and (iii) discourage complacency. The reduction in perceived independence arising from long tenure is shown by operator 'o'. However, as shown by operator 'p', there may be positive effects of tenure as it causes the incumbent auditors to be of greater benefit to the client since audit services are less costly and more efficient because they know the client well. This in turn gives rise to a reverse positive effect on tenure (operator 'q'). Shockley suggests that there is a negative link between MAS and independence as shown by the path 'dqo'.

4 Size of the audit firm (size)

We have already mentioned the possible effects of audit firm size on the impact of other factors such as the provision of MAS and competition. Shockley suggests that there are many arguments supporting the assertion that larger auditing firms are more likely to be independent, although he sees the research results as contradictory:

- A large firm is less dependent on a particular client because the client's fees represent a smaller proportion of total fees.
- Certain characteristics of smaller audit practices may be inherently dangerous to independence because, for instance, their relationship to clients is closer. They may be providing expertise lacked by the client in many areas (such as accounting and tax advice) and there is likely to be a greater emphasis on personal service.
- Large firms are better able to compartmentalize the audit and MAS functions.

It is worth mentioning in this context that individual auditing firms vary from the very small practice (with one practitioner or a small number of partners) to the very large (Big four) firms (with large numbers of partners and professional staff spread throughout the world and with many offices). In another contribution in this area Lee (1986) suggests that the independence problem depends upon the nature of the relationship between auditor and auditee and principally on the relative size of the participants. We show the effect of relative size in Table 3.3.

We return to this matter when we consider the ethical standards and codes relating to small entities later in this chapter.

5 Flexibility of accounting standards (accounting flexibility)

Accounting flexibility is said to make the auditor more dependent on the client because flexibility increases the probability that an auditor who does not agree with management will be replaced (operator 'f'). This is because an independent auditor favouring a particular accounting policy, might be rejected by the client in favour of another auditor who would accept the client's preferred policy where the accounting standard allowed a number of different treatments. However, Figure 3.2 shows there may also be a direct impact on the auditor's ability to withstand pressure (operator 'g') because flexibility makes it easier for the auditor to justify departures from accounting standards. The argument here is that the auditors may not hold to their own beliefs and may be swayed by management where accounting standards allow alternative treatments.

TABLE 3.3 Size and independence

Company		Audit firm
Small	Two pressures against independence: **1** Recurring audit fee loss often serious as related to economic survival and may be difficult to replace. **2** Close personal relationship with company, often providing many management services because of lack of resources/expertise in small company. But public interest not so high? Therefore, review not audit?	*Small*
Large	Major pressure against independence: fear of losing a substantial audit fee from a large client company. Principle is to be seen to be independent. Note that APB Ethical Standards sets limits on fees obtained from one client. Compare this with a United States proposal in the early years of the twentieth century that an audit fee should not exceed more than 1 per cent of the auditor's personal wealth.	*Small*
Small	In this case, the audit firm will probably be providing a high degree of management services. Firm may not be independent of systems installed by them. APB Ethical Standards state that there may be a management threat and suggests safeguards. There is little likelihood that the fee limits from one client will be breached.	*Large*
Large	On the face of it fewer problems but note: **1** Management advisory services likely. **2** Continuous auditing may breed familiarity and the treatment of audit staff almost as employees.	*Large*

In interpreting the data in Table 3.3 it should be remembered that in small companies many shareholders are frequently not remote from management as directors may be important shareholders. In large companies the directors often do hold shares in their company but these holdings are likely to be small in relation to the total shares in issue. Most shareholders of large companies will be remote from the directors. Remoteness, of course, is one reason why independence on the part of the auditor is important.

6 The degree of severity of professional sanctions and their application (professional sanctions)

Shockley observes that published codes of professional ethics support and enhance professional integrity but notes that the 'public needs some assurance that (auditors) will adhere to the code'. This assurance is provided by professional sanctions such as suspension or revocation of the right to practice, such sanctions increasing the auditor's perceived cost of inappropriate behaviour. This is shown by operator 'r' but its value will depend upon the degree of enforcement and the penalties incurred.

7 The extent of the auditor's legal liability to third parties (legal liability)

We discuss legal liability in Chapter 19.

The threat of legal liability to third parties is seen as a factor increasing perceived independence through operator 't'. We might note here that the United States is a more litigious environment than in the UK and Ireland, and Europe generally and that the Caparo case has reduced the likelihood of litigation for the auditors of public limited companies.

8 The fear the auditor might lose clientele and of losing his or her reputation (fear of losing clientele, reputation)

This factor relates to the belief that auditing firms would wish to avoid loss of reputation from adverse publicity of poor auditing, perceived to arise from lack of independence. This is because they believe that they would lose clientele as a result, as in the long run clients need the assurance given by a reputable audit report. This is shown by operator 's'.

Shockley suggests that factors 6, 7 and 8 all affect professional integrity by altering the perceived cost of unprofessional behaviour.

We have spent some time considering Shockley's model, as we believe that it puts many of the factors that may affect independence into a logical framework. As we have already mentioned, Shockley, himself, saw his conceptual model as an aid to researchers and regulators and he makes clear that the problem is not the identification of potential pressures on independence as such but the strength of the various effects (plus or minus) that must be determined.

ACTIVITY 3.4

If you were asked to explain auditor independence to someone who knows little about auditing, would you find Shockley's analysis useful? Explain why.

One of the problems is that the ideas discussed above appear to be contradictory. For each positive factor enhancing the perception of independence, there appears to be a negative effect, and it is not clear how strong the positive and negative effects are. From this point of view it may not be very useful for policy makers whether in the government or in the profession. However, the idea of respective power is a useful one and the arguments above certainly show that the question of independence is a complex one. We have discussed these ideas with students for many years and there was a strand of argument coming from many of them that independence, being a vital element, needs the tenure argument to be looked at more closely. New auditors would not necessarily be ineffective because of lack of knowledge of the client and indeed might well be more effective (enhancing the strength of their position) because they are looking at the client with a new eye (sometimes known as the 'New Broom' syndrome). We find it interesting that they were able to come up with arguments such as this, after being introduced to the ideas of Goldman and Barlev, and Shockley. On the whole, therefore we find the analysis useful.

PUBLISHED CODES OF ETHICS

Now that we have reviewed some of the academic work on independence, we shall introduce you to the Code of Ethics for Professional Accountants issued by the International Ethics Standards Board for Accountants (IESBA), an independent standard-setting body within the International Federation of Accountants (IFAC), and to the Ethical Standards (ESs) issued by APB in the UK and Ireland. We shall find that many of the matters raised by academics discussed above are reflected in the Code and Ethical Standards, which represent the regulators's answer to the intangible quality of objectivity and independence.

The Code of Ethics issued by IESBA was last revised in 2009. We refer to this as the IFAC Code in our subsequent discussion.

We shall approach this topic in the following manner:

- First, we give you a general introduction to the IFAC Code.
- Second, we move to a discussion of the structure underpinning the ethical control environment established for audit firms by reference to the IFAC Code and in the UK and Ireland by ES1 – *Integrity, objectivity and independence*.
- Third, we discuss the general principles regarding safeguards to threats to integrity, objectivity and independence, addressed by both the IFAC Code and the APB ESs.

IMPORTANT NOTE

Accounting bodies in the UK and Ireland have issued their own codes of ethics, derived from the IFAC Code of Ethics for Professional Accountants. Legislation has required the accounting bodies to adopt the Ethical Standards (ESs), issued by APB. Accordingly, when conducting audit engagements in the UK and the Republic of Ireland, professional accountants should comply with the requirements of ESs, but when performing audit engagements elsewhere, they should comply with the requirements of the section of the IFAC Code dealing with Audit and Review Engagements (Section 290). Furthermore, APB has stated in ISA 200 (UK and Ireland) that it is not aware of any significant instances where the relevant parts of the IFAC Code of Ethics are more restrictive than the ESs.

Paragraph A14-1 of ISA 200 (UK and Ireland) – *Overall objectives of the independent auditor and the conduct of an audit in accordance with international standards on auditing.*

GENERAL PRINCIPLES OF THE IFAC CODE

The fundamental principles identified by IFAC in paragraph 100.5 are:

> A professional accountant shall comply with the following fundamental principles:
>
> (a) **Integrity** – to be straightforward and honest in all professional and business relationships.
>
> (b) **Objectivity** – to not allow bias, conflict of interest or undue influence of others to override professional or business judgments.
>
> (c) **Professional competence and due care** – to maintain professional knowledge and skill at the level required to ensure that a client or employer receives competent professional services based on current developments in practice, legislation and techniques and act diligently and in accordance with applicable technical and professional standards.
>
> (d) **Confidentiality** – to respect the confidentiality of information acquired as a result of professional and business relationships and, therefore, not disclose any such information to third parties without proper and specific authority, unless there is a legal or professional right or duty to disclose, nor use the information for the personal advantage of the professional accountant or third parties.
>
> (e) **Professional behaviour** – to comply with relevant laws and regulations and avoid any action that discredits the profession.

Paragraph 100.6 of the IFAC Code.

This text is an extract from the *Code of Ethics for Professional Accountants*, of The International Ethics Standards Board for Accountants, published by the International Federation of Accountants (IFAC), published in June 2005, revised in July 2009, and is used with permission of IFAC.

> The IFAC Code then goes on to say that:
>
> The circumstances in which professional accountants operate may create specific threats to compliance with the fundamental principles. It is impossible to define every situation that creates threats to compliance with the fundamental principles and specify the appropriate action. In addition, the nature of engagements and work assignments may differ and, consequently, different threats may be created, requiring the application of different safeguards. Therefore, this Code establishes a conceptual framework that requires a professional accountant to identify, evaluate and address threats to compliance with the fundamental principles. The conceptual framework approach assists professional accountants in complying with the ethical requirements of this Code and meeting their responsibility to act in the public interest. It accommodates many variations in circumstances that create threats to compliance with the fundamental principles and can deter a professional accountant from concluding that a situation is permitted if it is not specifically prohibited.

We cannot overemphasize the desirability of adopting a principles-based approach (as adopted by IFAC) as opposed to a rules-based approach.

The IFAC Code and the codes of the accounting bodies expect professional accountants to identify threats to compliance with the fundamental principles. Based on an evaluation of those threats, if they determine that they are not at an acceptable level, they should determine whether appropriate safeguards are available and can be applied to eliminate the threats or reduce them to an acceptable level. They will have to exercise professional judgement and take into account whether a reasonable and informed third party would be likely to conclude that the threats would be eliminated or reduced to an acceptable level by the application of the safeguards, such that compliance with the fundamental principles is not compromised.

So the basic rule is for professional accountants to identify threats and if there are any, to ask if there are any safeguards that would eliminate or reduce the threat.

The IFAC Code identifies the following threats to compliance with the fundamental principles:

TABLE 3.4.1 IFAC potential threats to objectivity

Threat	Comment
(a) Self-interest threat	This might make you think 'If I do not report as they wish, I might lose this assignment.' The matter of self-interest is the central theme of Goldman and Barlev's (1974) work.
(b) Self-review threat	In this case you might have to form a view on your own work. The question is whether the auditor would find it easy to criticize (say) a system they have put in themselves.
(c) Advocacy threat	This threat arises where you support your client's views. An example is support for a particular accounting policy, not generally accepted by the profession.
(d) Familiarity threat	In this case, the auditor, through close association with management, might become accepting of their views, perhaps unknowingly.
(e) Intimidation threat	A typical situation might be a dominant personality on the board of directors making you feel that you have to behave in a way you know to be unprofessional. Think of domineering persons you know and ask yourself if you would like to audit a company run by them.

The APB Ethical Standard 1 (ES 1) identifies an additional threat to objectivity and independence in paragraph 28, and we add it to the list below.

Tables 3.4.1 and 3.4.2 are extracts from the *Code of Ethics for Professional Accountants*, of The International Ethics Standards Board for Accountants, published by the International Federation of Accountants (IFAC), published in June 2005, revised in July 2009, and is used with permission of IFAC.

TABLE 3.4.2 Additional threat to objectivity proposed by APB

Threat	Comment
(f) Management threat	Suppose that you have been giving advice on the introduction of a new IT system. It might be very difficult in these circumstances to avoid being involved in decisions, properly the responsibility of management. You might be in danger of supporting management at the expense of the impartiality required of an auditor.

Examples of threats under headings (a) to (e) above are given in paragraphs 200.4 to 200.8 of the IFAC Code and we consider these later together with heading (f) when we discuss the safeguards later in this section.

AUDIT FIRM'S CONTROL ENVIRONMENT

We examine the control environment within audit firms by reference to the IFAC Code and to APB's Ethical Standard 1 (ES 1) last revised in 2008, applicable in the UK and Ireland. We do this by introducing you to a professional firm performing audit and other assurance services, showing it diagrammatically in Figure 3.3.

In reading Figure 3.3 note that both the IFAC Code and ES1 draw a distinction between (1) the persons directly involved in the engagement and (2) the wider group of people, including those directly involved in the engagement team, who are in a position to influence the conduct and outcome of the audit. The IFAC Code calls the wider group 'the audit team' and in Figure 3.3 includes all those to whom we have given an asterisk. ES1 restricts the use of 'audit team' to audit partners, audit managers and audit staff.

Refer to the definitions of 'audit team' and 'engagement team' at the end of the IFAC Code, and to paragraph 16 of ES1 for a definition of those in a position to influence the conduct and outcome of the audit.

However, whatever the definitions used the principle is clear – it is not only those directly involved in the audit that are covered by the ethical codes, but all those who are in a position to influence the conduct and outcome of the audit.

The general principles are stated in paragraphs 15 and 18 of ES 1:

> 15. The audit firm shall establish policies and procedures, appropriately documented and communicated, designed to ensure that, in relation to each audit engagement, the audit firm, and all those who are in a position to influence the conduct and outcome of the audit, act with integrity, objectivity and independence.
>
> 18. The leadership of the audit firm shall take responsibility for establishing a control environment within the firm that places adherence to ethical principles and compliance with APB Ethical Standards above commercial considerations.

It is interesting to note that APB emphasizes the need for a proper control environment within the audit firm, a matter that we discuss in Chapter 7 as an important aspect of control in organizations. The IFAC Code does not refer specifically to the 'control environment' but does list safeguards that should exist in the 'work environment' of both the audit firm and the audited entity, and these are reflected in Figure 3.3.

Paragraphs 200.12 to 200.15 of the IFAC Code.

Paragraph 19 of ES1 refers to the importance of establishing the 'tone at the top'.

ACTIVITY 3.5

Explain in your own words what is meant by 'tone at the top'. You should refer to paragraph 19 as you perform this activity.

No doubt you have recognized that people within the firm are more likely to behave in an ethical way if they know that people in charge of the organization are themselves behaving ethically. Of course, the 'tone at the top' must be known to everyone throughout the firm, and to this end the leadership has to give 'clear, consistent and frequent messages, backed up by appropriate

FIGURE 3.3 Audit firm's control environment and elements to enhance ethical behaviour in a firm providing audit and other assurance services.

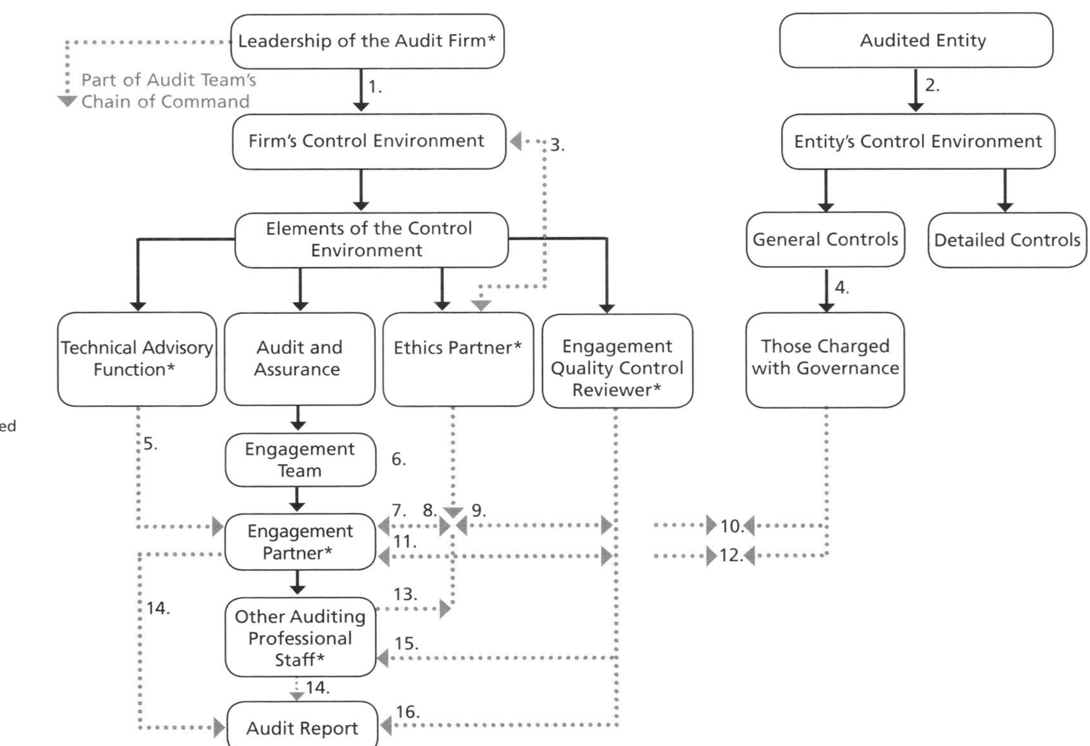

Notes

1. Leadership of the Audit Firm creates the Firm's Control Environment
2. Similarly, the Audited Entity creates the Entity's Control Environment
3. The Ethics Partner helps to create and maintain the Firm's Control Environment
4. An important element of the Entity's Control Environment comprises the role of Those Charged With Governance.
5. The Technical Advisory function gives advice on audit procedures and reporting to the Engagement team via the Engagement Partner.
6. The Engagement team comprises the Engagement Partner, Manager(s), Other Audit Staff, and Other Professional Staff (tax, IT, etc) providing services to the team.
7. The Ethics Partner communicates possible breaches of the firm's policies and procedures to the Engagement Partner.
8. The Engagement Partner evaluates and reports back to the Ethics Partner and course of action is decided
9. In the event of disagreement between the Engagement Partner and the Ethics Partner, the matter may be discussed with the Engagement Quality Control Reviewer and resolved
10. The existence of potential threats to objectivity and independence, and safeguards communicated to Those Charged With Governance at the Audited Entity.
11. The Engagement Partner and the Engagement Quality Control Reviewer discuss significant matters arising from the audit.
12. These matters also communicated to Those Charged With Governance at the Audited Entity.
13. Any member of the Engagement team are empowered to communicate with the Ethics Partner.
14. The Engagement Partner prepares the draft Audit Report on the basis of conclusions of the Engagement team.
15, The Engagement Quality Control Reviewer reviews individual procedures and conclusions of the Engagement team.
16. The Engagement Quality Control Reviewer reviews the draft Audit Report before it is finalized.

* The asterisk indicates all those persons who are in a position to influence the conduct and outcome of the audit. This includes some or all of the leaders of the audit firm. These are the people known collectively as the 'audit team' by the IFAC Code.

actions'. For instance, at times when the economic climate is poor, there may be undue pressures on the engagement team to agree to management wishes as regards accounting policies. The leadership should give guidance on how a threat of this kind should be addressed.

We list below the features of a strong control environment within the audit firm:

1 The establishment of a framework of responsibilities and reporting in the context of maintaining objectivity and independence of the audit firm and staff. This would include designating a member of senior management to oversee the adequate functioning of the firm's quality control system, as required by the IFAC Code. ES 1 gives the title of 'ethics partner' to this person (paragraph 21). We discuss the role of the ethics partner below.
2 The issuance of documented policies and procedures by the audit firm to be available to all staff involved in the provision of audit and assurance services.

We explain briefly the role of 'those charged with governance within the audited entity' a little later in this section.

3 The establishment of communication links to those charged with governance within the audited entity to ensure that the client is aware of:
   - threats that may affect objectivity and independence of the audit firm and staff.
   - safeguards to eliminate the threats or reduce them to acceptable levels.
   - action taken in the light of the threats and safeguards.

   The documented policies and procedures should include the following:

The IFAC and ES rules are more onerous for immediate family than those for close family. We discuss this later in this section.

(a) Partners and staff to report the following in respect of an audited entity:
   - family and other personal relationships, whether of immediate family: 'a spouse (or equivalent) or dependant', and close family: 'a parent, non-dependent child or sibling'.
   - financial interests in the entity.
   - decisions to join the entity.

(b) Clarification of the role of the engagement partner regarding maintenance of integrity, objectivity and independence in the following respects:

   The engagement partner is the person who is in charge of the engagement team and who signs the audit report at the end of the engagement. The integrity, objectivity and independence of this person is therefore of paramount importance.
   - Need to identify promptly possible or actual breaches of the firm's policies and procedures and communication of them to the relevant audit engagement partner.
   - Evaluation by the audit engagement partner of the implications of any identified possible or actual breaches of the firm's policies and procedures that are reported to them.
   - Consultation by the engagement partner with the member of senior management responsible for overseeing the adequate functioning of the firm's ethical control environment (the 'ethics partner' in ES1) to determine the adequacy of safeguards and to decide upon action to be taken.

- Apart from these specific matters, the engagement partner should carry out an ongoing review of any matters that may affect the integrity, objectivity and independence of themselves and their staff and to document the results of their ongoing review. This might include a review of the performance of non-audit services. They might also consider the desirability of rotating members of the engagement team, including themselves. 'Rotating' means that the personnel would be removed from the engagement team after a period of years on the audit assignment.

We emphasize the importance of documenting the judgments of the engagement partner and any person they consult in forming conclusions regarding the objectivity and independence requirements.

(c) Continual review of audited entities to ensure that all persons who are in a position to influence the conduct and outcome of the audit are independent of them.

As we noted above the IFAC Code and ES 1 identify the persons who are in a position to influence the conduct and outcome. If you refer to the definition of the 'audit team' in the IFAC Code and paragraph 16 of ES 1, you will see that the list of persons identified is pretty wide.

(d) Empowerment of staff to communicate to the ethics partner any issue of objectivity or independence that concerns them. Important in this respect would be:

- to establish clear communication channels open to staff and encouraging staff to use them.
- to ensure staff who use these channels are not subject to disciplinary proceedings as a result.

The ethics partner

The ethics partner is a partner in the audit firm with TWO particular responsibilities for:

(a) the adequacy of the firm's policies and procedures relating to integrity, objectivity and independence, its compliance with APB Ethical Standards and the effectiveness of its communication to partners and staff within the firm (this is a GENERAL responsibility); and

See paragraph 21 of ES 1.

(b) providing related guidance to individual partners (this is a SPECIFIC responsibility.

In a large firm the ethics partner may be supported by a compliance unit, staffed by a wide range of people with differing backgrounds and skills. In a small firm with three or fewer partners, it may not be practical to appoint an ethics partner. In these circumstances all partners will regularly discuss ethical issues amongst themselves. A sole partner might consult his or her professional body or other practitioners

Thus the ethics partner will be a key figure in helping to establish and maintain the control environment and, in addition will provide guidance to the engagement partner and other members of the engagement team and support staff. This latter role involves a two-way communication process between the engagement and ethics partner, the basic idea being to resolve any ethical matters that may affect the audit assignment. The ethics partner may also be called on to give advice should there be disagreement between the engagement partner and the engagement quality control reviewer (see below).

The ethics partner is the person to whom audit staff other than the engagement partner should be encouraged to raise ethical matters

ACTIVITY 3.6

The role of the ethics partner is clearly important. What kind of qualities do you think that this person should have?

In the first place the ethics partner must know what he or she is doing. This means that they should be very experienced in audit work and have the ability to recognize the threats to integrity, objectivity and independence that may arise. It would be important too to have a high status within the firm to give the authority to get his or her views accepted and to get the staff and other resources necessary to perform the role.

ACTIVITY 3.7

You are the ethics partner of George and Co, a firm of accountants and auditors. It has recently come to your attention that the engagement partner of Wormiston plc was asked some nine months ago if the senior in charge of the previous year's audit might be seconded to the company's IT development unit for a period of six months. Her role was to advise on the particular control features that should be in place for a new inventory control system. Her knowledge of Wormiston plc is extremely good and the engagement partner says he would like her to continue as senior in charge of the current year's audit. What advice would you give to the engagement partner?

It certainly looks as though there might be a threat to the independence of the audit senior in this case. In the first place, there is likely to be a self review threat, which may be very significant bearing in mind the likely materiality of the inventory figure in the financial statements. The senior has been involved in advising on the new inventory control system and may find herself reviewing her own work. Apart from this, she might have been involved in making decisions with regard to the adequacy of the controls, so there might be a management threat as well, in that these kinds of decisions are normally made by management. The other threat is the familiarity threat, as she will have been working closely with client staff, probably including those who are making decisions about the form and content of the financial statements.

Under these circumstances you would probably conclude that there were no safeguards that would reduce these various threats to independence, and that it would be desirable that the senior be removed from the engagement team.

Engagement quality control reviewer (EQCR)

ISA 220 and ISA 220 (UK and Ireland) – *Quality control for an audit of financial statements* requires the audit engagement partner in paragraph 19 to:

(a) Determine that an EQCR has been appointed;
(b) Discuss significant matters arising during the audit engagement, including those identified during the engagement quality control review, with the EQCR; and
(c) Not date the auditor's report until the completion of the engagement quality control review.

This requirement is principally for listed companies, but firms may decide to apply it to other engagements as well.

Paragraph 46 of ES 1 states that in these cases, the EQCR should:

(a) consider the audit firm's compliance with APB Ethical Standards in relation to the audit engagement;
(b) form an independent opinion as to the appropriateness and adequacy of the safeguards applied; and
(c) consider the adequacy of the documentation of the audit engagement partner's consideration of the auditor's objectivity and independence.

Apart from this the EQCR has another function – to 'perform an objective evaluation of the significant judgements made by the engagement team, and the conclusions reached in formulating the auditor's report'.

This will involve discussion of significant matters with the engagement partner, reviewing the financial statements and the proposed audit report, reviewing audit documentation where significant judgements have been made, and evaluating specific conclusions, and overall conclusions in formulating the proposed audit report. In the case of listed entities the EQCR would also evaluate the firm's independence in relation to the engagement, and consider whether the engagement partner has consulted with others when difficult or contentious matters have arisen. The reviewer would want to ensure that the conclusions appeared appropriate, and in addition that audit documentation generally supported any conclusions reached in respect of these and other matters.

See paragraphs 20 and 21 of ISA 220. We would call this work a 'hot review' as it is taking place when the engagement team is still in place.

Communication with those charged with governance

Both the IFAC Code and ES1 expect the audit firm to keep those charged with governance of the audit client informed with regard to potential threats to the auditor's objectivity and independence, the appropriateness of safeguards applied to eliminate them or reduce them to an acceptable level, and what action has been taken. The audit engagement partner would take a leading role in this respect, but the ethics partner and the engagement quality control reviewer would also be involved, where appropriate.

We shall discuss the role of those charged with governance later in this book, but note at this stage that these are the persons within an entity with responsibility for overseeing the strategic direction of the entity and obligations related to the accountability of the entity, including overseeing the financial reporting process. Members of the audit committee, independent of executive management, would be included among those charged with governance.

Overall conclusion at the end of the audit process

You might think that this is never-ending, but at the end of the audit process, when forming an opinion but before issuing the report on the financial statements, engagement partners have to reach an overall conclusion that any threats to objectivity and independence have been properly addressed. If they cannot make such a conclusion, they shall not report and the audit firm shall resign as auditor.

We have spent some time looking at ES 1, and relevant parts of the IFAC Code and ISA 220, but it is important to set the scene for a detailed consideration of the safeguards to mitigate the threats to integrity, objectivity and independence of auditors.

SAFEGUARDS TO COUNTER THREATS TO INTEGRITY, OBJECTIVITY AND INDEPENDENCE

The IFAC Code addresses the safeguards that may eliminate threats or reduce them to an acceptable level, splitting them into two broad categories:

(a) Safeguards created by the profession, legislation or regulation; and
(b) Safeguards in the work environment.

See paragraph 100.14.

Safeguards created by the profession, legislation or regulation

- Educational, training and experience requirements for entry into the profession.
- Continuing professional development requirements.
- Corporate governance regulations.
- Professional standards.
- Professional or regulatory monitoring and disciplinary procedures.
- External review by a legally empowered third party of the reports, returns, communications or information produced by a professional accountant.

The above text is an extract from the *Code of Ethics for Professional Accountants*, of The International Ethics Standards Board for Accountants, published by the International Federation of Accountants (IFAC), published in June 2005, revised in July 2009, and is used with permission of IFAC.

Safeguards in the work environment

The IFAC Code splits these into three categories:

See paragraph 200.12.

1 Firm-wide safeguards, such as leadership of the firm stressing the importance of compliance with the fundamental principles and establishing the expectation that members of an assurance team will act in the public interest. These safeguards are those that establish the 'tone at the top'.

See paragraph 200.13.

2 Engagement specific safeguards, such as having a professional accountant who was not a member of the assurance team review the assurance work performed or otherwise advise as necessary (the EQCR).

See paragraph 200.15.

3 Safeguards within the client's systems and procedures, such as the client has competent employees with experience and seniority to make

managerial decisions. (We shall see later that good control procedures within the client organization will reduce the risk that the auditor will form incorrect conclusions.)

Now let us take a look at specific threats to integrity, objectivity and independence and the safeguards that may eliminate them or reduce them to acceptable levels.

Financial, business, employment and personal relationships

These relationships are covered by ES2 and in Section 290 of the IFAC Code, and you should refer to these standards when performing the Activities below.

The general principle is that any relationships to the audited entity by those that have an influence on the conduct and outcome of the audit should be avoided because of the self-interest threat. This would include the immediate family of any person who can influence the conduct and outcome of the audit. In such cases no safeguard could eliminate or reduce the impact of the threat. Even where close family members have a relationship with an audited entity, a self-interest threat may arise, depending upon the significance of the relationship, and the position of the member of the engagement team. In the case of a junior member of the engagement team an appropriate safeguard might be for an independent person to review his or her work. A more important member of the engagement team or overall chain of command might have to be removed from any influence on the conduct and outcome of the audit.

We have seen above that the audit engagement partner plays an important role in identifying threats to objectivity and independence, and determining if safeguards exist to eliminate the threats or reduce them to an acceptable level.

ACTIVITY 3.8

It comes to your attention that the audit senior in charge of the audit of Mitchell plc holds 100 shares in the company. They have a current quoted value of £50 000, but represent only a tiny proportion of the total share capital of the company. What action would you take and why?

A holding of 100 shares with a market value of £50 000 might not be material in relation to the audit client, but could be very significant in relation to the total wealth of the audit senior. In these circumstances there are no safeguards which would reduce the threat to objectivity and would therefore require the audit senior to be removed from any involvement with the audit client, or for him or her to dispose of the shares in Mitchell plc.

ACTIVITY 3.9

A tax partner in your audit firm has a shareholding in a new audit client. What steps do you think that the audit firm should take?

The tax partner might not be involved directly in the audit of the new client company, but is part of the chain of command. In a case like this the audit firm would ask the tax partner to dispose of the shareholding as soon as possible. If there is any delay, the firm should ensure that the partner cannot influence the conduct and outcome of the audit – in this case in relation to the tax liability and charge, including deferred tax – either by exclusion from the audit or subjecting any work performed to the scrutiny of an independent partner of sufficient experience and authority.

ACTIVITY 3.10

You are a partner in an audit firm with a particular responsibility for performing a hot review of Grange Limited before the audit opinion is issued. Your father has recently informed you that he has a material (to him) shareholding in Grange Limited. What do you think you should do at this point?

Your father would be classified as a close family member and you should inform the engagement partner without delay. Although not the engagement partner, it might be desirable for you to withdraw from your current role in relation to Grange Limited, a course of action that the engagement partner might wish to discuss with the ethics partner.

ACTIVITY 3.11

You are a partner in your audit firm and trustee of a trust of which your daughter is beneficiary. One of the companies in which the trust holds shares has recently been taken over by an audit client of your firm. What issues do you think should be addressed in this case?

Trustees have a duty to protect the interests of trust beneficiaries and you would have to consider how material the investment in the audit client is to the trust, whether the trust is in a position to exercise significant influence over the audit client, and whether you had significant influence over the investment in the audit client. Depending on the outcome of your consideration of these matters, you might have to stop acting as trustee. This would also appear to be a matter that should be discussed with the ethics partner.

ACTIVITY 3.12

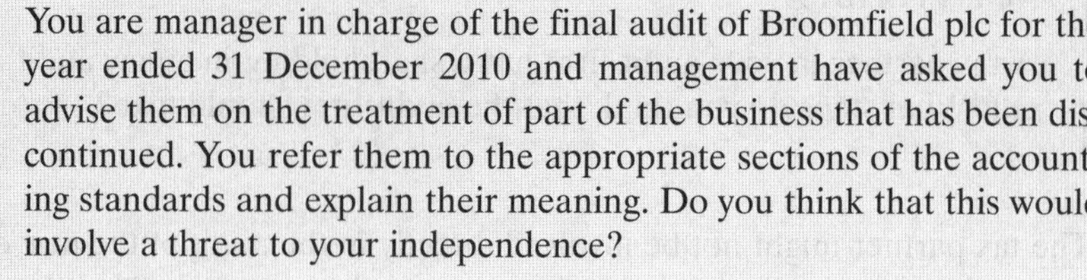

You are manager in charge of the final audit of Broomfield plc for the year ended 31 December 2010 and management have asked you to advise them on the treatment of part of the business that has been discontinued. You refer them to the appropriate sections of the accounting standards and explain their meaning. Do you think that this would involve a threat to your independence?

Auditors are frequently asked for advice on the application of accounting standards and it would be in order for you to refer them to the accounting standard and to explain the relevant sections. Provided that you went no further than this, there would probably not be a management threat to your independence.

If you went further and suggested actions that might enable the company to avoid treatment as a discontinued operation, that might be more dangerous. There might also be a self-review threat as you might be reviewing your own decisions about a particular treatment.

ACTIVITY 3.13

Robert Doig is a member of your staff, loaned to an audit client for a period of one year. How long a period of time should elapse before Robert becomes a member of the engagement team? You would rather like him to be on the team because of his knowledge of the company.

This question is like asking: 'How long is a piece of string?' The answer is: 'It depends.' It depends on how long he was with the client (a year is rather long) and on what level of responsibility he would have on the engagement team. You might decide that at least one year should elapse before he became a member of the team or even longer if he had become very involved in the management of the company.

ACTIVITY 3.14

James Black was engagement partner for the audit of Woodburn Limited up to the year ended 31 August 2009 and recently became a director of the company with effect from 1 January 2012. What issues would you consider in respect of this matter?

The basic rule in ES2 is that under circumstances where a partner has acted as engagement partner with the audit client at any time in the two years prior to appointment to a key position in the audit client, the audit firm should resign. In this case the two years have just elapsed, assuming that the AGM has been held before 31 December 2004, so the firm would not be required to resign. However, there may still be problems because the former engagement partner will probably know members of the present engagement team very well. Depending on his personality there may be an intimidation threat, and a familiarity threat is likely, and safeguards would have to be in place. Appropriate safeguards might be to ensure that key members of the engagement team had not worked closely with James Black in the past, or, if this is not possible, to have the audit work reviewed by a partner not involved in the audit, or even by another audit firm.

The audit firm might also consider changing audit emphasis to some extent, as the former partner is likely to know the firm's audit approaches very well.

The IFAC Code identifies the threats in the same way as ES2, and like ES2 requires audit firms to take remedial action, similar to those we mentioned above If Woodburn had been a public interest entity, paragraph 290.139 would only allow a key audit partner to join the entity if he or she had played no part in the audit for the 12 months to 31 August 2010.

A listed entity is regarded as a public interest entity, but other organizations may also be classified as such, if regulation or legislation demands it.

ACTIVITY 3.15

You are the engagement partner of Cardinal Limited, a small but growing company. A junior member of the engagement team has just told you that the audit senior appears to be in financial difficulty and that the client's chief accountant has offered to give him a temporary loan to tide him over the next few months. What are the threats in this case, are there any safeguards that you could put in place, and what action would you take?

The problem in this case is that a self-interest threat would arise, as the audit senior would not wish to upset the chief accountant. He might be willing to turn a blind eye to matters that should be reported to the engagement partner. He might also be subject to an intimidation threat if he came across a reportable matter that the chief accountant might wish to be kept secret Neither the IFAC Code or ES2 allow a loan of this nature and state clearly that there are no safeguards that would reduce the threats. In these circumstances the audit senior should be interviewed to discover the truth of the matter. If he or she has accepted a loan, even if temporary, removal from the engagement team would be the only option. The firm should also consider disciplinary procedures as the senior would clearly have acted in an unprofessional manner.

Long association with the audit engagement

These relationships are covered by ES3 and by sections 290.150 to 290.155 of the IFAC Code and you should refer to these standards when performing the Activities below.

The potential threat to objectivity and independence exists where audit engagement partners, key audit partners and staff in senior positions have served for a considerable length of time. The particular threats to objectivity and independence that may arise are self-interest, self-review and familiarity threats, but both the IFAC Code and ES 5 do recognize that there might be some ameliorating factors.

ACTIVITY 3.16

Identify ameliorating factors that might reduce the significance of the threat associated with long tenure.

There might be a number of factors that would reduce the significance of the threat. If a relatively junior member of the engagement team has been involved on the audit for some years, that would not be as significant as a long-serving manager or engagement partner. The threats are also likely to be more significant where the engagement partner or manager (say) are involved with the client for a large proportion of their time (ES3 refers to 'annual billable hours), as in such case, they might start to feel part of the client's organization. Threats might also be less significant where key personnel in the client's management team have changed, as the familiarity threat would be much reduced. In addition, where there is less complexity in the client's accounting system or where accounting estimates are less significant, the threats too are likely to be less significant. In such cases the engagement team will be less likely to be involved with difficult decision-making with the client's management.

ACTIVITY 3.17

Identify safeguards that might be available to reduce the significance of the threats arising from long tenure.

Both the IFAC Code and ES3 suggest that appropriate safeguards would include:

- Rotating the senior personnel (partners and managers) of the engagement team;
- Having a partner who was not a member of the engagement team review the work of the senior personnel; or
- Regular independent internal or external quality reviews of the engagement.

ACTIVITY 3.18

How long do you think that senior personnel on the engagement team should serve before being rotated?.

The period of time after which senior personnel should be removed is somewhat controversial and the IFAC Code and ES3 differ slightly on their approach. Both suggest that firms should evaluate the threats arising from long tenure, but ES3 (paragraph nine) puts a figure on it, suggesting that where an audit engagement partner has held this role for a continuous period of ten years, the firm should consider whether he or she should be rotated. If they are not rotated this would make the other safeguards listed above more important.

The IFAC Code and ES3 also differ slightly in the case of listed company clients, as shown in the following table.

IFAC Code	ES3
An individual should not be a key audit partner for more than seven years	No-one shall act as engagement partner for more than five years
After the seven years have elapsed they should not be involved with the team or client for a further two years	He or she shall not subsequently participate in the audit engagement until a further period of five years has elapsed.

The above IFAC Code text is an extract from the *Code of Ethics for Professional Accountants*, of The International Ethics Standards Board for Accountants, published by the International Federation of Accountants (IFAC), published in June 2005, revised in July 2009, and is used with permission of IFAC.

Both codes do allow service beyond the stated period if audit quality demands it, For instance ES3 relaxes the rule where a client company becomes listed, the engagement partner may continue to serve for a further two years, even if they have already served for four or more years.

We would emphasize that the basic approach for audit firms is that they should not apply the seven and five year periods without continuously reviewing the potential threats to objectivity and independence

NOTE ON MANDATORY ROTATION OF AUDIT FORMS

The IFAC Code and ES3 make no mention of mandatory rotation of audit firms, a specific way of improving independence that has been much opposed by accounting firms. Mandatory rotation would require audit clients to change their auditors periodically, the most common time period discussed being five or seven years. Arguments in favour are that it prevents the audit firm from developing too cosy a relationship with the client, and also provides an incentive for the audit firm to carry out work to a high standard because they know that the quality of their work will be observable to some extent when a new firm of auditors take over the audit. Detractors of the measure argue that if the audit firm were rotated after five years it would not give sufficient time to become fully acquainted with the audit client. Furthermore, having obtained a good knowledge of the company over several years the audit firm would be in a better position to offer valuable advice to the client. It is also argued that the auditor would have little incentive to spend much time determining the complexities of the audit client, as they know they will be replaced after a set period of time. Another argument for not endorsing mandatory rotation of auditors is that non-detection of fraudulent financial reporting is more likely when the audit firm is new to the audit and does not have the cumulative audit knowledge that is only obtainable after performing the audit for a lengthy period of time. Finally, it is argued that, since there are initially one-off start up costs involved in audit, the audit function would become more expensive if there were mandatory rotation. You might note, however, that rotation does take place when companies put their audits out to tender.

These matters are covered by ES4 and by sections 290.220 to 290.231 of the IFAC Code, and you should refer to these when performing the Activities below.

Fees, remuneration and evaluation policies, litigation, gifts and hospitality

The basic rules are as follows:

Fees: A proper audit has to be performed whatever the agreed fee, that is, corners should not be cut in performing audit work, even if a firm has submitted a fee proposal lower than its competitors. Nor should fees be contingent upon an expected or desired outcome. Threats to a firm's objectivity and independence may arise both in this case and where fees charged to a client represent a significant proportion of the firm's total income.

Remuneration and evaluation policies: The remuneration and progress of staff members through the firm should be soundly and fairly based and should not be dependent on the success of staff in selling non-assurance services to the audit client

Litigation: The existence of litigation between an audit firm and its client will damage the relationship between the engagement team and management and make the achievement of audit objectives extremely difficult if not impossible.

Gifts and hospitality: Unless the gifts and hospitality are insignificant in amount, they should not be accepted by any person in a position to determine the outcome of the audit. This would include gifts and hospitality to immediate family members.

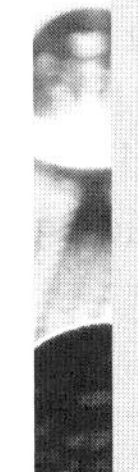

ACTIVITY 3.19

You are audit manager in charge of the audit of Denhead plc with a year-end of 31st December., and are explaining to the chief accountant how your firm's fees are calculated. The chief accountant tells you that it is important that the audit report be issued by 15th February 2011 and says he is willing to increase the audit fee by 10 per cent if you meet that deadline. What would you say to him?

The 10 per cent increase in audit fee would clearly be contingent upon the deadline being met. It might encourage your firm to cut corners, that is to omit some audit work, in order to meet the deadline. As such, self interest threats to the firm's objectivity and independence would be created and no safeguards could reduce the threats to an acceptable level. You would have to explain to the chief accountant that fees cannot be agreed on a contingent basis, but you would tell him that you would, of course, do your best to meet the deadline. You might suggest how Denhead itself might help by meeting its own internal deadlines for preparation of the financial statements, and by preparing schedules requested by the engagement team on a timely basis.

ACTIVITY 3.20

Both the IFAC Code and ES4 have rules to help firms decide if the amount of the regular fees charged to a client are significant in relation to the total income of the firm. Thus the IFAC Code suggests that 15 per cent of total income of the practice would be appropriate in the case of a listed client, whereas ES4 suggests that 15 per cent would be appropriate in the case of a non-listed client, and 10 per cent in the case of a listed client. Explain what kinds of threats to objectivity and independence would arise if fees to an individual client regularly exceeded these percentages? Would there be any safeguards that might reduce the threats to an acceptable level? If the percentage was 14.9 per cent or 9.9 per cent respectively would this mean that there was no threat?

Self-interest and intimidation threats are most likely where audit fees to a particular client are significant in relation to total income. If fees are significant, there would be a self-interest threat, as the audit firm would not wish to lose the client and may be more willing to accede to client wishes with regards to the application of accounting standards and to reporting. At the extreme the client might intimidate the engagement partner by threatening to move the audit elsewhere if he or she does not accede to their wishes. Important in this respect is that the engagement partner's own income is likely to be dependent on the total income of the audit firm.

Potential safeguards could include having an quality control review carried out by a person independent of the engagement team. Smaller firms might approach other local firms for advice on key audit judgements or ask their professional body for its opinion. The firm might also consider reducing the amount on non-assurance work that the firm performs on behalf the client.

It is important, of course, that the firm does not take the attitude that they are in the clear if the percentage of total income charged to an individual client is less than the 15 per cent or 10 per cent rules. Whatever the fee, the form should consider carefully whether any threats exist.

ACTIVITY 3.21

A partner in a small two-partner firm, established two years ago, tells you that in the first two years the fees charged to two audit clients both exceed 15 per cent of total income. This is expected to continue for the next two years until the fee income from other clients becomes significant. What advice would you give to the partner?

The basic rule is the same as we explained in Activity 3.20 above. The partners in the firm should make sure that audit work and reporting is soundly based, and if need be review each other's work or seek advice from other professional accountants or their professional body. It would be desirable to avoid audits of listed companies in the early years, but it is generally recognized that when new firms are seeking to establish themselves strict adherence to a percentage rule would be unfair.

The Audit Inspection Unit (AIU) of the Professional Oversight Board (POB) carries out periodic inspections of audit firms (the largest firms annually) and reported in 2009 that there was evidence in some cases that audit staff had been encouraged to identify opportunities to 'add value' to clients and that such efforts would be rewarded. We discuss the POB and AIU in greater detail in Chapters 4 and 20.

ACTIVITY 3.22

You are running a training course for your firm and you have been asked by a participant whether staff on an audit could expect to have their salary augmented if they were able to sell non-audit services to the client. He tells you that he has recently been able to make useful suggestions that will lead to efficiency savings for an audit client. What would be your response? What principles do you think would be relevant?

The basic principle is that the audit opinion should not be influenced by any non-audit services provided. If staff were encouraged to sell such services to an audit client, knowing that it might affect their remuneration or promotion prospects, this might indeed affect their independence and objectivity. For this reason the IFAC Code and ES 4 requires audit firms to establish policies and procedures to ensure that audit staff are not expected to sell non-audit services and to prevent staff remuneration and promotion prospects being influenced by success in selling such services.

Non-audit (or non-assurance) services provided to audit clients

These matters are covered by ES5 and by sections 290.156 to 290.219 of the IFAC Code, and you should refer to these standards when performing the Activities below. ES5 uses the term 'non-audit services', whereas the IFAC Code refers to 'non-assurance services'. We are using the term 'non-assurance services', unless 'non-audit' is contained in a quotation.

The performance of audit work gives audit firms excellent insights into the nature of the entities that they audit, and the problems faced by them. This puts firms into an excellent position to give advice and to provide services other than audit and assurance. Indeed, firms have traditionally provided a wide range of such services to their audit clients. The non-assurance services have become so significant that sometimes fees from these services exceed the fees charged for performing the audit. Providing non-assurance services may, however, create threats to the independence of the firm or members of the engagement team, and in this section we shall consider the nature of the threats and the safeguards that firms should have in place to reduce them to acceptable levels.

The general rule is that the audit firm should establish policies and procedures that require consideration of any threat to independence before a proposed non-assurance service is accepted. In Figure 3.3 we suggested a structure that a firm could establish to strengthen the firm's control environment. We noted that the engagement partner should be informed of any matters that might affect the independence of the firm and members of the engagement team. A specially designated person such as an ethics partner would give advice to the engagement partner, as appropriate. We saw also that an engagement quality control reviewer might be asked to intervene if there was disagreement between the engagement partner and the ethics partner. The matter that must be decided as the result of these deliberations is whether it would be appropriate not to undertake the non-assurance work or, alternatively, to withdraw from the audit engagement. We saw in Figure 3.3 that these matters should also be communicated to those charged with governance in the audited entity.

ACTIVITY 3.23

How do you think that those charged with governance in the audited entity would aid objectivity and independence of the auditor?

This is a good question. You will appreciate that if management in the audited entity asks the auditor to perform non-assurance services, they should be made aware of any threats to objectivity and independence of the audit firm and its staff and the safeguards that may reduce the threats. Some of those charged with governance will be independent of executive management of the client (such as members of the audit committee) and they can play a particular role in showing how the non-assurance services might affect objectivity and independence. They would, of course, have to be fully informed of the circumstances, including potential safeguards and decisions made by the engagement partner and others.

In this connection we refer you to a study by an ICAS working group titled 'The Provision of Non-Audit Services by Audit Firms to their Listed Audit Clients'. This study was published in January 2010. The working group concluded that there is no benefit to be gained from a complete prohibition on auditors providing non-audit services to their listed clients. However, and this is important, the working group did recommend an enhanced role for audit committees beyond that required by the present combined code provision c.3.2. This provision requires the audit committee to develop and implement a policy in respect of the auditor providing non-audit services, taking into account ethical issues. The ICAS paper makes the following specific recommendations:

- An audit committee should be required to publish its policy in relation to determining whether a non-audit service can be provided by the company's external auditor.
- The audit committee should clearly set out its policy on how any perceived conflicts of interest will be addressed in relation to the audit firm.
- A requirement of an audit committee to pre-approve all non-audit services above a set fee level should be introduced. This fee level would be established by the audit committee. Additionally, all non-audit services of an internal audit nature or which are procured on a contingency fee basis should also be subject to pre-approval by the audit committee.

The ICAS working group clearly sees the audit committee as performing an important role. We discuss the wider role of audit committees and review further recommendations of the ICAS working group on non-audit services in Chapter 18.

The IFAC Code does not use the term 'informed management', but the concept is described in paragraph 290.166.

Concept of 'informed management'

The concept of 'informed management' is very important in relation to the provision of non-assurance services. It is defined by the glossary to the ESs as: 'Member of management (or senior employee) of the audited entity who has the authority and capability to make independent management judgements and decisions in relation to non-audit services on the basis of information provided by the audit firm'. We quote paragraphs 26 and 27 of ES5 below to put it into context:

> 26. In determining whether a non-audit service does or does not give rise to a management threat, the auditor considers whether there is informed management. Informed management exists when:
>
> - the auditor is satisfied that a member of management (or senior employee of the audited entity) has been designated by the audited entity to receive the results of the non-audit service and has been given the authority to make any judgements and decisions;
> - the auditor concludes that that member of management has the capability to make independent management judgements and decisions on the basis of the information provided; and
> - the results of the non-audit service are communicated to the audited entity and, where judgements or decisions are to be made they are supported by an objective analysis of the issues to consider and the audited entity is given the opportunity to decide between reasonable alternatives.

27 In the absence of such informed management it is unlikely that any other safeguards can eliminate a management threat or reduce it to an acceptable level.

This means that, wherever there may be a management threat, the existence of informed management to make final decisions will be an important safeguard to eliminate or reduce the threat to an acceptable level. However, many audit clients may not possess sufficient expertise to make informed decisions about the acceptability and applicability of the non-audit service provided; in other words, there is no 'informed management'. If this is the case, there are unlikely to be safeguards to eliminate any threats to the independence of the auditors. In these circumstances, the non-assurance services should not be undertaken.

These comments on informed management are relevant wherever there is a management threat as identified in Table 3.5.

TABLE 3.5 Non-audit services and likely threats

Non-audit service	Some threats
Internal audit services	Self review; self interest; management; familiarity
Information technology (IT) services	Self review; self interest; management; familiarity
Valuation services	Self review; self interest; management
Actuarial valuation services	Self review; self interest; management
Tax services	Self-review, self interest; management; advocacy; self review
Litigation support services	Self review; self interest; management; advocacy
Legal services	Self review; self interest; management; advocacy
Recruitment and remuneration services	Management, self interest; familiarity; intimidation
Corporate finance services	Self-review, self interest; management; advocacy; self-review
Transaction related services	Management; self interest;
Accounting services	Management; self interest; familiarity

We discuss internal audit in Chapter 15.

Now let us consider the threats arising from specific non-audit services; we set these out in Table 3.5 and later we suggest appropriate safeguards.

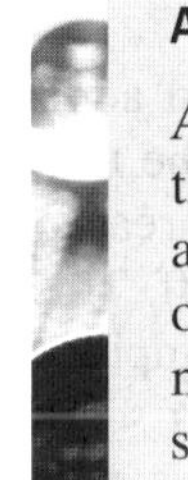

ACTIVITY 3.24

Audit firms often provide internal audit services to companies that they audit. This can be quite attractive to companies, as they can avoid the costs of maintaining an internal audit department of their own. However, in the table above we suggested that self review and management threats might result from the provision of internal audit services. Explain why this might be so and suggest safeguards that should be in place.

Internal auditors act on behalf of management and are often referred to as the 'longer arm of management'. They often work closely with management to come up with desired solutions. For instance, the internal audit function may be asked to advise on the desirability of acquiring a company or disposing of parts of a group. If an audit firm did provide services to management of this kind, it would be very difficult to avoid a management threat. There might be an impact on the financial statements if the firm has become so closely identified with management that they might accept management judgements and estimates with a less critical eye.

The self review threat arises from the fact that external auditors often use the conclusions of internal audit work in forming their own view on the efficacy of company systems and the accuracy and completeness of figures in the accounting records. If staff on the external engagement team also provided internal audit services, there would be a real danger that they would review their own work, and thus accept it without examining it in any detail.

This is exactly the sort of situation that the engagement partner should discuss with the ethics partner and with those charged with governance in the audited entity, and in particular with the audit committee, with a view to deciding the best course of action. To avoid the management threat it would be important for informed management of the entity to make any final decision on recommendations of the internal audit function.

Regarding the self review threat, an important safeguard would be to make sure that no person able to influence the conduct and outcome of the external audit should be involved in the internal audit work. In addition, if the internal audit work has any financial statement implications, you would expect the working papers prepared by the engagement team in respect of that part of the financial statements to be subject to special review by the EQCR. In some cases, such as banks and other financial institutions, the role of internal audit may be so important in ensuring that financial controls are strong, that the audit firm would be unable to find adequate safeguards and the internal audit assignment should not be undertaken.

ACTIVITY 3.25

We have shown self-interest as a threat in respect of all the non-assurance services listed in Table 3.5. Explain why this is the case.

The self-interest lies in the fact that non-assurance services bring in additional income to the audit firm. This means that it is in the interest of the firm to accept and perform the services, even though they might result in a threat to the integrity, objectivity and independence of the audit firm and its staff. This means that audit firms must be careful to analyse the independence implications of taking on a service, even though it brings in extra income. In some case, non-assurance services might be performed on a contingent fee basis, particularly in the case of tax services and corporate finance services. The self-interest threat might be heightened in these circumstances and would need particular vigilance in assessing their impact on objectivity and independence.

ACTIVITY 3.26

Advocacy is seen as a threat in respect of tax services, litigation support services, legal services and corporate finance services. What is meant by the advocacy threat and what safeguards may exist to mitigate the threat?

This can be illustrated by reference to tax services. When providing such a service members of the audit firm may suggest approaches to mitigate the tax charge, that is, they are advocating a particular method. They might even be asked to represent the audited entity in negotiations with the tax authorities. As the tax charge and liability will normally represent significant figures in the financial statements, there will be a threat that these figures will be accepted because members of the firm are closely connected with the tax computations.

Appropriate safeguards might include: (a) tax services being provided by staff not engaged on the audit; (b) review of tax services by a qualified person; (c) obtaining external independent advice in respect of tax work; (d) review of tax computations prepared by the engagement team by a qualified person not involved in the audit; (e) generally, an audit partner not involved in the audit should ensure that the tax work has been properly and effectively addressed in the context of the audit of the financial statements. In particular, to ensure the amounts of the tax liability and tax charge have not been affected by the subjective judgements made in providing the tax services. It might be advisable to reject requests to represent the audited entity in negotiations with the tax authorities.

ACTIVITY 3.27

In Table 3.5 we have singled out familiarity threats in each case where we have deemed that the service will involve staff of the audit firm being involved with client staff for longer periods of time. In the case of recruitment and remuneration services the familiarity threat may arise for other reasons. Now we would ask you to consider recruitment and remuneration services as a whole and to explain the particular threats that may affect the audit firm and its staff and to suggest safeguards that may mitigate the threat. You may refer to paragraphs 290.214 and 290.215 of the IFAC Code, or ES5 when performing this activity.

These services involve members of the audit firm in helping management to interview potential personnel of the audited entity and in giving advice on the remuneration of their employees. This could bring audit firm members into close contact with key personnel and involve them too in making decisions about that most personal matter – salaries and related remuneration. The thinking here is that if the firm had been involved in the appointment of key personnel, audit staff might be inclined to be less critical of the assertions made and explanations given by such staff. This is really an extreme example of the familiarity threat and the audit firm would have to seek appropriate safeguards, or, if there are none, to reject the non-assurance service. There might also be an intimidation threat, if audit staff are over-awed by staff who have been hired by their own firm.

In practice audit firms often provide recruitment and remuneration services for their audit clients, but great care should be taken before accepting a service of this nature. In the first place, to avoid the management threat, the audit firm should ensure that it is informed management that makes the final decision to hire a particular interviewee, albeit on the recommendation of audit firm personnel. It would also be desirable that the contract to provide the services should be completely separate from the engagement to provide the audit.

The IFAC Code and ES5 differ to some extent on their approach to restricting recruitment and remuneration services and we summarize the requirements in Table 3.6.

Although the IFAC Code is silent on the question of remuneration packages, it is clear that for public interest entities, including listed companies, audit firms should not provide recruitment and remuneration services relating to directors and key personnel. So the key safeguard here is: Don't do it. In the case of other employees such services are permitted as long as

TABLE 3.6

IFAC Code	ES5
The audit firm may generally provide recruitment services as reviewing the professional qualifications of a number of applicants and providing advice on their suitability for the post. In addition, the firm may interview candidates and advise on a candidate's competence for financial accounting, administrative or control positions.	The audit firm shall not undertake an engagement to provide recruitment services to an audited entity that would involve the firm taking responsibility for the appointment of any director or employee of the audited entity.
A firm shall not provide . . . recruiting services to an audit client that is a public interest entity with respect to a director or officer of the entity or senior management in a position to exert significant influence over the preparation of the client's accounting records or the financial statements on which the firm will express an opinion.	For an audited entity that is a listed company, the audit firm shall not undertake an engagement to provide recruitment services in relation to a key management position of the audited entity, or a significant affiliate of such an entity.
	The audit firm shall not undertake an engagement to provide advice on the quantum of the remuneration package or the measurement criteria on which the quantum is calculated, for a director or key management position of an audited entity.

The text in the left hand column above is an extract from the *Code of Ethics for Professional Accountants*, of The International Ethics Standards Board for Accountants, published by the International Federation of Accountants (IFAC), published in June 2005, revised in July 2009, and is used with permission of IFAC.

management, familiarity and intimidation threats can be kept to a minimum. One way to do this would be for recruitment and remuneration services to be kept completely separate from the audit function.

SMALL ENTITIES

The APB recognizes that some audit firms may find it difficult to comply with all of the ethical standards, particularly when auditing a small entity. The problem for many small entities is that they often do not have expertise within their organization, that would be available to larger organizations. In consequence they tend to be reliant on their auditor to provide a range of services that may conflict with the requirements of ES5 regarding advocacy and management threats. For this reason APB has issued a standard 'Provisions Available For Small Entities' (PASE) which relaxes some of the provisions of ES1 to ES5.

For instance, PASE allows the audit firm to undertake part of the role of management, provided that it discusses the objectivity and independence issues with those charged with governance, confirming that management accept responsibility for any decisions taken; and that it discloses the fact in the audit report.

Despite this and similar relaxations, audit firms are still required to exercise great care to ensure that their integrity, objectivity and independence are not adversely affected.

OTHER PRONOUNCEMENTS ON AUDITOR INDEPENDENCE

As we mentioned earlier in the chapter a number of international organizations concerned with the regulation of auditing have issued pronouncements relating to auditor independence. These pronouncements reflect an increasing concern in the last two decades with auditor independence. A major cause of this concern was the transformation of audit firms into multi-service organizations offering their clients a plethora of non-audit services, and, of course, the concern with independence was further heightened by the Enron scandal and the considerable criticisms levied at Arthur Andersen because of their apparent lack of independence from Enron Corporation. Apart from IFAC and APB the organizations issuing guidance have included: the European Commission, the International Organization of Securities Commissions (IOSCO), the Organization for Economic Cooperation and Development (OECD), the United States Securities and Exchange Commission (SEC) and various accounting bodies. In this chapter we cannot cover all of these, but instead will concentrate on the documents issued by the European Commission and the Securities and Exchange Commission.

The European Commission issued their recommendation on auditor independence in May 2002 in a document titled, 'Statutory Auditors' Independence in the EU: A Set of Fundamental Principles'. In this document the Commission recognized that there were differences within member states as to whom the scope of independence rules should apply; the kind of relationship, financial, business or other that an audit firm could have with its client and the type of non-audit services that can and cannot be provided by auditors. The Commission considered that issuing the document on independence was a step towards assuring audit quality by providing a benchmark for member states. It regarded independence as important because it was fundamental to the confidence the public had in the audit function. It added credibility to the financial statements and was therefore of value to investors, lenders, employees and other stakeholders. While recognizing that auditor independence contributed to the efficiency of the capital markets it was also considered that maintaining independence was costly. Costs include the creating, maintenance and enforcement of safeguards relating to independence. Thus, the Commission considered that when developing regulation on independence due emphasis had to be given to the costs as well as the benefits. Specifically, the Commission noted that while rules relating to independence might be suitable for public interest entities they might not be appropriate to small companies because the costs would outweigh the benefits.

Like the IFAC Code and the APB Ethical Standards the Commission document took a principles-based approach to its recommendations on independence. It did so because it believed it created a 'robust structure within which statutory auditors have to justify their actions'. By implication the European Commission believed that a rules-based system could not hope to cater for every conceivable situation that might be encountered and that a principles-based system allowed flexibility in meeting changes in business and the audit environment.

Paragraph 11.

Finally, let us now take a look at changes to the rules relating to independence issued in the United States by the Securities and Exchange Commission (SEC). The changes to the rules by the SEC can be seen as a direct consequence of the demise of the Enron Corporation and the laying of at least part of the blame for the scandal on the lack of independence between Enron and its auditors Arthur Andersen. As a result of investigation into the Enron scandal, in the United States a new act was passed, the Sarbanes-Oxley Act (2002), which contained many provisions relating to corporate and auditor behaviour and the regulatory structure. Among these were a number of requirements concerning independence of auditors and it is these measures, approved and adopted by the SEC, which are discussed below. The major changes were as follows.

It should be recognized that the rules issued by the SEC only apply to companies registered on a US stock exchange.

The Sarbanes-Oxley Act listed nine non-audit services that were considered to impair the independence of audit firms. These are:

- That an audit firm should not audit bookkeeping or accounting services provided by the same audit firm.
- The prohibition of work relating to the audit client's information system unless the work is unrelated to matters the subject of audit procedures.
- The prohibition of any appraisal or valuation services provided by the audit firm unless it can be shown that the results of the work will not be subject to audit procedures.
- The audit firm should not provide any actuarial service which is relevant to the determination of any amounts to be included in the financial statements unless it can be shown that the results of the work will not be subject to audit procedures during an audit.

- The banning of internal audit services provided by the audit firm that relate to the client's internal accounting controls, financial controls or financial statements unless the work will not be the subject of audit procedures.
- Members of the audit firm should not act temporarily or permanently as a director or employee of an audit client, nor should they perform any decision-making or supervisory function for the client. The accounting firm should not provide certain specified services relating to recruitment of senior personnel for the audit client.
- The audit firm should not act as a broker, dealer, investment adviser or investment banker for the client because it might result in them being perceived as acting in an advocacy role for the client.
- The audit firm should not provide legal service to the audit client where the service can only be provided by someone qualified to practise law.
- The audit firm should not provide an expert opinion on matters such as litigation or regulatory proceedings or investigation for an audit client because it might be perceived as acting as an advocate for the client.

In addition to the above prohibitions the SEC endorsed a number of other requirements of the Sarbanes-Oxley Act. Among these are:

- That the audit committee pre-approve any non-audit services provided by the auditor.
- The disclosure of non-audit services approved by the audit committee including details relating to the fees paid in respect of certain non-audit services.
- That the lead and concurring partner should rotate every five years and not be allowed to be involved in the audit of the same client for another five years. In addition other significant audit partners involved in the audit should rotate every seven years with a two year time-out period.
- That where an audit partner receives compensation based on procuring non-audit services from an audit client, the partner will be considered as not independent.
- That a member of the audit engagement team may not accept certain positions with an audit client until at least one year after they have left the employment of the audit firm. Where a former lead or concurring partner or certain other defined members of the engagement team is involved in financial reporting matters of a client within one year of leaving the audit firm then the audit firm will not be considered as independent of the audit client.

This is known as the cooling-off period.

- That the audit firm inform the audit committee of any critical accounting policies and practices used by the client; all material accounting treatments allowed by GAAP that have been discussed with management and the implications of each of these and which one was the preferred treatment of the audit firm; and finally other material written communication between the audit firm and the client's management.

You will have noticed that the recommendations of the European Commission are somewhat similar to the rules adopted in the United States by the SEC. However, there are a number of differences that are worthy of comment.

The SEC rules tend to be more detailed and prescriptive whereas the European Commission relies more on the application of principles. The SEC rules are also quite restrictive – for instance, those relating to the cooling-off period before members of the engagement team can join an audit client in a senior position. This might lead audit firms in the United States stipulating in their employees' contracts that they are prohibited from joining an audit client until at least one year has elapsed after they have left the employment of the audit firm. Although occasionally mentioned in the SEC rules, little emphasis is given to the concept of materiality and its implications for independence. In a number of places the SEC rules specify restrictions applied to members of the engagement team, which fail to recognize that the role of many individuals in the engagement team may have been inconsequential, and that their work will have been reviewed by other members of the team. The onus on communicating information to the audit committee seems to lie with the audit firm rather than the directors of the client. It might be argued that, in the first instance, the directors of the client should inform the audit committee of the issues mentioned by the SEC and that it would then be up the audit committee to discuss these further with the auditors. Finally, a major issue for accountants outside the US at the time that the Sarbanes-Oxley Act was passed in 2002 was the concern that the SEC rules extended to non-US based audit firms, auditing clients registered in the United States. Apart from the difficulties non-US audit firms might have in complying with the requirements of Sarbanes-Oxley there is a more general concern that it signals some sort of US imperialism, implying that US rules on independence are superior to those in other parts of the world.

The rules would also seem to extend to a non-US audit firm involved in auditing a substantial part of a group not located in the US but where the parent company is registered in the United States.

Summary

In this chapter we have addressed the question of auditor independence and have shown that a defining element of auditing is the independence of the person performing the function. We have seen too that the independent auditor has a role in achieving accountability, although we have left open at this stage whether the auditor has a present role as regards all forms of accountability. We looked at work by a number of academics in analysing the problems associated with independence, including Mautz and Sharaf (1961), Goldman and Barlev (1974) and Shockley (1982). We saw that the relative power of auditor and auditee is likely to affect independence and that a number of factors (as identified by Shockley and others) may either have a direct impact on perceived independence or affect it indirectly through their impact on relative power. We recognized, however, that much research is still required to determine which influences on perceived independence are strongest. We also looked at the IFAC Code and the APB Ethical Standards that identify potential threats to objectivity and suggest safeguards and procedures to reduce the impact of the threats. We saw that a useful feature was the identification of areas of risk. We discussed briefly the arguments for and against the mandatory rotation of auditors. The chapter concluded by widening the scope of the chapter to examine the rules that have been adopted in other countries or by other bodies. In particular, we looked at the European Commission's recommendations on auditor independence and we also discussed briefly detailed rules on independence adopted in the US by the Securities and Exchange Commission.

Key points of the chapter

- A fundamental principle of independent auditing is that auditors are objective and provide impartial opinions unaffected by bias, prejudice, compromise and conflicts of interest. Definitions of audit invariably include the notion of 'independence'. Independent audits help to secure accountability by adding credibility to the accountability document.

- There are five broad classifications of accountability: political; public; managerial; professional; and personnel. An important question is whether auditors are responsible for helping to achieve all classes of accountability.
- The need for independence derives from the 'remoteness gap' between managers and stakeholders.
- It is difficult to define independence precisely as it is very intangible and not easily observable.
- Mautz and Sharaf identified two types of independence: practitioner independence and profession independence. They suggested that: auditing suffers from 'built-in anti-independence factors' including (1) close relationship between the profession and business: (i) apparent financial dependence; (ii) confidential relationship; (iii) strong emphasis on service to management; (2) organization of the profession: (i) emergence of limited number of large firms; (ii) lack of professional solidarity; (iii) tendency to introduce ' salesmanship'.
- Watts and Zimmerman suggest that the probability of auditor reporting matters of concern is likely to be high because of adverse effects on reputation if their failure to report comes to light.
- Goldman and Barlev suggested that pressures affecting independence might arise because of conflicts between various parties associated with the audit client. An important element was emphasis on matters that increase or decrease respective power of managers and auditors.
- Shockley produced a conceptual model based on factors that may impact on the auditor's ability to withstand pressure: (1) MAS; (2) competition; (3) tenure; (4) size; (5) accounting flexibility; (6) professional sanctions; (7) legal liability; (8) fear of losing clientele, reputation.
- Lee suggests that independence depends on the nature of the relationship between auditor and auditee and principally on the relative size of the participants.
- The IFAC Code establishes the fundamental principles of professional ethics for professional accountants and provides a conceptual framework for applying those principles: (a) integrity; (b) objectivity; (c) professional competence and due care; (d) confidentiality; and (e) professional behaviour.
- Potential threats to integrity, objectivity and independence are: self-interest; self review; advocacy; familiarity; intimidation; and management threats.
- An important measure to ensure that audit firms have appropriate standards of integrity, objectivity and independence is the firm's control environment, which has a number of important elements, and, in particular the key roles of the engagement partner, the ethics partner and the engagement quality control reviewer (EQCR).
- Other important features of the firm's control environment is the establishment of links between key people in the audit firm and those charged with governance in the audited entity. Other important links are those between the engagement partner, the ethics partner and the EQCR, and also between members of the engagement team (who are empowered to do so) and the ethics partner.
- Safeguards to eliminate or reduce the threats are either created by the profession, legislation or regulation and in the work environment. They may be classified under four headings: (1) Financial, business, employment and personal relationships; (2) Long association with the audit engagement; (3) Fees, remuneration and evaluation policies, litigation, gifts and hospitality; (4) Non-audit (or non-assurance) services provided to audit clients.
- The general principle is that any relationships to the audited entity by those that have an influence on the conduct and outcome of the audit should be avoided because of the self-interest threat.
- A potential threat to objectivity and independence exists where audit engagement partners, key audit partners and staff in senior positions have served for a considerable length of time. The particular threats to objectivity and independence that may arise are self-interest, self-review and familiarity threats.
- *Fees*: A proper audit has to be performed whatever the agreed fee, nor should fees be contingent upon an expected or desired outcome. Threats to a firm's objectivity and independence may arise where fees charged to a client represent a significant proportion of the firm's total income.
- *Remuneration and evaluation policies*: The remuneration and progress of staff members through the firm should be soundly and fairly based and should not be dependent on the success of staff in selling non-audit services to the audit client.
- *Litigation:* The existence of litigation between an audit firm and its client will damage the relationship between the engagement team and management and make the achievement of audit objectives extremely difficult if not impossible.
- *Gifts and hospitality:* Unless the gifts and hospitality are insignificant in amount, including those to immediate family members, they should not be accepted by any person in a position to determine the outcome of the audit.
- A general rule is that the audit firm should establish policies and procedures that require consideration of any threat to independence before a proposed non-assurance service is accepted.
- The threats vary according to the nature of the non-assurance service provided, and safeguards must be found for each threat identified.
- Some audit firms may find it difficult to comply with all of the ethical standards, particularly when auditing a small entity because many small entities often do not have expertise within their organization and tend to be reliant on their auditor to provide a range

of services that may conflict with the ethical requirements. APB allows relaxation of the rules under some circumstances.

- Other pronouncements on auditor independence emanate from the European Union and under the terms of the Sarbanes-Oxley Act in the United States.

References

Commission on Auditors' Responsibilities (The Cohen Committee) (1978) *Report, Conclusions and Recommendations*, New York: AICPA.

Flint, D. (1988) *Philosophy and Principles of Auditing: An Introduction*, Basingstoke: Macmillan Education Ltd.

Goldman, A. and Barlev, B. (1974) 'Auditor-Firm Conflict of Interests: Its Implications for Independence', *The Accounting Review*, 49: 707–18.

Lee, T.A. (1986) *Company Auditing*, 3rd edition, London: Chapman & Hall.

Mautz, R.K. and Sharaf, H.A. (1961) *Philosophy of Auditing*, Sarasota, FL: American Accounting Association.

Shockley, R.A. (1982) Perceptions of Auditors' Independence: A Conceptual Model, *Journal of Accounting, Auditing and Finance*, pp 126–143.

Sinclair, A. (1995) 'The Chameleon of Accountability: Forms and Discourses', *Accounting, Organizations and Society*, 20 (2/3): 219–37.

Stewart, J.D. (1984) 'The Role of Information in Public Accountability', in Hopwood, A. and Tomkins, C. (eds), *Issues in Public Sector Accounting*, Philip Allan Publishers Ltd.

Watts, R.L. and Zimmerman, J.L. (1986) *Positive Accounting Theory*, Englewood Cliffs, NJ: Prentice-Hall.

Further reading

The following is an interesting article on individual auditor independence:

Miller, T. (1992) 'Do We Need to Consider the Individual Auditor When Discussing Auditor Independence?', *Accounting, Auditing and Accountability Journal*, 5 (2): 74–84.

Messner, M. (2009) 'The Limits of Accountability', *Accounting, Organizations and Society*, Vol. 34(8): 918–38.

It is important that you have a good knowledge of the Code of Ethics for Professional Accountants issued by IFAC's Ethics Committee and Ethical Standards issued by APB in the UK and Ireland.

Self-assessment questions (solutions available to students)

3.1 Consider the following situations:

(a) Assume that you are a partner in a two partner practice with total practice income of £250 000. One of your clients (a private limited company with a turnover of £10 million and with some 80 employees) pays ongoing fees to you amounting in total to £35 000. Do you think that your independence might be threatened? What steps would you take in a situation like this?

(b) Assume that you are partner in charge of an office of your firm. You are engagement partner of a major client whose fees of £150 000 represent 2 per cent of the total gross practice income of your firm, but 20 per cent of the income of your office. Consider the implications in the light of the IFAC Code and APB Ethical Standards

(c) Assume that you are a partner with a number of clients for whom you are personally responsible. One of these clients is much larger than the others and you have to spend about 40 per cent of your time on the assignment. The fees receivable represent about 4 per cent of the gross practice income of your firm. Your own income is not based on fees receivable from this client. Consider the implications of this situation.

3.2 Now that you have read the IFAC Code and the APB Ethical Standards do you think that they have been influenced by prior work on auditing theory? Justify a Yes or No answer.

3.3 You have been asked by your audit partner to be senior in charge of the audit of a small public limited company. Unbeknown to the partner, you hold 1000 of the 100 000 shares in the company. Do you think that you could remain unbiased in relation to this client?

3.4 You have just been telephoned by the chief accountant of a listed company client – Randerston plc – to tell you that there has been a computer breakdown and that some parts of the data concerning construction contracts have been lost. He asks if two senior members of the firm's engagement team could be loaned to enable reconstruction of the data to be made on a timely basis. The deadline would be in 30 days time when the draft financial statements are due to be finalized. What issues would you consider and what would be your response?

Self-assessment questions (solutions available to tutors)

3.5 In Table 3.3 we suggested pressures against independence in respect of small audit firms and small auditees. To what extent do you believe that the IFAC Code and ES1 to ES 5 and ES-PASE have been successful in dealing with the special circumstances of small audit firms and small entities. In your answer you may consider the problems identified in Table 3.3.

3.6 Discuss the arguments for and against requiring the mandatory rotation of auditors.

3.7 The following question is taken from the Pilot Paper for Paper F 8, Audit and Assurance of the ACCA. The year-end date has been changed.

You are the audit manager in the audit firm of Dark & Co. One of your audit clients is NorthCee Co, a company specializing in the manufacture and supply of sporting equipment. NorthCee have been an audit client for five years and you have been audit manager for the past three years while the audit partner has remained unchanged.

You are planning the audit for the year ending 31 December 2011

(i) NorthCee is attempting to obtain a listing on a recognized stock exchange. The directors have established an audit committee, as required by government regulations, although no further action has been taken in this respect. Information on the listing is not yet public knowledge.

(ii) You have been asked to continue to prepare the company's financial statements as in previous years.

(iii) As the company's auditors, NorthCee would like you and the audit partner to attend an evening reception in a hotel, where NorthCee will present their listing arrangements to banks and existing major shareholders.

(iv) NorthCee has indicated that the fee for taxation services rendered in the year to 31 Dcember 2009 will be paid as soon as the taxation authorities have agreed the company's taxation liability. You have been advising NorthCee regarding the legality of certain items as 'allowable' for taxation purposes and the taxation authority is disputing these items.

Finally, you have just inherited about 5 per cent of NorthCee's share capital as an inheritance on the death of a distant relative.

Required:

(a) Identify, and explain the relevance of, any factors which may threaten the independence of Dark and Co's audit of NorthCee Co's financial statements for the year ending 31 December 2011. Briefly explain how each threat should be managed. (10 marks)

Solutions available to students and Solutions available to tutors

These can be found on the website in the student/lecturer section at: www.cengage.co.uk/graymanson5.

Topics for class discussion without solutions

3.8 Figure 3.3 on page 81 is very useful in helping people to understand how objectivity and independence issues might be managed. Discuss.

3.9 The IFAC Code and the APB Ethical Standards contain many requirements and much advice on how auditors should behave. How should the professional bodies ensure that they are adhered to?

4 Audit regulation

LEARNING OBJECTIVES

After studying this chapter you should be able to:

- **Describe the form of regulation governing the work of auditors in the United Kingdom.**
- **Explain the role of the various bodies involved in the regulation of auditing.**
- **State and explain the requirements of the law on appointment, resignation and dismissal of auditors.**
- **Describe how the law attempts to strengthen the position of the auditor.**
- **Explain the professional guidance on appointment, resignation and dismissal.**

Learning objectives, 108
The need for regulation, 109
Company law regulation, 112
Historical overview of the UK regulatory system in force until 2003, 113
Monitoring audit firms' standards, 116
Present regulatory system, 116
Financial Reporting Council (FRC), 118
The Professional Oversight Board (POB), 119
Accountancy and Actuarial Discipline Board (AADB), 121
Auditing Practices Board (APB), 121
Accounting Standards Board (ASB), 126
Financial Reporting Review Panel (FRRP), 126
Audit monitoring, 126
Report of the Coordinating Group on Audit and Accounting issues (CGAA), 127
Further regulation of auditing by the law and accounting profession, 130
The statutory and practical relationships, 130
Rules on appointment, removal and resignation of the auditor, 133
Private companies, 145
Summary, 146
Key points of the chapter, 146
References, 147
Further reading, 148
Suggested solutions to tasks, 148
Self-assessment questions (solutions available to students), 150
Self-assessment questions (solutions available to tutors), 151
Topics for class discussion without solutions, 152

THE NEED FOR REGULATION

In the United Kingdom, as in many other countries, including the United States of America and Australia, auditors have considerable powers to determine how their work is performed. What this means is that the audit profession and its associated bodies, such as the Auditing Practices Board (APB) in the UK and Ireland, play a considerable role in shaping auditing, so that the auditing and accounting profession is largely self-regulated. This is not to say that government or the state leaves it completely to the auditing and accounting profession to determine all aspects of regulation, more that they delegate certain powers of regulation to the profession. In the UK the government can and does set regulations within which the profession operates.

Later in this chapter we shall consider particular aspects of regulation relating to: audit firms, admission to entry in the profession and the appointment, dismissal and removal of auditors. At this stage you may be wondering why there is a need for regulation and why the government is willing to delegate considerable authority in respect of regulation to the auditing profession.

If you are reading this book outwith the UK, you should take account of the special circumstances and regulations in your own country. Clearly, it would not be possible for us to consider regulation in detail throughout the world. Note, too, that while we generally refer to 'financial statements' in this book, we refer in this chapter to 'accounts' where we are discussing specific requirements in the UK.

ACTIVITY 4.1

List reasons why there is a need for regulation in auditing. Suggest why the government may delegate certain powers to the auditing profession.

In answer to the first part of this activity we would make the point that most professions, be they law or medicine, are regulated in some shape or form by their professional bodies and therefore self-regulation in auditing is not unique. You may have suggested that one role regulation plays is to provide some assurance to users or consumers of a service that certain standards are met. If regulation did not exist how would individuals know which audit firms they could trust to perform work for them? In this respect the audit profession acts as a kind of licensing authority. It sets standards which individuals must achieve before they are 'licensed' to act as auditors. In this way regulation exists to prevent anyone, regardless of their credentials, from portraying themselves as auditors. Another aspect of regulation is setting of standards, to which audit practitioners must adhere and which help ensure their work is conducted properly. In this regard it should be noted that these standards are increasingly set at an International level both by the European Union through the issue of Directives and the International Federation of Accountants (IFAC). Regulation, therefore, helps to reduce risk for users of the auditing service. Risk is mentioned many times throughout this book and is an important concept for auditors. In addition you might have said that regulation helps to enhance confidence and that it replaces the element of trust which may be lacking when a person is dealing with an individual of whom they know little.

The relationship between the audit function and trust is one which is expanded upon in an interesting book by Michael Power (1997).

The second part of Activity 4.1 is concerned with sharing responsibility for regulation between the state and the auditing profession. It is worth mentioning that the power the state cedes to a professional body may be dependent on the state's attitude towards a particular form of political economy. For instance, if the state believes in a *laissez-faire* form of economic system, it is more likely to consider it should avoid interference and delegate rule-making authority to professional organizations. Conversely, if the state is committed to collectivism they may be less likely to cede responsibility to private sector professional bodies. In most countries there are usually fairly strong and powerful groups in 'the business community', advising that business and its regulation should be left to operate as they see fit within certain prescribed parameters. This is sometimes termed the light touch to regulation. Of course, after financial or business scandals occur, as is the case in the first decade of the twenty-first century, there are also other voices recommending that regulation needs to be strengthened.

Another factor influencing the power the state delegates to a professional body will be the state's opinion of the expertise, integrity and state of development of the professional body. If the state believes the professional body is respectable and competent in rule making, it is more likely that it will allow the profession some role in regulating its members. You may also have mentioned that the state might believe that the profession has more expertise than itself in the subject of auditing and therefore is likely to be a better regulator. In addition, it is often argued that state regulation tends to be somewhat bureaucratic and that a (private) professional body is likely to be a more efficient regulator.

Finally, it should be remembered that although acting as regulator gives the professional body a certain amount of power, it also carries some risk. For instance, if the performance of auditing firms comes in for criticism, the public and the media may well accuse the regulator, that is, the professional body, of not being competent and/or criticize it for drafting inadequate regulation. If the state wishes to avoid such public criticism it may well believe its interests lie in delegating regulation to a professional body. In this respect the delegation of power also results in a reallocation of risk, that is, the risk of being blamed if things go wrong.

Up to this point we have assumed that the self-regulation function is performed by the auditing and accounting profession. However, as we will see later when we consider some of the committees that form part of the auditing regulatory regime a good number of their members do not originate from the auditing profession. There is no specific reason why the state could not delegate the responsibility to another specially constituted quasi legal body with powers to oversee the practice of auditing. The concept of self-regulation is common in the English-speaking world for good historical reasons, but not in many other parts of the world, principally on the continent of Europe. It is important to point out that the accounting bodies in the British Isles were established at a very early date (the first of the Scottish societies as early as 1854), at a time when there was little government intervention in the affairs of society. By the time the accounting profession was established in other parts of Europe (the German Institute, for instance, was not founded until 1932) government control was much tighter. Because of factors such as this, other parts of Europe have arrived at different solutions to the problem of monitoring. As an example of a different regulatory regime we show in Figure 4.1 the institutional environment of auditors in Germany from which you can see that there is a separation of powers between the two main professional bodies. The Institute of Public Auditors may be described as the liberal professional body, while the Chamber of Public Auditors is the monitoring body. Clearly, the legislator also has an important role in Germany. In 2005, following criticism of the effectiveness of the Chamber of Public Auditors, a new body was established – the Auditor Oversight Commission – to oversee the Chamber. The Commission is itself supervised by the Federal Ministry of Economics and Technology. A useful commentary on audit regulation in Germany by Köhler *et al.* is referenced at the end of this chapter. Figure 4.1 is taken from this book. Some commentators in the United Kingdom have suggested that professional accounting bodies should not be responsible for monitoring audit firms' activities on the grounds that an accounting body cannot both support its members and monitor them effectively. As we shall see, recent changes in the regulatory structures in the UK have moved the professional accounting bodies away from their monitoring function so that their emphasis is more on supporting their members. Further, as mentioned above, the regulation of auditing in the UK has been further complicated in recent years by the increasing role played by supra-national organizations. As you will have seen from earlier chapters APB is not free to set auditing standards but does so within the requirements of the International Auditing and Assurance Standards Board (IAASB). The role of IAASB is to serve the public interest by setting international standards on auditing and to facilitate the convergence of national standards.

We shall see in Chapter 20 that some academics and politicians have argued that it is inappropriate for the auditing profession to regulate its own members.

IAASB is a committee of IFAC which is the global organization for the accountancy profession. It currently works with its 159 members and associates in 124 countries.

At this stage you might care to pause and think how such a body can set standards that serve the public interest in a divergent set of countries, varying in terms of their stage of economic development, their political, cultural and social systems, language and so on. Indeed, one might go further and question how an organization decides what is in the 'public interest' and exactly how such a concept is constructed.

FIGURE 4.1 Institutional environment of auditors in Germany

COMPANY LAW REGULATION

We have stressed above why the auditing profession in the UK plays a major role in regulating auditing. This role was enhanced by certain provisions contained in the 1989 Companies Act and amended by the Companies (Audit, Investigations and Community Enterprise) Act 2004. Until the passing of the 1989 Act, the auditing profession had considerable autonomy in the way it regulated its members. The 1989 Act gave legitimacy to this by establishing in law two bodies: Recognized Supervisory Bodies (RSBs) and Recognized Qualifying Bodies (RQBs). To be recognized as a RSB it is required by the Companies Act 2006 (which superseded the 1989 Act) to have:

The Companies Act 2006 retained most of the previous legislation but made a few amendments.

- Rules and practices relating to the eligibility of a person for appointment as a company auditor, ensuring auditors are fit and proper persons and act with professional integrity and independence.
- Rules and practices on technical standards, maintaining competence and membership eligibility and discipline.
- Arrangements for monitoring and enforcement of its rules and the investigation of complaints (Schedule 10, Part 2).

In addition to the above the Companies Act 2006 Schedule 10, Part 3 also requires the RSB to be willing to participate in arrangements for:

- Setting standards relating to professional integrity and independence.
- Setting technical standards.
- Independent monitoring of audits of listed and other major bodies.
- Independent investigation for disciplinary purposes of public interest cases.

The latter four items were introduced by the Companies (Audit, Investigations and Community Enterprise) Act 2004 and paved the way for more independent regulation of members of the audit profession. Independence was further enhanced by requiring that the RSB as well as having no involvement itself in the above should play no role in appointing or selecting of individuals responsible for the above four tasks.

The role of the Recognized Supervisory Bodies (RSBs) is to:

> Maintain and enforce rules as to: (a) the eligibility of persons for appointment as a statutory auditor, and (b) the conduct of statuory audit work, which are binding on persons seeking appointment or acting as a statutory auditor either because they are members of that body or because they are subject to its control (s. 1217(1), CA 2006).

The role of the Recognized Qualifying Bodies (RQBs) is to enforce rules (whether or not instituted by the body) such as those relating to:

- Admission to or expulsion from a course of study leading to a qualification.
- The award or deprivation of a qualification.
- The approval of a person for the purposes of giving practical training or the withdrawal of such approval (s. 1220(2), CA 2006).

When the legislation was originally implemented all the main accounting bodies sought and achieved RSB and RQB status. It may be argued that the legislation resulted in a reduction in the level of pure self-regulation, as the accounting bodies had to work within a framework established in UK law.

Some commentators, for instance, Humphrey *et al.* (1992), have suggested regulation could be separated further from the professional bodies by setting up an independent Office for Auditing to oversee the framework for large company audit appointments, auditor remuneration and the audit practice of the major accounting firms. If this were done, this would clearly be a departure from the system of self-regulation.

HISTORICAL OVERVIEW OF THE UK REGULATORY SYSTEM IN FORCE UNTIL 2003

Over the last ten years there have been a number of important changes to the regulatory regime in the UK. To give some context to the system presently in place we first review the regulatory system that was in force for a few years prior to its demise in 2003. This is instructive because it will let you see the process of change that is occurring and the forces that are bringing about that change. Perhaps one of the most important aspects is the extent and the nature of the roles that the state and the accounting profession have played in the discussion about what is the most appropriate regulatory structure for accounting and auditing in the UK and the way the debate has been shaped by important financial scandals, such as the Enron debacle.

As a result of criticisms of audit regulation during the 1990s most of the main professional accounting bodies in the United Kingdom formed committees to investigate changes needed to the existing system. It was generally agreed that there were deficiencies in the regulatory structure that existed at that time. For instance, a paper, 'Audit Regulation in the Public Interest' (1995), produced by ICAS, listed the following weaknesses and limitations (p. 2):

- It burdened even the smallest practitioners with a demanding monitoring requirement, out of all proportion to the risks applicable in a typical small practice.
- It created, or could create, an inefficient interface between the Joint Monitoring Unit (JMU) and the Institute's own disciplinary processes.
- It confused practitioners as to whether their Institute was supporting them or confronting them.
- It gave the impression to some outsiders of being managed by the profession, for the profession, rather than the public interest.

We discuss the JMU later in the chapter.

As a result of the debate on regulation, the Department of Trade and Industry (DTI) issued a consultative document 'A Framework of Independent Regulation for the Accountancy Profession', in November 1998. After consultation, the Minister of State for the DTI, Ian McCartney, announced in April 1999 that he proposed implementing the new system. The purpose of the

From 'Independent Regulation of the Accountancy Profession: A Brief Outline of the New System', Accountancy Foundation, November 2002.

system was 'to ensure that the public interest in the way that the profession operates is fully met and thus to secure public confidence in the impartiality and effectiveness of the profession's systems of investigation and discipline, professional conduct and regulation'. The system of regulation is represented pictorially in Figure 4.2.

Six key principles were influential in developing the regulatory structure shown in Figure 4.2. These were:

1 *Independence*. External representation on the boards was necessary if they were to be seen to be independent.
2 *Public interest and integrity*. This would be more likely by inclusion of non-accounting members in the structure, and through public consultation.
3 *Transparency and openness*. The regulatory and disciplinary structures must be open to public scrutiny.
4 *Proficiency and commitment*. The effectiveness of the structures requires a balance to be struck between external participation and professional judgement.
5 *Relevance*. Procedures must be in place for monitoring the compliance of firms and practitioners with professional standards.
6 *Review*. There should be procedures to ensure that the regulatory structure is subject to both external and internal review.

Figure 4.2 shows that the regulatory regime consisted of a number of separate bodies reporting to the Accountancy Foundation. The purpose of these various bodies was as outlined below.

FIGURE 4.2 Regulatory system in force until 2003

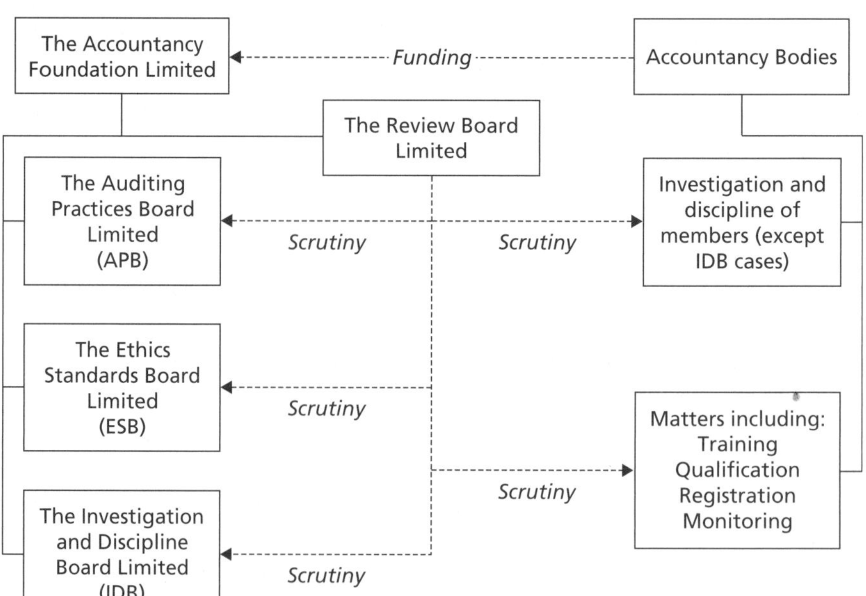

The Accountancy Foundation

The objective of the Accountancy Foundation was to maintain and enhance the standard of work performed by accountants and their conduct. It had three main functions:

- It appointed the members of the Boards of each of the Foundation's bodies.
- It acted as the channel for finance and ensured the system was adequately funded.
- It had an overarching responsibility for the success and good health of the new system and was the key point of contact with the government, the accountancy profession and others to this end.

The Accountancy Foundation was set up in 2000. The Auditing Practices Board reported to it, together with two other bodies established in 2001 – the Review Board and the Ethics Standards Board.

The Auditing Practices Board was part of this regulatory structure but because it is also in operation under the new structure we leave discussion of its role until later in the chapter.

The Review Board

The main purpose of this board was to monitor the regulatory structure and ensure that it was meeting the public interest. The Review Board consisted of eight part-time members and its constitution excluded the appointment of any practising accountant or any individual involved in the governance of any of the accountancy bodies. This body was seen as the most important element in the regulatory structure. This was because its remit was to oversee the work of the Auditing Practices Board, the Ethics Standards Board and the Investigation and Discipline Board. In addition it was charged with overseeing the responsibilities of the professional accountancy bodies. To fulfil this function the Review Board had access to documents and individuals in the three bodies. Because of its wide remit to investigate the three bodies at the inception of the new regulatory structure it was anticipated that the Review Board would play a key role in improving and developing regulation. As a first step in this process The Review Board issued in February 2002 a paper 'Protecting the Public Interest', in which as a first stage in exercising its role, it examined the approaches of the accountancy bodies to the public interest. In addition it also outlined its proposed work programme.

The Ethics Standards Board

The responsibility of this board was to develop ethical standards for all accountants, whether working in practice, industry or the public sector. The Board consisted of ten members of whom six had to be non-accountants. The Ethics Standards Board did not set the actual ethical standards; as that was left to the various accountancy bodies. Instead, the Board set the agenda and principles that provided the underpinning of the standards set. Before the accountancy bodies issued ethical standards, however, they had to be approved by the Ethics Standards Board. As a first step in fulfilling the above role the Board issued a consultation paper, 'Setting the Agenda for Ethics' in May 2002. The purpose of this paper was to help it 'gain an understanding of public opinion on the ethical issues involved in the work of accountants' by asking for responses to a number of questions on key topics. A further purpose of the paper was to 'promote thought and debate across the entire spectrum of ethical issues faced by all accountants.'

The Investigation and Discipline Board

However, under the new regulatory structures discussed below the Investigation and Discipline Board has come into operation. In 2007 the Board changed its name to The Accountancy and Actuarial Discipline Board (AADB) in recognition of the fact that its role had been enlarged to include certain disciplinary responsibilities in respect of the actuarial profession.

This board was expected to take over responsibility of the Joint Disciplinary Scheme and was therefore given the power to investigate members of the accounting bodies where there was a public interest element. Cases not involving the public interest continued to be the responsibility of the individual accountancy bodies. Although this body was seen as an important element in the regulatory structure, it never came into effect.

MONITORING AUDIT FIRMS' STANDARDS

In the old regulatory structure the monitoring of the performance of audit firms who were regulated by ICAEW, ICAS and ICAI was carried out by the Joint Monitoring Unit (JMU). The mode of operation of the JMU was to select a sample of firms to check that they were complying with good practice. During the year to 31 December 2002, the JMU started 1081 monitoring visits. Generally, large audit firms – some 20 accounting firms who audit the majority of listed companies – received some form of visit annually. Other firms auditing listed companies were expected to receive a monitoring visit every three years. The purpose of the visit was to ensure that companies were complying with audit regulations and auditing standards. The visit reviewed the audit firm's files and checked that audit work was being carried out in compliance with the firm's own audit procedures. In the case of large audit firms a full visit took up to 110 days with interim visits in the two intervening years taking up to 40 days. The visits included some to various offices of the audit firm. The duration of visits to smaller audit firms normally lasted for about three days. The JMU ceased to exist on 31 December 2003 and was replaced by a new monitoring system which is discussed later in the chapter.

We now outline the recent changes that have been made to regulatory structures, but before doing so we draw your attention to the limited lifespan of the previous regulatory regime. Effectively, it was only in operation for about two years before being replaced. This speedy replacement might cause one to question if sufficient thought had been given to the structures in the first place. We discuss this matter further in a later section.

PRESENT REGULATORY SYSTEM

A consultation document forming the basis for the recommendations included in the Review had been issued in October 2002.

The various scandals in the United States, such as Enron and WorldCom, caused concern regarding regulation of companies and auditors in the UK. As a result the government decided it was time to review the audit and accountancy regulatory regime and set up two major reviews. The first of these, 'Review of the Regulatory Regime of the Accountancy Profession' (RRRAP), published its report in January 2003 (DTI 2003b).

The second, the 'Co-ordinating Group on Audit and Accounting Issues' (CGAA), produced an interim report in July 2002 and a final report in January 2003 (DTI, 2003a) We deal first with the concerns of the RRRAP and then move on to the report of the CGAA. The purpose of the Review of the Regulatory Regime was to strengthen and simplify regulation of auditing and accounting in the UK. The review recommended significant changes that it felt would improve the system of regulation, although it also suggested there was no evidence that the system was substantially flawed. The main recommendations of the report were:

- The Financial Reporting Council (FRC) should take over from the Accountancy Foundation and become the overall 'independent regulator'.
- APB would become responsible for setting standards relating to independence, objectivity and integrity, which at the time were set by the individual professional accounting bodies.
- A new Professional Oversight Board (POB) should be formed whose function would be to oversee the audit function.
- An Investigation and Discipline Board should be set up for hearing significant public interest cases.

In November 2003 APB issued a consultation paper, 'Draft Ethical Standards for Auditors'.

We discuss each of these bodies in more detail below.

The new regulatory regime is shown in Figure 4.3 below.

Since the previous regulatory regime with the Accountancy Foundation as the main regulator had only been fully in operation since 2002, the obvious question to pose is why it was thought necessary to change it so soon after its inception. The main reasons given in the review for the proposed changes were:

- It was considered that the existing system was too complex and that the functions and responsibilities of the various boards overlapped.
- It was felt the Accountancy Foundation did not have 'a sufficiently authoritative voice'.
- The practical reality is that accounting and auditing are intertwined and therefore it would make sense and be beneficial for there to be one regulator covering both disciplines.

FIGURE 4.3 FRC Ltd Board

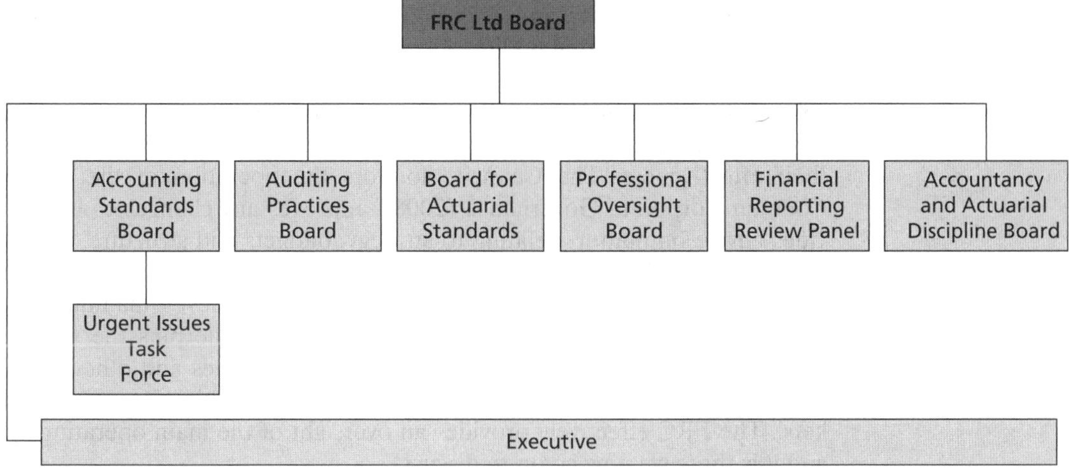

- It was considered that perception of independence of the regulatory regime could be improved by implementing a system that was clearly separate from the professional accounting bodies.
- Finally it was thought it would be beneficial to have the setting of both accounting and auditing standards under the remit of the same regulatory regime.

Dewing and Russell (2002) note that it is paradoxical that a regulatory system that was enthusiastically championed by the government should be called into question and eventually replaced in a very short space of time primarily as a result of an event, the scandal involving Enron Corporation, which occurred not in the UK but the US.

The Department of Trade and Industry has been re-constituted and is now known as the Department for Business Innovation and Skills.

Following publication of the review, the Department of Trade and Industry issued a consultation document in March 2003 containing legislative proposals on the *Review of the Regulatory Regime of the Accountancy Profession* (DTI 2003b). Following this, a number of the proposals aimed at ensuring the independence of the regulation of public interest audit work were enacted in the Companies (Audit, Investigation and Community Enterprise) Act 2004. It is interesting that generally the accounting profession welcomed the proposed changes. Austin Mitchell MP, a fierce critic of accounting regulation, also seemed to believe that the abolition of the Accountancy Foundation was a positive move stating that 'it has been a useless, inadequate substitute for independent regulation'. It should not, however, be thought that he wholeheartedly endorsed the changes; instead he considered that the new body (the Financial Reporting Council (FRC)) was the nearest thing to effective regulation that is available, but it is still limited, as running it will be left to the accounting profession, although the costs will be paid largely by the government. He thought that it would be 'another inadequate bodge'.

Accountancy, March 2003, p. 51.

FINANCIAL REPORTING COUNCIL (FRC)

The Financial Reporting Council has overall responsibility, in the UK, for the regulation of accounting, auditing and, from 2005/06, the actuarial profession. Its management consists of a board of directors with a chairman, a non-executive deputy chairman, seven non-executive directors and the chairs from each of the six operating bodies. The chair and deputy chair are appointed by the Secretary of State for Business, Enterprise and Regulatory Reform. The role of the board includes setting the overall strategy and priorities, making appointments to the various operating boards, such as APB, and ensuring their effectiveness. The Council monitors the operation of the Combined Code on Corporate Governance (2008), approves any changes to it, and provides advice on matters relating to strategy, budgets and structure. The membership of the Council is largely drawn from senior figures in the business, professional and financial community. The FRC believes maintaining high standards of corporate reporting and governance underpins the working of 'markets to the benefit of business, investors, employees and other interests', and enhances 'the UK's economic strength in competitive international markets'. The FRC effectively provides an oversight of the main operating boards and it is these we now go on to discuss.

THE PROFESSIONAL OVERSIGHT BOARD (POB)

Currently the Professional Oversight Board consists of 13 members, none of whom are presently employed within the auditing profession, although a few of them have had past association with large accounting firms. The role of the POB is to provide:

- Oversight of the operation and regulation of the auditing profession by the recognized supervisory and qualifying bodies.
- Monitoring the quality of the auditing function in relation to listed companies and other entities in which there is a major public interest.
- Reviewing various aspects of the regulatory procedures and processes of the professional accountancy bodies and making recommendations of how they might be improved.
- Reviewing the regulation and operations of the actuarial profession by the professional actuarial bodies and making recommendations of how they might be improved.

In this book we do not consider the POB's role in relation to the actuarial profession.

The CA 89 required regulation of auditing and supervision of the RSBs and RQBs, and gave this authority to the Secretary of State who in turn delegated it to POB. POB is required to make a report each year to the Secretary of State indicating how they have discharged their regulatory function. In discharging its responsibility, POB is concerned with the systems that RSBs have in place: to register audit firms, monitor their work, handle complaints about members, deal with disciplining members and ensure their competence. Regarding RQBs the main concern of POB will be the systems for registering and training students, provision of courses, training records and the setting, marking and moderation of examinations. In performing this function POB visits the various RSBs and RQBs to document, discuss and test their systems, and ensure they comply with statutory requirements. Its evaluation of the effectiveness of their systems includes their complaints and disciplinary procedures. In 2008/09 POB visited all RSBs and RQBs. POB also requires the RSBs and RQBs provide it with an annual regulatory report, including statistical information on their regulatory activities. An important function of the RSBs is to monitor audit firms which are registered with them for audit purposes. POB in turn supervises the monitoring activities of the RSBs to ensure that they are performing them effectively and, where necessary or appropriate, provides suggestions or recommendations to improve their activities. The Companies Act 2006 (in Schedules 10 and 11) specifies the requirements that bodies must meet if they are to be recognized as supervisory and qualifying bodies and POB has to ensure in its monitoring of the recognized bodies that they continue to meet the statutory requirements. The POB has under its control the Audit Inspection Unit (AIU).

The Companies Act 2006 maintained the requirement that RSBs and RQBs be monitored by POB. The Companies Act requirements were subsequently amended to incorporate the requirements of the Eighth Directive which were not originally contained in the Act.

The Big Four audit firms are all registered with the ICAEW as an RSB.

The role of the AIU is to monitor the audits of all listed and other major public interest entities, including large unquoted companies, major building societies, pension schemes, unit trusts and charities. Because of the concentration of the audit market most large listed companies are audited by one of the Big Four audit firms. For this reason, the AIU has focused predominantly on audits conducted by those firms with some emphasis on audits carried out by other 'significant' firms. The five other audit firms that carry out a significant number of audits (more than ten) within the remit of the AIU, comprise Baker Tilly, BDO Stoy Hayward, Grant Thornton, PKF and Horwath Clark Whitehill. While the Big Four will be subject to annual inspection the other major firms will tend to be investigated on a two year cycle. Other firms which carry out less than ten audits within the remit of the AIU will be subject to less onerous inspection, the AIU relying on the monitoring carried out by the body with which they are registered.

The AIU's approach is not only to evaluate the audit firm's audit approach but also the judgements exercised by the audit partners. The AIU characterizes its approach as follows:

- Focus on the quality of auditing, with recommendations to firms prioritized on this basis.
- Thorough, robust and challenging approach to inspection visits.
- Wide-ranging reviews of firm-wide procedures, including an assessment of how the culture within firms impacts on audit quality.
- Selection of major audits for review, which is largely risk-based.
- In-depth reviews of major audits, focusing on the quality of the group audit, including critical assessment of the key audit judgements made, particularly those that are pertinent to forming an audit opinion and compliance with auditing, quality control and ethical standards.
- Review of the quality of reporting to the Audit Committee.

The approach of the AIU with respect to the major audit firms is to review their overall policies and procedures in relation to such matters as leadership, human resources, independence, ethics, audit quality monitoring and methodological approach taken to audits. In addition when the AIU inspects particular audits their emphasis is on the quality of the audit judgements used in reaching an audit opinion and in the amount and relevance of the audit evidence collected. Although the AIU has only been in operation for a short period of time it is generally satisfied with the quality of the audits they have evaluated. In the AIU's report for 2008/09 they indicated that most of the audit firms had taken into account the economic downturn and therefore required greater emphasis on matters such as evaluating going concern. The AIU, however, also reported that the extent to which additional work was performed varied across the major audit firms and some were more timely than others in providing advice. Of particular relevance is the AIU's view that in certain instances the quality and quantity of evidence used to support going concern judgements could have been improved. They also noted in some instances that greater internal focus within the audit firms could have been given to client acceptance and retention decisions. Other issues raised related to the quality and sufficiency of audit evidence collected and lack of adaptation to take into account specific audit risk, including that of fraud. The AIU also noted that some firms' documentation seemed to suggest that audit staff would be appraised and rewarded on the basis of selling non-audit work to clients.

You will remember from Chapter 3 that rewarding staff for obtaining non-audit work from clients cuts across principles outlined in the Ethical Standards.

Though the AIU found some areas of concern and made a number of recommendations for improvement they considered the quality of auditing to be sound and recommended that the audit registration of these major firms be continued. Regarding other audit firms investigated, the AIU found not dissimilar issues as those relating to the major audit firms, but the extent of these and the proportion of audits where improvement was considered necessary was greater than for the major firms. In addition to publishing an overall or summary report of the work of AIU, for the last two years the FRC has also published the AIU's individual report on each of the major audit firms they investigated in that particular year.

ACCOUNTANCY AND ACTUARIAL DISCIPLINE BOARD (AADB)

This particular board had been proposed in 1998 under the regulatory regime discussed earlier but had never come into operation. The review envisaged that it should have authority to instigate cases involving public interest bodies proactively rather than simply waiting until cases are referred to them. Presently the board consists of eleven members of whom three are qualified accountants. The role of the body was expanded in 2007 to encompass cases involving the public interest arising from the actuarial profession. Its role is to act as an independent, investigative and disciplinary body for accountants and actuaries in the UK. Although cases involving the public interest will usually have been referred to the AADB from one of the accountancy bodies (or actuarial body) it has the power to look at cases where it sees the need, whether or not the case had been referred. At the time of writing the AIDB is investigating ten cases including the audit of the 2003 accounts of the MG Rover Group Limited and the 1999 accounts of Equitable Life Assurance Society. Since the AADB has only produced two tribunal reports it is too early to assess its effectiveness.

AUDITING PRACTICES BOARD (APB)

APB was established in 1991 and was an important element in the 'old' structure described above and remains relatively unchanged in the new one, though its remit has changed as we show later in the chapter. In the first part of this section we show how APB came into existence and 'fitted' into the old structure. Later in this section we discuss its place and role in the new regulatory regime.

Background

In the previous section we referred to powers of regulation that the state has delegated to the auditing profession. In the United Kingdom and the Republic of Ireland some of these powers are vested in APB, which was established by the Consultative Committee of Accountancy Bodies (CCAB) but now comes under the Financial Reporting Council. APB was not the first attempt by professional bodies at regulating the work of auditors. Prior to its formation the Auditing Practices Committee (APC), formed in 1976, had issued auditing standards and guidelines. Before this date the profession had taken little action to regulate the performance of auditing. You may be wondering why it was decided to replace APC with APB. To understand this, we must consider certain aspects of the audit environment in the 1980s. First, the audit

Note, however, from the early 1960s ICAEW issued advisory guidance on audit practice to its members in the form of 'U series statements'.

A clean audit report is without modifications signifying there was nothing amiss in the client company. See Chapter 16. To some extent we have a similar situation today with auditors being criticized for not alerting the public of concerns about the fragility of the financial statements of banks and the risks they were taking just prior to the credit crunch.

profession was criticized on a number of occasions, particularly when client companies collapsed, having previously received a clean audit report. Second, APC consisted largely of audit practitioners from big audit firms which led to criticism that it was less concerned with serving the public interest than with looking after the interests of those big firms. Third, the pronouncements of APC consisted mainly of guidelines and a few standards. The guidelines contained guidance on what was considered best practice but they were not as authoritative as standards. The Companies Act 1989 required RSBs to have rules and practices relating to technical standards to be applied in audit work and how those standards were to be applied in practice. It is difficult to decide, without obtaining legal opinion, if the guidelines produced by APC would have satisfied the requirements of the Act, but it did serve as a catalyst for the auditing profession to consider how it could best meet its requirements. The requirement of the 1989 Act for the accountancy supervisory bodies to have technical standards was retained in the Companies Act 2006, Schedule 10, except that the reference is now to 'statutory audit work' rather than 'audit work'. By implication, the ISAs adopted by APB ensure that the above requirement imposed on the RSBs is fulfilled. Finally, at about the same time, a review was carried out on the process of setting accounting standards, which resulted in the replacement of the Accounting Standards Committee (ASC) by the Accounting Standards Board (ASB). It is likely that the debate surrounding this change had some influence on how the auditing profession chose to develop rules governing the practice of auditing.

The objectives of APB

APB sets out its objectives in the statement 'Scope and Authority of Pronouncements (Revised)' (October 2009). These are stated as:

- Establish auditing standards which set out the basic principles and essential procedures with which external auditors in the United Kingdom and the Republic of Ireland are required to comply.
- Issue guidance on the application of auditing standards in particular circumstances and industries and timely guidance on new and emerging issues.
- Establishing standards and related guidance for accountants providing assurance services where they relate to activities that are reported in the public domain, and therefore within the 'public interest.'
- Establish ethical standards in relation to the independence, objectivity and integrity of external auditors and those providing assurance services.
- Participate in the development of any legislative or regulatory initiatives which affect the conduct of auditing and assurance services, both domestically and internationally.
- Contribute to efforts to advance public understanding of the roles and responsibilities of external auditors and the providers of assurance services including the sponsorship of research.

Although the above statement is not substantially different from the one issued in 2004 there are some changes in emphasis. Of particular note is that previously APB was to be involved in changes in accounting standards which might affect the work of auditors. However, as the International Accounting Standards Board (IASB) sets accounting standards and the International Auditing and Assurance Standards Board (IAASB) now has the primary responsibility for setting auditing standards, it may be argued that APB has a reduced role in the setting of standards.

Another interesting historical development is that in a previous 'Scope' statement issued by APB in April 2003, they acknowledged they had some responsibility to society when they stated the setting of standards is likely to lead to a framework for auditor judgement that will enhance 'the quality and relevance of auditing services in the public interest and public confidence in the auditing process' (Paragraph 1). It is interesting that APB laid some stress on the public interest and public confidence, which would seem to be an acknowledgement that they have some responsibility to user groups other than shareholders. Of equal interest is that both in the statement issued in December 2004 and its revision in April 2009 the emphasis given to the 'public interest' seems to be diminished. It may be that because an important part of APB's role in the issuing of auditing standards has effectively been taken over by the IAASB, they no longer can say they act as an autonomous body concerned with the public interest. It is also interesting that the objective to advance public understanding of the roles and responsibilities of auditors which was in the 2004 'Scope' statement has been retained, which seems to suggest that APB feels that the public still do not fully appreciate the role and responsibilities of auditors. In Chapter 18, where we discuss the audit expectations gap in greater detail, we examine whether the audit profession should be more responsive to the public and should go some way to meeting their concerns, rather than merely assuming various users need educating. Another interesting feature in the revised 'Scope' document is the continuing emphasis given to assurance services but this time only those where the resultant reports are in the public domain. Thus, assurance services provided by auditors to clients for the latter's own use do not have to comply with guidance or standards issued by APB.

The debate surrounding auditors' responsibilities to users of financial information will be taken up in Chapter 19.

We discuss assurance services in Chapter 15.

ACTIVITY 4.2

It is implicit in the requirements of the Companies Act 2006 and the objectives contained in 'The Scope and Authority of Pronouncements' that APB believes that setting standards will enhance the quality of auditing and the value of the audit. Suggest how the issuing of standards might achieve the above and what other measures might be taken by APB to enhance the value of the audit.

You might have suggested that the issuance of standards to be followed by auditors might enhance the quality of auditing and hence reduce the incidence of audit failure. If the likelihood of audit failure is reduced, this would, perhaps, increase the confidence with which users rely on audited financial information.

By audit failure we mean that the auditors' work has fallen below the standard expected from a professional person. Normally audit failure comes to the public's attention when a company fails and users suffer financial loss.

Another way in which the value of auditing might be improved is by extending the reporting requirements of auditors. An example would be to require auditors to report on the internal controls of a company. This report could be of value to both users and management of the company. The reporting on internal controls to directors was one of the recommendations of the preliminary report on corporate governance (the Hampel Report 1998). APB could also encourage extensions of the audit role that might be beneficial to clients. In an article in *Accountancy* (May 1996, p. 94) the Head of the Audit and Business Advisory practice at one of the Big Five (as they then were) stated that the value of audits can be enhanced by, for instance, guiding clients through 'the increasingly complex regulatory environment they are in'. It might be argued that this has been achieved to some extent by the increasing emphasis placed on assurance services. The extension of services into areas other than traditional audit might, however, have implications for auditor independence. Enhancing the value of audit was also considered in the APB (1996) publication, *The Audit Agenda – Next Steps*, which made a number of suggestions as to how the value of the audit could be enhanced. For instance, in respect of fraud detection it suggested that 'the accountancy bodies should review the education and training process to develop auditors' understanding of behavioural and forensic issues and undertake seminars discussing experience and means of detecting fraud' (Paragraph 4.2). It can be argued that APB in issuing and establishing statements on the principles and essential procedures with which auditors are required to comply in conducting audits has taken not only an effective but also a pragmatic step in enhancing the value of audit. Finally, APB has also sought to increase the quality of audit work by issuing practice notes and bulletins.

Auditing standards

Throughout this book we discuss many International Standards of Auditing (ISAs), issued by IAASB, adopted and augmented by APB for use in the United Kingdom and Ireland. Prior to the adoption of ISAs APB issued standards in their own right as Statements of Auditing Standards (SASs) but with harmonization as a principle APB decided to adopt in 2004 all the standards issued by the IAASB. They did so after reviewing the ISAs and adding extra material where they considered it necessary to meet specific UK regulatory requirements. Subsequently, the IAASB undertook the clarity project and arising from this a suite of revised ISAs was issued in October 2009. As well as incorporating the changes necessitated by the clarity project the IAASB also took the opportunity to revise a number of standards. The revised set of ISAs (UK and Ireland) are effective for audits ending on or after 15 December 2010. The only revised ISA APB did not adopt was ISA 700 which deals with audit reporting and we discuss that in Chapter 16. As their title suggests, standards contain prescriptions with which auditors are required to comply when performing their audit work. Each statement contains several standards setting out basic principles and essential procedures. In addition the ISAs contain explanatory material which is intended to help auditors in interpreting and applying the standards. The clarity project introduced two new innovations to the standards. First, each ISA includes an objective and second, the requirements of each ISA are separated from the application material.

We detail the structure of the ISAs in the Preface. See page xix.

The standards provide a minimum level of performance with which auditors must conform and therefore they help to ensure that all auditors' work complies with that minimum standard. If audit firms did not comply with the standards in their audit work, there would be a greater chance of the work falling below what the profession regards as acceptable. One of the purposes of issuing standards is to raise the general standard of audit work.

ACTIVITY 4.3

Suggest why the IAASB/APB issues auditing standards.

Auditing standards provide a benchmark by which the quality of audit work can be measured. This may be useful to a supervisory body when it is considering whether a particular audit firm should be subject to disciplinary sanctions. If the supervisory body finds that the firm's audit work falls below that specified, this would be prima facie evidence that the firm's audit work fell short of that required of a member of that body. Similarly, if an audit firm is charged with negligence, it is likely that a court of law would look to whether the firm's procedures complied with auditing standards (amongst other things) when deciding whether the firm has been negligent.

This is specifically stated in Paragraph 23 of the Revised APB 'Scope and Authority of Pronouncements' statement. It may not, however, always be easy to determine if a particular standard has been complied with. This will depend upon how specific the standard is and how open it is to interpretation.

Ethical standards

As we saw in Chapter 3, both IFAC and APB have issued codes of ethics. APB issued five ethical standards applicable to the UK and Ireland in October 2004 and these were revised in April 2008. Ethical Standard 3, 'Long Association with the Audit Engagement', was further revised in October 2009. Prior to APB being responsible for these, the various professional bodies had issued their own statements of independence, objectivity and integrity. The impetus to change came, as we mentioned above, from the RRRAP report which recommended that APB should take responsibility for setting the rules relating to ethical conduct. The motivating factor for the change was to improve independence by taking another element of the regulatory structure out of the hands of the professional accounting bodies and placing it under the control of an independent body. When revising the ethical standards APB took cognizance of the International Code of Ethics for Professional Accountants issued by IFAC and the change in legislation resulting from implementation of the EU's Statutory Audit Directive. Thus, in following APB ethical standards, auditors in the UK and Ireland will also be complying with international guidance.

Practice notes and bulletins

Practice notes are issued by APB to assist auditors in applying auditing standards in particular circumstances and industries. Examples of practice notes include: 'Auditing Complex Financial Instruments – Interim Guidance' (practice note 23 (revised), October 2009), and 'Attendance at Stocktaking' (practice note 25, January 2004). Bulletins are intended to provide auditors with timely advice on new or emerging issues. Examples of recent bulletins are: 'The Special Auditor's Report on Abbreviated Accounts in the United Kingdom', April 2008, and 'Developments in Corporate Governance Affecting the Responsibilities of Auditors of UK Companies', December 2009. The material included in practice notes and bulletins although intended to be persuasive rather than prescriptive is indicative of good practice.

ACCOUNTING STANDARDS BOARD (ASB)

ASB is concerned with issues relating to accounting standards, in particular, issuing new standards or amending existing ones, providing advice or clarification on extant standards and working with other standard setters, particularly the International Accounting Standards Board and appropriate EU bodies. Its board consists of up to ten members most of whom have a background in accounting, the accounting profession or the financial sector. In this book we mention a number of accounting standards and their implications for audit purposes, but apart from this, we do not give further consideration to the role of ASB, which you will examine in considerable depth during your accounting studies.

FINANCIAL REPORTING REVIEW PANEL (FRRP)

The FRRP is a UK body, concerned with the quality of financial reporting by public and large private companies. Its focus is on companies that do not follow or appear not to follow the requirements of the Companies Act 2006 or accounting standards. Since 2006 the FRRP has also reviewed Directors' reports. Using a risk-based approach the panel reviews a sample of annual accounts of companies in specific industry sectors, or in an area where it is expected accounting problems might arise. The panel also investigate areas of topical interest, for instance, accounting for derivatives. Other annual accounts may come specifically to their attention because of complaints. Generally FRRP will carry out an initial analysis to determine if some aspect of accounting regulation has not been followed and the importance of the non-compliance. If deemed sufficiently important FRRP will then perform a more extensive analysis involving a panel of members (normally of about five members) and the company concerned. The outcome of this might be an agreement with the company that the latter voluntarily takes some action, such as issuing a set of revised accounts or some form of clarification. If the panel and the company cannot reach an agreement, FRRP may apply to the courts to enforce some form of corrective action to the accounts. To date FRRP has not needed to apply to the courts, as matters have been settled by the company issuing revised accounts or FRRP and the company agreeing on an appropriate alternative course of action. Although FRRP is an important element in ensuring the quality of financial reporting, because it is not central to the concerns of this book, we do not discuss it further.

AUDIT MONITORING

Earlier in the chapter we discussed the role of the Audit Inspection Unit in monitoring the quality of auditing carried out in listed companies and other large entities in the UK, and noted that the RSBs retained a monitoring role. In this part we outline briefly the nature of the audit monitoring performed by the RSBs. Prior to the new regulatory structure ICAEW, ICAI and ICAS carried out their monitoring role through the joint monitoring unit (JMU) with the ACCA having their own monitoring mechanism. With the demise of the JMU on 31 December 2004, each of the above bodies now performs its own monitoring function. In this chapter we give you an overview of the nature of the monitoring process rather than a detailed account of the monitoring carried out by each professional body. Each of the bodies has a specialized unit consisting of individuals (reviewers or inspectors) who have experience of auditing to carry out the monitoring role. The objective of the monitoring is to ensure that the RSBs comply with the requirements first laid down for them in the Companies Act 1989 and subsequently superseded by the Companies Act 2006. In doing so the RSBs will be ensuring that registered audit firms adhere to appropriate standards and produce quality audits. As part of their monitoring the reviewers will check that the audit firms comply with audit regulations and auditing standards. Firms registered with each RSB complete an annual return that serves to give reviewers insight into the firms' processes and also enables them to identify risk factors which might need further investigation. The monitoring units will also select a sample of audit firms to visit for a more thorough examination of their processes. It will be normal for audit firms, not involved in the audit of listed companies or other significant entities, to be visited at least once about every six years. Audit firms involved in auditing listed companies or other significant entities will receive a visit more frequently. The frequency of visit is also partially determined by the monitoring unit's assessment of the risk involved and the results from its previous visit. At the visit the reviewers will discuss risk issues and other matters they have identified with key audit staff in the audit firm (normally audit firms will have a designated compliance partner) and review a number of audit files. The extent of the latter review will depend largely on the size of audit firms and how many audit clients they have. When examining files the reviewers will be interested in determining if audit staff have followed the procedures laid down by the audit firm and that critical issues are suitably documented. The reviewers will also want to ensure that the audit firm is complying with ISAs, UK GAAP, IFRSs and the International Standard on Quality Control 1, the Companies Act and any other specific regulatory requirements. At the end of the visit the reviewers will usually discuss their findings with audit firm personnel to give them a chance to correct any factual errors and also to give a response to the findings. As a result of the visit a report will be made to an Audit Registration Committee (ARC) in the RSB. Subsequently ARC will take a decision, normally that the audit registration should be continued, and give the audit firm an indication of the result of the examination. Where problems have been identified during the visit and these have not been satisfactorily resolved at the time of the meeting or in correspondence thereafter, follow-up action will usually be required. At the extreme, if the ARC has substantial doubts they may decide to withdraw audit registration or place conditions on its continuance.

The role of monitoring audit firms is also required by the EU Eighth Directive and therefore it does not just pertain to the UK.

Each of the RSBs have Audit Registration Committees which are concerned with matters such as audit firms eligibility and suitability to practice.

REPORT OF THE COORDINATING GROUP ON AUDIT AND ACCOUNTING ISSUES (CGAA)

Earlier in the chapter we mentioned that two major reports were produced on accounting and auditing and we now turn our attention to the second of those reports. The main concerns of CGAA were: auditor independence; corporate governance and the role of the audit committee; transparency of audit firms;

We have already discussed monitoring of audit firms earlier in this chapter. Page 126.

financial reporting: standards and enforcement; monitoring of audit firms and competition implications. CGAA noted that the various financial scandals that occurred in the UK in the 1980s and early 1990s had led to changes that improved the system of regulation and enabled them to declare 'that the UK can claim, with some justification, to be at the forefront of best practice. We [the Coordinating Group] do not subscribe to the more extreme views that have been canvassed; business and the professions have much to be proud of, and the great majority carry out their work with honesty, professionalism and skill.' This statement leaves no doubt that CGAA disagreed with the more vehement critics of audit which we mentioned earlier in the chapter. The main recommendations of CGAA were as follows:

page 5.

Auditor independence

CGAA concluded that audit partners should rotate and welcomed the decision by ICAS and ICAEW that the lead audit partner should rotate after five years and other partners after seven years. It is interesting that, while the CGAA accepted the case for partner rotation, they did not consider that audit firms should be rotated. The group accepted that there was a need to toughen the rules on the provision of non-audit services to ensure the independence of the auditor was maintained. It also accepted that a valuable first step was the implementation by ICAEW and ICAS of most recommendations of the European Commission in their report 'Statutory Auditors' Independence in the EU: A Set of Fundamental Principles' (2002). The group, however, also recommended that strengthening was required regarding the provision of internal audit services by external auditors. It was recommended that there should be a review of whether further safeguards were required when auditors supplied the following non-audit services: valuation services; taxation services; and the design and supply of IT and financial information technology systems. The group noted with approval the conclusions of the Smith report (Financial Reporting Council 2003) in respect of the role of audit committees, in particular their involvement in appointing auditors and their oversight of non-audit services. Non-audit services provided by audit firms remains a controversial issue and some commentators have suggested there may be a link between the provision of such services and the clean audit reports given to the accounts of banks. As you will be aware, shortly after the clean audit reports had been issued on some banks, in the aftermath of the credit crisis, they required an injection of funds from government in order to remain float. One final recommendation by the group in respect of independence was that a body separate from the professional accounting bodies should set independence standards.

We discuss some conclusions of the Smith report in Chapter 18.

Corporate governance and the role of the audit committee

In this part of the report CGAA noted with some satisfaction the conclusions and recommendations of the Higgs review (DTI 2003c) on the role and effectiveness of non-executive directors. The group also acknowledged the recommendations of the committee under the chairmanship of Sir Robert Smith designed to improve corporate governance and in particular the recommendations they had made regarding changing the Code of Best Practice (Financial Reporting Council 2003). One other issue the group considered was the introduction of a statutory approach to corporate governance rather than the present self-regulatory approach. They concluded that there appeared to be little evidence to support a statutory underpinning to corporate governance at present.

Transparency of audit firms

We discussed transparency reports in Chapter 2.

CGAA indicated that there was a need for greater openness from audit firms. They considered that, since auditors held a privileged position in society, in which the notion of trust was paramount, audit firms had a duty to be more transparent. They therefore recommended that relevant firms publish on a voluntary basis an annual report containing:

Relevant firms are those firms involved in the audit of listed clients. We discuss corporate governance in Chapter 18.

- Financial information: it was envisaged that the sort of financial information disclosed should be that required by the Statement of Recommended Practice for Limited Liability Partnerships.
- The governance arrangements of the audit firm: including the basis of partner remuneration, including that related to the provision of non-audit services.
- Quality: the audit firm should describe how quality of audit output was maintained, through, for instance, training of staff, quality control procedures and the procedures for monitoring quality.

After the CGAA report had been published the EU in article 40 of the EU's 8th Directive required that auditors of public interest entities publish on their website a transparency report giving information on matters such as their structure, governance and a description of their internal quality control systems. The recommendations were taken forward by POB in a consultation documentation which they issued in 2006. After due consultation POB issued regulations requiring auditors of public listed companies to publish on their website annual transparency reports. The regulations also stipulated the minimum requirements to be contained in the reports. The POB requirement had statutory backing as they invoked Section 1240 Companies Act 2006 which specifically gave the power to the Secretary of State to require audit firms to make available certain information.

The Secretary of State delegated this power to POB by Article 3(1)(b) of Statutory Instrument 2008/496 The Statutory Auditors (Delegation of Functions etc) Order 2008. We discussed the POB in relation to Audit Quality in Chapter 2 – see page 48.

Financial reporting: standards and their enforcement

CGAA welcomed the cooperation between world-wide standard setters and, in particular, the proposed adoption in the UK of International Accounting Standards by 2005. They also considered that standards should be firmly based on principles rather than on detailed rules. In this connection, note that, following the Enron scandal, one of the criticisms levelled at US standard setting is that it is rules-based rather than principles-based. As a result the SEC produced a report in 2003 entitled a 'Study Pursuant to Section 108(d) of the Sarbanes-Oxley Act of 2002 (SEC, 2003) on the Adoption by the United States Financial Reporting System of a Principles Based Accounting System'. A further important recommendation of CGAA was that FRC should become more pro-active in reviewing the accounts of listed companies.

See our discussion above on the workings of the FRRP.

Competition implications

The concern of CGAA in respect of competition was motivated in part by the demise of Arthur Andersen, which resulted in only four large firms, and by the fact that that these firms audited 76 per cent of all listed company audits in the UK. The small number of audit firms in the listed company market gave cause for concern that there was little competition and this might have adverse consequences. Because of this, the issue was investigated by the Office of Fair Trading. CGAA simply noted that the Office of Fair Trading had concluded that, as at 2002, there was no need for a Competition Commission referral but that they would keep the issue under review. However, the lack of competition in the listed company audit market is still of major concern in the UK and is a topic we will revisit in Chapter 20. For the remainder of this chapter we are concerned with Companies Act provisions in respect of the appointment, resignation and dismissal of auditors.

FURTHER REGULATION OF AUDITING BY THE LAW AND ACCOUNTING PROFESSION

For the purposes of your auditing examinations it is important to know the requirements of company law in respect of appointment, resignation and removal of auditors of limited companies. The relevant Companies Act 2006 sections are included on the publisher's website and this part of the book will draw your attention to important matters of principle. Understanding the principles behind the law will help you to retain the specific requirements in your memory. To aid understanding, we shall be using a case study to bring the main points to your attention. The basic approach will be to present you with a scenario and to invite your comments. The case scenarios will also be supported by diagrams and timescales.

If you are reading this book outwith Great Britain in a part of the world where the Companies Act 2006 does not apply, you will, we think, still find the case study in the next section of value in identifying important principles.

THE STATUTORY AND PRACTICAL RELATIONSHIPS

To appreciate the legal rules in relation to the appointment, resignation and removal of auditors, you need to have a firm understanding of the following concepts:

- The individuals and firms who are permitted to act as auditors.
- The period for which the auditor is appointed.
- The statutory relationships between auditors and shareholders.
- The statutory relationships between shareholders and directors.
- The practical relationships between auditors and directors.

The individuals and firms who are permitted to act as auditors

Sections 1209 to 1213 of the 2006 Companies Act concern those who may and may not act as auditors of limited companies in Great Britain and we set these out in Appendix 4.1 on the Cengage website, together with an explanation of the distinction between an RSB and an RQB. All such individuals and firms must be registered with an RSB.

Period for which auditor is appointed

The basic rules for appointment of auditors in private companies are laid down in s.485 and for public companies s.489(1) and (2) of the Companies Act 2006. s.489(1) states 'an auditor or auditors of a public company must be appointed for each financial year of the company' and s.489(2) 'the appointment must be made before the end of the accounts meeting of the company at which the company's annual accounts and reports for the previous financial year are laid'. It is important to know that a company's accounting year is determined by reference to the accounting reference period. The reference period in turn is determined by its accounting reference date in each year. The accounting reference date is the last day of the month in which the anniversary of the incorporation of the company falls (s.391(4). The first accounting reference period is the period greater than six months but not greater than 18 months beginning with the date of incorporation and ending with its accounting reference date (s.391(5). Later accounting reference periods are normally successive time spans of 12 months beginning immediately after the end of the previous accounting reference period and finishing at its accounting reference date. The company's accounting year begins with the day coming directly after the end of the previous financial year and ending normally on the last day of the next accounting reference period s.390(3). It is possible to alter the accounting reference date (s.392), but normally the accounting reference period will be for an accounting year. One other matter of importance is that the law requires accounts to be filed with the registrar within nine months after the accounting reference date for a private company and within six months for a public company s.442(2). In the case of a public company such accounts must be laid before the company in general meeting not later than the date for filing those accounts s.437(2).

For public companies the annual accounts are required to be sent to its members and debenture holders at least 21 days before the general meeting at which the accounts will be considered s.424(3).

For private companies, members and debenture holders must be sent copies of the annual accounts not later than the end of the period for filing the accounts or, if filed earlier, the date on which it actually filed its accounts with the registrar of companies s.424(2). This requirement is illustrated in Figure 4.4 below.

The relationships

In Chapter 3 we saw that the auditor was responsible for bridging the remoteness gap between management and the users of financial information. Figure 3.1 in Chapter 3, page 64 showed the relationship between auditor, management and users in very simple terms but we must now examine the relationships in greater detail. These relationships are described diagrammatically in Figure 4.5 which extends Figure 3.1. You should note in particular:

See page 133.

- *Shareholders* – legally appoint auditors.
- *Shareholders* – elect directors.

FIGURE 4.4 Period of auditor appointment, and accounting reference period and date

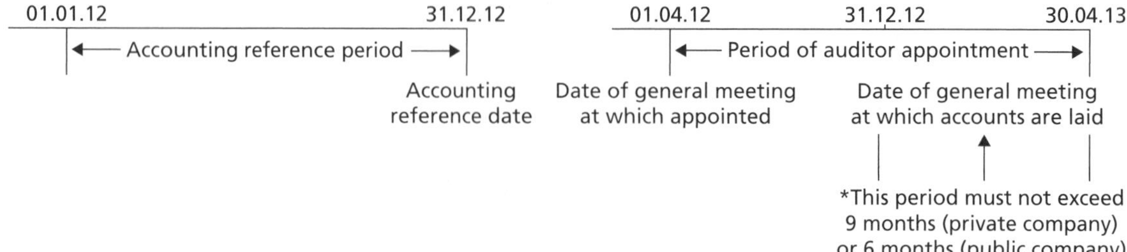

- *Directors* – are responsible for running the company on behalf of the shareholders. In listed companies the Board of Directors will normally consist of both executive and non-executive directors.
- *Directors* – are responsible for the preparation of accounts (giving a true and fair view of what they purport to show) for an accounting reference period and for laying them before shareholders in general meeting.
- *Audit committee* – a sub-committee of the main board comprising three (at least) independent non-executive directors. Its duties should include advising on the appointment of auditors and on their remuneration. It is responsible, among other things, for the effectiveness of the audit function, internal and external, and for reviewing the scope and results of the audit.

Where the company is listed but is not included in the FTSE 350 the audit committee should be established with at least two non-executive directors. We discuss audit committees in greater detail in Chapter 18.

- *Auditors* – have the duty to examine the accounts and to report to shareholders on whether the statements give a true and fair view and have been drawn up in accordance with legal and accounting requirements.
- *Auditors* – have the right of access to the accounting records and to receive information and explanations considered necessary from the directors and their representatives.
- *Other users* – have access to accounts and the auditor's report because these are published, or because they have a special relationship with the company (for instance, banks providing funds, or the inspector of taxes).

The legal relationships

- Shareholders elect directors and appoint auditors.
- Directors and auditors report to shareholders.

The practical relationships

We discuss some aspects of the close practical relationship in this chapter but extend the discussion later.

- The delegation of authority by directors to other management within the company.
- The close relationship the auditors must have with directors and other management when carrying out the audit process.
- The apparent reliance of other users of the accounts on the auditor's report.

We discuss auditor responsibility to third parties in Chapter 19.

We shall return to Figure 4.5 from time to time to put the legal requirements into proper context.

FIGURE 4.5 Legal and practical relationships between directors, the audit committee, other management, other user groups and the auditor

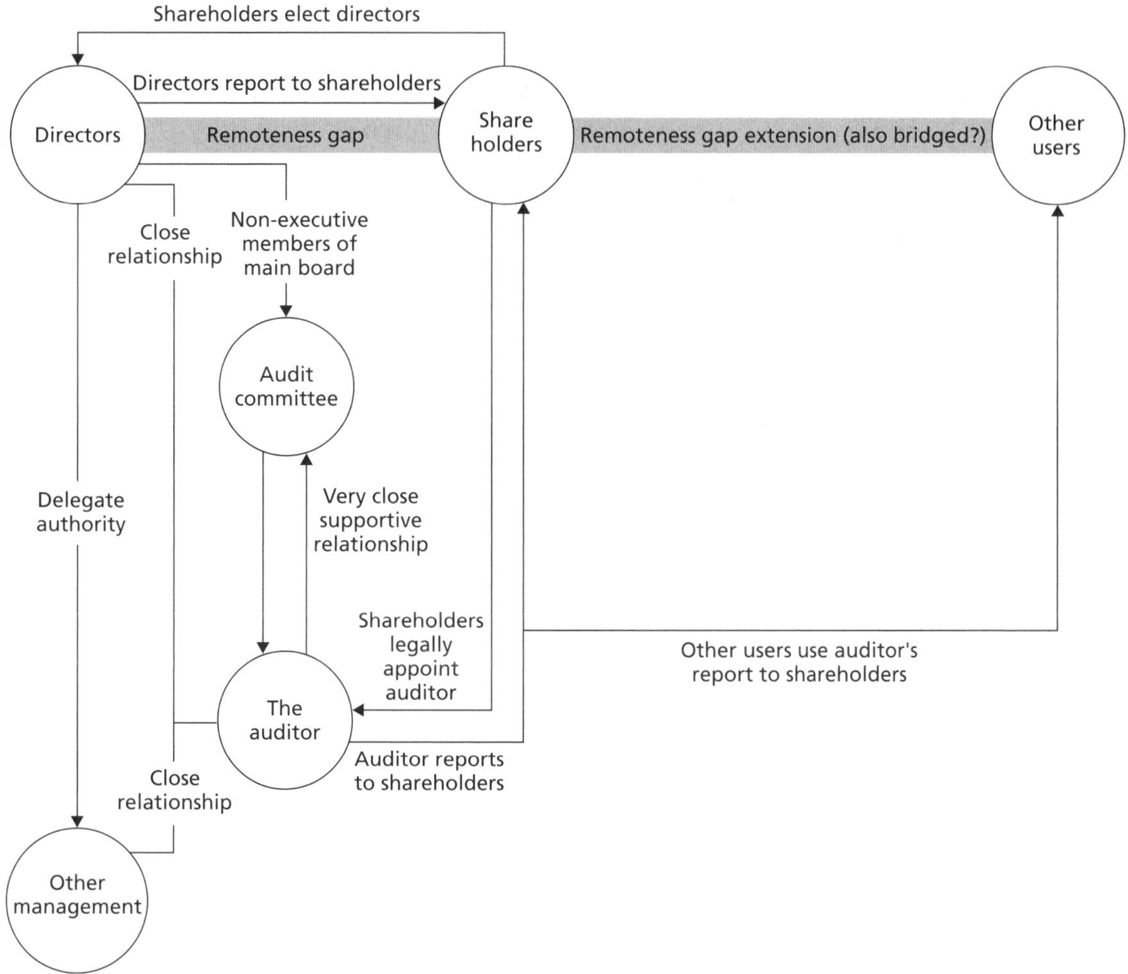

RULES ON APPOINTMENT, REMOVAL AND RESIGNATION OF THE AUDITOR

Following this discussion of the basic principles of appointment and of the legal and practical relationships we can now turn to the detailed rules. The case study, Rosedale Cosmetics plc, will be used to introduce you to the CA 2006 requirements on a number of matters affecting the directors and the auditor(s) of a company in the cosmetics industry. As the case proceeds you will be asked to inform yourself about the legal requirements. This book will assist you by directing your attention to particular sections of CA 2006 and, where appropriate, to professional rules on ethics. Note that the vast majority of auditor/client relationships are much happier than those portrayed in the Rosedale case. The various situations described, while all true to life, have been specifically introduced into one case to help you understand the law and professional requirements. You should turn to Figure 4.6 below whenever you need help in understanding the scenario. Now read Case Study 4.1, Rosedale Cosmetics plc, Part 1.

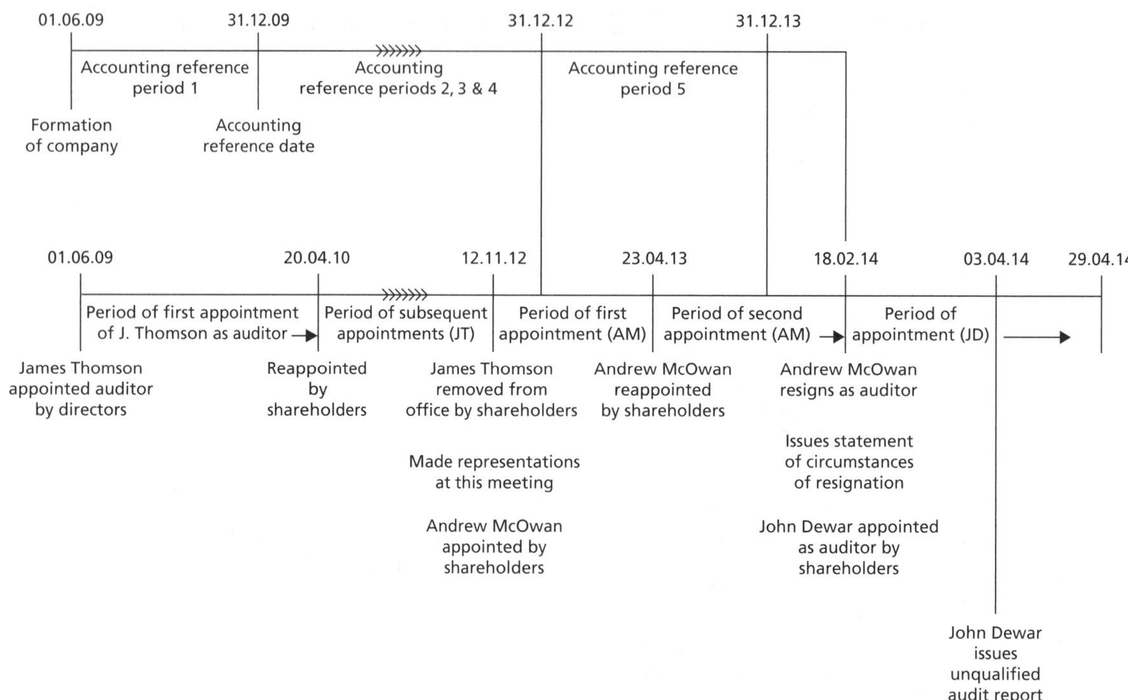

FIGURE 4.6 Appointment, removal and resignation of auditor of Rosedale Cosmetics plc

01.06.2009 James Thomson appointed auditor
20.04.2010 James Thomson reappointed by shareholders
12.11.2012 James Thomson removed from office by shareholders
James Thomson made written representations prior to the meeting at which he was removed
Andrew McOwan appointed by the shareholders
23.04.2013 Andrew McOwan reappointed by the shareholders
18.02.2014 Andrew McOwan resigned as auditor
18.02.2014 John Dewar appointed by shareholders

CASE STUDY 4.1

Rosedale Cosmetics plc, Part 1

Rosedale Cosmetics plc was formed on 1 June 2009, following the merger of a number of smaller companies in the cosmetics industry. There were some 25 shareholders, most of whom played no part in the management of the company. The chairman of the company was Sir Frederick Ashop who had a stated policy of growth through acquisition. Shortly after formation the company was given permission to have its shares dealt on the Alternative Investment Market (AIM).

> Before a company's shares can be traded on AIM the company must make certain disclosures. We will assume for the purposes of the question that Rosedale made the disclosures.

Try to answer Task 4.1 below and then look at the suggested solution on page 148.

TASK 4.1

Advise Sir Frederick on the following matters:	Relevant CA 2006 Sections
(a) The company's duty to keep accounting records.	386
(b) The directors' duty to prepare annual accounts. We are not specifically covering CA 2006 (s.399) requirements on group accounts in this book.	394
(c) The form and content of the annual accounts.	Accounts must be drawn up either in accordance with Companies Act 2006 or International Accounting Standards. The Companies Act formats for accounts are given in two statutory instruments issued in 2008 SI 2008/409 and 2008/410. The International Accounting Standards are those that have been adopted by the European Commission.
(d) The period in respect of which accounts must be prepared. Figure 4.4 will aid your explanation which should include advice on accounting reference dates and periods. Sir Frederick has already informed you that he wishes the accounting year-end to be 31 December.	390 to 392
(e) The directors' duties relating to laying the annual accounts before the company in general meeting. Draw also Sir Frederick's attention to ss. 454, 455 and 456, which describe the provisions relating to the revision of defective accounts and reports.	394, 396, 414, 423 and 437
(f) The directors' duty to prepare a directors' report.	415, its content 416, 417, 418 and approval 419
(g) The length of time allowed to elapse from the end of the accounting period to the date of the general meeting at which accounts are laid before	Approval of accounts 414, period allowed for filing accounts 442, time allowed for sending out accounts 424 and default in filing accounts 451

(Continued)

shareholders and the penalties for non-compliance. If the year-end is 31 December, by which date must accounts be laid before the company in general meeting? (Figure 4.6 will help)	
(h) Appointment of the first auditor and subsequent private companies and public companies re-appointment.	485 and 489 respectively
(i) Remuneration of the auditors: What is included and who fixes it?	492 also note 494 remuneration and disclosure of other services provided by auditor
Sir Frederick tells you he wishes to appoint James Thomson, a member of ICAEW as the first auditor of Rosedale Cosmetics plc and that he has already agreed fees of £75 000 with him. Read again ss.489 and 492 before you comment on whether this is permissible.	

Next, read Part 2 of the Case study. Try to answer Task 4.2 and then look up the suggested solution on page 149.

CASE STUDY 4.1

Rosedale Cosmetics plc, Part 2

After receiving your advice, Sir Frederick sent a letter to James Thomson, formally confirming his appointment as auditor and a few days later he received a letter, setting out the terms of the appointment as understood by James. The letter set out the duties of auditor and management, detailed services other than audit provided by James Thomson's firm and described the basis upon which fees would be charged. At the first meeting to discuss the audit Sir Frederick said that he would like to hold the AGM (annual general meeting, the general meeting at which accounts are laid before members) in April each year, putting it well within the six-month period required by CA 2006 s.442 and s.437. He also made clear to James Thomson that there was, in his view, little doubt that James would be re-appointed as auditor, as the shareholders 'will respect my judgement'. James received the impression that Sir Frederick was a very dominant personality within the company but felt that, with a little care and tact, he should be able to work with him. He requested the senior in charge of the audit to make sure that the assignment was carried out within the timescale requested by Sir Frederick. The audit of the accounts for the seven months to 31 December 2009 was somewhat problematic because the accounting systems of the individual components of the company had not been fully integrated. Despite having some doubts about the accounting records, however, James decided that the weaknesses were not grave enough to warrant mention in his audit report, particularly as Sir Frederick assured him that the problems encountered by the company would be solved when a new computerized accounting system was introduced. On 20 April 2010 the accounts at 31 December 2009 were laid before the company in general meeting, together with the directors' report and an unmodified auditor's report.

> We discuss audit reports in Chapter 16.

- Balance sheet at 31 December 2009.
- Profit and loss account for the seven months to 31 December 2009.
- Cash flow statement for the seven months to 31 December 2009.

> This statement is not required by CA 2006 but by Financial Reporting Standard 1 (FRS 1, revised 1996) cash flow statements. Small entities are exempt from the requirement to produce a cash flow statement.

- Notes to the accounts.

James Thomson and his staff did not find the audit work at Rosedale Cosmetics plc very easy. The senior in charge of the work found that the directors were frequently unavailable when he wished to raise audit matters with them, while Sir Frederick would only discuss the company's affairs with James Thomson. Despite this, however, the audit work revealed no major problems, the computerization of the accounting system was introduced in stages and James was generally satisfied with the way it was operating.

> Auditors often carry out larger audits in stages.

However, during the interim audit in September 2012 of the company for the year to 31 December 2012, the senior came across a letter from a customer in the company files. The customer had used a particular brand of face cream, which had caused her face – or so she claimed – to break out in unsightly spots. In her letter, which was dated 24 April 2012, the customer threatened legal action. The senior took a copy of the letter and discussed it with James Thomson who suggested to the senior that he ask the company's chief chemist for the periodic test reports on the company's products. He asked the chemist if he could see the reports for the face cream in question, but the chemist said Sir Frederick had those particular reports and suggested the matter be raised with the directors. The next day James Thomson received a telephone call from a very irate Sir Frederick who maintained that the auditors had exceeded their authority, that they had no right to poke their noses into company production and inspection reports. James defended his senior's actions, and said they were clearly carried out to determine whether there might be any pending legal claims against the company. He referred to FRS 12 – *Provisions, contingent liabilities and contingent assets* and said he would, as was his wont, write to Rosedale's lawyer requesting him to advise him of pending legal cases affecting the company, and their expected outcome. Sir Frederick said that the matter had not been referred to the company's solicitor and that, in any event, he took the view that the enquiries should not have taken place without his knowledge and that he had lost confidence in James and his staff. James Thomson made a number of attempts to resolve the issue with Sir Frederick over the course of the following two weeks and thought he was making some progress. He was, therefore, surprised to receive from the company on 9 October 2012 a copy of a resolution proposing his removal as auditor at a general meeting called for 12 November 2012. A second resolution proposed that Andrew McOwan, certified accountant, be appointed to replace James as auditor.

> Basically FRS 12 requires contingent liabilities, such as pending legal claims, to be disclosed in the accounts unless any possible settlement is judged to be remote.

TASK 4.2

Inform yourself as to the CA 2006 requirements on:	Relevant CA 2006 sections
(a) Removal of auditors.	510
(b) Auditor's right to attend company meetings.	502 and 513
(c) Notice required for certain kinds of resolution, including removing an auditor before the expiration of his term of office.	s.510(2), 511(1) and failure to reappoint s.515(2)
(d) To which persons must be sent copies of the aforementioned resolutions.	511(2) and if resolution to remove is passed 512
(e) Representations that the auditor proposed to be removed may make.	511(3)

Now move to Part 3 of the Case study.

CASE STUDY 4.1

Rosedale Cosmetics plc, Part 3

James was not surprised to receive a letter from Andrew McOwan on the following Monday (12 October 2012), stating he had been asked by Rosedale Cosmetics plc if he would be prepared to act as auditor of the company, and asking if James would inform him of any professional reason why he should not act. Andrew McOwan also said in his letter that he had discussed with Sir Frederick Ashop the requirement of his own professional body (ACCA) that he should communicate with the outgoing auditor, requesting all the information which ought to be made available to him to enable him to decide whether or not he is prepared to accept the appointment, and that Sir Frederick had agreed.

> Note that all the professional bodies have similar rules on changes in professional appointment. This is contained in their respective Code of Ethics. The permission to discuss is common to ACCA, ICAEW, ICAI and ICAS.

James was aware that auditors may be removed by the company in general meeting before the expiration of office. He was certain that the manner in which he and his staff had carried out the audit work was in accordance with the expected standards of his profession and felt that he should take advantage of CA 2006 s.511(3), which allows representations to be made by the auditor to the shareholders of the company. He decided to take this step to protect his own professional reputation, despite his belief that Sir Frederick had already obtained the support of the major shareholders.

James acknowledged receipt of the two resolutions from Rosedale Cosmetics and requested permission to discuss the affairs of the company with Andrew McOwan. He received a very brief letter from the company secretary giving this permission a day or two later. James decided to discuss the events leading up to his proposed removal as auditor with Andrew McOwan orally and arranged to meet him on 16 October 2012 in his own office.

At this meeting he described the audit enquiries made in respect of the prospective legal claim and stated his professional opinion that the enquiries were quite proper in the context of duties imposed by CA 2006.

Andrew McOwan told him that Sir Frederick Ashop had shown him the face cream test reports (which passed the cream as suitable for use by the public) and a letter from an independent medical doctor who gave her opinion that the customer suffered from an allergy which had caused the medical complaint. Andrew told James that Rosedale had made a small out-of-court settlement to the customer and Sir Frederick now considered the matter closed.

James told Andrew that he intended to make representations to the shareholders in respect of the matter and that he recognized that it was no longer possible for him to maintain a professional relationship with Rosedale Cosmetics. He also told Andrew that he would be submitting his note of charges for audit work carried out to date.

James submitted his representations to the company in writing on 19 October 2012. They were quite brief and he couched them in careful, professional language, knowing that CA 2006 s.511, not only requires them to be of reasonable length but also states that representations need not be sent out to shareholders or be read out at the meeting if the court decides that the rights were being abused to secure needless publicity for defamatory matter. These were sent to the shareholders prior to the general meeting on 12 November 2012. At this meeting, which was chaired by Sir Frederick, and prior to putting the two resolutions to the shareholders, James made a brief oral statement as permitted by CA 2006 s.502(2).

Also note s.513, giving the auditor the rights under 502(2).

As he expected, however, the resolutions were accepted by the shareholders, of whom only ten were present.

Note that CA 2006 s.510(3) states that nothing in the removal clauses should be 'taken as depriving the person removed of compensation or damages payable to him'.

If the auditor is simply not being re-appointed rather than removed, they have similar rights to the above.

At this stage you should, perhaps, ask yourself whether the Companies Act really gives the protection to the auditor that a cursory reading of the relevant sections would suggest. On the face of it, the law protecting the auditor from removal at the wish of directors does appear to be weighted in favour of the auditor. It must be said, however, that, in practice, few individual shareholders attend general meetings and that directors are often able to gain the support of sufficient supporters to carry the meeting in their favour. This should be a matter for concern to any person who sees the role of the auditor as important in society. By the time you have completed your study of auditing, you should be able to suggest steps that might be taken to make the position of the competent, independent and professional auditor secure, but you should start thinking about the problem now. At this stage it is worthwhile pointing out that changes in appointment are sufficiently important that they warrant guidance by the professional accounting bodies.

Changes in professional appointment

Each of the RSBs issue guidance on change of auditor appointment, for instance, Section 210 of the ICAS Code of Ethics deals with changes in a professional appointment. This statement provides guidance on the procedures that should be followed when a client decides to change its auditors. The statement makes clear that when a member is approached by a prospective client, the former should inform the latter that they have a duty to communicate with

Although the section below is based on guidance issued by ICAS, all the other professional bodies have issued similar guidance.

the existing auditors. In addition the client should be asked by the prospective auditors to give the existing auditors (preferably written) authority to discuss its affairs with the prospective auditors. If the client refuses to give the existing auditors the right to discuss the client's affairs with the prospective auditors the latter should normally not accept the nomination or appointment. Assuming the client does give permission, the prospective auditors should write to the existing auditors to determine any facts of which they should be aware which may influence their decision as to whether it would be appropriate to accept the appointment. The existing auditors should reply promptly stating that there are no matters which require to be brought to the attention of the prospective auditors or giving details of matters which should be brought to their attention. Matters which may warrant bringing to the attention of the prospective auditors include:

- where the existing auditors have serious doubts about the integrity of the directors/senior management;
- where the client is considered to have withheld information required by them or otherwise limited the scope of their work;
- where the existing auditors have unconfirmed suspicions that the client or its directors/employees have defrauded HM Revenue and Customs;
- where the existing auditors have faced opposition in their duties arising from substantial differences of opinion with the client in respect of principles or practices.

If the existing auditors have raised any matter, the prospective auditors should seriously consider whether it is appropriate for them to act as auditor. If the matter raised by the outgoing auditors relates to differences in opinion about an accounting policy or practice, the prospective auditors should ensure that they are satisfied as to the appropriateness of the client's position. Alternatively, where they do not concur with the client's views, they should ensure that the client accepts that they may have to express a contrary opinion. The need for this guidance arises from the practice of 'opinion shopping' by clients. This practice is where an auditor disagrees with a client about the treatment of a particular transaction or an accounting policy and the client then solicits opinions from other auditors in respect of the treatment or policy hoping that a firm of auditors will be found that agrees with them. The client can then proceed to instigate procedures to replace the existing auditors with these newly found auditors. Finally, where existing auditors do raise a matter with prospective auditors, it is unlikely that they can be sued by the client for damages for defamation. This holds even if what they say in any communication turns out to be untrue. For instance, the existing auditors may state in their letter to the prospective auditors that they have suspicions that some of the directors are defrauding HM Revenue & Customs. If this turns out to be false the existing auditors would not be liable for damages should an action be brought against them by the client as long as they made the statement without malice. It is unlikely that they will be found to have acted with malice as long as they stated only what they sincerely believed to be true and did not act recklessly in making such a statement. It would be wise, however, to record in the working papers or elsewhere, the reasons for the views they communicated to the incoming auditors.

It is generally now the case that if a listed, high profile company changes auditor it will attract some attention both from shareholders and the media who will be interested in the reasons for the change. This is particularly the case if the media believe that the existing auditors and their client may have clashed over presentation or disclosure issues in the accounts. The concern here is that the client is simply changing auditors to avoid conflict and potentially present accounts that are preferable to the directors. If the prospective auditors are suspicious that this might be the reason for the change, they have to give very serious consideration if they should accept the engagement. Finally, in listed companies one would expect members of the audit committee to be convinced of the need for a change in auditor before any such change was mooted by the executive directors.

A study by Beattie and Fearnley (1995) found that the most common reasons for a change in auditors were reputation and quality, acceptability to third parties, value for money and ability to provide non-audit services.

Now read Part 4 of the Case study. We move here to consideration of the law and practice relating to the resignation of auditors. Auditors may, of course, resign for many reasons including some which are entirely benign. For instance, many resign because of age and retirement, others for personal reasons unconnected with age, but some may resign for professional reasons, and it is the latter we shall be concentrating upon in this section.

CASE STUDY 4.1

Rosedale Cosmetics plc, Part 4

Andrew McOwan was not entirely happy about taking up the appointment as auditor but nevertheless decided to do so. His decision was influenced by his belief that the problems for the previous auditor were largely because of a personality clash. He recognized that Sir Frederick was not the sort of person who would accept criticism of his actions easily but felt that he could establish a professional relationship with him. During the audit to 31 December 2012, Andrew McOwan looked very carefully into the question of possible liabilities arising from legal claims. He satisfied himself that all the product inspection reports were complete and had been properly prepared. He also sought legal advice about the threatened claim by the customer and was assured that the out-of-court payment was accepted as final settlement. He signed his unqualified audit report on 12 March 2013 and the accounts were laid before the shareholders in general meeting on 23 April 2013.

Before you criticize Andrew McOwan for accepting the appointment, note he had not been involved in the audit and probably felt he *could* persuade Sir Frederick to accept his professional views.

Now read Part 5 of the Case study and then try to answer Task 4.3. Part of the answer to this Task is given in the text that follows but you will also find it helpful to refer to the suggested solution on page 150.

CASE STUDY 4.1

Rosedale Cosmetics plc, Part 5

Andrew McOwan became concerned during the final audit (in February 2014) for the year ended 31 December 2013 that inventories of certain products were slow-selling and should be valued at amounts considerably less than cost. The effect of the reduction in stock values he thought appropriate would have the effect of reducing profits for the year to 31 December 2013 by some £200 000. He discussed the matter with John Roberts, the chief accountant, who was clearly far from pleased with what Andrew had to say. Andrew was aware that the company was engaged in negotiations for the purchase of a majority holding in Arden Ltd, another company in the industry, and that consideration for the purchase consisted largely of shares of Rosedale Cosmetics plc. He also believed that, should the reported profits drop to any material extent below the sum of £1 500 000 shown in the draft accounts, the share price would drop and Rosedale's offer would become less attractive. Let us assume that the current price of Rosedale's shares was £2.00 per share but that, if the profits were £200 000 less than expected, the share price would drop to £1.80. If the terms of the offer for the Arden shares was two Rosedale shares for five Arden shares, then clearly at £2.00 per Rosedale share, a holder of five Arden shares would receive shares worth £2.00 × 2 = £4.00 while at £1.80 per Rosedale share, he would receive shares worth £1.80 × 2 = £3.60. To Andrew's surprise, the chief accountant told him (Andrew felt in a rather embarrassed way) on the following day that Sir Frederick Ashop, had found a purchaser for 50 per cent of the inventories in question. He produced several orders relating to the proposed purchase from a company called Lealholme Cosmetics Ltd. and copy invoices addressed to that company, dated 20 January 2014 for approximately 50 per cent of the inventories. Andrew felt that if the orders were genuine he would be satisfied that the relevant inventories at 31 December 2013 had been properly valued at cost. Andrew decided to find out more about Lealholme Cosmetics Ltd and after a number of enquiries discovered that the holders of more than 50 per cent of the shares were Sir Frederick Ashop and members of Sir Frederick's immediate family. He requested an urgent meeting with Sir Frederick to discuss the matter and during that meeting, which two other directors also attended, the results of his enquiries were confirmed. Furthermore, it became clear that the orders and invoices were bogus and that they had been raised merely to make Andrew assume that the inventories were saleable at above cost. Following the meeting Andrew realized that, despite his earlier hopes, the mutual respect that should exist between auditor and management was no longer present. He decided to offer his resignation as auditor and this was accepted.

TASK 4.3

Ask yourself the question: 'If I were responsible for drafting Companies Act sections to render the abuses described in the case less likely, what requirements would I introduce into the law?' In answering this question you should consider the following matters.

(a) Management had clearly tried to mislead the auditor. Does the law offer any remedies if the directors do this?

(b) Andrew obviously felt that if relations between management and himself had broken down, he had no choice but to resign. Does the law allow him to do so under these circumstances, or must he continue to act and use his report to explain his views to the shareholders?

(c) Andrew has resigned his position as auditor. Should CA 2006 or his professional body require him to take further action?

We are now moving to a discussion of CA 2006 s.516-518 (concerned with resignation of auditors), and s.501(1) (false statements to auditors). In your answer to Task 4.3 it is likely that you said the law should contain the following requirements:

1 That there should be penalties for those members of management who tell deliberate falsehoods to the auditor. Refer to s.501(2) and you will see that CA 2006 does indeed make it an offence (punishable by imprisonment and/or fine) to make knowingly or recklessly to the company's auditors 'a statement that … conveys … any information … which the auditors require, or are entitled to require … and is misleading, false or deceptive in a material particular'. (This requirement was first introduced into company law in CA 1976, largely as a result of the circumstances surrounding the failure of London and County Securities, a case, in which auditors were seriously misled.) Company law was further strengthened when the Companies (Audit, Investigation and Community Enterprise) Act 2004 added some further provisions. The 2004 Act:
   - entitled the auditor to require information and explanations from a wider group of people than in the original act, in particular from employees and not just company officers who tend to consist of managers and directors CA2006 s.499(2);
   - introduced a new offence, where a person fails to provide information or explanations required by auditors; see CA2006 s.501(3);
   - requires a statement in the directors' report to the effect that the directors are not aware of any relevant audit information of which the auditors are unaware and that each director has taken appropriate steps to ensure himself or herself are aware of any relevant audit information. Thus, directors will need to carefully consider if they have provided all the information necessary for a successful audit. CA2006 s.418

As indicated below the requirements of the 2004 Act were retained in the 2006 Act.

2 You may have suggested that the auditor should continue in office until the conclusion of term of office and inform the shareholders in the auditor's report of the facts. This is a very sensible suggestion but a reading of s.516 reveals that auditors are *not* required to continue in office if it is their wish to resign. However – and this is important – you will find that s.516(2) and s.519 state that an auditor's notice of resignation is not effective unless it contains either:
   In the case of unquoted companies; (s.519(1) and (2))
   - a statement that there are no circumstances connected with his or her ceasing to hold office which should be brought to the attention of the members or creditors of the company; or
   - a statement of any such circumstances.

   In the case of quoted companies; (s.519(3))
   - a statement of the circumstances connected with ceasing to hold office.

We can see from this requirement that the law does not allow auditors merely to 'walk away' from difficult audit situations such as those described in the case without taking action to make public the circumstances, if any, that caused them to resign. You should refer to the further description of the events in the case below to see the action that Andrew McOwan took on his resignation. Note further that the requirement to make a statement of circumstances was first introduced into law in CA 1976 after a notorious example of

Pinnock Finance (UK) Ltd.

The most likely reason for so few statements being lodged is because it avoids any possible legal complications or upsetting a former audit client and thus is effectively the easy option.

resignation without publicity. Interestingly, a study a few years ago by Moizer and Porter (2004) found that in a sample of 609 auditor changes (resignations and dismissals) only seven statements of circumstances were filed and of these only two disclosed meaningful information. The importance of auditor resignations is demonstrated in a study by Dunn *et al.* (1999) who found that when auditors resigned from a company there tended to be a negative reaction in the share price of the company. The Companies Act 2006 strengthened the preceding legislation by requiring auditors of quoted companies to lodge a statement with the company explaining the circumstances 'connected with his ceasing to hold office'. Furthermore, if such a statement is not lodged then, subject to certain exemptions, the auditor commits an offence punishable by a fine (CA2006 s.519(7)). Where a statement is lodged the company is required to circulate the statement, although the company can apply to the court not to circulate because the auditor is using the statement to 'secure needless publicity for defamatory matter'. Furthermore, where the auditor ceases to hold office in what the Act terms a 'major audit' the auditor is required to inform the appropriate audit authority that they have ceased to hold office and provide it with a copy of the statement of circumstances they have made and lodged with the company. If the statement says there are no circumstances that need to be brought to the attention of members or creditors, the auditor must supply a statement giving their reasons for ceasing to hold office. If the auditor ceases to hold office before the end of his or her audit term, no matter the size of the audit client, the audit authority must be notified. Where the audit is a major audit the appropriate audit authority is the Public Oversight Board (POB) and for all other cases it is the relevant supervisory body. Finally it should be noted that the audit authority is required to inform the accounting authorities and the Secretary of State of the auditor ceasing to hold office and may if it believes it appropriate provide a copy of any auditor's statement or statements. This provision is presumably to cover the situation, where the auditor is ceasing to hold office because of their concern about accounting irregularities occurring within the company that should be brought to the attention of the accounting authorities.

A major audit is essentially the audit of any listed company or a body 'in whose financial condition there is a major public interest.' CA2006 s.525(2). This is to prevent an auditor giving up an audit without bringing to the notice of members that they were dissatisfied with certain aspects relating to the audit of the client.

The accounting authority is the Financial Reporting Review Panel (FRRP).

You should now reread ss.516, 517, 518, 519 and 522 noting in addition the following points.

- Who is entitled to receive the auditor's notice of resignation and statement of circumstances (ss.517(1) 518(3) and 522(1) and (2)).
- The court may order that any statement of circumstances surrounding the auditor's resignation need not be sent out to individuals entitled to receive copies of the accounts if satisfied that the auditor is using the notice to secure needless publicity for defamatory material ((ss.518(9) and 520(4)).

A recent example invoking the above provision is *Jarvis plc* vs *PricewaterhouseCoopers (PwC)* (2000) (2000). In this case the defendants resigned as auditors of Jarvis plc and included a statement relating to their resignation explaining why they had resigned. Jarvis plc applied to the courts under CA85 s.394(3) to prevent the circulation of the statement to shareholders on the basis that the auditors were seeking needless publicity for defamatory matter. After some delay Jarvis, just prior to the court proceedings to consider the issue, withdrew their objection. However, in the intervening period they had appointed Ernst & Young as auditors and the day immediately after the

s.394 was the equivalent section in CA 85 prior to the superseding of that act by CA 2006.

discontinuance of the court proceedings sent a circular to the shareholders referring to the audit by Ernst & Young and giving an account of the dispute with PwC. It is obvious from the report on this case, which came before the High Court, that Jarvis had used the provisions of the Companies Act to delay the circulation of the statement by PwC, a delay enabling the company to appoint new auditors and for them to complete the audit thus somewhat defusing the potentially detrimental impact of the statement by PwC.

The report on this case is worth reading for the insight it gives into the conduct of a large plc and of its directors. It should also be noted in passing that the judge praised the behaviour of the auditors, PwC.

- The auditor also has the right to call for the directors to convene a general meeting of the company 'for the purpose of receiving and considering such explanation of the circumstances connected with his resignation as he may wish to place before the meeting' (s.518 (2)). The auditor may request that the company circulate its members with a written statement of the circumstances of their resignation:
  - (a) before the meeting convened at their request; or
  - (b) at which their term of office would have expired; or
  - (c) at which it is proposed to fill the vacancy (s. 518(3)). Again, the court may order that the statement need not be sent out if it decides it is defamatory (s. 518(9)).

PRIVATE COMPANIES

The Companies Act 1989 gave the government the opportunity to introduce certain provisions to reduce the burden of regulation on private companies. With some modification these provisions have been retained in the CA 2006. Of particular relevance to this chapter are the provisions contained in CA 2006 s.477, which provides that a small private company may elect not to have an audit. The criteria for being a small company is that it should in the current year not have a turnover exceeding £6.5 million and that the balance sheet total should not exceed £3.26 million. There is provision (CA 2006 s.476) whereby members holding not less than 10 per cent of the nominal share capital can, subject to giving due notice, require that an audit be carried out.

Based on data from Companies House in 2005 it is estimated that about 75 per cent of small companies take advantage of the provision.

To round off the story of Rosedale Cosmetics, read the final instalment of the Case study in Part 6.

CASE STUDY 4.1

Rosedale Cosmetics plc, Part 6

Andrew McOwan resigned as auditor on 18 February 2014 and on that day deposited a written notice to that effect at the company's registered office. Included in the notice of resignation was a brief statement of the circumstances of the resignation, in which he said that as he did not believe he was receiving from company officials 'full and adequate explanations regarding material matters', he was no longer able to act as auditor of the company.

> This would be a very serious step in view of the CA 2006 s.501 (1) and (2), penalties for making false statements to auditors. The auditor would have to be on very firm ground and management would normally wish to avoid the need for such a statement.

On the same date John Dewar was appointed auditor to fill the casual vacancy by the directors following separate meetings with Andrew McOwan and the directors. John Dewar was fully aware of the circumstances of Andrew McOwan's resignation and only took the appointment as auditor after the directors had forced the resignation of Sir Frederick Ashop. Before he commenced his audit, John Dewar had a meeting with the directors and they assured him that they had every intention of working in an open and informative manner with him.

The audit work carried out by John Dewar and his staff was completed on 3 April 2014 and his report bearing that date was issued a few days later. It was unmodified as the directors had accepted that the stocks of slow-moving inventories should be included in the accounts not at cost but at net realizable value. The AGM at which the accounts were presented to members took place on 29 April 2014.

Summary

In this chapter we examined first some of the reasons why auditing is regulated, the current and former regulatory structure and the role of the various boards reporting to the Financial Reporting Council. We examined the legal and practical relationships existing between auditors and the various groups within and outwith the company subject to audit. This discussion was supported by Figure 4.5. We then moved to a discussion of the Companies Act rules concerned with appointment, removal and resignation of auditors and considered also some of the relevant professional rules. This discussion was aided by a comprehensive case study and supporting diagram (Figure 4.6). Finally, you have been encouraged to read Companies Act sections and professional rules yourself. In fact you have started to use the Act and professional guidance in the way that a professional accountant uses them in day-to-day work. By now you should be feeling a great deal more confident in reading legal and professional rules. Now you can move to the self-assessment questions. When you are doing these you may find it necessary to refer to the Act and professional material referred to in the text.

Key points of the chapter

- In many countries such as the UK where the auditing profession has been long established there tends to be some form of self-regulation. The impact of company law and of international bodies such as the EU in the regulation of accounting and auditing and the introduction of international accounting and auditing standards has meant that powers of self-regulation have started to be taken away from the profession although some responsibilities still remain with the accounting bodies.
- Reasons for regulation in auditing include: (a) most professions are regulated in some form; (b) regulation provides some assurance to users that professional standards are met; (c) setting standards helps to reduce risk for users of the auditing service; (d) regulation helps to enhance confidence and replaces the element of trust.
- The power the state cedes to a professional body may be dependent on: (a) the state's attitude towards a particular form of political economy; (b) the state's opinion of the expertise, integrity and state of development of the professional body; (c) whether the state believes a private professional body is likely to be more efficient than a state body; (d) the state's wish to avoid public criticism when audit failure occurs.
- The role of the accounting bodies in regulating auditing was enhanced by CA 1989 that established in law two types of body – RSBs and RQBs. The main professional accounting bodies in the UK all have RSB and RQB status. CA 2006 retained these provisions. Summaries of certain provisions of the 2006 Act regarding the role of RSBs and RQBs are contained on the Cengage website
- Some commentators have suggested an independent Office for Auditing would improve existing systems of audit regulation for large company audits.

Overview of the UK regulatory system in force until 2003

- An ICAS paper in 1995 listed weaknesses/limitations in regulation: (a) demanding monitoring requirement; (b) inefficient interface between JMU and ICAS's disciplinary processes; (c) practitioners not clear if ICAS was supporting or confronting them; (d) gave the impression the process was not in the public interest.
- A new regulatory regime was introduced based on six key principles: (i) independence; (ii) public interest and integrity; (iii) transparency and openness; (iv)

proficiency and commitment; (v) relevance; (vi) review.

- A number of bodies were established to enforce the new regulatory system: (a) the Accountancy Foundation to which (i) a Review Board (ii) Ethics Standard Board and (iii) APB was to report; (b) an Investigation and Discipline Board overseen by the Ethics Standards Board to take over responsibility of the Joint Disciplinary Scheme and to investigate members of the accounting bodies where there was a public interest element.
- Cases not involving the public interest were to be the responsibility of the individual accountancy bodies. Under the new regulatory structure JMU ceased to exist.
- This regulatory structure was short-lived.

Overview of the UK regulatory system from 2003

- Following various scandals in the US, two major reviews were set up – *Review of the Regulatory Regime of the Accountancy Profession* (RRRAP), and *Co-ordinating Group on Audit and Accounting Issues* (CGAA).
- The main recommendations of RRRAP concerned the roles of (a) The Financial Reporting Council (FRC); (b) Auditing Practices Board (APB) (c) Professional Oversight Board (POB); (d) Investigation and Discipline Board. FRC was to become the overall 'independent regulator' of both accounting and auditing. POB would oversee the audit function, ensuring adequate monitoring by the RSBs and RQBs. A new Audit Inspection Unit reporting directly to POB, was concerned with review of audits of listed companies and public interest entities.
- Investigation and Discipline Board (now known as Accountancy and Actuarial Discipline Board) would hear significant public interest cases with authority to investigate on a proactive basis cases involving a public interest element.
- APB is a successor body to APC following criticism of the latter. APB issues auditing standards based on ISAs issued by the IAASB but with supplemental paragraphs to comply with specific aspects of the UK and Ireland environment.
- APB objectives indicate its wide role: (a) establish auditing standards, and provide guidance on their application; (b) provide guidance on new and emerging issues; (c) establish assurance standards; (d) contribute to public understanding of roles and responsibilities of auditors and assurance providers; (e) play a role in the development of statutes, regulations and accounting standards, affecting conduct of auditing both nationally and internationally; (f) establish ethical standards.
- *Auditing standards* contain prescriptions with which auditors are required to comply. They provide a minimum level of performance and provide a benchmark by which the quality of audit work can be measured. Practice notes are issued to assist application of auditing standards in particular circumstances and industries. Bulletins provide auditors with timely advice on new or emerging issues.
- The main reasons for the changes were: (a) existing system was too complex; (b) the Accountancy Foundation was not sufficiently authoritative; (c) one regulator should cover accounting and auditing; (d) regulatory regime should be independent of the accounting bodies.
- The Accounting Standards Board (ASB) and Financial Reporting Review Panel (FRRP) are concerned with accounting issues but the work of the former in issuing accounting standards has considerable implications for the work of auditors.
- Apart from the audit of listed companies and other large entities the monitoring of the work of the audit firm is performed by specialist units within the RSBs with which they are registered. Where the RSB has concerns about the quality of auditing carried out by an audit firm in the extreme, the Audit Registration Committee could impose conditions or even withdraw audit registration.
- The main concerns of CGAA were: (a) auditor independence; (b) corporate governance and the role of the audit committee; (c) transparency of audit firms; (d) financial reporting standards and enforcement; (e) audit monitoring; and (f) competition implications.
- Further regulation of auditing by the law and accounting profession includes provisions in CA 2006, the legal rules encompassing such matters as: (a) the individuals and firms who are permitted to act as auditors; (b) the period for which the auditor is appointed; (c) statutory relationships between auditors and shareholders; (d) statutory relationship between shareholders and directors.
- A major case study in six parts – Rosedale Cosmetics plc is used to provide a framework designed to aid understanding of the legal rules.
- Small and medium sized companies have modified audit and reporting criteria.

References

Beattie, V. and Fearnley, S. (1995) 'The importance of audit firm characteristics and the drivers of auditor change in UK listed companies', *Accounting and Business Research*, 25(100): 227–39.

Department of Trade and Industry, (2003a) 'Coordinating Group on Audit and Accounting Issues', *Final Report to the Secretary of State for Trade and Industry and the Chancellor of the Exchequer*, January.

Department of Trade and Industry (2003b) *Review of the Regulatory Regime of the Accountancy Profession, Report to the Secretary of State for Trade and Industry,* January.

Department of Trade and Industry (2003c) *Review of the role and effectiveness of non-executive directors*, The Higgs Report, January.

Dewing, I.P. and Russell, P.O. (2002) 'The new accountancy foundation: A credible form of regulation for UK listed company audits', *International Journal of Auditing*, 6: 231–48.

Dunn, J., Hillier, D. and Marshall, P. (1999) '*The market reaction to auditor resignations*', *Accounting and Business Research*, 29(2): 95–108.

Financial Reporting Council (2003) *Audit Committees Combined Code Guidance: A Report and Proposed Guidance by an FRC-appointed Group Chaired by Sir Robert Smith.* Available at http://www.ecgi.org/codes/documents/ac_report.pdf

Financial Reporting Council (2008) *The Combined Code on Corporate Governance*, June (available at http://www.frc.org.uk/documents/pagemanager/frc/Combined_Code_June_2008/Combined%20Code%20Web%20Optimized%20June%202008%282%29.pdf

Hampel Committee on Corporate Governance, Final Report (1998) London: Gee Publishing Ltd.

Humphrey, C., Moizer, P. and Turley, S. (1992) *The Audit Expectations Gap in the United Kingdom*, London: Institute of Chartered Accountants in England and Wales.

Institute of Chartered Accountants of Scotland (1995) *Audit Regulation in the Public Interest – A Framework for Public Accounting Practices*, June, Edinburgh.

Köhler, A.G., Marten, K.U.,Quick, R. and Ruhnke, K. (2008) 'Audit Regulation in Germany: Improvements Driven by Internationalization'. in Quick, R., Turley, S. and Willekens, M., *Auditing, Trust and Governance: Regulation in Europe*, Abingdon: Routledge.

Moizer, P. and Porter, B. (2004) *Auditor resignations and dismissals in the UK*, London: Institute of Chartered Accountants in England and Wales.

Power, M. (1997) *The Audit Society – Rituals of Verification*, Oxford: Oxford University Press.

Securities Exchange Commission (2003) *Study Pursuant to Section 108(d) of the Sarbanes-Oxley Act of 2002 on the Adoption by the United States Financial Reporting System of a Principles-Based Accounting System* (available at http://www.sec.gov/news/studies/principlesbasedstand.htm).

Further reading

This chapter concerns itself with certain aspects relating to the regulation of auditing and with the statutory and professional requirements affecting the appointment, removal and resignation of auditors. You should refer to the CA 2006 sections contained on the Cengage website. It would be useful to read the two reports issued by the DTI relating to the changes in the regulation of accounting and auditing. The article by Dewing and Russell is also a worthwhile read. A good deal of useful information is included on the financial reporting website located at: www.frc.org.uk.
A book we warmly recommend is Quick, R., Turley, S. and Willekens, M, (2008), *Auditing, Trust and Governance: Regulation in Europe*, Routledge, Abingdon. The chapters by Turley and Humphrey and Moizer are particularly relevant to this chapter. There are also a number of other chapters in the book which look at regulation in other countries which you might find useful. Finally you should read the professional accounting magazines, especially *Accountancy*, for articles on the regulation of accounting and auditing.

Suggested solutions to tasks

Task 4.1

It is not intended to review the sections of the law in detail as you can read these for yourself. The following particular points should be noted, some of which relate to the events in the Case study:

(a) All companies must keep accounting records. Make note of the characteristics that the accounting records must have as shown in s.386(1), (2), (3) and (4). Note that James Thomson used *judgement* in assessing whether proper accounting records had been kept (later in the case). Note that it is not possible to be dogmatic as to what is meant by 'proper accounting records'.

(b) Where and for how long records must be kept (s.388).

(c) Penalties for failure to keep proper records for the required length of time (s.389(4)).

(d) The directors have to prepare a profit and loss account and balance sheet (ss.394 and 396(1)).

(e) ss 395 and 396 are is a little difficult to understand at first reading. The basic logic of this section is as follows:

(i) Accounts must be drawn up in accordance with Companies Act 2006 or International Accounting Standards. The Companies Act formats for accounts are given in two statutory instruments issued in 2008 SI 2008/409 and 2008/410. The International Accounting Standards are those that have been adopted by the European Commission.

(ii) However, the overriding requirement is that the accounts should give a 'true and fair view'.

We discussed truth and fairness in Chapter 1, page 12.

(iii) In the case of a company preparing accounts under the Companies Act, if compliance with the Companies Act 2006 would not be sufficient to ensure a true and fair view is given, such additional information as is deemed necessary to give a true and fair view should be given in the accounts or the notes to the accounts (s.396(4)). This section (s.396(5)) also states that where compliance with any of the provisions of the Act would be inconsistent with giving a true and fair view, the directors must depart from the said provisions as far as is necessary. Any such departure should be fully explained in notes to the accounts. This provision is commonly called the 'true and fair override'. Details of extent and nature of disclosure required in notes to the accounts is given in FRS 18 – *Accounting Policies* (Paragraph 62). It is generally considered that invoking the true and fair override is mostly likely to occur when requirements of an SSAP or FRS are different from statutory requirements and will be an unusual event.

(f) It is permissible for the first accounting reference period to be fixed at less than one year after formation of the company, provided it is more than six months (but not more than 18 months) after incorporation (s.391(5). Sir Frederick may, therefore, set the accounting year-end at 31 December.

(g) The point to note particularly in s.394, s.414 and s.437 is that it is the *directors'* duty to sign (that is, take responsibility for) the accounts and to lay them before the company in general meeting.

(h) A further duty of the directors is to prepare a directors' report which contains, among other things, additional information about the company (for instance, a business review including a description of the risks and uncertainties facing the company) and about the directors (for instance, their names) (s.415, Schedule 5 SI 2008/409 and Schedule 7, SI 2008/410). There are certain exemptions for small companies and additional requirements for listed companies.

(i) Sir Frederick is quite correct (later in the Case study) that the date of the AGM he has decided upon (in April) is within the six months (nine months after the end of the relevant accounting period for private companies) required by CA 2006 (s.437(2) and s.442(2)).

(j) The directors are permitted by the law to appoint the first auditors of the company and to fix their remuneration, private companies s.485(3), public companies s.489(3) and fixing of their remuneration s.492(2)).

Task 4.2

(a) Note from s.512(1) that the registrar of companies must be informed when an auditor is removed. Also, although auditors can be removed before expiration of office, they are entitled to compensation for work performed.

(b) s.513((1) entitles the removed auditor to attend the meeting at which his or her term of office would have expired or the meeting at which it is proposed to fill the vacancy caused by his or her removal.

(c) Special notice, s.511, is required for the resolutions referred to in s.510(1), that is, removal of an auditor before the expiration of his or her term of office and appointing another person as auditor other than the retiring auditor.

Special notice is at least 21 days.

(d) s.511(2) and ss 514 and 515 (failure to re-appoint auditor) indicates that the auditor proposed to be removed; and the auditor proposed to replace such a person must be sent copies of the relevant resolutions. (ss. 514(3) and 515(3)).

(e) Note from s.511(3) to (6) that the removed auditor can make representations (not exceeding a reasonable length) to be sent to members or in certain circumstances to be read at the meeting but they must not be defamatory. Similar provisions apply to auditors not being reappointed. (ss. 514(4) to (7) and 515(4) to (7).

(f) When you come to read further in the Case study note that:

  (i) The Companies Acts requirements are supplemented by professional requirements. In many ways the latter are more stringent than the former.

  (ii) James was certain that he and his staff had acted correctly. If he were not so, it would have been difficult for him to have made representations.

  (iii) Note also that the decision to make representations was taken despite James's belief that he would be lucky to persuade the shareholders to allow him to stay in office.

  (iv) Interestingly, Andrew McOwan saw fit to tell James Thomson of the outcome of the medical complaint.

  You should remember two professional people are trying to resolve a difficult professional situation. Both would be required to treat the information that they had given to each other in strict professional confidence.

Task 4.3

The text answers all the questions posed. You should, however, note the following:

(a) John Dewar accepted the appointment when he knew that Sir Frederick had resigned. You must understand that the relationship between auditor and management is very important. Great care must be taken to ensure there is mutual respect on both sides.

(b) John Dewar's audit work confirmed the conclusions of Andrew McOwan. The remaining directors' decision to cooperate with John Dewar is an indication of awareness of their responsibilities following Sir Frederick's departure.

Self-assessment questions (solutions available to students)

4.1 Consider the following statements and explain why they might be true or false:

  (a) The directors may not appoint the first auditor, neither may they appoint an auditor to fill a vacancy caused by the death of the incumbent auditor.

  (b) The remuneration of auditors is not always fixed by the company in general meeting.

  (c) When auditors are dismissed during their term of office, remuneration may nevertheless be claimed.

  (d) Auditors who are dismissed have the right to make such representations to shareholders as they wish.

4.2 Janet Helmsley is auditor of Skiplam Ltd for the year ended 30 September 2010. She and her staff are examining the inventory figure in the accounts and have become concerned that the inventory count sheets are inaccurate because the test counts they had made at the year-end did not agree with the quantities on the inventory sheets prepared by the company. Also, as the inventory sheets had not been numbered, there was no way that they or the company officials could be certain that all sheets had been accounted for.

Required:

(a) State whether you think that this would be a reason for believing that the company had not kept proper accounting records (refer to CA 2006 s.386).

Apart from the above matter, Janet also concluded that the valuation of inventories could not be proved because the cost records were not complete. She duly informed the directors of Skiplam Ltd that she would have to inform the shareholders in her auditor's report that proper accounting records had not been kept and that, in consequence, she had not been able to determine if the accounts had been properly prepared. The directors were very annoyed about this and told her they would not be willing to put her name forward at the next annual general meeting for reappointment as auditor.

Required:

(b) Explain by reference to CA 2006 sections what Janet Helmsley's rights are as an auditor in the light of the directors' wish to dismiss her.

(c) State what Janet's rights are, should the directors refuse to pay her fee for her work in connection with the audit for the year ended 30 September 2010.

(d) If you were a member of a professional body of accountants and were asked by the directors if you would be prepared to act as auditor of Skiplam Ltd, state what action you would take and why.

4.3 You are auditor of a small building contractors with two partners, Thomas Murton and Ezra Byland. Neither of them have much accounting knowledge, although both are very good craftsmen. They have asked to see you because they believe they should consider forming a limited company, which they have heard would give them limited liability. They would, however, like to know what it would mean in practical terms, that is, could they continue to run the business in exactly the same way as they had been doing.

Required:

Advise them of their duties as directors and what the audit requirements would be. You should refer to the relevant CA 2006 sections as you are working through this question.

4.4 Consider the following statements and indicate if they are true or false:

(a) Auditors have the right of access at any time to any accounting records of the company they are auditing.

(b) The directors may not tell deliberate falsehoods to the auditor but they are allowed to withhold the facts if not directly asked for them.

(c) Notes to the accounts do not form part of the accounts subject to audit.

(d) The directors' report must be reported on by the auditor.

(e) The auditor's tenure of office runs from one accounting reference date to the next.

(f) Assuming an accounting year-end of a private company is 31 October 2009, the annual general meeting must be held by 31 July 2010.

Self-assessment questions (solutions available to tutors)

4.5 Your firm has recently been approached to act as auditor of an established company. The partner in charge of your firm wrote to the previous auditors, RAFT & Co., two months ago but no response has been received from them. The audit is due to commence in four weeks. In the circumstances outlined, what are the specific steps required to proceed with acceptance of the audit appointment. (ICAI, Final Admitting Examination, Autumn 2001, Paper 1, Auditing and the Reporting Accountant.)

4.6 It was indicated in the text that a study by Moizer and Porter (2004) found that in a sample of 609 auditor changes (resignations and dismissals) only seven statement of circumstances were filed and of these only two disclosed meaningful information.

Discuss whether you believe this indicates that the rights given under the Companies Act allowing auditors to make a statement when they resign is an irrelevant piece of legislation.

4.7 We noted in the chapter that often the directors of a company exerted a considerable influence in determining which firm of auditors should be appointed. Give reasons why this is not an ideal state of affairs and describe how this power might be reduced.

4.8 Describe the regulatory structure for auditing recently introduced in the UK and outline how it differs from the previous structure.

Solutions available to students and Solutions available to tutors

These can be found on the website in the student/lecturer section at: **www.cengage.co.uk/graymanson5**.

Topics for class discussion without solutions

4.9 Discuss the need for a different regulatory regime for small companies from that which applies to listed companies.

4.10 In this era of globalization it is no longer possible for there to be national regulation. For any regulation to be effective it must be done on a global basis. Discuss.

5

The risk-based approach to audit: audit judgement

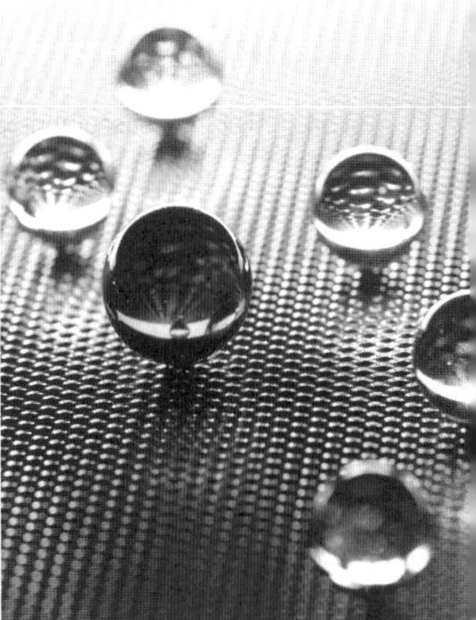

LEARNING OBJECTIVES

After studying this chapter you should be able to:

- **Define audit risk and suggest why risk-based approaches have become more important in recent years.**
- **Identify the components of audit risk and give practical explanatory examples.**
- **Identify risk in a number of practical scenarios and show how auditors approach risk.**
- **Define business risk, show how business risk approaches differ from audit risk approaches and whether they are relevant to the audit of companies of all sizes.**
- **Show how enhanced expectations of corporate governance has increased business risk.**
- **Explain why business risk approaches by auditors may widen the audit expectations gap.**
- **Explain why judgement is a vital aspect of accounting and auditing.**
- **Make the distinction between judgement and technical compliance with accounting standards.**
- **Explain the relationship between audit judgement and audit risk.**
- **Suggest what it is that enables successful audit judgements to be made.**

Learning objectives, 153
Why is a risk-based approach to audit an aid to the auditor?, 154
Broad approach to minimize audit risk, 156
A practical example, 167
Other practical matters, 169
Business risk approach to audit, 178
Business risk and inherent risk approaches: similarities and dissimilarities, 181
The business risk approach and smaller clients and smaller audit firms, 184
Analytical review as a risk analysis tool, 185
Judgement in accounting and auditing and its relationship to risk, 186
Management of the audit process, 189
The terms of reference provide the audit framework, 190
Planning the assignment, 194
Summary, 202
Key points of the chapter, 203
References, 204
Further reading, 204
Self assessment questions (solutions available to students), 207
Self assessment questions (solutions available to tutors), 210
Topics for class discussion without solutions, 211

WHY IS A RISK-BASED APPROACH TO AUDIT AN AID TO THE AUDITOR?

ISA 200 – *Overall objectives of the independent auditor in accordance with international standards on auditing*
ISA 315 – *Identifying and assessing the risks of material misstatement through understanding the entity and its environment*

Before we can answer this question, we have first to define risk and decide why it is important for the auditor. We approached this question in Chapter 2 when we identified risk as an important auditing concept. There are three important International Standards of Auditing in the area and you should have these to hand as you read this chapter: ISA 200, ISA 315 and ISA 330.

ISA 200 sets the scene by stating in paragraph 5 that:

> ISAs require the auditor to obtain reasonable assurance about whether the financial statements as a whole are free from material misstatement, whether due to fraud or error. It is obtained when the auditor has obtained sufficient appropriate evidence to reduce audit risk … to an acceptably low level.

ACTIVITY 5.1

There are two terms in the above extract from ISA 200 that need further explanation: 'reasonable assurance' and 'material misstatement'. We have not discussed these matters in detail yet, but try to explain what is meant by these terms.

When you see the word 'reasonable', it must make you think that the auditor is not expected to give absolute assurance, that a guarantee that the financial statements give a true and fair view is not required or possible This may imply a limitation in audit, but, knowing as you do, that there is considerable uncertainty in the application of accounting principles, you would not expect auditors to give absolute assurance.

Turning to 'material misstatement' you have no doubt decided that this must mean a misstatement that, if not corrected, is significant enough for the financial statements not to give a true and fair view. We discuss materiality briefly below and in detail in Chapter 11, but you are now in a position to consider audit risk.

The primary objectives of the audit risk ISAs are for auditors to identify and assess the risks of material misstatement at the financial statement level and at the assertion level for classes of transactions, account balances and disclosures. It is important that you understand what is meant by risk at 'financial statement level' and at 'assertion level':

- Risks of material misstatement at the financial statement level refer to risks of material misstatement that relate pervasively to the financial statements as a whole and potentially affect many assertions.
- Risks of material misstatement at the assertion level refer to risks of material misstatement of individual transactions, account balances and disclosures. The risks of material misstatement at the assertion level consist of two components: inherent risk and control risk.

We introduced you to the role of assertions in Chapter 2, where we suggested that assertions about headings in the financial statements enables the auditor to set objectives for their work as the basis for the seach for evidence. This is supported by paragraph A4 of ISA 330 which states:

The auditor's assessment of the identified risks at the assertion level provides a basis for considering the appropriate audit approach for designing and performing further audit procedures.

In Chapter 2 we suggested assertions that might be made about the inventory figure in the financial statements and also considered some audit steps to prove the assertion 'the inventories exist'. See page 39.

ACTIVITY 5.2

You are auditing Bowhouse Limited and are concerned that a major problem facing the entity in the current year is that its customer base has dropped by some 50 per cent as a result of competition from a new entrant to the market. What risks would face Bowhouse at the financial statement level and what risks might arise at the assertion level as a result?

The auditor might be concerned about the overall viability of Bowhouse, which at the extreme causes doubts about the going-concern status of the entity. This would represent a major risk at the financial statement level and the auditor would have to assess whether the company was likely to survive in the foreseeable future. In such circumstances, however, the auditor would also be concerned about heightened risk at the assertion level. For instance, has cut-off been manipulated to increase recorded sales and trade receivables; have inventories been over-stated to make the company's asset base look more healthy; has the company made insufficient provision for bad and doubtful debts; have trade payables been understated to make the company look more liquid than it really is. You can readily see, we think, that risk at the financial statement level might increase risk at the assertion level for a wide range of transactions and balances. If you go to Appendix II of ISA 315 you will find a number of conditions and events that may indicate risks of material misstatement at the financial statement level and therefore at the assertion level.

In this chapter we address the matters discussed in ISA 315, namely understanding the entity and its environment and assessing risks of material misstatement and discuss audit approaches to the auditor's procedures in response to assessed risks later in this book,

ISA 315 addresses both business risk as well as audit risk, so we shall start by comparing the definitions of each, before discussing them in greater detail.

Audit risk – The risk that the auditor expresses an inappropriate audit opinion when the financial statements are materially misstated. Audit risk is a function of the risk of material misstatement (or simply, the risk that the financial statements are materially misstated prior to audit) and the risk that the auditor will not detect such misstatement ('detection risk').

Business risk – A risk resulting from significant conditions, events, circumstances, actions or inactions that could adversely affect an entity's ability to achieve its objectives and execute its strategies, or from the setting of inappropriate objectives and strategies. ISA 315 is most concerned with those business risks that may cause material misstatement (paragraph 11 (d) of ISA 315), reflecting the fact that not all business risks will cause material misstatement and heighten audit risk. For instance, failure to attain a desired share of the market, while resulting in a turnover somewhat less than desired, does not necessarily heighten risk of misstatement. This is reiterated by paragraph A31 of ISA 315, which also notes that most business risks will eventually have financial consequences.

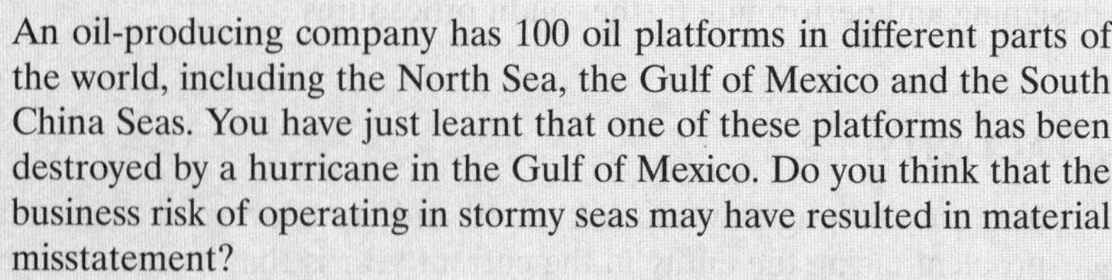

ACTIVITY 5.3

An oil-producing company has 100 oil platforms in different parts of the world, including the North Sea, the Gulf of Mexico and the South China Seas. You have just learnt that one of these platforms has been destroyed by a hurricane in the Gulf of Mexico. Do you think that the business risk of operating in stormy seas may have resulted in material misstatement?

Of course, if there was a disaster involving an oil rig on the scale of that faced by BP in the Gulf of Mexico in 2010, the matter would be very serious indeed, and might even place the survival of the company in doubt.

Of course, you would have to take all the circumstances into account. The destruction in 2010 of an oil well owned by BP in the Gulf of Mexico caused considerable pollution at a cost to the company, which would have to be reflected as a charge in its financial statements. At the time of writing the costs have not been determined.

See page 43.

Destruction of oil platforms in this manner might rightly be regarded as a business risk, but the auditor must decide if the destruction of one from 100 significantly affects the financial statements if it is not removed from non-current assets. Of course, we would expect management to recognize that there has been impairment of the oil platform, although it is probably not material in itself. The auditor would probably also conclude that the going-concern status of the company would not be affected by the destruction of this one platform.

This means that when we are considering business risk, auditors always have to ask the question: Does this risk, even if it becomes real, have such an effect on the financial statements that we will be faced by a significant audit risk?

You will remember from Chapter 2 that the risk of material misstatement has two entity components: inherent risk and control risk, and one a function of the effectiveness of an audit procedure and of its application by the auditor – detection risk.

ACTIVITY 5.4

Recall the definitions of the components of audit risk that we gave you earlier in this book.

The definitions are as follows:

- *Inherent risk*. Inherent risk is the susceptibility of an assertion to a misstatement that could be material, assuming that there are no related controls.
- *Control risk*. Control risk is the risk that a misstatement that could occur in an assertion and that could be material will not be prevented or detected and corrected on a timely basis by the entity's internal control.
- *Detection risk*. Detection risk is the risk that the auditor will not detect a misstatement that exists in an assertion that could be material. Detection risk is a function of the effectiveness of an audit procedure and of its application by the auditor.

BROAD APPROACH TO MINIMIZE AUDIT RISK

We shall now consider how auditors assess inherent and control risk and what impact their assessment of risk has on the way they perform their audits and the extent of the tests and procedures designed to reduce detection risk.

It is vital for the auditor to fully understand the entity and its external and internal environment, the latter including its control environment and related detailed internal controls. You will remember that we introduced you to some features of the external and internal environment in our discussion of layers of regulation and control in Chapter 2 (see Figure 2.3 on page 53). We also referred to the audited entity's control environment in Chapter 3 when we discussed the structures in place to ensure objectivity and independence in an audit firm (see Figure 3.3 on page 81).

Paragraphs 11 to 24 of ISA 315 set out the aspects of the entity and its environment, including its internal control, which the auditor must understand, and Appendix 2 gives a fairly exhaustive list of conditions and events that may indicate risks of material misstatement. We summarize below the approach that the auditor should adopt. We show the various risks facing the auditor in Figure 5.1 to which you should refer while you are reading this part of the chapter. As a practical point, audit firms often classify clients according to the degree of identified risk, of which listed entities would be placed in the highest risk category.

The lines in Figure 5.1 indicate related risks.

FIGURE 5.1 Components of audit and business risk

Business risk	Audit risk						
The risk that the entity will fail to achieve its objectives.'	The risk that auditors may give an inappropriate audit opinion on financial statements						
	Engagement risk	Inherent risk (IR)		Control risk (CR)	Detection risk (DR)		Independence in fact risk
		At the financial statement level	At the assertion level		Materiality risk and Sampling risk	Quality control risk	
Examples of objectives: Attaining a certain level of profitability; Maximising shareholder wealth'; Ensuring efficiency and effectiveness of operations; Meeting a desired market share; Giving customer satisfaction, however that might be measured; Maintaining a desired level of liquidity; Maintaining reputation; Meeting the challenge of changes affecting the entity as they occur; Adherence to accepted principles of corporate governance, including adherence to predetermined measures of environmental protection.	The risk that the competitive tendering process has forced auditors to accept an unreasonably low fee, thus restricting time available to perform an effective audit (audit quality) and/or increasing pressures on independence in fact. A further engagement risk is that auditors may accept clients whose inherent risk at the entity level is unduly high, because, for instance, of management with low integrity.	*Examples of relevant factors:* Management integrity; Management experience and competence; Unusual pressures on management; Nature of entity's business; Nature of industry; Complex computer systems	*Examples of relevant factors*: Susceptibility to misstatement or loss; complexity; judgment in determining; quality of accounting systems; completion of unusual or complex transactions, particularly at or near year-end; transactions not subjected to ordinary processing.	*Factors increasing CR:*(1) Inherent limitations: trade-off between cost and benefit; not directed to non-routine transactions; human error; collusion to circumvent controls; overriding internal controls; controls not keeping pace with change. (2) Complex computer systems. *Factors reducing CR*: good control environment; specific controls over account balances and classes of transactions	Materiality risk arises when the auditor fails to set performance materiality at an appropriate level. Sampling risk includes risk that sample is not representative of the population and that the results are misinterprete d - judgment risk.	The auditor fails to collect sufficient appropriate audit evidence and/or to evaluate it properly. Includes judgment risk by staff and reviewers	The risk that, even though the auditors' procedures have detected misstatements that cause the financial statements NOT to give a true and fair view, the auditor may fail to report the misstatement because of lack of independence in fact.

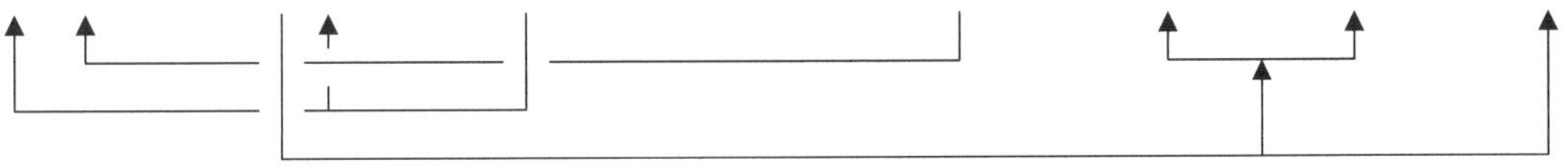

1. Investigating the legitimacy of the entity and the integrity and competence of its management before acceptance of the audit assignment, and before commencing each subsequent audit

In recent years it has become increasingly important for audit firms to decide if there is any risk in accepting a particular engagement. In particular, firms wish to ensure that the potential client entity is engaged in legitimate activities and not in fraudulent activity, such as money laundering. This means that they look for evidence from independent sources, such as trade associations and Companies House. Similarly, they would try to determine the background of key members of management to see if they are likely to behave in an ethical way. The risk of accepting a client that is not genuine and is engaged in fraudulent activities is known as engagement risk. Lack of integrity or competence in management would be inherent risk factors.

We look again at engagement risk when we discuss the business approach to auditing later in this chapter.

When the audit engagement is long-standing, auditors will know many of the risk factors that increase audit risk, leading to modification of audit procedures to reduce risk. In the case of a new engagement, the incoming auditor has little in-depth knowledge, although they are likely to have some as a result of initial contact with directors, or as a result of a tender process. This lack of knowledge, particularly of inherent risk factors, is likely to enhance risk, particularly if they have not become aware of management deficiencies and unusual pressures on management.

This kind of initial investigation is particularly important when the client has not been audited by the firm before. However, considering the legitimacy of the entity and its management should be done on a continual basis and at least once every year. For instance, there may have been changes in management during the period, or there might be unusual pressures on directors, such as tight reporting deadlines, market expectations or other circumstances that might predispose them to misstate the financial statements, particularly if the entity is close to breaching borrowing covenants.

2. Considering the independence of the audit firm and its staff in relation to the entity before acceptance of the audit assignment, and before commencing each subsequent audit

We considered independence in depth in Chapter 3, and you know that the engagement partner must consider his or her own independence and that of other members of the engagement team, often together with the ethics partner.

This is done prior to acceptance of an audit assignment, during the later stages of the audit process, and also on a continual basis from year to year. In Figure 5,1 we have referred to 'independence in fact risk' as one important risk that might inhibit achievement of audit objectives. This risk is the risk that auditors (either the individual engagement partner or the audit firm) may fail to report material misstatements in the financial statements because they lack independence in fact.

This is different from the appearance of independence, which is an important factor when deciding whether reliance might be placed on the auditors' report.

There are also risks deriving from the process by which firms tender bids to become the entity's auditors. Tendering for audit services has become important in recent years and has until recently been accompanied by considerable lowering of audit fees. It is important to note in this respect that many directors see little value (for themselves) in the audit process and report, and they have sought lower fees in consequence. Reduction in audit fees in some cases has resulted in poor remuneration for audit work and we suggest might result in policies to reduce the amount of audit work undertaken. It is known, for instance, that there has been a considerable reduction in the amount of audit work on systems in the recent past with the potential for not detecting control risk. Some firms justify this reduction in systems work by reliance on higher level controls, often in conjunction with the business risk approach that we discuss below. There has also been considerable reduction in sample sizes and in substantive tests of detail, which some argue might increase audit risk. The other risk factor resulting from lower audit fees is that auditors become more reliant on non-assurance services with a consequent threat to independence, leading to the suspicion that auditors might be unwilling to report misstatements in financial statements because this might put the non-assurance income at risk. It is well to consider in this respect that there is some evidence from the POB's Audit Inspection Unit reports that the success of individual partners and the remuneration of other audit staff may depend to some extent on their success in obtaining non-assurance work. Certainly this is one of the pressures on individual partners and staff that firms should think about when they are considering measures to maintain independence.

We discussed the POB in Chapter 4. See page 119.

We discuss systems work in Chapters 7 and 8, sampling in Chapter 11 and substantive procedures in Chapter 10. Note at this stage that a substantive procedure is defined in paragraph four of ISA 330 as 'An audit procedure designed to detect material misstatements at the assertion level'. Substantive procedures comprise:

(a) tests of details (of classes of transactions, account balances and disclosures); and

(b) substantive analytical procedures.

We refer you also to the Important Note on page 342 of Chapter 9.

Two academic papers that have addressed these issues are 'Auditor independence and audit risk in the UK: A Reconceptualization' by Fearnley *et al.* (2005), and 'Auditor changes and tendering: UK interview evidence' by Beattie and Fearnley (1998).

3. Understanding the nature of the entity and the environment in which it operates before commencing any detailed audit work

Initially, the audit firm will know little about a new client, apart from the investigations to minimize engagement risk. The auditors start collecting the necessary information to set the scene for the audit at a series of preliminary meetings with those charged with governance of the audited entity and with leading members of support functions. These preliminary meetings are of the utmost importance as they enable the auditor to get a first impression of the qualities of members of the management team and of others involved in assuring good governance of the entity. If you refer to paragraph six of ISA 315, you will see that risk assessment procedures include (a) inquiries of management within the entity who in the auditor's judgement may have information that is likely to assist in identifying risks of material misstatement due to fraud or error; as well as (b) analytical procedures and (c) observation and inspection. What this means is that risk assessments will be made at all stages of the audit process.

In the case of an existing client, much of the information needed to understand the entity and its environment will be contained in permanent files prepared in previous years. However, discussions with personnel of the entity must be held each year in order to update the information held about the entity.

IMPORTANT NOTE

Some factors in the environment will be common to all clients. For instance, the economic crisis in most parts of the world in 2008 and following years has had a considerable impact on many organizations, this impact including difficulty in obtaining bank finance, and of maintaining revenue streams in time of recession. Audit firms should make sure that all audit staff are aware of the heightened inherent risk during the crisis and consider audit approaches to reduce the impact of the risk. In particular, auditors should discuss with management of the entity, and others charged with governance, how they are addressing the specific problems arising from the crisis.

Typically, the auditors will meet with responsible people in the entity, including:

- Members of the executive board, including the finance director.
- Members of the audit committee (an important element of those charged with governance), who have an interest in the effectiveness of controls to reduce the impact of business risk and inherent risk.
- Head of the internal audit function which plays an important role in identifying risk and represents in itself an important part of the control environment. A good internal audit function can also provide support to members of the audit committee.

The bulk of audit inquiries will take place later in the audit process, as indeed will observation and inspection, but these initial meetings give the auditor the chance to discover the nature of the organization, how it manages and controls itself in broad terms, and about the quality of management and other key personnel. Regarding analytical procedures paragraph A7 of ISA 315 states:

> Analytical procedures performed as risk assessment procedures may identify aspects of the entity of which the auditor was unaware and may assist in assessing the risks of material misstatement in order to provide a basis for designing and implementing responses to the assessed risks. Analytical procedures performed as risk assessment procedures may include both financial and non-financial information, for example, the

relationship between sales and square footage of selling space or volume of goods sold.

These analytical procedures will usually form the basis for further discussions with management.

Information at the early stage of the audit process should be gathered in respect of the following matters. Initially this information will be gathered in broad terms and later subjected to detailed examination.

(a) The nature of the entity and its environment

- What industrial or commercial sector does the entity occupy and what particular business and other risks are common in its sector?
  For instance, some industries, such as the water industry and the pharmaceutical sector, are highly regulated and may need special controls to maintain quality of its product. Pharmaceutical entities might face greater regulation of product testing, thereby increasing costs or even making some products less viable in the marketplace. In others the valuation of inventories may require a high level of estimation, for instance where long-term construction contracts are involved. In the public sector, management may be required to prove that they have achieved value for money.
- Is the industry or commercial sector subject to technological change?
  The more volatile the sector, the greater the business risk will tend to be, and the greater the inherent risk for the auditor. For instance, new production technologies are likely to change cost patterns, as production times decrease and the balance between labour cost, material cost and overheads change and product output and quality change. New technology may affect sales systems as well. We shall see later in this book that organizations are having to adapt sales and information systems to deal with selling through the Internet. We discuss information systems in detail in Chapters 7 and 8, but note here that the growth of e-commerce has significantly changed the ways in which internal controls operate. In particular, it has made security of customer details held on file of much greater significance.
- Is the entity a public interest entity?
  If it is a public interest entity, including a listed entity with a wide ownership, how does it manage its affairs in the public interest? Corporate governance issues will be important for both the entity's management and the auditor.

We discuss corporate governance in Chapter 18.

- Is the company growing or declining?
  Rapid growth might well result in overtrading and poor liquidity, which at the extreme might put the going-concern assumption at risk. In Chapter 17 we consider auditors' approach to going concern in greater detail. Where the entity is operating in a declining market, its non-current assets may be under-used or idle and management and auditor might have to consider whether impairment of assets has occurred.
- What are its objectives, how does it try to achieve them and what are the business risks that may inhibit the achievement of its objectives?

Different entities in a sector may adopt different strategies to achieve their objectives; for instance one might trade in high quality high priced products, whereas another might go for the cheaper end of the market. Changes of fashion or an economic downturn might affect one entity more than another.

- Is the entity financed predominantly by equity or is outside financing high in relation to equity?
  If an entity is highly geared it may face the risk of illiquidity if it has difficulty in acquiring additional finance to meet short-term cash flow short falls. If short-term financing is significant, (say) by means of bank overdrafts, this may also put its going-concern status at risk.
- What are the nature of its transactions?
  For instance, some companies might sell principally on credit terms, others might sell on an immediate payment basis. This will affect the kind of controls the entity would have to put in place. Cash transactions, for instance, may be subject to misappropriation. To make a sale on credit needs a control to make it likely that the trade receivable will be paid.
- Does the entity invest in other entities, either as subsidiaries, associated companies or investments and how does it seek to manage its relationships with these entities?
  On the whole business and inherent risk will be higher for these other companies, as they are more distant from the parent entity. This may be particularly so where the entity has foreign subsidiaries, as foreign conditions may be very different from those in the home country. Communication lines may not be as good and there will be added risks from foreign exchange exposure, which enhance business risk and related financial statement risk.
- How experienced is the management of the entity and how long have key personnel been with the entity?
  Less experienced or new personnel in key positions may increase business risk and may have a direct bearing on inherent risk and control risk. New personnel, for instance, may need some time before they have an understanding of the internal controls in force. There may also be problems where the entity has been restructured, particularly where downsizing has taken place with the intention of reducing costs. The problem with this kind of restructuring is that the entity often loses in the process its older and more experienced staff, often with important supervisory roles. At the same time, reducing the staff base makes segregation of duties more difficult. We shall see later in this book that supervision and segregation of duties are important elements of internal control.

Having completed the initial investigations described in heading (1) above, auditors should be aware of the major business risks faced by the entity and the inherent risks faced by themselves. Later in the course of the audit, the auditors may come across other risk factors not detected at the initial stage. If this is the case they would have to reconsider the overall audit risk and possibly amend their approach and the extent of their procedures.

(b) The entity's internal control

The next basic matter is for the auditor to determine how the management of the entity seek to reduce the impact of business risk and inherent risk. From the auditor's point of view it is important to find out how the entity organizes its internal environment, including its control environment and related detailed controls to ensure that risks of misstatement at the assertion level are avoided or minimized.

We discuss internal control in greater depth in Chapters 7 and 8, but at this stage the major factors considered by the auditor are those discussed in paragraphs 12 to 24 of ISA 315:

(i) The entity's control environment

When we discussed the control environment of the audit firm in relation to objectivity and independence we emphasized the importance of establishing 'tone at the top'. The same applies to audited entities, the argument being that, if a culture of honesty and ethical behaviour is established by those charged with governance, there will be a solid foundation for other components of internal control. These other components include the audit committee, the internal audit function and the allocation of responsibilities for the supervision of the entity's activities. The effectiveness of these individual components would be undermined if an ethical tone at the top is not established in the first place.

(ii) The entity's risk assessment process

Controls are put in place by management to address the business risks and inherent risks facing the entity. This means that a risk assessment process must be established to ensure that risks are identified, and auditors have an interest in determining how effective the process is in minimizing the risk of significant misstatement of the financial statements. The entity's risk assessment process must include estimating the significance of the risks, assessing the likelihood of their occurrence, and deciding what action should be taken to address the risks.

If management decides that a significant risk is likely to occur, appropriate action would be to introduce a control to reduce the impact of the risk.

ACTIVITY 5.5

Dreel plc has a large number of non-current assets in course of construction. On completion, they are transferred from 'assets in course of construction' to the relevant non-current assets account. What risk would the entity's management have to assess in this case and what action should they take?

The risk in this case is that the entity would fail to identify which assets had been completed in the period (with subsequent understatement of depreciation and overstatement of the asset). Suitable controls might include reporting by informed people of the stage of completion of projects particularly at the year-end, backed up by expert reports.

If the entity's risk assessment process had not identified this particular risk, the auditors would be concerned that this important process is deficient and would discuss the matter with management to discover why the risk had not been identified. The auditors might conclude that there has been an unfortunate human error in this one case so that the breakdown of the control might not be so serious. If, however, the auditors conclude that the risk assessment process is fundamentally flawed, this would mean there was a significant deficiency in internal control, and the auditors would have to consider extending their own risk assessment procedures and detailed testing of transactions and balances.

(iii) The entity's information system
The auditor is most interested in that part of the entity's information system relevant to financial reporting. The auditors would obtain an understanding of how transactions significant to the financial statements are processed by the IT and manual systems and how these systems capture the balances for inclusion in the financial statements. The auditor would wish to know how the information systems ensure that transactions and balances reflected in the financial statements are genuine, accurate and complete. An important element of the information system in this respect is how the system captures the information needed for the preparation of the financial statements, including significant estimates and disclosures. At the year-end, management will prepare journal entries to ensure that such matters as cut-off and accruals are properly reflected in the financial statements. Auditors would wish to ensure that the system provides management with all the necessary information on a timely basis.

We discuss the assertions concerning transactions, balances and disclosure in greater detail in Chapter 12 – see page 442 but you may refer to paragraph A111 of ISA 315 for a list of specific assertions.

(iv) The audit committee and the internal audit function
We mentioned the internal audit function in (a) above as an important element in the control environment. We discuss internal audit in detail in Chapter 15, but note here that the function is established by management to act on their behalf in a number of different areas, including the review of the entity's control systems. The external auditors are interested in the effectiveness of internal audit. The function can, if properly set up, provide vital support to members of the audit committee, who, we have noted before, represent an important element of those charged with governance.

We discuss the nature and role of audit committees in Chapter 18.

(v) Control activities relevant to the audit
The matters discussed in (i) to (iv) above are broad controls, but the auditors will also be interested in the controls at assertion level relating to specific figures in the financial statements. Again, we discuss these matters at greater length later (in Chapters 7 to 10 in particular), but note here that modern IT systems are so complex, that often the auditor has to rely on the controls built into the systems. The auditors would expect to see such matters as physical controls over assets, segregation of duties to ensure that no one person can see a transaction through from

beginning to end, and authorization of transactions by responsible management. The auditors would also expect management to continually monitor the effectiveness of controls that they have established.

4. Planning by the auditor to minimize risk of failing to detect material misstatement at the financial statement and assertion level

Once the auditors have identified the significant inherent risks and considered in broad terms the efficacy of the controls established by management to minimize the impact of risk, they have to plan their own procedures to minimize detection risk. Audit planning is the subject of ISA 300 – *Planning an audit of financial statements.* Paragraph 2 of ISA 300 explains that:

> Planning an audit involves establishing the overall audit strategy for the engagement and developing an audit plan. Adequate planning benefits the audit of financial statements in several ways, including the following:
>
> - Helping the auditor to devote appropriate attention to important areas of the audit.
> - Helping the auditor identify and resolve potential problems on a timely basis.
> - Helping the auditor properly organize and manage the audit engagement so that it is performed in an effective and efficient manner.
> - Assisting in the selection of engagement team members with appropriate levels of capabilities and competence to respond to anticipated risks, and the proper assignment of work to them.
> - Facilitating the direction and supervision of engagement team members and the review of their work.
> - Assisting, where applicable, in coordination of work done by auditors of components and experts.

The auditor would hope to achieve a good overall knowledge of the company at an early stage to avoid later significant changes to audit strategy. We come back to planning at various stages throughout the book, including the need for detailed planning of the work and supervision of audit staff and documentation of the overall audit strategy in the audit plan. At this stage you should be aware that planning work usually takes up a large proportion of audit time as will become clear if you review the appendix to ISA 300 which gives a list of considerations in establishing the overall audit strategy. We shall see later in this chapter that the large firms have adopted a business risk approach to audit,

It is clear from our above discussions that the auditors wish to ensure that they have detected material misstatements, whether caused by fraud or error. We have already asked you to consider the meaning of 'material misstatement' in Activity 5.1 above, but materiality is so important to the planning process that we must mention the concept here. Here is a definition of materiality contained in ISA 320:

ISA 320 – *Materiality in planning and performing an audit.*

> Misstatements, including omissions, are considered to be material if they, individually or in the aggregate, could reasonably be expected to influence the economic decisions of users taken on the basis of the financial statements.

You might think that this is somewhat vague. Nevertheless at the planning stage the auditors have to decide what level of misstatement would be regarded as material. For instance, if the profit in the draft financial statements was £1 000 000, would they regard an overstatement of inventories of £50 000 as material or not? Would a figure of £100 000 be the benchmark? There is a lot more to materiality than this simple example, but auditors have to plan to find the misstatements in excess of the materiality level, in excess in fact of what is known as 'tolerable error'. In practice auditors set what is known as 'performance materiality' at a level lower than materiality for the financial statements as a whole. This is to reduce to a low level the probability that the total of misstatements exceed materiality. The auditors' assessment of risk of misstatement is closely bound to that of materiality, as it is 'material misstatements' that they wish to detect. Assessment of inherent and control risk and materiality at the planning stage is important as they influence the conduct of the audit and the procedures that auditors perform.

5. Design of the audit approach on the basis of what is now known about the audit client and the setting of performance materiality; forming an engagement team with the required experience and skills

The engagement team carry out the detailed audit procedures, including recording and testing the internal control systems, and substantive procedures to ensure within reason that transactions, balances and disclosures are genuine, accurate and complete. The team members have to have the experience and skills to handle the complexity of the client's systems and accounting information on which the financial statements are based. For instance, if the client is engaged in e-commerce the team would need to include a person with the special knowledge of the problems associated with the control and recording of the activity.

The engagement team needs direction and supervision and this is the responsibility of the engagement partner with the support of the manager in charge of the assignment. The overall audit approach will be included in the audit plan, including the decision as to whether reliance is to be placed on the entity's internal controls or whether there should be extended testing of transactions and balances (known as the substantive tests of detail approach).

6. Design of audit programmes to obtain the evidence necessary to form conclusions at the assertion level, leading to an opinion on the truth and fairness of the financial statements taken as a whole

In Chapter 10 we explain how auditors set objectives in particular audit areas and show how they prepare detailed audit programmes to search for evidence to meet these objectives. In Chapter 6 we discuss audit evidence in detail, basically to set the scene for detailed audit work described in later chapters. Audit programmes have to be properly designed if detection risk is to be minimized.

IMPORTANT NOTE FOR STUDENTS IN THE EXAMINATION ROOM

Clearly, the first stage must be to identify significant business risks. The second stage will be to decide whether the identified business risks will give rise to potential misstatements of the financial statements, that is, to audit risk. Examiners of auditing papers frequently provide scenarios affecting audit clients and ask candidates to identify audit risks. It is not sufficient, when confronted with a question like this, merely to state the business risks – the further step, to identify the related audit risk, is essential. For instance, damage to oil platforms in the Gulf of Mexico because of hurricanes may indeed be a business risk leading to loss of assets and a reduction in income, but, unless you go that step further and discuss the potential misstatements in the financial statements, you will fail to gain any marks. Note in particular that a reduction in income, while not desired, is not itself an audit risk, unless it is indicative of omission of sales transactions.

If you refer to the examination questions on the Cengage website (**www.cengage.co.uk/graymanson5**) you will find a question that asks you to identify audit risk – Question 1.1 (Island Ltd), and another that asks you to identify principal business risks – Question 2.1 (Medix Ltd. Taurus Traders Limited).

A PRACTICAL EXAMPLE

To help you to understand the three components of audit risk and the relationships between them, we shall introduce you first to a company in the property industry and suggest risks that may be associated with its environment, transactions and balances. We will follow this case with a company in the fashion industry and ask you to work a number of activities. Both cases will lead you through an analysis of risk and procedures to identify and alleviate audit risk.

CASE STUDY 5.1

Edengrove Limited

You are auditing Edengrove Limited, a company in the property commercial sector (buying, selling and managing property, the latter including letting to tenants and collecting rents, on behalf of others).

ACTIVITY 5.6

This appears to be a fairly simple scenario, but there are a number of risks associated with this kind of company and we ask you to identify the business risks, which will include industry and economic risk factors.

The major business risk in the industry is the volatility of the property market, often occasioned by unexpected changes in interest rates. In the United Kingdom, there have been at least three periods in the last 50 years in which the property market has virtually collapsed. If the property company is highly geared, having borrowed heavily to finance its purchases of property, it could be at risk if property prices drop. Even if not highly geared, the company may be left with properties on its hands, which it cannot sell without making a loss. This is clearly of significance for the auditor as companies may either be at risk of collapse (making its going-concern status doubtful) or they may have properties with a realizable value below cost. This kind of risk is inherent risk arising from the nature of the environment in which the company operates.

Apart from the inherent risk arising from the environment in which the entity operates, there is another kind of inherent risk attaching to the nature of the transactions and balances. Thus, in its lettings activity, Edengrove Limited faces the inherent risk that tenants will fail to pay the rent on the due dates or fail to pay at all, or the company may not be able to fully let properties during an economic downturn.

If you refer to the definition of inherent risk again, you will note that it exists '*assuming that there are no related controls*', implying that one reason for having controls is to reduce the impact of inherent risk. For instance, a useful control to reduce risk in the lettings activity would be the vetting of potential tenants for creditworthiness before acceptance. This is a specific control. Later, we shall see that a good control environment, including good corporate information systems and higher level controls, will provide a framework within which specific controls are embedded.

ACTIVITY 5.7

Suggest controls that Edengrove Limited might introduce to increase the likelihood that the tenants in the managed properties will pay and on time.

Controls might include the following:

(a) Allocation of responsibility to identified responsible persons for such matters as checking the credentials of potential tenants and for chasing up payment when due.

(b) Vetting by responsible persons before letting to tenants, such as requiring prospective tenants to give bankers references and character references from reliable individuals.

(c) An accounting system recording amounts due and the issue of timely reminders if tenants fall behind with their rent.

(d) Requiring tenants to pay by bank standing order.

(e) Giving discounts for timely payments.

The controls needed to reduce the impact of inherent risk in the property buying and selling part of the company's business is more problematic. The auditor will be concerned that the company might be at risk if borrowing was high and property was being held on a speculative basis. One control the company might introduce would be careful review of economic indicators by knowledgeable, trustworthy and experienced people to detect whether the economy might be overheating and that interest rates might in consequence rise. This might allow timely withdrawal from the more speculative property market. Careful review of borrowing requirements, to keep them to a minimum, and the use of forecasts, including cash forecasts, are examples of further controls.

There is, of course, a risk that controls may not operate properly and fail to reduce the impact of inherent risk. Thus, if the manager responsible for vetting potential tenants goes on sick leave for a period of three months, there might be a breakdown in controls during this period, resulting in tenants being accepted who are poor credit risks. If controls do not function in the way intended, or do not exist, or are poorly designed in the first place, this will enhance control risk.

OTHER PRACTICAL MATTERS

You will appreciate that financial statements are prepared by the very people who will be judged by the view presented by them. We have already seen that integrity of management is a matter considered by the auditor, not only at the point of accepting the assignment but on a continuous basis over the years. One of the major problems is the nature of the accounting process itself which requires estimates to be made in respect of many of the figures appearing in the financial statements. Paragraph A3 of ISA 200 puts it succinctly:

> The preparation of the financial statements requires management to exercise judgement in making accounting estimates that are reasonable in the circumstances, as well as to select and apply appropriate accounting policies.

ACTIVITY 5.8

Give examples of significant estimates in the preparation of financial statements and suggest why the need for management to exercise judgement in respect of them would increase audit risk.

You will already be aware that management estimates include estimates of such matters as the saleability of inventories, the collectability of trade receivables and the useful life of non-current assets. However, some industries or particular circumstances may be particularly prone to uncertainty, making the assessment of the reasonableness of accounting estimates particularly difficult. Here are some examples:

ISA 540 – *Auditing accounting estimates, including fair value accounting estimates, and related disclosures* is the principal ISA dealing with accounting estimates, although they are also referred to in many other ISAs.

- The estimation of the likely profitability of long-term construction contracts.
- The estimation of reserves in the mineral oil industry.
- The estimation of future cash flows where there is some doubt about the going-concern status of the entity.

- The estimation of the effect of technological change on the value of current inventories or the impairment of non-current assets.
- The estimation of the amount of significant accrued liabilities such as pension obligations.
- Judgement about fair values.
- Judgement about the outcome of litigation in respect of claims against the entity.
- Estimates of the realizable value of property or equipment held for disposal.

Clearly, uncertainty surrounding estimates will increase the possibility of misstatements at the assertion level, or even the financial statement level. This makes the experience and integrity of management of great significance. If inherent risk arising from the nature of the industry in which the entity operates is high, management experienced in handling the industry risks may counterbalance the risk. Risk would also be reduced if the directors of the company possess high integrity and their strong ethics are communicated to the rest of management. Equally, inexperienced management or directors with low integrity would increase risk. Auditors will pay much attention to factors such as these. Clearly, if management feel that it has to meet market expectations or the requirements of borrowing covenants, they may be under pressure to make the company look more profitable than it really is (by, for instance, taking up more profit on long-term contracts than is justified, or by capitalizing expenditure than should really be charged against profit). Management could make the company look more liquid by not taking up all liabilities, such as trade creditors, outstanding at the end of the financial year.

Auditors would look to the controls designed to aid management in making the necessary judgements about the estimates they have to make, and for ensuring that the information needed to make the judgements are complete and accurate. Typical controls would include:

- An information system to keep them informed of technological developments.
- Budgetary systems to warn of funding requirements.
- A reliable system for allocating costs to inventories and long-term construction contracts.
- The existence of skilled personnel to assess such matters as actuarial computations of pension obligations.

In some cases management will have to turn to outside experts, such as actuaries, lawyers (in respect of litigation) and surveyors (in respect of long-term construction projects).

Clearly, if auditors are to reduce audit risk, they would need not only to ensure that the controls are effective, but also that the estimates are soundly based and are not just ‘plucked out of the air’. In other words, the auditors would perform both systems work and substantive procedures in respect of the estimates made by management. They might choose to recalculate the estimates themselves. They certainly would wish to ensure that any outside experts employed by the company were properly skilled and had been properly instructed by management.

Now have another look at the definition of control risk – 'the risk that a misstatement that could occur in an assertion and that could be material will not be prevented or detected and corrected on a timely basis by the entity's internal control'.

In practice the auditors make an initial assessment of control risk. If the assessment is positive, that is, that the controls are seen to be effective, they will design and perform tests of controls as explained in ISA 330:

> The auditor shall design and perform tests of controls to obtain sufficient appropriate audit evidence as to the operating effectiveness of relevant controls if:
>
> (a) The auditor's assessment of risks of material misstatement at the assertion level includes an expectation that the controls are operating effectively (that is, the auditor intends to rely on the operating effectiveness of controls in determining the nature, timing and extent of substantive procedures); or
>
> (b) Substantive procedures alone cannot provide sufficient appropriate audit evidence at the assertion level.

Paragraph 8.

Basically, in planning the audit, auditors obtain and document an understanding of the accounting system and control environment sufficient to determine their audit approach. The auditor records the system in use and tests it to ensure the record is valid and then makes a final assessment of control risk. If control risk is deemed to be low, the auditors will be able to reduce the substantive procedures they perform. Examples of substantive procedures include analytical reviews, detailed tests of transactions and balances and external confirmations from credit customers, actuaries, lawyers and others. Paragraph 18 of ISA 330 states in this connection:

> Irrespective of the assessed risks of material misstatement, the auditor shall design and perform substantive procedures for each material class of transactions, account balance, and disclosure.

You should note this requirement reflects the facts that (a) the auditor's assessment of risk is judgemental and so may not identify all risks of material misstatement; and (b) there are inherent limitations to internal control, including management override. Management override means that certain members of management might be able to 'switch off' a control. For instance, they might be able to insert additional inventory count sheets, thereby increasing stated amount of inventories, even though a control is supposed to be in force to ensure that all count sheets returned from count teams reflect those issued to them.

The substantive procedures carried out by the auditors are designed to reduce detection risk, which you will remember means: 'the risk that the auditor will not detect a misstatement that exists in an assertion that could be material. Detection risk is a function of the effectiveness of an audit procedure and of its application by the auditor'. If they conclude that controls are weak, they will increase the level of substantive procedures. In the management override case suggested above, the auditor would observe the inventory count and make sure that inventory count sheets were pre-numbered and that they had recorded the numbers of those issued to count teams. This would be followed up by reconciling the record of those recorded with those purporting to be the record of the actual counts. Any discrepancies would be investigated. Observing the inventory count and testing that the counts have been properly performed is another example of a substantive procedure.

This brief discussion has revealed that there are clear relationships between the three components of audit risk. This is shown in the following formula:

Audit Risk (AR) = Inherent Risk (IR) × Control Risk (CR) × Detection Risk (DR)

We emphasize that DR is closely related to the confidence that auditors wish to obtain from substantive procedures. If the auditor needs a low detection risk, more transactions and balances will require to be tested substantively than where detection risk can be allowed to be high (because control risk is low, for instance). The more transactions and balances that are tested in terms of sample size and scope, the greater the confidence the auditor will have that all the transactions/balances are valid. If the desired DR is low, the confidence level required from testing will be high, confidence level being defined as 100 minus detection risk, expressed as a percentage. Thus if DR is 10 per cent and transactions and balances are selected on that basis, the confidence level will be 90 per cent which means that the auditor wishes to be 90 per cent confident that the sample of transactions or balances used in substantive tests of detail will be representative of the total of such transactions and balances. The basic idea is that the auditors have to decide initially what level of audit risk is acceptable. In the following table we have assumed that a 5 per cent risk of error is acceptable. The point to remember is the only risk that the auditors have under their control is detection risk, so that if both IR and CR are high, the auditor will have to take steps to ensure that DR is low (and confidence level from substantive tests of detail therefore high). We show this in Table 5.1.

We discuss confidence level in statistical sampling in Chapter 11.

Auditors may, of course, seek to reduce control risk by recommending that management implement tighter controls.

TABLE 5.1 Calculation of Detection Risk (DR) and confidence level

AR	= IR	× CR	× DR	100% – DR (confidence level)	Comment
5%	= 100%	× 50%	× 10.0%	90.0%	Low DR and high confidence level because IR is high and CR relatively high. If high confidence (and 90% is high) is required, the auditor would have a level of testing to provide that confidence.
5%	= 100%	× 30%	× 16.7%	83.3%	IR is again high, but CR is lower (controls are better), so that confidence level need not be so high, resulting in a lower level of testing.
5%	= 50%	× 40%	× 25%	75.0%	IR is lower, but CR is somewhat higher, possibly because the company considers that tight controls are not necessary. Net effect is that confidence level required is lower than the previous case.

A formula might lead you to believe that audit risk can be easily determined and that one has only to multiply three factors together. Unfortunately it is not as easy as that, as the measure of each component of risk is difficult to determine and is very subjective. Some auditors recognize this and assess risk in qualitative terms – low, medium and high. Often controls are themselves influenced by the inherent risk so that they are not independent of each other. For instance, we noted in the Edencroft case that management experienced in handling the industry risks would counterbalance the risk. Nevertheless, the principle is clear, if you wish audit risk to be low and you know that inherent risk and control risk are both high, detection risk will have to be low. Similarly, if inherent risk is high but management has put in good controls and has a good control environment, auditors will be able to perform fewer substantive procedures and live with a higher level of detection risk. You can work out this for yourself if you insert figures. In Table 5.1, we have assumed that you wish audit risk to be no more than 5 per cent when you come to give your opinion on the truth and fairness of the financial statements.

We shall see in Chapter 11 that AR can be equated with the level of tolerable error.

Now that we have established some basic principles concerning audit risk, let us examine another case.

CASE STUDY 5.2

Kemback Limited, Part 1

Kemback Limited is a company manufacturing clothing for young people. Forty per cent of its sales are on credit to a variety of outlets and 60 per cent are through its own shops. The managers are normally marketing graduates and receive training in the company's products and philosophy before being put in charge of a shop. Other personnel in the shops are young and enthusiastic individuals, chosen for their knowledge of the young persons' fashion scene.

Shops send weekly reports to head office, containing details of goods received from/returned to head office, inventories on hand at the close of business each Friday, and daily bank deposits, together with requests for delivery of goods from head office. Shops prepare profit and loss statements weekly and these statements are also included in the reports and reviewed by head office staff for reasonableness and to assess shop performance.

Goods are invoiced by head office to shops at cost plus a mark-up to cover head office administration charges. Shop managers have some freedom to purchase goods locally if they think they will sell well, but are required to prepare a report justifying their action and to keep track of how well these goods are selling. Each shop has a cash float of £500 and managers are required to bank all takings intact. Shop expenses (except minor petty cash expenditure) are paid through head office. The company's internal audit department is expected by management to visit each shop on a surprise basis at least once each year.

You are senior auditor in charge of the Kemback Limited assignment and are accompanied by an assistant auditor whose work you are expected to supervise.

We have given you quite a lot of information about the company and we shall now take you through a number of activities related to the risks involved.

ACTIVITY 5.9

Explain to your assistant the inherent risks that may arise from the entity's environment or because of the nature of its transactions and balances. Suggest appropriate controls to reduce the impact of inherent risk.

You should first explain to your assistant what is meant by inherent risk and show that the environmental risks affecting Kemback Limited will include the following:

1 Manufacture of clothing for young people – a group notorious for its lack of consumer loyalty and wide swings of fashion. Consequent risk that stocks will prove unsaleable
2 Part of the company's philosophy is that shop staff should not only be 'trendy' but also have a marketing background. Possible risks are that staff with this background will fail to apply company rules on control, such as depositing takings in the bank intact, or that they will commit the company to the purchase of goods that may not prove saleable. This would appear to be a control risk factor, but it is really an inherent risk that makes supervisory control important (see below).
3 The distance of the shops from head office represents a particular kind of inherent risk associated with the structure of the company itself.

Appropriate controls might include:

1 Market research to identify fashion trends and to reduce danger of unsold stocks.
2 Appointment of staff following careful interview and receiving character references, to increase the likelihood that they will preserve the company's image and follow company policies.
3 Training for shop managers to ensure they exercise properly their supervisory role and maintain the enthusiasm of staff.
4 Training of staff in accounting and control matters and in company policies.
5 The impact of inherent risk associated with the distance of shops from head office is reduced by the system of weekly reporting as described, as backed up by the visits by the internal auditors.

We might mention again the difficulty of distinguishing between inherent and control risk. Thus, there is an inherent risk that staff will not be competent and will not possess integrity, but the existence of staff with ability and integrity will make more certain the correct application of company controls. The impact of inherent risk in this case might be reduced by proper appointment and training procedures.

ACTIVITY 5.10

Identify controls present in the shops reducing control risk and hence mitigating inherent risk.

You would first explain to your assistant the kinds of inherent risk that might affect transactions (such as sales transactions for cash) and balances (such as inventories on hand). Particular controls and related inherent risks in the shops include the following:

- Invoicing shops at fixed mark-up and preparation of weekly profit and loss statement mitigates inherent risk of loss of assets (principally inventories and cash). Reviewing the profit and loss statement might prompt such questions as 'Why are margins lower than expected?' and lead to investigations to discover if irregularities have occurred. Such investigations might discover poor accounting or even misappropriation of cash or inventories and inappropriate buying by shop managers.
- Weekly reporting of sales (and sales returns) will mitigate the inherent risk that a shop is underperforming without being detected. Head office should be able to identify trends that will enable them to pin-point problems, such as slow-moving inventories and excessive returns of inventories.
- Weekly counting of inventories will mitigate the inherent risk that attractive inventories could go missing. You might suggest that the weekly statements would only be valid if inventories are properly counted and care should be taken to ensure that shop managers supervise the counts. This is a good example of a supervisory control.
- The fact that cash is required to be banked intact and that a cash float is maintained separately mitigates the inherent risk that takings will not be fully recorded and helps to minimize loss of cash. Although not mentioned in the question, the use of an imprest system for control of the cash float would be useful. Banking intact is a useful control as it means that the till rolls should always be in agreement with the bankings.

In an imprest system a float is established, in this case £500. Initially, the float will be in cash, but as it is used, the cash element will be reduced, the remainder of the £500 being represented by vouchers. Periodically, the cash element will be reimbursed by the total of the vouchers, these then being filed. Thus, at any point of time, the imprest float will amount to £500 in the form of cash or vouchers.

- Rotational surprise visits by internal auditors will mitigate a number of inherent risks, such as records not being properly maintained, inventories not counted properly, and reports not in accordance with the facts. The following kinds of work would be carried out at these visits:
  (a) Review of weekly returns, including weekly profit and loss statements to seek explanation for trends and to highlight unusual matters, such as poor sales record, turnover of staff and shortfalls in inventories or cash.
  (b) Observe counts of inventories and calculate value. Reconcile to previous counts of inventories carried out by shop personnel.
  (c) Count cash in shop – tills and float. Reconcile till cash to till rolls. Check that cash is banked intact by reconciling till rolls and bank deposits on a test basis.
  (d) Check receipts of inventories to head office records and test cut-off at time of count of inventories.

ACTIVITY 5.11

Internal auditors visit the shops on a surprise basis at least once annually. How do you think that internal audit work may reduce control risk and detection risk and thereby aid the external auditor?

We consider the work of internal auditors in some depth in Chapter 15.

You will have noted that the internal auditors would be performing work not only to detect whether controls appear to be working properly, but also whether reported transactions and balances were reliable. Internal auditors increasingly have much wider duties than this kind of work, but this is an area where the work of external and internal auditors should be coordinated, as both are concerned with the reliability of control systems and information.

In the context of this chapter, the existence of a good internal audit department reduces control risk and mitigates the impact of inherent risk. However, as you can imagine, before you accept the work of internal auditors, you need to be satisfied about the adequacy of the work performed and their independence in the performance of their duties. Once you have done this you would find it useful to read and follow up on matters raised in internal audit reports. External auditors do not rely entirely on the work of internal auditors and perform themselves the kind of work set out above.

You should by now have a good appreciation of the meaning of inherent, control and detection risk and the relationships between them.

See page 208.

To reinforce this we suggest that you work self-assessment question 5.1, Fine Faces plc, a company in the cosmetics industry.

CASE STUDY 5.2

Kemback Limited, Part 2

Before we discuss other aspects of risk, we will move you forward a little in time and consider a number of problems that have arisen at three of the shops visited by you or your assistant.

> Auditing is very much a problem-solving exercise.

Problem 1. On arriving at two of the ten shops visited by you during the year you discover that they had received no visit from the internal audit department in the previous 15 months.

Problem 2. Your assistant had visited a shop on a surprise basis as it opened on a Monday morning and asked the cashier to count the cash in the till and in the float. The cash float was correct but the cash in the till was less than the till record suggested, because the shop assistant had taken some money out of the till to pay for some goods, not in the company's normal range, but which he thought might sell well. The details of this transaction had not been included in the previous Friday's weekly return.

Problem 3. In one other shop visited by you, you compared goods received records over a three-month period with the deliveries to the shop recorded in the central warehouse. Your work revealed that, in the case of five deliveries out of 13, the shop records showed significantly lower quantities than those despatched. On average the shortfalls represented some 20 per cent of the invoiced amounts.

ACTIVITY 5.12

Write a note in which you explain the issues arising from the matters coming to your attention and suggest audit actions you would take. In each case, state whether the problem is significant in terms of the risk of giving an inappropriate opinion.

Let us look at each problem one by one, decide what the implications are, and form a view on what the auditor should do.

- *Problem 1.* It seems that the internal audit department is failing to meet management's requirements. The external auditor would be concerned that general control risk is higher than expected and the impact of inherent risk in the company had not been mitigated. The reasons for not visiting should be determined and steps taken to discover how many shops had not been visited for some time.

  The external auditor would have to decide if audit staff should visit more shops, thus altering audit scope. If concerned generally about the work of the internal auditors, the external auditor might have to review overall reliance on internal audit. In other words a general extension of scope might become necessary.

'Audit scope' indicates the extent of work on transactions and balances the auditors judge is needed to achieve the objective of the audit. We discuss this further in Chapter 10.

- *Problem 2.* It appears that company procedures have not been applied and the auditors would investigate the circumstances. One step would be to ascertain whether invoices were available to support the purchases that the cashier claims to have made, to see the inventories on hand, and to discover if any sales had been made in respect of the goods in question. If there is no record of any transaction, there may have been simple misappropriation of cash. A further possibility is that the assistant has been selling the inventories and taking the proceeds for him/herself. The auditor should determine how long the assistant has been employed and the extent to which his or her work has been supervised. The auditor would discuss the matter with management and discover their attitude to this type of occurrence. One recommendation might be to tighten the manager's supervisory work. Another might be for management to state that infringement of company procedures would result in disciplinary action.

  The auditor might feel that detection procedures should be extended, but this would depend on discussions with management and the internal auditors. If the matter is a one-off, it is unlikely that it would be seen as increasing control risk.
- *Problem 3.* The initial impression must be that this is a grave matter, as one would expect it to be picked up at head office during the review of weekly reports. However, you should first establish the facts. You should review internal audit reports on the shop and head-office records and the weekly reports to see if the matter has already been brought to the attention of management. If this is not so, you should examine head-office despatch records and ensure that copy despatch notes support issues of inventories. A further step in head office would be to check the sequence of despatch note numbers in the three-month period to ensure that there is no break in sequence. A comparison of copy despatch notes with the original despatch notes held in the shop should then follow.

  In a worst-case scenario you might discover that despatch notes are not pre-numbered or that there are breaks in sequence, not detected at head office and that the despatch notes held in the shop are not in agreement (bear different reference numbers and are for different quantities). In this case, control risk would be high and the auditor would probably extend detection procedures widely, that is, not just for the shop in question. The auditor would wish to discover if significant losses of inventories had occurred.

There might, of course, be more benign reasons for the differences. For instance, the shop might have asked head office to deliver direct to certain customers and this had been charged to the shop instead of direct to the customer. If this is so, you might merely bring the matter to the attention of management and take no further action, having concluded that control risk in this case is low.

BUSINESS RISK APPROACH TO AUDIT

See paragraph 11 (d) of ISA 315.

We noted earlier in this chapter that ISA 315 requires the auditors to obtain an understanding of the entity and its environment, including its objectives and strategies, and the related business risks that may result in material misstatement of the financial statements. We have looked at a number of business risks in two case studies and have considered the related audit risks and the procedures that auditors might adopt to reduce audit risk to acceptable proportions. Auditors will always consider business risks as part of their risk assessments, but some audit firms (all the Big Four and some other larger ones) are now trying to add value to the audit, while collecting enough appropriate audit evidence to express an opinion on published financial statements, by using the so-called business risk approach to the audit. It is argued that this approach is sufficiently different from the audit risk approach to cause changes in the audit methodologies of the firms using it. In this section we shall describe the main features of the business risk approach, compare it with the audit risk approach, and discuss the implications of the two approaches.

You may find the following paper to be of interest: Lemon, Tatum and Turley, *Developments in the Audit Methodologies of Large Accounting Firms* published by ICAEW in May 2000.

ACTIVITY 5.13

'Business risk' may be defined as 'the risk that the entity will fail to achieve its objectives'. Make a list of possible objectives that an entity might have.

You have probably come up with quite a lot of objectives that an entity might have, including the following:

This list is by no means exhaustive.

- Attaining a certain level of profitability.
- Maximizing shareholder wealth.
- Ensuring efficiency and effectiveness of operations.
- Meeting a desired market share.
- Giving customer satisfaction, however that might be measured.
- Maintaining a desired level of liquidity.
- Maintaining reputation.

- Meeting the challenge of changes affecting the entity as they occur.
- Adhering to accepted principles of corporate governance, including adherence to predetermined measures of environmental protection.

If you refer to Figure 5.1 you will see that we have listed these objectives there. It can be seen from this list that business risk is broader than audit risk, so firms using this approach would be looking at wider issues than just the truth and fairness of the financial statements. That this is relevant to the audit report may become clearer if you note that management may adopt more aggressive accounting policies to ensure that their objectives are met. For instance, taking up a higher level of profits on a long-term construction contract to improve stated profitability.

Let us take a look at a brief example.

ACTIVITY 5.14

Kellie is a rapidly growing company providing advertising copy to a variety of individuals and companies. It currently has 10 per cent of the market but its management has as one of its objectives to increase this to 20 per cent within the next two years. Management is of the view that this will be necessary if its desired level of profitability is to be maintained and if they are to retain and attract high-quality staff.

Do you think that this information about the business is of relevance to auditors required to give an opinion on the company's financial statements at the end of the current year? What are the matters that you would wish to discuss with management about their declared objective? Do you think that you might be able to give management any helpful advice?

In practice the auditors would have much more information about the company to put this objective in perspective. But taking the desire to increase market share to 20 per cent on its own, there is one matter of significance that might have a bearing on the financial statements of the current year: that the company is already growing rapidly and has a culture of growth. Before the auditors direct their attention specifically to the financial statements, they would discuss with management the following matters:

- Why does management believe that increase in market share will benefit the company? They say it is necessary if its desired level of profitability is to be maintained and if they are to retain and attract high-quality staff, but there may be other reasons.
- Why do they think that increase in market share improves profitability?
- Does the company have or expect to have the financial resources to fund continued growth?
- Does the company have a view on how changes in the economic climate are likely to affect the company?

- Does the company presently have, or have a reasonable expectation of having, the human resources (artists, graphic designers, copy-writers) to allow growth of this magnitude?
- Who are your major competitors and how are they reacting to your presence in the market and your rapid growth? For instance, is there any evidence that any of your best people are being attracted to competitors?
- What kind of feedback are you getting from customers and potential customers? Are they positive about the work you are doing for them? Do you know whether their advertising budgets are likely to remain constant, expand or decrease in size?

We think you will agree that these are all questions pertinent to the continued success of the business. You might be able to advise management on ways to obtain additional finance, and suggest how to retain quality staff. The economy and the size of advertising budgets are likely to be directly linked and you might discuss with management the propriety of expanding at such a high rate at the present critical time. You may well have come up with further points of relevance to the business risks facing the company.

The other important matter is whether the above matters are of significance to the current financial statements. Here are some that might be of direct significance:

We discuss audit approaches to going concern in Chapter 17.

- Is the company overstretching itself financially? It might be over-trading if it cannot find additional finance to fund the growth of the company. At the extreme, there might be doubts about the going-concern status of the company and the auditors would need to direct audit effort to satisfying themselves that the company is likely to continue in existence for the foreseeable future.
- Rapid expansion normally means that the company's customer base is expanding. This in itself can cause problems as the company may be extending credit to individuals and companies that are new to them. The auditor might wish to extend tests of the company's credit control system.

What this example suggests is that auditors can achieve audit aims as well as helping management to achieve company objectives of only indirect significance to the financial statements. We shall now turn our attention to a comparison of business risk and inherent risk and ask why auditors have started to adopt business risk approaches. We shall also consider whether the business risk approach might be applicable to the smaller audit firm as well as the Big Four and the other larger firms. Before that, however, we shall address the issue of income smoothing.

Income smoothing

We have not mentioned 'income-smoothing' as an entity objective, even though managements might prefer their stated profits not to swing significantly from year to year, as it is not an approach allowed by the Companies Acts or accounting standards. However, it is worth noting that there has been an increased incidence in recent years of income smoothing that can be achieved by understating assets such as trade receivables in a year when profits are high and reversing the understatement in years where profits are low. The same effect can be achieved by manipulating liabilities such as trade creditors, but in the opposite direction. We shall find – when we come to discuss 'provisions' in Chapter 14 – that IAS 37 – *Provisions, contingent liabilities and contingent assets* has restricted considerably the ability of companies to make provisions (which could be easily reversed in future years if they are not genuine). Income smoothing is not specifically referred to in the IASs or IFRSs, although the IASB Framework for the preparation and presentation of financial statements notes in Paragraph 37, among other things, that 'the exercise of prudence does not allow, for example, the creation of hidden reserves or excessive provisions, the deliberate understatement of assets or income, or the deliberate overstatement of liabilities or expenses'. IASB is on the point of publishing as part of its Conceptual Framework, a revised Objective and Qualitative Characteristics of Financial Reporting and the problem of income smoothing may be specifically highlighted in this. However, income smoothing is discussed in FRS 18 – Accounting policies, applicable in the UK and Ireland and we refer you to paragraph 14 of Appendix IV, which says that deliberate understatement of assets and gains, and overstatement of liabilities and losses 'are no longer seen as a virtue' (presumably because this was confused with 'being prudent'). Auditors should keep an eye open for evidence that income smoothing might be attempted by management and the attitude of the directors to fairness in financial reporting determined. FRS 18 treats prudence as one aspect of the overall objective of reliability (in financial statements) and the last sentence of Paragraph 37 reads as follows: 'In conditions of uncertainty, appropriate accounting policies will require more confirmatory evidence about the existence of an asset or gain than about the existence of a loss, and greater reliability of measurement for assets and gains than for liabilities and losses.' Paragraph 38 then goes on to say:

The comparable UK and Ireland standard is FRS 12 – *Provisions, contingent liabilities and assets* which is substantially identical to IAS 37.

> However, it is not necessary to exercise prudence where there is no uncertainty. Nor is it appropriate to use prudence as a reason, for example, creating hidden reserves or excessive provisions, deliberately understating assets or gains, or deliberately overstating liabilities or losses, because that would mean that the financial statements are not neutral and therefore not reliable.

We refer to this question when we are considering individual assets and liabilities in Chapters 12, 13 and 14.

BUSINESS RISK AND INHERENT RISK APPROACHES: SIMILARITIES AND DISSIMILARITIES

Let us first consider the implications of the business risk approach, noting that management have always tried to counter the risks that might prevent them from achieving company objectives. Business risk assessment is a management technique that involves senior management establishing business objectives. Objectives may of course change as circumstances change, so this kind of assessment should be made regularly. Establishment of business objectives is clearly vital before the next stage – that of determining the business risks that may prevent the objectives from being achieved. To take the Kellie example discussed in Activity 5.14, the company objective of achieving 20 per cent of market share may be inhibited by such risks as competition from other companies in the advertising sector, or lack of funds to support the enlargement of the company.

We have seen in the Kellie example that the auditors might discuss such risks with management and offer advice on how the risks might be countered and we have seen that this work might also be of relevance in reducing audit risk. Thus, the business risk approach by management has been adapted to allow auditors to provide business risk assessments as a consultancy exercise to audit clients, an important spin-off being improvement of the auditors' knowledge of the company's business. This allows auditors to direct audit effort towards high risk areas in the company from an operational perspective. This kind of approach may detect areas that might lead to the financial statements being misstated, such as liquidity problems threatening the going-concern status, and would help the auditor to comply with auditing standards. Another important spin-off is that the auditors' business risk assessment may well identify areas where less audit work is needed than historically has been the case. A further important spin-off is that the assessment may highlight areas where business risk has not been controlled and where the auditors can advise management, reducing business and audit risk in the future. This kind of work also has the advantage that it increases the value of audit as far as management is concerned and also provides a potentially lucrative source of additional income for the audit firm.

You might at this point suggest that you can see little difference between business risk and inherent risk, so we shall now address this question, asking you to refer to Figure 5.1 as we do so.

Similarities

1 Approaches to business risk and inherent risk, whether by management or auditor, use a 'top-down' approach in that, initially, management/auditors consider the entity in its entirety before they decide what steps are necessary to prevent the company achieving its objectives or – in the case of auditors – to decide what procedures must be performed to ensure that the financial statements give a true and fair view of results and financial position.

2 The factors that increase inherent risk, such as management inexperience and lack of skills and other negative entity level factors may well make it less likely that business objectives will be obtained.

3 The factors that serve to increase control risk, such as a poor control environment may also inhibit the achievement of business objectives.

We have shown the influence on business risk of the factors under (2) and (3) above in Figure 5.1.

4 Analysis of business risk and inherent risk may help the auditors in work designed to prove that financial statements give a true and fair view. Both kinds of analysis give auditors a better understanding of the entity and its operations.

Dissimilarities

1 The major dissimilarity is that auditors consider inherent risks in relation to the impact that they may have on the financial statements, whereas the

business risk approach considers those risks that inhibit the company in achieving its objectives. Many company objectives may have little bearing or only an indirect bearing on the financial statements. It is true that maintaining company reputation may have an impact on the financial statements in that it may positively affect the saleability of products, for instance, but an objective such as this has only an indirect effect on the financial statements for any particular year. In many cases, auditors may bear only inherent risks affecting the financial statements in mind, and adopt a bottom-up approach to account balances and classes of transactions, identifying risks that may cause them to be misstated, unless appropriate controls are in place. By doing this auditors would be adopting a traditional inherent risk approach without reference to the wider business objectives of the entity.

2 While it is true that factors that fail to reduce the impact of inherent risk may also fail to reduce the impact of business risk, business and audit objectives are so dissimilar that the factors cannot be regarded as creating a similarity.

Now let us consider the impact that a business risk approach might have on the audit process, where it is adopted. Here are some suggested benefits that may help us:

1 It is argued that it improves the basic audit of the financial statements and makes it less likely that erroneous conclusions will be reached about the state of the company's affairs and its results of operations.
2 It makes the audit more efficient and therefore more profitable.
3 It expands the potential for giving assurance to management beyond traditional audit and is felt to 'add value' to the audit from the client perspective and thereby to create additional sources of income.
4 The expanded audit has potential to contribute to corporate governance arrangements and disclosures because of the broader understanding of the business and its risks.
5 Better understanding of a client's business and its risks will reduce the audit firm's own 'business risk' – sometimes referred to as 'engagement risk'.

Figure 5.1 suggests that financial statement level factors may affect engagement risk.

One further issue that you might consider is that advances in application of information technology have resulted in company records being inherently less likely to contain routine error so they are more reliable – leaving more scope for higher level audit assessments.

One thing that you may have noticed about the discussion with management of Kellie Limited is that it would need to be carried out by experienced staff at partner and manager level within the auditing firm. This is likely to increase the cost of audit, particularly at the planning stage and when you are obtaining knowledge of the business environment of the client. We have already suggested that planning work usually takes up a considerable proportion of audit time, but the business risk approach normally results in even more time being spent at this stage because of the need to find out much more about management (are they skilled and trustworthy), how management views the company (what are its objectives) and how they control it (to make more certain that its objectives will be obtained).

This early evidence gathering leads to another important development. As more knowledge is gained about management and their objectives and the business risks faced by them, the auditors will form views on the reliance that they can place on management. This may result in reduction in detailed tests of transactions and balances (substantive tests of detail), more reliance being placed on qualitative evidence such as the effectiveness of the control environment and on analytical evidence. Auditors are increasingly using the computer in the audit process, creating large databases and other information to provide industrial, economic and competitor data used to form conclusions about the client company. Firms adopting business risk approaches recognize that the change has far-reaching consequences with more reliance on experienced staff *and* on assessments of management competence and integrity. There may, however, be a danger that auditors become so closely aligned to management that they lose their independence. It might also be that business risk approaches cut down the likelihood of over-auditing in non-risk areas, but that under-auditing may result in audit failure. If auditors fail to test enough sales transactions, for instance, they may fail to discover that sales invoices have not been calculated properly. However, if properly managed, reducing the risk of over-auditing in a non-risk area can be a positive advantage, as it will release audit time for addressing risk areas.

THE BUSINESS RISK APPROACH AND SMALLER CLIENTS AND SMALLER AUDIT FIRMS

The business risk approach was developed by the larger firms, but we should consider whether it can be used effectively in the audit of smaller companies by smaller audit firms.

ACTIVITY 5.15

Now that you know what the business risk approach involves, do you think that it can be applied in the audit of smaller companies by small audit firms?

For a general discussion about the impact of business risk approaches you might read the report by Lemon, Tatum and Turley already referred to above. There is an interesting discussion of an actual case of the audit of a bank in the Czech Republic in Eilifsen, Knechel and Wallage, 'Application of the Business Risk Audit Model: A Field Study', *Accounting Horizons,* September 2001.

Smaller firms might be at a disadvantage in adopting a business risk approach as it clearly needs a wide variety of expertise within the firm to enable business risks to be identified and to allow a dialogue on equal terms to be conducted with experts in the client company. If this is the case you might argue that the business risk approach is most appropriate in the audit of large multinational companies by the Big Four audit firms.

However, you might equally argue that the business risk approach is about an attitude of mind on the part of the auditor involving the acquiring of knowledge about the rationale behind the business. It is likely that the smaller audit client will not have wide expertise and smaller audit firms may usefully discuss business risks with management as an aid to them. This means that firms other than large firms might be able to use the business risk approach.

Of course, this wider approach will probably be more expensive and management would have to be persuaded that it would be to their advantage and that benefits exceeded costs.

Later, we provide you with case material to help you to assess business risk and the impact on the audit process. Whether such an approach will receive wide acceptance cannot be assessed yet, but you should note that it took a long time for firms to adopt changes in the past – for instance the moves to a systems-based approach to audit and the use of statistical methods of selection of items for testing.

Finally, students should note the discussion on the business risk approach when we assess corporate governance issues, and when we consider auditor liability for negligence. We also consider whether the audit expectations gap might widen as the result of increased expectations of the business risk audit.

ANALYTICAL REVIEW AS A RISK ANALYSIS TOOL

Analytical procedures are useful when auditors are deciding where risk areas in the client company lie. Analytical procedures are defined in ISA 520 – *Analytical procedures*, Paragraph 4 as:

We discuss analytical review in detail in Chapter 12. Some audit firms refer to these procedures as 'diagnostic procedures'.

> Evaluations of financial information through analysis of plausible relationships among both financial and non-financial data. Analytical procedures also encompass such investigation as is necessary of identified fluctuations or relationships that are inconsistent with other relevant information or that differ from expected values by a significant amount.

We have already seen earlier in this chapter that ISA 315 explains that analytical procedures are important risk assessment procedures used during the process of obtaining an understanding of the entity and its environment'.

You will remember that head office staff review the financial statements of the shops of Kemback Limited for reasonableness and to assess performance. This is an example of an analytical procedure. The auditors of Kemback would perform similar reviews. Here is a further brief example.

ACTIVITY 5.16

You are auditing a company and have obtained the information in Table 5.2 from a variety of sources.

The liquidity ratio is calculated as (current assets less inventories)/current liabilities and is a measure of the ability of the company to pay its short-term liabilities as they fall due. Gearing is calculated as: long-term debt/net assets employed × 100.

Gearing may be calculated in a number of ways but this ratio shows the extent to which net assets are financed by outside long-term debt.

Both liquidity and borrowings are factors that need to be considered in assessing risk. The question is whether the company looks more of a risk for the auditor in the current year compared with last year? How would the information above affect your planning? What specific additional information would you seek as part of your audit procedures?

TABLE 5.2 Liquidity and gearing ratios

	Company		Industry average	
	Current year	Last year	This year	Last year
Liquidity ratio	0.6 to 1	0.7 to 1	0.75 to 1	0.74 to 1
Gearing ratio	45%	35%	35%	35%

You will have noted that the company is not only less liquid than last year, but is also less liquid than the industry average in both years. The poor liquidity is compounded in the current year because higher gearing would make it more difficult to obtain additional funds to improve liquidity. You would clearly need to direct your attention to the reasons for poorer liquidity, to discover if there are any ameliorating factors and what actions management intend to take to improve liquidity. Examples of additional specific procedures might include:

1 Reviewing the bank overdraft limit in relation to the bank balance.
2 Discovering the attitude of the bank to the poorer liquidity of the company.
3 Checking whether poorer liquidity has been accompanied by infringement of creditors' payment terms to any significant extent.
4 Whether debtors are paying more slowly than in the previous year.
5 Review of cash budgets to discover movements in liquidity in the subsequent period.

Analytical procedures are an important aid in reducing overall audit risk and in particular reducing detection risk. Analytical review will be of particular value in determining if the company is a going concern or likely to have going-concern problems. We shall see that they are used at several points in the audit process, including the planning stage when the initial decisions on inherent risk are taken.

JUDGEMENT IN ACCOUNTING AND AUDITING AND ITS RELATIONSHIP TO RISK

In performing the above work you were seeking information to help you make judgements about risk. You will remember from Chapter 2 that judgement is one of the 'enduring principles of auditing' developed by the Auditing Practices Board. So what is judgement and what do you need as auditor to exercise it? Judgement, like many aspects of human activity is intangible in its nature. One of the authors remembers the partner in charge of his firm's training programme telling groups of trainees that 'next year judgement will be taught in the classroom', and going on to say that, in fact, they would have to learn to exercise it over years and years of bitter experience. This is all too true, but, if you think about it, you are making judgements about whether to do one thing or another, many times every day. Even if it is just a question of whether you should wear a raincoat; you are making judgements as to whether it is likely to rain or not. You may not necessarily make the right decision, but you will have based your assessment on your previous experience, aided perhaps by evidence provided by the weather forecast. This is what auditors do. They assess available evidence, call on their experience of dealing with similar matters in the past, assess risk and then make a decision as to whether they have been persuaded to accept or reject evidence. An experienced auditor can often assess the integrity and competence of management fairly quickly. In your own personal life you are probably able on the basis of your experience to assess whether you can trust someone or not.

The relationship between audit judgement and risk is direct, as it is exercised in the context of risk. In forming judgements the auditor makes initial risk assessments and then modifies those assessments on the basis of controls in existence and of the validity of figures in the accounting records. Any assessment of risk involves judgement to a greater or lesser extent. We shall give two examples at this point, but return to the question of judgement throughout the book.

ACTIVITY 5.17

Wedel Limited operates a city-centre restaurant specializing in fast food. During the audit you discover that a customer has sued the company for personal injury caused by food poisoning. The amount claimed is £100 000, but management has told you that the company has good defences against the claim. You are aware that judgement cannot be exercised in a vacuum and that you require evidence before you can make a decision. Describe the evidence that you think you require. In doing this give consideration to matters that you might have considered at the planning stage.

A major inherent risk in the catering industry is that of food poisoning. At the planning stage, therefore, you would have obtained information about the hygiene regulations affecting the restaurant and would have questioned management on the cleanliness and cooking regime that had been installed and on the controls to ensure compliance with hygiene regulations. If you were satisfied that company procedures were good, you might have concluded that control risk was low and controls had mitigated the high inherent risk. In forming your conclusions you would have exercised judgement.

The court case might cause you to revise your initial judgement, but first you would have to obtain the facts. Useful evidence would be a doctor's certificate confirming food poisoning and evidence that the customer had consumed a meal at the restaurant. If the customer had bought the food as a carry-out there might be reasonable doubt as to the stage that contamination had taken place. You should obtain the previous reports of the hygiene inspector on the restaurant and discuss the circumstances with management. One important step would be to obtain the view of the company's lawyer as to the likelihood of the case being successful. Judgement by the auditor would be difficult as the court case has not yet been heard and there would be a measure of uncertainty. Nevertheless, the auditor would have to exercise

The testing of a specific assertion regarding financial statement figures involves substantive procedures and we discuss this matter in Chapter 10 at greater length.

judgement based on the available evidence. One further matter is that you will have exercised judgement regarding audit risk in two different contexts. The first is at the planning stage and the second at the stage of forming a view on a particular management assertion – that no provision in respect of the claim is necessary.

ACTIVITY 5.18

You have been performing a cut-off test at 31 December 2010 to satisfy yourself that purchases are recorded in the proper period. You have compared the pre-numbered goods received notes (GRNs) with purchase invoices to ensure that the invoices are recorded in 2010 where the GRN has been issued up to the end of December. You judged initially that purchase invoices were recorded in the proper period. However, you had written to some creditors to confirm amounts owed to them at 31 December and some had confirmed higher amounts owing than had been recorded by your client.

Do you believe that you, as auditor, are at risk? How would you exercise professional judgement in respect of this matter?

Clearly, your initial judgement had been too hasty, but you had decided to seek corroborative evidence. Before you form a final judgement you would have to carry out additional work, testing purchase invoices shown by creditors as owing at the balance sheet date to goods received notes. If these notes are missing, this may mean that goods have been received without being recorded and you would have to extend your detection procedures in this area. You might decide to send out confirmation requests to more creditors, asking them to provide you with details of transactions just prior to and just after the year-end date.

Before we leave this topic we wish to draw a distinction between the exercise of judgement and technical compliance with auditing standards. There may be an element of judgement as to whether a specific element of an accounting standard is applicable or not, for instance, is this long-term construction contract sufficiently complete to allow profit to be taken up on it, but for many accounting standards the rules are so tight that it will be clear which treatment is acceptable and which not. There would be little room for argument, for instance, on the application of IAS 20 or SSAP 4 on the treatment of government grants. So, when we use the word 'judgement' we do not mean the application of a straightforward rule, but apply it to situations where the amount of a valuation or provision, for instance, can be interpreted in different ways and the auditor has to decide that the amount is appropriate in the circumstances of this particular company.

We discuss long-term construction contracts in Chapter 13. See Table 1.1 on page 16 and Figure 6.3 on page 230, both of which provide an overview of the whole audit process.

This has been a very brief discussion of judgement, but we shall return to it from time to time. The basic thing to note is that auditor judgement is exercised in the context of audit evidence collected and carefully evaluated.

MANAGEMENT OF THE AUDIT PROCESS

Now that we have introduced you to audit and business risk, it is time to consider how the auditor manages the audit process. In this section we consider primarily the preliminary stages of the audit, but before we do this, we wish to remind you that the audit firm may be seen as a group of people with differing responsibilities and experience, with perhaps two basic objectives, both of which are related:

- *Objective one* is that of meeting the professional aim of reaching a carefully formed opinion on financial statements as required by law or by special instruction and requires the audit firm to act effectively and to perform professional work of high quality. There are two International Standards of Auditing, which address quality control:
    1. International Standard on Quality Control 1 (ISQC1) – *Quality control for firms that perform audits and reviews of financial statements, and other assurance and related services engagements*.
    2. ISA 220 – *Quality control for an audit of financial statements*.
- *Objective two* is that of making a profit in carrying out your professional duties, sufficient to give fair remuneration for the imaginative and demanding work required in the audit process and for the professional risk involved. This objective requires the audit firm to act efficiently as well as effectively.

We have seen earlier that auditors adopting a business risk approach may have another objective in mind – that of expanding the potential for giving assurance to management beyond traditional audit and thereby to create additional sources of income.

We have already seen in Chapters 2 and 3 that there may be conflict between the two objectives and that there might be a risk that professional corners will be cut to meet the objective of profitability. We suggest that the only way to prevent this is to manage the audit process efficiently and effectively.

The starting point for effective management is to create a logical structure within the audit firm and to allocate special responsibilities to each person working in it. We have already considered such a structure in Figure 3.3 in which we showed how creating a proper control environment within the firm would be a prerequisite for ensuring objectivity and independence in the performance of the audit. We also saw that the firm's technical advisory function supports engagement teams through the engagement partner on such matters as the application of accounting and reporting standards. We also saw that the engagement quality control reviewer (EQCR) performs an objective evaluation of the significant judgements made by the engagement team, and the conclusions reached in formulating the auditor's report. As we saw in Chapter 3, this will involve discussion of significant matters with the audit engagement partner, reviewing the financial statements and the proposed audit report, reviewing audit documentation where significant judgements have been made, and evaluating specific and overall conclusions in formulating the proposed audit report.

Other key people in the audit firm are the partners in the chain of command, including the engagement partner for the individual audit assignment. We shall now take a closer look at the responsibilities of individual members of the engagement team.

- *The engagement partner* is responsible as we have seen for ensuring objectivity and independence issues are considered, but also for planning

We discuss audit evidence in Chapter 6 and take an overall look at audit documentation in Chapter 14, once we have covered the audit process in detail. ISA 230 – *Audit documentation* is relevant here.

Auditors normally record information of continuing value in permanent files, but inevitably much will reside in the memories of audit staff engaged on the audit assignment in current and prior years.

and overall conduct and control of individual audit assignment, and for making certain that sufficient appropriate evidence has been gathered to enable the audit opinion to be soundly based. The engagement partner has considerable interest in this respect, as he or she signs the audit report. Much of the planning and control work will be delegated to managers.

- *Managers* are thus responsible for the delegated planning and overall conduct and control of individual audit assignments and for the overall quality of the work performed. They bear, together with the engagement partner, responsibility for the effective and efficient conduct of the audit, including maintaining cumulative client knowledge. Cumulative client knowledge is an important aspect of quality control, comprising all the knowledge about the client firm of value for the conduct of the audit. We shall return to the question of cumulative client knowledge in this and later chapters but gathering information is a costly exercise and it should be recorded to ensure that it remains useful and that you will not have to collect it again next year.
- *Seniors* are responsible for the day-to-day conduct, control and quality of the individual audit assignment. Unlike managers they will normally be present in the client company during virtually the whole of the audit process. They will also bear some responsibility for the maintenance of cumulative client knowledge, including descriptions of company systems, used in the audit process.
- *Assistant auditors* are the people who carry out much of the day-to-day detailed audit work. Their experience depends upon the time they have spent in professional life and normally the seniors will subject their work to considerable supervision and control. Some firms have a grade – semi-senior – between assistant auditor and senior.

ISA 220 defines a network firm as a firm that belongs to a network (i) that is aimed at cooperation; and (ii) that is clearly aimed at profit or cost-sharing or shares common ownership, control or management, common quality control policies and procedures, common business strategy, the use of a common brand name, or a significant part of professional resources.

The people on an individual audit assignment, including the engagement partner, manager, seniors, assistant auditors and appropriate staff, such as tax and IT experts, form together the engagement team. The engagement team is defined in ISA 220 as: 'All partners and staff performing the engagement, and any individuals engaged by the firm or a network firm who perform audit procedures on the engagement.' Note that, if the firm employs external experts, such as lawyer or actuaries, they would not be regarded as part of the engagement team.

THE TERMS OF REFERENCE PROVIDE THE AUDIT FRAMEWORK

In this section we shall introduce you to the engagement letter which sets the scene and determines the terms of reference, the criteria by which the audit is carried out. Let us start with a brief case. See Case Study 5.3.

ACTIVITY 5.19

What conclusions do you think can be drawn from Case Study 5.3?

You will observe that the business risk approach to audit was not taken in this case. You will probably be concerned that what has happened is a classic

CASE STUDY 5.3

Hughes Electronics Limited

You have been asked by a partner to carry out the audit of a new client – Hughes Electronics Limited. You spend three weeks on the audit (one week longer than budgeted) and on completion return to your firm's offices with draft accounts and a set of working files for review by the partner. During the review he asks why you spent longer on the assignment than planned and you admit that you had become concerned that the person in charge of the petty cash fund at the company was misappropriating sums from the fund. You had extended the work done in an attempt to prove that this was the case. You had finally concluded that, although the system was weak, there was no evidence that the weaknesses had resulted in loss to the company.

The partner asks you why you had spent so much time on the matter as the petty cash fund was £100 only, an insignificant amount in the context of the financial statements taken as a whole and the additional work would result in higher fees to the client company. Later, the directors of Hughes Electronics Limited refuse to pay your firm's fees of £4 000 because it exceeded the fee originally agreed by £1 000 and they had not authorized a fraud investigation. The correspondence file reveals that a letter of engagement had been received from Hughes Electronics and this is reproduced below:

HUGHES ELECTRONICS LIMITED
BUTTERBURN, SHANK END
24 May 2010

Messrs Smith, Smythe and Gow
Accountants and Auditors
High Street, Butterburn, Shank End

Dear Sirs,

With reference to the recent meeting between our Mrs Alston and your Mr Haughton, we hereby appoint you to act as our auditors. Please let us know when you will be able to start your work. We understand that your fee will not exceed £3 000.

Yours faithfully,

Janet Alston (Mrs)
Finance Director

---

case of over-auditing, although you might make the point that misappropriations over time could far exceed the £100 float. At the same time there are other matters of concern:

- The letter of engagement is not clear as to what is required of the auditor. Audits can vary considerably and may encompass statutory audits (leading to an opinion on the truth and fairness of financial statements), audits of systems to detect strengths and weakness in them, audits to detect fraud and audits of management decision-making processes. The letter of engagement should have spelled out the kind of audit that was required. If this is not done, work may be performed that is not desired and directors may, quite rightly, refuse to pay the fees for the unnecessary work. It could be argued that as many business people are not aware of what an audit entails, it is up to the auditor to explain this to the client company.
- The engagement partner should have made clear to the staff member what kind of work was required. Generally, statutory auditors have the right to obtain from management the information and explanations they believe are

necessary for the performance of their duties, but this does not mean that the auditor can do work peripheral to the main audit purpose. The correct course of action would have been to explain to the directors that there were weaknesses in the system of control surrounding petty cash, that petty cash was not important enough in the financial statements to warrant further audit work, but if management wished, the audit firm could investigate the matter.

The letter of engagement: role and contents

Now that you have considered the above scenario and it's consequences, we can turn to the letter of engagement, which is the subject of ISA 210 – *Agreeing the terms of audit engagements*. We do not discuss this standard in detail, but you should read it and refer to an example of an audit engagement letter given in an appendix to ISA 210. We comment below:

To whom the engagement letter is addressed

The letter should be addressed to a person having management authority in the entity; ISA 210 refers to 'those charged with governance'.

Objectives and scope of the audit

This section identifies the financial statements and states that the audit will be conducted with the objective of expressing an opinion on the statements.

'Scope of audit' means what the auditor will be doing in order to form reasonable conclusions in the course of an audit of the financial statements of the company. We use the term 'true and fair view scope' if auditors are carrying out an audit to form an opinion on whether or not the financial statements give a true and fair view. Often auditors will carry out work with different scope. For instance, if management suspected that fraud was taking place in the company and asked the auditors to investigate, the nature and extent (that is, scope) of the work would be very different.

The responsibilities of the auditor

There is a reference to the ethical standards to which auditors must adhere.

There is an explanation of the audit process, including planning, and a reference to the fact that the audit is about obtaining reasonable assurance whether the financial statements are free from misstatement.

We discuss audit evidence in Chapter 6.

There is a reference to how the audit will be conducted – adhering to ISAs, selection of procedures to obtain audit evidence, that the procedures selected depend upon auditor's judgement, including assessment of risk, and that the auditor evaluates the appropriateness of accounting policies selected and of estimates made by management.

There is a reference to the limitations of audit and of internal control and that there is an unavoidable risk that some material misstatements may go undetected – even though the audit is properly planned and performed.

There is a disclaimer regarding the entity's internal control – that the auditor will not report on its effectiveness – though considering internal control relevant to the entity's preparation of financial statements when designing audit procedures. There is also a statement that the auditors will communicate to management any deficiencies in internal control that come to their attention.

Responsibilities of management and those charged with governance

The auditors inform management and those charged with governance of their responsibilities and ask them to acknowledge and understand that they have responsibility for preparing financial statements that are fairly presented in accordance with IFRSs (including IASs). As part of this responsibility they are required to establish internal controls they consider necessary to enable them to prepare financial statements free of material misstatement, whether due to fraud or error.

It is vital that management understand that the preparation of the financial statements is their responsibility.

Management are also informed of the responsibility they have to give the auditors access to all information they know is relevant to the preparation of the financial statements, plus any additional information that the auditors request from management for the purpose of the audit. Management must also agree to give unlimited access to persons within the entity from whom the auditors determine it is necessary to obtain evidence.

One wonders if Sir Frederick Ashop of Rosedale Cosmetics (See Chapter 4) bothered to read the engagement letter before signing it.

Management are also informed that the auditors will request from them and those charged with governance written confirmation of representations made to the auditors in connection with the audit.

We discuss written representations from management in Chapter 14. ISA 580 – *Written representations* is the relevant ISA.

Finally in this section the auditors say they look forward to full cooperation with the staff of the entity. You might note here that an audit without cooperation of management and staff would be well nigh impossible. Sir Frederick Ashop of Rosedale Cosmetics is a good example of lack of cooperation.

Audit reporting

There might be a reference here to the fact that the form and content of the audit report would depend on the outcome of the audit work performed, and that the draft audit report would be discussed with management before issuance.

We discuss audit reporting in Chapter 16.

Fees

Normally, the letter will contain details of how audit fees are calculated, based on time spent by members of the engagement team, rates depending on their responsibility and skill and experience required of them. This section would normally contain reference to billing as work progresses.

Recurring audits

There might be a statement here that the terms of the engagement letter would be effective for the current and future years, until such time as circumstances change. The auditors might send a new letter if circumstances change, such as new management or in the size and complexity of the entity, or where it becomes clear that management have misunderstood the objective and scope of audit. You might refer to paragraph A28 of ISA 210 in this connection.

Finally

Two copies of this letter of engagement would be sent to the management (the addressee) with the request that one be signed to indicate agreement and returned to the audit firm.

It is vital that management and auditors are aware of their respective responsibilities and it is the engagement letter that sets the scene for the relationship between them. It can prevent subsequent disagreements if things go wrong.

FOR READERS IN THE UK AND IRELAND

Note that the form of the engagement letter for use in the UK and Ireland is similar to that described above. However, there are a number of additional features and you should refer to Appendix 2 of ISA 210 (UK and Ireland) for appropriate wording of the engagement letter. For instance ISA 210 (UK and Ireland) inserts into the letter a statement that the audit firm 'shall not be treated as having notice, for the purpose of audit responsibilities, of information provided to members of our firm other than those engaged on the audit' These other members might have been engaged on accounting, taxation or other services.

You should note too that The Financial Services and Markets Act 2000 in the United Kingdom, and a number of Acts in the Republic of Ireland, allow auditors under certain circumstances to report direct to regulators. The engagement letter should explain this matter. You should note that ISA 250 (UK and Ireland), Section B – *The auditors' right and duty to report to regulators in the financial sector*, requires auditors to report direct to a regulator information which comes to the auditor's attention in the course of the work undertaken in the auditor's capacity as auditor of the regulated entity. Matters to be reported in this manner might include suspected money laundering offences or failure to keep clients' monies separate from office monies. A report of this nature may be given without informing management, despite the general requirement for confidentiality.

Before we leave this section you should be aware that auditors may feel the need to emphasize certain other matters in the engagement letter. Examples are:

- Companies are increasingly providing users with financial statements and other information about the company on the Internet. The engagement letter in these circumstances should state that the directors should seek consent from the auditors before any opinion by them is made public in this way.
- Some firms have started to issue disclaimers in their audit reports, stating that the report has been made solely to the company's members as a body and that they will not accept responsibility to anyone other than the company and the company's members as a body. Some auditors may feel that this policy should be highlighted in the engagement letter.
- The engagement letter may also be used to flag up auditors' duties with respect to corporate governance. Note in this respect that ISA 260 – *Communication with those charged with governance,* contains the matters that should be communicated by the auditor to those charged with governance of the entity. ISA 260 also sees communication as being very much a two-way process.

This followed the Bannerman case in Scotland in 2002, which we discuss at greater length in Chapters 16 and 19.

We discuss corporate governance in Chapter 18.

We might also mention at this point, that if the audit firm is providing non-assurance services, it would be appropriate to prepare a separate engagement letter.

PLANNING THE ASSIGNMENT

To give you some insight into the matters considered at the planning stage we shall introduce you to a Case study of a company in the hotel industry.

CASE STUDY 5.4

County Hotel Limited, Part 1

Imagine that it is 31 May 2010 and that you have been called into the office of John Gunn, a partner in your firm of professional accountants. John Gunn tells you that David Jones, the managing director of County Hotel Limited, catering for both tourists and business people, has asked the firm to act as auditor for the year ending 31 December 2010. He has already been in touch with the previous auditors to ensure that there is no professional reason why the assignment should not be accepted. This assurance has been received in writing and a letter of engagement duly signed by management included in the permanent audit file. John Gunn asks you to be manager in charge of this assignment. He tells you, as the result of previous discussions with the client, that the company is large enough to have a good accounting system and enough staff to operate a good system of control. He suggests that you apply a business risk approach to the audit so that management will see that the firm is considering their needs as well as forming an opinion on the financial statements of the entity.

Study of the business

Introduction

John Gunn has already obtained some information in broad terms but you will have to gather much more before you can plan the audit work. In the case of companies audited in prior years, much information needed for planning should be available in the working paper and other files, but in the first audit more time will be devoted to this phase.

You should have ISA 300 – *Planning an audit of financial statements* – to hand when you are performing the tasks relating to this case study.

Before we study County Hotel Limited, we ask you to consider the hotel industry in broad terms. We have chosen this industry because we think you will be familiar with hotels to some extent and will have some notions of possible problems faced by management and of the operations of a hotel even if your knowledge has been obtained as a guest.

The external environment

It is important for auditors to understand the industry within which their client operates, so they can appreciate the kinds of competition the client might face and the problems and risks of concern.

TASK 5.1

Make a note of the following matters:

- Typical kinds of hotel and the competition they might expect.
- The major business and inherent risks in the industry and controls that might be introduced to reduce the risks.

We want you to put yourself in the position where you will be able to discuss the industry, its problems and solutions with management in a credible manner. Think about the business risks that a company running a hotel might face. Do not forget our previous advice that being well informed usually means it is easier to become better informed. When you have given careful thought to the two matters noted above, turn to the end of the chapter, page 205, for the suggested solution to the task.

The internal environment

It is often difficult to separate the internal environment from the external, as many internal features of hotels are there because of a response to the external world. However, we ask you now to consider what goes on in a hotel and why knowledge of this will be useful to you.

TASK 5.2

Make a note of the following:

- The broad functions you would expect to find in hotels, such as portering and housekeeping.
- Typical sources of income of hotels (be imaginative).
- Typical kinds of expenditure in hotels.
- The kinds of records that hotels would have to keep and the sort of evidence that should be available to the auditor of a hotel.
- The sort of information that management might need to run the hotel profitably and effectively.

When you have considered the above matters, turn to the end of the chapter, page 206, for the suggested solution to the task.

Now that you have an appreciation of the hotel industry, we shall look at County Hotel Limited, find out its special features and consider how management runs the hotel. First remember that the basic idea of ISA 315 is that only by fully understanding the business of the client will an auditor be able to form a view on its risks and controls. You may want to have Appendix 2 to ISA 315 to hand when you are reviewing the case. This appendix provides a list of matters to consider when assessing risks of material misstatement in relation to understanding the entity and its environment. You may also find it useful to refer to Appendix 1 – *Internal control components*.

CASE STUDY 5.4

County Hotel Limited, Part 2

You arrange to visit the hotel and, during discussions with David Jones (managing director) and with the chief accountant, Mrs Carol Henshaw, you elicit the following information about the hotel.

Accommodation

The hotel has 60 rooms, classified as shown in Table 5.3. The room usage figures are an important measure of success. On average the hotel rooms have been occupied in the 12 months to 30 April 2010 for 74 per cent of the time. Remember that an empty room in an hotel is like a rotten tomato in a greengrocer's shop. Neither generates any income. Management is concerned because accommodation rates have dropped from 76 per cent in the 12 months to 30 April 2009. Usage varies throughout the year, from 50 per cent during the winter months to 90 per cent in the spring/summer and early autumn months.

TABLE 5.3 County Hotel Accommodation

	No	Daily rate £	% usage
Single rooms with bath	15	100	75
Single rooms with shower	10	85	77
Single rooms with washbasin	5	60	81
Total single rooms	30		
Double rooms with bath	17	120	70
Double rooms with shower	9	100	77
Double rooms with washbasin	4	70	82
Total double rooms	30		
Total rooms	60		74

Each room contains a remote control television set, tea/coffee-making equipment, clothes press and telephone.

- The basic daily rates are as indicated above but these rates may be departed from for the following reasons:
  (a) special rates for weekends and reduced weekly rates;
  (b) if single rooms are not available, double rooms may be charged at single rates;
  (c) special seasonal rates.
- The management of the County Hotel is planning to provide baths for those rooms with washbasins only and the work is likely to commence in the current financial year.
- Mrs Henshaw tells you the room-letting side of the business breaks even (2009 room-letting income was some £1 500 000).

Restaurant

The hotel has a restaurant with 60 tables. Management informs you that most guests take breakfast in the hotel, but that usage of the restaurant by residents in 2009 was approximately 20 per cent at midday and 65 per cent in the evening. The hotel admits non-residents and most diners at midday do not stay in the hotel. Management estimates that the restaurant breaks even when operating at 55 per cent of capacity, but wishes to improve usage of restaurant capacity (which was 75 per cent in 2009, including residents and non-residents). They are restructuring the menu and have recently engaged a new chef who specializes in food traditional to the neighbourhood. Income from the restaurant was some £3 400 000 in 2009, including income from breakfasts. Mrs Henshaw tells you that the hotel makes most of its profit from the restaurant and is advertising the new menu and specialities in the local press. One of the reasons for attention being currently devoted to the restaurant is because of competition from Bellbank Hotel, a recently modernized hotel nearby, which has been successful in attracting business from the County Hotel, not least because of its attractive restaurant.

Kitchen

Management has taken steps to reduce waste in the kitchen. They have introduced stricter portion control and have recently given the responsibility for buying food to the new chef, under the general supervision of Mrs Henshaw.

Bar

There are three bars in the hotel and a wide range of drinks is available to both residents and non-residents. One of the bars is in the functions room, which also serves as a residents' lounge when functions are not taking place. This is a profitable part of the business.

Functions

The hotel offers complete facilities for wedding receptions, small business meetings, and discussion groups.

Accounting system

The hotel's accounting system is computerized. The company has a small network of desktop computers that cost £36 000, some two years ago. The desktop computers are at reception, in the restaurant, in the bar, in the manager's office and in the office of the chief accountant. The system uses programs purchased as complete packages from a reputable software house. One person runs the computer system, but Mrs Henshaw also has computer knowledge and supervises the operation of the system.

The most important accounting record relating to residents is the reception record that is entered into the computer system when the guest arrives. The room number is used to record any services the guest uses. Thus, when a resident has a meal in the restaurant, the room number is entered on the meal document signed by the guest.

Restaurant

The important control record in the restaurant is the numbered menu, which is contained on a master file in the computer system, together with standard prices. Each waiter has a four-part order pad, one part going to the kitchen, one to the restaurant cash desk, one to the accounts office and one being retained by the waiter. The waiters enter the number of orders for a particular meal at each table, using the menu numbering system, and notes the room number of guests resident in the hotel. The restaurant manager uses the restaurant desktop computer to enter details of all meals served in the restaurant, distinguishing between those paid in cash and those that are to be recorded in the resident's record. Meals paid for in cash are entered in the cash till in the restaurant.

Bar

The important control in the bar is a programmed till which contains pre-set prices for drinks and requires the barman to enter the number of drinks ordered and cash paid, the system automatically calculating the change. There are regular inventory counts by an external inventory taker.

Hotel structure and personnel

The organization chart of the hotel is shown in Figure 5.2.

FIGURE 5.2 Organization chart of County Hotel Limited

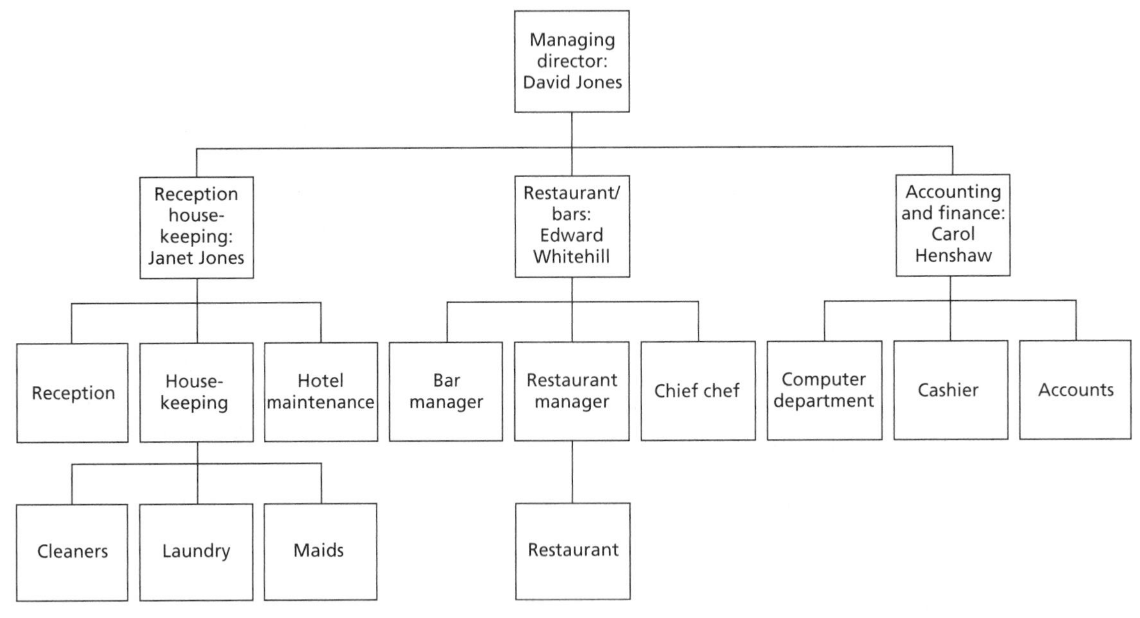

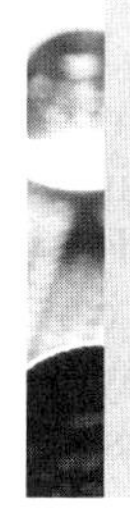

ACTIVITY 5.20

Do you think that during the course of the above discussions you would be able to form an impression of the competence and integrity of David Jones and Carol Henshaw? What would you be looking for in particular? What do you think management would expect from you?

It does depend on how long you spend with them, but if you have been with them for some length of time, you should be able to form a fairly firm opinion. You will see later that we are suggesting a planning and fact finding visit to the hotel by the manager lasting one week. Things you would be looking for are willingness to cooperate, to discuss problems faced by the hotel openly, and to give you access to important management information, such as room and table usage, how they intend to meet the threat of competition, what plans they have in force to deal with disruption during the building programme and so on.

Management would expect you to say how you intend to approach the audit in general terms, for instance, whether you would expect to do a lot of detailed testing or whether you would rely on the company's systems and control environment. They would expect too that you would be willing to discuss their problems and to suggest solutions either immediately or after an agreed length of time. They would also in all likelihood expect to be given an estimate of fees to be charged and how they might be kept to a minimum.

Preparation of audit planning memorandum

You are now better informed about the hotel industry in general and about County Hotel Ltd in particular. As auditor, you would need much more information about the company than you have obtained in this brief survey, but you should have obtained enough to be able to plan in global terms whether there are any matters that need special attention and whether the accounting system seems adequate. Paragraph 12 of ISA 300 explains what should be included in the audit planning documentation:

12. The auditor shall include in the audit documentation:

(a) The overall audit strategy;

(b) The audit plan; and

(c) Any significant changes made during the audit engagement to the overall audit strategy or the audit plan, and the reasons for such changes.

And paragraphs A16 to A18 explain the meanings of these headings:

> A16. The documentation of the overall audit strategy is a record of the key decisions considered necessary to properly plan the audit and to communicate significant matters to the engagement team. For example, the auditor may summarize the overall audit strategy in the form of a

> memorandum that contains key decisions regarding the overall scope, timing and conduct of the audit.
>
> A17. The documentation of the audit plan is a record of the planned nature, timing and extent of risk assessment procedures and further audit procedures at the assertion level in response to the assessed risks. It also serves as a record of the proper planning of the audit procedures that can be reviewed and approved prior to their performance. The auditor may use standard audit programs or audit completion checklists, tailored as needed to reflect the particular engagement circumstances.

Paragraph A18 reflects the fact that as the audit progresses the auditor may well come across matters that make it necessary to change the initial plan.

> A18. A record of the significant changes to the overall audit strategy and the audit plan, and resulting changes to the planned nature, timing and extent of audit procedures, explains why the significant changes were made, and the overall strategy and audit plan finally adopted for the audit. It also reflects the appropriate response to the significant changes occurring during the audit.

Auditors formulate the general audit strategy in an overall audit plan, which sets the direction for the audit and provides guidance for the development of the audit programmes. The audit programmes set out the detailed procedures required to implement the strategy.

TASK 5.3

We realize that you may be as yet somewhat inexperienced in auditing but we ask you now to prepare a memorandum detailing the areas to which you would pay particular attention during the audit of County Hotel Limited. When you have given careful thought to the matters noted above, turn to the end of the chapter, page 206 for the suggested solution to the task.

You will observe that the matters contained in the memorandum all relate to areas of difficulty and risk for management and auditor. In fact, the main point of audit planning is to direct attention to those difficult areas and to assess the degree of risk involved. Remember how risk was approached in the Kemback Ltd case earlier in this chapter and make sure that you understand the distinction between inherent risk, control risk and detection risk. You should also remember the distinction between audit risk and business risk and recognize that business risk and inherent risk may be similar in nature in many respects.

Refer also to Fine Faces plc in Self-assessment question 5.1.

You can see that planning is concerned both with the efficiency of the audit process and generally with making the process effective. It is good practice to back up the audit-planning memorandum by staff briefings prior to the commencement of audit work. Staff briefings are a two-way process in that a senior person in the team directs the attention of staff to critical features, but also gives staff members the opportunity to seek clarification of matters of interest. Note in this connection Paragraph A8 of ISA 300:

> The process of establishing the overall audit strategy assists the auditor to determine, subject to the completion of the auditor's risk assessment procedures, such matters as:

- The resources to deploy for specific audit areas, such as the use of appropriately experienced team members for high risk areas or the involvement of experts on complex matters;
- The amount of resources to allocate to specific audit areas, such as the number of team members assigned to observe the inventory count at material locations, the extent of review of other auditors' work in the case of group audits, or the audit budget in hours to allocate to high risk areas;
- When these resources are to be deployed, such as whether at an interim audit stage or at key cut-off dates; and
- How such resources are managed, directed and supervised, such as when team briefing and debriefing meetings are expected to be held, how engagement partner and manager reviews are expected to take place (for example, on-site or off-site), and whether to complete engagement quality control reviews.

The Appendix to ISA 300 lists examples of considerations in establishing the overall audit strategy.

Returning briefly to County Hotel Limited, it is clear that all the points in the audit memorandum affects the way the audit will be carried out. Thus, knowledge of competition from Bellbank Hotel will help to put accommodation and restaurant income into context. The same may be said for further information the auditor might be able to obtain regarding social habits in the town (for instance, whether it is part of the local culture to 'eat out') or about levels of unemployment in the town, which might affect the level of income of people in the town. You might also note that the work involved in preparing the special purpose report on room and restaurant table usage and the assurance report on the efficiency and effectiveness of the computer systems will also help to understand how the company is performing and how its accounting and control systems work.

What we intended to give you in this section is a practical understanding of the need for determining the needs and objectives of management, the objectives of the audit, of the context in which the audit will take place and the importance of risk analysis and planning in an informed way. You should now read ISA 300 again and relate it to the matters we have discussed in this chapter. We shall return to planning from time to time as it is rare for an audit plan to remain unchanged during the audit process and planning feedback is required to ensure amendment to the plan when necessary. You will note references to planning feedback in Figure 6.3 on page 230 in Chapter 6

Preparation of time and fee budgets

One final matter we wish to discuss with you is the time budget and fee budget, both of which are directly dependent upon the auditor's evaluation of risk. This is because the risk evaluation will determine the extent of substantive procedures performed. The amount of work carried out involves of course the use of resources, the most important of which will be the time of partners and staff of the audit firm. What we are suggesting is that the time budget should be designed to provide sufficient time for audit risk to be reduced to acceptable levels.

TASK 5.4

You have been asked to prepare the time and fee budget. You may assume that as a result of your discussions with David Jones and Carol Henshaw, you have decided on the following timescale for the audit:

- Interim examination: two weeks, for systems work and transactions testing (one senior and two assistant auditors).
- Final examination: two weeks, for final work preparation and the final work itself (one senior and one assistant auditor).

In addition to the time of the field staff it will also be necessary to budget for the time of the partner and of the manager. As a rule of thumb we suggest that partner time should be 2.5 per cent and manager time 7.5 per cent of time spent by seniors and assistant auditors. However, you are to budget for 40 hours of manager time and eight hours of partner time in evaluating business risks, determining management objectives and how they go about controlling the risks.

How realistic these percentages are will depend on the structure of the firm and the allocation of responsibilities.

You may assume that a computer auditor will attend for two working days of eight hours each (charge-out rate £135 per hour) during the interim examination. A member of the tax department (charge-out rate £135 per hour) will spend one day on the engagement team (as a tax auditor) during the final examination. Other hourly charge-out rates for calculating fees are:

Partner	£190
Manager	£145
Senior	£110
Assistant auditors	£75

These figures are very rule of thumb. Some firms charge more, other less. There also seems to be a move to charging an audit fee for the whole assignment rather than splitting it up in the way indicated here.

When you have prepared the time and fee budget, turn to the end of the chapter, page 208 for the suggested solution to the task.

We have now reached the end of the preliminary stages of the audit process. It would be normal for your firm to discuss the estimated fee budget with the client and, perhaps, to arrange for payments on account at the completion of audit stages. The timing of the audit stages would be discussed with management, so they can arrange for their staff to discuss systems, audit problems and other matters with the audit staff, as required.

Summary

In this chapter we have set the scene for the conduct of the audit. We introduced you to the risk-based approach to audit and have defined both audit and business risk and exemplified inherent risk, control risk and detection risk. We have suggested approaches to business risk and why a business risk approach is being adopted by some firms and the consequences of so doing. We have shown that there is an important link between risk and judgement, and that analytical procedures represent an important tool of risk analysis and aid the exercise of audit judgement.

We have also introduced you to the engagement letter as an important vehicle for establishing the relationship between auditor and auditee, for setting out responsibilities of management and auditor, and the basis of charging fees.

To aid understanding of the basic rule that the client must be understood in terms of its internal and external environment, we have introduced you to the hotel industry and to an entity running a hotel. The discussion of the hotel entity was designed to show what impact the knowledge of company problems and management responses would have on subsequent audit work.

Having identified the audit problems we then showed that the time budget would be designed to provide sufficient time for audit risk to be reduced to acceptable levels.

Key points of the chapter

- Auditors must obtain reasonable assurance about whether the financial statements are free from material misstatement. The auditor does not give a guarantee. A material misstatement is one that causes financial statements not to give a true and fair view.
- Auditors identify and assess risks of material misstatement at the financial statement level and at the assertion level. The risks of material misstatement at the assertion level are inherent risk and control risk. To assess such risks the auditor must understand the entity and its environment.
- There is a distinction between audit risk and business risk. Audit risk is the risk that the auditor expresses an inappropriate audit opinion. Business risk is the risk that an entity will fail to achieve its objectives and may result in audit risk.
- Audit risk comprises three components: inherent risk, control risk and detection risk.
- Broad approach to minimize audit risk comprises: 1. Investigating the legitimacy of the entity and the integrity and competence of its management before acceptance of the audit assignment; 2. Considering the independence of the audit firm and its staff before acceptance of the audit assignment; 3. Understanding the nature of the entity and the environment in which it operates before commencing any detailed audit work; 4. Planning by the auditor to minimize risk of failing to detect material misstatement at the financial statement and assertion level; 5. Design of the audit approach and the setting of performance materiality; forming an engagement team with the required experience and skills; 6. Design of audit programmes to obtain the evidence necessary to form conclusions at the assertion level, leading to an opinion on the truth and fairness of the financial statements taken as a whole.
- Tools for understanding the entity and assessing risk include initial inquiries with responsible people in the entity and analytical procedures. Initially information will be gathered in broad terms and later subjected to detailed examination. Understanding the entity includes its nature, environment and internal controls.
- The nature of the entity and its environment, includes the risks facing its industrial or commercial sector; subjectivity to technological change; whether it is a public interest entity; whether the entity is growing or declining; the entity's strategies to attain its objectives; how the entity is financed; the nature of the entity's transactions; whether the entity invests in other entities; the experience of management.
- The entity's internal control includes: (a) The control environment; (b) The risk assessment process; (c) The information system: (d) Specific controls relevant to the audit; (e) The audit committee and the internal audit function.
- Planning an audit involves establishing the overall audit strategy and developing an audit plan to minimize the risk that material misstatements remain undetected. Misstatements, including omissions, are considered to be material if they could reasonably be expected to influence the economic decisions of users taken on the basis of the financial statements.
- Audit engagement team members must have experience and skills to enable them to handle the complexity of the client's systems and accounting information on which the financial statements are based. The engagement team is directed and supervised by the engagement partner with the support of the manager in charge of the assignment.
- Auditors set objectives and prepare detailed audit programmes to search for evidence to meet these objectives.
- A major problem in the context of risk is the nature of the accounting process itself which requires estimates to be made of many of the figures appearing in the financial statements. Uncertainty surrounding estimates increases the possibility of misstatements. Auditors look to the controls designed to aid management in making the necessary judgements about the estimates they have to make.
- In planning the audit, auditors obtain and document an understanding of the accounting system and control environment sufficient to determine their audit approach, recording the system in use and testing it to ensure the record is valid and making a final assessment of control risk. If control risk is deemed to be low, the auditors reduce substantive procedures, but substantive procedures always have to be performed. Substantive procedures are designed to reduce detection risk.
- Audit risk (AR) = Inherent risk (IR) × Control Risk (CR) ×Detection Risk (DR), but the measure of each

component of risk is difficult to determine and is very subjective.
- The existence of a good internal audit department reduces control risk and mitigates the impact of inherent risk.
- Many audit firms adopt a business risk approach to audit on the assumption that auditors can achieve audit aims as well as helping management to achieve company objectives.
- One particular risk is that management may engage in income smoothing. IASB and APB are attempting through accounting standards to ban this activity.
- Business risk and inherent risk are similar in some respects and dissimilar in others.
- The business risk approach may also be applied by smaller audit firms to the audit of smaller entities.
- Analytical procedures are useful when auditors are identifying risk areas by evaluation of financial information through analysis of plausible relationships in both financial and non-financial data.
- There is a direct relationship between audit judgement and risk.
- The starting point for effective audit management is to create a logical structure within the audit firm. Creating a proper control environment within the firm is a prerequisite of ensuring objectivity and independence in performance of the audit. It is important to allocate responsibilities to all persons involved in the achievement of audit objectives.
- The engagement letter sets the scene and determines the terms of reference, the criteria by which the audit is carried out.
- Case Studies 5.4 and 5.5 provide practical examples of how to plan the assignment, how to structure the audit process and prepare an audit planning memorandum and time and fee budgets.

References

Beattie, V. and Fearnley, S. (1998) 'Auditor changes and tendering: UK interview evidence', *Accounting, Auditing & Accountability Journal*, 11(1): 72–98.

Fearnley, S., Beattie, V. and Brandt, R. (2005) 'Auditor independence and audit risk in the UK: a reconceptualization', *Journal of International Accounting Research*, Vol.4(1): 39–71.

Further reading

A general article on risk, which you might find useful to supplement your reading in this chapter is:

Colbert, J.L. (1987) 'Audit risk: tracing the evolution', *Accounting Horizons*, September: 49–57.

Other useful articles on business risk are:

Lemon, W.M., Tatum, K.W. and Turley, W.S. (2000) *Developments in the Audit Methodologies of Large Accounting Firms*, published by APB in May.

Eilifsen, A., Knechel, W. and Wallage, P. (2001) 'Application of the business risk audit model: a field study', *Accounting Horizons*, 15(3): 193–207.

Other interesting articles on risk are:

Gwilliam, D. (2003) 'Audit methodology, risk management and non-audit services', Centre for Business Performance Briefing 05.03, ICAEW.

Khalifa, R., Sharma, N., Humphrey, C. and Robson, K. (2007), 'Discourse and audit change: Transformations in methodology in the professional audit field', *Accounting, Auditing and Accountability Journal*, Vol.20(6): 825–54.

The accounting journal *Accounting, Organizations and Society* (2007) 31: 4–5 contains a number of articles on business risk. You are specifically recommended the articles by Power, Knechel, and Peecher, Schwartz and Solomon.

There are a number of ISAs relevant to this chapter and you should read these carefully:

ISA 200 – *Overall objectives of the independent auditor and the conduct of an audit in accordance with international standards on auditing.*

ISA 210 – *Agreeing the terms of audit engagements.*

ISA 260 – *Communication with those charged with governance.*

ISA 300 – *Planning an audit of financial statements.*

ISA 315 – *Identifying and assessing the risks of material misstatement through understanding the entity and its environment.*

ISA 320 – *Materiality in planning and performing an audit.*

ISA 330 – *The Auditor's responses to assessed risks.*

ISA 520 – *Analytical procedures.*

A book that takes a slightly wider perspective on risk is Michael Power, *Organized Uncertainty: Designing a World of Risk Management* published by Oxford University Press in 2007. Chapter 2 is particularly relevant to the issues discussed in this chapter.

Suggested solutions to tasks

Task 5.1

The suggestions below are unlikely to be complete, and you may have others on your list.

1 Typical kinds of hotel:

(a) Residential hotel, often small.

(b) Hotels catering for sales representatives.

(c) Hotels catering for business people, including conferences.

(d) All-purpose hotels, catering for a cross-section of guests, providing wedding and other receptions, meetings facilities, etc.

(e) Hotels catering for the holiday trade or guests attending festivals in the locality.

(f) Very large international hotels, providing every imaginable kind of facility from hairdressing to surfing.

(g) Boutique hotels offering an individualistic approach and high quality service.

Generally, hotels of similar type and size will compete with each other. It is unlikely that a small hotel catering for sales representatives will see itself as competing with a large international hotel. The basic facilities of the hotel, such as baths, showers, dial-out telephones and television sets in every room, will often be good selling points that attract custom. The attitude towards young children may attract guests with or without young children. Part of your work would be to find out from management what they were doing to make their hotel attractive to potential clientele.

2 Business risks in the industry include the following:

(a) The risk that hotels will attract insufficient guests to cover high fixed costs. Controls to mitigate this risk include:

- The use of statistical analyses of room and restaurant table usage to enable management to react to trends by (say) special pricing at different times of the year/month/week.
- The use of records of bookings so that the hotel always knows whether rooms/tables are available.

(b) The risk of failing to collect all amounts due from transitory and short-stay guests.

The most important control in this case would be an accounting system that allows rapid, accurate recording of food and drink consumed and services used, combined with regular comparison of usage records and income recorded.

(c) The risks associated with casual staff, many with low basic pay. The main risks are that such staff may not be fully committed to the organization, particularly if low-paid. We do not wish to give the impression that casual staff members are by nature unreliable, but they will need supervision to ensure that they adhere to company policy and are efficient and behave honestly. An important control would be checks on the background of staff before appointment.

(d) The risk of losing moveable and attractive assets, ranging from cutlery to food and towelling.

Most hotels will accept certain levels of loss of such assets, but important controls would include:

- Company policy on such matters as consumption of food. (Most hotels allow staff to have meals on the premises, but frown on the removal of food.)
- Analysis of restaurant results and investigation of high food consumption.
- Regular stock counts of hotel moveable assets.
- Investigation of unacceptably high levels of loss.

Apart from the above risks that might be accompanied by specific controls designed to reduce their impact, there are a number of other general risks that are less easy to control. These might include:

(e) The risk that an economic downturn might make it less likely that people will use hotels.

(f) The risk that competitors might open a hotel in the area with more modern facilities and that key staff such as a highly regarded chef might be tempted away.

Possible management responses to threats of this nature might be to seek ways of making the hotel more attractive such as ensuring:

- that it is modernized when necessary;
- that standards of cleanliness and service are maintained;
- that conditions for key staff are such that they are unlikely to move.

Of course, if the two suggested threats did materialize, management would have to respond but the auditor could enquire of management what contingency plans they had in mind if they did. Keeping a careful eye on the trade press would be useful in this respect for both management and auditor.

Task 5.2

1 The broad functions that may be found in a hotel include: (a) reception, (b) portering, (c) housekeeping, (d) maintenance, (e) restaurant, (f) bar and wine cellar, (g) kitchen, (h) finance, accounting and management control.

2 Typical sources of income in a hotel include: (a) accommodation charges, (b) restaurant income, (c) telephone charges, (d) bar income, including drinks served with meals and in rooms, (e) income from other services, depending on whether they are provided, for instance, laundry, hairdressing, newspapers, special charges for use of tennis courts, swimming pool, parking, etc.

3 Typical kinds of expenditure include: (a) food and drink, (b) wages, salaries and other labour costs, (c) laundry expense, (d) housekeeping supplies, (e) cleaning expense, (f) flowers, (g) stationery and printing, (h) telephone, (i) replacement of crockery, cutlery, linen, glasses, (j) repairs and maintenance, (k) power and light, (l) insurance.

4 Kinds of records. There can be many of these but will include the following:

   (a) Arrival and departure lists for each day. These list the expected arrivals and departures of guests.

   (b) Reservation lists, showing reservations made by expected guests.

   (c) Registration lists, showing guests in the hotel and room occupied.

   (d) File of individual bills for each guest, containing details, price and value of each service used to date. This means that guests can receive their bill at short notice.

   (e) Room occupancy schedules, actual and projected. This is vital management information and is used to support budgets and management action to control occupancy levels.

   (f) Menus, recipes and yield (that is number of portions) for ingredients used. This is an important control over food usage.

   (g) Food and beverage stocktaking reports. These are used to highlight any losses in food and beverages.

5 Management information. The management information needed to run a hotel has already been indicated to a certain extent. Vital management information includes: (a) long-term projections of room occupancy and restaurant usage, (b) short-term and medium-term records of room and restaurant bookings to enable management to accept or reject further bookings, (c) restaurant and kitchen and bar costing to fix restaurant and bar prices, (d) food usage reports to control food cost and losses.

Task 5.3

Audit Planning Memorandum, County Hotel Limited, 31 December 2010

Basic requirements:

Management letter: including a special purpose report on room and restaurant table usage	31 October 2010
Assurance report on the efficiency and effectiveness of the computer systems in use	30 November 2010
Audit report	1 April 2011

Key audit dates:

Manager fact finding and planning	1 week from 29 May 2010
Interim examination	Two weeks from 9 October 2010
Trade receivables' circularization	At 30 September 2010
Inventory count	31 December 2010. Count commences at 8 a.m.
Final examination	Two weeks from 18 March 2011

Time budget and audit fee estimate
(See separate memorandum)

Key matters:

- The hotel is large enough to allow segregation of duties, and systems are likely to be reliable. This has been confirmed in general terms following a one-day visit to discuss basic procedures with hotel officials. This will have an impact upon our risk assessment and should be reflected in the amount of detailed work performed. This year we shall have to spend time recording and testing the systems in use and the final risk assessment will be made thereafter.
- Computerized systems in use possess sophisticated control features such as standard menus in a master file and bar prices in a programmed till. The company has a small network of desktop computers that cost £36 000, some two years ago. The computers are at reception, in the restaurant, in the bar, in the manager's office and in the office of the chief accountant. The system uses programs

purchased from a reputable software house. One person runs the computer system and we shall have to look at the controls in force, noting, in particular, the role of Mrs Henshaw who has computer knowledge and supervises the operation of the system. The engagement team should include a computer auditor.

- New bathrooms are being installed in nine rooms during the year and this is likely to disrupt the day-to-day work of the hotel. The interim examination has been scheduled to take place after installation. Particular audit attention should be directed towards testing transactions in the installation period as controls may not have been so effective and control risk may be high. We must also test the costs of installation, ensuring that all costs have been completely and accurately recorded and that the capital/revenue decision has been properly made.
- There is some concern on the part of management as to room usage and low usage of restaurant capacity. Some audit work should be directed to management decision-making in the area and information on break-even points and costs and income. We should consider whether management statistics on room usage and usage of restaurant capacity are reliable as this may be the best way to satisfy ourselves that income is properly stated. The same applies to budgets of accommodation and restaurant costs, including food preparation. If they are carefully prepared estimates of expected costs, rather than goals to be achieved, we might be able to use them to compare with actual costs.
- There have been portion control and purchasing problems in the recent past and we should direct attention to food costs and management's solutions to improve control. It is not known how material this matter is in relation to the true and fair view, but we could look into it if management wish. If so, the work would be billed separately and a separate engagement letter prepared.
- There are a large number of different billing rates for rooms and inherent risk is correspondingly high. Our tests should be directed to ensuring within reason that rates are being properly applied as part of our work on accommodation income.

John Ruddons, 14 June 2010

Apart from the matters discussed above, comments would also be included on individual balance sheet and profit and loss account positions and the specific inherent and control risks affecting them at the assertion level.

Task 5.4

The time budget and fee calculation are given in Table 5.4. The charge-out rates may or may not be realistic; they depend largely on location, some places being much more expensive than others. Note that we have assumed that typing and secretarial time is not charged out separately but the charge-out rates include typing and secretarial overhead.

Note that the decision might be taken to allocate some partner and manager time to the special purpose and assurance reports. In view of the amount of time spent in planning it might be possible to reduce some of the senior and assistant time because of reduced substantive procedures. Reducing assistant time by half would enable the amount charged to be reduced by £12 000 to £46 700. Suggest an audit fee of £40 000 after charging £6 700 of partner and manager time to the other reports.

Self-assessment questions (solutions available to students)

Task 5.9

In this question we are taking you through various scenarios and will ask you to perform a number of activities.

Case Study 5.5 Cosmetics company: Fine Faces plc

You are engaged in the audit of Fine Faces plc, a cosmetics company that manufactures and sells a range of lipsticks, deodorants, after-shave lotions and perfumes. The products are manufactured according to secret formulas that the company has developed over time.

5.1, Activity 1

Think about the nature of a cosmetics industry and then ask yourself what business risks would be faced by this kind of business.

We are sure that you have seen that the cosmetics industry is in the fashion industry and that a major problem is the difficulty of assessing future fashion trends, so that what sold well in the past

TABLE 5.4 John Gunn and Co: County Hotel time budget and fee

	Planning	Interim	Final	Total	Rate	£
Partner						
J Gunn	8	6	4	18	190	3420
Manager						
J Ruddons	40	20	12	72	145	10400
Senior						
R Denhead		80	80	160	110	17600
Assistants						
C Lamont		80	80	160	75	12000
J Bianchi		80	80	160	75	12000
Computer auditor						
M Lethan		16		16	135	2160
Tax auditor						
C Kenley			8	8	135	1080
						58700

may not do so in the future. For the auditor this can be problematic. At the extreme, if the company gets future fashion trends wrong, the whole company might be at risk of losing its going-concern status. Even if this risk does not exist, the auditor might be worried that the company has inventories on hand that will prove to be unsaleable.

5.1, Activity 2

Now that you have considered a major business risk associated with the industry in which Fine Faces is placed, think about controls the company might have in place to meet the risk of changes in fashion. You should also decide what specific work the auditor might perform in respect of the control to make sure that control risk is minimized. Consider the information that the company may require.

The most obvious control that the company would introduce is market research to establish current fashion trends and to determine if planned company ranges are likely to go down well with a somewhat fickle public. The auditor would wish to find out from management how they conduct market research and how often. This might involve face-to-face interviews, questionnaires and soundings with fashion leaders, the results of which should be subjected to analysis by company staff and a record made of the decisions taken. As changes in fashion may happen quickly, the company would have to ensure that it is kept informed of trends. The auditor will determine that the process has been satisfactory and will examine the market research reports, minutes of market research committee meetings and directors minutes. A review of the trade press might also reveal whether the company had got it right or not. You would also be influenced by how successful Fine Faces plc management had been in forecasting fashion trends in prior years, and also if sales analysis enables them to determine trends. Remember that your prime objective is to determine if the control is working properly, with the objective of reducing control risk, but you might also be interested in advising management on critical matters.

At this stage, you are aware of the major business/inherent risk and the main control in force. However, being a good modern auditor you adopt an attitude of professional scepticism and ask management how they keep track of how well products are performing in the marketplace. You discover that the company prepares projections of sales and production at the beginning of the year, keeps monthly records of sales budgets per line and makes monthly comparisons of budgeted with actual sales. Auditors might in practice make a comparison themselves for planning purposes to decide if inherent risk is high, but also to determine if controls in force are adequate. The audit programme might read: 'Obtain the budgets for year to date and compare with actual sales.' Any significant discrepancy between the two might reveal timing differences (sales turning up later than expected or vice versa) but more seriously might reveal that the anticipated sales had failed to materialize.

5.1, Activity 3

Assume that you have discovered a serious discrepancy between projected and actual sales. One brand of lipstick shows projected sales of £500 000, but no actual sales. This would seem to suggest that a problem exists for both Fine Faces and the auditor. Obviously, you now have to decide what you would do. Make a list of the actions that you think might be appropriate.

Your immediate reaction might have been to go to the chief accountant and raise the matter with him or her. However, one of the basic rules of auditing is to be sure of your ground before you take any matter further. Here are some suggested procedures you might adopt:

1 Review the market research report again to confirm the company's view that this particular type and colour of lipstick would achieve good sales in the current year.
2 Examine the production reports to confirm that the product has been put into production.
3 Take a look at the inventory records to confirm that the finished stock of this lipstick has been received in the stores.
4 Confirm that the inventory on hand agrees with the inventory records.

At this point you can go to the chief accountant with information that backs up your previous concern, that one of the products might turn out to be unsaleable. When you raise the matter, it will be almost certain that the chief accountant already knows about it. You may be somewhat concerned that you have not been told about it, knowing that integrity of management is important to the auditor. However, at this point it will be important for you to discover the background to the problem and what action the company is intending to take.

5.1, Activity 4

Assume that the chief accountant, faced with the wealth of information you have obtained, tells you that the problem of the unsold stock had arisen because of a buying problem. The buyer had purchased inappropriate raw materials, but this had been compounded by the failure of the inspection process when the materials had been received. The result was that, during the production process, the finished product could not be produced to a satisfactory standard. The company had tried to rectify the problem by purchasing new raw materials, but by the time they had passed through the production process, their competitors had captured the market.

Bearing in mind that we are considering the risk that the auditor might draw wrong conclusions on the basis of audit work performed, what would concern you at this stage? What conclusions could you draw?

The main concern would be that you had failed to detect the problems in the buying and receipt of goods areas of the company before you stumbled on it as the result of detection procedures in another part of your audit. There was, of course, failure also of company control systems in respect of purchasing and the inspection of goods on receipt. The worry would be whether this had implications for other production lines as well.

Audit actions as a result of identifying the control risks discussed above would be an expansion of audit procedures to ensure that detection risk was low, bearing in mind high inherent risk at the boundary (between the entity and the outside world) and the high control risk at the same boundary. Examples of procedures might include tests on quality of raw materials and finished goods, examination of correspondence between suppliers, customers and the entity. The extent of your tests would depend on your judgement as to whether the breakdown in controls was a one-off breakdown or something more serious.

> There are, of course, also internal boundaries, such as those between the raw material store and the factory floor.

Apart from the audit risk matter that we have discussed we have also seen that the entity's controls have failed to reduce the impact of an important business risk – that products manufactured will fail to meet the standard expected, thus ensuring that the company is failing to meet at least one of its objectives – an acceptable level of profitability. You have also discovered that management has failed to inform you of this important matter, so much so, that at the extreme you might wonder if you should seek reappointment as auditor. This means that we have come across another reason for adopting a business risk approach – to aid you in the decision as to whether you should accept or extend appointment.

5.2 Consider the following statements and whether they might be true or false. Provide explanations with your answers.

(a) The directors of the client company sign the audit engagement letter.

(b) The auditor must always discover fraud and other irregularities.

(c) Fees of the auditor are based on the time taken and the grade of staff involved in the assignment.

(d) A business risk approach by auditors is wider than the audit risk approach.

5.3 The audit firm consists of a collection of individuals with varying degrees of experience and expertise. Briefly describe the role that individual staff members play in achieving audit objectives.

5.4 You are the senior in charge of the audit of a local newspaper and have been asked by your audit assistant to explain what kinds of income and expenditure can be expected to arise in the company. She is also anxious to know if there are any particular problems that might be faced by management and, therefore, the auditor. Think of problems such as reporting on circulation of the newspaper to government or independent bodies and maintenance of circulation.

5.5 Discuss briefly the following statements (in doing this, try to go beyond the text of this chapter and use your imagination to explore the statement).

(a) Audit risk is the risk that control systems will not detect material misstatements in the financial statements subject to audit.

(b) Cumulative client knowledge enables the auditor to be more efficient and aids effectiveness in the audit process. Explain what you understand by cumulative client knowledge. Ask yourself what information about an organization would be useful to you on a permanent basis.

(c) The letter of engagement is of little value, as most clients will not understand what it means.

Self-assessment questions (solutions available to tutors)

5.6 Take another look at both the County Hotel and Fine Faces and discuss the proposition that auditors are so willing to help management that they might forget that their primary duty is to form an opinion on the financial statements issued to and used by third parties.

5.7 What are the main practical differences between the audit risk approach and the business risk approach to auditing?

5.8 'It is very easy to apply the audit risk model. All you have to do is to multiply figures together to determine the amount of testing you have to do.' Discuss this statement.

5.9 Explain to your assistant what is meant by audit judgement and give examples of its application. How certain can you be that your judgement has produced the right answer?

Solutions available to students and Solutions available to tutors

These can be found on the website in the student/lecturer section at: www.cengage.co.uk/graymanson5.

Topics for class discussion without solutions

5.10 The exercise of judgement is key to attaining audit objectives. Discuss.

5.11 The business risk approach endangers the independence of the auditor. Discuss.

6

The search for evidence explained

LEARNING OBJECTIVES

After studying this chapter you should be able to:

- **Explain why the audit evidence search is a central concept of auditing.**
- **Identify the stages of the audit process and show that evidence has to be collected in different ways at each stage.**
- **Explain the relationship between audit evidence and audit risk.**
- **Show that there are different grades of audit evidence and that evidence may be upgraded or downgraded.**
- **Explain the relationship between audit evidence and the application of audit judgement.**
- **Show to what extent the evidence-gathering process might be affected by a decision by the auditor to rely on the directors and the control environment they have introduced.**
- **Form conclusions on the basis of evidence available in selected scenarios.**
- **Explain the difference between an audit, a limited assurance engagement, a compilation engagement and an engagement involving agreed upon procedures and suggest how the evidence-gathering process may differ between them.**

Learning objectives, 212
The audit defined as a search for evidence to enable an opinion to be formed, 213
Forming conclusions on the basis of evidence: the exercise of judgement, 216
Reliability of audit evidence (grades of audit evidence), 220
The business risk approach to gathering audit evidence, 228
The stages of the audit process and the evidential requirements at each stage, 229
Limited assurance and compilation engagements and agreed upon procedures, 232
Conclusion, 234
Summary, 234
Key points of the chapter, 235
References, 236
Further reading, 236
Self-assessment questions (solutions available to students), 236
Self-assessment questions (solutions available to tutors), 237
Topics for class discussion without solutions, 239

THE AUDIT DEFINED AS A SEARCH FOR EVIDENCE TO ENABLE AN OPINION TO BE FORMED

Introduction

In this chapter we will show you that the whole audit process is essentially a search for evidence to enable the auditor to form an opinion. In the external audit context the opinion is formed from a whole series of conclusions in pursuit of the main audit objectives of:

- Verifying the accuracy and dependability of the accounting records.
- Giving an opinion on the truth and fairness of financial statements.
- Being satisfied that legislation and accounting and reporting standards have been complied with.

This chapter is important because we are using it to set the scene for future chapters where we shall discuss the evidence search in detail. We shall refer back to this chapter from time to time because it is here that we are discussing the basis of the evidence search and the principles you should know to aid the search in practice. The evidence search may differ somewhat in emphasis if the auditor is adopting a business risk approach rather than an audit risk approach, but the general principles will be the same.

The relevant ISAs in the area are ISA 500 – *Audit evidence*, ISA 501 – *Audit evidence: specific considerations for selected items,* and ISA 330 – *The Auditor's responses to assessed risks*. Paragraph 1 of ISA 500 states that the ISA:

> Explains what constitutes audit evidence in an audit of financial statements, and deals with the auditor's responsibility to design and perform audit procedures to obtain sufficient appropriate audit evidence to be able to draw reasonable conclusions on which to base the auditor's opinion.

We shall have to take a close look at some of the words in this paragraph, and in particular at the meaning of the words 'sufficient' and 'appropriate', but first let us define 'audit evidence':

> 'Audit evidence' is the information used by the auditor in arriving at the conclusions on which the auditor's opinion is based. Audit evidence includes both information contained in the accounting records underlying the financial statements and other information.

See Paragraph 5 (c) of ISA 500.

To start our discussion of audit evidence we would like to make several basic points before we go further:

1 Sufficient, appropriate audit evidence has to be obtained to reduce audit risk to an acceptably low level, and thereby enable the auditor to draw reasonable conclusions on which to base the auditor's opinion on the financial statements.

  We have already seen in Chapter 5 that 'reasonable assurance' or 'reasonable conclusions' mean that the auditor cannot give a guarantee that the financial statements give a true and fair view. We shall see in this chapter that the auditor has to exercise judgement in deciding that the audit evidence collected is sufficient and appropriate and that most of the time the evidence will be persuasive rather than conclusive in forming audit conclusions. Because much audit evidence is merely persuasive auditors seek evidence from different sources to support the same assertion. In other words, the auditor seeks corroborative evidence. A number of ISAs address this question of persuasive evidence. For instance paragraph 7 (b) of ISA 330 states that the auditor should 'Obtain more persuasive audit evidence the higher the auditor's assessment of risk', and paragraph A 19 expands on this by saying:

> When obtaining more persuasive audit evidence because of a higher assessment of risk, the auditor may increase the quantity of the evidence, or obtain evidence that is more relevant or reliable, for example, by placing more emphasis on obtaining third party evidence or by obtaining corroborating evidence from a number of independent sources.

We expand on relevance and reliability below and on corroborative evidence later in this chapter when we discuss Figure 6.2 on page 227.

Another important point to be made here is that collecting audit evidence is like making a picture. It is cumulative in nature in that as the auditor collects audit evidence the final picture of the validity of an assertion gradually emerges.

2 Audit evidence is not merely collected within the audited entity but also from sources outwith the entity and independent of it. We shall see later in this chapter that independent sources can provide evidence of high quality, such as that from lawyers. You will remember that in the Andrew and James case in Chapter 1 the 'value' of the lorry was obtained from an independent source.

See page 6.

Refer to paragraphs A10 to A25 of ISA 500.

3 Auditors collect audit evidence using a number of different procedures, including:
   - Inquiry
     Inquiry will normally not be sufficient on its own, but we have already seen in Chapter 5 that inquiry of key people in the entity at the initial stage of understanding the organization was an important means of obtaining audit evidence. Inquiry would be particularly important where evidential matter appears to be contradictory. An example might be inquiries made when comparison of inventory records with quantities counted reveal material discrepancies.
   - Inspection
     The auditor inspects documents and accounting records for a number of different reasons, but to give one example the auditor might inspect inventory records and compare them with records of inventory counted, possibly as a test of a control. Auditors also inspect assets, such as equipment or inventories to satisfy themselves that they exist.

ACTIVITY 6.1

Explain why inspection of a piece of equipment in the entity's factory would not give evidence that it belonged to the entity.

Proving existence is one thing, proving ownership is another. The entity might have hired the equipment for a short space of time. This means that the auditor would have to inspect documents to prove that it had been bought by the entity and perhaps see if it had been included in the non-current assets budget at some point before purchase and was included in the non-current assets register. This shows that auditors use a number of procedures when collecting audit evidence.

- Observation
  Auditors often observe processes and procedures carried out by entity staff to obtain evidence that the process is being properly performed. A good example of this is observation of inventory counts performed by client staff. Observation would also be combined by inspection, as auditors would select a number of inventory items for inspection to ensure that they had been properly counted, doing this by counting them themselves and then checking that their count results agreed with that of the client's staff.
- Confirmation
  Confirmations from third parties external to the entity can be a very valuable source of auditor evidence to support trade receivables and from such people as lawyers and actuaries. Confirmation is stronger evidence than inquiry to the client's staff as it is in written form and from independent sources.

ISA 505 – *External confirmations* deals with the rationale for confirmations from third parties and audit procedures in relation to them.

- Recalculation
  Recalculation would be a useful procedure when assessing whether documents and records had been properly prepared, recalculating either manually or electronically, for instance, figures appearing on sales invoices. Another example might be the recalculation of a bank reconciliation statement.
- Reperformance
  An example would be the use of the computer to reperform the ageing of trade receivables We discuss the use of CAATs (computer-assisted audit techniques) in Chapters 9 and 10.
- Analytical procedures
  We have already seen in this book that analytical procedures represent an important tool for assessing risk. But they are also used throughout the audit process to establish whether the figures in the accounting and financial records make sense. This is done by analysing relationships among both financial and non-financial data. The auditor would determine what factors were used by the entity as a measure of success and use analytical procedures to investigate significant trends.

Sufficient appropriate audit evidence

Now let us consider the question of 'sufficient appropriate audit evidence'. Basically, sufficiency is a measure of the *quantity* of audit evidence, while appropriateness is a measure of its *quality*.

We discussed confidence level in Chapter 5 in relation to detection risk and discuss it in greater depth in Chapter 11.

1 'Sufficient' means that enough evidence has to be obtained by the auditor to meet audit objectives, a major factor being the degree of confidence required. Note that there is a link between persuasiveness of audit evidence and quantity as auditors seek to be persuaded that their objectives have been met by accumulating evidence. (See Table 6.1 below in this respect).
2 'Appropriate' has two elements and means that the evidence is:
   - Relevant (the evidence must be pertinent to the matter in hand, to a management assertion you wish to prove).
   - Reliable (the evidence must be trustworthy. You will find, however, that there are many grades of evidence, some being more reliable or trustworthy than others).

We show these relationships in Figure 6.1.

Note at this point that sufficiency and appropriateness are related, as the higher the quality of the audit evidence the less may be required. For instance, if tests of quantity of inventory on hand reveal that inventory records are accurate, the auditor will be able to reduce the number of inventory items counted. On the other hand if the quality of audit evidence is poor, obtaining more evidence will probably not give greater satisfaction to the auditor. For instance if the quality of information in the accounting records is low, extended analytical procedures are unlikely to give the audit the evidence required.

Later in this book we shall show that before the search for audit evidence commences, the auditors will set objectives, based on management assertions, that they hope to achieve. We shall see that auditors need to determine what evidence is needed to meet the objective in question.

FIGURE 6.1 Audit evidence supporting reasonable conclusions

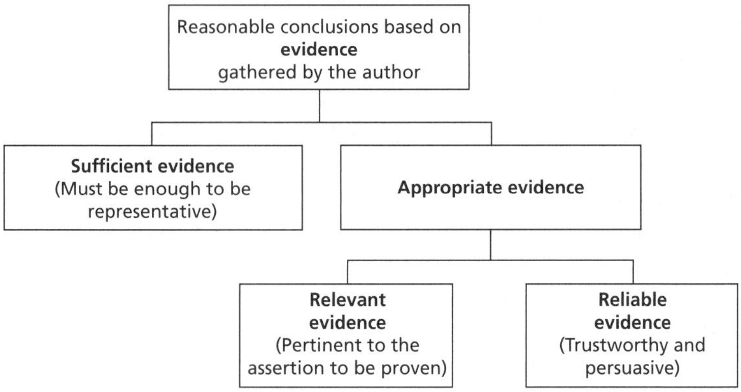

FORMING CONCLUSIONS ON THE BASIS OF EVIDENCE: THE EXERCISE OF JUDGEMENT

It is important you understand that evidence is the cornerstone of the audit process and that it is a prerequisite for forming an opinion. No rational person would argue that, without evidence, it would be possible to come to a reasoned conclusion about anything. You should not assume that the search for audit evidence is an easy matter. It needs the exercise of considerable imagination and the relevant evidence is frequently difficult to find, being often concealed, intentionally or unintentionally. Auditors are wont to use the term 'the search for scarce evidence', to indicate this. Before we discuss the audit process in detail, we will examine the idea that evidence will provide you with the basis for believing whether a statement is true or false. Imagine you have read in the local newspaper that 10 per cent of all private motor vehicles are dangerous because their tyres lack tread of sufficient depth (less than 1 mm) and that you have tested this assertion by examining the tyres of 100 vehicles in your neighbourhood, selected randomly, with the results shown in Table 6.1.

Let us assume that you have decided beforehand that you had selected 100 vehicles because you needed this number to make the vehicles selected representative of all private motor vehicles in your area. Your work would seem to bear out the statement that 10 per cent of vehicles have a tyre tread of less than 1 mm, although at first you may have had some doubts because after the selection of 30 vehicles, poor tread rates exceeded 10 per cent. The question as to whether the vehicles are, as a consequence, unsafe is a more difficult matter to prove; nevertheless this example does give us some help in showing how people generally, and auditors in particular, try to form conclusions. Note that if you had only selected 30 vehicles you would have been wrongly persuaded that 13 per cent of vehicles had a tread of less than 1 mm, giving support again to the idea that quantity of evidence is important. As you progressed towards testing 100 vehicles, your view is likely to have strengthened towards acceptance of the statement.

TABLE 6.1 Tyre tread data

	Batch size	Total examined	Poor tread this batch	Poor tread cumulative	This batch (%)	Cumulative (%)
First 10 vehicles	10	10	2	2	20	20
Next 10 vehicles	10	20	1	3	10	15
Next 10 vehicles	10	30	1	4	10	13
Next 10 vehicles	10	40	0	4	0	10
Next 10 vehicles	10	50	0	4	0	8
Next 10 vehicles	10	60	2	6	20	10
Next 10 vehicles	10	70	1	7	10	10
Next 10 vehicles	10	80	2	9	20	11
Next 10 vehicles	10	90	0	9	0	10
Next 10 vehicles	10	100	1	10	10	10

Whilst you may start off with a position of neutrality in relation to a statement (an assertion relating to a set of accounts, for instance), as you collect evidence, you begin to form conclusions as to whether you should accept or reject the assertion. When you feel you have collected enough evidence, you should be able to state with confidence whether the statement or assertion is acceptable to you. In practice, as we have already suggested, the auditor has to consider relevance and reliability as well as a sufficiency of evidence. Thus, although we have said that the sample has to be large enough to be representative, it will only be reliable if it has been selected on a random basis, giving each item (all vehicles in the neighbourhood in the case of our example) an equal chance of being selected. We must also be sure that the evidence is relevant. Thus, we have already posed the question as to whether at least 1 mm of tread, ensures that the vehicle is safe. If it does not our evidence collection could hardly be described as relevant to the question of safety.

Before we move to some practical examples we consider the kinds of assertion management make in respect of classes of transactions and events during the period, and about account balances at the end of the period. Of course, auditors will be far more likely to accept that management assertions, implied or otherwise, are true if they believe that management are competent and possess integrity. Identification of these assertions is important for the auditor as they form the basis for audit objectives and we set them out in Table 6.2.

These are stated in paragraph A111 of ISA 315.

We find the general headings of genuine, accurate and complete to be useful and have indicated these in Table 6.2. You should note that these assertions are interrelated. If inventory exists (a genuineness assertion), it will make the assertion that valuation is proper (an accuracy assertion) more likely. If a company has entered into an obligation (a genuineness assertion), as they would if they had purchased goods on credit, we would expect that obligation to be correctly valued (an accuracy assertion). We shall refer to Table 6.2 from time to time throughout this book.

Let us now turn to a financial statements example. Directors are required to state that the published financial statements prepared by them give a 'true and fair view' of what they purport to show. This is a general assertion by management. In practice auditors break down this general assertion into a whole series of separate representations or assertions. To do this, they split the financial statements into components, an example being recorded trade receivables in the balance sheet. Directors make the implicit assertions that trade receivables are genuine, accurate and complete. Below are some specific assertions about trade receivables.

- The persons or entities owing the trade receivables exist and have an obligation to pay the amounts stated in the entity's trade receivables ledger (this is basically a genuineness assertion). In this case relevant evidence could be sales invoices supported by pre-numbered sales despatch notes and sales orders, combined with controls such as independent checking of completeness of despatch notes and sales orders. This would enhance the likelihood that credit sales are not only genuine but have been accurately and completely recorded. If credit sales are genuine, accurate and complete, trade receivables should also be genuine, accurate and complete, assuming that receipts from customers have been properly recorded as well.
- Trade receivable balances are fully collectible, and if not, an appropriate provision for bad and doubtful debts has been made (this is an accuracy assertion). Relevant evidence in this case would be very different from that required for the previous assertion above. The auditor might, for instance, examine trade receivable ageing statements to see which amounts are significantly overdue. Another source of relevant evidence might be trade receivable balances exceeding credit limits, or amounts paid by credit customers since the year-end.

- All amounts owed by credit customers are included in the amount attributed to trade receivables in the financial statements and relate to the correct period (this is a completeness assertion). Relevant evidence in this case might include cut-off tests to ensure that sales on credit are reflected in the right period and to make sure that trade receivables include all amounts owed at the year-end. Similar tests would be carried out on cash received from credit customers to ensure that amounts received before the year-end are deducted from trade receivable balances. You will note that we also considered completeness of despatch notes in the first assertion also.

TABLE 6.2 Assertions used by the auditor

General category	Specific category	Our general heading
(a) Assertions about classes of transactions and events for the period under audit	(i) Occurrence – transactions and events that have been recorded have occurred and pertain to the entity.	Genuine
	(ii) Completeness – all transactions and events that should have been recorded have been recorded.	Complete
	(iii) Accuracy – amounts and other data relating to recorded transactions and events have been recorded appropriately.	Accurate
	(iv) Cut-off – transactions and events have been recorded in the correct accounting period.	Accurate
(b) Assertions about account balances at the period end	(i) Existence – assets, liabilities, and equity interests exist.	Genuine
	(ii) Rights and obligations – the entity holds or controls the rights to assets, and liabilities are the obligations of the entity.	Genuine
	(iii) Completeness – all assets, liabilities and equity interests that should have been recorded have been recorded.	Complete
	(iv) Valuation and allocation – assets, liabilities, and equity interests are included in the financial statements at appropriate amounts and any resulting valuation or allocation adjustments are appropriately recorded.	Accurate
(c) Assertions about presentation and disclosure	(i) Occurrence and rights and obligations – disclosed events, transactions, and other matters have occurred and pertain to the entity.	Genuine
	(ii) Completeness – all disclosures that should have been included in the financial statements have been included.	Complete
	(iii) Classification and understandability – financial information is appropriately presented and described, and disclosures are clearly expressed.	Accurate
	(iv) Accuracy and valuation – financial and other Information are disclosed fairly and at appropriate	Accurate

This kind of thinking can be very useful in the examination room where you have a question that asks you to design audit tests in a particular area. A good way to gain marks is to identify assertions first and then formulate tests to address them.

As we mentioned above, this sort of approach can be very useful for auditors as it enables them to set objectives more easily and places the evidence search into a suitable context.

You will note that we mentioned controls in the first assertion and having read Chapter 5 you will have a good appreciation of their role in reducing control risk. Clearly, if sales despatch notes and sales orders were not pre-numbered, control risk would be high because the inherent risk that goods despatched might not be invoiced would not have been mitigated by an appropriate control.

Now take a look at Paragraph A29 of ISA 500, which states:

> Tests of controls are designed to evaluate the operating effectiveness of controls in preventing, or detecting and correcting, material misstatements at the assertion level. Designing tests of controls to obtain relevant audit evidence includes identifying conditions (characteristics or attributes) that indicate performance of a control, and deviation conditions which indicate departures from adequate performance. The presence or absence of those conditions can then be tested by the auditor.

Thus, appropriate evidence in seeking to prove that controls over completeness of recording sales are adequate, would be tests on the sequence of the numbering of the relevant documents.

It is worth mentioning at this point that the only way that auditors can keep audit risk to acceptable proportions is to seek evidence to prove that management assertions are reasonable in the context of the subject of the audit.

RELIABILITY OF AUDIT EVIDENCE (GRADES OF AUDIT EVIDENCE)

Guidelines for assessing evidence reliability

Before we look at a particular case, we first introduce some guidelines to help in assessing the reliability of evidence. In this connection you should refer to Paragraph A31 of ISA 500, which suggests that certain generalizations about the reliability of audit evidence may be useful. This paragraph does warn, however, that care has to be taken in assessing reliability, giving the example of audit evidence obtained from sources external to the entity. External sources independent from the entity are generally regarded as providing reliable evidence, but if the source is not knowledgeable or is not as independent as it appears to be, the evidence derived from it may not be reliable at all. We comment on each generalization below.

1. The reliability of audit evidence is increased when it is obtained from independent sources outside the entity

Assume you are the auditor of a timber importation entity and that the timber is held in bonded warehouses until required by the entity for manufacture and sale. The auditor would normally regard a letter from the management of the bonded warehouse confirming that they hold the timber on behalf of your client as good evidence, provided that the warehouse company is of good reputation. Another example would be a letter from a bank manager confirming bank balances in the name of the client, overdraft limit, charges on entity assets in the name of the bank and so on.

We do, however, make a distinction between evidence provided by independent third parties acting in a professional capacity (the bank manager referred to above, for instance, or lawyers, or other qualified accountants) and evidence from third parties such as customers and suppliers in the business contact group. We are not suggesting that a letter from a credit customer confirming that the amount due from him/her, correctly recorded in the books of the client entity is not useful. We believe it to be very useful, but generally, nonprofessional business contacts such as customers may have a closer, more dependent relationship to the entity. Neither can the auditor be certain that the credit customer's accounting and control systems are reliable.

For the reasons discussed above we will restate this basic rule as follows:

> Evidence from independent sources outside the entity is more reliable, particularly when received from persons acting in a professional capacity.

Note that we are not trying to classify evidence in a rigid manner. We are merely suggesting that, taken on their own, some kinds of evidence are better than others in that they are more reliable. Furthermore, much evidence may be available that came originally from third parties but, being in the hands of management, may have been manipulated in some way.

Typical third party evidence in the hands of the audited entity are: invoices from suppliers, sales orders received from customers and bank statements received from banks. On the whole, such evidence is of good quality from the point of view of the auditor but as it has been in the hands of company officials, it may have been manipulated or, at the extreme, may even be false. The auditor cannot accept such evidence at face value and must take other steps to confirm its accuracy. A bank statement should, for instance, be confirmed by obtaining a confirmation direct from the bank.

2. The reliability of audit evidence that is generated internally is increased when the related controls, including those over its preparation and maintenance, imposed by the entity are effective

An example will show clearly the meaning of this generalization. Let us assume that the auditor wishes to verify the existence of plant and machinery stated at cost in the accounting records. One way to do this would be to take the entity's non-current assets register, containing information about the asset including reference number and location, and reconcile it (perhaps on a test basis) to the non-current assets actually held by the company. In this case we are using the non-current assets register as a source of evidence for existence of non-current assets. However, it will be much enhanced as evidence if it is maintained by officials separate from those who have custody of the actual non-current assets. And, if those officials (perhaps in the accounting department) reconcile the register to the assets periodically. The auditor will test the entries in the non-current assets register to ensure that it is a complete and accurate record. The register would be even better as a source of evidence if the control environment included regular training of staff to make them aware of the reason for the controls that they are performing.

What the auditor is hoping to achieve by using the non-current assets register is to substantiate the figures relating to non-current assets and depreciation in the balance sheet and profit and loss account. In this case, the assertions are that the figures for non-current assets, accumulated depreciation and depreciation charge of the year are genuine, accurate and complete. In particular we wish to ascertain that the non-current assets exist, that the entity has the right to the assets, that all such assets are recorded and that the accumulated depreciation has resulted in an appropriate value. The non-current assets register can be used to substantiate the figures, but it is only reliable if the controls over its preparation are adequate.

3. Audit evidence obtained directly by the auditor (for example, observation of the application of a control) is more reliable than audit evidence obtained indirectly or by inference (for example, inquiry about the application of a control)

If you are sitting in a chair when you are reading this book, touch the chair with your free hand and ask yourself if it is there (does it exist?). If it isn't there you are in trouble, but we imagine that you will very easily be able to confirm its existence. The auditor uses this kind of evidence when counting inventories on hand to compare later with inventory records.

Furthermore, analysis and observation carried out by auditors is good evidence. Although more intangible than the evidence concerning inventories mentioned above, analysis of audit evidence collected by auditors, making sure that it supports other evidence collected, will normally produce very good evidence. Another kind of analysis that is useful to auditors is analytical review of accounting information performed by auditors themselves, resulting in reliable evidence, or at least a reliable basis for further questioning of management. One note of caution in respect of analytical review is that interpretation is frequently a difficult matter. Also, although analytical review can be very valuable to the auditor, a ratio, for instance, is only as good as the figures used to calculate it.

4. Audit evidence in documentary form, whether paper, electronic, or other medium, is more reliable than evidence obtained orally (for example, a contemporaneously written record of a meeting is more reliable than a subsequent oral representation of the matters discussed)

During an audit, the auditor will receive a wide variety of oral evidence from officials of the client. Much of this oral evidence will be reflected in the working files of the auditor and this act of recording does have the effect of making the evidence more useful and more reliable. As a matter of policy audit firms should require staff members to record immediately in the working files (whether computerized or manual) minutes of meetings held with the client's staff. Some of the oral statements made by management will be included in a formal letter of representation from management to the auditor, thus putting this guidance on evidence into effect. An example of a representation would be 'There have been no legal cases affecting the company other than those of which you have been informed'.

ISA 230 – *Audit documentation* states that the auditor shall prepare audit documentation on a timely basis. We discuss management representations at greater length in Chapter 14.

5. Audit evidence provided by original documents is more reliable than audit evidence provided by photocopies or facsimiles, or documents that have been filmed, digitized or otherwise transformed into electronic form, the reliability of which may depend on the controls over their preparation and maintenance

The reason for this generalization is clear. It would be very easy to manipulate a photocopy or facsimile.

Apart from the above five generalizations we suggest that the following four matters are also of importance.

6. Evidence created in the normal course of business is better than evidence specially created to satisfy the auditor

Let us suppose that the auditor needs evidence to prove (say) that inventories held at the year-end have a net realizable value above cost. Up-to-date order books and market research reports, prepared for day-to-day use in the business, will provide the auditor with good evidence of saleability of inventory. Such evidence will be better than evidence collected on an *ad hoc* basis. The point is, of course, that information collected on a day-to-day basis is less likely to be biased than specially created evidence. If you refer to the County Hotel case we discussed in Chapter 5, hotels clearly need to keep detailed records of occupancy for management purposes. This sort of information has to be accurate so they can tell a potential customer if a room is available or not, or which times of the year need special rates to encourage visitors. It will have greater value than evidence produced 'just to satisfy the auditor'.

7. The best-informed source of audit evidence will normally be management of the company but management's lack of independence reduces its value as a source of such evidence

Let us give a simple example. During the analytical review, an auditor notes that trade receivables represent 60 days sales in the current year compared with 45 days in the prior year and becomes concerned that this might indicate the need to increase the bad or doubtful debts provision. On enquiry, the chief accountant says that this is the result of a policy decision on the part of the directors, taken as a result of increased competition in the industry of which the entity forms a part. The statement by the chief accountant is a good example of well-informed internal comment and one that the auditor would seek to corroborate. Possible sources of corroborative evidence might include:

- Directors' minutes of the meeting at which the policy decision was taken.
- Instructions issued on a routine basis to credit control staff in the entity.
- Commentaries in the financial press and trade press confirming the increased competition in the industry and the steps taken as a result.

8. Evidence about the future is particularly difficult to obtain and is less reliable than evidence about past events

Auditors frequently have to consider future events in the course of their duties. Examples of such events are:

- Outcome of potential legal claims.
- Net realizable values of inventories.

- Collectability of trade receivables.
- Useful lives of non-current assets.

Although it may be more difficult for the auditor to obtain evidence about the future, its main feature being the uncertainty associated with it, there are ways in which the future may be made less cloudy. Generally speaking, the auditors' view of future events is likely to be coloured by their opinion of the reliability of management, the extent to which management has proved able to anticipate the future in the past and the means by which management itself attempts to control the future. Good company-generated evidence about the future might include budgets for control purposes, forecasts of profits and up-to-date price lists for the post-balance sheet period. Other evidence about the future which must be treated with great care might include:

- Government reports about the state of the economy.
- Comments by industry leaders.
- Reports in the trade and financial press.

9. Evidence may be upgraded by the skilful use of corroborative evidence

We have already seen that other evidence may corroborate statements by client officials and that evidential material may be rendered more useful by the source from which it is derived being subjected to adequate control. The idea of upgrading of evidence is very important in the audit process, as, indeed, is the rejection of evidence as the result of downgrading and we discuss this aspect below. When reading the next section you should remember that corroborative evidence is evidence that is consistent with the data or information you have already collected. Note that when you find evidence that corroborates another piece of evidence, both pieces of evidence are much enhanced, so that taken together they are more valuable than the sum of their individual values. This is one case where two + two may indeed equal five.

It has been our intention in this section to introduce you to a few basic rules for evaluating audit evidence. Evaluation of evidence requires in practice the use of considerable judgement on the part of the auditor but rules, sensibly applied, can be very useful in aiding judgement. We shall invite you to refer to this section from time to time in later chapters of this book.

The use of corroborative evidence and the upgrading process

Now let us look at a brief case in which the ideas we have discussed above will be put into context.

CASE STUDY 6.1

Ridgewalk plc

Assume that you are auditing Ridgewalk plc, a trading entity, which markets a wide range of goods (some 1000 in number). The sales are all on credit and the entity has some 1000 customers. In the year to 30 June 2010, Ridgewalk issued approximately 50000 sales invoices using a computerized sales system. The company maintains (also on the computer) a detailed inventory record system. Some relevant figures for the current and prior years are as follows:

	2009	2010
	£	£
Sales	6 250 000	4 500 000
Gross profit %	50	48
General ledger entry	800 000	600 000
Inventories	500 000	350 000

You have been asked by the senior in charge of the audit assignment to satisfy yourself that the sales figure for 2010 amounting to £6 250 000 is true and fair in the context of the financial statements taken as a whole.

Let us suggest a fruitful way to approach this task, by asking a series of questions.

1 Would you say that the copy sales invoices (all 50 000 of them) represent useful evidence?

Probably not, in themselves. Copy sales invoices by their nature can easily be reproduced and it looks as though you will have to look further to satisfy yourself that they represent genuine sales. There are also rather a lot of them and even if you only spent one second on each one, it would take approximately two working days to complete the checking of them.

2 Do you think that it would be sufficient to look at a sample of the invoices in detail?

It is, in fact, common for auditors to do this but before you decide how big the sample should be, you would have to consider other matters, such as the degree of confidence you wish to obtain from the sample and materiality limits.

See our comments on detection risk in Chapter 5, pages 155–167. See also our discussion of sampling in Chapter 11.

3 Do you think that the number of invoices you would have to test in detail could be reduced to manageable proportions if:

(a) The company's control environment is good?

(b) The company system for preparing the invoices was a good one?

(c) The sales figure in the accounts makes sense in terms of what you know about the company?

The 50 000 sales invoices will all have passed through a sales system. If you as auditor can satisfy yourself that the control environment is satisfactory and that the system is designed to produce complete and accurate recording of sales, and you have tested and evaluated its operation yourself, this will provide you with useful persuasive evidence to support a conclusion on the sales invoices themselves.

You will remember from our discussion of audit risk in Chapter 5 that assessment of control risk has a direct impact on the number of transactions and balances tested. We shall discuss the control environment at greater length in Chapter 7.

The 50 000 sales invoices should, of course, all be reflected in the sales figure in the financial statements. If your review of the statements, your discussions with management and other work reveals that sales are reasonable in relation to (say) prior years' sales, to cost of sales, to trade receivables, inventories, etc., this will also be evidence enabling you to form a conclusion on the sales invoices.

We shall discuss systems work and analytical review in greater detail in Chapters 7, 8 and 12. We have introduced the topics very briefly here to show you a number of aspects of the evidence search. In brief, the auditor will be able to reduce the detailed testing of the sales invoices if the systems work (including that on the control environment) and analytical review produce supportive evidence. This supportive evidence corroborates the rather weak evidence of the copy sales invoice and, in so doing, strengthens it. We shall consider the impact of this after we have considered a number of other factors.

4 Every sale causes a movement in goods to occur. Do you think you could use this fact in the circumstances of this company to find additional supportive evidence for the sales invoices?

We have been told that the company operates a computer-based inventory records system. If our sample sales invoices are all shown as movements in the inventory records, we shall have gone a step further in validating them, particularly if we work in the opposite direction, take an additional sample of inventory record movements and check that they are all included as sales. We do have to take care, however, not to jump too quickly to conclusions. If people independent of sales invoicing prepare the inventory records, they will be able to corroborate the sales invoices and thereby increase their value as evidence. If not, they will be less capable of providing corroborative evidence. This is one of the reasons that it is so important for the auditor to evaluate the control systems established by management.

5 Can you think of any way in which the inventory records themselves can be corroborated by good evidence?

We are sure you can. You will remember that one of the generalizations we discussed above was that *audit evidence obtained directly by the auditor* was a reliable form of evidence. If the auditor compares a sample of inventory record balances with actual inventory on hand and finds there is agreement between the two, a further important step has been taken to corroborate the sales invoices, although the trail is now somewhat longer:

- If quantities of inventory on hand are the same as those shown in the inventory records, the inventory records are likely to be a reliable record of inventory issues also.
- If the inventory record issues are in agreement with sales invoice quantities, this will be persuasive evidence that sales invoice quantities are accurate.

6 Bearing in mind that Ridgewalk plc sells only on credit, is there any other way that you could obtain satisfaction that the sales invoices represent genuine transactions?

We mentioned above that *the reliability of audit evidence is increased when it is obtained from independent sources outside the entity.* Clearly, Ridgewalk's sales will have flowed through trade receivable ledger personal accounts. If the auditor can obtain confirmation of balances and movements on the sales ledger accounts from credit customers, then additional evidence will have been obtained to support the sales invoices we wish to prove form a complete and accurate record of sales during the year. The auditor would clearly wish to ascertain that the trade receivables selected to confirm balances were genuine. Typical procedures to increase this possibility would be for the auditors to post letters to credit customers themselves, to have replies sent directly to the auditor's office, to examine postmarks on reply envelopes carefully, to examine correspondence with selected customers and so on.

We hope that we have not made the audit process appear too easy and the corroboration of the sales invoices too neat. In practice, it might be more difficult than we have suggested. For instance, there might be no inventory records, the company sales might be for cash, the company systems might be poor and the figures in the accounts might not make sense. If this is so the auditor will have to be even more imaginative. What we have tried to show is that auditors must actively seek corroborative evidence if they are to be successful in obtaining audit objectives. We show the corroboration process described below in Figure 6.2.

You should take a careful look at Figure 6.2 and note the relationships between documents and records and the manner in which the auditor uses them. We have extended the diagram to include the corroborative evidence process as it relates to bank transactions.

There is one final point of great importance. If you have selected a sample representative of *all* sales invoices, the upgrading of the sample will have the effect of upgrading *all* the invoices, provided of course that no errors are discovered during tests of sales invoices and supporting documentation.

It is vital that you remember the ultimate audit objective in the sales area – that of establishing the veracity of the figure for sales appearing in the financial statements. In testing the sample of sales invoices you have as an objective, therefore, not merely that of forming an opinion on those invoices in the sample but also on all sales invoices.

FIGURE 6.2 Evidence corroboration and upgrading in a sales system

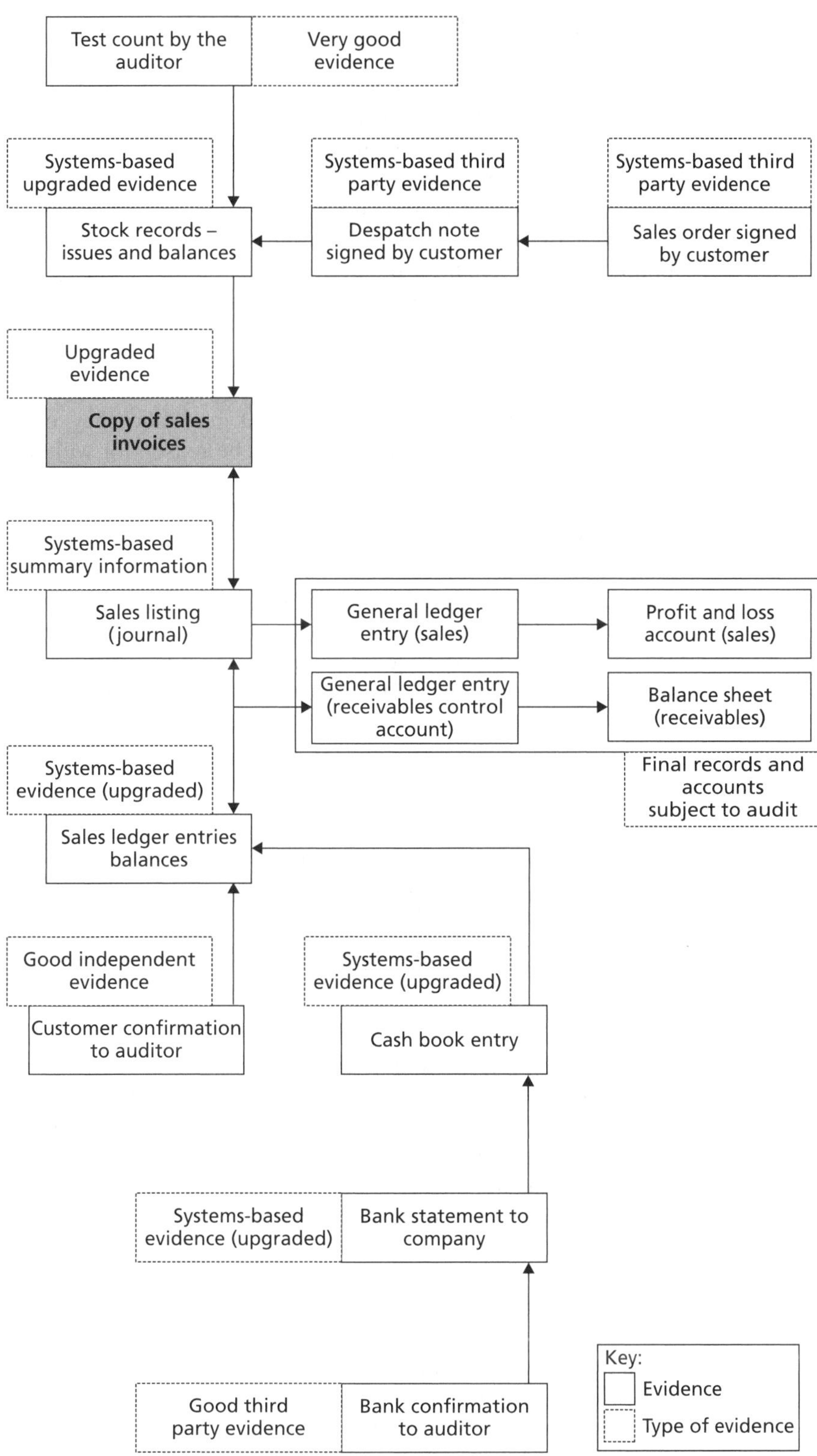

THE BUSINESS RISK APPROACH TO GATHERING AUDIT EVIDENCE

When we discussed risk in Chapter 5 we saw that the auditor concentrates on critical features of the company and that at an early stage would form views on the competence and integrity of management. Clearly, if auditors have formed a good impression of management, evidence emanating from them may well be relied on by the auditor to a much greater extent than if the contrary were the case. Auditors have always done this, but the business risk approaches have heightened a desire to rely on management as far as possible. The approach suggests that as auditors align themselves more with management, they get to know individual members of the management team very well, to the extent that engagement partners feel they can judge their integrity. Protagonists of the business risk approach argue further that close involvement of the audit team with management may show they, either individually or as a whole, lack integrity, which would be reason for withdrawing from the engagement. The point to note here is that trust in the integrity and competence of management of the company will have important consequences for the evidence gathering process. It would mean, for instance, that the auditor would trust the assurances of management about the efficacy of the control environment and of the individual controls to reduce the impact of business/inherent risk. This would lead to a decision to reduce the level of substantive tests of detail and a consequent reduction in audit cost to counterbalance the increased cost of partner and manager time at the planning stage of the audit.

Companies with suspect managements may find it difficult to appoint an audit firm among the larger firms, including the Big Four. There is an article in the April 2003 issue of *Accountancy* (pp. 26–7) by Peter Williams which touches on this topic.

ACTIVITY 6.2

Think about these matters and decide if it is wise to trust management in the way that the protagonists of the business risk approach to auditing believe is possible. Before you do this, go back to Chapter 1 and reread what we had to say about agency theory on pages 9–10.

You will have seen from Chapter 1 that one of the basic ideas of agency theory is that the providers of resources cannot trust managers to use resources on their behalf and may suspect that they are diverted to the benefit of the managers. In the light of Enron, WorldCom, Parmalat and Satyam, you might feel that the agency theorists are right and that it would be very unwise for auditors to accept the word of management, without obtaining considerable corroborative evidence from elsewhere. However, as we all know from our personal lives, trusting other people is the only way for society to operate. Thus, we might agree that it would be unwise to put complete trust in people in charge of resources belonging to other people, but equally the auditor cannot start from a presumption that managements lack integrity. An interesting study was carried out by three academics, Vivien Beattie, Glasgow University, and Stella Fearnley and Richard Brandt, both Portsmouth University, in which they conducted a number of interviews with finance directors of selected companies and engagement partners in charge of the audits of the financial statements of those companies. A number of interesting facts came out of the study, but one of the most important seemed to be the evident integrity of the people involved, both from management and the audit firms.

There was one clear exception where an inexperienced engagement partner was faced by an older and much more experienced financial director. We reference their study at the end of this chapter.

A major issue is clearly that the business risk approach will bring the auditor close to management ('aligning' the auditor with management is a term that suggests this) so that independence may be threatened or, at the very least, appear to be so threatened. As you are aware from Chapter 3, very wide-ranging discussions are presently taking place between regulators and the profession in different parts of the world. Anyone interested in the future of the auditing profession, and we assume that this includes you, will follow these developments very closely. In the meantime, we believe that it would be wise for auditors to consider very carefully the extent to which they are prepared to rely on management. However, you should note that the protagonists of the business risk approach suggest that most audit failures are not because the auditor failed to perform tests of detail, but because they missed clear indicators of impending catastrophe, that might have been discovered by a more intelligent use of procedures, such as analytical review.

We discuss analytical review in greater detail in Chapter 12.

THE STAGES OF THE AUDIT PROCESS AND THE EVIDENTIAL REQUIREMENTS AT EACH STAGE

It is our contention that the auditor gathers audit evidence at all stages of the audit process. We believe, therefore that we should introduce you to the whole of the audit process in broad terms at this stage, bearing in mind that we shall discuss it in greater detail as we proceed through the book. In Figure 6.3 we set out in diagrammatic form the various stages of an external audit, in each case indicating the sort of evidence that will be relevant in achieving audit objectives and the main audit purposes that the auditor has at each stage. The stages we have identified are relevant to all sizes of external audit assignment but we would emphasize that whereas in the case of larger audits, the various stages will normally be separated in time, for the audit of small organizations they may be carried out at the same period. Figure 0.1 in the Preface summarizes Figure 6.3 and shows in which chapters we discuss the various stages of the audit process. You should also refer to Figure 9.5 on page 344 which provides you with a more detailed explanation of walk-through tests, tests of control and substantive procedures and the conclusions and decisions that are made in respect of them.

We think you will find Figure 6.3, of value throughout this book, as supplemented by Figure 9.5, and we suggest that you refer to them from time to time to put audit work into an understandable framework.

Timing of the audit process

We suggested a typical timetable for an audit of a company, Gilsland Electronics Limited, in the first year the audit is carried out in Table 1.1 and you should refer again to that table to see in detail the kind of work that will be carried out at each date and in each period. You should pay particular attention to our comments, but note that the timetable in Table 1.1 assumes that Gilsland is a new audit. In the case of second year and subsequent audits, much information of value to the auditor will have been recorded in permanent audit files, correspondence and other files.

See page 16.

FIGURE 6.3 The audit process: audit stages, evidence-gathering process and main audit

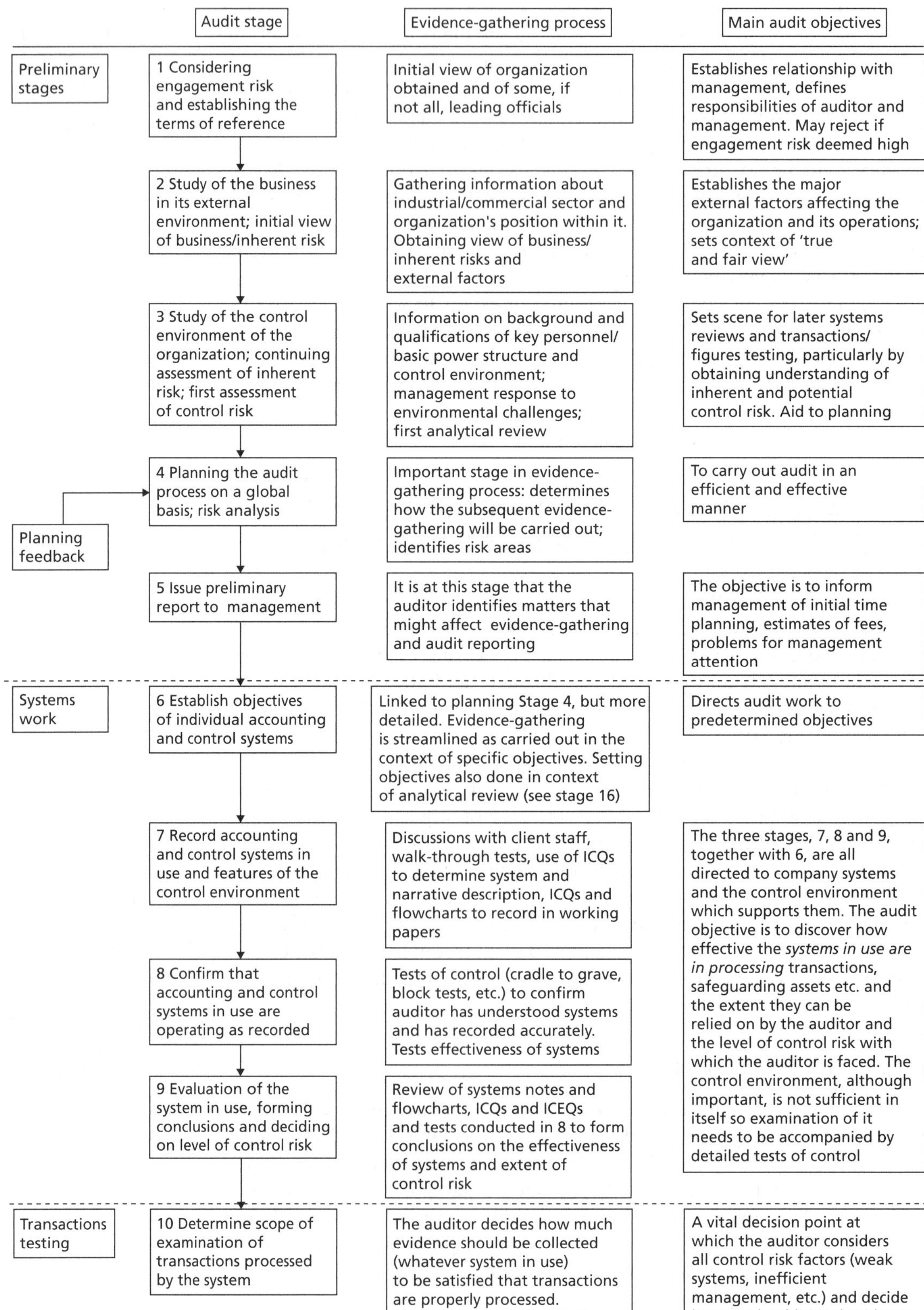

FIGURE 6.3 (Continued)

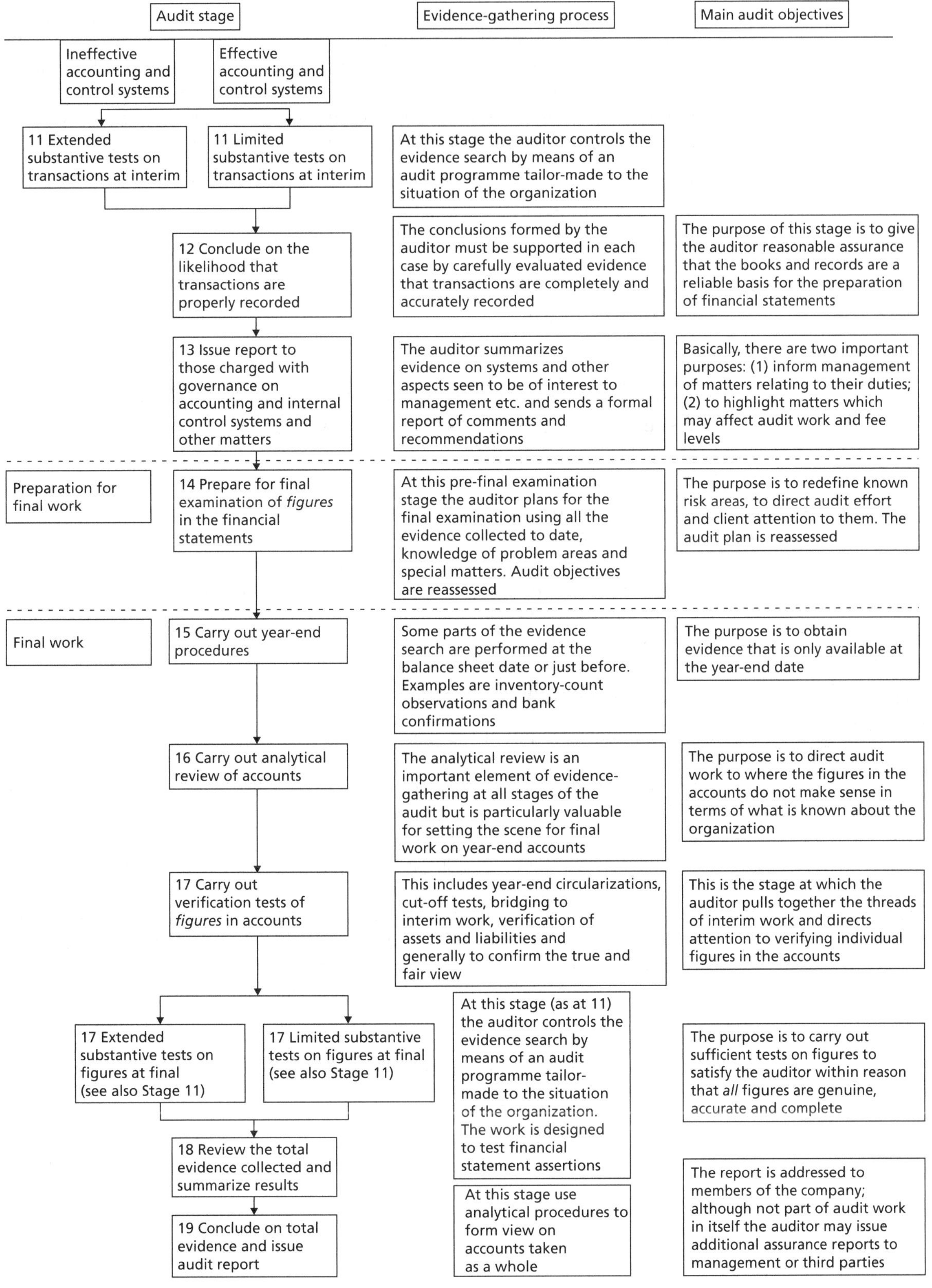

We appreciate we have not discussed in detail the work that would be carried out at each date, in each period and at each stage. This is the subject of the rest of this book. What we hope you have been given by this brief review, is a feel for the audit process in practice and a recognition of the importance of planning if each stage is to be successfully carried through. Auditors today spend a great deal of time in the planning process, mainly because of the current emphasis on identification of risk and the emphasis on risk areas. Other matters we would wish to emphasize (or re-emphasize) at this stage are:

- The importance of personal contact with management.
- In view of this close personal contact, the vital importance of maintaining an independent attitude and of keeping in mind the duty to shareholders and other outside users.
- The whole audit process is essentially a search for evidence to accomplish the audit objectives.

LIMITED ASSURANCE AND COMPILATION ENGAGEMENTS AND AGREED UPON PROCEDURES

This book, as you can see from the title, is about the *audit* process, but professional accountants do carry out other kinds of engagement in relation to financial statements. In this chapter about audit evidence, we wish to suggest the different evidential approaches to three particular kinds of engagement: the compilation engagement; the limited assurance engagement; and agreed upon procedures engagement.

We shall meet up with these kinds of engagement again in Chapter 15 when we discuss assurance engagements as defined by the International Framework for Assurance Engagements, issued by IAASB for IFAC in January 2004. Under the framework, engagements such as those discussed here are either not classified as assurance engagements or give only limited assurance to users because the evidence collected is not sufficient to give reasonable assurance.

The compilation engagement

Professional accountants in this case are engaged to prepare financial statements on the basis of data and information given to them by management, often of a small company that does not possess staff with the necessary skills. This kind of engagement might be requested for the purpose of preparing financial statements for submission to the tax authorities. In this case the professional accountant will issue a compilation report, sometimes known as an accountant's report. The accountant is not required to give any assurance as regards the truth and fairness of the information presented, nor compliance with the Companies Acts and accounting standards. The report will therefore contain a disclaimer stating that an audit has *not* been carried out.

As you would expect the evidence gathering is at a very much lower level than for an audit. However, the accountants do add some credibility to the financial statements, even though an audit has not been carried out, and they would normally carry out the following procedures:

- Find out what accounting principles and practices are common in the entity's industry.
- Get a general understanding of the business, the risks facing it, the nature of the transactions entered into, the accounting principles used and the presentation and content of the financial statements.

- Generally review the financial statements using limited analytical procedures and discuss them critically with management.
- Obtain a letter from management saying that they have been given all the books and records and other information pertinent to the preparation of the financial statements.

The limited assurance engagement

This again is not a full audit but the professional accountant aims to obtain limited assurance that the financial statements comply with the legislation and accounting standards. It is the kind of engagement that a group auditor might require in respect of a subsidiary whose financial statements are not material in the group context, but where a lower level of assurance is required none the less. The review report will state that the review consisted primarily of enquiries of management and analytical procedures related to the financial statements and other information and data, but because the work performed was considerably less than that required to give a full audit opinion, no such opinion is expressed. The report would then give a negative form of opinion stating that, based on the review, the accountant is *not* aware of any material amendments that should be made to the financial statements to make them conform with the requirements of the Companies Act and accounting standards.

The evidence gathering procedures would be broadly as follows:

- Find out what accounting principles and practices are common in the company's industry.
- Get a good understanding of the business, how it is organized, its operating characteristics, the risks facing it and how their impact is reduced by controls, the nature of the transactions entered into and of its assets and liabilities. This work will go much further than the compilation engagement work, although there will be very little in the way of detailed tests.
- Apply analytical procedures to identify any relationships between figures that appear unusual and discuss them with management. The work may involve advising management on appropriate adjustments to the financial statements.
- Obtain a letter of representation from management confirming the significant oral representations made by management during the review. The letter should be signed by persons responsible for the preparation of the financial statements.

We discuss management letters of representation at greater length in Chapter 14.

- At the completion of the review read the financial statements to ascertain that they appear to conform to the requirements of the Companies Act and accounting standards.

You can see that the evidence gathering requirements are again much less than required for a full-scale audit, but that the enquiries of management and the review of information and the analytical procedures performed are much more wide-ranging than is the case with a compilation review. There would, however, be little in the way of detailed tests of transactions and balances unless it would help to clarify matters discussed with management.

The agreed upon procedures engagement

This kind of engagement would be similar to a review except that certain detailed procedures would be performed – as agreed with management. For instance, management might ask the accountant to discuss contingencies, such as pending court cases, with the company's lawyers, or they might be asked to review inventory-taking instructions for reasonableness or even to attend the inventory-take of selected high-value items. The report would indicate the detailed procedures carried out but would again disclaim a full audit opinion.

Clearly, the agreed procedures would require the accountant to seek evidence that the items subject to the agreed procedures (such as the stated contingencies, or the inventory figure) have been stated appropriately.

ACTIVITY 6.3

Now that we have introduced you to the above engagements, do you believe that they will be of value to users?

We think you will agree that the three engagements described above are likely to be of some value to users, even though a full audit opinion is not given. In all cases there has been some evidence gathering and a report prepared by a professional person who would be expected to have performed the work with due care.

CONCLUSION

This has been a very important chapter as it has set the scene for the rest of this book. Our intention has been to introduce you to some ideas about audit evidence and about the audit process itself. You should now read the whole of ISA 500 – *Audit evidence*, and also take note of ISA 501 on *Audit evidence – specific considerations for selected items*, and ISA 505 – *External confirmations.*

ISA 500 is fairly short but you will see that it refers to many of the matters that we have discussed in this chapter. We have considered the impact of the business risk approach on the evidence-gathering process and have also discussed the way in which evidence gathering is restricted where less than a full audit is carried out.

Summary

In this chapter we have attempted to show that evidence is required to give the auditors assurance that they are forming proper conclusions. We see evidence as the cornerstone of the whole audit process and for this reason we described the audit process as an evidence-gathering process. This was shown diagrammatically in Figure 6.3. The audit process was, however, placed within a context as we wished to recognize that evidence gathering does not take place in a vacuum but in real organizations and with the participation of real people. We see this timescale as being important for our later discussions of planning.

In this chapter we have also approached the question of the sufficiency and appropriateness (relevance and reliability) of audit evidence and we considered the different factors that might affect reliability in some detail. An important feature of the chapter has been the section on upgrading and downgrading of audit evidence and the effect that consistent audit evidence has on the conclusions of the auditor.

Key points of the chapter

- The audit process is a search for evidence to enable the auditor to form conclusions about the accuracy and dependability of the accounting records, about the truth and fairness of financial statements and that legislation and accounting and reporting standards have been complied with.
- The auditor's responsibility is to obtain sufficient appropriate audit evidence to be able to draw reasonable conclusions on which to base the audit opinion. The evidence search is designed to reduce audit risk to an acceptably low level. Audit evidence is persuasive and not conclusive and needs to be corroborated. It is cumulative in nature. Audit evidence is collected within the audited entity and from independent sources outwith the audited entity.
- Auditors collect audit evidence using a number of different procedures, including: Inquiry, Inspection, Observation, Confirmation, Recalculation, Re-performance and Analytical procedures.
- In terms of 'sufficient appropriate audit evidence', 'sufficiency' means that enough evidence has to be obtained to meet audit objectives. 'Appropriate' means that the evidence is both relevant and reliable. Sufficiency and appropriateness are related.
- The search for audit evidence needs the exercise of considerable imagination and judgement. Auditors may start off with a position of neutrality in relation to an assertion relating to a set of accounts, but as evidence is collected they begin to form conclusions as to whether they should accept or reject the assertion.
- Management assertions are made about classes of transactions and events for the period under audit, about account balances at the period end, and about presentation and disclosure. They may be classified as 'genuine', 'accurate' and 'complete'.
- Tests of controls are designed to evaluate the operating effectiveness of controls in preventing, or detecting and correcting, material misstatements at the assertion level.
- The reliability of audit evidence is increased when it is obtained from independent sources outside the entity
- Evidence from independent sources outside the entity is more reliable, particularly when received from persons acting in a professional capacity.
- The reliability of audit evidence that is generated internally is increased when the related controls, including those over its preparation and maintenance, imposed by the entity are effective.
- Audit evidence obtained directly by the auditor (for example, observation of the application of a control) is more reliable than audit evidence obtained indirectly or by inference (for example, inquiry about the application of a control).
- Audit evidence in documentary form, whether paper, electronic, or other medium, is more reliable than evidence obtained orally (for example, a contemporaneously written record of a meeting is more reliable than a subsequent oral representation of the matters discussed).
- Audit evidence provided by original documents is more reliable than audit evidence provided by photocopies or facsimiles, or documents that have been filmed, digitized or otherwise transformed into electronic form, the reliability of which may depend on the controls over their preparation and maintenance.
- Evidence created in the normal course of business is better than evidence specially created to satisfy the auditor.
- The best-informed source of audit evidence will normally be management of the company but management's lack of independence reduces its value as a source of such evidence.
- Evidence about the future is particularly difficult to obtain and is less reliable than evidence about past events.
- Evidence may be upgraded by the skilful use of corroborative evidence.
- Business risk approaches result in greater reliance on management, but enables auditors to judge the integrity of individual managers, and to reduce substantive procedures.
- One of the basic ideas of agency theory is that the providers of resources cannot trust managers to use resources on their behalf and that it would be unwise for auditors to accept the word of management, without obtaining considerable corroborative evidence from elsewhere.
- A major issue is that the business risk approach may affect audit independence.
- The auditor gathers audit evidence at all stages of the audit process. Figure 6.3 sets out in diagrammatic form the various stages of an external audit, in each case indicating the sort of evidence that will be relevant in achieving audit objectives and the main audit purposes that the auditor has at each stage. Figure 6.3 is supported by Figure 9.5.

- Professional accountants carry out other kinds of engagement in relation to financial statements, requiring different levels of evidence, and opinions that are at a lower level than reasonable assurance. Three particular kinds of engagement are the compilation engagement; the limited assurance engagement; and agreed upon procedures engagement.

Reference

Beattie, V., Fearnley, S. and Brandt, R. (2001) *Behind Closed Doors: What Company Audit is Really About*, Basingstoke: Palgrave. (Based on research sponsored by The Institute of Chartered Accountants in England and Wales.)

Further reading

The ISAs in the area are:

ISA 500 – *Audit evidence*

ISA 501 – *Audit evidence: specific considerations for selected items,* and

ISA 505 – *External confirmations* are essential reading.

Self-assessment questions (solutions available to students)

6.1 Consider the truth or falsity of the following statements:

(a) Sufficient evidence for the auditor means having enough to form a conclusion that an assertion made by management may be accepted.

(b) Relevant evidence for the auditor would include the following:

  (i) The dates that the chief accountant goes on holiday.

  (ii) A file of recognized suppliers.

  (iii) The place that the chief accountant chooses for his or her holiday.

  (iv) Credit limits of customers buying on credit

(c) Reliable evidence means evidence that has been vetted by the company's directors.

(d) Written evidence from a bank manager is reliable evidence.

(e) Written evidence from within the company is not reliable.

(f) If differing types of evidence are consistent with each other, the auditor can reduce the amount of evidence collected and examined.

(g) Physical inspection by the auditor of a non-current asset provides the auditor with reliable evidence as to its existence, but not as to its ownership, cost or value.

6.2 You are the auditor of Oakshaw Ltd and are searching for evidence to prove that the figures for purchases and related creditors are true and fair in the context of the accounts, taken as a whole. You have extracted the following information from the accounts at 31 December 2010:

		2010	**2009**
	£	**£**	**£**
Turnover		1 500 000	1 400 000
Opening stock	200 000		
Purchases	1 100 000		
	1 300 000		
Closing stock	250 000		
Cost of goods sold		1 050 000	994 000
Gross profit		450 000	406 000

Your audit work has revealed the following:

(i) Discussions with management and other tests show that selling prices have been increased by more than the cost of purchases with the result that gross profit has improved by 1 percentage point.

(ii) The company maintains the following records:

- *Purchase requisitions* from stores to the purchasing department (this is the request that goods be purchased).
- *Purchase orders* made out by the purchasing department on the basis of purchase requisitions and files of information about suppliers (the purchase

order is a request to a supplier of goods to deliver them).

- *Goods received notes* made out by the goods receiving department when goods are received.
- *File of purchase invoices* received from a supplier.
- *Inventory records* showing quantities of receipts, issues and balances of inventory on hand.
- *Purchase journal* in which all invoices are recorded.
- *Purchase ledger* containing personal accounts for each supplier.
- *General ledger accounts*, containing, among other things, purchase accounts and trade payables control account.

(iii) As a result of your systems work you have concluded that each of the above records are held by different people and that they are carefully and properly controlled.

Required:

(a) In Figure 6.4 fill in the blanks to show the relationship between the above records and the purchases and trade payables figures in the accounts. You should refer to Figure 6.2 on page 227 while you are doing this.

(b) Describe the kinds of evidence that can be used to upgrade the various documents and records.

(c) Explain how the systems work and the review of the accounts may help you to accept the figure of 'purchases'.

6.3 Below is a list of sources of audit evidence:

(i) The chief accountant, who is a member of CIMA, explains why inventory levels are higher at the end than at the beginning of the year.

(ii) A storeman in the main store explaining how the store control system operates.

(iii) An invoice from a supplier of electricity.

(iv) A trainee accountant, presently studying for professional accounting examinations, explaining the reason why telephone charges were lower this year than last.

(v) A letter to the auditor from a lawyer confirming that, as far as he is aware, there are no legal matters of material significance.

(vi) A confirmation from a credit customer agreeing that a balance in the books of the entity is correct.

(vii) A calculation of tax charge and liability made by the auditor.

(viii) Inventory count sheets, the count having been observed by the auditor.

(ix) The company's order book, showing orders received from customers. This book is required for company planning purposes.

(x) Estimates of useful life of newly acquired plant, made by the production director.

Required:

(a) Suggest which sources may be regarded as reliable, explaining why this is so.

(b) Suggest how you might upgrade the evidence, if required.

6.4 Explain the meaning of the following terms:

(i) Interim examination.

(ii) Final examination.

(iii) Inconsistent audit evidence.

(iv) Systems-based evidence.

(v) Third-party evidence.

(vi) Persuasive evidence.

Self-assessment questions (solutions available to tutors)

6.5 An important objective of the business risk approach is to make the audit more profitable by cutting down on the amount of evidence obtained by substantive tests of detail. Discuss.

6.6 You are the engagement partner of an audit assignment with an entity specializing in the provision of information technology services and software. At the beginning of the financial year the company entered into a contract with the government of China and you have been discussing the implications of the contract, including the investment in necessary new technology and amounts receivable from the Chinese government. What evidence would you look for to satisfy yourself that business risks have been considered and that the company has taken reasonable steps to reduce the risks? Would this work be useful in ascertaining that management is competent and trustworthy? Assume this is not a new client.

6.7 Explain how a review engagement differs from an audit engagement. Explain why a report on a review engagement might be useful to the person requesting that the engagement be carried out.

6.8 Audit evidence is required to be both sufficient and appropriate. Explain what is meant by this statement giving appropriate examples.

FIGURE 6.4 Oakshow Ltd purchases and related creditors (to be completed)

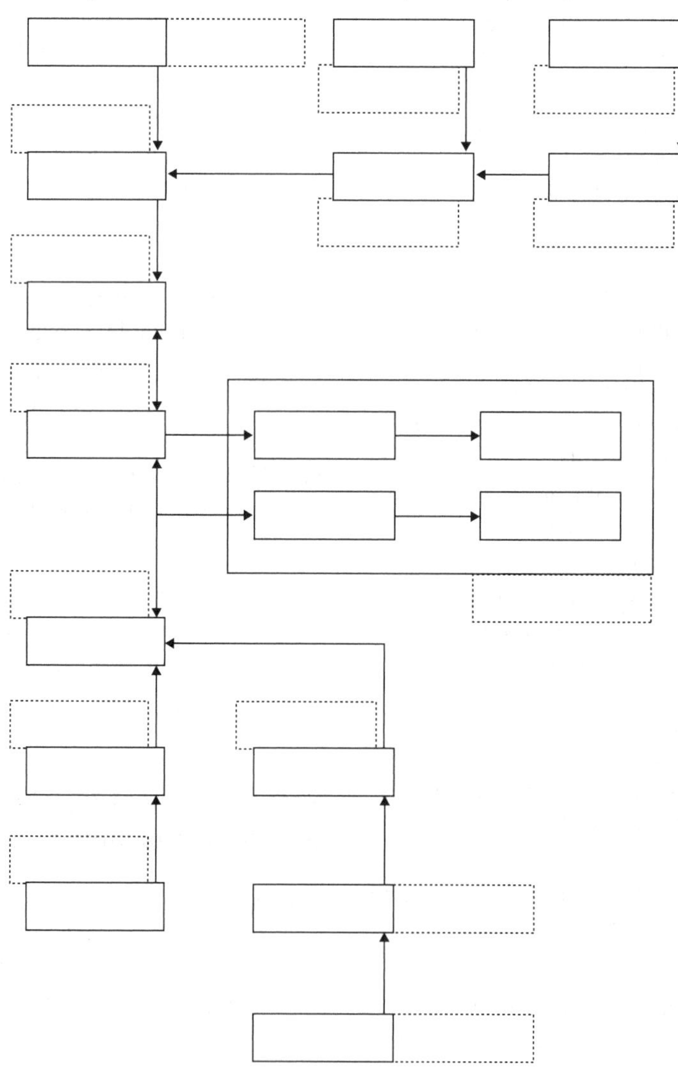

Topics for class discussion without solutions

6.9 There is a direct relationship between audit risk and the audit evidence search. Discuss.

6.10 Explain why audit judgement is a vital element of obtaining sufficient, appropriate audit evidence.

These can be found on the website in the student/lecturer section at: www.cengage.co.uk/graymanson5.

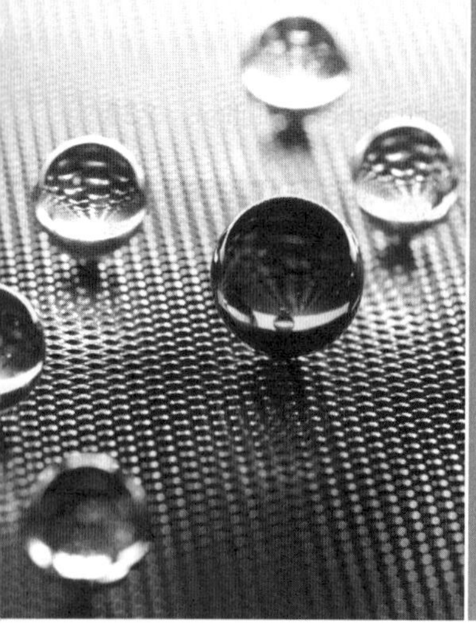

7

Systems work: basic ideas 1

LEARNING OBJECTIVES

After studying this chapter you should be able to:

- **Explain the significance of the layers of regulation and control.**
- **Define internal control and explain the significance of the control environment and related components, and accounting and quality assurance/control systems.**
- **Explain the nature and role of systems development/maintenance controls and describe the main features of these controls.**

Learning objectives, 240
Introduction, 241
Layers of regulation and control expanded, 243
Accounting and quality assurance/control systems, 258
General controls, 260
Summary, 281
Key points of the chapter, 281
References, 283
Further reading, 283
Self-assessment questions (solutions available to students), 283
Self-assessment questions (solutions available to tutors), 283
Topics for class discussion without solutions, 284

INTRODUCTION

In Chapter 5 we showed that organizations try to reduce the impact of risk by introducing accounting and control systems. We saw that auditors seek to minimize their own risk by identifying business/inherent risks, and examining and evaluating the control environment and individual control systems, followed by a choice of detection procedures. We saw too that the nature and extent of detection procedures depend on such factors as the integrity and competence of management. We now examine accounting and internal control systems in greater detail.

We have reached the point where we consider stages 6 to 9 of the audit process shown in Figure 6.3. In this chapter we discuss the control environment and its related components in greater depth than we did in Chapter 3. In Chapter 8 we consider more detailed controls and the related audit objectives and procedures. We discuss testing and evaluation of systems in Chapter 9 (including the use of computers in systems work), and in Chapter 10 we consider stages 10 to 13 of the audit process, including the use of the computer in the audit of transactions processed by systems.

The main interest of the external auditor at stages 6 to 13 is that the accounting records are genuine, accurate and complete, the basic presumption being that if the accounting and control systems are good and the general control environment is satisfactory, it is likely that the accounting records will be reliable.

See Table 6.2 on page 219 for an explanation of 'genuine, accurate and complete'.

The effectiveness of accounting and control systems is closely related to control risk and the assessment of such risk will have a bearing on the extent of audit tests carried out by the auditor. Thus, ISA 315 states in paragraph A42:

ISA 315 – *Identifying and assessing the risks of material misstatement through understanding the entity and its environment.*

> An understanding of internal control assists the auditor in identifying types of potential misstatements and factors that affect risks of material misstatement, and in designing the nature, timing and extent of further audit procedures.

ISA 500 – *Audit evidence* also notes that audit evidence to draw reasonable conclusions on which to base the auditor's opinion is obtained by performing tests of control (see paragraph A10).

It is important to understand the relationship between tests of controls performed by auditors and the extent of substantive procedures. The transactions of the entity will have passed through the accounting system and account balances will be held by it; controls are imposed on the accounting system to ensure within reason that it is operating effectively. If the auditors conclude that the system is properly designed and controls are effective, they can conclude that the transactions and balances are likely to be properly recorded. A corollary of this conclusion is that they can reduce the amount of substantive tests of detail. Note, though, that the auditors, in testing controls, will perform some tests similar in form to those carried out when substantive testing, but with a different objective, that of ensuring the effectiveness of controls. We discuss this matter in great depth in Chapter 9 and you may refer to Table 9.1 on page 341 and Figure 9.5 on page 344.

Remember that substantive procedures are 'audit procedures performed to detect material misstatements at the assertion level; they include: (a) tests of details of classes of transactions, account balances, and disclosures, and (b) substantive analytical procedures.'

The nature of the entity's operations do, however, need to be taken into account. Let us look at a simple example involving sales and trade receivables:

Sales invoices processed during the year	10 000
Total value of those invoices	£10 000 000
Value of trade receivables at the year-end	£1 250 000
Number of customers	three

This is an interesting situation for auditors. Should they record and test the system that has processed the 10 000 sales invoices or should three letters be sent to customers asking them to confirm sales made to them in the year and the amount owed to the entity at the year-end? In other words carry out a substantive procedure. We would like more information before we made a decision, but we have introduced this example to put systems work into context and to remind you that, above all, the auditor must be imaginative in approach.

NOTE ON BUSINESS RISK APPROACH TO AUDIT

In Chapter 5 we saw that many audit firms use business risk approaches to audit, involving the auditors gaining knowledge about management, their objectives and business risks faced by them. We suggested this approach would enable auditors to form views on the reliance they can place on management, resulting in reduced tests of control and substantive tests of detail; more reliance would be placed on qualitative evidence such as the effectiveness of the control environment and on analytical evidence. We discuss the control environment and related components below. This emphasis on the control environment represents a significant switch in recent years from detailed testing. However, while it is true that many auditors are spending less time examining systems in detail, we cannot avoid a discussion of systems and their control and the detailed tests of controls that auditors perform. Auditors are becoming more selective in the detailed work they carry out, concentrating on those systems that are critical to their ability to form an opinion and on identification of control points within systems. It is worth noting too that the internal audit function within companies has developed in quality and scope in recent years and that much detailed work may be carried out by that function. We shall see too that many large companies establish a quality standards group to ensure that systems and data derived from them are of high quality and are reliable. When reading our comments on systems work in this and subsequent chapters, bear in mind that work of this nature may be performed by functions other than external audit. The external auditor will naturally wish to assess the effectiveness of these other functions.

We discuss the role of a quality standards group in this chapter and of internal audit in Chapter 15.

We turn now to a discussion of control over systems. We shall consider general controls first and then break down systems into subsystems and discuss the controls associated with each.

LAYERS OF REGULATION AND CONTROL EXPANDED

In Chapter 2 we discussed a number of external influences on entities, including general expectations of corporate governance, regulatory response and commercial pressures, under the general heading of 'the external environment'. These influences we summarized in Figure 2.3. We are now turning our attention to the internal environment of entities and have expanded Figure 2.3 to show in Figure 7.1 the elements of control introduced by management internally under the general headings of:

See page 53.

- The control environment and related components.
- Accounting and quality assurance/control systems.

External relationships are often complex, but internal relationships can be equally complex. It is a mistake to think that entities and their management are always pulling in the same direction. Different managers and staff will have their own personal agendas and it is a mark of good management to get disparate groups within the entity to work together for common objectives. You should bear this in mind when reading the rest of this chapter.

NOTE ON NATURE OF CONTROLS

Controls are to prevent, detect or correct events that the entity does not wish to happen:

- *Prevention*. Proper training of staff will make it less likely that such events will occur.
- *Detection*. Entry of a credit customer's account number that did not exist could be detected by the system provided that the computer program compares the entry with the database of customer numbers.
- *Correction*. Listing items rejected by the computer program in exception reports will enable the entity to take rapid corrective action. Furthermore, analysis of these reports will show entity staff why errors are occurring, enabling action to make errors less likely in the future.

However, not all data is required to be completely accurate, so there is some leeway as to what is meant by a correct event. For instance, data used by management for strategic decision making, such as projection of historical data into the future for planning purposes, will be acceptable if it is timely and reasonably based. On the other hand, the entity will require its trade receivable records to be accurate. Such records are used to ensure collection of amounts owing to the entity and, for instance, to estimate cash flows in the short and medium term.

We have linked control systems to quality assurance systems and later in the chapter we shall find that adherence to standards of quality is an important objective of management. These quality standards may relate to systems in use, including ease of use and efficiency and also to information derived from the systems.

FIGURE 7.1 Layers of regulation and controls – as extended (see Figure 2.3).

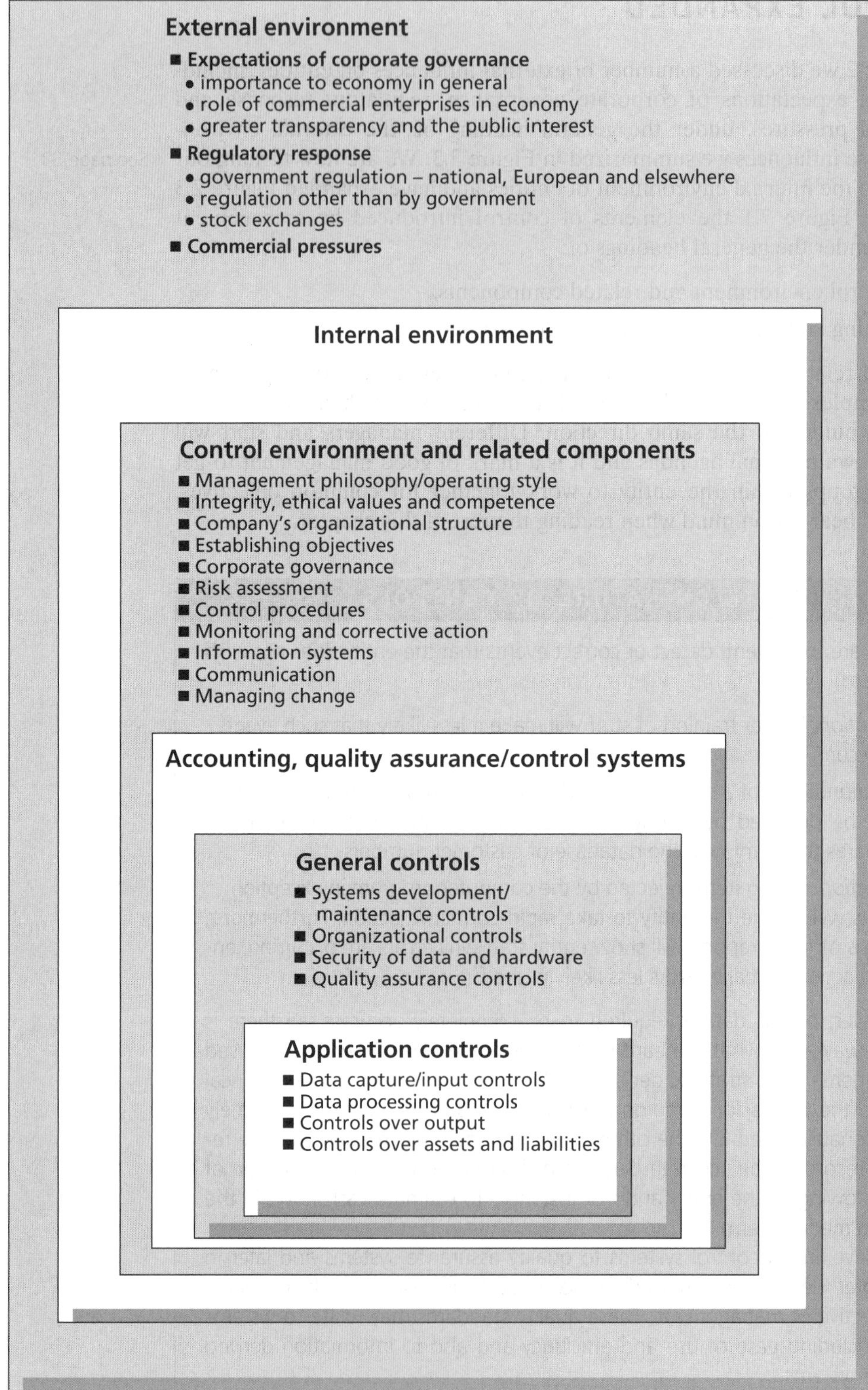

External environment
■ Expectations of corporate governance
• importance to economy in general
• role of commercial enterprises in economy
• greater transparency and the public interest
■ Regulatory response
• government regulation – national, European and elsewhere
• regulation other than by government
• stock exchanges
■ Commercial pressures
Internal environment
Control environment and related components
■ Management philosophy/operating style
■ Integrity, ethical values and competence
■ Company's organizational structure
■ Establishing objectives
■ Corporate governance
■ Risk assessment
■ Control procedures
■ Monitoring and corrective action
■ Information systems
■ Communication
■ Managing change
Accounting, quality assurance/control systems
General controls
■ Systems development/ maintenance controls
■ Organizational controls
■ Security of data and hardware
■ Quality assurance controls
Application controls
■ Data capture/input controls
■ Data processing controls
■ Controls over output
■ Controls over assets and liabilities

Internal control and related components

Internal control is defined in Paragraph 4 (c) of ISA 315:

> The process designed, implemented and maintained by those charged with governance, management and other personnel to provide reasonable assurance about the achievement of an entity's objectives with regard to reliability of financial reporting, effectiveness and efficiency of operations, and compliance with applicable laws and regulations. The term 'controls' refers to any aspects of one or more of the components of internal control.

You can see that this definition of internal control is in the context of the reliability of financial reporting and compliance with applicable laws and regulations. There is also, however, a reference to wider objectives of effectiveness and efficiency of operations. Clearly, good internal control is seen as an important element in ensuring that financial statements give a true and fair view of what they purport to show. It is important, therefore, that auditors obtain an understanding of internal control and particularly those elements that are relevant to the audit.

Limitations in internal control

Before we discuss internal control in detail, we must explain that there are limitations in internal control that may result at best in only reasonable assurance being given about achieving the entity's financial reporting objectives. We set out some reasons why internal controls may be less effective than desired by the auditor in Table 7.1. These factors would be taken into account by the auditor when identifying the risks of material misstatement because of error and fraud.

See paragraphs A46 to A50 of ISA 315.

We have already discussed internal control in Chapter 5 in the context of risk, but we now need to look at it again in the context of the auditors' procedures to prove its effectiveness. Here are the components of internal control suggested by ISA 315:

The components of internal control are discussed in paragraphs A69 to A104 of ISA 315.

- The control environment.
- The entity's risk assessment process.
- The information system, including the related business processes, relevant to financial reporting, and communication.
- Control activities.
- Monitoring of controls.

We discuss each of these components below.

Control environment

Definition

The word 'environment' suggests that the control environment represents the general conditions in which the risk assessments are made, the information system operates, and the controls are performed and monitored. In fact, without a strong control environment the other activities would fail to achieve

TABLE 7.1 Potential limitations in internal control.

Limitation	Comment
1 Design of controls may be faulty or there has been inadequate consideration of changes in circumstances; human error can cause breakdown in controls.	For instance, controls, such as supervision by top management, might become inadequate as an entity grows. Or credit limits may not be reviewed as circumstances change. A control such as timely review of exception reports to correct errors may seem adequate on paper, but if staff do not understand why it is important they may not carry out the procedure making the control ineffective.
2 Controls can be rendered ineffective if two or more people collude to circumvent a control; or if management is in a position to override controls.	Refer to 'A word about collusion' on page 80. Note too that if a manager can intervene to prevent such reporting, the control would again be ineffective. In a small firm with an owner-manager, the latter may be more able to override controls because the system of internal control is weaker.
3 Management may recognize that a risk exists, but decide not to implement controls if they judge them to be too expensive. in the circumstances.	For instance, auditors may suggest that inventories be counted at month ends to ensure that inventory records are accurate on a continuous basis. Management may decide that this would be too costly and rely only on year-end counts.
4 An important internal control is segregation of duties to ensure that transactions cannot be completely processed by one person. Smaller entities often have insufficient numbers of employees to make segregation of duties practicable.	We shall see later that in a small owner-managed entities the owner-manager may be able to exercise more effective oversight than in a larger entity (see Case Study 7.1 on page 163). You would expect the owner-manager to have other controls, such as a good information systems to enable the oversight to be effective.

their purposes. Here is how paragraph A69 of ISA 315 defines control environment:

> The control environment includes the governance and management functions and the attitudes, awareness and actions of those charged with governance and management concerning the entity's internal control and its importance in the entity. The control environment sets the tone of an organization, influencing the control consciousness of its people.

An important element of the control environment is that it provides a framework for effective internal control and a sense of discipline and structure. We have already referred to the importance of 'tone at the top' in Chapter 3 in relation to audit independence (see page 80) and Chapter 5 in relation to risk (see page 163).

Elements of the control environment

We discuss below the elements of the control environment that should be evaluated by the auditor and determined how they have been incorporated into the entity's processes.

- *Communication and enforcement of integrity and ethical values*
  It almost goes without saying that the effectiveness of controls is dependent on the integrity and ethical values of the people who create, administer and monitor them – those charged with governance. Those charged with governance should communicate the required ethical standards by policy statements and codes of conduct to staff responsible for the day-to-day operation of the accounting and control systems. Two very important aspects of ensuring ethical approaches by staff in practice are:
  (a) By the example of top management. If top management is seen to be guilty of sharp practice or of issuing false statements on such matters as quality of goods offered to the public, it is unlikely that staff lower in the organization will take policy statements on ethics seriously.
  (b) By the removal or reduction of incentives and temptations that might prompt personnel to engage in dishonest, illegal, or unethical acts. For instance, if bonuses are based on the profitability of the whole or parts of the entity, which is often the case, there might be a temptation to manipulate the accounting records.
- *Commitment to competence*
  If accounting systems and controls are to be effective and entity objectives are to be obtained, it is essential that individuals have the knowledge and skills necessary to make their work effective. This means that management has to consider the competence levels required for particular jobs and how requisite skills and knowledge can be acquired and maintained. Practical consequences are that directors set criteria for the appointment and retention of high-grade staff and to train staff properly for the jobs they are required to do. This may not be an easy task. In circumstances of rapid technological change it is often difficult for management to assess how competent IT staff are and whether they possess the necessary integrity.
- *Participation by those charged with governance*
  In many jurisdictions, including the UK and Ireland, those charged with governance include both executive and non-executive management who have responsibility for overseeing the strategic direction of the entity and obligations related to the accountability of the entity. This includes overseeing the financial reporting process. You should draw a distinction between (a) the responsibility of the whole board for establishing an effective control environment and (b) the control roles of individual directors within their respective spheres of activity. For instance, sales directors will, apart from having overall responsibility for the management of the sales function, be responsible for supervising the various elements of the sales system. They might, for instance, be responsible for ensuring that sales commissions paid are reasonable in relation to sales, probably aided by computerized analytical procedures.

  Similarly, non-executive directors comprise an important element of the control environment, because of their independence from executive

See paragraph 10 (a) of ISA 260 – *Communication with those charged with governance.*

management, as you can see from paragraph A70 (c) of ISA 315. Apart from independence other important factors are the degree to which difficult questions are raised and pursued with executive management and their interaction with internal and external auditors. In this respect they perform an important role on the audit committee, as we have indicated in Figure 4.5 in Chapter 4 (see page 133). We saw too in Chapter 3 that they play a role in enhancing the independence of external auditors (see Figure 3.3 on page 81). The duties of the audit committee can be wide-ranging but it will be responsible, among other things, for reviewing the adequacy of the internal control system and in ensuring the effectiveness of the internal audit function. It will review not only reports of internal auditors but also of external auditors, and generally ensure that the work of internal and external audit are integrated as far as possible. Integration of internal and external audit does not mean that the audit committee will interfere with the scope of external audit work, but there may be many areas where internal and external audit might usefully be coordinated, for instance, visits to entity branches and other locations. It is clear that the general effectiveness of the audit committee will be dependent on the qualities of its members, including their experience, reputation and general status. Also important is how well informed they are about the entity and its accounting and control systems and the extent to which they achieve understanding of the activities of the organization.

We discuss audit committees in the context of corporate governance in Chapter 18. We also show how they interact with internal auditors in Chapter 15.

The internal audit function plays an important role in making the audit committee effective. Its members have access to all parts of the organization and in consequence can provide audit committee members with insight into the way the entity is run and the effectiveness of the accounting system and internal controls. For this reason you would expect the chief internal auditor to have a direct line of contact to the audit committee. We shall find that external auditors report regularly to the committee too.

Other responsibilities of non-executive directors include oversight of the design and effective operation of whistleblower procedures. Whistleblowers are members of staff who become so concerned about underhand activities within the organization or about poor controls that they make their concerns public, perhaps even outwith the organization. Whistleblowers often have very genuine concerns and it is important, therefore, that organizations set up systems to allow them to report their concerns to people who have the standing to investigate such concerns and take corrective action.

A good example of a whistleblower is Sherron Watkins who, reports say, expressed concerns about practices at Enron to Ken Lay, the chairman and CEO, who then conducted a bogus investigation and misrepresented Enron's problems to the public.

Audit committees are often required to consider the public interest as well as the narrower interests of their company, although public and company interests may well coincide. A case in point is one we asked you to consider in Activity 2.10 in Chapter 2, where we introduced you to Annets Limited, a company producing and storing toxic waste and suggested measures the company could take to control the waste. We noted that the company had to have control and information systems to reduce harm to the public, an important accounting control being to have proper records of toxic waste held and to measure the waste regularly for comparison with the amount shown in the records.

See page 54.

- *Management's philosophy and operating style*

  This includes management's approach to managing business risks, and management's attitudes and actions toward financial reporting, information processing and accounting functions and personnel. You will have noted by now that the elements of internal control we are discussing here are all interrelated in one way or another. Management philosophy and operating style is no exception, comprising, as it does, the way that directors set objectives, approach business risk and manage change. It is about the way that management assigns authority and responsibility and how they organize and develop people (see below) and how they balance the needs of various stakeholders of the business from shareholders to employees, from business associates to customers and so on. Management philosophy also includes the way in which integrity, ethical values and competence are encouraged throughout the organization, elements that we have discussed above. Management philosophy should also include a professional approach to financial reporting and compliance with generally accepted accounting practice.

  Appendix 1 to ISA 315 recognizes this, and makes a further important point about financial reporting – that this may be influenced by conservative or aggressive selection from available alternative accounting principles, and conscientiousness and conservatism with which accounting estimates are developed. This means that in considering whether the financial statements give a true and fair view, auditors must decide whether the directors are being unduly conservative (calling it prudence) or whether they use alternative accounting principles to enhance the appearance of profitability and liquidity. The same applies to the way that management make accounting estimates (about the profitability of long-term construction contracts, for instance).

- *Organizational structure*

  The organizational structure creates a framework within which the entity's activities for achieving entity-wide objectives are planned, executed, controlled and reviewed. It aids employees' understanding of their responsibilities and enables an appropriate delegation of authority.

  In practice, managements have a number of different organizational structures to choose from, such as functional specialization, as expressed in the County Hotel case in Figure 5.2 on page 198, or geographical, product or service specialization. Matrix structures may be suitable where an organization has clearly defined projects with specific goals, such as the development and launch of a new product or delivering a service. In such cases a functional line of authority may be combined with a project line of authority, the project leader liaising with functional leaders, from whom they can draw expertise and facilities as required. An example of a matrix structure is given in Figure 7.2.

  Auditors should be aware of the nature of the organizational structure when deciding if it is effective. For instance, in a matrix structure it may be difficult to decide who has authority in a particular area – the project head or functional leader – and whether entity resources are being properly allocated. If there is lack of clarity as to where authority lies it may be difficult to allocate accountability, with a resultant increase in risk.

FIGURE 7.2 Example of matrix organizational chart

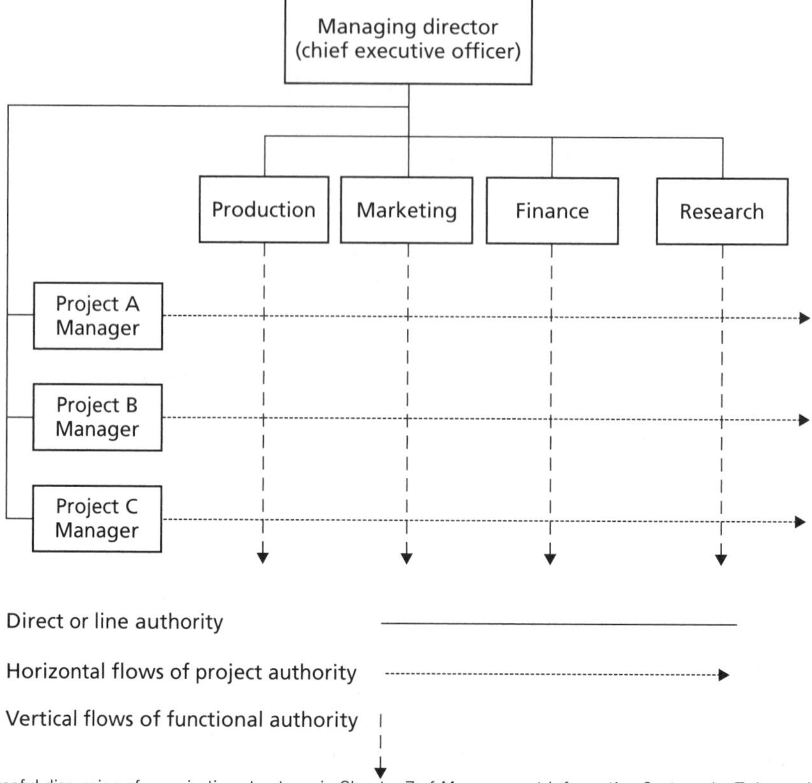

Source: There is a useful discussion of organization structures in Chapter 7 of *Management Information Systems* by T. Lucey (2004) 9th edition. The above figure has been taken from this text.

- *Assignment of authority and responsibility*
  We have already discussed the question of authority and responsibility in relation to organizational structure above, but you should note that this factor also includes policies relating to appropriate business practices, knowledge and experience of key personnel, and resources provided for carrying out duties. It includes policies and communications directed at ensuring that all personnel understand the entity's objectives, know how their individual actions interrelate and contribute to those objectives and recognize how and for what they will be held accountable.
- *Human resource policies and practices*
  Human resource policies and practices are relevant to all organizations, including professional firms of accountants and auditors. Organizations on the whole are only as effective as the people that they employ, so it is not

ACTIVITY 7.1

If you were responsible for deciding what your organization expected from new recruits, what would you be looking for and what would help you decide? How would you ensure high performance of people within the entity?

only important to recruit the right people but also to keep their level of performance as high as when they joined the organization.

Clearly you would want to bring new employees into your organization who would aid it in achieving its objectives and who would possess integrity and the ethical standards expected. Structured interviews of candidates would enable experienced staff to evaluate them in this context, but you would also be looking at their educational background and experience in previous employment and whether they have any particular skills that would make them suitable for your organization. Integrity and ethical attitudes are, of course, very intangible attributes, but interview techniques should be developed to discover how they would approach ethical dilemmas.

Recruiting properly qualified staff with high integrity is vital, but policies should be in place to keep level of attainment high. This would include training not only in technical matters (that is, how to do the job efficiently) but also in respect of expected behaviour, such as attitude to customers, suppliers and fellow members of staff.

A further important element in making employees effective would be proper remuneration policies and clear and open policies on promotion through the organization. One effective way is to conduct periodic performance appraisals. One of the authors remembers writing performance appraisals for staff and discussing the appraisals with them before passing them to the personnel partner of the firm.

Entity's risk assessment process

We discussed business and inherent risk at length in Chapter 5 and we will not repeat the discussion here. We emphasize, however, that entities should consider the likelihood of business risks crystallizing and the significance of the consequent financial impact on the business. Once this has been done suitable controls should be introduced to reduce risks to an acceptable level. To take the toxic waste example again, there is a clear risk to the entity that the public may suffer as a result of contact with the waste, but it may not be clear how likely it is that contact will occur. It may also not be clear initially what losses the entity might suffer in such a case but the entity analysis should include consideration of such matters as claims from the public for damage caused, and from national and/or local government for infringement of environmental legislation. The entity would have to decide how to reduce the likelihood that it would suffer such losses, including the recording and measurement controls suggested above. We would, of course, also expect the entity employees to have an awareness of the risks faced by the entity so that they could react properly as they arise.

Other risks that should be considered include such matters as:

- The health of employees using computer keyboards. Repetitive strain injury is a new condition for office workers, but its incidence can be reduced by introducing proper rest periods and mixing activities.
- Another relatively new risk in relation to computer systems is the possible failure to maintain privacy of individuals. This is a human rights matter that the Data Protection Act has tried to address. Furthermore as more

business is conducted on the Internet (e-commerce), the security of customer data, including credit card details, becomes of added significance.

- Potential losses from computer abuse, such as hacking, viruses and misuse of entity facilities by employees and others. We discuss controls to reduce risks of this nature in Chapter 8.
- Management of change. Managing change is about responding effectively to new risks and opportunities. For instance, if a competitor introduces a new and improved product, the entity will have to decide quickly how to respond. If new computer technology becomes available – and competitors are using it – the entity has to decide quickly if it can afford not to adopt it. Many companies too are faced with the e-commerce revolution and are having to make decisions as to whether they should set it up as an adjunct to their existing organizations, as a separate activity, or whether it would be better to integrate it fully with their existing systems. Many, perhaps most, people tend to be resistant to change so management needs to consider how to communicate the need for change to staff.

The Data Protection Act was passed in the UK in 1998 and lays down rules for holding data on individuals.

Rowley (2002) defines e-commerce as doing business electronically across the extended enterprise. It covers any form of business or administrative transaction or information exchange that is executed using any information and communications technology. Others are more restrictive and apply the term only to sales via the Internet, electronic purchasing and electronic payment. We discuss e-business and associated audit problems in Chapter 8.

Information system, including the related business processes, relevant to financial reporting and communication

Relevant and timely information about internal activities and external factors is essential if an entity is to be successful. For instance, the hotel company we looked at in Chapter 5 required information on accommodation and restaurant usage to control its affairs properly. This sort of performance indicator allows management to monitor the key business and financial activities and risks, to assess the progress towards financial objectives and to identify developments that require intervention. It is not always easy to determine how successful an organization is. A railway entity, for instance, might be judged not only on profitability of its individual activities but on the degree of satisfaction given to its passengers, based on such matters as cleanliness of carriages, time-keeping, and quality and availability of food in the buffet.

See paragraphs A81 to A87 of ISA 315.

Key performance indicators (KPI) are used by many different organizations as an aid to measuring how successful an entity has been in achieving its objectives.

What is important is that information systems should have in-built controls enabling entity officials to respond properly to any deficiencies or to information that appears contradictory. For instance, were there to be a significant difference between toxic waste recorded and waste actually on hand, what steps should be taken to determine what has happened? It could be something as simple as a despatch not being properly recorded, but equally it could mean that waste has been lost into the external environment. A less emotive example would be information to sales managers on price reductions by competitor companies to enable decisions to be made about pricing on a short- and long-term basis. Modern information systems make considerable use of IT and we discuss these later in this chapter and the management structures that are necessary as a result. IT systems do not merely consist of physical hardware and software, but also require people to be properly trained to ensure that data is valid, completely processed and properly classified. Data and information held in computer files must be secure and accounting records accurate enough not only for the day-to-day running of the business, but to allow financial statements to be properly prepared.

Paragraph 18 of ISA 315 lists the aspects of an entity's information system that the auditor should understand.

We cannot overstate the importance of communication as an element of information systems. Exchange of information is essential if the entity is to attain its objectives and maintain good control systems. We would expect directors to foster open discussion on issues, problems and concerns arising within the organization. There is, of course, a danger of information overload and the entity should establish a policy for ensuring that individuals get the information they need for the role they play in the organization. Thus, sales clerks would need to have information about such matters as sales prices, delivery times, availability of inventory and discounts for particular customers. They would not need to know about non-current assets budgets over the next ten years.

Communication is important in all kinds of organization. In small companies it can be informal, but in large companies, formal codes and standards will be more important.

Later in this chapter we shall see that effective communication means that the roles of individuals must be well understood. For instance, IT staff will have different roles and responsibilities – and different information needs – than users of the system, such as those responsible for receiving data and entering them into the system. We shall also make clear later in this chapter that all personnel must understand how their activities in the financial reporting information system relate to the work of others, including reporting exceptions to normal processing to responsible officials in the entity. An example would be reporting instances of credit limits being exceeded by customers, with the added requirement that reported exceptions are corrected.

Control activities

See paragraphs A88 to A97 of ISA 315.

We discuss control activities to reduce business and audit risk later in this chapter but note at this stage that they include:

- *Authorization*. This would include authorization by responsible officials of such matters as access to assets of the entity and giving permission to enter into transactions.
- *Performance reviews*, very often using analytical procedures comparing actual performance with budgets and forecasts, with prior period performance and with performance of competitors.
- *General and application controls over information processing*. Later in this chapter we discuss information systems, in particular in relation to modern computer systems. Risks arising from IT are referred to in paragraphs A95 to A97 of ISA 315.
- *Physical controls*. These activities include physical security of assets and restriction of access to data and programs held on computer files.
- *Segregation of duties*. Basically this means that duties are segregated in such a way as to prevent individuals seeing transactions and their recording from the beginning to the end.

You should also note at this stage that the auditor has to decide what controls are relevant to the audit. For instance, a vital control is the counting of inventory by qualified and properly supervised staff, supported by clear instructions.

ACTIVITY 7.2

Name two objectives of the inventory count.

Two specific objectives of the inventory count are:

(1) to check there have been no significant losses of inventory – a control designed to safeguard an important asset.

(2) to establish quantities to form the basis of the inventory figure. Clearly the auditor has an interest in the inventory count being effective in establishing the inventory quantities which, when valued, will be reflected in the financial statements.

There are other objectives, which we discuss later in this book.

Monitoring of controls

See paragraphs A98 to A104 of ISA 315.

The basic task under this heading is to assess the performance of controls and their adequacy and relevance over time. Monitoring may be a special responsibility of a quality standards group, internal audit or even external audit.

The monitoring process should provide reasonable assurance that there are appropriate control procedures for the entity's significant business activities and that timely monitoring reports are prepared to enable corrective action to be taken. Reports from the internal audit function or from independent accountants may usefully be considered by executive management and others charged with governance. In large and complex organizations, a formal monitoring process will normally be vital to ensure that control systems are continuing to operate as intended. A properly resourced internal audit function, coordinated with external audit and reporting to a suitably competent and independent audit committee of non-executive directors would be of great value in ensuring proper monitoring.

In some countries directors may be required to make regular reports on the effectiveness of internal control within their organizations. This is a controversial matter and in the UK and Ireland and throughout the European Union, such reports are not required. However, in the United States, post-Enron, auditors are now issuing reports on management's assessment of the effectiveness of internal controls. These reports refer to the fact that the auditor had planned and performed the audit of the entity to obtain reasonable assurance about whether effective internal control over financial reporting was maintained in all material respects, and that the audit provided a reasonable basis for the opinion on the financial statements. They refer to inherent limitations in internal control over financial reporting, but include an opinion on the management's assessment that the entity maintained effective internal control over financial reporting, stating, if the auditors have formed this opinion, that the assessment is fairly stated, in all material respects, based on criteria established in 'Internal Control – Integrated Framework' issued by the Committee of Sponsoring Organizations of the Treadway Commission (COSO). It seems that there have been many instances of the reporting of internal control weaknesses by management in the United States since the introduction of the new requirements. Since the collapse of Enron, there has been an increase in restatements of financial statements in the United States, although it is not clear whether this is the result of increased scrutiny of control systems, or merely because auditors have been more assiduous in examining the application of accounting principles. Auditors in the United States are required to consider the financial statement amounts or total of transactions exposed to any material deficiency in internal controls and the volume of activity in the account balance or class of transactions exposed to the deficiency that has occurred in the current period or that is expected in future periods.

This requirement is stated in Paragraph 135 of Public Company Accounting Oversight Board Bylaws and Rules – Standards – AS2.

Cases

Having discussed these matters, let us consider two cases, one of them a small supermarket run by two shareholders and a company in the financial services sector giving advice to people about such matters as pensions, life assurance and investments in bonds and securities.

CASE STUDY 7.1

High Quality Limited (small independent supermarket)

High Quality Limited is an entity with two shareholders who take an active part in the business, employing two assistants in a small independent supermarket. The entity has a simple accounting system and uses a micro-computer with bought-in software to record:

- Expenses, such as wages, rent and insurance.
- Purchases of fresh produce, tinned food and household products.
- The products' subsequent sale (the different products are bar-coded where possible and a detailed list of purchases is provided to each customer; a detailed analysis of sales can be made daily and weekly).

Expenses and purchases are supported by two ring binders of 'paid' and 'unpaid' invoices from suppliers and the sales by till rolls. The computer system records types of goods purchased, other expenses and types of goods sold and can be prompted to produce daily and weekly analyses of purchases, expenses and sales made.

The company advertises its fresh produce (vegetables and fruit) as being grade A and prides itself on meeting the needs of its customers.

Required

1 How relevant do you believe the matters we discussed above are to the management of this small company? What kind of objectives could the business have?

2 If you were the proprietors how would you ensure that sales and purchases were fully and accurately recorded?

We discuss this below but before you read further, make a few notes of your own ideas. While you are doing this activity you may like to refer to paragraphs A71 to A104 of ISA 315, some of which contain comments on application of internal control components to small entities.

1 Control environment and related components

We can be sure that the two shareholders, who also manage the company, have certain objectives in mind. You might have come up with some or all of the following, though there may be others in addition to those listed:

1 That the produce sold is of a certain quality (in this case class A for fresh produce).
2 That the assets of the business are safeguarded.
3 That the records of transactions, amounts owed and assets held (such as cash) are complete and accurate.
4 That you know the likely demands for produce on any particular day or in a particular period so purchases can be made on an informed basis.
5 That the business is profitable.
6 That the business remains financially viable.

We are sure you will agree that integrity is of relevance. If, for instance, the greengroceries are advertised as being Class A, the goods should be of that quality to maintain an honest relationship with customers. There is clearly a corporate governance issue here. If members of the public become aware that quality is less than that advertised, the shop may lose clientele and become less profitable, thus failing to meet one of its objectives. Competence is clearly demanded too if objectives are to be met. For instance, the maintenance of records to assess likely consumer demand requires particular skills and would also make necessary the existence of an information system to keep track of customer demand on certain days of the week and at certain times of the year.

It would be essential too for managers to create an environment to ensure that shop staff know how to handle the goods so that losses are reduced. Integrity in staff would be a vital factor in keeping reputation high and in ensuring within reason that shop produce does not go missing.

We started by thinking about possible objectives of the business. The setting of objectives is clearly a vital feature of a control system, as the controls should be designed to ensure that the objectives are met. For instance, to ensure that losses resulting from deterioration of fresh produce are kept to a minimum, or to ensure that inventories of tinned products and household goods are kept at an optimum level, an information system is necessary to tell the proprietors how much to purchase on certain days.

We have made a key feature of this book the identification of business/inherent risk in businesses. A major risk in this kind of business will be losses arising from the deterioration of inventory and this will confirm the need not only for the information system referred to above, but also for careful buying to ensure that produce purchased in the market is fresh.

The software used by the business does allow the proprietors to analyse trends of sales, cost of sales and expenses, enabling them to determine such matters as necessary level of purchases, profitability, etc., and there is therefore a facility available to provide the needed information.

Control procedures that would aid the safeguarding of the assets of the business might include:

- Close supervision of the assets (for instance cash in the till and produce on the shelves) by the directors.
- Prompt banking of takings to reduce the likelihood of cash going missing.

Regarding communication, this is obviously important for the business. Good shop assistants will keep track of customer enquiries, for instance, 'I am looking for fresh basil. Do you stock it?', 'I have seen a new brand of washing up liquid advertised on TV. Do you keep it?' Likewise the shop assistants should be made aware of management policy with regard to customer needs.

You might think that managing change would not be of great significance for a small independent supermarket. Just think, however, of the need for change if a newly opened shop in the neighbourhood provided close competition for the first time. The proprietors might have to consider how to retain their customers, including the introduction of special offers and new ranges.

In a small shop a sophisticated monitoring system would probably not be necessary but this does not mean that monitoring has no place. The proprietors themselves should monitor through supervisory controls. This monitoring would be much enhanced by using trends shown by computer printouts. If the proprietors lacked accounting knowledge, they might employ a qualified accountant to exercise a monitoring role for them.

The example given is of a fairly simple business, but it is interesting how relevant a good control environment is, even in this case.

2 Record of sales and purchases

The accounting system is in itself an important aspect of control, as we have seen above, but on its own is not enough to ensure that the assets of the company are safeguarded and that all transactions are genuine, accurately and completely recorded. Controls will be needed to ensure a sale is recorded each time a customer pays for goods and that all invoices are filed in the invoice files and paid on a timely basis. We suggest that the following controls would be helpful (some we have already mentioned above in relation to the control environment).

Sales:

- Personal supervision of the two assistants by the directors, at least one director to be in the shop during opening hours.
- Comparison by the directors of actual daily takings with those expected.
- Comparison of actual and expected gross profits on (say) a four-week basis. In making such comparisons, changes in gross profit percentage might occur because of seasonal changes in produce sold and because of changes in sales mix.
- A review of the sales analysis will give the directors a good indication of popular and less popular lines and will aid purchase decisions.

Purchases:

- Purchases of goods by the directors to ensure that inventory is of the desired quality. This would be particularly important for the fresh produce.
- Invoices to be numbered on receipt to ensure that all invoices are filed in the invoice files, this control supported by periodic sequence checks. A sequence check is to ensure that a sequence of numbers is complete. Thus, if invoice numbers 1, 2, 3, 5, 6 are in the file, invoice number 4 can be seen to be missing and steps taken to recover it. We shall see later that sequence checks are also used in sophisticated computer systems.

CASE STUDY 7.2

Entity in the financial services sector: Caiplie Financial Services

Caiplie Financial Services is an entity giving advice to individuals about such matters as personal pensions, life assurance and investments in bonds and securities.

Required

What policy features would be relevant in a business such as this and what kind of controls might be particularly important? Remember that the entity is advising people about some of the more important investment decisions they will make during their lives.

In a business such as this, it would be most important that the specific needs of individual clients are carefully considered when being given financial advice. One might expect to see each investment decision checked by an independent person within the entity after the investment scheme has been drawn up by the primary advisor. You would also expect the rights of clients be made known to them, particularly the right to reverse the investment decision within a certain period of time. However, of equal, perhaps greater importance would be the establishment by the directors of an environment that would encourage investment advisors to put the interests of clients at the forefront. This would include such features as ethical policy guidelines, proper training for advisors and other sales staff, and a system for calculating commission that would discourage the sale of inappropriate investments and provide a structure for control. As the entity is in a highly regulated sector, there would also be a strong emphasis on complying with regulation.

See ISA 250 – *Consideration of laws and regulations in an audit of financial statements.* You might also refer to the Financial Service Authority regulations.

Specific information to be made available to advisors so that they can give proper advice to clients would be the various investment opportunities that are available and the pros and cons of each. We would expect to see a system to ensure that communication lines to and from staff provide them with the information they require. Companies of this kind often have this information available through computer networks, in which case it would be vital that the networked information was up to date. This might include details of current share prices, examples of expected returns, special schemes for pensioners or retired individuals, house buyers and so on.

ACCOUNTING AND QUALITY ASSURANCE/ CONTROL SYSTEMS

We now move to a discussion of more detailed elements of entity control procedures. You will note from Figure 7.1 that we have split these procedures into two sections under the headings 'General controls' (which we discuss in this chapter) and 'Application controls' (which we discuss in Chapter 8). As you read, take into account the discussion of the control environment and related components of internal control earlier in this chapter.

It will be useful for you to distinguish between accounting systems and systems of internal control. The accounting systems are required to record all the transactions that an entity engages in from inception to completion. It also holds the records of balances resulting from those transactions, such as aggregate sales and trade receivables records, which eventually are reflected in the financial statements of the entity.

The accounting system is clearly an important part of the overriding control system instituted by management to achieve their objectives, one of which is to ensure that the information they use for their own internal purposes and that they publish for the benefit of interested outside users is genuine, accurate and complete. The important point is that other controls are necessary apart from the accounting system itself. Thus, management will introduce an accounting system to record, for instance, credit sales made, but in addition will introduce other controls to ensure within reason, that credit customers will pay for goods or services received.

ACTIVITY 7.3

Make a note of the kind of controls that might make it more likely that credit customers will pay for goods or services received. Remember that outstanding balances for such customers will be included in the figure for trade receivables, normally a material figure in the financial statements.

Here are a few suggested control procedures:

- Obtain bankers references for new customers.
- Set credit limits for all customers.
- Prepare regularly trade receivables ageing statements showing the age of outstanding balances.
- Regularly review credit limits on the basis of payment records and ageing statements.
- Introduce a system for reminding credit customers of outstanding balances.

In this chapter and Chapter 8 we are concerned with the practical assessment of internal control required to allow the auditor to form a view on control risk. Internal control and related systems are not static and evolve over time. Internal control is essentially a process for achieving objectives that should be identified beforehand. Furthermore – and this is important – internal control gives reasonable but not absolute assurance that the control objectives mentioned in the above definition (such as adherence to internal policies and safeguarding assets) are met. Normally, directors will only introduce controls if the costs are less than the perceived benefits.

We emphasize that it is not the accounting and control systems in which users of information are primarily interested. They are concerned above all in the information derived from the systems and its reliability and in whether the records from which information is compiled are accurate and complete. We show this diagrammatically in Figure 7.3.

FIGURE 7.3 Raw data to information

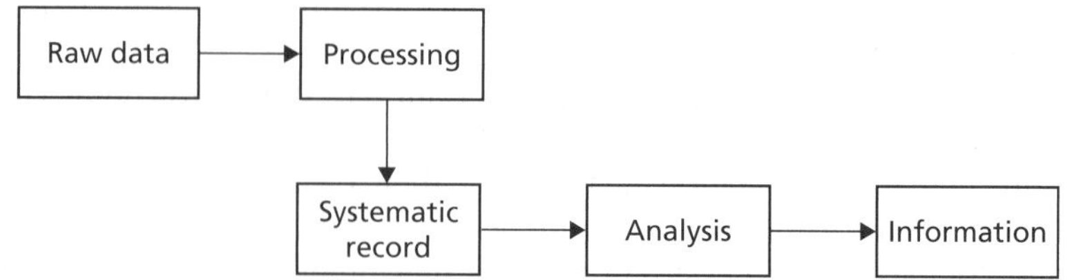

An example of raw data in a sales system is the sales order. The systematic record could be typified by the record of sales in a sales journal or in a computer sales transactions file, and information by a summary of sales for a period according to product or sales person. Information may be described as useful data that has gone through processing and analysis stages. Clearly, analysis of sales can be useful to management in the running of the business and also to outside users when assessing the results of operations. Even at the lower level, that of systematic recording, the data is useful to management. The raw data that produced the sales record also produced the trade receivable records, used to protect the important asset – amounts due from credit customers – by ensuring the entity knows who owes money to it and can collect it. The receivables record can become more useful to management by further analysis, such as an analysis by age, enabling decisions on future cash flows and provision for bad debts to be made.

We discuss application controls in Chapter 8.

Now let us take a look at the first category of control procedures, namely, general controls.

GENERAL CONTROLS

General controls are controls over the environment in which the entity operates and therefore form an extension of the control environment. The term is normally applied to computer systems, but it is really of general significance. Their important role is to ensure that applications are trouble free and that they prevent, detect or correct events that management do not wish to happen. Basically, application controls are those designed to ensure within reason that an individual application, such as processing of sales orders to create despatch notes and sales invoices, runs smoothly and accurately. The distinction between general and application controls can be exemplified in a non-computer context in an accounting and auditing practice. The individual audit assignment equates with an application, rendered efficient and effective by the existence of general controls, such as controls to ensure quality of staff, including careful appointment procedures, training of staff and audit manuals. The individual audit assignment (application) does, of course, need application controls in place, such as the allocation of appropriately experienced staff to audit areas.

Systems development/maintenance controls

Rigorous control of the development of systems, to get it right at the beginning, makes it easier to control individual applications. We saw that High Quality Limited had established authority and supervisory levels to safeguard assets. Computer systems are, of course, more inflexible than manual systems. You can say to a person at any time: 'Please make sure that you compare the trade receivables balance with the customer's credit limit before you issue a sales order', and expect the control to be put into effect immediately (assuming the credit limits have been established). A similar control in a computer system, however, needs careful planning at the development stage.

See Case study 7.1 on page 255.

A development programme for computer routines in large systems is suggested in Figure 7.4 and we comment below on a number of important elements.

FIGURE 7.4 Programme for the development of computer applications in a large-scale system

Action at conclusion of stage	Stages	Parallel development and subsequent maintenance
High level decision to perform feasibility study	1 Preliminary survey and analysis of users' needs	During the system development process, including the testing period, it is vital that the people who will be running the system are aware of the impact that the new system will have on their working practices, and that they are properly trained to run the system when it is implemented. The following points should be noted: • User department personnel should be closely involved in the design of user department procedures and putting together the detailed instructions for data preparation and user department personnel. • User department personnel should also have a close involvement in the design of user interfaces. • Careful consideration should be given to design of control procedures, including setting of degrees of access, preparation of control data, such as hash totals, and database administration procedures. • There should be carefully designed procedures to ensure conversion of files to the new system is complete and accurate.
High level authorization to proceed	2 Feasibility study; application of cost/benefit criteria	
	3 System design, including user interfaces, files to be used, processing to be performed; drafting of program specifications	
Testing by programmers; program manager confirms in writing that stage is complete	4 Programming–designing, coding, compiling and documenting of programs	
	5 Preparation of operating instructions; designing of forms for user use	
Testing by systems analysts to ensure in line with specifications; systems manager gives written agreement	6 System review and testing by systems analysts; in complex systems may be done on a modular basis	
User departments test the operation of the whole system, paying particular attention to the user interfaces; user department heads give written agreement	7 System review and testing by user departments	
Internal audit and/or external audit testing of controls and completeness of information/audit trail	8 System review and testing by auditor (internal or external)	
Written approval by: • operations manager • user departments • internal/external audit • board of directors	9 System accepted as operational by key officials	After initial implementation, it is necessary to maintain the system. It is essential that a reliable system is in place for reporting system malfunctions and program bugs, and inefficiencies of user and computer department personnel. Internal and external audit may play an important role in this process.
	10 Conversion–changeover from old to new system	
	11 Implementation	
	12 Operation and maintenance	

1 An organizational structure is required to manage the project and to ensure that high standards are applied during the development. Some entities set up an information technology (IT) committee comprised of interested parties to manage a development. The following should be included in the main committee, although there may be sub-committees to consider different subsystems:

- A member of the board which has final responsibility for how information systems will be used. In some companies this board member will be directly responsible for detailed planning and control of the system and might have the title 'information systems director'.
- Member of systems analyst group, responsible for the design, implementation and maintenance of systems.
- Member of programming group, responsible for programming new systems and maintaining existing systems.
- Member of group responsible for the control of data from collection of input, to processing and distribution of output.
- Representative(s) of important user groups.
- Member of management with specific responsibility for quality assurance to ensure that systems conform to quality standards established by management.
- Member of management with specific responsibility for security of data, software and hardware.
- Member of management responsible for operations with specific responsibility for planning and control of applications.
- Member of the database administration department, responsible for design of the database and its content and establishing controls over access to and use of the database.

Internal auditors are often included on IT committees to provide an independent view on controls and on potential deficiencies as the development process proceeds or on whether there are serious gaps in the information/audit trail. The counter argument is that the independence of internal auditors may be threatened by being too closely associated with the development process and that it would be difficult for them to give an objective appraisal of a system in use if they have aided its development.

We discuss the information/audit trail below.

The committee would be responsible for receiving the preliminary survey report and feasibility study and for recommending action to the main board. Internal or external audit intervention might be appropriate to ensure a proper evaluation of the costs of controls had been made. It might be useful to have audit committee involvement at this stage as well.

2 Documentation of the development process should be complete enough to allow an informed person to understand what had gone on during the process and how the system works. It should include such matters

as written preliminary and feasibility studies, system flow charts, data flow diagrams, program specifications, program logic, test records, summary of problems encountered and how these were overcome, controls to ensure that the effect of system breakdowns can be minimized and so on. The development documentation should also cover controls over distribution of output, bearing in mind that it should only be distributed to authorized personnel. Personnel should only be authorized on the basis of need, particular care being taken with confidential information.

3 Testing at each stage before permission is given to proceed to the following stage. Thus testing takes place at stages 4, 6, 7 and 8 by programmers, systems analysts, users and auditors respectively.

4 Persons involved in the development process take responsibility by confirmation in writing. This is extended beyond stages 4 to 8, when at stage 9 agreement is given to final acceptance of the new system by the operations manager, user departments and internal/external audit.

5 It is also vital that parallel developments take place alongside the main technical development. These developments include staff training, preparation of forms and file conversion procedures. The human factor has to be taken into account, as it is people who will be running the system.

6 A reliable system for reporting system malfunctions should be in place after implementation. Any changes to the system, other than very minor modifications, should go through the same rigorous development process as described above. The organization should certainly have laid down standards so that everyone involved is aware of agreed processes, including the need for proper authorizations.

This is another example of the important role that communication plays in internal control.

7 Related to 6 above is the need to ensure that unauthorized changes are not made to programs. There should be controls to ensure such changes are prevented and that any changes made are detected, including those made in error (perhaps during operation, testing or maintenance) as well as deliberate changes. Staff involved in these activities should be trained and properly supervised; official changes should be fully documented and authorized. Master copies of programs should be held in a secure location outside the computer facility and regular comparisons by responsible officials made with programs in use. We consider organization controls and security further below.

We emphasize the importance of user agreement at the development points, where users are affected. It is the users who are responsible either for running the system or using the information derived from it and it is users who will be concerned that interfaces between them and the system are friendly. You will note that Figure 7.4 includes audit intervention at all points where controls are being considered and tested. We shall see later that auditors will test for existence of controls and the proper processing of data as part of their normal audit work, but clearly testing by them at the development stage may make costly errors less likely at a later stage. In large systems

Remember that interfaces are the points at which users interact with the system. When you visit a website on the Internet, you see a user interface. If it is 'friendly' you will be able to access other pages with ease, but if it is not, you may choose not to visit that site again. Good design of user interfaces is vital in any information system.

internal auditors might play an important role, but smaller organizations would benefit from the advice of external auditors.

ACTIVITY 7.4

Suggest how the development programme shown in Figure 7.4 might be modified for a small system, using bought-in software. When you are doing this, remember that a small entity will rarely have qualified computer personnel in-house.

In a small system, the process would be much truncated. When an entity uses bought-in software as does High Quality Limited (Case 7.1) the programming would not be carried out in-house. However, the preliminary survey and feasibility stages would still be important. The proprietors of the supermarket would want the system to record transactions and balances completely and accurately and to provide them with information to help them run their business efficiently and effectively. The feasibility study will include a cost/benefit analysis of acquiring computer equipment and bought-in software. Careful assessment is necessary of the needs of the business and testing of the software before purchase by both auditors and users within the entity to ensure that it does what is claimed of it. Many small companies are now using computers in the running of their business, but they may have very little knowledge of the features they need or how to keep it up and running. For this reason, many audit firms advise their clients of the controls that should be built into the system, such as passwords to control access. It is also common practice to advise clients on staff training and file conversion. In High Quality Limited, access to the database of sales prices and products should be restricted to directors. The directors would also need advice on maintaining the system after it has been introduced and on the need to keep back-ups of critical data.

The main features of the development process shown in Figure 7.4 would be valid for small systems, but some parts would have a different emphasis.

The information/audit trail

In purely manual systems, it may be easy to trace the various elements of a transaction from inception to its final disposition, for instance from sales order to sales despatch note to recording in sales ledger and subsequent receipt of cash from the credit customer. However, in computer systems it is often difficult to establish the information/audit trail. In some cases it may be impossible without sophisticated techniques. To help you understand the information/audit trail we look first at a manual system for receipt of cash from credit customers. This manual system might be designed to ensure completeness and accuracy of cash received before it becomes input to a computerized trade receivables system. We want to use this system to introduce you to the idea of an information/audit trail, before we look at the need to establish such a trail in a heavily computerized system.

We refer in this book to cheques, postal orders, bank notes and coins as 'cash' unless it is appropriate to use the specific term.

CASE STUDY 7.3

Cash received system: Horton Limited

All mail received at Horton Limited is opened by two people in the accounting department, neither of whom have cashier or sales ledger duties. If the mail contains cash, one person lists the amounts and the names of the persons from whom received in a 'Cash received book', and totals the columns. The other person checks that the amounts and names entered in the cash received book and the total are accurate. Both persons initial the book to show they are in agreement.

The cheques are stamped 'Not negotiable', crossed restrictively to Horton, and sent with the cash received book to the cashier, John Wiston. The cashier enters amounts and names in the cash book and bank paying-in book and deposits all the cash received in the bank daily.

Periodically, a member of the accounts department (not the cashier) checks the cash received book with the cash book and bank paying-in book. Monthly, the cashier reconciles the cash book and bank statement balances, this reconciliation being checked and initialled by the chief accountant.

The sales ledger clerk (not the cashier) makes the entry of the cash received in the sales ledger accounts. Monthly, credit customer statements are prepared by the sales ledger clerk and these statements, after checking by an accounts clerk, are mailed by that clerk.

The relationship between the various records mentioned above is shown in Figure 7.5.

ACTIVITY 7.5

Read carefully the description of the system Horton Ltd uses for controlling and recording cash received from credit customers, referring to Figure 7.5 as you do so. When you have done this, ask yourself the following questions:

1 Would it be possible in your opinion for anyone involved with the operation of the system to misappropriate cash? Consider arrangements for:
   - Receipt of cash.
   - Banking of cash.
   - Entry in the cash book.
   - Preparation of the bank reconciliation statement.
   - Entry in the sales ledger account.
   - Sending the statement to the credit customer (the statement is a reminder of the amount due to the entity).

List the reasons why you think it would or would not be possible for misappropriation to take place. Are there any further questions you would like to ask as auditor?

See the note on collusion on page 374.

We think that it would be very difficult to misappropriate cash *without* collusion for the following reasons:

(a) *Receipt of cash* is controlled by two people. Not only are there two persons present when the cash is received, both check each other's work. Also, the cash is *recorded immediately* on receipt in the cash received book so that loss or misappropriation of cash is rendered more difficult subsequently. Furthermore, the cheques and postal orders are all

FIGURE 7.5 Information trail/audit trail flowchart

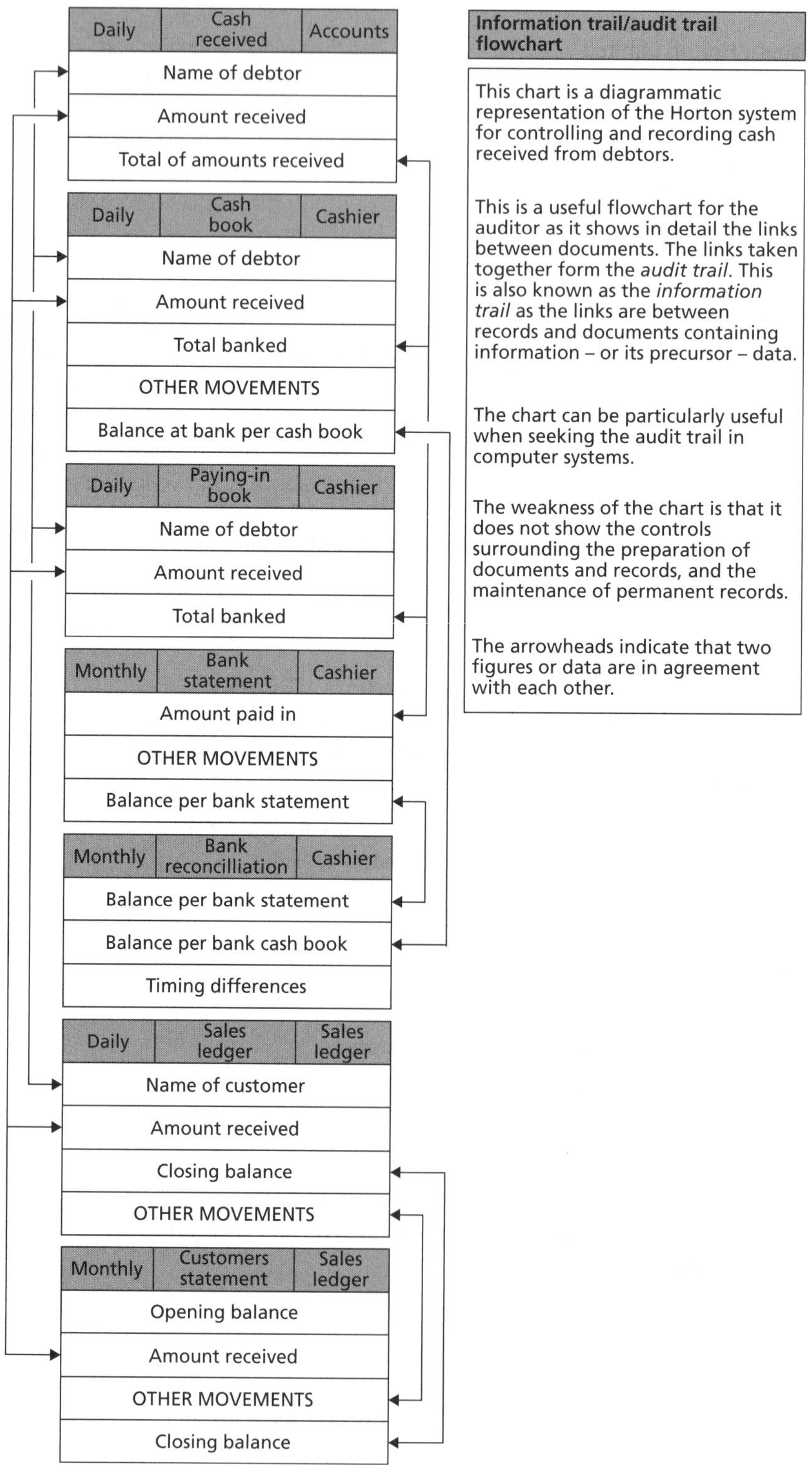

stamped 'Not negotiable' on receipt, which means that they cannot be passed to other people as a form of near cash.

(b) *Preparation of paying-in book, banking of cash, entry in the cash book and preparation of bank reconciliation* are in the hands of one person, the cashier. This may suggest initially that the cashier might be in a position to misappropriate cash. However, the cheques and postal orders are stamped 'Not negotiable' so the risk of misappropriation is reduced. Also you will have noticed that:

- An independent person in the accounts department compares the cash received book entries with those in the cash book and bank paying-in book. Any amount not banked should be obvious as the paying-in book is a reliable record (it will bear the stamp of the bank).
- The bank reconciliation is checked and initialled by the chief accountant (who will check the balances on the bank statement and in the cash book and also trace the subsequent clearance of unpresented cheques).

(c) *The entry in the sales ledger account and the sending of the statement to the credit customer.* The cash received from the credit customer is entered in the sales ledger account by a person independent of the cashier, that person also taking the credit customer's statement to the post. This means that the cashier cannot prevent statements being sent out as he might wish to do, had cash been misappropriated.

All in all we believe that it would be difficult to misappropriate cash received by Horton.

One major question you should ask as auditor, before you finally formed your conclusion, would be: 'Is the system as described the one that is actually in operation all the time?' Supplementary questions you could ask are: 'What happens when staff are ill or when they go on holiday?', 'Does the cashier ever carry out duties such as receiving cash when others are absent?' and so on.

We think that you will agree that Figure 7.5 shows the link between all the documents and records and we would suggest, therefore, that the information/audit trail is intact as you can trace entries backwards and forwards from any point. We will now consider a computerized trade receivables system where there appears to be a break in the information/ audit trail. In computerized systems, particularly in real-time systems, entries are often held in electronic form only and hardcopies of data produced only periodically. The example we are illustrating is from an 'open items' trade receivables system. In such a system, the unpaid invoices are held on file as open items, the invoices cleared by payment, discount or credit being removed from the system.

Assume that at 1 April 2010, the open items relating to Robert Brown, a credit customer, were as follows:

23:02:2010	Invoice	£74.55	
02.03.2010	Invoice	£25.76	
15.03.2010	Invoice	£36.99	£137.30

During April 2010, the following transactions took place: Invoice of 23:02:2010 cleared by cash on 16:04:2010. A cash receipt of £99.84 and cash discount of £2.04 on 30:04:2010 clear an invoice issued on 02:04:2010 for £101.88. The entity prints the trade receivables open items list at the end of each month. The open items list for Robert Brown at 30 April 2010 would be as follows:

02.03.2010	Invoice	£25.76	
15.03.2010	Invoice	£36.99	£62.75

All entries for the invoice of 02:04:2010 (invoice of £101.88, cash receipt of £99.84 and cash discount of £2.04) will, on this basis, never appear in the open items listing. This is an example of a break in the information/audit trail and the auditor (and indeed management) would wish to reconstitute the trail, if possible, as proper accounting records require it to be complete. It might be possible to print the open items listing after each transaction run, but this would be costly. Another solution would be to leave clearing items as open items for a period of (say) one month. If this were done, the open items for Robert Brown at 30 April 2010 would be as follows:

23:02:2010	Invoice	£74.55	
02.03.2010	Invoice	£25.76	
15.03.2010	Invoice	£36.99	
02:04:2010	Invoice	£101.88	
16:04:2010	Cash	−£74.55	
30:04:2010	Cash	−£99.84	
30:04:2010	Discount	−£2.04	£62.75

Do not think that maintenance of the audit trail is easy. In modern e-business systems it is common for instructions to be entered through a website, sales orders, for instance, to be input by completion of a form shown on the screen. This means that systems design must ensure that all events are recorded and that their disposition is clear. Thus, details of the order placed through the website must be recorded on receipt, together with the record of customer information (including credit card details), despatch, entry in sales record and payment (at receipt of order or later). We shall return to a discussion of audit trail at various points when we look at application controls in Chapter 8.

ACTIVITY 7.6

How long do you think that the information/audit trail should be maintained by the organization?

There is no firm answer to this question, as you will have recognized. Some information may have to be retained for a period required by law. Other types of information may have to be maintained for a very long time, depending on the type of data and type of entity. Think of the long timeframe of companies in the pensions industry or of financial institutions such as building societies lending on a long-term basis. The auditor should ensure that the entity has a clear policy with regard to this matter.

Organizational controls

We have already come across organizational controls earlier in this book. For instance, an important feature of system development/maintenance was the allocation of responsibility for particular aspects of the development system to particular individuals. This was also important in the Horton Limited manual system for recording and control of cash received. Allocating responsibility gives individuals in the entity an understanding of their duties and to whom they are responsible, particularly when backed up by job descriptions.

Organization chart

An organization chart is usually the starting point for allocating responsibilities and is a good example of an organizational control. An example of a functional organization chart is given in Figure 5.3 (the County Hotel Limited) and a matrix organization chart in Figure 7.2 in this chapter.

It is also important that the information/computer system be properly organized with clear roles for each element and appropriate segregation of duties. Before we discuss segregation of duties and other organizational controls, we suggest in Figure 7.6 a suitable organization chart for a computer department in a large organization and its place within it, as a service department that must possess independence and sufficient authority to perform its role properly.

We comment specifically on segregation of duties below.

Comments on Figure 7.6 include the following:

- This entity is large enough to have a director with specific responsibility for the entity's information systems.
- It has clearly been decided that quality of systems and information is a priority and that the quality standards group should be independent of the computer department.
- The *manager of the computer department* has a wide-ranging responsibility, but has an overall control role over the staff responsible for detailed development and operation of systems.
- The *systems analyst group* is responsible for designing new and evaluating existing systems and considering their redesign. Specific design work

FIGURE 7.6 Organization chart of the computer department and its place in a large entity

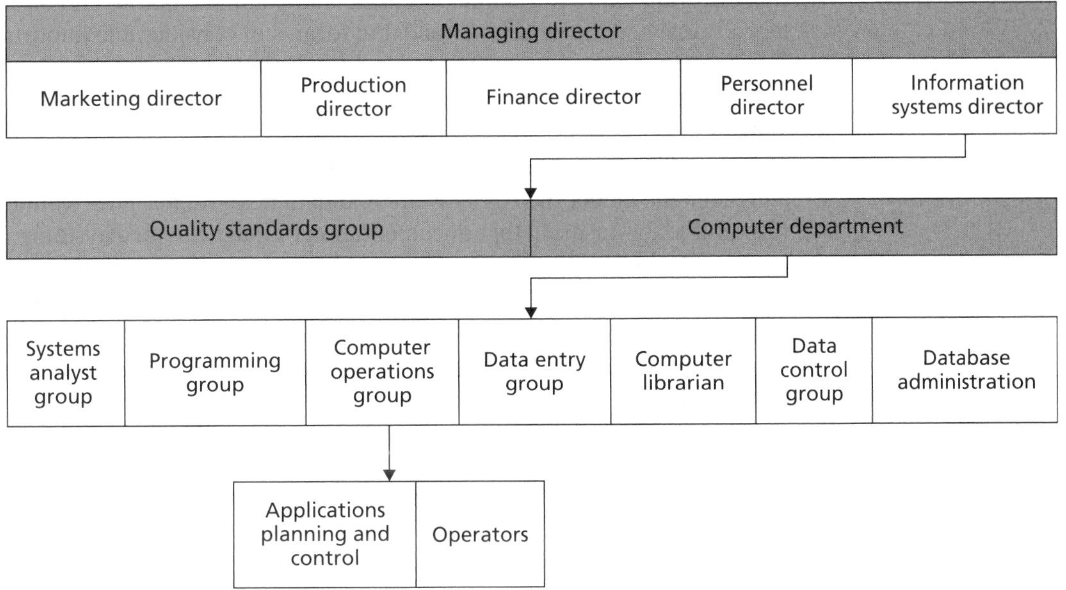

includes designing user interfaces to enable easy access to data by authorized users, deciding what data files are to be used in processing and the procedures to be performed on the data. As we saw above an important duty is the preparation of detailed program specifications to form the basis of the work by the programming group.

- The *programming group* is responsible for the preparation of programs based on requirements of program specifications set by systems analysts. We would expect programs to process data accurately and completely and efficiently all the time, even where conditions are unusual, such as abnormal overload, but the programming group also has other duties. We have already mentioned the importance of good user interfaces, but it is the programming group that is responsible for putting them into effect. Programmers should ensure that the logic of programs is clear, that they are well documented and that they are easy to maintain. Good maintenance will be aided by good documentation, showing, among other things, why programmers chose to adopt certain approaches.
- We have split the *computer operations group* into two, separating day-to-day operations from planning and control of operations. *Operations planning and control* staff would be involved in development and maintenance of systems. Their closeness to day-to-day operations would mean that they have a good awareness of such problems as poor user interfaces and abnormal incidence of rejected data. The *operators* are responsible for execution of programs using detailed operating instructions prepared during the development process and amended by responsible persons as day-to-day problems are resolved. Operators would be responsible for reporting bugs in programs and other problems to operations planning and control staff. They would also be responsible for proper use of computer hardware and general maintenance.
- *Data entry* might be the responsibility of a specific group or of individual user departments. We have shown it separately to highlight the fact that ensuring data are genuine, accurate and complete before and after being translated into machine readable form is of considerable importance. It is at the data entry point that control totals (both hash and value) might be prepared for subsequent checking to output processed by the system.
- *Computer librarians* would be responsible for safe keeping of documentation and magnetic media such as software and data held offline. They would be responsible for ensuring that documentation or magnetic media is only removed from the library with proper authority *and* that an accurate and complete record of movements in documentation and media is maintained.
- The *data control group* is responsible for ensuring that data is properly received by the system, is accurately and completely processed and that output is received by users in useable form. Control group staff will be in close contact with data entry staff, operators and users. They will have specific responsibility for ensuring that error messages are properly dealt with and that exception reports are followed up. Other specific responsibilities will be to reconcile control totals of output to predetermined control totals at the data entry point.

- The *database administration department* (the database administrator) is responsible for ensuring that the database operates efficiently and effectively. The department's staff will provide assistance to users as required and will maintain control over access. At the development stage the department will be responsible for design of the database and its content.

In smaller systems, some of these duties may be amalgamated, but this may increase the risk of unauthorized manipulation of data. We comment on segregation of duties immediately below.

Segregation of duties

An important principle of internal control is segregation of duties (we have seen examples in Figure 7.6). Auditors have traditionally given prominence to effectiveness of segregation when considering the efficacy of control systems, although we suggest below that auditors may gain more satisfaction from supervision by higher management. That division of duties is important can be seen if we imagine a system where a cashier received cash, banked it, entered it in the cash book, prepared the bank reconciliation, kept the sales ledger and sent out statements to credit customers. The possibility of error here would be increased because another person does not check the work of the cashier. You need not assume that people in industry and commerce are generally dishonest, but it would be possible to misappropriate cash, perhaps on a temporary basis, and to hide it by *teeming and lading.* It would also be easy to send out false statements (showing the balances the credit customers would expect).

See marginal note on 'teeming and lading' on page 43 of Chapter 2.

The first basic rule of division of duties is that there should be segregation of the functions as far as possible of:

- Authorization of transactions.
- Execution of transactions.
- Custody of assets.
- Recording of transactions and assets.

In modern computer systems this is often not possible. All the above functions might be controlled by computer programs that authorize a purchase, for instance, when a minimum inventory level has been reached; they might then execute the transaction by automatically issuing an order to a supplier, whose details are recorded in a master file. There would have to be human intervention at some stage – for instance, setting reorder levels, agreeing which suppliers are to be selected and entering the invoice when received. Even the latter might be done automatically if the invoice is received electronically, in which case the program might carry out the matching of the purchase invoice with order and make the entry in the stock records and purchases and accounts payables records.

This means that there is a *second basic rule of division of duties*, namely, that when traditional segregation of functions is not possible, additional control devices must be in operation – or a rethink of segregation. It becomes important to consider where decision-making lies in the following circumstances:

(a) Operation of a program should be segregated from the ability to change it. For instance, an operator running a payroll program should not be able to change the program to avoid them manipulating salaries paid. A further practical point is that programmers should not test programs during actual processing of data, as programmers know how programs operate and data is processed and it might be easy for them to make unauthorized changes to data. Similarly, we would expect clear separation of duties between system analysis and programming. In small companies it may be difficult to prevent access by programmers during operations and such companies frequently amalgamate systems analysis and programming. The auditor should be aware of increased control risk in these circumstances and to introduce audit procedures, such as enhanced substantive procedures to reduce its impact.

(b) Alteration of master file data should be in the hands of a responsible official. A master file consists of standing data used every time that a program is run. A good example is a personnel file containing details of everyone employed by the entity, such as name, department, basic rate of pay, overtime rate of pay, tax code, deductions and so on. A transactions file, on the other hand, represents transactions in a particular period of time, such as sales transactions in this period and year to date. Because master files are so important, we would expect only authorized persons to update them with, for instance, changes in tax codes.

In the case of automatic generation of an order to a supplier, the entity would have to ensure people independent of computer and stock holding personnel enter stock reorder levels and details of suppliers on the suppliers master file. Also reorder levels should be reviewed periodically by responsible officials, as well as review of prices and terms of suppliers and analysis of the suppliers used over a period of time.

The third basic rule of division of duties is that where control is dependent on segregation of duties within a particular function, management should allocate duties appropriately. An example is where a chief accountant keeps a trade receivables control account independent of the person keeping the sales ledger itself. Of course, both the control account and sales ledger might both be maintained on computer file, in which case we would expect regular review of control accounts to be carried out by responsible people independent of computer personnel.

If sales ledger clerks did keep both, the control account would merely be a means for them to control their own activity and would be more properly called a total account.

The fourth basic rule of division of duties is that there should, where practical, be rotation of duties at appropriate intervals. This means that personnel should not have responsibility for the same activity, for instance, reviewing and changing customers' credit limits for a long period of time, but that it should be passed on to other personnel. This becomes particularly important in a database system where data may not *belong* to any specific user or user group, and the database administration department exercises a vital control role with an overriding duty to maintain the integrity of the database. In order to perform this role, the department has to know everything about the database – nature of data stored, which programs can access the data, when they will do so, the built-in controls and so on. This means that rotation of duties within the department is essential.

We would also expect to see systems for independent review of data for reasonableness, either manually or computer-aided analytical reviews.

Authorization and approval

Closely linked to segregation of duties is authorization and approval by appropriate responsible persons, the limitations to whose authority is specified. You will come across the words, 'appropriate responsible person' often in relation to internal control systems. To give an example from a sales system, a sales order sent to the goods despatch department as authority for release of goods from the stores prior to despatch to customers should bear the signature of an authorized sales order clerk and of the credit controller. In the case of more modern computer systems authorization would be given by an authorized person with a personal password to access the system, in which case there have to be strong controls over the issue and use of passwords. The store person should be instructed not to release inventories unless authorized personnel have intervened to give appropriate authority. The store person could also be instructed that deliveries over a certain quantity should be authorized by a person higher up the organization. Clerk A might be able to authorize despatch of (say) 1000 items, but 100 000 would have to be authorized by the sales manager and 1 000 000 by the sales director. The creditworthiness check might be performed by a computer program that compares credit limit with the balance owing after the current sales transaction. In this case, the point at which authorization was given would be shifted to the point where the credit limit was authorized, in which case access controls should be present to ensure that only an authorized person can access the database of credit limits. We might note that allocation of authority and responsibility becomes difficult where many users share a single database. If corruption of data occurs it may be difficult to decide who is responsible. We shall discuss particular control problems of database systems in Chapter 8.

We discuss access controls below.

Supervision controls

Supervision controls can be classified as higher level controls as they are carried out by responsible management at a high level within the organization. Any system of internal control should include supervision by responsible officials of day-to-day transactions and their recording. Thus, perusal of the payroll for reasonableness by the chief accountant before payment to employees is a good example of a supervisory control. Similarly, if management accounts are reviewed for reasonableness by a qualified accountant the auditor would gain a high level of satisfaction from this. We do not wish to downplay the importance of segregation of duties. What we are suggesting here is that the auditor may in some circumstances gain more satisfaction from the existence of controls carried out at a high level than they will from segregation itself. Of course, auditors would consider whether the people carrying out higher level controls possess integrity and are competent.

Other examples of supervisory controls are:

- An office supervisor of sales invoicing staff would be responsible for ensuring that staff performed their duties properly and had someone to turn to if problems arose.
- Supervision of staff accepting orders via an e-commerce system would need to ensure that staff are performing their work efficiently and politely.
- Sometimes, supervisory controls may be performed electronically, for instance, the automatic preparation of 'customers' credit limits exceeded'

listings. It is also common practice to record employee activity, such as interventions from specific terminals. There would, of course, have to be human controls at some stage, for instance, scrutiny of computer-prepared listings.

Further important organizational controls relate to the way that data is collected, prepared for entry to the system and actually enters the system at the entry interface for processing and we shall discuss this aspect when we take a look at boundary and input controls below.

A WORD ABOUT COLLUSION

Case study 7.3 gives good examples of segregation of duties to ensure that no one person can control a transaction from beginning to end or is in a position to interfere with the proper processing of data. Clearly, segregation is an important element of internal control, whether in a manual or computer system. This is because different people are responsible for different parts of the process or for checking the work of another. The value of segregation of duties and this kind of checking does depend, naturally enough, on whether the people performing the duties are genuinely independent of each other. If they work together – *collude* – to defeat the object of the control, it is as though the control does not exist. Thus, *collusion involves two or more employees agreeing to take common action to override a control.* For instance, if employee A keeps inventory and employee B is required to count it and compare it with inventory records, this would be an important control to safeguard assets. If A misappropriates inventory and B helps to hide it by stating that there are no differences between physical and book inventories, this would exemplify collusion. Both auditor and management are in a difficult position if collusion is occurring, but as a general principle, the auditor should ensure that management checks outputs for reasonableness and that duties are rotated periodically. The work of people who never take holidays should be particularly investigated, as this may be because they wish to cover up their activities. Procedures to ensure within reason that directors and other employees act with integrity are clearly important.

This is one reason that fraud is so often difficult to detect. The system may look as though there is proper segregation of duties but where collusion exists, two people act as one.

Security

This heading includes security of the assets of the information system, whether they are:

- Physical, such as hardware (computers, terminals or printers, etc.), other facilities, documentation, or negotiable instruments, such as cheques. Because of health problems associated with computer use (such as repetitive strain injury), we include people, such as terminal operators in this category.
- Software (systems and applications software) and data on master files and transactions files.

Security risk assessment

In considering security of these important assets, the auditor would confirm that the entity has a sensible security plan in place, that they have identified the assets at risk, the potential threats to them and also the likelihood of occurrence.

Review of the entity's security plan is an important step in the auditor's risk assessment.

Potential threats might include some that are accidental (but can be avoided with careful planning) such as fire, flood damage and other natural hazards or misuse by staff such as spilling coffee over keyboards. Other threats might be classed as deliberate, such as hacking, introduction of destructive viruses and Trojan horses and other kinds of deliberate sabotage, both internal and external. Having identified the threats, the auditor would also expect to see careful analysis of the controls needed to reduce potential losses from the identified threats, bearing in mind that it would normally be prohibitively expensive to reduce those losses to zero. Important physical controls to reduce losses to acceptable proportions include the following:

One of the authors attended a computer course in Paris some years ago and was invited to count the computer installations nearby that were proudly installed openly on ground floors behind plate glass. There were quite a number. Companies have since learned to be more careful.

Using fire extinguishers in computer installations can be problematic as some fire suppressants such as water can damage equipment while others are harmful to human beings or to the environment.

- Fire damage is a considerable threat in computer installations. The auditor would expect to see the installation itself made as safe as possible by siting in buildings resistant to fire and structurally sound, the use of fire resistant materials in computer rooms and regular and rapid clearing of waste. We would expect to see strategic placing of fire alarms with a central control panel showing the location of any alarm triggered, and automatic and manual fire extinguishers. It would also be important for staff to be trained to recognize potential fire risks.
- Water damage. We have already mentioned in the margin note above that water can damage computer equipment, but there are some sensible precautions that can be taken. Putting computer installations into buildings sited away from areas subject to flood, an increasing hazard as global warming takes place, is desirable or at least on the upper floors of buildings. Apart from this companies should have an alarm system that would allow appropriate action to be taken, have an easily accessible and known master switch for turning off water mains, and site facilities where water might be used (such as a canteen) away from computer facilities.
- Energy variations may occur taking the form of power surges that can damage equipment and software, or power failure. Companies may consider the use of back-up energy sources to prevent losses through power loss. The impact of power surges can be reduced by the use of voltage regulators or circuit breakers.
- Pollution, such as dust, can be a major cause of damage to disk drives and companies should install appropriate air-conditioning systems and ensure that installations are regularly cleaned.
- Intrusion by unauthorized personnel can be dangerous as intruders may cause physical damage or steal important documentation, portable equipment and data on portable media. Even hard disks and computer chips may be vulnerable. Physical controls to prevent intrusion include securing doors and windows and restricting entry through ventilation ducts. Alarm systems and cameras to detect unauthorized entry are other possibilities. Entry to computer installations might be restricted to authorized holders of cards with identification data encrypted on them.

The authors used word processing and spreadsheet packages and were perhaps overcautious in saving work done regularly and keeping back-up copies as writing proceeded. To lose many hours of work does not add to human happiness, so we arranged to have virus protection too.

Security of data

Just as important as physical assets are the data (remember that data and information are the life-blood of an organization) and data and programs must be protected against loss and unauthorized use and unauthorized change.

Security risk assessment

Again, the auditor would expect management to assess the risks that the entity may lose vital data and information. In particular management should identify the most important data, without which the entity could not survive and then introduce controls to protect such data.

ACTIVITY 7.7

Would you consider that an entity's sales ledger would be vital to the continued existence of the entity?

As we saw above in relation to assets, the auditor would, as a first step in identifying data security risks, review the entity's security plan, which should also describe the controls to reduce these risks.

Clearly trade receivables represent a very important asset, and one that normally will be converted into cash at a relatively early date. If the entity's sales ledger was destroyed, it would be necessary to reconstruct the ledger at a considerable cost of time, and in the meantime, the entity's cash flows would probably be seriously diminished. The entity's continued existence might even be put at risk, and the auditor faced with going-concern problems.

Controls over the security of data include some features that we have already discussed and others that we shall discuss later. They include:

- Restriction of access to data. We discuss this in relation to boundary and input controls in Chapter 8.
- Maintenance of information/audit trails.
- Maintenance of file and program libraries under the control of a responsible official.
- Holding data and programs in a secure place outside the computer complex.
- Use of grandfather, father, son (GFS) system or file dumping. An example of a GFS system is shown in Figure 7.7. File dumping is used for similar reasons and involves the copying of a file or of files after or before processing so that if the working file is corrupted during processing, the process can be started again using the copy of the file(s). These systems require files to be identified and the recording on the file(s) of control totals may also be used to ensure that the correct files and programs are being used in current processing.

Now work Activity 7.8, which contains a description of the files used to update a master file, together with a system flowchart showing the same thing diagrammatically.

ACTIVITY 7.8

Troston plc manufactures high-quality specialist equipment for dental hospitals and practices. It maintains data for all personnel employed on a master file held on hard disk. This master file forms important input to the company's payroll routine. The master file update run is shown on the computer systems flowchart below (Figure 7.8). The input to the run is as follows:

- Existing master file.
- New contracts of employment for joiners.
- Termination notifications for leavers.
- Agreed wage rate listings.
- Agreed bonus rate listings (the bonus is calculated on the difference between standard and actual time for batches of components or equipment assembled).

Output from the run is:

- Updated master file.
- Hard copy of personnel files.
- Hard copy of changes.

Required:
Suggest controls to ensure that the master file is, and remains, complete and accurate.

Important security controls in the area would include the following:

- A rigorous grandfather/father/son system to ensure that master files can be reconstructed in the event of a system crash. We discuss this matter at greater length in relation to run-to-run controls in Chapter 8.
- Copies of all master files to be held in a secure location outside the computer room.
- All master files to be identified internally by, for instance, date or control totals. External labelling to ensure selection of the correct file would also be important.
- Master files to be updated by persons not connected with the execution or processing of transactions. To ensure this a password system should be in operation.
- Careful validation of input data to the master file updating run to ensure that the master file is not corrupted.
- Checking of all input data (new employee contracts, termination notifications, new wage and bonus rates) to hard copy personal files by the person inputting the data and an independent person. Ideally there should be exception reporting and check digit controls in force. Remember that errors in the master file would cause systematic errors to occur every time the payroll is prepared.

FIGURE 7.7 An example of a grandfather, father, son (GFS) system

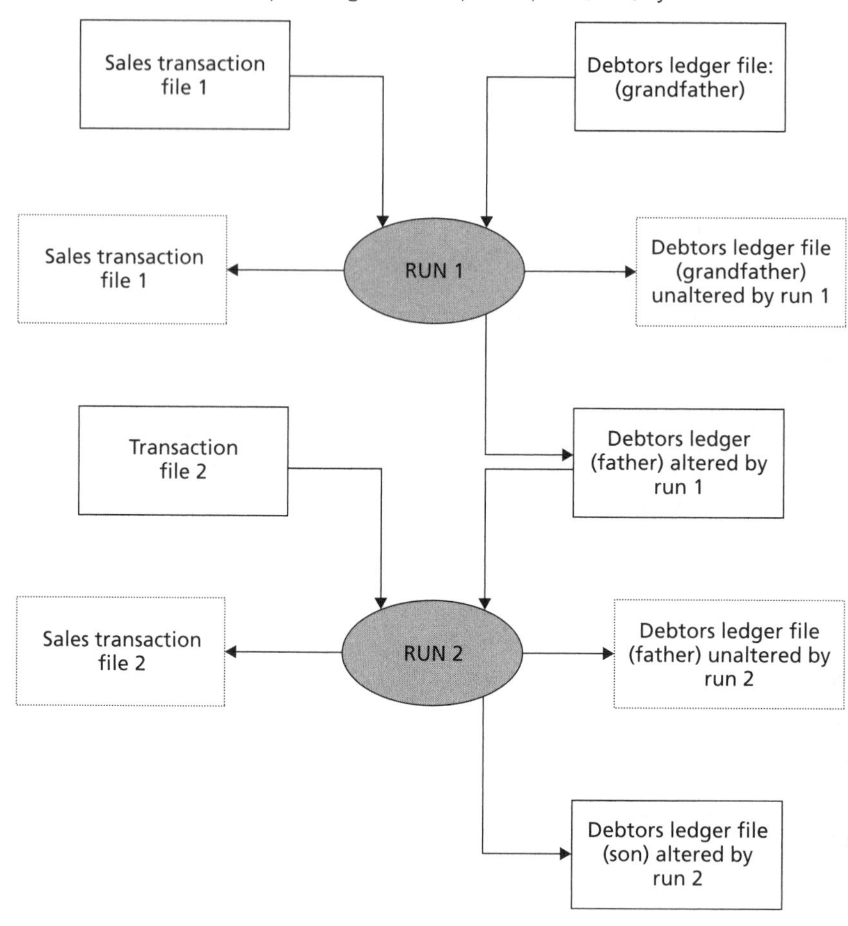

We discuss data capture/ input controls in Chapter 8.

We have discussed controls over the updating of master files under the heading 'Security', but they could be just as easily classified as input controls.

Quality assurance

See page 269.

In Figure 7.6 we showed an organization chart of the computer department and its place in a large entity, and included a quality standards group, responsible to the information systems director and independent of the computer department. It is this group that would ensure at the development stage that quality standards are incorporated into the design of the system and that they are maintained thereafter. The quality standards function should be independent of development, maintenance and operations. As far as auditors are concerned, the existence of such a function gives greater confidence that controls over development, maintenance and operations are reliable with a consequent impact on the amount of substantive procedures required. In smaller organizations the quality control function might be in the hands of internal audit, which will also possess the necessary degree of independence. Naturally, the external auditor will have to be confident that the quality control function, however set up, is itself of high quality.

We discuss external audit work to establish quality of internal audit in Chapter 15.

FIGURE 7.8 Troston payroll master file update

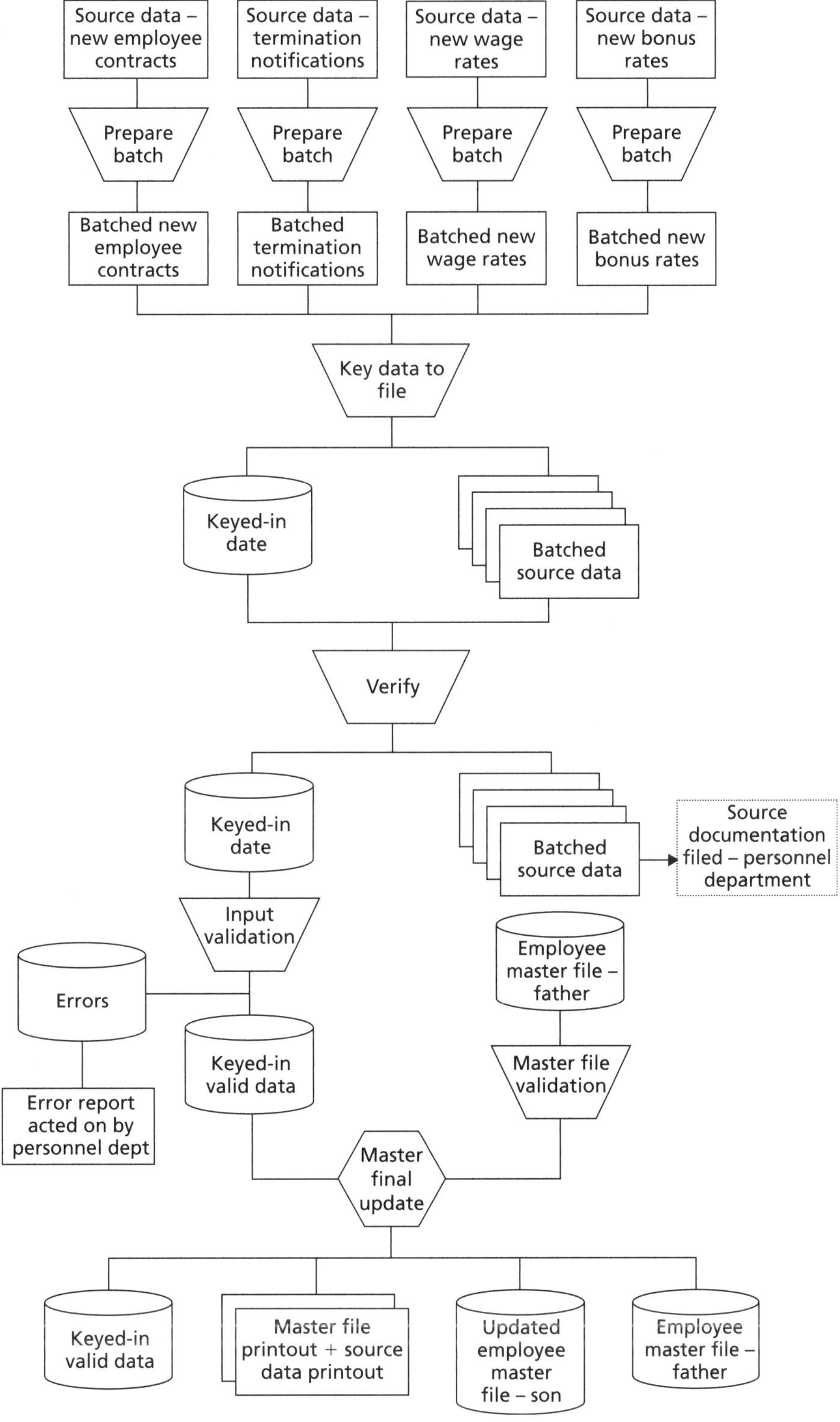

The basic matters with which the quality standards group will be concerned is whether the developed software will meet user needs, how reliable it is, its ease of use, whether it is efficient in terms of the resources used and how easy it is to maintain. Clearly, the quality standards function will also be concerned with such matters as the clarity and completeness of documentation of the system and the training and effectiveness of staff.

There are a number of reasons why there has been an increased interest in quality. In the first place, information/computer systems have become critical to an organization's survival. Imagine what losses an organization might suffer if it lost critical information on its customer database, such as trade receivable balances and their make-up. Some software, such as that used in air traffic control systems, is critical for human safety. Users are also becoming more demanding as they become used to the technology and are less willing to put up with the frustration caused when computer systems operate slowly or crash. This is particularly important when organizations are engaged in e-commerce. Poorly designed web pages and slow response times will soon cause potential customers to move elsewhere. Companies are also becoming aware of the impact that poor information systems and inadequate user interfaces have on staff morale and the general effectiveness of systems and their control.

For these reasons, auditors will be interested in the effectiveness of the quality assurance function.

ACTIVITY 7.9

Suggest general factors that might make a quality assurance function effective. How do you think that auditors should satisfy themselves that the function is effective?

In general terms we suggest the following general factors would enhance effectiveness of the function:

- Support of top management and a clear statement from management of the importance of quality of systems and information.
- High status within the organization. The function's position within the organization as shown in Figure 7.6 would seem to indicate high status. If it is not perceived to have high status its work and recommendations will tend not be taken seriously.
- As a corollary to this, it would be important that management took action on the recommendations made by the function, including those made during the development process.
- Adequate resources to perform the function properly, including staff with wide skills. A paramount skill would be their ability to work with a wide range of other professionals. Diplomacy and tact, combined with firmness would be essential attributes. The function's staff would have to be able to hold their own with other highly skilled managers and technicians within the entity.

As the function is such an important element of control, the auditor would have to assess its effectiveness. Discussion with management on the function's role would be important, backed up by examination of documentation making the role known to people within the organization affected by its work. Examination of reports by the quality assurance group at both the development stage and thereafter would help to disclose the nature of their work and whether their recommendations had been accepted. Discussion with major users would also be necessary to determine how effective the group's work is from user perspectives. Regarding quality of staff the auditor should examine the educational and experience background of staff. As there are very fast-moving developments in technology, the auditor would also ascertain what steps were taken by the entity to keep staff up to date. We shall see in Chapter 15 that this sort of audit work would also be carried out in respect of the work of the internal audit function.

This chapter has been an important one, as we have been considering the way in which organizations control their activities so that their business objectives can best be obtained. As we have seen, the auditor is very interested in the effectiveness of controls as a means of reducing control risk. We shall consider further aspects of control systems in Chapter 8.

Summary

This chapter was concerned with the control environment and other components of control systems internal to organizations. Most of these controls are designed to aid companies in achieving business objectives in the face of an external environment that is often of high risk. In addition, we saw that the general controls have to be in place to ensure that applications are, within reason, error free.

An important element was the discussion of the control environment and its components and we used a small company running a small independent supermarket to show that even a small business requires an accounting system and a control system. We also discussed the elements of more formal systems and used them to explain the importance of information/audit trails, and of segregation of duties and other important control features.

We introduced you to general controls over the internal environment (systems development/maintenance controls, organizational controls, security and quality assurance). We shall consider controls over individual applications in Chapter 8, together with a discussion of a number of different ways in which auditors record and evaluate systems, covering narration, visual descriptions and questionnaires and checklists.

In Chapter 9 we describe a number of systems used by companies, which use the computer with varying degrees of intensity. We shall also take the opportunity to discuss in greater depth how auditors test systems and evaluate how effective they are.

Key points of the chapter

- In establishing overall audit strategy the auditor considers the important factors that will determine the focus of the engagement team's efforts, including whether the auditor may plan to obtain evidence regarding the effectiveness of internal control.
- Auditors obtain an understanding of the accounting system and control environment. If they decide that control risk is low, they may be able to reduce the extent of substantive procedures.
- Controls are designed to prevent, detect or correct events the entity does not wish to happen, and to ensure that data and information are valid. Basic elements are (a) control environment and related components; (b) accounting and quality assurance/ control systems.
- Internal control is the process designed to provide reasonable assurance about the achievement of an entity's objectives with regard to reliability of financial reporting, effectiveness and efficiency of operations, and compliance with applicable laws and regulations.
- There are potential limitations in internal control.

- The components of internal control are: (a) control environment; (b) entity's risk assessment process; (c) information system; (d) control activities; and (e) monitoring of controls.
- The control environment includes governance and management functions and the attitudes, awareness and actions of those charged with governance and management concerning the entity's internal control and its importance in the entity. The control environment sets the tone of an organization, influencing the control consciousness of its people.
- Elements of the control environment are: (a) communication and enforcement of integrity and ethical values; (b) commitment to competence; (c) participation by those charged with governance; (d) management's philosophy and operating style; (e) organizational structure; (f) assignment of authority and responsibility; (g) human resource policies and practices.
- Entities should consider the likelihood of business risks crystallizing and the significance of the consequent financial impact on the business, and introduce suitable controls to reduce risks to an acceptable level.
- Relevant and timely information about internal activities and external factors is essential if an entity is to be successful; information systems should have in-built controls so that entity officials can respond properly to any deficiencies or to information that appears contradictory.
- Effective communication is an important element of information systems if the entity is to attain its objectives and maintain good control systems.
- Control activities to reduce business and audit risk include: authorization, performance review, information processing, physical controls, segregation of duties.
- Monitoring of controls is to assess the performance of controls and their adequacy and relevance over time. Monitoring may be a special responsibility of a quality standards group, internal audit or external audit.
- There are two broad control classifications: (a) general controls over the environment in which the entity operates; (b) application controls, to ensure an individual application runs smoothly and accurately. General controls include: (a) systems development/maintenance controls; (b) organizational controls; (c) security; (d) quality assurance.
- If systems development/maintenance controls are strong, it is easier to control individual applications. Important elements are: (a) organizational structure to ensure high standards during development; (b) documentation of development process; (c) testing at critical stages; (d) agreement in writing at each stage; (e) parallel developments, including staff training; (f) reliable system for reporting system malfunctions after implementation; (g) steps to prevent unauthorized changes to programs; (h) user agreement at critical development points. The same principles apply also to smaller systems but the process is truncated.
- The information/audit trail allows transactions to be traced forwards and backwards through the system.
- Organizational controls include: (a) organization charts; (b) segregation of duties; (c) authorization and approval; (d) supervision controls.
- Segregation of duties includes: (a) segregation of (i) authorization of transactions; (ii) execution of transactions; (iii) custody of assets; (iv) recording of transactions and assets; (b) in modern computer systems, segregation includes: (i) operation of programs segregated from ability to change them; (ii) alteration of master file data by responsible officials; (c) where control is dependent on segregation of duties within a particular function, management allocates duties appropriately; (d) rotation of duties within departments.
- Authorization and approval is closely linked to segregation of duties to responsible persons. Allocation of authority and responsibility is difficult in modern computer systems.
- Supervision controls are classified as higher level controls as they are performed by responsible management at a high level within the organization.
- If people work together to circumvent the system–collude – segregation of duties may be ineffective, often making fraud difficult to detect.
- Security of information system assets is vital, whether physical assets or software and data. The entity should have a security policy and identify assets at risk and the likelihood of risks occurring. Security controls include: (a) physical controls; (b) controls over data.
- Physical controls include controls to reduce impact of: (a) fire damage; (b) water damage; (c) energy variations or power failure; (d) pollution; (e) intrusion by unauthorized personnel.
- Controls over security of data include: (a) restriction of access; (b) information/audit trails; (c) file and program libraries; (d) holding data and programs in secure places; (e) use of grandfather, father, son or file dumping systems.
- The quality assurance function is to ensure developed software meets user needs and that documentation is clear and complete and staff are effective. Effectiveness factors include: (a) support of top management; (b) high status within the organization; (c) adequate resources to perform the function properly.

References

Lucey, T. (2004) *Management Information Systems* (9th edn), Cengage Learning.

Rowley, J. (2002) *E-business: Principles and Practice*, Basingstoke: Palgrave.

Weber, R. (1999) *Information Systems Control and Audit*, New York: Prentice Hall.

Further reading

The important ISA in the area is ISA 315 – *Identifying and assessing the risks of material misstatement through understanding the entity and its environment*. You may also refer to ISA 330 – *The auditor's responses to assessed risks*.

You may also refer to the revised Turnbull guidance on internal control: **http://www.frc.org.uk/documents/pagemanager/frc/Revised% 20Turnbull%20Guidance%20October% 202005.pdf**

We discuss this revised guidance in Chapter 18.

Self-assessment questions (solutions available to students)

7.1 Explain the importance of internal control within organizations. What are the main elements and what is the auditor's interest in them?

7.2 Integrity and ethical values are important factors in ensuring that internal control, including the control environment, is effective in reducing risk and in helping management to achieve objectives. Do you think that these are just meaningless words or are they really important in the business context? Why do you think that auditors look for integrity and ethical values in management and throughout the organization?

7.3 You have recently become auditor of a small trading entity whose system is based on a series of networked microcomputers, using bought-in software for basic accounting functions. During the initial meeting with management, the managing director told you that he is really scared of all 'this computer stuff', particularly as there is no one in the entity who has any specialized knowledge of computers. How would you advise him? What do you think might be the key risks in such a entity?

Self-assessment questions (solutions available to tutors)

7.4 Figure 7.1 showed that there are two broad levels of regulation and control relating to the external and internal environment. Assume that you are the auditor of an entity providing advice to clients on financial matters. You are aware that there have been serious reductions in the value of shares quoted on stock exchanges throughout the world and that this will have a negative impact on pensions in the future. Explain how management of the entity should react to this external factor. Consider the control environment of the entity and auditors' interest.

7.5 As organizations have become more dependent on the reliability of information systems, they have become more aware of the need to maintain quality of systems and the data/information derived from them. If you were asked to set up a quality standards group, what role do you think it should have and what steps should be taken to render it effective?

7.6 Segregation of duties is a basic requirement of a good control system. Explain what is meant by this statement and show how 'segregation of duties in a modern computer system might differ from that in a manual system.

Solutions available to students and Solutions available to tutors

These can be found on the website in the student/lecturer section at: www.cengage.co.uk/graymanson5.

Topics for class discussion without solutions

7.7 The existence of a quality standards group within an entity's control system, like the internal audit function, is a vital element of the control environment. Discuss.

7.8 Audit staff have to be skilled and experienced enough to understand the complexities of modern control systems. Discuss how this might be achieved.

8

Systems work: basic ideas 2

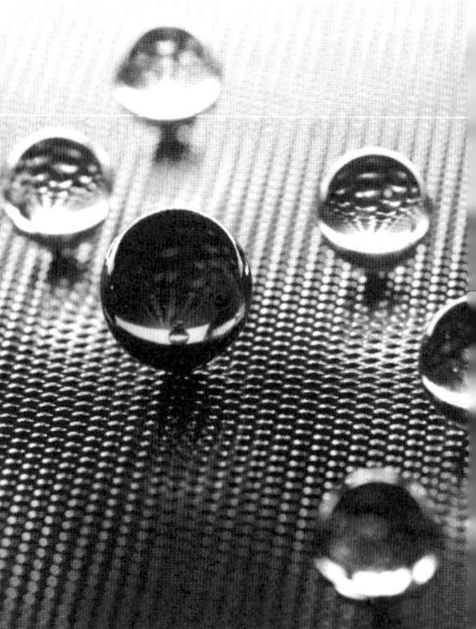

LEARNING OBJECTIVES

After studying this chapter you should be able to:

- **Explain the nature and role of application controls and describe the main features of these controls.**
- **Distinguish between systems-development/maintenance controls and application controls.**
- **Show how the auditor breaks down systems into components as an aid to understanding the systems.**
- **Explain how the auditor records systems in use.**

Learning objectives, 285
Introduction, 286
Application controls, 286
Data capture/input controls, 287
Processing controls, 294
Output controls, 296
Database systems, 297
E-commerce, 299
Audit approaches to systems and controls, 305
Summary, 326
Key points of the chapter, 326
Further reading, 327
Self-assessment questions (solutions available to students), 327
Self-assessment questions (solutions available to tutors), 328
Topics for class discussion without solutions, 328

INTRODUCTION

In Chapter 7 we discussed the significance of layers of regulation and control in an organization. We defined internal control and explained the significance of the control environment and related components. We also discussed the nature and role of systems development/maintenance controls, looked at their main features and noted that general controls provide a secure environment within which applications can take place. In this chapter we turn our attention to application controls, but before doing this, let us remind ourselves that computerized systems are so important for modern businesses that their failure or significant inefficiencies in them will be a major business risk. Auditors will have to satisfy themselves that controls over applications are strong, particularly where they are used to process transactions and create balances reflected in the financial statements.

APPLICATION CONTROLS

Before we discuss application controls we will ask you what the major objectives of applications might be, bearing in mind that they transform input data into further data and information for users.

ACTIVITY 8.1

List the major objectives of computer applications in general terms.

You may have listed the following major objectives:

- Data collected prior to input should be genuine, accurate and complete. An important supporting objective is that all input data should be properly authorized.
- Data accepted by the system should be processed in such a way that it remains genuine, accurate and complete.
- Data stored temporarily or permanently should be genuine accurate and complete.
- Output data/information is genuine, accurate and complete and goes to the intended recipient.
- All transactions and balances processed by the system can be traced back to their source and forward to their final destination, that the information/audit trail is complete.

We have used the phrase ‘genuine, accurate and complete’ four times in our list of objectives. We remind you that this phrase means that all transactions or balances should be based on real events; for instance, a sales order should be the result of a real order by a customer; that a trade receivable balance should have resulted from real transfers of goods or services (genuine).

In addition, all data items should be properly calculated, for instance, that sales invoices contain amounts charged to customers on the basis of agreed prices and quantities and that casts are correct and VAT properly calculated (accurate). Furthermore, that all the data have been input and processed and made available to users, that none are missing (complete). You should remember these objectives as you read about application controls below.

In this chapter we discuss application controls under the following headings:

We refer you again to Table 6.2 on page 219 for an explanation of 'genuine, accurate and complete'.

- Data capture/input controls
- Processing controls
- Output controls
- Database systems
- E-commerce.

DATA CAPTURE/INPUT CONTROLS

In this section we consider the controls at the point where data are captured at the boundary or interface of the system and subsequent entry by operators. They are particularly important at the boundaries or interfaces as risk is high as boundaries are crossed.

ACTIVITY 8.2

A sales clerk receives a telephone order from a customer, Harry Smith, who asks for a delivery of 100 units of a product, at a price of £5 per unit.

What is particularly risky about this transaction and what procedures would be appropriate to reduce the risks to an acceptable level?

A major risk is that the customer will receive goods or services and not pay for them. Other risks include despatch of goods other than those requested, despatches to wrong addresses, despatch at prices or terms other than those agreed, or promising delivery when goods are not available, thus threatening good relations. No doubt there are other risks, but these are enough to be going on with.

These risks can be reduced if the entity has systems for identifying the customer, for checking the order, for checking credit worthiness, for determining terms for that kind of customer and for checking inventory availability. If Harry Smith is an existing customer, he may identify himself by giving details known only to himself, such as mother's maiden name, or identification word (banks frequently use identification systems like this). For existing customers, the system might allow comparison by the clerk of current balance outstanding as updated by current transaction and credit limit. New customers might be asked for credit card details that will establish that credit is available, or may be asked to pay before the goods are delivered. The information system should allow the clerk to check on availability of inventory and delivery times. The other risks mentioned probably all result from incorrect recording. To make such errors less likely, the screen format for sales orders should be designed for ease of use and the system should not allow the order to proceed unless all fields of the form on the screen are completed. The clerk should also be trained to read the details of the order back to the customer. A copy of the order might be emailed or sent by post to the customer.

Now let us consider data capture and input controls in detail.

Boundary controls

These are the controls over the interface between the user and the system. They have tended to become more important as systems have been distributed to distant locations. At one time such controls were not so necessary as users were well known, most computing activities were centrally located and access could be restricted by physical controls such as locked doors. When users became dispersed and e-commerce became an important means of conducting business, it became necessary to establish the identity of users, to restrict their use of data and information and to ensure users got the data/information desired by them. This is a very complex area and we cannot do more than give a flavour of some of the controls in use and to expand on those more commonly used. Boundary controls include the following:

- *Cryptographic controls*, which make data unreadable except to authorized users, who possess the means to make them readable.
- *Plastic cards* are a means to identify users and may contain information about them, which can be used to prove that they are genuine. There should be controls over application for the card, over its preparation, issue and cancellation. They are more secure if they are used in conjunction with PINs.
- *Personal Identification Numbers (PINs).* The use of PINs will be well known to you because banks and retailers use them to prove that the user is genuine. Of course, if the PINs are not held separately from the plastic card, neither cards nor PINs will provide the needed control if both are lost in the same wallet. Careful control has to be maintained over generation of PINs and their alteration, over their issue and receipt by users. Most systems allow only a few attempts to enter a PIN and this is obviously a good control, even if it is annoying if you have a poor memory.
- *Digital signatures.* We often sign documents to give our agreement to a contract or when we send a letter. These are known as analogue signatures. Increasingly, however, people using computer systems are required to give their agreement to documents and contracts using digital signatures which are encrypted and may be read by someone with the appropriate facility when the document is received.
- *Passwords and firewalls.* The above controls are largely to do with making data unusable by unauthorized users, either by making the data unreadable or by requiring identification and authentication of the person attempting to cross the boundary. However, perhaps the most widely used controls to prevent or restrict access are passwords and firewalls.

Passwords

We would expect a password system to have the following features:

- Establishment of degrees of access, giving users an identifying number, and an access status that tells what data they are allowed to access and the functions they can perform. These functions would include a range of possible actions affecting data – 'read only'; 'read and add new data'; 'read and amend'; and 'read and delete': and, of course, 'no access' or 'access denied'. Thus, a sales order clerk might be allowed to read information on the trade receivables file – balance and credit limits, for instance – but not alter them. Other more senior users might be allowed to alter such data.
- Passwords with at least eight alphanumeric digits, but combinations easy to remember.
- Avoidance of passwords that have an association with the person using them.
- Staff training to ensure that staff are aware that passwords are secret.
- Regular and frequent changes in passwords.
- Shutdown of terminals when an incorrect password has been entered (say) three times.

Access controls are particularly important when distant terminals are used to transmit data to a computer at a central location:

(a) At one time terminals were kept in a separate room, but this is not relevant today when in most organizations they are on desks of employees for use when required. This means that a password system is an important control in systems using distant terminals.

(b) Another important control in systems using terminals is to limit their use so that, for instance, some terminals might be used to access the sales accounting system only. This would make it more difficult for unauthorized persons to obtain access to confidential data (such as payroll) or to data for which they have no need. (The goods received department might not be allowed to access sales analyses, for instance.)

(c) A useful technique is to have a system that records which terminals and which employees are accessing the system and at what times. Such a control needs to be backed up by review of the access record by a responsible person and enquiry made when there appears to have been access from unauthorized terminals or by unauthorized employees.

(d) A further useful control is to restrict the use of terminals to normal working hours unless special authorization is given by a responsible person. This might not be appropriate in the e-commerce environment where the facility might be online for 24 hours.

In many instances companies use the national telephone system for transmitting data to computer installations. Where this is the case we would expect to see the following additional controls in force:

- The telephone numbers used should be ex-directory and not made public. This would make it more difficult for 'hackers' to gain access. This feature can be strengthened by making the telephone numbers known only to computer software and not to users of terminals. The central computer system would only allow access when the identity of the employee has been verified.

- It is possible to hire private lines from the telephone operator, which would be used by the organization only and no one else. Such lines would be more secure.
- The use of telephone numbers can be restricted to certain parts of the computer system so that, for instance, the sales system could only be accessed using 'sales' numbers.
- A call-back system can be used to ensure that calls to the main computer system are genuine. Such a system would disconnect the terminal and the central computer system would then call the terminal back and connect it. This is to prevent unauthorized access from a location outside the organization.
- Where data are being transmitted over telephone lines, encryption might be particularly important if they are to be secure.

Firewalls

Firewalls are created and maintained by specially designed systems to protect computer networks from unauthorized intrusion. Many businesses have established networks (known as intranets) to provide a variety of services such as email to employees. There is no doubt that email has much improved communication within organizations and has also allowed easy transfer of data between parts of the system. Networks are often expanded to include people and organizations outwith the organization, such as customers and suppliers, in which case they are known as extranets. The problem with networks such as these is that they may become vulnerable if they are too open to the outside world. Data might be corrupted from an outside source and companies have had to find ways to protect themselves from such intrusions. A firewall is a system that controls access from or to the Internet or between two or more networks, even within the same organization, while allowing free communication within the network. Some of the features of firewall control are similar to those we have already discussed, such as requiring identification of data being transmitted and of the person or organization transmitting it. Some networks are very tight, not allowing any transmission through the firewall without the control mechanism being primed. This may, however, be too restrictive for effective communication, so many companies adopt open methods for some forms of communication and more rigorous methods where data is being transferred or where privacy is paramount.

An intranet might be set up for the use of top management, other parts of the organization not having access to it.

Initiation of the information/audit trail

It is at the point of access where the user crosses the boundary at the user interface that the first records of the trail must be made. The identity and the authenticity of the user would first be recorded.

ACTIVITY 8.3

Bearing in mind our discussion above, what other data about users and related actions should be recorded?

Clearly, the system should record the data to which access is requested, but in addition/the actions that the user wishes to take with respect to the data (for instance, a sales clerk requiring access to credit customers' details and inventory availability). The system would also record the terminal at which access is being sought, as this would indicate the location of the user. After access has been requested, a record should be made of the access decision with regard to the data and the degree of access. Other matters that might be recorded would be the number of sign-on attempts and the time of starting and finishing. All of this seems very logical, but clearly if these steps were not taken the entity and auditor would find it difficult if not impossible to reconstruct the sequence of events and to determine if security at the user interface was satisfactory.

Input controls

Boundary controls and input controls are clearly interrelated as controls at the interface will help to ensure that data entering the system is valid. However the input subsystem is the one that brings the data to the application system for processing. The application system also requires the correct programs to be verified and loaded, so the input subsystem is responsible for ensuring the validity of software in use as well.

Some input controls over data must be in place before the data passes the user interface. Examples of such controls are:

- *Design of source documentation*. We suggested above that screens should be properly designed to reduce errors at the user interface, but we would also expect to see the use of pre-printed and pre-numbered source documents and subsequent sequence checking. Such checking is an aid to completeness of collection – and later processing – as a break in sequence may indicate missing input data. Other design features include clear headings and layouts to aid completion. Fields should also be designed to ensure that product, customer, supplier codes, dates and so on are complete by standardizing length of entry and providing the appropriate number of boxes on the form. An important objective is ease of entry at the keyboard. Even documents originating from outside the organization may be made easier to read by prior highlighting of key data, such as order number, price, value, VAT and so on. One of the authors remembers seeing a computerized payments system that used the German Post Office giro account number of the supplier as the supplier's computer-account number. One person in the office seemed to spend his entire day underlining the giro account number on the face of suppliers' invoices in green ink, so the operator would be able to find it easily. He seemed to be happy in his work, doubtless because he knew he was exercising an important control function.
- *Design of product, customer and other codes*. Codes are important means for the application system to identify the subject of data entry. Clearly, if wrong codes have been entered, processing will be inaccurate, so ways have to be found to ensure codes are likely to be entered correctly – or that wrong entries are detected at an early stage. Some are fairly simple, such as keeping codes as short as possible or grouping parts of a code into short blocks, grouping alpha characters and numeric characters separately, ensuring that codes do not need shift key movements on the keyboard and avoiding the use of letters that might be mistaken for numbers.

- *Use of check digits* to make detection of entry errors more likely, thus ensuring that the correct employee details are entered or the correct customer is charged or the correct inventory movement is recorded. Check digits are digits that are included in the code number and bear a mathematical relationship to the rest of the digits, which is checked by the program. Check digits must be carefully designed as some kinds of error, such as transposition, might not be detected by the more simple systems. Furthermore, as the use of check digits takes up computation time, many companies restrict their use to fields deemed to be critical, such as inventory codes.
- *Sequence checking*. We noted above that sequence checking would enable the system to detect whether a data item is missing. Clearly, there must be a system to allocate numbers to documents or to data read or entered directly at the user interface. A sequence check by the input subsystem might reveal missing data items at an early stage, but we would expect to see sequence checking during processing as well.
- *Limit or reasonableness tests*. These are programmed controls that detect data items that do not meet certain criteria. For instance, if hours worked were entered incorrectly as 64 in a week instead of 46, the input system might detect this by checking input to a predetermined limit of (say) 50 hours and request re-entry.
- *One-for-one checking*. Some data items are so critical that they need to be checked manually to source documentation. This might apply to changes to the personnel master file that has to be correct if the payroll is to be accurate.
- *Batch controls*. Batching of documents and transactions is a good way of controlling input, particularly if combined with appropriate organizational controls. Let us take a look first at a simple, document batch system in an entity with a centralized data entry system, as shown in Figure 8.1.

FIGURE 8.1 Interface between data preparation and computer room

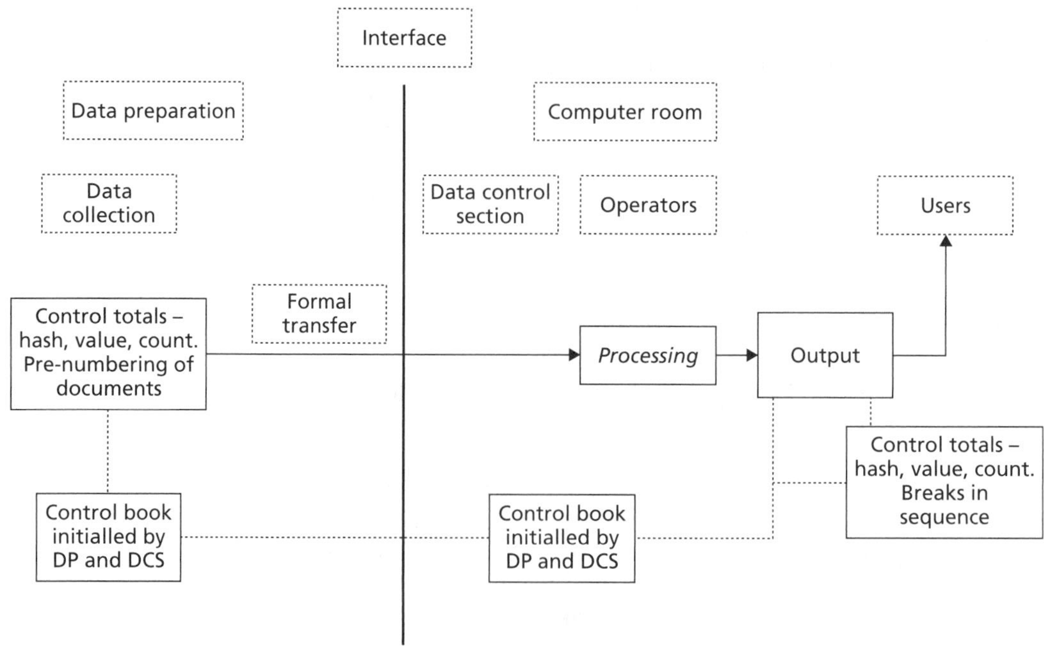

Organizational controls in this entity include formal transfers of data between data preparation departments and the data control section and early verification of inputs. In this kind of system we would expect to see:

- Segregation of user departments and the computer department.
- User department retention of control over data (in database systems, where the database is updated from numerous sources, this is normally not possible). Control is aided by the use of control totals prepared by data preparation departments, whether hash, value or count. Hash totals are meaningless in themselves. For instance, they might be a summation of quantities of different products sold, but can be used to check that outputs after processing are accurate and complete. The value total is the currency value of data entered. The count is the number of documents in the batch and is a means to ensure that all documents have been processed. You will observe too that the documents are pre-numbered, allowing the program to check that there is no break in sequence. The number of the document would be entered with the other data.
- Formal transfer of data between data preparation departments and the data control section in the computer department. This would reduce the risk of unauthorized processing.
- Maintenance of control logs by both data preparation and the data control section of the computer room.
- Investigation of differences between pre-determined control totals and actual totals initially by the data control section but with review of exception reports and decision on action by data preparation departments.
- Early verification of inputs. In non real-time systems there can be a pause between input and processing and input validation can be carried out prior to processing.

The data control section is responsible for ensuring input documentation is complete on receipt, passed to operators and that computer-prepared control totals agree with pre-determined totals. In offline systems and online (not real-time) systems, data preparation staff have ultimate responsibility for completeness and accuracy of input data and should have the final decision about corrective action if control totals do not tally.

In database systems, batching cannot be used in the way shown in Figure 8.1, because data will be entered by a number of different users, probably in dispersed locations. This means that the data preparers lose control of the data. However, batch systems can still be used, although the batch may be very different in nature, in that it does not consist of a batch of documents but a batch of actions. It might be all the data entries made by a particular clerk or all entries through a particular terminal during the day. Clerks will prepare control totals of their transactions during the day and these control totals will be transmitted to the data control section, together with the date the entries were made, for after-the-event comparison between the clerks' control totals and those produced by the processing subsystem. So, if Clerk A has sent sales orders from a terminal in a distant location, with a self-prepared hash total of £10 903, the output total for Clerk A should be the same. Of course, Clerk A has to be identified at the user interface. In this kind of system, the input clerks do remain in control of their data, but this would not be the case if only the terminal control totals were recorded.

Input data should be verified as soon as possible as it is expensive to correct errors at a later stage, say after processing, and in the meantime there is a danger that the data, whether on the database or elsewhere, has been corrupted. This means that the input subsystem should put the data through a validation run to check input data before it proceeds to final processing, that the checking routine should produce an exception report of such matters as incomplete sequence, and non-existent product/customer codes. The system should then route details of errors back to the original preparer of the data for correction. In more modern systems, the input subsystem will report the error to the preparer at the time of entry, giving a sound warning and describing the type of error (for instance 'invalid product number') on the screen.

ACTIVITY 8.4

What kind of data on the information/audit would you like to see recorded?

The information/audit trail as input goes through the input subsystem to be readied for processing is similar to that recorded at the data interface, but with additional data concerning transaction and master file data to be updated, number of batch to which data item is attached, time and date of capture and so on.

Basically enough information is required to trace data items back to source and forward to output.

PROCESSING CONTROLS

CPU, main memory and operating system

CPUs and main memory have a reputation for high reliability, but the entity should ensure that their elements are tested from time to time and that backup facilities are available when needed. Some companies run two identical computer installations and transfer operations from one to the other on a regular basis. Other organizations have agreements with entities with similar configurations should problems occur.

With regards to the operating system, it has to be capable of preventing corruption of data, bearing in mind that in modern systems many users may be using the system at the same time. If things do go wrong, such as an unexpected power failure, it must control operations so that losses of data and software are minimized. It must protect itself from unauthorized intrusion, bearing in mind that clever hackers have found ways in the past to fool operating systems that they are legitimate users. Auditors should ensure that the entity has a monitoring system to reduce the likelihood of unauthorized intrusion as far as possible.

Controls over applications

There are a number of particular control matters that should be observed regarding processing. These are:

(a) There should be continuity in processing, with run-to-run controls to ensure correct transaction and master files have been selected for processing. Thus, if an entity keeps 'sales transactions to date' and 'trade receivables ledger' on file, the program should check whether the files it is updating are the previously updated ones. In other words the 'father' files should be used, together with current transactions, to produce the 'son' 'sales transactions to date' and 'trade receivables ledger' files. Clearly, updating 'grandfather' files would produce the wrong result. One way to do this would be to record the date of last processing and related control total on files at the end of each processing run. The update program would check that the master files were as expected and then use the control totals on master files and new transactions file to check on the accuracy of the processing. Where files are stored on secondary storage, such as external disks, the secondary storage medium should contain an external label as well as an electronic identifier, such as date of last update and control totals. The program would reject any file where the electronic identifier was different from that expected. For security purposes it is necessary to dump contents of disks and the database from time to time and control totals may be set up then.

(b) Data on master files used by all runs of a particular kind of transaction must be genuine, accurate and complete. Take another look at the Troston system flow chart in Figure 7.8 and remind yourself that master file data and transactions form input to the updating computer run. Clearly, master files must be up to date, but authorization procedures should be in force, coupled with segregation of duties, when updating these files. It is preferable, for instance, for individuals in the personnel department, independent of payroll preparation, to update payroll master files. It is so important that master files are genuine, accurate and complete that all new entries should be checked for accuracy after initial entry. In the Troston system the output from the master file update run includes hard copy personnel files and these could be checked with input data. Control totals can be set up for testing each time the file is used. Auditors, both internal and external, will test completeness and accuracy of master files.

See page 279.

(c) Processing in computer systems is performed using programmed instructions, so it is vital that programs are tested at the development stage *and* on a continuing basis to ensure that they continue to perform as planned. Errors arising automatically because of program errors are known as 'systematic errors' and are dangerous because they automatically arise every time the program is run or the master file used.

(d) As far as the information/audit trail is concerned the auditor would expect to see a record of all processing actions from the time the input data is received to the time that it is despatched as output.

ACTIVITY 8.5

Assume that in an entity you are auditing, a inventory order is automatically prepared when a minimum inventory level has been reached. What kind of data would you like to see recorded in the preparation of the purchase order?

In circumstances such as this the record should identify the reasons for the action, the results of the action, and the part of the program that triggered it. We would expect to see a record of the logical decision – actual free inventory quantity is below minimum quantity and also details of re-order quantity; new free inventory quantity; selected supplier; date; order number; and so on. The subroutine of the program that caused the action should also be recorded.

Clearly, auditors seeking to use the recorded audit trail must have a means of interrogating it and producing a report of the data that they wish to trace. We discuss auditor use of the computer in audit testing later, but the audit objective must first be established when carrying out work like this. In this case it might be to establish that purchase orders issued had been properly authorized and had been triggered as a result of a real need for the goods in question.

Chapter 10.

(e) If a system failure occurs during processing, the control system should ensure that no data is lost or corrupted. We are sure that all of you at one time or another have lost part of an essay or other written work because a PC has failed. There are ways to protect work in the course of completion – either by saving regularly or having built-in save routines. In large-scale computer systems, companies will install systems that will tell, in the event of a processing failure, which data has been successfully processed and which has not. Auditors will wish to ensure that such systems are reliable and that the details of broken and restarted processing is recorded in the information/audit trail.

(f) Other processing controls include the following:

- Sequence checks. We discussed sequence checks in input controls, but in this case the purpose would be to ensure completeness of data processed.
- Limit or reasonableness tests. These tests are also useful for testing the accuracy of data after processing. To take a payroll example again, if a wage, after processing, exceeds a pre-determined amount, the processing subsystem would cause the item to be recorded on an exception report.
- Casts and cross-casts. Some groups of data items can be tested for accuracy by checking that cross-casts agree with vertical casts. This kind of test could be carried out on a payroll or on sales reports.

OUTPUT CONTROLS

The two purposes of output controls are to ensure that outputs are genuine, complete and accurate and that they are distributed to those who need them.

The basic rule on distribution of outputs is that they should be designed to give the information that users need for their work and that the users should be formally authorized. Particular care should be taken with outputs containing confidential information.

In Chapter 7, page 263 – we noted that decisions regarding distribution of output should be made at the development stage and fully documented.

We have already suggested a number of controls to ensure genuineness, completeness and accuracy of input and processing of data. Clearly, if access controls, batch control and rapid correction of errors are present, the likelihood that outputs will be complete and accurate will be much enhanced. The exception report is a special kind of output, important in the context of control. In modern systems we would expect errors to be detected and corrected rapidly, but, if for any reason correction is delayed, there should be proper follow-up of the reasons for delay and investigation of errors, their analysis and confirmation that rejected items have been corrected within a reasonable timescale. Another vital control is accounting by user departments for all stationery, particularly if valuable, for instance, pre-printed cheque stationery.

ACTIVITY 8.6

Assume that you use monthly sales analyses derived from the entity's information systems as one tool to determine the marketing strategy. What do you think you should first do before you take any action in respect of the analyses?

It may sound obvious but users of output data and information (in this case sales analyses) should be trained to review the output for any obvious errors. Actual results might be compared with estimates or what is the norm for a particular set of data or information. Similarly, one would not expect payroll totals to vary to a great extent in the normal course of business. A salary or wage on a payroll might stand out as being abnormal, although we would expect such abnormal items to be picked up by programmed limit or reasonableness checks. The auditor would be interested in this kind of user activity as it represents a further control over the accuracy of data and the effectiveness of systems.

DATABASE SYSTEMS

We have already mentioned database systems from time to time, but now wish to summarize important database controls. A database may be defined as 'a collection of data that is shared and used by a number of different applications for different purposes'. We have already seen the prime advantage of database systems is that they provide the same data to everyone in the entity having authority to access them, but we did note that there are security and integrity problems associated with databases and these we address below:

(a) There is loss of control over data by data preparation personnel. This is because the database may be updated from a number of different sources, often over telephone lines from distant locations. Data preparers thus cease to 'own' the data they initiate, leading to loss of responsibility on the part of the key data preparers.

ACTIVITY 8.7

How do you think the entity should re-establish control? When you are considering this matter assume that a sub-schema on the database contains data for all personnel in the entity. Suggest what the auditor's interest might be in this area.

We have already considered the update of personnel master files in Activity 7.8 on page 277. One way to solve the control problem in database systems is to give ownership of a particular sub-schema to designated users, who have specified rights (such as read, add, amend, delete) with regard to data (in this case the personnel standing data). Other users might also be allowed to access data in a sub-schema but with restricted rights, such as 'read only' rights, or not being allowed to access data with certain characteristics, such as details of employees with salaries in excess of a specified amount.

(b) After-the-event authorization may become a necessary feature of database systems. In our comments on non-database systems we suggested that input data should be authorized before processing takes place. In real-time database systems this becomes difficult as input data updates the database immediately. The database administrator wants only valid data to enter the database and one way of achieving this is to program control totals, and sequences for all entries from individual input clerks or individual terminals. These control totals and sequences would be checked by the input subsystem and a report, containing perhaps a complete listing of their inputs for a certain day, together with control totals, returned to the clerks concerned. This could be a feature of the personnel standing data update routine referred to in Activity 8.7. Retrospective agreement to the listing is known as 'after-the-event authorization'. The auditor should ensure that this authorization process is in place.

(c) Excessive power in the hands of the database administrator. As data preparation personnel lose control over data, this control passes to the database administrator. In small systems the database administrator may be one person, but in larger systems may be represented by a department. The database administrator is responsible for managing the database management system, including access control and security, back-up and recovery. We saw earlier in this chapter that the database administrator is also represented on the IT committee. To operate the database system, the database administrator has to have an intimate knowledge of the structure of the database, details of the data required by specific programs, when the data must be made available and so on. In these circumstances, segregation of duties becomes more difficult to achieve. It is argued that the very existence of large companies could be put at risk because so much power lies in the hands of a small group.

In consequence, the auditor would expect to see controls over personnel within the data administration department, including supervision of their activities, segregation of duties and periodic rotation of duties. A record of all actions by personnel affecting the database should be maintained, and supervision should include regular review of such records. This might be aided by programmed analysis of interventions by individual persons within the department. Proper arrangements should be made for taking holidays and taking over the duties of personnel during holiday periods.

(d) Technical features to secure safety in processing tend to reduce control. For instance, file dumps may be made before processing, so that if something is going wrong, it is possible to 'roll back' to the previous position and process again. It does not need much imagination to realize that unauthorized 'rolling back' could easily result in the destruction of data.

(e) The information/audit trail is particularly important in respect of a database. We would expect to see the same kind of records as we have discussed in relation to other parts of the system, namely, a record of all interventions affecting data on the database, the name and location of the user concerned, the degree of access requested and given, the program used to read, add, amend or delete data, the time and date of intervention, and a record of the data item before intervention and after.

We would also expect to see a means of reading the whole audit trail of an event affecting the database.

E-COMMERCE

In Chapter 16, we discuss the use of the Internet to publish financial information and the kind of controls necessary to ensure that it remains valid.

We gave you a definition of e-commerce earlier in this chapter. We are now turning to a discussion of business carried out electronically through the Internet. There has been considerable hype about e-business using the Internet and many of the original dot.com companies collapsed without making any profit. However, that does not mean that there is no scope for generating business over the Internet. In some cases it may be possible to integrate systems with business partners to take advantage of such matters as 'just-in-time' supply arrangements. There is an EU directive in the area designed to provide legal certainty for business and consumers alike. It is gradually being put into effect by members of the EU, and the UK adopted it in 2006. We will not consider the terms of the directive in detail, but note that it covers the following areas: sale of goods or services to businesses or consumers on the Internet or by email; advertising on the Internet or by email; or conveying or storing electronic content for customers or providing access to a communication network.

In this section we consider the business risks faced by companies using the Internet and other public networks and how companies attempt to reduce the impact of those risks. We consider also important matters for auditors.

Typical means of communication over the Internet are email, web pages, file transfers, chat-rooms and news groups. Risk is enhanced by the very openness of the Internet. To understand risk in this context it is important that you know how the entity uses the Internet for business purposes. The following are four degrees of Internet use:

1 Using the Internet as a means of making information available to outsiders about the entity and its products and services.

2 Exchanging information with customers and other trading partners. There may be links to other information and search engines may help potential customers to find a particular product or service.
3 Using the Internet to transact business, such as e-shopping. At this point there may be security concerns about such matters as protection of personal data.
4 The most sophisticated use of the technology fully integrates business systems with e-business conducted through the Internet. Companies might allow customers to have access to databases, to such information as availability of inventory, and details of products and prices. At this stage access controls such as those already discussed will assume importance.

Some types of business have embraced the use of Internet in commerce more than others and the impact of associated risks is therefore greater.

ACTIVITY 8.8

From your own personal experience, suggest business sectors that are heavily involved in e-commerce.

There are quite a few sectors involved in e-commerce, but your suggestions probably include banking and financial services, books and recorded music, computer software and hardware and the travel and holiday industry. There have also been attempts by central government in the United Kingdom to increase the use of electronic communication in local government and for submission of tax returns. They have in fact been successful in persuading one of the authors to submit his tax return electronically.

Management strategy and business/inherent risks

There are two publications relevant to this section and you may care to read them: *E-business: Identifying Financial Statement Risks*, issued by APB in April 2001 (Bulletin 2001/3); *Electronic Commerce: Effect on the Audit of Financial Statements*, issued by IFAC in October 2001 (International Auditing Practice Statement 1013).

At stages 3 and 4 above, management has to decide whether business conducted over the Internet is regarded as separate from the entity's main business or whether it is fully Integrated. If fully integrated, Internet transactions will have direct impact on the entity's records, with, for instance, immediate update of inventory records, trade receivables' and creditors' records and so on. If this is the case, business and inherent risks will be much higher. For this reason it is vital that auditors determine at an early stage management strategy with regard to e-business and, very importantly, what steps they have taken to identify risks and to introduce controls to reduce their impact. Remember that controls are not cost free and it will be important for managers to decide what level of risk is acceptable in its e-commerce activities by balancing the losses that may arise from potential risks against the estimated cost of added controls and the management of risk. Particular risks that should be addressed are detailed below.

Security risks

Because the Internet is so open, particular care has to be taken to avoid outside intervention for malicious purposes or for personal advantage. Particular threats to security of data and systems include corruption of data and destruction of systems by viruses and interventions by hackers. There is a real threat to privacy of personal data, such as bank account and credit card details provided by customers when making payment over the Internet. Unless companies have controls to prevent such details being read by unauthorized persons, the latter may be able to gain access to customer funds, the entity facing losses because of customer claims. Companies engaged in selling products such as software or recorded music over the Internet have been suffering considerable losses because outsiders have been able to infringe intellectual property rights. There has also been a worrying increase in the amount of unwanted communication, either in the form of offensive material or email 'spam'. The latter is even threatening the use of email as a rapid communication device. Organizations providing websites for the use of a wide variety of organizations may be particularly threatened by offensive material, as legislators attempt to make website owners liable for material provided by others. Clearly, auditors have to be aware of the risks affecting companies engaged in e-commerce. Controls to reduce the impact of these risks include security policy, firewalls, private networks and information/audit trails.

Security policy

In our discussion of internal control in Chapter 7 we suggested that management should have firm policies to control risk and that communication of management philosophy and approaches to staff is vital. In the context of our present discussion, the auditor should determine if the entity has a security policy, clearly communicated to all staff. The policy should be firmly based on an analysis of what data and information is critical to the entity and should include a statement of the controls needed to protect them. Many, perhaps most, system failures are caused by human failure. For instance, if the entity security policy includes a system of rapid reporting of successful hacking, but staff are either not trained or too busy or lazy to do so, the threat to data integrity will be high. Clearly, staff must be trained to recognize threats to security when they occur. We have already mentioned the importance of passwords to restrict access, but security can be endangered if passwords become public knowledge. We have all heard of individuals who write their passwords on a note attached to the side of the VDU because they cannot remember it. The entity's security policy should, therefore, include design of passwords to aid recall and to keep the number of passwords to a minimum, but with regular changes to passwords. The security policy should also include:

See page 247.

- guidelines on the use of email. Many organizations have come to realize that a potential threat to their reputation is the use of inappropriate language in emails by staff and it has become common practice to include a disclaimer at the end of each email.
- requiring staff to log off if they leave a terminal unattended (to prevent unauthorized access).
- virus-checking of files from outwith the entity (and regular updating of virus checking software).
- preventing use of unauthorized copies of software.

Firewalls

Firewalls are particularly important in an e-commerce environment and auditors should ensure they are suitable for the organization, that they are updated continuously and that the entity has a system of regular monitoring to detect any signs the firewall might be breached. The auditor should check whether there is a system for reporting problems as they arise, and for regular independent review of the quality of the firewall systems. Such reviews might be carried out by the quality standards group or by the internal audit function and should include an assessment of likely exposures and an analysis of attempted entry by unwanted individuals. Some organizations even employ known skilled hackers to determine the effectiveness of firewalls and other security measures.

Private networks, such as intranets and extranets

Private networks protected by secure firewalls can be a useful way of reducing risk of inappropriate intervention. An intranet can provide a secure environment within which entity staff can communicate, provided that the firewall itself is secure. An extranet that extends beyond the immediate organization and includes external people and organizations, perhaps even competitors, with whom the organization has regular business dealings, can be particularly useful as it is like an extended marketplace that only allows recognized traders within it to buy and sell services. It is important, of course, that all individuals and organizations allowed entry abide by the rules of the market and that they do not allow unauthorized individuals or organizations to climb over the wall (come through the boundary of the extranet). Auditors should determine entity policy for admitting individuals or organizations to the extranet and find out what controls are in force to restrict access.

Information/audit trails

We have already discussed information/audit trails and how they can be maintained, but they are equally important in the e-commerce environment. The auditor should ensure that integrity of transactions is maintained, and that details of transactions are recorded from inception of a sales order (say) to despatch of goods and payment received. This is particularly important where e-commerce is integrated with all other entity systems. We would expect to see a record, for instance, of why a inventory movement or cash movement or an entry in a creditor's record occurred. If contracts have been entered into by electronic means the auditor would expect to see a system to verify electronic signatures and the place where the contract would be considered legally binding. We discuss legal and taxation matters below.

Other security measures

Page 288.

We have already discussed security measures such as encryption of data above but they become very important as more business is conducted over the Internet. Much e-business is dependent on the use of credit cards by customers, and companies must have systems to authenticate the customer and to check validity of credit card information. Linked to identification and authentication is the need to require new business partners such as customers to register and to provide identification and authentication information. It is important to establish means of contacting the business partner and the degrees of access they are allowed to have. There are systems available to protect personal details and the auditor should determine the nature of the systems, their reliability and whether they are updated as circumstances change.

Legal and taxation matters

ISA 250 – *Consideration of laws and regulations in an audit of financial statements* states in paragraph 13:

> The auditor shall obtain sufficient appropriate audit evidence regarding compliance with the provisions of those laws and regulations generally recognized to have a direct effect on the determination of material amounts and disclosures in the financial statements.

The Internet is international in nature and transactions may be entered into by a national of one country with a national of another country, and the question arises as to which legal jurisdiction the transaction belongs. To make matters more complex some transactions may be conducted over the website of an entity located in yet another country. One way to deal with such matters would be to state at the time the transaction is entered into, which jurisdiction, such as that of England, applies. Some companies might try to restrict business to the residents of particular legal jurisdictions. Clearly, the auditor should be aware of entity policy and procedures with regard to contracts entered into via the Internet. For instance, there should be a system to ensure that all boxes of a contract, including acceptance by the user appearing on a screen, are completed before it is accepted by the system. In addition, it is important to determine how the entity verifies the validity of electronic or digital signatures given by the other party to the contract.

There has been publicity recently of so-called 'carousel fraud' which depended on the ability of criminals legitimately to import goods free of VAT from within the European Union, but who then charged VAT when they sold the goods, but did not hand it over to the tax authorities. The losses multiplied when the goods were re-exported, allowing the final trader to reclaim VAT they had paid. The name 'carousel' was given because the goods went round and round in an elaborate circle through several countries.

As regards taxation, there may be doubt as to which tax jurisdiction is allowed to tax the income derived from a transaction, including value added tax. This is not a new question, of course, as trading over national boundaries has always occurred. However, where transactions do not involve a physical transfer of goods from one location to another, where the services or products are digital in nature, it may be difficult for the provider or governments to say where the customer is located. The auditor should ensure that the entity is applying consistent rules for determining the location of transactions and the tax law applicable to them. The auditor would need to consider the arrangements for double tax relief where transactions overlap tax jurisdictions.

Practical business and accounting problems

An entity carrying on business over the Internet may act either as a principal or as an agent. In the latter case only the commission on the contract should be recorded as income, whereas in the former, gross sales should be recorded. The auditor should discuss contractual arrangements with management and ensure that the status of the entity is clear in the contractual arrangements with third parties. Other accounting matters include:

These accounting matters apply to business other than e-commerce. However, unless the audit trail is clear and the contractual arrangements equally clear, there may be a lack of transparency making it difficult to determine appropriate accounting treatments.

- *Cut-off.* The auditor would wish to know when the transaction is deemed to have occurred – when the transaction is entered into and when goods and services change hands. It would be necessary to ensure that terms of trade are agreed before an order is placed, including timing of the payment for the goods or services. In many (most) cases payment may be required at the time of placing the order and it would be important to determine if property passed at the same time (that is, before goods or services are made available to the customer), in which case the entity may have goods on hand that really belong to the customer. The auditor would also wish to know whether the transaction is stopped if the credit card of the customer is not accepted. Another cut-off issue might be repudiation of a transaction or some of its terms by a customer. The auditor would wish to know if there are controls to prevent repudiation once a contract has been agreed.

- *Return of goods and claims under product warranties*. Clearly, there should be a system allowing return of faulty goods and for handling claims under product warranties. Such a system should include checks that the claims are justified under the terms of the contract and in the case of returned goods that physical inspection takes place.
- *Bulk discounts and special offers.* The auditor would discuss contractual arrangements for giving bulk discounts to customers and when they become payable. It is not uncommon for introductory offers to be made, allowing the provision of free or heavily discounted goods. There may be inventory pricing issues if net realizable values are lower than cost.
- *Payment other than by monetary transfer.* Sometimes, suppliers take advertising space on a entity's website and offset advertising cost against amounts due to them. Again, the auditors should discuss the contractual arrangements with management.
- *Browsing*. A common feature of websites is to allow customers to browse before placing an order. The auditor would expect to see controls to ensure that browsing is not confused with placing an order.
- *Follow-through of transactions*. When a transaction occurs there should be proper follow-through of all aspects of the transaction, including instructions to despatch goods, evidence of despatch, adjustment of inventory records, adjustment of cash records or trade receivables' records and so on. Details of the transaction must be communicated to other parts of the system to enable proper actions and accounting to take place. The transfer of such details forms part of the audit trail. Systems to control actions and recording in other parts of the system are known as 'back office' systems and it is important that they are integrated with the e-commerce transaction interface. Some systems allow automatic follow-through, but this is often not the case and transaction details may require human intervention. Automatic updating would probably reduce cut-off problems and would make it more likely that companies will meet performance and delivery obligations, particularly when demand is unpredictable.

The Internet never sleeps

Because the Internet is worldwide, companies engaged in e-commerce should have systems that operate efficiently and effectively for 24 hours. Customers will not expect a website to close down just because it is night time in the United Kingdom, and the entity's reputation would suffer if the service is broken intermittently. This may have staffing implications and will mean that reliable technology should be in place. Auditors should ensure that systems are robust enough to work properly throughout the 24-hour period.

Crisis management

All businesses should have systems to ensure that losses are minimized when things go wrong. However, e-commerce depends on sophisticated technology and companies may suffer losses that could affect the entity's going-concern status if systems or infrastructure failures occur. System failures could arise from failure of servers, corruption of disks or failure of software, whereas infrastructure failures are normally outwith the entity control but nevertheless may be significant. Infrastructure failures include power failures or breakdown of telephone line communication. Possible consequences of such failures include loss of reputation, loss or corruption of data and information and significant reductions in positive cash flows.

The auditor should discuss with management the steps they have taken to prevent such failures, and to minimize their impact if they occur by ensuring business continuity. Appropriate measures would include back-up of important data, installing emergency power supplies, regular review of system quality by independent persons and regular maintenance and testing of systems in use.

AUDIT APPROACHES TO SYSTEMS AND CONTROLS

In Chapter 7 we introduced you to the control environment and its components and to detailed general controls. We explained why the auditor would be interested in the effectiveness of such controls and suggested that the auditor should discuss with management their approach and the system and control measures in force. Discussion with management is always a good way of getting to know what is going on but, to be effective, auditors must have a structured approach to examining systems and clear objectives before they start detailed discussions with management. Before we look at audit approaches to controls we emphasize that auditors today tend to be very selective in the systems that they examine in detail.

IMPORTANT NOTE ON AUDIT APPROACHES TO SYSTEMS AND CONTROLS

In earlier chapters we discussed the business risk approach to auditing adopted by many audit firms, an important feature of which is to identify areas of significant risk and to concentrate on them. An important practical aspect of this approach is that auditors during the planning process identify balances in the financial statements that are significant and concentrate their detailed work on them. The corollary is that the auditor will restrict work on non-significant balances, such as petty cash, or areas perceived to be low risk from the auditor's point of view, such as payroll, perhaps placing more reliance on analytical reviews and cutting out detailed tests of control and reducing substantive tests of detail. We shall return to this issue when we discuss the audit of particular balances later in this book, but you should bear this note in mind when you read our remarks on system testing below.

Page 255.

Systems objectives are audit objectives

When we considered High Quality Limited in Chapter 7, we noted that setting objectives is an important element of control. The objectives we discussed were fairly broad, but we discuss now systems objectives in greater detail, and shall then move to a discussion of how the auditor finds out about systems, records them in the working papers and evaluates them. In the process we shall find that management objectives are the same or very close to audit objectives. We use a sales system to show what we mean by this, noting again that it is useful to break down the process into stages.

ACTIVITY 8.9

Identify six stages in a sales system where important events happen.

We suggest that the six stages in a sales system might be as follows, although we do recognize that some of the stages might be accomplished at the same time. For instance, stages 4, 5 and 6 might occur simultaneously

1 Receipt of order.
2 Authorization of order.
3 Despatch of goods and entry in inventory records.
4 Invoicing of goods despatched and entry in sales record.
5 Entry in trade receivables' ledger or bank records.
6 Entry in general or nominal records.

The entity will have objectives for all these stages, many of which should be apparent from previous discussions in this chapter. The detailed objectives of auditors are framed as key questions, but before we discuss the objectives of each stage let us first consider the assertions that management might implicitly be making in respect of the sales and related figures appearing in the financial statements.

ACTIVITY 8.10

Sales account		Trade receivables		Bank account	
P&L 2 500	Goods 2 500—>	2 500	Op. bal->	4 750	
			Bank 1 125—>	1 125	
			Cl. bal 1 375		Cl. bal 5 875
2 500	2 500	2 500	2 500	5 875	5 875

(all figures in thousands of pounds sterling.)

The three accounts show transactions and resulting balances in a credit sales system. We can see that recorded sales on credit are

£2 500 000, receipts from trade receivables are £1 125 000 and closing trade receivables amount to £1 375 000.

What basic implied assertions do you believe that management is making about these figures? Consider whether the transactions and balances are genuine, accurate and complete.

Once again we mentioned the importance of transactions and balances being genuine, accurate and complete and do so again later, particularly in Chapters 12 and 13.

We have referred to assertions by management on several occasions so you should have been able to identify some relating to the above figures. The basic assertions are likely to be as shown in Table 8.1. 'Genuine' in the sales and trade receivables context means that the sales have been made (they have occurred in the name of the company) and that the trade receivables balances are valid, that is, they represent a genuine sale on credit, resulting in a right pertaining to the company, that has not been cleared at the year-end. Accuracy means that the sales transactions have in each case been properly calculated and the trade receivables balances also, taking into account a potential bad debt provision. Completeness means that we have recorded *all* sales made in the year and *all* trade receivables have been identified and are recorded in the accounting records in the proper period.

We discussed audit approaches in general terms when we considered audit risk in Chapter 5, but now we look at these in greater detail. Remember that the basic approach to any audit area can be summarized as follows:

1 Identify the components.
2 Identify the assertions relating to those components.
3 Identify the inherent risks associated with each assertion.
4 Identify the controls associated with the component.
5 Estimate the level of control risk.
6 Determine the audit detection procedures necessary to reduce total audit risk to acceptable proportions.

This approach is relevant whatever system is in force, although more complex systems will need different kinds of control from those in simpler systems. Clearly, High Quality Limited needs different controls from a large entity with a database accessed from a number of terminals.

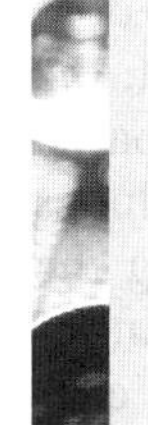

ACTIVITY 8.11

Consider the following assertion relating to sales: 'The sales represent goods whose title has passed to a third party'. This can be rephrased as an inherent risk: 'There is an inherent risk that recorded sales do not represent goods that have passed to a third party'. Under what circumstances do you think that inherent risk might be high in relation to this assertion?

There are a number of possible reasons why inherent risk could be high for this assertion. An important one might be that the client is experiencing

TABLE 8.1 Assertions in the Activity 8.10 figures

	Genuine (real)	Accurate	Complete
Sales (£2 500 000)	The sales represent goods whose title has actually passed to a third party. The terms on which goods have been delivered have been authorized by responsible persons.	The sales transactions have been accurately calculated. Sales have been recorded in the proper period (cut-off).	All sales have been recorded. Sales are recorded in the proper account.
Receipts from customers (£1 125 000)	The cash has really been received.	Receipts have been accurately recorded, taking into account such matters as discounts and foreign exchange. Receipts have been recorded in the proper period (cut-off).	All receipts have been recorded. Receipts have been recorded in the proper accounts.
Trade receivables (£1 375 000)	Trade receivables represent amounts actually due to the company.	Trade receivables represent amounts that are collectable (provisions for bad and doubtful debts are appropriate). Trade receivables represent amounts due at the balance sheet date (cut-off).	All trade receivables are recorded. Trade receivables have been properly summarized for disclosure in the financial statements.

difficult trade conditions and is inclined to insert sales transactions to bolster apparent profitability and to improve apparent liquidity. Adding credit customers that do not exist (are not genuine) would, of course, also have an impact on risk associated with trade receivables as stated in the balance sheet.

We can also look at the above assertions in terms of the natural stages in the creation and recording of a sale. Figure 8.2 is a simplified overview flowchart of the basic stages in a manual system. Think of the chart as a visual description of document flows (shown by continuous lines) and of information flows (shown by dotted lines). Note too that the chart shows who does things and where documents are filed, and, in one instance in this chart, the fact that two documents (sales order and sales despatch note) are compared before another (sales invoice) is prepared. There is clear segregation of duties in this system. Basically, what is happening is that the person receiving the sales order makes out a pre-numbered sales order in triplicate when an order is received from a customer. The sales order pack is sent to the credit controller to check creditworthiness and agree that the customer can be supplied with the goods on the terms stated on the sales order. The sales order clerk keeps one of the orders and passes one to the despatch department (as authority to despatch) and another to the invoicing department. When the goods are despatched a pre-numbered sales despatch note is prepared in triplicate, one going with the goods to the customer, one being retained by the despatch department and the other going to the sales invoicing department. The sales department compares sales order and sales despatch note to ensure what has been despatched has been ordered and then prepares the sales invoice in duplicate. One invoice goes to the customer and the other is retained and forms the basis for entry in the sales journal and sales ledger and eventually in total in the sales and trade receivables accounts in the general ledger.

ACTIVITY 8.12

Examine Figure 8.2 (on next page) and identify points where there should be control actions.

There are a number of points where there should be control actions. You have probably identified the following:

- Sales orders and sales despatch notes are pre-numbered so a sequence check would be possible at later critical points. For instance, the invoicing department should check the sequence of these documents before invoices are prepared.
- The person receiving the original sales order from the customer should scrutinize it and ensure that it is complete and that inventory is available before preparing the pre-numbered sales order (which would be signed by the sales order clerk).
- There is a control following receipt of the sales order as the credit control department checks for credit worthiness before orders are passed to the despatch department. If an order is rejected at this stage, there will be a break in sequence of sales orders and the invoicing department should be informed of the break, thus maintaining the information/audit trail.
- The despatch department should ensure that all sales orders bear an authorization signature from the sales order clerk and credit controller.
- Other controls would include review of the sales journal, sales ledger and general ledger by an independent person for reasonableness. A sales ledger control account should also be maintained independent of anyone involved in the process.

We have started to show you how the auditor will record systems before forming views about their efficacy. The above system was a purely manual system, but now let us assume that the system has been computerized. In this system we have assumed that customers, wishing to purchase items in the entity's catalogue, contact one of the sales clerks by telephone and that this clerk enters the details of the order and customer into a terminal. The order may be

FIGURE 8.2 Sales system: simplified overview chart

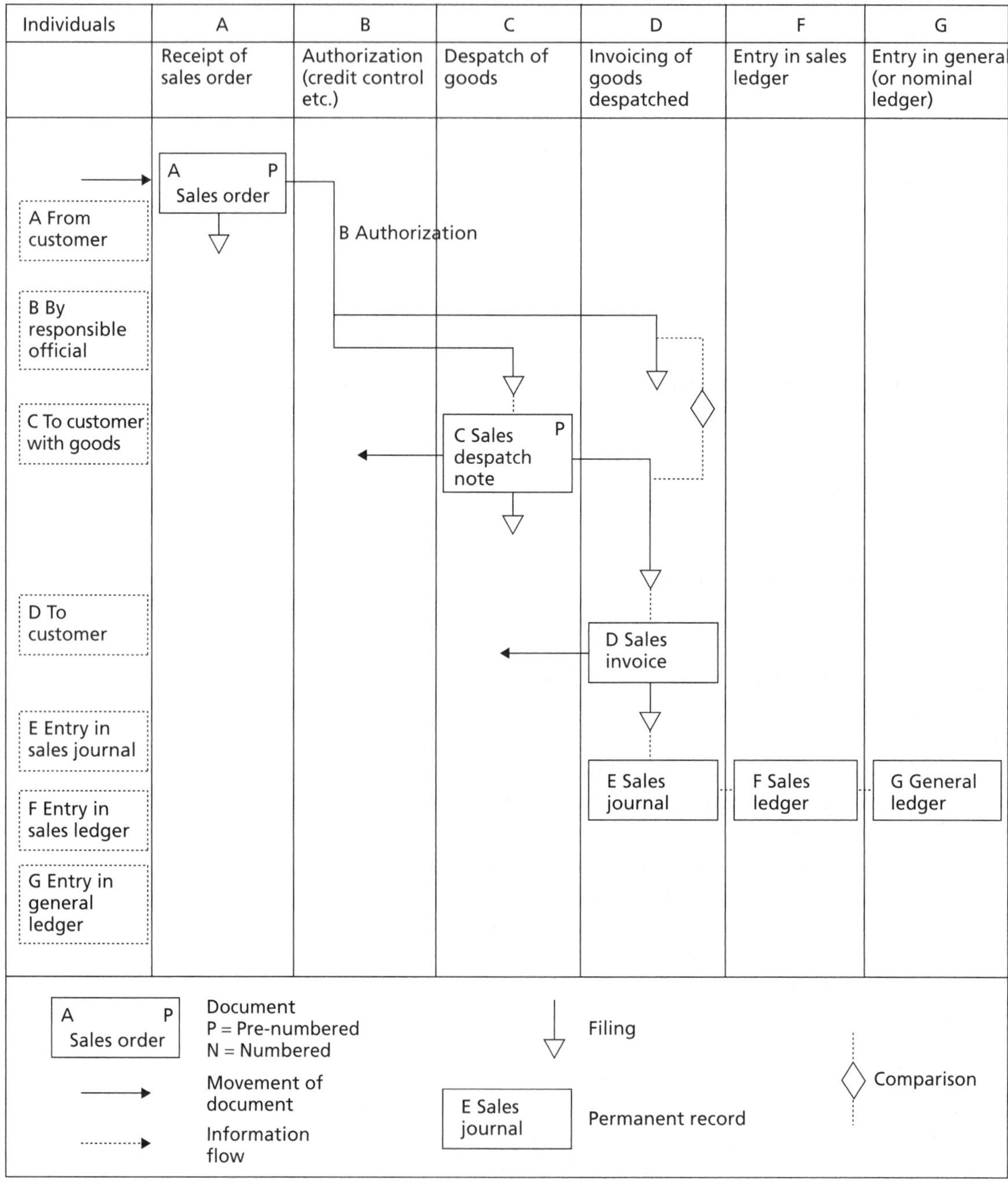

either accepted or rejected by the input subsystem (perhaps the credit card details are suspect, or customers have exceeded credit limits). If orders are rejected customers are immediately informed and told that they will receive rejection letters giving reasons for non-acceptance. If orders are accepted by the input subsystem they will be passed for processing and the following outputs prepared:

- Instructions to update accepted and rejected orders record.
- Instructions to prepare sales invoices and update sales record and trade receivables accounts.
- Instructions to despatch goods and update inventory record.
- Instructions to prepare order rejection notifications.

Figure 8.3 (on next page) shows you how the system works by means of a data flow diagram. In this system, so much is happening internally, that a document flowchart would not be very useful.

ACTIVITY 8.13

Now do the same as you did in Activity 8.12, that is, identify points where there should be control actions in the data flow system shown in Figure 8.3.

We have discussed controls in a system like this earlier in this chapter. You have probably identified the following:

- At the interface we would expect to see a properly designed form on screen to be completed by the sales clerks. The system does make a check for completeness and this is an important feature. A further important feature would be the allocation of a consecutive number to the order for the particular sales clerk so the system can check for completeness of processing later. Clerks would enter identification details as well, so daily control totals could be prepared for them.
- The customer should provide identification and authentication information. New customers would provide data about themselves, which would be used for identification and authentication at later dates. They might only be allowed to place an order initially if a credit card is used for immediate payment. We would expect the credit card to be checked for validity before proceeding with the order.
- The first data for the information/audit trail would be recorded when sales clerks enter customer and order details at the interface. All subsequent actions should also be recorded.
- Controls to ensure that prices and other terms are in accordance with entity policy are important. Such data forms an important element of standing data and should only be entered or changed by people with requisite authority.
- Customers are informed by sales clerks of invoice amounts after they have been calculated. Customers should be allowed to withdraw from or make

FIGURE 8.3 Data flow diagram: customer order system

The customer gives sales clerk personal and order details by telephone.

Sales clerk enters details at the terminal (user interface).

Input subsystem checks the order is complete.

System calculates invoice amount and customer told order is being processed.

System compares customer credit limit with sales ledger balance as adjusted for invoice amount.

System updates orders accepted record and orders not accepted record.

System prepares invoice and updates sales ledger. Sales invoicing department sends invoice to customer.

System prepares despatch note and sends to storeroom who sends copy out with goods.

If order is rejected, an order not accepted letter is prepared in standard format, giving reasons for rejection and suggesting that any outstanding balance be paid. Letter is sent to sales department for forwarding to customer.

Physical people or documents

Electronic data or information

Computer actions

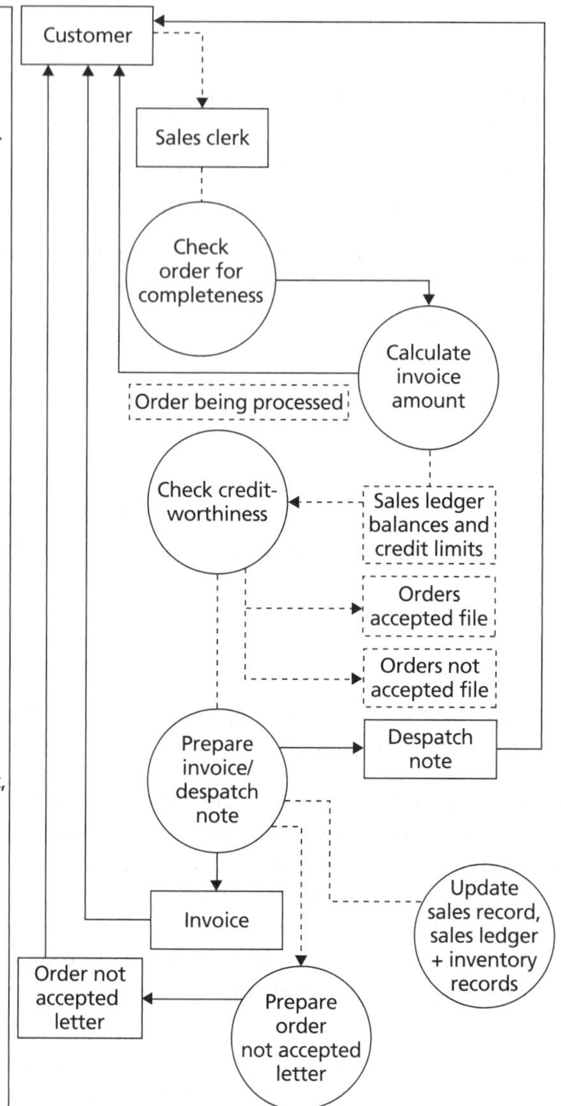

amendments to the order at this stage. This is an important stage as it makes it more likely that orders will be error-free.

- The credit limit plays an important role in the creditworthiness decision. Again, credit limits should only be input to customer master files by persons with appropriate authority.
- When preparing invoice and despatch note and updating sales record, trade receivables ledger and inventory records we would expect to see controls to ensure that the correct files are being updated (run-to-run controls) and that the correct customer's account and inventory record are updated. The entity might use check digits for this purpose.
- Control totals generated after processing should be compared with control totals prepared at sales clerks' terminals. This is an example of after-the-event authorization.
- Finally, there should be regular reviews of outputs. Some of these will be programmed, such as reasonableness and validity checks, and control totals and sequence checks of orders, despatch notes and sales invoices should also be used. There should also be human intervention if output seems not to make sense. Thus perusal and analysis of sales records, review of sales ledger control accounts and of the inventory records might reveal matters needing investigation. A further control over inventory records would be periodic physical inventory checks and comparison of physical quantities with the records, followed by investigation if differences are significant to determine reasons for them.

There may be other controls in a system like this but the above list does give a good flavour of controls and the reasons for them.

Recording accounting and control systems

Before we look at recording systems in use, you will appreciate that the collection of information about the system needs in practice the exercise of considerable powers of enquiry and, in complex systems, much technical ability as well. The information is collected by asking entity staff how the system operates and this means going into the sales order department, into the stores, on to the factory floor and observing procedures. It means that auditors discuss the system in use, not only with systems analysts or chief accountants but also with input staff at the interface, with data control staff and with users receiving output and taking action on exception reports. The basic rule is that auditors should not assume that the system is operating in the way intended. The practical way to approach the work is:

The larger auditing firms employ many different kinds of expert who may be called on to examine technically complex areas.

1 Find out which persons operate the system by enquiry.
2 Interview each person, asking them what they do, what documents they prepare, what documents they receive from other people during their work and how often they carry out particular actions. For instance, if you are talking to a sales clerk at the interface, the auditor should find out what kind of information is received from the customer, whether they have a means to establish control totals in respect of data they have entered, and

whether there are any differences between their totals and those generated by the system. The auditor can ask sales clerks what data about themselves are entered when they log in, how often passwords are changed, what kind of secrecy rules are in practice and if anything goes wrong during processing.

3 Note how many copies of each document (for instance, sales order, sales despatch note, sales invoice) are raised and to whom they are distributed. Find out what entries are made in permanent records as a result of the transactions and construct the information/audit trail. It is at this stage that auditors use what are known as 'walk-through tests', a stage which involves selecting a few transactions and tracing them through the system with the objectives of understanding the system, recording it and seeing if the entity appears to have appropriate controls in force. In subsequent years walk-throughs may be performed to see if the system is still operating in the same way as in the past. This is what paragraph A13 of ISA 315 says about walk through tests in an existing client:

> The auditor is required to determine whether information obtained in prior periods remains relevant, if the auditor intends to use that information for the purposes of the current audit. This is because changes in the control environment, for example, may affect the relevance of information obtained in the prior year. To determine whether changes have occurred that may affect the relevance of such information, the auditor may make inquiries and perform other appropriate audit procedures, such as walk-throughs of relevant systems.

There are a number of ways that auditors record systems and their associated controls, the recording being a prelude to their evaluation:

- Narrative description.
- Visual description.
- Questionnaires and checklists.

Narrative description

The auditor prepares a written description of the system, as we did when we described the Horton Ltd cash receipts system (Case study 7.3) and the two systems in Activities 8.11 and 8.12. Descriptions of this nature can be useful in small systems but are of limited use in complex systems. Narrative descriptions are a useful support, however, to other means of recording.

Visual description

The auditor uses charts of one kind or another to make the system more visual and easier to understand. These include:

Organization charts We have already seen that organization charts can be important features of the control environment. They show flow of authority through the organization and are vital if segregation of duties is a means of control. We saw, for instance, that the place of the quality standards group alongside the computer department, both responsible to the information

See Figure 7.6 on page 269.

systems director, indicated an important independent role. We saw too that the organization chart of the County Hotel reflected the complexity of various functions within the hotel. We offer one word of warning about organization charts though – they do not always show the power structure actually existing in the organization. The auditor can use the chart as a guide, but needs to find out whether, for instance, the quality standards group is really independent of the computer department. Or whether a strong personality on the board is pulling the entity in a particular direction, even though that person appears to be at the same level as other directors.

See Figure 5.3 on page 198.

Flow charts Flowcharts showing flows of documents or data are used extensively both by management and auditor to gain a better understanding of systems and the controls imposed on them. They include:

- Information trail/audit trail flow chart. We have seen that in manual systems it is relatively easy to trace the data and we used the Horton Case study to show what the information/audit trail means. In computer systems it is much more difficult to trace data and the way it is changed and in our previous discussions we have shown what kinds of record should be maintained. An information/audit trail flowchart may be useful in this context, particularly in showing where breaks in the trail occur.

See Figure 7.5 on page 266.

- Document flowchart. We have already given an example of a document flowchart earlier in this chapter, albeit in a somewhat simplified form. As its name implies it shows where documents are prepared, who prepares them, their characteristics (for instance, are they pre-numbered), where they are filed, how many copies are prepared, where they are sent, the action taken on their basis, how they are modified (for instance signed and by whom) and so on. The value of the chart lies in the fact that a visual description is often easier to understand than a long narrative. However, we did note that document flowcharts have become less used and less useful, as so many actions that were taken by different people and functions now take place electronically and are not visible to the naked eye. They may still be useful, however, for an understanding of the system before and after the computer system and where, as is still often the case, systems are not fully computerized. One of the authors used them extensively when questioning entity staff about their part of the system, often discovering that staff were very well informed about what they themselves did, but knew little about other parts of the system, for instance, what happened to a copy of a document after it had left their hands.

See Figure 8.2 on page 310 above.

- Data flow diagram. This chart, as we saw earlier, is a useful means of determining what happens to data when it is entered at the interface by users and passes through various subsystems. When we looked at the data flow diagram for the sales order entry and subsequent processing, we saw that it can be extended to show control points – the points at which data is subjected to checks of one kind or another. For instance, the system checked the order entered at the interface for completeness, and we suggested such controls as identification and authentication routines to prove the customer credentials. This kind of flow diagram will be prepared by systems analysts and programmers and can be used by the auditors, provided they are confident that the diagram is the most up-to-date

See Activity 8.13 and Figure 8.3 on page 312.

version. Auditors may be forced, however, to draw their own charts based on entity documentation, and their observation of systems, backed up by their own tests.

We gave an extract from a system flowchart in Figure 7.8 on page 279 and provide you with further examples, albeit in simplified form, later in the book.

- System flowchart. This also shows the flow of data through a system, but concentrates more on the way that data is affected by the various programmed routines and how it relates to other data input to the routines from a variety of media. Such flowcharts do not tell us much about the logic applied within the routines but they do give a very good overview and may be accompanied by notes highlighting main control features.
- Program flowchart. This kind of flow chart shows detailed decision making internal to programs, such as 'If employee hours exceed 40 go to overtime routine'. Auditors may well examine such flowcharts and test them to make sure that the routine works as intended. However, we shall not look at flowcharts of this nature in detail.

The program instructions would be more complex than this.

Now that you have had some exposure to flow charting, we suggest below some advantages and disadvantages of the technique. Advantages include:

1 Aids understanding of accounting and internal control systems by the following individuals:
   - The person carrying out the detailed work.
   - Persons reviewing the work of that person, including seniors, managers and partners.
   - Client staff at a variety of levels. The flowchart is an excellent means of explaining to clients where strengths and weaknesses lie.
2 To draw a flowchart properly the auditor must understand the system in use. It is thus a technique that forces the auditor to understand how the entity controls its operations.
3 Apart from detecting strengths and weaknesses, flowcharts may pinpoint unnecessary procedures or documents. Documents that do not seem to be used for any particular purpose are not uncommon.

In very complex situations, flowcharting may be the best way to understand what is going on in an organization.

Disadvantages include:

1 Flowcharts can be time-consuming to prepare and may be very difficult to alter, although computerized flowcharting has made this much easier.
2 In simple systems, narrative descriptions may be more appropriate.
3 Individual firms may have unified symbols, but there is considerable variation of symbols generally.
4 Flowcharts require experience to prepare them properly and to enable proper interpretation. They may not, therefore be appropriate in the hands of inexperienced audit staff.
5 In complex situations flowcharts may be too simplistic to aid genuine understanding.

Questionnaires and checklists

Although unstructured interviews with client staff have their place, audit firms have developed pre-determined sets of questions, which, when answered, will enable auditors to form views about the system in use in a more logical way.

The auditor uses a variety of questionnaires for recording and/or assessing the effectiveness of systems:

Internal control questionnaire (ICQ) ICQs are used to record details of the system. They can be useful in recording small systems, and, although not of great use for recording complex systems, you should be aware of their nature and role. A suitable questionnaire for the Horton Limited cash receipts system is given in Figure 8.4.

FIGURE 8.4 Receipts of cash system

Client name: Horton Limited					**Date:** 31 October 2010	
Audit area: Receipts of cash						
No.	Question	Answer	Strong	Weak	Audit programme reference	Action taken
A. Collections: Remittances received by post						
1	Who opens the mail?	Two people in the accounts dept.				
2	Are they (is he/she) independent of cashier and sales ledger personnel?	Yes	*			
3	Are all cheques stamped 'Not negotiable' and crossed restrictively to the client immediately on receipt?	Yes	*			
4	Is a cash received book kept by the person(s) opening the mail in which is recorded: (a) cheques and postal orders? (b) cash?	 Yes Yes	 * *			
5	Is the cash received book signed by both persons opening the mail?	Yes	*			
6	Are all monies received paid into the bank intact?	Yes	*			
7	Are bankings made daily?	Yes	*			
8	Is the cash received book checked with the cash book and paying-in book by a person other than the cashier? State by whom.	Yes accounts clerk	*			
9	Are entries in the cash book compared with paying-in book by a person other than the cashier? State by whom.	Yes accounts clerk	*			
10	What is the name of the cashier?	John Wiston				
11	Does he ever make entries in records other than the cashbook or paying-in book?	No	*			
12	Who prepares the bank reconciliation?	John Wiston				
13	If prepared by the cashier, is the reconciliation checked by an independent person? State by whom.	Yes, chief accountant	*			
14	Are statements to debtors prepared monthly and mailed by persons other than the cashier?	Yes	*			
					Overall conclusion	Strong

ACTIVITY 8.14

See page 317.

Take another look at the description of the Horton Limited receipts of cash system and ask yourself the following questions after you have reviewed the ICQ in Figure 8.4.

- Has the form made it easier to record and interpret the system for cash remittances received through the post?
- Do you still agree with the analysis of the system we made above?

We think you will agree that the ICQ has made it easier to record and interpret the system. Note in particular that the form is designed to prompt your memory as to the matters of importance in the cash receipts system. The form not only expects you to indicate whether individual parts of the system are strong or weak, but also to form an overall conclusion. It may be that there are weaknesses in the system but because of strengths elsewhere, it will be possible to form the conclusion that the *overall* system is strong.

Some firms of auditors are still using paper-based ICEQs and EDP/IT checklists (see below), but larger firms are increasingly using computer-generated information in conjunction with expert systems to highlight areas of weakness needing attention by the auditor.

Internal control evaluation questionnaire (ICEQ) ICEQs are not used to record the system, but to evaluate it after recording by other means. They set objectives for auditors, these objectives being phrased as *key questions*. An example of a key question in a sales system would be: 'Does the system of credit approval ensure that all potential customers submitting orders are given appropriate credit approval before the order is accepted?' These key questions can often only be answered by asking other questions and, in Table 8.2 we set out a suitable questionnaire containing key questions and suggested *subsidiary questions* in the sales and debtors area.

TABLE 8.2 Key and subsidiary questions in a sales system

Stage or component	Key questions	Subsidiary questions
1	**Receipt of sales order** Are all orders received and processed in such a way that keeps errors to a minimum in acceptance of the order, filling the order and in pricing, delivery and payment terms?	(a) Are the persons responsible for preparation of sales orders independent of credit control, of custody of inventories and recording of sales transactions? (b) Are they responsible persons authorized to prepare sales orders? (c) Are standard forms used to record orders in hard copy or on screen? (d) If not, is there a written record of sales orders in every case?

TABLE 8.2 *(Continued)*

Stage or component	Key questions	Subsidiary questions
		(e) Are sales orders pre-numbered or automatically numbered by computer system? (f) Do the sales order clerks take steps to ensure that the customer is genuine? (g) Do sales order clerks ensure that the goods ordered are available in the quantity and quality desired? (h) Are up-to-date standard prices, delivery and payment terms provided for the use of sales order clerks? (i) Are special orders (special qualities, quantities, prices) authorized by a responsible official? (j) Are sales orders prepared by one person checked by another or by computer program?
2	**Credit control** Are potential customers submitting sales orders checked for creditworthiness before the order is accepted?	(a) Is the credit controller independent of the sales order clerks? (b) Are new customers wishing to buy goods on credit vetted for creditworthiness by reference to independent persons or organizations or by means of credit card? (c) Are orders from existing customers checked for payment record, sales ledger balance and credit limit? (d) Are credit limits set by responsible officials on the basis of reliable data? (e) Is the credit approval evidenced on the sales order by the signature of a responsible official or by programmed code? (f) Is the work of the credit control clerk checked by another?
3	**Despatch of goods** Are goods only despatched to customers after proper authorization by responsible officials outside the warehouse and goods despatch department?	(a) Is warehouse/despatch department independent of sales order preparation, credit control and invoicing? (b) Do warehouse personnel release goods from the warehouse on the basis of orders signed by authorized sales order and credit control personnel or on the basis of despatch notes derived from a controlled computer system?

TABLE 8.2 (*Continued*)

Stage or component	Key questions	Subsidiary questions
		(c) Is the despatch of goods evidenced by the preparation of a goods despatch note? (d) Are the goods despatch notes pre-numbered or automatically numbered by the computer system? (e) Are control totals following despatch note routine compared with predetermined totals? (f) Are two copies of the goods despatch notes sent to the customer, with one returned as evidence of receipt? (g) Is a copy of the despatch note sent to a inventory control department to update inventory records or are the inventory records updated on the basis of despatch notes derived from a controlled computer system? (h) Are inventory records periodically compared with inventory on hand and any differences investigated?
4	**Invoicing of goods despatched** Does the system ensure that all goods despatched are invoiced at authorized prices and terms?	(a) Is sales invoicing independent of sales order preparation, credit control and warehouse and despatch departments? (b) Does sales invoicing receive a copy of the sales order or is a sales invoice derived from a controlled computer system? (c) Does sales invoicing carry out a sequence check on sales orders or does a controlled computer system check the sequence of all documents, including sales order, despatch note and sales invoice? (d) Does sales invoicing carry out a sequence check on goods despatch notes? (e) Are control totals following sales invoicing routine compared with predetermined totals? (f) Does the system match sales invoices with goods despatch notes and sales orders – and chase up unmatched orders?

TABLE 8.2 *(Continued)*

Stage or component	Key questions	Subsidiary questions
		(g) Does the invoicing clerk have details of up-to-date prices, terms and conditions, including special agreements with particular customers, and are the terms and conditions master file kept regularly up-to-date by responsible officials?
		(h) Are the sales invoices checked independently for reasonableness by despatch?
5	**Entry in sales ledger** Are all sales invoices properly recorded in individual customers' accounts in the sales ledger?	(a) Is the sales ledger clerk independent of sales order preparation, credit control, goods despatch department and sales invoicing, or is the sales ledger kept updated by a controlled computer system?
		(b) Are sales ledger control totals checked for accuracy before the updating routine is accepted?
		(c) Is the sales ledger control account maintained independently of the sales ledger clerk and are differences between extracted list of sales ledger balances and control account balance investigated by a responsible official, or is a computer-derived control account reviewed by a responsible official?
		(d) Are statements of amounts outstanding prepared at least monthly and despatched to customers?
		(e) Is an ageing statement prepared, reviewed by a responsible official other than the sales ledger clerk and any old balances investigated to determine reasons for slow payment?
		(f) Are sales ledger balances made up of identifiable sales invoices and other movements?
		(g) Are adjustments to the sales ledger accounts, such as bad debt write-offs and discounts authorized by a responsible official other than the sales ledger clerk?

TABLE 8.2 *(Continued)*

Stage or component	Key questions	Subsidiary questions
6	**Entry in general (or nominal) ledger** Are all sales revenues and receivables properly determined, analysed and disclosed in the accounts?	(a) Are sales invoices properly coded to enable analysis as required by management, for instance, by geographical area, type of product, etc.? (b) Do responsible officials compare sales of the current period with sales in earlier periods of the year and with the same period in the prior year? (c) Are steps taken to ensure sales are properly allocated to the year in which the sales occurred (that is, does a responsible official check that cut-off is accurate between sales/receivables and inventories)? (d) Do responsible officials check that sales appear reasonable in the light of gross profit and other relevant ratios? (e) Does a responsible official review receivables for collectability and are appropriate adjustments and provisions authorized by that official?

Electronic data processing (EDP) or IT checklists Although we have assumed that most companies use computer-based systems, the degree of use varies to a great extent, from the kind of system that High Quality Limited uses through traditional batch control systems to sophisticated information and e-commerce systems. Clearly the auditor has to find out the kind of technology in use and the general and application controls in force. Checklists, known as EDP or IT checklists, have been developed to help the auditor assess the quality of computer systems. We give an example of an EDP/IT checklist in Figure 8.5. This EDP/IT checklist has been completed for general controls: development controls and organizational controls and security for Burbage Limited whose sales system is described in Case study 9.4 in Chapter 9.

See page 338.

One final word in this section. In practice, a combination of narrative description, flowcharts and questionnaires and checklists will be used. Each method has its value.

FIGURE 8.5 EDP IT checklist of development, organizational and security controls (Burbage Limited).

Name of company: Burbage Limited **Year-end: 31 December 2010**
Section 1: Details of computer installation
Section 2: Details of computer department personnel
Section 3: Details of hardware, including peripherals
Section 4: Details of file media

Section 5: General and application controls

A. General controls: development controls

Question	Answer	Evaluation	Management letter	Scope decision
1. Is a preliminary survey and feasibility study carried out for all new developments and for modifications by qualified personnel?	Yes, but not documented	Weak	Yes 29.10.2010	See notes on scope decision on working paper XXX
2. In making the study are the following matters covered: A Need for new system or modification? B Alternative courses of action? C Costs and benefits of all alternatives? D Consultation with user departments? E Consultation with internal auditors? F Consultation with external auditors? G Timescale	 Yes Yes Yes Informal Yes No Yes	Generally OK but formal user and external audit agreement essential	Yes 29.10.2010	
3. Is authorization given at an appropriate level?	Yes	S		
4. In carrying out the system design stage are there written procedures for: A System design? B Behavioural aspects? C Program specifications? D Programming? E Testing? F File conversion?	 Yes No Yes Yes Program Yes	Generally OK but testing of whole system needs to be more formalized	Yes 29.10.2010	
5. Does system design include the following: A Narrative description and flowcharts? B The nature and form of input? C Description of input controls? D The nature and form of output? E Description of output controls? F Description of processing routines, including programmed controls and exception reporting? G Master files?	 Yes Yes No Yes No Yes Yes	Weak because not enough attention paid to control, particularly validation	Yes 29.10.2010	
6. Programming A Are standards for program specifications formally established? B Do programmers formally accept program specifications? C Are standards for program writing or modification established to include: (i) Programming approach? (ii) Programming logic and block diagrams? (iii) Documentation standards? (iv) Programming controls? (v) Program testing standards? (vi) Operator instructions?	 Yes Informally Yes Yes Yes Too late Yes Yes	 S Weak S S S See 5 above S S	 Yes 29.10.2010 See 5 above	

Question	Answer	Evaluation	Management letter	Scope decision
7. Testing				
A Are all programs and program amendments tested using all anticipated transaction types?	Yes	S		
B Are all programmed controls tested for proper operation?	See 5 above	See 5 above	See 5 above	
C Are program test results fully documented and retained?	Yes	S		
D Do programmers give written assent on completion of programming stage?	No	Weak	Yes 29.10.2010	
E Are complete systems exhaustively tested by both systems analysts and users?	No	Weak	Yes 29.10.2010	
F Are new systems run in parallel with the old system and are the live results compared?	Yes	S		
G Are system test results fully documented and retained?	Partially	Weak	Yes 29.10.2010	
H Do systems analysts and users give written assent on completion of systems testing?	No	Weak	Yes 29.10.2010	
I Is internal and/or external auditor required to test controls and give written consent?	No	Weak	Yes 29.10.2010	
8. File conversion:				
A Is file conversion properly planned?	Yes	S		
B Are file conversion standards laid down in writing?	Yes	S		
C Are the converted files compared in detail with the original files and discrepancies investigated?	Yes	S		
9. Operator and user instruction:				
A Are all operators and users given adequate training on a timely basis?	Yes	S		
B Are people in the organization affected by the system changes kept properly informed at all stages?	No	Weak	Yes 29.10.2010	
10. Final review and acceptance: Do the following carry out a final review of the new system and do they give formal acceptance in writing before implementation:				
A Operations manager?	Yes	S		
B Representatives of user departments?	No	Weak	Yes to B & C 29.10.2010	
C Internal/external auditor?	No	Weak		

B General controls: organizational controls and security

Question	Answer	Evaluation	Management letter	Scope decision
1. Organizational:				See notes on scope decisions on working paper XXX
A Does IT department report to board of directors?	Yes	S		
B Is IT department independent of user departments for whom it processes data?	Yes	S		
C Is there a formal transfer of data between user departments and IT department?	No	Weak	Yes 29.10.2010	
D Do all staff in the IT department possess adequate competence and are they properly supervised?	Yes	S		

Question	Answer	Evaluation	Management letter	Scope decision
E Is an organization chart in existence for the IT department and does it show clearly lines of authority?	Yes	S		
F Are job descriptions in existence for each staff level and are they reviewed regularly?	Yes	S		
G Are the following duties segregated in the IT department: (i) Systems analysis and design? (ii) Programming? (iii) Operations? (iv) Control?	No	Weak	Yes 29.10.2010	
2. Security of the physical environment:				
A Is the building housing computers and other equipment sited to avoid floor and other natural hazards?	Yes	S		
B Is the building protected against unauthorized entry?	Yes	S		
C Are the fire precautions adequate?	Yes	S		
D Are steps taken to ensure constant and adequate electricity supplies?	Yes	S		
E Is hardware adequately serviced?	Yes	S		
F Is access to the computer restricted to authorized personnel?	Yes	S		
G Is there adequate insurance of the computer installation, including network and peripherals?	Yes	S		
3. Security of data:				
A Are copies of programs and documentation held in a secure location outside the IT installation?	No	Weak	Yes 29.10.2010	
B Is there a program and file library?	Yes	S		
C Is the library controlled by a librarian?	No	Weak	Yes 29.10.2010	
D Are all programs, master files and transaction records files all labelled internally and externally?	Yes	S		
E Are back-up copies of data files held in a location outside the computer installation?	No	Weak	Yes 29.10.2010	
F Are magnetic disks retained until the third processing run after creation (grandfather-father-son) and are hard disk files dumped frequently and regularly?	Yes	S		
G Is access to data held on computer file determined on the basis of need?	Yes	S		
H Have grades of access been determined: no access, read only, read and add, read and delete?	Yes	S		
I Is access restricted by password?	Yes	S		
J Are passwords carefully designed, protected and changed regularly?	No	Weak	Yes 29.10.2010	
K Are proper controls in force to detect unauthorized access and to enable counter-action?	No	Weak	Yes 29.10.2010	
L Are console logs maintained and are they regularly reviewed by a responsible official?	Yes	S		
M Is the information/audit trail adequate to ensure compliance with law against data loss?	Yes, but debtors' list only monthly	S	OK as can create as desired	
N Is there adequate insurance against data loss?	Yes			
O If the nature of the organization or method of processing prevents adequate division of duties or restricted access, are there other procedures in force to prevent loss or manipulation of data?	Yes, good supervision in computer room	S		

Note 1: An 'S' denotes strong controls: Note 2: If this checklist was on an expert system the initial evaluation might be suggested by the computer program, but would have to be reviewed manually before a final conclusion was reached

Summary

We have considered application controls, including those related to data capture/input, processing, output, database and e-commerce. We have discussed the nature and purpose of password controls and the use of firewalls to protect intranets and extranets. We reviewed particular problems and related controls in database and e-commerce systems.

Throughout the chapter, we considered how the information/audit trail can be made and the reason for so doing. We saw that this was generally important but particularly so for companies engaged in e-commerce.

We addressed the audit approaches to recording and evaluation of systems, and considered the advantages and disadvantages of the various recording and evaluation means.

Key points of the chapter

- Broad objectives of application controls are: (a) data collected is genuine, accurate and complete; (b) data accepted is processed so it remains genuine, accurate and complete; (c) data stored temporarily or permanently is genuine, accurate and complete; (d) output data/information is genuine, accurate and complete and goes to the intended recipient; (e) information/audit trail is complete. Application controls include: (a) data capture/input controls; (b) processing controls; (c) output controls; (d) database controls; (e) e-commerce controls.
- Data capture/input controls include boundary controls, such as passwords and firewalls.
- Password systems have the following features: (a) degrees of access; (b) at least eight alphanumeric digits and combinations easy to remember; (c) avoidance of passwords associated with users; (d) staff training on keeping passwords secret; (e) regular and frequent changes; (f) shutdown of terminals when incorrect passwords entered. Other controls include: (a) limit the use of terminals to particular functions; (b) record which terminals and employees access the system; review by responsible persons; (c) restrict use of terminals to normal working hours where possible. Additional controls are necessary where the national telephone system is used to transmit data.
- Firewalls are created and maintained by specially designed systems to protect computer networks from unauthorized intrusion. Networks may be intranets or extranets. Some firewalls are very tight, but many companies adopt open methods for some forms of communication.
- The first records of the information/trail are at the boundary where identity and authenticity of the user is first recorded. Records include all actions taken in respect of data.
- Input subsystem accepts data and ensures software is valid.
- Batch controls are supported by appropriate organizational controls.
- Input data to be verified as soon as possible as it is expensive to correct errors later and data held may be corrupted. The input subsystem should produce exception reports and route details of errors to the original preparer of the data for correction.
- An information/audit trail is maintained by input subsystem on transaction and master file data to be updated.
- Processing controls include controls over CPU, main memory and operating system, and controls over applications.
- CPU and main memory should be tested periodically and back-up facilities made available.
- Controls over applications include: (a) run-to-run controls; (b) identification of secondary storage media; (c) master file data must be genuine, accurate and complete before processing; (d) programs must be tested at the development stage *and* on a continuing basis; (e) the information/audit trail should be updated to record all processing actions from time input data is received to time it is despatched as output; (f) sequence checks; (g) limit or reasonableness tests; (h) casts and cross-casts.
- Output controls have two purposes: (a) outputs are genuine, accurate and complete; (b) outputs are distributed to those who need them.
- Database systems provide the same data to all applications, but special controls are needed, including: (a) ownership of sub-schemas to designated users; (b) after-the-event authorization; (c) supervision and rotation of DBA staff essential; (d) complete record of use; (e) information/audit trail, including record of all interventions.
- E-commerce presents particular control problems, but degree of risk depends on how the organization uses Internet. Particular risks relate to: (a) security; (b) residence for legal and taxation purposes; (c) business and accounting risks; (d) risk arising from e-commerce as a 24-hour business; (e) risks associated with complex technology.
- Controls to reduce the impact of e-commerce risks include: (a) security policy; (b) firewalls; (c) private networks; (d) information/audit trails.
- Companies engaged in e-commerce should have systems that operate efficiently and effectively for 24 hours.
- Crisis management may be particularly important in the e-commerce environment.

- Auditors must have a structured approach with clear objectives when examining systems. Systems objectives are broken down into stages and objectives determined. The audit approach to the financial statements comprises: (a) identification of components and related assertions, inherent risks and controls; (b) estimating level of control risk; (c) determination of audit detection procedures to reduce total audit risk.
- Collection of information about systems needs considerable powers of enquiry. Auditors interview a wide range of people involved with the system. Recording of systems may be by narration, visual description or questionnaires and checklists.
- Narrative description can be useful in small systems and may be useful support to other means of recording.
- Visual descriptions include; (a) organization charts; (b) flowcharts of various kinds, including information/audit trail flowcharts, document flowcharts, data flow diagrams, system flow charts and program flowcharts
- The advantages of flowcharts are: (a) enable understanding of systems; (b) forces the auditor to understand how the entity controls operations; (c) pinpoint unnecessary procedures/documents. Disadvantages of flowcharts include: (a) can be time-consuming to prepare and alter; (b) in simple systems, narrative descriptions may be more appropriate; (c) considerable variation in use of symbols; (d) may not be useful in the hands of inexperienced audit staff; (e) in complex situations flowcharts may be too simplistic.
- Questionnaires and checklists enable auditors to form views about the system in use in a logical way. They include: (a) internal control questionnaires; (b) internal control evaluation questionnaires; (c) EDP/IT checklists.

Further reading

The important ISA in the area is ISA 315 – *Identifying and assessing the risks of material misstatement through understanding the entity and its environment.*. You may also refer to ISA 330 – *The auditor's responses to assessed* risks. We have also made mention of ISA 250 – *Consideration of laws and regulations in an audit of financial statements*.

Two useful texts are:

Rowley, J. (2002) *E-business: Principles and Practice*, Basingstoke: Palgrave.

Weber, R. (1999) *Information Systems Control and Audit*, New York: Prentice Hall.

Self-assessment questions (solutions available to students)

8.1 Consider the following statements and explain why they may be true or false:

(a) ICQs are questionnaires used to record the system in use.

(b) ICQs are questionnaires used to evaluate the system in use.

(c) ICEQs are questionnaires used to record the system in use.

(d) The basic requirement of an accounting system is that it meets the needs of the business for which it is designed.

(e) In a small organization it is impossible to have a good system of internal control.

(f) In modern systems, a data flow diagram is more useful than a document flowchart.

8.2 Assume that Ann Paterson, an established customer, has telephoned asking that she be supplied with three recently published books. She has been passed to a sales clerk who deals with her order. Suggest controls that should be in force before her order is accepted.

8.3 Assuming that the order is accepted and that the books will be supplied on credit, explain what records will be affected by the transaction and the information/audit trail details that should be recorded.

8.4 In Table 8.2 we provided you with key and subsidiary questions in a sales system. Two key questions in a purchases system are:

(a) Are all requisitions for goods and services initiated and approved by authorized responsible officials?

(b) Are all purchase orders based on valid, authorized requisitions and are they processed in a manner to ensure that prices, conditions, quantity, quality and suppliers are appropriate to the business?

What subsidiary questions might you ask, assuming that in this system the order is automatically generated by the computer system?

Self-assessment questions (solutions available to tutors)

8.5 Refer to questions 8.2 and 8.3 above and explain how a data flow diagram would help the auditor to understand how the entity's order entry system is operating. Why would a data flow diagram be better than a document flowchart for this purpose?

8.6 Set out in Figure 8.6 is a systems flowchart for a production payroll system and we ask you now to explain what is happening in the two routines 'transaction file update' and 'salary run'. In addition, explain the kinds of control, programmed or manual, that should be in force to ensure that the payroll is genuine, accurate and complete. Explain what is meant by 'genuine, accurate and complete' in this context.

8.7 Describe the nature of an extranet and explain why it might be a useful means of achieving business objectives.

Assume that you are auditor of an entity carrying on business using an extranet and explain what controls you would expect to be in force to protect it.

Solutions available to students and Solutions available to tutors

These can be found on the website in the student/lecturer section at: www.cengage.co.uk/graymanson5.

Topics for class discussion without solutions

8.8 Where a client company fully integrates business systems with e-commerce conducted through the Internet, particular problems arise for the auditor. Explain why this is so.

8.9 The cost of audit has increased dramatically in recent years. Explain why this is the case and what approaches auditors have adopted in consequence.

FIGURE 8.6 Computer systems flowchart for a payroll system

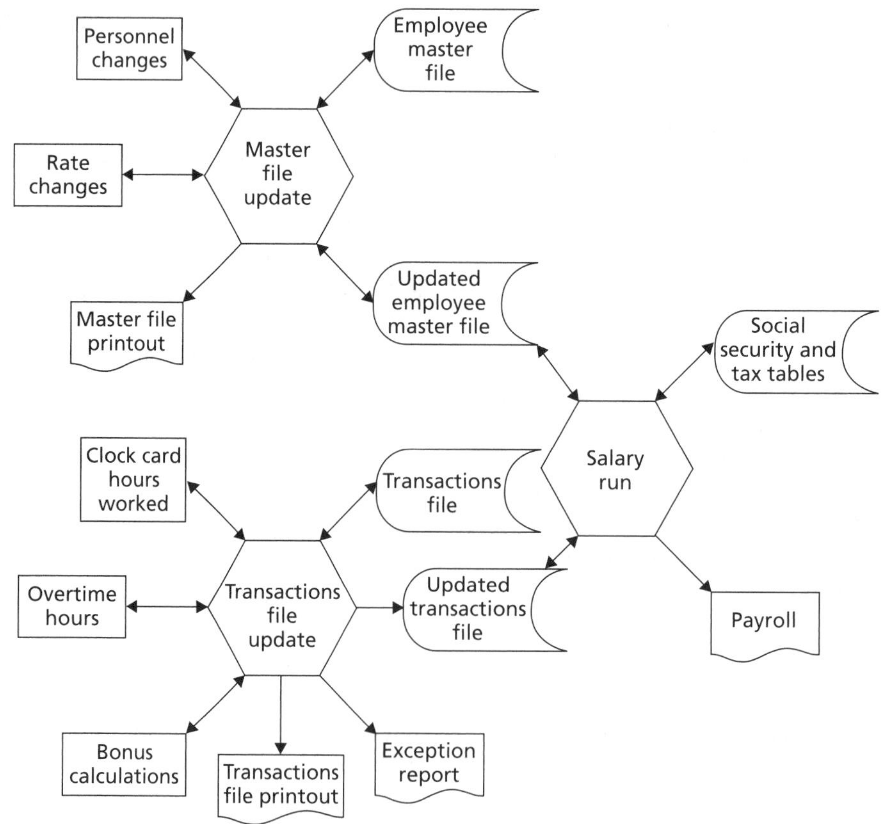

9

Testing and evaluation of systems

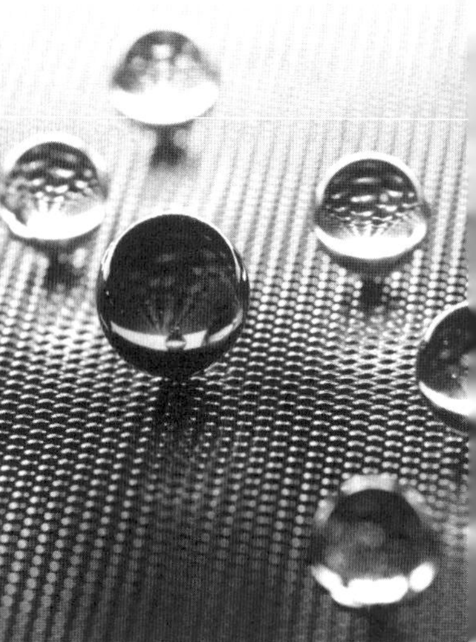

LEARNING OBJECTIVES

After studying this chapter you should be able to:

- **Suggest audit and systems objectives for selected components of the financial statements.**
- **Evaluate systems in use in selected areas and draw up audit conclusions.**
- **Explain the role of tests of control, and in particular those used to test computer systems.**

Learning objectives, 329
Introduction, 330
Sales and debtors system, 330
Payroll system, 333
Purchases and creditors system, 335
General and application controls in a sales system, 338
Tests of control, 341
Evaluation of systems and audit conclusions, 353
Summary, 355
Key points of the chapter, 355
Reference, 355
Further reading, 355
Self-assessment questions (solutions available to students), 355
Self-assessment questions (solutions available to tutors), 356
Topics for class discussion without solutions, 357

INTRODUCTION

In Chapters 7 and 8 we introduced you to the control environment and related components, and detailed controls over systems, particularly computer systems. We suggested ways that auditors might record systems prior to testing and how they might approach evaluation of systems. In this chapter we shall ask you to look at a number of scenarios in which companies use computer technology in several different ways. These are similar in some respects to auditing examination questions, so should provide useful practice. We summarize the Case studies below:

- Case study 9.1 Broomfield plc: integrated computerized sales, trade receivables, cash and inventory system.
- Case study 9.2 Troston Limited: integrated production and production wages system.
- Case study 9.3 Broomfield plc: part of computerized purchases and trade creditors system, one feature being the automatic generation by computer of purchase orders.
- Case study 9.4 Burbage Limited: sales order processing system and identification of application controls.

In each case we introduce you to components of the financial statements and ask you to suggest systems and audit objectives in relation to them.

SALES AND RECEIVABLES SYSTEM

CASE STUDY 9.1

Broomfield plc: sales and debtors system

Figure 9.1 shows a data flow diagram describing the sales and debtors system in use.

The company

Broomfield plc is a large company manufacturing and selling furniture and beds through its own department stores. Some goods are available for immediate delivery, but to keep inventories low, some ranges are manufactured to order, the stores having examples of main lines. Customers choose goods from catalogues on display, and sales people in the stores take the orders. Smaller items of furniture may be collected at once from the showroom store; other goods are kept in Broomfield's main store, and the customer is informed of availability by telephone or post. The company uses company vans to deliver if requested by the customer. No charge is made for delivery within a five-mile radius of the department store, but for greater distances, a charge is made for the service.

In recent years the company has experienced problems arising from a recession in the economy, and inventory levels were reduced to improve liquidity. Profit margins have also been adversely affected.

Sales and trade receivables system

1 Showroom customers may buy for cash or on credit. Credit customers must give bankers' references and other private information. The credit controller sets credit limits and authorizes a person in the credit control department to input them to customers' master files. The credit control department is independent of showroom staff. Customers without a credit limit are informed that goods will only be supplied by immediate payment by credit card or cheque.

2 Goods in the department stores are labelled with price, description and reference number and the catalogues give a range of prices for selected materials and designs. Sometimes goods are reduced in price and in such cases the original price, percentage reduction and new price are all displayed. Customers fill in showroom order forms for items they require.

FIGURE 9.1 Data flow diagram for Broomfield plc sales and receivables system

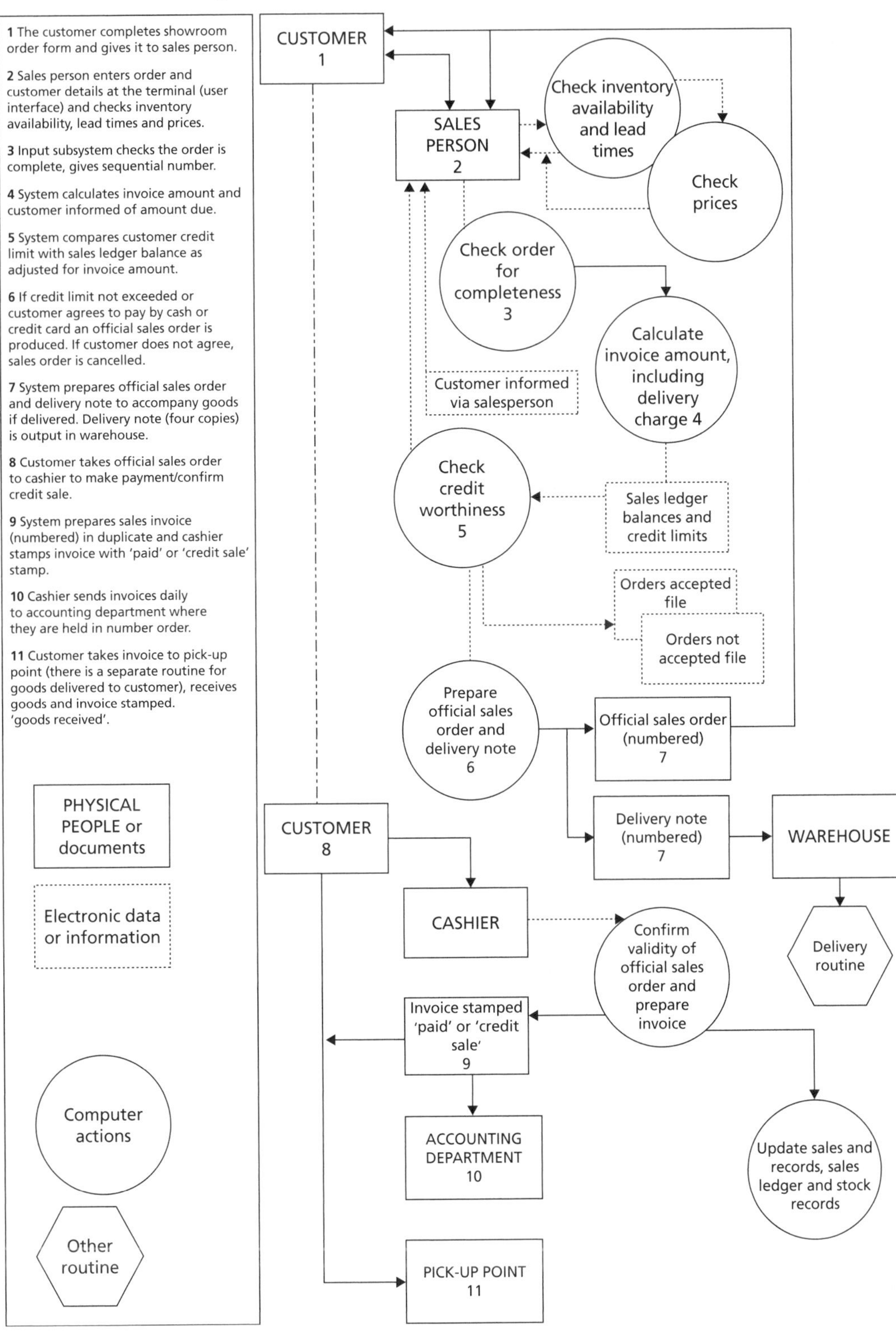

1 The customer completes showroom order form and gives it to sales person.
2 Sales person enters order and customer details at the terminal (user interface) and checks inventory availability, lead times and prices.
3 Input subsystem checks the order is complete, gives sequential number.
4 System calculates invoice amount and customer informed of amount due.
5 System compares customer credit limit with sales ledger balance as adjusted for invoice amount.
6 If credit limit not exceeded or customer agrees to pay by cash or credit card an official sales order is produced. If customer does not agree, sales order is cancelled.
7 System prepares official sales order and delivery note to accompany goods if delivered. Delivery note (four copies) is output in warehouse.
8 Customer takes official sales order to cashier to make payment/confirm credit sale.
9 System prepares sales invoice (numbered) in duplicate and cashier stamps invoice with 'paid' or 'credit sale' stamp.
10 Cashier sends invoices daily to accounting department where they are held in number order.
11 Customer takes invoice to pick-up point (there is a separate routine for goods delivered to customer), receives goods and invoice stamped. 'goods received'.
PHYSICAL PEOPLE or documents
Electronic data or information
Computer actions
Other routine
CUSTOMER 1
SALES PERSON 2
Check inventory availability and lead times
Check prices
Check order for completeness 3
Calculate invoice amount, including delivery charge 4
Customer informed via salesperson
Check credit worthiness 5
Sales ledger balances and credit limits
Orders accepted file
Orders not accepted file
Prepare official sales order and delivery note 6
Official sales order (numbered) 7
Delivery note (numbered) 7
WAREHOUSE
Delivery routine
CUSTOMER 8
CASHIER
Confirm validity of official sales order and prepare invoice
Invoice stamped 'paid' or 'credit sale' 9
ACCOUNTING DEPARTMENT 10
Update sales and records, sales ledger and stock records
PICK-UP POINT 11

3 Salespersons access inventory availability reports and lead times for goods not immediately available and compare prices displayed on the furniture to computer records. Salespersons enter their identification code and details of customer and order at a terminal in the showroom, using a form on the screen. A sequential transaction number for the salesperson is entered automatically by the system. The order details include inventory reference number, price, payment terms, delivery code (immediate or delayed delivery) and expected delivery date. The system checks the order for completeness, calculates delivery charge, if any, on the basis of postal code, and total invoice value, and checks that the customer details are accurate. If the credit limit would be exceeded by the new invoice the customer is given the opportunity to pay for the goods immediately. If the credit limit is not exceeded or the customer agrees to pay immediately, an official sales order is produced (numbered by the system) in duplicate, and signed by the sales person and customer. The 'orders accepted' and 'orders not accepted' files are updated. These files are used as part of the audit trail and to assess levels of activity and reasons for orders not being accepted. If delivery is to be made the system routes a request to the warehouse to deliver goods and prepares four copies of the delivery note (sequentially numbered), for use by the warehouse. The salesperson keeps one copy of the official sales order, attaches the salesroom order form to it and files it in number order.

4 The system keeps a record of sales order input and quantity hash totals and invoice totals for each salesperson. The customer takes the official sales order to the cashier in the store. The cashier confirms the validity of the sales order at the terminal and a sales invoice is prepared in duplicate, retaining one copy and giving the other to the customer. If the customer pays by cash or credit card, the invoice is stamped 'paid'. If the sale is on credit, the cashier confirms the credit rating at a terminal (read only facility) and stamps the invoice with a 'credit sale' stamp. Sales, cash, inventory and trade receivable records are updated automatically. The retained invoices are kept in number order and are sent daily to the accounting department.

(Note: We are not considering the routine where goods are not immediately available and have to be ordered from head office.)

5 Goods are only released by personnel at a pick-up point (attached to the warehouse) on production of the invoice by the customer. On taking delivery, the invoice is stamped 'goods received', the customer retaining the invoice.

6 Where delivery is to be made, the warehouse prepares the goods and despatches them on the agreed date. The delivery-person is given three copies of the delivery note (one copy is held by the warehouse), one for own records in the despatch department, one to be retained by the customer and one to be signed by the customer and returned to the accounting department at the store. The delivery-person stamps the invoice held by the customer 'goods received'. Accounting department personnel compare the delivery note signed by the customer with their copy of the sales invoice and both documents are filed in sales invoice number order.

> This system is today somewhat out of date. Many companies now make use of electronic pads for signature by the customer, resulting in automatic production of the delivery note.

Required

1 What do you think are the objectives of this system? Phrase them as audit objectives. Consider all components of the financial statements that are altered when a transaction takes place.

2 Identify control points in this system and suggest controls that should be in force.

3 Refer to the suggested key and subsidiary questions for receipt of sales order and credit control and decide how you would evaluate the parts of the system relating to these aspects. If you feel that the information given is not sufficient, describe the controls you would like to see.

4 There are at least two matters that might affect the inventory figure appearing in the financial statements. Identify these matters and suggest how the company might overcome them. Consider the timing of events and inventory values.

The suggested solution for this Case study is contained in suggested solutions to self-assessment questions (available for students) at **www.cengage.co.uk/graymanson5**.

Working a question like this should give you a better insight into the critical matters that auditors consider when forming a view about the effectiveness of systems. We emphasize the need to determine objectives. If you do not do this, it will be very difficult to know if they have been achieved. The above Case study was in the sales area, but the same principles can be applied when approaching any system.

PAYROLL SYSTEM

We introduce you now to a wages payroll system and will ask you to suggest key questions and to form conclusions about the system. We have already introduced you to Troston plc in Chapter 7, where we asked you to consider controls over the personnel master file. We now ask you to take a look at other parts of the payroll system. We suggest that you review the computer systems flowchart (somewhat simplified) shown in Figure 9.2 for the production payroll system of Troston plc as you read the narrative description below. As we mentioned in Chapter 8, many firms regard payroll as a low-risk area in relation to other components of the financial statements, such as inventory, trade receivables and long-term contracts, and have reduced audit work in consequence. However, we think that it will be useful to consider company objectives and control procedures in respect of payroll, as it represents an area where considerable outflows of financial resources occur and where fraud has been prevalent in the past.

CASE STUDY 9.2

Wages payroll: Troston plc

You are the auditor of Troston plc, a manufacturer of high-quality specialist equipment for use in dental hospitals and practices and incorporating a large number of components in the assembly of the final product. The factory has two main sections: 'Component manufacture' and 'Equipment assembly'.

The calculation of wages

There are 175 employees and their pay is based on basic hourly rate, overtime payable at 1.5 times the basic rate and group bonus. The standard week is 40 hours and employees record time by inserting a personal encoded plastic card (issued by the personnel department) into a card reader close to the factory office. All employees are allocated a personal code and a code showing the group to which they belong and these details are included on the card. The card reader is under observation by officials in the factory office. Daily, the factory office prints the recorded times, checks them for reasonableness and downloads the data to the central computer payroll system. Overtime is paid for weekly hours exceeding 40. Hours in excess of eight hours daily are authorized by the head of the production control department (PCD), and are recorded on overtime authorization forms (OAFs), which are initialled by the head of PCD. OAFs are held in PCD and details are entered into an overtime file in the department desktop computer. This file is downloaded daily to the central computer payroll system. Overtime requests come from PCD or from group forepersons. The bonus is calculated on the difference between standard and actual time for batches of components or equipment assembled. A batch/equipment ticket (BET) containing details of budgeted time as shown in the daily production report accompanies each batch/piece. The tickets (pre-numbered) and daily production reports are prepared by PCD. Actual time taken is recorded on the BET by the group forepersons and initialled by them and counter-initialled by the employee. On completion of a batch/piece, the BET is signed by the inspection clerk to show the goods are of the quality required. BETs are passed to PCD to enter actual times in the daily production reports (also held on computer file) and to record standard and actual times for each group. These times are downloaded daily to the central computer payroll system.

FIGURE 9.2 Computer systems flowchart for production payroll system of Troston plc

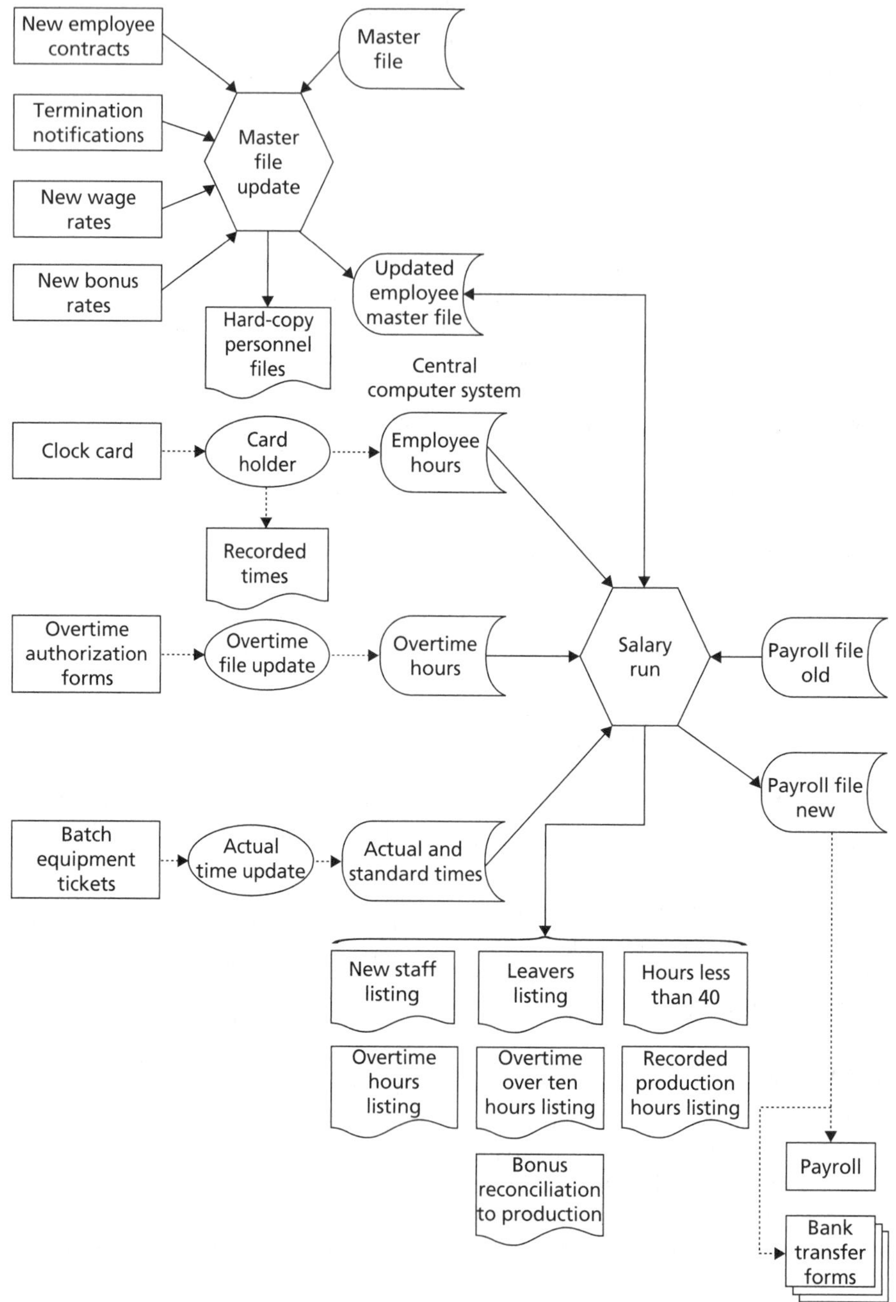

The personnel department

This department is responsible to the production director and comprises a personnel manager and one assistant. A personnel file is kept for each employee in computer master files and also in hard copy. Master files are updated by the assistant on the basis of:

- New contracts of employment for joiners.
- Termination notifications for leavers.

- Wage rate forms.
- Bonus rate forms.

All forms, contracts and termination notifications are signed by the personnel department head. The production director reviews the files periodically. He signs all contracts of employment.

The wages department

The wages department staff (two employees) are responsible to the chief accountant and are independent of the personnel department. They are responsible for preparing the payroll from the data held in the central computer payroll system. However, before preparation of the payroll they run an input validation run, the output from which is an exception report, containing the following:

(a) Staff whose hours are less than 40 per week.
(b) Overtime hours per employee.
(c) Staff whose overtime exceeds ten hours per week.
(d) Total recorded production hours and total possible payroll hours and shortfall.
(e) Bonus calculation and reconciliation to production report.
(f) New staff employed since the last payroll.
(g) Staff departed since the last payroll.

Listings (f) and (g) above are checked to the master file by the personnel department. Listings (a) to (e) are sent to the PCD for review and checking to the underlying records. The personnel department and PCD give their approval to the wages and salaries department and the preparation of the payroll and bank transfer forms are then automatically prepared by the central computer payroll system. The two employees in the wages and salaries payroll department review the payroll and both sign it for approval. They compare the bank transfer forms to the payroll and both payroll and forms are then sent to the chief accountant.

Payment of wages

The chief accountant reviews the payroll for reasonableness and initials it as evidence of approval. He signs the bank transfer forms before sending them to one of the directors for counter-signature. The cashier takes the bank transfer forms to the bank.

Required

(i) State the broad objectives of the wages system.
(ii) List the key questions in the wages area.
(iii) Review the payroll system of Troston plc and comment on the strengths and weaknesses you have identified.

The suggested solution for this case study is contained in suggested solutions to self-assessment questions (available for tutors) at **www.cengage.co.uk/graymanson5**.

PURCHASES AND CREDITORS SYSTEM

We shall now return to Broomfield plc. You have already been introduced to this company in Case study 9.1. You will notice that the purchases system requires considerably more human intervention than the sales system. In at least one case management claims that a computerized procedure has proven not to be working satisfactorily.

A flowchart of the system is given in Figure 9.3, showing flow of documents and interaction of users with the computer system. The sentence in italics in point three is not reflected in the flowchart below, which had not been updated from the previous year.

FIGURE 9.3 Document flowchart for the purchases systems of Broomfield plc

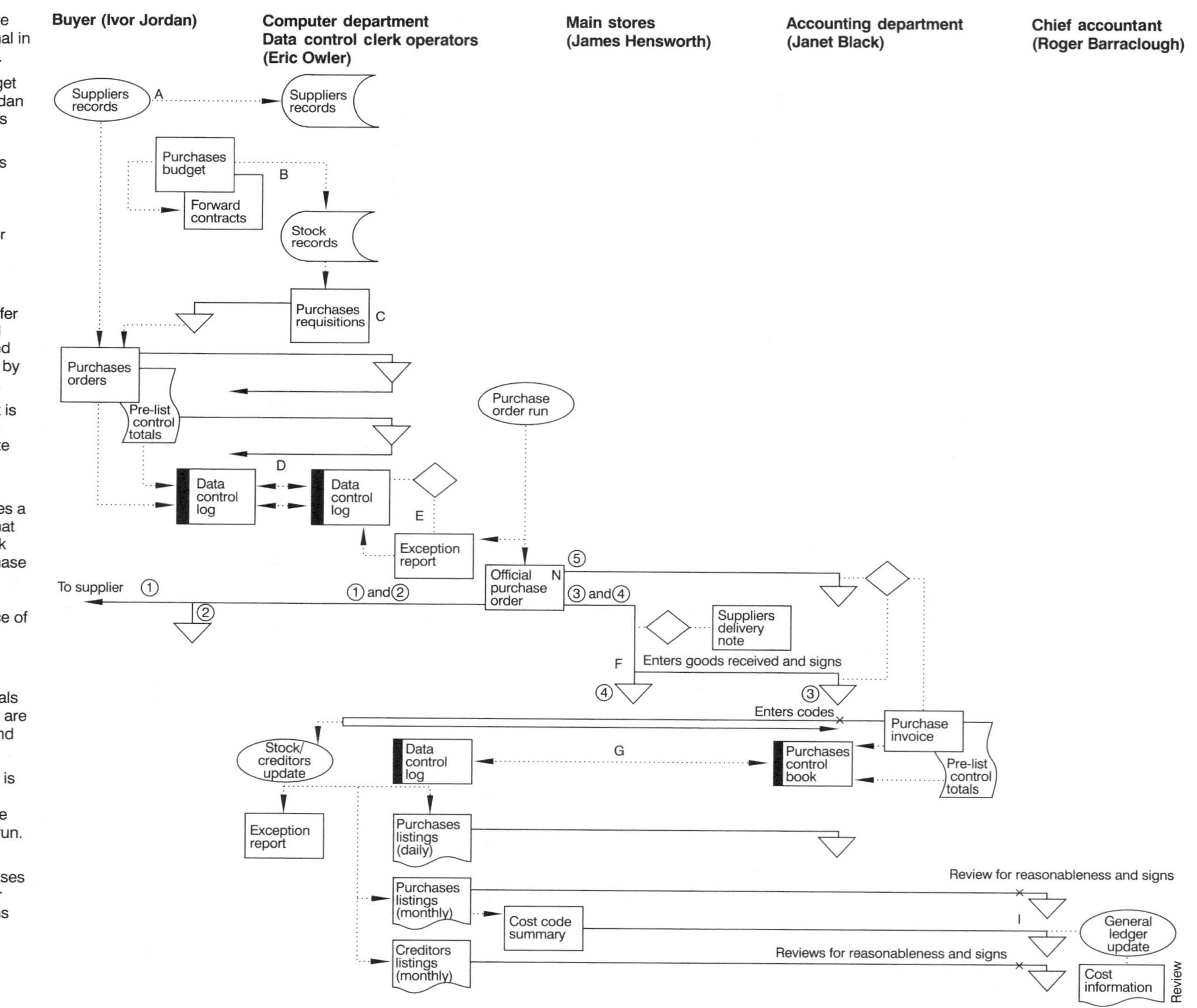
A. Suppliers records are updated using a terminal in the buying department.
B. The purchases budget is prepared by Ivor Jordan and stock reorder levels set (annually).
C. When reorder level is reached the computer automatically prepares purchase requisitions which form the basis for preparation of the purchase order by Ivor Jordan.
D. There is formal transfer of purchase orders and control totals pre-list and control logs are signed by both Jordan and Owler.
E. The exception report is used by Owler to make corrections in a separate purchase order run.
F. Copy 4 of the official purchase order becomes a goods received note, that is passed to Janet Black for matching with purchase invoice. She enters supplier and general ledger codes on the face of the invoice.
G. There is a formal transfer of purchase invoices and control totals pre-list and control logs are signed by both Black and Owler.
H. The exception report is used by Owler to make corrections in a separate stock/creditors update run.
I. The chief accountant reviews monthly purchases and creditors listings for resonableness and signs to indicate approval. Likewise he reviews the information for reasonableness.
Buyer (Ivor Jordan)
Computer department Data control clerk operators (Eric Owler)
Main stores (James Hensworth)
Accounting department (Janet Black)
Chief accountant (Roger Barraclough)
Suppliers records
A
Suppliers records
Purchases budget
B
Forward contracts
Stock records
Purchases requisitions
C
Purchases orders
Pre-list control totals
Purchase order run
Data control log
D
Data control log
E
Exception report
Official purchase order
N
5
To supplier
1
1 and 2
2
3 and 4
Suppliers delivery note
F
Enters goods received and signs
4
3
Enters codes
Purchase invoice
Stock/ creditors update
Data control log
G
Purchases control book
Pre-list control totals
Exception report
Purchases listings (daily)
Review for reasonableness and signs
Purchases listings (monthly)
Cost code summary
I
General ledger update
Reviews for reasonableness and signs
Creditors listings (monthly)
Cost information
Review

CASE STUDY 9.3

Broomfield plc: part of purchases and trade creditors system

1 The company has some 50 suppliers, whose records are held on computer master file, kept updated by the buyer, Ivor Jordan, using a terminal in his department.

2 Ivor prepares a purchases budget annually on the basis of a sales budget and estimated minimum inventory levels and suppliers lead times. The budget is agreed by the board at an annual budget meeting, but is updated from time to time as circumstances change. It is used by Ivor to negotiate contracts with suppliers.

3 The budget is also used to set minimum inventory levels for each type of inventory. Inventory records are computerized and purchase requisitions are produced automatically in duplicate when inventory balances reach re-order levels. The requisitions are sent to Ivor Jordan who decides whether it is appropriate to send out an order to suppliers. [*If he decides it is not necessary he notes 'rejected' on the requisition and changes the minimum inventory level on the inventory records file. Management recently gave this authority to him after orders were sent out despite a slowing in economic activity and a management decision to reduce inventory levels.*]

4 Ivor batches purchase orders, and calculates quantity hash totals and record count. A data control log is kept both by Ivor Jordan and Eric Owler, the data control clerk in the computer department, and the control totals, together with date and run number are entered in the logs by Ivor and Eric respectively. When the purchase orders and control pre-list are given to Eric Owler, both Ivor and Eric sign the respective control logs. The orders and prelist form are input to a computer run which produces five copies of the official purchase order, which are sent to Ivor Jordan (two copies, one being sent to the supplier), James Hemsworth in the main stores (two copies) and Janet Black in the accounting department. Official purchase orders are sequentially numbered. A further output is an exception report that contains control totals and details of rejected items. Eric Owler is responsible for making the necessary corrections of rejected items and putting them through the computer system in an additional run. When the control totals are in agreement with his control log, he informs Ivor Jordan. The purchase orders and pre-list are returned to Ivor Jordan.

5 Goods are received in the main stores by James Hemsworth who checks the purchase order to the supplier's delivery note and the goods and enters the goods received on his copies of the purchase orders which then become goods received notes (GRNs). He signs these for approval and sends one copy to Janet Black.

6 Purchase invoices are matched against purchase orders and goods received notes by Janet Black. She checks calculations, enters the supplier and general ledger code, pre-lists invoice values and records the total and document count in her purchases control book.

7 The invoices and pre-list are sent daily to Eric Owler who enters control totals in the data control log and both he and Janet initial the logs for agreement. The invoices form input for an inventory records and trade payables ledger update run. This run also produces a weekly listing of invoices. Rejected items appear on an exception report. Eric compares the machine-generated control totals with the pre-determined totals, reviews the exception report and arranges for input errors to be corrected. The purchase invoices and control totals pre-list are returned to Janet Black.

8 At the end of each four-week period the following are printed:

- List of creditors (individual invoices and total for each supplier).
- List of invoices for the period and summary per cost code.

The chief accountant, Roger Barraclough, reviews the listings for reasonableness and uses the creditors' listing as the basis for payment decisions. He posts the cost summary totals to the general ledger file, using the VDU in his office and prints cost information prior to preparing management accounts for the period.

Required

(a) State the broad systems objective of a purchases and related trade payables system.

(b) Redraft the part of the flowchart to reflect the fact that Ivor does not always send out an order on the basis of the requisition and has the authority to change inventory reorder levels.

(c) Suggest key questions in the following areas:

- Requisitioning.
- Purchasing.
- Receipt of goods and services.
- Processing of suppliers invoices.
- Entry in purchases ledger.
- Entry in general ledger.

(d) Evaluate the system you have recorded. (In doing this it may be desirable for you to think of subsidiary questions to help you to answer the key questions.)

The suggested solution for this Case study is contained in suggested solutions to self-assessment questions (available for students) at **www.cengage.co.uk/graymanson5**.

See Figure 8.5 on page 323.

We are now looking at another sales system, that of Burbage Limited, and are providing you with a document flowchart in Figure 9.4 to help you understand what is going on. We will ask you to consider, in particular, general and application controls. We have not given you much information about development controls but in Chapter 8 we provided you with part of an EDP/IT checklist covering this part of the company's control system. You will note that the system is not totally integrated and that a batch control system is in force.

GENERAL AND APPLICATION CONTROLS IN A SALES SYSTEM

CASE STUDY 9.4

Burbage Limited

Burbage Limited is a trading company selling a range of bought-in goods on credit. You have discussed the system with Mr Moscar, the chief accountant and Mrs Houndkirk, the data-processing manager, who have provided you with narrative description and flowcharts illustrating the sales and debtors routine:

The numbers in square brackets in the Case are references to the flowchart in Figure 9.4.

- Sales orders are received daily from customers via salespersons who forward them to the sales order department. The sales order clerks use a terminal with a 'read only' facility to determine inventory availability and then prepare a sales order with the following data:

(a) Customer name, address and reference/account number (used for updating the sales ledger).

(b) Product name and code (used for updating inventory records).

(c) Quantity required and price.

(d) Sales code (used for analysing sales).

Sales orders are initialled by sales order clerks and sent to the computer department for processing. Customer numbers and product codes are

FIGURE 9.4 Sales order processing (Burbage Limited)

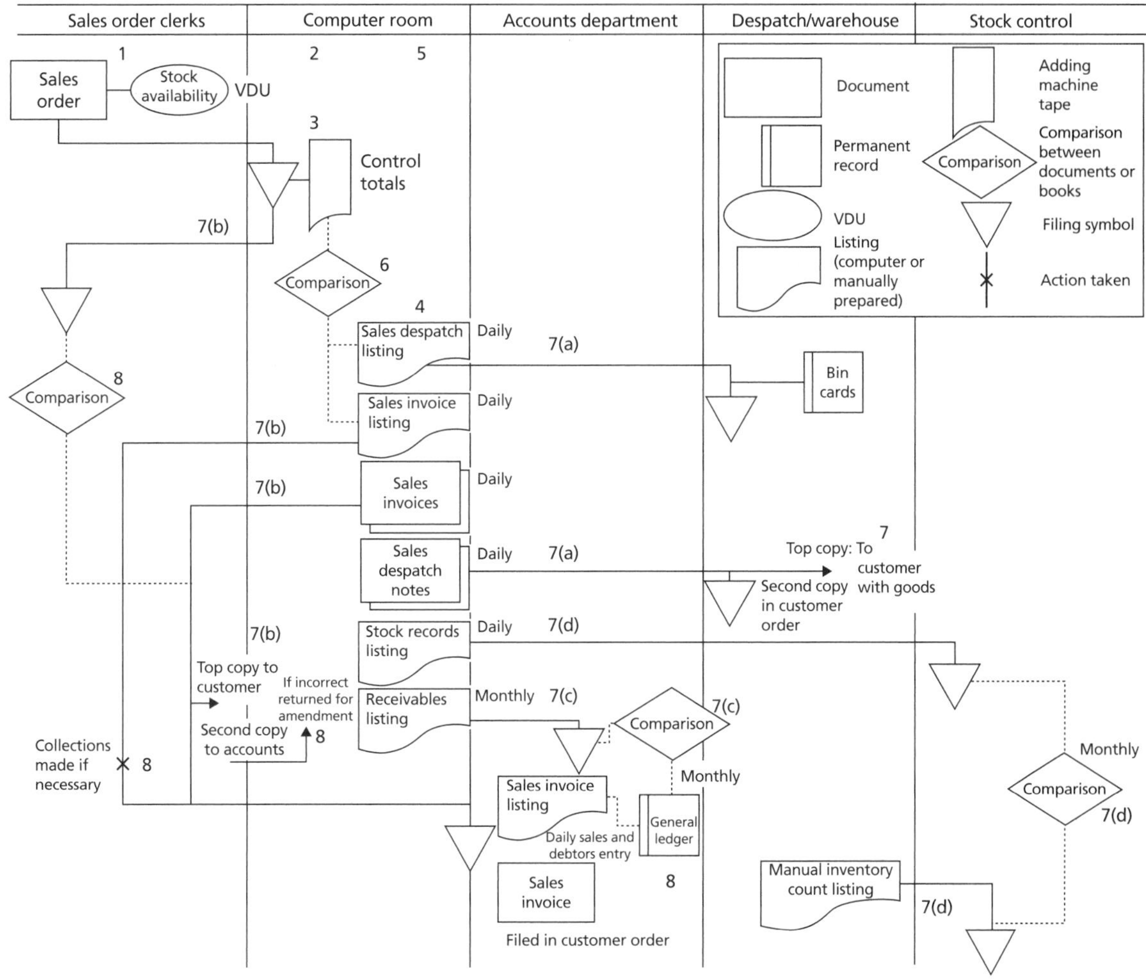

computer-generated under the control of Mrs Houndkirk; they contain check digits in each case. New customers are allocated a number from a list held by the sales order clerk. [1]

- Computer department staff are Mrs Houndkirk (a trained systems analyst and programmer), an assistant programmer (acting at peak times as operator) and two operators (both are attending programming courses at a local college). A reputable software house supplied the computer software but it was subsequently modified by the computer department staff in conjunction with the software house and the computer manufacturer, following informal discussions with staff involved in the system. Documented test results following modification of software are held by Mrs Houndkirk. Only computer department staff members are allowed to enter the computer room. [2]
- On receipt of the sales orders the operator produces a quantities hash total and document count that he/she enters on a control sheet. [3]
- Daily the operator loads the sales ledger and inventory record files held on a fixed disk, types in transaction details from the sales orders on the computer keyboard and the computer updates the sales ledger and inventory records on the disk. The following are printed output: (a) Sales despatch listing; (b) Sales invoice listing (day book);

(c) Sales invoices (two copies); (d) Sales despatch notes (two copies); (e) Updated inventory record listing. At the month-end the operator enters an additional instruction and the computer prints an outstanding trade receivables listing showing total of balances and, for each customer, uncleared invoices (open items) and the total of those invoices. Receipts from customers are input separately. [4]

- Mrs Houndkirk is very security conscious and daily the hard disk files are dumped on to a back-up disk held in the file library next to the computer room. Mrs Houndkirk operates a grandfather-father-son system for the disks that contain header and trailer labels and are also identified manually. Burbage Limited has no file librarian but computer department staff have been instructed to sign and enter date and time in the library control book when files are moved. [5]
- After the daily run the operator compares the control totals on the sales invoice and despatch listings with the control sheet totals and takes corrective action if there is a lack of agreement. The operator also takes corrective action on items in the exception report. (Typical exceptions are non-existent customer numbers and inventory codes, customer credit limit exceeded, orders exceeding pre-determined values.) [6]
- Documents and listings are distributed as follows:
  - (a) Despatch notes and sales despatch listing to despatch department as authority to despatch, one copy of the despatch note being sent to the customer with the goods and the other held in despatch.
  - (b) Sales invoices (both copies), sales invoice listing and original sales orders to sales order clerks who compare sales orders with the listing and invoices. The customer receives a copy of the invoice.
  - (c) The monthly list of trade receivable balances is sent to the accounts department for comparison with the sales ledger control account in the general ledger.
  - (d) The daily inventory records listing is sent to the inventory control department where it is used as the basis for ordering inventory. (Monthly, warehouse staff count inventory and send details of inventory on hand to inventory control where they are compared with the month-end inventory records listing.) [7]
- If sales order clerks find differences between the sales orders and sales orders/sales order listing, the invoice is amended by hand and both copies sent back to the computer room for correction during the next run. The sales invoice listing (containing details of individual invoices in customer number order and a summary of individual sales code allocations) and remaining second copies of the sales invoices are then sent (the sales invoice listing amended appropriately by hand) to the accounts department. Here it is used to update sales ledger control account in the general ledger and to post individual sales accounts. [8]

Required

Analyse the Burbage Limited sales order processing system and identify areas of significant weakness in internal control and suggest steps the company should take to rectify any weaknesses. Your answer should be framed under the following headings (we covered development, organizational and security controls for this company in Figure 8.5).

- application controls
  - (a) input
  - (b) processing
  - (c) output
- other matters

The suggested solution for this Case study is contained in suggested solutions to self-assessment questions (available for tutors) at **www.cengage.co.uk/graymanson5**.

TESTS OF CONTROLS

In Table 9.1 we remind you of three important definitions, which we have expanded to some extent.

See Glossary of terms and paragraph 4 of ISA 330 – *The auditor's responses to assessed risks.*

When we discussed flow charting in Chapter 8 we said that auditors need to obtain information about how systems work, although we also suggested that they would only do this if they had decided that related balances in the financial statements were significant. We saw that this process involves discussions with a wide range of individuals from quality control staff to users at the system interfaces, and that one important audit objective was to confirm completeness of the information/audit trail. To record how the system works, auditors use walk-through tests to inspect a limited number of documents and transactions from inception to final entry in the permanent records. However, as the scope of this work is limited, it is unlikely that, on the basis of such work, the auditor can be sure that the system operates at all times in the manner recorded.

For this reason, as we have already seen in Chapters 5 and 6, the auditor carries out tests of controls to support a risk assessment and to provide evidence that the system is working as expected. Paragraph A4 of ISA 330 states in this respect:

> The auditor's assessment of the identified risks at the assertion level provides a basis for considering the appropriate audit approach for designing and performing further audit procedures. For example, the auditor may determine that:
>
> (a) Only by performing tests of controls may the auditor achieve an effective response to the assessed risk of material misstatement for a particular assertion;
>
> (b) Performing only substantive procedures is appropriate for particular assertions and, therefore, the auditor excludes the effect of controls from the relevant risk assessment. This may be because the auditor's

TABLE 9.1 Objectives of walk-through tests, tests of control and substantive procedures

Procedure	Objective	Using
Walk-through tests	To understand the system, to record it and to see if the entity appears to have appropriate controls in force.	Tracing a few transactions through the financial reporting system.
Tests of controls	To evaluate the operating effectiveness of controls in preventing, or detecting and correcting, material misstatements at the assertion level. (They are used to determine level of control risk.)	A variety of tests (see below), but usually involving selecting a greater number of transactions – and balances, if appropriate.
Substantive procedures, comprising: (a) substantive analytical procedures, (b) substantive tests of detail.	To detect material misstatements at the assertion level. (To enable conclusions to be formed as to the validity of recorded transactions, balances and disclosures.)	Analytical procedures and/or a sample of transactions and balances, the extent of which is determined by the level of control risk.

risk assessment procedures have not identified any effective controls relevant to the assertion, or because testing controls would be inefficient and therefore the auditor does not intend to rely on the operating effectiveness of controls in determining the nature, timing and extent of substantive procedures; or

(c) A combined approach using both tests of controls and substantive procedures is an effective approach.

However paragraph 18 of ISA 330 notes that:

> Irrespective of the assessed risks of material misstatement, the auditor shall design and perform substantive procedures for each material class of transactions, account balance, and disclosure.

Paragraph A43 then goes on to say:

> Depending on the circumstances, the auditor may determine that:
>
> - Performing only substantive analytical procedures will be sufficient to reduce audit risk to an acceptably low level. For example, where the auditor's assessment of risk is supported by audit evidence from tests of controls.
> - Only tests of details (a substantive procedure) are appropriate.
> - A combination of substantive analytical procedures and tests of details are most responsive to the assessed risks.

IMPORTANT NOTE ON RECORDING SYSTEMS. TESTS OF CONTROL AND SUBSTANTIVE PROCEDURES

Students sometimes find it difficult to distinguish between the tests that auditors make when they are recording systems, when they are testing controls in the systems and when they are performing substantive tests to prove that a management assertion is valid. We believe that this is because although the objective of the tests differ, the actual procedures may be similar. There are basically three stages to this part of the audit with different objectives as shown in Table 9.1. We also show in Figure 9.5 the decisions that are made at each stage.

We have discussed analytical procedures and substantive procedures briefly earlier in this book, but do not do so in detail until Chapters 13 and 10 respectively. At this point, however, we want to highlight the different objectives of the audit tests. We shall refer you back to this note as we proceed through this book.

1 When auditors are determining how the systems work and what controls appear to be in place they carry out 'walk-through tests', which, as we see from Table 9.1 involves tracing a few transactions through the financial reporting system. For instance, they might select a sales order from a credit customer, whether manual or computerized, and trace it to a decision to grant credit, to the despatch note, to the sales invoice, and to the entries in the trade receivables account and the inventory movement record. The objective in this case is not to prove that all transactions are properly recorded but to understand the system, to record it, and to see if the entity has appropriate controls in place.

You will remember from Chapter 8 (see page 314) what paragraph A13 of ISA 315 says about walk through tests in an existing client:

The auditor is required to determine whether information obtained in prior periods remains relevant, if the auditor intends to use that information for the purposes of the current audit. This is because changes in the control environment, for example, may affect the relevance of information obtained in the prior year. To determine whether changes have occurred that may affect the relevance of such information, the auditor may make inquiries and perform other appropriate audit procedures, such as walk-throughs of relevant systems.

2 Whether the client is new or existing, the auditors have to decide if the system *appears* to be strong enough for them to rely on it in arriving at conclusions, that sales and trade receivables appear to be controlled satisfactorily. However, the auditors then have to perform tests of control to satisfy themselves that their initial conclusion is valid. So, the auditors might select (say) 20 sales despatch notes and trace them to the customer order, to the recorded credit limit decision, to the sales invoices and to the entries in the trade receivables accounts and inventory movement records. The objective in this case is to enable them to decide whether they can in fact rely upon the system and controls.

We emphasize that the auditor wishes to ensure that the transactions selected have been authorized by someone in authority. In manual systems this will be by signature (for instance of the credit controller confirming that the transaction will not cause the credit limit to be exceeded). In computer systems the authorization will be evidenced by the recorded intervention of the credit controller using an authorized password. In this connection you may refer to Figure 9.1 on page 331 to see where authorizations are being given.

3 The auditors should then be able to make a decision as to the level of control risk, leading to a decision as to the level of substantive procedures they should perform to enable them to form a conclusion at the assertion level, as to the validity of recorded sales, recorded inventory movements and of trade receivable accounts. Depending on the level of control risk, the auditors will adopt the procedures identified in Paragraph 43 of ISA 330:

(a) if the control risk is low, to perform an analytical review of sales and trade receivables to see if these figures make sense in the light of what is known about the company.

This would mean that the auditor would rely on substantive analytical procedures, although if the item was material, auditors might well perform some substantive test of detail as well.

(b) If the control risk is high, the auditor may decide not to rely on the controls and use tests of detail only, such as those referred to in **2** above, selecting in this case (say) 100 sales despatch notes or more and tracing them to the other records.

This would be a substantive test of detail.

(c) If the system is weak, but the auditors decide they are going to rely on it to some extent, they might select a combination of substantive analytical procedures and tests of detail, as described in **2** above.

A further important point to note here is that tests of controls and substantive tests of detail may be carried out at the same time. This is known as a dual purpose test because two objectives are being sought at the same time (see paragraph A23 of ISA 330).

In some cases, only tests of controls will give the needed audit satisfaction because effective substantive tests cannot be designed. This might be the case in complex IT systems with little documentation of transactions (see paragraph A24 of ISA 330).

FIGURE 9.5 Walk-through tests, tests of control and substantive procedures: conclusions, decisions and extent of tests and procedures

Notes
Walk-through tests at stage 1
Conclusion after stage 1
Decision after stage 1
Tests of control at stage 2
Conclusion after stage 2
Decision after stage 2
Substantive procedures at stage 3
Types of substantive procedure at stage 3

WALK-THROUGH TESTS
No or very poor controls
Auditor does not rely on controls
SUBSTANTIVE PROCEDURES
Substantive analytical procedures
Tests of detail
Controls are in place
Auditor relies on controls
TESTS OF CONTROLS
Controls are excellent
Low control risk
SUBSTANTIVE PROCEDURES
Substantive analytical procedures
Controls are weak in places
High control risk
SUBSTANTIVE PROCEDURES
Substantive analytical procedures
Tests of detail

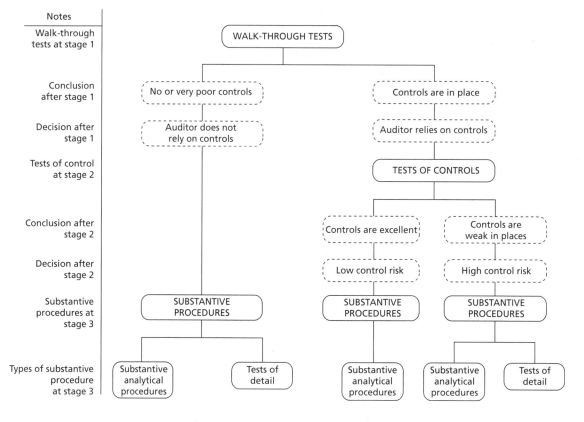

We discuss inventory count procedures in detail in Chapter 13 and cut-off in Chapters 12 and 13.

ACTIVITY 9.1

Rummond Limited is a trading company and performs an inventory count at the end of the year to be satisfied about the following:

1 quantities of recorded inventories are correct;
2 physical condition of inventories is such that they are saleable;
3 purchases and sales of inventories are recorded in the correct period (this is known as establishing correct cut-off).

The auditors (a) examine the inventory count instructions; (b) at the count observe the count procedures being carried out by Rummond staff, testing a few of the items counted themselves; and (c) select items counted at random and record them in the working files for comparison later with the quantities recorded in the inventory valuation sheets.

Refer to the important note on recording systems, tests of control and substantive testing and explain what the audit objectives are at each stage (a), (b) and (c) above.

(a) When the auditors examine the inventory count instructions they are assessing whether the count has been properly planned by the entity, the count being an important control. (The auditor would, of course, perform tests to ensure that the instructions were being applied.) The objective is to find out how the entity plans to perform the count, the instructions representing the system in force. The auditors would recommend changes to the instructions if they considered it was necessary. The instructions would be filed in the audit working files and would be later transferred to the permanent audit files as part of cumulative client knowledge.

(b) Observing the count and selecting some items to count themselves would be a test of controls. Remember that the count is itself an important control. The objective would be to assess whether the inventory count was being properly performed.

(c) By selecting a number of stock items at random, counting them and recording the results for later comparison with the inventory valuation sheets is an example of a substantive test.

Examples of tests of controls

See Activity 9.1 starting on page 344.

When you are looking at these examples, remember that they may be performed at the walk-through stage and tests of controls stage, as well as at the substantive testing stage. You should refer to the Important Note on page 342 and Table 9.1. We elaborate further below:

- *Tests of the audit/information trail.* The auditor selects transactions from various stages of the system and tests them to supporting evidence. Relevant audit procedures in this case would be inquiry, backed up by inspection of records and documents. In complex computer systems with little in the way of hard-copy documentation, it would probably be necessary to establish the completeness of the audit trail (re-performance) using the computer. As we have seen the information/audit trail may be difficult to establish, but clearly, a complete record of transactions from first capture to final recording will aid the auditor in determining that transactions have been properly processed.

We discuss computer-assisted audit techniques later in this chapter.

- *Testing of outputs.* On a restricted basis the auditors might test the outputs from systems to source documentation, possibly in conjunction with establishing the validity of the audit information trail. They might also obtain satisfaction that the system is working properly by analytical review of outputs, re-performing in fact the supervisory control that should have been performed initially by company staff.

- *Block testing.* This sort of testing can be used to test one aspect of the system. For instance, in the Broomfield sales system, you were told that salespersons and customers both signed the official sales order. An easy way to test this assertion would be to take a block of 200 standard orders (in other words testing records and documents) and flip quickly through them to see that all are signed.

We shall see in Chapter 11, however, that block testing is not a statistically valid selection method. See page 401.

- *Interviews with company staff (inquiry).* Auditors talk to a wide range of people during their work and it is essential that entity staff, even highly trained experts, have respect for them. Auditors must have a clear idea of their objectives and role and must also develop an interviewing style that is conducive to getting people to be open with them. Audit objectives are to find evidence to form conclusions about the efficacy of systems and the data/information derived from them. They should keep an eye open for contradictory statements by staff members. For instance, management might tell you that passwords are kept private, but the auditor may find that accounting department staff have access to each other's passwords. They may do this for convenience, but it can cause real security problems.
- *Observing staff at work (observation).* This is not so difficult as you might assume. We do not mean that auditors should hover menacingly over client staff, but they should certainly keep their eyes open and not assume that staff will always operate in the manner they have told you they do.
- *Re-performance of control procedures.* We have already mentioned re-performance above in relation to checking the completeness of the audit/ information trail, and testing the validity of outputs. Auditors frequently perform procedures that client staff have already performed. Another example would be when auditors prepare bank reconciliations to test that client reconciliations are properly prepared. Clearly, if client and auditor reconciliations are in agreement, there will be greater confidence that client control procedures are adequate.
- *Examination of management reviews.* Management is responsible for ensuring that control systems are operating properly and as expected, and have a duty to keep systems under review for signs of deterioration. Some management interventions will be in the form of supervisory controls, which are part of the control system, and auditors look for evidence of such interventions and supervisory controls exercised by them. For instance, auditors should examine minutes of management meetings at which financial results are reviewed and corrective action decided on, such as setting lower prices when there has been a sales downturn.
- *Testing the reliability of budgets prepared by management.* Budgets represent an important control to aid planning and to protect assets of the entity. For instance, a sales budget will be used by management to determine desired inventory levels and other budgets such as purchasing budgets, labour input budgets, financing requirements and so on. The auditor may be very interested in the reliability of company budgets. For instance, when assessing the saleability of year-end inventories, the auditor may decide to

rely on projected sales in the sales budget of the following year. Budgets would also be an important tool in assessing the going-concern status of the entity.

ACTIVITY 9.2

If the auditors are to use the entity sales budget in the way suggested above, what tests would they perform on the budget before relying on it?

One way of testing the reliability of budgets is first to discuss with management how they use them. Are they a target that they would like to achieve or are they soundly based on expectation of what is likely to happen?

The auditors would also find out whether the entity has a system of comparing budget figures with actual figures. In the case of the sales budget, did the sales actually materialize, and does the entity investigate variances between budgeted and actual sales?

If the entity has a good system of budgetary control in the sales area, including variance analysis, the auditors will be able to rely on budgeted sales in forming a view of the saleability of inventories. The auditors would of course examine management's comparison of budgeted with actual sales, and inspect the entity's variance analyses. Basically, if management has been good at preparing budgets in the past, auditors will be much more inclined to rely on current budgets.

Refer to paragraph A 22 of ISA 330.

Before we discuss how auditors test the operation of systems let us first take a look at possible approaches to computerized systems and the auditor's use of the computer in auditing.

Auditing round, through and with the computer

Auditing round the computer

In the early days of computer auditing, auditors tended to see the computer as a black and somewhat mysterious box into which input (after collection and preparation) was deposited and from which output was ejected and distributed at the other side. Audit activity concentrated on ensuring that source documentation (the basis of input) was subjected to proper controls outside the computer room to ensure it was genuine, accurate and complete (we still do this of course). Outputs were subjected to normal analytical review techniques and, on a test basis, were compared with input documentation (and vice versa). What happened in the actual computer processing was largely ignored, this approach being known as 'auditing round the computer'. In comparing output with input, the auditor used control totals kept by the data control section as a guide, but had little further contact with the computer installation and its staff. To some extent this approach was acceptable in the early stages of computer development, as the computer was used in many instances as though it was a fast and reliable human being, rather than in the integrative

These so-called early days are not in fact so far distant, being only some 50 years in the past.

manner that it is today. In the mid-1960s computer processing was normally offline and was broken down into a number of runs, which made it easier to maintain the information/audit trail. Today, however, computer systems are complex, processing is online and/or in real-time and, as we have seen, this means that special measures have to be taken to maintain the information/audit trail. As computer systems developed in complexity, auditors started to 'audit through the computer'. Figure 9.6 shows the difference between the two approaches.

Even today, auditing round the computer may be appropriate if the engagement team decides that controls within the system are very good.

Auditing through the computer: computer assisted audit techniques (CAATs)

When auditing through the computer, the computer is seen as a tool in the hands of the auditor and the audit is said to be computer assisted. Paragraph A16 of ISA 330 highlights their importance:

> The use of computer-assisted audit techniques (CAATs) may enable more extensive testing of electronic transactions and account files, which may be useful when the auditor decides to modify the extent of testing, for example, in responding to the risks of material misstatement due to fraud.

FIGURE 9.6 Auditing round and through the computer

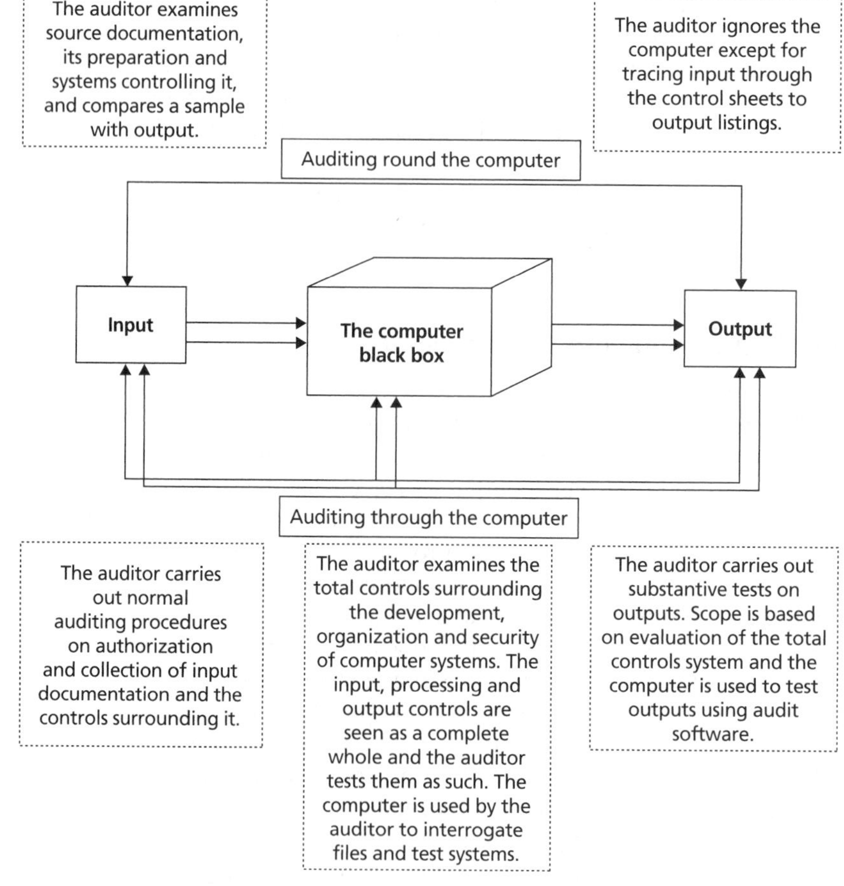

Such techniques can be used to select sample transactions from key electronic files, to sort transactions with specific characteristics, or to test an entire population instead of a sample.

Generally, the computer may be used for:

- Testing the system and the manner in which the computer processes data (tests of controls).
- Testing data (transactions and balances) held on computer file (substantive tests of detail).

If the auditor intends to use the computer, the audit planning stage becomes more important, as computer files and programs are not retained indefinitely and management must be approached to allocate computer time for audit purposes.

A great-grandfather file can only be tested when it is still a grandfather. Programs may also be amended before the auditor can test them unless testing is done on a planned basis.

We discuss the use of the computer to test the system below and substantive testing of data on computer files in Chapter 10.

Auditing with the computer

Management of the audit process with the aid of the computer is becoming widespread. Time and billing records are computerized and auditors are provided with desktop and laptop computers for such matters as designing audit programmes, keeping working schedules and performing analytical reviews. We call this 'auditing with the computer'. We shall discuss this matter at greater length in Chapter 10.

See page 383.

Specific tests of control in computer systems

Auditors' tests of controls in computer systems should not just be directed to controls surrounding specific applications, but also to proving that general, environmental controls are effective.

We have already discussed the general principles of control in computer systems in Chapters 7 and 8. We suggested that auditor intervention during development is desirable to ensure that controls are strong, whether over the development process itself, or whether they are organizational, security or application controls. Being involved at the start is, of course, not enough as auditors have to be sure that the controls are operating at all times and they will therefore test systems whenever they intend to rely upon them.

There are a number of ways in which auditors test the operation of computer systems and these we summarize under the following headings:

- Program code review.
- Use of test data.
- Use of program code comparison.
- Continuous review of data and their processing.
- Integrated test facility (ITF).
- Systems control and review file (SCARF).

Program code reviews

In testing the system the auditor is trying to determine if there are defects in programs that will cause data to be incorrectly processed. One way to test for defects is to carry out code reviews of programs they believe to be critical, although such reviews do tend to be costly in time and need expert knowledge. It would be important for auditors to determine that at the development stage programming standards are high and that test procedures by programmers, systems analysts and others are rigorous.

An example of invalid data would be a inventory transaction possessing a non-existent inventory number; potentially invalid data might be a sales transaction for an unusual quantity such as 10 000 pounds weight of 2 inch brass screws (when 10 pounds weight might be more normal). It would also be possible to create test data with both correct and incorrect batch control totals to see if the programme picks up the lack of agreement.

Use of test data

Another way to prove that the program is operating properly is to pass test data through the system to determine if it is processed in the way expected. Test data is data assembled by the auditor, some valid and some invalid (which should give rise to exception reporting). The process of assembling test data can also be very time consuming and, like program code reviews, will tend to be used to test critical programs, on which the auditor wishes to rely. It is important that test data are representative of real data passing through the system. If they are not, they will not provide the degree of satisfaction that the auditor requires. Good design of test data involves systematically analysing the nature of real data passing through the system; auditors need to consider all possible kinds of data and controls that they wish to test. This means: (a) that the design stage will be the most important in using test data; and (b) auditors must have a clear idea of why they are testing a particular part of the system. Some auditors have started to use computer-generated test data, perhaps even copying live data for reuse as test data. In such cases, the auditor would have to specify the kind of data they require, such as overtime hours at a reasonableness boundary (say, eight hours in any one week), lower than that and higher than that. Or they may ask for copies of high volume live data and then make comparisons between performance of the system at high load and low load, to see if the former results in system crashes.

Test data may either be processed during normal processing runs ('live' test data) or outside normal processing ('dead' test data). The auditor calculates the expected results from processing the data manually, listing all items that should be detected by the validation or edit checks and that should be printed out on the exception report. As we saw earlier, systems analysts, programmers and users use test data to test systems prior to implementation so the technique is of proven value. There are, however, a number of problems for auditors to which they must seek solutions:

- If used during normal processing runs, the test data will corrupt company files unless corrective action is taken. One way to do this is to identify test data with special codes that allow immediate reversal. Alternatively a reverse data run could take place under careful control, although this would be much more time consuming.
- If used outside normal processing, the results may be artificial because of the difficulty of creating normal conditions, not least because of the small volume of test data transactions. However, auditors are increasingly

processing data on a replica of the client's system on their own systems and this allows greater flexibility.

Use of program code comparison

An important concern for the auditor is the uncertainty that the program tested is the one normally used. For this reason, auditors may compare program codes of the program being tested with those of a program they know to be the authorized version. There is special software in existence that compares two sets of program codes and prints out any difference between the two. Clearly, interpreting the results will need considerable expertise, but the discrepancies might reveal that unauthorized changes have been made to programs. The technique does not, of course, tell the auditor that the authorized program is not defective, so it is best used in conjunction with the other techniques we have mentioned above.

Continuous review of data and their processing

See Weber (1999), Chapter 18.

Continuous reviews of this nature are sometimes referred to as 'concurrent auditing techniques'. These techniques involve embedding audit facilities that allow continuous review of the data and their processing. Embedded audit facilities are programs created by the auditor and placed within the client's computer system and designed to collect audit evidence while processing is taking place. They should only be capable of amendment by the auditor or by the client under conditions imposed by the auditor. Because such facilities are embedded in the client's system, they are sometimes known as 'auditing within the computer'. Such facilities can result in immediate flagging of a critical event (say, an excessive order to a particular supplier). The facility may cause a message to be transmitted to a monitor in the auditor's own office, or it may store the evidence collected in a file for subsequent review. One of the reasons for the use of such continuous review is that the information/audit trail is increasingly difficult to trace, certainly in hard copy. The auditor might use the company's own systems for recording the information/audit trail, but in critical areas may wish to establish it for themselves. One of the problems for the auditor is that systems are highly integrated with automatic updating of files controlled by a multiplicity of application systems, with the result that it can be exceedingly difficult to walk through the system as suggested above.

As we have noted in relation to test data, there is a danger that the auditor has not taken all data types and conditions into account in setting up the embedded audit facility. This means that there must be continuous updating of data types and conditions used. Embedded audit facilities may, however, be programmed to detect unusual transactions for review by the auditor. Furthermore, the whole system should be tested and not merely a single program or a partial suite of programs. We describe briefly below two kinds of embedded audit facility, integrated test facility (ITF) and systems control and review file (SCARF).

Integrated test facility (ITF)

When using this technique the auditor creates simulated transactions (identified by a special code to enable later removal) that are then mixed with

Auditors must be certain that reversals have not removed genuine data erroneously and that simulated transactions do not end up on a genuine account, so they must review simulated results with great care, ensuring that all transactions are accounted for.

genuine transactions. All transactions (simulated and genuine) are processed on the client's system and the results are analysed by the auditor. For instance, simulated sales orders may be input and the auditor will subsequently check that sales despatch notes and invoices have been prepared and fictitious inventory and trade receivable accounts set up by the auditor on the database have been correctly updated.

Clearly, reversal of the process is essential, hence the need for special identifying codes, but the auditor must ensure that reversal has taken place properly, and that company staff are aware that their control totals may be incorrect in respect of the fictitious data. Auditors would use this facility to test that input, processing and output controls are operating effectively. The facility has the advantage that it tests the actual operation of the client's system. In addition, It is possible to spread the use of the facility on a random basis throughout the year to give assurance that the systems in use are operating effectively in the whole period. The main problem with the use of ITF (apart from ensuring that genuine data are not corrupted) is that computer personnel may easily identify the codes used for simulated transactions and cause them to be processed in a manner other than that used for genuine data.

Systems control and review file (SCARF)

This technique is more complex than ITF and involves continuous monitoring of transactions passing through the company's systems using embedded audit software. The auditor has to decide which parts of the system are critical enough to require continuous monitoring. SCARF records data/information collected on a special file and prepares reports for audit purposes. It can report on both transactions and program logic. When used to audit transactions the auditor puts a code or parameter into the program so that every transaction that meets certain criteria is selected for examination. It can be described as auditing by exception as all transactions that meet the criteria are examined. An example might be the identification of all sales orders over a certain amount (say £10 000), together with the audit/information trail associated with them. Tests on the validity of the transactions would help the auditor to assess whether the system was operating properly and in particular whether the programmed controls on customers exceeding their credit limit had been overridden or not.

SCARF may also be used to test program logic by checking whether the program operates properly when a particular circumstance exists. For instance, the auditor might wish to test the automatic preparation of a purchase order or the printing of cheques in a selected period. SCARF would identify each time the computer made the decision to raise an order or print a cheque and the auditor would check that the decision was valid.

There are downsides to the use of ITF and SCARF. They are expensive and need considerable expertise. There is also a danger that auditor intervention might cause transactions to be improperly processed or for program logic to be disturbed. On the whole auditors tend to use these techniques in high-risk situations. The automatic printing of cheques is a good example, as there is a danger that assets are not being safeguarded.

Note, however, that SCARF may be used for selection of items for substantive testing on a continuous basis.

This has been a very brief summary of techniques that the auditor may use to test computer programs and the data processed by them. They tend to be costly or of limited use and the auditor is increasingly using substantive testing approaches to computer systems by developing special computer software. We discuss audit software for substantive testing in Chapter 10.

EVALUATION OF SYSTEMS AND AUDIT CONCLUSIONS

We have encouraged you to determine systems objectives before commencing systems work and suggested that auditors should identify key issues for each component of the system. In this chapter we asked you to work four case studies involving evaluation of systems and in three of them we asked you to identify the systems and audit objectives. It is important that audit staff record a formal conclusion on the efficacy of systems they have investigated.

We now turn to formal conclusions on systems, and shall give you an example based on the Broomfield plc sales and trade receivables system, described in Case study 9.1. In preparing this conclusion we have taken note of the system objectives we asked you to identify. If objectives have been properly set, and evidence properly collected, concluding on the results of systems work should follow logically. The audit conclusion should refer both to original objective(s), and to work done. Because this is an integrated system, the conclusion covers aspects of the inventory system as well. In the conclusion below the **bold** letters and figures are working file references:

At stage 9 in Figure 6.3, you will see a reference to stage 6.

> On the basis of the work carried out on the sales and trade receivables system of Broomfield plc (see working file containing the record of that system on **M/A** and compliance testing work on **M 100** to **M 105**), I can conclude that the system is designed to ensure that:
>
> (a) Customers receive the goods that they require at advertised prices and quality.
>
> (b) Customers receive goods on credit only if they are likely to pay for them.
>
> (c) Recorded sales are genuine, accurate and complete.
>
> (d) Trade receivables accounts are debited with sales on credit, which are genuine, accurate and complete.
>
> (e) All cash received is recorded in full before banking.
>
> (f) Inventory records reflect genuine movements in correct quantities, except for the matters listed on **M 10**.
>
> (g) There is a full audit trail of transactions and impact on balances, except for the matters listed on **M 10**.
>
> The matters listed on **M 10** will result in extension of scope (see scope decision on **M 1**) but reliance upon the system remains appropriate. The initial assessment of control risk (see **M 10**) has been confirmed as the result of this work.
>
> Extract from **M 10:**
>
> (i) Some goods are sold below normal prices. Our work has shown that these prices are below cost. At year-end we must consider company procedures to identify these inventories and their net realizable values.

In using this kind of conclusion auditors are not only stating that audit objectives have been achieved (with possible exceptions) but is also saying how they have been able to form conclusions. Staff members have indicated actions to resolve problems coming to their attention.

(ii) We noted delays between issue of sales invoice and physical transfer of inventory to customers (see details on **M 104**). To avoid cut-off problems at the year-end, the company is to identify goods belonging to customers (those invoiced but not collected) and transfer them to a special part of the storeroom. We shall test cut-off in this respect at year-end.

These two matters have been discussed with the chief accountant and will be included in the management letter.

(iii) We noted in one case that there was a difference between the control total of transactions input by a salesperson (Robert Black on 26 March 2010) and the final sales record of his input. The company says that the salesperson's code became detached from one transaction (it is not known why) but that the salesperson failed to notice the difference between control totals. The invoice was, however, processed correctly. We extended our tests of control totals as a result but discovered no further errors. This matter is to be mentioned in the management letter.

ACTIVITY 9.3

See Cengage website (**www.cengage.co.uk/graymanson5**).

We have not yet introduced you to substantive testing of transactions and balances in detail. However, take a look at the weaknesses that we highlighted in the solution to Case study 9.3 and suggest in broad terms what you might do as a result of the weaknesses that were found in the purchases system.

In broad terms the auditor might consider performing tests in the following areas:

- Review of exception reports to ensure appropriate corrective action has been taken.
- Check coding of purchase invoices to ensure within reason that costs have been charged to appropriate cost and expense accounts. Support this work by analytical reviews of costs.
- Check interventions to amend inventory master files using information/audit trail as an aid.
- Match purchase orders and purchase invoices to ensure prices and terms are in agreement.
- Check on reasonability of prices charged by suppliers.

See Chapter 15.

Some of this work might be carried out by the internal audit function, in which case the work of the internal auditors should be reviewed by the external auditors.

Summary

In this chapter we have given you the opportunity to evaluate a number of systems and have shown you the importance of setting objectives and how auditors formulate their conclusions. We discussed the role and significance of walk-through tests, tests of controls and substantive procedures, and gave examples of specific tests that auditors would use in respect of computer systems.

Key points of the chapter

- Auditors identify components of financial statements/related systems and identify control points and assess the appropriateness of controls, using key and subsidiary questions.
- Auditors obtain information to record systems by discussing their operation with a wide range of individuals and by inspecting a limited number of transactions as a walk-through test. The auditor performs tests of controls to decide whether or not internal controls are satisfactory and whether controls can be relied on. Substantive tests are designed to enable auditors to form conclusions at the assertion level, as to the validity of recorded figures in the financial statements.
- Depending on circumstances auditors may choose to rely on tests of controls or may decide to perform only substantive procedures. But a combined approach using both tests of controls and substantive procedures may be an effective approach.
- Irrespective of the assessed risks of material misstatement, the auditor designs and performs substantive procedures for each material class of transactions, account balance and disclosure. They may decide to perform only substantive analytical procedures (unless the item is material, in which case some substantive tests of detail may be performed as well), or only tests of details, or a combination of substantive analytical procedures and tests of details.
- Tests include (a) walk-through tests of the information/audit trail; (b) block testing one aspect of the system; (c) interviews with company staff; (d) observing staff at work; (e) re-performance of control procedures; (f) examination of management reviews.
- Approaches to auditing computer systems include: (a) round the computer; (b) through the computer; (c) with the computer. The computer may be used for: (a) testing the system; and (b) testing data held on compute file. The audit planning stage is important.
- Specific tests of computer systems include: (a) program code reviews; (b) test data; (c) program code comparison; and (d) concurrent auditing techniques.
- Code reviews are designed to determine if there are defects in programs that will cause incorrect processing of data.
- Test data are used to ascertain if the system operates as expected. Either 'live' or 'dead' test data may be used, usually only in systems critical for the auditors. Test data must be representative of real data. Problems are: (a) if used during normal processing the test data will corrupt entity files and need corrective action; (b) if used outwith normal processing, the results may be artificial.
- Program code comparison is used to compare the program being tested with a program known to be the authorized version.
- Concurrent auditing techniques involve embedding audit facilities that allow continuous review of data and their processing. Programs created by the auditor flag critical events as they occur for immediate or delayed review. Two types of embedded audit facilities are: (a) integrated test facility (ITF); and (b) systems control and review file (SCARF).
- When forming conclusions on systems the auditor states the consequences of particular strengths or weaknesses in the system and may suggest changes in scope in respect of them.

Reference

Weber, R. (1999) *Information Systems Control and Audit,* New York: Prentice Hall.

Further reading

Weber (1999), see above, contains a useful summary of procedures for testing controls in computer systems. Relevant ISAs are ISA 315 – *Identifying and assessing the risks of material misstatement through understanding the entity and its environment*. and IAS 330 – *The auditor's responses to assessed risks.*

Self-assessment questions (solutions available to students)

Two questions are placed within the text: (9.1) Case study 9.1 Broomfield plc: sales and trade receivables system; (9.2) Case study 9.4 Burbage Limited.

9.3 The balance sheets of Carnbee Limited, a trading company, at 31 August 2010 and 31 August 2009, together with profit and loss account extracts are as follows:

		2010		2009
Fixed assets: cost		500 000		500 000
Accumulated depreciation		150 000		100 000
		350 000		400 000
Inventories	150 000		100 000	
Trade receivables	160 000		150 000	
Petty cash	500		500	
	310 500		250 500	
Trade payables	200 000		160 000	
Bank overdraft	40 000		10 000	
	240 000		170 000	
Net current liabilities/assets		70 500		80 500
Net assets		420 500		480 500
Turnover		900 000		1 000 000
Cost of goods sold		650 000		700 000
Gross profit		250 000		300 000
GP%		27.8%		30.0%
Inventory turnover		84 days		52 days
Trade receivables days		65 days		55 days
Trade payables days		112 days		83 days
Acid test ratio		0.67		0.89

You are planning your audit approach for the year ended 31 August 2010. What areas would you regard as being of low risk and of high risk? Are there any areas where you might be inclined to spend restricted or no systems work?

Self-assessment questions (solutions available to tutors)

Two questions are placed within the text (9.4) Case study 9.2 Wages payroll: Troston plc; (9.5) Case study 9.3 Broomfield plc: part of purchases and trade creditors system.

9.6 You are auditing a company engaged in the development and sale of games software over the Internet. You are satisfied that the software is of high quality and are now directing your attention to the controls over the sale of their products. You have confirmed that the company's systems are fully integrated and that sales automatically update bank and trade receivable records (depending on whether the sales are by credit card or on credit) and quantity inventory records. Your initial discussions with management have satisfied you that the control environment is good and you have classified control risk as 'medium'. (Your firm asks audit staff to classify control risk as 'high', 'medium' and 'low'.)

Required:

(a) Explain what the three control risk classifications probably mean in practice.

(b) What basic controls would you expect to see to ensure that sales are genuine, accurate and complete, that the risk of bad debts is low, and that inventory movements resulting from sales are genuine, accurate and complete?

Suggest suitable tests of control.

Solutions available to students and Solutions available to tutors

These can be found on the website in the student/lecturer section at: www.cengage.co.uk/graymanson5.

Topics for class discussion without solutions

9.7 Explain the objectives of walk-through test, tests of control and substantive tests and give examples of each.

9.8 Audit working files show why the audit team have reached its conclusions. Discuss.

9.9 We mention frequently in the text the term 'genuine, accurate and complete'. Explain what the term means.

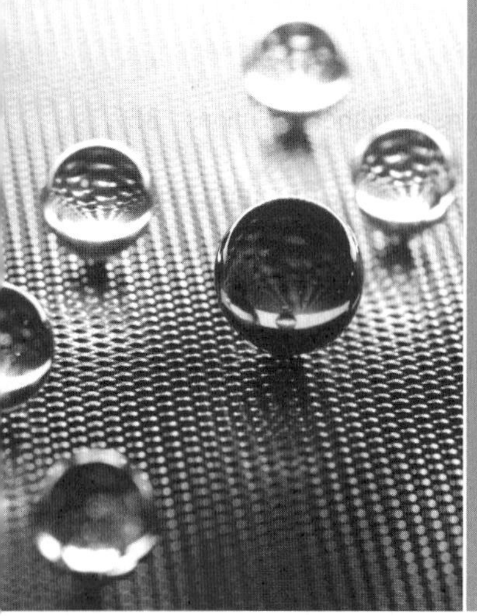

10

Substantive testing, computer-assisted audit techniques and audit programmes

LEARNING OBJECTIVES

After studying this chapter you should be able to:

- **Describe the substantive procedures an auditor would perform to prove that recorded transactions and figures are genuine, accurate and complete.**
- **Explain the purpose of selecting a sample when performing substantive procedures.**
- **Draft suitable conclusions after substantive procedures have been performed.**
- **Draft a management letter, containing recommendations on internal control and other matters of interest to management and others charged with governance, and to the auditor.**

Learning objectives, 358
Introduction, 359
Substantive testing of transactions, account balances and disclosures, 359
The use of audit software, 364
Directional testing, 373
Substantive audit programmes for wages, 375
Substantive audit programmes for cash and bank balances, 377
Communication of audit matters to those charged with governance (management letter), 378
Audit management with the computer, 383
Summary, 385
Key points of the chapter, 385
Reference, 386
Further reading, 386
Self-assessment questions (solutions available to students), 386
Self-assessment questions (solutions available to tutors), 387
Topics for class discussion without solutions, 388
Appendix 10.1: substantive audit programme for production wages: Troston plc, 389
Appendix 10.2: substantive audit programme for cash/bank: County Hotel Limited, 392

INTRODUCTION

In Chapters 7, 8 and 9 we explained how auditors approach accounting and internal control systems established by management to process transactions and record them in the accounting records. We saw that auditors determined objectives at an early stage to put their work into context and to help them to form conclusions. In earlier Chapters (5 and 6) we saw that the evidence search to be efficient and effective has to be performed in the context of risk evaluation, having identified business/inherent and control risks for each management assertion.

In this chapter we look principally at how auditors use substantive procedures to test that transactions, processed and controlled by accounting and control systems, are genuine, accurate and complete.

SUBSTANTIVE TESTING OF TRANSACTIONS, ACCOUNT BALANCES AND DISCLOSURES

We have already discussed the relationship between audit work on recording systems, and tests of control and substantive testing in Chapter 9 and we suggest that you reread the section on tests of controls on pages 341 to 347, including the Important note and Activity 9.1.

Let us remind ourselves yet again of the definitions of 'substantive procedure' and 'test of control' taken from paragraph 4 of ISA 330:

(a) Substantive procedure – An audit procedure designed to detect material misstatements at the assertion level. Substantive procedures comprise:
  (i) Tests of details (of classes of transactions, account balances and disclosures); and
  (ii) Substantive analytical procedures.
(b) Test of controls – An audit procedure designed to evaluate the operating effectiveness of controls in preventing, or detecting and correcting, material misstatements at the assertion level.

ACTIVITY 10.1

What do you think is the difference between substantive 'tests of detail' and 'substantive analytical procedures'?

It may sound obvious but tests of detail involve detailed testing of transactions and balances, such as selecting goods despatch notes (GDNs) and checking that they have always resulted in a sales invoice being prepared. The auditors might also select customers orders and check that GDNs have always been prepared for sales orders accepted. A further substantive test might be to select trade receivables balances for confirmation by the customer. If the customer agrees that the balance is correct, that proves too that the sales invoices have been properly raised. We discussed this in Chapter 6 and you may care to take a look at Figure 6.2 on page 227 once more. The audit objective would be to ensure that turnover included all despatches of good during the year.

A substantive analytical procedure would not be so concerned with detail. In this case, the auditor might check if the gross profit percentage appeared to be what was expected, turnover being an important element in its calculation. They would check whether trade receivables appeared to be reasonable in relation to turnover; trade receivables are often expressed as 'number of days sales' and the auditor would query any significant change in this figure compared with previous periods and what is known of current trends. The argument here is that, if the analytical review results are as expected in the light of what is known about the company, the auditor might accept that the entity's controls ensure that sales are genuine, accurate and complete.

We discuss analytical procedures in Chapter 11. ISA 520 – *Analytical procedures* provides guidance on the application of analytical procedures during an audit.

Of course, the auditors would only restrict substantive tests to analytical procedures if they were satisfied that the company controls in the area were strong. If they were deemed to be weak, analytical procedures on their own would not be sufficient (see paragraph 43 of ISA 330 as detailed in Chapter 9, page 342). Note too that substantive analytical procedures are generally more applicable to large volumes of transactions that tend to be predictable over time. Thus these analytical procedures would be more useful in obtaining audit satisfaction about large volume sales transactions of a similar nature in a stable entity than would be the case for a company with a smaller number of high value one-off sales transactions, dissimilar in nature.

See paragraph A42 of ISA 330.

There are two important reasons why substantive tests should always be performed:

1 Because the auditor's assessment of risk is judgemental and may not be sufficiently precise to identify all risks of material misstatement.
2 There are inherent limitations to internal control including management override.

If you refer to Figure 6.3 on page 230 you will see that we have taken the auditor on a different path at stage 11 depending on whether the accounting and control systems are deemed to be ineffective or effective. What is meant by limited is a matter of judgement and it may include some tests of detail as well as analytical procedures. The implication is that stages 6 to 9 may be omitted if systems are very unreliable and the auditor decides to pass directly to substantive procedures. In a first-time audit the auditor would normally assess systems, however unreliable, but in subsequent years (although assessing systems would continue to be desirable) would probably pass quickly to substantive testing. This assumes that no positive changes have been made to an unreliable system since the last visit.

See stage 4 in Figure 6.3.

Planning feedback

As the audit progresses, more knowledge of the company is gained. For instance, during discussions with management and when recording and testing systems, or carrying out substantive procedures, audit risk assessments may change and affect the scope of examination, resulting in planning feedback. This is recognized in Paragraphs 31 and A 130 of ISA 315, to which you may refer.

Setting objectives before designing a programme of substantive tests

As you are aware from your reading of ISA 330, substantive tests should be designed to prove the validity of financial statement assertions of material account balances and transaction classes. This means that auditors must be clear as to what they wish to achieve before designing a programme of substantive tests. We can illustrate this by a case study based on an ACCA auditing paper of some years ago. The case is not particularly computer oriented, but it does give some good pointers to the principles behind the design of substantive audit programmes.

CASE STUDY 10.1

Powerbase plc: the substantive audit programme for purchases

You are engaged in the audit of the purchases figure in the financial statements of Powerbase plc, a company producing power tools. The company's purchases and trade payables system is computerized, the goods received note (GRN) prepared by stores forming the source documentation for updating the inventory records. The purchase invoices, on receipt from suppliers, are matched with purchase orders and GRNs in the accounting department and these form the input to the purchases transactions and trade payables updating runs. The following interim financial results have recently been published in the financial press:

	12 months to 31 May 2010		6 months to 30 November 2010	
	£m	£m	£m	£m
Sales		95.2		50.4
Cost of sales		54.8		24.8
Gross profit		40.4		25.6
Administrative expenses	22.3		10.1	
Selling expenses	10.5		4.7	
		32.8		14.8
Net profit before taxation		7.6		10.8

You are the audit senior in charge of the interim audit of Powerbase plc and have satisfied yourself that the systems for recording purchase orders, inventory movements and updating purchases and trade payables are satisfactory. You asked Bill Chivers, a junior member of staff who has only recently joined your firm of auditors, to prepare substantive audit programmes in the purchases and trade payables area and you are reviewing the programmes (set out below) prepared by him.

Purchases: interim audit

- *Cheque payments*. Select a sample of cheque payments for purchases of raw materials and check as described below:
  - (a) Agree to invoices for goods received.
  - (b) Agree to goods received notes.
  - (c) Check calculations and additions on invoices.
- *Purchase daybook*
  - (a) Select entries at random and examine invoices and credit notes for price, calculations and authorization, etc.
  - (b) Check postings of entries to trade payables ledger.
- *Purchase ledger*
  - (a) Select a sample of accounts and test check the entries into the books of prime entry, checking the additions and balances carried forward.
  - (b) Enquire into all contra items.
- *Conclusions*

Note any conclusions covering any weaknesses and errors discovered during the above tests for possible inclusion in a management letter.

ACTIVITY 10.2

Discuss the extent to which the interim audit programmes should take account of the interim results of Powerbase plc.

Audits are not carried out in a vacuum and auditors need as much information as possible if the work is to be effective. Let us see whether the figures in the case might be helpful in forming a view about the required scope of substantive tests. As we look at the figures remember that the auditor's interest is in forming an opinion on the validity of the figures. It will be useful first to extract a number of ratios:

	31.5.2010	30.11.2010
Gross profit to sales	42.44%	50.79%
Administration expense to sales	23.42%	20.04%
Selling expense to sales	11.03%	9.33%
Net profit to sales	7.98%	21.43%

You will agree that the changes in these ratios are significant. They may of course represent genuine changes resulting from management decisions and commercial factors. The auditor, however, would direct the audit work towards determining whether this is the case and with the intent of subjecting high-risk areas to greater audit emphasis. In the context of purchases, the auditor would want to ascertain that the system was processing transactions properly. In Powerbase plc, the increased gross profit percentage may be an indication that purchases have been omitted or not recorded in the right period. We might also wonder whether the system was properly allocating costs to administrative and selling expenses in view of the significant reductions in percentage relationship to sales. It would clearly be desirable for interim audit work to test the operation of the purchases system, despite your initial conclusions that the system is satisfactory. Your main aim is to satisfy yourself as to the validity of purchases recorded in the first half of 2010/2011. Many substantive procedures are carried out at interim dates because of the tightness of year-end reporting deadlines.

Later you will use your conclusions on the purchase figure for the first half of the financial year in forming your opinion on the figure for the whole year, although you will want to assure yourself that the figures for the second half of the year are reasonable.

Let us now look at the purchases audit programme that your assistant has drafted.

ACTIVITY 10.3

Critically examine the audit programmes set out above, taking into account the implied assertions that management is making and the related audit objectives. When you are reviewing the assistant's programme, ask yourself: 'What is this programme step proving to me?' Remember that Bill is new to auditing and it is your responsibility to give him good training under your supervision.

You should first tell Bill that his work should be put in context and that, as he is auditing an actual company – Powerbase – he should tailor-make the programme to the circumstances of the company. An important first step is therefore the analytical review of the interim figures as they relate to purchases, and the programme should contain a requirement to carry out the review. We now turn to criticism of the programme steps suggested by Bill:

- *Cheque payments*. Selecting a sample of cheque payments and tracing to supporting invoices and goods received notes proves only that cheque payments are valid. It does not prove that all purchases are complete and accurate and represent a proper charge.
- *Purchase daybook*. Likewise, selecting entries in the purchases daybook and testing to invoices and credit notes proves only that entries in the daybook are supported by those documents. It does not prove that the daybook is a complete and accurate record of purchase costs incurred by the company.
- *Purchase ledger*. Selecting a sample of purchase ledger accounts and testing entries to daybook, cash book, etc., proves only that the entries are in agreement with the books of prime entry. It does not prove that the ledger accounts represent all entries that should have been entered.

In other words, the first serious weakness of the detailed audit programme is that it has failed to identify the objective of testing and to select on the basis of what is to be proven. The second serious weakness is that it gives no indication of scope of examination, referring only to selection of a sample and not its size. In addition, Bill has ignored some aspects of processing entirely, namely, the updating of the inventory records, which is an important output of the purchases routine.

You should explain to Bill that it is important to decide where the starting point should be if the programme objectives are to be met. Thus:

- If you wish to prove that all goods received have been matched with an invoice and included in the purchases daybook and purchase ledger, the appropriate starting-off point would be to select a representative sample of GRNs.
- If one wished to prove that all goods received had been properly approved for purchase, the above selection of GRNs should be traced to purchase orders and approval of those orders checked.
- If you wish to prove that all purchase orders had resulted in goods being received promptly and in the correct quality and quantity, the correct procedure would be to take a random selection of purchase orders and trace to goods received notes and purchase invoices.

There is a further basic rule, however, relating to the reliability of the document or record chosen to prove the management assertion. In the case we are considering the auditor would wish to ensure that the GRNs are themselves genuine, accurate and complete. The auditor might consider the following steps as part of the substantive procedures:

The GRNs are vital documents as they are records of goods received and normally signify that liabilities have been accepted.

1 Check the sequence of purchase orders to ensure that there are no breaks and trace a random selection of (say) 20 of them to goods received notes, enquiring into any order that has apparently not resulted in goods being received. This would help to verify the goods received notes.

2 Check inventory records for accuracy by test counting quantities on hand and comparing with the records. This would help to prove the inventory records.

3 Check a random selection of entries in the inventory records (say 20) to GRNs. This would be a further test on GRN validity.

In steps 1, 3 and 4 we suggested that 20 items be selected for testing in each case. This is a scope decision and would be influenced by what you thought of the system.

4 Check sequence of GRNs (helping to prove their completeness) to ensure there are no breaks and trace a random sample (say 20) to invoices, checking product description and quantities. This would be an important test on the completeness and accuracy of purchases, although there would have to be additional tests on the invoices (such as prices and calculations).

In carrying out work of this nature, it is necessary to use such records as are available. If, for instance, the purchase order were the source document for preparation of goods received note and inventory movements, the auditor would pay more attention to the controls surrounding the preparation of the purchase order. Two further matters are worthy of mention before we leave this case:

- The step that Bill put under the heading 'Conclusions' is also very weak. It is true that conclusions on weaknesses and errors should be noted for inclusion in a management letter. However, the primary concern for the auditor is forming a conclusion on the adequacy of the purchases system and the genuineness, accuracy and completeness of the purchases transactions. The programme drafted by Bill does not require such a conclusion and this should be remedied.
- The audit process must be as efficient and effective as possible. There is considerable pressure on audit fees and this means that audit tests should be carefully designed to meet audit objectives within a limited timeframe. This case shows how to design tests to achieve the predetermined objectives We set out a suitable purchases audit programme for Powerbase plc in Figure 10.1, incorporating the ideas we have discussed above.

IMPORTANT NOTE

This has been a very important case not only from the point of view of the audit process but because this approach can be very useful in the examination room. Many auditing questions provide the candidate with an audit scenario and then ask for suitable tests of control or tests of details. The key to success in a question like this is to determine the implied management assertion for each identified financial statement component, to set objectives and to devise tests that will meet the objectives. We gave you this advice in Chapter 2 also, but it is worth repeating here.

THE USE OF AUDIT SOFTWARE

They may also be used in testing controls in computer systems as we noted in Chapter 9.

In Chapter 9 we gave examples of techniques used by auditors to test operation of computer systems. We now discuss the use by auditors of specially

FIGURE 10.1 Powerbase plc purchases audit programme

Purchases audit programme for the six-month period to 30 November 2010	Ref.	Done by
Financial statement assertions to be verified by this programme: 1. The purchases figure as included in cost of sales is a complete and accurate record of purchases for the six months to 30 November 2010 2. The accounts payable represent all trade creditors balances outstanding at 30 November 2010		
Programme step 1: Carry out an analytical review of detailed management accounts at 30 November 2010 and ascertain that the purchases and trade creditors components make sense in relation to the prior year and budgeted figures. Carry out further analysis to discover reasons for significant variations in the figures for the period.		
Programme step 2: On the basis of the evaluation of the purchases and accounts payable system carried out previously and of the analytical review performed in step 1, establish scope of examination (extent of audit procedures). (*Note*: The engagement partner would be the final arbiter of scope of examination, but the audit team would be expected to make recommendations.)		
Programme step 3: (designed to prove the accuracy of goods received notes) (a) Check the sequence of purchase orders to ensure that there are no breaks and check a random selection of (say) 20 in detail to goods received notes, enquiring into reason for any order that has apparently not resulted in goods being received or amount/quality of goods received differing from the order. (b) Check a random selection of 20 receipts in the inventory records and test to goods received notes. (*Note*: the accuracy of the inventory records has been tested by count of stock items and checking to the records.)		
Programme step 4: (this represents a completeness test, when taken with programme step 3) Check the sequence of goods received notes to ensure that there are no breaks. If there are breaks in the sequence enquire into reasons.		
Programme step 5: Conclude on the completeness of the goods received notes.		
Programme step 6: (this represents a reperformance of the matching operation that should already have been carried out by company personnel) Select 30 goods received notes on a random basis and trace details to: (a) purchase order (confirm also that the order has been signed by an appropriate responsible official) (b) stock records (c) purchase invoices (confirm also that the invoices contain a completed box showing that all matching steps have been carried out by an appropriate responsible official).		
Programme step 7: (this represents a further test on the accuracy of the invoice and is done in conjunction with programme step 6) On the invoices selected check that all calculations and additions have been properly made.		
Programme step 8: Trace the invoices selected to: (a) purchase daybook (check amount and cost allocation) (b) trade payables ledger (check amount and name of supplier) (c) cash book entry on subsequent payment (check also to cheque book stub and entry in bank statement).		
Programme step 9: (this represents a further test on completeness and accuracy of purchase transactions, but also that trade payables are properly stated at the circularization date) Select 30 suppliers' balances on a random basis and request the company to ask the suppliers concerned to confirm direct to us (the auditor) the balances in their books relating to the company at 30 November 2010. *The date of 30 November 2010 in programme step 9 has been selected for illustrative purposes only.* The auditor might prefer to select a circularization date nearer to the balance sheet date.		
Programme step 10: Conclude on the completeness and accuracy of the purchases transactions in the six months to 30 November 2010		

designed audit software for substantive tests of details. There are several different types of software developed for use by the auditor including:

- Generalized audit software.
- Software developed for use in specific industries.
- Statistical analysis software.
- Expert system software.

Generalized audit software and software developed for specific industries

For instance, audit software can be used to confirm that there are no blank fields in customer data. The existence of blank fields might mean that procedures for identifying and authenticating customers at the interface were faulty.

Generalized audit software and software developed for specific industries are essentially interrogation tools used to access and examine and even manipulate data and information held on file. Although they are designed primarily as tools for substantive testing to prove the validity and quality of data on file, they can also be used to confirm that systems from which the data are derived are operating satisfactorily, and that development and systems maintenance staff, including quality standards personnel, are themselves of high quality. Such software can be used to interrogate data held on a company's own files, but it has also been developed to interrogate data downloaded from company files to the auditors' own systems, including microcomputer systems.

The main reason for developing generalized audit software was that external auditors were faced with a wide variety of hardware and software among their clients. To develop software for individual clients would have been extremely expensive, and generalized software was seen as the answer, even if less efficient in operation. An advantage of generalized audit software is that audit staff can be more easily trained in its use. The software designed for use in specific industries is similar to generalized audit software but have additional functions. For instance, in the audit of a building society, the auditor would wish to ensure that interest on borrowers' and members' accounts has been properly calculated. Industry specific audit software has been developed to test such calculations.

Before we look at some examples of the use of generalized audit software let us consider what such software can do:

- It can access files with many different characteristics and can manipulate the data on them, for instance by sorting files and merging different files.
- It can select data on the basis of predetermined criteria and can perform arithmetical functions on data selected (such as: add, subtract, multiply, divide).
- It can analyse selected data statistically and can stratify data into desired categories.
- It can cause files to be created and updated from the company's own files.
- It can produce reports for the auditor in desired format.

We will not look at all these functions in detail but we want you to know how audit software can be used to achieve audit objectives. Note that all the actions require the auditor to exercise judgement.

Of course, to interrogate a file you have to have a good idea not only of what you want to achieve, but also what is on the file.

ACTIVITY 10.4

Let us assume that a trading company client (buying and selling goods) keeps its inventory records on computer file and these records contain the following details for each line of inventory:

- Receipts (quantities and purchase cost); goods received note number; date of receipt.
- Issues (quantities); despatch note number; date of issue.
- FIFO cost per item (calculated automatically by computer).
- Selling price.
- Maximum inventory level.
- Minimum inventory level.
- Balance on hand (quantities and total FIFO cost).
- Adjustments to actual inventory following count (quantities and value); date of adjustment.

Bearing in mind that the auditor can only apply audit software to data and information held on computer file, how do you think the above information could be used to form conclusions about the inventory figure in the balance sheet of the company? (Think of three different uses and explain the implied management assertion in each case.)

There are many uses that could be made of this data. Here are three suggestions:

1. Comparison between FIFO cost and selling price adjusted for selling and distribution cost still to be incurred. This test would be useful for determining if inventory should be valued at net realizable value rather than FIFO cost. The implied management assertion might be: 'All inventory is stated at cost, except in the reported cases where net realizable value has been used.' The test would be a substantive test of detail.
2. Details of all inventory items where there has been no outward movement in the last (say) 90 days with the objective of identifying slow moving inventory where special provision may be required. The implied management assertion might be: 'All inventory is saleable in the normal course of business.' This is also a substantive test of detail.
3. Details of inventory exceeding maximum inventory level. This may be an indicator of a breakdown in the control system or failure to meet expected sales. The implied management assertion being tested is: 'No inventory is held in excess of predetermined maximum inventory levels.' (The test in this case might be seen as a test of control but it might also be a substantive test of detail if it reveals material amounts in excess of predetermined levels, prompting the question: 'Will you be able to sell this excess inventory?')

Taking the first example above, the software would identify the FIFO cost for each item, then identify selling price and adjust for expected selling and distribution cost still to be incurred and compare FIFO cost with net realizable value. If net realizable value were lower, the total amounts at FIFO cost and net realizable value could be calculated. In practice you might not be interested in small excesses of cost over net realizable value, so the auditor might build in an instruction that items should only be printed out if (say) cost exceeded net realizable value by 5 per cent of cost. Now let us consider further ways in which audit software might be used.

ACTIVITY 10.5

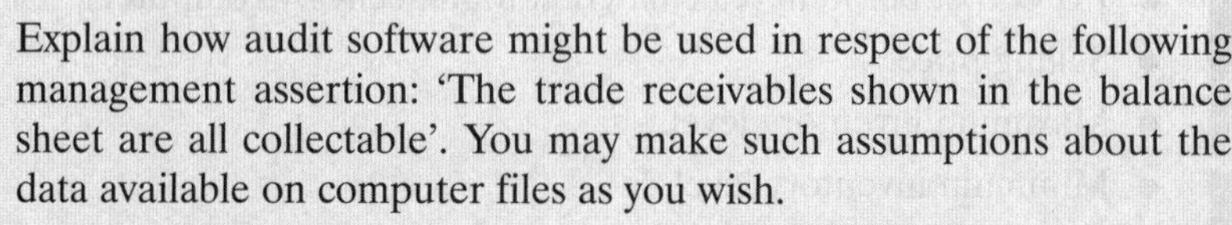

Explain how audit software might be used in respect of the following management assertion: 'The trade receivables shown in the balance sheet are all collectable'. You may make such assumptions about the data available on computer files as you wish.

In answering this question you should first consider what indicators the auditor would use in forming a view about the collectability of debtors. We suggest that two indicators are the age of items included in the balances and whether credit limits have been exceeded. Thus, if the date of each open item is on the trade receivables computer file, it will be a relatively easy matter to use audit software to select items less than 90 days old or lying between 90 days and 120 days and so on. The technique can, therefore, be used to check the validity of a trade receivables ageing statement. Similarly, if the trade receivables file contains details of credit limits, it will be possible, using audit software, to obtain a schedule of all balances exceeding the credit limit by (say) 20 per cent.

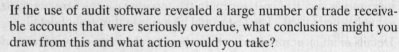

ACTIVITY 10.6

If the use of audit software revealed a large number of trade receivable accounts that were seriously overdue, what conclusions might you draw from this and what action would you take?

There are two kinds of action that the auditor might take, one directed towards the trade receivables figure in the financial statements and the other directed towards the system in force and the company staff operating it.

- *Trade receivables figure in the financial statements*. Overdue accounts may not be collectable and the auditors, in conjunction with management, would review these accounts with a view to deciding if the provision for bad and doubtful debts needed to be increased. Past history of payments by slow payers should be reviewed. If there are many overdue customers, the initial review might first be made by internal audit, followed by review of their work by the external auditor. Clear decisions concerning collectability should also be made by management.

- *System in force and company staff*. Many overdue accounts might reveal that the system and the staff operating it are inadequate. The auditor might ask how often the system produces reports of overdue accounts, and whether there is an adequate system for reminding customers of amounts outstanding. As far as credit limits are concerned these should be reviewed by company staff on a regular basis; if they are unreasonably high, credit might be granted to bad risk customers; if too low, the company might lose sales to good customers.

ACTIVITY 10.7

Explain how audit software might be used in respect of the following management assertion: 'All purchase invoices have been recorded in the correct period, so that cut off is accurate.' You may again make such assumptions about the data available on computer files as you wish.

Let us assume that goods received data are held on a goods received computer file (File A), containing the date of receipt of the goods. It might be possible, using audit software, to reconcile the data on this file with the computer file (File B) containing purchase invoices recorded in the period to the balance sheet date. If there were items in File A not in File B, this might indicate unrecorded purchases and liabilities.

It must be clear to you by now that audit software used for substantive testing can tell us a great deal about systems in use. The same applies to a technique known as parallel simulation, whereby the auditor creates a program to reprocess critical data, the audit software being used to compare the results of the company system with those of the auditor's own program. For instance the company might have a routine for calculating net realizable values of inventory for comparison with calculated cost of inventory items. The auditor might use parallel simulation in critical areas such as this.

Statistical analysis software

We shall discuss analytical review in greater detail in Chapter 12 but as we noted in our discussion of the Powerbase Case study, such reviews form an important element in substantive testing performed by the auditor. We mention it here because generalized audit software can be used to extract important ratios and balances from the company records for comparison with previous periods and external data. There are also software packages available with regression analysis capabilities, which enable auditors to form a view about company trends in relation to several prior years and the industry average.

Generalized audit software can be used to select data on a statistically sound basis. It might be used, for instance, to select customers for circularization, possibly stratifying the population of trade receivables before making the selection. The software's report writing facility might be used to prepare summaries of customers selected and the circularization forms to be sent to customers. The software might be used to prepare a list of open items to be included on the forms.

ACTIVITY 10.8

Assume that the auditor wishes to select inventory for physical observation. How might a statistical facility in audit software be used by the auditor in this respect?

Auditors would have to decide if there were any particular inventory items whose count they wished to observe. For instance, high-value items might be selected, or items that had not moved for a particular period of time, or they might wish to select inventory items on a random basis. They might wish to know the location of inventory of particular kinds. The reporting facility might be used to list selected items in a manner that would facilitate the auditors' own count procedures. For instance, inventory selected might be shown under location headings within the storeroom and in other locations. The software might also provide supplementary data about inventory items, such as dates and details of last movement.

The use of generalized audit software in such ways is a very useful supplement to statistical sampling techniques. We shall see in Chapter 11 that statistical sampling seeks to provide a sample which is representative of the total population of transactions or balances. Audit enquiry packages, apart from those used for statistical selection purposes, do the exact opposite, an unrepresentative sample is the desired result. They audit by exception, interrogating the file and pulling out those items possessing the characteristics the auditor has selected. The auditor uses the listing of items possessing (or not possessing) the selected characteristics to assess whether the management assertion about the file is valid. Paragraph A16 of ISA 330 puts it: this way:

> The use of computer-assisted audit techniques (CAATs) may enable more extensive testing of electronic transactions and account files, which may be useful when the auditor decides to modify the extent of testing, for example, in responding to the risks of material misstatement due to fraud. Such techniques can be used to select sample transactions from key electronic files, to sort transactions with specific characteristics, or to test an entire population instead of a sample.

Provided its use is properly controlled, it may be possible for auditors to use enquiry software supplied by the manufacturer. This would reduce cost considerably but auditors must be sure it is suitable for their purposes.

Audit software is particularly useful when there are large amounts of data. The major disadvantage is the cost of developing it, but, once developed, it can be economical in audit resources and can achieve quick results. It is argued by some that too much time must be devoted to obtaining understanding of system and files, a possible disadvantage from the efficiency, although not from the effectiveness point of view. There are other disadvantages that you should know about:

1 Generalized audit software can only be used after the event, that is, it is very useful when interrogating data on computer files, but cannot be used concurrently in the same way that SCARF (systems control and review file) can be used in testing data moving through the system.

2 Although we have seen that systems weaknesses can be discovered using audit software, it is difficult to assess the likelihood of error using it. Note

too that as audit software is not used continuously, any system weaknesses may not be discovered on a timely basis. Also audit software would not be very useful in detecting where system breakdowns are likely, for instance, when there is system overload.

We set out below a number of potential uses for audit software. In each case you may assume that the client company is large and that using audit software would be an economical way of carrying out substantive tests.

Computer-assisted audit techniques: examples

Sales and trade receivables.

1 Listing large sales transactions for special investigation.
2 As part of cut-off tests matching dates of despatch notes and sales invoices; similarly matching dates of goods returned notes and credit notes.
3 Listing prices that differ from the official price lists and discounts exceeding a certain percentage. Recalculating sales discounts.
4 Analysing sales per product line.
5 As part of completeness of recorded sales test, listing quantities despatched and quantities invoiced.
6 Listing write-off of customer balances.
7 Listing credit note transactions, particularly those of high value or near the year-end.
8 Testing additions on invoices and trade receivable accounts.
9 Testing that sales have correctly entered the costing record.

Inventories and production cost.

1 Listing material changes in standard costs from previous year or period.
2 Comparing finished inventory records with sales data.
3 Identifying obsolete inventory by calculating inventory turnover statistics.
4 Identifying abnormal usage or costs.
5 Testing overhead cost allocations.
6 Comparing production usage with issues of raw materials and components from inventory.
7 Comparing proportions of materials, components, labour and overheads included in production costs with those included in inventories.
8 Comparing inputs to production processes with outputs (this might be useful in the case of a refinery inputting crude oil and additives to produce a range of mineral oil products).

Purchases and trade payables.

1 Listing large purchases of goods and services for later examination.
2 Analysing purchases of goods and services for each month or for the year.
3 Comparing goods received data with recorded purchase invoices as part of the cut-off test.

4 Listing details of new suppliers.
5 Comparing outputs from financial accounting records of purchases to inputs to costing records.

Wages and salaries.

1 Listing details of new or dismissed/resigning employees for later checking to supporting records.
2 Comparing date of first entry or last entry of employees on the payroll with date of appointment/leaving in personnel records.
3 Testing mathematical accuracy of tax, social security and other deductions.
4 Testing payroll casts and cross-casts.
5 Testing outputs from financial accounting records of wages and salaries to inputs to costing records.
6 Comparing records on personnel and payroll files for consistency.

Non-current tangible assets.

1 Retrieval of non-current asset records to check that records for assets known to be in existence, themselves exist.
2 Analysing assets by type, age and location.
3 Listing details of fully depreciated assets.
4 Testing reconciliation of assets recorded in non-current assets accounts to non-current assets register.
5 Reconciling non-current asset budget entries with subsequent purchases and printing material variances.

Investments.

1 Testing that income from all assets held is complete and accurate.
2 Listing changes in investment balance sheet values.
3 Comparing costs with investment market values.

Taxes on income

1 Identifying and analysing repairs above a certain amount to check validity of the capital/revenue decision.
2 Listing subscriptions and donations to check for allowability as a charge against taxable income.
3 Listing motor vehicle usage by, and pension scheme contributions on behalf of, individuals for checking to benefits in kind calculations.

Expert systems

Expert systems can be useful when a system or other area can be broken down into a series of rules. One of the first ways that expert systems were used was in respect of value added tax (VAT), which has a number of very clear rules to assess the amount of VAT payable. A VAT expert would determine all the rules and express them in the form of questions, such as: 'Does annual turnover exceed £x' (being the turnover at which a company must be registered for VAT); 'If so, is the company registered for VAT', and so on. Staff members would answer the questions presented to them by the computer program and if there were any critical matters, such as not being registered for VAT when required, the program would prepare a report containing details of action required. Expert systems have also been developed for audit purposes and checklists that in the past had been paper based have been turned into a rules-based expert system. We have already mentioned this in Chapter 8 when we introduced you to an EDP/IT checklist for Burbage Limited. Essentially, expert systems make expertise available to persons who are not experts themselves. They are used both for evidence collection and evaluation of the evidence, once collected. Expert systems have been devised to evaluate risk (for instance, is the company likely to face going-concern problems?); to evaluate strength of systems (for instance, are any serious breaches in security likely?); to suggest appropriate audit programme steps based on evaluation of systems (for instance, what steps would be appropriate if there are serious breaks in information/audit trail?); to check that legislation and accounting standards have been complied with (for instance SSAP 21 and IAS 17 have a number of quite complex disclosure rules for leased assets).

See Figure 8.5 on page 323.

DIRECTIONAL TESTING

Another kind of substantive procedure is that of 'directional testing'. You will recall from our discussion of the true and fair view in Chapter 1 that auditors wish to prove that there are no material over- or understatements in the financial statements. This means that substantive procedures should be designed to test for such over- or understatement, the auditor's aim being clearly twofold in nature. Many auditors suggest that the best way to achieve the twofold aim is to direct tests of *debit* items (such as expenses, cash receipts and assets) to detecting overstatement and to direct tests for *credit* items (such as income, cash payments and liabilities) to detecting understatement. As double entry is itself twofold in nature, adopting the directional tests will result in tests in two directions (to detecting over- and understatement). Let us take an example of a company purchasing and selling goods on credit, the entries being shown in Figure 10.2.

We consider the sales and trade receivable entries first. The argument runs that the auditor would test the trade receivables figure (£1 375 000) for overstatement by such procedures as confirming balances with credit customers, by testing sales/trade receivables/ inventory cut-off and by reviewing ageing statements to obtain satisfaction that trade receivables are recoverable at the stated amount.

The sales credit entry (£2 500 000) would be tested for understatement by tests designed to ensure that sales are genuine, accurate and complete. Auditors might, for instance, include the following in their programme:

- Test sales orders for completeness by checking sequence and enquiring into reasons for any missing orders.
- Select a representative sample of orders and vouch to sales delivery notes.

FIGURE 10.2 Directional testing example (all figures in thousands)

Sales account

P&L	2 500	Goods	2 500
	2 500		2 500

Trade receivables

	2 500		
		Bank	1 125
		Cl.bal	1 375
	2 500		2 500

Bank account

Op.bal	4 750		
	1 125		
		Cl.bal	5 875
	5 875		5 875

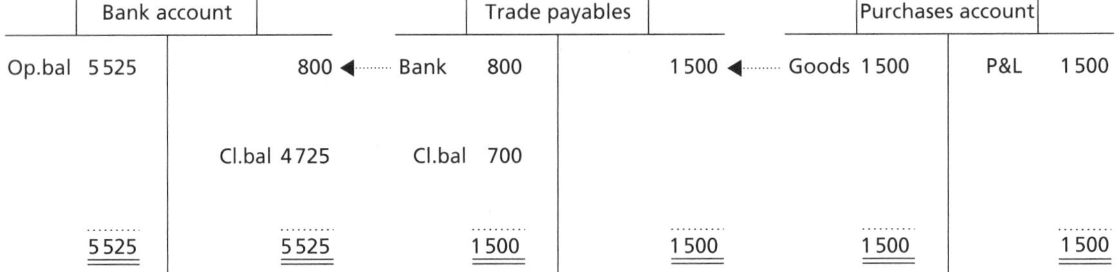

Bank account
Op.bal 5 525
800
Cl.bal 4 725
5 525
5 525
Trade payables
Bank 800
Cl.bal 700
1 500
1 500
1 500
Purchases account
Goods 1 500
P&L 1 500
1 500
1 500

- Test sales delivery notes for completeness by checking sequence and enquiring into reasons for any missing notes.
- Select a representative sample of sales delivery notes, check that they bear the customer's signature and test to sales invoice and inventory movement records.
- Perform a sequence test on sales invoices.
- Check inventory movement records to the delivery notes and sales invoices.

These tests are examples of tests of details. However, it would also be appropriate to perform analytical procedures, such as testing that margins on sales are as expected, that inventory turnover and trade receivable days outstanding appear reasonable.

The objective of these tests is to ascertain that sales invoices have been properly raised for all goods despatched. The auditor would also test pricing

ACTIVITY 10.9

Now suggest directional tests for purchases (£1 500 000) and trade payables (£700 000) and explain your answer.

and calculations. An important point is that by testing debits (trade receivables) for overstatement you are also confirming that sales are not overstated, because of the nature of double entry.

The objective of the testing of credits (in this case, trade payables) is to check that there is no material understatement of liabilities. This may be difficult as it is likely to be more problematic to test for something that is not there than something that is recorded in the accounting records. Tests of detail could include:

- Examine the purchases record, cash book and trade payables ledger after the year-end and search for items that appear to relate to the previous period but are not recorded as a liability.
- Write to selected suppliers and ask them to tell the auditors the amount owed to them by the company at the year-end date and the invoices issued (say) 15 days before and after the year-end.

The objective of testing of debits (in this case, purchases) is to ensure that there is no material overstatement of purchase cost. Tests of details could include:

- Check that recorded purchases are all supported by purchase orders and GRNs in proper sequence.
- Test that purchases/inventory cut-off has been correctly performed.

Apart from these tests of details, analytical procedures are required, such as testing that sales and cost of sales are reasonable in relationship to each other (checking sales margin again) for sales lines and in total. Testing inventory levels for reasonableness in relation to cost of sales will also be a useful procedure.

Testing for overstatement of assets and understatement of liabilities could result in detecting over-statement of income.

The directional testing approach is useful as it introduces an organized element to setting audit objectives. However, a global approach should also be adopted to ensure that the debits and credits (expense/assets and revenue/liabilities) give a true and fair view when taken together. The profit and loss account figures should be given as much attention as those in the balance sheet. This means that directional testing should be supplemented by other kinds of tests.

SUBSTANTIVE AUDIT PROGRAMMES FOR WAGES

In Chapter 8 we noted that many auditors regard payroll as a low-risk area, with the consequence that they tend to carry out limited tests of control or substantive tests of detail. However, as we noted then, payroll has traditionally been an area where frauds have occurred and it is also an area relatively easy to understand and through which to explain principles. So we suggest a substantive audit programme for wages in Appendix 10.1 to this chapter. You may assume that payroll is regarded as a significant figure in the Troston financial statements, not least because of the complexity of the allocation of labour cost to products. We might mention that observation of wages pay-outs have become increasingly rare, and in the case of Troston are unnecessary because payments are made direct to the employees' bank accounts. However, the auditor might select a sample of forms signed by the employee authorizing transfer to the bank of their choice.

See page 305.

See page 389.

We reproduce below the general comments in Appendix 10.1 to put the audit of wages into context:

> *Directional tests* that should be incorporated into the audit programme are principally as follows:
>
> - Tests to ensure there is no overstatement of gross wages.
> - Tests to ensure there is no understatement of deductions from wages.

The auditor checks both calculations of gross wages and deductions to confirm that the gross wage cost (including any employer's share of social security contributions) has been properly calculated and distributed to wage earners, tax authorities, social security offices, and so on.

In drawing up appropriate audit programmes for production wages for Troston plc, we have made assumptions about the size of sample and the basis of selection in carrying out substantive tests. We discuss sample size and basis of selection in Chapter 11.

Programme objectives should be clearly stated.

Suitable objectives for a production wages programme would be to determine:

- That the financial accounting and costing records contain an accurate, complete and valid record of production wages, including proper allocation within the costing system to revenue expense, non-current assets and inventories.
- That the money paid out by the company for production wages and related costs and described as such in the financial accounting and costing records reached the persons for whom it was intended.
- That the wages paid have been made for services performed for the benefit of the company.

You should note in particular the following matters:

(a) The programme includes programme objectives, as it is important for auditors to be constantly aware of what they wish to achieve. Having set objectives, prepared the audit programme and carried out tests of details in accordance with the programme, the auditor should be able to form conclusions about the accuracy, completeness and reliability of the accounting records (stage 12 of the audit process shown in Figure 6.3 on page 230).

(b) The auditor's approach is dependent on the sophistication of the computer system in place.

(c) Regarding global tests, in preparing the audit programme we have assumed that the auditors would prepare statistical information but, if this information is available in the company's computerized information system, they might download it to their PC and review it there. Troston produces a listing of recorded production hours and these could be used for reconciliation purposes. We assume that the company keeps all information in computer files, including back-up, so that the auditor might be able to use computer software to interrogate these files. We have incorporated into the programme a number of steps using the computer for selection and comparison.

(d) The programme refers to documents and records in existence in the company (for instance, batch/equipment tickets) and reflects the processing system in use, indicating that it has been tailor-made to the organization.

(e) Although many firms of auditors do not regard the wages and salaries area as high risk in itself, production cost and its relation to inventory appearing in the financial statements may well be high risk and the auditor will normally wish to be sure that labour costs have been properly determined.

(f) Note in particular that the system is the one in operation at the present time and not the system that may be in existence in the future because of any recommendations the auditor may care to make.

(g) Appendix 10.1 includes a detailed schedule of work performed as shown in Figure 10.5, which would form the basis for the auditors' conclusions.

SUBSTANTIVE AUDIT PROGRAMMES FOR CASH AND BANK BALANCES

We have included in Appendix 10.2 to this chapter, again placed on the Cengage website, (**www.cengage.co.uk/graymanson5**) the major features of a cash and bank audit programme for the County Hotel Limited (see page 392). The reason we have chosen this business is because cash control is particularly important in the hotel industry because of the number of cash points where cash and cheques may be collected. We have chosen to consider major features in the accommodation income instead of reproducing a complete programme of cash testing for the hotel because we believe this will highlight the approach the auditor should adopt to problem areas. The auditors will have concluded that a significant figure in the financial statements of the County Hotel was that of accommodation income.

You were first introduced to the County Hotel in Case study 5.4 on page 196.

In preparing the audit programme in Appendix 10.2 we have directed our attention in the first place to the proper recording of income and expense as control over cash received and cash paid is best achieved by accurate and complete recording of such income and expense. The audit objective is to test that cash as an asset is being properly safeguarded. The audit steps are classified under two broad headings:

- Complete and accurate recording
  Accommodation income will be collected in cash immediately or charged to a customer's account for subsequent collection. The control procedures to ensure accurate and complete recording of accommodation income are an important element in the control of cash. You will agree that the easiest way to misappropriate cash will be not to record it in the first place. The particular problem for the auditor (and management) in relation to accommodation income is the variety of rates and the fact that rooms may be let at rates other than standard.

  Note that the programme uses management information and statistics and requires the audit team to discuss with management the reasons for changes, including the drop in room usage from 76 per cent in 2009 to 74 per cent in 2010.
- Proper safeguarding of cash
  Proper recording of the transactions forming the basis for cash payment and receipt is a prerequisite of cash control, although it is not sufficient in itself. The auditor also tests to ensure that payment is made to the right individuals and that receivables are in fact received.

In Chapter 12 we refer to the procedures that auditors adopt for obtaining confirmation of bank balances and other related matters.

See page 425.

COMMUNICATION OF AUDIT MATTERS TO THOSE CHARGED WITH GOVERNANCE (MANAGEMENT LETTER)

We discuss communication of audit matters to those charged with governance in Chapter 16, but this is an appropriate place to discuss one aspect of such communication. There is an International Standard on Auditing in the area, ISA 260 – *Communication with those charged with governance*. Paragraph 9 of ISA 260 sets out below the objectives of communicating with those charged with governance, one of which is:

> (c) To provide those charged with governance with timely observations arising from the audit that are significant and relevant to their responsibility to oversee the financial reporting process.

There are many matters that auditors communicate to those charged with governance at various stages of the audit process, including scope of examination, comments on the entity's accounting policies, material risks and uncertainties, and expected modifications to the audit report. Here we are considering only one aspect of matters that would be communicated to those charged with governance.

During their audit auditors often come across matters that may have a significant impact on the financial statements and they would be failing in their duty if they did not inform the directors and others charged with governance (including the audit committee), about these matters. We are raising this matter here as tests of control and substantive testing performed at the interim examination will have given the auditors insight into the effectiveness of controls and into whether transactions and balances are being properly recorded. You will appreciate that the directors and others charged with governance have a duty to ensure internal controls are adequate This means that they have to be informed as soon as possible of any weaknesses. Apart from this, it will help auditors considerably in fulfilling their duties if weaknesses are remedied. Furthermore, weaknesses are likely to result in an increase in audit time and directors and others charged with governance should be informed.

At this stage we discuss the communication concerning internal control, which has traditionally been referred to as 'the management letter'. ISA 265 – *Communicating deficiencies in internal control to those charged with governance and management* and you should refer to this ISA when you are reading Figure 10.3 which is a specimen management letter sent to those charged with governance in Broomfield plc. You will notice that we have referred to certain efficiency matters as well. When you are reading it, note particularly the following features:

- The management letter has a title and the intended recipients are clearly stated.
- The introduction tells the recipient the circumstances in which the letter came to be written and the reasons it is being submitted to those charged with governance. It also states that the main purpose of the audit is not to detect all weaknesses and efficiency matters that may exist in the systems and company generally, thus warning that there may be other matters that a more rigorous examination might reveal.
- The responsible officials with whom the memorandum has been discussed, stating that their view has been included where they did not agree with the auditor. It is vital that the internal control matters be discussed with management with the authority to take remedial action before the issue to be certain there have been no misunderstandings and to ensure that the recommended remedial action is appropriate.

FIGURE 10.3 Communication of audit matters to those charged with governance (internal control section) at Broomfield plc

JOHN GUNN & Co, Public Accountants

The directors and chair of audit committee of Broomfield plc

MEMORANDUM ON INTERNAL CONTROL AND OTHER MATTERS OF INTEREST TO THOSE CHARGED WITH GOVERNANCE ARISING FROM OUR INTERIM EXAMINATION

As you are aware we have recently been carrying out our interim examination of the books and records of Broomfield plc for the year ended 31 December 2010. As part of our examination we reviewed and tested the company's systems of accounting and internal control. We did this to the extent we considered necessary to evaluate the systems with the objective of establishing the nature and extent of our audit procedures necessary to express an opinion on the truth and fairness of the financial statements at 31 December 2010. We also performed a special examination of the system for the control of purchases and trade creditors in accordance with your instructions dated 24 June 2010.

During our review and testing of the aforementioned systems certain matters came to light which we believe should be brought to your attention to assist you in your duty of safeguarding the assets of the company and of maintaining reliable accounting records for the preparation of financial statements required by law to give a true and fair view.

We have discussed the internal control matters contained in this memorandum with your chief accountant, Mr Philip Moscar, and he is in agreement with our comments unless otherwise stated. We would mention that none of the comments made below should be taken as questioning the integrity of any member of the staff of your company.

SUMMARY OF WEAKNESSES IN INTERNAL CONTROLS
A. Purchases and trade payables
MAJOR FINDINGS
1. The system should be programmed to produce the official purchase order rather than the requisition note and the opportunity taken to strengthen the controls over setting and changing minimum inventory levels (see findings 2. a) and 2. b).
2. a) A responsible official outside the buying department should be authorized to change minimum inventory levels.
2. b) Budgets and minimum inventory levels should be reviewed regularly to ensure that they are still valid. Significant changes should be authorized by the board.
3. Bids should be sought from suppliers to ensure best prices and terms are obtained.
4. The buying department should decide how the items on the exception report should be dealt with after the purchase order run.
Similarly the accounting department should decide on the disposition of items on the exception report after the inventory/trade payables update run.
5. The buying department should compare official purchase orders with the initial orders as there is a risk that official orders are incorrect.
6. Accounting department staff should have 'read-only' access to current prices and terms of suppliers to enable an independent check of their validity.
7. Coding of purchase invoices should be independently checked.

DESCRIPTION OF WEAKNESS, POSSIBLE CONSEQUENCES AND RECOMMENDATIONS
1/2. *The system should be programmed to produce the official purchase order rather than the requisition and the opportunity taken to strengthen the controls over setting and changing minimum inventory levels.*

This is an efficiency as well as a control matter. Currently, purchase requisitions are automatically prepared by the program when minimum inventory levels are reached, such requisitions forming the basis for the preparation of the purchase order in the buying department. The requisitions are sent to Ivor Jordan who, having decided whether it is appropriate, prepares a purchase order which is the source document for the purchase order run and the preparation of the official purchase order. In our view this is a very long-winded procedure, which may result in time delays and transposition errors, and we believe that it would be appropriate to change your system so that the official purchase order is prepared automatically when minimum inventory levels are reached.

FIGURE 10.3 (Continued)

However, before a change of this nature is carried through we believe that changes are required to your system for determining minimum inventory levels and for authorizing and changing reorder limits. As you are aware minimum inventory levels forming the basis of reorder limits are based on the purchases budget (prepared by Ivor Jordan and agreed by the directors). However, during the year it became clear that goods were being reordered when not really required, as minimum inventory levels had been set too high at the time that the budget had been prepared. In consequence, Ivor Jordan has been given authority to disregard a requisition if he believes that the goods are not really required and, in addition, has been allowed to change minimum inventory levels on the inventory master file. However, no independent responsible official reviews the new minimum inventory levels or the adjustments to them on the inventory master file, with the result that inappropriate amendments may be made.

Recommendations

1. We believe that you should consider changing your existing purchase order routine to allow for the official purchase order to be automatically prepared once predetermined minimum inventory levels have been reached.
2. Coupled with this recommendation are two further recommendations:

a) A responsible official outside the buying department should be authorized to change minimum inventory levels and that a review be made of all changes to the inventory master file during the current year.

b) Budgets and reorder limits should be reviewed regularly to ensure that they are still valid. Significant changes should be authorized by the board.

3. *Bids should be sought from suppliers to ensure best prices and terms are obtained.*

It is not clear that best prices, terms and qualities are obtained from suppliers as the company does not require them to make written bids before orders are placed with them. In consequence, the company cannot be sure it is obtaining the goods it requires on the most advantageous terms.

Recommendation

We would advise you to introduce a system requiring potential suppliers to submit bids before they become recognized suppliers, such bids to include details of prices at various order quantities, purchase rebates and payment terms, including cash discounts. We recommend that the chief buyer and a responsible official from production review the bids before acceptance and that goods be tested as being suitable for production as part of the process. You already keep suppliers' details in a suppliers' master file and we suggest that you consider the feasibility of automatic selection of the most appropriate supplier at the time that the purchase order is prepared. In the meantime we suggest that suppliers selected by the buying department are reviewed by an independent official.

4. *The buying department should decide on disposition of the items on the exception report after the purchase order run. Similarly the accounting department should decide on the disposition of items on the exception report after the inventory/trade payables update run.*

5. *The buying department should compare official purchase orders with the initial orders as there is a risk that official orders are incorrect.*

Currently, Eric Owler, the head of the data control section is responsible for reviewing the exception reports forming part of the output of the purchase order run and the inventory/payables update run. Neither the buyer (Ivor Jordan) nor the accounting department (Janet Black) receive copies of the exception reports and play no role in the correction of errors, even though they have a considerable interest in the accuracy of data emanating from their departments. While it is true that some errors may be the result of incorrect keying in the computer department, there may be other errors, such as non-existent inventory or supplier number, that should be reviewed by Ivor Jordan and Janet Black. In this connection we noted that Ivor Jordan does not currently compare official purchase orders with the original purchase orders that he has prepared. In consequence, he has no chance to pick up potential differences between original and official purchase orders, particularly as he does not see the exception reports that contain the control totals.

Recommendation

We recommend that exception reports be passed to Ivor Jordan and Janet Black for checking control totals, for comparison with source documentation and for a decision as to disposition. If you decide to put in the new system discussed in 1/2 above, we would recommend that Ivor Jordan review purchase orders for reasonableness before they are sent to suppliers.

FIGURE 10.3 Communication of audit matters to those charged with governance (internal control section) at Broomfield plc (Continued)

6. *Accounting department staff should have 'read-only' access to current prices and terms of suppliers to enable an independent check that these are in order.*
We noted that Janet Black kept her own database of suppliers' terms, culled from previous purchase invoices, and that she used this database to check suppliers' terms on current invoices. This can hardly be regarded as a satisfactory procedure as her database may not be up to date and may contain errors.

Recommendation
We strongly recommend that Janet Black in the accounting department be given 'read-only' access to suppliers' prices and other terms on the suppliers' master file. We would remind you in this connection that one of the advantages of a database is that everyone in the company is using the same data. We recommend that you ensure that the use of personal databases is kept to a minimum.

7. *Coding of purchase invoices should be independently checked.*
Janet Black is currently responsible for entering general ledger codes on the face of the purchase invoice prior to processing. However, the coding is not independently checked and errors might not be brought to light by the review of purchase invoice listings and cost summaries by the chief accountant.

Recommendation
We recommend that an independent official within the accounting department check that the purchase invoice cost codes are accurate. The review of listings and summaries by the chief accountant should continue but the independent check will in our view give a heightened sense of security that the figures are reliable.

B. Other areas (not discussed here)

CONCLUSION
The above matters we believe to be of sufficient importance to be put into effect as soon as possible. In our view, your system of control over purchases and related trade payables and also the general efficiency of your company would be much improved if our recommendations were to be put into effect. We are willing to discuss these matters with you further if you wish. We should be pleased if you would let us know your decisions in due course. We would mention that it would help our work at the final examination if the recommendations were put into effect before the year-end. A number of other minor matters came to our attention during our examination and these we have discussed with company officials.

- If the auditor has no reason to doubt the integrity of client officials, a comment to that effect.
- A section stating the main conclusions. This is done because a clear statement of main points will make the conclusions more understandable. We auditors are not in the Sherlock Holmes business of impressing Doctor Watson in the last reel of the film.
- The main conclusions are then followed by detailed comments, each comprising a brief description of the system in use, possible consequences and recommendations.
- Minor matters already cleared with management should not be allowed to clutter the report, although brief mention in the letter of their existence would be appropriate.
- In the concluding paragraph the auditors indicate their willingness to discuss the matters at greater length with those charged with governance and asks for a response to the recommendations.

There are many possible styles that may be adopted in the writing of management letters dealing with internal control matters, but we think the above suggestions are sensible ones.

In the examination room a good writing style where a report is required may earn you an extra mark or two.

We shall highlight a number of other matters discussed in ISA 265 after you have worked Activity 10.10.

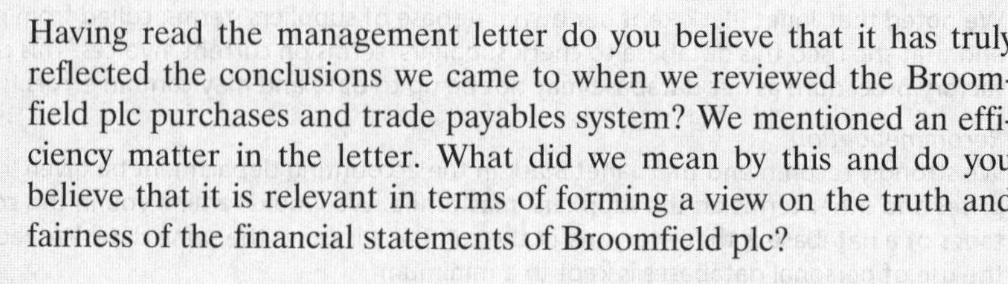

ACTIVITY 10.10

Having read the management letter do you believe that it has truly reflected the conclusions we came to when we reviewed the Broomfield plc purchases and trade payables system? We mentioned an efficiency matter in the letter. What did we mean by this and do you believe that it is relevant in terms of forming a view on the truth and fairness of the financial statements of Broomfield plc?

We tried to write the letter in such a way that the reader will understand the points that we are making. For this reason we gave a brief summary of the system as it is, the description of the weakness and then recommendations following our previous discussion. We couched the letter in a more formal and less chatty way than we might have done in the internal worksheet and in some cases we gave slightly more information about the matter being discussed. On the whole we believe that the letter reflects our major concerns closely. The efficiency matter relates to the somewhat long-winded system that the company has in place for the preparation of purchase orders. It is of relevance to the auditor, as an efficient system is likely to be less prone to error. Not only is the present system inefficient, it also lacks some basic controls over access to master files and updating of budgets. The emphasis on efficiency might encourage management to accept our recommendations more readily. An important point is that we are not auditing this year the system that we hope will be in force next year if our recommendations are accepted. That means that weaknesses such as we identified would have to be evaluated for their potential impact on the financial statements. For instance, would we have to carry out some additional substantive work on allocation of cost codes? (this might be important from the inventory valuation point of view).

Further matters of importance relating to the management letter

1. There may be circumstances where it would not be appropriate to discuss findings direct with management, if their integrity or competence is in question. For instance, if senior management have been overriding controls to commit fraud, the auditor might wish to raise the matter direct with the audit committee.
2. In smaller entities with insufficient staff to have full segregation of duties, the management letter might emphasize the importance of supervision by management.
3. The auditors report internal control matters that have resulted in misstatements in the financial statements, and potential significant misstatements.
4. If no remedial action has been taken in respect of significant weaknesses in internal control raised in previous management letters, the current letter should refer to it and the auditor should ask why no remedial action has been taken.
5. Auditors of public sector entities may have special responsibilities for reporting internal control matters, such as compliance with regulations of legislative authorities.

AUDIT MANAGEMENT WITH THE COMPUTER

Earlier in this chapter we considered approaches to the audit of computer systems. There is, however, another aspect of computing – the way it is used by the auditor in the management of the audit process. We have already mentioned the use of expert systems in completing EDP/IT questionnaires and highlighting potential problem areas for the client and auditor following completion. We have mentioned too the use of packages for preparation of flowcharts. There are, however, a range of other ways in which the computer has had an impact on the activities of the auditor, all designed to increase audit efficiency and effectiveness at a time when there is much pressure on audit fees. The general term 'audit automation' is the term given to the use of IT in the audit process, the basic idea being that it frees up staff to carry out judgemental work rather than being engaged in repetitive activities. We mention also that the highly visible use of IT on the premises of a client can enhance the prestige and reputation of the audit firm. We comment on some ways in which audit automation is used, noting both pros and cons.

The Institute of Chartered Accountants in England and Wales has identified the following benefits from audit automation:

> The use of computers in the management, planning, performance and completion of audits to eliminate or reduce time spent on computational or clerical tasks, to improve the quality of audit judgments, and to ensure consistent audit quality.

('Audit Automation', *IT Briefing Number 4*, Chartech Books, ICAEW, 1993). A useful reading is Manson, *et al.* 1997.

Risk assessment, planning and allocation of staff and other resources to the audit assignment

We have not discussed analytical review procedures in detail yet, although we saw their value in identifying risk in the Powerbase Case study. These procedures using spreadsheets and other statistical techniques, such as regression analysis, can be much aided by the use of IT. Spreadsheets are ideal for carrying out analytical reviews of prior year, budgeted and current year financial information and data. Their value lies in their ability to calculate ratios and trends and in preparation of 'what-if' scenarios. They may also be used to compare company ratios with industry averages. At a more sophisticated level expert systems have been developed to carry out audit risk analysis at the important stage of audit planning.

The computer is also being used to record time spent by each grade of staff on various sections of the audit and in total. The time spent on training on the job may also be separately recorded. Comparisons with budgeted time may also be made and, apart from being useful for planning purposes in future years, enables the auditor to pinpoint budget overruns. The audit firm will be able to compare times recorded centrally with times recorded on the assignment and this will help to validate both sets of times. Audit planning memoranda are now frequently prepared by audit staff using word processing software, rather than putting it through the rather long-winded process of office typing on the basis of hand-written drafts. Much of the work now being carried out by computer would not have been possible manually.

Information retrieval and analysis

Audit firms are increasingly transferring data and information from client computer files to their own computers, which can then be used to analyse the data transferred. Thus they might be able to determine a high incidence of returned goods from certain customers or to certain suppliers. A common use of this technique is to read a computerized trade receivables ledger and to select a sample of balances for circularization on a scientific basis.

We discuss statistical sampling in Chapter 11 and shall delay commenting on how the computer might be used for selecting transactions and balances for testing.

Interpretation and documentation of results

Working papers are being increasingly automated and recorded on computer file. Thus a selection of items (say sales invoices) for detailed testing might be recorded on spreadsheet and the results of the tests (correctness of calculations, checking to sales despatch notes, checking to sales orders, checking to inventory records and so on) similarly recorded (see Figure 10.5 on page 392). Word processing can also be used in a number of ways, including recording audit working papers, such as lead schedules, various checklists and ICEQs. Many of these checklists may be available as templates on central computer files and can be downloaded by audit staff for completion.

Review and reporting activities

Audit reports, such as management letters (see Figure 10.3 on page 380) and reports to partners and managers on important matters arising from the audit, points for future visits, etc., can easily be prepared by audit staff using word processing software. Audit firms are increasingly using templates of memoranda, reports and letters so that a common style is used throughout the firm. Spreadsheets may also be used to analyse the final accounts before the audit report is finally issued.

Manuals and checklists on computer file

The firm's audit manual and guidance on particular problem areas, including solutions to common accounting/audit problems, may be made available on computer file, together with checklists, such as audit completion checklists, and Companies Acts and Accounting Standards checklists. This makes it unnecessary to carry weighty guidance and checklist material from assignment to assignment, formally a common complaint of audit staff.

We discuss audit documentation at greater length in Chapter 14.

A strong word of warning must be interjected at this point. All we had to say about computer security above applies equally to data held by the auditor on computer file. Access controls should be in place to make corruption of data less likely and to prevent files falling into the wrong hands, including client staff. Back-up copies of audit documentation should be made to avoid loss of data.

Particular words of warning are necessary in respect of spreadsheets. Spreadsheets can be an invaluable tool but their preparation needs careful control. The purpose of the spreadsheet must always be clearly stated and layout must be carefully thought out. It is good practice, for instance, to designate particular parts of the spreadsheet as 'work areas' and other parts for such matters as description of the spreadsheet and what its intended purpose is. The use of macros must always be carefully explained. It must not be forgotten that spreadsheets are a mixture of programming and data and that the programming should be documented and tested in the way we suggested earlier in this book. How many of our readers have returned to a spreadsheet after some time and wondered for what it was designed or have failed to test the operation of a spreadsheet containing erroneous formulas, thereby producing false results? The authors of this book have certainly found themselves in this unfortunate position and very annoying it is too. Once the spreadsheet is up and running it will be vital that any formulas are protected, although of course they can be easily unprotected unless the 'unprotection' facility is subject to access controls.

Summary

We have now reached the end of the interim stage of the audit. In doing this we have introduced you to a number of different organizations, which is, of course, typical of the life of an auditor in public practice. Unlike internal auditors, external auditors are not concerned only with one organization and their experience is likely to encompass a wider selection of differing organizations.

> Internal auditors may, of course, meet many different organizations if they work for a large group or a company with several disparate divisions. On the whole, however, external auditors will encounter a greater variety of organizations and managements.

The auditors by this stage should be well informed about the organization, its problems, management responses to them, and should know how reliable the entity's systems and accounting records are. If auditors have established good but professional relations with management officials and others charged with governance they should have persuaded them to keep them informed of developments and potential problems affecting the annual accounts as they occur. Auditors should also keep management informed of relevant matters, such as changes in legal requirements or accounting standards. The relationship with the client should be as constant as the size and complexity of the company makes necessary.

In this chapter we have directed attention to the way in which the auditor attempts to prove the completeness and accuracy of the accounting records and considered in particular the use of audit software. We showed you that following evaluation of the systems in use, the auditor made a scope decision, reflected in tailor-made audit programmes designed to obtain the predetermined audit objectives. We made a particular point of showing that the auditor has to have clear objectives when drafting audit programmes and to identify the point at which testing should commence. We discussed the nature and use of directional testing as an element of substantive testing.

We also discussed the management letter as one aspect of communication to those charged with governance, basing its contents on a review of controls of a company to which we introduced you in Chapter 9. Finally, we discussed audit management using the computer.

Key points of the chapter

- A substantive procedure is an audit procedure designed to detect material misstatements at the assertion level. Substantive procedures comprise: (i) tests of details and (ii) substantive analytical procedures.
- There are two important reasons why substantive tests should always be performed: 1. Because the auditor's assessment of risk is judgemental, and 2. There are inherent limitations to internal control including management override.
- As more knowledge of the company is gained audit risk assessments may change and affect the scope of examination, resulting in planning feedback.
- Auditors must set objectives before designing a programme of substantive tests.
- The Powerbase Case study shows that salient features of the audit programme include: (a) financial statement assertions to be verified, providing audit objectives; (b) analytical review of figures and assessment of control risk as a basis of scope of examination; (c) selection of items for testing on a random basis; (d) conclusions at various points in the testing procedure and a final overall conclusion.
- The use of CAATs may enable more extensive testing of electronic transactions and account files. Several different types of audit software are used by the auditor including: (a) generalized audit software; (b) software developed for use in specific industries; (c) statistical analysis software; (d) expert system software.
- Generalized audit software and software developed for specific industries are interrogation tools used to access and examine and even manipulate data and information held on file. They can be used for both tests of control and for substantive testing. Such software can: (a) access files with many different characteristics and manipulate data on them; (b) select data on the basis of predetermined criteria and can perform arithmetical functions on data selected; (c) analyse selected data statistically and can stratify data into desired categories; (d) cause files to be created and updated from the company's

own files; (e) produce reports for the auditor in desired format.

- To interrogate a file you must know not only what you want to achieve, but also what is on the file.
- Generalized audit software can be used to extract important ratios and balances from the company records, and can be used to select data on a statistically sound basis Software packages are available with regression analysis capabilities and with report writing facilities
- The use of generalized audit software can be a useful supplement to statistical sampling techniques. They enable the auditor to audit by exception, interrogating the file and pulling out those items possessing the selected characteristics.
- Audit software is particularly useful when there are large amounts of data. The major disadvantage is the cost of developing it, that it can only be used after the event and it is difficult to assess the likelihood of error using it.
- Expert systems can be useful when a system or other area can be broken down into a series of rules, and have been developed for audit purposes, such as aiding conclusions based on checklists.
- Directional testing is a form of substantive testing, which tests debits for overstatement and credits for understatement.
- An important measure to improve audit effectiveness is to have a good system of communication of audit matters to those charged with governance by means of the timely issue of management letters. Such letters are designed to provide those charged with governance with timely observations arising from the audit that are significant and relevant to their responsibility to oversee the financial reporting process. In this chapter we considered a management letter concerning internal control.
- Auditors are using the computer to manage the audit process, including (a) risk assessment, planning and allocation of staff and other resources; (b) information retrieval and analysis; (c) interpretation and documentation of results; (d) review and reporting activities; (e) manuals and checklists on computer file.

Reference

Manson, S., McCartney, S. and Sherer, M. (1997) *The Use of Information Technology in the Planning, Controlling and Recording of Audit Work*, ICAS Research Report, Institute of Chartered Accountants of Scotland, March.

Further reading

Weber, R. (1999) *Information Systems Control and Audit*, New York: Prentice Hall contains a useful section on the nature and use of audit software.

The following book provides a bit more discussion on some of the issues covered in this chapter.

Cascarino, R.E. (2007) *Auditor's Guide to Information Systems Auditing*, John Wiley & Sons.

Apart from this, as IT and computer auditing are developing in a very volatile manner, you are advised to read articles in IT and accounting/auditing journals.

ISAs referred to in the chapter are:

ISA 260 – *Communication with those charged with governance*

ISA 265 – *Communicating deficiencies in internal control to those charged with governance and management*

ISA 315 – *Identifying and assessing the risks of material misstatement through understanding the entity and its environment*

ISA 330 – *The auditor's responses to assessed risks*

Self-assessment questions (solutions available to students)

10.1 Consider the following statements and explain why they may be true or false:

(a) Tests of controls are those tests designed to check that the accounting and control systems are effective.

(b) Substantive tests are different in nature from tests of controls.

(c) Audit programmes should be designed to take account of the strengths and weaknesses of the individual entity.

(d) Audit programmes are developed before the scope decision is made.

(e) Directional tests are tests of controls.

10.2 In this chapter we showed in Figure 10.1 a purchases substantive audit programme, but we did not include the use of audit software. Suggest how audit software could have been used in programme steps 3, 4, 6, 8 and 9. In doing this, state the data on computer file which you would be able to use.

10.3 In Appendix 10.2 on page 392 and on the Cengage website (**www.cengage.co.uk/graymanson5**) we suggest steps that could be included in the audit programme for accommodation income of the County Hotel Ltd received in cash. Re-read this appendix and now suggest steps that should be included in the audit programmes for restaurant income received in cash. Explain the reasons for the tests.

10.4 Assuming that your audit programme for the purchase of non-current assets has been completed and that your programme objectives have been met, draft a suitable audit conclusion for audit work carried out in respect of the period from 1 January 2011 to 30 September 2011.

Self-assessment questions (solutions available to tutors)

10.5 In Appendix 10.2 on the Cengage website (**www.cengage.co.uk/graymanson5**) we suggested steps that could be included in the audit programme for accommodation income of The County Hotel Ltd. received in cash. Re-read this appendix and now suggest steps that should be included in the audit programmes for bar income received in cash. Explain the reason for the tests.

10.6 You are auditing a manufacturing company and have drafted a management letter that contains reference to matters to increase the efficiency of company systems and the general profitability of the company. Your audit assistant has asked you if this is appropriate as she understands that the auditor's duty is to provide an opinion on the truth and fairness of financial statements. How would you respond to your assistant's question?

10.7 This question is taken from a past paper of the Final Admitting Examination of ICAI. Only the dates have been changed.

You are undertaking the fieldwork for the audit of the financial statements of CAREFREE Limited for the year ended 31 December 2010. CAREFREE owns and operates a network of six private nursing homes, each with facilities for up to 50 patients. In each home some of the patients are temporary patients recuperating from acute illness, while others are long term. The company has expanded rapidly, following a change in ownership and management in March 2009, prior to which it had only two nursing homes in operation for several years.

Each home is under the control of a matron, who authorizes all admissions; the staff consists of part-time and full-time nursing staff, as well as part-time employees dealing with areas such as catering, cleaning and maintenance. Before the change in ownership and management, each of the two homes arranged the billing of its own clients (usually relatives of the patients have responsibility for payment) and dealt with all queries and collections. As the business expanded, it was considered necessary to recruit an accountant/administrator who, as well as dealing with payroll matters, has implemented a centralized PC-based billing system for income and trade receivables.

You have noted the following aspects of the billing system:

1. There is a standard daily residential charge (which may differ from home to home), which is used as a basis for monthly bills. Each matron has a limited discretion to allow reductions from the standard charge in cases of exceptional hardship.
2. Matrons are expected to notify the accountant/administrator by telephone on a daily basis of all changes in occupancy.
3. The accountant/administrator should be notified by telephone on a weekly basis of all costs for medical attendance or prescription medicines.

The accountant/administrator has found it difficult to ensure that the necessary information is received from the matrons within the appropriate timeframe. She/he has also found that there has been an increasing number of complaints from clients, concerning such matters as:

- Rates used for billing residential charges differing from rates advised by the relevant matron to the patients' relatives.
- Fees for medical attendance not coinciding with information about doctors' visits supplied to the patients' relatives.

In most cases, complaints are received by the accountant/administrator, who frequently has difficulty in ensuring that the matrons investigate the complaints and report any adjustments to the bills which may be required. Most queries are resolved eventually, but one of the side effects of the problems experienced is that bills are outstanding on average for 50 days as opposed to 22 days in 2009. In a small number of cases, the period of arrears is substantial, but CAREFREE finds it virtually impossible to have patients removed, and very difficult to press too hard for payment given the recent history of errors in the billing procedure.

Requirement

(a) Draft a management letter for the Board of CAREFREE and to the head of the Audit Committee, making suggestions as to how the billing system might be improved, both from the point of view of control and to increase operational efficiency.

14 marks

(b) Specify two aspects of the audit of trade receivables in the financial statements for the year ended 31 December 2010 which will require particular attention in view of any weakness that you have identified.

6 marks

Total 20 marks

10.8 Munro Limited is a small company with two divisions. One division trades in specialized equipment for walkers and mountaineers, and the other sells artists' materials. The company has acquired rights of access to a rocky area near a major city, where it runs weekend schools for climbers and groups of artists. The school is staffed by one full-time member of the company's staff and a number of university students and local artists on a part-time basis. The company sells equipment and materials on both cash and credit terms and also rents equipment to student climbers on a daily basis and to experienced climbers for longer periods of time. People attending the schools pay a fee on the spot as the weather does not always allow schools to take place. The company receives a grant from the local authority for running the weekend schools.

State basic controls you would like to see to ensure that fees received for weekend schools are completely and accurately recorded and tests of details you would perform to satisfy yourself that this is so.

Solutions available to students and *Solutions available to tutors*

These can be found on the website in the student/lecturer section at: www.cengage.co.uk/graymanson5.

Topics for class discussion without solutions

10.9 Communication by the auditors with those charged with governance other than management makes the audit process more effective. Discuss.

10.10 Explain the difference between substantive analytical procedures and substantive tests of detail.

APPENDIX 10.1: SUBSTANTIVE AUDIT PROGRAMME FOR PRODUCTION WAGES: TROSTON PLC

The detailed audit programme production wages of Troston plc set out on pages 390 and 391 but you may note the following general points:

General point

This programme incorporates tests of detail, but we draw your attention to the following paragraph A7 of ISA 520 – *Analytical procedures:*

> In some cases, even an unsophisticated predictive model may be effective as an analytical procedure. For example, where an entity has a known number of employees at fixed rates of pay throughout the period, it may be possible for the auditor to use this data to estimate the total payroll costs for the period with a high degree of accuracy, thereby providing audit evidence for a significant item in the financial statements and reducing the need to perform tests of details on the payroll. The use of widely recognized trade ratios (such as profit margins for different types of retail entities) can often be used effectively in substantive analytical procedures to provide evidence to support the reasonableness of recorded amounts.

Directional tests that should be incorporated into the audit programme are principally as follows:

- Tests to ensure there is no overstatement of gross wages.
- Tests to ensure there is no understatement of deductions from wages.

The auditor checks both calculations of gross wages and deductions to confirm that the gross wage cost (including any employer's share of National Insurance contributions) has been properly calculated and distributed to wage earners, tax authorities, Social Security Offices and so on.

In drawing up appropriate audit programmes for production wages for Troston plc, we will make assumptions about the size of sample and the basis of selection in carrying out substantive tests. We shall discuss sample size and basis of selection in Chapter 11.

Programme objectives should be clearly stated. Suitable objectives for a production wages programme would be to determine:

- That the financial accounting and costing records contain an accurate, complete and valid record of production wages, including proper allocation within the costing system to revenue expense, non-current assets and inventories.
- That the money paid out by the company for production wages and related costs and described as such in the financial accounting and costing records reached the persons for whom it was intended.
- That the wages paid have been made for services performed for the benefit of the company.

The detailed programme for production wages of Troston plc is set out in Figure 10.4. Read carefully through the audit programme and the explanatory notes, noting that they are designed to meet the objectives we set out above and are tailor-made to the company.

> The programme shown in Figure 10.4 is designed to give you a flavour of the kind of work carried out and is not necessarily complete.

You should note in particular the following matters:

(a) The programme includes programme objectives, as it is important for auditors to be constantly aware of what they wish to achieve. Having set objectives, prepared the audit programme and carried out tests of details in accordance with the programme, the auditor should be able to form conclusions about the accuracy, completeness and reliability of the accounting records (stage 12 of the audit process shown in Figure 6.3 on page 230).

(b) The auditor's approach is dependent on the sophistication of the computer system in place.

FIGURE 10.4 Audit programme for substantive tests of production wages (Troston plc)

Troston plc Year ended 31 December 2010	
Objectives are to determine: • That the money paid out by the company for production wages and related costs and described as such in the financial accounting and costing records reached the persons for whom it was intended. • That the wages paid have been in return for services performed for the benefit of the company. • That the financial accounting and costing records contain an accurate, complete and valid record of production wages, including proper allocation within the costing system to revenue expense, fixed assets and stocks.	
Global tests	**Done by/ref**
1. Summarize the labour costs for production wages by reference to departmental reports in terms of number of employees and amount for the year to date, the corresponding period last year and total for the whole of last year, the labour costs to be analysed as to grades of staff, amounts paid on a time basis and amounts paid for bonus, and incidental costs such as employer's social security contributions.	
2. Review the above information and obtain explanations from management on trends and changes, where systems work has not provided the required insights.	
3. Obtain summaries of production reports from the production control department and estimate total production wage costs on the basis of known labour content of production cost and compare that estimate with total of actual production wages to date.	
4. Estimate production bonus on the basis of normal production quantities and actual production quantities and bonus agreement, and compare with actual production bonus to date.	
5. Apply known wage percentage increases to corresponding period basic production wages total and compare to the same period in this year, after adjusting for known changes in numbers.	
6. Review the labour costs for selected products appearing in the costing records and enquire into any significant changes in costs as compared with previous periods this year and last. Review the company's variance analyses in conjunction with this work.	
Tests of detail	
(a) Select four weekly payrolls in the period to date on a random basis and check the gross amounts to the wages control account and the general ledger expense account. Check the net totals to the cash book entry.	
(b) Confirm that the selected payrolls have been signed by the two wages and salaries personnel and by the chief accountant.	
(c) Scrutinize the general ledger accounts containing entries emanating from the payroll (checked in (a) above) and enquire into any postings of an unusual nature, particularly those originating in the payroll.	
(d) Select two of the payrolls on a random basis and using audit software (CAAT 1) recreate the following listings: i) new staff ii) leavers iii) hours less than 40 iv) overtime hours v) overtime over ten hours vi) recorded production hours and total possible payroll hours and shortfall vii) bonus calculation and reconciliation to production report. CAAT 1 to include producing reports of new or dismissed/resigning employees for comparison with supporting documentation, and comparing date of entry on payroll with date of appointment or leaving (using data on separate files).	

FIGURE 10.4 (Continued)

(e) For the two payrolls check the casts and crosscasts and reconcile to recorded times using audit software (CAAT 2).	
(f) For the two payrolls check the mathematical accuracy of deductions using audit software (CAAT 3).	
(g) For selected employees (20) check names to tax cards and social security documentation.	
(h) For the selected employees check hours worked per the payroll to recorded times listing. (Note: This work should be backed up by proving the validity of the encoded clock cards of the selected employees held by them.)	
(i) Check listings (d) i) and ii) to the personnel master file hard copy. Back up this by checking the master file to the hard copy on a random basis, and for the selected employees check to employee contracts, and wage and bonus rates, ensuring that these are properly authorized.	
(j) Check listings (d) iii) to vii) to overtime authorization forms and production reports and related BETs, checking that OAFs have been approved by the head of PCD and that BETs bear the signatures of group heads, employees and inspector. (Obtain specimen signatures for the purpose of this work.) Check sequence of the BETs. (Note: It may be possible to use audit software to test the reconciliations to the production reports and costing records generally.)	
(k) Review the accounting records for deductions in the general ledger and check: i) That the details agree with returns submitted to the departments and bodies entitled to the deductions. ii) That payments appear to be on a timely basis. iii) That reconciliations are regularly made between returns and the relevant accounting records.	
l) For the selected employees, check to copies of the bank transfer forms and to entries in the cash book and bank statements.	

(c) Regarding global tests, we have assumed that the auditors would prepare statistical information but, if this information is available in the company's computerized information system, they might download it to their PC and review it there. Troston produces a listing of recorded production hours and these could be used for reconciliation purposes. We assume that the company keeps all information in computer files, including back-up, so that the auditor might be able to use computer software to interrogate these files. We have incorporated into the programme a number of steps using the computer for selection and comparison.

(d) The programme refers to documents and records in existence in the company (for instance, batch/equipment tickets) and reflects the processing system in use, indicating that it has been tailor-made to the organization.

(e) Regarding level of testing, you may have asked how we decided to make our selection of payrolls and employees. In Chapter 11 we discuss statistical sampling in detail but note at this stage that the important matters to be taken into account when selecting transactions or balances for detailed testing are:

- Designing the sample, including its size, to meet your desired objectives.
- Selecting the sample – which items are to be tested individually.
- Examining the sample – testing, for instance, for accuracy.
- Sample evaluation – forming conclusions about the population based on the sample.

(f) Many firms of auditors do not regard the wages and salaries area as high risk in itself. However, production cost and its relation to inventory appearing in the financial statements may well be high risk and the auditor will normally wish to be sure that labour costs have been properly determined.

(g) Note in particular that the system is the one in operation at the present time and not the system that may be in existence in the future because of any recommendations the auditor may care to make.

Note at this juncture that accounting records form the basis for the preparation of the accounts upon which the auditor is reporting so forming conclusions on their acceptability is vital. The audit conclusions following substantive procedures must be based on good evidence recorded in the working files. It is normal practice for auditors to prepare audit depth test schedules for this purpose and we set out an example for Troston plc production wages in Figure 10.5. This kind of schedule would be typically prepared using a spreadsheet.

APPENDIX 10.2: SUBSTANTIVE AUDIT PROGRAMME FOR CASH/BANK: COUNTY HOTEL LIMITED

We set out below a number of detailed audit programme steps that would be suitable for some aspects of the audit of cash/bank transactions in the County Hotel Limited. We will first direct our attention to the proper recording of income and expense as control over cash received and cash paid is best achieved by accurate and complete recording of such income and expense. We shall consider the programme steps to test that cash as an asset is being properly safeguarded.

> You should refer to Case study 5.4: County Hotel Ltd, to help you understand our suggested steps.

Complete and accurate recording

Accommodation income

This income will be collected in cash immediately or be charged to a customer's account for subsequent collection. The control procedures to ensure accurate and complete recording of accommodation income are an important element in the control of cash. You will agree that the easiest way to misappropriate cash will be not to record it in the first place. The particular problem for the auditor (and management) in relation to accommodation income is the variety of rates and the fact that rooms may be let at rates other than the standard.

Programme step. Review the accommodation income work programme and confirm that our work has enabled us to conclude that *such income is genuine and fully and accurately recorded.*

FIGURE 10.5 Audit depth test: production wages (Troston plc)

Employees		Rates basic OT		Hrs		Bonus		Gross		Tax		NIC		Trade union		Deduction		Net	Personnel records	Tax cards	NIC records	Payroll no.
Hanwell	✓	8.00	×	40	<	59	α	499.00	α	93.40	α	29.94	γ	4.00	>	127.34	>	371.66	β	β	β	3
W	✓	12.00	×	10																		
Hassan	✓	6.00	×	40	<	41	α	353.00	α	60.20	α	21.18	γ	4.00	>	85.38	>	267.62	β	β	β	10
R	✓	9.00	×	8																		
Sykes	✓	7.00	×	35	<	38	α	283.00	α	41.70	α	16.98	γ	4.00	>	62.68	>	220.32	β	β	β	25
E	✓	10.50	×	0																		
Popat	✓	5.00	×	40	<	25	α	277.50	α	42.20	α	16.65	γ	4.00	>	62.85	>	214.65	β	β	β	31
A	✓	7.50		7																		
Nelson	✓	5.00	×	40	<	24	α	261.50	α	38.60	α	15.69			>	54.29	>	207.21	β	β	β	48
A	✓	7.50	×	5																		

✓ Checked to pay agreements
× Checked to recorded hours list and OAFs
< Checked to bonus agreement and BETs
α Checked calculations
γ Checked to personnel files (agreement to have TU dues deducted from salary)
> Checked crosscasts
β Checked to records indicated

The audit programme in the accommodation income section should include the following steps (assuming that you have already concluded that the accounting and internal control systems are adequate:

- Review accommodation income for the year to date and the corresponding period last year and enquire into any significant changes in total income and room usage.
- Using management information and statistics, discuss with management the reasons for the changes (in particular the drop in room usage from 76 per cent in 2009 to 74 per cent in 2010). Enquire into correlation between restaurant income and accommodation income.
- Trace reception record details to accommodation records, including copy invoices, invoice register and housekeeping records.
- Select 30 entries at random from the housekeeping records of room usage and check to reception record register and accommodation income records.

Note that apart from these audit programme tests, forming part of other audit programmes, when performing a cash audit programme, the auditor will normally test from the bank documentation backward to the source documentation. For instance, a payment to a supplier of lamb or beef for the kitchen will be traced back to invoices, goods received notes, orders, etc. In other words, the auditor will choose to approach transactions from the point of view of the movement on the bank account and will attempt to verify that all movements selected (receipts and payments) are properly supported. This is because the auditor at this point wishes to verify the validity of recorded cash transactions.

Proper safeguarding of cash

Proper recording of the transactions forming the basis for cash payment and receipt is a prerequisite of cash control, although it is not sufficient in itself. The auditor also tests to ensure that payment is made to the right individuals and that receivables are, in fact, received. For this reason the following tests should be carried out:

- Review cash receipt and payment records for unusual items and enquire into them. For instance, the auditor of the County Hotel Ltd should pay particular attention to payments made on account or finally to the building firm carrying out the bathroom conversions.
- Compare totals of cash collected at the various cash points in the hotel – reception, restaurant, bars, etc. – with the amounts recorded in the bank paying-in book and bank statement. Enquire into any discrepancy.

> In the Horton Ltd example in Chapter 7, the company required *all* cash received to be deposited in the bank. This is a very useful general rule for cash control: *all monies received should be banked intact*, and is particularly important where coins and banknotes are received. They should not be used to pay expenses or costs merely because it seems easier to do so, as this will make reconciliation between monies received and cash banked more difficult.

- Test the accuracy of individual cash receipts as recorded (for instance, receipts from customers for a wedding reception held in the hotel) by checking remittance advices, paying-in slips and posting to the customer's account. The auditor would in this instance be testing that no teeming and lading was occurring. Note that this kind of test may be performed on a surprise visit basis, the auditor checking cash receipts before they have been banked, enabling names on cheques received to be compared with the customer's account.
- Banks no longer return cheques to customers but on occasion auditors may wish to obtain selected cancelled cheques for audit purposes.

> This would normally be at the request of the client.

The cancelled cheques should be tested as follows:

(a) Check signatures on the cheques to list of authorized cheque signatories. (This would highlight any apparently unauthorized signing of cheques.)

(b) Compare payees, amounts and dates to the cash book and creditors ledger entries and other supporting documentation.

- The next two audit tests are typical year-end verification tests but may be performed at interim examinations as part of the programme for checking the record and safeguarding of cash is satisfactory:

Such tests are outlined in some detail in Chapters 12 and 13.

(a) Cash counts: in the County Hotel example, in view of the large number of cash points, it would be necessary to arrange for sufficient audit firm staff to visit the hotel at the same time so that no transfers can be made between cash points to hide deficiencies. It is usual for such cash counts to be carried out on a surprise basis, having identified all cash items under the control of various custodians. Matters to which the auditor should pay particular attention are:

(i) Comparison of counted cash with the record of cash balances.

(ii) Count to be carried out in the presence of the custodian of the cash, a written record of the count details and that no other funds are held to be signed by the custodian at the close of the count.

(iii) Check that cash held temporarily prior to deposit in the bank is deposited in the bank intact.

(iv) Check that petty cash balances held are reasonable, review the petty cash book and ascertain that a responsible official checks that receipts and payments appear reasonable.

We have already noted that many auditors do not observe petty cash counts because they are not material in the context of the financial statements. However, where large quantities of cheques and bank notes have been received from customers, it may be a useful step to count and compare with the records of income received.

(b) Confirmation from the bank of balance on hand and such matters as overdraft limit, accounts opened and closed in the year, guarantees by and for third parties, security for overdraft and so on.

In this section we have covered some major matters that should be included in a cash audit programme during the interim examination. The main matter to emphasize is that the programme should be specifically designed to meet the programme objectives determined by the auditor before the detailed work commences. Set out below is a suggested audit conclusion for cash and cash transactions.

On the basis of the work performed on cash balances and handling as set out in the cash audit programme on working paper C100, as supported by working papers C101 to C131, I can conclude that, within reasonable limits; (i) all cash which the County Hotel should receive, has been received and safeguarded; (ii) payments are only made on the instructions of authorized officials of the company as the result of proper documentation produced by the accounting system; and (iii) that the accounting records can be relied upon to give a true record of the cash balances and transactions. Note that the audit programme was prepared on the basis of scope decisions recorded in working paper C10, supported by systems notes in the permanent audit files (section C).

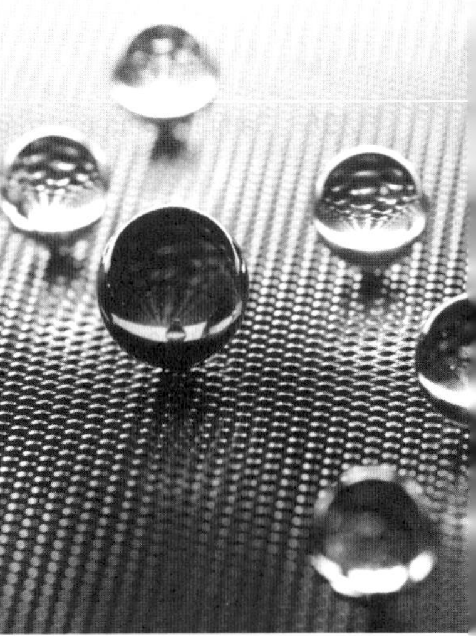

11

Sampling and materiality

LEARNING OBJECTIVES

After studying this chapter you should be able to:

- **Discuss the importance of audit sampling.**
- **Distinguish between non-statistical and statistical sampling.**
- **Describe the key steps and data required for the auditors to perform statistical sampling.**
- **Discuss the importance of the concept of materiality.**
- **Explain the role of materiality in relation to the financial statements.**
- **Describe how the auditors set the materiality level and use it in various stages of the audit.**

Learning objectives, 395
Introduction, 396
What is sampling?, 396
Designing and selecting the sample for testing, 397
Sample selection methodology, 400
Evaluation of test results, 404
Monetary unit sampling (MUS), 405
Comparative advantages of statistical and non-statistical sampling, 407
Alternative statistical sampling methods, 407
Materiality, 408
Summary, 419
Key points of the chapter, 419
References, 420
Further reading, 421
Self-assessment questions (solutions available to students), 421
Self-assessment questions (solutions available to tutors), 422
Topics for class discussion without solutions, 422

INTRODUCTION

You will remember from our discussions in Chapter 6 that evidence must have the qualities of sufficiency and appropriateness, the latter encompassing relevance and reliability.

In this chapter we introduce the related topics of materiality and audit sampling. Audit sampling is one of the methods auditors use to gather evidence to reach an opinion on the financial statements. As you have already seen in earlier chapters, whenever auditors select transactions, documents or accounts balances for testing they take a sample of them, using audit sampling as a technique. Materiality is a concept that is vital when the auditors seek to determine if a company's financial statements give a true and fair view. Without some notion of what level of misstatement in the financial statements would be misleading, auditors would not be able to evaluate the importance of any misstatements they discovered during audit testing. The two concepts are related because when auditors assess the significance of errors or misstatements they find in their sample, they are in effect putting into operation the concept of materiality.

WHAT IS SAMPLING?

We saw in Chapter 6 that the audit process is a search for evidence to enable auditors to form an opinion. We noted that, in carrying out the evidence search, auditors are expected to be both efficient and professionally effective. In other words, they are expected to carry out sufficient appropriate work to be reasonably certain that audit conclusions are soundly based but at a reasonable cost. Auditors have developed a number of procedures to achieve both aims, one of which – audit sampling – involves the auditors in selecting a sample for testing from the entire set of data (called the 'population').

This section is not intended to be a complete review of the theory and practice of audit sampling, but to cover some of the important ideas concerning sampling and the audit process. There is an International Standard of Auditing on this topic, ISA 530 – *Audit sampling*, and we have taken note of its contents in writing this chapter. Paragraph 4 of ISA 530 states that the objective of sampling 'is to provide a reasonable basis for the auditor to draw conclusions about the population from which the sample is selected'. It describes audit sampling as involving the application of audit procedures to less than 100 per cent of items within a population of audit relevance such that all sampling units have a chance of selection (para 5(a)). This enables auditors to obtain and evaluate audit evidence about the characteristics of the items selected, thus assisting them in forming a conclusion concerning the population from which the sample is drawn.

This ISA has been recently revised and is effective for periods beginning on or after 15 December 2009.

It should be recognized that auditors can obtain evidence in a number of different ways by using, for instance, analytical review and observation, so that audit sampling is just one procedure among many. When deciding which procedure to use auditors must bear in mind the objective(s) they are trying to achieve, the persuasiveness of the evidence they will obtain by using the particular procedure and the costs of applying the various procedures. At the outset auditors must decide what approach they are going to use and when it might be appropriate to use audit sampling. It is worth noting that the criteria of sufficiency, relevance and reliability that we apply to audit evidence generally can be applied also to audit sampling. Thus, we would ask in relation to audit sampling, questions such as: 'Is the sample large enough to be representative of the total population?' 'Is taking a sample relevant in the circumstances of this population?' 'Are the selection procedures designed to achieve a sample representative enough to make it a suitable basis for assessing the reliability of the population from which it is drawn?'

DESIGNING AND SELECTING THE SAMPLE FOR TESTING

If auditors can extract a sample of balances or transactions, which is *representative* of the total population of balances/transactions, the testing of the sample should enable audit conclusions to be extended to the total population. A major incentive to using sampling is that it reduces audit costs. If, however, the sample size is smaller than it should be because the auditors have underestimated the level of risk involved or if the sample is unrepresentative, they will have failed to collect sufficient, appropriate evidence.

It is important to recognize that audit sampling may be conducted either on a non-statistical or on a statistical basis. If auditors use statistical sampling they use probability theory to determine sample size and random selection methods to ensure each item or £1 value of the population has the same chance of selection as any other, thus providing a valid basis for the evaluation of the sample results. Non-statistical sampling is more subjective than statistical sampling, typically using haphazard selection methods and placing no reliance upon probability theory. Sometimes non-statistical sampling uses random selection, but usually even in these instances statistical methods are not used for evaluation nor for determining sample size.

In some textbooks, including this one, non-statistical sampling is often referred to as judgemental sampling.

We have emphasized in this book the importance of the planning stage of the audit process and the setting of objectives and we wish now to emphasize that careful planning of the sampling process is essential. The reasons for this are twofold:

1 Taking a sample rather than testing all items in the population increases the risk that the auditors will fail to detect matters of significance. It will be clear that in deciding to test less than 100 per cent of the transactions or balances, the auditors do accept a certain amount of risk. This risk must be carefully evaluated by the auditors to decide whether it is acceptable in the circumstances of the company and its audit.

We call this risk 'sampling risk' which is part of detection risk.

2 Characteristics of the population must be clearly identified before a sample is taken from it. For instance, in selecting employee salaries from a payroll for testing the auditors would wish to ensure that all grades of employee were tested. To do this the auditors would analyse the payroll (the population) before the sample is selected. There is a further example of identification of population characteristics in the Broomfield plc example in Case study 11.1 on page 398.

Judgemental sampling

We mentioned above that judgement has to be exercised in statistical and in non-statistical sampling. However, as mentioned above, the term *judgemental sampling* is frequently used as a synonym for non-statistical sampling because in this case *all* aspects of the sampling require the exercise of judgement.

CASE STUDY 11.1

An example of judgmental sampling: Broomfield plc

Broomfield plc has 500 trade receivables at 30 September 2010 with a total amount outstanding of £4 352 636.

During your audit work you have analysed the trade receivables according to size as shown in Table 11.1. This work is an example of an analytical procedure.

TABLE 11.1 Broomfield plc: analysis of trade receivables

Number of trade receivables	% of total	Value of trade receivables	% of total value
105	21	233 562	6
70	14	298 110	7
80	16	339 726	8
58	12	364 145	8
70	14	343 973	8
48	9	408 733	9
28	6	433 151	10
18	4	550 355	13
18	3	636 986	14
5	1	743 895	17
Total 500	**100**	**4 352 636**	**100**

ACTIVITY 11.1

Suggest how a sample should be selected from trade receivables shown in Table 11.1, with the purpose of confirming that Broomfield plc's sales and trade receivables system is operating properly and that the trade receivables' balances recorded in Broomfield's accounting records are accurate and complete.

The trade receivables listed are the result of transactions passing through the sales and related receivables system. Auditors have a twofold interest in relation to receivables: first, that the system for recording them is sound (tested by means of tests of control) and second, that the receivables figure is valid (tested by substantive procedures). A useful test for auditors to perform, which achieves *both* ends is a circularization of a sample of receivables. In making our selection of the sample we decided first to analyse the receivables. Note the following:

- 44 per cent of receivables in value are represented by 8 per cent of the receivables in number (being 41 receivables with an average balance of £47 103);
- the remaining 459 receivables, 92 per cent of the receivables in number (with an average balance of £5 275), represent 56 per cent of the balances.

We have already mentioned external confirmations in Chapter 6 where we discussed audit evidence. The role of such confirmations, including confirmations from debtors in respect of accounts receivable balances is discussed in ISA 505.

The auditors clearly have to judge how many receivables should be selected. In the audit conclusion on the Broomfield system in Chapter 9 on page 353 there was a reference to an extension of scope owing to certain weaknesses in the system, which would influence the auditors in deciding on the size and selection of sample. The auditors know that if they write to 41 credit customers *and they all confirm their balance in Broomfield's books is accurate* they will have substantiated 44 per cent of the receivables, but on the basis of experience and detailed knowledge of the company may conclude it is only necessary to send requests to 20 of these credit customers.

We discussed size of sample in Chapter 5 (Table 5.1) where we discussed risk, in Chapter 6 (Case study 6.1) where we discussed audit evidence, in Chapter 8 where we discussed control systems and in Chapter 10 where we showed that audit programmes should reflect the agreed level of testing.

The auditors also know that the amounts making up the receivables' balances have all been processed by the system and the auditors may test the operation of the system by selecting a sample of them. If these receivables (and some of them may be credit balances or be as low as £1) all confirm their balance in Broomfield's books is accurate, the auditors would obtain evidence through this test of control that the company's systems appear to be operating properly. Again using knowledge and experience, the auditors may conclude that a sample of 30 receivables for circularization will be sufficient to meet the objective of performing tests of control.

In total the auditors would select 50 debtors to meet both substantive and test of control objectives.

Statistical sampling

Now we have discussed judgemental sampling, we will turn our attention to statistical sampling methods. We shall find that judgement still has to be exercised in statistical sampling, but that, in some respects, there is a reduction in the amount of judgement required.

Let us first look at the need for homogeneity in the population before we move to discussing how the auditors might achieve a representative sample. We consider first some examples of factors leading to lack of homogeneity:

A population is said to possess homogeneity or be homogeneous if the items included in it, for instance, sales transactions or trade receivables possess the same characteristics.

- Transactions that have not been subjected to the same internal controls throughout the relevant period should not be treated as being homogeneous. For instance:
  - (a) It may be that some kinds of sales transactions are controlled in different ways, large transactions treated differently from small ones.
  - (b) The chief accountant, exercising important controls, may have been ill during part of the period with the result that some transactions have been strictly controlled, others not.
- Balances in a population may have widely different values. For instance:
  - (a) In the Broomfield example we saw some receivables balances were large, representing a high proportion of the total, others, the majority, being small.

We met with this company in Chapters 7, 8, 9 and 10.

(b) Inventories may represent either items with low value or high value individually. If we were to tell you that the inventories stated in the balance sheet of Troston plc included on the one hand components for dental equipment and on the other hand dental gold for making dental crowns and bridges, we are sure you would wish to test the transactions and balances relating to the gold much more carefully than the other components. The reason for this, we suggest, is that the degree of inherent risk, and possibly control risk, is perceived as being greater in the case of the gold than of the components.

Stratification of the population is discussed in Appendix 1 of ISA 530.

Because of the lack of homogeneity in populations, it is common practice to stratify them and to treat the different strata as different populations, each subpopulation being either homogeneous or closer to homogeneity than the original (total) population. Thus, having discovered that sales transactions at Broomfield over a certain amount were subjected to special controls exercised by senior officials, the auditors might decide to stratify the total population into two, and to take a sample from each.

Before we look at different kinds of sample, let us make a further important point – a sample can only be truly representative if it is taken from the whole population. If auditors select items for testing from one week in March, they are testing that week but not the whole year. The auditors cannot assume the transactions in March are representative of the whole year and must take a sample from the whole year's transactions.

SAMPLE SELECTION METHODOLOGY

These are outlined in Appendix 4 of ISA 530.

Sampling methods

Let us now have a look at various ways a sample can be selected and see how closely they approximate the requirements for statistical sampling.

Random sampling

This method tries to ensure that each item in the population has the same chance of selection as any other item. This is a statistical method of selection and is required for statistical sampling, but can also be used with non-statistical sampling methods. The auditors allocate an individual identifier to each sampling unit and then use random procedures to determine which of the sampling units to select for testing. The procedures most commonly used include random number generator tables and special computer random selection programs.

Systematic or interval sampling

This is a method possibly employing a random starting point and thereafter selecting every *n*th item. It does provide cover throughout a population and can have the same effect as random sampling if the errors are spread randomly throughout the population. If they are not spread randomly, systematic sampling may not result in a representative sample. For instance, selecting every tenth employee on a payroll may result in all the charge-hands being selected.

Block or cluster sampling

This method makes no attempt to select a representative sample, but involves the selection of a block of transactions (say) and testing for the existence of some criteria. The auditors may use this method when testing a system. For instance, the auditors may have been informed that the credit controller initials each sales order as evidence that creditworthiness checks have been carried out. A selection of a 'block' of 100 sales orders might prove or disprove this claim. This sort of sample selection method can be quite useful and is relatively efficient in that a sample can be selected fairly quickly but it is a non-statistical sampling method. Appendix 4 of ISA 530 suggests that it is not an appropriate method of selection to use when the objective of the audit test is to draw valid inferences about the population from the sample.

Haphazard sampling

In this case samples are selected by such methods as using blindfolds and pins or spouses' birthdays. The problem is that it is not mathematically valid as the sample may be biased. It may not, therefore, provide a sample from which conclusions can be drawn about the whole population. It is a non-statistical method of selecting a sample.

Size of sample

We have emphasized previously that auditors should collect *sufficient* audit evidence. This means that sample size is important. There are, however, a number of important judgemental factors to be considered in determining the size of samples for detailed testing. These include the level of confidence sought by the auditors and the expected and acceptable error or deviation rate.

We use the term 'deviation rate' when engaged in tests of controls, and 'error rate' when engaged in substantive tests of detail. In our subsequent discussion we use the term 'error rate' to cover both errors and deviations.

Appendix 2 of ISA 530 gives examples of factors affecting sample size for tests of controls.

The level of confidence auditors set for their statistical sampling tests

The extent of confidence auditors require will be influenced by factors, such as assessment of inherent and control risks. The judgement of inherent risk will influence how confident they are of misstatements arising in the transactions or balances prior to the application of internal controls. The initial assessment of the company's internal control system will influence the extent to which they believe misstatements exist in the transactions or balances after being processed by the company and having been subject to its internal control procedures. This initial assessment will be based on a number of factors including (a) the auditors' evaluation of the control system after conducting tests of controls; (b) conducting other relevant audit tests, such as analytical review; (c) the auditor's previous experience with the client and the particular aspect of the system (or balance) being tested. If the auditors have obtained evidence from other relevant audit tests they have performed on the control system or balances they are testing, the degree of confidence they require from their sampling is correspondingly reduced. Other tests may include detailed analytical review or scrutiny of large or unusual transactions.

The expected error rate in the population

The expected error rate is an important determinant of sample size. When testing a company's internal controls the auditors use what is termed attribute sampling. In attribute sampling there are two responses to a test: *yes* the control has been applied correctly or *no* the control has not been applied. Hence, what auditors seek to determine in attribute sampling is the rate of non-occurrence of the internal control procedure being applied. When testing an account balance, auditors are concerned with determining if the balance is correctly stated. The greater the expected error rate, the greater the sample size must be for them to conclude that the actual error rate is less than the tolerable error rate.

The tolerable error rate set by the auditors

The auditors have to determine the tolerable error rate in the population. This is the maximum error rate the auditors are prepared to accept when deciding whether their initial evaluation of control risk is valid or whether total recorded transactions or balances may be regarded as accurate and complete. When testing controls using attribute sampling the tolerable deviation rate is the maximum deviation rate in the sample the auditors are willing to accept and still conclude that their initial evaluation of control risk is valid. When testing for amounts the tolerable error is related to the level of materiality set by the auditors. The lower the tolerable error rate set by the auditors the greater the sample size.

We discuss materiality later in this chapter.

You may have wondered why we have not mentioned the size of the population as a determinant of size of the sample. This is because with the normal population sizes with which auditors are working, population size has very little effect on sample size. Therefore, normally, auditors do not need to consider size of the population.

Although the statistics of how the sample size is calculated is beyond the scope of this book we will show you below how that sample size is calculated by applying the following formula:

$$\text{Sample size} = \frac{\text{Reliability factor}}{\text{Tolerable error rate}}$$

The reliability factors in the above equation are obtained from specially prepared tables, a portion of which we show in Table 11.2.

The values in these tables are derived from the Poisson statistical distribution and are dependent on the auditors' required confidence level and their expectation of the likely number of errors/deviations.

TABLE 11.2 Reliability factors (extract)

Number of sample errors	Confidence levels				
	70%	80%	90%	95%	99%
0	1.21	1.61	2.31	3.00	4.61
1	2.44	3.00	3.89	4.75	6.64
2	3.62	4.28	5.33	6.30	8.41
3	4.77	5.52	6.69	7.76	10.05

Example

The auditors have decided to perform a statistical sampling test on an internal operation in the purchasing system of a company. They have obtained some assurance from other relevant tests and therefore decide that for the purposes of the present test they will set the confidence level at 70 per cent. They have set the tolerable deviation rate for this test at 3 per cent. This is the maximum deviation rate they are willing to accept in the sample and conclude that their initial assessment of control risk is still appropriate. Based on their previous experience and their assessment of the strength of the internal control system the auditors expect to find one error. The appropriate reliability factor is obtained at the intersection of the 70 per cent confidence level column and the one sample error row, that is, 2.44. Therefore:

$$\text{Sample size} = \frac{2.44}{0.03} = 81$$

ACTIVITY 11.2

Calculate the sample size using the following data:

- maximum risk auditors are willing to accept = 20 per cent;
- expected number of errors = 1;
- tolerable error rate 4 per cent.

So far our discussion has been in terms of confidence levels required by the auditor. However, it is important to appreciate that risk is simply the complement of the confidence level. Thus a confidence level of 90 per cent is equivalent to a risk level of 10 per cent. You will sometimes see this risk referred to as 'sampling risk'. The risk is effectively the probability the auditors fail to detect an error rate greater than the tolerable error rate.

The first thing to notice in this example is that the confidence level is not stated. However, as we mentioned above, risk and confidence are the complement of each other. Therefore, the risk level given translates into a confidence level of 80 per cent. The appropriate reliability factor is 3.00. Therefore the sample size is:

$$\frac{3.00}{0.04} = 75$$

We introduced you to these ideas when we discussed audit risk in Chapter 5, page 172. Paragraphs 12 and 13 of ISA 530 deal with the nature and cause of deviations and misstatements.

After determining sample size the auditors will select the sample using random sampling and perform their test. Before we become too carried away with technical details we should remind you that it is important that the auditors select the sample from an appropriate population. The population identified should be the one that is consistent with the objective of the audit test. For instance, if the auditors' objective is to prove the genuineness, accuracy and completeness of sales, a suitable population from which to draw the sample might be the sales despatch notes. For each despatch note selected the auditors could check that a sales invoice has been properly prepared. We discussed this issue in some depth in Chapter 10 when we commented on the audit programme for Powerbase plc in Case study 10.1. After selecting the sample and performing the test the next stage in the process is to evaluate the test results.

EVALUATION OF TEST RESULTS

The first stage in evaluation is to determine the number of errors occurring in the sample. This requires the auditor to define what an error is before an error rate can be established. For instance, if they are checking the control procedure 'All purchase invoices are signed as authorization for payment' and they find an invoice that has been initialled rather than signed, should they count that as a deviation from desired practice? In this example, if the auditors are satisfied that the initials are those of a member of staff who has the authority to sign the purchase invoices then they would not consider this instance as a deviation. What, however, this example does indicate is that auditors are likely to come across situations where it may not always be clear-cut whether or not an error has occurred.

The next stage in the process is for the auditors to estimate on the basis of the sample results, at their given level of confidence, the upper error rate in the population. This is known as 'projecting errors'. To do this requires the auditors to use the table and formula shown above.

Example

Using the data from Activity 11.2 let us assume that the auditors find two errors in their sample of 75. The upper error rate can be found by rearranging the above formula to give:

$$\text{Upper error rate} = \frac{\text{Reliability factor}}{\text{Sample size}}$$

At the confidence level the auditors are using (80 per cent), the reliability factor associated with two errors/deviations from the tables is 4.28. Thus, the upper error rate is calculated as follows:

$$\text{Upper error rate} = \frac{4.28}{75} = 5.7\%$$

This amount is above the tolerable error rate that the auditors at the outset had identified as acceptable. The auditors could determine the confidence limit commensurate with finding two errors in a sample of 75. To do this they would first determine the appropriate reliability factor. This is the tolerable error rate times the sample size (0.04×75) so that the reliability factor would be 3.00. Turning to the reliability factor table we can see from the row corresponding to two sample errors that the confidence level is below 70 per cent. To determine the exact confidence level would require a fuller set of reliability factor tables.

The auditors have to decide on appropriate action on the basis of the sample results. In this example, the auditors may reduce the amount of reliance they will place on the particular part of the control system they were testing. As a consequence, they may extend the scope of the substantive procedures performed on the relevant balance sheet or profit and loss amounts to which the control being testing pertained.

We would not wish to give you the impression that auditors conduct the evaluation in a mechanistic fashion. They would also be concerned with the nature of the errors they identified. Although they may all be classified as errors, some errors may be more important than others. For instance, the errors may provide grounds for suspicion of the possibility of fraud, or they may indicate the possibility of a systematic type of error.

ACTIVITY 11.3

Using the data from the activity above find the upper error rate if the auditors in their sample of 75 items did not find any errors.

From the reliability factor table the factor corresponding to a confidence level of 80 per cent and finding 0 errors is 1.61. Therefore the upper error rate is calculated as follows:

$$\text{Upper error rate} = \frac{1.61}{75} = 2.14\%$$

What this result means is that the auditors can state with 80 per cent confidence that there will be no more than just over two errors, or deviations from a control procedure, out of every 100 items in the population.

Since the results indicate that the tolerable error rate is less than 4 per cent, the auditors can continue to place (at minimum) their planned reliance on the control procedure they have tested. Indeed, they could calculate, using the above formula, what confidence level is commensurate with finding no errors and a tolerable error rate of 4 per cent. This confidence level will be somewhat above their required confidence level of 80 per cent. Another perspective on this is to say, given that no errors were found, what sample size is commensurate with a confidence level of 80 per cent. This can be found by rearranging the above formula:

$$\text{Sample size} = \frac{1.61}{4\%} = 40$$

What this suggests is that the auditors could have obtained the appropriate level of confidence by selecting a sample of approximately 40 rather than 75. Effectively, the auditors have over-audited the population. This has occurred because they have found fewer errors than expected. This illustrates the importance of auditors making as best an estimate as they can of the expected number of errors.

In the above examples we have been concerned with attribute sampling and the testing of internal control systems. Although this is important, of greater importance is the amount by which an account balance is in error. In the next section we will consider monetary unit sampling which is the most popular statistical sampling method used to estimate the amount by which an account balance is in error.

MONETARY UNIT SAMPLING (MUS)

You may refer to Appendix 1 of ISA 530 under the heading 'Value-weighted selection'.

In the final analysis, auditors wish to be confident that errors in the population are not great enough to cause the accounts to depart from truth and fairness. This means they are not only interested in error rates but also in the monetary effects of these errors. First, the auditors clearly have to decide in relation to the account balance being tested what would be regarded as material, that is, the maximum value of errors in the account balance they would be prepared to accept. MUS is a method of sampling which allows auditors to estimate for the population being tested the amount of the most likely error (MLE) in monetary terms and the likely upper error limit (UEL) also in monetary terms. There are two basic ideas underlying MUS:

In MUS the upper error limit is sometimes referred to as monetary precision.

- The population is divided not into transactions (such as a sales invoice) or balances (such as trade receivables) but £1 units, the auditors selecting from those units. Thus, trade receivables of £35 million would be assumed to consist of 35 million £1 units.
- Should an error be found in the transaction or balance to which the £1 is attached, the transaction or balance is held to be 'tainted' by the percentage of error in the value of the transaction or balance. Thus, if a balance is recorded at £100 but its true value is £80 then the balance is held to be tainted by 20 per cent.

This section is based in part on Chapter 13 of *Current Issues in Auditing* (Manson, 1997).

Monetary unit sampling can only be used when the population can be specified in terms of £1 monetary amounts and a cumulative total of these amounts can be calculated. Thus, if auditors are selecting trade receivables for circularization, a monetary cumulative running total of the amounts owed will be required, and within that total the allocation of specific monetary units to particular trade receivables. Since the population is in £1 units this means that the sample selected will consist of specific £1 units from the population. These £1 units are, however, only a hook for the individual trade receivables that are to be audited. Based on the specific £1 units selected the auditors obtain a sample of trade receivables to be circularized. The determination of the sample size proceeds as follows.

The auditors must first specify the confidence level, and the tolerable error – the amount of error in the account being audited, which when combined with errors in other accounts would lead to the financial statements being misleading. Using the confidence level, the tolerable error and an estimate of the likely error together with suitable statistical sampling tables they can determine the appropriate sample size.

When evaluating the sample results the auditors first calculate a point estimate corresponding to the most likely error in the population. This is supplemented by calculating an estimate of the upper error limit in the population. Using these the auditors are able to make a statement of the most likely error and, at the confidence level being used, the upper error limit in the population. If the upper error limit is less than the tolerable error, the auditors can accept the population. If the opposite is the case, the auditors may adjust the upper error limit for any errors found – assuming the client is willing to agree to the adjustment – to determine if that reduces the upper error limit to below the tolerable error. If the upper error limit remains above the tolerable error, the auditors should carry out additional procedures, such as extending detailed testing or performing alternative audit procedures.

The calculation of the most likely error and the upper error limit involves extrapolating from the errors found in the sample using their level of tainting, that is, the percentage by which they are in error.

COMPARATIVE ADVANTAGES OF STATISTICAL AND NON-STATISTICAL SAMPLING

To finish this section on sampling it is worthwhile comparing the advantages and disadvantages of non-statistical and statistical sampling. An advantage of statistical sampling is that it requires auditors to make explicit their judgements on matters such as confidence level, expected error rate and tolerable error rate. This requirement helps ensure that they adopt a methodical approach to their sampling work. The sample size is calculated based on statistical principles and therefore can be justified. The determination of the sampling risk and the evaluation of results, in particular the upper error rate, is quantified and more precise.

Statistical sampling does, however, have a number of disadvantages. It is usually more time-consuming, and hence more costly than non-statistical sampling. It requires documents, such as invoices or account balances, to be held in a manner that enables each of them to be separately identified for the purposes of selection. This task is undoubtedly easier when the client's records are computerized. It may be argued that statistical sampling is more difficult to understand. As a counter argument, since audit firms tend to use specialized computer statistical sampling packages which determine sample size and evaluate results, audit staff do not need to understand the mathematical theory underlying the statistical sampling process. We should mention here that since the early 1990s the use in practice of statistical sampling appears to have decreased. Where it is used today it is more likely to be in specialized audit situations such as the audit of banks or insurance companies. The reason for the decrease in the use of statistical sampling techniques can, at least partly, be attributed to increased use of risk-based auditing which has resulted in reorientation in the types of testing performed in auditing. In particular, greater emphasis is given to analytical review and the investigation of large or unusual transactions or balances, which may have been detected using audit software. The reduction in emphasis is particularly acute in attribute sampling and again this is probably because of changes in the audit process, in particular the move away from the detailed checking of numerous documents and transactions to placing emphasis on other aspects of control such as evaluating the effectiveness of the control environment. It is also noteworthy that the rise in popularity in statistical sampling was partially because it was seen as bringing a scientific approach to auditing. This is particularly true in the USA where quantification and scientism appear to be privileged. This is less so in the UK where greater emphasis is placed on qualitative and less visible aspects such as auditor judgement.

ALTERNATIVE STATISTICAL SAMPLING METHODS

In addition to attribute sampling and monetary unit sampling there are a number of other statistical sampling methods, two of which we mention briefly below.

Discovery sampling

There may be circumstances where the discovery of one error or irregularity may be vitally important and result in special further investigation. This may be the case where fraud is suspected (for instance, an employee in a sensitive position may be unaccountably enjoying a higher standard of living than his or her salary level would allow) and the auditors are asked (as a special exercise) to investigate and find out if fraud is in fact taking place. In this form of sampling the auditors' sampling plan is devised to have a high probability of detecting a population which has an error rate above what auditors would normally consider acceptable. As soon as an error is detected the auditors cease sampling and conclude at a certain level of confidence that the population has a higher than acceptable error rate. Because of its design and the fact that sampling ceases as soon as an error is found, this type of sampling is relatively efficient in the sense that sample sizes tend to be small. Normally in discovery sampling the occurrence of one irregularity of the predetermined type will set the auditors on further extensive enquiry.

Variables sampling

This form of statistical sampling consists of a number of different but related types of sampling which have a common foundation. In one variant (*mean per unit method*) the auditors select a sample of items that have some numerical value attached to them, for instance, sales invoices, and from that calculate the mean and standard deviation of the sample values. The auditors can use the normal distribution to extrapolate from the sample and estimate, at some confidence level, the population value and a standard deviation. The auditors can compare the calculated range of values with the value in the company's books or financial statements. If the book value lies outside the calculated range, the auditors will have to implement a fuller investigation of the figure in the company's books and records.

In another method (*ratio and difference method*) the auditors select a sample and compare the audited value of the item with its book value to identify any differences. These differences can then, by extrapolation, be used to estimate the most likely error in the population and the standard deviation. Thus the auditors can conclude on the basis of their sample at a particular confidence level that the amount of error in the population is within a certain range. The auditors can then decide on the acceptability of this range of error. This type of variables sampling is only suitable where auditors anticipate a large number of errors. Variables sampling is not very common in practice, mainly because one needs large sample sizes to generate the population estimates, which makes it an inefficient method of sampling.

In the next section we consider the related topic of materiality. We shall see there is a connection between tolerable error allocated to an account balance in sampling and materiality.

MATERIALITY

Introduction to materiality

You will be aware from what we have said in earlier chapters that auditors need to come to a view about the truth and fairness of the financial statements and their compliance with Companies Act requirements. In respect of the former requirement this suggests that auditors need to have some way of determining when financial statements do not give a true and fair view. Since the term 'true and fair' is subjective in nature and not capable of being couched in objective terms, identification of departures from it can be problematic, even though auditors contend with such identification in their day-to-day practice. In this section we are concerned with how auditors try to identify whether or not financial statements give a true and fair view.

As a starting point it is worth noting that most auditors would probably agree that the true and fair view cannot be reduced to a mechanistic formula. Nevertheless, they would probably also contend that they are able to identify those occasions when the financial statements do *not* give a true and fair view. That is, they are able to identify departures that are of such significance that they result in a deviation from what the auditors perceive to be an appropriate benchmark of truth and fairness. You may think that this seems rather vague and gives little guidance as to the practical application of the true and fair view concept. However, in practice there are no easy answers, even though accounting standards setters have issued many accounting standards designed to aid the achievement of truth and fairness. Unfortunately accounting standards are as yet incomplete and may never be sufficiently extensive to cover all eventualities, with the result that auditors, unable to resort to a rule or guide, will have to make use of their professional judgement. We have stressed throughout this book that auditors frequently make judgements about sufficiency and appropriateness of audit evidence and many other matters. The decision as to whether the financial statements give a true and fair view is just another example of a situation where auditors have to exercise judgement.

We made reference to materiality in Chapter 2 when considering audit concepts. Now it is time to consider it in greater detail as materiality and truth and fairness are interrelated. We shall start by reminding you of the definition of materiality included in the International Auditing Standard 320 – *Materiality in planning and performing an audit*:

See ISA 320, paragraph 2

> Misstatements, including omissions are considered to be material if they, individually or in the aggregate, could reasonably be expected to influence the economic decisions of users taken on the basis of the financial statements. Judgments about materiality are made in light of surrounding circumstances, and are affected by the size or nature of a misstatement, or a combination of both.

It is apparent from this definition that the words 'materiality' and 'size' are related but allow factors other than size to determine if an item is material. The definition above highlights a number of important issues that we discuss in the next sections.

Materiality and decision making

The above definition of materiality emphasizes that it is the effect on users' decisions that is important in determining whether an item is material. This would seem to imply that the auditors must have some notion of whom the users are and to what use they are likely to put the financial statements.

Although many different groups use the financial statements it is generally thought that shareholders are the primary user group and this is emphasized in ISA 320. What, auditors have to determine, therefore, is the extent to which the financial statements can be misstated before they would alter a shareholder's decision in one way or another. In this respect the ISA takes it as given that users have a reasonable knowledge of business and accounting, work hard to understand the financial statements, understand that the financial statements are prepared using the concept of materiality and recognize that the statements contain uncertainties and that judgements are involved in their preparation (para 4, ISA 320). Thus it would seem that the type of investor the auditor should be considering is a sophisticated and knowledgeable investor, not someone who is unsophisticated or naive. Ultimately, it would be for the courts to decide the type of investor that should be considered by auditors when determining the appropriate level at which to set materiality. In adopting this approach we are attempting to identify the link between a shareholder's decision and the financial statements. In respect of listed companies considerable research has been conducted attempting to identify the link between accounting numbers and share price. Research has also been conducted into the investor decision-making process. Although both types of research have produced interesting results, none has proved particularly helpful to auditors when attempting to identify the materiality level for a specific company. What is certain is that at the outset of the audit, and particularly during the planning period, the auditors have to decide what level of error or misstatement could occur in the financial statements before an investor's decision would be influenced. We discuss this matter in the next section.

Materiality in the financial statements

In this section we are concerned with the measurement of materiality in respect of the financial statements. Research in the financial management literature and that concerning the effect of accounting data on a company's share price and investor decision making, has confirmed the importance of the profit figure to investors and the financial community, including financial analysts. You can confirm this by looking at the financial section of a newspaper and seeing the kinds of comments journalists tend to make about companies. Often financial journalists refer to a company as having met, exceeded or not met analysts' forecast profits for the period. Given the amount of attention the market pays to profit, one would expect that the stated profit is also a figure to which auditors would direct attention when determining the materiality level. From your previous studies in accounting it should, of course, come as no surprise that such emphasis is given to the profit figure. The profit figure is often seen as encapsulating a company's performance for the period.

As an aside, some commentators would argue that too much attention is paid to a company's profit for a period and too little attention to other aspects of a company's performance or position.

In practice auditors, when setting materiality levels, often do so in terms of a percentage of a company's profit figure for the period. Materiality figures quoted in the auditing literature vary from between 1 per cent and 10 per cent of the profit figure. Taking 10 per cent as an example, this means that if a misstatement were to affect profit by 10 per cent or more, it would be considered as material by the auditors. Auditors may in practice use a slightly more complicated decision process than this. For instance, a decision rule might take the following form: if misstatements affect profit by more than 10 per cent, they are material; if they affect profit by between 5 and 10 per cent, the auditors have to look at their nature and the context surrounding the company before they take a final decision about the materiality of the misstatements. More prudent auditors might set the materiality level at 1 per cent, in which case, if misstatements affect profit by 1 per cent or more, they would be deemed to be material. At what level auditors set materiality again comes down to professional judgement. It should, however, be recognized that the materiality level set and the amount of evidence auditors need to acquire are related. The basic relationship is that the lower the materiality level the greater the quantity of evidence that auditors must acquire. Since evidence gathering has a cost, other things being equal, the lower auditors set the materiality level the greater the cost of the audit work. An audit firm may, however, be under pressure from its clients to reduce audit fees and it also faces competition from other audit firms, which tends to force audit fees downwards. You can see that auditors face a dilemma to which there is no easy answer. In the end, however, auditors may be answerable for the quality of their work in a court of law and therefore the materiality level they set is likely to be highly influenced by what they believe can be justified in a court.

This far we have not specifically considered what profit figure auditors should use when setting materiality levels: profit before tax, profit after tax, or retained profit for the year. Based on the authors' experience we believe the most common choice among auditors is profit before tax or profit before tax from continuing operations. Once again, however, auditors would have to use their judgement about which profit figure is most appropriate in setting materiality levels for a particular company.

We do not wish to give the impression that auditors are only concerned about the profit figure. It is likely that they will also attempt to set materiality levels for other figures. For instance, turnover, total assets and net assets are often cited as other items in the financial statements for which the auditors set materiality levels in terms of percentage amounts. Indeed, if the profit of a company in a particular year was very low then calculating say 5 per cent of that figure would give a very low materiality level. In this instance the auditors may believe a more appropriate figure for materiality would be obtained if the auditors used turnover or net assets, although auditors might also use average profit figures over a number of years. In practice, auditors would normally calculate materiality levels based on a number of different criteria and then decide on appropriate materiality levels for different aspects of the audit. For instance, if they were auditing expenses they might use a materiality level based on profit whereas if they were auditing trade receivables they are likely to use a materiality level based on net assets.

You might think that auditors would be more concerned with overstatements of profit than understatements because they would suffer more adverse publicity if the profit figure in the financial statements was overstated rather than understated, and that this might be translated into different materiality levels for under- and overstatements, or at least influence the audit approach. However, great care must be taken by auditors to ensure that they give the same stress to under- and overstatements.

ACTIVITY 11.4

We have indicated above that auditors may consider using a certain percentage of profit as the materiality level. Suggest other matters relating to profit that auditors may consider when setting materiality levels.

Other aspects of materiality in relation to profit that you might have mentioned include the following:

- *The trend in profits over the last few years.* If profits have been showing a steady increase or decrease, the auditors may wish to consider at what levels of profit for the current year the trend would look unusual or appear to be exceptional. In effect, auditors form an expectation of what would be the normal profit for the year and if the company's draft profit figure exceeds or is less than this by a 'considerable' amount, the auditors would take that into account when setting the materiality level.

The auditors would have to use their judgement about what is a 'considerable' amount after taking into consideration their knowledge of the company and its circumstances.

- *The effect of the profit figure on important ratios.* The profit figure is often used as a numerator in a number of important financial ratios, such as the gross profit and net profit ratios. The auditors could examine how these would be affected in the current year for a number of different profit levels (assuming the denominator remains constant or varies by some amount set by the auditors). They would then have to make a decision about whether the ratios looked unusual or exceptional. At this point they could use the deviation from expectation as a guide to what level of profit would be regarded as material. Both of the above depend upon there being some figure of expected profit from which deviations are measured and used to assist in determining the materiality of profit.
- *External influences.* If the auditors are aware of particular circumstances pertaining to the company, for instance, rumours that it is a potential takeover target or that it is likely to be raising additional capital from the stock market, this may influence where they set materiality levels for profit. This is because the auditors realize that in these situations the client's profit is likely to come in for greater scrutiny than normal. They are also aware that, should the profit figure turn out to be incorrect, the chances of being sued for negligence may also be increased. In these circumstances auditors have an incentive to set a lower materiality level and the audit partner and manager will give more serious consideration to its appropriateness. Other circumstances where the auditors would show an above average concern about the materiality level include poor performance and difficulties in raising finance, giving rise to concerns about the going-concern status of the company.

At this stage we have only been concerned with materiality at financial statement level and more generally have approached it from an accounting perspective. Below we discuss the relationship between materiality and individual components in the financial statements.

Materiality at the planning stage

Auditors will normally set materiality levels at the planning stage of the audit. They will do this on the basis of draft or management accounts supplied by the audit client. Since these are draft financial statements, it may be that at a later date the draft statements change, which may require the auditors to reassess the materiality levels set originally.

The main reason auditors consider materiality at the planning stage is to help them put audit risk into context. They have to consider what level of misstatement in the financial statements would cause them not to show a true and fair view. They then have to make an assessment of what audit risk they are prepared to accept if they fail to detect such misstatement. As you might expect, if auditors wish to avoid complaints that inappropriate audit opinions have been issued, the desired audit risk expressed as a percentage is likely to be a fairly low figure. In addition, they will consider what individual items in the financial statements are material. It almost goes without saying that ex-post (that is, after the audit) audit risk will be high if the auditors have failed to discover material misstatements and that these misstatements are more likely to occur in financial statement items that are themselves material in amount. Clearly there is a strong relationship between risk and materiality. Although there are some general risks affecting companies, as we indicated above, most risks relate to specific financial statement headings and auditors must therefore consider the various components of the financial statements and assign a materiality level to each. For instance, auditors may assign a materiality level to inventory of (say) £100 000, so that if inventory was either under- or overstated by less than this amount because of (say) calculation errors, they would not consider it material. Conversely, if inventory was under- or overstated by more than this amount this would constitute a material misstatement. When deciding the materiality for each component auditors have to consider a number of factors.

ISA 320 considers the relationship between materiality and audit risk in Paragraph A1.

ACTIVITY 11.5

What factors do you think are likely to influence auditors when determining a materiality level for components of the financial statements?

You may have mentioned some of the following factors.

- *The importance of the heading in the financial statements.* For instance, if inventory constitutes 40 per cent of the net assets of the company it is likely it would be considered an important component that may influence auditors when setting the materiality level for inventory. If on the other hand the amount of inventory held by the company was negligible, then the auditors would be less concerned by the amount by which it was under- or overstated. In general, the greater the amount at which an item is stated in the financial statements the greater the emphasis auditors will place on setting an appropriate materiality level.
- *The nature of the item.* For instance, auditors may believe that users consider the cash balance more important than the deferred tax balance.

Consequently, if both of these are stated at similar amounts in the balance sheet auditors may allocate a smaller materiality level to the cash balance than to the deferred tax balance.

- *The auditors' past experience with the audit client.* If in previous years the auditors have found a number of misstatements in a particular account balance, they would set a lower materiality level for that account than if there had been no misstatements in previous audits.

In general the higher the inherent risk and control risk in respect of an account balance the lower the auditors will set the materiality level.

- *The trend in the account balance.* If a particular account balance has remained relatively constant or increased by a relatively constant amount each year but in the current year there is a departure from this, the auditors would consider setting a smaller materiality level than they would otherwise set.

It is interesting that ISA 320 says very little about the materiality of individual items in the financial statements, suggesting that setting an overall or global materiality level for the financial statements is of prime importance. However, we believe that it is also important the auditor gives some consideration to setting a materiality level for individual financial statement items. ISA 320 does lay some stress on setting what it terms 'performance materiality'. Performance materiality recognizes that individually a misstated amount in an account balance may be immaterial, but if combined with other uncorrected misstatements *and* undetected misstatements, it may give rise to a total amount that exceeds the materiality for the financial statements as a whole, or the materiality amount set for an individual balance in the financial statements. When setting the performance materiality level auditors need to take into account their risk assessment and the type and extent of misstatements found in previous audits. Thus in setting performance materiality for an individual account balance the auditor is trying to reduce to an acceptable level the probability that, after conducting their tests, the total amount of undetected misstatements and uncorrected misstatements in that account balance is greater than the set materiality level. This would mean setting performance materiality level lower than the assessed materiality level, and thus increasing sample sizes.

See ISA 320, paragraph A12

In an earlier section we noted that auditors set materiality levels in respect of global figures in the financial statements, for instance, percentages of net profit or net assets. You will no doubt be wondering how global or financial statement level materiality is related to individual account balance materiality levels. There is no easy answer to this question. Some authors consider that the overall materiality level should be split between the individual account balances. For instance, if the auditors believe that the overall materiality level for net assets should be £200 000, they would need to allocate this between the various items composing net assets, such as inventories, trade receivables, trade payables and so on. To accomplish this, audit firms may use simple decision rules to aid them. Alternatively, the audit firm may allocate overall materiality on a rule of thumb basis to arrive at a materiality level for each of the components, perhaps decreasing the component materiality level if inherent and/or control risk is high for the component concerned. In this case the sum of the individual component materiality levels may differ somewhat from the overall materiality level. Note, however, that the materiality level set for an individual item in the financial statements will be less than the overall materiality level. In the end, the allocation process comes down to the auditors using professional judgement, taking into consideration aspects we have highlighted above, such as the inherent and control risks of the particular account balances. The setting of individual materiality levels is an important task because it influences the nature and scope of work the auditors will perform on individual account balances. The lower the materiality levels the greater the amount of audit work the auditors will have to perform and vice versa. These materiality levels might become the tolerable error level that auditors use in their substantive testing. This is particularly the case where auditors use statistical sampling which requires an estimate of tolerable error for evaluation purposes.

We suggested above that auditors *might* use the materiality level for the component as the tolerable error. This is not necessarily the case, however, because audit firms sometimes arbitrarily adjust (usually reduce) the component materiality level when arriving at tolerable level. This might be done for a variety of reasons, such as prudence or because of evidence arising from other tests relating to the same item. No matter how the auditors arrive at the materiality levels they should always record the levels and reasons for the levels in their audit files. In particular, at the planning stage they should document decisions relating to materiality in the audit planning memoranda.

Materiality during the audit

See ISA 320, paras 12 and 13.

During the audit the auditors may have to change their views about the appropriate materiality level for a particular account balance. This may occur, for instance, when at the commencement of the audit the auditors find that changes have been made to the draft accounts. If the profit figure has changed, or inventory or trade receivables figures have been amended, the auditors will have to consider the implications of the changes and decide if their original materiality levels require amending. Evidence gathered during audit testing might also result in reassessment of materiality levels. For instance, if the auditors find during their audit of inventory a larger number of errors than they expected, they may decide that the materiality level should be reduced. Alternatively, they may discover that the method of recording inventory, valuing inventory or the personnel in charge of inventory has changed. If this has occurred the auditors have to decide if the changes have any implications for their assessment of materiality. As a result of this reassessment the auditors may also decide to change the nature and scope of audit testing.

Materiality at the evaluation stage

After auditors have conducted their audit tests the effect of any misstatements found have to be evaluated. This requires the auditors to determine the amount by which each of the components of the financial statements may be misstated and to calculate the sum total of all misstatements. At this point the auditors have a value for the misstatements or errors they have found. What they do not have is a value for the misstatements or errors their audit tests have *not* discovered, but may exist in the total population. The next stage in this process therefore is for the auditors to estimate the amount of potential errors in the components of the financial statements and in the financial statements taken as a whole. This is not an easy task and requires the auditors to extrapolate from the test results. The estimation of the misstatements that

See our earlier discussion on performance materiality.

they have not identified but which may exist in the total population relies again on the auditors' professional judgement. The closer the value of the misstatements found as a result of audit tests is to the set materiality level, the more likely it becomes that the sum of the detected and undetected misstatements will exceed the materiality level.

If as a result of their estimation process the auditors find that their estimate of misstatements is less than the various materiality levels they have set, they can conclude that the financial statements are not materially misstated. However, if the auditor's evaluation of uncorrected and estimated undetected misstatements is close to the materiality level then the auditor may decide to extend their audit tests to reduce the possibility of the materiality level being exceeded.

If the auditors' estimate of the misstatements exceeds one of the materiality criteria, we must ask what steps auditors should take in respect of misstatements they have discovered as a result of audit testing. The auditors will consider their nature, discuss them with management, and determine if management intend to adjust the components of the financial statements for the errors. Assuming there is nothing contentious about the misstatements, management should be willing to make the necessary adjustments. If after discussion, management is not willing to adjust the financial statements the auditors must ascertain the reasons for this, and decide on an appropriate course of action. One of the reasons why management may not be willing to alter the financial statements is that they do not accept that there is a misstatement. For instance, the auditors may believe that management's estimate of the bad debt provision is too low, but management do not agree and believe that the auditors' estimate is too high. If the difference between the two estimates is not material and the auditors remain convinced that their estimate is the appropriate one, the auditors may simply treat it as an unadjusted misstatement. Alternatively, the auditors may extend the scope of their audit tests and obtain additional evidence pertinent to the bad debt provision. They might, for instance, do further work such as reviewing after date receipts from trade receivables to discover if old receivables balances remain uncleared. If these tests confirm the auditors' belief in their estimate of the bad debt provision they may approach management again and try to convince them to adjust the provision. It is important that the auditor documents in their working files all misstatements above a trivial amount which have been corrected and uncorrected by management. Where management indicate they do not want to adjust for a particular misstatement and the auditors believe it is an important item, then it should be brought to the attention of the audit committee where one exists. It would also be beneficial for the audit committee to receive from the auditors a list, perhaps in summary form, of the misstatements that have been found during the audit and corrected by management.

See paras 8 and 9 of ISA 450.

The schedule compiled of uncorrected misstatements will usually be one of the items included in the Letter of Representation (see Chapter 14).

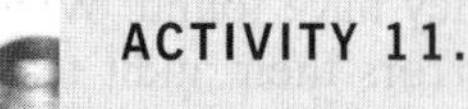

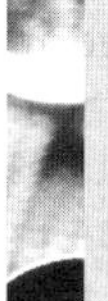

ACTIVITY 11.6

In the above paragraph, we said that auditors would have to consider the nature of the misstatements found. Suggest aspects of the nature of misstatements the auditors may wish to consider when performing their evaluation.

The auditors may well be interested in the following features.

- *The size and incidence of any errors or misstatements they have discovered.* For instance, have they discovered a large number of small errors or a small number of large errors?
- *Whether the errors or misstatements exhibit some pattern.* For instance, the majority of the errors may have occurred during a particular period of the year. Thus, a large number of them may have occurred when the accountant was on holiday and checking was rather haphazard. In this case, the auditors would discuss the issue with the accountant and probably ask for assistance in evaluating the extent of the errors during his holiday period. Alternatively, if the misstatements were all close to the year-end, this might indicate that the client is attempting to manipulate their financial statements.
- *Whether the errors or misstatements relate to factual matters or to matters of opinion.* For instance, the provision for bad debts mentioned above is a matter of opinion, whereas errors in counting stock quantities are factual.
- *Whether the misstatements found relate to matters that are illegal.* For instance, the auditors might have discovered sales invoices without VAT for payment in cash or small illegal payments, such as backhanders to local authority officials to gain advantage in commercial relationships. These misstatements may not themselves be significant in amount, but the potential costs if they come to the attention of tax authorities and regulators, for instance, may be high.
- *Whether there is any suspicion that some of the misstatements may have arisen because of fraud being perpetrated by employees in the company.* For instance, under-pricing of invoices may be done in collusion with customers.
- *Whether similar misstatements have been discovered in previous years' audits of this client.* This may be an indicator of poor management practices, particularly if the auditors have included the matter in the previous year's management letter.
- *Whether the misstatements affect only balance sheet items or whether they affect the profit and loss account.* For instance, the auditors might have discovered that a significant purchase on credit of fixed assets has occurred near the end of the year but has not been recorded in the books of the company. If depreciation is calculated using a low depreciation rate, the effect on profit may not be material, but the impact on liquidity ratios may be substantial because of the missing liability.

When we discuss audit reports in Chapter 16 you will see that auditors do not disclose in the audit report the level of materiality. The lack of disclosure has been criticized by Roberts and Dwyer (1998) who suggest it is symptomatic of a paternalistic approach taken by auditors. They argue that auditors, when assessing materiality, are effectively calculating the level of errors and misstatements that are likely to be considered material by users. However, having done this they do not inform the users what level of materiality they have used. An alternative perspective put forward by the same authors is that the non-disclosure of the materiality level is intentional in order to maintain a certain amount of mystification about the work they perform. The authors conclude by stating that the auditors, by not disclosing the materiality level, are not fulfilling their public interest duties but instead are acting in their own self-interest. We can see that consideration of materiality is not just about making quantitative comparisons between the materiality level and the expected amount of misstatements but also involves qualitative issues. To further emphasize this in the next section we discuss a number of other issues related to materiality.

Qualitative issues

A number of matters other than size that might affect the materiality of an item are listed in para A16 of ISA 450.

Thus far the discussion has been in terms of the misstatement of financial statement items or components. This would include those occasions where items are omitted from the financial statements. In addition the auditors need to have regard to the following considerations:

- *Whether the item is required to be disclosed by law or by professional requirements*. For instance, disclosure of directors' remuneration and capital commitments are required by the Companies Act 2006, and disclosures concerning leases should be in accordance with SSAP 21 and IAS 17. In these situations because they are concerned with legal or accounting standard requirements the auditors would ask the client company to change the disclosures to ensure compliance with the regulations.
- *Improper disclosure of accounting policies.* Improper disclosure may mislead the reader. For instance, a statement that the company exercises significant influence over certain companies, when it is clear that such influence does not, in fact, exist. In this type of example, the auditors would have to discuss the misleading policy with the directors and ask them to amend the wording so that it is clearer.
- *Improper classifications in the financial statements.* For instance, including certain expenses as part of the costs from discontinued operations when they are, in fact, part of the costs from continuing operations.

Conclusions on materiality

We discuss audit reports in Chapter 16.

After performing audit tests and having arrived at an estimate of the expected level of misstatement, the auditors have to form a conclusion about whether their amount or nature is material. This would normally be done after the client has adjusted for any errors found during the audit. If the remaining unadjusted misstatements plus the estimated undetected misstatements amount to less than the various materiality levels, the auditors would give an unmodified audit report, assuming of course that there are no other issues. However, if the materiality level is exceeded the auditors would have to enter into discussions with management about what should be done. It may be that auditors can perform additional audit tests to determine if their estimate of the extent of the misstatements is too high. If the misstatement relates to a difference in opinion about the amount that should be provided in respect of unrecorded liabilities or provision for bad debts it may be that the directors and the auditors will reach a compromise that will satisfy them both. Alternatively, if the problem is of a qualitative nature, such as the wording of an accounting policy, management may be prepared to reword the disclosed policy. If after discussion and further work the auditors are still concerned about what they believe is a material misstatement in the financial statements, they should consider modifying the audit report. Obviously, this is a last resort and in practice most differences of opinion between auditors and client companies are sorted out before this extreme action is taken. As a final word, auditors should resist altering their materiality levels upwards to such an extent that the misstatements are no longer material.

Summary

In this chapter we have discussed the twin concepts of audit sampling and materiality. We have shown how audit sampling may be classified as non-statistical sampling and statistical sampling. We highlighted the important factors that determine sample size, such as confidence level and expected error rate. In respect of statistical sampling we discussed two types in detail: attribute and monetary unit sampling. We emphasized that the former is mostly used in assessing whether a company's controls are working satisfactorily, whereas the latter is used to determine the extent of potential errors or misstatements in account balances. In respect of materiality we described how materiality in financial statements is related to the use made of financial statements by users. We discussed a number of factors, both quantitative and qualitative, which influence auditors when arriving at a materiality level. We also described how auditors use materiality at the planning stage, during the audit and in the evaluation stage of the audit.

Key points of the chapter

- Auditors seek sufficient appropriate evidence to be reasonably certain that audit conclusions are soundly based and at a reasonable cost. At the outset they decide when it is appropriate to use audit sampling.

Sampling

- Audit testing of a sample *representative* of the total population should enable auditors to conclude on the total population. If sample sizes are too small, auditors will have failed to collect sufficient, appropriate evidence.
- In statistical sampling probability theory determines sample size and random selection ensures each item or £1 value has the same chance of selection as any other. Non-statistical sampling typically uses haphazard selection and placing no reliance on probability theory.
- Careful planning of the sampling process is essential to reduce 'sampling risk'. The characteristics of the population must be clearly identified.
- Non-statistical sampling is often termed judgemental sampling. Judgement is a feature of statistical sampling too, but there may be a reduction in judgement required.
- A population is homogeneous if all items have the same characteristics. Factors causing lack of homogeneity include: (a) transactions not subjected to the same internal controls; (b) balances with widely different values. It is common practice to stratify populations and to treat each stratum as a different population.
- A sample is taken from the whole population and may be selected in various ways: (a) random; (b) systematic or interval; (c) block or cluster; (d) haphazard sampling.
- Audit evidence must be *sufficient*, so sample size is important. Size of samples is dependent on: (a) level of confidence required; (b) expected error rate; (c) tolerable error rate.
- Level of confidence is influenced by assessment of inherent and control risks, and may be reduced by evidence from other relevant audit tests, such as analytical review.
- The greater the expected error rate, the greater the sample size needed. Auditors must define an error or deviation beforehand.
- Tolerable error rate or amount is the maximum error rate or amount auditors are prepared to accept. The lower the tolerable error rate or amount the greater the sample size.
- Population size has little effect on sample size.
- Sample size may be calculated using reliability factors and tolerable error rate. Reliability factors are dependent on required confidence level and expectation of likely number of errors.
- The first stage in evaluation is to determine the number of errors in the sample. The next is to estimate the upper error rate (UER) in the population, using reliability factors and sample size. Auditors decide on appropriate action on the basis of sample results.

Auditors are also concerned with the nature of the errors identified.

- Attribute sampling tests internal control systems whereas monetary unit sampling is used to estimate the amount by which an account balance is in error. MUS is used to estimate the most likely error (MLE) and the likely upper error level (or monetary precision) in monetary terms. MUS divides the population into £1 units. Errors found taint the transaction or balance to which the £1 is attached. Confidence level and tolerable error and estimate of likely error, are used to determine the appropriate sample size.
- When evaluating sample results auditors calculate Most Likely Error, supplemented by calculating an estimate of Upper Error Level. If UEL is less than tolerable error, the auditors can accept the population. If UEL remains above the tolerable error, the auditors carry out extended or alternative procedures.
- Advantages of statistical sampling are; (a) requires auditors to make explicit their judgements; (b) Sample size is based on statistical principles and evaluation of results is quantified and more precise.
- Disadvantages of statistical sampling are: (a) time-consuming and costly; (b) requires documents or account balances to be separately identified; (c) more difficult to understand for non-statistician.
- Since the early 1990s the use of statistical sampling has decreased and is more likely to be used in specialized audit situations. There has been an increased use of risk-based auditing using audit software, and more emphasis on evaluating the effectiveness of the control environment.
- Other statistical sampling methods include: (a) discovery sampling; (b) variables sampling, including: (i) mean per unit method; (ii) ratio and difference method.

Materiality

- Auditors have to judge when misstatements or omissions are material enough to cause financial statements not to give a true and fair view.
- 'Materiality' is an expression of the relative significance or importance of a particular matter in the context of the financial statements as a whole; a matter is material if its omission or misstatement would reasonably influence the decisions of a user of the financial statements.
- Auditors often direct attention to the profit before tax figure when determining materiality level, but look at nature and extent of 'errors' and company context before taking a final decision about materiality. The lower the materiality level the greater the quantity of evidence required.
- Auditors set materiality levels for other figures such as turnover and total assets and normally calculate materiality levels based on several criteria and then decide on appropriate materiality levels for different aspects of the audit.
- Auditors must ensure that they give the same stress to under- and overstatements.
- Auditors may also consider: (a) trend in profits; (b) effect of profit figure on ratios; (c) external influences; (d) poor performance and difficulties in raising finance.
- Auditors set materiality levels at the audit planning stage to put audit risk into context.. Most risks relate to specific financial statement headings and auditors assign a materiality level to components of the financial statements based on: (a) importance of the heading; (b) nature of item; (c) auditors' past experience; (d) trend in the account balance. Auditors record and explain materiality levels.
- Auditors may change their views about materiality levels because of: (a) changes to draft accounts; (b) evidence gathered during audit testing.
- The effect of any misstatements are evaluated and an estimate made of the amount of potential errors in the components of the financial statements and in the financial statements taken as a whole.
- If management decides not to adjust the auditors should determine the reasons. If errors may be material they extend the scope of audit tests. In evaluating misstatements they consider: (a) size and incidence;(b) if 'errors' exhibit a pattern; (c) if 'errors' are factual or matters of opinion; (d) if the 'errors' relate to illegal matters; (e) if there is suspicion of fraud; (f) if similar 'errors' were discovered in previous year; (g) whether misstatements affect only balance sheet items or the profit and loss account too.
- Qualitative issues should also be considered, such as: (a) whether the item is required to be disclosed; (b) whether accounting policies are improperly disclosed; (c) where there is improper classification.
- When management refuse to correct a misstatement the auditor should consider including details in the letter of representation.
- Where an audit committee exists the auditors will provide them with details of uncorrected misstatements and some summary details of corrected misstatements.
- Some commentators believe auditors should disclose level of materiality in the audit report.

References

Manson, S. (1997) 'Audit Risk and Sampling', Chapter 13 in Sherer, M. and Turley, S. (eds), *Current Issues in Auditing*, third edition, London: Paul Chapman Publishing Ltd.

Roberts, R.W. and Dwyer, P.D. (1998) 'An Analysis of Materiality and Reasonable Assurance: Professional Mystification and Paternalism in Auditing', *Journal of Business Ethics*, 17, No.5: pp.569–78.

Further reading

You should inform yourself of the content of The International Auditing Standards ISA 530 – *Audit sampling*, ISA 320 – *Materiality in planning and performing an audit* and ISA 450 – *Evaluation of misstatements identified during the audit.*

If you wish to know about the technique and application of monetary unit sampling you should read the draft audit brief, *Audit sampling*, published by the Auditing Practices Committee in 1987.

Two articles which examine the rise in the use of sampling by auditors, both of which are very interesting, are:

Carpenter, B. and Dirsmith, M. (1993) 'Sampling and the Abstraction of Knowledge in the Auditing Profession: An Extended Institutional Theory Perspective', *Accounting, Organizations and Society*, 18(1): 41–63.

Power, M.K. (1992) 'From Commonsense to Expertise: Reflections on the Prehistory of Audit Sampling', *Accounting, Organizations and Society*, 17(1): 37–62.

A good review of research into materiality is given in:

Iskandar, T.M. and Iselin, E.R. (1999) 'A Review of Materiality Research', *Accounting Forum*, 23(3), September: 209–39.

Self-assessment questions (solutions available to students)

11.1 Consider the following statements and explain why they may be true or false:

(a) Statistical sampling methods do not require auditors to exercise judgement.

(b) Tolerable error is the amount of error auditors expect to find in an account balance.

(c) Monetary unit sampling is a form of statistical sampling that enables auditors to estimate both the most likely monetary error in an account balance and the upper error limit.

(d) Auditors only use the concept of materiality at the final stage of an audit when considering whether the financial statements give a true and fair view.

(e) The most important factor influencing the materiality of an item in the financial statements is its monetary value.

(f) When setting a materiality level for the financial statements an important factor influencing the auditors' decision is likely to be the company's profit for the year.

11.2 It is important to recognize that audit sampling may be constructed on a non-statistical basis. If the auditors use statistical sampling, probability theory will be used to determine sample size and random selection methods to ensure that each item or £1 in value of the population has the same chance of selection. Non-statistical sampling is more subjective than statistical sampling, typically using haphazard selection methods and placing no reliance upon probability theory. However, in certain circumstances statistical sampling techniques may be difficult to use. The auditors will review the circumstances of each audit before deciding whether to use statistical or non-statistical sampling.

Required:

(a) List three situations where the auditors would be unlikely to use audit sampling techniques.

(b) Explain what you understand by the following terms:

- attribute sampling;
- monetary unit sampling.

(c) Describe the factors which auditors would consider when determining the size of a sample.

(d) Describe to what extent statistical sampling enhances the quality of audit evidence. (ACCA, Paper 6 Auditing, June 1993)

11.3 Leslie Ltd has had a trend of profits in the past five years as set forth below:

Year to 31 December	£
2006	100 000
2007	125 000
2008	150 000
2009	175 000
2010	200 000 (per draft accounts)

During the year to 31 December 2010, you discover that inventories have been overstated by £5000 and that, in consequence, profits have been overstated by the same amount. Would you consider that the accounts should be adjusted for the error of £5000?

11.4 During the audit of Leven Ltd for the year ended 31 March 2010, your audit tests reveal that trade receivables include £30 000 for a customer who went into liquidation shortly before the end of the financial year. Leven's profits for the year amount to £190 000 and receivables shown in the balance sheet are stated at £585 000. The directors do not wish to reduce the stated profits to £160 000 and the receivables to £555 000 and suggest that the accounts will still give a true and fair view if the notes to the accounts explain that the debtor has gone into liquidation and that no amount is expected to be received from the liquidator. Do you agree? What would you say to the directors?

Self-assessment questions (solutions available to tutors)

11.5 On page 417 of this chapter we noted that Roberts and Dwyer (1998) appear to suggest that auditors should disclose the level of materiality they have used when conducting the audit. Can you suggest any reasons why auditors may be unwilling to follow this suggestion?

11.6 In this chapter we have referred to the term non-sampling risk. Outline what you believe the term means and give some examples of what you consider to be a non-sampling risk.

11.7 Give some examples of qualitative characteristics an auditor might take into account when deciding if a particular item in the financial statements is materially misstated.

Topics for class discussion without solutions

11.8 Discuss the assertion that the use of statistical sampling by auditors is in decline.

11.9 Sampling and materiality are both related to audit risk. Discuss

11.10 When setting materiality levels it is crucial that the auditor considers the external environment. Discuss

12

Final work: general principles, analytical review of financial statements, non-current assets and trade receivables

LEARNING OBJECTIVES

After studying this chapter you should be able to:

- **Explain the importance of planning the year-end examination on the basis of interim work and other information about the organization.**
- **Describe the kind of work carried out on or near the balance sheet date.**
- **Show how audit techniques discussed earlier can be applied during the final work on selected assets and related profit and loss account headings.**
- **Describe specific matters, including risk assessments, relating to audit of selected financial statement headings.**
- **Explain why the auditor analyses financial statements before and after performing detailed audit work.**
- **Describe the techniques employed by the auditor in analysing financial statements.**

Learning objectives, 423
Introduction, 424
Pre-Final work, 424
Balance sheet date work, 425
Bridging work between conclusion of interim work and the balance sheet date, 427
Analytical procedures, 428
Detailed final audit work: general matters, 441
Tangible non-current assets and depreciation, 448
Trade receivables and sales, 464
Summary, 480
Key points of the chapter, 480
Further reading, 482
Self-assessment questions (solutions available to students), 483
Self-assessment questions (solutions available to tutors), 483
Topics for class discussion without solutions, 484

INTRODUCTION

In this book we have adopted the general timescale of the audit year. We have now completed interim work, when we formed conclusions about the operation of systems and whether transactions processed by those systems were genuine, accurate and complete. The next stage is to plan the final work needed to form an opinion on the financial statements taken as a whole. In this chapter we consider the work auditors perform to prepare for final work and then move to examination of selected assets and related income and expense. As in previous chapters we assume that the audit client is sufficiently large to allow the audit year to be planned in the way suggested in Figure 6.3 on page 230. The amount of work that the auditor deems necessary on final balances will depend on two factors:

1 The inherent and control risk related to the balances.
2 The significance of the balances in the context of the truth and fairness of the financial statements.

PRE-FINAL WORK

By the time the interim examination is complete, auditors will have collected much information about the client and should be aware of the main problems management are likely to encounter in preparing the year-end financial statements. Auditors will also have adapted the audit plan in the light of risks related to problem areas not anticipated at the initial planning stage. For instance, the management of County Hotel had expected that new bathrooms would be installed in the year to 31 December 2010. If the work had been completed it would be relatively easy to determine final cost, but if in fact work will not be completed before the year-end, management should ensure that:

See the planning memorandum on page 199.

- Costs incurred have been properly collected.
- Assets in course of construction account have been correctly debited.
- Payments in advance are properly reflected in the financial statements.

This may not be difficult, but auditors should address the new circumstances and advise management about the disclosure and accounting treatment. If unforeseen circumstances arise, the audit firm may have to re-schedule the work programme. For instance, a staff member experienced in inventory valuation might be attached to the audit team if the interim examination has revealed some lines are not selling well and pricing at net realizable value might be appropriate. The audit firm should plan to re-plan if this proves necessary, which it will, more often than not. Apart from this, discussions with management will normally be desirable to ensure that preparation of financial statements runs smoothly and timetables are met. It is vital that auditors maintain regular contact with management to detect problems at an early date and to take steps to solve them. We set out below a typical agenda for such discussions:

- Matters arising from interim examination, such as incomplete work on bathrooms and slow movement of some inventory lines.

- Preparation by management of inventory count instructions – the system for determining inventory quantities.
- Timetable for preparation of year-end financial statements. It is normal practice to set a deadline for completion of audit work as the annual general meeting is fixed in advance. Just as important, however, are management deadlines for such matters as inventory valuation, balancing of trade receivables and payables ledgers, preparation of accruals schedules, and so on. Failure to meet internal deadlines may make it difficult for auditors to meet their deadlines and they should be discussed in advance.

We discuss the auditor's observation of inventory counts in Chapter 13.

- Accounting and reporting standards. Most accounting standards require considerable disclosure and management should plan to collect the required information in advance of the year-end. The auditor would wish to ensure the company has a system to collect the necessary information.

We comment briefly on the audit implications of accounting standards below.

- New legislation. New companies and tax legislation requirements, and stock exchange requirements are examples of matters that should be discussed with management.
- Auditing standards. Auditing standards have an impact on the auditor's work and it may be necessary to discuss them with management. ISA 315 – *Identifying and assessing the risks of material misstatement through understanding the entity and its environment* is an example of a standard with considerable impact on audit work.

We now turn to work specifically performed at or near the year-end.

BALANCE SHEET DATE WORK

Certain classes of audit work can only be performed at the year-end, some, such as inventory count observations, because of the nature of the work, and others, such as obtaining confirmations from banks, because special agreements make year-end work necessary. We discuss typical audit work at the balance sheet date below.

- *Bank confirmations*. In Chapter 6 we discussed various kinds of audit evidence and concluded that evidence from independent third-party/external professional persons is good evidence. As part of their verification procedures, auditors obtain confirmation from bank managers of bank balances and other matters at the year-end. We do not discuss the requirements in detail, but APB Practice Note (PN 16) – *Bank reports for audit purposes in the United Kingdom (revised),* issued by the APB in 2006, describes arrangements agreed between the APB and the British Bankers Association. Other countries may have similar requirements.

  The requirements are basically a sensible attempt to make life easier for both banks and auditors. The information requested from banks does not merely relate to details of bank accounts held in the entity's name but also such matters as customer's assets held, either as security or for safe custody, of contingent liabilities, bank overdraft limits and certain other information. Appendix 1 to PN 16 contains templates for auditor request forms. Appendix 2 is an example of authority by the client for the bank to disclose information. Appendix 3 contains guidance to bankers.

See Chapter 6, pages 220 to 224. Refer also to Figure 6.2 (page 227).

One important matter is that PN 16 suggests that bank letters be sent to banks one month in advance of the period-end date. Large organizations, particularly those with a large number of overseas subsidiaries, are likely to have many bank balances in different branches. Overseas bank balances will require to be translated at the appropriate rate at the year-end.

- *Inventory count observation*. Companies perform inventory counts to confirm the existence and condition of inventories and to help ensure there is a proper relationship to purchases and sales (cut-off). Auditors perform both tests of control and substantive auditing procedures when they are present at inventory counts.
- *Long-term construction contracts*. Companies involved in long-term construction contract work have a number of important matters to consider in respect of long-term construction contracts, including stage of completion and amount of profit to be taken up before completion. Stage of completion should clearly be determined at the year-end. We discuss the accounting for and audit of long-term construction contracts in Chapter 13.
- *Non-current assets in course of construction*. Non-current assets in course of construction should be transferred to appropriate asset accounts on completion and management should have procedures to ensure that state of completion is known at the year-end. The auditor may decide to observe significant assets at the balance sheet date.

We discuss confirmation of trade receivables in greater detail below. ISA 505 – *External confirmations* discusses confirmations requested from the third-party individuals and groups mentioned here.

- *Circularization of customers and suppliers*. It is the practice for auditors to ask the client to write to customers and suppliers asking them to confirm balances in their books direct to the auditors and this may be done at interim or final examination. If at the latter, it will be desirable to send the letters just prior to the balance sheet date if replies are to be received by the date the audit report is required.
- *Letters to other professionals*. Professional people with special expertise may also be sent letters near to the balance sheet date, asking for confirmation of matters known to them, including:
  - (a) Surveyors: stage of completion of long-term construction contracts.
  - (b) Lawyers: legal matters affecting the company.
  - (c) Actuaries: matters relating to pension schemes.
  - (d) Valuers: non-current assets revaluation.
  - (e) Geologists: quantification of mineral reserves.

Work done at the pre-final and balance sheet date is vital because tight deadlines for issue of audit reports mean that as much work as possible must be carried out prior to the final examination. The auditor who has planned properly, carried out substantial portions of the work prior to the final examination and kept in regular touch with management officials, should not expect to find major problems during the period leading up to the giving of the opinion. This is not to say that unexpected problems will not arise, but they should be unlikely.

We remind you that the final examination is performed in the context of the interim and pre-final work and the conclusions formed earlier:

- Conclusions on the operation of accounting and control systems – following tests of controls.

- Conclusions on whether the assets are being safeguarded and whether transactions and balances recorded in the accounting records are genuine, accurate and complete – following substantive procedures.
- Discussion with management of the known problems affecting the organization and the solutions that appear to be most appropriate in the circumstances – pre-final work.
- The auditors have amended the audit plan for matters not contained in the original plan. Audit and company deadlines will also have been discussed – pre-final work.
- The auditors have, near or at the balance sheet date, carried out certain audit procedures which can only be performed at that time, such as inventory count observation.
- The auditors have carried out an analytical review of the financial statements to put their work in context.

BRIDGING WORK BETWEEN CONCLUSION OF INTERIM WORK AND THE BALANCE SHEET DATE

We call it bridging work because it bridges the period from the interim to year-end and beyond.

As suggested above, the auditor will have formed judgements about many matters at interim dates and will use these judgements in supporting conclusions at the final examination. However, some time normally elapses between interim and final examinations and the auditor should ascertain that the conclusions formed earlier are still valid. Thus, before starting the final examination, the auditor pauses and considers carefully the results of previous work. In particular, the auditor reconsiders strengths and weaknesses in accounting and control systems and performs so-called bridging work for the period between the interim examination and the balance sheet date. This is to ensure that systems operated as expected during the whole year and not merely for part of it. If the auditors had made recommendations to improve systems, they should determine if they had been effected as this may colour their views on the reliability of accounting records. For instance, if the Broomfield plc directors have introduced our recommendations, the auditor might be prepared to accept the system as basically reliable. The auditor might decide to perform some tests of control and carry out substantive procedures on transactions and balances in the intervening period. Typical substantive procedures include:

Refer to the management letter set out in Figure 10.3 on page 380.

- Reviewing sales records to ensure there are no significant departures from expectation. For instance, if there had been material returns from customers in the period between the conclusion of the interim work and the year-end, it would trigger inquiry:
  - (a) Had there been a breakdown in production inspection procedures? Is it likely that trade receivables contain irrecoverable amounts as a result?
  - (b) Had there been problems in purchasing goods of the requisite quality? Is it likely that inventories include goods of poor quality that should be valued at a figure lower than cost?

- Review of non-current asset purchases in the intervening period and comparison with budget to ensure that company controls over the purchase of non-current assets appear adequate.

ANALYTICAL PROCEDURES

We assume that you have already covered interpretation of financial statements in your other studies. In this section we shall ask you to apply existing knowledge to auditing and perhaps enhance your appreciation of interpretation of financial statements in the process. Paragraph 4 of ISA 520 – *Analytical procedures* defines them as:

> Evaluations of financial information through analysis of plausible relationships among both financial and non-financial data. Analytical procedures also encompass such investigation as is necessary of identified fluctuations or relationships that are inconsistent with other relevant information or that differ from expected values by a significant amount.

We have made clear that an audit is a search for evidence and we have given you many examples of how the search is conducted. Not only must the search be on a global and detailed basis but also within a clearly understood risk context. For instance, in the textbook publishing sector, competitors may be publishing texts in the same area as those written by the company's own authors. Auditors of a publishing company would have to understand the nature of different texts and what makes them attractive, the market to which they appeal and how up to date they are. Without this knowledge auditors would find it difficult to interpret sales trends and saleability of books on hand. Auditors should also consider the logic of the figures. In a notorious case in the United States in the 1960s (The Salad Oil Case) the inventories of salad oil stated in the records of the company exceeded the entire inventories of salad oil in the United States at a particular point in time and this was not picked up by internal auditors or the warehousing company supposedly managing the company's tank farm. Informed analysis of information can be a valuable tool for setting the scene and pinpointing areas of risk. We shall now put analytical procedures on to a more formal basis and start with a number of general observations:

Some auditors use the term 'diagnostic procedures' to describe analytical procedures.

First, long before the auditors give their opinion on the financial statements, they use analytical procedures at the planning stage to pinpoint critical areas where audit risk may be high. This is suggested by paragraphs A7 and A8 of ISA 315:

> A7. Analytical procedures performed as risk assessment procedures may identify aspects of the entity of which the auditor was unaware and may assist in assessing the risks of material misstatement in order to provide a basis for designing and implementing responses to the assessed risks. Analytical procedures performed as risk assessment procedures may include both financial and non-financial information, for example, the relationship between sales and square footage of selling space or volume of goods sold.
>
> A8. Analytical procedures may help identify the existence of unusual transactions or events, and amounts, ratios, and trends that might indicate matters that have audit implications. Unusual or unexpected relationships that are identified may assist the auditor in identifying risks of material misstatement, especially risks of material misstatement due to fraud.

If you refer to Figure 6.3 you will see mention of analytical review at preliminary stage 3, and at stage 16 analytical procedures were used to set the scene for, and to aid planning of, the final work on year-end financial statements.

Second, analytical procedures are also used as substantive procedures when responding to the risk of material misstatement at the assertion level. Thus they are used at stage 10 in Figure 6.3 during audit of specific transactions or figures (such as purchases). It is always useful to know how important particular figures or sets of transactions and balances are when discussing audit matters with management. You will remember that analysis of interim figures of Powerbase (discussed in Chapter 10) was useful in directing detailed substantive procedures. Clearly analytical procedures may be regarded as substantive procedures in their own right, in so far as they confirm the reasonability of the figures. We discuss this matter at greater length below.

Third, analytical procedures are used just before the end of the audit as paragraph 6 of ISA 520 makes clear:

> The auditor shall design and perform analytical procedures near the end of the audit that assist the auditor when forming an overall conclusion as to whether the financial statements are consistent with the auditor's understanding of the entity.

At stage 19 the analytical procedures are performed in the context of conclusions drawn from detailed audit evidence. In other words the auditors have already formed views on individual figures in the financial statements, but need to see that the figures are reasonable taken together. Specifically, auditors try to determine whether in their opinion:

(a) The financial statements have been prepared using consistent accounting principles (unless the effect of material change is disclosed) and are appropriate to the company's circumstances.

(b) Information published in the financial statements and other information issued with them are compatible with the auditor's knowledge of the company and with each other.

(c) Presentation and disclosure in the financial statements are as required by law and by regulatory bodies and in particular aid the achievement of truth and fairness.

(d) Conclusions drawn from other tests, together with those drawn from the overall review of the financial statements, enable an opinion to be formed on those statements.

(e) In performing the overall review the auditor compares the financial statements or individual pieces of information with other available data. For the review to be effective the auditor needs to have sufficient knowledge of the activities of the enterprise and of its business to determine whether particular items are abnormal.

Fourth, the auditor has to be sure of the reliability of the figures used in performing analytical procedures. For instance if the auditors are comparing actual figures with budgeted figures, they have to ensure that the budgets are reliable estimates of future activity. They also have to be sure that, if they are using statistical information prepared by management, that the controls over the preparation of the statistics are designed to ensure completeness, accuracy

See paragraph A12 of ISA 520.

and validity. For instance when we prepared the audit planning memorandum for the audit of County Hotel we included the following:

See page 199.

> We should consider whether management statistics on room usage and usage of restaurant capacity are reliable as this may be the best way to satisfy ourselves that income is properly stated. The same applies to budgets of accommodation and restaurant costs, including food preparation. If they are carefully prepared estimates of expected costs, rather than goals to be achieved, we might be able to use them to compare with actual costs.

In Chapter 6 we suggested that 'Evidence created in the normal course of business is better than evidence specially created to satisfy the auditor.' Hotels need to keep detailed records of occupancy for management purposes and this information has to be accurate so they can tell a potential customer if a room is available or not, and whether parts of the year need special rates to encourage visitors. Statistics on room and restaurant usage can be helpful in substantiating accommodation and restaurant income. If auditors are satisfied that they are reliable, analysis of such statistics will become an integral part of substantive procedures.

Fifth, if the auditors are using only analytical procedures as substantive tests rather than tests of detail, they have to be quite sure that control risk is low. We have already observed in relation to payroll that auditors may restrict their substantive procedures to analytical reviews of the payroll. They may use such measures as: (a) trends of employee numbers; (b) relationship between employee numbers to sales and cost of sales excluding labour cost; (c) employee numbers multiplied by average wage for comparison with total wage bill; (d) employer contribution to social security checked globally by application of expected percentage of wage bill.

In this chapter we are still at stage 10 and we shall see that analytical procedures are used to direct audit effort in relation to classes of transactions and balances. Auditors like to ask if the figures make sense, as they look for inconsistencies in the figures in the light of what they know about the organization.

Do the figures make sense? A question to direct audit effort

We have seen that auditors seek background information to aid planning and to place audit work in context. During the audit, auditors acquire further detailed knowledge about such matters as management integrity, management objectives, accounting and control systems in place and performance of the company. They use this knowledge when assessing whether the figures in the financial statements make sense. Apart from this knowledge (described earlier as cumulative client knowledge), the auditor uses analytical procedures to aid analysis of the figures. Considerable experience and imagination is needed for this task and normally the work is performed by experienced staff. This is costly in fee terms, but a skilled review should result in time-savings as a major objective of analytical review is to direct audit effort towards risk areas and the reduction of audit effort elsewhere. Skilled analytical review may well reduce the extent of tests of detail.

All staff should, however, be encouraged to adopt an analytical approach.

Audit approach to analytical review of data

Auditors use ratio analysis and other interpretative tools in performing analytical procedures in a manner similar to investment analysts seeking to understand organizations on the basis of published financial statements. The big difference is that auditors, even external auditors, are really insiders and can obtain information not readily available to the investment analyst. In fact, the objective of the analytical review at any stage where the auditor is searching for evidence is to direct audit effort towards the evidence needed to form audit conclusions. For instance, if the financial statements showed that trade receivables represented 50 days' sales instead of 45 days', the auditor would be led to enquire about the reasons. These might include:

- *Errors* – (say) incorrect cut-off, overstating sales and trade receivables.
- *Changes in accounting practice*, such as special sales being shown in a separate heading of the financial statements instead of being included in general sales as previously.
- *Changes in management policy* – (say) a decision to allow customers to take extended credit.
- *Changes in general commercial factors*, such as worsening in the business climate resulting in poorer cash flows in the customers' businesses and hence an inability to pay on time. This might prompt the auditor to suggest a higher provision for bad and doubtful debts.
- *Changes in commercial factors affecting the client only* – (say) the company has a higher proportion of sales on credit so that trade receivables represent a higher proportion of total sales, despite little change in collectability. Normally collectability should be assessed in relation to credit sales, but we mention the point to emphasize the need for care in the use of data and information.
- *Fraud* – if, for instance, an employee has misappropriated cash received from customers on a significant scale, trade receivables may be overstated in the accounting records. We have already asked why the auditors of WorldCom failed to detect the very significant capitalization of items that should have appeared as an expense in the income statement.

The six headings above are a useful guide to factors the auditor should consider when investigating apparent inconsistencies in figures. All the examples relate to sales and trade receivables but examples could have been taken just as easily from other areas. Case study 12.1 contains financial statements of Kothari Limited. Although still in draft, they will form the basis of your final examination.

CASE STUDY 12.1

Kothari Limited: analytical review

The following information for the year to 30 April 2010 has been extracted from the accounting records of Kothari Limited, a manufacturing concern, together with comparative figures for 2009:

		2010		2009
	£000	£000	£000	£000
Turnover		4 600		3 000
Raw materials: Opening inventory	400		350	
Purchases	3 000		1 500	
Closing inventory	−800		−400	
Materials used	2 600		1 450	

		2010		2009
	£000	£000	£000	£000
Labour and factory overheads	1 550		750	
Production cost	4 150		2 200	
Work in progress: Opening	300		400	
Closing	−1 000		−300	
Factory cost: finished goods	3 450		2 300	
Finished goods: Opening inventory	500		550	
Closing inventory	−150		−500	
Cost of sales		3 800		2 350
Gross profit		800		650
Selling expenses	150		70	
Administrative expense	100		90	
Depreciation not yet allocated to headings	300		150	
		550		310
		250		340
Non-current assets		3 050		1 840
Current assets				
Stock of raw materials	800		400	
Work in progress	1 000		300	
Finished goods	150		500	
	1 950		1 200	
Trade receivables	1 650		750	
Trade payables	−700		−340	
Net current assets		2 900		1 610
Net assets employed		5 950		3 450
Financed by				
Share capital and reserves		3 500		3 000
Long-term borrowings		2 450		450
Net capital employed		5 950		3 450

ACTIVITY 12.1

Examine the draft financial statements of Kothari Limited and, without calculating any ratios, note matters of significance in the context of planning the final examination.

Before commenting on the information in the financial statements, we emphasize the following.

Approach to analytical review, particularly in the examination room

We believe that students in the examination room spend too much time calculating ratios, many of little value. We think that the best approach is as follows:

- Look at the figures broadly, before calculating any ratios. Ask the question: 'Are there any matters requiring further investigation?' For instance, you might note sales are higher (or lower) than the previous year, that gross profit looks high (or low) and stock levels look high (or low) this year compared with last year. Do not immediately suspect that fraud is taking place.
- The next step would be to calculate selected ratios to see if your initial impression was valid. For instance, you might wish to look at sales trends, to calculate gross profit percentages and turnover of stock. Leave the calculation of ratios until they are necessary. In the exam room, you will not have time to calculate inappropriate ratios. Be selective.
- Remember that many ratios are interrelated. For instance, poor liquidity may not be grave if low gearing and good profitability make practical a further injection of capital. Liquidity ratios should be interpreted in the light of inventory turnover (the rate at which inventory is converted to more liquid assets) and of trade receivables collectability and trade payables payment period. The gearing ratio may also be a useful guide to the ability of a company to raise additional funds.
- Bear in mind that analysis of financial statements is designed to direct audit effort and to prove that the financial statements do, in fact, show a true and fair view of what they purport to show.

Now let us comment on Kothari's draft financial statements:

- The first noticeable matter is the increase in sales from £m3000 to £m 4600 and you would ask why. You might decide that sales increases would only be likely if prices have reduced, so make a note to calculate gross profit percentage. You notice that selling expenses have increased considerably so you may decide initially that part of the increase is because of a sales push in the current year. (Make a note to check ratio of selling expense to sales.)
- Second, there seems to be strange developments affecting inventories and you note in particular that raw materials stocks have doubled (purchases likewise), but that finished goods inventory is much diminished (from £m500 to £m150). Work in progress too has shown a substantial increase (£m300 to £1000). You might decide that production activity has increased, but that this has not translated itself into finished goods, whose level suggests that existing inventory has been disposed of.
- The third matter of interest is that non-current assets have increased, another indicator of expansion. (You make a note to calculate non-current assets turnover ratio, but think that care should be taken with this ratio as the new non-current assets may not have been on-stream during the whole of this year.) Ask how the increase in non-current assets and working capital levels have been financed and make a note to take a look at the cash

We are not giving you the cash flow statement, but you might decide to take a look at liquidity and gearing ratios.

flow statement. However, it is clear from the financial statements that the increase in assets has been funded partly by shareholders but mainly by long-term borrowings.

You may have noted other matters but these seem to be the salient features.

ACTIVITY 12.2

Now that you have obtained a global view, select ratios that would support or refute the above observations. Do not overdo it. Remember that you wish to arm yourself with relevant information before you go to see the chief accountant.

We have calculated ten ratios. Have we overdone it?

We have calculated the following ratios to help us in our discussions with management.

	2010	2009
Increase in sales in %	53.33	
Fixed assets turnover ratio	1.51	1.63
Raw materials stock in days usage	112	101
Work in progress in days (in relation to factory cost)	106	48
Finished goods in days (in relation to cost of sales)	14	78
Gross profit %	17.39	21.67
Selling expense to sales (%)	3.26	2.33
Acid test ratio	2.36	2.21
Collectability of debtors in days	131	91
Total assets financed by non equity holders (%)	47.36	20.84

The above ratios confirm what we have already noticed in our first global analysis, although they do give some additional insights:

- The increase in non-current assets exceeds that of sales and this is borne out by the decrease in non-current assets turnover ratio from 1.63 to 1.51. You would want to find out from company management their thinking behind the programme of expansion and whether the non-current assets really contributed to this year's increase in sales.
- Selling expenses have increased in relation to sales and the auditor should discover what kinds of expense were included. For instance, the expansion in sales might have been partially triggered by an advertising campaign. At the same time we note that gross profit percentage has dropped by more than four points and this may have played a role. Clearly the auditor would wish to know more about the company's pricing policy.
- The acid test ratio appears to be high, but the company may still not have completed its expansion programme. Of course, we do not know what is a 'normal' ratio in this company's industry. One worrying feature that we did

not address above was the reduced collectability of trade receivables (the company is waiting for more than four months for payment) and you would want to find out why this is so. Poor collectability of trade receivables might hinder an expansion programme. There may of course be good reasons for poorer collectability

- The raw materials inventory position and the enhanced production cost seem reasonable in view of the expansion of the company. The finished inventory position looks strange, but it may be that the company is clearing out old lines at low prices (hence the lower gross margin) and starting to manufacture new lines which have not yet been completed and reflected in finished goods inventory.
- Gearing is clearly higher and this will mean higher interest charges in future years. The auditor would wish to know what the terms of the borrowings are, such as interest rates and repayment dates. It will probably be desirable to discuss long-term cash flows with management.

We hope that this example has given you insight into how analytical procedures can be used to direct audit effort and to prompt further questioning of management. As we mentioned above, we think that this approach can be useful in the examination room.

We have introduced words of warning at various stages in this book and we cannot proceed without a comment on the limitations of ratios. Ratio analysis can be a useful analytical tool, but ratios are meaningless unless they are compared with other ratios, such as ratios from the previous period, expected ratios as projected in budgets prepared by the company or the auditor, ratios of other parts of the business, ratios of other organizations in the same industry.

The comparison with other organizations in the same industry may be particularly useful and industrial/commercial sector statistics are available from a number of sources. However, the auditor must ensure that such statistics have been prepared in the same way as the ratios used for the company. Thus, paragraph A12 of ISA 520 states, among other things:

> The reliability of data is influenced by its source and nature and is dependent on the circumstances under which it is obtained. Accordingly, the following (is) relevant when determining whether data is reliable for purposes of designing substantive analytical procedures:
>
> (b) Comparability of the information available. For example, broad industry data may need to be supplemented to be comparable to that of an entity that produces and sells specialized products

Auditors should also be aware of special measures of success or performance indicators used in a particular industry. For instance, 'sales per square metre' and 'sales per employee' are important measures in the supermarket sector. This is an example of a relationship between financial and non-financial data.

Paragraph A2 of ISA 520 gives the example of the relationship between payroll costs and number of employees.

At the same time ratios must be handled with great care. If, for instance, non-current assets have been revalued during the year, comparison of non-current assets turnover ratios must take this into account. Ratios are only useful in the hands of an informed person. Do not imagine either that there is a magic acid test ratio that all companies should adhere to. Thus, it is common for supermarket companies to have an acid test ratio well below one, whereas companies in the furniture industry might only be safe with a ratio of well over one.

We emphasize that the auditor is concerned with obtaining insight into the reasons for deviations from expectation or for lack of deviation, when deviation is expected, and that frequently analysis will need to be carried out in great detail. For instance, details of gross profits may be available for individual products or product lines. This would clearly give more insight than a global review although the latter may pinpoint the need for greater analysis.

Other analytical tools

Apart from ratio analysis there are a number of other analytical tools that may be used by auditors:

- Graphs (similar to flowcharts in that they show detail visually). Graphs can be a useful tool when discussing audit results with clients.
- Regression analysis and multiple regression analysis. Analyses of this kind using past and projected data may aid the auditor by providing evidence of expectation in the light of which actual results may be interpreted.
- Use of Z-scores, a sophisticated and controversial form of ratio analysis. The score is produced from a number of financial ratios (appropriately weighted) and if the calculated score is very different from a benchmark figure there may be a heightened chance that they will face serious financial problems within a relatively short time period.

Substantive analytical procedures

In the case of Kothari we performed analytical review in the context of planning, the basic idea being to direct the auditor's attention to where audit work might be performed in critical areas. However, in Case study 12.2 we consider the use of substantive analytical procedures. If the analytical procedures suggest that the likelihood of misstatement of figures in the financial statements is low, this might allow the auditors to reduce the extent of detailed tests. Of course, if the likelihood of misstatement is high, the detailed tests might be extended.

ACTIVITY 12.3

You are manager in charge of the audit of Art Aid Limited for the year ended 28 February 2011 and you have obtained draft financial statements prepared by the accountant, as set out below. You are aware that there are some areas of particular risk in the company and have decided to use a combination of analytical procedures and tests of detail in forming a view of figures in the financial statements at the assertion level. You think too that there is likely to be scope for discussion of the company's business risks and the management's approach to them.

CASE STUDY 12.2

Art Aid Limited: analytical review

Art Aid Limited

Profit and loss account for the year ended 28 February 2011

	Total	Café	Gallery	Shop
Turnover	6 734 770	1 079 520	735 250	4 920 000
Costs				
Wages and commission, including directors' remuneration	1 630 000	400 000	200 000	1 030 000
Materials and artwork sold at cost	2 960 200	315 200	125 000	2 520 000
Sundry establishment expenses	530 000	30 000	250 000	250 000
Insurance	415 000	40 000	200 000	175 000
Bad debts	190 000	0	0	190 000
Fixtures depreciation	105 000	10 000	45 000	50 000
Sundry other expenses	460 000	150 000	200 000	110 000
Total costs	6 290 200	945 200	1 020 000	4 325 000
Operating profit	444 570	134 320	−284 750	595 000
Operating profit %	6.60	12.44	−38.73	12.09
Long-term interest	150 000			
Profit after interest	294 570			
Dividends	50 000			
Profit retained	244 570			
Retained profit b/f	−49 570			
Retained profit c/f	195 000			
Balance sheet at 28 February 2011				
Fixtures				
Cost			1 050 000	
Accumulated depreciation			630 000	
			420 000	
Current assets				
Inventories		2 500 000		
Trade receivables		240 000		
Cash		10 000		
		2 750 000		
Current liabilities				
Accounts payable	160 000			
Accrued expenses	15 000			
Bank overdraft	300 000	475 000		
Net current assets			2 275 000	
Assets employed			2 695 000	
Financed by:				
Share capital			1 000 000	
Retained profit			195 000	
			1 195 000	
Long-term loan			1 500 000	
Capital employed			2 695 000	

Art Aid Limited: analytical review

Art Aid Limited is a company providing services to local artists, including running art galleries and cafés in ten locations. Admission fees to the galleries vary depending on the reputation of the artist. The company has a policy of reduced admission fees for students, senior citizens and the unwaged. Attached to each gallery is a shop selling artists materials and providing a framing and hanging service. The shops sell paintings and sculptures, about 60 per cent of which are sold on commission on behalf of local artists. The rest of the work in the shops has been purchased by the company on a speculative basis, one of the directors, Brandon Smythe, being an art critic, who has an 'eye' for what might sell. The board has five members, including Brandon Smythe and John Leslie, a qualified accountant. The company employs a gallery manager and café/shop manager (both full time) for each location. The accounting department has two full-time staff as well as John Leslie. All other staff are part time. The galleries and cafés are open seven days per week.

Review the financial statements of Art Aid Limited and, using a risk-based approach, show with reasons why you would wish to pay particular attention to the following areas:

(a) Liquidity and gearing.

(b) High inventory levels.

(c) Gallery results.

(d) Treatment of the work of local artists displayed in the shop and the commission paid by them.

You may consider matters other than those in the financial statements, and ask yourself what additional information you would like to have.

Suggest substantive procedures to satisfy yourself that management assertions about the above four areas are valid in the context of the financial statements.

Remember that audit problems in one area may be linked to those in other areas, so look at the figures holistically and try to identify the real concerns in this particular organization.

We discuss the four areas below:

Art Aid appears to be in a poor liquid position (the acid test ratio is 0.52 to 1) coupled with high gearing (62 per cent of total assets are financed by sources other than equity). The acid test ratio looks low in view of the high gearing and the speculative nature of the inventories on hand. We discuss the inventories below.

Liquidity and high gearing are closely related, as companies may borrow (increasing gearing) to improve liquidity. However if gearing is high the only option may be to increase equity, which may not be possible if profitability is poor. On the face of it, the return to shareholders looks quite good (about 25 per cent of year-end equity) but there may be concerns about the saleability of artwork and the auditors would wish to determine how robust the profits are.

Detailed audit work would include the following:

- Determine terms of the overdraft and long-term loans and, in particular, the agreed overdraft limit, repayment terms and charges (if any) against assets and guarantees (if any) by directors and others.
- Review correspondence between the company and the bank and, in particular, examine any cash flow information (actual and forecast) at the time the overdraft was agreed.
- This work should be backed up by analytical review of the original forecasts and the subsequent actual flows. The reasons for any significant variances should be established.
- The current attitude of the bank to the overdraft facility should be determined (this may be evident from correspondence) and company plans to reduce it and to repay the long-term loans.
- Regarding long-term loans, the auditors should determine when repayments will commence so that they can assess the risk the company is facing. If the overdraft limit has been exceeded and loan repayments are imminent, the company may be facing going-concern problems. If on the other hand there is a comfortable buffer between bank overdraft and limit and the long-term loans are not due to be repaid for some time, the auditor may be willing to accept that the going-concern basis for preparing the financial statements is valid.

However, in this company inventory represents a major problem area, having a considerable bearing on the question of liquidity. The auditor would not come to firm conclusions about the going-concern status of the company until the work described immediately below has been performed.

High inventory levels

Inventories are high compared with sales and, mainly representing artwork, is clearly speculative. This is of particular concern because of poor liquidity. There may be a high risk that the work will not sell above cost, or at least not on a timely basis and this may also affect profitability.

Audit work on company inventories will include the following:

- Artwork should have been recorded in a register but also described on the work itself (on the rear of canvases, for instance). The auditor should observe the inventory count and check selected items to the register. In the process, the auditor would observe how artwork is displayed.
- Confirm the success of Brandon Smythe in identifying artwork that sells well. The auditor could review records of work purchased (cost) and sold (selling price). Review of the register would reveal how long works have been held.
- Confirm that the artwork is by the stated artists and also check the reputation of the artists whose work has been purchased by Brandon Smythe. This is a case where the auditor might consider using the work of an expert, although the conclusions might be somewhat subjective.

- Obtain Brandon Smythe's estimate of how quickly artwork on hand can be sold. The auditor would determine whether work is sold only through the gallery or shop or through Smythe's contacts.
- Insured amounts might be a broad indicator of value.

We consider how the auditor reports uncertainty in Chapter 16.

This is a difficult area for the auditor because of high subjectivity. If there is a high degree of uncertainty the auditors may have to refer to the matter in their report.

Gallery results

The gallery is not covering costs and, although one would expect that café and shop sales are dependent on the gallery and should therefore bear a part of gallery overheads, there must be concern that the gallery is not pulling in enough people.

Audit work will include the following:

- Compare this year's figures with prior years and with expectation of attendance for particular exhibitions. This is a difficult area as exhibitions may not be strictly comparable.
- Information is required on the breakdown of turnover and in particular how much is at full rate and how much at reduced rate. Enquire into reasons for any change in mix of people viewing this year compared with last.
- Compare ticket sales (supported by admission stubs) with actual receipts on a representative sample basis.
- Check that ticket sales are banked intact. More information is needed on how the system operates.
- Normal work on allocation of costs and income to activities is required.

The work of artists on display but not owned by the company

This work should not appear in the company's balance sheet and the auditor should ensure that such work is separately identified. Substantive tests of detail will be necessary to prove who actually owns inventories held:

- The company should have a register of all work held for sale on behalf of artists. It would be a strange artist that would not ensure that their work is identified on the work itself as being their own. The auditors should observe an inventory count of such work, check on a test basis to the register, using identification details on the work itself.
- The auditors might consider asking selected artists to confirm the work as belonging to them but held by the company.
- More information is required on contractual arrangements with artists, including length of time work will be held before being returned.
- Analytical review of commissions received would include comparing commissions this year and last and with budget.
- Select individual contracts on a representative basis and check commission rates; enquire into any variations in rates between individual artists.

- Obtain information on how local artists' work is checked in and out. Take representative selection of these movements and ensure that there is good reason for no record of commission when a painting is removed. Check that period held before sale, or without sale, is reasonable.

Art Aid is an interesting company but one that appears to suffer considerable business risks and, in particular, its lack of liquidity and the speculative nature of some of its business both give rise to concern about its status as a going concern. The auditor should discuss the future of the company with the board of directors and how they intend to realize inventory and secure sufficient funds to continue in operation.

Concluding remarks on analytical procedures

In this book we encourage you to see audit work as requiring skill and imagination. Analytical procedures form a vital tool in the hands of the auditor and we hope that we have shown the value of such a review for setting the audit scene and directing audit effort. You will have noted that analytical reviews should take into account the performance measures that are appropriate to the industry or commercial sector within which the organization is placed.

DETAILED FINAL AUDIT WORK: GENERAL MATTERS

For the rest of this chapter and Chapter 13 we discuss principles for the audit of assets and liabilities. We concern ourselves too with related costs and income.

Audit implications of accounting and reporting standards

Accounting and reporting standards issued by the ASB and IASB have a bearing on the measurement and disclosure of assets and liabilities and related costs and income. Auditors must be aware of the implications of accounting standards as they are designed to aid the achievement of truth and fairness. Paragraph 10(b) of the Foreword to Accounting Standards issued by ASB is relevant, as it deals with the responsibilities of members who act as auditors and reporting accountants:

> Where members act as auditors or reporting accountants, they should be in a position to justify significant departures to the extent that their concurrence with the departures is stated or implied. They are not, however, required to refer in their report to departures with which they concur, provided that adequate disclosure has been made in the financial statements.

The members referred to here are members of the member bodies of the Consultative Committee of Accountancy Bodies (CCAB). IASB have issued a similar framework, one of its objectives being 'to assist national standard-setting bodies in developing national standards'.

You will note from this paragraph that departures from accounting standards may be appropriate under certain circumstances, normally if departures are necessary to secure the true and fair view. Auditors must report departures from accounting standards if they feel they are not justified in the circumstances of the company.

Assets and related profit and loss account headings: general matters

We suggested earlier that auditing is rendered more efficient and effective if auditors first identify management assertions and then consider the inherent and control risks associated with each. Some assertions relate to accounting and control systems, but others relate to the figures in the financial statements. These latter assertions are known as 'financial statement assertions' and you will remember that auditors design tests to determine that there are no material misstatements at the assertion level.

Page 219.

In Chapter 6 we suggested that one approach to figures in the financial statements was to ascertain whether they were genuine, accurate and complete and we gave examples of what these headings mean. For assets and liabilities these three words prompt questions about existence, condition, ownership, valuation and disclosure/presentation in the financial statements. In Table 12.1 we show basic assertions for selected assets, liabilities and related income and expense.

This is an extension of Table 8.1 on page 308.

TABLE 12.1 Examples of financial statement assertions for selected assets, liabilities and related profit and loss account entries.

	Genuine (real)	Accurate	Complete
Non-current assets	Acquisitions are properly authorized. (Occurrence) Recorded acquisitions represent non-current assets that have been received or for which title has passed. (Occurrence) The recorded non-current assets physically exist. (Existence) The risks and benefits of holding the asset rests with the company. (Rights) Recorded non-current assets are used in the business. (Occurrence) Disposals of non-current assets represent the transfer of the risks and benefits (Rights) in them to third parties. Disposals have been properly authorized. (Occurrence)	Acquisitions of non-current assets are correctly calculated in accordance with relevant accounting principles and the proper capital/ revenue decision. (Valuation) Disposals have been correctly calculated. (Valuation) Non-current assets reflect all matters affecting their underlying valuation (whether cost or revalued amount) in accordance with relevant accounting principles. (Valuation) All acquisitions are recorded in the right period. (Cut-off)	All acquisitions are recorded, excluding any revenue items in the relevant non-current asset account. (Complete) All non-current assets owned by the company are recorded. (Complete) All disposals have been recorded. (Complete) Non-current assets have been properly summarized for disclosure in the financial statements. (Classification)

TABLE 12.1 *(Continued)*

	Genuine (real)	Accurate	Complete
		All disposals are recorded in the right period. (Cut-off)	
Depreciation	The depreciation charge is in respect of non-current assets in existence and for which the risks and benefits of ownership accrue to the company. (Existence and rights)	Depreciation is correctly calculated using appropriate depreciation methods and useful lives. (Valuation) The accumulated depreciation serving to reduce the amount attributable to non-current assets is appropriate in the light of changed circumstances, if any. (Valuation) Depreciation is allocated to the right period. (Cut-off)	All depreciation is recorded in the accounting records and costing records. (Complete) The depreciation charge has properly entered the costing records and is included under appropriate headings in the profit and loss account. (Classification) Accumulated depreciation is properly summarized for disclosure in the financial statements. (Classification)
Trade receivables	Trade receivables represent amounts actually due to the company, taking into account: • the actual performance of services for the customer or • transfer of title in goods transferred to the customer. • cash received or other genuine credit entry. (The entity holds the rights to the recorded trade receivables)	Trade receivables reflect all matters affecting their underlying valuation (including changes in foreign currency exchange rates) in accordance with relevant accounting principles. (Valuation) Trade receivables represent amounts that are collectable. (Provisions for bad and doubtful debts are appropriate) (Valuation) Trade receivables represent amounts due at the balance sheet date. (Cut-off)	All trade receivables are recorded. (Complete) All necessary disclosures about trade receivables have been made in the financial statements. (Classification)
Sales	The sales represent goods whose title has actually passed to a third party. The terms on which the goods have been delivered have been authorized by responsible persons. (Occurrence; right transferred to credit customer)	The sales transactions have been accurately calculated. (Accuracy) Sales have been recorded in the right period. (Cut-off).	All sales have been recorded in the accounting and costing records. (Complete) Sales have been appropriately disclosed in the financial statements. (Classification)

TABLE 12.1 *(Continued)*

	Genuine (real)	Accurate	Complete
Trade payables and accruals	Trade payables and accruals represent amounts actually due by the company, taking into account: • the actual performance of services for the company or • transfer of title in goods transferred to the company. • cash payments or other genuine debit entry. (Obligations)	Trade payables reflect all matters affecting their underlying valuation (including changes in foreign currency exchange rates) in accordance with relevant accounting principles. (Valuation) Accruals though not formally agreed have been estimated on a sound basis. (Valuation) Trade payables and accruals represent amounts due at the balance sheet date. (Cut-off)	All trade payables and accruals are properly recorded in the accounting records. (Complete) Trade payables and accruals have been properly summarized for disclosure in the financial statements. (Classification)
Provisions	Though uncertain in timing and amount, there is a present obligation as a result of a past event and it is probable that a transfer of economic benefits will be required to settle the obligation. (Occurrence and obligation) The past event is an obligating event, that is, it can be enforced by law or gives rise to a constructive obligation arising from valid expectations in other parties that the entity will discharge the obligation. (Occurrence and obligation)	Reliable estimates based on a range of possible outcomes can be made of the present obligation as a result of the past event. (Valuation) The provision relates to the correct period. (Cut-off)	All provisions are properly and separately disclosed, including brief descriptions of their nature, and indications of the uncertainties about amounts and timing. (Complete and classification)
Contingent liabilities	The events giving rise to the contingent liabilities have actually occurred. (Occurrence and obligations)	The possibility that an outflow of economic benefits will occur is remote or not probable has been reasonably assessed. (Valuation) Estimates of financial effects, uncertainties and possible reimbursements are reasonably based. (Valuation) The contingent liabilities have been recorded in the correct period. (Cut-off)	All contingent liabilities have been identified. (Complete) Contingent liabilities are properly disclosed in the financial statements, including brief description of nature, estimate of financial effect, indication of uncertainties, possibility of any reimbursement. (Classification)

TABLE 12.1 *(Continued)*

	Genuine (real)	Accurate	Complete
Contingent assets	The events giving rise to the contingent assets have actually occurred. (Occurrence and rights)	The decision that the inflow of economic benefits is probable, but not virtually certain is reasonably based. (Valuation) Estimates of financial effects are reasonably based. (Valuation) The contingent assets have been recorded in the right period. (Cut-off)	All contingent assets have been identified. (Complete) Where it is probable that there will be an inflow of economic benefits, the contingent assets are properly disclosed in the financial statements, including brief description of their nature, and estimate of their financial effect. (Classification)
Purchases	Purchases represent goods which have been received or for which title has passed and services which have been received. (Occurrence and obligation) Purchases of goods and services are properly authorized. (Occurrence and entry into obligations)	Purchases of goods and services are correctly calculated. (Remember foreign currency) in accordance with nature of the transaction and relevant accounting principles. (Valuation) Purchases of goods and services have been recorded in the right period. (Cut-off)	All purchases of goods and services have been recorded and in the proper accounting and costing records. (Complete)
Inventories	Inventories exist, are in good condition, and are owned by the company. (Existence and rights)	Inventories have been properly priced at cost to bring them to present condition and location (cost of materials and costs of conversion, including labour and overheads). (Valuation) Inventories have been valued at the lower of cost determined above and net realizable value, and provisions have been made to take account of condition. (Valuation) Inventories bear proper relationship to movements in the period. (Cut-off)	All inventories have been recorded in the underlying accounting records that are in agreement with the figure for inventories in the financial statements. (Complete) The policy for valuing inventories has been properly disclosed and disclosure has been made of sub-classifications required by the Companies Act 2006. (Classification)
Production cost	The recorded costs (of materials, labour and overheads) are	The production costs (of materials, labour and overheads) have been	All production costs have been identified and recorded in the

TABLE 12.1 *(Continued)*

	Genuine (real)	Accurate	Complete
	properly attributed to production cost. (Occurrence)	correctly calculated. (Valuation) Production cost has been properly allocated to inventories (see above) or to cost of sales in accordance with relevant accounting principles. (Valuation) All production costs have been allocated to the right period. (Cut-off)	appropriate accounting records. (Complete)
Consolidated accounts	Financial statements of undertakings over which dominant control is exercised are fully consolidated. (Rights) Financial statements of undertakings over which significant control is exercised are accounted for on an equity basis. (Rights) Financial statements of undertakings over which neither dominant nor significant influence is exercised are accounted for as investments. (Rights) Consolidation adjustments, including adjustments to fair value, are made on the basis of real transactions or occurrences. (Occurrence)	The underlying financial statements of undertakings included in one form or another, in the consolidated financial statements have been properly prepared on a consistent basis throughout the group. (Valuation) Consolidation adjustments (including those relating to foreign currency) are correctly calculated in accordance with relevant accounting standards. (Valuation) All consolidating adjustments have been made in the proper period. (Cut-off)	The consolidated financial statements reflect all of the underlying financial statements and necessary consolidation adjustments. (Complete and classification)

We discuss these in detail in this chapter and Chapter 13. We shall now remind you of the meaning of genuine, accurate and complete.

- *Genuine* can mean different things depending upon the kind of asset or liability or income/expense, but it basically means that figures in financial statements are supported by real transactions and real assets and liabilities, that something has happened or exists to support the figures. Thus, taking trade receivables as an example, 'genuine' means that they represent amounts actually due to the company, that a service has been performed on behalf of a customer or title in goods has passed to a third party. It also means that cash or some other credit entry has not cleared the balance. In the case of 'provisions' the event, giving rise to the obligation, has actually taken place.
- *Accurate* means that figures in financial statements have been properly calculated, taking into account all relevant factors. Taking trade receivables as an example again, this means they consist of open items whose valuation

reflect such matters as proper pricing and calculation of invoices and changes in foreign currency exchange rates. The valuation should be in accordance with relevant accounting principles. Accuracy also means that trade receivables represent collectable amounts, that is, that provisions for bad and doubtful debts are appropriate. They must also represent amounts due at the balance sheet date, that is, that cut-off is accurate. In the case of provisions, although the amount is an estimate, accuracy means that the estimate is soundly based on a careful consideration of a range of possible outcomes.

- *Complete* means that figures in financial statements include all relevant balances. In the case of trade receivables, 'complete' means that all trade receivables have been recorded and that they have been properly summarized for disclosure in the financial statements. In the case of provisions, completeness means that all necessary provisions have been accounted for; in particular that all the information required to understand the nature and amount and probable outcome has been disclosed.

We address the following assets and liabilities and related headings in the profit and loss account:

- Tangible non-current assets and depreciation.
- Trade receivables and sales.

In Chapter 13 we shall consider the audit of:

- Trade payables and accruals, and purchases.
- Stocks and work in progress.
- Long-term construction contracts.

In Chapter 14 we consider the audit of provisions.

There are, of course, other headings in financial statements, but we shall demonstrate the principles using these major headings. For each heading our discussion takes the following form:

- The nature of the asset or liability, where we consider what makes the particular asset or liability different from others.
- Inherent risks affecting the asset or liability, where we give examples of critical areas for consideration by the auditor.
- Controls to reduce the impact of inherent risk, where we give examples of particular measures taken by management to safeguard assets and control activities.
- Analytical procedures, using a case study to highlight risk.
- Suggested substantive approaches to prove that figures are genuine, accurate and complete. We do not provide detailed audit programmes, but suggest substantive approaches and give examples of programme steps.

Income smoothing

You will remember that in Chapter 5 we referred to the increased incidence in recent years of income smoothing, a practice that involves manipulation of assets and liabilities with consequent impacts on stated income. FRS 18 condemns this practice and suggests that deliberate understatement of assets and overstatement of liabilities should not be confused with application of the

See page 180.

prudence concept. We ask you to remember this when you are reading this chapter and Chapter 13.

TANGIBLE NON-CURRENT ASSETS AND DEPRECIATION

In this section we use Case study 12.3: Pykestone plc to illustrate our comments.

CASE STUDY 12.3

Pykestone plc: non-current assets

You are given the following details of the non-current assets of Pykestone plc, a company manufacturing and selling timber boarding and timber products, such as doors, window frames and furniture:

	Freehold land and buildings	Plant and machinery	Motor vehicles	Total	Profits/losses on disposal	
	£	£	£	£		£
Cost					Freehold land and buildings	484 380
Balance at 1 January 2011	1 000 000	2 749 400	760 000	4 509 400	Plant and machinery	−267 340
Additions	500 000	1 952 000	200 000	2 652 000	Motor vehicles	2 000
Disposals	−25 000	−614 600	−230 000	−869 600		219 040
Balance at 31 December 2011	1 475 000	4 087 800	730 000	6 291 800		
Depreciation						
Balance at 1 January 2011	250 000	904 010	488 000	1 642 010		
Charge	18 440	415 750	146 000	580 190		
Disposals	−9 380	−269 760	−214 000	−493 140		
Balance at 31 December 2011	259 060	1050 000	420 000	1 729 060		
Net book value						
At 1 January 2011	750 000	1 845 390	272 000	2 867 390		
At 31 December 2011	1 215 940	3 086 800	310 000	4 562 740		
Repairs and maintenance charges:	2011	2010				
Buildings	97 000	35 000				
Plant and machinery	43 000	25 000				
Motor vehicles	25 000	15 000				

The directors have entered into contracts for purchase of plant and machinery for £500 000 and have decided to purchase further plant and machinery amounting to £450 000, although contracts have not yet been placed for these. The directors have also decided that the freehold land and buildings should be revalued at £3 000 000 (on an existing use basis) as at 31 December 2011. The valuation has been carried out by a professional valuer. Depreciation rates are:

- Buildings: over 40 years straight line.
- Plant and machinery: from 7.5 per cent to 15 per cent straight line.
- Motor vehicles: 20 per cent straight line.

The nature of tangible non-current assets

Tangible non-current assets are defined by IAS 16 – *Property, plant and equipment* as:

> Tangible items that (a) are held for use in the production or supply of goods or services, for rental to others, or for administrative purposes; and (b) are expected to be used during more than one period.

It is therefore important to estimate the time over which economic benefit accrues from use of the asset so accounting periods can be properly charged with usage.

Non-current assets may also be intangible, such as goodwill, brands and trademarks. There is generally more subjectivity attached to the valuation of intangible assets and the accounting profession throughout the world has not yet come to an agreed position on their valuation.

IAS 16 and the comparable UK and Ireland standards FRS 11 and 15 contain much material and in the space available to us we cannot do more than refer to matters we believe to be of particular significance to the audit of non-current assets.

Tangible non-current assets vary in nature, not only within companies (motor vehicles differ from a mainframe computer) but also between industries. Thus, non-current assets of a company drilling for oil differ from those of a company running a chain of supermarkets. An oil rig in the North Sea may have a limited useful life (if the oil runs out, it may not be possible to use it elsewhere). A supermarket building on the other hand is likely to be useful for a long period and the land on which it is situated may have a variety of other uses. The non-current assets of Pykestone plc will include buildings with a controlled atmosphere for the storing of timber products, showrooms and machines for the measuring, cutting, drilling and shaping of timber and specialist craftsmen's machinery and tools for making doors, window frames and furniture. Associated costs such as depreciation, maintenance and insurance also vary in nature but their existence often help to prove the existence, condition and valuation of the asset itself. Thus, resharpening costs and replacement of circular saw blades proves the existence and use of circular saw equipment.

Inherent risks affecting tangible non-current assets

We give below some examples of inherent risk factors affecting tangible non-current assets:

- Technological changes affecting the industry, rendering the assets obsolete.
- Closure of part of the business so the assets may have to be stated at net realizable value.
- Difficulties in making estimates of useful lives for calculating depreciation so the assets may be over- or understated.
- Revaluation of tangible non-current assets has taken place with consequent subjectivity.
- The company owns a significant number of idle non-current assets.
- The company has significant non-current assets in the course of construction with consequent uncertainty about stage of completion and point of coming on stream.
- The company has capitalized some of its own costs of construction of non-current assets.
- The existence of moveable, high-value assets, such as desk top PCs, with high risk of loss.

We remind you at this point that income smoothing might be achieved by manipulating such matters as the capital/revenue decision and the calculation of useful lives and depreciation.

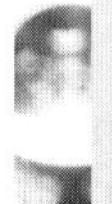

ACTIVITY 12.4

Explain why capitalization of own costs of construction of tangible non-current assets might be regarded as an inherent risk factor.

If a company purchases a non-current asset from a third party, it is relatively easy to ensure costs are genuine, complete and accurate. However, building a non-current asset using own labour is more problematic as a wide variety of individual costs, including overheads, must be properly collected and determined. Auditors would be alert to the existence of inherent risk and would test and evaluate company controls and perform substantive procedures on costs.

Controls to reduce the impact of inherent risk affecting non-current assets

We discussed control environment in Chapter 7. Remember that the general control environment needs to be supported by controls in individual areas, and it is these specific controls that we discuss in this chapter and Chapter 13.

Apart from a satisfactory control environment generally, we would expect to see controls in the following areas, if control risk is to be minimized:

- Acquisitions, revaluation and impairment of non-current assets.
- Safeguarding non-current assets owned/held by the company.
- Disposals of non-current assets.
- Maintenance and insurance of non-current assets.
- Authorization of depreciation charges and accumulations.

Acquisitions of non-current assets

The main control document for acquisitions of non-current assets is the non-current assets budget. Many organizations prepare long-, medium- and short-term budgets and these should reflect carefully argued need and be authorized at an appropriately high level. The final authority should lie with the board of directors, but non-current assets budgets should only be approved after consultation with production personnel and after consideration of known constraints, such as available labour at appropriate skill levels and estimated demand for products. Directors should minute approval of the planned expenditure and its timing. Once approved, the budget becomes authority to purchase, although we would expect further confirming authorizations at appropriate levels to ensure that the asset is still required prior to ordering. It is good practice for different authority levels to be established within the company. An important control is regular comparison of budget with actual expenditure and enquiry into any significant variations. Computerized budgets can be programmed to show budgeted expenditure not yet incurred and this can also be a useful control.

One of the authors used to get a laugh from students when he told them that he had authority to purchase no more than a new stapler.

An important question at the acquisition stage is the capital/revenue decision and management should ensure that purchased items are properly treated as non-current assets and not as repair/maintenance expenditure, and vice versa. For instance, if the company has purchased a site containing a building for development, the company should have clear policies as to which costs, such as the cost of clearing the site, should be included in the cost of the final non-current asset. The basic rule is that only costs that are directly attributable to bringing the asset into working condition for its intended use should be included in its measurement. Examples are: acquisition costs (such as stamp duty), the cost of site preparation and clearance, initial delivery and handling costs, installation costs and professional fees (such as legal, architects' and engineers' fees).

Remember that WorldCom is accused of treating much repair/maintenance expenditure as capital assets.

Other important areas where controls should exist are those over revaluation of non-current assets, such as selection of a qualified valuer (see below), and identification of non-current assets that have suffered impairment (there should, for instance, be a system for identifying idle assets).

IAS 16 and FRS 15 deal with valuation of non-current assets and IAS 36 and FRS 11 with impairment of non-current assets. We discuss these topics in greater detail below.

Safeguarding non-current assets owned/held by the company

The main accounting record for non-current assets is the non-current assets register. To be a good control document it should be kept and accessed by persons independent of those using and having custody of the non-current assets. We would expect the register to be compared periodically with physical assets and vice versa. Further essential procedures if the register is to be an effective control over non-current assets include: (a) assets should have unique numbers affixed to them, the register containing the same number; (b) the register should contain all the details necessary to control the individual assets, including:

- Name
- Technical specifications
- Location
- Identification number
- Estimated useful life
- Depreciation method
- Depreciation per year
- Accumulated depreciation
- Maintenance record
- Residual value
- Notes on condition
- Manufacturer's name
- Date of purchase
- Invoice number
- Asset budget number
- Cost
- Revalued amount (if any) and revaluation date
- Insured amount
- Note on whether owned or leased.

Non-current assets should be reconciled by the company at least annually to cost/valuation, accumulated depreciation and depreciation charge figures in the financial statements. In large and complex companies the non-current assets register may be the only way to control assets. Identification number and location details are used when reconciling non-current assets entries to assets physically in existence. Significant differences between the register and physical assets or between the register and general ledger entries would suggest high control risk and differences should be investigated by the company. The relationship between the non-current asset and other records of Pykestone plc is shown in Figure 12.1. This figure shows the flow from budget preparation to procedures for the purchase of non-current assets, preparation of non-current assets register, calculation of depreciation and entries in the balance sheet and profit and loss account. The figure shows the kind of documentation that you would expect to see, whether Pykestone's records, including non-current assets budget and purchase daybook, are computerized or not.

Physical controls over high-value, especially moveable, assets are particularly important, including stamping with the company name, restricting access

FIGURE 12.1 Pykestone non-current assets recording system

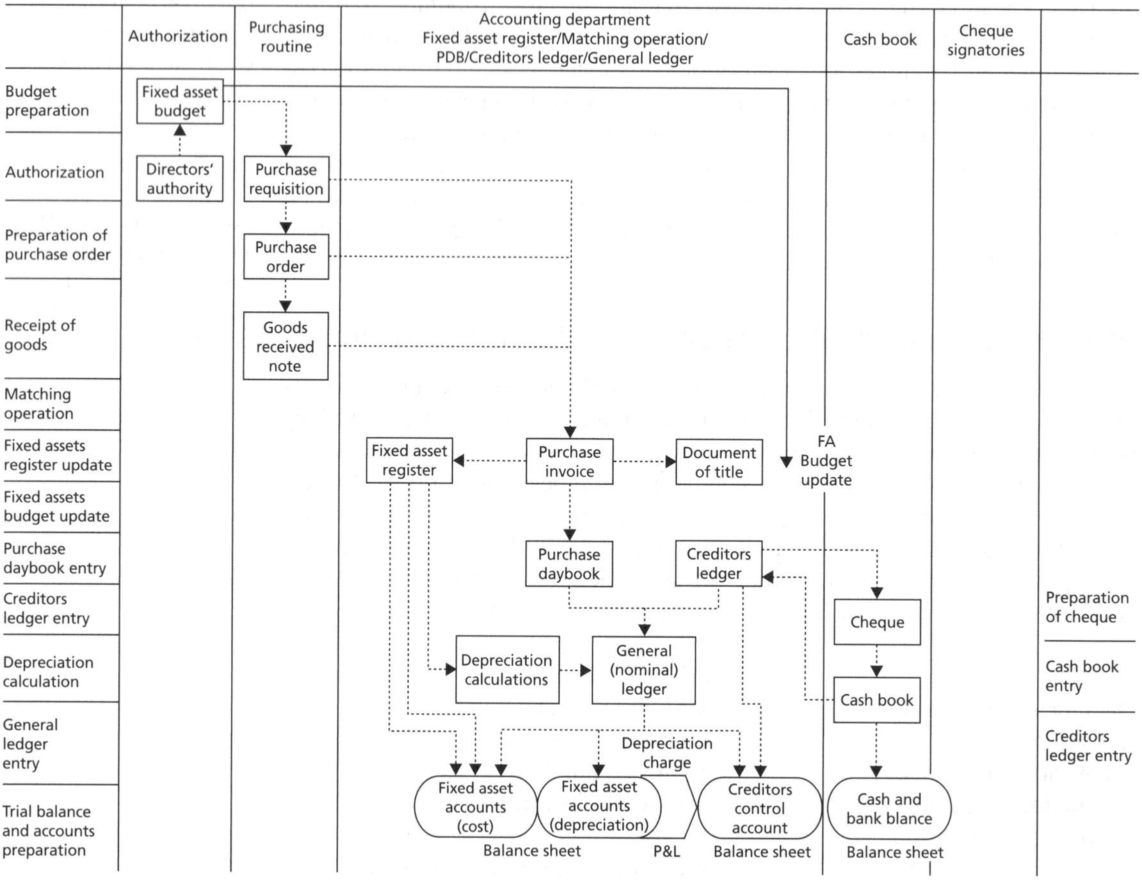

and securing machines to desks. If a non-current assets register is not kept or the register is found to be subject to error, control risk will be increased and the auditor may have to extend substantive tests of detail.

Disposals of non-current assets

Proceeds of sale can easily be misappropriated if controls are not in place. Disposals should be authorized by individuals with appropriate authority after careful assessment of the continuing value of the asset, taking into account company policy, which may have rendered assets surplus to requirements. The directors should issue guidelines for making such assessments. Disposal requests should be written (with reasons), and approval evidenced by signature.

Maintenance, insurance and other charges associated with non-current assets

Proper maintenance and insurance are necessary if the assets of the company are to be safeguarded and regular maintenance is likely to maintain or extend useful economic lives. The maintenance record and insured amounts should be included on the register. We would expect repairs and insurance to be approved on the basis of expert recommendation within or outwith the company. The capital/revenue decision is important in relation to repairs (are they revenue or capital items?) and we would expect approval to include instructions on accounting treatment. If maintenance and repairs expenditure has changed significantly compared with the previous year, this might indicate that control risk is high. This should be discussed with management.

Further matters to be emphasized are the treatment of profits and losses on disposal of non-current assets and how to account for changes in useful lives. These are discussed briefly below.

Authorization of depreciation charges and periodic review of accumulated depreciation

Depreciation is a measure of economic benefits of the tangible non-current asset consumed during the financial period. Such consumption reflects the reduction of economic useful life arising from use, passage of time or obsolescence because of changes in technology or demand for the goods and services produced. The calculation of economic benefit is based on the depreciable amount which may be original cost or the revalued amount. The auditor would expect to see a system of approval of economic useful lives and depreciation method. The approval should not be just at the point of purchase, but there should be rolling approvals of remaining useful lives annually to ensure that the carrying amount does not exceed the higher of its net realizable value or its value in use, that is, its recoverable amount. The assumption is that if economic useful lives are reviewed annually and depreciation is based on amended useful lives, it is unlikely that material impairment losses will arise. You should be aware though that unexpected changes in the estimate of the recoverable amount, may cause impairment losses to arise and such losses would need to be reflected in the financial statements. This means that the auditor should keep an eye open for events or circumstances that might cause a sudden reduction in the estimate of recoverable amount, such as current period operating losses, significant decline in a non-current asset's market value, obsolescence and departure of key employees.

ACTIVITY 12.5

Clatto plc has a subsidiary whose draft financial statements at 31 December 2011 show the following picture of its tangible and intangible assets:

	£
Goodwill	1000 000
Patents	150 000
Tangible fixed assets	2000 000
	3150 000

During the current financial year, a competitor introduced a new improved product, and the company suffered its first loss in ten years. Average annual operating profits in the ten years to 31 December 2010 were £2 500 000, but in the year to 31 December 2011 the draft financial statements show an operating loss of £1 100 000.

Explain how you would address the problems facing the company from an audit point of view. You may assume that the company's going-concern status is not at risk. Consider the intangible as well as tangible assets.

This company has clearly been profitable, but new circumstances suggest that the tangible and intangible assets may be impaired. The patents may be worthless if they relate to products or processes that are out of date and there may be considerable doubt about the value of goodwill. Auditors should discuss the future of the company with the directors of the holding and subsidiary company. We are told that the going-concern status of the company is secure, but we would wish to confirm this. It may be that it has some new lines that could become profitable and create a positive cash flow fairly quickly, but any goodwill that they generate would not be relevant as far as the present goodwill figure is concerned. In these circumstances it may be necessary to write off £1 150 000 in respect of goodwill and patents. The 'value' of tangible non-current assets might be difficult to determine. Those assets that are specific to products that have been affected by the new competition, may have to be written down to net realizable value, while others, such as buildings, that have a future value in use, might retain their stated value or be reduced only to a certain extent. This is a very subjective area as assets only have a value in use if they generate cash flows in the future. Auditors would review management forecasts, consider industry comment and projections and examine any evidence from experts, such as external valuers. If tangible non-current assets were deemed to have a value in use of £1 150 000 only, £850 000 should be recognized in the profit and loss account unless it arises on a previously revalued non-current asset.

If the asset has been revalued IAS 36 states that any impairment loss should be treated as a revaluation decrease and identified, if material, in the statement of changes in equity – as shown in the implementation guidance to IAS 1. FRS 11 requires the loss to be recognized in the statement of total recognized gains and losses until the carrying amount of the asset reaches its depreciated historical cost and thereafter in the profit and loss account.

Analytical procedures

Case study 12.3 contains numerical information about Pykestone's non-current assets figure and we now review it.

ACTIVITY 12.6

Carry out an analytical review of the information in Case study 12.3 and prepare a working paper in which you list (with reasons) the matters that will need further explanations from management.

The following are the matters requiring investigation:

Additions to non-current assets during the year and planned

Non-current asset additions represent a significant investment (at 31 December 2011 they are 42 per cent of total assets) and investments in the coming year will increase the new investment further. Generally, new or significant transactions or events tend to suggest areas of increased risk, especially when they involve the future.

Disposals of non-current assets

Disposals of plant and machinery represent approximately 32 per cent of additions indicating that there has been a major change to the composition of the non-current assets. This significant change is an indicator of enhanced risk.

Depreciation rates and losses on disposal

The average rates of depreciation on cost are as follows:

- Freehold land and buildings: 1.25 per cent.
- Plant and machinery: 10.17 per cent.
- Motor vehicles: 20 per cent.

These rates reflect global depreciation rates in the information given. Further information is needed, however, on the proportion of land (not being depreciated) in the cost of land and buildings. Losses on disposal of non-current assets might indicate that useful lives have been overestimated in the past. There may be a good reason for losses (for instance, forced disposals because of the introduction of new technology) – obsolescence is of course one of the matters indicating that impairment may have occurred – but this is a risk area requiring investigation. In particular, the auditor would wish to ensure that current useful economic lives have been determined on a reasonable basis.

Significant profit on disposal of freehold land and buildings

Profit on disposal of freehold land and buildings may not be unexpected because of the low original cost of the asset. This matter is linked to revaluation of existing assets (see below), which represents a significant risk factor because of its subjectivity.

Revaluation of freehold property

The auditor would wish to enquire further into the decision of the directors to revalue the land and buildings. As suggested above, risk is high because of subjectivity and the auditor would wish to consider carefully the valuation procedures, the qualifications of the valuer and the instructions they were given.

Repairs and maintenance charges

Higher repairs and maintenance charges in 2011 suggest that the capital revenue decision might have been wrongly made. If a responsible company official approves repairs and maintenance expenses and makes the capital/revenue decision, the auditor may decide that control risk is low and that substantive tests may be reduced.

Substantive approaches to prove that figures are genuine, accurate and complete

We now discuss general enquiries you would make, followed by substantive approaches to ensure that non-current assets are properly stated, using Pykestone as the basis of our discussion. We give examples of appropriate substantive tests. In respect of the revaluation of non-current assets, you should read ISA 620 – *Using the work of an auditor's expert*.

Additions to non-current assets

Class of assertion	Assertions
Genuine	Acquisitions are properly authorized (Occurrence) Recorded acquisitions represent non-current assets that have been received or for which title has passed. (Occurrence)
Accurate	Acquisitions of non-current assets are correctly calculated in accordance with relevant accounting principles and the proper capital/revenue decision. (Valuation) All acquisitions are recorded in the right period. (Cut-off)
Complete	All acquisitions are recorded, excluding any revenue items in the relevant non-current asset account. (Complete)

The auditor would ask the directors of Pykestone to explain the thinking behind the investment programme, including impact on profits (actual and potential). Find out when the assets were acquired and when the contribution to profits commenced. The effect of the acquisitions and proposed acquisitions on liquidity would also be of interest.

Substantive procedures include:

- Check board minutes to confirm directors' approval of the non-current assets budget. Review memoranda and related budgets supporting the non-current assets budget to ensure it is soundly based. A review of budgeted expenditure not yet incurred should be made to see if the company has the necessary funds, including finance of additional working capital.
- Review management analyses of variances between budgeted and actual acquisition cost and determine that any significant variances are legitimate and have been approved in the same way as the original budget. This would be one test of the accuracy of acquisition cost.

Refer to Chapter 10, page 372 and note that we suggested the use of audit software in the area: 'Reconciling non-current asset budget entries with subsequent purchases and printing material variances'.

- Select major items in the budget on a random basis and trace to acquisition documentation: purchase requisition, order (ensuring it has been properly approved), GRN (check date is before the balance sheet date), invoice (check all details) and entries in the non-current assets register and purchases journal (a typical depth test that would prove that budget items have been properly processed). The auditor may select a representative sample of acquisitions in the purchases listing and test to the budget and supporting documentation, a test helping to ensure recorded acquisitions and entries in the non-current assets register are genuine, accurate and complete.
- For each selected item check that the capital/revenue decision has been properly made. For instance, Pykestone may have incurred material costs for reorganizing the production process on the purchase of the new machinery and it may be legitimate for such costs to be capitalized.

Revaluation of non-current assets

Freehold land and buildings have been revalued on 31 December 2011. The net book value before the revaluation was £1 215 940 and a gain on revaluation of £1 784 060 has arisen. The auditor will have to be satisfied that the accounting figures and treatment are valid.

ACTIVITY 12.7

We have not referred to assertions respecting revaluation of non-current assets. Suggest suitable assertions under genuine, accurate and complete headings. You may refer to IAS 16 and FRS 15.

Suitable assertions would include the following:

- *Genuine*. The basic idea is that revaluation of non-current assets takes into account real conditions within the company, so you have to consider the nature of the asset before you can conclude on what would be a fair value, based on actual market conditions. This means that we have to ask whether management intends to continue using the asset within the business or whether it intends to dispose of it in the near future. The basic rules are as follows:
  (a) Intending to retain the asset within the business – use existing value use (EVU).
  (b) Intending to dispose of the asset – use open market value (OMV). Properties surplus to requirements should be valued on an OMV basis as an exit value, presumably because the likelihood is that the asset will be disposed of.

  In some cases it may be impossible to determine an EVU because the assets are very specialized and in this case it would be appropriate to use depreciated replacement cost (DRC) or a basis using the income derived from the asset, if this can be determined. Specialized assets such as oil refineries should be valued using DRC because there is unlikely to be an open market.
- *Accurate*. The calculation of current value of non-current assets appropriately reflects their underlying value in accordance with relevant accounting principles. This means that there must be proper selection and calculation of EVU, OMV, DRC or income basis as appropriate.
- *Complete*. All non-current assets in a particular class have been revalued. This means that if one asset of a particular class is revalued, then all items in that class of non-current asset must be revalued. This is a requirement of both FRS 15 and IAS 16.

See margin note on page 454 above.

Before we take a look at substantive procedures to satisfy the auditor that the revalued amounts are not misstated we ask you to refer to ISA 620 – *Using the work of an auditor's expert.* This ISA considers the use by the auditors of an expert where the auditors are not themselves expert in the field, such as revaluation of non-current assets. However, it also considers what the auditor should do when a management's expert has already given expertise to the company, as has been the case in Pykestone. Paragraph A9 of ISA 620 gives guidance in this respect:

> When management has used a management's expert in preparing the financial statements, the auditor's decision on whether to use an auditor's expert may be influenced by such factors as:
>
> - The nature, scope and objectives of the management's expert's work.
> - Whether the management's expert is employed by the entity, or is a party engaged by it to provide relevant services.
> - The extent to which management can exercise control or influence over the work of the management's expert.
> - The management's expert's competence and capabilities.
> - Whether the management's expert is subject to technical performance standards or other professional or industry requirements
> - Any controls within the entity over the management's expert's work.
>
> ISA 500, paragraph eight, includes requirements and guidance regarding the effect of the competence, capabilities and objectivity of management's experts on the reliability of audit evidence.

Substantive procedures would include the following:

- Determine that the valuer is properly qualified, including such matters as:
  - (a) Membership of professional body.
  - (b) Experience and reputation.
- Determine that the valuer is independent of the company (an internal valuer would be less reliable from the audit point of view than an external valuer).
- Ensure that the valuer's scope of work is appropriate. Written instructions to the valuer should be examined and attention paid to the following matters:
  - (a) Objectives and scope of the valuer's work. The auditor would determine, for instance, if a physical inspection is merely cursory or is detailed enough. The basic rule is that a valuation should take place if it is likely that there has been a material change in value. IAS 16 and FRS 15 suggest fuller valuations be carried out at intervals of three or five years.
  - (b) Clear statement of the matters the expert is to examine. For instance, if the property is intended to have a change of use, whether the valuer is required to consider this issue.
  - (c) Why the work is being carried out. For instance, if it is intended that the asset is to be sold on the basis of the valuation, the valuer should have been informed of this fact.
  - (d) The information provided to the valuer and its reliability. A full valuation of non-specialized property normally involves detailed inspection of the interior and exterior of the property and inspection of locality. Physical inspection, if carried out competently, is a reliable source of evidence for the valuer. Apart from physical inspection, enquiries of

independent third parties would also be relevant and reliable: (i) enquiries of local planning and similar authorities, which should be independent and therefore reliable; (ii) enquiries of client officials and solicitors (these sources are not necessarily independent but are likely to be well informed about the property). Other information that might be available to the valuer would include market transactions of similar properties, identification of market trends and the application of these to the property under consideration.

(e) Assumptions and methods used. The auditor must ensure that the assumptions made and methods used by the valuer are reasonable. For instance, the valuer may have made assumptions about the length of useful economic life of the asset.

(f) Timing of valuation. The auditor should ensure that if the valuation has happened some time before, it is still valid.

- The auditor should review the working papers of the valuer and make such tests of the data used to prove that the valuer's conclusions are valid.
- Where the amounts involved are significant, the auditor may feel that an auditor's expert should be engaged. The same criteria would apply as in (a) to (f) above. The auditor's valuer may be either internal or external to the audit firm.

Disposals of non-current assets

Class of assertion	Assertions
Genuine	Disposals of non-current assets represent the transfer of the risks and benefits (Rights) in them to third parties.
	Disposals have been properly authorized. (Occurrence)
Accurate	Disposals have been correctly calculated. (Valuation)
	All disposals are recorded in the right period. (Cut-off)
Complete	All disposals have been recorded. (Complete)

The auditors would first discuss the high level of disposals with Pykestone's management and determine if the losses on disposal have arisen because of rationalization. The non-current assets may have been disposed of earlier than originally expected at a lower price than would normally have been the case. The auditor should enquire if it is necessary to consider the need for an impairment review and to reassess useful lives generally (see depreciation below). The high level of disposals is closely linked to acquisitions. It may be that disposals look right in the light of management policy on acquisitions.

Substantive procedures would include the following:

- Check number sequence of disposal approvals as one test helping to prove completeness.
- Select a random sample of approvals and check authorization signature. Trace approvals to sales despatch notes (check date is before year-end

date), sales invoices (check calculations) and non-current assets register (check removal from the register). This would help to prove authorization, accuracy and proper cut-off.

Non-current assets balances

Class of assertion	Assertions
Genuine	The recorded non-current assets physically exist. (Existence)
	The risks and benefits of holding the asset rests with the company. (Rights)
	Recorded non-current assets are used in the business. (Occurrence)
Accurate	Non-current assets reflect all matters affecting their underlying valuation (whether cost or revalued amount) in accordance with relevant accounting principles. (Valuation)
Complete	All non-current assets owned by the company are recorded. (Complete)
	Non-current assets have been properly summarized for disclosure in the financial statements. (Classification)

We comment as follows:

- Work on acquisitions and disposals will help to prove that non-current assets balances are genuine, accurate and complete, but it is not enough just to prove transactions are in order. Acquisition transactions may have caused non-current assets figures to come into existence, but figures should be verified at the period end to prove they are still valid. If a disposal has been made the asset should have been removed from the records.
- Existence, condition and ownership checks may be either direct or indirect. Direct tests include physical examination of assets selected from the non-current assets register after the register has been proven to be a reliable record, and examination of title deeds. Auditors can, however, also obtain indirect evidence of the existence and condition of the asset, such as:
  (a) Smooth flow of production suggests that the assets are functioning. If an oil refinery is producing heating oil and other products in accordance with a refinery plan, that is persuasive evidence that the refinery non-current assets are working well. If sulphur is being produced as a by-product, that suggests that the de-sulphurization unit is working satisfactorily.
  (b) Costs associated with assets, such as in Pykestone resharpening costs. Auditors can also use records required for insurance companies and health and safety authorities. Companies will normally keep detailed maintenance records to control assets and to ensure that machinery is kept in good working condition. The auditor may be able to use such records.
- Possession does not necessarily indicate ownership and auditors would wish to look for appropriate evidence. Title deeds and land registry certificates

should be inspected in the case of freehold property. Generally speaking, if the company is bearing all normal costs of ownership, this is prima facie evidence that non-current assets should appear in the balance sheet. You will know from your accounting studies that leased assets should be accounted for as a non-current asset of a lessee company if the lessee has the rights and duties of ownership. Motor vehicle registration documents are not in themselves documents of title, but should also be inspected to ensure they are in the name of Pykestone.

- As far as accuracy is concerned, the auditors' duty is to ensure that cost/valuation at the year-end is properly stated. An important vehicle for achieving this purpose is to prove and use the non-current assets register (see below).
- Disclosure and presentation. If you take a look at the non-current assets note in a set of published financial statements you will see that disclosures in respect of non-current assets are substantial, even more in fact than we have shown in the Pykestone example in Figure 12.2. The auditor's task is to ensure that the disclosures and presentation are such as to give a true and fair view in the context of the financial statements taken as a whole.
- Testing validity and making use of the non-current assets register.
  - (a) Prove that the non-current assets register is complete and accurate in all respects. This could be done by checking to the register representative samples of: (i) physical assets (but see comment on moveable assets and property below); (ii) acquisition documentation (see above); (iii) disposal documentation (see above).
  - (b) Check company reconciliations between the register and amounts recorded in the financial records. This would be a completeness check.
  - (c) Ensure that the register has been kept by person(s) independent of the persons using and having custody of the non-current assets throughout the period and inspect the company's schedules comparing the register with physical assets and physical assets with the register.
  - (d) Ascertain how frequently non-current assets are reconciled to and from the non-current asset register and enquire particularly as to any significant deviations discovered by those carrying out the inspection. The condition of the asset would, in a good system, be noted in the non-current asset register. This would be an existence and condition check.
  - (e) Select a representative sample of entries in the non-current assets register and check recorded data to supporting documentation, such as purchase invoices, title deeds and motor vehicle documents. An important check on the risks of ownership would be to ensure that the selected assets appear on insurance documentation. These would be valuation and ownership tests.
  - (f) For the same sample check for physical existence and condition, using location, identification number or motor vehicle registration number as appropriate.

These tests are not exhaustive but do represent a logical programme. Remember that you should be able to explain why each test is being performed.

- Assets charged as security for loans given to the company. It is common practice to secure loans from banks or long-term loans on non-current assets, particularly freehold land and buildings (which would then be 'encumbered'). Auditors should ensure that full disclosure is made of charges as this will normally be necessary to achieve the true and fair view.
- Capital commitments. The auditor should examine directors' minutes to determine commitments entered into, both for contracts placed and for contracts not yet placed. In the case of Pykestone the directors have entered into contracts for the purchase of plant and machinery for £500 000 and have decided to purchase further plant and machinery for £450 000. Where contracts have been placed they should be examined. Remember that Pykestone's commitments will have been entered into within the context of a planned expansion or replacement programme.
- *Other tests* would include the following:
  (a) Check production records to determine if there has been any significant downturn in production, which might indicate the existence of an idle plant.
  (b) Some assets are moveable and special arrangements may be necessary. Ships on the high sea, motor vehicles and earth-moving equipment are all examples of non-current assets that may not be immediately observable, if at all. The auditor should ascertain the methods the company takes to prove their existence. Invoices for costs associated with non-current assets may be of help in this respect. For instance, invoices for petrol for company motor vehicles may refer to the vehicle registration number, indeed the company should ask that such invoices always contain identification for control purposes. Clearly, the vehicle registration number will be a useful means of identification.
  (c) The auditors should make an inspection visit to freehold land and buildings of Pykestone. In 2011, they would be particularly interested in the additions to and disposals of land and buildings. If the addition represents an extension to existing property, the reasons for the extension should be ascertained and note made of how it is used since it was built. The auditors of the County Hotel might do the same at the company's premises. In the latter case, there would be a particular interest in the progress of work on new bathrooms. If a company has such property at a number of locations, the auditor may inspect on a rotation basis.
  (d) For non-revalued properties enquiries as to their value should be made as disclosure of their current value is required if there is a significant difference between such value and the amount shown in the balance sheet.
  (e) Check disclosures required by company legislation and accounting standards. These include revalued assets: where assets are revalued, legislation may require certain disclosures to be made, including name and qualifications of the valuers, bases of valuation and dates/amounts and similar disclosures are required by IAS 16 and FRS 15.

Sundry matters affecting depreciation

Class of assertion	Assertions
Genuine	The depreciation charge is in respect of non-current assets in existence and for which the risks and benefits of ownership accrue to the company. (Existence and rights)
Accurate	Depreciation is correctly calculated using appropriate depreciation methods and useful lives. (Valuation)
	The accumulated depreciation serving to reduce the amount attributable to non-current assets is appropriate in the light of changed circumstances, if any. (Valuation)
	Depreciation is allocated to the right period. (Cut-off)
Complete	All depreciation is recorded in the accounting records and costing records. (Complete)
	The depreciation charge has properly entered the costing records and is included under appropriate headings in the profit and loss account. (Classification)
	Accumulated depreciation is properly summarized for disclosure in the financial statements. (Classification)

Audit work on depreciation is closely allied to work on the non-current assets themselves. We have already noted that the non-current assets register should contain details of estimated useful economic life, depreciation method, depreciation per year and accumulated depreciation as well as cost/valuation and residual values. For Pykestone we have seen that the significant losses on disposal may indicate that depreciation in the past has been inadequate, possibly because useful economic lives have been underestimated.

Useful economic lives of non-current assets and appropriateness of depreciation method Useful lives may be difficult to determine because the future is uncertain. Some assets reduce in value pro rata over a period of time (leasehold property, for instance). For others, reduction in value may depend on usage rather than effluxion of time (a machine usage rate may be more appropriate than a straight-line basis, in which case the useful economic life will be estimated hours in use). The auditor should examine written evidence of management annual reviews of useful lives, paying particular attention to identification of idle or unproductive plant and machinery. The auditor will ascertain the appropriateness of depreciation methods and their consistent application. Auditors should satisfy themselves that management reviews are performed in sufficient depth. In the case of Pykestone, the auditor should approach production staff (with hands-on experience of the assets) as well as the chief accountant and ask why losses on disposal had arisen. The auditor is likely to have knowledge of the industry and local conditions and this would help to assess the reasons for the losses.

A further matter concerning Pykestone is the materiality of additions to non-current assets. Audit work should be directed to ensuring that proper consideration has been given to useful lives of the new machinery. Useful lives of existing or previously owned machinery may not be a good guide to lives of the acquisitions, particularly if the new machinery has features such as electronic gadgetry, not possessed by the old machinery. It may be that electronic features will increase the usefulness of the machinery without increasing length of useful life. The latter may even be reduced. The auditor should discuss this question with the production manager and look for corroborative evidence in the form of manufacturer's specifications and trade press. A useful substantive procedure would be examination of memoranda prepared at the time the new purchases of non-current assets were mooted, as these should include estimated useful lives.

Both IAS 16 and FRS 15 contain a discussion on residual values and you should read the paragraphs in question.

Residual values Auditors would expect management to review residual values annually and should seek evidence to prove any changes in these values, discussing them with management, including the production director. Any changes in useful lives and residual values should be recorded in the non-current assets register.

Depreciation on revalued non-current assets On revaluation the revalued amount becomes the depreciable amount and following revaluation current and future depreciation should be based on revalued amount.

Substantive tests of details would include reconciling depreciation charges and accumulated depreciation per the non-current assets register to the total charge and accumulation in the non-current assets note. For selected non-current assets, check calculations of depreciation charge and accumulated depreciation using useful lives and depreciation method. Analytical review of each class of asset would help to prove the depreciation charge in total.

TRADE RECEIVABLES AND SALES

The nature of trade receivables together with comments on sales

Trade receivables balances are normally classified as current assets, as they are receivable in the short term. They are not tangible in the sense that many non-current assets are (a lathe, for instance), but, if genuine, they are receivable from real people or organizations. They come into existence as the result of the sale of goods or the performance of a service by the company. It is important that the point at which the property in the goods is transferred or the service is performed is carefully defined. In earlier chapters we considered the objectives of systems for recording and control of sales and related trade receivables and suggested evidential matter the auditor would use to prove that sales and trade receivables are properly reflected in the accounting records and financial statements.

See Figure 6.2, page 227 for evidence corroboration and upgrading process in the sales and trade receivables area and Case study 9.1 on page 330 for a discussion of the auditor's approach to a sales system.

Sales of goods and services may either be on credit or for cash, so sales will either cause trade receivables to come into existence or will increase cash balances. The practical effect is that audit work on sales cannot be divorced from work on the assets accounts and vice versa. Where sales are on credit it will normally be easier to find evidence to prove the sale, if only because companies selling on credit will need to maintain trade receivable records. The problem is greater where sales are made for cash as there is no need to keep records of amounts owed. Often cash sales will be listed on cash registers, in which case the auditor should ensure there is control over access to the register and listing operation. If cash sales are not so recorded the auditor should ensure that documentation is adequate in other ways, for instance, whether sales slips are pre-numbered and supervisory controls suitable. Another example would be a newspaper; the auditor could reconcile classified advertising receipts to expected page income.

We considered control of cash sales in the County Hotel in Chapter 5. The accuracy and completeness of sales were aided by standard menus in master files and by a programmed till in the bar.

Inherent risks affecting trade receivables

An important rule is that new or material transactions or events often result in increased risk. Here are some indicators of inherent risks that may affect trade receivables:

- Large number of new customers, so there is little prior history regarding them.
- Significant changes in the collectability of trade receivables.
- New products have been introduced, so little is known about potential claims for poor quality.
- Competitors have introduced new product lines, so sales may diminish or profit margins be adversely affected.
- The norm in the industry or commercial sector within which the company operates is for sales on a 'sale or return' basis, making it difficult to determine when title has passed.
- The company has a history of above average returns of goods sold, so trade receivables and sales may be overstated.
- New staff in the sales, sales accounting and credit control section.
- Complicated computerized accounting system.

We remind you again that income smoothing could be achieved by manipulating stated values of trade receivables by erroneous cut-off and unnecessary bad debt provisions.

Controls to reduce the impact of inherent risk in the sales and trade receivables area

Apart from a satisfactory control environment generally, we would expect to see controls in the following areas:

- Creation and clearance of trade receivables balances.
- Safeguarding of the asset – trade receivables.

Creation and clearance of trade receivables balances

We covered in Chapters 8 and 9 many of the controls expected in the sales area, and emphasize the following points:

- We would expect the company to have a policy on when title in goods pass to third parties and when services rendered are deemed complete. We noted in Chapter 8 that this is particularly important when the

Page 299.

company uses e-commerce to conduct business on the Internet often between people in different countries.

- The policy should be included in the terms of trade, given in writing to all customers, on sales order confirmations, despatch notes, sales invoices or shown clearly on websites.
- If goods are delivered to customers on sale or return, obligations of customers should be clearly stated. For instance, if goods have been damaged in the customer's hands before sale to a third party, it should be agreed who bears the consequent loss. We would also expect to see a system for early notification of any sales made.

Safeguarding the assets – trade receivables

Trade receivables balances are clearly an important asset as they must be turned into cash relatively quickly to maintain the company's liquidity. Safeguarding procedures include:

- *Rapid billing of customers.*
- *Regular preparation of statements and reminder letters to chase up outstanding amounts.* We would expect to see a system for preparing statements regularly and reminding customers that balances are overdue in increasingly strong language as the balance becomes older. Statements and reminders should be approved and despatched by individuals not associated with maintaining the trade receivables ledger.
- *Offer of cash discounts to encourage early payment.* This should certainly be considered, although it can be quite expensive. It may be accepted practice in some sectors.
- *Approval of entries reducing the stated amount of trade receivables' balances.* These entries include cash transactions, discounts and credit notes, and write-off of bad debts. We looked at the system for control of cash receipts from credit customers at Horton Ltd. Cash receipts should be matched with open items in the trade receivables ledger and independent responsible persons should approve that matching is correct. If the customer has claimed discount, this should also be authorized and care taken to ensure that it is in accordance with company terms. Credit notes for returned goods or claims by customers should be investigated and reasons for returns and claims recorded. No goods should be accepted for return without full inspection and claims should only be allowed after investigation to discover the merits of the claim. Any write-offs should be authorized by a person who has no responsibility for day-to-day matters relating to the sales and trade receivables system.

See Case study 7.3 on page 265.

- *Ageing statement.* An important control over trade receivables is the ageing statement. It should be prepared regularly and carefully reviewed and appropriate action taken to collect outstanding open items and to ensure that write-offs are soundly based. Part of an ageing statement is shown in Case study 12.4 and we ask you to perform an activity in respect of it later in this section.

CASE STUDY 12.4

Sterndale plc: ageing statement

Part of the ageing statement of Sterndale plc at 30 November 2010 is set out below.

Credit customer's name	Credit customer's number	Address	Date	Transaction type	Open items	Balance £	Current £	1+ month £	2+ months £	3+ months £
Adams, A.	20/1284	36 Muir Street	01.07.10	Invoice	1 000					
		Carlton	15.09.10	Invoice	500					
			22.10.10	Invoice	600					
			15.11.10	Bank	−1 000	1 100		600	500	
Adcock, J.	20/1296	78a Milner	29.11.10	Invoice	250	250	250			
		Gate, Rufford								
Airton, A.	20/1489	38 Beaumont	20.02.10	Invoice	700					
		Ave. Derwent	20.03.10	Invoice	1 050	1 750				1750
Allen, T.	21/1234	356 East Road,	10.09.10	Invoice	9 000					
		Ashbury	11.09.10	Return	−4 500					
			14.09.10	Invoice	12 500					
			31.10.10	Invoice	6 500					
			07.11.10	Invoice	5 500					
			21.11.10	Bank	−16 575					
			21.11.10	Discount	−425	12 000	5 500	6 500		
Alvey, P.	21/1546	2 West Lane	17.01.10	Invoice	10 500					
		Barnstane	21.02.10	Invoice	9 000					
			08.03.10	Invoice	8 500					
			19.07.10	Bank	−4 000					
			20.08.10	Bank	−4 000					
			19.09.10	Bank	−4 000					
			20.09.10	Invoice	3 500					
			20.09.10	Bank	−3 500	16 000				16 000
Other balances						9 140 134	5 273 206	2 338 589	1 344 734	183 605
Total trade receivables balance						9 171 234	5 278 956	2 345 689	1 345 234	201 355

- *Credit limits*. A means to ensure that sales are made to customers likely to pay and that trade receivables represent (within reason) collectable amounts. It is usual to set credit limits at a low level until payment history is established but they should be periodically reviewed and approved for changes by responsible persons. In a computer system we would expect credit limits to be input to the trade receivables account and for an exception report to be prepared where transactions cause credit limits to be exceeded. Where manual override allows the transaction to be processed, an independent person should authorize. Sometimes, companies set credit limits somewhat lower than the real limit, allowing transactions to be processed, but informing sales personnel by exception report that a customer is close to exceeding the real limit.

Analytical procedures

The sales and trade receivables figures in the financial statements do not stand on their own but are affected by other transactions and bear direct relationships to other figures. As we have seen, the auditor can form conclusions by analysing figures and relationships in the financial statements and directing attention to the areas where the figures do not make sense. To give you experience in analysing trade receivables figures we give you Case study 12.5, Sterndale plc, and the related Activity 12.8. The Case study is based on an ACCA question of some years ago.

ACTIVITY 12.8

Review the figures for Sterndale's sales and trade receivables and prepare a working paper showing:

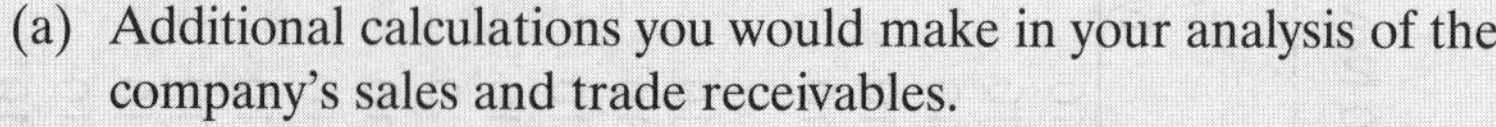

(a) Additional calculations you would make in your analysis of the company's sales and trade receivables.

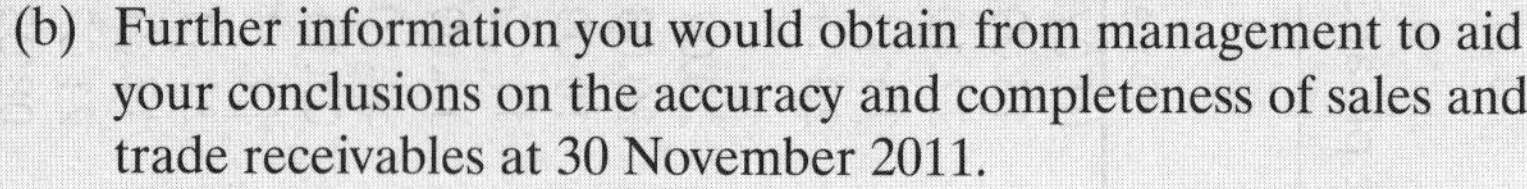

(b) Further information you would obtain from management to aid your conclusions on the accuracy and completeness of sales and trade receivables at 30 November 2011.

Sterndale plc

Additional calculations to aid analysis

We have extended the information on Sterndale's sales and trade receivables for 2011 and 2010 by calculating the percentage relationships in Figure 12.2. You should refer to this figure as you read our suggestions for further useful information:

- Percentage relationship between cash sales and credit sales for each product group and in total. This has highlighted the higher proportion of cash sales for each product group and in total.

CASE STUDY 12.5

Sterndale plc: analytical review of sales and trade receivables

Sterndale plc is a large company manufacturing a range of tools of various qualities and prices, which it sells to a variety of retail outlets from supermarkets to specialist shops and general stores. Its trade receivables ledger and sales records are kept on computer files and you have obtained a computer print-out of individual trade receivables and certain summarized information relating to sales for the nine months to 30 November 2011 and debtors at that date, three months before the company's year-end. You are also given comparative figures for the period to 30 November 2010.

	2011 £	2010 £
Sales: Product group 1 (Prices below £5)		
Cash	3 330 059	766 966
Credit	18 870 333	14 572 357
	22 200 392	15 339 323
Product group 2 (Prices £5 to below £50)		
Cash	2 148 425	973 254
Credit	15 755 117	11 192 416
	17 903 542	12 165 670

	2010 £	2011 £
Product group 3 (Prices £50 to below £100)		
Cash	1 260 409	476 048
Credit	10 197 858	7 458 085
	11 458 267	7 934 133
Product group 4 (Prices from £100 upwards)		
Cash	401 039	174 551
Credit	19 650 928	17 280 541
	20 051 967	17 455 092
Total sales	71 614 168	52 894 218
Total cash sales	7 139 932	2 390 819
Total credit sales	64 474 236	50 503 399
	71 614 168	52 894 218

Debtors at 30 November 2011/2010	No.	Value £	No.	Value £
Zero balances	950	0	900	0
Credit balances	85	−496 100	40	−234 770
£1 to £1 000	4 836	3 134 789	4 554	1 468 600
£1 001 to £10 000	290	525 600	300	376 500
£10 001 to £20 000	78	1 701 200	100	1 206 900
Over £20 001	36	4 189 956	30	2 719 010
Sundry trade receivables with collection agencies	32	115 789	76	349 856
Total	6 307	9 171 234	6 000	5 886 096

- The increase in the value of sales in the nine months to 30 November 2011 compared to the same period in the previous year (for each product group and in total). This has shown more clearly that the general increase of some 35 per cent results from increases of 44 per cent to 47 per cent in the three lower-priced groups and a lower increase (15 per cent) for the higher priced product group.
- The percentage relationship of individual product sales to total sales. This has confirmed that the importance of the higher priced products has decreased, representing 5 per cent less of total sales.
- Further information of value to the auditor is the number of transactions for each product group and in total. We have made assumptions in calculating the relevant figures but have included the additional information to show you the extent of increase in workload.

We made a number of assumptions in preparing the statistical information, principally that:

- Sales were made pro rata throughout the year (in calculating collectability ratios).
- Average sales prices lay in the middle of the range (in calculating average number of sales transactions on a nine months and weekly basis).

Further information required from management

Examples of the additional information auditors would obtain from management are:

- Auditors should ascertain if the higher proportion of cash sales was intentional, for instance, has the company offered lower price terms for cash customers, or is it for reasons outwith the control of the company?
- The auditor would wish to know if changes in product mix (lower proportion of high-value sales) resulted from company policy or whether it was outside its control.
- Are trade receivable accounts with zero balances retained indefinitely on computer file or are they removed periodically after it is clear there will be no further business with the customer?
- Why do credit balances arise, particularly in light of their high value? Is it common for customers to be suppliers also, the credit balance resulting from set-off?
- At which point are slow-paying trade receivables referred to collection agencies? Is this done automatically when the debt is a certain age or does it result from careful analysis?
- The trade receivables appear to be much slower-moving than in the previous year (12 days longer, taking the relationship of trade receivables to credit sales and ignoring credit balances). Why is this? Is it the result of problems facing the commercial sector not existing last year or are there other reasons? Are some groups of trade receivables slower-moving than others. For instance, are the large trade receivables better or worse payers than the average?

Further comments on the Sterndale plc example

The review has given the auditors the opportunity to obtain additional information from management by providing a basis for discussion that may elicit reasons for changes in the figures. It has also provided useful information to put audit work in context. The number of sales transactions processed weekly, for instance, tells auditors about the workload of client staff and also gives an indication of the size of population. It is also significant that 36 credit customers represent more than 45 per cent of the total value of trade receivables. This may suggest to the auditor that confirming those trade receivables (perhaps by circularization) may be a useful substantive test of details and an efficient way of meeting audit objectives. We comment below also on other information that may be of value to the auditor:

- The increase in cash sales would lead the auditor to pay greater attention to control of cash.
- The changes in sales mix (lower proportion of high-priced items) will help the auditor to place changes in gross profitability in context. If, for instance, Group 4 products had a bigger gross margin than the other groups, this might explain a downturn in global gross profitability.
- The large increase in sales transactions may have caused considerable pressure on personnel processing them. In such circumstances it is not uncommon for accounting and control systems to break down, and auditors would be set upon enquiry as a result. In a proper control environment management should have taken steps to maintain the effectiveness of controls.
- The large and increasing number of zero balances may give auditors cause for concern as a significant number may be dormant accounts. As a general rule, but particularly in computer systems, it is undesirable for dormant accounts to be retained in easily accessible records as they could be used for fraudulent purposes, such accounts not usually being subjected to the same degree of scrutiny as other accounts.
- The considerable reduction in trade receivables in the hands of collection agencies would lead auditors to enquire if there had been a genuine reduction or whether the company had been less assiduous in following up slow-paying trade receivables. This might be a matter for particular concern as credit customers seem to be paying some 12 days slower than in the previous year (now taking more than seven weeks to pay on average). The auditors' work would be directed to an examination of credit control procedures and an analysis of the trade receivables ageing statement to provide further information about the scale of the problem.
- Credit balances are substantial and have increased considerably since the previous year. Credit balances may arise for a number of reasons, but the auditors should ensure they are genuine. In particular, they would check if they had arisen because payments had been credited to the wrong accounts, or invoices posted to the wrong accounts or not raised at all.

Substantive approaches to prove that figures are genuine, accurate and complete

Creation of trade receivables balances

We discussed sales systems and related tests of controls in Chapters 8 and 9 and looked at substantive testing to prove that sales are genuine, accurate and complete in Chapter 10. We do not think it necessary to cover this ground

See Case study 9.4 Burbage Limited Computerized sales, trade receivables and stock records on page 338.

FIGURE 12.2 Sterndale plc: analysis of sales and trade receivables

	%	2011 £	%	Average sales transactions 9 months	Weekly	%	2010 £	%	Average sales transactions 9 months	Weekly	% incr
Sales											
Product group 1											
Cash		3 330 059	15				766 966	5			
Credit		18 870 333	85				14 572 357	95			
	31	22 200 392	100	8 880 157	227 696	29	15 339 323	100	6 135 729	157 326	44.7
Product group 2 (£5 to £50)											
Cash		2 148 425	12				973 254	8			
Credit		15 755 117	88				11 192 416	92			
	25	17 903 542	100	651 038	16 693	23	12 165 670	100	442 388	11 343	47.2
Product group 3 (£50 to £100)											
Cash		1 260 409	11				476 048	6			
Credit		10 197 858	89				7 458 085	94			
	16	11 458 267	100	152 777	3917	15	7 934 133	100	105 788	2713	44.4
Product group 4 (£100 to £500)											
Cash		401 039	2				174 551	1			
Credit		19 650 928	98				17 280 541	99			
	28	20 051 967	100	66 840	1714	33	17 455 092	100	58 184	1492	14.9
Total sales	100	71 614 168	100			100	52 894 218				35.4
Total cash		7 139 932	10				2 390 819	5			
Total credit		64 474 236	90				50 503 399	95			
		71 614 168	100				52 894 218	100			

Trade receivables at 30 November	No. 2011	%	Value	%	Ave.	No. 2010	%	Value	%	Ave.
Zero balances	950	15.1	0	0	0	900	15.10	0	0	0
Credit balances	85	1.3	−496 100	5.4	−5 836	40	0.7	−234 770	−4.0	−5 869
£1 to £1 000	4836	76.7	3 134 789	34.2	648	4 554	75.9	1 468 600	25.0	322
£1 001 to £10 000	290	4.6	525 600	5.7	1 812	300	5.0	376 500	6.4	1 255
£10 001 to £20 000	78	1.2	1 701 200	18.5	21 810	100	1.7	1 206 900	20.5	12 069
Over £20 001	36	0.6	4 189 956	45.7	116 388	30	0.5	2 719 010	46.2	90 634
Sdy drs with coll agent	32	0.5	115 789	1.3	3 618	76	1.3	349 856	5.9	4 603
Total	6 307	100.0	9 171 234	100.0	1 454	6 000	100.0	5 886 096	100.0	981

Days collectability	2011	2010
Total sales: total trade receivables	47 days	41 days
Credit sales: total trade receivables	52 days	43 days
Credit sales: receivables not in hands of collection agencies and ignoring credit balances	54 days	42 days

again except to remind you that if the sales figure is valid, this is a good starting point for ensuring that trade receivables are created on a sound basis.

Proving that the asset trade receivables is fairly stated

The auditors interest is in determining not only that trade receivables represent genuine, accurate and complete initiating transactions, but also that they represent balances that have not been cleared by the balance sheet date. The basic assertions are as follows:

Class of assertion	Assertions
Genuine	Trade receivables represent amounts actually due to the company, taking into account: ● the actual performance of services for the customer or ● transfer of title in goods transferred to the customer. ● cash received or other genuine credit entry. (The entity holds the rights to the recorded trade receivables)
Accurate	Trade receivables reflect all matters affecting their underlying valuation (including changes in foreign currency exchange rates) in accordance with relevant accounting principles. (Valuation) Trade receivables represent amounts that are collectable (Provisions for bad and doubtful debts are appropriate). (Valuation) Trade receivables represent amounts due at the balance sheet date. (cut-off)
Complete	All trade receivables are recorded. (Complete) All necessary disclosures about trade receivables have been made in the financial statements. (Classification)

We comment on these assertions below.

Relationships between trade receivables/sales and other figures in the financial statements

We have already seen that relationships between figures are investigated as part of substantive analytical procedures. Thus, changes in gross profit percentage might indicate that sales are misstated (and trade receivables likewise). However, it might equally indicate that purchases are misstated. This leads us to one of the fundamental accounting concepts – the matching or accruals concept. It is important to check that there is proper matching in the sales area. For instance, auditors of a company selling computer software would wish to ensure that potential initial servicing costs have been provided for. The same consideration applies to the sale of products where there is a history of claims by customers, such claims affecting the validity of both sales and trade receivables figures. A good example is a company selling and laying floor coverings that must be laid carefully if they are to be usable. In such circumstances the auditors should consider whether a provision for potential claims is necessary in respect of sales of the period. The auditor would examine claims in the past, determine the reasons for them and discuss with management the likelihood of future claims. Useful audit checks would include obtaining confirmation from legal advisors of the company that no claims had been received, reviewing customers' correspondence files and enquiring of management.

Is cut-off accurate?

A means to achieve matching is accurate cut-off, which is important in relation to many balance sheet and profit and loss account positions. However, it is particularly crucial for sales/trade receivables, purchases/trade payables and inventories. Accurate cut-off is necessary if transactions are to be matched to periods and we cover this aspect of cut-off when we consider inventory cut-off in Chapter 13. Note, however, that trade receivables/bank cut-off is also important, as trade receivables and bank balances should be in proper relationship to each other. Let us assume that Whygate's trade receivables control account shows a balance of £300 000 and the bank balance per the cash book is £180 000. During the audit the auditor discovers that cash for £50 000 had been received from a credit customer on 31 December 2011, but this had not been recorded in the cash book until 3 January 2012. This transaction would not affect the profit figure but it may affect the view given by the balance sheet. If the item is material (and £50 000 does represent 28 per cent of stated bank and 17 per cent of stated trade receivables) the auditor would have to consider if the trade receivables should be reduced by £50 000 and bank balance increased by the same amount.

Clearing entries: cash receipts

We shall now ask you to devise a number of substantive procedures for the receipts from credit customers of Horton limited.

ACTIVITY 12.9

See Figure 8.4 on page 317.

You already know a lot about the control of cash receipts from credit customers in Horton Ltd. Assume that Horton keeps its trade receivables ledger on an open items computer system and that input to the cash receipts updating run are drawn from entries in the cash receipts book. You will remember that:

(a) There is tight control over this book, which is signed by two members of the accounting department staff independent of the cashier and the person holding the trade receivables ledger.

(b) An accounts department member (not cashier) periodically checks the cash received book with the cash book and bank paying-in book and, monthly, the cashier reconciles cash book and bank statement balances, the reconciliation being checked and initialled by the chief accountant.

You have been asked to find evidence to prove that cash receipts have been properly entered in the cash records and the trade receivables ledger accounts. Suggest appropriate substantive procedures.

Our conclusion on the Horton system for controlling cash receipts from credit customers was that it was very reliable. This means that the extent of substantive procedures can be reduced provided that tests of controls have confirmed initial conclusions. Your substantive programme should refer to this scope decision.

Suggested tests of details include:

- Select cash receipts in the cash received book on a random basis and test for entry in bank paying-in book, cash book and in trade receivables ledger, checking in each case that names as well as amounts are correct. This test would be directed to proving that cash receipts had entered the records properly and would in particular help to detect teeming and lading fraud, not that it is likely in the Horton system. You could also test back to the cash received book from the trade receivables ledger to prove that individual entries in the ledger are supported by earlier entries. Of particular relevance is the company procedure to offset cash received against the correct original invoice.
- Select a number of cash book bankings and check to bank statement. This test would prove that the recorded bankings had been banked, and would be useful as the bank statement comes from an external source. It should be backed by confirmation of the bank balance direct by the bank, including confirmation that there were no other accounts at the bank during the year.
- Test the accuracy of the bank reconciliation statement at the balance sheet date and at the latest date one has been prepared.
- Test the entries in the trade receivables control account and confirm that the balance on this account agrees with the detailed list of trade receivables. The sum of the latter may be tested by audit software.

As you know there are other matters the auditor would ask the bank to confirm. See page 425.

Clearing entries: claims for cash discount

Auditors should ensure that for the items selected above, discount has been approved in line with company policy.

Clearing entries: credit notes for returned goods or claims by customers

Auditors should review the company's analysis of returns and claims. This is an important substantive test of detail for proving provisions for claims are accurate and that credit notes have been issued for good reasons. Auditors should back up this global test by selecting credit notes randomly and checking to GRNs, ensuring that goods were inspected on receipt and that the company had investigated the customer's claim before issuing a credit note.

Clearing entries: write-offs of trade receivables' balances

Auditors would select major write-offs and the remainder on a random basis and check that in each case an independent responsible official has given approval in writing. If the debts have been in the hands of a collection agency, the reports of the agency should also be examined.

Are accounting methods used for determining sales and related trade receivables acceptable and applied consistently with previous years?

Tests in this area are accuracy tests, as they are designed to prove the value of sales and trade receivables has been determined on the basis of appropriate accounting principles.

Consistency is a fundamental accounting concept and auditors must ensure that accounting methods are consistently applied. For instance, if a company had been taking up sales on the basis of transfer of a product to customers (this would be normal) but decided in the current year to record sales only when cash was received from customers, the auditor would ensure:

- The new method was appropriate to the circumstances of the company.
- The effect of the change was disclosed in the notes to the financial statements.

Company management might decide to record trade receivables net of cash discount, rather than gross as had been done in the past, on the ground that discounts were always granted. The effect of this would be to take up an expense earlier than would otherwise have been the case. Again auditors should ensure that the new method was appropriate and the effect disclosed.

Do trade receivables represent customers who exist and represent amounts owed to the company?

ISA 505 – *External confirmations* recognizes that 'audit evidence in the form of external confirmations received directly by the auditor may be more reliable than evidence generated internally by the entity'. But note that doubts about the trustworthiness of replies and the fact of 'no replies' does mean that other substantive procedures should be adopted as well.

We suggested above that proving that sales are genuine, accurate and complete is an important first step in proving trade receivables. However, at the balance sheet date the auditor must prove not only existence of the customer, but that ownership of the trade receivable lies with the company. One way of doing this is for the auditor to circularize credit customers; another is to test after-date receipts – a test that may be more useful as:

- replies from credit customers may not always be trustworthy, as there is no certainty that their own systems are adequate, and in any event many reply without proper consideration of the items making up the balance;
- credit customers may not even reply (modern computer systems may make it difficult to determine a balance at a particular date).

It is common practice for auditors to carry out circularizations of trade receivables at interim dates, as there is often insufficient time at the final examination to carry out the whole process. There are, however, some ground rules to be observed:

- If the results of the circularization are to be relied upon when forming conclusions about the year-end trade receivables, the date of the circularization should not be too distant from the year-end. Three months prior to the year-end is probably about the maximum permissible.
- Auditors must be satisfied that the company's internal control system for sales and trade receivables is sound. If the system is weak, it may be necessary to circularize credit customers at the year-end.
- Auditors should review the trade receivables ledger and control account between the interim and year-end date and obtain explanations for material changes affecting trade receivables in that period.

- If the results of the circularization are unsatisfactory (for instance, significant differences have been revealed, or replies have been received from a low number of credit customers), auditors may make a further circularization at the year-end date. They may decide to circularize some credit customers at the year-end as a matter of course to reduce identified audit risk (for instance, the auditor may have doubts that cash receipts are all being recorded).

ACTIVITY 12.10

Assume that the auditor circularized 60 credit customers of Sterndale. Do you think that this is too many? What would cause you to think that a lower number of credit customers might be selected, say 30, or even ten?

This is a good question, and one that you cannot really answer, unless you had much more information about the company. If you had adopted a business risk approach to this client, you might have formed the view that management is trustworthy and have established a good control environment – and that control risk was low. If this was the case you might feel that selecting 60 credit customers was unnecessary, particularly if you can get audit satisfaction from simpler procedures such as examining after-date receipts from credit customers. A credit customer who has paid a balance would certainly appear to be in agreement with it. Auditors might decide to circularize a restricted number of high-value balances to get good coverage of the trade receivables figure in the balance sheet.

We cannot leave the subject of existence and ownership of trade receivables without mentioning factoring, a procedure involving the sale of trade receivables' balances to a third party. Auditors would wish to ensure the trade receivables transferred were excluded from the financial statements, as ownership has passed to a third party, even though the initial sales transaction had been with the company. The auditor would examine the factoring agreement and test the system for recording factored trade receivables. It might be desirable for the auditor to obtain confirmation from the third party of balances transferred. The auditor should also determine the procedure if trade receivables sold turn out to be bad and also whether payments made to the company were net of retentions payable at a later date.

Does the trade receivables figure represent amounts that will be collected?

This question is concerned with the value at which trade receivables are stated. Current assets should be at realizable value if this is less than the amount at which originally stated. You will remember that a key control in the sales and trade receivables area is for credit worthiness to be checked before the order is accepted. If auditors are satisfied that credit control is adequate, this will be persuasive evidence that the trade receivables stated in the balance sheet are collectable.

See Table 8.2 on page 318.

It will normally be necessary, however, for auditors to carry out substantive tests at the final examination to provide evidence that the recorded trade receivables are all collectable or that adequate provision for bad and doubtful debts has been made. However, the scope of detailed substantive tests will depend, as we saw in Chapter 10, on the auditor's evaluation of the system of control over credit given. Procedures for assessing collectability are discussed below.

Audit tests for collectability

A good way to assess the collectability of trade receivables is to examine an ageing statement, showing for each debtor the total outstanding and the ageing of each open item in bands (say) of 30 days. You have already seen part of the ageing statement of Sterndale plc in Case study 12.4 on page 467. We shall now ask you to perform an activity in respect of it.

ACTIVITY 12.11

Review the extract from the ageing statement of Sterndale plc and list the matters you would raise with management. You are interested in ensuring that the trade receivables have the realizable value stated in the financial statements, taking into account the provision for bad and doubtful debts.

General comments on Activity 12.11

The trade receivables' balances of Sterndale plc at 30 November 2011, ignoring credit balances and trade receivables in the hands of collection agencies are summarized below:

	£	%	%	Suggested provision £
Current amounts	5 278 956	57.56	2	105 579
One month old	2 345 689	25.58	4	93 828
Two months old	1 345 234	14.66	6	80 714
More than three months old	201 355	2.20	12	24 163
Total	£9 171 234	100.00	3.32	304 284

This statement gives some additional information. About 2 per cent of trade receivables are more than three months old and the auditor should ensure that a decision is properly taken as to collectability. It may be desirable to provide for some trade receivable balances in full, but to make a general provision for bad and doubtful debts based on past experience and expectation. The summary above assumes that no specific provision for doubtful debts is deemed necessary (but see our comments below).

Specific comments on Activity 12.11

Adams, A.	The debtor is paying with a delay of more than four months. The auditor should ascertain if a delay of this nature was common for this debtor. If so, a provision may not be necessary.
Adcock, J.	Appears in order.
Airton, A.	Both open items are more than eight months old and the auditor should consider the balance for 100 per cent provision, unless management know of good reasons why they believe it to be collectable.
Allen, T.	The debtor has taken discount for the payment in November of the September invoices and the auditor should ascertain if this is in accordance with company terms. If the debtor is taking discount whenever payment is made, the auditor may wish to see a provision for discount on open items in the accounts.
Alvey, P.	The debtor is paying round-sum amounts – always a danger sign. Further, no round-sum payments have been made in October and November and the auditor should determine why, particularly as the company now appears to supply goods to the customer on immediate payment of cash. The balance is now more than eight months old. In the circumstances the auditor may wish to see a provision of the majority of the balance.

Audit software may be used to interrogate files to extract information useful to the auditor. If the company does not prepare ageing information in sufficient detail, it may be possible to extract the further information required. A further use of audit software in assessing collectability might be a comparison of outstanding balance with credit limits to ensure that such limits have not been materially exceeded. This CAAT may be used as a test of the adequacy of credit control as well as providing evidence as to collectability. However, you should not take things at face value. A credit limit being exceeded may not be evidence that a debt is bad (although it may be) nor that the credit control procedures are poor (although they may be). A basic rule of auditing is that all parts of an equation must be tested, so if you wish to use credit limits to assess collectability, you must ensure the credit limits have been properly determined in the first place. We have suggested elsewhere in this book that systems are only as good as the people who control them so, although the existence of a credit limit would be evidence of strong control, the failure to update regularly would negate the control and its value to the auditor.

A further procedure to prove collectability is testing post-balance sheet receipts from credit customers, although as we noted above it can also prove genuineness and accuracy. It is good practice to include in the working papers a summary of trade receivables, showing, among other things, the amount and proportion received from credit customers since the balance sheet date up to the time when the final field work is complete.

In Chapter 14 we discuss the auditor's responsibility in relation to post-balance sheet events.

Is there proper disclosure of: (a) trade receivables receivable in the short, medium and long term?; (b) trade receivables subject to encumbrances?

This heading relates to disclosure and presentation and is therefore a completeness matter. Generally, trade receivables will be receivable within one year. If the term is longer, the auditor should ensure that the debtor is reported as being long term in nature. Audit checks would include review of contracts with credit customers and enquiry as to normal commercial practice. For instance, it may be common practice in Pykestone's industry to retain part of the contract consideration until elapse of a predetermined period to ensure no serious building faults exist.

Regarding potential encumbrances, trade receivables may be subject to a floating charge to secure bank and other loans and the auditor should refer to loan agreements. If trade receivables are charged this should be disclosed in the notes to the financial statements.

Summary

In this chapter we have discussed the pre-final planning process and have considered typical audit work performed by the auditor at or near the balance sheet date. We have considered the role of analytical procedures and have introduced you to approaches to analytical review. We concentrated in particular on ratio analysis as the main analysis tool and emphasized the need to analyse in detail as well as in global terms. We highlighted the fact that auditors are insiders in terms of the information they have the right to obtain and that more detailed information is thus available to the auditor than would be to investment analysts.

We have considered general matters of importance to the auditor relating to non-current assets and trade receivables and related income and expense, highlighting in particular the need to determine if figures in the financial statements are genuine, accurate and complete. We considered tests of existence, condition, ownership, valuation and disclosure.

Key points of the chapter

- Pre-final work is directed to (a) resolving known problems; (b) stocktaking instructions; (c) timetable for preparation of year-end financial statements; (d) circularizations; (e) requirements of accounting, reporting and auditing standards; (f) new legislation;
- Balance sheet date work includes (a) bank confirmations; (b) stock count observation; (c) stages of completion of long-term contracts/assets in course of construction; (d) letters to other professionals.
- Auditors should not expect to find major problems at final examination if interim and pre-final work is carefully performed. Bridging work between interim and final examinations is required.
- Analytical procedures are 'evaluations of financial information through analysis of plausible relationships among both financial and non-financial data. Analytical procedures also encompass such investigation as is necessary of identified fluctuations or relationships that are inconsistent with other relevant information or that differ from expected values by a significant amount.'
- Analytical procedures are used: (a) at the planning stage to obtain an understanding of the entity and its environment; (b) as substantive procedures when responding to the risk of material misstatement at the assertion level; (c) just before the end of the audit when forming an overall conclusion as to whether the financial statements as a whole are consistent with the auditor's understanding of the entity.
- Analytical procedures involve analysis of relationships: (a) between items of financial data, or between items of financial and non-financial data; or (b) between comparable financial information from different periods or different entities – to identify consistencies and predicted patterns or significant fluctuations and unexpected relationships.
- Auditors use ratio analysis and other interpretative tools. Significant changes in figures revealed by analytical review may result from: (a) errors; (b) changes in accounting practice; (c) changes in management policy; (d) changes in general commercial factors; (e) changes in commercial factors affecting the client only; (f) fraud.

- Our advice:(a) look at the figures broadly, before calculating ratios; (b) calculate selected ratios to confirm initial impression; (c) remember many ratios are interrelated.
- Ratio analysis can be useful, but ratios are meaningless unless compared with other ratios. Industry statistics may be useful but must have been prepared in the same way as company ratios. Some industries have special measures of success or performance indicators.
- Other analytical tools include: (a) graphs; (b) regression analysis and multiple regression analysis; (c) z-scores.
- The auditor's substantive procedures at the assertion level may be derived from tests of details, from substantive analytical procedures, or from a combination of both. Analytical procedures may be more effective or efficient than tests of details in reducing the risk of material misstatement at the assertion level.
- It may be efficient to use analytical data prepared by the entity, provided they have been properly prepared. Budgets are only of value if they are established as results to be expected rather than as goals to be achieved.
- Accounting standards are designed to aid the preparation of financial statements that give a true and fair view.
- Financial statement assertions in respect of assets, liabilities and related revenues and costs are grouped under the headings 'genuine', 'accurate' and 'complete', prompting questions about existence, condition, ownership, valuation and disclosure/presentation in the financial statements.
- *Genuine* means that figures in financial statements are supported by real transactions and real assets and liabilities, that something has happened or exists to support the figures. *Accurate* means that figures have been properly calculated, taking into account all relevant factors. *Complete* means that figures include all relevant balances and disclosures.

Non-current assets

- Tangible non-current assets are (a) held for use in the production or supply of goods or services, for rental to others, or for administrative purposes; and (b) expected to be used in more than one period. Inherent risk factors relate to: (a) technological changes; (b) closure of part of business; (c) determining useful lives; (d) revaluations; (e) idle assets; (f) significant assets in course of construction; (g) own construction of non-current assets; (h) moveable, high-value assets.
- Specific controls are necessary over: (a) acquisitions, revaluation, impairment; (b) safeguarding; (c) disposals; (d) maintenance, insurance; (e) authorization of depreciation charges and accumulations.
- Main control documents for acquisitions are non-current assets budgets – long, medium and short term
- The non-current assets register is an important control document but must be held by persons independent of those using and having custody of the assets, comparing it periodically with physical assets and vice versa. If a non-current assets register is not kept or is found to be subject to error, control risk will be increased and auditors may have to extend substantive tests of detail.
- Disposals should be authorized in writing by individuals with appropriate authority.
- Proper maintenance and insurance are necessary if assets are to be safeguarded; regular maintenance maintains or extends useful economic lives. Capital/revenue decision is important.
- Depreciation is a measure of economic benefits of the tangible non-current asset consumed during the financial period, reflecting the reduction of economic useful life arising from use, passage of time or obsolescence because of changes in technology or demand for the goods and services produced by the asset.
- Economic useful lives is approved at point of purchase and annually. Amended annual economic useful lives and depreciation based thereon makes it unlikely that material impairment losses will arise. Unexpected changes in estimate of recoverable amount, may cause impairment losses. Impairment is the reduction in the recoverable amount of a non-current asset or goodwill below its carrying amount. The *recoverable amount* is the higher of net realizable value and value in use.
- Significant profits or losses on disposal of non-current assets may indicate failure to identify useful economic lives.
- Analytical procedures on non-current assets might be directed to significant additions and disposals, profits/losses on disposal, revaluations, significant repairs and maintenance charges.
- Substantive procedures on additions include: (a) determine thinking behind investment programme; (b) review board minutes and non-current assets budget; (c) review management analyses of variances between budgeted and actual acquisition cost; (d) trace major items in budget to acquisition documentation; (e) check the capital/revenue decision.
- On revaluation of non-current assets, financial statement assertions include: *Genuine:* revaluation of non-current assets takes into account real conditions within the company; selected basis is appropriate; *Accurate:* the calculation of current value of non-current assets appropriately reflects their underlying value in accordance with relevant accounting principles; *Complete:* all non-current assets in a particular class have been revalued.

- If a management's valuer and/or an auditor's valuer is used, they must be properly qualified and scope of work appropriate. Valuer objectives and the matters to be examined must be clearly stated. The valuer must know why work is being carried out and be given reliable information. Assumptions and methods used must be clearly stated and justified in valuers' reports. The timing of the report may be important.
- Significant disposals of non-current assets – determine the reasons and whether impairment of remaining assets is necessary. Substantive procedures include (a) checking disposal approvals and removal from the non-current assets register; (b) tracing to authorized sales despatch notes.
- Non-current assets balances: (a) work on acquisitions and disposals help to prove non-current assets balances are genuine, accurate and complete; (b) existence, condition and ownership checks may be proved by direct tests, such as physical examination, and indirect evidence such as smooth flow of production and costs associated with assets; (c) supporting evidence of ownership, including deeds of title; (d) tests to ensure validity of cost/revalued amount; (e) tests on disclosures and presentation; (f) testing validity of non-current assets register.
- Depreciation: audit work is closely allied to work on the non-current assets. Specific matters of interest are: useful economic lives and appropriateness of depreciation method; residual values; depreciation on revalued non-current assets.

Trade receivables

- It is important to determine the point at which the property in goods is transferred or service performed. Audit work on sales cannot be divorced from work on the trade receivables.
- Inherent risks may be enhanced by: (a) large number of new customers; (b) significant changes in collectability; (c) new products; (d) new products from competitors; (e) sales on 'sale or return' basis; (f) above average returns; (g) new staff; (h) complex computerized accounting system.
- The auditor would expect to see controls over: creation, clearance and safeguarding of trade receivables.
- Controls over creation and clearance of trade receivables include: (a) policy on title passing to third parties, especially in e-commerce environment; (b) policy included in written terms of trade; (c) clear statement on obligations of customers if goods delivered on sale or return.
- Important elements safeguarding trade receivables are: (a) rapid billing of customers; (b) regular preparation of statements and reminder letters; (c) offer of cash discounts; (d) approval of entries reducing the stated amount of trade receivables' balances, including write-off of bad debts; (e) ageing statement; (f) credit limits.
- Analytical procedures are directed to the relationship between sales and trade receivables and other transactions and balances.
- Substantive approaches cover: (a) creation of trade receivables; (b) proving trade receivables are genuine, accurate and complete; (c) proving reasonable relationships between trade receivables/sales and other figures in the financial statements; (d) checking cut-off; (e) proving clearing entries are genuine, accurate and complete, especially write-offs; (f) proving accounting methods are acceptable and consistent; (g) proving that trade receivables represent customers who exist and amounts owed to the company; (h) proving collectability; (i) checking proper disclosure in the short, medium and long term, and those subject to encumbrances.
- Two useful tests are to circularize credit customers and to test after-date receipts. However, replies from credit customers may not always be trustworthy and credit customers may not even reply.
- Factoring causes ownership of receivable to pass to a third party, The factoring agreement should be examined, the system for recording factored trade receivables tested, and confirmation from the third party obtained of balances transferred. The factoring agreement should contain procedures if trade receivables sold turn become bad and whether payments made to the company are net of retentions.
- Audit software may be used to test ageing statements, to compare balances with credit limits, and to test adequacy of credit control procedures.

Further reading

Useful articles on analytical reviews to supplement your studies include:

Higson, A. (1991) 'The Rise of Analytical Auditing Procedures', in Sherer, M. and Turley, S. (eds), *Current Issues In Auditing*, second edn, London: Paul Chapman Publishing.

Higson, A. (1997) 'Developments in Audit Approaches: From Audit Efficiency to Audit Effectiveness', in Sherer, M. and Turley, S. (eds), *Current Issues In Auditing*, third edn, London: Paul Chapman Publishing.

ISAs that you should read in conjunction with this chapter are:

ISA 505 – *External confirmations*

ISA 520 – *Analytical procedures*

ISA 620 – *Using the work of an auditor's expert*

Accounting standards referred to in the text are:

IAS 1 – *Presentation of financial statements*

IAS 16 – *Property, plant and equipment*

IAS 36 – *Impairment of assets*

FRS 11 – *Impairment of assets and goodwill*

FRS 15 – *Tangible fixed assets*

Self-assessment questions (solutions available to students)

12.1 Consider the following statements and explain why they may be true or false.

- (a) The audit approach to any asset will involve the auditor in a consideration of condition.
- (b) If the analytical review discloses no variations from the previous year, the auditor need not enquire further.
- (c) Analytical review is an evidence-gathering procedure performed as part of substantive procedures.
- (d) Planning feedback means that audit plans are altered to take account of changed circumstances.
- (e) A genuine transaction is one that has been authorized by an independent responsible official.

12.2 Turn to the Pykestone example (Case study 12.3) and draft an audit programme for:

- (a) Non-current asset additions during the year.
- (b) Non-current asset disposals during the year.
- (c) Non-current assets held at 31 December 2011.
- (d) The depreciation charge of the year.

12.3 Draft a request for confirmation of a trade receivables balance in the accounting records of a company audited by you, explaining why you have included each item.

12.4 Consider the following items of income and expense and state: whether they bear a relationship to each other or not; if they are related in any way, in what way they should move in relation to each other; the reasons for your answer in each case.

- (a) Sales of manufacturing concern:
  - Bank interest
  - Administrative expense
  - Commission to sales personnel
  - Distribution cost
  - Production royalties
- (b) Cost of production of a manufacturing concern:
  - Trade receivables
  - Cost of non-current assets in use
  - Loss on disposal of factory equipment
  - Inventory levels
  - Directors' emoluments
- (c) Gas company income
  - Number of units of gas used
  - Temperature in winter months
  - Electricity company prices
  - Number of employees.

Self-assessment questions (solutions available to tutors)

12.5 Consider the following items of income and expense and state: whether they bear a relationship to each other or not; if they are related in any way, in what way they should move in relation to each other; the reasons for your answer in each case.

- (a) Newspaper advertising income
  - Number of rolls of newsprint used
  - Circulation revenue
  - Number of column classified advertising inches
- (b) Fuel costs of a bus company
  - Number of passengers carried
  - Depreciation on bus fleet
  - Drivers' wages

(c) Fees of a practising accountant
- Quantity of stationery purchased
- Charge-out rates
- Office rental.

12.6 'If management review useful lives annually, impairment reviews will rarely be necessary.' Give your views on this statement. What audit procedures should you carry out to see if an impairment review is necessary?

12.7 You ask your audit assistant to carry out a review of after-date receipts from credit customers. Explain to them the reason for such a review and show how it should be performed. What kind of conclusion might they be able to form after carrying out such a review?

Topics for class discussion without solutions

12.8 Auditing is a logical process. Discuss, in the light of our discussion of check this numbering the audit of non-current assets and trade receivables in this chapter.

12.9 Analytical procedures represent an important tool in the hands of the auditor. Discuss.

13

Final work: Specific problems related to inventories, construction contracts and trade payables

LEARNING OBJECTIVES

After studying this chapter you should be able to:

- **Apply the general principles for determining the validity of the amount attributed to inventories, construction contracts and trade payables.**
- **Describe the inherent risks affecting inventories, construction contracts and trade payables and explain the control introduced by management and the detection procedures carried out by the auditor to keep audit risk to acceptable low levels.**
- **Evaluate a company's system for the determination of physical existence, condition and ownership of inventories and construction contracts.**
- **Explain how identification by the auditor of judgements by management in relation to inventories, construction contracts and trade payables helps to direct audit effort to critical areas.**
- **Draft audit programmes to test the amounts attributed to inventories, construction contracts and trade payables.**

Learning objectives, 485
Introduction, 486
Inventories, 486
Analytical procedures, 491
Valuation of construction contracts, 509
Trade payables and purchases, 515
Analytical procedures, 518
Summary, 526
Key points of the chapter, 526
Further reading, 527
Self-assessment questions (solutions available to students), 527
Self-assessment questions (solutions available to tutors), 529
Topics for class discussion without solutions, 529

INTRODUCTION

In this chapter we use the same general approach as we adopted in Chapter12, discussing first the nature of the asset or liability concerned and then moving to identification of inherent risks and expected controls in the area. We discuss substantive procedures in the context of financial statement assertions, using cases and analytical procedures as appropriate and suggest substantive programme approaches and tests.

INVENTORIES

IAS 11 – *Construction contracts* is the international accounting standard relevant to construction contracts which we discuss in a later section of this chapter. SSAP 9 complies in all material respects with IAS 2 and with IAS 11. We use the term 'construction contacts' in this chapter.

In this section we look at the work the auditor performs on inventories. The amount attributable to inventories has a significant impact on measurement of income of manufacturing and trading concerns. IAS 2 – *Inventories* is the international accounting standard relevant to inventories, while SSAP 9 – *Stocks and long-term contracts* is valid in the UK and Ireland. We do not discuss the accounting standards in detail but cover the main matters of interest to the auditor.

The nature of inventories

Inventories normally represent a significant asset of manufacturing companies and has a direct effect on the profit and loss account, any under- or overstatement of inventories resulting in an under- or overstatement of profit.

Inventories vary as much in character as non-current assets and pose a variety of problems for auditors who must adapt their procedures to the nature of the product. If the auditor is checking existence and value of mineral oil products, for instance, different procedures will be needed than if the company is manufacturing and selling television sets. We discuss the major differences in audit procedure for these two examples below.

Mineral oil

Crude oils vary greatly in quality, some being more suitable for production of lighter products and others for heavier products.

- *Cost*. Mineral oil products vary considerably in nature, ranging from butane and naphtha (both light products) through petrols and heating oils to bitumen, a very heavy product. All these products are produced from crude oil, input to the refining process. Production of one product results also in a range of other products, so management is faced with the difficulty of allocating costs to products in a typical joint cost situation. In determining cost of individual product throughputs, management may have to use arbitrarily determined figures as a key for allocating cost. Thus throughputs might be valued at net realizable value and the resultant figures used to allocate actual costs to products. Having determined total cost in this way, cost per litre of throughput can be determined and this cost used to value inventories at the year-end.

Some crude oils are viscous and are kept heated to retain liquid form.

- *Quantities and qualities*. Mineral oil products are normally liquids and stored typically in tanks or underground storage. In determining quantities management take the following factors into account:
  (a) The capacity of the tank in which the product is stored must be known and, in particular, the conversion factor from millimetres to litres, so if

the depth of oil in the tank is known (in millimetres) it will be possible for management to determine cubic volume (in litres).

(b) The temperature of the product in the tank must be known as the higher the temperature, the greater the recorded quantity. It is common practice to determine quantities at a constant temperature of 60 degrees Fahrenheit.

(c) One product may look much like another. Petrol with high octane content may not be easily distinguished from low octane petrol. Most people would probably not be able to distinguish light heating oil from medium heating oil. Thus, mineral oil companies take samples of products from each tank at the time of counting and conduct laboratory tests to be certain of the nature and quality of the product.

Television sets

- *Cost*. Television sets are manufactured from a predetermined number of components, some manufactured by the assembler, but many bought in. The television set manufacturer has all the normal accounting problems of allocation of direct and indirect costs to individual products and of determining stage of completion of work in progress. However, although there may be some subjectivity in allocating costs, essentially it will be possible to determine the cost of manufacture and assembly with fair accuracy.
- *Quantities*. Unlike liquids, television sets and components can be counted in a straightforward manner. The uninformed person might have some difficulty in identifying many of the components but there are not the same identification problems as those in the mineral oil industry, particularly if the company ensures components are properly labelled and segregated.

These two examples show that auditors must adapt audit procedures to the nature of inventories. In the case of a mineral oil company, for instance, auditors take samples of products and send them to an independent laboratory for analysis. In the case of the television set manufacturer, they may need to examine bills of materials and costing records to determine component usage and manuals to determine nature and use of components.

In Chapter 7 we emphasized the need for a sound control environment within which the company operates, designed to ensure that the controls in particular areas will be effective.

The costing system plays an important role in determining cost of inventories and construction contracts and auditors pay particular attention to ensuring that costs are genuine, accurate and complete. The auditor will normally concentrate first on financial accounting records and then ensure that costs have entered the costing system properly. Integration of the financial accounting and costing system would be important and auditors would check reconciliations between the two.

Many management accountants believe management accounting has tied itself too much to historical financial accounting records. This may be true, but auditors have different objectives and reconciliations help ensure completeness and accuracy of costs used for calculating inventory values.

In determining cost of inventories, some costs are fairly easily allocated. However, overheads may have to be allocated on an arbitrary basis. The auditors will determine that the methods used to allocate overheads to production are reasonable in the circumstances. For instance, if application of overheads is based on labour cost content of units of production when labour cost represents only (say) 10 per cent of prime cost, the auditor might consider that allocation on another basis (such as material cost content or machine hour basis) that is more reasonable. We have already seen that joint production, as in the mineral oil industry, may make arbitrary allocation necessary. Some products might be recognized as 'main' products, whereas others might be treated as by-products, their income on disposal being treated as reduction in cost of the main products. Another problem is that IAS 2 and SSAP 9 require overheads to be allocated to inventories on the basis of normal production levels, and auditors will enquire carefully into management estimates of future activity.

Remember that the basic valuation rule for inventory is 'the lower of cost and net realizable value'.

The other element of inventory valuation – net realizable value – may also cause problems for the auditor. Net realizable value may not be easily determinable because inventories in existence at the balance sheet date may not be used or sold until after audit field work is completed, so there may still be doubt about amounts realizable on disposal. For partly completed goods there is the added problem of assessing the cost of completing the manufacture and assembly of products.

Construction contracts require a longer period to complete and are likely to extend over the balance sheet date. We shall pay attention to auditor decision-making and evidence search in relation to construction contracts later in this chapter.

Inherent risks affecting inventories and work in progress

We give below examples of inherent risk factors in the area. One particular problem with inventories is that they are continually acquired, used or disposed of. While purchase and sale of inventories result in entries in the double entry system, inventories themselves are not normally readily determinable from accounting entries. This means that inherent risk in the inventory area will be high as inventories normally have to be determined by count. Other inherent risk factors are:

- Demand for the company's products may alter significantly, so some product lines might become less saleable.
- Production levels may have changed significantly, so new 'normal' levels have to be established and new optimum inventory levels determined.
- Defects in product lines may have come to light, so saleability or usability is threatened and the company's reputation may be generally under threat.
- Inventories are attractive and easily transportable, making attempted theft likely.
- The production process is complex so cost allocations are rendered difficult.
- The company's production process produces joint products, so cost allocations are arbitrary.
- There have been significant variances from standard costs.
- Competitors have provided a more risky environment by introducing new products or existing products at lower prices so there is doubt about saleability of company inventories.
- Complex calculation of overheads.

Apart from these factors there are others that relate to the assertion that inventories exist. These include:

- Reliability of inventory recording systems, including those that determine the stage of completion of work in progress.
- Where inventories are not counted at year-end the reliability of records used to roll forward from count date to year-end date.
- Sometimes inventories are at locations not under the control of the organization, such as inventories on consignment, inventories held in bonded warehouses and inventories in transit.
- Poor physical controls particularly over high-value items and those subject to deterioration unless protected.
- Independence and experience of inventory counters and their supervisors.
- Degree to which inventory levels fluctuate.
- Inventories requiring special procedures to count and identify both quantity and quality, such as the mineral oil products mentioned above.

We discuss counts at dates other than year-end below.

ACTIVITY 13.1

Explain why significant variances from standard costs are an inherent risk factor.

Variances between actual cost and standard cost suggest either that actual cost has been wrongly determined or that the standards are invalid. The latter would be particularly relevant if the company is using standard costs as an approximation to actual cost of inventories. The existence of variances would therefore set auditors on enquiry, the first line of enquiry being the company's own variance analysis.

Variances can arise for a number of reasons but – very important – the auditor should determine if the variances have arisen for ongoing reasons, such as changes in product prices, material usage or labour efficiency. Variances which have arisen because of 'disasters', such as one-off strikes or political crises may be ignored, unless they are likely to recur. Important variances are those that represent changed permanent circumstances and these should be adjusted by management in determining inventory values for financial statement purposes.

Controls to reduce the impact of inherent risk

As suggested above, inventory has characteristics that make it difficult to control, so periodic inventory counts will often be necessary to establish inventory quantities, condition and ownership and the accuracy of inventory records, if any. Apart from a satisfactory control environment, we would expect to see controls in the following areas, if control risk is to be minimized:

Proper cut-off will help to establish ownership.

- Acquisitions of inventory.
- Safeguarding inventories.

- Disposals of inventories whether by sale or otherwise.
- Determining existence, condition and ownership at period-end dates.
- Valuation of inventories.

Acquisitions of inventories

Remember this is particularly important in an e-commerce relationship.

As with sales, the point at which title in the inventory item passes must be known, this time from the supplier to the company, bearing in mind that inventories may be transferred into the possession but not ownership of the company. Particular controls are needed to identify such inventories and we discuss these when we address observation of inventory counts below.

Safeguarding inventories

We would expect the company to have physical safeguards over inventories. How secure these physical safeguards should be, is dependent on the nature of the inventories. Clearly, controls over inventories of sand at a builders merchant will be of a different order from controls by a jeweller holding inventories of diamond bracelets or from controls over electronic software. Basically, controls will be tighter the more valuable an item is, the more moveable and accessible it is, and we would expect the jeweller's inventories to be kept in a safe in a protected room with access restricted by such measures as double keys. Slipping a diamond ring into a pocket is much easier and worthwhile than hiring a truck to move a load of sand. The builders merchant might need no more than a low wall as protection. Electronic software would have to be protected by computer security measures such as access controls and secure back-up.

Apart from direct controls we would expect to see restriction of access via documentation, as it is important that inventory should only be released if properly authorized. Thus, jewellers would only allow a diamond bracelet to be released if absolutely certain about the credentials of the customer. The same would apply to those firms offering electronic software over the Internet. The builders merchant might only allow a customer to remove sand through the gate on production of an invoice or delivery note signed by staff in the accounting department.

Apart from these access controls we would expect the company to keep inventories in an environment which prevents deterioration and allows easy identification. Thus, inventories of butter and meat products will be kept in refrigerated stores and inventories of components for an assembly process should all be carefully labelled. This would be important for selection as needed and would aid counting.

Disposals of inventories whether by sale or otherwise

We have covered sales of inventory in a number of previous chapters and shall not discuss normal sales here. Inventories may, however, be disposed of outwith the normal sales system for reasons such as specialist sales, very large sales and sales of scrap. Such disposals or disposals where manual override takes place, should receive special approval at an appropriate level. Thus, disposal of slow-moving or obsolete inventory should only occur after careful inspection and informed decisions as to disposal prices have been taken, possibly after inviting bids from potential customers. Disposal decisions should be recorded in writing and be evidenced by signature of the person giving approval. No adjustments to inventory records should be made without approval at a high level, as failure to do so may enable individuals to hide misappropriation of inventory.

Determining existence, condition and ownership at period-end dates

We would expect to see adequate procedures for physical inventory counts and timely reconciliation of quantities counted to inventory records, if any, followed by investigation of any significant differences. The existence of significant differences would be a control risk factor. Physical inventory counts do not merely prove existence of inventory, but are also used to identify inventories in poor physical condition and to help clarify ownership. Proving ownership is a more difficult matter than proving existence and additional procedures, including cut-off procedures, will have to be performed. We discuss inventory count and cut-off, and the auditor's duties in respect of them below, including inventories counted on a rotating basis rather than at the year-end. Using inventory quantities recorded in inventory records rather than year-end count may heighten control risk and would only be acceptable if the inventory records are reliable.

Valuation of inventories

The basic principle for determining amounts at which inventory is stated is the lower of cost and net realizable value. This means there should be controls to ensure the costing and other records are reliable and will produce inventory values prepared on a consistent basis. Standard costs may be used if they are close to actual cost, so we would also expect analysis of variances and adjustment of standards as appropriate. Failure to amend standard costs or the existence of variances not investigated would be control risk factors. We discuss audit approaches to inventory valuation below.

ANALYTICAL PROCEDURES

We shall now move into a Case study in the inventories area (Case study 13.1).

CASE STUDY 13.1

Billbrook Limited: analysis of inventory, Part 1

You have been provided with the following lead schedule information for the year to 31 December 2010 concerning inventories, which you are about to audit. The company only commenced trading on 1 January 2010, so you have little company history to help you. However, the company has provided you with budgeted information prepared before commencement of trading.

	Actual	**Budget**
Sales	3 965 000	5 580 000
Production cost	4 815 000	4 868 760
Less: Closing inventories	1 049 050	597 465
Cost of sales	3 765 950	4 271 295
Gross profit	199 050	1 308 705

ACTIVITY 13.2

Look at the figures in the Case study and give your initial impressions. Remember that your review is intended to set the scene for your substantive testing procedures of inventories.

Your first impression will be that sales are well below expectation, that production cost has just about met budgeted levels but that inventory is nearly double the expected levels. The first conclusion might be that production has continued at budgeted levels despite lower than expected sales with the result that inventory levels are high. There might be severe doubts about saleability of inventories. Three relevant ratios are:

- Sales decrease from budget: 29 per cent.
- Increase in days inventory held from 51 days per the budget to 102 days actual results.
- Decrease in gross margin from a high 23.5 per cent to a low 5 per cent, which may indicate the company has been forced to drop selling price (or not to increase despite higher production costs).

This would set the auditor on enquiry to discover where the problem lies. Assume that you have asked the company to give you more detailed information about the results of individual product lines (there are seven of them) and this is set out in Case study 13.1 (Part 2).

CASE STUDY 13.1

Billbrook Limited: analysis of inventories, Part 2

Actual results	**A**	**B**	**C**	**D**	**E**	**F**	**G**	**Total**
Direct cost per unit								
Raw materials	5	7	4	9	11	2	3	
Labour content	15	2	1	10	5	3	7	
Other direct costs	3	4	2	6	3	1	4	
	23	13	7	25	19	6	14	
Units produced	40 000	60 000	80 000	10 000	15 000	90 000	70 000	365 000
Selling price	20	16	10	30	25	8	15	
Units sold	21 000	55 000	75 000	6 000	8 000	70 000	65 000	
Indirect overhead	54 795	82 192	109 588	13 699	20 548	123 288	95 890	500 000
Direct production cost	920 000	780 000	560 000	250 000	285 000	540 000	980 000	4 315 000
Total production cost	974 795	862 192	669 588	263 699	305 548	663 288	1 075 890	4 815 000
Unit production cost	24.37	14.37	8.37	26.37	20.37	7.37	15.37	
Inventories on hand	19 000	5 000	5 000	4 000	7 000	20 000	5 000	65 000
Inventories at cost	463 030	71 850	41 850	105 480	142 590	147 400	76 850	1 049 050

Summary trading accounts								
Sales	420 000	880 000	750 000	180 000	200 000	560 000	975 000	3 965 000
Production cost	974 795	862 192	669 588	263 699	305 548	663 288	1 075 890	4 815 000
Less: Closing inventories	−463 030	−71 850	−41 850	−105 480	−142 590	−147 400	−76 850	−1 049 050
Cost of sales	511 765	790 342	627 738	158 219	162 958	515 888	999 040	3 765 950
Gross margin	−91 765	89 658	122 262	21 781	37 042	44 112	−24 040	199 050
Inventory turnover in days	330	33	24	243	319	104	28	102

Budgeted results	**A**	**B**	**C**	**D**	**E**	**F**	**G**	**Total**
Direct cost per unit								
Raw materials	4	6	4	8	10	2	3	
Labour content	11	2	1	8	4	3	6	
Other direct costs	2	3	2	6	3	1	4	
	17	11	7	22	17	6	13	
Units produced	50 000	70 000	80 000	12 000	17 500	90 000	80 000	399 500
Selling price	25	18	11	30	25	9	17	
Units sold	40 000	65 000	75 000	10 000	15 000	80 000	70 000	355 000
Indirect overhead	68 493	95 890	109 589	16 438	23 973	123 288	109 589	547 260
Direct production cost	850 000	770 000	560 000	264 000	297 500	540 000	1 040 000	4 321 500
Total production cost	918 493	865 890	669 589	280 438	321 473	663 288	1 149 589	4 868 760
Unit production cost	18.37	12.37	8.37	23.37	18.37	7.37	14.37	
Inventories on hand	10 000	5 000	5 000	2 000	2 500	10 000	10 000	44 500
Inventories at cost	183 700	61 850	41 850	46 740	45 925	73 700	143 700	597 465
Summary trading accounts								
Sales	1 000 000	1 170 000	825 000	300 000	375 000	720 000	1 190 000	5 580 000
Production cost	918 493	865 890	669 589	280 438	321 473	663 288	1 149 589	4 868 760
Less: Closing inventories	−183 700	−61 850	−41 850	−46 740	−45 925	−73 700	−143 700	−597 465
Cost of sales	734 793	804 040	627 739	233 698	275 548	589 588	1 005 889	4 271 295
Gross margin	265 207	365 960	197 261	66 302	99 452	130 412	184 111	1 308 705
Inventory turnover in days	91	28	24	73	61	46	52	51

ACTIVITY 13.3

Analyse the information in Case study 13.1 (part 2) and ask yourself, if it has changed your perceptions. What areas, in your view, require special audit emphasis? Do not spend too much time in very detailed analysis, just pinpoint areas of concern in relation to inventory quantities and values. We suggest also that you look at allocation of overheads.

There is much detailed information in the Case study, but as in real life we shall try to identify the important matters. These appear to be:

1 Most products show that quantities produced are lower than expectation, the exception being product lines C and F.

2 Most selling prices are below expectation, the exceptions being D and E.
3 Direct costs are in most cases much higher than expectation.

Taking 2 and 3 together, this has resulted in the big drop in gross margin from expectation.

4 Quantity inventories on hand are higher in most cases, only B and C equalling expectation and only G having levels lower than expectation.
5 The following are of great concern: (a) products A and G are being sold at a gross loss; (b) inventory turnover of A, D and E is very low (representing 11, 8 and 11 months sales respectively).
6 Overheads appear to have been allocated on the basis of quantities produced (a very arbitrary method on the face of it).

You will know from your accounting studies that allocation of overheads for inventory valuation purposes should be made on the basis of normal production levels.

We consider overhead allocation later in this chapter.

We discuss net realizable values at greater length later in this chapter.

The auditors should ensure overheads are allocated on a reasonable basis and would ask management to justify the method. A more appropriate basis might be direct costs incurred, but discussions with management might cause you to change your mind. There is also a problem of whether budgeted amounts are normal levels of activity or whether actual levels in this first year should be regarded as normal. You will note that total quantities actually produced were 365 000 units compared with budgeted 399 500, some 9 per cent lower than budget. Thus, it could be argued that 9 per cent of overhead (£45 000) should not be allocated to production and inventory. The impact would reduce inventory values and profits.

The other matter of concern relates to products A and G as their cost may exceed net realizable value. The auditor might be uncertain about this until the most appropriate overhead allocation method is determined. This area will have to be looked at carefully, particularly as management may not even be able to achieve current selling prices in the coming year. You would ask management what measures they will take to reduce inventory quantities to acceptable levels. If this involves price reductions, the reductions to net realizable values may represent material amounts.

Suggested substantive approaches to prove figures are genuine, accurate and complete

In this section we shall consider in particular inventory and work in progress. We set out financial statement assertions in the area below. Note that we have combined inventory assertions and production cost assertions as production costs will be the basis for calculating cost of inventory.

Class of assertion	Assertions
Genuine	Inventories exist, are in good condition, and are owned by the company. (Existence and rights)
	The recorded costs (of materials, labour and overheads) are properly attributed to production cost.(Occurrence)
Accurate	Inventories have been properly priced at cost to bring them to present condition and location (cost of materials and costs of conversion, including labour and overheads). (Valuation)

	Inventories have been valued at the lower of cost determined above and net realizable value, and provisions have been made to take account of condition. (Valuation)
	Inventories bears proper relationship to movements in the period. (Cut-off)
	The production costs (of materials, labour and overheads) have been correctly calculated. (Valuation)
	Production cost has been properly allocated to inventories (see above) or to cost of sales in accordance with relevant accounting principles. (Valuation)
	All production costs have been allocated to the right period. (Cut-off)
Complete	All inventories have been recorded in the underlying accounting records that are in agreement with the figure for inventories in the financial statements. (Complete)
	The policy for valuing stocks has been properly disclosed and disclosure has been made of sub-classifications required by the Companies Act 2006. (Classification)
	All production costs have been identified and recorded in the appropriate accounting records. (Complete)

We discuss these matters individually under the two headings 'Do inventories exist, are they in good condition and owned by the company? Is cut-off accurate?' and 'Have all production costs and inventory values been properly determined?'.

Do inventories exist, are they in good condition and owned by the company? Is cut-off accurate?

It is normal audit practice to attend inventory counts to ensure the system of inventory-taking is operating satisfactorily and to carry out tests of control and substantive tests during the count. You will remember from Chapter 6 that the existence of physical objects confirmed by auditors themselves is good evidence. We call this work 'observation of inventory counts', a matter referred to in Paragraph A17 of ISA 500 in the following terms:

> Observation consists of looking at a process or procedure being performed by others, for example, the auditor's observation of inventory counting by the entity's personnel, or of the performance of control activities. Observation provides audit evidence about the performance of a process or procedure, but is limited to the point in time at which the observation takes place, and by the fact that the act of being observed may affect how the process or procedure is performed.

APB has issued Practice Note (PN25) on Attendance at stocktaking.

There is an International Standard on Auditing in the area, ISA 501 – *Audit evidence: specific considerations for selected items* and you should read it carefully before you work the next example, requiring you to review and evaluate inventory-taking instructions. It should be read with other auditing standards in mind, and in particular, ISA 315 – *Identifying and assessing the risks of material misstatement through understanding the entity and its environment,* and ISA 500 – *Audit evidence*. You should refer to the inherent risk factors relating to the 'existence assertion' we listed above. You might also like to reflect on the fact that because of the nature of inventories it is very easy to manipulate the quantities and amounts attributable to them and the auditor should be aware of ways in which such manipulation might take place. Consider the following:

- Recording false sales where no movement has taken place, such sales cancelled in the following period.
- Moving inventories between locations with different inventory-taking dates, as might occur when subsidiaries have different year-ends from the parent company.
- Manipulation of cut-off.
- Alteration of inventory count records after the count has taken place, or insertion of additional count records not reflecting reality.
- Over-optimistic estimations, on such matters as stage of completion.

Before we move to the Greenburn example (Case study 13.2), we emphasize the nature and importance of cut-off in the context of completeness, but note that cut-off is also concerned with establishing to whom ownership belongs at the balance sheet date.

Cut-off

We mentioned cut-off briefly in Chapter 12, but have left the main discussion to this chapter. We use the term 'cut-off' to highlight the fact that the balance sheet date divides one accounting period from another, the balance sheet date being the 'cut-off point'. All transactions on both sides of that point must be correctly allocated to the period to which they relate. If goods costing £5 000 have been received on 31 December 2011 and have been included in inventory at that date, it is vital the purchase invoices are recorded in the period ending on 31 December 2011 and not in the subsequent period. The basic rule may be summarized in the following diagram, assuming that debtors and trade payables remain uncleared:

Purchases prior to the year-end	Include in purchases	Include in trade payables or deduct from cash if cash purchases	Include in inventory
Sales prior to the year-end	Include in sales	Include in trade receivables or cash (if cash sales)	Take out of inventory

If this is not done profits will be under- or overstated as can be seen from the following example:

	As originally stated		As restated	
	£	£	£	£
Sales in year to 31 December 2010		100 000		100 000
Opening inventory	20 000		20 000	
Purchases	70 000		75 000	
	90 000		95 000	
Closing inventory	−25 000		−25 000	
Cost of goods sold		65 000		70 000
Gross profit		35 000		30 000

The above example shows that gross and net profit have both been initially overstated by £5000. There is inherent risk that purchases and sales will be allocated to the wrong period and management should ensure there are procedures to ensure that cut-off is accurate. The auditor, in assessing control risk, should test that cut-off procedures are sound. In the above example we addressed external cut-off only, but there are many cut-off points internal to the organization too. In a manufacturing concern, the following cut-off points would be typical:

- Purchase of raw materials and components.
- Requisitioning of raw materials by production.
- Requisitioning of components by assembly.
- Transfer of finished goods from production and assembly to finished goods store.
- Sale of finished goods.

These cut-off points represent either external or internal boundaries. Inherent risk is highest at any boundary. We would expect movements over boundaries to be recorded by the accounting system and for controls to be in force to ensure recorded movements are accurate and that control risk is minimized.

ACTIVITY 13.4

Calculate the effect on profits of the following matters:

(a) Goods with a cost value of £10 000 were transferred from raw materials store to production on 31 December 2011. They were not included in inventory in the raw materials store, but erroneously were not counted in the factory either. The goods were used in production on 2 January 2012.

(b) Finished goods costing £15 000 were transferred to the finished goods store at 12.30 p.m. on 31 December 2011. The inventory count team had completed the count in the finished goods store at 12 noon and did not commence counting inventory in the factory until 2.00 p.m.

(c) Goods with a sales value of £30 000 were despatched to customers on 2 January 2012 but were invoiced at 31 December 2011. The goods had been included in inventory in the finished goods store and valued for accounting purposes at £20 000.

It is useful to think your way through audit problems of this nature. Auditors in practice frequently have to demonstrate to clients what the effect of non-observance of principles will have on the financial statements. The cut off matters referred to would have the following effects on reported profits and on assets:

(a) Raw materials understated by £10 000 and profits understated by £10 000.

(b) Finished goods understated by £15 000 and profits understated by £15 000.

(c) Sales and debtors overstated by £30 000 and profits overstated by £30 000.

We shall now introduce you to the procedures management perform to ensure accurate cut-off. One of the problems in the above cases was uncontrolled movement of goods during the inventory count and for this reason it is common practice for management:

- To appoint an individual with special responsibility for ensuring that cut-off is accurate.
- To restrict movement of goods as far as possible during the count.
- If movements cannot be avoided, to ensure that the responsible individual is consulted on the proper treatment, so that appropriate action can be taken, for instance, retaining goods received in the goods receiving bay and counting separately; holding goods completed in the factory and counting separately; and so on.

The problem in (c) above was that goods were despatched in one period and invoiced in another. The same can happen when goods are received. They may have been received in one period but the invoice dated and recorded in another. For this reason, it is good practice for management to make note of the last goods received note (GRN), the last goods despatch note (GDN) and last requisition note numbers prior to the count. Later, management should ensure that purchases, sales and other movements reflected in the accounts all relate to movements prior to the last recorded movement.

The auditors test the operation of these procedures and check all movements are recorded in the proper period. Auditors also note the numbers on GRNs etc. at the time of the count observation. They should ensure that inventory movements are restricted during the count and that a responsible official makes appropriate decisions where movements do occur. In the Greenburn example (Case study 13.2), the inventory-taking instructions contain references to cut-off and you should note the above remarks in forming conclusions as to their adequacy.

CASE STUDY 13.2

Greenburn Limited: inventory taking instructions

Greenburn Limited is a trading company dealing in a range of 200 hardware products purchased from 30 suppliers, all well-known companies. It sells on credit to large stores and hardware shops. The company's inventory records are on computer file, the main source documentation for updating the inventory records being GRNs, sales dispatch note and goods returned notes (to suppliers and from customers).

You are presently preparing the agenda for a meeting to discuss arrangements for the final examination of the financial statements of Greenburn at 31 December 2011. This meeting will be on Friday 16 December 2011 and one item on the agenda is the company's inventory taking instructions for the count which is to take place on Saturday 29 December and Sunday 30 December 2011. As in previous years, members of your firm will observe the count under your supervision.

You are informed that goods may be received from suppliers and may be sent to customers up to 13.00 on Saturday afternoon 29 December 2011.

The inventory taking instructions are as follows:

- The chief accountant, Janet Wedder, has overall responsibility for the inventory count and inventory taking teams report directly to her. Her second in command is the inventory control clerk (Philip Cross) and he is responsible for ensuring the stores are neat and tidy before the count commences. He is also to ensure as far as possible that goods to be dispatched before the end of the year are packaged before the count commences and moved to the goods despatch bay.
- The stores occupy one large building and individual products are stored in racks by type. Five inventory count teams have been set up, each team being responsible for particular product groupings:

Team number	**Team members**	**Product groups**
Team 1	C. Newhouse, sales order dept, and E. Arkney, stores	Product groups a and b
Team 2	J. Whiteside, accounting dept, and C. Abingdon, stores	Product groups c and d
Team 3	E. Tippet, accounting dept, and A Drummond, stores	Product groups e and f
Team 4	D. Lamb, accounting dept, and J. Chapel, stores	Product groups g and h
Team 5	M. Thornhill, accounting dept, and L. Brown, stores	Product groups i and j

- The count is to start at 07.30 on Saturday 29 December 2011 and is expected to be completed by noon on Sunday 30 December 2011. Each count team will be given pre-numbered inventory sheets, sufficient to record product groups they are to count and at the conclusion of the count will be required to account to Janet Wedder for all sheets issued. The sheets contain names and reference numbers for each product in the group, a column for entering quantities and one for comments. There is at the foot of each sheet a space for the signatures of the two members of the count team.
- The leaders of count teams are those persons whose names appear first above. Both members of the count team are to count the inventory items independently and, in the event of discrepancy between the two figures, further counts should be made until agreement is reached, at which point the quantity is to be entered in the inventory sheet.
- Goods which appear to be of poor quality are to be counted and included on the inventory sheets, but details of condition and quantity involved noted in the comments column of the sheets.
- If goods are received during the count they are to be retained in the goods receiving bay. Any goods in the goods receiving and goods despatch bay at noon on 30 December 2011 are to be entered on a special inventory sheet by count team 1.
- Philip Cross is responsible for noting the numbers of the last (GRN) and goods despatch note (GDN).
- Following the count the inventory sheets will be passed to Amvar Hussain in the data control section for processing. He is responsible for checking the completeness of inventory sheets before passing them to operators for the inventory count run. The output from this run is a listing showing, for each inventory line, quantity counted, balance per the inventory record and difference between the two.
- Philip Cross and Jack Chapel are responsible for investigating any significant discrepancies between inventory records and physical quantities counted as shown on the inventory listing prepared by the computer department.
- Any queries during the count are to be referred to Janet Wedder or to representatives of our auditors, John Gunn and Co.

Signed: J: Wedder, 8 December 2011

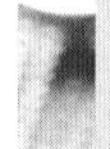

ACTIVITY 13.5

Review the inventory-taking instructions and list those features:

- That would serve to ensure that the inventories were properly counted and recorded.
- That might be regarded as weaknesses in the system for counting and recording the inventories.

Features which would serve to ensure the inventory was properly counted and recorded include the following:

- The issue of inventory-taking instructions increases the likelihood that inventory was properly counted.
- The chief accountant is responsible for the overall control of the inventory count and all personnel connected with the count report directly to her. This is an important feature as she is independent of the stores personnel.
- Further to the last point, the inventory count teams are composed of representatives from non-stores departments as well as stores personnel and the former are the team leaders. This not only keeps the count teams independent of stores but also ensures that personnel knowledgeable about the products are involved in the count.
- Arrangements are in place to ensure the stores are neat and tidy before the count commences.
- The arrangements for cut-off seem to be good:
  - (a) Philip Cross has arranged to have goods to be despatched before the year-end moved to the goods despatch bay and to count any goods not despatched by identified personnel at the close of the count.
  - (b) Goods received during the count are to be held intact in the goods receiving bay and are subject to separate count arrangements by identified personnel.
  - (c) Arrangements have been made to have adjustments made to inventory for movements on 30 December 2011 by a responsible official (Philip Cross), independent of stores.
  - (d) Philip Cross is to note the number of the last GRN and GDN for subsequent cut-off check.
- The issue of pre-numbered inventory sheets to count teams and the requirement that each team is to account for all inventory sheets issued to them at the conclusion of the count. A sequence check will ensure that all inventory sheets have been returned.
- The inclusion of inventory names and reference numbers on the inventory sheets will help to ensure that no products are missed. This may not be foolproof, however, if the system for recording inventory names and reference numbers is weak and this will need to be tested by the auditor before accepting this feature as a strength.

- Two members of the count team are to count the inventory independently of each other and further counts made until agreement is reached.
- Count sheets are required to be signed by both members of the count team, thus ensuring they take responsibility for the details entered on the sheets.
- Count teams are required to comment on items of inventory that appear to be in poor condition. This requirement does not ensure that all unsaleable items are recorded at the time of the count (items in good physical condition may be unsaleable for economic reasons), but it will help when the inventory comes to be valued for the purposes of the preparation of financial statements.
- The official responsible for inventory control (Philip Cross) and the storeman (Jack Chapel) are to investigate any significant discrepancies between inventory records and physical quantities counted. Discrepancies may arise because of inaccurate recording in inventory records or because of inaccurate counts. It may be necessary to recount certain products and, should the investigation reveal extensive count errors, it might be desirable to recount completely.

Features which might be regarded as weaknesses in the system for counting and recording the inventory include the following:

- Count teams are each responsible for two product groups. While this may be appropriate, it is unlikely that the product groups will be the same in nature and volume. The auditor should investigate this matter and advise that the count burden be allocated evenly.
- As mentioned above, the system of recording inventory names and reference numbers will help to ensure all items are counted, but only if the system for recording names and numbers is satisfactory. If not, the system as described may cause unlisted products to be ignored.
- There appears to be no system for test counts to be carried out by Janet Wedder or Philip Cross. This is a serious weakness as inaccurate counting may not be detected early enough.
- A further serious weakness is that the instructions do not state how goods that have been counted are to be marked to prevent double counting. It would be appropriate to tag goods already counted, indicating name, reference and quantity. This would also aid the test count procedures by Janet Wedder or Philip Cross discussed above.
- No reference is made to goods held for third parties or to goods owned by Greenburn in the hands of third parties. Regarding the former, such goods should be segregated, separately counted but not included in the company's inventory. The latter should be counted separately.
- Although efforts have been made to restrict deliveries during the count, the instructions fail to state the procedures to be adopted should an urgent delivery to a customer be necessary.
- The auditors should not take part in the formal inventory count procedures. In practice members of the audit team will be available for advice but it is important that they do not offer advice independently of

Janet Wedder. If the auditors do detect a problem they should inform her and ensure that the same advice is given to all count teams.

- The instructions do not refer to briefing sessions with members of the count teams to ensure the instructions are properly understood. This is normally vital.

The inventory count observation, purposes and procedures

The auditors do not conduct the count, but attend the count to determine if the client's staff are performing their instructions properly, thus providing reasonable assurance that the inventory-taking will be accurate. They perform test counts to satisfy themselves that procedures and internal controls relating to the inventory-taking are working properly. The auditor in this case performs a test of control. Auditors may also perform substantive tests of details on inventory quantities, condition and cut-off. This means that when carrying out test-counts, the auditors select items both from count records and from the physical inventories and check one to the other to gain assurance as to the completeness and accuracy of the count records. Particular consideration would be given, when substantive testing, to those inventories which they believe to have a high value either individually or as a category of inventory. The level of substantive tests of details is dependent, of course, on the auditor's view of the quality of the inventory-taking instructions and the way they are put into effect.

You should note that many organizations with sound systems of control and adequate inventory records determine inventory quantities from the records instead of conducting a count at the balance sheet date. This can be attractive to management as it may save time and effort of staff at a busy time of year. The auditor may accept inventory determined on the basis of inventory records provided:

- The system of control over the inventory records is adequate.
- The inventory records are proven to be accurate and complete by means of regular, properly controlled inventory-taking procedures. The frequency of count will depend on the nature of the inventories and their turnover. Normally, this would be done on a continuous basis, different classes of inventory being counted at differing times of the year.
- Any significant differences between inventory records and quantities counted are investigated and corrected.

Auditors must be satisfied that company procedures and records are satisfactory and should carry out tests and procedures to this end. Audit procedures would include the following:

- Observe inventory count observation procedures during the year.
- Test the accuracy of inventory records by comparing test count results with the records.
- Test for cut-off at the count date *and* the balance sheet date.
- If considered necessary, conduct a restricted test count at the balance sheet date.

Work in progress at the balance sheet date, including construction contracts

Some inventory items in a manufacturing concern may be incomplete at the balance sheet date. We distinguish between short-term 'work in progress' and construction contract balances. There are particular problems from the existence and condition point of view as the company and auditors will have to assess the stage of completion and whether costs are properly charged according to the stage reached. The problem for the auditors is that they may not have sufficient expertise to determine the stage of completion and they may have to rely on the work of an expert, particularly in the case of construction contacts.

Refer to ISA 620 – *Using the work of an auditor's expert*, particularly when we come to look at construction contracts later in this chapter.

Inventories held at third parties

Such inventory may be significant and if the auditors feel that a certificate from the third party is not sufficiently reliable evidence, they may wish to observe the count where it is held. If the inventories are in a location where the auditor does not have an office, another auditor may be asked to perform this work, in which case ISA 600 – *Special considerations: audits of group financial statements (including the work of component auditors)* will be of relevance.

We do not discuss ISA 600 in detail, but we suggest that you note its contents. ISA 600 is principally concerned with the relationship between principal auditors and other auditors examining significant parts of a group.

Inventory held at branches

The client may have branches at which quantities of inventory are held. In such cases auditors should ensure inventory-taking instructions issued to branches are clear and just as carefully drafted as those used at head office. It would be good practice to put a member of head office accounting department staff in charge of the count. Auditors may not feel it necessary to visit every branch but decide to observe the count at selected branches. This is a good example of rotational visiting. If inventory at individual branches is not significant but the total held at branches is, the auditor may feel justified in visiting the branches over (say) a three-year period. The auditor may also suggest that some of the inventory count observation work at branches be carried out by internal auditors.

Refer to Chapter 15 for a discussion of the work of internal auditors and the extent to which external auditors may rely on them.

Have all production costs and inventory values been properly determined?

Inventory valuation is covered in your accounting studies, but the auditor's work in this area is so important that we must cover the major features. We will support the discussion with examples that will help you to come to grips with the audit process in relation to inventories.

The basis of inventory valuation

IAS 2 (paragraph 9) and SSAP 9 (paragraph 26) both require inventories to be valued at the lower of cost and net realizable value (NRV). The effect of valuing at NRV is that the reduction from cost is charged against profits of the current year, despite the fact that the sales of inventory will be made in the following year.

The auditor needs to be aware of the definitions of cost and NRV and must devise audit procedures to determine that both elements have been properly calculated. We discuss Cost and NRV below.

Rules for calculation: cost

The basic rules are:

- Cost is calculated for different categories of inventory and not for the inventories as a whole.
- Cost comprises cost of purchase and costs of conversion, including:
  (a) direct costs, such as direct material and labour costs.
  (b) variable production overheads that vary according to level of production, such as indirect materials and indirect labour.
  (c) fixed production overheads, such as the cost of factory management and administration and depreciation of factory buildings and equipment, based on normal level of activity taking one year with another, and
  (d) other overheads incurred in bringing the product or service to its present location condition.

Refer to IAS 2, paragraphs 9 to 18, and SSAP 9, paragraphs 16 to 20.

Let us consider the audit considerations and tests that might be appropriate in determining if the cost of different inventory lines had been properly established. We will do this in a series of activities.

ACTIVITY 13.6

Suggest audit procedures that would be appropriate to satisfy you that direct material costs had been applied appropriately to inventory. You may assume that the purchases system had recorded the direct material costs in the financial accounting records, including import duties, transport and handling costs and other direct costs, less cost reductions such as trade discounts and purchase rebates. (see Chapter 12).

The first step would be to determine that the direct material costs transferred to the costing system were genuine (representing costs that had occurred), accurate and complete (including appropriately classified). The auditor should therefore test the reconciliation of the financial and cost accounting records and test on a sample basis that the monetary amounts attributed to specific raw material and components by the costing department were accurate. Specific matters to be tested would be the accuracy of cost calculations by reference to the stated method (FIFO, weighted average cost) and purchase invoices, goods inwards documentation, duties paid documentation, etc.

The second step would be to determine that direct material costs had been appropriately allocated to products in the production process. Raw materials and components would typically be requisitioned from the raw material and components stores using requisition documents and charged to production cost sheets on the basis of the costs determined by the costing department.

The auditor would test the following:

- Raw materials and components entries on production and assembly cost sheets to requisitions (ensuring that the latter have been properly authorized), and vice versa.

- Completeness of batch cost sheets by carrying out a sequence check on sheet numbers.
- Batch cost sheets to bills of materials for selected ranges of goods and enquiring into reasons for significant variances.
- Variance analyses prepared by the company that might indicate abnormal amounts of wasted materials. Abnormal wastage should be reflected in the profits of the year and not carried forward to the following year in inventory values.

If production and assembly cost records and requisition details are both held on computer file, audit software could be used to identify requisitions that have not been charged to production and assembly batches. Another possible use would be to compare bills of materials with materials charged to batches to highlight any excessive use of materials.

The third step would be to determine that the costs of products allocated to inventory items held at the year-end were those recorded in the costing records. Let us assume at this stage that those inventory quantities had been determined by count observed by the auditors and that they had concluded that inventories were in good physical condition and that cut-off was accurate. The auditor would test entries in the inventory valuation record by reference to the values recorded in the cost records.

ACTIVITY 13.7

Suggest audit procedures that would satisfy you that production overheads had been appropriately allocated to products, based on normal level of activity taking one year with another. You may assume that these overhead costs had been appropriately entered in the financial accounting records and transferred to the costing records and individual products. We would like you to show how the auditor would approach the requirement that production overheads should be allocated to products on the basis of normal level of activity taking one year with another.

In the case of a company in a stable industry with no serious fluctuations from year to year, there should be no problem. The auditor might look at trends of production activity over the years and examine sales and production forecasts for the coming year. However, let us assume that production levels have dropped by 25 per cent from year 1 to year 2 as a result of a similar drop in turnover. If production overheads remained at the same level as the previous year, application of these overheads to the lower production levels would mean a higher production overhead per individual product. The question for the auditor is whether it is expected that production levels will return in year 3 to the levels of year 1, or whether year 2 might be regarded as the new norm. This means that the auditor has to consider the future and should adopt the following approach:

- Discuss future plans with management and in particular with the production director, determining the reasons for the downturn in production and if they are temporary.
- Review books and records in search of evidence to support the representations of management, including:
  - (a) Directors' minute book.
  - (b) Budgets and forecast accounts for the current year and for the two following years. Determine if they are realistic in the light of what is known about the economic outlook and other pressures in the external environment. Consider in this connection how successful the company has been in the past in making forecasts and preparing budgets.
  - (c) Trade or financial press.
  - (d) Events subsequent to the year-end as shown in such records as production and assembly reports.

If the auditor forms the view that production levels in year 3 are likely to be the same as in year 1, it would be appropriate to reduce production overhead in year 2 inventories to year 1 levels, the consequence being that overhead not applied to inventory would be charged against profits of the year. If production in year 3 and subsequent years were likely to stay at year 2 levels, it would be appropriate to apply the higher production overhead to inventories in year 2. Year 2 would then be accepted as the new norm.

ACTIVITY 13.8

Other overheads incurred in bringing the product or service to its present location condition may also be included in inventory values. Explain what this means.

Any expenses incurred in readying the inventory item for sale may be included in inventory values. Thus, the cost of inventories manufactured in Hamburg and transported to a depot in Inverness will include transportation costs from Hamburg to Inverness.

However, costs of distributing to customers and selling expense would normally be charged direct to the profit and loss account and not carried forward to the following year in the inventory figure. Administrative costs that do not contribute to bringing inventories to their present condition and location would also be charged direct against profits.

Audit work would therefore be directed to analysing other overheads included in inventory and discussing with management their justification for including them.

Rules for calculation: net realizable value (NRV)

The basic rule is that NRV is actual or estimated selling price less all further costs of production (to complete) and costs yet to be incurred in marketing, selling and distributing the inventory. Thus for products A and B:

		A	B
Selling price		100	70
Less: further production costs to completion		10	10
		90	60
Less: Marketing cost	5		
Selling expense	3		
Distribution cost	7		
		15	15
Net realizable value		75	45
Cost		60	60
Value at		60	45

ACTIVITY 13.9

There are a number of important matters in respect of the above basic rule and we ask you to consider the following:

(a) Explain why the audit of NRV value is more problematic than the audit of inventory cost. What specific steps might the auditor take to check whether valuing at NRV would be appropriate?

(b) What audit procedures would the auditor use in determining whether costs of production to complete work in progress at the balance sheet date are appropriate?

(c) What matters would the auditor consider in respect of costs yet to be incurred in marketing, selling and distributing the inventory. What audit procedures would be appropriate?

These are all good questions and matters to consider. We comment as follows:

(a) The reason that NRV of inventory items is more problematic for the auditor than their cost, is that NRV lies in the future whereas cost has been incurred in the past. This means that the auditor has to look for evidence of conditions that are likely to occur in the period after the balance sheet date. Of course, some actual evidence will be available about this period as the final audit work is taking place after the balance sheet date and actual data will be available as well as (we hope) budgeted information about the future.

We discuss post balance sheet events in Chapter 14.

The auditor will review inventory turnover of all inventory lines to identify those that appear to be slow moving and determine trend of sales and inventory turnover; in particular, are trends of sales and inventory turnover moving up or down within the year and subsequent period?. Rising inventory levels may suggest that realizable values lie below cost, although the auditors would be wise not to take this at face value (rises in inventory levels may occur because of genuine management decisions to increase inventories, a matter that might be discussed with management during discussions of business risk).

The auditor should proceed as follows:

- Ascertain whether the company is maintaining production levels for slow moving lines. If so, this might indicate that management believes that sales will turn upwards. If they are still slow-moving in the post balance sheet period, the auditor should discuss the position with management with the aim of establishing what management intends to do. You would need to find out whether the inventory items in question would only be saleable at much lower prices. The auditor would also ask for detailed forecast management accounts; these should indicate sales levels in the coming year. Apart from these detailed checks, the auditor would look for external evidence, such as general economic conditions, and the trade press.

  If inventory levels do appear unacceptably high in relation to sales budgets, management should be asked how they intend to reduce inventories (for instance, do they intend to sell at lower prices or with increased sales effort?).
- Test movements and prices in the period after the balance sheet date.
- Check inclusion of inventory lines in current price lists. If not included, this may be evidence that management regards them as obsolete. Not only should auditors consider a provision for obsolete finished inventory but also for raw materials and components of the affected lines. Discussions should be held with management to determine realizable values, including scrap values.
- Review directors' minutes to obtain written evidence of directors' decisions in the area.

  Once this work has been done the auditor will be in a better position to judge whether lower selling prices might cause net realizable values to drop below cost. In the case of Product B above, the lower selling price, other things being equal, would result in the inventory item being valued below cost at NRV of 45.

(b) The first step would be to establish the stage of completion of the work in progress. In the case of significant items the auditor might rely on the work of an auditor's expert (or of a management's expert if the auditor can prove the credentials of the expert) It might also be appropriate to discuss the stage of completion with production personnel. This work would determine the stages not yet complete.

The second step would be to determine the costs of the stages not yet complete and the auditor would inspect the costing records and extract the direct costs and overhead costs that had not yet been allocated to production of the work in progress concerned. At the time of the inventory count, the auditor would make a note of the last requisitions for raw materials and components and the last labour allocations to the work in progress. Reference to the bill of materials and budgeted labour cost would form the basis of these direct costs still to be incurred. Budgeted overhead allocations should also be inspected as a basis for determining overheads still to be applied.

(c) The first thing that the auditor would be concerned about is whether the marketing, selling and distribution cost are those costs designed to bring the product to the point of sale. They should not normally include general administration costs, although in certain circumstances such costs specific to the product might be included.

The costs in question again lie in the future. The auditor might try to find out if the future costs are likely to be the same as in the past, in which case it might be appropriate to apply the same percentage relationships to selling price. The auditor would wish to find out, however, if cost patterns are the same for all products or whether some products bear a higher proportion of (say) marketing costs. Examination of detailed costing records would be useful in this respect. Again discussions with management would be necessary to discover if additional costs may arise. For instance, there might be increased marketing expense to move the slow-moving inventory items, which would serve to reduce NRV even further.

As you can see, a fair amount of imagination, examination of available records about the future and close contact with management will be necessary on the part of the auditor.

Disclosure of the effect of changes in basis of valuation

The effect of changes in bases can normally be determined. If, for instance, the company changes its basis of allocating overheads, the effect would normally be determinable and would require disclosure.

Have all calculations affecting inventory valuation been properly made?

This heading is self-explanatory. All calculations on inventory sheets and detailed valuations should be tested to ensure they have been properly made.

Can the inventories be freely disposed of by the company?

Finished inventories are assets held for resale and it would be rare, where a company is a going concern, to encounter encumberment that would prevent resale. However, it is not uncommon for inventories to be the subject of floating charges to secure bank or other lending and such charges should be disclosed. If the company's continued existence is dependent upon bank facilities being maintained, creditors and other users of published accounts may need to know of the charge as this may affect their rights.

VALUATION OF CONSTRUCTION CONTRACTS

Construction contracts may be defined as 'contracts entered into for the design, manufacture or construction of an asset or provision of a service or a combination of related assets or services such that the contract activity usually falls into different accounting periods'. A duration exceeding one year is not an essential feature of a construction contract, but the basic idea is that turnover and attributable profit should be accounted for in such a way as not to distort the period's turnover and results shown in financial statements purporting to give a true and fair view. It is important that the chosen accounting policy should be applied consistently within the reporting entity and from year to year.

We assume you have already some knowledge of the accounting entries from your financial accounting studies, but you may find that this activity will help to refresh your memory.

You will know from your accounting studies that the major problem regarding construction contracts is that their period of construction usually overlaps accounting periods. This means that a decision must be made as to whether profits and losses not realized at the balance sheet date should be reflected in the profit and loss account before completion of the contract. This matter is subjective and the auditor will have to be skilled in assessing the validity of management judgements. In this section we discuss the auditor's approach in terms of identification of judgement areas and suggest audit procedures in each case. Financial statement assertions for construction contacts are similar to those for inventories and work in progress, but in particular it is useful to recognize that each judgement area discussed below carries with it a management assertion, somewhat more detailed than the more general ones identified earlier.

CASE STUDY 13.3

Graves Limited: construction contracts

Graves Limited is a building company specializing in the construction of hotels. The company values long-term contracts in accordance with accounting standards and takes up profit on contracts which are one-third complete, using costs of contracts certified as complete in relation to estimated total costs. All stages of the contracts are equally profitable. At 31 March 2008, the company has three major contracts in progress – Currie, Kiefer and Hals. You are in charge of the audit assignment and are examining the valuation, presentation and disclosure of the contracts in the financial statements at 31 March 2008. You have extracted the following information from the accounting records:

	Currie	Kiefer	Hals
	£000	£000	£000
Costs of stages completed	500	800	300
Costs of work not yet completed	100	150	50
Estimated total costs	750	1 500	1 800
Contract price	1 000	1 275	2 250
Invoiced work certified by surveyors	650	700	350
Progress payments received	450	810	400

Raw material cost is allocated to contracts on the basis of stock requisitions from central stores, some deliveries being made direct to the site by suppliers. All requisitions are signed by the site manager, the name of the contract being shown on the face of the requisition. All deliveries from suppliers are recorded in central store computerized stock records in quantity and at invoice cost, whether delivered direct or not and all issues are priced at FIFO value, such value being recorded on the face of the requisition note. Labour costs are charged to contract accounts using time allocation sheets prepared by site personnel. Fixed assets are charged to contracts at a value determined by head office, less the deemed value at the end of each period. Overheads are allocated to contracts on the basis of direct labour cost. They include canteen costs and costs of central service departments, such as research and development, design, accounting and administration.

Required

- Identify the detailed assertions (implied or otherwise) made by management in respect of long-term contracts. We believe that there are nine major assertions in areas where management would exercise judgement.) To aid you we set out below our workings and suggested disclosures in the profit and loss account and balance sheet.

Graves Limited Accounting entries

	Currie	Kiefer	Hals	
Raw data	£	£	£	
Costs of stages completed	500	800	300	
Costs of work not yet completed	100	150	50	
Estimated total costs	750	1500	1800	
Contract price	1000	1275	2250	
Invoiced work certified by surveyors	650	700	350	
Progress payments received	450	810	400	
Stage of completion				
Costs of stages completed	500	800	300	
Estimated total costs **(assertion five)**	750	1500	1800	
Percentage completed	66.67	53.33	16.7	
Estimated profits (losses)				
Contract price **(assertion six)**	1000	1275	2250	
Estimated total costs	750	1500	1800	
Estimated profit (loss)	250	−225	450	
Company takes up profits/losses as follows (assertions seven, eight and nine)				
Currie (66.67% of 250)	167			
Kiefer (full estimated loss)		−225		
Hals (nil as not sufficiently complete)			0	
Contract balance				
Total costs incurred to date **(assertion one)**	600	950	350	
Transfer to cost of sales **(assertion two)**	−500	−800	−300	
Long-term contract balance	100	150	50	
Cost of sales (long-term contracts)				
Transfer from contract balance	500	800	300	
Transfer to profit and loss account	−500	−800	−300	
	0	0	0	
Turnover (long-term contracts)				
Transfer to debtors **(assertion three)**	−650	−700	−350	
Profit and loss account	650	700	350	
	0	0	0	
Profit and loss account initial entries				Total
Turnover	650	700	350	1700
Cost of sales	−500	−800	−300	−1600
Profit (loss) initially recorded	150	−100	50	100
Adjustment to profit taken up	17	−125	−50	−158
Adjusted profit (loss)	167	−225	0	−58
Debtor's balance (long-term contracts)				
Turnover (invoices issued)	650	700	350	
Cash received **(assertion four)**	−450	−810	−400	
Balance receivable from debtor	200	−110	−50	
Adjustment to debtors turnover	17	−125	−50	
	217	−235	−100	

- Having identified management assertions, describe the substantive audit tests you would carry out in respect of the long-term contracts.

We have identified nine major management assertions, whether implied or not, in respect of construction contracts:

- *Assertion one*: costs incurred to date are genuine, accurate and complete (£600 000, £950 000 and £350 000 for Currie, Kiefer and Hals respectively).
- *Assertion two*: stages of completion and costs of such stages have been properly determined (£500 000, £800 000 and £300 000 for Currie, Kiefer and Hals respectively).
- *Assertion three*: invoices issued to customers in respect of construction contracts are properly calculated in accordance with the contract and are in respect of all stages completed certified by the surveyor (£650 000, £700 000 and £350 000 for Currie, Kiefer and Hals respectively).
- *Assertion four*: cash received from debtors is genuine, complete and accurate. In particular, cash received has been properly allocated to contracts (£450 000, £810 000 and £400 000 for Currie, Kiefer and Hals respectively).
- *Assertion five*: the estimated total costs, used to estimate profits or losses on contracts, are genuine, accurate and complete (£750 000, £1 500 000 and £800 000 for Currie, Kiefer and Hals respectively).
- *Assertion six*: contract prices also used to estimate profits or losses on contracts, are genuine accurate and complete (£1 000 000, £1 275 000 and £2 250 000 for Currie, Kiefer and Hals respectively).
- *Assertion seven*: when attributable profits on contracts are taken up in the profit and loss account, the contract is sufficiently complete to give adequate assurance that the outcome of the contract is certain. Losses on construction contracts should be provided for as soon as they are recognized.
- *Assertion eight*: the profitability of different stages of the contract has been properly determined.
- *Assertion nine*: the method employed in taking up profits is not only consistent with prior years, unless the effect of any change is disclosed, but is also appropriate.

In this example we are not looking in detail at the disclosures regarding figures in the profit and loss account and balance sheet, but clearly there will be a number of financial statement assertions about disclosure as well.

Now that we have identified the major assertions, we can move to substantive audit tests to prove the validity of the assertions (which are now audit objectives).

Audit objective one: costs incurred to date are genuine, accurate and complete (£600 000, £950 000 and £350 000 for Currie, Kiefer and Hals respectively)

Work in respect of this objective would be directed to proving first, that materials, labour cost and overhead costs had been properly determined; second, that they had properly entered the costing records; and third, that they had been properly allocated to contracts. We have already discussed audit work to prove proper determination of financial accounting entries and the need to reconcile financial accounting and costing records (to prove the latter are genuine, accurate and complete). Typical audit work on allocation of costs to contracts includes:

- Check sequence of requisition notes.
- Randomly select issues of raw materials in central stores inventory records and check to requisition notes (to prove accuracy and completeness of requisition notes and occurrence of genuine movement of inventory).

- For the selected issues, check calculation of FIFO cost and test materials received to purchase invoices.
- Select a representative sample of requisitions and test that amounts allocated to contracts are correct, by reference to the signature of the site manager and the contract name on the face of the requisition.
- For selected employees check that worksheets prepared by them reconcile to total time worked per the payroll records.
- For selected worksheets check that time has been properly allocated to contracts, and test that labour cost has been properly calculated, taking into account employer's portion of social security contributions.
- Check that overheads can legitimately be charged to contracts. We know that they include canteen costs and costs of central service departments, such as research and development, design, accounting and administration, but the auditor should ensure that they are directly attributable to contracts. Contract work often requires the use of fixed assets such as dumper trucks and diggers. In such cases it is common practice to charge the contract with an amount representing the use of the asset and the auditor should ensure that the charge is fair and includes no element of profit.
- Ensure that it is appropriate to charge overheads to contracts on the basis of direct labour costs. The same rules on normal levels of activity apply as we discussed above in relation to inventories and the auditor would seek assurance that overheads are not over-allocated to contracts where a temporary downturn of activity has occurred.
- For all costs cut-off must be correct, particularly where a stage has been completed and the costs associated to the stage, now invoiced, are transferred to cost of sales.

If you work for a firm of accountants you will know that you allocate your time to clients and other activities. This enables the firm not only to charge clients properly but also to calculate the value of work in progress.

Audit objective two: stages of completion and costs of such stages have been properly determined (£500 000, £800 000 and £300 000 for Currie, Kiefer and Hals respectively)

This objective is important as these costs will be charged to the profit and loss account as cost of sales. Returning to our discussion above, costs should not be just allocated to contracts but also to stages of contracts. It is normal practice for surveyors to review costs incurred before certifying completion of a particular stage and it may be desirable to obtain assurance from the surveyor that costs are valid.

Auditors would compare actual cost of stages completed with budgeted cost. This might give satisfaction that costs appear to make sense, but if budgets have been much exceeded it might cause doubts about the estimated profits on the contract (see below).

This is another case where auditors use the work of a management's expert or an auditor's expert and you should refer again to ISA 620.

Audit objective three: invoices issued to customers in respect of construction contracts are properly calculated in accordance with contract and are in respect of all stages completed certified by the surveyor (£650 000, £700 000 and £350 000 for Currie, Kiefer and Hals respectively)

The auditor should ascertain that the surveyor has given authority for invoices to be issued for the stages of completion concerned and also that the issue of such invoices was according to the terms of the contract.

Audit objective four: cash received from clients is genuine, complete and accurate. In particular, cash received has been properly allocated to contracts (£450 000, £810 000 and £400 000 for Currie, Kiefer and Hals respectively)

You might think that this test would be accomplished by checking to the bank paying in book and other records, but the auditors would also test that all cash received has been recorded. Apart from testing the system for recording cash received (a compliance test) they could circularize clients to ensure that payments by them had been properly recorded.

Audit objective five: the estimated total costs are genuine, accurate and complete (£750 000, £1 500 000 and £1 800 000 for Currie, Kiefer and Hals respectively)

Profit is taken up on the basis of contract price and estimated total costs, so estimates of cost must be reliable. The closer to completion (see assertion seven above) the more certain management should be about the outcome. However, we are looking into the future at this point and there is bound to be some uncertainty. If the company has a history of reliable forecasts and estimates, the auditor will be more likely to accept the estimate. An important step is to compare budgeted expenditure at each stage to ensure that the budgeted costs are not being significantly exceeded. Discussions with management, including those on the sites, on the progress of contracts would be important. Much might be gleaned from inspecting directors' minutes or examination of forecasts of profit and cash flows for the coming year.

Care must be taken in estimating profits on construction contracts, particular note being taken of rectification and guarantee work and estimated inflation affecting costs. It is important to identify penalties for late completion of contracts. The auditor should inspect the contract and ascertain if deadlines are being met at each stage. If contracts are late, it may be necessary to increase estimated costs to completion by expected penalties.

Audit objective six: contract prices are genuine, accurate and complete (£1 000 000, £1 275 000 and £2 250 000 for Currie, Kiefer and Hals respectively)

If contract prices are fixed it will be easy to determine them from contracts. However, contracts often include clauses allowing upward revisions of contract prices if cost inflation has occurred. Note that cost inflation should not include additional costs because of inefficiencies on the part of contractors. This matter may have to be discussed with the expert surveyor. A further matter that may cause concern is where there are variations to the contract but the amended contract price has not been finally determined. In this case management may have to make estimates of the changes and the auditor will have to assess the reasonableness of the estimates.

Audit objective seven: when attributable profits on contracts are taken up in the profit and loss account, the contract is sufficiently complete to give adequate assurance that the outcome of the contract is certain

The basic rule is that the company should be careful in taking up profits on construction contracts. You will note that Graves takes up profit on contracts which are one-third complete, using costs of contracts certified as complete in relation to estimated total costs. Auditors should make sure that the rule is not being applied too rigidly. It may be perfectly in order to take up profit when the contract is only one-third complete if the hotel is being constructed in accordance with the design of a previously built hotel in an unproblematic location. This may be totally inappropriate if the hotel is being built on a hillside with underground streams, as there may be many unexpected costs.

Audit objective eight: the profitability of different stages of the contract has been properly determined

Graves' management has said that all stages are equally profitable, but this may not be the case. For instance, the stage where fittings are installed, may be more profitable than others. If this profitable stage has not been reached, it would be inappropriate to take up any profits in respect of it. The auditor should examine costings and agreed terms for the issue of invoices.

Audit objective nine: the method employed in taking up profits has been comparable with prior years, unless the effect of any change is disclosed and is also appropriate

Comparability is one of the objectives against which an entity should judge the appropriateness of accounting policies and the method of taking up profits and losses on contracts should be consistently applied, and if not, the effect should be disclosed. Any attempt to take up profits earlier or later than in the past would require particular justification, but the auditor should also keep an eye open for changes in the allocation of overheads, particularly when the overhead burden for some contracts has been reduced at the expense of others. The auditor should ensure that this is not done to reduce losses being recognized in the financial statements.

TRADE PAYABLES AND PURCHASES

The nature of trade payables together with comments on purchases

Trade payables are normally classified as current liabilities, as amounts payable in the short term. Like trade receivables they are not tangible, but, if genuine, they are payable to real people or organizations. They come into existence as the result of purchase of goods or performance of services by third parties. Because they are intangible the auditor relies on documentary evidence to a greater extent than for tangible assets. As for trade receivables and sales, the company should define the point at which title in goods transfers or services are performed.

As trade payables come into existence as the result of purchase of goods or services, audit work on purchases cannot be divorced from that on trade payables. We noted that where sales are made on credit it will normally be easier to find evidence to prove the sale. This is equally the case for purchases on credit.

Purchases may be for cash and these cash purchases will cause cash to decrease rather than liabilities to increase.

Inherent risks affecting trade payables

Remember the overriding rule – new or material transactions or events often, perhaps normally, result in increased risk. Here are some indicators of inherent risks affecting trade payables:

- Material variances from standard costs, which suggest either that standard costs are unrealistic or that actual costs are over- or understated because trade payables are under- or overstated.
- Suppliers are experiencing difficulties which may mean that supplies are threatened. (Possible difficulties include financial difficulties and labour problems.)
- Significant changes in the terms of trade with suppliers, so comparisons with previous periods are less valid.
- Material increase in the age of trade payables, which may indicate that the company is in financial difficulties.
- Major changes in the nature of purchases, so there is little past history of the product and services acquired.
- The company has a history of above average returns of goods purchased, so trade payables and purchases may be overstated at the year-end.

Controls to reduce the impact of inherent risk in the purchases and trade payables area

Apart from a satisfactory control environment, we would expect to see controls in the following areas:

- Creation of trade payables' balances.
- Recorded trade payables at the year-end.
- Payment of trade payables' balances.

Creation of trade payables' balances

We have covered many controls in the purchases and trade payables area in previous chapters, but we would expect to see the following in particular:

- The preparation of a purchases budget, integrated with other budgets, such as production, sales, finance and inventories. The company should have a system for investigating any significant variances from budget or from standard costs, and for enquiring into significant build-ups of inventories as this may indicate purchases in excess of production requirements.
- The company should record the point at which the title of goods acquired pass to it and at what point services rendered by third parties are deemed to be complete.
- If goods are accepted on a sale or return basis, there should be a clear statement as to the company's obligations to suppliers. For instance, if goods have been damaged in the hands of the company before sale to a third party, it should be agreed who bears the loss. We would also expect to see a system for notifying suppliers when sales have been made of goods on

a sale or return basis. Goods held on sale or return basis should not be included in inventory.

- In some cases title to goods supplied by a supplier may technically remain the property of the supplier until payment is made. There may be special disclosure requirements, although normal practice would be to treat these transactions as purchases with a corresponding liability if on credit.
- Purchases not in the normal purchases system should be kept to a minimum, but where special purchases are not processed in the normal way, they should be specially authorized.
- Investigation of reasons for returns to suppliers by independent responsible officials as the basis for corrective action.
- Cut-off procedures at period ends and particularly in respect of any period where financial statements are being published.

We have discussed cut-off above in relation to inventories.

Recorded trade payables at the year-end

Procedures include the following:

- *Appropriate division of duties.* Personnel responsible for holding or updating the trade payables ledger should not have any responsibility for authorizing or creating documentation for any movement on the trade payables ledger accounts, including:
  (a) Approval of purchases transactions, including the matching operation, such as comparing purchase invoices with goods received notes and purchase orders.
  (b) Approval of payments to suppliers.
  (c) Approval of purchases returns.
  (d) Holding inventory for resale.
  (e) Approval of any adjustments to trade creditor balances.
  (f) Reconciliation of trade creditor listings to the control account in the general ledger.

  You will remember from Chapters 8 and 9 that in computer systems it is important to identify where responsibilities lie. Basically, authorization of transactions (whether before or after the event) should be outwith the computer installation, such approval being aided by the use of control totals checked independently by data collection personnel. Reconciliation of trade payables listings should not be made by persons responsible for transactions affecting the trade payables ledger. There should be access controls over standing data and a strict limit on persons allowed to update data.

Refer to Case study 9.3 Broomfield plc: purchases and trade payables system on page 336.

- *Regular review of statements from suppliers.* We would expect to see a system for enquiry into differences. Persons negotiating with suppliers should be independent of the persons responsible for input to or processing of the trade payables ledger.
- *A system for ensuring that supplier credit limits are adhered to and for renegotiating such limits as necessary*. Credit limits are often set low until the supplier has built up a picture of customer reliability. Normally after a relatively short time higher limits may be negotiated, particularly if orders are of a size that makes it easy to exceed limits.

- *A system for detecting unrecorded liabilities*. This search would be aided if the company has a system to identify liabilities at the balance sheet date. Accounting personnel need to be informed of important charges and liabilities affecting the financial statements. An example would be identification of contingent liabilities, say legal cases. A specific procedure in the area would be testing of purchases cut-off at the year-end.
- *A system for enquiry into unusual features*. An example is debit balances in the trade payables ledger. They may be valid, but may arise because of erroneous double payments or postings of cash to the wrong account, suggesting breakdown in control and heightened control risk.

If any of the features described in the above two sections and in the section below, are not present or are operating ineffectively, control risk would be increased and increased substantive testing would become necessary.

Payment of trade payables' balances

In sophisticated computer systems, a complete information/audit trail may be the only way to match these documents.

- The most important control over payments is the matching operation performed by a person with no responsibility for authorizing transactions, executing them, and holding assets affected by them. The matching operation involves the detailed checking of purchase invoices received with purchase orders, goods received notes and price agreements.
- Apart from matching, all calculations on the purchase invoices should be checked for accuracy, including extensions, casts and VAT calculations.
- The above controls should be evidenced, perhaps by a check box on the invoice.
- When paying by cheque or bank transfer, the signatories (preferably two) should see supporting documentation and check that matching etc. has been properly performed.
- There should be a strictly applied rule that blank cheques are never signed, even if it is more convenient to do so.

ANALYTICAL PROCEDURES

See Kothari Limited (Case study 12.1) on page 432 and Powerbase plc (Case study 10.1) on page 361.

We have already seen that analytical procedures involve investigation of relationships between figures in the financial statements and detecting those that seem not to make sense. We have looked at some cases where we felt (initially at least) that purchases and trade payables figures were suspect and required further investigation. In Chapter 12 when we discussed trade receivables and sales, we saw that the auditor must check that sales and cost of sales, including purchases, are properly matched. If a sale of goods has been made but the purchase cost of these goods is not included in cost of sales, matching will not have taken place. For this reason, 'genuine, accurate and complete' tests of purchases and trade payables should be carried out by the auditor. Material unrecorded purchases/trade payables would cause ratios such as gross margin and trade payables days outstanding to vary from expectation and would prompt the auditor to be particularly careful. We suggest below steps that the auditor might take in carrying out a search for unrecorded liabilities, but do not address analytical review of purchases and trade payables specifically in this section; however, you should attempt Self-assessment question 13.4 at the end of this chapter.

Suggested substantive approaches to prove that figures are genuine, accurate and complete

Creation of trade payables' balances

We have discussed purchases systems, suitable compliance tests, and substantive tests to prove that purchases are genuine, accurate and complete in previous chapters. We shall not cover this ground again except to remind you that if purchases are genuine, accurate and complete, this is a good starting point for ensuring that trade payables are created on a sound basis.

Look again at Case Study 10.1 Powerbase plc: the substantive audit programme for purchases.

Recorded trade payables at the year-end

The auditor's interest is to determine not only that trade payables have come into existence as a result of genuine, accurate and complete transactions, but that they represent all the balances owed by the company, not cleared by the balance sheet date. The basic assertions are as follows:

Class of assertion	Assertions
Genuine	Trade payables and accruals represent amounts actually due by the company, taking into account: • the actual performance of services for the company, or • transfer of title in goods transferred to the company. • cash payments or other genuine debit entry. (Obligations)
Accurate	Trade payables reflect all matters affecting their underlying valuation (including changes in foreign currency exchange rates) in accordance with relevant accounting principles. (Valuation) Accruals though not formally agreed have been estimated on a sound basis. (Valuation) Trade payables and accruals represent amounts due at the balance sheet date. (Cut-off)
Complete	All trade payables and accruals are properly recorded in the accounting records. (Complete) Trade payables and accruals have been properly summarized for disclosure in the financial statements. (Classification)

Search for unrecorded liabilities

It is often not easy to determine if everything that should have been recorded has been recorded. For instance, if your task is to prove that a creditor for £10 000 is truly a liability at the year-end date, you can examine the supporting documentation such as correspondence, GRNs, inventory records, etc. If, however, your intent is to prove whether a creditor exists that has not been recorded, you will have to institute a search. Such a search represents work to prove completeness but would also be made to prove that transactions at the year-end are genuine and accurate. The auditor's work would include the following:

- *Perform an analytical review in the purchases and trade payables area*. The auditor analyses profit and loss account cost and expense headings and related trade payables and ensures they are reasonable in the light of what is known about the company. Let us assume that the review has revealed that gross profit percentage (at 40 per cent) is higher than expected, trade payables payment in days (at 22 days) is much lower than expected and the acid test ratio is much higher than expected (see the first column of figures in Figure 13.1). This would set you upon enquiry as both cost of sales and trade payables may be understated, prompting the auditor to make a search for unrecorded liabilities. In Figure 13.1 we have assumed that trade payables were in fact understated by £60 000. Note that correction of the error has a material impact on a number of ratios by looking at the final column in Figure 13.1.

Analytical procedures may also reveal that liabilities are understated. For instance, they might show that quantity rebates have not been taken up. The auditor would examine purchase contracts to ensure that rebates have been taken up in the correct period, and audit software might be used to identify suppliers with whom the company has had material transactions during the year. The same considerations apply to potential claims against suppliers for poor workmanship or other problems after delivery or completion of work. In some industries (for instance, the building industry), it is common practice

FIGURE 13.1 Extract from profit and loss account and balance sheet

	Original	Amendment	As restated
	£	£	£
Sales	1 000 000		1 000 000
Cost of sales	600 000	60 000	660 000
Gross profit	400 000		340 000
Inventories	115 000		115 000
Trade receivables	123 000		123 000
Cash	10 000		10 000
	248 000		248 000
Trade payables	36 000	60 000	96 000
	212 000		152 000
Gross profit %	40.00		34.00
Inventories turnover	69.96 days		63.60 days
Debtors collectability	44.90 days		44.90 days
Creditors payment	21.90 days		53.09 days
Acid test ratio	3.69 times		1.39 times

to retain part of the purchase consideration for a period after completion of the work until passed by a surveyor. These tests help to prove the accuracy of the purchases and trade payables figures.

- *Discuss with management the steps they have taken to ascertain that all liabilities have been recorded*. We have discussed systems for controlling transactions earlier, but the company should also have systems for establishing figures in company records. For instance, department heads should be required to report any liabilities known to them at the year-end. Such a step will help the auditor in forming conclusions in the area, although, like any system, it will need testing to see if it is operating satisfactorily. If, for instance, auditors find that the chief accountant takes no action when department heads do not reply, they will not be able to rely upon the system and a useful source of evidence may not be available.
- *Review purchases record in the period subsequent to the year-end*. When performing this work the auditor looks for invoices recorded after the year-end with a delivery date before the year-end.
- *Review payment record in the period subsequent to the year-end*. The auditor will review the bank records and test entries in the period after the year-end to ascertain if there are any payments for liabilities arising in the previous period. The objective is to discover if there are any liabilities cleared in the new period that existed but were not recorded in the former period.
- *Review goods and services received record prior to the year-end*. The auditor checks that all entries in goods and services received record has resulted in a recorded invoice in the period prior to the year-end. (This is really a cut-off matter and we discuss it further below.)
- *Inspect suppliers' statements*. In Chapter 6 we saw that suppliers' statements come into the category of systems-based third-party evidence and as such may be regarded as useful evidence for the auditor, provided that care is taken to assess the system that supports it. Inspection of suppliers' statements will be an important audit step, as they provide not only evidence of balances outstanding but also serve to prove purchases.

Refer to Figure 6.5 (the Oakshaw example) in Chapter 6 for the evidence corroboration and upgrading process in the purchases and trade payables area.

- *Circularize suppliers*. Earlier we discussed circularizations of credit customers. It is also practice to circularize suppliers and companies may ask selected suppliers to inform the auditors of the amount recorded in their books. This would aid auditors' search for unrecorded liabilities. It is also good practice to ask suppliers to give details of transactions in a period (say, fourteen days) before and after the year-end to help ensure that they have been recorded in the correct period.

Consistency in application of accounting standards

Consistency, as we have seen before, is an important element of achieving comparability in financial statements, and auditors must ensure that accounting methods are consistently applied. For instance, if a company had been recording purchases at gross amount, only taking up cash discounts when actually received, but decided in the current year to reduce purchases value in the accounts by normal discounts, the auditor would wish to ensure that:

- The new method was appropriate to the circumstances of the company. (Was it likely that the discount would be received?)
- The effect of the change, if material, was disclosed in the notes to the financial statements.

Is cut-off accurate?

We have already discussed trade payables cut-off in relation to inventory earlier in this chapter. Cut-off of bank transactions affecting trade payables would also be tested to ensure that payments to suppliers before the year-end are all deducted from trade payables in arriving at year-end figures. Remember that cut-off tests are completeness tests.

Disclosure of trade payables payable in the short, medium and long term

Most trade payables are payable in the short term (that is, within 12 months of the balance sheet date) and should be disclosed as payable within one year. It may be common in some industries, however, for amounts to be payable at a date later than one year. For instance, Pykestone may have completed a contract for Hagshaw plc priced at £100 000 on 21 September 2011, £80 000 being payable after 30 days and £20 000 on 31 October 2012. In Hagshaw's financial statements at 30 September 2011, £800 000 would be shown as payable within one year and £20 000 as payable after one year.

We discuss contingent liabilities in detail in Chapter 14.

Examples of specific disclosure in the liabilities area include significant contingent liabilities, that is, liabilities that will come into existence as a consequence of a future event, the outcome of which is not certain (such as a court case).

Payment of trade payables' balances

If the matching operation has taken place properly and the person giving authority for payment is independent of the cashier, the purchase ledger clerk, the buying department and stores, the auditor will have greater confidence in the payment process. Audit steps in the area might include re-performance of the matching operation and checking that invoices have been properly cleared by cash and discount transactions.

Purchases and trade payables audit programme at the year-end

We shall not give you a long list of audit procedures in the purchases and related trade payables area. However, we give you below a number of short audit situations affecting purchases and trade payables and ask you to devise audit steps to solve the problems arising.

We comment as follows:

See Activity 13.10 on page 522

ACTIVITY 13.10

- *Situation 1*: company A is a glass manufacturer and requires high quality sand from Australia for its production of special precision glass products. At the year-end, sand is on board a ship in the middle of the Indian Ocean. What audit steps would you take to ensure related liabilities have been properly recorded and reflected in the financial statements?

- *Situation 2*: the audit programme for purchases and trade payables of company B includes the following: 'Examine the company's reconciliations between suppliers' statements and purchase ledger balances'. You discover that company B has not made such reconciliations and on selecting suppliers' statements for comparison with purchase ledger balances you find many material differences between the two. Suggest further audit steps.
- *Situation 3*: you are investigating debit balances in the trade payables balances of company C. What audit steps would you take to ensure the debit balances are valid?
- *Situation 4*: company D has listed unmatched GRNs and goods returned forms (GRFs) at the year-end date, valued them and included the amounts in purchases accruals. What steps would you take to satisfy yourself that the accruals are acceptable?
- *Situation 5*: as part of your audit work you have reviewed the forecast accounts to 31 December 2011 prepared by company E six months prior to that year-end date. You note that trade payables in the forecast accounts are about 25 per cent higher than those shown in the draft financial statements at 31 December. Describe the audit tests you would take to satisfy yourself that the trade payables in the draft financial statements are acceptable.

Situation 1

The first step for the auditor would be to determine who owns the sand on board ship in the middle of the Indian Ocean, by examining the contract of sale and the bill of lading. There are a number of possible kinds of agreement for the transport of goods by sea, including:

- Free on board (FOB). In this case the seller has to place the goods over the ship's rail at a port mentioned in the sales contract. The seller pays all transport to the quayside and the cost of loading on board the ship.
- Cost insurance and freight (CIF). In this case the seller has to place the goods on board a ship at a port mentioned in the sales contract and is responsible for paying for insurance of goods in transit as far as the named port. The seller pays all transport to the quayside, cost of loading on board and insurance of goods in transit.

The following matters should be considered in determining liability at the year-end:

- The cost of the sand. The auditor should determine what costs are included in the supplier's invoice. If the cost is all-inclusive, the verification work will

The terms are part of a set of internationally agreed definitions (known as Incoterms), used to set out the rights and obligations of parties for the transport of goods. The auditor must confirm which Incoterm is being used. If the property in the sand passed to the company when loaded onto the ship, it should be included in the balance sheet as a current asset at the year-end, together with corresponding liability.

be relatively simple. If not, the auditor will have to consider the following matters.

(a) Cost of loading in Australia.
(b) Agents' charges in Australia and in company A's own country.
(c) Carriage, insurance and freight.
(d) Supplementary port charges including such items as demurrage. (The auditor would wish to ensure that such costs fall on company A and are not the responsibility of the carrier.)

'Demurrage' is a charge payable to the port authorities if there has been undue delay. For instance, the vessel may be longer in port than expected because of unloading problems not the fault of the port authorities.

- The cost of bank facilities such as export credit guarantees. In performing this work the auditor would seek evidence to support conclusions, including:
  (a) The costs of previous deliveries of sand.
  (b) Invoices from suppliers of goods (sand) and services (carriers, port authorities, agents).
  (c) Bank and finance company confirmations for cost of finance.

The other matter to be considered is whether the sand should be valued at the total cost to be incurred in respect of its material value and all other costs, including those, such as port dues in the country of destination, which have not yet been incurred. Our view is that the inventory should be valued at the cost of buying and transporting the sand to the destination in the country towards which it is proceeding on the ground that the company will pay these costs to make it useful to it. If this is done the company will have to include costs not yet theoretically incurred in trade payables and accruals.

Situation 2

When a company reconciles suppliers' statements to purchase ledger balances, it has a system to determine the accuracy of figures in the records and auditors would test its adequacy by checking some of the reconciliations. Company B has no reconciliations, so the auditors have no system that can be relied on and should ask the company to perform the reconciliations without delay. They might suggest that the company write to those suppliers who have not sent statements at the year-end, asking them to do so. The company should be requested to prepare an adjustments schedule and the auditors should test its accuracy. A trade payables circularization might be appropriate in the circumstances.

Situation 3

Debit balances on creditor ledger accounts would not be the norm and the auditor should investigate them. They may arise for a variety of reasons including:

- Mis-posting of purchase invoices so that the subsequent correct posting of cash payments produces a debit balance on an account.
- Mis-posting of cash payments so that a debit balance appears on the account to which it is posted. In these two cases the auditor would wish to know why the mis-posting had occurred and why it had not been picked up by the company.

- Sales ledger offset resulting in a debit balance on the trade payables ledger. The auditor would ask why the trade payables ledger balance was not transferred to the sales ledger account instead.
- Payment in advance by company B. The auditor would wish to know why payments in advance were made and also to ascertain at what point the goods or services provided by the supplier were eventually received.
- Double payments of suppliers' invoices. The auditor would wish to know why this had occurred as, on the face of it, the accounting and control system has broken down. In particular, the auditor would check that invoices were cancelled after payment to reduce the possibility that they were presented for payment on more than one occasion.
- Return of goods. The auditor would wish to know why the goods originally supplied had been paid for when the goods turned out not to be required. It may be that there has been a systems breakdown and goods were not properly inspected on arrival. To be fair, however, it may not be known that some materials are unsuitable until entering the production process.

You can see from our comments above that the auditor should adopt a questioning attitude to debit balances on the trade payables ledger. Some of the work may result in adjustments while others may lead to the auditor recommending changes to company procedures.

Situation 4

Auditors should ascertain that there is a system for matching purchase invoices and credit notes to GRNs and GRFs (this would be easier if they were pre-numbered), test invoices received from suppliers and ensure that accruals are in respect of genuinely unmatched GRNs and GRFs. Furthermore, auditors would compare accruals with invoices and credit notes subsequently received. If they have not been received the auditor may test to inventory records, purchase orders and other supporting documentation.

Situation 5

Comparison of forecast accounts with draft financial statements is a normal analytical review procedure. If company E had forecast trade payables to be 25 per cent higher than they turned out to be in the draft financial statements, the auditor would seek an explanation, and discuss with management the expectations of the company at the time the forecast was prepared and the extent to which they were fulfilled. This sort of approach can be useful as it enables the auditor to understand the problems of management. If a business risk approach is adopted, auditors would already know of risks affecting the forecast accounts. Perhaps activity in the six months has been less than expected and purchases of goods and services and related trade payables correspondingly reduced. If the figures made sense in this way, the auditors might not extend detailed testing.

Summary

In this chapter we have shown how the general principles relating to the audit of balance sheet headings should be applied to the audit of inventories, including construction contracts, and trade payables. In the process we have considered related profit and loss account headings and the audit approaches to them. In each case we have conducted the discussion in terms of management assertions and audit objectives appropriate to each asset or liability and have related this discussion to matters we considered in previous chapters such as systems work, the use of computers and analytical review.

Key points of the chapter

Inventories

- Inventories vary in character and pose a variety of problems for auditors.
- Auditors pay particular attention to the costing system for ensuring costs are genuine, accurate and complete. Overheads must be allocated on a reasonable basis, and on the basis of normal production levels. Products may be 'main' or by-products.
- Net realizable value not easy to determine because inventories may not be used, sold or completed until after audit field work is complete.
- Inherent risks include: (a) changes in demand; (b) changes in production levels; (c) defects in product lines; (d) inventories attractive and transportable; (e) complex production process; (f) joint products; (g) significant variances; (h) new competitors; (i) complex calculation of overheads.
- Inherent risks affecting the existence assertion include: (a) reliability of recording systems; (b) reliability of records where inventories are counted before year-end; (c) inventories are at third party locations; (d) poor physical controls; (e) independence and experience of inventory counters/supervisors; (f) fluctuation of inventory levels; (g) specialized inventories.
- Acquisitions: important to determine point at which title passes, particularly in e-commerce relationships; *safeguarding inventories*: includes physical safeguards and restriction of access via documentation; *disposals of inventories*: normal sales more likely to be controlled than abnormal disposals; *determining existence, condition and ownership*: physical inventory counts, reconciliation to records and investigation of significant differences; *valuation of inventories*: basic principle is the lower of cost and net realizable value, Costing and other records must be reliable and prepared consistently.
- Substantive testing include analytical procedures and tests to address: (a) existence; (b) condition; (c) ownership; (d) cut-off; (e) recording of production costs; (f) allocation of production costs to inventories.
- Inventories might be manipulated by: (a) recording false sales; (b) moving inventories between locations; (c) manipulation of cut-off; (d) alteration of inventory count records; (e) over-optimistic estimations.
- Auditors attend inventory counts to ensure system is operating satisfactorily and to perform tests of controls and substantive tests. Cut-off procedures performed at external and internal cut-off. Company procedures to ensure accurate cut-off: (a) individual responsible for cut-off; (b) restrict movement during count; (c) decision on treatment of unavoidable movements by responsible official; (d) note number of last movement document.
- Inventory-taking instructions are important for staff to follow in determining physical existence, condition, ownership and cut-off.
- Procedures to ensure inventory is properly counted and recorded: (a) inventory-taking instructions; (b) person with overall responsibility, independent of stores personnel; (c) balanced inventory count teams; (d) stores neat and tidy; (e) cut-off arrangements; (f) use of pre-numbered inventory sheets and completeness check; (g) inventory names and reference numbers on inventory sheets; (h) count team members count inventory independently; (i) count sheets signed by two members of count team; (j) count teams comment on items in poor physical condition; (k) investigation of significant differences between inventory records and count; (l) count teams responsible for manageable quantities; (m) logical system for recording; (n) test counts by responsible officials; (o) marking inventory counted; (p) identification of goods held for or by third parties; (q) auditors available for advice; (r) briefing sessions with count teams.
- Auditors attend count to check if instructions properly followed, and to make test counts, particularly of high value inventories. Level of substantive tests depends on quality of instructions and how applied. Inventory counts carried out during the year and inventory quantities taken from records only if: (a) controls over inventory records are adequate; (b) inventory records are accurate and complete; (c) significant differences are investigated and corrected. Audit procedures include: (a) inventory count observations during year; (b) test accuracy of inventory records; (c) test for cut-off at count date *and* balance sheet date; (d) if necessary, restricted test count at balance sheet date. Particular problems affecting work in progress, inventories held at third parties and at branches.
- Basis of inventory valuation is lower of cost and net realizable value. Basic rules for calculating cost include: (a) for individual categories of inventory; (b) comprises cost of purchase and conversion;

(c) cost of purchase comprises direct costs, less cost reductions; (d) cost of conversion comprises: (i) direct costs; (ii) production overheads based on normal level of activity; (iii) overheads incurred in bringing product or service to its present location and condition; (e) costs may be allocated to production using a method, such as FIFO. Selling price less an appropriate percentage mark-up may be acceptable.

- Net realizable value is actual or estimated selling price less all further costs of production and costs yet to be incurred in marketing, selling and distributing.
- Other inventory valuation matters: (a) disclosure of changes in basis of valuation; (b) all calculations affecting valuation properly made; (c) disclosure of encumbered inventories.

Construction contracts

- Construction contracts defined as 'contracts entered into for the design, manufacture or construction of an asset or provision of a service or a combination of related assets or services such that the contract activity usually falls into different accounting periods'.
- Decision must be made as to whether profits and losses should be taken up before completion. This is subjective and auditors assess validity of management judgements in relation to: (1) costs incurred to date; (2) stages of completion; (3) invoices issued to customers in accordance with contract and certified by the surveyor; (4) cash received from customers; (5) estimated total costs; (6) contract prices; (7) taking up of attributable profits and losses; (8) profitability of different stages of the contract; (9) comparability of the method of taking up profits and losses.

Trade payables and purchases

- Audit work on trade payables closely associated with work on purchases and related assets.
- Inherent risks include: (a) new or material transactions or events; (b) material variances from standard costs; (c) suppliers experiencing difficulties; (d) significant changes in terms of trade; (e) material increase in age of trade payables; (f) major changes in nature of purchases; (g) above average returns of goods purchased.
- Creation of trade payables – expected controls include: (a) preparation of integrated purchases budget and investigation of variances; (b) record point at which title passes or services rendered are complete; (c) clear statement of company obligations regarding goods on sale or return; (d) identification of purchases where title remains with the supplier; (e) purchases not in the normal purchases system to be specially authorized; (f) investigation of significant returns; (g) cut-off procedures.
- Recorded trade payables at the year-end – expected controls include: (a) appropriate division of duties; (b) regular review of suppliers' statements; (c) system for determining supplier credit limits; (d) system for detecting unrecorded liabilities; (e) system for enquiry into unusual features.
- Payment of trade payables balances – expected controls include: (a) independent matching operation; (b) calculations on purchase invoices; (c) evidence of controls performed; (d) cheque signatories to see supporting documentation; (e) blank cheques never to be signed.
- Substantive approaches cover analytical procedures and tests of (a) matching operation; (b) recorded trade payables at year-end; (c) search for unrecorded liabilities: (i) proving reasonable relationship between trade payables/purchases and other figures; (ii) discussions with management; (iii) review post year-end purchases and payments; (iv) review goods and services received record prior to the year-end; (v) inspect payables' statements; (vi) circularize payables; (vii) check consistency of accounting policies; (viii) check cut-off; (ix) check disclosure of trade payables and contingent liabilities.

Further reading

This has again been a very practical chapter and you should work the examples in an imaginative way, again trying to visualize the situation in the various cases. Relevant accounting standards are SSAP 9 – *Stocks and long-term contracts*, IAS 1 – *Presentation of financial statements*, IAS 2 – *Inventory* and IAS 11 – *Construction contracts*. Auditing standards are ISA 500 – *Audit evidence*, and ISA 501 – *Audit evidence: specific considerations for selected items*. You may also refer to Practice Note 25 – *Attendance at stocktaking* – issued by APB.

Self-assessment questions (solutions available to students)

13.1 Consider the following statements and explain why they may be true or false:

(a) The omission of a short-term liability from the balance sheet will result in the acid test ratio showing that the company is less liquid than it really is.

(b) Trade payables may be regarded as complete once auditors have carried out their search for unrecorded liabilities.

(c) Accurate cut-off means that trade payables are genuine.

(d) In valuing inventories it is permissible to include an element of administrative expense.

(e) In planning work on construction contracts the auditor should identify the points where management is exercising judgement.

13.2 You are auditing a company that operates a computer-controlled warehouse. There is no human entry to the warehouse except when essential maintenance is carried out and products are taken into the store and taken out on pallets controlled by an operator using a desktop computer. Suggest how you might approach that section of your audit where you are seeking to prove existence and condition of inventory.

13.3 The following is a record of inventory movements and recorded sales of Whygate Ltd, a company buying and selling products on credit with a December 2011 year-end. Consider these figures and then attempt the following questions.

Value	Despatch note number	Inventory despatched	Sales record
£25 000	1456	27 December 2011	30 December 2011
£12 550	1457	27 December 2011	3 January 2012
£9 000	1458	30 December 2011	27 December 2011
£7 500	1459	30 December 2011	31 December 2011
£6 000	1460	31 December 2011	6 January 2012
£5 600	1461	3 January 2012	31 December 2011
£9 750	1462	3 January 2012	3 January 2012
£6 240	1463	6 January 2012	3 January 2012
£5 995	1464	31 December 2011	3 January 2012

(a) Assuming that inventory was determined by count at 31 December 2011 state the adjustment required to sales and debtors and indicate the effect on profits of the adjustment.

(b) Assuming that inventory was determined on the basis of recorded inventory movements, state the adjustment required to sales and trade receivables and indicate the effect on profits of the adjustment. The company carries out periodic inventory counts.

You may assume in both cases that purchases have been recorded in the correct period.

(c) What action would you take as auditor to prove that sales/inventory cut-off was accurate?

13.4 You are responsible for the audit of trade payables and purchases of Powerbase for the year ended 31 May 2011. You carried out interim audit work on purchases and trade payables at 30 November 2010 and concluded that purchases were being properly processed although you were somewhat concerned that delays in processing were occurring. Your concern was heightened by a comment by a member of the accounting staff: 'I don't know what you are worried about. If we haven't recorded a liability, the supplier will soon remind us!' You have now been given the following figures (including some ratios) and aim to ensure that the purchases and trade payables at 31 May 2011 are fairly stated. Design substantive programme steps that will help you to accomplish this aim. You should refer to our comments on the Powerbase Case study (10.1 on page 361).

		Year to 31 May 2010		Year to 31 May 2011
		£m		£m
Sales		95.2		110.0
Cost of sales		54.8		51.0
Gross profit		40.4		59.0
		(42.44%)		(53.64%)
Administrative expenses	22.3		20.2	
Selling expenses	10.5	32.8	9.4	29.6
Net profit before taxation		7.6		29.4
Inventory	11.3 75 days		11.7 84 days	
Trade receivables	11.7 45 days		12.8 42 days	
Trade payables	9.01 60 days		8.2 59 days	

Self-assessment questions (solutions available to tutors)

13.5 Blackford Ltd is a company engaged in two diverse activities: the manufacture of lawnmowers and trading in the hardware sector, selling its lawnmowers through its own hardware outlets. The company decided to discontinue its loss making lawnmower operation from 31 May 2011 (one month before the year-end date). Many people in the workforce were accepted for transfer to the hardware sector, but others are taking early retirement and accepting redundancy payments. Redundancy payments are based on length of service and wage/salary levels in the last year of service, provided the employee has been at least two years with the company. The company has provided for redundancy costs of £200 000. Identify management assertions and suggest audit steps you would perform to satisfy yourself that the provision for redundancy cost is accurate.

13.6 Question taken from ICAEW Audit and Assurance Paper December 2001. You have conducted analytical review procedures on the draft accounts of Blunt Limited for the year ended 31 October 2011. Two of your findings are as follows:

1. The gross margin has decreased from 29 per cent for the previous year to 23 per cent for this year.
2. The current ratio has decreased from 1.6 at the previous year-end to 1.2 at this year-end.

The directors had expected a decrease in both these measures but not by as much as shown above. Indicate what errors might be incorporated within the draft accounts to produce these unexpected variations, and in which areas you would carry out extra audit work in order to reach a conclusion.

13.7 Explain why it is so important for auditors to identify the points at which management is making judgemental decisions about accounting matters. Give examples.

Topics for class discussion without solutions

13.8 It is easier to prove that trade receivables are genuine, accurate and complete than is the case for trade payables.

13.9 Identify important controls surrounding inventory counts by the entity.

14

Final review: post-balance sheet period, provisions, contingencies, letter of representation

LEARNING OBJECTIVES

After studying this chapter you should be able to:

- **Describe the nature of the work the auditor performs immediately prior to preparation of the audit report.**
- **Detail the specific procedures the auditor performs in respect of post-balance sheet events.**
- **Explain the nature of provisions, contingent liabilities and contingent assets and detail audit procedures in respect of them.**
- **Describe the final working paper review procedures performed by the auditor prior to forming the final audit opinion.**
- **Explain the nature and role of the management letter of representation, in the context of the evidence search.**

Learning objectives, 530
Introduction, 531
Post-balance sheet events, 531
Provisions, contingent liabilities and contingent assets, 537
Going concern, 546
Audit work to detect post-balance sheet events and contingencies, 547
Management letter of representation, 549
Audit documentation, 554
Role of the final review, 558
Summary, 559
Key points of the chapter, 559
Further reading, 561
Self-assessment questions (solutions available to students), 561
Self-assessment questions (solutions available to tutors), 562
Topics for class discussion without solutions, 563

INTRODUCTION

We have now reached stage 18 of the audit process shown in Figure 6.3. In this chapter we discuss a number of matters the auditor specifically considers at this advanced stage in the audit process. The auditor is still engaged in the search for audit evidence, but at this stage is pulling evidence gathered together, reviewing conclusions made earlier and trying to form a view on the financial statements taken as a whole. Apart from this we have also to review a number of new topics which you need to know about and which will help you to understand the audit process. These are:

See Chapter 6, page 230.

- Post-balance sheet date work, including that relating to contingent liabilities and contingent assets.
- Audit work on provisions.
- Final working file review.
- Consideration of the validity of the going-concern concept. (We discuss audit approach to going concern in Chapter 17.)
- Management letter of representation – an important record of evidence from management sources.

POST-BALANCE SHEET EVENTS

In our discussions we have noted a number of instances where the auditor considers the period after the end of the financial year-end. We give examples below:

- The provision for bad and doubtful debts is based on an assessment of amounts that will be collected in the subsequent period.
- The decision as to whether inventories are to be valued at cost or lower net realizable value must take note of prices and costs expected to exist in the new period.
- The useful lives of fixed assets, which are important for determining depreciation rates, are based on an assessment of the future.
- The search for unrecorded liabilities takes place in the period subsequent to the balance sheet date.

This means that the post-balance sheet period needs to be considered during the detailed substantive testing work on a number of balance sheet and profit and loss account items.

Post-balance sheet period

Apart from the above matters, however, it is important that the auditor should specifically review the post-balance sheet period as a whole to ascertain whether there are any matters which should be reflected in the accounts or referred to in the audit report. There is an International Accounting Standard in the area, IAS 10 – *Events after the reporting period.* The relevant

International Standard of Auditing is ISA 560 – *Subsequent events*. Paragraph 4 of this states the objectives of the auditor clearly:

(a) To obtain sufficient appropriate audit evidence about whether events occurring between the date of the financial statements and the date of the auditor's report that require adjustment of, or disclosure in, the financial statements are appropriately reflected in those financial statements in accordance with the applicable financial reporting framework; and

(b) To respond appropriately to facts that become known to the auditor after the date of the auditor's report, that, had they been known to the auditor at that date, may have caused the auditor to amend the auditor's report.

Definition of subsequent events

Paragraph 3 of IAS 10 defines subsequent events as: 'those events, favourable and unfavourable, that occur between the balance sheet date and the date when the financial statements are authorized for issue. Two types of event can be identified:

(a) those that provide evidence of conditions that existed at the balance sheet date (adjusting events); and

(b) those that are indicative of conditions that arose after the balance sheet date (non-adjusting events).'

ACTIVITY 14.1

Read again the objectives of the auditor as stated in ISA 560 and the definition of subsequent events as stated in IAS 10. What differences are there between the two as regards the period of time after the balance sheet date?

We discuss below the relevance of the date that the directors sign the financial statements and the date of signing the audit report.

Clearly the major difference is that IAS 10 ends the post balance sheet period at the date when the financial statements are authorized for issue. This would be the date when the directors sign the financial statements and the date of the auditor's report. However, paragraph 4 (b) of ISA 560 expects the auditors to look beyond the date of the auditor's report to consider events that might have caused the auditors to amend their report had the events been known at the date of signing.

The period after the balance sheet date may be divided into a number of sub-periods, all of which have their own characteristics and provide different problems for the auditor. We show this diagrammatically in Figure 14.1.

Examples of post-balance sheet events

In Figure 14.1 we have assumed that five post-balance sheet events (one of which is the discovery of a fact concerning the allocation of overheads to inventory) have occurred, each in a different period:

- In the period between the balance sheet date and the date of completion of draft accounts.

FIGURE 14.1 Accounting reference period and post-balance sheet period

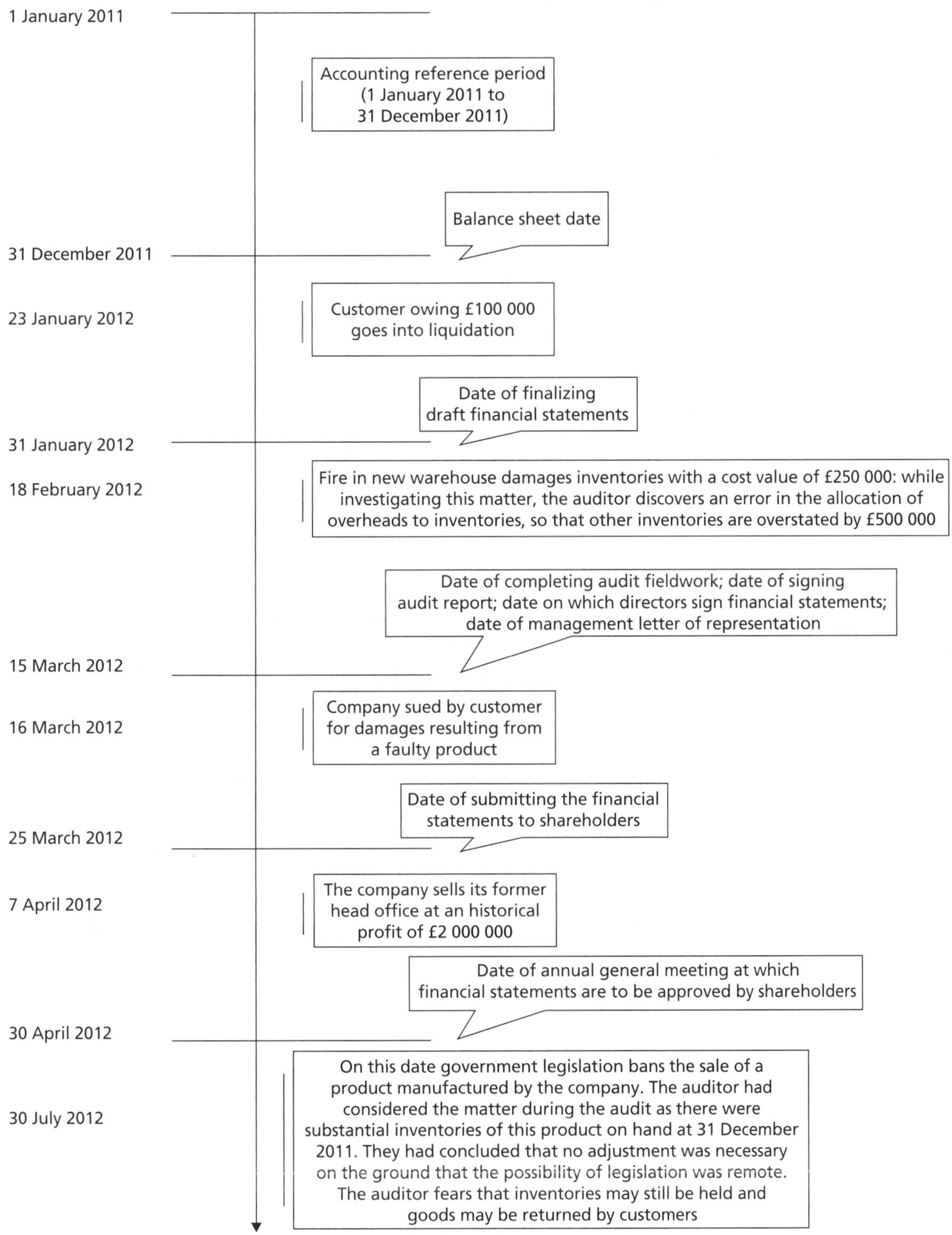
1 January 2011
Accounting reference period (1 January 2011 to 31 December 2011)
Balance sheet date
31 December 2011
23 January 2012
Customer owing £100 000 goes into liquidation
Date of finalizing draft financial statements
31 January 2012
18 February 2012
Fire in new warehouse damages inventories with a cost value of £250 000: while investigating this matter, the auditor discovers an error in the allocation of overheads to inventories, so that other inventories are overstated by £500 000
Date of completing audit fieldwork; date of signing audit report; date on which directors sign financial statements; date of management letter of representation
15 March 2012
16 March 2012
Company sued by customer for damages resulting from a faulty product
Date of submitting the financial statements to shareholders
25 March 2012
7 April 2012
The company sells its former head office at an historical profit of £2 000 000
Date of annual general meeting at which financial statements are to be approved by shareholders
30 April 2012
30 July 2012
On this date government legislation bans the sale of a product manufactured by the company. The auditor had considered the matter during the audit as there were substantial inventories of this product on hand at 31 December 2011. They had concluded that no adjustment was necessary on the ground that the possibility of legislation was remote. The auditor fears that inventories may still be held and goods may be returned by customers

- In the period from completion of draft accounts and the date upon which audit fieldwork was completed.
- In the period from the completion of audit fieldwork and date of submitting the financial statements to the shareholders.
- In the period after the financial statements have been submitted to shareholders but before the AGM.
- In the period after the date of the AGM.

IAS 10 provides examples of adjusting and non-adjusting events.

We discuss the significance of these periods and whether the events would be treated as post-balance sheet events after we have considered their nature in the light of IAS 10. To put the events into context you are informed that operating profits in the draft financial statements amount to £1 000 000.

23 January 2012: customer owing £100 000 goes into liquidation

ACTIVITY 14.2

How do you think this matter should be reflected in the financial statements? Explain your answer.

This item would seem to be an adjusting event in terms of IAS 10, which defines such an event as a post-balance sheet event which provides evidence of conditions that existed at the balance sheet date. The amount also appears to be material in relation to the stated profit. The argument would be that the balance owing by the customer was really uncollectable (that is, it possessed the condition of uncollectability) at 31 December 2011 and the event has merely confirmed this, although the reasons for the liquidation might have to be determined to be certain. The auditor would also wish to ascertain whether the liquidator is likely to make partial payment of the amount owing.

18 February 2012: fire in the new warehouse damages inventory with a cost value of £250 000; while investigating this matter, the auditor discovers an error in the allocation of overheads to inventory so that inventories, other than those lost in the fire, are overstated by £500 000

ACTIVITY 14.3

There are two events here. Identify them and state how they should be treated in the financial statements, giving reasons.

The two events are the fire and the discovery of the inventory overstatement. The fire would seem to be a non-adjusting event in terms of IAS 10, which defines such an event as a post-balance sheet event which is indicative of conditions that arose after the balance sheet date. Although the value of the inventory appears to be material, it is unlikely to be significant enough to cast doubts on whether the company is a going concern, and this would appear therefore to be a disclosure matter rather than an adjusting event. The auditor would wish to ascertain whether the company was insured against this sort of loss and damage. The discovery of the fact that inventories are overvalued by £500 000 as the result of misallocation of overheads is an adjusting event as it gives information about a condition existing at the balance sheet date. It is certainly material in relation to the stated profit.

See Paragraph 14 of IAS 10.

16 March 2012: company sued by customer for damages resulting from faulty product

We shall discuss this event when we discuss contingent liabilities later in the chapter.

7 April 2012: The company sells its former head office at an historical cost profit of £2 000 000

This event tells us nothing about conditions existing at the balance sheet date and we would not therefore expect the exceptional profit to be taken up in the financial statements. However, it does seem to be a matter of some significance and would be regarded as disclosable.

30 July 2012: government legislation bans the sale of a product manufactured by the company

This event would have an immediate effect on the saleability of the product concerned. It may be seen as an adjusting event if it can be seen as providing proof that the product was dangerous (at the balance sheet date) but more information would have to be sought by the auditor.

Now we have formed some conclusions about the nature of the events themselves, let us consider the dates upon which they occurred.

The significance of the periods in which post-balance sheet events occur

23 January 2012

The company is in the course of preparing the financial statements at 31 December 2011 and should have a system for detecting events after the year-end to be reflected as an adjustment or disclosure in the accounts. At this date the accounts have not even been finalized in draft and we would expect the liquidation of the debtor to result in a provision to reduce the trade receivable to collectable value. Even at this stage there may be some indication from the liquidator of the amount likely to be payable to claimants.

The auditors would be presumed to have knowledge of this event because it occurred before completion of fieldwork. Naturally, they will need to devise procedures to ensure that such events come to their attention.

We suggest procedures to detect material post-balance sheet events below.

18 February 2012

This date occurs in the period after the draft financial statements have been prepared, but before the directors have signed them and the auditors have issued their report. The financial statements do not legally come into existence until they have been formally signed by the directors, so one would expect the same situation to apply as to the event of 23 January 2012. A problem for the auditor might be that management may have made expected results known to other insiders or even to outsiders and may, therefore, be reluctant to make any necessary adjustments or disclosures. In the case of the fire causing loss of inventory, the auditor should ask for details of inventory damaged and an estimate of realizable value. The overstatement of inventory because of misallocation of overheads might set the auditor on enquiry, as it might cast doubt on the competence or integrity of management.

As an event in this period occurs before the end of the auditors' fieldwork, they would be presumed to have knowledge of it and the post-balance sheet procedures should cover this period also.

16 March 2012

We are concerned here with the period for which the auditor has responsibilities, demarcated by the date of the audit report. It is clearly important that the audit report should be dated.

This event has occurred after the directors have signed the financial statements and after completion of audit fieldwork, but before the financial statements have been submitted to shareholders. The question we have to address is whether the auditors have any responsibility, bearing in mind that they are no longer actively looking for post-balance sheet events and will not know of the event unless somebody tells them. Paragraph 10 of ISA 560 clearly states that the auditor has no obligation to perform any audit procedures after the date of the auditor's report. However, if the auditor becomes aware of a fact that, had it been known to him or her at the date of the report, may have caused the report to be amended, ISA 560 requires the auditor to:

(a) Discuss the matter with management and, where appropriate, those charged with governance.

See Paragraph 10 of ISA 560.

(b) Determine whether the financial statements need amendment and, if so,

(c) Inquire how management intends to address the matter in the financial statements.

There are two possibilities:

1 Assuming that the directors decide to amend the financial statements, they will issue new statements and sign them on the new date of issue. The consequence for the auditors is that they will be required to issue a new report with the additional consequence that further audit procedures will be necessary to obtain evidence of material subsequent events and their impact up to the date of the new report. Appropriate action in this case might be to identify any potentially faulty products in inventory, as well as considering whether the case against the company is likely to succeed.

2 If the directors do not amend the financial statements, when the auditors believe they should, the auditors should express a qualified or adverse opinion. If the audit report has already been released to the company, those charged with governance should be asked not to submit the financial statements and audit report to third parties. If, however, the directors still do not wish to amend the financial statements, paragraph A16 of ISA 560 suggests that the auditor's course of action depends on legal rights and obligations. Consequently, the auditor may consider seeking legal advice.

We discuss qualified and adverse opinions in Chapter 16.

7 April 2012

This event has taken place after the financial statements have been submitted to shareholders, but before the AGM. Again, the auditors would have no obligations to perform any audit procedures, although the event would be known to the directors and one would expect them to inform the auditors. However, the auditor still has responsibilities similar to those in the previous period. They certainly should discuss with management and with others charged with governance the impact on the organization of selling its head office for such a material sum, pointing out that, while it is not an adjusting event, it is significant enough to require disclosure.

The auditors might suggest that they could address the AGM to inform the shareholders of this non-adjusting event. If the directors decide to withdraw the financial statements (which is unlikely) the auditor would carry out additional post-balance procedures up to the time that the amended financial statements were issued. This would mean a new audit report dated at the time that the procedures were complete and that steps should be taken to ensure that anyone who had received the previously issued financial statements are informed of the situation. The auditors would make clear that their original audit report should no longer be relied upon.

30 July 2012

This event has occurred after the AGM itself. Clearly the auditors will not be expected to be aware of the event, but, if they do learn of it, the matter should be discussed with management and those charged with governance, and action, if any, they intend to take determined. If the auditors have a good working relationship with management it is likely that significant post-balance sheet events in this period will be brought to their attention. This may not always happen, of course, and if, say, they learned about a major post-balance sheet event from press reports, the directors and those charged with governance should be contacted immediately. The auditor might consider whether they should continue as auditor, particularly as, in the case in point, the possibility of legislation had been considered but the view taken that the possibility was remote. Legal advice would appear to be particularly desirable in this case.

ISA 560 does not specifically mention the period after the AGM, but the suggestions under this heading appear reasonable.

PROVISIONS, CONTINGENT LIABILITIES AND CONTINGENT ASSETS

A number of the events discussed above clarified conditions that really existed at the balance sheet date, while others were in respect of events that could be clearly interpreted, even though they did not concern conditions that existed at the balance sheet date. Only one of the events – the company being sued by a customer for damages resulting from a faulty product – was uncertain as to its outcome and both management and auditors might be hard-pressed to determine the amount of any loss and whether it will occur anyway. In this section we consider events, occurring either before or after the balance sheet date, that have uncertain outcomes.

Provisions

The nature of provisions

Both FRS 12 and IAS 37 – *Provisions, contingent liabilities and contingent assets* were introduced to stop the practice of using provisions to smooth profits (by creating them when profits were good and releasing them when profits were less good). In doing so they tried to put a stop to the creation of provisions where there was no obligation, that is, there was no liability. These standards also tried to put an end to so-called 'big bath accounting', which also involved putting through big provisions and/or large asset write-downs at critical points, such as just before or after a take-over or merger, or just after a new management had taken over. This practice had very little to do with fair value accounting, but it was often done to make the new management 'look good' in subsequent years when the provisions and write-downs were written back. Sometimes big bath accounting was used when management was already facing a big loss in a particular year and made the provisions bigger than necessary to make it look as though they had turned the company round subsequently. Clearly, auditors should consider these matters when deciding if financial statements give a true and fair view.

There are a number of exemptions for certain kinds of contract and financial instruments and in respect of matters covered by other accounting and reporting standards.

FRS 12 and IAS 37 state that a provision should be recognized when an entity has a present obligation (legal or constructive) as a result of a past event, it is probable that a transfer of economic benefits will be required to settle the obligation, and a reliable estimate can be made of the amount of the obligation. Unless these conditions are met, no provision should be recognized.

The qualities of genuineness, accuracy and completeness will also be sought in relation to provisions, just as they are in the case of assets and other liabilities.

Class of assertion	Assertions
Genuine	Though uncertain in timing and amount, there is a present obligation as a result of a past event and it is probable that a transfer of economic benefits will be required to settle the obligation. (Occurrence and obligation) The past event is an obligating event, that is, it can be enforced by law or gives rise to a constructive obligation arising from valid expectations in other parties that the entity will discharge the obligation. (Occurrence and obligation)
Accurate	Reliable estimates based on a range of possible outcomes can be made of the present obligation as a result of the past event. (Valuation) The provision relates to the correct period. (Cut-off)
Complete	All provisions are properly and separately disclosed, including brief descriptions of their nature, and indications of the uncertainties about amounts and timing. (Complete and classification)

You should read the relevant accounting standard as we discuss these matters below.

A present obligation arises from a past event when all the available evidence suggests that it is more likely than not that a present obligation exists at the balance sheet date. There is clearly some judgement to be exercised here.

ACTIVITY 14.4

Re-read our comments on the toxic waste scenario described in Activity 2.10 on page 54. Assume that one month before the year-end, a lorry carrying waste on behalf of Annets Limited hit the gatepost of the depot, and that the waste spilled and ran into a river running through the nearby town. What matters would you consider in deciding if a present obligation exists?

It would be necessary to consider the following:

- How serious is this matter from the technical point of view? Has the spill contaminated the local water supply? Is there a threat to the health of local residents? The auditors would expect the company to use management's experts to assess whether the answers to these questions is yes or no or maybe. They might also employ auditor's experts if the matter was regarded as significant.
- What is the likelihood that the local residents will take action against the company? We already know that the people living in the town have recently expressed doubt about the safety of the storage facility, so it is likely they will take action.
- What do the government regulations have to say about control of toxic waste? If they are tightly drawn, the likelihood that a present obligation exists will be much enhanced. The auditor might seek legal advice on interpretation of the regulations and other cases of a similar nature.

See ISA 620 – *Using the work of an auditor's expert.*

As regards whether settlement of the obligation can be enforced by law or if the parties involved have valid expectations that the company will discharge the obligation arising from the event, expectations can be rendered valid and a constructive obligation arise if company actions in the past would reasonably suggest that it would continue to settle obligations of this nature.

ACTIVITY 14.5

What actions do you think that the auditor should take to decide if there is a legal or constructive obligation?

We have already suggested above that the auditors might wish to seek legal advice on interpretation of the law, whether of statute law or case law. In this respect, expected future events can be taken into account in measuring provisions, including possible new legislation that is 'virtually certain to be enacted'. The example given in the standards is measurement of the costs of cleaning up a site some years in the future where it is known that existing technology will result in reduced costs in future years. The auditor would need to discuss the application of technology and expected efficiencies with experts within or outwith the company. They should also seek advice on the likelihood of legislation being enacted that might increase expected costs.

The question of whether a constructive obligation has arisen may be a difficult one. However, the auditors should determine if the company has a published policy, or whether some other authoritative statement from management has been made in the past for dealing with matters such as that of toxic waste *and* if the company has honoured its stated policy in the past. This would involve the auditor in discussions with management and perusal of other sources of evidence such as directors' minute books. Of course, if the company has started to clean up the toxic waste spilled, this might be seen as an admission that it intends to finish the job, although there might be doubts as to what is meant by 'finish the job' and whether this would be an admission that it owes a duty of care to people who might have been affected by the spillage. The auditor should visit the site to see if clean-up is taking place. That this is a difficult area can be seen from the reluctance of railway track maintenance companies in the United Kingdom to admit liability following recent train disasters. However, the auditor should examine any contracts that the company have entered into in respect of any clean-up and if the company is undertaking the work itself, to examine internal documentation, including bills of materials and time sheets of staff engaged. The auditor should also ask management to make written representations about their intentions with regard to the clean-up.

We discuss the letter of management representations later in this chapter.

As regards the issue of whether a reliable estimate can be made of the amount of the obligation, this again is a problematic area as there may be no certainty as to potential costs, whether they are for the clean-up operation itself, or for claims made by persons suffering loss as a result of the event. Potential losses arising from claims for damage to health and/or property may be particularly difficult to ascertain.

ACTIVITY 14.6

What audit steps would you take to determine the amount of the obligation, if any?

In this toxic waste example the clean-up would probably take a relatively short time, but, as we noted above, where the provision relates to a site being contaminated over a long period of time, future costs of clean-up may be reduced by future changes in the application of existing technology. Clearly, this area is very subjective.

If it becomes clear there is an obligation in respect of the event, management would be required to estimate the amount of the provision (measured before tax), and the auditor would seek evidence to support the estimate. Some of the costs might be relatively easy to determine, such as clean-up costs. The auditor would examine documentation supporting the estimate and test its reliability by examination of contracts and the company's own records if it intends to clean up the spillage itself. The auditor would consider how reliable company estimates have been in the past and how reliable management is, based on past experience. Experts in the area might be called on if there are doubts about management estimates. The claims by local people for damage to health and property values would probably have to be tested in relation to similar claims in the past and the degree of success expected in the courts. In this case legal expertise might be called on. Lawyers might be able to put a reasonable estimate on potential successful claims and the probability that the claims will be successful. This would include consideration of management policies as well as government regulations and case law. If the probability that the obligation will crystallize is high, it would be appropriate to treat the event as one giving rise to a provision.

ACTIVITY 14.7

Assume that the company had decided to set up a provision of £1 000 000 at 31 December 2011 for obligations arising from the toxic waste spillage (the event). How should this matter be disclosed? You may assume that you have satisfied yourself that the provision is justified. What actions would you take as auditor? Read the accounting standard before performing this activity.

To meet the criteria of completeness, the provision must be properly disclosed in accordance with the requirements of FRS 12 or IAS 37. The auditors would perform sufficient work to satisfy themselves that disclosures were adequate to allow the reader to understand the nature of the obligation, the expected timing of any resulting transfers of economic benefits, and the uncertainties about the amount or timing of those transfers. This suggests that the company should disclose separately clean-up costs and costs arising from damage to property and health of third parties. It suggests that, if costs have already been incurred during the current year, these should be disclosed too.

ACTIVITY 14.8

During the year to 31 December 2011, it becomes clear that there has been an over-provision at the previous year-end of £500 000, but the company has decided to set other costs against the provision, which are not related to the toxic waste matter. How would you advise management about this matter? Assume that you have satisfied yourself that the amount of the over-provision has been properly determined. Would you be concerned that the estimates at the previous year-end had turned out to be substantially wrong?

It is the nature of estimates that they are estimates, and are unlikely to be completely accurate. However, the auditor would want to find out why half of the provision at the previous year-end is not required. It might be that some of the assumptions about such matters as the number of people likely to claim for damages, were too pessimistic. The auditors would examine the previous year's working schedules to remind themselves of what was known at the time of the audit. Provided that the decisions were reasonably based, there should not be a problem as far as the auditor is concerned. However, they would be less happy about management's proposed course of action. Any provision no longer required should be reversed and separately disclosed. In particular, a provision should only be used for expenditures for which the provision was originally recognized.

We are not covering all provisions of the accounting standard in detail, but the above are some of the significant ones relating to provisions. Clearly the auditor has to have a good knowledge of accounting standards of relevance to any audit area.

Contingencies

If the event does not give rise to a present obligation, or there is no *probable* outflow of economic benefits or it is not possible to evaluate the timing and amount of the obligation (that is, the matter cannot be treated as a provision), the question arises as to how it should be treated. If an event does not meet the criteria for a provision, it may give rise to a contingent liability. FRS 12 and IAS 37 discuss how contingent liabilities and contingent assets should be accounted for. Contingent liabilities and contingent assets are defined as:

Contingent liability

(a) A possible obligation that arises from past events and whose existence will be confirmed only by the occurrence of one or more uncertain future events not wholly within the entity's control; or

(b) A present obligation that arises from past events but is not recognized because:

   (i) it is not probable that a transfer of economic benefits will be required to settle an obligation; or

   (ii) the amount of the obligation cannot be measured with sufficient reliability.

Contingent asset

A possible asset that derives from past events and whose existence will be confirmed only by the occurrence or non-occurrence of one or more uncertain future events not wholly within the entity's control.

Accounting for contingencies

'Possibility' is not as strong a word as 'probability', which suggests that there is a high degree of uncertainty in both contingent liabilities and contingent assets. Contingencies, like provisions, are problematic for the auditor because of the aspect of uncertainty and of varying degrees of certainty from remote to probable. We discuss now the accounting treatment of contingencies, but note first that events giving rise to contingencies may occur in periods before and after the balance sheet date. This means that post-balance sheet reviews should include work to determine the existence and nature of contingencies. Thus, paragraph A9 of ISA 560 – *Subsequent events*, gives a number of examples of specific enquiries which may be made of management, including: 'whether there have been any developments regarding contingencies'.

There are a number of matters to help you to appreciate the work of the auditor in relation to contingencies:

- Directors are expected to consider the estimate of the outcome and financial effect of contingencies up to the date they approve the financial statements.
- Directors should, therefore, review events occurring after the balance sheet date up to the date they approve the accounts.
- The accounting treatment of the contingency is dependent upon its expected outcome and its nature.

Before we take a look at contingent liabilities, below are the basic assertions about them.

Class of assertion	Assertions
Genuine	The events giving rise to the contingent liabilities have actually occurred (Occurrence and obligations)
Accurate	The possibility that an outflow of economic benefits will occur is remote or not probable has been reasonably assessed. (Valuation) Estimates of financial effects, uncertainties and possible reimbursements are reasonably based. (Valuation) The contingent liabilities have been recorded in the correct period. (Cut-off)
Complete	All contingent liabilities have been identified. (Complete) Contingent liabilities are properly disclosed in the financial statements, including brief description of nature, estimate of financial effect, indication of uncertainties, possibility of any reimbursement. (Classification)

FRS 12 and IAS 37 do not allow contingent liabilities to be recognized, meaning that they should not be the subject of adjustment in the financial statements. However, contingent liabilities should be assessed continually to determine whether a transfer of economic benefits has become *probable*. In this case it would be recognized as a provision in the period in which the change in probability has occurred, unless no reliable estimate can be made (said to be rare). This is why ISA 560 suggests that the auditor should enquire of management whether there have been any developments regarding contingencies.

If the transfer of economic benefits is *remote*, the contingency is not even required to be disclosed. However, if the transfer of economic benefits is neither probable nor remote, the contingent liability should be disclosed in accordance with FRS 12 and IAS 37, that is a brief description of the contingent liability and, where practicable:

- an estimate of financial effect;
- an indication of the uncertainties relating to the amount or timing of any outflow; and
- the possibility of any reimbursement.

What this means is that management and auditor have to assess degrees of possibility or probability that the contingent liability will result in transfers of economic benefits – remote, probable, or somewhere in between.

The effect of contingent liabilities may be reduced by counterclaims against third parties and any accrual or disclosure should reflect such counter-claims, if any.

See page 533

Let us take a look at Figure 14.1 again and consider the event that occurred on 16 March 2012 – company is sued for damages resulting from faulty product.

ACTIVITY 14.9

What kind of event is this and how would the matter be treated in the financial statements? What audit steps do you think might be appropriate?

The auditor would need to know more about the circumstances and basis of the claim. Let us assume the product is a child's toy and that a child of the person bringing the court case has suffered damage as a result of putting the toy into his mouth. The auditors would wish to know what defences the company has and what are the views of the company's lawyers as to whether an outflow of economic benefits is probable. The lawyers may conclude on the basis of previous cases and careful labelling of the toy specifying age ranges of children, that it is unlikely that the company will be found liable. If this is so, there would appear not to be a present obligation as a result of a past obligating event, and management and auditors would have to decide if the event has given rise to a contingent liability, the outcome of which would only be known when the court case is heard. If the chances of the court case being found against the company is regarded as remote, the contingency would not need to be disclosed. Clearly the auditors would discuss the matter with management and its lawyers, and may even seek legal advice themselves. If the conclusion is that the outcome, though uncertain and not probable, is not remote, the auditor would expect to see full disclosure as a contingent liability in the terms of the accounting standard.

ACTIVITY 14.10

Do you think that news of the court case might affect the saleability of the inventory of toys held by the company at the year-end? What matters, including inventory accounting, would the auditor consider? Read the scope paragraph of FRS 12 or IAS 37.

News of the court case rather than its outcome (which is likely to lie some time in the future) may indeed affect public confidence in the company's products, and may result in a severe drop in sales not only of the toy the subject of the case, but other toys as well. You will know from our discussion in Chapter 13 and from your accounting studies that the valuation rule for inventories is: 'the lower of cost and net realizable value'. In this case the provisions of FRS 12 and IAS 37 do not apply, as specific requirements in IAS 2 and SSAP 9 will take precedence. We have covered inventories in Chapter 13 and will not go through the detailed evidence searches to prove that the inventories of toys have been properly valued, except to observe that it may not be clear whether the event will have a serious impact on the saleability of the company's products. The auditor might wish to consult with marketing experts as well as discussing the saleability of the toys with management and carrying out work on inventory movements since the court case became public knowledge.

Now let us take a brief look at contingent assets, before we do so here are the basic assertions about them:

Class of assertion	Assertions
Genuine	The events giving rise to the contingent assets have actually occurred. (Occurrence and rights)
Accurate	The decision that the inflow of economic benefits is probable, but not virtually certain is reasonably based. (Valuation) Estimates of financial effects are reasonably based. (Valuation) The contingent assets have been recorded in the right period. (Cut-off)
Complete	All contingent assets have been identified. (Complete) Where it is probable that there will be an inflow of economic benefits, the contingent assets are properly disclosed in the financial statements, including brief description of their nature, and estimate of their financial effect. (Classification)

Both IAS 37 and FRS 12 state bluntly that contingent assets are not to be recognized. This is because recognition of the asset could result in the recognition of profit that may never be realized. However, if the realization of a profit becomes *virtually certain*, then the related asset is not a contingent asset and its recognition is appropriate. Where the inflow of economic benefits is *probable* (but not *virtually certain*) the contingent asset should be disclosed, giving a brief description of its nature, and, where practicable, an estimate of its financial effect.

So again, both management and auditor have to make decisions about probability: '*virtually certain*' and '*probable*' in this case. Clearly, a contingent asset whose realization is only *possible* should not even be disclosed.

The event seems to be the application requesting the grant. This is a difficult matter for the auditor as a decision has to be made about probability. The difficulty is made more serious by the fact that non-receipt of the grant might

ACTIVITY 14.11

Blebo Limited is a small company that publishes books of poetry. In the past, the company has applied for grants to cover costs of publication from the local arts council and has been successful six times out of ten. The company has now published a selection of twentieth century poems in English and Gaelic and has applied for a grant to cover one-third of the costs, amounting to £50 000. It has shown the grant as a receivable in the financial statements on the grounds that it is virtually certain that it will be made available by the arts council. What issues would you consider in this case and what audit actions would be appropriate? You are aware that the company would be at risk if the grant is not received. You may assume that in the context of Blebo Limited the amount involved is material.

affect the company's going-concern status, and the auditor might be concerned that treating the item as an actual asset might be an attempt to improve the look of the balance sheet. The fact that the company has only been successful in 60 per cent of applications in the past might suggest that it is not 'virtually certain' that it will be successful this time, and that including the grant as a receivable would lead to overstatement of assets. However, the company may have been in negotiation with arts council officials and may have received assurances, written or oral or both, that the chances of receiving a grant are very good. The auditor should examine correspondence between the company and the arts council, discuss the matter with management, and examine the justification for the grant in the application, including the summary of expected costs, the reasonability of which should be tested by the auditor. The auditor might also consider discussing the matter with arts council officials and with individuals in the arts scene.

If discussions reveal that the chance of receiving the grant are not virtually certain, but in the light of past experience are probable, then disclosure only would be appropriate. The disclosure should include a description of the grant application and the amount applied for. The disclosure should not give a misleading impression of likelihood of the grant being received.

GOING CONCERN

You will be aware from your other studies that most financial statements are prepared on the assumption that the organization will continue in existence for the foreseeable future. During the final review period the auditor has to consider the validity of assuming that the company is a going concern. We shall not discuss the auditor's duties with respect to going concern here as we consider the concept and audit approaches at length in Chapter 17.

AUDIT WORK TO DETECT POST-BALANCE SHEET EVENTS AND CONTINGENCIES

We have already made some suggestions above about the kind of work that auditors would carry out on post-balance sheet events and contingencies, but we summarize below audit work that would be appropriate in the period up to the signing of the audit report. As you consider the points below, you should remember that the effect of the events or potential events may not be entirely certain with the result that audit work may not be conclusive. We suggest too that the subsequent events procedures should be contained in a special subsequent events programme to support conclusions on their existence and impact. Paragraphs 6 and 7, and A6 to A10 of ISA 560 are relevant in this respect, and you should read them in conjunction with the matters we discuss below.

Company procedures

As the directors have the prime responsibility for the preparation of the financial statements, the auditor should find out what procedures they have instituted to detect material post-balance sheet events and contingencies as they occur. For instance, has the legal department, if there is one, been given instructions to inform the accounting department of important legal matters arising in both the accounting reference period and the post-balance sheet period? It would also be useful for the auditor to enquire into the success or failure of company procedures in detecting post-balance sheet events and contingencies in prior years.

Minutes of shareholders and those charged with governance, including minutes of executive committees and audit committees

Minutes of such meetings are not always very informative, but they may be a useful means of detecting matters arising in the post-balance sheet period or matters giving rise to contingencies, and the auditor should certainly review them. Where minutes are not yet available, enquiries should be made of those present to determine the matters discussed.

Management accounts and accounting records

The usefulness of such accounts and records depends on how up to date they are. The date of signing the audit report of the company above is 15 March 2012 and, assuming the company prepares monthly accounts, the monthly accounts for January 2012 are likely to have been prepared. The auditor's perusal of the January management accounts should have revealed the loss arising from the liquidation of the customer on 23 January, assuming of course, that the company has provided for the loss in these accounts. If the February 2012 accounts have not been prepared by 15 March, the fact of the warehouse fire may not be readily apparent and the auditor would hope to become aware of it from other sources.

Profit and cash flow forecasts for the period subsequent to the balance sheet date

It is unlikely that the four events in the period up to the date of the AGM (see Figure 14.1) would have been included in the forecast accounts and cash flows if such forecasts had been prepared prior to the year-end. On the other hand, assuming that the company had been, for instance, sued by a customer some time prior to the year-end, the fact that the company had anticipated a loss relating to the court case in forecast accounts may be a good indication of the directors' views as to the likelihood and quantification of the outcome. Cash flow forecasts may be very useful when considering the validity of the going-concern assumption.

Enquiry of the organization's legal department and external legal representatives

The auditor should also make direct enquiries with the company's legal department, if it has one, and its external lawyers to determine if there is any litigation affecting the organization and potential outcomes.

Known risk areas and contingencies arising from the nature of the business

In some businesses certain risks may be very common. We have already cited the case of a company selling floor tiles, requiring the exercise of skill in laying them. A normal risk of this kind of business might be remedial work in the post balance sheet period and the auditor should pay particular attention to the reports of company inspectors and correspondence from customers in that period as a result.

Correspondence and memoranda in the post-balance sheet period

The auditor should review correspondence to and from third parties for matters of significance. Such correspondence is often held in the personal files of suppliers and customers and it may therefore be a time-consuming process. It is, however, likely that important matters will be collected in special files held by the chief accountant and the auditor should ask to have sight of them.

Confirmation from third parties direct to the auditor

See Chapter 12 page 426.

You will remember that in Chapter 12 we suggested the auditors should ask the company's legal representative to inform them of any legal matters of significance affecting the company. Communications from bankers may also be of value, particularly when considering going-concern matters. There might also be a case for arranging a meeting with bankers if the auditor believes the company can only remain in existence if bankers continue to provide financial support.

Information in the public domain

If the company is in a sector with a trade press, the auditor should review recent issues to detect any matters of relevance to the company. The same applies more broadly to national and local press.

Last-but-not-least: management interviews

Examples of matters that should be discussed with management are:

- Developments regarding known risk areas, including additional information that might be available about accounting estimates or other areas where there was some uncertainty.
- New commitments entered into by the company, including new borrowings and guarantees given.
- Significant acquisitions or disposals of assets, including subsidiary or associated organizations.
- Matters that might affect the going-concern status of the organization, such as new or planned share or debenture issues.
- Significant losses of assets, whether by appropriation by government, or by fire or flood.

The auditor should discuss the business of the company with management, if possible at the time the management letter of representation is being prepared. We discuss management letters of representation below, but note here that the letter will normally contain a paragraph on litigation affecting the company (or lack of it) and a specific reference highlighting the importance of the post-balance sheet period.

One thing to remember once again is that audits are not carried out in a vacuum and that the auditor should already be aware of the significant matters of subjective judgement. These matters would include not only saleability of inventory or collectability of trade receivables but also legal outcomes. As time goes by and the balance sheet date recedes into the past, matters that may have been subjective at that date may have been clarified, at least to some extent. Management may also have taken steps to solve particular problems, such as problems of liquidity, which might have given concern about the going-concern status of the company. Knowledge of the areas of judgement and those that are problematic will provide a framework within which subsequent procedures take place.

MANAGEMENT LETTER OF REPRESENTATION

In Chapter 6 we noted that an important source of audit evidence is management itself, being well informed about the company as they are. We noted too in Chapter 5 that the engagement letter details the responsibility of management 'for preparing financial statements that are fairly presented in accordance with IFRSs, including IASs, and for giving the auditors access to all information they know is relevant to the preparation of the financial statement, plus any additional information that the auditors request from management for the purpose of the audit.'

See Chapter 6, page 220, and Chapter 5, page 190.

Paragraph A1 of ISA 580 suggests that a request for written rather than oral representations, may prompt management to consider the matter more carefully, thereby enhancing the quality of the representation.

At the end of the audit, management are asked to confirm in writing their responsibilities and to confirm too assertions or representations that they have made to the auditors. This is regarded as important evidence in the hands of the auditor, especially as it is written. The relevant ISA is ISA 580 – *Written representations* and paragraphs quoted in this section refer to this ISA unless otherwise stated. Here is what paragraph 6 has to say about the objectives of the auditor:

(a) To obtain written representations from management and, where appropriate, those charged with governance that they believe that they have fulfilled their responsibility for the preparation of the financial statements and for the completeness of the information provided to the auditor;

(b) To support other audit evidence relevant to the financial statements or specific assertions in the financial statements by means of written representations if determined necessary by the auditor or required by other ISAs; and

(c) To respond appropriately to written representations provided by management and, where appropriate, those charged with governance, or if management or, where appropriate, those charged with governance do not provide the written representations requested by the auditor.

Who should be asked to make written representations?

Paragraph A2 of ISA 580 suggests that appropriate people from whom representations may be requested are the entity's chief executive officer and chief financial officer, or other equivalent persons in entities that do not use such titles. However, as paragraph A4 suggests, representations might be obtained from others within the entity with specialized knowledge, such as actuaries, engineers and lawyers.

What are the representations required from management?

There are two broad category of representation:

1 Representations about management's responsibilities:

(a) *Preparation of the financial statements*. Management is requested to provide a written representation that it has fulfilled its responsibility for the preparation of the financial statements in accordance with the applicable financial reporting framework.

It may be necessary, of course, to remind management what those responsibilities are, including the requirement that the financial statements are to give a true and fair view of what they purport to show.

(b) *Information provided and completeness of transactions.* Management is requested to provide a written representation that: (a) it has provided the auditor with all relevant information and access as agreed in the terms of the audit engagement, and (b) all transactions have been recorded and are reflected in the financial statements.

Auditors can never be entirely certain that they have been made aware of all matters relevant to their audit. For instance, whether they have knowledge of all bank accounts in the company's name. Our discussion of trade payables in Chapter 13 has also shown that the search for unrecorded liabilities can be far from conclusive. Paragraph A11 also suggests that auditors might like to have written representation that management has communicated to the auditor all deficiencies in internal control of which it is aware. So the written representations under (b) as to the completeness of information and transactions is important audit evidence in the hands of the auditor.

2 Other written representations

(a) *Additional written representations about the financial statements.* These are representations that are more specific than those referred to in 1 (a) above, and include such matters as whether the selection and application of accounting policies are appropriate and whether certain matters have been accounted for properly, such as plans or intentions that may affect the carrying value or classification of assets and liabilities.

For instance, management might have decided to close part of their operations, a decision that might affect the value of inventories, and might result in additional liabilities such as redundancy payments to employees.

(b) *Written representations about specific assertions.* As you know there are many areas of judgement that have to be exercised in respect of figures in the financial statements. For instance, management of a company in the mineral oil business may be storing large quantities of heating oil in underground salt caverns under high pressure to meet EU requirements for strategic oil reserves. The auditors might need specific written representations from company geologists that the heating oil will be easily recoverable when needed and whether additional costs will be incurred to make the products marketable when released from storage.

One important point to be made here is that auditors receive many oral representations from management during the course of the audit. Not all of these will require written representations from management, and the auditors should consider communicating to management a threshold for purposes of the requested written representation (see paragraph A14).

Written representations required by other ISAs

Written representations are required by a number of other ISAs, including from ISA 240, acknowledgement by management and those charged with governance of their responsibility for the design, implementation and maintenance of internal control to prevent and detect fraud; and from ISA 450, whether they believe the effects of uncorrected misstatements are immaterial to the financial statements as a whole. For a complete list of these ISAs refer to Appendix 1 of ISA 580.

ISA 240 –*The auditor's responsibilities relating to fraud in an audit of financial statements*; ISA 450 – *Evaluation of misstatements identified during the audit.*

What period should the written representation cover? (See paragraph A16 and A17)

Basically, the written representations should cover all periods referred to in the auditors' report. This may mean that specific representations may be required about prior periods, even if it is just a statement that there have been no changes to written representations that have been made about those prior periods.

It is good practice to tell management that written representations will be required about specific assertions as it becomes clear during the audit that representations will be required.

Date of the written representations (See paragraph A15)

ACTIVITY 14.12

Explain why the management letter of representation should bear them same date as the audit report.

The management letter of representation is clearly an important source of audit evidence, and it needs to be as up to date as possible when the auditor signs the audit report. It would be most unwise for the auditor to accept a management representation letter dated a month (say) before the completion of audit fieldwork.

It is good practice to date the letter of representation at the same date as the directors sign the financial statements and the auditors sign the audit report.

Illustrative representation letter

Appendix 2 to ISA 580 contains an illustrative representation letter.

What do the auditors do when they have doubts about the reliability of written representations, or where written representations are not provided? (paragraph 16)

ACTIVITY 14.13

What do you think the consequences would be if management refused to sign the letter of representation or if they wished to exclude a matter that the auditors regarded as important?

We discuss audit reporting in Chapter 16.

We have not covered the audit report as yet, but in such a case, the auditor would be lacking important evidence, and be faced with a limitation of scope. In these circumstances the auditor would consider qualification of the audit report for limitation of scope, leading to a disclaimer of opinion.

ACTIVITY 14.14

What do you think the consequences would be if the auditors have doubts about the reliability of written representations?

The auditor might have doubts about the reliability of the representations if they are inconsistent with other audit evidence. For instance, if management of Fine Faces (see Chapter 5, page 208) state that there are no inventories that have to be valued at net realizable value, lower than cost, but the auditors' tests have revealed significant inventories (in this case lipstick) are not selling and are not likely to sell, this would cast doubt on their integrity and on the value of any other representations they have made, written or oral. This could lead to a qualification of the audit report and at the extreme a disclaimer of opinion. (See paragraph 20.)

Informing those charged with governance

ISA 260 *Communication of those charged with governance* requires the auditor to communicate with those charged with governance the written representations which the auditor has requested from management. This is to enable those charged with governance to fulfil their duty of overseeing the financial reporting process

Paragraph 16 (c)(ii).

Note for readers in the UK and Ireland

In the UK and Ireland those charged with governance are responsible for the preparation of the financial statements, that is, not just management. This means that those charged with governance must acknowledge their collective responsibility for the preparation of the financial statements and have approved the financial statements. Written representations that are critical to obtaining sufficient appropriate audit evidence are to be provided by those charged with governance rather than the entity's management (see paragraph A2-1 of ISA 580)

Communications by the auditor to those charged with governance with regard to written representations are made in the UK and Ireland before those charged with governance approve the financial statements to ensure that they are aware of the representations on which the auditors intend to rely in expressing their opinion on the financial statements (paragraph A22-1 of ISA 580).

It is an offence under company law in the UK and Ireland to mislead the auditor, and the auditor may also wish to take the opportunity to remind the directors of this fact.

When reading ISA 450, note that the auditor is required to seek a written representation from those charged with governance that explains their reasons for not correcting misstatements brought to their attention by the auditor.

Let us finish this section on letters of representation with two activities:

ACTIVITY 14.15

During an audit you come across a sales transaction with a company, in which the auditee has a 20 per cent interest, at a sales price lower than transactions with third parties. What action would you take and would you wish to include the matter in the letter of representation?

This transaction is clearly with a related party and management is responsible for the identification and disclosure of such transactions and for implementing adequate internal controls to identify such transactions. The problem for the auditor is that it may be very difficult to detect all transactions with related parties and it would be necessary to refer to the matter in the letter of representation in the following terms: 'The identity of, and balances and transactions with, related parties have been properly recorded and adequately disclosed in the financial statements.'

ACTIVITY 14.16

Does the management letter of representation change the liability of management and auditors in any way?

This is an important question. It is clear that auditors take full responsibility for their opinion on the financial statements. Written representations from management are a valuable source of evidence, but, like any other evidence, they have to be corroborated. From this point of view the representations do not reduce the liability of auditors, although they may help auditors to form conclusions. We can also say that representations made by management do not increase the liability of management who have a duty to prepare financial statements that show a true and fair view, a duty that cannot be reduced in any way.

AUDIT DOCUMENTATION

We have referred to audit documentation from time to time earlier in this book, but now is the place to discuss it more fully. ISA 230 – *Audit documentation* sets out the nature and purpose of audit documentation in paragraphs 2 and 3:

2. Audit documentation that meets the requirements of this ISA and the specific documentation requirements of other relevant ISAs provides:
   (a) Evidence of the auditor's basis for a conclusion about the achievement of the overall objectives of the auditor; and
   (b) Evidence that the audit was planned and performed in accordance with ISAs and applicable legal and regulatory requirements.
3. Audit documentation serves a number of additional purposes, including the following:
   - Assisting the engagement team to plan and perform the audit.
   - Assisting members of the engagement team responsible for supervision to direct and supervise the audit work, and to discharge their review responsibilities in accordance with ISA 220.
   - Enabling the engagement team to be accountable for its work.
   - Retaining a record of matters of continuing significance to future audits.

ISA 220 – *Quality control for an audit of financial statements.* See paragraphs 15–17.

- Enabling the conduct of quality control reviews and inspections in accordance with ISQC 1 or national requirements that are at least as demanding.
- Enabling the conduct of external inspections in accordance with applicable legal, regulatory or other requirements.

ISQC 1 – *Quality control for firms that perform audits and reviews of financial statements, and other assurance and related services engagements.* See paragraphs 32–33, 35–38, and 48.

Thus, there are two major purposes of audit documentation:

First – to record the audit evidence to form the basis of conclusions and opinion, and

Second – to increase the efficiency and effectiveness of the audit and to allow quality control and other reviews to take place. One of the efficiency and effectiveness elements relates to the recording of matters that will make future audits more efficient and effective.

We have already referred to the importance of cumulative client knowledge in Chapter 5 – see page 190 – Clearly, keeping a record of relevant information about the client will be important for an effective and efficient audit.

You should note at this point that audit documentation may be recorded on hard copy or in electronic form, but the basic principle is that the working files must be secure and the information in them easily accessible. The following are important features of audit documentation:

1 The basic rule is that the audit documentation should be sufficient to enable an experienced auditor, having no previous connection with the audit, to understand the following:

(a) The nature, timing and extent of the audit procedures performed to comply with the ISAs and applicable legal and regulatory requirements;

(b) The results of the audit procedures performed, and the audit evidence obtained; and

(c) Significant matters arising during the audit, the conclusions reached thereon, and significant professional judgements made in reaching those conclusions

ISQC 1 – *Quality control for firms that perform audits and reviews of financial statements, and other assurance and related services engagements*, and ISA 220 – *Quality control for an audit of financial statements.*

You should note in this respect that audit documentation will be reviewed by persons having no connection with the audit, such as partners independent of the audit team with responsibility for conducting quality control reviews and inspections in accordance with the quality control standards ISQC 1 and ISA 220. This is important because audit firms will wish to ensure that any poor quality work or unsatisfactory conclusions on work performed is detected as soon as possible. Furthermore, accounting bodies monitor the work of their members from time to time to ensure their work is at a standard expected by the profession and those interested in the quality of professional work. The audit documentation and discussions with audit team members will form the basis of these so-called 'cold reviews'.

Reviews carried out after the audit has been finalized are known as 'cold reviews', whereas reviews carried out before the audit report is finalized are titled 'hot reviews'.

Apart from these cold reviews the engagement quality control reviewer (EQCR), as we observed in Chapter 3 (see Figure 3.3 on page 81) will carry out hot reviews prior to the audit report being finalized. It is worth noting too that the engagement partner and even the audit manager who are connected to the audit, but who do not have day-to-day contact with the client will also want the audit documentation to be understandable enough to enable them to form the final opinion on the financial statements.

We discussed the role of the engagement quality control reviewer in Chapter 3. See page 85.

2 Some practical matters:

(a) There must be a referencing system to enable anyone interested to find their way through the files. For instance, non-current tangible assets might be given a reference letter A with working sheets at the final examination labelled A1, A2 and so on. Substantive testing of tangible assets might be labelled AI 1, AI 2 and so on. This would enable a staff member working on the tangible assets figure in the financial statements to reference to the conclusions drawn following substantive test that might have performed at the interim examination.

In addition, any items or matters tested during the audit should be clearly identified so that it can be easily traced, if need be.

(b) There should be no delay in preparing audit documentation. In particular, minutes of meetings with management, including conclusions and action points, should be recorded immediately after the meeting. Names of client staff involved in discussions should also be recorded.

(c) You must know who has prepared audit documentation and when it was prepared.

(d) You must know who has reviewed audit documentation prepared by subordinates and the extent of the review and the date the review was performed.

(e) You must know what action has been taken as a result of reviews by superiors

(f) Once the audit has been completed no-one should be allowed to change or remove any part of the documentation, that is, not until an agreed period of years has elapsed (this is known as the 'retention period').

As regards (c) to (f) above, modern computerized systems have been developed to record and hold audit documentation. Clearly, audit staff will need to receive careful training to ensure that computerized audit working papers are a complete and accurate record of the audit. In practice firms now allocate passwords to individual members of staff and to the audit assignment, so that engagement team members can access the system using their own password, carry out audit work and record it on an electronic worksheet and sign off the work using their own personal 'signature'. An important feature would be to prevent alteration of working schedules, so that staff who have not prepared a schedule would have 'read only' access to it. The worksheet prepared by an individual becomes part of the assignment worksheets; it can be reviewed by more senior auditors using the assignment password and signed off by them, again using a personal 'signature'.

(g) The audit file containing the audit documentation should be finalized as soon as possible after the date of the audit report. This needs to be done quickly before members of the audit team leave to form the audit team of another assignment.

To aid your understanding of audit documentation we set out in Figure 14.2 a diagram showing the link between audit documentation of various kinds and the sort of information that should be included in them.

FIGURE 14.2 Audit documentation: relationships and contents

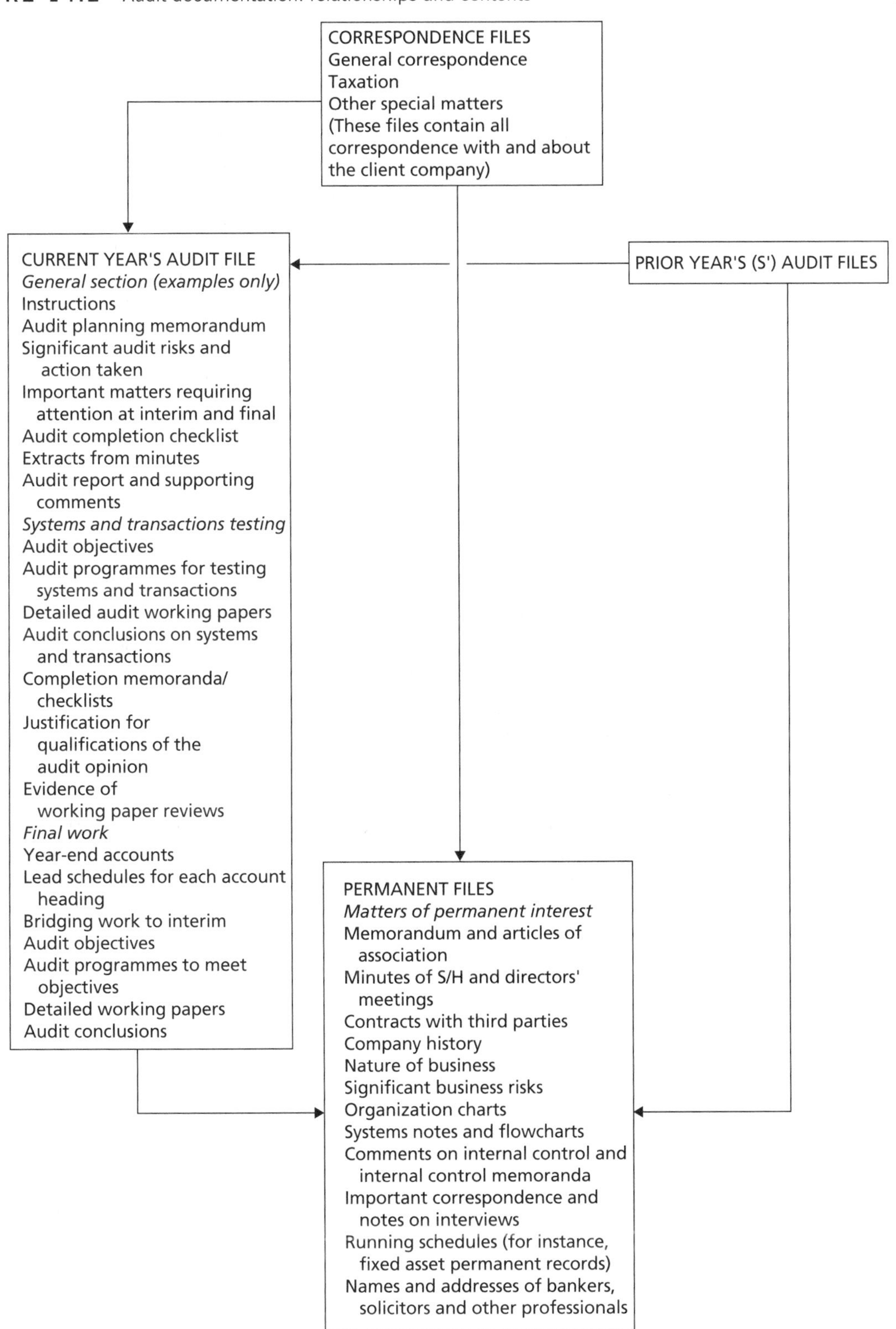

ROLE OF THE FINAL REVIEW

The final review takes place immediately before the audit report is finalized. It is very important, as at this stage all the audit work is put into context and a view reached as to the truth and fairness of the financial statements taken as a whole. For instance, if there are doubts about the entity's status as a going concern, the auditor would wish to ensure that management and those charged with governance have considered the viability of the entity and that their view of the future has been communicated to the auditors, together with supporting evidence. This might include profit and cash forecasts and the results of discussions with the entity's bankers and other providers of finance. At this final stage the auditors would review all the evidence and might consult with the bankers and providers of finance themselves

Generally, it is important that a final review of audit documentation be carried out. Remember that the detailed audit work will normally have been carried out by a person or persons other than the person actually signing the audit report. The final working sheet review should therefore be carried out by the engagement partner. Normally the audit documentation will have been reviewed by the senior auditor in charge of the day-to-day audit fieldwork and by the manager in charge of the assignment and the final review can usefully be carried out by the partner in the presence of the other two so that questions can be answered immediately. The objective of this review is to ensure that:

- All routine matters that should have been covered have been dealt with (for instance, has the impact of company legislation, accounting standards and Stock Exchange requirements been considered?).
- There are no outstanding matters in the audit documentation. Notes such as: 'Two major debtors still outstanding at 13 March 2012 – discuss with chief accountant', should not be left open but a conclusion formed and recorded in the files.
- The financial statements have been reviewed at conclusion of the audit process and a decision made that in the light of the interim and final work carried out, they *do* make sense and *do* show a true and fair view – with the exception of qualifications in the audit report. The objective of the review at the conclusion of audit work is to ensure that:
  (a) All important matters have been covered by audit work.
  (b) The accounts as a whole show a true and fair view and not merely that the disparate elements of the accounts are fairly stated.

The auditor records a number of matters at the final review stage:

Refer to Chapter 12.

- Results of analytical review, including ratio analysis.
- Conclusions on each balance sheet and profit and loss account heading. Remember that we encouraged you to write conclusions at the end of systems and transactions testing work. The same applies to figures in the year-end accounts.
- A memorandum commenting on any major account headings greater than or less than the previous year by a predetermined percentage. For instance, a firm of auditors might have a rule that reasons for accounts headings

varying by 10 per cent from the previous year should be detailed in the audit documentation. Thus, if the sales of Product 1 made by Greenburn Ltd in 2011 are recorded as £1 000 000 and last year they amounted to £1 300 000, the reason for the decrease would be noted in the audit documentation. This would clearly be a useful procedure for the engagement partner as well as for the audit staff.

We came across Greenburn plc in Case study 13.2. See page 498.

- Whether evidence recorded in the audit documentation supports the conclusions reached. The audit documentation should be a complete synopsis of the audit and should be self-explanatory. For instance, if the auditors have formed the conclusion that there are no significant post-balance sheet events, that conclusion should refer to the post-balance sheet events audit programme and that programme should, in turn, refer to audit documentation supporting the conclusion. It is particularly important that the background to any qualifications in the audit report should be clearly stated.
- The management letter of representation (discussed above).

Summary

In this chapter we have discussed a number of important audit steps that are performed prior to signing the audit report, including the final review of audit documentation and the preparation of the letter of representation.

Specific topics discussed in some detail were post-balance sheet events, provisions for liabilities of uncertain timing and amount, and contingent liabilities and assets, and the auditor's responsibilities and work in relation to them. We referred briefly to going concern but have delayed discussion of this topic until Chapter 17.

Key points of the chapter

- At stage 18 of the audit process auditors pull together evidence gathered and conclusions arrived at earlier to form a view on the financial statements as a whole. They also perform other final procedures.

Post balance sheet events

- Auditors review the post-balance sheet period to ascertain whether any matters should be reflected in the accounts or disclosed in the audit report.
- Two types of subsequent event can be identified: (a) adjusting events, providing evidence of conditions that existed at the balance sheet date; and (b) non-adjusting events, indicative of conditions that arose after the balance sheet date.
- The period after the balance sheet date may be subdivided: (a) between balance sheet date and completion of draft financial statements; (b) from completion of draft financial statements to completion of audit fieldwork; (c) from completion of audit fieldwork to date of submitting financial statements to shareholders; (d) after the financial statements have been submitted but before the AGM; (e) after the AGM.
- Events occurring in periods (a) and (b) are known by both directors and auditors. Regarding (c) the auditors have no responsibility to perform audit procedures after the date of the audit report, but directors do have a responsibility to inform the auditors of any facts that may affect the financial statements. If the auditor becomes aware of any material facts they decide what action to take, whether or not the directors decide to amend the financial statements. Those charged with governance may be involved. Regarding (d) auditors have no obligation to perform procedures, but if they become aware of an event which might have caused them to issue a different report, they should consider whether the financial statements need amendment and the implications for their report. Regarding (e) auditors will not be expected to be aware of events after the AGM, but, if they do obtain knowledge of an event they should discuss with management and those charged with governance.

Provisions, contingent liabilities and assets

- Some events have uncertain outcomes – provisions and contingencies. A provision should be recognized (with some exemptions) when an entity has a present obligation (legal or constructive) as a result of a past event, it is probable that a transfer of economic benefits will be required to settle the obligation, and a reliable estimate can be made of the amount of the obligation.

- FRS 12 and IAS 37 were introduced to stop the use of provisions to smooth profits and 'big bath accounting' by a tight definition of provisions. Judgement has to be exercised when deciding if a provision is appropriate.
- Provisions must be disclosed sufficient to enable the reader to understand the nature of the obligation, the expected timing of transfers of economic benefits, and the uncertainties about amount or timing.
- If the event does not meet the requirements for a provision, it may be treated as a contingency.
- Contingencies are problematic because of the varying degrees of certainty from remote through possible to probable.
- An entity should not recognize a contingent liability, but, if not remote, it should be disclosed in the financial statements. An entity should not recognize a contingent asset, but if the realization of a profit becomes *virtually certain*, the related asset should be recognized. Where the inflow of economic benefits is *probable* (but not *virtually certain*) the contingent asset should be disclosed.

Going concern

- During the final review period the auditor considers the validity of assuming that the company is a going concern.

Audit work to detect post-balance sheet events and contingencies

- Appropriate audit work: (a) determine company detection procedures; (b) examine minutes of shareholders and those charged with governance; (c) examine management accounts/accounting records; (d) examine forecasts; (e) review known risk areas; (f) enquire of the organization's legal department and external lawyers; (g) review correspondence; (h) gain confirmation from third parties; (i) review information in the public domain; (j) conduct management interviews.

Management letter of representation

- At the end of the audit management confirm in writing its responsibilities and assertions they have made to the auditors during the engagement.
- Management give written representations from management and those charged with governance regarding their responsibility for the preparation of the financial statements and for the completeness of information provided to the auditor; Representations support other audit evidence relevant to the financial statements or specific assertions in the financial statements. Auditors respond appropriately to written representations by management and those charged with governance, or if management or those charged with governance do not provide the written representations requested by the auditor.
- Appropriate people from whom representations may be requested are the entity's chief executive officer and chief financial officer, or similar, and from others within the entity with specialized knowledge.
- There are two broad category of representation: 1. About management's responsibilities for (a) preparation of financial statements and (b) information provided and completeness of transactions; 2. About (a) broad aspects of the financial statements, such as selection and application of appropriate accounting policies; (b) specific assertions.
- Written representations are required by other ISAs shown in Appendix 2 of ISA 580.
- The written representations should cover periods referred to in the auditors' report.
- The management letter of representation should be dated at the same date as the directors sign the financial statements and the auditors sign the audit report.
- If the auditors have doubts about the reliability of written representations, or where written representations are not provided they would consider qualification of the audit report for limitation of scope, leading to a disclaimer of opinion. The auditor might have doubts about the reliability of the representations if they are inconsistent with other audit evidence.
- The auditor communicates with those charged with governance the written representations which the auditor has requested from management.
- There are additional requirements for the UK and Ireland.

Audit documentation

- There are two major purposes of audit documentation: 1. to record the audit evidence to form the basis of conclusions and opinion, and 2. to increase the efficiency and effectiveness of the audit and to allow quality control and other reviews to take place. One of the efficiency and effectiveness elements relates to the recording of matters that will make future audits more efficient and effective.
- Audit documentation may be recorded on hard copy or in electronic form.
- Audit documentation should be sufficient to enable an experienced auditor, having no previous connection with the audit, to understand: (a) nature, timing and extent of the audit procedures performed; (b) the results of the audit procedures performed on the basis of audit evidence obtained; and (c) significant matters arising during the audit, the conclusions reached and significant professional judgements made.
- Reviews of audit documentation may be hot reviews or cold reviews.
- Practical matters include: (a) a referencing system; (b) no delay in preparing audit documentation;

(c) preparer of audit documentation and when it was prepared; (d) reviewer of audit documentation, the extent of the review and the date of the review; (e) action taken as a result of reviews by superiors; (f) once the audit has been completed no-one should be allowed to change or remove any part of the documentation; (g) modern computerized systems have been developed to record and hold audit documentation, but controls must be in place; (h) the audit documentation should be finalized as soon as possible after the date of the audit report.

Role of final review

- The final review takes place immediately before the audit report is finalized, and is performed to ascertain (a) all routine matters dealt with; (b) there are no outstanding matters in the audit documentation; (c) the financial statements have been reviewed at conclusion of the audit process.
- The objective of the review at the conclusion of audit work is to ensure that: (a) All important matters have been covered by audit work; (b) The financial statements as a whole show a true and fair view.
- The auditor records a number of matters at the final review stage: (a) results of analytical review; (b) conclusions on each balance sheet and profit and loss account heading; (c) comments on major account headings greater than or less than the previous year by a predetermined percentage. (d) whether evidence recorded in the audit documentation supports the conclusions reached. (e) the management letter of representation.

Further reading

This has been another very practical chapter. Relevant ISAs and accounting standards are:

ISQC 1 – *Quality control for firms that perform audits and reviews of financial statements, and other assurance and related services engagements.*

ISA 220 – *Quality control for an audit of financial statements.*

ISA 230 – *Audit documentation.*

ISA 560 – *Subsequent events.*

ISA 580 – *Written representations.*

IAS 10 – *Events after the reporting period.*

FRS 12 and IAS 37 – *Provisions, contingent liabilities and contingent assets.*

Self-assessment questions (solutions available to students)

14.1 Consider the following statements and explain why they may be true or false:

(a) Audit working sheets should be a record of all evidence collected by auditors in forming the audit opinion.

(b) Auditors' responsibility ceases at the date they sign the audit report.

(c) The financial statements signed by directors on or slightly before the date of the audit report must be identical with the financial statements submitted to shareholders.

(d) Oral evidence from management that can be confirmed from other sources need not be acknowledged in writing in the letter of representation.

(e) If management refuse to sign the letter of representation, auditors will be unable to form an opinion as to whether the financial statements give a true and fair view.

(f) FRS 12 and IAS 37 apply to provisions for accrued electricity and telephone usage and provisions for doubtful debts.

14.2 Show how the following events should be reflected in the accounts at 31 December 2011 and describe audit procedures you would carry out to verify them:

(a) Company A estimated that the profits on a construction contract that was 75 per cent complete at 31 December 2011 would amount to £100 000 and had taken up £75 000 in the profit and loss account on the portion of the contract certified as complete by a qualified surveyor. On completion on 21 February 2012, company records show profit on the contract amounted to £30 000.

(b) Company B acquired non-current assets for £500 000 on 31 January 2012. The financial statements at 31 December 2011 showed non-current assets at cost less depreciation amounting to £250 000.

(c) Company C has shown in its financial statements at 31 December 2011 an investment in another company at cost of £750 000. On 1 March 2012 there is a significant decline in prices on the Stock Exchange resulting from unexpected foreign exchange movements.

(d) Company D is in dispute with a supplier as to the quality of goods supplied and has provided for the amount it believes to be correct (£100 000). The supplier has sued for the full amount invoiced (£150 000) but on 12 March 2012 the company and supplier agree the liability out of court at £120 000.

(e) Company E had prepared draft financial statements at 30 November 2011, showing an acid test ratio of 0.85 to 1. (The normal acid test ratio in its industry is 1 to 1.) Shortly before 31 December 2011, the company sold trade investments for £450 000, incurring a loss of £100 000 and this had the effect of increasing the acid test ratio to 0.98 to 1. On 16 January 2012, the company repurchased the trade investments for £500 000.

14.3 Bandon Limited acquired a subsidiary, Gateside Limited, ten years ago and goodwill on consolidation is being written off over 20 years. Gateside made good profits until two years ago, but in the year to 31 December 2010, made a small loss and in the year to 31 December 2011 made a significant loss. Do you think that this would provide good grounds for an impairment review? What audit steps would you perform to satisfy yourself that the results of the impairment review are valid?

14.4 During an audit of the cost records of Roberton Ltd at 31 March 2011 you discover that Prospect Limited has sued the company, claiming that it is using a manufacturing process which has been patented by Prospect. However, the directors of Roberton say that the manufacturing process used is sufficiently different from the one patented and that no disclosure of any potential liability is required. Discuss the accounting and auditing implications of this matter.

Self-assessment questions (solutions available to tutors)

14.5 Lundin plc operates a number of divisions, but the board of directors has been considering closing those that no longer fit into the future plans of the company. On 30 November 2011 (year-end is 31 December 2011), the board decided to close two of the divisions (Division A and Division B), make the employees redundant and to realize the assets of the divisions as quickly as possible. A detailed plan for closing down Division A was published by the board on 12 December 2011, letters were sent to customers and suppliers informing them of the closure and redundancy notices were posted to employees. In the case of Division B, although a detailed plan of closure had been agreed by the board on 30 November 2011, no action had been taken to effect the closure of the division and no notifications had been sent to business associates and employees.

You are auditor of Lundin plc. How would you expect these matters to be accounted for, and how would you audit any estimate of the amount of the obligation, if any?

14.6 Your audit assistant on the Greenburn Ltd assignment has asked you where the following working schedules should be filed:

(a) Summary of the details of a construction contract for the supply of goods to a customer.

(b) Letter to the company from the company's bankers during the year to 31 December 2011 stating that they were prepared to extend overdraft facilities to £500 000, but did not wish this amount to be exceeded without prior discussion.

(c) Working paper containing a depth (cradle to grave) test in the sales area showing that a number of despatch notes could not be traced by company officials.

(d) Note that arrangements should be made to discuss inventory taking procedures with the company at an earlier date than in the year to 31 December 2011.

(e) Results of the analytical review of the company's draft financial statements at 31 December 2011.

(f) Purchases systems notes prepared during the interim examination.

(g) Replies from credit customers circularized at the interim examination and at 31 December 2011.

14.7 Dunino Limited is a company manufacturing, selling and laying carpet tiles, currently preparing financial statements at 31 December 2011. Under the terms of sale, Dunino gives a warranty, whereby it agrees to make good manufacturing or laying defects that become apparent within three years after the date of laying. Independent inspectors would determine if making good was best done by repair or replacement. On the basis of past experience the company expects that 3 per cent of sales will be the subject of a claim for making good, of which two-thirds will result in repair or replacement.

State whether you believe the above matter would give rise to a provision under FRS 12 and IAS 37, giving your reasons. If a provision is recognized, what work would the auditor perform to ensure that it is the best estimate of costs to be incurred?

Topics for class discussion without solutions

14.8 The management letter of representation is a key piece of audit evidence. Discuss.

14.9 Describe the key features of audit documentation.

15

Assurance engagements and internal audit

LEARNING OBJECTIVES

After studying this chapter you should be able to:

- **Explain the nature and role of assurance engagements.**
- **Describe the characteristics that should be possessed by an assurance engagement.**
- **Explain the degrees of assurance that may be given for different kinds of assurance engagement.**
- **Describe typical work carried out by the internal audit function.**
- **Explain the relationship between internal and external audit and show the extent to which the latter can use the work of the former in achieving audit objectives.**
- **Suggest ways in which the audit function as a whole may be rendered more useful.**

Learning objectives, 564
Introduction, 565
Assurance engagements, 565
Internal audit, 584
How to make the internal audit function effective, 591
Reliance on internal audit by the external auditor, 594
Outsourcing of internal audit work, 596
Auditing in the public sector, 599
Summary, 603
Key points of the chapter, 603
Further reading, 605
Self-assessment questions (solutions available to students), 605
Self-assessment questions (solutions available to tutors), 607
Topics for class discussion without solutions, 608

INTRODUCTION

We have already shown that many external auditors are now using a business risk approach, involving close contact with top management, with a twofold purpose:

1 To enable them to determine where real risks lie that may affect the view given by the financial statements.

2 To enable them to provide services to the company, aiding management in the performance of their duties, and, in addition, providing another source of income for the auditors themselves.

Many of these services come under the general heading of assurance engagements and in the first part of this chapter we explain the nature and role of such engagements. In the second part we direct our attention to internal audit and shall find that many services now being provided by the audit function – either by external auditors or internal auditors – are very similar in nature, ranging from financial statement work to engagements giving a lower level of assurance. We consider the extent to which external auditors use the work of internal auditors, particularly where the latter are testing the efficacy of systems and the genuineness, accuracy and completeness of transactions and figures. We show that internal auditors perform a substantial range of work beyond that related to systems, transactions and figures, work that is valuable to management in the performance of its duties.

ASSURANCE ENGAGEMENTS

It is clear from our discussion so far that a statutory audit is about collecting sufficient appropriate audit evidence to enable reasonable conclusions to be drawn on which to base the audit opinion. We have not yet discussed audit reporting but note at this stage that an audit opinion provides a reasonably high level of assurance about the truth and fairness of the view given by the financial statements, thus increasing their usefulness to readers of the statements. Clearly it would be possible to issue reports that give a level of assurance lower than 'reasonable assurance', such as those given in respect of review, compilation and agreed upon procedures engagements, mentioned in Chapter 6 (see page 232). We noted that such work does not normally include detailed tests of control or substantive tests of detail, such as observation of inventory counts, or detailed tests of transactions, but would normally involve analytical review of information, and in-depth discussions with management at various levels throughout the organization. Work of this nature would enable the practitioner to give 'negative assurance', which, although limited, can be useful to recipients of the report and be relied on by them if the review has been carried out by a skilled and independent professional. Both audits and reviews are sometimes called 'attestation services', as the auditor or reviewer is attesting to the validity of information to one degree or another.

The standard audit report uses the phrase 'reasonable assurance that the financial statements are free from material misstatement' See Chapter 16.

We give an example of negative assurance later in this chapter. See page 574.

ACTIVITY 15.1

Explain why the external auditor can only give '*reasonable* assurance' that the financial statements are free from material misstatement'? Do you think that you might apply the term '*limited* assurance' to the assurance given to a review engagement?

You will have noted from our comments in Chapter 6 that even the best audit evidence is persuasive rather than absolute, so, although auditors may possess a high degree of certainty that management assertions are valid and that misstatements are unlikely, they can never be completely sure. This means that the highest degree of assurance that they can give is 'reasonable assurance'.

The kind and amount of evidence collected during a review engagement does not allow reasonable assurance to be given, but the reporting accountants will have satisfied themselves that, within the limitations of the evidence collected, the subject matter is plausible. So it is appropriate to apply the term 'limited assurance' to the assurance given. These terms are both suggested by the International Framework for Assurance Engagements, issued by IAASB (the Framework). IAASB also issued an international standard on assurance engagements, ISAE 3000 – *Assurance engagements other than audits or reviews of historical financial information* in 2005.

There is no standard comparable to ISAE 3000 in the UK and Ireland. ISAE 3000 is to be read in the context of the Framework.

This Framework defines an assurance engagement as:

> An engagement in which a practitioner expresses a conclusion designed to enhance the degree of confidence of the intended users other than the responsible party about *the outcome of the evaluation or measurement of a subject matter* against criteria.

This text is an extract from the International Framework for Assurance Engagements, of the IAASB, published by the International Federation of Accountants (IFAC), published after January 2005, and is used with permission of IFAC.

The wording in italics is described in the Framework as 'subject matter information' and may be regarded as the 'assertion' about the subject matter. Thus subject matter might be the timeliness of arrival of trains at their destination and a statement by rail company management (the responsible party) that trains arrive on time is an assertion that might be proven by measuring the times that trains actually arrive. The Framework explains in paragraph 8 what is meant by the various elements of the above definition by putting it into the context of a set of financial statements (the authors have added bold emphasis):

We look at this example of trains arriving on time at greater length later.

> The recognition, measurement, presentation and disclosure represented in the financial statements (**outcome**) result from applying a financial reporting framework for recognition, measurement, presentation and disclosure, such as International Financial Reporting Standards, (**criteria**) to an entity's financial position, financial performance and cash flows (**subject matter**).

This text is an extract from the International Framework for Assurance Engagements, of the IAASB, published by the International Federation of Accountants (IFAC), published after January 2005, and is used with permission of IFAC.

The Framework distinguishes between direct reporting engagements and assertion-based engagements, each of which have a responsible party and subject matter information upon which the practitioner reports to the intended users in the assurance report. The main difference between an assurance engagement and a direct reporting engagement is that in the former a responsible party makes an assertion which is reported on by the practitioner, whereas in the latter, the practitioner directly performs the evaluation or measurement of the subject matter, and then reports on the matter. An example of a direct reporting assignment might be where a potential investor in a company wishes to receive some assurance about such matters as its performance, actual or anticipated, about the risks facing the company and key employees. The practitioner in this case might consider assertions by management about such matters as the reliability of the financial information provided, but would make a direct report to the potential investor (known as the 'engaging party').

The Framework identifies five elements of an assurance engagement:

(1) a three-part relationship involving a practitioner, a responsible party and intended users.

(2) an appropriate subject matter;

(3) suitable criteria;

(4) sufficient appropriate evidence; and

(5) a written assurance report in the form appropriate to a reasonable assurance engagement or a limited assurance engagement.

These elements are all to be found in Figure 2.1. See page 37.

1 The *practitioner* may be requested to perform assurance engagements on a wide range of subject matters, much wider than audits or reviews of historical financial information. The *responsible party* may be responsible for the subject matter or for the subject matter information or both. The *intended users* are the person, persons or class of persons for whom the practitioner prepares the assurance report. The responsible party can be one of the intended users but not the only one.

Paragraphs 21 to 30 of the Framework discuss the three-part relationship.

2 The *subject matter* is:

(a) identifiable and capable of consistent evaluation or measurement against the identified criteria; and

(b) such that the information about it can be subjected to procedures for gathering sufficient appropriate evidence to support a reasonable assurance or limited assurance conclusion, as appropriate.

Paragraphs 31 to 33 of the Framework.

3 *Criteria* are the benchmarks used to evaluate or measure the subject matter, including, where relevant, benchmarks for presentation and disclosure. Criteria need to be available to the intended users to allow them to understand how the subject matter has been evaluated or measured.

Paragraphs 34 to 38 of the Framework. Think again about financial statements (the subject matter). The users could not evaluate them properly unless they are aware of the accounting policies (part of criteria) that have been applied.

4 We have discussed the need to obtain *sufficient appropriate evidence* in Chapter 6 and in numerous other parts of this book. The same applies to practitioners in an assurance engagement. They need to obtain evidence with these qualities to support their conclusion. The framework also emphasizes the need to perform the assurance engagement with an attitude of 'professional scepticism' and that materiality and assurance engagement risk need to be considered.

The framework addresses the elements of sufficient appropriate evidence in paragraphs 39 to 55.

5 The practitioner provides a written report containing a conclusion that conveys the assurance obtained about the subject matter information. It may be in positive form for a *reasonable assurance engagement* and in a negative form for a *limited assurance engagement*.

Paragraphs 56 to 60 of the Framework.

ACTIVITY 15.2

Suggest subject matter other than financial statements that users might wish to be reliable and likely subject matter information. Ask yourself if experts in particular fields other than external auditors could provide assurance to users.

KPI are clearly those measurements that provide users with the means to evaluate assertions about the subject matter.

Paragraph 31 of the framework gives examples of subject matter and subject matter information.

This text is an extract from the International Framework for Assurance Engagements, of the IAASB, published by the International Federation of Accountants (IFAC), published after January 2005, and is used with permission of IFAC.

COSO = 'Internal Control – Integrated Framework' The Committee of Sponsoring Organizations of the Treadway Commission; CoCo = 'Guidance on Assessing Control – The CoCo Principles' Criteria of Control Board, The Canadian Institute of Chartered Accountants.

There are many kinds of matter that users might wish to rely on, other than financial statements. We have already seen that auditors might be required to report on local authorities' statements about the cleanliness of its streets. In this case the subject matter information might be selected key performance indicators (KPI) used, such as the number of street cleaners employed and number of times cleaned per month or number of complaints. We saw too in Chapter 5 that hotels use a number of performance indicators as a measure of their success, such as usage of accommodation capacity, and usage of restaurant tables. Companies might assess customer satisfaction by the number of complaints received over a period of time, or the level of repeat purchases by existing customers. Clearly all of these matters can be examined by auditors to decide if they are a proper measure of performance. For instance, is the number of street cleaners employed a good indicator of whether streets are clean or not?

Other subject matters that assurance engagements might address are systems and processes (such as, efficacy of internal controls, and measures to reduce risk in e-commerce) and organizational behaviour (for instance, the degree to which companies address corporate governance issues, whether a company is complying with regulations, such as those designed to reduce pollution, whether an organization is applying practices that conform to human rights legislation, whether a company is complying with contractual terms). The subject matter information in these cases might be assertions by management about effectiveness or compliance.

The Framework explains in paragraph 8 what is meant by the various elements of an assurance project on the efficacy of internal controls:

> An assertion about the effectiveness of internal control (outcome) results from applying a framework for evaluating the effectiveness of internal control, such as COSO or CoCo (criteria) to internal control, a process (subject matter).

External auditors are not the only ones who could provide useful degrees of assurance to users. Apart from internal auditors providing a wide range of services to management, other bodies or persons can add to the value of information to users, provided that they possess the quality of independence. In Scotland, for instance, the Scottish Environment Protection Agency (SEPA) is an independent body that reports on water quality at bathing beaches used by members of the public. Another example is the Consumers' Association, a not-for-profit organization, which has been researching and campaigning on behalf of consumers since it was founded in 1957. One of its publications is *Which?* magazine, giving independent advice on products and services.

ACTIVITY 15.3

Explain what is meant by the responsible party. Do you think that the responsible party might be one of the intended users?

The responsible party is clearly the person(s) responsible for the subject matter information and/or the subject matter. Responsible parties might be those responsible for preparation of performance indicators, for assertions that newly developed computer systems are suitable for use, for statements on corporate governance, for statements that water quality is high. It is an interesting idea that the responsible party might be one of the users, but this might indeed be the case. For instance, top management of a company engaged in e-commerce might want assurance that computer systems developed by a lower level of management protect the identity of customers. In this case both top management and the customers would be the intended users. The senior executives of a local authority might want assurance that performance indicators developed by their subordinates are suitable for publication to users of the local authority's services. You should note though that the framework states that although the responsible party can be one of the intended users, it cannot be the only one, presumably because it would then just be an internal report.

Let us turn now to the question of suitable criteria. In Chapter 2, we identified a postulate that stated:

> Standards of accountability, for example, conduct, performance, achievement and quality of information, can be set for those who are accountable: actual conduct, etc. can be measured and compared with these standards by reference to known criteria and the process of measurement and comparison requires special skill and judgement.

We also saw, in the context of financial reporting, accounting standards, such as FRSs and IASs, had been developed to enable accountability to be achieved, that is, they are a means to enable accountants to measure financial position and results and to allow auditors to form an opinion about position and results.

ACTIVITY 15.4

The Framework suggests that characteristics of suitable criteria are: relevance, completeness, reliability, neutrality and understandability. What do you think that these characteristics mean? Illustrate your answer by reference to performance indicators on punctuality issued by train operators. For instance, '95 per cent of trains operated by North South Railway Company arrived on time during the month ended 31 August 2011'.

See Paragraph 36.

Some of these characteristics overlap somewhat but we comment as follows:

- *Relevance.* Criteria will only be relevant if they contribute to conclusions that assist decision making by intended users. Potential passengers might use them to decide whether to travel by this company or another one and government bodies might use them to determine public policy, such as level of public funds to be made available. On the face of it, the punctuality of trains does appear to be relevant.
- *Completeness*. Criteria are sufficiently complete when relevant factors that could affect the users' decisions are not omitted. Thus, punctuality might be only one of the factors to be considered when deciding to travel by this company or determining levels of public funding, so we have to consider the question of *completeness*. For instance, it might be useful to know how many complaints have been received about cleanliness of the trains or about the politeness and helpfulness of staff. This means that we must go beyond asking whether a particular piece of information is relevant, and ask in addition: Have we got *all* the information that we need to make informed decisions? That would lead us to ask what the needs and objectives of the users might be and how the information might be presented and how often to make it useful for decision making.
- *Reliability.* Users would ask the question: Are the criteria used in preparing the information used consistently and presented in the same way? In the case we are considering we would wish to know if the information about punctuality is prepared on a basis that allows genuine decisions to be made and if all the train companies prepare the data on the same basis. Users could legitimately ask what is meant by the term 'on time'. Does it mean that the train was either early or arrived exactly at the publicized time of arrival or do they define as 'on time' as no more than (say) ten minutes late? If the company prepares the information at variance from an established norm, it can hardly be said to be reliable. To make the information reliable it would need to be accompanied by disclosure of the definitions adopted.
- *Neutrality.* Neutral criteria contribute to conclusions that are free from bias. For instance, we would not expect the criteria to be amended in the interests of management, such as changing definitions without warning to save face in the management team. Thus, if a train company states month by month that it is adhering to company regulations on testing for faulty rails, that might be regarded by the user as being satisfactory. However, if the company had fallen behind with its work so that rails were being tested only once every year instead of six months, but it had changed its regulations without telling anyone, the criteria would clearly be biased and the subject matter information is not be of value to the user.
- *Understandability*. Understandable criteria contribute to conclusions that are clear, comprehensive and not subject to significantly different conclusions. This means that the criteria are so clear and unambiguous that all users will interpret them in the same way. Thus, 95 per cent punctuality means that 95 out of 100 trains of this company arrive within ten minutes of the publicized time. This seems understandable enough, although commuters might regret that they always seem to be passengers on the 5 out of 100 trains that are always late. They might be happier, however, if an auditor or reviewer assured them that the company's statement was valid.

One further point on criteria is that they can be specially developed for a particular engagement or they may be established criteria embodied in laws or regulations or issued by recognized bodies of experts. Thus, if auditors or reviewers are asked to provide assurance that a new computer system is working properly, it would be necessary for them to work together with management to establish criteria by which 'working properly' can be judged. It might be necessary, for instance, to establish a desired speed of access to the system and its files. Clearly, no one engaged in the provision of an assurance engagement will be able to report effectively if criteria have not been established beforehand. This means that practitioners should not accept an assurance engagement if suitable criteria are not available or cannot be established. A corollary to this is that users of any assurance report must be aware of the criteria used, either in the report or by other means.

Engagement acceptance and letter of engagement

Before practitioners enter into an assurance engagement there are a number of factors they should consider based on their knowledge of the engagement circumstances:

- The relevant ethical requirements are met, including independence and competence.
- Whether the engagement possesses the following characteristics:
  - (a) Appropriate subject matter.
  - (b) Suitable criteria available to intended users.
  - (c) Availability of sufficient appropriate evidence to support the desired conclusion.
  - (d) The practitioners' conclusion will be contained in a written report.
  - (e) A rational purpose for the engagement, including an appropriate scope of examination. Practitioners must also be certain that their name is associated with the subject matter in an appropriate manner.

We discussed letters of engagement in Chapter 5, and clearly they will be just as important in the case of any assurance engagement. Basically we would expect the letter to contain a mention and explanation of the following matters:

See page 192.

- A description of the engagement objective (either prescribed by law or by the person appointing the practitioner) and of the subject matter and subject matter information.
- The scope of work to be performed by the practitioner, explaining the nature and extent of procedures for obtaining evidence, specifying in the case of a limited assurance engagement that the procedures will be limited to inquiry and analytical procedure, unless a matter comes to the attention of the practitioner that may indicate the subject matter does not conform in all material respects with the identified criteria.
- The form of report that will be given, including a brief description of work performed, and comments on the subject matter and criteria as seen fit, and highlighting the fact that a positive or negative form of conclusion will be given, as the case may be.

- The assurance given by the report – either 'reasonable assurance' or 'limited assurance'.
- Restrictions (if any) on the use of reports, including availability to third parties.
- Fees and billing arrangements.
- Any other matters of relevance to the engagement being carried out, including timetables and deadlines.

Evidence-gathering procedures

We have already discussed audit evidence in Chapter 6 and have drawn the distinction above between the kind of evidence required for an audit and that required for a review. What is clear is that the amount and quality of evidence obtained will determine the conclusions that practitioners can form and the kind of report that they can issue in the light of the engagement risk they face. The appendix to the Framework outlines the difference between reasonable assurance engagements and limited assurance and we reproduce it in Table 15.1. As well as describing the evidence-gathering procedures, the appendix also indicates the level of engagement risk, the kind of conclusion in the assurance report and the assurance obtained and conveyed.

Content of assurance report

These elements are those shown in paragraph 49 of ISAE 3000 – *Assurance engagements other than audits or reviews of historical financial information.*

The assurance report should contain the following basic elements:

- A title that clearly indicates the report is an independent assurance report.
- An addressee.
- An identification and description of the subject matter information and, where appropriate, the subject matter.
- Identification of the criteria.
- Where appropriate a description of any inherent or significant limitation associated with evaluation or measurement of the subject matter against the criteria.
- When the criteria used to evaluate or measure the subject matter are available only to specific intended users, or are relevant only to a specific purpose, a statement restricting the use of the assurance report to those intended users or that purpose.
- A statement to identify the responsible party and to describe the responsible party's and practitioner's responsibilities.
- A statement that the engagement was performed in accordance with ISAEs (International Standards on Assurance Engagements).
- A summary of the work performed.
- The practitioner's conclusion. Where appropriate the conclusion should inform the intended users of the context in which the practitioner's conclusion is to be read. In a reasonable assurance engagement, the conclusion should be couched in the positive form – 'In our opinion internal control is effective, in all material respects, based on XYZ *criteria'*

You will see in Chapter 16 that a positive form of opinion is given in the standard unqualified statutory audit report. When we introduce you to the standard audit report, we suggest you compare it with the content of the limited assurance report, described here.

TABLE 15.1 Differences between reasonable assurance engagements and limited assurance engagements

Type of engagement	Objective	Evidence-gathering procedures	The assurance report
Reasonable assurance engagement	A reduction in assurance engagement risk to an acceptably low level in the circumstances of the engagement, as the basis for a positive form of expression of the practitioner's conclusion.	Sufficient appropriate evidence is obtained as part of a systematic engagement process that includes: • Obtaining an understanding of the engagement circumstances. • Assessing risks. • Responding to assessed risks. • Performing further procedures, using a combination of inspection, observation, confirmation, recalculation, reperformance, analytical procedures and inquiry. Such further procedures involve substantive procedures including, where applicable, obtaining corroborating information and, depending on the nature of the subject matter, tests of the operating effectiveness of controls. • Evaluating the evidence obtained.	Description of the engagement circumstances and a positive form of expression of conclusion.
Limited assurance engagement	A reduction in assurance engagement risk to a level that is acceptable in the circumstances of the engagement, but where that risk is greater than for a reasonable assurance engagement as the basis for a negative form of expression of the practitioner's conclusion.	Sufficient appropriate evidence is obtained as part of a systematic engagement process that includes obtaining an understanding of the subject matter and other engagement circumstances, but in which procedures are deliberately limited relative to a reasonable assurance engagement.	Description of the engagement circumstances and a negative form of expression of conclusion.

or 'In our opinion *the responsible party's* assertion that internal control is effective, in all material respects, based on XYZ *criteria,* is fairly stated.' In a limited assurance engagement, the conclusion should be expressed in the negative form – 'Based on our work described in this report, nothing has come to our attention that causes us to believe that *the responsible party's* assertion that internal control is effective, in all material respects, based on XYZ *criteria,* is not fairly stated.'

- The assurance report date.
- The name of the firm or the practitioner, and a specific location, which ordinarily is the city where the practitioner maintains the office that has responsibility for the engagement.

Before we leave this topic we give some examples in Table 15.2 of different levels of assurance that may be given by practitioners. Certain of them do not meet the definition of an assurance engagement and are not covered by the Framework – agreed-upon procedures, compilation of financial and other information, preparation of tax returns where no conclusion conveying assurance is expressed, and consulting engagements. The Framework does suggest, however, that some consulting engagements may meet the definition of an assurance engagement. Where an engagement does not meet the definition of an assurance engagement the Framework makes clear that the practitioner should avoid using certain wording that implies compliance with the Framework and certain other international standards.

TABLE 15.2 Levels of assurance

Levels	Examples
No assurance	*Compilation report.* We discussed this kind of report briefly in Chapter 6. This kind of engagement involves practitioners in acquiring an understanding of the accounting principles and practices of the client's industry. Practitioners would also acquire an understanding of the client's business, the nature of its transactions and the accounting records maintained. They would consider the quality of accounting personnel and review the financial statements. On this basis the practitioner would prepare the financial statements, state in their report that they have done so, but would also state that they have *not* carried out an audit or a review.
	Preparation of tax returns but no conclusion given on their acceptability.
Limited assurance	*A report on review of interim financial statements.* As we have seen above, practitioners would make enquiries and perform analytical reviews of the subject matter. They would then issue a negative assurance report – which would be a form of disclaimer.
	Agreed-upon procedures. In this case practitioners would carry out procedures that have been agreed upon by them, the responsible party and the intended users of the report. These procedures would not normally be sufficient to allow the practitioner to give positive assurance. The report would state the agreed-upon procedures, give the results of the procedures, but would also state that an audit has not been carried out. The proposed international framework on assurance engagements does not regard an agreed-upon-procedures engagement as an assurance engagement because it does not meet the definition, presumably because the report is intended for a responsible party who is the only user.

TABLE 15.2 *(Continued)*

Levels	Examples
	Consulting engagements where the nature and scope of the work is agreed between the practitioner and management. The engagement is normally for the benefit of management only and is likely to be in the form of a long-form report containing much detail. The work performed is usually an analytical process often evaluating alternative courses of action and the development of recommendations and suggested courses of action.
	Report on a company's corporate governance statement. In this case (as we shall see in Chapter 16) practitioners review the directors' statements concerning corporate governance matters. The review is normally not sufficient to express an opinion on the effectiveness of internal financial control or corporate governance procedures nor on the ability of the company to continue in operational existence. Practitioners then give an opinion that the directors have complied with identified rules and that the directors' statements are not inconsistent with the information of which they are aware from audit work on the financial statements. They then go on to say that based on their enquiries of certain directors and officers of the company and examination of relevant documents, the directors' statements appropriately reflect compliance with identified criteria. Some of these conclusions are expressed in positive form, but in a very limited way, in that practitioners are merely stating that certain rules have been adhered to.
	Comfort letters. These are frequently issued by practitioners in relation to financial statements included in new share issues. The practitioner may have given a full true and fair opinion on the statements, but carries out an extended subsequent events review from the issue of the audit report to the date of the prospectus issue. The practitioner would describe the procedures performed and issue a negative assurance report.
Long-form and short-form reports on the effectiveness of internal control	*Report on internal control using generally accepted auditing standards.* The report might indicate that there are inherent limitations in any internal control system and that such systems may deteriorate over time. The practitioner may then give assurance on the management assertion that the internal control system is effective, except for any weaknesses identified, and acknowledging the inherent limitations. In 2001, the APB issued a briefing paper entitled 'Providing Assurance on the Effectiveness of Internal Control'. This briefing paper highlights inherent limitations in internal control and suggests that a long-form narrative report would be necessary to enable users to understand the context in

TABLE 15.2 *(Continued)*

Levels	Examples
	which the opinion is given or the judgements that have to be made in reaching the conclusion and the reasons underpinning those judgements. The briefing paper seems to indicate that there can be a number of different types of assurance provided and therefore auditors will match their wording to the nature of the engagement. The question of reports on the effectiveness of internal control is very controversial. You should note that in the United States, post-Enron, auditors are now issuing short-form reports on management's assessment of the effectiveness of internal controls in accordance with criteria established in *Internal Control – Integrated Framework* issued by the Committee of Sponsoring Organizations of the Treadway Commission. Note that this is not a direct reporting engagement but an engagement leading to a report on a management assertion. A typical management assertion would be: 'XYZ Inc. maintained effective internal control over financial reporting as of 31 December 2011.' The US standard notes that there may have been weaknesses in internal control in the period up to the date (in this case 31 December 2011) and that management could only make this assertion if those weaknesses have been eliminated before the quoted date. The assurance is limited in the sense that the reports state that systems of internal control have inherent limitations. See our comments in Chapter 7.
Positive assurance	*Statutory audit of financial statements,* using the techniques and procedures described earlier in this book. The practitioner would assess the evidence gathered and give a positive assurance on the view shown by the financial statements. If the evidence gathered does not support the true and fair view assertion or evidence is not available, the practitioner will 'qualify' the report. We shall discuss qualifications in audit reports in Chapter 16.

Paragraph 165 of public company accounting oversight board bylaws and rules – standards –AS2

Why have assurance engagements become more common?

Before we take a look at assurance cases it will be useful to consider why assurance engagements have assumed such importance in the portfolios of auditing firms in recent years. There are a number of factors:

- Many entities have merged with the result that the number of large audit clients has reduced considerably.

- Many smaller companies are no longer required to have an annual audit, with the result that more assurance is required by interested parties.
- At various times in the past there has been substantial downward pressure on audit fees.
- Business has become significantly more complicated, and therefore more risky, as a result of merger activity (creating groups and companies that encompass a wide range of activities) and of such factors as the technological revolution and the use of complex financial instruments.
- Audit firms also saw the opportunity to open up new markets for their services and hence increase their profitability. In this respect it might be said that the audit firms themselves assisted in the creation of the demand for assurance services.

As a result of such factors, audit firms have started to adopt strategies to reduce audit risk and have, as mentioned earlier, adopted a business risk approach. As you know, this approach involves gaining a deep understanding of the company and its industry, of company objectives, of the business risks that may inhibit achievement of objectives, and the way in which management attempt to reduce the impact of those risks. As this brings auditors into very close contact with management, it often results in the identification of problem areas that the firm can address and may lead to the provision of assurance engagements. For instance, a particular business risk faced by many organizations is that their objectives may be hindered because of environmental considerations. Auditors may be called upon to advise how environmental matters may be handled and subsequently to prepare assurance reports in the area. Case study 15.1 will help us to show what an assurance engagement might involve.

CASE STUDY 15.1

Protecting the environment in an area of scenic beauty

You are the auditor of a local authority in an area of scenic beauty with a long coastline. The authority is keen to attract visitors, as it believes this will benefit local traders, and has decided that it needs to take steps to protect the environment and to publicize the steps that it has taken. In discussions with the chief executive of the authority it becomes clear that the county's coastline is regarded as one of its most attractive features and that the authority is concerned that the path along the coast has become overgrown and that rubbish has collected in places – rubbish that is not only unsightly but may also be detrimental to the seabirds and waders that nest and feed in the area. Apart from these environmental matters you learn that the authority wishes to make the coastal path more attractive to visitors, although there are restrictions on the amount of money available for such a programme.

What kind of advice would you give to the local authority? It is worth stating at the outset that auditors of local authorities have a duty to ensure that programmes of the authority give value for money. In advising the authority, therefore, costs and benefits of the programme should be considered.

Your advice might encompass the following matters:

The environmental problem

- Determine the extent and gravity of the problem. If the rubbish is non-toxic, it will be less serious than toxic material. Some of it might have been dropped by visitors, while some might have been deposited on the coast from the sea. Your first piece of advice would be for a qualified environmental expert to walk the path and to determine the nature of the rubbish.

- Following the expert's report, the local authority would need to consider appropriate action. You should advise that any toxic waste discovered should be removed without delay. There might be local authority or government regulations relating to the impact of toxic waste on the environment and you should discuss any such regulation with management. This might mean that some of the scarce funds should be earmarked not only for clearing the waste immediately but to ensure also that there are regular patrols to ensure that such waste is identified quickly in future. You would advise the authority to detect the source of waste to prevent it in future, and to obtain compensation, if possible. These steps are clearly necessary as the public would be concerned about their own personal safety and that of wildlife.
- If the rubbish is non-toxic, but merely unsightly, you would advise regular patrols to clear it. The authority might contact local walking and bird-watching groups to see if they would participate in such patrols and cleaning operations. One of the authors occasionally meets a public spirited woman near where he lives who picks up any small-scale rubbish as she takes a walk along rural paths. Another useful action might be to ask visitors by means of occasional notices to take care of the environment.

Making the coastal path more attractive

The first step to make the path more attractive is to deal with the environmental matters, discussed above. However, there are a number of other steps the local authority could take:

- Publicizing the existence of the path and the measures taken to make it attractive. This could be done by asking the Highways Authority and Rail Authorities to indicate its existence on nearby roads and at railway stations. Other kinds of publicity might include descriptions of the path on the local authority website and at national and local tourist offices.
- Showing the course of the path on publicity material and by placing of signs along the path. It would be useful for visitors to know how long particular stretches are and whether the stretch is easy or hard-going. As the path is currently overgrown in places, grass and other vegetation should be cut before making decisions about ease of access and passage. Some parts of the path might cross land on which cattle are grazing, and visitors should be made aware on which parts of the path cattle might be encountered. Parents should also be informed whether children should be accompanied or not.
- In view of the large number of seabirds and waders that are to be seen along the path, the local authority might aid identification by putting up pictures and descriptions of birds and their behaviour where they might be found.

> In this part of the coastal path, the following birds are frequently to be seen: Cormorants and Shags (on the rocks extending into the sea); Oystercatchers, Curlews, and Redshanks (in the shallow water among the rocks at the sea edge); Sanderling (on the long stretch of sand about quarter of a mile ahead – at the water edge); Stonechats (on the hedges to the left of the path); Dunlin in the fields to the left and among the rocks. Occasionally, Herons may be seen standing on the rocks or in the fields. They nest in the trees on the brow of the hill.

- Local farmers might also be encouraged to provide information about farming activities alongside the path, together with requests for visitors not to leave the path because of the danger of passing disease to livestock.
- A positive feature of informing visitors in the ways suggested above is that they are more likely to take the environment seriously themselves. The notices about birds might also warn that plastic bags can be a serious danger to birds and other wildlife.

There might be other matters that you could consider, but these recommendations would form a useful basis for establishing a policy.

ACTIVITY 15.5

Assume that the local authority has decided to put the above recommendations into effect and that they now wish to issue a document informing potential visitors of the existence of the path and its attractions and stating that it is safe for use by the public, provided that notice is taken of the information concerning the ease of use of the path. The local authority has asked you to issue an assurance report confirming that the document issued by the local authority is acceptable in all material respects.

Do you think that the engagement will meet the definition of an assurance engagement? Is this the sort of engagement that a practitioner might be willing to undertake? What would be the issues that you would wish to consider? Do you think that you could give a positive or negative form of conclusion? Explain your answer. Finally, if you have been involved in advising the local authority about their policy in the first place, do you think that you would be a suitable person to perform the assurance engagement?

It does seem that there is in this case (i) a practitioner (in this instance, you); (ii) a responsible party (the local authority); (iii) intended users – potential visitors to the coastal path. Whether you would accept the engagement depends on the factors that we discussed above:

- Is the subject matter identifiable, capable of consistent evaluation or measurement against identified, suitable criteria and in a form that can be subjected to procedures for gathering evidence to support that evaluation or measurement? The subject matter in this case is clearly the document issued by the local authority informing potential visitors of the path and its attractions and that it is safe to use provided that notice is taken of the ease of use. The assertion about safety is clearly subject matter information.
- The criteria to be used are suitable and are available to intended users You will remember that criteria should have the following characteristics – relevance, completeness, reliability, neutrality and understandability. The criteria could be quite subjective in some cases. That the path is well marked and accurately delineated is a question of fact, as well as the existence of the birds and other physical features. Whether the path is easy to use is somewhat subjective but the question of safety may be problematic. What does 'safe' mean in this context? You would have to determine if this has been defined in the document. For instance, there might be requirements that visitors keep to the delineated path, that children below a specified age should be accompanied by an adult, that livestock be treated with respect, that suitable footwear be worn over the more difficult stretches and that such stretches are clearly indicated.
- Sufficient appropriate evidence to support the practitioner's conclusion is available. As suggested above, some of the statements in the document might be quite easy to confirm. Visual inspection would be enough to prove

that the path is clearly delineated, for instance. The birds might be more difficult as they tend to fly around, but talking with local bird-watching groups would confirm their existence and what times of the year they would be best seen. The question of safety is more difficult to prove, particularly as some times of the year might be safer than others. In the winter or any rainy season or at times when tides are high, the path might be more difficult to walk, and, if so, the document should state this fact. You might be able to obtain sufficient evidence by visual inspection at different times of the year or talking to local walking groups to prove that the subject matter is generally valid.

Regarding the form of conclusion – positive or negative – this depends on whether the evidence gathered was adequate or not. You might decide that there are so many variable factors that you could only give a negative form of opinion. The variable factors would include differing conditions at different times of the year, the nearness to the sea, the fact that ease of access would depend on the local authority keeping the path clear and that a continuous eye has to be kept on material washed up from the sea. Your conclusion report might describe the evidence that you had sought, but your conclusion on safety might be along the lines of: 'Nothing has come to our attention that would lead us to believe that the statements on safety made by the local authority in the document are not reliable.'

The last question is about your ability to prepare an engagement report if there were doubts about your independence of mind. This is a difficult question to answer. It depends on whether you had been involved in the detail of creating the policy to the extent that you were exercising management functions. If this were the case, it would be difficult for you to prepare an independent report. It might be advisable for you to pass the assurance engagement to a fellow partner not involved in the advisory activity. At the extreme, another firm might be better placed to carry out the assurance engagement. If, on the other hand, you had not been involved in the detail of policy formulation, but had confined yourself to broad issues such as adequate publicity, reducing environmental pollution and considering the safety of the path for all users, you might be able to give an independent assurance report.

CASE STUDY 15.2

Gilling Limited

Gilling Limited is a company based in a coastal village. It owns a pleasure boat and during May to October each year uses it to take visitors to an island some five miles offshore, known for its historical interest, ancient lighthouse and for seals and puffins, some 70 000 pairs of which nest there each year in spring and early summer. The boat carries a maximum of 82 passengers and leaves its home port daily, at varying times depending on the tide, and provided at least 12 passengers are aboard. There are two crewmen, one of whom serves refreshments to passengers. The fare is £14 (£12 for certain classes of people) and £6 for accompanied children. The trip to and from the island takes one hour each way and passengers spend three hours ashore. There is a small museum on the island, next to the seabird research station, but there are no other facilities, apart from clearly marked paths. The administrator and ferrymen are part time, being employed also in a local boatyard. The company is licensed by the local authority and pays an annual licence fee of £2000.

The company cannot meet demand in June, July and August and has decided to acquire another (second-hand boat), similar to the one the company is already running, for £150 000 and has prepared the following forecast profit and loss account for the second boat. The company has applied to the local authority for a further licence.

Ferry income		100 000
Refreshment income	25 000	
Less refreshment costs	–8 500	
		16 500
		116 500
Wages of ferrymen	25 000	
Wages of administrator	5 500	
Fuel	1 000	
Insurance	10 000	
Annual refurbishment and certification	4 000	
Sundry admin	3 000	
Licence	2 000	
Harbour dues	2 000	
Depreciation of ferry	5 000	
		57 500
Operating profit		59 000
Less interest expense		–15 000
Profit after interest		44 000

The company has applied to its bank for a loan of £100 000 to be repaid over a period of ten years and has provided the bank with the forecast financial statements set out above.

ACTIVITY 15.6

1 Identify the principal business risks that might be faced by a company of this nature and suggest measures that the company might adopt to reduce their impact.

2 Describe the major matters you would consider when forming a view on the validity of the forecast profit and loss account.

3 In your opinion would the engagement be an assurance engagement as defined on page 566?

4 Explain whether you would be able to give a reasonable or limited assurance to the bank on the figures in the forecast financial statements.

1 The principal business risks facing Gilling Limited include:

(a) The risk that passengers or crew may suffer injury during trips or in embarking or disembarking, with resulting claims or loss of company reputation, because of failure to adhere to health and safety legislation. To reduce the impact of this risk, passengers should be made aware of safety regulations and emergency procedures. Crew should be trained to take appropriate action in the event of emergency and to distribute life jackets in an orderly fashion. There should be sufficient life jackets on board, including those suitable for children. The boat should have signalling and radio equipment on board so coastal authorities can be informed of problems on a timely basis. There should be strict control of numbers on board and a register of names taken at point of payment.

(b) The risk that bad weather may prevent sailing or cause people not to visit the village or take a trip in the company's boats. The company will not be able to change the weather, but it should have a system of informing customers on a timely basis if the trip is not to take place. If landing on the island is not possible because of heavy swell, the crew might be trained to run the boat round the island, pointing out nesting sites and other interesting features.

(c) The risk that other operators might enter the market. The company does seem to be profitable and there will always be a risk that competitors will enter the market. The best strategy for the company might be to make the trips as interesting and informative as possible. There seems to be little in the way of facilities on the island, and it may be better that it stays like that, but the company might arrange for seabird research personnel or museum staff to give talks about birds nesting on and visiting the island, and some of the history of the island. As far as the second boat is concerned, management might consider alternative destinations if demand for trips to the island turn out to be less popular than expected.

(d) The risk that crewmen might be lost to other activities along the coast. Clearly, the company should pay personnel well and give them training to enhance their work. It seems that staff work part time in a local boatyard and it may be desirable to train other people in the boatyard to take the place of crewmen, either because they have left or are sick.

(e) The risk that the operating licence may not be renewed. We are not informed of the terms of the licence, but the company should make sure that they are adhered to. The terms might include the health and safety procedures mentioned above and annual or more regular inspections and overhaul.

2 The first step might be to consider the reasonableness of the projected income, and to do this by estimating the full-capacity income on an assumed mix of passengers. Let us assume that discussions with management reveal an average mix of full paying adults 65 per cent, concessionary adults 10 per cent and accompanied children 25 per cent. On this basis the total income from full capacity trips would be:

	Adults	**Concessions**	**Children**	**Total**
Percentages	65%	10%	25%	
Numbers one trip	53	8	21	82
Fare	£14	£12	£6	
Total fares per trip	£742	£96	£126	£964
Total trips				184
Maximum fare income				£177 376

The income projected by the company is slightly above 56 per cent of total capacity on this basis – which looks conservative on the face of it. You should enquire of management how they had calculated the figure of £100 000 and you may find that they have assumed the boat would be running at lower capacity in May, September and October. The same kind of analytical work would be carried out on the refreshment income. The company has assumed a gross margin on refreshments of 66 per cent, and you should discuss this with management. You are told that the boat the company wishes to acquire is similar to the existing boat and you will be able to compare the projected figures with the actual figures for the existing boat.

One important point that you should discuss with management is whether the second boat will need any refurbishment to bring it up to the standard required by the local authority and health and safety regulations. You should ask the company to prepare a cash flow forecast to accompany the forecast profit and loss account, as this might reveal that, initially at least, the company might need to borrow more than £100 000. On the basis of the forecast profit and loss account, the company would seem to have a projected positive operating cash flow in the year of £49 000 (profit £44 000 plus depreciation £5000). You would need to review the projected costs carefully to ensure none are missed, and in calculating cash flow, calculate tax charge, the amounts that the directors' remuneration might be, and dividends expected by shareholders. Particular attention should be paid to annual refurbishment and certification. As the boats are no longer new, annual refurbishment might include steps to reduce toxic emissions, and to meet ever more stringent health and safety requirements.

3 It does seem to be an assurance engagement. Gilling Limited is the responsible party. The bank is clearly the prime user, although there may be other interested parties as well – the local authority, the health and safety authorities, the public. The subject matter is the forecast profit and loss account – and if you have your way – a forecast cash flow statement. The subject matter information is the assertion by management that the forecasts are a fair representation of anticipated profits and cash flows. The criteria are those elements of the forecasts that will enable the bank (and the other potential users if they get involved) to make soundly based decisions, and they do have to have characteristics of relevance, completeness, reliability, neutrality and understandability. We can agree that the forecast profit and loss account and cash flow statements are relevant. You might argue that completeness would be achieved by inclusion in the subject matter of the major assumptions made by Gilling – such as numbers likely to use the boat. Your report will have added a degree of reliability and the use of known accounting principles consistent with those used by the company in the past will add neutrality and understandability. There is a practitioner – in this case you – and you have collected evidence to enable you to prepare an assurance report

4 Forecast financial statements and cash flow statements are intended to illuminate the future. The problem is uncertainty about the future. Although the future is not clear, the practitioner can test the reasonableness of the assumptions in determining income levels and costs, and they can ensure that the accounting principles used are acceptable and that calculations are accurate. In your report you can describe the criteria and discuss important elements of the subject matter. You would explain the nature of the evidence that you have examined, but it is doubtful that you could give an audit-level opinion. In other words, for this kind of engagement only limited assurance would be possible and you would give a negative form of expression.

INTERNAL AUDIT

From time to time we have mentioned internal audit and this is an appropriate point to discuss its function and its work in greater detail. Internal auditors may not be practitioners in the terms of the proposed international framework we discussed above, and management may be the single user of their services, but we shall find that internal auditors provide assurance to management on a range of matters of interest to the company. In addition, because their work frequently covers areas of interest to external auditors, the latter may use their work in achieving their own objectives. We made the same point earlier with regard to the work of the quality standards function.

See page 278 in Chapter 7.

ACTIVITY 15.7

What do you think is the common feature of internal audit and the quality standards function, identified in Chapter 7, which might enable the auditor to rely on their work?

An important feature of internal audit and the quality standards function is their independence from day-to-day management. The auditor would have to decide if they were truly independent, but we did suggest in Figure 7.6 that quality standards personnel should be independent of the computer department, making them more reliable from management's point of view.

See page 269.

We shall now turn to a discussion of the work of internal auditors and why it might be appropriate for auditors to rely on the function. Here is the definition of internal auditing issued by the Institute of Internal Auditors (1999):

ISA 610 – *Using the work of internal auditors*, contains in paragraph A3 a list of objectives of the internal audit function. We cover the activities of internal auditors below.

> Internal auditing is an independent, objective assurance and consulting activity designed to add value and improve an organization's operations. It helps an organization accomplish its objectives by bringing a systematic, disciplined approach to evaluate and improve the effectiveness of risk management, control, and governance processes.

This definition has some common elements with external auditing. Thus, there is a reference to independence and also to assurance, risk and governance, all terms of significance to external auditing. However, the definition would seem to suggest two major differences between internal and external audit:

1 The internal audit function, as its name suggests, is established within the organization and its independence should be judged with this in mind.
2 A prime objective is to improve an organization's operations.

External auditors do, as we have seen, often provide services to management designed to improve the organization's operations in the context of the business risk approach, but this is as a by-product of the audit process rather than a main objective.

The aim of statutory auditing is to establish whether financial statements have been drawn up in *compliance* with regulatory requirements, some of them legal, others professional and others required by regulatory bodies such as the Stock Exchange. For this reason the statutory audit process is sometimes described as 'compliance auditing'. Internal auditing, however, although still concerning itself with compliance auditing, is moving into other fields where it acts as an 'arm of management' in obtaining greater efficiency and effectiveness in all operations of the organization. We shall see later that the increasingly wide range of work performed by internal auditors has made some commentators suggest that the internal audit function might play an important role in the way that companies govern themselves.

We discuss corporate governance in Chapter 18.

Because internal audit often directs its attention to the efficacy of internal control systems it may be regarded by external auditors as an important part of the control system itself. We shall find that external auditors assess the quality and effectiveness of internal audit work and frequently use the work of internal auditors in attaining their ends.

Types of internal audit

We shall use a simple example (Case study 15.3) to help you understand different types of internal audit, including compliance, efficiency and effectiveness auditing. Later we shall discuss the different kinds of subject matter on which it might provide assurance.

CASE STUDY 15.3

Greenburn Limited: fleet of vans

The management of Greenburn Ltd, as part of its marketing policy, operates a fleet of vans to distribute products to customers. The fleet consists of some 50 vehicles of varying size with an average cost of some £30 000.

Compliance auditing

Compliance auditing would be concerned with determining:

- Whether the company's systems to control and record distribution costs were operating as laid down by management.
- Whether distribution cost had been properly determined and disclosed in the financial statements.

A typical compliance audit aim would be to determine whether the costs of the fleet of vans were genuine and had been completely and accurately recorded, not whether the costs could have been lower or the company's customers better satisfied.

Efficiency auditing

Efficiency auditing determines whether resources (personnel, property, etc.) are used optimally within the bounds of what is feasible. In Greenburn, the efficiency auditor would go beyond compliance auditing and ask the question: 'Is the fleet of vans being operated as efficiently as possible?' Audit work might be directed towards establishing whether vans were being regularly serviced to keep costs over time to the minimum. The auditor might check whether van routes were planned to reduce unnecessary mileage and to control distribution costs. In other words, the auditor would be more interested in determining whether costs were higher than they should have been. This kind of audit would, however, not be directed towards determining whether a fleet of vans was the best way to meet company objectives.

Effectiveness auditing

Effectiveness auditing determines whether resources are being used to proper effect. Again taking the Greenburn example, the auditor might go beyond efficiency auditing and ask the question: 'Is the ownership of a fleet of vans by the company the best way to achieve the objectives of the organization?' This kind of auditing would consider the costs of alternative distribution policies and the benefits to be derived from them. The auditor would consider whether reduced cost from using third-party distributors would be desirable, bearing in mind that customers might be less well served or that the image of the company might suffer as a result of change in policy.

The auditor might also consider the feasibility of leasing the motor vehicles instead of buying them or purchasing different kinds of vehicles.

Several other terms are also used in the context of internal audit and these we briefly describe below:

- *Operational auditing* is a term used to show that modern internal auditing is concerned with the whole organization and not merely with finance and accounting; consequently it audits operations in general, including production, personnel, advertising, and research and development. Operational auditing encompasses both efficiency and effectiveness auditing.
- *Management auditing* is another term used to describe audit work performed by internal auditors. In many ways management auditing is similar to effectiveness auditing in that the audit aim is to ascertain whether management is acting effectively. Auditors direct attention to the formulation of management objectives and to the extent to which they had been met. The setting of objectives is in itself a means to improve management and auditors would be concerned to see that the management objective-setting process had been properly carried through. Some kinds of management activity can be easily audited. For instance, if management has prepared budgets to control activities the auditor can compare budgeted and actual figures and enquire into the reasons for material differences. To audit a management decision such as a decision to run a loss-making railway line in (say) the north of Scotland is much more difficult because of intangible social and cultural factors that have to be considered.
- In *value for money auditing (VFM)* auditors enquire into the economy, efficiency and effectiveness of the organization and its component parts. Efficiency and effectiveness we have exemplified above. By economy is meant avoidance of unnecessary waste, such as the use of protective clothing for the van drivers instead of high-cost uniforms. VFM auditing goes far beyond the traditional compliance audit, which the majority of statutory audits are. If you refer back to the suggested definition of auditing, you will see that it is somewhat restrictive as we referred to the audit effort being directed to establishing the reliability of information, whereas audit objectives in economy, efficiency and effectiveness auditing may be quite different. In the public sector in the UK, including local authorities and the National Health Service, both external and internal auditors are required to address VFM issues and to report on them to certain stakeholders.

See page 23 in Chapter 1.

- *Evaluation* as traditionally practised has developed along different lines from auditing. Independence is not such an important feature and the evaluator's role is to bring together a number of interested stakeholders to a programme to which resources have been given in an attempt to find a mutually acceptable solution to achieving success. Thus, a programme examined by the National Audit Office (NAO) was one designed to increase the number of jobs in Wales, with a wide range of stakeholders, including the Welsh Office, central government, political parties in Wales, the unemployed in Wales, people interested in the Welsh language and so on. This was a difficult arena for the NAO as they were carrying out a VFM study in a politically charged area. It was not clear whether they were carrying out an audit or an evaluation. However, it may be that 'holding the ring' between various stakeholders will be an important way forward for internal audit (and indeed external auditors in the public sector). We shall say more about this when we discuss participative auditing below.

The distinction between an audit and other forms of evaluation is one taken up by Michael Power in his various writings which we discuss in Chapter 20.

CASE STUDY 15.4

Photocopy costs in an educational institution

You are internal auditor of an educational institution and have been asked to carry out a value for money audit of photocopying costs. Your initial enquiries reveal the following:

- Management informs you that photocopying in the college is carried out on machines rented from the manufacturer and that the cost of photocopying one sheet of A4 paper is 4p per sheet.
- The college also has a print room and official policy is for print runs of more than 20 sheets from a single original to be undertaken by the print room, as print room costs are lower when print runs above 20 are undertaken. This policy was introduced following a study carried out five years previously.

You decide initially to find out if this policy is being adhered to and a visit to the print room during the spring term reveals the following:

- The print room records show that the average print run is 100 and that no run below 20 is accepted.
- A notice was displayed on the door to the print room stating that staff could expect a six-day delay in the processing of print requests.
- You discuss the question of delay with print room staff and are informed that at some times of the academic year, there is a flood of print requests, normally at the start of each term. At other times (in the summer term during the examination period, for instance) the print room can satisfy requests at very short notice.

A visit to one of the teaching departments reveals the following data. (Your request that you should watch the photocopying in progress for one day is acceded to.)

- The department has purchased a photocopying machine from its own budget. You are told by the head of department that the machine had cost £20 000 and that it can copy in reduced and normal size with facilities for collating and stapling and with a variety of options including double-sided copying. The cost per sheet including depreciation is 2.5p per original sheet if normal size and 1.25p per sheet if reduced. Costs are reduced if copies are double sided.
- During the day you noted that the average number of copies made of an original was 25 and that approximately 40 per cent of these were reduced size print.
- On about ten occasions staff members copied more than 100 copies from one original.

ACTIVITY 15.8

Review the above information and suggest matters that would require further investigation. Justify your answer. When you have done this, compare your answer with that in the 'Solutions available to students' section at www.cengage.co.uk/graymanson5.

We do acknowledge that external auditors are extending their work into areas other than compliance auditing. Note also our comments on VFM auditing above.

Our intention in describing the different kinds of audit activity has been to broaden your perspective of auditing. We also want you to recognize that the external auditor must have an understanding of internal audit activity if reliance is to be placed upon internal audit work.

We will now take you through a Case study (Case study 15.5 Barnton plc) which will give us the opportunity to consider a number of important aspects of modern internal auditing.

CASE STUDY 15.5

Barnton plc

Barnton plc is engaged in manufacturing, marketing and distribution of goods and services for companies in the building and engineering industry. Each division of the company is run as a separate subsidiary, but the company also has investments in associated undertakings in which it has significant control. A major activity is construction contract work for the government. The company has an internal audit department that has developed in recent years from being principally concerned with internal control and checking the validity of transactions and balances to operational auditing and close involvement with management decision making. The internal audit department has ten staff composed of the head of internal audit (John Michael), an audit manager, two senior auditors, a computer auditor and five assistant auditors.

The internal audit department reports to the chief executive of the company but all reports are reviewed by the audit committee consisting of three non-executive directors. Apart from this formal review activity, the audit committee has also established informal lines of communication with the head of internal audit and it is made aware on a timely basis of potential audit problems, including significant weaknesses in internal control. The board of directors sees internal audit as an important element of management planning. This seems to be in line with the definition of internal audit set out on page 584, which states that internal audit is designed to add value and improve an organization's operations. John Michael has been head of internal audit for four years and expects to be promoted to senior executive management shortly. He tells you that the internal audit department has placed a number of staff members in senior management posts.

Audits of internal control systems, of subsidiaries prior to consolidation and examination of construction contracts

We suggested above that statutory external audit is classified as compliance auditing. The audits of subsidiaries by Barnton's internal audit department seem to have the specific objective of ensuring that their financial statements may be included in the consolidated financial statements and this kind of auditing may also be classified as compliance auditing. As Barnton is engaged in construction contracts for the government, one objective of the internal auditors might be to ensure that no breach of contract is occurring. Obviously, if government auditors were to discover that contracts had been breached, Barnton might lose future government works. In any event, internal audit is properly classified as compliance auditing in this respect as the objective is to ensure that Barnton is complying with the terms of the contract. If internal audit work includes such matters as examining the effectiveness of group procedures for making estimates for determining contract prices, they will be moving more into an advice role.

Financial auditing, including audits of financial systems at Barnton subsidiaries, periodic joint audits of associated undertakings (with internal auditors of other companies holding a significant interest), and post-completion audits of major capital expenditure projects (directed to completeness and accuracy of records)

We should perhaps not be too pedantic about headings as the audit of systems might be classified as compliance auditing (that the systems as operated comply with expectation) but Barnton internal audit department clearly find it useful to distinguish between financial control systems and other control systems. The audit of financial systems at subsidiaries would underpin the audit of the financial statements of those subsidiaries. The periodic joint audits of associated undertakings is of interest and it might be legitimate to ask if the associated undertakings have their own internal audit departments and to whom each group of auditors report (see below). Regarding post-completion audit of the major capital expenditure projects, typical work carried out by the internal auditors would include ascertaining that the actual recorded income and expenditure figures were genuine, accurate and complete, and also whether there were any significant variations from expectation. Again this kind of audit could just as easily be classified as compliance auditing.

Management auditing, including efficiency and effectiveness of information processing throughout the group and the efficiency and effectiveness of investment appraisal process in the company

This kind of auditing is moving into more difficult areas of efficiency and effectiveness. To be successful these audits require measures of efficiency and effectiveness to be determined. Efficiency generally means that the auditor asks: 'Has this part of the group achieved its objectives at minimum cost – or alternatively – at this input cost have the outputs been optimized?' Barnton appear to have many subsidiaries and types of business and it might be possible for the auditors to compare unit costs of different subsidiaries, provided that outputs are similar. The auditors could then try to determine why some parts of the group are low or high cost. Effectiveness may be a more difficult matter and might mean that the auditors would have to determine users' perceptions of the adequacy and speed of data processing.

The audit of the investment appraisal process is an interesting area. You will know from accounting studies that investment appraisal involves estimating input costs and output benefits of different investment projects and choosing projects with optimum results. What many organizations fail to do is to audit the projects after they have been put into operation (this is why this kind of audit is known as post-audit) to discover if the projected costs and benefits, including allocation of overheads, met expectation. In performing post-audit engagements, auditors are doing more than merely assessing whether costs and benefits met expectation, they are also assessing how effective the investment appraisal process has been with the objective of improving it in the future. Internal auditors might wish to investigate whether there is a proper system for ensuring that *all* potentially viable projects are considered by senior management, rather than being filtered out at a lower level. Incidentally, it appears that Barnton internal auditors carry out this work on their own, whereas some organizations put together a composite team, comprising personnel from head office (finance, production and marketing) and the original development team as well as internal audit. If this were to be the case the audit could be classified as participative auditing (see below).

Participative auditing, including audits of companies prior to acquisition, leading to management decisions to proceed

A composite post-audit team would mean that the internal auditor was participating in a management process. At this point we are far removed from the traditional view of audit, as the internal auditors could hardly be regarded as totally independent, although if properly trained and provided the department takes a strong ethical stance, they may add an element of objectivity to the work of the post-audit team. The same applies to the audits of companies ear-marked for possible acquisition. This kind of audit is about advising management on whether they should buy a company. Of particular interest would be audit work designed to assess how the newly acquired company would fit into the group and whether its costs and income might change as a result of change of ownership. Similar audits might be carried out prior to disposal of part of the group that no longer meets group criteria. If the audit report is the basis of a management decision to buy (or not buy) or to sell (or not sell), internal auditors will be very close to acting as part of the management team.

One-off audits, including audit of funds set up for specific purposes, fraud investigations and other special reviews and projects

Special audits all appear to be audits of special concern to management and will tend to be one-off audits such as investigation of potential or actual fraud. Fraud audits might be instigated after concerns have been voiced by external auditors, on the initiative of the internal auditors themselves or by special request of senior management. As fraud investigations can be costly it might be appropriate for internal auditors to perform this work rather than external auditors. One point worth mentioning is that the very presence of the internal auditors, knowing that they are likely to examine your area of activity, may serve as a deterrent to fraudulent behaviour. In other words the internal auditor (external auditor as well, for that matter) may well serve to deter fraud as well as detecting it. In this connection, internal auditors may be able to show management on a timely basis that controls in certain areas are weak and suggest additional controls to deter and detect fraud.

Now that you have seen the kind of work carried out by the internal auditors at Barnton, we refer you to paragraph A3 of ISA 610 which sets out objectives of the Internal Audit Function:

> The objectives of internal audit functions vary widely and depend on the size and structure of the entity and the requirements of management and, where applicable, those charged with governance. The activities of the internal audit function may include one or more of the following:
>
> - Monitoring of internal control. The internal audit function may be assigned specific responsibility for reviewing controls, monitoring their operation and recommending improvements thereto.
> - Examination of financial and operating information. The internal audit function may be assigned to review the means used to identify, measure, classify and report financial and operating information, and to make specific inquiry into individual items, including detailed testing of transactions, balances and procedures.
> - Review of operating activities. The internal audit function may be assigned to review the economy, efficiency and effectiveness of operating activities, including non-financial activities of an entity.
> - Review of compliance with laws and regulations. The internal audit function may be assigned to review compliance with laws, regulations and other external requirements and with management policies and directives and other internal requirements.
> - Risk management. The internal audit function may assist the organization by identifying and evaluating significant exposures to risk and contributing to the improvement of risk management and control systems.
> - Governance. The internal audit function may assess the governance process in its accomplishment of objectives on ethics and values, performance management and accountability, communicating risk and control information to appropriate areas of the organization and effectiveness of communication among those charged with governance, external and internal auditors, and management

We think that you will agree that the work carried out by internal auditors, such as those at Barnton and suggested above, is very wide-ranging. Their assurance and consulting activity, if properly resourced and supported, is likely to add value and improve an organization's operations. One important factor in enabling them to do that is their independence and objectivity. We have seen in Chapter 3 that independence and objectivity are prerequisites of an effective audit process and we have seen too that these qualities must be fostered and encouraged.

Let us now look at measures designed to make the internal audit function effective.

HOW TO MAKE THE INTERNAL AUDIT FUNCTION EFFECTIVE

Barnton's internal auditors clearly have a wide and demanding remit. In this section we consider how to make the internal audit department effective and suggest that the following factors are important:

- *Support of top management*. This would appear to be the case at Barnton, in view of the large area of activity covered by the department and the value apparently placed on their work. This support should include:
  - (a) the appointment of a good leader to the internal audit department, responsible for ensuring that high standards are maintained.
  - (b) ensuring that the role of internal audit and its powers are well understood within the organization.
  - (c) ensuring that there is a strong ethical culture in the company and the internal audit department. Clearly the head of internal audit would play a vital role in this respect in both the wider company and the internal department itself.
  - (d) ensuring that there are good *communication links with the external auditors.* This is an important factor as good communication links with the external auditor can enhance the status of the internal audit function. We shall see later that effective communication links will help the external auditors to judge whether the work of the internal auditors is likely to be adequate for the purposes of their external audit. Paragraph A4 of ISA 610 goes further and suggests that 'Communication between the external auditor and the internal auditors may be most effective when the internal auditors are free to communicate openly with the external auditors'.

  Internal audit is as useful as management allows it to be. Thus, if internal audit issues reports critical of certain parts of the organization and management takes no action for political reasons, this would tend to undermine the function and reduce its effectiveness. Management may also reduce the role of internal audit by restricting it to compliance auditing or by involving it only in day-to-day checking procedures rather than independent audit work. A decision to combine efficiency auditing, effectiveness auditing and operational auditing generally with compliance auditing would indicate a positive attitude by top management towards internal audit. If internal auditors are able to initiate work without reference to the person(s) to whom they are responsible, this would tend to increase status and effectiveness. To the extent that their recommendations are put into effect, there would be a similar effect. Important in this respect is that it should be known within the entity that management has acted on internal audit recommendations.

We saw in Chapter 7, page 247, that a strong ethical culture is a prerequisite of a good system of internal control.

See paragraph A4 of ISA 610 – bullet point 6.

- *Independence of the internal auditor* from the parts of the organization subject to audit, both in terms of area of work and to whom responsible (that is, physical independence). Thus, if the internal auditor is investigating the efficiency of operations within the accounting department, it would be inappropriate for the auditor to report to the chief accountant (who may be the prime cause of inefficiencies). In recent years audit committees have become an important feature of corporate governance. You will note that Barnton's internal auditors have established useful formal and informal links with the audit committee and that the committee is likely to increase the independence and status of the internal audit department. Note in this respect that ISA 610 suggests that the objectivity of the internal audit function will be enhanced if it has direct access to those charged with governance.

See paragraph A4 of ISA 610. We discuss the role of audit committees in Chapter 18. They have an interest in good lines of communication between internal and external auditors.

- *Appointment of motivated staff with good educational background, combined with continuing education and training.* Internal auditors have to have enquiring mindsets and an ability to communicate well and to get on well with people of widely differing backgrounds. In view of the diverse range of activities in which internal auditors are involved, staff members should possess a suitable range of skills. For instance, if the company is an engineering company you would expect to see staff with an engineering background on the team. Continuing education and training enhance general efficiency and effectiveness of internal audit.

See paragraph A4 of ISA 610 on technical competence.

  We would also expect to see an *appraisal system* that ensures that good work is properly rewarded, including promotion. Paragraph A4 of ISA 610 suggests that those charged with governance should have a role in overseeing employment decisions related to the internal audit function.

  A further important point here is that steps should be taken to ensure high job satisfaction. This might include giving staff the chance to work on more interesting tasks such as making decisions on acquisition of companies and disposal of parts of the organization, even if this might be in a junior capacity initially.

  In the past when internal auditors were concerned principally with compliance auditing there was often a perception of conflict between auditor and auditee. People in organizations often held unfavourable images of internal auditors who tended to have lower job satisfaction than middle level managers and external auditors. Low job satisfaction clearly would be a factor limiting effectiveness particularly if the person being audited makes the auditor feel unwelcome. However, a move from compliance to efficiency and effectiveness auditing causes a shift from an inspection style to an advisory and participative teamwork approach with management. This clearly does not mean that conflict will disappear but the argument is that internal audit would be seen as performing a useful and effective role within the organization. We saw above that participative auditing was an important element of the Barnton internal audit remit. We have already noted that this approach may appear at first sight to conflict with the ideas of independence, but provided the dangers of bias in mental attitude are recognized by auditors it may well lead to greater effectiveness.

- *Steps to ensure that staff behave in a professional way.* This is linked to the previous bullet point, as well-informed and competent auditors with high status will be better able to recognize the dangers of mental dependence, and to recognize the importance of acting with due professional skill. Their training should include showing that maintaining an independent state of mind adds to effectiveness even where the auditor is involved in participative auditing. Independence in mental attitude is difficult to measure but it is clear from our discussions in Chapters 2 and 3 that it is a critical aspect of auditor effectiveness, whether internal or external. Internal auditors are often members of professional accounting bodies, that expect their members to develop their professionalism and to behave with honesty and integrity in matters pertaining to their work. The Institute of Internal Auditors promotes the qualification of 'Internal Auditor' and operates an examination scheme leading to qualification as an internal auditor. One would expect membership of professional bodies to be a factor enhancing the status of internal auditors.

You may refer again to paragraph A4 of ISA 610.

ACTIVITY 15.9

You will have noted that John Michael, the head of internal audit at Barnton, expects to be promoted to senior executive management shortly and that the company appears to draw a number of its senior staff from the internal audit department.

What do you think about this apparent policy? Do you think that it shows that the internal audit department is staffed by high-quality people and that it will enhance the status and effectiveness of internal audit?

The fact that senior management staff have come up through the internal audit department does suggest that the department is staffed by high-quality personnel. However, we have to ask whether Barnton is putting individuals identified as potential top managers into the internal audit department for them to learn how the business operates. If this is the case and after a relatively short period of time they are moved into managerial roles, this may have a detrimental effect on the internal audit department for at least two reasons:

- They will only be a short time in the department before moving on and internal audit may not receive much benefit from them, with a possible adverse effect on remaining staff morale.
- Short-stay staff, knowing that they will soon be part of the management team, may feel that they should not offend future colleagues with a detrimental effect on their independence.

This is the so-called 'short-stay syndrome' and is likely to weaken the internal audit function because it is seen as a way of training managers rather than seeing it as an important function in its own right. It is, however, important that internal auditors are considered for promotion within the wider organization from a staff morale point of view. It should be made clear to the directors though that individuals joining the internal audit department should prove themselves in the audit function and stay long enough to make a good contribution to the function. While noting the possible detrimental effect of the 'short-stay syndrome', provided that it is known that staff must prove their mettle in the department before being promoted elsewhere, the potential for promotion will add to staff morale among internal auditors.

RELIANCE ON INTERNAL AUDIT BY THE EXTERNAL AUDITOR

We have briefly described the sort of work carried out by internal audit and the factors enhancing or detracting from its effectiveness, as we wished you to understand the nature and role of the function before we considered the extent to which external audit may rely upon it. You should refer to ISA 610 – *Using the work of internal auditors*, as you read what we have to say here.

Internal audit as an element of internal control

In our discussion of internal audit above we suggested that it could provide a dynamic role within organizations provided the function had been properly established. This is clearly the case at Barnton, despite our doubts about the short-stay syndrome. External auditors accept that the scope of internal audit is expanding but tend to concentrate on its internal control aspect. Bearing in mind that external auditors are interested in the soundness of internal control, it is clear that they will be interested in the internal control role of internal audit. The argument is that, because of the similarity of certain of their objectives, the external auditor may be able to rely upon the work of the internal auditor.

Planning the extent of reliance on internal audit

Assessment of effectiveness of internal audit

We have already discussed above the general factors used to judge the effectiveness of the internal audit function. Clearly the external auditors will not wish to use the work of the internal audit function if they have doubts about the objectivity, competence and the exercise of due professional care by the internal auditors. However, before deciding to use the work of the internal auditors, some specific factors have to be considered

Extent of reliance

The auditor's decision as to whether reliance should be placed upon the work of the internal auditor is a scope decision. An internal audit function lacking independence or with staff of a low level of competence would represent a weak element in the system of internal control. Less reliance would therefore be placed upon it.

As a general rule the external auditor should audit all material matters in the financial statements, particularly where there is significant risk of misstatement. This does not mean that no reliance should be placed on internal audit in these circumstances, providing external auditor involvement is sufficient to enable them to form conclusions with certainty. For instance, if a company holds inventories in ten locations, internal audit staff might observe the count in two locations, provided the external auditor observed sufficient inventory counts in other locations.

If external auditors decide to place reliance on some aspects of internal audit work, they should agree the timing and extent of the work with the chief internal auditor and record the decision (with reasons) in the audit files. It is usual for internal audit departments to plan their audit year in advance of the commencement of the financial year. Thus, for the year ending 31 December 2012, the internal audit plan might be complete by 30 September 2011 and the external auditor should arrange to meet the chief internal auditor about then. However, it would be important not only to have periodic meetings with internal auditors, but to review internal audit reports to ensure that they are kept up to date on important developments. Paragraph 6 (b) of ISA 610 states in this connection that an objective is: 'If using the specific work of the internal auditors, to determine whether that work is adequate for the purposes of the audit.' We discuss this matter immediately below.

Specific work of the internal auditors

The external auditors may use the work of internal auditors in obtaining evidence in respect of specific assertions relating to the financial statements. If they are to do this the external auditors must first consider the risks of material misstatement at the assertion level for the particular classes of transactions, account balances and disclosures. They would then consider what kind of work the internal auditors were going to perform in the area, and the degree of subjectivity involved in evaluating the audit evidence.

See paragraph 10 of ISA 610.

Let us consider two scenarios:

1 The internal auditors have been asked by management to form a view on the validity of the amount shown in the financial statements in respect of construction contracts. During their work they considered the appropriateness of the amounts of profit and loss taken up in the statements in respect of those contracts.

2 The internal auditors have performed work on cut-off at the year-end date, including testing that goods received before the year-end had been included in inventory, if not used or sold, and in recorded purchases.

ACTIVITY 15.10

The above internal audit work has clearly been done in respect of matters of great interest to the external auditors. To what extent would it be appropriate for the external auditors to use their work?

You will know from our discussion of construction contracts in Chapter 13 that the degree of risk and subjectivity in respect of construction contracts is very high. This is particularly the case of the amounts of profit or loss on contracts to be taken up in the financial statements. The external auditors might have discussed the methodology that the internal auditors would use in performing the work on construction contracts (see paragraph A5 of ISA 610) and subsequently discuss the results of their work with them and examine their working schedules. However, the area is so risky and subjective that the external auditors would carry out their own extensive tests.

As regards scenario 2 on purchases and inventory cut-off, although this matter is important, it does not carry the same degree of risk and subjectivity as the case of construction contracts. The external auditors might well rely quite heavily on the work of the internal auditors, once they were satisfied that the work was being properly performed. They might restrict their own tests to testing a sample of the tests that the internal auditors have performed. In this connection we would ask you to refer to paragraphs 11, 12 and A6 of ISA 610.

Documentation of effectiveness

See paragraph 13 of ISA 610.

In Chapter 6 we discussed audit evidence at length. Naturally, if external auditors decide to rely upon evidence collected by internal audit the assessment and conclusions with regard to these matters should be fully documented in the audit files.

The responsibility of the external auditor when relying upon the work of internal audit

When auditors rely on other specialists they still have full responsibility for the audit opinion. Thus, if external auditors decide to rely on the work of internal audit, it does not take away any responsibility for the audit opinion and it is for the external auditor to judge extent of reliance on the work of internal audit. Paragraph 4 of ISA 610 states:

> Irrespective of the degree of autonomy and objectivity of the internal audit function, such function is not independent of the entity as is required of the external auditor when expressing an opinion on financial statements. The external auditor has sole responsibility for the audit opinion expressed, and that responsibility is not reduced by the external auditor's use of the work of the internal auditors.

OUTSOURCING OF INTERNAL AUDIT WORK

A recent phenomenon has been the use of professional audit firms to perform internal audit work, a form of outsourcing. Organizations might feel that the cost of setting up and maintaining an internal audit function of high quality is excessive. This is prompting some organizations to employ professional firms who possess the necessary expertise and have the structures to provide an audit function whether external or internal. Whether professional firms will be effective in providing the wide range of services demanded of modern internal auditors remains to be seen.

Apart from this latter point, you should note that the performance of internal audit work by the external auditors is very controversial. In the United States a list of services (issued by SEC) which cannot be provided by a company's auditors includes internal audit functions. You should note too that the ICAS Working Group on Non-Audit Services came to the conclusion that the provision of internal audit services by external auditors to their listed clients should be specially approved by the audit committee. Indeed, the Working Group's report reproduced an extract from Taylor Wimpey's 2008 report stating that the audit committee had determined that internal audit outsourcing services should not be undertaken by the (external) auditors

NOTE FOR READERS IN THE UK AND IRELAND

For listed companies in the UK and Ireland, 'The Combined Code on Corporate Governance', published by the FRC) contains guidance to assist company boards in making suitable arrangements for their audit committees.

Paragraph A6-1 concerns arrangements the external auditor should make when obtaining direct assistance from individuals from the internal audit function. For instance, an internal auditor might take part in the inventory count observation, reporting direct to the external auditor in charge of the observation.

We discuss the Combined Code on Corporate Governance in detail in Chapter 18.

We have included this section on internal audit as we believe that you should understand the similarities and differences between external and internal audit. The above discussion should have shown you that auditing has many facets, that internal auditing particularly and external auditing to some extent is moving into areas much broader in scope than traditional compliance auditing and that external audit can use the work of internal audit provided that its work is relevant and reliable and that internal auditors have retained their independence, despite their close association with management.

Ideally, the external auditor should be in close touch with internal audit throughout the audit year and audit committees can be useful vehicles for formalizing this contact.

In Case study 15.6 we provide you with some information about the internal audit department at Troston plc to give you some experience in evaluating internal audit.

CASE STUDY 15.6

Internal audit at Troston plc

The company is already known to you from Activity 7.7 in Chapter 7. We set out below details of the company's internal audit department.

Staffing

Head of internal audit, John Hazely, is an ICAEW member and has been head of department for some five years. Prior to that he had been with a number of other departments in the company, including accounting and finance. He has five staff members in his department:

- Andrew Howgill, a recently qualified certified accountant who joined the company three months previously.
- Janet Greensett, a computer expert who has been in the department for some five years. She has been called on by Troston to give advice to the IT committee in respect of new developments and significant changes to existing computer applications.
- Alex Gayle and Derek Carlton, two experienced but professionally unqualified auditors, members of the department for some eight years.
- Anthony Newby, a graduate of a North of England university, two years with the company and one year with internal audit. He is shortly to join the production control department, as assistant to the head of that department. He is to be replaced by a recently appointed graduate, Richard Watson.

Reporting responsibility

John Hazely reports to the finance director who also has the financial accounting, management and costing and finance departments under his control. Internal audit reports are prepared at the end of each assignment. The report is reviewed in each case by

FIGURE 15.1 Position of the Troston plc internal audit department within the organization

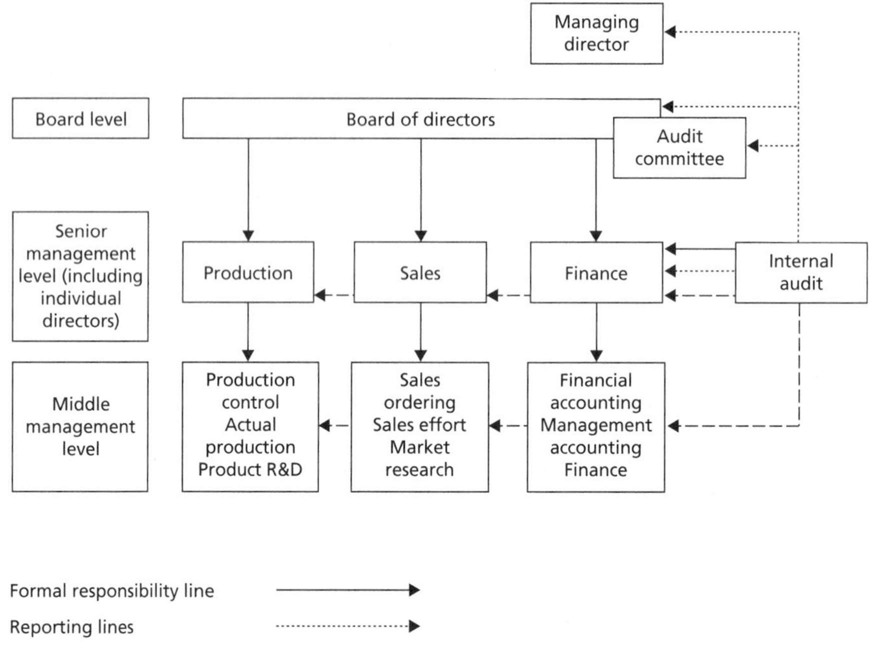

John Hazely. Comments by the head of the department subject to audit are incorporated into the report in each case. Copies of reports are sent to each member of the board of directors and to the appropriate department head.

Copies are also sent to the chairperson of the audit committee. The audit committee was formed three years ago and comprises three non-executive directors, all of whom are executive directors of other companies. It is normal practice for members of the audit committee to meet the head of internal audit and other audit staff to discuss reports that they believe are of particular importance. The position in the organization of internal audit is shown in Figure 15.1.

Audit task as planned

For the year to 30 June 2011 the internal audit head has drawn up the following broad plan. (In practice, the plan would be detailed, showing allocation of work to individual staff members and the dates on which the work would be performed.)

- Accounting and finance:
  - (a) Production wages.
  - (b) Sales and related trade receivables.
  - (c) Purchase and related trade payables.
  - (d) Non-current assets and depreciation.
- Production (at request of production director):
  - (a) Efficiency of the production process.
  - (b) Appropriateness of allocation of production costs to products.
  - (c) Effectiveness of production control department.
- Computer operations:
  - (a) Review of systems with particular attention to completeness and adequacy of documentation of new developments.
  - (b) Participation in new development of production wages system.
  - (c) Review of production costs system in conjunction with production work above.
- Personnel, including review of staff training and other measures to increase staff productivity.
- Sales and market research.
  - (a) Market research VFM study
  - (b) Validity of sales statistics (on initiative of internal audit).
  - (c) Sales department VFM study (completion of work started last year).

- Inventory control
  - (a) Inventory records completeness and accuracy.
  - (b) Inventory count observations (including year-end counts in conjunction with external auditors).
- Research and development
  - (a) Review of activity (on initiative of internal audit – as the basis for further in depth studies).

Coordination with external auditors

The detailed plan is discussed annually with the external audit manager and amendments made to allow coordination with the work of the externals.

Progress reports

John Hazely prepares a progress report for the board at six-monthly intervals. This report is given to the external auditors and the manager in charge of the external audit assignment meets with the internal audit head to discuss it shortly after it has been prepared. On occasion the external auditor's advice is sought on the contents of the report.

Required

Review the description of the internal audit department at Troston Ltd and note matters which you believe might add to or detract from its effectiveness. Consider also if the work of internal audit could be extended to make it more useful.

When you have done this, compare your answer with that in the 'Solutions available to students' section at www.cengage.co.uk/graymanson5.

AUDITING IN THE PUBLIC SECTOR

The public sector employs a large number of people throughout the world and provides services of considerable significance. In the UK and Ireland there are a number of bodies with specific responsibility for auditing in the public sector, including the National Audit Office (NAO), responsible for the audit of central government bodies in the UK, The Audit Commission for Local Authorities and the National Health Service in England, Audit Scotland, providing services to the Auditor General for Scotland, and the Accounts Commission for Scotland (similar to the Audit Commission in England).

Other bodies responsible for audit of the public sector in the UK and Ireland include The Wales Audit Office, The Northern Ireland Audit Office, Office of The Comptroller and Auditor General (Republic of Ireland).and Local Government Audit Service (Republic of Ireland).

These bodies may carry out audits on their own behalf but private sector firms are also engaged in public sector audit. The kind of work carried out by auditors of the public sector includes:

- *Financial audits*, to determine if the published financial statements give a true and fair view.
- *Legality audits,* to determine if an authority is allowed to engage in a particular activity. There have been cases, for instance, where local authorities have engaged in interests rate swaps, subsequently found by the court to be illegal.
- *Regularity audits*, to determine if monies have been spent as elected representatives intended. For instance, if councillors of local authorities vote to expend funds on the provision of local sports facilities, have they been so spent?
- *Systems examinations*, to determine that an authority or National Health Service body has good systems in place. This would be similar to the kind of systems examination we have already discussed. The auditor would wish to ascertain, among other things, that systems for recording transactions and balances and for monitoring activities were adequate.

- *Probity audits*, to determine if public monies were well cared for and that the possibility of fraud and other irregularities were minimized, that travel claims, for instance were well supported, that purchasing officers' decisions on placing of orders were properly based and so on.
- *Value for money audits.* We mentioned above that in the local authorities and the National Health Service, external auditors are required to address VFM issues and to report on them to certain stakeholders. Bodies controlling public sector audits such as The Audit Commission in England and Wales and Audit Scotland carry out VFM studies, the results of which are communicated to local authorities and their auditors with the objective of making good practice more widely known. Basically VFM audits would be directed to determining if resources are being used economically, efficiently and effectively.
- *Performance audits*, directed to ascertaining whether authorities have proper procedures for specifying and measuring their own performance. For instance, are the published statements about the cleanliness of streets and the measures adopted to keep them clean, valid?

In the Summer of 2010 the government announced that the Audit Commission in England and Wales was to be abolished. Students should keep an eye open for developments in the area.

Apart from external audit, internal auditors also have an important role in the public sector and many of the audited bodies also have audit committees with an interest in ensuring that the total audit function, internal and external, is both efficient and effective.

It is worth noting at this point that neither external nor internal auditors are allowed to question matters of policy. However, this is a very difficult area and if a policy is patently not working, auditors may find themselves moving dangerously close to criticizing policy.

Management letters in the public sector

In Chapter 10 (see page 378) we discussed the role of the management letter as required by ISA 265 in bringing deficiencies in internal control to the attention of management and those charged with governance. Management letters are also issued by external auditors of public sector bodies, but they are much more extensive than management letters in the private sector, containing as they do comments and recommendations covering all or many of the areas referred to above under italicized headings. They contain a wealth of detail about the financial state of an authority, on how well the authority is managed and on the audit process itself. In this respect we refer you to paragraph A27 of ISA 265, which states, among other things:

> Legislation may require public sector auditors to report on broader internal control-related matters than the deficiencies in internal control required to be communicated by this ISA, for example, controls related to compliance with legislative authorities, regulations, or provisions of contracts or grant agreements.

We might mention, however, that a study carried out by Bowerman and Gray in 1999 concluded that management letters issued by external auditors of local authorities in England could be made more useful. A major conclusion of the report was that the local authority management letter has the potential to strengthen accountability to back-bench members and to the

'Local Government Management Letters', ACCA Occasional Research Paper No. 27, Bowerman and Gray, 1999.

public, but that it would not do so if it was not made available to a wider group of interested parties.

Audit committees in the public sector

A further important matter is that audit committees play an important role in public sector bodies. A report issued by CIPFA in Edinburgh in 2004 considered the role of audit committees in Scottish local government. The main audit committee principles identified in the report were:

1 *The control environment*: Independent assurance of the adequacy of the risk management framework and the associated control environment within the authority;

   Suggested good practice was as follows:

   Consideration of internal audit plan and strategy; Monitoring of achievement of the internal audit plan; Review of audit reports, main issues arising and implementation of recommendations; Ensuring that risk assessment has been carried out by the head of internal audit; Review of annual report and assurance statement to committee from the head of internal audit; Existence of strong/effective relationship between external audit, inspection agencies and internal audit; Ensuring that the value of the audit process is actively promoted.

2 *Risk related performance*: Independent scrutiny of the authority's financial and non-financial performance to the extent that it affects the authority's exposure to risk and weakens the control environment; and

   Suggested good practice was as follows:

   Consideration of the effectiveness of the corporate risk assessment process; Consideration of significant risk related performance issues raised by auditors or other inspectors; Monitoring of implementation of improvement action plans.

3 *Annual accounts and the external auditor;* Assurance that any issues arising from the process of drawing up, auditing and certifying the authority's annual accounts are properly dealt with.

   Suggested good practice was as follows:

   Review of audit certificate and consideration of matters arising from audit; Consideration of annual report to members from external auditor and monitoring the implementation of agreed action plans; Consideration of external audit reports, main issues arising and implementation of recommendations.

In 2008 the Scottish Government published an Audit Committee Handbook which also contains good practice principles, some of which are similar to those mentioned in the CIPFA report:

Principle 1: the role of the audit committee: The Audit Committee should support the Board and Accountable Officer by reviewing the comprehensiveness of assurances in meeting the assurance needs of the Board and Accountable Officer, and reviewing the reliability and integrity of these assurances.

Principle 2: membership, independence, objectivity and understanding: The Audit Committee should be independent and objective; in addition each member should have a good understanding of the objectives and priorities of the organization and of their role as an audit committee member.

Principle 3: skills: The Audit Committee should own corporately an appropriate skills mix to allow it to carry out its overall function.

Principle 4: scope of work: The scope of the Audit Committee's work should be defined in its Terms of Reference, and encompass all the assurance needs of the Board and Accountable Officer. Within this, the Audit Committee should have particular engagement with the work of Internal Audit, the work of the External Auditor, and Financial Reporting issues.

Principle 5: communication: The Audit Committee should ensure it has effective communication with the Board and Accountable Officer, the Head of Internal Audit, the External Auditor and other stakeholders. In addition, the role of the Chair and provision of appropriate secretariat support are important elements in achieving Audit Committee effectiveness.

References in the ISAs to the public sector

The ISAs recognize that the organizations in the public sector are often different from those in the private sector and many of them contain paragraphs to highlight the differences. To give you a flavour of the considerations relevant to the public sector, we set out paragraphs from selected ISAs below:

> ISA 200 – Overall objectives of the independent auditor and the conduct of an audit in accordance with International Standards on Auditing (paragraph A57): The ISAs are relevant to engagements in the public sector. The public sector auditor's responsibilities, however, may be affected by the audit mandate, or by obligations on public sector entities arising from law, regulation or other authority (such as ministerial directives, government policy requirements, or resolutions of the legislature), which may encompass a broader scope than an audit of financial statements in accordance with the ISAs. These additional responsibilities are not dealt with in the ISAs. They may be dealt with in the pronouncements of the International Organization of Supreme Audit Institutions or national standard setters, or in guidance developed by government audit agencies.
>
> ISA 220 – Agreeing the terms of audit engagements (paragraph A30): In the public sector, a statutorily appointed auditor (for example, an Auditor General, or other suitably qualified person appointed on behalf of the Auditor General), may act in a role equivalent to that of engagement partner with overall responsibility for public sector audits. In such circumstances, where applicable, the selection of the engagement quality control reviewer includes consideration of the need for independence from the audited entity and the ability of the engagement quality control reviewer to provide an objective evaluation.
>
> ISA 265 – Communicating deficiencies in internal control to those charged with governance and management (paragraph A27): Public sector auditors may have additional responsibilities to communicate deficiencies in internal control that the auditor has identified during the audit, in ways, at a level of detail and to parties not envisaged in this ISA. For example, significant deficiencies may have to be communicated to the legislature or other governing body. Law, regulation or other authority may also mandate that public sector auditors report deficiencies in internal control, irrespective of the significance of the potential effects of those deficiencies.

> ISA 315 – Identifying and assessing the risks of material misstatement through understanding the entity and its environment (paragraph A65): Public sector auditors often have additional responsibilities with respect to internal control, for example to report on compliance with an established code of practice. Public sector auditors can also have responsibilities to report on compliance with law, regulation or other authority. As a result, their review of internal control may be broader and more detailed.
>
> ISA 520 – Analytical procedures (paragraph A11): The relationships between individual financial statement items traditionally considered in the audit of business entities may not always be relevant in the audit of governments or other non-business public sector entities; for example, in many public sector entities there may be little direct relationship between revenue and expenditure. In addition, because expenditure on the acquisition of assets may not be capitalized, there may be no relationship between expenditures on, for example, inventories and fixed assets and the amount of those assets reported in the financial statements. Also, industry data or statistics for comparative purposes may not be available in the public sector. However, other relationships may be relevant, for example, variations in the cost per kilometer of road construction or the number of vehicles acquired compared with vehicles retired.

We have only been able to give you a brief look at the audit of bodies in the public sector., which really needs a whole book to do it justice. However, the public sector does provide different challenges and opportunities for the auditor and it might be well for you to consider whether the private sector has much to learn from it.

Summary

In the first part of this chapter we discussed assurance engagements and considered the various characteristics that they possess, basing our analysis on the International Framework for Assurance Engagements. We also addressed the degree of assurance that can be given by practitioners carrying out assurance engagements, ranging from 'no assurance' to 'limited assurance' and 'reasonable assurance'. We drew a distinction between reasonable assurance and limited assurance engagements and suggested levels of risk and suitable forms of report for each. We also suggested reasons for the increasing provision of assurance services by audit firms.

In the second part of this chapter we introduced you to a definition of internal audit and discussed the factors leading to its effectiveness. To aid your understanding of internal audit we discussed typical work carried out by the function and showed that it covers compliance, efficiency and effectiveness auditing. We used the Barnton Case to show the kind of work an internal audit department performs in practice and the reporting and responsibility lines of the head of internal audit, including those to the audit committee. We considered the factors the external auditor should take into account in deciding whether the work of the internal auditor could be relied upon.

Finally, we considered the special features of auditing in the public sector.

Key points of the chapter

- Standard audit reports give 'reasonable assurance that financial statements are free from material misstatement'. Review and other reports give a lower level of assurance', using a negative expression of opinion because evidence gathering is limited.
- An assurance engagement is: 'an engagement in which a practitioner expresses a conclusion designed to enhance the degree of confidence that intended users other than the responsible party can have about

the outcome of the evaluation or measurement of a subject matter (subject matter information) against criteria'.

- The main difference between an assurance and a direct reporting engagement is that in the former a responsible party makes an assertion on which the practitioner reports, whereas in the latter, the practitioner directly performs the evaluation or measurement of the subject matter, and then reports.
- Five elements of an assurance engagement are: (1) three-part relationship involving a practitioner, responsible party and intended users; (2) appropriate subject matter; (3) suitable criteria; (4) sufficient appropriate evidence; (5) the written assurance report giving reasonable assurance or limited assurance.
- Assurance might be given on: (a) effectiveness of local authority programmes; (b) systems and processes; (c) corporate governance issues; (d) environmental matters; (e) compliance with legislation; (f) compliance with contractual terms. The subject matter information might be performance indicators or assertions by management about effectiveness or compliance.
- Parties other than external auditors can provide useful degrees of assurance to users.
- The responsible party is the person(s) responsible for the subject matter information and/or the subject matter and may be one of the users, but cannot be the only one.
- Characteristics of suitable criteria are: relevance, completeness, reliability, neutrality and understandability.
- Amount and quality of evidence determines conclusions practitioners can draw and the report they can issue.
- Basic elements of assurance report: (a) title; (b) addressee; (c) identification and description of subject matter information and subject matter; (d) identification of criteria; (e) description of inherent or significant limitation; (f) a statement restricting use of the assurance report; (g) statement to identify responsible party and to describe responsible party's and practitioner's responsibilities; (h) statement that the engagement was performed in accordance with ISAEs.
- Reports may give different levels of assurance, ranging from no assurance to positive assurance.
- Before accepting an assurance engagement consider: (a) relevant ethical requirements; (b) whether the engagement has: (i) appropriate subject matter; (ii) suitable criteria available to intended users; (iii) availability of sufficient appropriate evidence to support the desired conclusion; (iv) practitioners' conclusion that will be contained in a written report; (v) rational purpose for the engagement. Letter of engagement should be obtained.
- Assurance engagements have assumed greater importance, partly as a result of the business risk approach to auditing.
- An important feature of internal audit is its independence from day-to-day management, but the auditor has to decide if it is truly independent.
- Internal auditing is an independent, objective assurance and consulting activity designed to add value and improve an organization's operations. It helps an organization accomplish its objectives by bringing a systematic, disciplined approach to evaluate and improve the effectiveness of risk management, control, and governance processes. (IIA – 1999)
- Types of internal audit include compliance, efficiency and effectiveness auditing, Value for money auditing
- Evaluation has developed along different lines from auditing. Independence is not such an important feature and the evaluator's role is to bring together a number of interested stakeholders to find a mutually acceptable solution.
- ISA 610 notes that the objectives of internal audit functions vary widely and depend on the size and structure of the entity and the requirements of management and those charged with governance. The activities of the internal audit function may include: (a) monitoring of internal control; (b) examination of financial and operating information; (c) review of operating activities; (d) review of compliance with laws and regulations; (e) risk management; (f) governance.
- Effectiveness of the internal audit function depends on (1) support of top management, including (a) the appointment of a good internal audit leader; (b) ensuring role of internal audit and its powers are well understood within the organization; (c) ensuring there is a strong ethical culture in the company and the internal audit department; (d) ensuring that there are good communication links with the external auditors. (2) independence of the internal auditor from the parts of the organization subject to audit. (3) appointment of motivated staff with good educational background, combined with continuing education and training; (4) appraisal system and steps to ensure high job satisfaction; (5) steps to ensure that staff behave in a professional way; (6) avoidance of short-stay syndrome.
- In planning the extent of reliance on internal audit the external auditor considers the general effectiveness of internal audit
- The external auditor should audit all material matters in the financial statements particularly where there is significant risk of misstatement.
- If external auditors decide to place reliance on internal audit work they should agree the timing and

extent of the work with the chief internal auditor and record the decision (with reasons) in the audit files. They should determine whether that work is adequate for the purposes of the audit.

- In using the work of internal auditors in respect of specific assertions, external auditors consider the risks of material misstatement at the assertion level. They also consider the degree of subjectivity involved in evaluating the audit evidence.
- If external auditors decide to rely upon evidence collected by internal audit the assessment and conclusions should be fully documented in the audit files.
- Reliance on internal audit does not take away any responsibility for the audit opinion.
- A recent phenomenon has been outsourcing of internal audit to external auditors, but this is very controversial and in some jurisdictions it is banned. In the UK and Ireland audit committees may determine that internal audit outsourcing services should not be undertaken by the external auditors.
- There are many different bodies throughout the world responsible for audit of the public sector.
- Auditing in the public sector includes: financial audits, legality audits, regularity audit, systems examinations, probity audits, value for money audits and performance audits.
- Management letters issued by external auditors of public sector bodies, are more extensive than private sector management letters, containing a wealth of detail about the financial state of an authority, on how well the authority is managed and on the audit process itself.
- The main principles of audit committees in the public sector authorities are: 1. Independent assurance of the adequacy of the risk management framework and the associated control environment; 2. Independent scrutiny of financial and non-financial performance to the extent that it affects exposure to risk and weakens the control environment; 3. Assurance that any issues arising from the process of drawing up, auditing and certifying the annual accounts are properly dealt with.
- other identified principles relate to the role, membership, independence, objectivity and understanding of audit committees. Also, appropriate mix of skills of audit committee members, scope of work, and communication with stakeholders.
- Many ISAs contain considerations relating to the public sector.

Further reading

Roberts, S. and Pollitt, C. (1994) 'Audit or Evaluation? A National Audit Office VFM Study', *Public Administration*, 72: 527–49.

The ISA in the area is ISA 610 – *Using the work of internal auditors*.

We have also referred in the text to the International Framework for Assurance Engagements and ISAE 3000 – Assurance engagements other than audits or reviews of historical financial information, issued by IAASB. There is currently no UK or Irish statement on assurance engagements.

J.P. Percy saw assurance services as important to the future of the auditing profession in Percy, J.P. (1999) 'Assurance Services – Visions for the Future', *International Journal of Auditing* 3: 81–7.

'Local Government Management Letters', ACCA Occasional Research Paper No. 27, Bowerman and Gray, 1999.

Selim, G. Woodward, S. and Allegrini, M. (2009) 'Internal Auditing and Consulting Practice: A Comparison between UK/Ireland and Italy', *Journal of International Auditing* 13(1): 9–25.

Spira, L.F. and Page, M. (2003) 'Risk management: The reinvention of internal control and the changing role of internal audit Accounting', *Auditing and Accountability Journal* 16(4): 640–61.

'The Provision of Non-Audit Services by Audit Firms to their Listed Audit Clients, Report by a Working Group established by the Institute of Chartered Accountants of Scotland ', ICAS, January 2010.

Self-assessment questions (solutions available to students)

15.1 This question is placed within the text (Case study 15.4: Photocopy costs in an educational institution).

15.2 This question is placed within the text (Case study 15.6: Internal audit at Troston plc).

15.3 The information on page 606 is taken from a public notice displayed at Billowness Beach, Anstruther, Fife, Scotland:

ENCAMS Seaside Awards

A beach may fly a Seaside Award Flag when it meets specific criteria for management and cleanliness and the bathing water reaches the overall legal minimum microbiological standards the previous year. The Seaside Award which is only valid for one year recognizes two categories of beach:

Resort beaches
have a range of facilities including supervisors, first aid, toilets and easy access for all. They restrict dogs from the main section of the beach during the season. The flag is flown when all 29 of the criteria are being met.

Rural beaches
are quieter and are often more remote than resort beaches. They will not have the same range of facilities as resort beaches and may allow dogs. The flag is flown when all 13 of the criteria are being met.

Billowness Anstruther
Fife Council

Rural category Seaside Award 2003
This beach has reached the standards necessary for this award of distinction.
It fulfils 13 criteria under the following general headings:

- water quality
- management
- safety
- cleanliness
- information.

Information
This beach operator cares for the coastal environment. Please help look after this beach and the surrounding environment by disposing of your rubbish carefully, cleaning up after your dog and observing the Waterside Code.

Tourist information	Fife Council
St Andrews	Community Services

Regular feedback is vital to check and maintain standards. Please contact the beach operator immediately if you discover a problem. For further information about the Seaside Awards, or to send your comments about this beach please contact ENCAMS Seaside Awards office, Norwich.

Management and cleanliness
Dogs
Dogs may be banned from certain areas of this beach from May 1 to September 30. Special bins are provided for dog refuse on all adjacent areas where dogs should be kept on a leash at all times

Litter
Litter bins are provided at regular intervals along the seafront. PLEASE DISPOSE OF YOUR LITTER CAREFULLY.

Vehicles
Vehicles are not permitted on this beach without authorization from the local authority.

Watercraft
Watercraft users should refer to the map for appropriate zoning.

Safety
Lifeguards
Lifeguard facilities are available from Billowness (no further information given).

First Aid
First Aid facilities are available from Billowness (no further information given).

Hazards
To keep your family safe, follow the Water Safety Code:
Beware of the dangers – rip tides, offshore winds, breakwaters, pipes, rocks.
Follow advice – look out for signs and listen to the lifeguard.
Never swim alone or after food or alcohol.
Take note of the following hazards (None listed).

Flags

- Red: Danger no bathing
- Orange and Yellow: area patrolled by lifeguards
- Dark green and light green: surfing area
- No inflatables

Contact telephone numbers – for doctor, hospital, police, coastguard, veterinary surgeon, beach cleaning, head of community services, dog warden, area team leader, area supervisor, ranger service, training officer.

Bathing water quality		Definitions
13 May 2003 5 June 2003 10 June 2003 18 June 2003 23 June 2003 2 July 2003 8 July 2003 11 July 2003	Poor standard Excellent standard Good standard Excellent standard Excellent standard Excellent standard Excellent standard Excellent standard	Excellent standard: the sample met European Union Guideline Standards: less or equal to 500 colliforms per 100 ml of water or 100 faecal colliforms per 100 ml of water. Good standard: the sample met European Mandatory Standards: less or equal to 10 000 colliforms per 100 ml of water or 2 000 faecal colliforms per 100 ml of water. Poor standard: the sample failed to meet European Mandatory Standards.
Year 2000 Year 2001 Year 2002	Excellent standard Excellent standard Excellent standard	Excellent standard: At least 80% of samples were excellent and at least 90% of samples met a standard of 100 streptococci per 100 ml. Good standard: At least 95% of samples are good or excellent. Poor: The good or excellent yearly standards were not met

Tests are performed by the Scottish Environment Protection Agency (SEPA), Edinburgh Office, Clearwater House, Heriot Watt Research Park, Riccarton, Edinburgh. SEPA is an independent body responsible to the Scottish Executive (of the Scottish Parliament).

The map of Billowness indicates the position of toilets, life saving equipment, disabled access, public telephone, litter bins, dog waste bins.

More information and historical data about this beach can be found at www.sepa.org.uk

Required:

Examine the information contained in this notice and

(a) identify the following:
   (i) the person or body exercising the role of practitioner
   (ii) responsible party
   (iii) intended users
   (iv) subject matter
   (v) criteria
   (vi) report of practitioner.

(b) State whether a positive or negative conclusion has been given.

(c) State whether you think that the subject matter provided by the responsible party is of value to the intended users. Do you think that the report provided by the independent third party will have enhanced the confidence of the intended users in the subject matter?

Self-assessment questions (solutions available to tutors)

15.4 Consider the truth or falsity of the following statements:

(a) The same standards of independence need not be applied in assurance engagements as in the statutory audit of financial statements.

(b) A review engagement results in a conclusion in the assurance report that gives limited assurance.

(c) An assurance engagement need only have two parties involved – the practitioner and the responsible party.

(d) If criteria is said to be complete, this means that the intended user will be able to rely on the subject matter of the assurance report

(e) A conclusion in an assurance report that takes the form of a negative form of expression is of little value to the intended user.

15.5 You are a member of an internal audit department and have been asked the following questions by an audit assistant:

(a) Why is it that we check all purchases invoices daily to goods received notes and purchase orders when the definition of internal audit states that internal audit is an appraisal function?

(b) The production director has asked internal audit to investigate the high incidence of poor-quality steel used in the production process. Is this really part of our work, can we do it and how do we go about it?

(c) Why is it that the external auditors are allowed to look at our working papers but we are not allowed to look at theirs?

(d) Some management consultants have been appointed by the company to review and report on the effectiveness of the research and development programme. Are they auditors, and, if so, why does the internal audit department not do this work?

15.6 Your firm has been external auditor of Elgol plc for some years. Elgol has an internal audit department, engaged in both compliance and operational auditing. You have a high opinion of the quality of internal audit work and have established a good relationship with John MacLean, the head of internal audit. He has asked you to give a talk to the members of his department during their annual training week. He would like your views on the different roles of external and internal auditors, the type of work that each carry out and their reporting responsibilities.

Required

(a) Draft the lecture notes that you will use when giving your talk, paying particular attention to the differences and similarities of the following features of external and internal auditors:
   (i) general role;
   (ii) independence;

(iii) the work carried out on systems of internal control and operations;

(iv) reporting responsibilities.

(b) Explain what evidence you would seek as external auditor to satisfy yourself that you can rely on the work of the internal auditors.

(c) Give three examples of internal audit activity that might be used by the external auditor.

Topics for class discussion without solutions

15.7 A properly constituted audit committee enhances the role of both external and internal audit. Discuss.

15.8 Assurance services provided by the external auditor, other than the audit of financial statements, are far more useful than the latter. Discuss.

16

The auditors' report

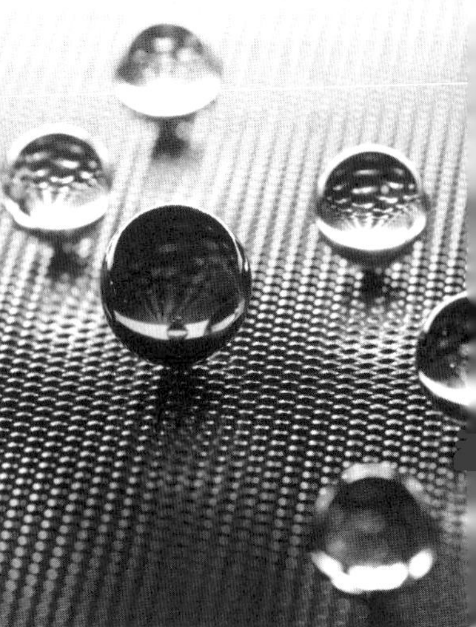

LEARNING OBJECTIVES

After studying this chapter you should be able to:

- **Explain the nature and importance of the audit report.**
- **Describe the various components of the audit report.**
- **Discuss when an 'emphasis of matter' or 'other matter' paragraph might be required in the audit report.**
- **Discuss the various forms of modified opinions and identify the circumstances under which each type would be issued by auditors.**
- **Outline the reason why auditors have started to include a disclaimer to third parties paragraph in the audit report.**
- **Outline auditors' responsibilities for reporting on corporate governance issues.**
- **Outline the procedures the auditor will undertake to review the corporate governance statement.**
- **Describe the implications of electronic publication of the audit report.**

Learning objectives, 609
Introduction, 610
The unmodified opinion, 611
The modified audit opinion, 626
Disclaimer of responsibility, 637
Reporting on corporate governance issues, 638
Electronic publication of auditors' reports, 646
Summary, 648
Key points of the chapter, 648
Further reading, 649
Self-assessment questions (solutions available to students), 650
Self-assessment questions (solutions available to tutors), 651
Topics for class discussion without solutions, 653

INTRODUCTION

We discuss the various forms the audit report may take later in the chapter.

Signing the audit report is generally regarded as the completion of the audit process, as it is through the report that auditors give their opinion on the financial statements. Giving a signature to the report is a responsible task and a duty that auditors should not take lightly. The report is effectively the means by which auditors communicate satisfaction or dissatisfaction with the financial statements to the shareholders. If they are satisfied that the statements do give a true and fair view and comply with all relevant legislation, they will give an unmodified or clean opinion. If they are dissatisfied, however, they will have to consider whether a modified opinion will be appropriate. In ISA 700 – *Forming an opinion and reporting on financial statements* a modified opinion is used to describe any opinion other than one that is unmodified. It therefore encompasses qualified opinions, adverse opinions, and disclaimers of opinion.

The role of the audit report has come under recent scrutiny as a result of the banking crisis. Why, critics ask, did none of the banks that later needed financial assistance receive a qualified audit report?; why were users of the financial statements not warned about the huge risks that these banks were taking? Critics argue that at the time of greatest need, when some sort of health warning should have been added by auditors to the financial statements, they remained silent. Defenders of the audit profession do not accept these criticisms as justified, indeed the then chairman of the Financial Reporting Council, Paul Boyle, went out of his way to state that the critics misunderstood the role of the audit report. While parties to this debate have failed to reach agreement, it does serve to highlight the importance placed on the audit report.

We will revisit these debates in Chapter 20.

As we mentioned in Chapter 4 APB recently adopted the auditing standards issued by IAASB. The one exception to the adoption was ISA 700 which is concerned with audit reporting. Instead APB revised and issued a clarified version of ISA 700 for use in the UK and Ireland in October 2009. The original version of ISA 700 had been issued in December 2004 and replaced SAS 600 which itself had been introduced in May 1993 as part of the new set of auditing standards developed by APB at that time. The form of the new audit report in both SAS 600 and ISA 700 was substantially different from the previous report, containing considerably more information instead of being brief and concise. It is interesting that one of the reasons why APB did not adopt ISA 700 issued by IAASB was because feedback from a consultation process indicated that respondents wanted a more concise audit report. The aim of APB might indeed have been a more concise audit report, but it is still notably longer than the so-called 'short form' audit reports of the 1980s and early 1990s. Later in this chapter and in Chapter 20 we discuss some of the reasons why it was thought necessary to revise the audit report, in particular to lengthen it, but for the moment we will proceed with discussing the form, content and meaning of the unmodified report. Before doing so you should note that, although APB did not adopt the IAASB's ISA 700 they did adopt ISA 705 – *Modifications to the opinion in the independent auditor's report* and ISA 706 – *Emphasis of matter paragraphs and other matter paragraphs in the independent auditor's* report. We discuss their requirements later in the chapter.

THE UNMODIFIED OPINION

Example of an unmodified opinion

In Figure 16.1 we give you an example of an unmodified audit opinion for a publicly traded company taken from APB Bulletin 2009/02 – *Auditor's Reports on Financial Statements in the United Kingdom*, which was issued in April 2009. We have framed it as a report to the members of Greenburn Plc on the assumption that all audit problems have been resolved. We have added labels and other comments to each paragraph to aid our discussion below. In the following sections we shall discuss some of the issues raised by the report shown in Figure 16.1. In the Appendix material to Chapter 16 on the Cengage website we have drafted the audit opinion using the version of ISA 700 issued by IFAC, to allow you to make comparisons between it and the example in ISA 700 (UK and Ireland). In this connection, you should obtain an unmodified audit opinion in your own legal jurisdiction to see how IFAC's ISA 700 has been changed to take account of your own local circumstances.

available on the Cengage website

Title

The audit report normally uses the term independent auditor as being the preparer of the audit report. This is done to distinguish it from reports that might be issued by other parties.

To whom the report is addressed

In the case of companies the audit report is normally addressed to the members of the company, which would usually be its shareholders. It is a requirement that directors send a copy of its annual accounts to every member and in a *public company* that they lay accounts before the company in a general meeting and that those accounts be audited.

The Companies Act 2006 does not require private companies to lay the annual accounts before the members at a general meeting.

Refer to CA 2006 s.423, s.437 and s.475 and to Case study 4.1 on pages 134 to 146.

This does not necessarily mean that the audit report will be valueless to other users, but the auditors do not owe them a statutory duty. If you refer back to Figure 4.5 on page 133, you will note that auditors can be said to bridge the remoteness gap for other users as well as for the shareholders. In Chapter 19 we show that, in general, auditors are only likely to be responsible to shareholders as a group rather than to individual shareholders except in certain specified circumstances. Furthermore, auditors will not usually be liable in negligence cases to third parties. When the auditors report on group accounts the addressees will be the parent company shareholders. Those shareholders of other companies (such as subsidiaries and associated companies) within the group have to look to the audit report on the financial statements specifically prepared for the company in which they hold an interest. In other instances, such as financial statements prepared for charities or trade unions, the audit report will be addressed to people other than shareholders, the members or trustees of the charity, for instance, or members of the trade union. In the UK where shareholders have indicated they do not want to receive a full annual report and accounts, the company may send them summary financial statements (Ss 426-428 CA 2006 and SI 2008 No.374). Those summary financial statements must contain a statement by the auditor that they are consistent with the full financial statements, and whether their audit opinion was modified or unmodified. If it was modified they have to provide

FIGURE 16.1 Example of an unmodified audit opinion for a publicly traded company

INDEPENDENT AUDITORS' REPORT TO THE SHAREHOLDERS OF GREENBURN PLC	Title and addressee (to whom the audit report is addressed)
We have audited the financial statements of Greenburn Plc for the year ended 31 March 2011 which comprise the profit and loss account, the balance sheet, the cash flow statement, the statement of total realized gains and losses, the reconciliation of movements in shareholders funds and the related notes. The financial reporting framework that has been applied in their preparation is applicable law and United Kingdom Accounting Standards (United Kingdom Generally Accepted Accounting Practice).	This paragraph is known as the scope paragraph and serves to identify the subject matter of the report. This paragraph is suitable where a company publishes its financial statements on the Web or in pdf format. If it is published in hard copy or in non-pdf format, rather than list the various statements, they may simply refer to the financial statements by reference to the page numbers in the annual report where they are contained.
Respective responsibilities of directors and auditors	
As explained more fully in the directors' responsibility statement set out on page X the directors are responsible for the preparation of the financial statements and for being satisfied that they give a true and fair view. Our responsibility is to audit the financial statements in accordance with applicable law and International Standards on Auditing (UK and Ireland). These standards require us to comply with the Auditing Practices Board Ethical Standards for Auditors.	We give an example of a directors' responsibility statement on page 612.
Scope of the audit of the financial statements	
An audit involves obtaining evidence about the amounts and disclosures in the financial statements sufficient to give reasonable assurance that the financial statements are free from material misstatements whether caused by fraud or error. This includes an assessment of: whether the accounting policies appropriate to the company's circumstances and have been consistently applied and adequately disclosed; the reasonableness of accounting estimates made by the directors; and the overall presentation of the financial statements.	The auditors have three options in this section. They can either include an audit scope statement as done in this example or they can either (1) state that a description of the scope is given on the APB's website at **WWW.frc.org.uk/apb/scope/UKP** or (2) they can refer to the page in the annual report where the scope statement is set out.
Opinion on the financial statements	
In our opinion the financial statements: ● give a true and fair view of Greenburn's affairs as at 31 March 2011 and of its profit for the year then ended; ● have been properly prepared in accordance with United Kingdom Generally Accepted Accounting Practice; and ● have been prepared in accordance with the Companies Act 2006.	
Opinion on other matters prescribed by the Companies Act 2006	
In our opinion: ● the part of the directors' remuneration report to be audited has been properly prepared in accordance with the Companies Act 2006; and ● the information given in the directors' report for the financial year for which the financial statements are prepared is consistent with the financial statements.	Statutory Instrument 2008, No. 410 states the information in the directors' remuneration report that is subject to audit. This is a requirement of s.496 Companies Act 2006.
Matters on which we are required to report by exception	
We have nothing to report in respect of the following: Under the Companies Act 2006 we are required to report to you if, in our opinion:	These requirements are set out in s.498 of the CA 2006. We discuss these aspects later in the chapter.

● Adequate accounting records have not been kept or returns adequate for our audit have not been received from branches visited by us; or ● the financial statements and the part of the directors' remuneration report to be audited are not in agreement with the accounting records and returns; or ● certain disclosures of directors' remuneration specified by law are not made; or ● we have not received all the information and explanations we require for our audit. Under the listing rules we are required to review: ● the directors' statement set out on page X, in relation to going concern; and ● the part of the Corporate Governance Statement relating to the company's compliance with the nine provisions of the June 2008 Combined Code specified for our review.	
Signature Sherlock Holmes (Senior Statutory Auditor) **Address** For and on behalf of Houndogs LLP, **Date** **(Statutory Auditor)**	We noted in Chapter 14 that the date of the audit report is the date of the end of audit field work.

the report in full. In the remainder of this chapter we are solely concerned with the audit report on the full financial statements. The form of the auditors' statement on summary financial statements is given in the Appendix to APB Bulletin 2008/03 – *The auditor's statement on the summary financial statement in the United Kingdom.*

For comparison with the UK version of the audit report we have included an example audit report from ISA 700 in Appendix material to Chapter 16 on the Companion Website.

Identification of statements upon which the auditors are reporting

Many companies publish information in their 'reporting package', which is not subject to audit, such as pictorial displays of its product range, ten-year results summaries, and chairperson's report. It is therefore very important that the auditors carefully identify that part of the total information upon which they are reporting. In the example above we have listed the statements and related notes that are subject to audit. The auditors will check that other information contained in the annual report does not conflict with the view given by the financial statements or contain factual errors or inaccuracies. Indeed it is a statutory requirement (s.496 CA 2006) that the auditors check that the information contained in the directors' report is consistent with the financial statements and state such in their audit report. ISA 720 – *The auditor's responsibilities relating to other information in documents containing audited financial statements*, also specifically requires auditors to read the other information, such as the chairperson's statement or names of directors, and identify if there are any material inconsistencies with the financial statements. If they believe there is an inconsistency or that the other information in incorrect in some way, the auditors should consider whether an amendment to either the other information or financial statements is required. Having established that an inconsistency exists, the auditors should discuss it with the directors of the

Later in this chapter we discuss the nature of the modification arising from a disagreement between the auditors and the directors.

company and seek to resolve the matter. If the auditors believe the other information needs to be amended and the directors refuse, the auditors will consider the need to add an Other Matter paragraph to their audit report or taking some other form of action such as resignation from the audit assignment or making a statement at a general meeting of the company's members. If the inconsistency is of such a nature that it requires the financial statements to be adjusted and the directors refuse to do so, the auditors should consider issuing a modified opinion. Where the client is listed and has an audit committee and the directors refuse to adjust either the other information or the financial statements, the auditors would normally discuss the matter with the committee. The auditor would also undertake similar action where the other information contains a material misstatement of fact rather than being inconsistent with the financial statements. It should be apparent that, if the directors refuse to make changes to the other information, this is likely to influence the auditor's perception of the nature of their relationship with the client and the risk associated with the engagement. In the extreme the auditor may have to consider withdrawing from the engagement.

Where the auditors consider that the directors' report is inconsistent with the financial statements they should follow a similar procedure to that outlined above for an inconsistency in other information. In particular they should discuss the matter with the directors and try to get them to adjust either the directors' report or the financial statements to remove the inconsistency. If the directors' report needs amending and the directors refuse and the auditors believe the inconsistency is material, the auditor is required to describe the inconsistency in a separate paragraph in their report. The auditors would state that, except for the matter described, the directors' report was consistent with the financial statements. This paragraph would be placed after the opinion paragraph perhaps headed up 'material inconsistency between the financial statements and the directors' report'. If the inconsistency required the financial statements to be adjusted and the directors refuse, the auditor would need to consider issuing a modified opinion. In both the above situations where the auditors believe there is an inconsistency, they should ensure they adequately document the matter and their discussions with the directors. In the case of the directors' report they should also document the procedures (and the results of those procedures) undertaken to check that it was consistent with the financial statements.

The directors' responsibility statement, although it could be included in the audit report, is in practice invariably located elsewhere in the annual report.

Responsibilities paragraph

Statement of auditor's responsibilities

You may remember that ISA 700 is the one exception to this where APB has chosen not to adopt the auditing standard issued by IAASB.

This section states that the auditors' work is in conformance with auditing standards. Auditing standards, as we have seen in previous chapters, contain pronouncements on key auditing issues, and are prepared by IAASB. They are modified where appropriate by APB for use in the UK and Ireland. They are, in effect, primarily codifications of best practice and auditors, by including the above statement in their audit report, are conveying to the reader that the financial statements have been audited to the standard used by competent practitioners. In consequence, the readers' expectations will be that they can place greater reliance on the statements than would otherwise be the case. The issue of auditing standards can be viewed as an attempt to standardize auditing practice or at least to ensure that audits are conducted to an acceptable standard across the countries that adopt them. As far as the audit report is concerned, the objective is to make it more understandable and therefore more useful to the reader. It must be said that originally many members of the profession viewed the issue of auditing standards with some trepidation, as it was felt that the courts would look to them to see if best professional practice had been followed in negligence cases. If you look at APB's statement '*Scope and authority of pronouncements (Revised)*' you will see that Paragraphs 22 and 23 specifically state:

- 'Auditors who do not comply with auditing standards when performing company or other audits make themselves liable to regulatory action which may include the withdrawal of registration and hence of eligibility to perform company audits' (paragraph 22) and
- 'All relevant APB announcements and in particular auditing standards are likely to be taken into account when the adequacy of the work of auditors is being considered in a court of law or in other contested situations' (paragraph 23)

We noted in the Preface that the ISAs contain both Requirements and Application and other explanatory material, the latter containing paragraphs with 'A' prefixes. If auditors can show in court that the requirements in the auditing standards have been followed, this would be prima facie evidence that they have carried out their audit duties in a competent fashion and should not be found negligent. It can be argued that the standards are too general to provide detailed guidance as to expectations but they do give a framework for the audit process, highlighting, among other things, such important questions as:

- The planning of audit work.
- The assessment of audit risk.
- The sufficiency and appropriateness of audit evidence.

It, must, however, be recognized that standards considered satisfactory by the profession will be dependent upon the circumstances surrounding a particular case and that apparent compliance with auditing standards may not always be enough to prove that the auditors have not been negligent. For instance, Paragraph 2 of ISA 300 – *Planning an audit of financial statements,* suggests that one of the roles of planning in an audit assignment is to assist the auditor in devoting appropriate attention to important areas of the audit. There is a clear message in the standard that auditors should plan their work, although it is possible to imagine a situation in which they have planned the work but have nevertheless been negligent in failing to devote sufficient attention to an important area.

The responsibilities statement also makes it clear that the work of the auditor is governed by ethical standards. This reinforces the notion that the audit report is being given by a professional person who must comply with certain rules and regulations relating to his or her conduct.

Statement of directors' responsibilities

The preparation of the financial statements on which the auditors report is the responsibility of the directors. This paragraph also refers to the page in the annual report where a fuller description of the directors' duties can be found. APB Bulletin 2009/02 gives an example of the directors' responsibilities statement. The example provided is that of a large non-publicly traded company which prepares its financial statements under UK GAAP. If the company prepared its financial statements using International Accounting Standards the wording would have to be changed to reflect this. If we were dealing with a listed company, the statement would need to refer to the specific listing rules and regulations with which it has to comply. If the company was either small or medium sized there would also need to be minor amendments to the statement. The example given of a directors' responsibility statement in the Bulletin is worded as follows:

STATEMENT OF DIRECTORS' RESPONSIBILITY

The directors are responsible for preparing the directors' report and the financial statements in accordance with applicable law and regulations.

Company law requires the directors to prepare financial statements for each financial year. Under that law the directors have elected to prepare the financial statements in accordance with United Kingdom Generally Accepted Accounting Practice (United Kingdom Standards and applicable law). Under company law the directors must not approve the financial statements unless they are satisfied that they give a true and fair view of the state of affairs of the company and of the profit or loss for that period. In preparing these financial statements, the directors are required to:

- select suitable accounting policies and then apply them consistently;
- make judgements and accounting estimates that are reasonable and prudent;
- state whether applicable UK Accounting Standards have been followed, subject to any material departures disclosed and explained in the financial statements;
- prepare the financial statements on the going-concern basis unless it is inappropriate to presume that the business will continue in business.

The directors are responsible for keeping adequate accounting records that are sufficient to show and explain the company's transactions and disclose with reasonable accuracy at any time the financial position of the company and enable them to ensure that the financial statements comply with the Companies Act 2006. They are responsible for safeguarding the assets of the company and hence for taking reasonable steps for the prevention and detection of fraud and other irregularities.

Source: Appendix 11, Bulletin 2009/02 Auditor's Reports on Financial Statements in the United Kingdom

There are a few points worth making about the above example. First, you may have noticed that the directors also have to be familiar with the concept of truth and fairness because they have the primary responsibility for ensuring that the financial statements do give a true and fair view. Second, the statement emphasizes that the financial statements involve judgements and the making of estimates; in other words their preparation is not a simple mechanical exercise. When directors make these judgements and estimates they must be reasonable and prudent, suggesting that the directors should not take an unjustified optimistic view when determining or making them. Finally, we draw your attention to the fact that the directors are required to safeguard the company's assets and take reasonable steps to prevent and detect fraud and other irregularities. Use of the term 'reasonable steps' suggests that it is not possible to prevent and detect all fraud and error, and that the directors have to make a judgement on when it is not appropriate to commit additional resources to their prevention and detection because the costs are likely to outweigh the benefits.

The objective of including responsibilities statements was to make clear to readers of the financial statements the extent and scope of the respective responsibilities of the directors and auditors. It was thought necessary to include such statements because it was considered that users were confused as to the extent of auditors' responsibilities.

ACTIVITY 16.1

The inclusion of responsibility statements was seen as a way of educating users and in the process helping to eliminate the audit expectations gap. List any misconceptions users may have had about the respective responsibilities of the auditors and directors.

We discuss the audit expectations gap in more detail in Chapter 18.

You may have mentioned some of the following points in your answer to this activity:

- Users may have believed that the auditors are guaranteeing the accuracy of the financial statements. By stating that they have adhered to ISAs auditors are conveying that they have followed best auditing practice. This is followed in the opinion part of the audit report where it is clear they are giving an opinion on the financial statements and that they are not guaranteeing accuracy.
- Users may have believed that the auditors are responsible for the preparation of the financial statements. By stating specifically in the directors' statement that it is the directors' duty to keep proper accounting records and prepare financial statements which give a true and fair view this should help eliminate this misconception.
- Users may have thought that the auditors had prime responsibility for detecting fraud and error. The reference in the directors' responsibility statement to their duty to take appropriate steps to prevent and detect fraud and other irregularities should make it clear to users that the auditors' responsibility in respect of fraud and other irregularities is less than is commonly perceived.

Scope of the audit of the financial statements

The auditors, in this section, refer to their responsibility for the detection of fraud and error. It is made clear that this is in the context of collecting sufficient, appropriate evidence to give reasonable assurance that the amounts and disclosures in the financial statements are not materially misstated. Two important issues are raised. First, that the auditors' evidence collection process is influenced by what is needed to give them reasonable assurance. The use of the term 'reasonable assurance' should inform users that the auditors are not guaranteeing that the company's accounts are free from fraud or error. This should lessen users' expectations of the auditors' responsibilities for detecting fraud or error. It may well be asked what is meant by reasonable assurance. The audit report standard does not give any guidance on this issue, which suggests that it will be left to the courts to decide what should be reasonably expected of auditors in respect of detecting fraud and error. It may be presumed that, if the fraud is ingenious, well concealed and perhaps involves senior management, the courts may well consider that it would be unreasonable to expect the auditors to detect the fraud. This suggests that what is reasonable will depend on the circumstances and nature of the fraud or error. The second issue raised in the audit report is that the auditors' responsibility only relates to detecting misstatements that are material to the financial statements. This should ensure that users are aware that the auditors are not responsible for detecting *all* frauds and errors.

You will remember that we have already discussed levels of assurance in Chapter 15. We discuss in more detail the auditors' responsibility for the detection of fraud in Chapter 17.

In an effort to reduce the length of the audit report APB has given auditors the option of providing their scope of audit statement elsewhere in the annual report or to simply refer to a standard statement available on the APBs website. There are two statements available on the website, one for a UK publicly traded company and the other for a UK non publicly traded company. It is interesting that the APB chose to provide not only a scope statement, but also a narrative on a number of other matters, for instance, the auditors' responsibility for other information contained in the annual report.

The example for a publicly traded company is available on the FRC website at: http: //www.frc.org.uk/apb/ scope/ UKP.cfm.

ACTIVITY 16.2

The scope paragraph also states that the auditor has to ensure that accounting policies chosen by the company are appropriate, and significant accounting estimates made by the directors are reasonable.

Suggest why these two matters are important and the issues they pose for auditors.

You may have suggested something along the following lines:

Accounting rules and standards may allow directors some flexibility in their choice of accounting policies, thus giving them an incentive to choose the policies that suit their objectives, even if they may not be the most appropriate in the circumstances of the company. The determination of a particular set of policies may have considerable influence on, for instance, the earnings figure and the auditors must ensure that this figure is justified by how the company actually performed during the period. The scope statement also makes it clear that the policies chosen must be consistently applied and adequately disclosed. Again, the concept of adequate disclosure is one where there may be some scope for debate and may give rise to differences in perception between the auditors and the directors.

Furthermore, accounting estimates by their very nature require the exercise of judgement and may therefore give rise to differences of opinion between the auditors and the directors of a company. In some instances there may only be circumstantial evidence available, making it difficult for the auditors to convince the directors that they should change their mind on the disputed matter. What this serves to highlight is that the accounts cannot be totally objective, as the exercise of judgement is subjective.

The opinion

The first thing to make clear is that the auditors are expressing an opinion and not giving a guarantee. As we have stressed above, the preparation and audit of financial statements is not merely a mechanical exercise; it requires the exercise of judgement and the critical evaluation of the appropriateness of alternative accounting treatments. To give a guarantee would be to imply that auditors are infallible and will never make errors of judgement. In a process such as auditing, requiring the collection and evaluation of evidence and the judging of assumptions such as the expected useful lives of plant and machinery, this is never likely to be the case. The environment in which a company operates is by its very nature uncertain and events may turn out differently from expectation. The company's directors and auditors may concur at the year-end as to the value of stock or investments, but with the passing of time and changes in circumstances the valuation may turn out to be incorrect. The investments may lose material value owing to a decline in Stock Exchange prices or because the company in which the shares are owned goes into liquidation. What the user would wish to know is whether at the time of the signing of the audit report any of the above events should have been detected by the auditors. It is easy with the advantage of hindsight to say: 'Yes, the dramatic fall in the value of the investments owing to the liquidation of the company should have been anticipated'. It is more difficult to put oneself into the auditors' shoes at the time of the audit, with only the information available at that time, and to state unequivocally that the event should have been anticipated. We are not of course suggesting that the opinion is of no value merely because it is an opinion and not something stronger. Users can and do expect high standards because the opinion given by auditors is not an opinion without weight. It is accepted that in the vast majority of cases it is an opinion of independent and competent experts who are being compensated for their expertise in the form of the audit fee. In everyday life we rely very frequently on expert opinion. For instance, we rely on the doctor, who diagnoses illness, even though we are aware that occasionally doctors diagnose incorrectly. Although incorrect diagnoses are regrettable it is a price, as a society, we are willing to pay because the costs stemming from the alternative, that is, not to have doctors or not to consult them, are outweighed by the perceived benefits. Never to trust expert opinion would make life intolerable, although, of course, every step should be taken to ensure that the opinion is, in fact, being given by an expert. It would seem inappropriate to abandon the audit requirement merely because some audit opinions have turned out to be invalid. You may wish to dwell on how the capital markets would react to the increased uncertainty surrounding financial statements that had not been audited or how confident bank managers would be to lend money on the basis of financial statements that had not been the subject of independent scrutiny.

Not unnaturally, we should be concerned with the frequency that auditors fail to detect material misstatements. If this were to be the norm, auditing would lose its credibility and could result in the extreme to the abandonment of the audit function. Clearly, in the final analysis auditing can only exist if it is seen to be providing a useful function in providing an opinion on: (a) the truth and fairness of the financial statements; (b) compliance with whatever accounting framework is being used, for instance, UK GAAP or IFRS; and (c) compliance with Companies Act 2006.

Finally, you will notice the opinion is signed by the senior statutory auditor. A requirement of the Companies Act 2006 is that where an audit firm is appointed as auditor, the audit report must be signed, and dated, in the name of the senior statutory auditor, for and on behalf of the audit firm. This requirement ensures that a named individual within the audit firm takes responsibility for the audit. The term 'senior statutory auditor' has the same meaning as the term 'engagement partner'. Where in exceptional occasions this person is not available to sign the audit report, the audit firm will have to make provision for another person to be responsible for the audit and sign as senior statutory auditor.

Possible circumstances here include the audit partner being seriously ill or leaving the audit firm.

The truth and fairness of the accounts

We have already discussed truth and fairness in accounting in Chapters 1 and 4. Note, however, that an audit opinion need not always use the term 'true and fair view'. For instance, in local authority accounts in England and Wales the requirement is whether the accounts 'present fairly' the financial position of the authority. In 2008 the Financial Reporting Council obtained a new counsel's opinion on the meaning of the true and fair view, there having been a previous counsel's opinion by Mary Arden in 1983. The opinion in 2008 was given by the Queen's Counsel, Martin Moore. The reason for obtaining a new opinion was because of the many changes that had occurred since the original opinion in 1983. These changes include a new Companies Act, the issuing of new standards and the preparation of financial statements using international accounting standards. In this respect it should be noted that while the term 'true and fair' is used in the UK and Ireland, many other countries use the term 'fair presentation'. Counsel considered that the term 'true and fair' was still relevant and that it was indistinguishable from 'fair presentation'. He also noted that there was not one true and fair view, in other words, a company's financial statements could be prepared in a number of different ways but each set might still give a true and fair view. Counsel also considered that what was true and fair was a matter of judgement and was an overarching concept. He also considered that in most instances companies would need to adhere to accounting standards for a true and fair view to be given. Thus, it would only be in exceptional circumstances that a company could depart from accounting standards in preparing its financial statements and for them to still show a true and fair view.

This is discussed further below.

Compliance with CA 2006 and accounting standards

To give a true and fair view it is likely that the financial statements will have been prepared in accordance with accounting standards. This requirement has been given some legal backing in the UK by the requirement of Schedule 1, Para 45 of the statutory instrument SI 2008/410 – *The large and medium-sized companies and groups (accounts and reports) regulations 2008* which says that companies should state whether the accounts have been prepared in accordance with applicable accounting standards. It goes on to state that where there has been a material departure from those standards particulars should be given together with the reasons for the departure. Thus, where there have been departures from regulations or the financial reporting framework the auditors will have to consider whether they are justified and adequately explained in the financial statements if they are to give an unmodified opinion. Finally, the auditors have to determine if the non-compliance results in the financial statements not giving a true and fair view, in which case the auditors would have to issue a modified audit opinion. In very exceptional circumstances companies may consider it appropriate to depart from a provision of the Companies Act 2006 or accounting standards in order that a true and fair view be given. On those occasions the reasons for the departure and its effect should be included in the notes to the accounts (Section 396(5) and 404(5) CA 2006). Further details of what should be included in the notes to the accounts are given in FRS 18 – *Accounting policies*. This states that:

There are similar provisions to FRS 18 in International Accounting Standard 1 Presentation of Financial Statements.

- Details should be included of the treatment the Act normally requires and the actual treatment adopted.
- A statement should be included giving the reasons why compliance with the provision(s) of the Act or standards would not give a true and fair view.
- A description should be given of how the financial statements are affected by departure from the provisions of the Companies Act or an accounting standard. Normally this requires quantification of the effect of the departure.

Where the directors have departed in some way from Companies Act 2006 or accounting standard provisions, the auditors will have to arrive at an opinion whether the departure is necessary for the accounts to give a true and fair view.

The Companies Act also makes it clear that where compliance with the provisions of the Act would not be sufficient for a true and fair view to be given, such additional information as is deemed necessary should be given in the accounts or in the notes to the accounts (s.396(4) CA 2006). If the auditors are satisfied that the accounts do give a true and fair view and they comply with the Companies Act 2006, they will issue an unmodified report.

In the above discussion we have alluded to the fact that companies may prepare their financial statements using alternative frameworks. In the example given in Figure 16.1 it was assumed the company prepared its financial statements using UK Generally Accepted Accounting Practice. This served to indicate that the company complied with UK Accounting Standards in the form of SSAPs and FRSs. Alternative frameworks are allowed by the Companies Act 2006. Thus, a company may use either UK GAAP or International Financial Reporting Standards (IFRS) as adopted by the European Commission

(EU adopted IFRS). However, there is an EU regulation that requires companies listed on a recognized exchange to prepare their consolidated financial statements using EU adopted IFRS. Since, however, this only applies to the consolidated financial statements it leaves the option open for the parent company (and subsidiaries) to prepare their own financial statements using UK GAAP. The majority of companies in the United Kingdom still prepare their financial statements using standards issued by the ASB. Thus a listed company's consolidated financial statements may have been prepared using International Accounting Standards and the UK parent company may have used UK GAAP. As you might gather from the above, the position is quite complex and the auditor's opinion might have to reflect that the consolidated financial statements have been prepared using EU adopted IFRS whereas the parent company accounts have been prepared using UK GAAP. A further complication is that International Accounting Standards are issued by the International Accounting Standards Board (IASB). However, the EU did not adopt all the pronouncements of the IASB and therefore some companies, primarily those who are listed on an US exchange, might prepare their financial statements using the complete set of IASB standards and their opinion would have to reflect this fact. Although over time the standards have been converging, having two accounting standard frameworks makes matters unduly complicated and it would be beneficial therefore if a move was made towards using one accounting (IAS) framework. In furthering this objective the FRC has issued proposals which look at the future of UK GAAP. In the next section we turn our attention to modifications of the audit report.

The parent company and UK subsidiaries have the option of using IFRS as do non-listed UK companies.

There is also another set of standards for small enterprises.

Emphasis of matter paragraphs and other matter paragraphs

There may be occasions when the auditor believes that certain matters need to be brought to the attention of users but which do not warrant the auditor expressing a modified opinion. These include matters where the auditors do not disagree with the client about its disclosure or presentation. However, the auditors may feel that the matter is of such significance that awareness of it is fundamental to users' understanding of the financial statements and therefore users should be specifically directed to the matter. Alternatively, there could be some matter which has not been reported or disclosed in the financial statements because it was not required, but nevertheless the auditors believe it is sufficiently important to a user's understanding that it needs to be brought to their attention. These matters are dealt with in ISA 706 – *Emphasis of matter paragraphs and other matter paragraphs in the independent auditor's report.*

ISA 706 (paragraph A1) provides a number of examples where an emphasis of matter paragraph may be appropriate:

- An uncertainty relating to the future outcome of exceptional litigation or regulatory action.
- Early application (where permitted) of a new accounting standard that has a pervasive effect on the financial statements in advance of its effective date.
- a major catastrophe that has had, or continues to have, a significant effect on the entity's financial position.

An example of an uncertainty that could relate to future outcomes is an event which might cast some doubt on the company's ability to continue as a going concern. The auditors would wish to determine if the matter and its potential effect on the going-concern status of the company was adequately disclosed in the financial statements. If they were satisfied on this matter, the auditor would not issue a modified opinion but would instead consider including an emphasis of matter paragraph. However, it needs to be stressed that ISA 706 (paragraph A3) makes it clear that an emphasis of matter should not be used as a substitute for a modified audit report. Furthermore, paragraph A2 makes the important point that a widespread use of emphasis of matter paragraphs diminishes the effectiveness of the auditor's communication of such matters. Where an emphasis of matter paragraph is deemed necessary, the auditors will place it immediately after the opinion paragraph and title it 'emphasis of matter'. They should be clear in the paragraph about the nature of the matter and where the disclosures relating to it can be found in the financial statements. The auditors should also make it clear that their opinion is not modified (qualified) in respect of the matter.

As an historical note, the ability to add an emphasis of matter paragraph has been available to auditors for some considerable period of time. A number of years ago its frequency of use gave some cause for disquiet among the audit profession because it was felt that auditors were using it rather than giving a modified opinion. ISA 706, however, makes it clear that it can only be used on certain specified occasions and therefore its frequency of use is likely to be low except for those instances where it is being used to flag going-concern issues.

ISA 706 states that use of an Other Matter paragraph is restricted to occasions where some issue has not been communicated in the financial statements. The ISA gives a number of situations where an other matter paragraph might be used. These include:

- Where the auditor has been unable to obtain sufficient evidence because of a limitation of scope imposed by management which is regarded as pervasive but has not withdrawn from the audit engagement (which would be the normal course of action) the auditors should disclaim giving an opinion and explain in the Other Matter paragraph why it was not possible for them to withdraw from the engagement. (See paragraph A5).
- Where an entity prepares two sets of financial statements, one perhaps in compliance with the National Accounting Framework and the other in compliance with an International Accounting Framework and the auditor is engaged to report on both sets of accounts. If both frameworks are appropriate the auditor may include an Other Matter paragraph in their audit report stating that they have issued an audit report on another set of financial statements but one which was prepared using a different accounting framework and that they issued an audit report on those statements. (See paragraph A8).

The placement of an other matter paragraph will vary depending on what it is reporting and may be after the opinion paragraph and emphasis of matter paragraph or alternatively where the matter referred to is related to other reporting responsibilities it may be included in a section headed 'Report on other Legal and Regulatory Requirements'.

See Appendix 5.

APB Bulletin 2009/2 – *Auditor's reports on financial statements in the United Kingdom,* published in April 2009 provides two examples of an emphasis of matter paragraph. The first of these relates to a situation where the going-concern status of the company is in doubt and the company has disclosed this in a note to the accounts, and the second example relates to the situation where the company is being sued and the determination of the legal case against them has not been decided. Again the company has disclosed details of the case in the notes to the accounts and the auditor concludes that a qualification is not necessary but that the matter needs to be brought to the attention of users of the accounts and therefore include an emphasis of matter paragraph directly after the opinion paragraph. We give below the wording of that emphasis of matter paragraph:

EMPHASIS OF MATTER – POSSIBLE OUTCOME OF A LAWSUIT

In forming our opinion on the financial statements, which is not qualified, we have considered the adequacy of the disclosure made in note [x] to the financial statements concerning the possible outcome of a lawsuit, alleging infringement of patent rights and claiming royalties and punitive damages, where the company is the defendant. The company has filed a counter action, and preliminary hearings and discovery proceedings on both actions are in progress. The ultimate outcome of the matter cannot properly be determined, and no provision for any liability that may result has been made in the financial statements.

Example 12 Bulletin 2009/02 Auditor's Reports on Financial Statement in the United Kingdom

There are a number of important points to note in respect of the suggested wording above. First, the auditors make it clear that the paragraph describing the uncertainty should not be considered as a qualification of the audit report. Second, reference is made to the note in the accounts where details of the uncertainty can be found. Third, it gives some indication of the nature of the significant uncertainty. Lastly, no assessment is given of the potential implications of the uncertainty because the outcome cannot be determined. Prior to determining that an emphasis of matter paragraph rather than a qualification is appropriate the auditor would have carried out a considerable amount of detailed work. They would need to have familiarized themselves with the details of the case and seen all legal correspondence relating to it. They may also have sought independent legal advice on the likelihood of the courts finding against their client. As a matter of course they would have discussed the issue with the directors and where one exists, the audit committee of the company, and it would be one of the items the auditor would specifically examine in their post-balance sheet events review prior to signing the audit report.

You will remember we discussed post-balance sheet events in Chapter 14.

ACTIVITY 16.3

Why do you believe it was thought necessary for ISA 706 to advocate that auditors should refer to a 'fundamental' uncertainty relating to a future event in their audit report?

The main reason is to draw shareholders' attention to an event that could have significant implications for the company and therefore the value of and risk to their investment in the company. If no mention was made of such an event in the audit report, and the outcome turned out to be significantly detrimental to the company, users would probably complain that it should have been drawn to their attention by the auditors. It is important to emphasize that the notes in the accounts have to make disclosure sufficient to secure the true and fair view. The argument goes that if the note disclosure is adequate, a qualification of the audit report will not be necessary. To some extent inclusion of the description of the significant uncertainty in the audit report can be seen as a defensive mechanism by the auditors to protect themselves from adverse criticism. We have assumed above that the auditors agree with management's treatment and that adequate and proper disclosure has been made in the notes to the accounts. Where the auditors believe that the directors' disclosures in the notes to the accounts relating to the matter are inadequate, they will have to consider issuing a modified opinion. In these circumstances the auditors are disagreeing with the directors and will have to consider issuing a modification indicating disagreement.

Inclusion of details relating to the uncertainty is also likely to be of use to other users of the accounts, such as present or potential lenders.

We discuss the form of modified audit opinion that would be given below.

IMPORTANT NOTE FOR STUDENTS

You should note that an emphasis of matter is likely to be rare, except where it is being used to flag going-concern issues. This means that in the exam room you should great care not to suggest its use to highlight all instances of uncertainty. For instance, a court case against the company might be pending, but legal advice received points to good defences by the client, and the auditor is satisfied that the matter is properly disclosed in the notes to the financial statements. There are, after all, many examples of uncertainty in the preparation of financial statements, including collectability of trade receivables and the saleability of inventories, and if audit procedures reveal nothing untoward, there would be no point in putting an emphasis of matter into the audit report. You should never suggest its use where there is disagreement between the auditors and management (see below). Do not forget that readers of the auditors' report may well be misled into believing that the auditors are qualifying a matter when they are not doing so. Many users of financial statements are very unsophisticated and the auditor should bend over backwards to ensure that they are not unnecessarily misled. We know that the auditor will introduce the emphasis of matter by saying: 'Without qualifying our report . . .', but if the material matter is properly treated in the financial statements and the available audit evidence suggests that the uncertainty will not crystalize, there is no need to confuse people by putting in an emphasis of matter when it is not necessary.

THE MODIFIED AUDIT OPINION

There is an ISA covering this issue, ISA 705 – *Modifications to the opinion in the independent auditor's report* which was issued in October 2009. The ISA states there are three forms of modification; a qualified opinion, an adverse opinion and a disclaimer of opinion. Though the ISA makes this distinction all three types are often referred to as qualifications.

Modifications by their very nature indicate that there are matters contained in the financial statements, about which the auditors are not completely satisfied. This dissatisfaction could result for one of two reasons. First, there may have been limitation in the scope of the auditors' examination. Second, the auditors may disagree with the treatment or the disclosure of an item in the financial statements. Before the auditors issue a modified opinion they will have come to a judgement about the materiality of the item with which they are concerned. If the item is so material, that is, important enough, to make it inappropriate for the auditors to issue an unqualified report, they would issue a modified opinion. We show below that not all types of modification are on a par or have the same degree of severity associated with them. The notion that there are grades of modification originally adopted in SAS 600 has been retained in ISA 700 and provides a framework the auditors can use in determining the type of modification to their opinion on a company's financial statements. Before issuing a modification to the audit report the auditors should have fully discussed the contentious item with the directors of the company and, if possible, convince them where it (say) related to non-compliance with a SSAP, FRS or IAS that they should change their policy and comply thus avoiding a modified opinion.

Forms of modification

The various forms of modified opinion can be represented using the matrix shown in Figure 16.2. This matrix shows that the form of modification can range from the relatively mild 'except for' to the extreme and, it is to be hoped, infrequent 'disclaimer' and 'adverse' opinions. In the next few sections we shall examine the constituents of the matrix.

FIGURE 16.2 Forms of qualification matrix (adapted from figure in paragraph A1, ISA (UK and Ireland) 705.

Nature of matter giving rise to the modification	Auditor's judgement about the pervasiveness of the effects or possible effects on the financial statements	
	Material but not pervasive	Material and pervasive
Financial statements are materially misstated (Disagreement)	Qualified – Except for opinion	Adverse opinion
Inability to obtain sufficient appropriate audit evidence (Limitation of Scope)	Qualified – Except for opinion	Disclaimer of opinion

The form of the modification given is dependent on the importance of the matter under consideration. If the auditors find that the petty cash is in error by £2.00, this would not be a matter for a modified audit opinion. However, if the auditors conclude that stock is overvalued by £30 000 (total stock being stated at £100 000) then this appears as though it would be a modification matter. Once again, we are dealing with the concept of materiality. The auditors have to use their judgement in deciding when a particular matter is material and when it is not. Generally, the overriding concern will be whether the non-adjustment or nondisclosure of the matter would mislead a user and whether knowledge of the matter would cause the user's decision to change. The auditors must take into account the nature of the item under consideration and might have to consider questions such as the following:

- Is it more misleading for an asset to be overstated or for a liability to be understated by the same amount?
- Is there a conceptual difference between stock being overstated and cash at bank being overstated?
- Does it matter that some of the administrative expenses have been misclassified and included in cost of goods sold?

There is no definitive answer to the above questions but we believe you should understand the importance of questions of this kind, with which auditors must come to terms as a matter of course during their audit work. Other examples of matters that must be considered are:

- The amounts involved, both absolute and relative. For instance, an understatement of £100 000 in the stocks figure may only have a 1 per cent effect on profit before tax.
- The current economic position of the company. For instance, is the company suffering from liquidity problems?
- The importance attached by analysts to certain key figures or ratios, such as gross profit percentage (which would, of course, be affected by the stocks matter mentioned above).
- The importance attached by users to the profit and loss account as compared with the balance sheet.

It is no easy matter for the auditors to stand back in a detached manner and consider if users would alter their decisions as a result of an item being adjusted to a 'correct' value. There is no single user and no single decision model and while some users would change their decision, for other users additional knowledge may merely reduce the confidence with which they make their decision. Auditors may seem to be faced with an impossible task, but it is one to which they must apply expert knowledge of financial and other affairs. There may be matters that are not material in financial terms in the context of the financial statements as a whole, but which are nevertheless important items. In Figure 16.1 we noted that the auditor has certain responsibilities in respect of the directors' remuneration report. Thus, if might be that directors' remuneration was understated by £50 000, in circumstances where that amount is not material in the context of the financial statements taken as a whole. The auditors may regard the £50 000 as not material in purely financial terms, but important because it is

See page 612

specifically required by legislation to be disclosed and accurately stated. The auditors would have to consider issuing a modified opinion but this would only be done after discussions with the directors to correct the misstatement.

We have already emphasized the importance of the concept of materiality when determining if an audit opinion should be modified. ISA 700 further refines the concept by distinguishing between two situations. The first is where they believe the matter is material but not pervasive and the second is where the matter is both material and pervasive. ISA 705 (see paragraph 5) gives some guidance on the issue of pervasive by stating:

- It is not confined to one item or matter in the accounts.
- If it is confined to one item then it concerns a matter that is a substantial proportion of the financial statements.
- If the matter relates to disclosures then those disclosures are fundamental to the users' understanding of the financial statements.

ACTIVITY 16.4

Suggest examples of the three factors above that might cause the auditor to conclude that the matter is pervasive.

A good example of a matter that would quite likely affect more than one item in the financial statements might be a misstatement of revenue, affecting not only the turnover figure, but also the profit from operations and the trade receivables figure, and potentially also the inventories figure and other important headings in the financial statements too.

An example of the second category might be a failure to take up expected losses on construction contracts, thus seriously overvaluing the construction contract figure in the financial statements. The matter would be pervasive if the construction contract figure represented a significant proportion of the total assets of the company.

An example of the third category might be a failure to disclose in the notes to the financial statements the circumstances of a fundamental uncertainty concerning the going-concern status of the company.

In the next section we consider the two main reasons why financial statements may be modified. The modification can arise because of what is known as limitation of scope or because of a disagreement.

Limitation of scope

This will arise if auditors are not able to obtain all the evidence required to issue an unmodified opinion. This could be because information is not in existence or at least is not available for the auditors because of reasons outside the client's control or has not been supplied by management. Evidence in the form of accounting records may not be available because they have been stolen or destroyed, perhaps by fire or flood. Alternatively, the auditors may have been unable to gain access to audit an important overseas subsidiary because of political strife in the country in which it is located. These two examples are extreme in nature but, at a more mundane level, auditors may feel that they have not received sufficient or satisfactory explanations from management. For instance, the auditors may be unable to prove whether stock has been properly valued because management refuses to give access to costing records. Where the limitation of scope prevents the auditors gathering what they consider to be sufficient evidence and it relates to a material but not pervasive issue, they will issue a qualified audit report known as an 'except for' opinion. Where the possible effect of limitation of scope is so material and pervasive that they cannot form an opinion, they will have to issue a disclaimer of opinion. ISA 705 makes a distinction between those factors that are imposed on the auditors by management, (for instance, not allowing access to all the records) and those that are outwith the control of auditors or directors (termed in the ISA 'imposed by circumstances'). An example of the latter would be where the timing of the auditors' appointment prevents them from being able to attend the company's inventory count. ISA 705 stresses that where the limitation in scope on their work is imposed by management the auditors should request the removal of the limitation. If management refuse to withdraw the limitation and it is both material and pervasive then they should, if possible, withdraw from the audit. If withdrawal from the audit is impractical, the auditors could undertake the audit for the year in question but issue a disclaimer of opinion and give full details relating to the circumstances surrounding their qualification in their audit report. The auditor may not withdraw from the audit because they have substantially completed the audit work thus making it impractical to withdraw or because there are legal requirements preventing them from withdrawing.

If auditors do withdraw from the audit engagement because of a limitation imposed by management they will indicate this in the statement that is required by the Companies Act 2006 (ss.519 and 521) on ceasing to hold office. Even where the management withdraw the limitation and provide the auditors with the required information the auditors may feel that the issue is symptomatic of wider problems, such as a lack of integrity on the part of the directors, and therefore they may decide not to seek re-appointment as auditors after the completion of the audit. When management impose a limitation, it will normally be regarded by auditors as a serious issue and one they would want to report and discuss with the audit committee where one exists.

You will remember that we discussed this in Chapter 4.

When considering whether a qualified opinion should be issued because of a limitation of scope, the auditors will consider a number of issues. They will identify the evidence they would normally expect to be available to verify the item(s) where there is no limitation of scope. This will be compared with the evidence actually available to them to enable them to judge the extent of the limitation of scope. The auditors will also consider the materiality of the item for which there is insufficient evidence and in particular the possible effect any misstatement of the item(s) would have on the financial statements. As a disclaimer of opinion is only issued where the auditors are unable to form an opinion it is likely that the limitation of scope affects a number of items in the financial statements or if it affects only one item, its financial consequences must be very great in relation to the financial statements as a whole. ISA 705 also gives the example of the auditor obtaining sufficient appropriate audit evidence for a number of uncertainties but concludes that cumulatively the possible effect of the uncertainties is such that they cannot express an opinion. The auditor will issue a qualified 'except for' qualified opinion when, based on the audit tests performed, they are unable to obtain sufficient appropriate evidence to verify the item(s) in the accounts but they are able to conclude that the possible effect of any undetected misstatements are or may be material but not pervasive. Although an 'except for' opinion is more likely to be issued where the limitation of scope affects only one item in the financial statements, it is also possible where the limitation of scope affects a number of items and the possible financial consequences of each item is not particularly large in relation to the financial statements. Where a limitation of scope exists but the auditor is able to obtain alternative evidence for the item or items in questions and that evidence satisfies the requirements of the auditors, they will not need to modify their opinion.

As you have probably gleaned from the above discussion there is no firm line or test available that allows an auditor to distinguish between when a limitation of scope should lead to a disclaimer and when it should lead to an 'except for' opinion. ISA 705 does not provide any firm guidance (other than the matters we have considered above) as to how auditors should make the decision on whether a modification is necessary or on the type of modification. This is a further issue where auditors have to exercise their judgement. ISA 705 and Bulletin 2009/02 provide an example of each type of modification caused by limitation of scope and we consider them in turn.

Disclaimer of opinion

Unless there were particular reasons for the limitation of scope imposed by the directors it is likely that the severity of this type of limitation would cause the auditors to consider if they should continue with this engagement.

trade receivables

The example of a disclaimer given in Bulletin 2009/02 concerns the position where the directors imposed a limitation of scope on the auditors which prevented them from gathering sufficient evidence to confirm the value of inventories and trade receivables (note that the Bulletin uses the terms 'stock(s)' and 'trade debtors') The wording used in the opinion part of Example 19 is reproduced below:

OPINION: DISCLAIMER ON VIEW GIVEN BY THE FINANCIAL STATEMENTS

The audit evidence available to us was limited because we were unable to observe the counting of physical stock having a carrying amount of £X and send confirmation letters to trade debtors having a carrying amount of £Y due to limitations placed on the scope of our work by the directors of the company. As a result of this we have been unable to obtain sufficient appropriate audit evidence concerning both stocks and trade debtors.

Because of the possible effect of the limitation in evidence available to us, we are unable to form an opinion as to whether the financial statements:

- give a true and fair view of the state of the company's affairs as at . . . and of its profit [loss] for the year then ended;
- have been properly prepared in accordance with United Kingdom Generally Accepted Accounting Practice; and
- have been prepared in accordance with the requirements of the Companies Act 2006.

Opinion on other matter prescribed by the Companies Act 2006

Notwithstanding our disclaimer of an opinion on the view given by the financial statements, in our opinion the information given in the directors' report for the financial year for which the financial statements are prepared is consistent with the financial statements.

Matter on which we are required to report by exception

In respect solely of the limitation of our work referred to above:

- we have not obtained all the information and explanations that we considered necessary for the purpose of our audit; and
- we were unable to determine if proper accounting records have been kept.

We have nothing to report in respect of the following matters where the Companies Act 2006 requires us to report to you, if in our opinion:

- returns adequate for our audit have not been received from branches not visited by us; or
- the financial statements are not in agreement with the accounting records and returns; or
- certain disclosures of directors' remuneration required by law are not made.

[Signature]
John Smith (Senior Statutory Auditor) ***Address***

For and on behalf of ABC LLP, Statutory Auditor ***Date***

Source: This extract is taken from Example 19 of APB Bulletin 2009/02

There are some points worth stressing in respect of this audit report. First, the disclaimer relates to the true and fair view, compliance with UK GAAP and the Companies Act 2006. For all of these the auditors are disclaiming an opinion and therefore sending a very clear signal to users that they should not rely on the financial statements. Second, the auditors by stating that they are unable to determine if proper accounting records have been held and that have not received all the necessary explanations and information, are drawing attention to the fact that the company is not complying with two of the major requirements if financial statements are to be successfully prepared and audited. Finally, the auditors have indicated that the lack of evidence relates to stock and debtors and the monetary value of these items in the financial statements.

'Except for' opinion arising from a limitation of scope

The example of an except for opinion arising from limitation of scope given in APB Bulletin 2009/02 relates to the situation where the auditors were unable to observe the stocktake and therefore unable to verify the amount of stock held by the company. In addition, the auditors were unable to find other evidence that could used to verify the stock. The opinion section of the audit report for this example is reproduced below:

QUALIFIED OPINION: LIMITATION ON SCOPE – AUDITOR NOT APPOINTED AT THE DATE OF THE STOCKTAKE

With respect to stock having a carrying amount of £X the audit evidence available to us was limited because we did not observe the counting of the physical stock as at 31 December 20X1, since that date was prior to our appointment as auditor of the company. Owing to the nature of the company's records, we were unable to obtain sufficient appropriate audit evidence regarding the stock quantities by using other audit procedures.

Except for the financial effects of such adjustments, if any, as might have been determined to be necessary had we been able to satisfy ourselves as to physical stock quantities, in our opinion the financial statements:

- give a true and fair view of the state of the company's affairs as at 31 December 20X1 and of its profit [loss] for the year then ended;
- have been properly prepared in accordance with the United Kingdom Generally Accepted Accounting Practice; and
- have been prepared in accordance with the requirements of the Companies Act 2006

Opinion on other matter prescribed by the Companies Act 2006

In our opinion the information given in the directors' report for the financial year for which the financial statements are prepared is consistent with the financial statements.

Matter on which we are required to report by exception

In respect solely of the limitation on our work relating to stock, described above:

- we have not obtained all the information and explanations that we considered necessary for the purpose of our audit; and
- we were unable to determine if adequate accounting records had been kept.

We have nothing to report in respect of the following matters where the Companies Act 2006 requires us to report to you, if in our opinion:

- returns adequate for our audit have not been received from branches not visited by us; or
- the financial statements are not in agreement with the accounting records and returns; or
- certain disclosures of directors' remuneration required by law are not made.

[Signature]
John Smith (Senior Statutory Auditor) **_Address_**

For and on behalf of ABC LLP, Statutory **_Auditor_** **_Date_**

As can be seen in the above example the auditors not only describe the cause of the limitation of scope but also refer to the carrying amount in the financial statements of the items that been subject to a limitation of scope.

Disagreement

A disagreement arises when the auditors can form an opinion on a specific matter but this differs from the opinion of management. The disagreement is likely to result in the financial statements being misstated and the auditors have to determine if that misstatement is material enough to warrant a modified opinion. The misstatement may relate to the amount an item is stated at in the financial statements, its presentation, classification or issues relating to its disclosure. ISA 705 (paragraph A3) states that a material misstatement in the financial statements can arise because of:

- the appropriateness of the selected accounting policies;
- the application of the selected accounting policies; or
- the appropriateness or adequacy of disclosures in the financial statements.

Where the auditors consider that the financial statements of a company need to be modified because of disagreement, they have to determine the type of modified opinion to give. If you look at Figure 16.2 again, you will see that two types of qualification are available – an 'adverse' opinion or an 'except for' opinion. The ISA does not specifically indicate when an adverse opinion should be given but states:

> The auditor shall express an adverse opinion when the auditor, having obtained sufficient appropriate audit evidence, concludes that material misstatements, individually or in the aggregate, are both material and pervasive to the financial statements (ISA 705 para. 8).

On other occasions, where there is a disagreement which is material but not pervasive the auditors should issue an 'except for' opinion. As with the limitation of scope matter we discussed above, the severity of the disagreement qualification given is dependent on the auditor's judgement of the effect of the matter on the financial statements, that is, on how material it is. A disagreement can arise for a number of reasons; various examples of which are discussed below.

The company may use an accounting base, which the auditors believe is inappropriate in the circumstances. You are aware that many accounting areas are the subject of an SSAP, FRS or IAS and, if there is a standard on a particular accounting matter, it will be normal for the company to follow the treatment outlined in the standard. Indeed paragraph 45 in part 3 of Schedule 1 of Statutory Instrument 2008/410 – *The large and medium sized companies and groups (accounts and reports) regulations 2008* requires companies to state that they have followed UK accounting standards and if it has not, details and reasons for not following a standard must be given. If the company does not follow a particular standard in respect of a material matter, the auditors will usually have no alternative but to qualify their opinion on the financial statements. For instance, SSAP 9 – *Stocks and work in progress* and IAS 11 – *Construction contacts*, make it clear that where a company engages in long-term/construction contracts and it is anticipated that some of those contracts will make a loss, those losses should be provided for in full as soon as they become

There is a similar provision for companies that prepare their accounts using International Standards.

We discussed construction contracts in Chapter 13.

known. If the company does not provide for the losses, then, subject to materiality considerations the auditors should qualify the financial statements.

In certain exceptional cases the company may not comply with a particular standard but the auditors may agree that in the circumstances non-compliance with the standard is the correct course of action. In this instance the auditors would not need to qualify the accounts but should ensure that there is full and proper disclosure of the matter in the accounts. The disclosure would include the financial effects of the departure unless this would be impracticable or misleading. The auditors must, however, be able to justify the departure from the standard. They should not merely concur to avoid upsetting their relationship with the company's management, and they should attempt to maintain their independence and not bow to managerial pressure. Throughout, they must use the concept of truth and fairness as their guiding light. When standards are drawn up care is taken to ensure that as far as possible their provisions will have wide acceptability and be appropriate in most circumstances. However, one cannot hope to legislate for every conceivable situation and so there may be occasions, albeit rare, when application of the standard will not be appropriate. Where there is no standard that covers the particular matter affecting the company's accounts, the auditors should use their judgement as to the appropriateness of the selected accounting base. In forming their opinion the auditors must have regard to the industry the company is in and the usual policy adopted by companies in that industry. It may be desirable for the auditors to discuss the matter (without infringing confidentiality) with other members of the accounting profession or other practitioners or the practitioner advisory departments of their accounting body before forming a definitive conclusion. Where a particular accounting treatment used by the directors is generally acceptable but is considered by the auditors to be not the most appropriate treatment in the particular circumstances of the company this can give rise to conflict between the directors and the auditors. It is likely that the directors will argue that the treatment they have selected does not infringe legislation or accounting standards and hence there is no need for the auditors to modify their opinion. The auditors may acknowledge that the treatment adopted is one that does not infringe the terms of any standard but be of the opinion that the particular treatment selected is not the most appropriate in the context of the true and fair view. This kind of situation can be a very difficult and tricky one to manage and can easily cause considerable friction between the auditors and the directors. The auditors should try to convince the directors that the more appropriate treatment should be adopted, as it will more accurately reflect the reality of the company's situation. If the directors do not comply the auditors are then faced with the difficult decision of deciding whether the treatment adopted, although strictly acceptable, does or does not result in the accounts giving a true and fair view. It is obviously better for relations between the directors and the auditors if they can reach some compromise but, if they cannot, the auditors should not simply refrain from giving a modified opinion to remain on good terms with the client's directors. It is on occasions like this that the auditors should remember that they are employed to serve shareholders and not the directors. Finally, where specific disclosures are required for a matter, the auditor has to ensure that these are sufficient to give users an understanding of the issue and are not misleading in any way. This requires auditors to consider both the nature and extent of the disclosures.

'Except for' opinion arising from a disagreement

It is not uncommon for auditors to disagree with the client as to facts or amounts contained in the financial statements. For instance, the company may only have provided £60 000 for bad debts whereas the auditors believe that a figure of £100 000 is more appropriate. If the difference of £40 000 is material, the auditors would have to consider giving a qualification. An example of this type of disagreement and the except for qualification it gives rise is included as Illustration 1 in ISA 705, an adapted extract from which is reproduced below:

BASIS FOR QUALIFIED OPINION

The company's inventories are carried in the balance sheet at £XXX. Management has not stated the inventories at the lower of cost and net realizable value but has stated them solely at cost, which constitutes a departure from International Financial Reporting Standards. The company's records indicate that had management stated the inventories at the lower of cost and net realizable value, an amount of £Y would have been required to write the inventories down to their net realizable value. Accordingly, cost of sales would have increased by £Y and corporation tax, net income and shareholders' equity would have been reduced by £A, £B and £B respectively.

Qualified opinion

In our opinion, except for the effects of the matter described in the Basis for Qualified Opinion paragraph, the financial statements:

- give a true and fair view of Greenburn's affairs as at 31 March 2011 and of its profit for the year then ended;
- have been properly prepared in accordance with IFRSs as adopted by the European Union; and
- have been prepared in accordance with the Companies Act 2006

There are a few points worth making about the above qualification. First, you will notice that details are given about how the qualification has arisen and that it is because of a departure from an IFRS. Second, details are given of the financial implications of not following the standard. Lastly, note that in ISA 705 the details of the disagreement are given under a separate heading, 'Basis for qualified opinion' with the opinion section merely stating that an 'except for' opinion has been given. ISA 705 specifically states in paragraph 16 that there should be a separate paragraph with its own appropriate title, giving details of the matter giving rise to the modification.

Adverse opinion arising from a disagreement

For the sake of completeness we set out below an example of an adverse opinion, which has been adapted from Illustration 2 in ISA 705. This example concerns a situation where a company has failed to consolidate a subsidiary and this has resulted in a material misstatement in the consolidated financial statements which is deemed to be pervasive. The auditor has not been able to calculate the impact of the non-consolidation of the subsidiary on the financial statements. The company prepares its financial statements using IFRSs.

BASIS FOR ADVERSE OPINION

As explained in Note X, the company has not consolidated the financial statements of subsidiary XYZ company it acquired during 20X1 because it has not yet been able to ascertain the fair value of certain of the subsidiary's material assets and liabilities at the acquisition date. This investment is therefore accounted for on a cost basis. Under International Financial Reporting Standards, the subsidiary should have been consolidated because it is controlled by the company. Had XYZ been consolidated many elements in the accompanying financial statements would have been materially affected. The effects on the consolidated financial statements of the failure to consolidate have not been determined.

Adverse opinion

In our opinion, because of the significance of the matter discussed in the 'Basis for Adverse Opinion' paragraph, the consolidated financial statements do not give a true and fair view of the financial position of ABC Company and its subsidiaries as at 31 December 20X1 and of their financial performance and their cash flows for the year then ended in accordance with International Financial Reporting Standards.

Within the UK context the auditors would probably want to add an additional paragraph to the above stating in other respects the financial statements have been prepared in accordance with the requirements of the Companies Act 2006.

The auditors, as well as being concerned with the amounts in the accounts, need to consider the way in which information is presented and disclosures made. The auditors need to ensure that the information is presented in a way that is not misleading. They have also to be aware that, if the information presented is incomplete, the value of the disclosure may be reduced. For instance, if the company has funds in a country that does not allow export of its currency, the fact that there are restrictions on the funds may be relevant information requiring disclosure. You can see from the examples cited above that a disagreement arises because the auditors and the directors differ in their judgement as to the appropriateness of an accounting estimate, the appropriateness of the chosen accounting policy or disclosures required. Because they all involve judgement the auditors need to present as well argued a case as possible to the directors if they wish the latter to adopt the suggestions made by them. Skills of persuasion are important assets for auditors wishing to convince the directors to change the item, giving rise to the disagreement, but the argument must also be logical as well as competently presented.

DISCLAIMER OF RESPONSIBILITY

A recent innovation to the wording of the standard audit report is the addition of a paragraph disclaiming responsibility to third parties. The reason for the addition of an extra paragraph was as a result of the decision in a Scottish legal case, *Royal Bank of Scotland* vs *Bannerman, Maclay and Others,* where a lender brought an action against a firm of auditors claiming that they owed them a duty of care. In this case the Royal Bank of Scotland lent money to ABC Limited and as part of the lending agreement the company was required to supply the bank with its annual audited accounts. Subsequently, the company went into receivership and, with a major fraud having been committed, the bank claimed that the financial statements misstated the company's financial position. It was thought audit procedures concerned with assessing going concern should have made the auditors aware of the loan facility and the fact that the company had to supply the bank with its audited accounts. On the basis of the facts the court decided that the auditors had assumed a responsibility towards the bank and therefore allowed the case to proceed to determine if the auditors had been negligent. This recent case has raised concerns about the extent to which auditors may be liable to third parties, and, in particular, banks. It is recognized that banks often provide funds to companies by way of loan finance, so, if it was accepted that auditors did owe a duty to lenders, it could have substantial consequences for them. As a result the Audit and Assurance Faculty of the ICAEW issued a technical release – *The audit report and auditors' duty of care to third parties,* in January 2003.

The technical release recommended the inclusion of an additional paragraph just before the paragraph on auditors' responsibilities. The suggested wording (slightly amended) is as follows:

> This report is made solely to the company's members, as a body, in accordance with Chapter 3 of Part 16 of the Companies Act 2006. Our audit work has been undertaken so that we might state to the company's members those matters we are required to state to them in an auditor's report and for no other purpose. To the fullest extent permitted by law, we do not accept or assume responsibility to anyone other than the company and the company's members as a body, for our audit work, for this report, or for the opinions we have formed.

Chapter 3 concerns functions of the auditor.

Even though the recommendation to insert an additional paragraph was only issued in January 2003, at the time of writing, the inclusion of such a paragraph appears to have become common practice among the Big Four audit firms. The rationale for this appears to be that, although the insertion of the disclaimer will not prevent third parties suing auditors, it should reduce the probability of such actions being successful. This, however, does not appear to be the view held by the ACCA council. In the ACCA factsheet 84, giving advice on the Bannerman case, it was suggested that it did not change or enlarge the auditors' responsibility beyond that determined by the Caparo case. For this reason the ACCA has not recommended that its members include a disclaimer paragraph in their audit reports. Furthermore, the Association appeared to suggest that such a response was not appropriate in that it would not help regain the confidence of investors as it might give the impression that auditors were attempting to evade their responsibilities. However, given the actual judgement handed down in the Inner House of the Court of Session in 2005, it would appear prudent for the risk adverse audit firm to include a disclaimer to limit the possibility of being found liable to a claim for negligence by a third party.

This concludes our discussion of the audit report but we will return to it again in Chapter 20 when we consider its limitations and whether it could be improved.

REPORTING ON CORPORATE GOVERNANCE ISSUES

Over the last 15 or so years corporate governance has become of great importance in a large number of countries in the world as well as in the United Kingdom, particularly in respect of listed companies, and this has had implications for the responsibilities of auditors. The development of the reporting rules in the UK has been a rather long-winded process and we set out below an historical summary of how it took place.

The listing rules are now issued by the Financial Services Authority.

In the UK the additional burden on auditors commenced with publication of the *Cadbury Report on Corporate Governance* in 1992. Subsequently, the requirements of the Cadbury Report were appended to the listing rules of the London Stock Exchange. These listing rules required the directors of all UK listed companies to disclose certain information in respect of corporate governance in the annual report. The listing rules also required auditors to review some of the corporate governance matters disclosed by the directors. Of particular importance was the requirement for auditors to review whether the information in respect of going concern and internal control was appropriately disclosed. The Cadbury Code contained 19 provisions upon which the directors had to report and the auditors were required to review 11 of them. The provisions of the Cadbury Committee were modified by the publication of the *Hampel Report* which resulted in the issue of a revised Combined Code in 1998 and the *Greenbury Report* which resulted in listing rules on directors' remuneration. The Hampel Combined Code was superseded by a new Combined Code on corporate governance issued in July 2003. The main reason for issuing a new Combined Code in 2003 was to incorporate the Guidance on Audit Committees (known as the *Smith Guidance*) and the guidance contained in the Review of the Role and Effectiveness of Non-executive Directors produced by the *Higgs Committee*. Both of these were published in January 2003. Subsequently, a new Combined Code with a few minor modifications was issued in June 2006. There was a further review of the Combined Code in 2007 which resulted in a couple of changes and a new code was published in 2008. The review in 2007 generally considered that the Combined Code was working well but with some concern that the directors' explanation of how they complied with the code was not as useful to investors as it should be. This was perhaps because the explanation was somewhat general in tone and the hint that perhaps a boiler plate approach was being taken by companies.

We discuss the Smith Guidance in Chapter 18.

At the time of writing the Combined Code is once again being reviewed and we will discuss aspects of this in Chapter 20.

The listing rules were given additional scope when EC Directive 2006/46 on company reporting was published, which requires companies whose securities are admitted to trading on a regulated market disclose a corporate governance statement. The requirements of this directive were enacted in *Disclosure and*

Transparency Rules issued by the Financial Services Authority and by minor amendments to the Companies Act 2006. The specific requirements in respect of the content of the corporate governance statement are set out in *Disclosure and Transparency Rule (DTR) 7.2*. Although the requirements are in most respects similar to that required by the listing rules, there is a specific option allowing the corporate governance statement to be published either; (i) as part of the directors' report; (ii) as a separate report published with the annual report; or (iii) by means of a reference in the directors' report to the company's website where the corporate governance statement can be found. Where the company takes the second option, the auditor has to confirm in the audit report that the information in the corporate governance statement in respect of DTR rules 7.2.5 and 7.2.6 is consistent with the accounts (CA 2006 s.497A). Rule 7.2.5 refers to a description of the main features of the company's internal control and risk management systems in relation to the financial reporting process. Rule 7.2.6 refers to matters relating to share capital structures. Where the company opts to use the third option, the auditors will have to amend their audit report and refer to the Web address where the corporate governance statement can be found and also state that the information contained in it in respect of DTR 7.2.5 and 7.2.6 is consistent with the financial statements.

There is some discussion of the above in Bulletin 2009/04 – *Developments in corporate governance affecting the responsibilities of auditors of UK companies.*

We now return to the specific requirements of the Combined Code and the listing rules. The Combined Code and the listing requirements set the framework for the directors' and auditors' responsibilities in respect of corporate governance. As we mentioned above, the Combined Code is given additional force because its requirements are included as part of the listing rules issued by the Financial Services Authority. The listing rules require that the directors of a listed company set out in the annual report how they have applied the principles required by the Combined Code in a way that is useful and understandable to shareholders. The directors must also include a statement on whether they have complied with the requirements of the Combined Code. Where they have not complied with certain provisions they must state which provisions those are and explain why they did not comply.

The listing rules provide that the auditors must review the nine provisions contained in the companies' statement of corporate governance in respect of the items listed in Table 16.1. The Combined Code (see Provision C.1.1) requires that auditors describe their reporting responsibilities and this will usually be included as part of the audit report. An example of how they might report this is as follows, example 3 of bulletin 2009/02 placing the statement just above the auditors name, signature and address.

APB Bulletin 2009/02 – *Auditor's reports on financial statements in the United Kingdom*.

> Under the listing rules we are required to review:
>
> The directors' statement set out on page X in relation to going concern; and
>
> The part of the Corporate Governance Statement relating to the company's compliance with the provisions of the June 2008 Combined Code specified for our review.

TABLE 16.1 Requirements of the listing rules

Combined Code provision	Requirement
C. 1.1	The directors should explain in the annual report their responsibility for preparing the accounts and there should be a statement by the auditors about their reporting responsibilities.
C. 2.1	The directors should, at least annually, conduct a review of the effectiveness of the group's system of internal controls and should report to shareholders that they have done so. The review should cover all material controls, including financial, operational and compliance controls and risk management systems.
C. 3.1	The board should establish an audit committee of at least three, or in the case of smaller companies two, independent non-executive directors. In smaller companies the company chairman may be a member of, but not chair, the committee in addition to the independent non-executive directors, provided he or she was considered independent on appointment as chairman. The board should satisfy itself that at least one member of the audit committee has recent and relevant financial experience.
C. 3.2	The main role and responsibilities of the audit committee should be set out in written terms of reference and should include: • To monitor the integrity of the financial statements of the company, and any formal announcements relating to the company's financial performance, reviewing significant financial reporting judgements contained in them. • To review the company's internal financial controls and, unless expressly addressed by a separate board risk committee composed of independent directors, or by the board itself, to review the company's internal control and risk management systems. • To monitor and review the effectiveness of the company's internal audit function. • To make recommendations to the board, for it to be put to the shareholders for their approval in general meeting, in relation to the appointment, re-appointment and removal of the external auditor and to approve the remuneration and terms of engagement of the external auditor. • To review and monitor the external auditor's independence and objectivity and the effectiveness of the audit process, taking into consideration relevant UK professional and regulatory requirements. • To develop and implement policy on the engagement of the external auditor to supply non-audit services, taking into account relevant ethical guidance regarding the provision of non-audit services by the external audit firm; and to report to the board, identifying any matters in respect of which it considers that action or improvement is needed and making recommendations as to the steps to be taken.
C. 3.3	The terms of reference of the audit committee, including its role and the authority designated to it by the board, should be made available. A separate section of the annual report should describe the work of the committee in discharging those responsibilities.
C.3.4	The audit committee should review arrangements by which staff of the company may, in confidence, raise concerns about possible improprieties in matters of financial reporting or other matters. The audit committee's objective should be to

TABLE 16.1 *(Continued)*

Combined Code provision	Requirement
	ensure that arrangements are in place for the proportionate and independent investigation of such matters and for appropriate follow-up action.
C.3.5	The audit committee should monitor and review the effectiveness of the internal audit activities. Where there is no internal audit function, the audit committee should consider annually whether there is a need for an internal audit function and make a recommendation to the board, and the reasons for the absence of such a function should be explained in the relevant section of the annual report.
C.3.6	The audit committee should have primary responsibility for making a recommendation on the appointment, reappointment and removal of the external auditors. If the board does not accept the audit committee's recommendation, it should include in the annual report, and in any papers recommending appointment or re-appointment, a statement from the audit committee explaining the recommendation and should set out reasons why the board has taken a different position.
C.3.7	The annual report should explain to shareholders how, if the auditor provides non-audit services, auditor objectivity and independence is safeguarded

Source: Financial Reporting Council: Combined Code on corporate governance (June 2008)

Where a company does not comply with a particular Combined Code requirement, coming within the scope of the auditors' review, but have properly disclosed that fact in their corporate governance statement, the auditors would not be required to make any reference to non-compliance. Bulletin 2006/05 suggests that the auditor does not need to perform any additional procedures to determine the appropriateness of the reasons given for nondisclosure of a particular provision but merely that the directors' description of the non-disclosure is adequate. Where, however, the auditors do not believe the disclosure of a departure from a provision of the code has been adequate, they would need to report this fact in their audit report. This would not normally constitute a qualified audit report but would simply be included after the opinion paragraph in an other matter paragraph. As a matter of course the auditor would read the directors' complete statement on corporate governance and ensure that it is consistent with other information the auditor has obtained during their audit and that to the best of their knowledge does not contain any misstatements. Where the auditors believe some element of the corporate governance disclosures contains an inconsistency they would seek to resolve this with the directors. In the next part of this section we discuss the typical evidence auditors may gather in respect of the nine provisions for which they have specific responsibility, to support the assertions being made by the directors in their corporate governance statement.

APB Bulletin 2006/05 The Combined Code on corporate governance: requirements of auditors under the listing rules of the Financial Services Authority and the Irish Stock Exchange.

Prior to discussing the specific procedures it is important to recognize that the auditors will already have accumulated a considerable amount of evidence in verifying other aspects of the financial statements and therefore should

The various procedures that should be adopted by the auditor are discussed in APB Bulletin 2006/05 – *The Combined Code on corporate governance: requirements of auditors under the listing rules of the Financial Services Authority and the Irish Stock Exchange.*

already have a considerable knowledge about some of the matters required by the Combined Code. For instance, they will as a matter of course have examined board minutes and the minutes of sub-committees of the board and have discussed various matters with the directors of the company. The main specific procedures adopted by the auditors to verify compliance with the Combined Code provisions include:

Code Provision C.1.1

The auditor would check that the directors have in fact explained their responsibility in a statement contained in the annual report.

Code Provision C.2.1

This is probably the most difficult aspect of the code that the auditor has to review and also probably the one that requires most thought and work on the part of the directors. It is in recognition of this that the Financial Reporting Council issued guidance to directors in the revised Turnbull Guidance – *Internal Control: Revised Guidance for Directors on the Combined Code,* published in October 2005. Perhaps the most contentious part of the code provisions relates to directors reporting that they have conducted a review on the effectiveness of the company's system of internal control. Although auditors will normally, as part of their audit, have evaluated the company's system of internal control, it must be stressed that the code provision goes beyond financial controls. More generally, to review the directors' statement on internal controls, auditors would normally have to undertake some additional work, including:

Initial guidance on the implementation of this requirement was contained in the publication *Internal Control and Financial Reporting: Guidance for Directors of Listed Companies Registered in the UK*, The Turnbull Guidance, published by ICAEW in 1999.

- Determining the process by which the directors reviewed the effectiveness of the system of internal control and comparing that with the statement the directors make on internal control.
- Reviewing the documentation prepared for the directors and evaluating if it supported the directors' statement.
- Determining if the directors' statement accords with the auditors' knowledge of the system of internal control obtained from their audit procedures and with knowledge of the company.
- Ensuring that the directors' statement covers the financial year and the period to the date of approval of the annual report and financial statements.
- In respect of internal control aspects of significant problems disclosed in the annual report, the auditors should discuss the issue with the directors and evaluate any disclosures the directors have made in respect of processes implemented to deal with those internal control aspects of the problem. This is likely to be a difficult and very judgemental area for both directors and auditors since revised Turnbull gives little guidance as to what is meant by a significant problem and in identifying whether there are any internal control aspects related to the problem.

The Board is also required by Paragraph 36 of the FRC publication – *Internal Control: Revised Guidance for Directors on the Combined Code* to confirm in their corporate governance statement that the necessary actions have been taken or are underway to remedy any significant weaknesses highlighted by their review of the effectiveness of internal control. In respect of this the auditors should:

- Review documentation relating to the identified significant weaknesses.
- Discuss with the directors any actions they have taken or are considering in respect of the weaknesses.
- Compare the directors' statement on this aspect with their knowledge of the company.

Where the directors do not review the effectiveness of the system of internal control they must disclose this, giving the reasons why they have not done so. The auditors would have to check that the directors' explanation for the failure to carry out a review is adequate and is consistent with their understanding. Where the auditors undertake the additional work above and conclude, for instance, that the description of the process used to review the effectiveness of the internal controls is inaccurate or that the description of the process implemented by the directors is inaccurate in some way, they should report as such in an other matter paragraph in their audit report

It should be apparent that the disclosures by the directors relating to the effectiveness of a company's system of internal control and the reviewing of that statement by the auditors can be controversial. It should, however, be noted that the original Cadbury Committee Code had suggested that the directors should report on the effectiveness of the company's system of internal control and that auditors should review that statement. Unfortunately there were significant problems in the implementation of this provision particularly in respect of the requirement to report on effectiveness. Most annual reports at that time contained rather general and vague comments on the company's system of internal control, particularly when it came to reporting on their effectiveness. Perhaps, because of the lack of general acceptance of this provision of the code, the Hampel Committee Code suggested that, instead, the directors should, at least annually, conduct a review of the effectiveness of the group's system of internal controls and should report to shareholders that they have done so. This requirement is still in force.

We point this out because a similar requirement to the Cadbury requirements was implemented in the United States where it has created considerable controversy.

ACTIVITY 16.5

Outline how you think the auditor would verify that the company has complied with Code provision C.3.1.

You might have suggested that in the first instance the auditor would need to check that there is an audit committee and that it is composed of three independent non-executive directors and they are identified as such in the annual report. This should be a fairly routine task and just requires the auditor to check relevant documentation. The auditors would also need to check how

Two non-executive independent directors if the listed company is not included in the FTSE 350.

the company determined that the directors were independent and review any available evidence to support this assertion. The Combined Code lays down guidance on non-executive director independence. The auditors do not have any direct responsibility to verify that the criteria are met, but if, as a result of their audit work, they believe any of the non-executive directors named as independent do not meet the criteria, they should discuss the matter with the directors of the company. Similarly, the auditor should review how the company has arrived at the conclusion that at least one of the directors has recent and relevant financial experience. Obvious evidence here that might support the board's assertion would be if one of the non-executive directors had recently held the post of finance director at a plc and was a qualified accountant. APB Bulletin 2006/05 emphasizes the main concern of the auditor is to ensure that the board has procedures in place that allow them to make the statement required by the Combined Code.

Code provisions C.3.2,C.3.3 and C.3.4

The obvious starting point to verify compliance with this part of the code is to obtain a copy of the terms of reference. The next stage would be for the auditor to ensure that it contains reference to the various matters referred to in this code provision. To verify compliance with code provision C.3.3 the auditor would check that the terms of reference are available, for instance, on the company's website and that it contains details of the work of the audit committee. The auditor, as part of their audit procedures when verifying other information contained in the annual report, would ensure that there is a description of how the audit committee discharges its responsibilities.

The auditor's responsibilities for other information contained in the annual report is discussed in ISA 720.

ACTIVITY 16.6

Can you identify any issues that might arise if employees alert management or other authorities to possible improprieties?

The raising of concerns about possible improprieties can be a controversial issue since the person alerting authorities outwith the company may feel that they are being disloyal. Indeed at one time there was a bit of a stigma attached to employees who blew the whistle on a company or its employees engaged in improprieties. This was particularly the case where the improprieties were carried out by senior management. It also needs to be recognized that business sometimes can involve being engaged in practices that are close to being or actually are illegal, such as the payment of sweeteners or bribes, the obtaining of privileged information about a competitor's strategy and so on. It should also be remembered that a practice that is frowned upon in one country may be an accepted part of business practice in another. Although the issue of whistleblowing can be contentious, in the last ten years or so companies have begun to grapple with it, many companies now having in place codes of conduct and procedures about how concerned employees can alert senior management. In terms of audit procedures the auditor should review available documentation about any concerns that have been raised by employees. This would include reviewing audit committee minutes to ensure that there is evidence that the audit committee has considered the arrangements for staff to raise concerns in respect of possible improprieties. The auditor may also discuss this issue with members of the audit committee.

Code provision C.3.5

The procedures followed here are likely to be similar to those involved in code provision C.3.4, that is, reviewing relevant documentation and discussion with appropriate members of the audit committee. Since it is likely, where there is an internal audit function, that the auditor will have made use of their work and been concerned about issues, such as whether the audit committee takes their reports seriously, reviewing compliance with this part of the code should be relatively straightforward. If the company does not have an internal audit function, the auditor will seek to verify, using minutes of the audit committee meetings, that they consider annually whether an internal audit function should be established, making a recommendation to the board in this respect. The latter should be verifiable from the board minutes. The auditors would also check that the company explains in the annual report why there is no internal audit function.

Code provision C.3.6

The auditor should examine the audit committee's terms of reference to ascertain that certain matters relating to the employment of the auditor come within its remit. If there is no mention in the terms of reference, other documentation should be sought to determine that the audit committee is responsible for the matters coming with in this provision. Any recommendation from the audit committee to the main board should be verifiable from both the audit committee's minutes and those of the main board. Similarly, where the audit committee's recommendations are not accepted, the auditor would check that the annual report contains an explanation of why the board decided not to accept the committee's recommendation.

Code provision C.3.7

Where the auditor provides non-audit services they will check that the annual report contains a statement by the company outlining how auditor independence and objectivity is maintained. Again, because the auditor is likely to have considerable communication and discussion with the audit committee about this matter, verification should be relatively unproblematic. The provision of non-audit services was one of the issues raised in debates concerning the recent banking crisis and it is therefore important for the auditor to have engaged in discussions with the audit committee about maintenance of independence where they provide other services.

In addition to the above, the listing rules also place an onerous responsibility on both the directors and the auditors in listing rule 9.8.6 (3). This rule requires a statement by the directors that the business is a going concern along with supporting assumptions or qualifications; this statement must be prepared in accordance with the guidance issued by the FRC in their document *Going concern and liquidity risk: guidance for directors of UK companies* published in October 2009. The auditors' duty will be to ensure that the directors'

We discuss the issue of going concern further in Chapter 17.

statement is consistent with their knowledge of the business and that it meets the requirements of rule 9.8.6 (3). Where the auditors disagree with the directors about the appropriateness of using the going-concern basis or about the adequacy of disclosures required, they will either issue a modified opinion or include appropriate disclosures in their audit report.

We have discussed above the reporting of corporate governance matters and the auditors' duties in respect of such reporting. In Chapter 18 we discuss a number of other matters contained in the Combined Code, including the appointment of non-executive directors and the composition and role of audit committees. Finally, in addition to the above provisions that the auditor is required to review, the listing rules require that the scope of the auditors' report on the financial statements must cover the disclosure of certain items. A summary of the main items coming within this provision is given below:

Listing rule	Disclosure requirement
9.8.8R (2)	Details of the remuneration package for each director (by name), any compensation for loss of office, any significant payments made to former directors and information on share options for each director.
9.8.8R (3), (4) and (5)	Details of any long-term incentive schemes and the interests of each director (by name) in such schemes at the start of the period under review and any entitlements awarded during the year.
9.8.8R (11)	For money purchase pension schemes details of the contribution or allowance payable or made by the company in respect of each director during the period under review.
9.8.8R (12)	Details for defined benefit pension schemes of the amount of any increase for the period under review and the accumulated total amount at the end of the period in respect of the accrued benefit to which each director would be entitled on leaving service.

Where, in the auditors' opinion, the directors have not complied with any of the above disclosure requirements, they must state so in their report. Furthermore, they must also include in their report, where they are reasonably able to do so, a statement giving the required disclosure details. It is likely, where the directors do omit certain disclosures, that the auditors will provide such information in an emphasis of matter paragraph, but will not modify the audit report. However, before this stage is reached the auditors would have discussed the matter with the directors of the company and attempted to persuade them to include the necessary information.

ELECTRONIC PUBLICATION OF AUDITORS' REPORTS

In recent years it has become common for companies to place financial information, or indeed their annual report, on the World Wide Web. This method of making the accounts available was furthered by the Companies Act 2006 (s.430) making it a requirement of quoted companies that the annual accounts and reports should be made available on a website. This raises particular problems for auditors for three main reasons:

APB issued guidance on this topic in Bulletin 2001/1 – *The electronic publication of auditors' reports* which was issued in January 2001.

- *Information on the Web is more easily changed or altered.* Where financial information is published on the Web, auditors should encourage the directors to indicate clearly in their statement of responsibilities that they are responsible for maintaining the integrity of the information placed there. It should be apparent that, where directors make use of the Web, they should install control systems that prevent the unauthorized alteration of the information published there. Where the auditors consider it necessary, they may include a statement after the audit report, clearly indicating that the directors are responsible for the maintenance of the information on the Web and that the auditors are not responsible for any changes to the financial statements that have occurred since the information was initially posted.
- *It may not be readily apparent what information included on the Web has been subject to audit.* As we have seen in this chapter, auditors may indicate in their audit report the information that has been audited by referring to the appropriate page numbers of the company's reporting package. When published on the Web, the page numbers may not be so readily apparent, particularly if they are posted using HTML rather than PDF format. In the audit report appended to the electronic version of the financial statements, rather than referring to page numbers, the auditors may refer to the actual financial information that has been subject to audit. The auditors should encourage the directors to adopt an electronic presentation that makes the reader aware of what information has been audited and what has not been audited. For instance, they may include a watermark with the message AUDITED on pages where the information has been subject to audit.
- *The information on the Web can be accessed in many different countries.* The bulletin recommends that the auditors specifically identify in their audit report the nationality of the auditing standards they have used and sufficient information enabling the reader to identify the country in which the auditors are located.

Where a client intends to distribute its financial statements electronically the bulletin suggests auditors should undertake the following procedures:

- Review the process by which the financial statements to be published electronically are derived from the financial information contained in the manually signed accounts.
- Check that the proposed electronic version is identical in content with the manually signed accounts.
- Check that the conversion of the manually signed accounts into an electronic form has not distorted the overall presentation of the financial information, for instance, by highlighting certain information so as to give it greater prominence.

Summary

In this chapter we have discussed the way in which auditors report the results of their audit investigation to members of the company. We described the main components of the audit report as given in ISA 700 (UK and Ireland) – *The auditor's report on financial statements*. It was noted that the audit report contains some text explaining auditors' responsibilities and the nature of the audit work they perform. It was also noted that the auditor, as well as reporting if the financial statements give a true and fair view, also states if they are in compliance with the Companies Act 2006 and with whatever accounting framework has been used in their preparation. We saw that there may be occasions where the auditors agree with the directors on an issue, but nevertheless believe that because of its nature that it should be brought to the attention of shareholders by using either an 'emphasis of matter' or 'an other matter' paragraph. Following this we considered the topic of the modified audit opinion and described how a modification can arise either because of a 'limitations of scope' or a 'disagreements'. We showed that, corresponding to each of these categories, auditors can give one of two forms of modified audit opinion, the precise form depending on the severity of the 'limitation of scope' or 'disagreement'. Where the disagreement or limitation of scope is material, the audit report would be qualified using the term 'except for'. If the disagreement or limitation in scope is material and pervasive, the audit report would be an adverse or disclaimer of opinion respectively. Since the early 1990s auditors' reporting responsibilities have been expanded by the requirement that they report on certain corporate governance issues. We outlined in some detail the contents of the Combined Code of Corporate Governance issued by the Financial Reporting Council and its incorporation along with previous code requirements of the Cadbury Committee in the Financial Services Authority listing rules. We also briefly discussed some of the implications for auditors of the implementation of EC Directive 2006/46 and the issuing of Disclosure and Transparency Rules by the FSA. This was followed by a discussion of the implications for auditors of companies using electronic means, such as the Web, to publish financial information.

Key points of the chapter

- Auditors communicate views on financial statements in the audit report. If satisfied they give a true and fair view and comply with legislation, they give an unmodified opinion; if dissatisfied, a modified opinion may be appropriate. Auditing standards require 'reasonable assurance', other engagements may give only 'limited assurance'. The current audit report is a 'long-form' report.
- A clean unlisted company audit report has a number of sections: (a) title; (b) addressee; (c) identification of the financial statements; (d) responsibilities; (e) scope of audit; (f) opinion; (g) opinion on other CA 2006 matters; (h) matters reported by exception; (i) date of audit report; (j) location of auditor's office; (k) auditor's signature.
- Auditors identify the published information and check that information not audited does not conflict with the financial statements. If there is inconsistency or incorrect information auditors consider amendment to the other information or financial statements.
- Auditors state their responsibility is to form an opinion on the financial statements. Directors' responsibilities include: (a) preparation of financial statements giving a true and fair view; (b) selection of suitable consistent accounting policies; making reasonable judgements/estimates; following applicable accounting standards; determining appropriateness of the going-concern assumption; (c) ensuring proper accounting records; safeguarding assets; taking action to prevent and detect fraud and other irregularities.
- Responsibilities statements are to make clear the extent and scope of the respective responsibilities of the directors and auditors.
- Auditors make a statement of the scope of audit in three possible ways.
- Auditors express an opinion and not a guarantee. The opinion is directed towards three basic matters: (a) truth and fairness; (b) compliance with CA 2006; (c) proper preparation in accordance with identified accounting framework.
- Information in the directors' report must be consistent with the financial statements.
- For large and medium-sized companies auditors report that the part of the directors' remuneration report subject to audit has been properly prepared.
- CA 2006 requires companies to state financial statements have been prepared using applicable accounting standards; if not, details of and reasons for material departure from standards, together with financial effect, are given. Companies may depart from a provision of the CA 2006 to give a true and fair view, but reasons and effect should be disclosed.
- Emphasis of matter and other matter paragraphs are not qualification matters, but matters the auditor

wishes to bring to the attention of shareholders. Emphasis of matter may be used where there is uncertainty regarding the outcome of litigation or regarding the going-concern status. Directors must make appropriate disclosures and auditors must concur with their judgement and the disclosures made by the directors. Emphasis of matter should not be used where the auditors disagree with the directors' assertion that the company is a going concern.

- Qualifications in the audit report indicate there are material but not pervasive matters about which the auditors are dissatisfied because of (a) limitation in audit scope; (b) disagreement with treatment or disclosure.
- Limitation of scope arises if auditors are unable to obtain sufficient appropriate evidence. If the possible effect is material but not pervasive auditors issue an except for opinion. The audit report includes a description of factors leading to a qualified opinion.
- Disagreement arises when the auditors form an opinion that differs from the opinion of management. Where the effect of the disagreement is material but not pervasive, the auditors issue an except for opinion. Disagreement can arise for a number of reasons, including selection of an inappropriate accounting policy, or one inappropriately applied, and where disclosures are inadequate.
- If the possible effect of the limitation in scope is material and pervasive the auditor will issue a disclaimer. If the limitation in scope has been imposed by management, the auditors would normally withdraw from the assignment, but the auditor should try to persuade management to remove the limitation.
- Where there is a disagreement and the effect is both material and pervasive, the auditors issue an adverse audit opinion.
- If an opinion is modified for disagreement the auditors should include reasons for the modification and the effect on the financial statements.
- A paragraph disclaiming responsibility to third parties, arising from the Bannerman case, is common practice among the Big Four.
- There have been numerous reports on corporate governance and different versions of a corporate governance code.
- The listing rules require auditors to review certain Combined Code provisions that directors are required to include in their statement of corporate governance.
- The auditors do not have a responsibility to check the application of the directors' statement on the Combined Code.
- Auditors must: (a) determine how directors reviewed the effectiveness of internal control; (b) review and evaluate documentation prepared for the directors; (c) determine if the directors' statement accords with the auditors' knowledge of internal control and of the company; (d) enquire how the company has dealt with significant internal control weaknesses.
- Auditors' corporate governance review will include: (a) reviewing board and board committee minutes; (b) reviewing relevant documentation; (c) discussing relevant matters with appropriate directors; (d) attending meetings of the audit committee when considering annual report and corporate governance statement; (e) checking the terms of reference of the audit committee, (f) reviewing relevant documentation of the audit committee.
- Listing rules require companies to state that the business is a going concern with supporting assumptions or qualifications; auditors ensure the directors' statement is consistent with their knowledge of the business and that it meets the listing rule requirements.
- Companies in Great Britain often post financial reports on the Web, raising problems for auditors because: (a) information is easily changed; (b) may not be apparent what information has been subject to audit; (c) information can be accessed in many different countries.
- Where a client publishes financial statements on the Web, auditors should check (a) how the electronic financial statements are derived; (b) the proposed electronic version is identical to the manually signed accounts; (c) conversion of the manually signed accounts has not distorted overall presentation.

Further reading

The obvious starting point for reading on this chapter is ISA 700 (UK and Ireland) – *The Auditor's report on financial statements*, issued by the Auditing Practices Board in October 2009.

ISA 705 – *Modifications to the opinion in the independent auditor's report* and ISA 706 – *Emphasis of matter paragraphs and other matter paragraphs in the independent auditor's report,* both published in 2009.

See also Chapter 10, 'Audit Reports' by David Hatherly published in *Current Issues In Auditing*, 3rd edn, Michael Sherer and Stuart Turley (eds), London: Paul Chapman Publishing, 1997.

On corporate governance students are recommended to read the Combined Code issued in June 2008 available at http://www.frc.org.uk/documents/pagemanager/frc/Combined_Code_June_2008/Combined%20Code%20Web%20Optimized%20June%202008(2).pdf and Internal Control: Revised Guidance for Directors on the Combined Code available at http://www.frc.org.uk/documents/pagemanager/frc/Revised%20Turnbull%20Guidance%20October%202005.pdf

You may also find it useful to check the following website, **http://www.ecgi.org**, which contains much information on corporate governance worldwide.

You will also find it useful to read the APB Bulletins:

Bulletin 2006/05 – *The Combined Code on Corporate Governance: requirements of auditors under the listing rules of the Financial Services Authority and the Irish Stock Exchange*

Bulletin 2009/02 – *Auditor's reports on financial statements in the United Kingdom*

Bulletin 2008/6 *The 'senior statutory auditor' under the United Kingdom Companies Act 2006*

Bulletin 2009/4 *Developments in corporate governance affecting the responsibilities of auditors of UK companies*. All the bulletins are available at **http://www.frc.org.uk/apb/publications/bulletins.cfm**.

Self-assessment questions (solutions available to students)

16.1 Consider the following statements and explain why they may be true or false.

(a) If a company fails to comply with the provisions of a specific SSAP, FRS, or IFRS the company's auditors would have no alternative but to issue a qualified report.

(b) Although auditors may find a number of errors in an audit investigation, these will only result in a qualified report if they are material.

(c) Auditors' reporting duties on a company's annual report only extends to the financial statements and relevant notes.

(d) Auditors will only sign and date their audit report when satisfied sufficient audit evidence has been gathered and the reporting partner has reviewed the audit file.

(e) Where auditors disagree with a particular accounting policy adopted by a client and consider that the implementation results in a material effect but does not result in the financial statements being seriously misstated or misleading, they should issue an 'except for' opinion.

16.2 The following question is an adapted and updated version of a question from the ACCA December 1994 Paper 6, Audit Framework.

ISA 700 (UK and Ireland) – *The auditor's report on financial statements*, issued in October 2009, provides guidance on when a modified opinion is appropriate.

Your firm audits the following two companies, and you have been asked to consider the form of qualified or unqualified audit report which should be given.

Gamston Burgers plc has a loss-making branch and it has included fixed assets relating to this branch at £710 000, after deducting a provision for permanent diminution in value of £250 000. The directors believe that if operating changes are made and economic conditions improve, there is a reasonable probability of the branch trading satisfactorily, which will result in the current value of tangible fixed assets exceeding £710 000. However, under the current circumstances, the directors consider the extent of any permanent diminution in value to be uncertain. You have obtained all the evidence you would have reasonably expected to be available. If trading conditions do not improve, your audit investigations have concluded that the branch will have to close. If the branch closes, the tangible fixed assets will be worthless, as the property is leased and the cost of moving any tangible fixed assets will be more than their net realizable value. If the tangible fixed assets are worthless, you have concluded that the effect will be material, but it will not result in the financial statements being misleading.

Keyworth Supermarket Limited sells food to the general public and customers pay in cash or by cheque. Your audit tests reveal that controls over cash takings and the custody of stock are weak, and you have not been able to obtain sufficient evidence to quantify the effect of any misappropriation of stock or cash takings. You have concluded that:

(i) if the uncertainty relates to all the company's sales, it could result in the financial statements being misleading; and

(ii) if the uncertainty relates to only the sale of fresh fruit and vegetables, which comprise ten per cent of the company's sales, it will have a material effect on the financial statements but it will not result in them being misleading.

Required

(a) List and briefly describe the contents of an unqualified audit report. (8 marks)

(b) Consider and describe the form of an unqualified or qualified audit report you would give in each of the following situations:

- On Gamston Burgers plc's financial statements if you agree with the directors' statements about the uncertainty relating to the value of the tangible fixed assets of the branch.
- On Gamston Burgers plc's financial statements if you have come to the conclusion that trading conditions will not improve and the company will have to close the branch. Thus, the tangible fixed assets will be worthless.
- On Keyworth Supermarket Limited's financial statements if the uncertainty about the misappropriation of stock and cash takings relates to *all* the company's sales.
- On Keyworth Supermarket Limited's financial statements if the uncertainty about the misappropriation of stock and cash takings relates only to the sale of fresh fruit and vegetables which comprise ten per cent of the company's sales. (12 marks)

Note: In part (b) the marks are divided equally between each of the four parts.

Tutorial note: In answering this question you may assume that any provisions that may be required satisfy the terms of FRS 12.

16.3 Write brief notes of the following topics:

(a) Discuss the extent to which you believe that the inclusion of a scope paragraph and a brief description of the auditors' responsibilities in the extended audit report is useful.

(b) Briefly outline the merits and limitations of the extended audit report.

(c) Discuss the arguments for and against auditors reporting on the effectiveness of a company's internal control systems.

(d) Comment on the extent to which you believe the auditors' responsibilities as contained in the Combined Code on Corporate Governance provides useful information to users of the financial statements.

Self-assessment questions (solutions available to tutors)

16.4 The following question, slightly adapted, has been taken from the ICAEW, Professional Stage Examination, Audit and Assurance paper of December 2002.

Described below are situations which have arisen in three audit clients of your firm. The year-end in each case is 30 September 2011.

Vista plc

Vista plc, a supplier of retail display equipment, has included in its profit and loss account immediately below net profit after tax an exceptional loss of £3.7 million on the sale of a trade investment. The accounting treatment is not in accordance with FRS3 – *Reporting financial performance*, which requires the loss to be taken into account in arriving at the profit or loss on ordinary activities before taxation. The pre-tax profit of Vista plc for the year ended 30 September 2011 is £694 000.

Expo Ltd

Expo Ltd exports a significant amount of its products and has a major distribution centre in an overseas country in which there has been a military coup. As a result of travel restrictions imposed by the military junta, it was not possible for your firm to attend the year-end stocktake. The stock at the overseas distribution centre at 30 September 2011 represented 75 per cent of Expo Ltd's stock.

Pharm plc
Pharm plc, a company engaged in the manufacture of pharmaceutical products, has extensive interests in an overseas country which requires pharmaceutical products to be registered. The regulatory situation in that country is undergoing considerable change and Pharm plc does not expect to obtain drug registration as quickly as originally anticipated. However, after carrying out the appropriate review, the directors have decided that Pharm plc has enough resources to continue for the next 12 months. Additional funding will be required from that point, and the directors believe that this can be achieved by a further issue of shares within the next 12 months.
The directors have included a note to the accounts explaining this situation.

Required

(a) List the conditions of the Companies Acts which have to be satisfied before an unmodified audit report on annual financial statements can be issued.

(b) In respect of the situations outlined above, reach a conclusion on whether or not you would modify each audit report. Give reasons for your conclusions and describe the potential effects on each audit report.

16.5 Presently, the audit report issued with the financial statements tends to have standardized wording following the examples in APB Bulletin 2009/02 – *Auditor's reports on financial statements in the United Kingdom*. Discuss the arguments for and against auditors having a free hand in the wording of the audit report.

16.6 The following question has been adapted from a question in the ICAEW, Professional Stage Examination, Audit and Assurance paper of December 2002.

Described below are situations which have arisen in four audits. The year-end in each case is 31 March 2011.

Mercury Ltd
On 21 March 2011, the Inland Revenue commenced a major enquiry into all aspects of the tax affairs of the company. Until the enquiry is completed, it is not possible to estimate, with any reasonable degree of certainty, any ultimate liability which may fall upon the company. Consequently, no liability in respect of this matter has been included in the financial statements. The directors have included a note to the accounts explaining the situation.

Pluto Ltd
Included in the balance sheet at 31 March 2011 are fixed assets at cost of £2.5 million which have been constructed by the company during the year. The costs include own labour capitalized of £180 000. The labour costs have been based on the directors' estimates of time spent by employees on the construction work, which are unsupported by time records. There are no satisfactory audit procedures to confirm that labour costs have been appropriately capitalized. The pre-tax profit of Pluto Ltd for the year ended 31 March 2011 is £650 000.

Neptune Ltd
In January 2011, the company received a government cash grant of £1.6 million in respect of assistance with the acquisition of fixed assets which have estimated useful economic lives of between five and ten years. The £1.6 million has been credited directly to the profit and loss account for the year ended 31 March 2011. The directors insist on continuing with this treatment despite having been informed that this is not in accordance with SSAP4 – *Accounting*

for government grants, which requires such grants to be credited to profit and loss over the useful economic lives of the assets to which the grant relates. The pre-tax profit of Neptune Ltd for the year ended 31 March 2011 is £1.1 million.

Jupiter Ltd

On 16 May 2011 a receiver was appointed at Saturn Ltd, a major customer of Jupiter Ltd. The balance due from Saturn Ltd on 31 March 2011 was £242 000. In addition, work in progress included £520 000, the cost of customized work relating to Saturn Ltd. The directors refuse to make a provision for the debt on the grounds that the receiver was appointed after the balance sheet date. They also refuse to make any provision in respect of work in progress because they are planning to convert it to finished goods at an estimated cost on completion of £260 000 as another customer has agreed to buy it for £700 000. Final audit materiality has been set at £250 000 for Jupiter Ltd for the year ended 31 March 2011.

Required

In respect of each of the situations outlined above, reach a conclusion on whether or not you would modify your audit report. Give reasons for your conclusion and describe the effect on your audit report.

Topics for class discussion without solutions

16.7 Discuss the extent to which you believe the audit report does not provide enough insight about the findings derived from an audit.

16.8 The value of the auditor's involvement in reviewing certain of the Combined Code requirements would be much enhanced if the auditors actually provided an opinion on the nature of the disclosures made by the directors rather than just ensuring that directors have made the relevant disclosures. Discuss.

16.9 The audit report is a rather crude device to inform shareholders about the auditors' satisfaction, or dissatisfaction, with the view given by the financial statements and their compliance with the Companies Act and with the accounting framework used in their preparation. It would be beneficial to shareholders and other users if the auditor graded the financial statements using a number of attributes, somewhat along the lines of a school report card. Discuss

17

Fraud and going concern

LEARNING OBJECTIVES

After studying this chapter you should be able to:

- **Describe auditors' and directors' responsibilities for deterring and detecting fraud.**
- **Outline the factors which may indicate a higher than usual risk of fraud.**
- **Discuss suggestions made by the audit profession in respect of auditors' responsibilities to detect fraud.**
- **Describe auditors' reporting requirements when they suspect fraud has occurred.**
- **Be aware of some recent financial scandals involving auditors.**
- **Outline the auditors' responsibilities for considering compliance with law and regulations.**
- **Describe the importance of the going-concern concept.**
- **Describe the information sources directors and auditors may use to determine if a business is a going concern.**
- **Discuss the potential implications for auditors where there is some doubt over whether a client is a going concern.**

Learning objectives, 654
Introduction to fraud, 655
Responsibility for fraud detection, 656
Recent debates relating to fraud, 667
Case law relating to fraud, 670
Auditing scandals, 672
Consideration of law and regulations, 674
Introduction to going concern, 676
Directors' and auditors' responsibilities for going concern, 677
Reporting on going concern, 683
Summary, 684
Key points of the chapter, 684
References, 686
Further reading, 686
Appendix 17.1, 687
Self-assessment questions (solutions available to students), 687
Self-assessment questions (solutions available to tutors), 688
Topics for class discussion without solutions, 689

INTRODUCTION TO FRAUD

The auditors' responsibility for detecting fraud is an issue that has generated considerable controversy. Although auditors have attempted over many years and in a number of different ways to suggest to the public that their responsibility for fraud detection is limited, there nevertheless remains a popular belief that auditors are responsible for detecting fraud. Although auditors would nowadays maintain that their prime function is not to detect fraud, this has not always been the case. In the 1800s and early 1900s the detection of fraud and error was seen as one of the most important, if not the most important, function of audit. This change in function can be traced to the increasing size of companies, the separation of ownership from management and the changing emphasis in the role of accounts from stewardship to decision making. All these factors have no doubt played their part, but in the final analysis the audit profession would argue it is not now economically viable for them to be responsible for the detection of fraud and error. The old type of audit carried out in the late 1800s and early 1900s was very different from that of today, concerned as it was with vouching transactions to attest to their accuracy and checking the honesty of management. Today, there has been a reduction in vouching and auditors concentrate more on assessing the integrity and competence of management, the effectiveness of internal control systems, the use of analytical procedures and largely restricting detailed audit work to high-risk areas identified during the planning and planning feedback process.

This disparity in opinion about the nature and extent of auditors' duties is partially responsible for the expectations gap, which we discuss in Chapter 18.

Before proceeding further it is worthwhile defining the term 'fraud'. A useful definition is included in ISA 240 – *The auditor's responsibilities relating to fraud in an audit of financial statements*:

> An intentional act by one or more individuals among management, those charged with governance, employees or third parties, involving the use of deception to obtain an unjust or illegal advantage.

See paragraph 11(a)

You will notice that the definition includes within its scope employees, management and those charged with governance. The distinction between fraud carried out by management or those charged with governance and fraud carried out by employees has a number of implications. In particular, it may be argued that managerial fraud or fraud by those charged with governance is likely to be more important in the context of the financial statements and that it may be the more difficult for the auditors to detect. You will also note that the definition recognizes that fraud in a company can involve the participation of third parties. An example of this would be an arrangement between a customer and a member of staff, such as the customer submitting false or inaccurate invoices to the company, these being authorized by the employee.

Importance of fraud

Before we discuss some of the issues relating to fraud it is worthwhile considering the dimension of losses associated with fraud to demonstrate its importance:

- A report by KPMG estimated that £1.1 billion of fraud came before the courts in 2008, the second highest amount in the last 21 years. Fraud perpetrated by managers, employees and customers trebled from the previous year. Of these groups, managers accounted for the greatest amount, £127 million, in 2008.

- In a survey conducted in 2009 by PricewaterhouseCoopers, 75 per cent of the companies with more than 5000 employees who responded to their survey reported that they had been victims of economic crime in the preceding 12 months. The same survey found that the most common type of economic fraud in UK organizations was asset misappropriation followed by accounting fraud and that money laundering was the third most common type of fraud.
- In a survey by Ernst & Young covering 33 countries conducted in 2007 and 2008, they found that 25 per cent of their respondents had encountered an occurrence of bribery or corruption in the previous two years.

These figures clearly indicate that fraud is now a major cost to industry and therefore in turn to society.

RESPONSIBILITY FOR FRAUD DETECTION

As we indicated above, it is nowadays accepted doctrine, at least within the auditing profession, that the main responsibility for fraud detection lies with management and those charged with governance, and not with the auditors. If you refer to auditing standard ISA 210 – *Agreeing the terms of audit engagements* (sample engagement letter in the appendix 1), you will see that this view is made known where it is stated that management are responsible for such internal control that they determine 'is necessary to enable the preparation of financial statements that are free from material misstatement, whether due to fraud or error'. This view on the responsibility for fraud is emphasized in ISA 240, where it is stated that the objectives of the auditor are: 'To identify and assess the risks of material misstatement of the financial statements due to fraud' and 'to obtain sufficient appropriate audit evidence regarding the assessed risks of material misstatement due to fraud, through designing and implementing appropriate responses' (para. 10).

See also paragraph 6(b)(ii)

The above quotation serves to indicate that the incidence of fraud is seen as another part of the audit where the auditor is concerned with managing their risk exposure to ensure that planned audit risk is at an acceptable level. The ISA, however, stresses that the main responsibility for the prevention and detection of fraud lies with management and those charged with governance (para. 4). This is also implied in certain of the audit procedures suggested in ISA 240. The standard emphasizes the importance for auditors to obtain from management their estimate of the extent to which financial statements are materially misstated because of fraud. Auditors should also determine the procedures they have in place to identify fraud, how they respond to the risks of fraud and the tone they set in the company regarding fraud. In larger companies, where there are individuals who are not involved in management, the auditors will want to know how they exercise oversight over the processes installed by management.

For instance, members of the audit committee in a listed company.

The importance of taking fraud into account during the audit planning process is emphasized in the ISA where it is stated that no matter the auditors' experience with a particular client, they should maintain an attitude of

See paragraph 12

professional scepticism. In other words, at the very outset, they should consider the possibility of fraud having occurred. The ISA specifically requires that a discussion among the engagement team 'shall place particular emphasis on how and where the entity's financial statements may be susceptible to material misstatement due to fraud, including how fraud might occur.' (para. 15). 'Paragraph A10 highlights the benefits of discussing the susceptibility of the entity's financial statements to material misstatement due to fraud with the engagement team.' It is interesting to note the emphasis placed in the ISA on the possible occurrence of material misstatement arising from fraud. Following from this, although auditors may not accept detection of fraud as the prime objective of the audit, they will nevertheless plan and conduct the audit tests in such a way as to limit the possibility that material fraud goes undetected. This process, as stressed above, will start at the planning phase of the audit when auditors are considering the company and its environment. For instance, the auditors will be aware that certain assets, such as cash, are more susceptible to fraud than others and, in conducting the audit of a concern where cash is important (such as a retailing concern), their planning will take account of this factor. Similarly, if the company is in financial difficulties, the auditors should take particular care in judging whether the directors may attempt to paint a better picture of the company than exists, or in the extreme case does not enter into irregular transactions as a means of taking money out of the business and defrauding creditors who will suffer loss if it goes into liquidation.

Auditors would argue that they can never hope to guarantee the detection of all frauds. This is because of a number of factors, including:

- Inherent limitations in the techniques and tests performed by the auditors, remembering that auditors make considerable use of samples in forming a view on the whole population of transactions and balances.
- The use of deceit, collusion and other means to conceal fraud (often by individuals occupying a responsible role in the company) can mean that its detection is very difficult.
- The fact that auditors are only required to arrive at an opinion on the financial statements rather than give a guarantee means that the evidence they gather in terms of persuasiveness is necessarily limited to that required to form an opinion.

It should also be recognized that no matter how strong a company's system of internal control, there is always a chance of it not detecting some errors and frauds. Furthermore, when members of management or those charged with governance comprise the group who perpetrate the fraud, it is more likely that it will go undetected by the company's internal control system and the auditors. This is because they have greater scope to override controls and conceal the fraud. Thus, it should be recognized that where fraud is well planned and executed, involves collusion and is complex in nature, it may remain undetected for a considerable period of time. As an aside we would point out that many large accounting firms offer another form of audit, separate from the statutory audit, known as a forensic audit, one aim of which is to detect if fraud is taking place in a company.

Earlier in the chapter we quoted the definition of fraud contained in ISA 240. After defining fraud the standard goes on to distinguish between the risk of material misstatement caused by fraud at the financial statement level and at the individual assertion level. If the auditors believe there is a high risk of material misstatement at the financial statement level they will have to ensure they have an appropriate audit team in terms of expertise and experience and that they focus sufficient audit effort on areas where there is scope for manipulation. For instance, risk of manipulation may be highest in areas of subjectivity or where alternative accounting treatments are available. At the individual assertion level the auditor should design their audit tests in such a way as to minimize the risk of fraud going undetected.

Fraudulent financial reporting can be achieved by:

- Manipulation, falsification (including forgery), suppression or alteration of accounting records or supporting documentation.
- Misrepresentation or intentional omission of transactions, events and significant information.
- Misapplication of accounting principles.
- Inappropriate classification or disclosure in the accounts.

See paragraph A3

ACTIVITY 17.1

Suggest occasions when a company's directors may want to suppress records or documents of the company.

There are a number of occasions when a company's directors might want to conceal documents or records. For instance, if the company is being sued for a considerable sum of money, they may not wish to disclose this fact in their financial statements since the appropriate action could well be the recording of a liability. Documents showing that a company's assets are not worth as much as they are stated in the balance sheet may also be suppressed by the directors. Briefly, it is likely that a company's directors will attempt to conceal a matter where it will have an adverse effect on the company's financial statements. There may, of course, also be occasions when directors do not disclose matters that might improve a company's profit figure. For instance, directors might be intent on 'income smoothing', or shareholder directors in smaller companies may wish to minimize their profits for tax reasons.

ACTIVITY 17.2

Can you suggest any types of transactions that might be recorded but are without substance?

The most obvious example is where the company's directors wish to overstate an aspect of the financial statements either to boost profit or the net assets of the company. The boosting of profit could be achieved by recording fictitious sales; company assets could be overstated by the recording of bogus purchases of stock, thus inflating stocks. Income smoothing might be achieved by setting up unnecessary provisions and releasing them later. These are just three of a number of devices companies can use to manipulate their financial statements by fictitious or unnecessary recording. FRS 5 – *Reporting the substance of transactions* – is an accounting standard that specifically addresses transactions that are not real (that is, have no substance).

There is currently no IAS on this subject.

It should be apparent that a common thread runs through the examples listed above – an intention to misrepresent the assets, liabilities or profits on the part of employees or directors. In addition, the motive for fraud may also involve individual financial gain, such as where there is misappropriation of assets or theft or where, for instance, misrepresentation of financial information might give rise to excessive bonuses for directors or cause unjustified changes to share values.

Identification of motives can be an important step for auditors in developing indicators of potential significant fraud. An example of this is when the company directors wish to portray the company's performance as better than it actually is. Pressure to misrepresent financial performance may be high under the following circumstances:

- When the company has performed badly, perhaps even making a loss.
- Where the company is under pressure from markets expecting a certain level of profits from the company.
- Where the company has shown considerable growth in profits over a number of years, the directors may wish to show that growth as continuing.
- Where the company has been expanding by acquiring other companies, directors have an incentive to show the policy has resulted in the group of companies continuing to be profitable – to demonstrate, for instance, that previous acquisitions have been successful – or to sustain the share price of the company so they can continue successfully to acquire other companies.
- Where the company has liquidity problems and the directors do not want shareholders or the markets to become aware of this.

We are not suggesting that these are the only occasions when management have an incentive to distort the financial statements, but have listed them to demonstrate that it is possible to identify where the risk of fraud is higher than normal. In Appendix 1 to ISA 240 the risk factors that might be related to a higher likelihood of the incidence of fraud are further categorized by the condition that is likely to be present when a material misstatement occurs. These are:

- *Incentives/pressures*. Where a company has had a period of continuous growth, there may be a pressure on management to manipulate the financial statements to ensure that apparent growth continues to meet the market's expectations.
- *Opportunities*. Where a company engages in complex transactions, perhaps involving overseas linked parties, this may provide an opportunity for management to engage in fraudulent financial reporting.
- *Attitudes/rationalization*. Where it is known that a company has in the past been guilty of breaking the law or engaging in unscrupulous practices, this would be an indicator that management's attitude towards such activity is

that they be more likely to engage in fraudulent activity. You may also note that management who engage in this sort of activity also signal more generally to the auditors their lack of ethical values which is likely to put the auditor on alert from the commencement of the audit.

The prime focus of the auditor, no matter the source of fraud, is to identify situations where there is a higher than usual risk. It is only then that the auditor will be in a position to change the audit approach to reflect the higher risk. The importance of risk assessment by the auditor is emphasized in ISA 240 which lays stress on a number of factors, including:

- Auditors having discussions with management and those charged with governance about the processes they exercise to fulfil their responsibilities in respect of fraud detection. The auditor would be particularly interested in management's assessment of the risk that material fraud may occur and what procedures they have adopted to minimize the likelihood of fraud. This includes the potential risk of fraud affecting particular account balances or classes of transactions. In addition, the auditor would identify the ethical attitudes management communicate to other employees in the company or group.
- The auditors should also ascertain from management and the internal auditors if they are aware of any fraud that has occurred or have any suspicions that fraud may be taking place. As management may be the group most likely to be involved in fraudulent financial reporting and therefore unlikely to alert auditors, it will be useful for the auditors to speak to a range of employees who may provide them with valuable information.
- The auditor will want to ascertain if the internal audit function has conducted work specifically aimed at detecting fraud and to determine the results of their testing. Where the internal auditors have identified weaknesses in controls that give rise to the possibility of fraud, the auditors will be interested in the response of management to any related recommendations made by them.
- The auditor should also enquire of those charged with governance how they determine what processes and procedures have been used by management to identify the risks of fraud occurring and how the latter have responded to specific risks by the development of internal control procedures to lessen the possibility or risk of fraud.
- The auditor, when performing their risk assessment procedures, should also consider if any fraud risk factors exist. To a large extent these procedures are likely to be an extension of the work the auditor performs when assessing the inherent risk of an engagement, but with a greater focus on factors that may influence the incidence of fraud. The ISA notes that when performing their analytical review the auditor may identify some unexpected relationships which might suggest the possibility of material misstatement because of fraud. It is interesting, however, that a US study by Cullinan and Sutton (2002) suggested that the move away from auditors conducting tests of detail and placing a heavier reliance on analytical procedures might result in an audit that is less effective in detecting fraud.

We discussed risk in Chapter 5.

Paragraph 22.

Where the auditor has identified the risk of a material misstatement in the financial statements arising from fraud they should adjust their audit procedures accordingly. This might entail:

- Increasing the scope and variety of tests they perform. If the material misstatement is likely to arise because of a weakness in internal controls the auditor will concentrate on testing the effectiveness of the controls that exist through compliance testing and by carrying out tests of detail on the transactions or balances subjected to those controls. The auditors should also inform those concerned with governance of any significant internal control weaknesses they have detected and recommend that they be rectified. If the fraud is likely to occur in the misstatement of a particular account balance, the auditor might increase testing of that balance and may seek to obtain higher grade evidence, such as third-party evidence, as far as possible, rather than relying on internally generated evidence.
- Ensuring that suitably qualified staff are assigned to the audit. If the fraud is likely to involve computer systems, the auditors should have a suitably qualified staff member attached to the audit team. The engagement partner would also communicate to the audit manager and the senior in charge of the job the need to provide adequate supervision to other audit staff.
- Adapting their audit tests to ensure they contain an element of unpredictability. This unpredictability might relate to the timing of the audit tests or the nature of tests performed. This would be a required response especially where the auditor has carried out the engagement for a number of years and may be concerned that client staff have a good grasp of the audit tests that are likely to be performed during the audit and when they are likely to be performed.
- Concentrating on areas that are subjective, might involve management judgement or where management may exert a considerable influence. Thus, for instance, the ISA stresses the need for auditors to investigate very carefully journal entries and unusual significant transactions. As senior management normally determine the accounting policies adopted in the preparation of the financial statements the auditor must ensure that these policies are not selected in such a way to (say) maximize the reported income of the company.
- Giving sufficient attention to areas which might be subject to override of internal controls by senior management. Because of the control senior management wield, they are in a strong position to commit fraud and the auditors need to take that into account during their audit planning. An example where management have the opportunity to commit fraud is in recording inappropriate journal entries. Auditors should always inspect large journal entries being put through the company's books especially those towards the year-end.

Although the ISA tends to focus on the risk of the financial statements being misstated because of fraud, it is well to remember the fairly obvious point that fraud is conducted by individuals. This means that an examination of the characteristics of personnel, the management team and how it is structured in a company may also provide helpful indicators as to when and where a fraud is more likely to occur. Examples of these characteristics include:

- Where particular directors or the chief executive or other senior personnel are autocratic and authoritarian.
- Where the staff are poorly qualified or lacking in motivation.
- Where individuals are paid according to results.
- Where individuals are allowed too much authority or power.
- Where there is a high turnover of staff.

The above are typical situations where the incidence of fraud is more likely. In such situations it is possible that any fraud perpetrated by the individual(s) may lead to either a misstatement of the financial statements or the misappropriation of assets. The nature of the individuals themselves and their particular circumstances may also influence the likelihood of fraud.

ACTIVITY 17.3

Suggest characteristics of individuals, which might influence their susceptibility to commit fraud.

There are a number of characteristics you may have thought of and we list a selection below:

- The integrity of the individual and whether they seem to have a strong sense of ethics. Although a difficult characteristic to assess, the behaviour of individuals and their opinions on issues may provide important evidence to assist the auditors in assessing this characteristic.
- The extent to which the individuals appear to be motivated by greed. Again, a difficult characteristic to assess but the individual's concern with money and consumer goods may provide some clues about this.
- The degree of loyalty exhibited by the individual. If the individual has been with the one firm a long time this may indicate a certain level of satisfaction with their employment and perhaps reduce the likelihood of them committing fraud. You should, however, also be aware that experienced employees, because they are trusted, might have a greater opportunity to commit fraud.

In their forensic work KPMG have found many instances of fraud involving seemingly trusted employees.

The ISA highlights the auditor's main concern is whether there is misstatement of the financial statements, but notes that fraud can also result in misappropriation of assets. It is possible that misappropriation might result in the misstatement of the financial statements, especially if committed by senior management, but very often the amounts involved will be relatively small. This type of fraud (which can take the form of theft of assets, the pocketing of cash receipts, entering into relationships with third parties with a view to gaining some advantage) can be committed by a range of employees in the company. Where management is the perpetrator or where collusion is involved, it can be difficult to detect.

One of the main ways that management attempt to minimize the risk of this type of fraud is through the implementation of a robust system of internal control.

ACTIVITY 17.4

List reasons why weaknesses in the design and operation of accounting and internal control systems and problems in obtaining sufficient audit evidence may increase the likelihood of fraud and error occurring.

The reasons why weaknesses in the design and operation of accounting and internal control systems may increase the likelihood of fraud and error occurring include the following:

- The auditors rely, at least to some extent, on the information derived from the accounting and internal controls systems. If there are deficiencies in these systems, the reliability of the accounting information may be reduced. An example of this is where the company does not reconcile the payables ledger to the payables control account or does not reconcile payables statements. The lack of such controls may mean the payables figure cannot be relied upon.
- Specific deficiencies lend themselves to the possibility of employees taking advantage of them to commit fraud. An example would be lack of controls at the point where employees book materials or components out of stores (an internal boundary) giving them the opportunity to misappropriate.
- If deficiencies allow management specific opportunities to avoid or override controls this increases the likelihood of fraud. An example of this is where expenditure by management is not subject to authorization controls, allowing them, perhaps, the opportunity to buy items for personal use.

Similarly, we suggest the following reasons for why problems in obtaining sufficient appropriate evidence increase the risk of fraud or error occurring:

- Where external or auditor-generated evidence is not available, this presents auditors with particular problems in assessing the reliability of evidence. An example of this would be substantial payments paid into foreign bank accounts being payments to agents to help ensure that overseas contracts were obtained by the company. The sensitivity of transactions of this type may make it very difficult for the auditors to obtain evidence to verify the validity of the transaction. As an aside, the auditors would also wish to determine whether the payments were legal.
- Where the lack of evidence relates to material transactions this would be particularly worrying for the auditors. An example of this arose in the BCCI case where fictitious loans were made by that company and the audit evidence used to confirm them were audit confirmations signed by the chairman of the company purportedly receiving the loans. Unfortunately, the loans did not exist and the audit confirmations were signed to deceive the auditors.

We discuss the BCCI case later in the chapter.

- Where the lack of audit evidence relates to unusual or complex transactions, this again presents particular problems for auditors and raises the risk of error or fraud having occurred. An example is where the company enters into a complex financing arrangement with an offshore bank located, for instance, in the Bahamas. There may be specific difficulties in the auditors obtaining evidence from the bank to verify the arrangement.

- Lack of evidence as a result of management action would cause the auditors to be concerned. An example is where management deliberately conceals customer complaints about a product to minimize the provision that would be required in the accounts to make good the defects in the product.

One change in the current ISA from the previous standards on auditing (SASs) is the greater emphasis that the ISA gives to material misstatements of the financial statements rather than misappropriation of assets. There seems to be an implicit acknowledgement here that, except perhaps in exceptional circumstances, the greater risk to the auditor lies in the failure to detect a material misstatement in the financial statements rather than the failure to (say) detect the theft of inventories or cash. Undoubtedly this is probably because the auditor believes that in most circumstances the misappropriation of assets is unlikely to be sufficiently material to distort the truth and fairness of the financial statements. This focus is forcefully made in the ISA in respect of revenue recognition where it is emphasized that material misstatements in the financial statements often arise from the overstatement of revenue. This overstatement may arise from the recording of fictitious sales or through bias in the selection of accounting policies by management, resulting in early recognition of revenue. The ISA notes that, since material misstatement of the financial statements often arises because of revenue recognition issues, it would be normal for the auditor to flag this as an area of high risk.

See Chapter 13 where we considered this aspect in relation to recognition of revenue on long-term contracts.

Reporting fraud and error

Once auditors have ascertained that there is a possibility of fraud taking place they have to decide upon appropriate action. The first course is to make sure that they are aware of all the facts and that they have understood the situation correctly. It should be reasonably obvious that they do not want to suggest that a fraud has taken place where they have simply misinterpreted some facts or events. They should fully inform themselves of the situation, including the nature of the fraud and its likely magnitude. They will be particularly concerned if the fraud is material in relation to the financial statements. Determination of the likely magnitude may require auditors to perform additional audit tests, the extent of which depends on their judgement as to the likelihood of a fraud and its potential magnitude. The auditors also need to determine the extent to which further audit tests will reveal additional information about the fraud.

Having obtained all the necessary evidence, the auditors should discuss the fraud with senior management, the directors or the audit committee. Which of these groups the auditors first inform will depend on the auditors' estimate of the amount of the fraud or error and whom they suspect is involved. If the auditors discover material fraud affecting the financial statements, they should ask senior management or the directors to consider changing the draft financial statements to reflect the financial impact of the fraud. In addition, they may ask management to carry out further work to determine if they, the auditors, have identified the full extent of the fraud. The auditors will also need to assess the impact of the fraud on their other audit work. For instance, if the auditors found that the fraud occurred because certain internal controls had not been applied properly, they would need to reassess the level of control risk and the reliability that they had placed on internal controls. If the auditors suspect that management other than the directors may be implicated in fraud, they should discuss the matter with the directors of the company. A more difficult problem arises where the auditors believe that individuals charged with governance of the company, such as executive directors, may be involved in the fraud. The auditors would, in this instance, have to consider reporting their suspicions about the fraud to the audit committee, where one exists. Where there is no audit committee or the auditors believe there may be problems in reporting to it, they should consider obtaining legal advice. The latter might be the position where the auditors have suspicions about the integrity of all parties charged with the governance of the company. There are also some circumstances, noted below, where it may be appropriate to report their suspicions to third parties.

Once they have reported their suspicions of fraud or error, the auditors would normally expect to see those charged with governance take appropriate action. If the auditors consider that management or the directors appear to be relatively unconcerned or do not investigate the issue as thoroughly as they would like, this can also present problems for the auditors. The auditors will be concerned that, if management do not investigate the issue thoroughly, it may be difficult to determine the full extent of the fraud. This is important because, if it is material, it could have implications for the audit report. Indifference on the part of management to fraud or error may also cause the auditors to re-evaluate the integrity of management and the control environment. In the extreme where the auditor has detected material fraud, and senior management or those charged with governance do not take the actions the auditor considers necessary or are involved in the fraud, the auditor may have to consider withdrawing from the engagement.

In all of the above situations auditors should ensure that they document the process until its satisfactory resolution. This documentation should include: the initial grounds for their suspicion; the additional audit work they performed to substantiate their suspicions; details of what, when and to whom they reported their suspicions; management's response to the stated suspicions; any action taken by management; the implications for audit work and changes in risk assessment and final conclusions.

Finally, if the auditors believe the fraud involves false documents, such as sales invoices, they should obtain copies of those documents. Clearly if those perpetrating the fraud were to destroy the evidence before the matter is resolved, it might be difficult to pursue it further.

Responsibilities of the directors

We noted above that the view of the auditing profession is that it is not the auditors' duty to detect fraud. If this view is accepted, the obligation must fall, as we mentioned at the beginning of the chapter, on the directors, both executive and non-executive, who are normally charged with the governance of a company. It is an established principle in law that one of the duties of directors is to exercise reasonable care, skill and diligence. Furthermore, the Companies Act 2006 requires the company to keep adequate accounting records (s. 386) and prepare financial statements which give a true and fair view. ISA

240 also emphasizes the responsibilities of the directors in stating that the auditor should obtain written representations from management that 'they acknowledge their responsibility for the design, implementation and maintenance of internal control to prevent and detect fraud' (para. 39). The Combined Code on Corporate Governance (2008) also notes that one of the board of director's responsibilities is to 'maintain a sound system of internal control to safeguard shareholders' investment and the company's assets' (Code Main Principle C.2). This would seem to indicate that the directors have responsibility for preventing and detecting fraud and error. The question then arises how they can best discharge that duty. It is suggested that the following would assist the directors and senior management:

- Developing an appropriate control environment. The directors and senior management set the tone in respect of how seriously employees view control procedures. It is important that, if the directors wish employees to take controls seriously, they themselves do so and allocate sufficient resources to the development of control systems.
- By establishing a strong and effective system of internal control in the company. As you have seen in Chapters 7 and 8, this would entail proper division of duties, training and employing suitable personnel. The system of internal control should, where appropriate, include an internal audit function.
- By encouraging a strong ethical environment in the company and developing a code of conduct. This will only be effective if the directors adhere to it. If they are seen to indulge in shady business practices or act unfairly in respect of their dealings with employees it is hardly setting employees a good example. The code of conduct should include guidance on whistleblowing. It should be made clear in the code that whistleblowing is not frowned upon and that whistleblowers will not be disciplined or unfairly prejudiced within the company. Unfortunately, in the last few years there have been examples of whistleblowers being disciplined for reporting aspects of a company and/or its employees' practices. The publication *Taking Fraud Seriously* published by The Audit Faculty of the ICAEW emphasizes that one of the factors that has encouraged the growth of fraud has been attitudinal change. That is, the perception that fraud has somehow become acceptable and does not have the same opprobrium that was once associated with it. In this context note that the Combined Code (2008) recommends that where a company has an audit committee, it 'should review arrangements by which staff of the company may, in confidence, raise concerns about possible improprieties in matters of financial reporting or other matters' (Code Provision C.3.4).

Whistleblowing is the term used to describe the situation whereby employees report perceived wrong or unjust practices of colleagues (or certain aspects of company policy) to management or some outside agency.

- The establishment of an audit committee to whom the auditors can report any incidence of suspected fraud.

We discuss audit committees in greater detail in Chapter 18.

- By the directors following the Combined Code provision C.2.1 and conducting at least annually a review of the effectiveness of the company's internal control system and reporting to shareholders that they have done this. Although it might be argued by critics that the Combined Code provision does not go far enough, the increased focus on internal control and the requirement to provide some form of report or information should ensure that it is taken seriously by the directors and senior management.

At this point it is useful to remind you that the Combined Code requirements relating to corporate governance apply only to listed companies.

If the directors accept and diligently apply the above it would undoubtedly be of benefit to the auditors who would know that management had put in place procedures relating to internal control. It would enable the auditors to reduce the time taken on assessment of control risk and give some assurance that the directors have attempted to reduce the likelihood of fraud and error.

Reporting to third parties

ISA 240 notes that in certain circumstances it may be necessary for auditors to report to a third party that they have found a fraud, or suspect it is taking place, in a client organization. They would do this when they consider that reporting the fraud or suspected fraud is required by specific legislation. One of the reasons why auditors take seriously the reporting of fraud by themselves is because they owe a duty of confidentiality to their clients. This is a duty they do not like to breach and it will only be done when they have reached the conclusion that it is their duty under legislation to report the matter. In this respect it should be noted that the definition of money laundering is a wide one and includes a criminal offence that gives rise to some benefit. Although it is likely that most criminal offences detected by the auditor have been committed by their client, the legislation also covers the situation where the auditors become aware of a criminal offence conducted by a third party.

The example given in the UK and Ireland version of ISA 240 is where the auditor is suspicious that a criminal offence which falls within the anti-money laundering legislation is taking place.

We will end this section by discussing the case of *Sasea Finance Limited (in liquidation)* vs *KPMG* (2000) which is an example involving fraud and the auditors' duty to report to a third party. In this case two dominant figures, one of whom was a director of Sasea Limited, were involved in a massive fraud and as a result the financial statements were misstated. Sasea duly went into liquidation and the liquidator brought an action against the auditors, KPMG, on the ground that they should have detected and reported the fraud. The court decided KPMG had a case to answer and that in this instance the auditors' duty to report the fraud to a third party overrode the duty of confidentiality to the client. In arriving at this decision the court took into account:

- the extent to which material losses would be borne by any one person or a large number of persons.
- the likelihood of the fraud being repeated if it was not disclosed.

The court was specifically concerned with the reporting to third parties because some of the management were implicated in the fraud and therefore would not have been the appropriate party to whom the auditor could report.

In the Court of Appeal the issue under consideration was whether KPMG had a case to answer, it being assumed for this purpose that KPMG had not acted with the requisite degree of care and skill.

It was regarded at the time that a possible implication of the Sasea case was that it might result in a greater number of cases being brought against auditors for failing to detect and report frauds, perpetrated in their clients.

RECENT DEBATES RELATING TO FRAUD

The topic of fraud and the extent of the auditors' responsibility to detect it is a controversial one that has produced much discussion in the accounting profession. Although these discussions have been superseded to some extent by the publication of ISA 240 it is useful to review the debates that have taken place to gain some insight into the accounting profession's approach and attitude to the topic.

The issue of fraud was specifically addressed in *The Audit Agenda: Next Steps* published by APB in 1996. It did not propose any changes in auditors' responsibilities for detecting fraud, but it did contain a number of proposals in respect of fraud. Specifically it recommended that:

- Auditors should report to the board and audit committees of listed companies their observations on the appropriateness and adequacy of the control systems to minimize the risk of fraud. This recommendation is now in essence required because of the implementation of the Combined Code and the guidance given in the Turnbull Report and Smith Report.
- Attention should be given to the training and education of auditors to improve their understanding of fraud.
- The professional bodies should hold seminars to discuss experience and means of detecting fraud.
- The board of directors should consider commissioning, on a periodic basis, a forensic audit. You will recall that we mentioned in a margin note above that many of the large accounting firms do offer forensic audit, one aim of which is to detect if fraud is taking place in a company.

The Audit Agenda: Next Steps also highlighted how difficult it can be for auditors to detect fraud that is well planned, ingenious or involves collusion, or top management. It is at least partly because of these attributes that the profession believes it would not be cost-effective to include fraud detection in the auditors' responsibilities. The auditors can, of course, contribute to the prevention of fraud by informing management of weaknesses in their control systems, which could be exploited for fraudulent purposes. Another interesting point made in *The Audit Agenda* is the somewhat limited nature of the penalties, which can be inflicted on directors if they mislead auditors. Indeed, recently in the wake of various scandals there has been considerable attention given in the media to the following:

- The cost of prosecuting directors or officers of companies who have been involved in fraudulent activity.
- The limited nature of the penalties that can be imposed on such individuals.
- The difficulty of obtaining a successful conviction.

The law relating to fraudulent activity by directors and officers of companies was developed a number of years ago and does not reflect the massive cost and suffering that can result from fraudulent activity. There appears to be something of a mismatch between the seriousness of the crime and the penalties that can be imposed, though it should be noted that the recent Fraud Act has increased the maximum term of imprisonment that can be imposed for certain offences coming within the remit of the Act. We have already mentioned the publication of *Taking Fraud Seriously* in 1996 by the ICAEW Audit and Assurance Faculty which recognized, *inter alia*, that the public's perception of the auditors' responsibilities for detecting fraud and the auditors' own perception were somewhat different. They recommended that auditors take a more active role in detecting fraud. In addition, they suggested that auditors should have knowledge of:

- The definition of fraud.
- The characteristics and typical methods of management and employee frauds.

- Risks in industry and commerce.
- Forensic skills.

Recognizing that fraud is now a major problem they suggested that a coordinated response was necessary to fight fraud. To this end they advocated the establishment of a Fraud Advisory Panel. This panel was envisaged as being composed of a number of bodies with an interest in fraud and would be responsible for:

- Better defining the extent of fraud.
- Increasing awareness of trends in frauds.
- Advising on counter measures of all kinds.
- Encouraging improved cooperation between the government, law enforcement and the private sector.

The Audit and Assurance Faculty followed this up with a further publication in 2003, *Fraud: Meeting the Challenge through External Audit*. This document provided a ten-point plan which it was considered would improve current audit procedures and practices. Many of the recommendations contained in the plan were subsequently included in ISA 240. The latest pronouncement from APB on fraud came in November 1998 when it issued a discussion document: *Fraud and Audit: Choices for Society.*

The document noted that the more radical proposals in respect of the prevention and detection of fraud put forward in *The Audit Agenda* and *The Audit Agenda: Next Steps* had, in general, received a negative reaction. APB also admitted that it was very difficult to detect management fraud. Although the tone of the initial discussion in the document is somewhat negative about what auditors can do to detect management fraud, later in the document they propose ways in which the audit could potentially be made more effective. These proposals included reviewing key auditing standards; radical change in the professional auditing attitude and emphasis; an expansion of role of audit; and changes to corporate law.

Although APB considered that reviewing and updating auditing standards would be helpful in improving detection of management fraud, they indicated that achievement of a significant increase in the likelihood of detecting such fraud would require more radical change. These changes included:

- Increased emphasis on professional scepticism.
- Tighter rules for what is regarded as acceptable audit evidence.
- Reporting any material matters in the financial statements that are only supported by management representations.

APB also considered that expanding the auditors' role could be helpful in preventing and detecting fraud. This could be achieved by:

- Reporting to boards and audit committees on controls to prevent and detect fraud.
- Forensic fraud review.
- More reporting of suspected frauds.

Finally APB suggested a number of ways in which corporate law and governance could be changed which would help in preventing and detecting fraud.

Although the APB suggested that the proposals listed above would help in the fight against fraud, the final arbiter would be whether they, in fact, reduced the incidence of fraud, particularly those involving management.

It is useful at this point to consider the above developments and the extent to which change has taken place since the various recommendations alluded to were made. In ISA 240, as with a number of the other ISAs, there has been a greater emphasis on audit risk. In ISA 240 this takes the form of auditor identification of aspects of the environment that might lead to fraud being perpetrated and also ensuring that directors are informed about possible internal control risks, followed by action to remedy any deficiencies in internal control. The ISA also notes that one of the key elements in identification of fraud is professional scepticism. While the ISA discusses audit procedures that should be undertaken where there is a risk of misappropriation of assets, it is clear from the text that the main responsibility for detecting this type of fraud lies with company management. The focus in ISA 240 is on the auditor being alert to ways in which the financial statements might be misstated through management choice of inappropriate accounting policies or the incorrect recording of revenue. It is clear that the main concern is with detecting high level material fraud and in that respect it might be argued that the public's belief that the auditor should be responsible for detecting all types of fraud is misplaced. Furthermore, the COSO report found that about 90 per cent of financial statement fraud resulted from the alteration and manipulation of financial information and only about 10 per cent from misappropriation of assets. The emphasis on director responsibility for maintaining an effective system of internal control that can both deter and detect fraud is reaffirmed in the Combined Code. In conclusion, it might be argued that auditors have adopted changes that would make it more certain that they would detect misstatement of the financial statements. However, in responding to claims that they should have greater responsibility for fraud detection, the auditing profession still maintains that the primary responsibility lies with management.

Reported in Rezeaa (2005).

CASE LAW RELATING TO FRAUD

We discuss in some detail more recent case law relating to auditors responsibilities in general in Chapter 19.

In this part of the chapter we consider some historical case law relating to fraud with which auditing students should be familiar.

One of the earliest cases concerned with auditors' duties to detect fraud was *Re Kingston Cotton Mill Co (No. 2)* (1896). In this case it was held that it was not the auditors' duty to count inventories and that they were not negligent in accepting a certificate signed by the company's officials as long as they had no suspicion of fraud. Lopes L.J. gave his famous and much overquoted dictum that the role of the auditor is that of 'a watch-dog not a bloodhound'.

Lopes went on to say:

> Auditors must not be made liable for not tracing out ingenious and carefully laid schemes of fraud where there is nothing to arouse their suspicion, and when those frauds are perpetrated by tried servants of the company and are undetected for years by the directors.

We would observe again in this connection that fraudulent actions by the directors themselves may be particularly difficult to detect. The notion that the auditors may be responsible for the detection of fraud if their suspicions are aroused was the focus of attention in *Irish Woollen Co. Ltd vs Tyson and Others* (1900). In this case the auditors were found to be negligent for failing to detect fraud owing to lack of reasonable care and skill. In particular the audit tended to be conducted in a rather mechanical fashion and the auditors failed to question entries that were raised after the end of the period but dated prior to that date. The duty of care and skill was also a feature in *Re Thomas Gerrard & Son Ltd* (1967). In this case the profit of Thomas Gerrard & Son Ltd was manipulated through the use of incorrect cut-off procedures. Specifically, certain purchase invoices which were received prior to the year-end were post-dated and included in the following year's purchases, but the purchases were included in closing inventory and hence profit was overstated. The audit team was aware of the alteration of the invoices but accepted the managing director's (Mr Croston's), word that this was done because it was more convenient. The judge held that it was not enough to rely on the honesty and integrity of a person, even where, as in this case, the managing director was a person of repute. They must obtain sufficient audit evidence before an audit opinion should be given; in this case the auditors neither attended the inventory take nor reconciled or obtained independent evidence of the amount owed to suppliers even though they were aware of the alterations.

Stone & Rolls Ltd (in Liquidation) v Moore Stephens (a Firm) [2009] UKHL 39

In a recent legal case Moore Stephens, a firm of accountants, had to defend themselves against an action by a company, Stone and Rolls Ltd, which was in liquidation. The background to this case was that a Mr Stojevic was the main person in charge of the company which he used as a vehicle to defraud banks by obtaining letters of credit. Subsequently, one of the banks brought an action against Stone and Rolls Ltd and Mr Stojevic which was successful and brought about the liquidation of the company. Later, the liquidator sued the auditor Moore Stephens for carrying out a negligent audit in failing to detect the fraud. The reason the liquidator sued the firm of accountants was to try and gain some money for the creditors of Stone and Rolls Ltd. Moore Stephens argued that Stone Rolls Ltd had perpetrated the fraud and therefore could not rely on its own illegal act to mount an action. The liquidator, however, argued that the fraud was carried out by Mr Stojevic and should not be attributed to the company. In this particular case, because Mr Stojevic and the company were effectively one and the same, the judges decided by a majority that the illegality defence was sound and held that Moore Stephens should not be liable to pay damages. It might be thought here that, when it is the directors who conduct the fraud, the auditors might be excused responsibility; however, it is likely that this will only apply in the case of 'a one man firm' type of situation.' It does, however, raise the intriguing question of what would happen if (say) a company had four directors and all four of them in collusion had conducted a fraud; would the illegality defence be a sound defence? The dissenting judges in the Stone and Rolls case also made the observation that it was the innocent creditors who lost out through not being able to recover amounts owed to them, while the auditors who failed to detect the fraud escaped financial punishment.

AUDITING SCANDALS

In recent years there have been a number of high profile scandals involving fraud with attention focussed on why the auditors did not detect the fraud and prevent losses being inflicted on shareholders and lenders. It is noticeable that a number of these cases have involved companies in the financial services sector, for instance, Barlow Clowes, Nick Leeson and Barings Bank, and BCCI. We do not have enough space to go into detail about all the above scandals but considering the specific case of BCCI is interesting because it highlights a number of important issues related to auditing.

BCCI was founded by a Pakistani banker, Agha Hasan Abedi, in 1972 and, although a considerable amount of its business was based in London, it was incorporated or domiciled in Luxemburg. This had considerable consequences because it meant that BCCI was not subject to the full scrutiny of the Bank of England, but instead was subject to the more lax rules relating to banking in Luxemburg. Another key feature in BCCI was the considerable financial support of its operations from the ruler of Abu Dhabi, Sheik Zayed bin Sultan al-Nahyan. In 1990 the auditors, Price Waterhouse, reported to the Bank of England that BCCI had lending problems and that they suspected fraudulent activity. Despite these problems, Price Waterhouse issued an unqualified audit report on the 1989 accounts. It would appear that the Bank of England had concerns about BCCI but thought the situation was manageable and that a modified audit opinion might have a detrimental effect. In addition it was thought that the bank would receive a capital injection from the ruler of Abu Dhabi sufficient to keep the bank afloat. Subsequently in 1991, Price Waterhouse prepared a report on BCCI that showed the company had considerable debts, made some illegal acquisitions in the US, incurred considerable losses from its treasury activities and manipulated its accounts. As a result of this, bank regulators including the Bank of England, forced BCCI into bankruptcy in 1991 with debts of over £9 million. Such was the scale of the bankruptcy it resulted in an official report in the UK by Lord Bingham and in the US by Senator John Kerry. Both of these reports found a number of failings, particularly relating to the regulatory regime, the Bank of England coming in for special criticism. Price Waterhouse was sued for negligence by the liquidator of BCCI and apparently made a settlement in 1998 of about $95 million. Price Waterhouse were also investigated under the Joint Disciplinary Scheme which operated at that time and reportedly fined £150 000, incurring costs of £825 000. From the official reports on BCCI it is clear that there were a number of warning signs; for a period of time Price Waterhouse were joint auditors mainly with Ernst & Young but with neither set of auditors having access to complete information; the main regulatory agency was situated in Luxemburg and even though a substantial amount of the bank's operations were conducted in the UK, the Bank of England was reportedly reluctant to take an enlarged role in regulating the bank. Some of the operations of the bank were situated in the Cayman Islands, a location noted for the lack of transparency in the reporting of financial transactions. There was apparent occurrence of fraud in the company, known to the auditors, and deficiencies in internal control. In passing, we would note that a study of uncorrected misstatements by Keune and Johnstone (2009) found that there appeared to be a greater risk of

unmodified

these occurring in highly regulated industries such as banking, insurance and real estate.

We would want to emphasis at this point that corporate scandals are not just a UK phenomenon. For instance, as we mentioned in Chapter 1, there has been the major Parmalat scandal in Italy. Parmalat was about the eighth biggest industrial company in Italy with approximately 35 000 employees operating in about 30 countries. The company was founded by a Calisto Tanzi who for many years leading more or less up to the time the scandal started was the main figure in the company. In 2003 the Bank of America declared that a document showing a deposit from Parmalat of about 4 billion Euros held in a Cayman Islands bank was fictitious. Subsequently, it was discovered that the extent of fraud and deception was much greater, involving a number of financial instruments and offshore companies. The purpose of the complex corporate and financial structures that operated in the group was to hide the extent of Parmalat's financial liabilities whilst at the same time overstating profits. The company was forced into bankruptcy and in the investigation that followed, it was found that the fraud had been going on for many years. It was also found that considerable resources of the company had been diverted to companies associated with the Tanzi family. The auditors of Parmalat were criticized for not detecting the fraud and for their lack of independence, two partners in the audit having been involved in the audit for many years. It was also found that the auditors had relied on documentation relating to the bank deposits that had come to them via Parmalat rather than direct to the auditors, thus giving the former the opportunity to forge the documents. The case is interesting because it illustrates a number of important issues, including the poor governance structures in the company, the use of a complex financial and corporate structure, the use of financial instruments, expansion fuelled by a large number of acquisitions and a dominant chief executive. All of these should serve as a signal to auditors that they need to exercise professional scepticism when carrying out their audit work.

Another more recent case of fraudulent accounting, also mentioned in Chapter 1, is Satyam Computer Services, an Indian company. In this case the founder and chairman of the company Romalinga Raju resigned in January 2009. On his resignation he stated that the profits of the company had been overstated for many years and that 94 per cent of the company's stated cash asset, about 1 billion dollars, was fictitious. One of the methods used in the fraud was to create false sales invoices and receivables, thus inflating turnover and trade receivables. The extent of the fraud and the number of years involved prompted the question of why the auditors, an affiliate of PricewaterhouseCoopers (PwC), did not detect the fraud. Following an investigation into the company's affairs two partners in PwC along with some corporate officers in Satyam were charged with criminal conspiracy and subsequently jailed. One of the individuals was released about one year later, but at the time of writing the other person remains in jail. In a related action the US accounting regulator, PCAOB, has also intervened by barring another two senior members of staff in a firm associated with PwC from being associates of a public registered accounting firm. The reason PCAOB took this action was because the individuals were not cooperating with its fraud investigation. What these two cases show is that fraud is global and remains a major issue for audit firms.

CONSIDERATION OF LAW AND REGULATIONS

In this section we are referring principally to legislation in the UK, but the principles may be applied in any legal administration. You should note that Section B of ISA 250 is applicable only in the UK and Ireland.

In addition to the auditing standard on fraud there is a further relevant standard, ISA 250 – *Section A Consideration of law and regulations in an audit of financial statements* and *Section B The auditor's right and duty to report to regulators in the financial sector*, which we briefly discuss below. There are numerous laws and regulations with which an entity must comply, some of which are directly related to items in the financial statements and others with only an indirect bearing. Where law and regulations relate directly to the financial statements, the auditors are required to obtain audit evidence that the client has complied with them. The main law and regulations that bear directly on the financial statements are contained in certain Companies Act sections. In some commercial sectors, for instance the financial service sector, there are other laws and regulations related to the financial statements and with which the auditors should check compliance. ISA 250 provides guidance on areas to which the audit team should focus their attention, thus, the auditor's procedures should be designed to:

> 'Obtain sufficient appropriate audit evidence regarding compliance with the provisions of those laws and regulations generally recognized to have a direct effect on the determination of material amounts and disclosures in the financial statements.' and 'To perform specified audit procedures to help identify instances of non-compliance with other laws and regulations that may have a material effect on the financial statements.' (ISA 250, para. 10)

The specific audit procedures the auditor is likely to undertake include:

- Obtaining an understanding of laws and regulations relating to the entity and industry and determining what the entity does to ensure compliance with them.
- Inspecting any correspondence with regulatory or licensing authorities.
- Discussing with management if they are aware of any non-compliance with law and regulations.
- Where the regulation has a direct effect on the amounts appearing in the financial statements, for instance, specific Companies Act requirements, the auditor will gather sufficient appropriate audit evidence to give them assurance that the entity has complied with the legislation.
- Obtaining from the directors written confirmation that they have disclosed all known actual or possible non-compliance with law and regulations with potential implications for the financial statements.

When the auditors become aware of information that indicates the possibility of non-compliance they should fully inform themselves of the nature of the event and its potential effect on the financial statements. Subsequent to this and assuming that the auditors have satisfied themselves that the entity may not have complied with certain laws or regulations, they should discuss the issue with management. These discussions are undertaken with the objective of determining whether in fact the entity has complied with the law and regulations and management's attitude to the matter. The auditors may wish to consult with the entity's legal representatives to assist in determining if infringement has occurred. Management's attitude towards the issue may provide important information for the auditors. For instance, if management were aware of the infringement, their attitude to it may influence the auditors' judgement of management's integrity. The auditors also have to reach a conclusion about the potential effect of non-compliance on the financial statements. Under certain circumstances, for instance, where the effect of the non-compliance is material and it has not been adequately reflected in the financial statements, the auditor may have to issue a modified audit opinion. Where there is uncertainty about the potential financial impact of non-compliance on the financial statements, but the auditors consider the non-compliance could be significant, they should ensure that the matter is fully disclosed in the notes to the accounts and refer to it in an explanatory paragraph in their audit report. Where the auditors disagree with management about either the accounting treatment or disclosure in the financial statements in respect of a non-compliance issue which they consider material, they should issue an 'except for' (or an adverse) opinion. If, because of limitations in the scope of their work imposed by the entity, they are unable to determine whether non-compliance has occurred, they should issue an except for opinion or a disclaimer of opinion. Normally, because of confidentiality considerations, the auditor is precluded from disclosing information derived from the audit work to third parties. This requirement is, however, overridden where the auditor is under a statutory duty or is required by law to report an incidence or suspected incidence of non-compliance with the law. As indicated earlier in this chapter, this may arise in the UK where a criminal offence has been committed, which comes within the remit of the money laundering legislation. Alternatively, where the audit being conducted is of a pension fund which is governed by pensions legislation or a financial services entity acting under the Financial Services and Markets Act 2000, the auditor has certain duties under the legislation to report non-compliance with the law or legislation. Finally, auditors may also report actual or suspected non-compliance with law and regulations to a third party (some appropriate authority) where they believe it is in the public interest. Detailed guidance on the reporting of non-compliance with legislation is contained in ISA 250. Perhaps, the most important recent development relating to this is in the area of money laundering. As indicated earlier the ambit of this legislation is wide and extends not just to proceeds arising from drug-trafficking or terrorist activities but extends to 'possessing, or in any way dealing with, or concealing, the proceeds of any crime'. Thus, where the auditor has knowledge of or reasonable grounds for suspicion that money laundering is taking place within a client organization, they have a duty to report internally to the firm's designated Money Laundering Reporting Officer (MLRO) who in turn has to decide on the basis of the report if the matter should be reported to the Serious and Organized Crime Agency (SOCA). Failure to do so could result in the auditor, partners and staff being guilty of a criminal offence and hence possibly subject to criminal penalties. Media reports of major cases of money laundering and the introduction of regulation – 'The Proceeds of Crime Act 2002' amended by 'The Serious and Organized Crime and Police Act 2006', 'The Money Laundering Regulations 2007' and the Terrorism Act 2000 and Proceeds of Crime Act 2002 (Amendment) Regulations 2007' – have focused increased attention on the issue of money laundering. The new legislation places additional responsibilities on accountancy firms. These include:

APB Practice Note 12 (Revised): Money laundering – interim guidance for auditors on UK legislation, March 2008.

- Appointing a money laundering reporting officer (MLRO) who is required to receive money laundering reports from other members of the accountancy firm and report to the Serious and Organized Crime Agency.
- Training employees of the firm on the requirements of the new legislation and how to react to a potential money laundering situation and how they should report to the MLRO.
- Verifying the identity of new clients and keeping records of the evidence obtained.
- Establishing internal procedures to forestall and prevent money laundering.

It should be apparent from the above that the new legislation has important implications for accounting firms. Two examples of this are:

- The interim guidance for auditors stresses that the requirements relate to the performing of accountancy services which encompass not only audit but other services accounting firms may provide, such as taxation advice or planning and insolvency services.
- The legislation can apply in certain situations to activities conducted overseas, but which would be considered an offence if conducted in the United Kingdom. Thus, if the auditors come into possession of information of a reportable offence occurring in the overseas subsidiary of a UK company client, this might give rise to a requirement to report the information that has come into their possession.
  Clearly, the reporting of noncompliance with legislation and money laundering regulations is a complex area and one where the auditor might have to seek advice from their legal advisor.

INTRODUCTION TO GOING CONCERN

See page 546.

You will recall that in Chapter 14 we said that the validity of the application of the going-concern concept was a matter that would be considered by the auditors during the final review prior to preparing the audit report. In this section we address the auditors' responsibilities for determining if an entity is a going concern and the procedures they use to enable them to identify entity's that may not be going concerns. FRS 18 – *Accounting policies*, states in Paragraph 22 that:

The concept of going concern is also referred to in Paragraphs 25 and 26 of IAS 1.

> The information provided by financial statements is usually most relevant if prepared on the hypothesis that the entity is to continue in operational existence for the foreseeable future. This hypothesis is commonly referred to as the going-concern assumption. Financial statements are usually prepared on the basis that the reporting entity is a going concern because measures based on break-up values tend not to be relevant to users seeking to assess the entity's cash-generation ability and financial adaptability.

This means in particular that there is no intention to liquidate the entity or to cease trading. Going concern is one of the most important concepts underlying financial reporting. The assumption that an entity is a going concern directly affects the financial statements. In particular, if it was considered that a company is not a going concern, the assets of that company would need to be valued on a different basis from that of depreciated historical cost or revalued amount assuming continuing use in the business. As indicated in FRS 18 the valuation basis used would most likely be a variant of break-up value or liquidation values. It is likely that in most situations the carrying values of fixed assets and current assets, such as stock and debtors would need to be reduced. In addition, it is likely that long-term liabilities and fixed assets would require reclassifying as current liabilities and current assets respectively. Financial statements prepared using the going-concern basis are likely to be substantially different from those prepared on the assumption that the company is not a going concern. It should also be noted that the listing rules applying to listed companies in the UK require company directors to make a statement in the financial report that the company is a going concern together with supporting assumptions or qualifications.

The vast majority of financial statements are prepared on the going-concern basis and users assume from this that the company is going to survive beyond the short term. In other words, users tend to take for granted that if there is no comment to the contrary, either by the directors in the annual report or by the auditors, the company will survive. If the company should subsequently fail these users may readily ask why they were not forewarned about the potential failure of the company. Auditors have indeed often come under criticism when a company has failed and there has been no indication in its annual report either by the directors or the auditors that the company had any going-concern problems.

The difference in perception between users and auditors concerning going concern is one of the reasons for the audit expectations gap. We discuss the gap in some detail in Chapter 18.

DIRECTORS' AND AUDITORS' RESPONSIBILITIES FOR GOING CONCERN

ISA 570 – *Going concern* makes it clear that one of the responsibilities of those charged with the governance of a company is to determine if the application of the going-concern assumption in the preparation of the financial statements is appropriate. Thus management will have the prime responsibility for determining the appropriateness of preparing financial statements using the going-concern basis. The auditors' responsibility is to satisfy themselves that the use of the going-concern basis by the company is appropriate and its use has been adequately disclosed in the financial statements. This is emphasized in Paragraph 6 of ISA 570 where it is stated that the auditors shall:

In the UK and Ireland those charged with governance are responsible for the preparation of financial statements and the assessment of the entity's ability to continue as a going concern.

> Obtain sufficient appropriate audit evidence about the appropriateness of management's use of the going-concern assumption in the preparation of the financial statements and to conclude whether there is a material uncertainty about the entity's ability to continue as a going concern.

For this purpose:

(i) the auditor shall determine whether management has already performed a preliminary assessment of the entity's ability to continue as a going concern; and

(ii) if such an assessment has been performed, the auditor shall discuss the assessment with management and determine whether management has identified events or conditions that may cast significant doubt on the entity's ability to continue as a going concern and, if so, management's plans to address them;

(iii) if such an assessment has not yet been performed, the auditor shall discuss with management the basis for the intended use of the going-concern assumption, and inquire of management whether events or conditions exist that may cast significant doubt on the entity's ability to continue as a going concern.

Refer to paragraph 10 of ISA 570.

Appropriate financial information

In the discussions with management referred to above the auditors will be assessing the logic, rationale and strength of information that the directors have used to form a view on the going-concern status of the entity. In many instances, because the company is profitable, has a strong resource basis and is located in a relatively stable industry there may not appear to be too much risk that the company will experience financial problems. In this case the directors and auditors may not have to spend much time considering whether the company is a going concern.

ACTIVITY 17.5

Suggest audit activities that auditors perform at the planning stage that should provide the auditors with information in assessing if a company is a going concern.

Particular activities that we think would be of benefit to auditors in assessing going concern are:

- Assessment of business/inherent and to a lesser extent control risk.
- Analytical procedures.

The first of these activities – assessment of business/inherent risk – requires auditors to be knowledgeable about the company, its products, main suppliers, competitors and the environment in which it operates. All of these characteristics are necessary pieces of information, which auditors evaluate when assessing going concern. The assessment of control risk is important because it can give the auditors some guidance on the confidence with which they can rely on both historical and budgeted financial information.

The use of analytical procedures provides important information about the present profitability and financial strength of the company, which the auditors can use when assessing going concern. Auditors may also use bankruptcy prediction models to aid them in identifying if a company is at risk of failing. These models, commonly known as Z-score models, require the auditors to calculate the values of about five or six ratios. Each of these ratios is then multiplied by a coefficient and then added together to give a score – the Z-score. This score is then compared with some benchmark that enables the auditors to gauge the extent or likelihood of the company failing. The model, including coefficients and the benchmark, is usually purchased from a commercial supplier who specializes in developing bankruptcy prediction models.

One of the major problems in assessing going concern is that it requires the auditors (and the directors) to look into the future. By its nature the future is uncertain and therefore any judgements about the future by auditors and directors could turn out to be incorrect. Normally, however, companies do not throw themselves completely into the hands of the future but instead attempt to anticipate as much as they possibly can what is going to happen. To help them plan for the future, companies normally gather information which enables them, albeit incompletely, to predict what is going to happen in the future.

It may be argued that an important attribute of good management is the ability to predict future trends and then react accordingly.

ACTIVITY 17.6

Suggest accounting information that a company may prepare, which is concerned with the future and should help directors and thus auditors in assessing the going concern of the company.

Among other items, you may have mentioned some of the following.

- *Cash flow budgets or forecasts*. These statements enable directors and auditors to assess the likelihood of the company having sufficient cash resources to remain in business.
- *Forecast profit and loss accounts and balance sheets*. The first of these, the forecast profit and loss account gives directors and auditors an awareness of the profit of the company in the forecast period. While profit by itself does not ensure that a company will survive, the ability to generate profit is usually directly related to a company's survival prospects. The forecast balance sheet allows the directors and auditors to identify the financial strength of the company and its likely liabilities. The auditors will not examine each of these statements in isolation but consider them as a totality. They will in particular be concerned to ensure that they are consistent with one another, so that one would expect the sales figure in the profit and loss account to be the basis of cash inflows in the cash flow budget and for the anticipated bank balance in the cash budget to be that in the forecast balance sheet at the appropriate dates. In addition to the above information the company may also prepare detailed information relating to forecast sales, costs and product information, perhaps broken down into product lines.

Auditors do not blindly accept these forecast statements but check them to ensure they are consistent with their knowledge of the business. If the company's sales and profit have been static in the current year, it would be somewhat unexpected if the company forecast substantial growth in the forecast period. If the forecast figures are unexpected the auditors would need to determine how the company intends to achieve them. In other words they will want to know what assumptions underlie the forecast statements and try to assess if management have been realistic in their estimates of, for instance, future sales. They will also need to examine the sensitivity of the forecast statements to changes in, for instance, economic conditions. Given the difference in size and complexity of firms the evidence available to assess going concern need not always be sophisticated and include such items as multi-period forecasts and budgets. The information a company prepares is dependent upon its needs and if management consider it possible to plan and control using relatively simple methods, sophisticated forecasts may not be available when considering going concern. This is more likely in smaller companies where management may be more dependent on their personal knowledge of the business and its environment when planning. Sophisticated forecasts may also not be necessary where the business operates in a relatively stable environment. Where the company does not have sophisticated planning systems, the auditors will have to use what information is available, supplemented by discussions with management about their plans for the future.

The evidence management and auditors need to come to a conclusion about a company's going-concern status is dependent on the extent to which it is clear that the company is a going concern. The less clear, the greater the amount of information and evidence that must be examined to come to a final conclusion about whether the going-concern status is valid. Thus, if a company is profitable and has a positive cash flow position, the industry and the environment in which it operates is stable, it is likely that very little additional evidence will be needed to arrive at an assessment of going concern. The converse situation is one where auditors and management have to spend a considerable effort to arrive at a final conclusion about the use of the going-concern basis. Where the auditor does have concerns about the applicability of the going-concern concept, they should adequately document those concerns.

ACTIVITY 17.7

List indicators that might suggest that a company is having going-concern problems.

You may have mentioned some of the following:

- The company is generating negative cash flows.
- The company has made significant losses.
- The company has substantial debts which it is having trouble servicing.
- The company has a substantial overdraft and on occasion is close to or exceeding its overdraft limit.
- The company has current net liabilities.
- The company has had to renegotiate loan repayments or overdraft facilities with its bankers.
- The company has reduced its dividends.
- The company is taking a longer period to pay its trade payables who are becoming increasingly irritated by the failure of the company to pay on time.

- The company has made a number of its employees redundant and/or has had to reorganize/rationalize its operations.
- The company is in a declining market and/or manufactures or retails products which are out of fashion.
- A number of the major customers of the company have gone bankrupt.
- The company has been forced to sell some of its non-current assets.

As you can see there are a number of potential indicators that can be useful when considering whether a company is a going concern, indeed you may have mentioned others. It is important, however, to stress that these are only indicators and do not prove that the company is having going-concern problems. They serve as a signal to the auditors that there may be problems and that they should investigate further. At the root of a company's going-concern problems is usually a lack of financial resources to cover financial commitments. Major providers of financial resources are often banks from whom companies obtain loans or overdraft facilities. Where the auditors have concerns about going concern, it is likely that they will have to satisfy themselves about the continuation of, or the supply of, additional funds from the company's bankers. The auditors will be particularly concerned where the company is close to its overdraft limit and correspondence between the bank and the company would seem to indicate that the former is reluctant to increase the overdraft facility. Where the company's present bankers appear unwilling to extend further loan or overdraft facilities, the auditors will have to discuss with the directors what contingency plans they have, should they need additional financial resources. If the firm is dependent on the continuation of loan or overdraft facilities from their bankers, the auditors may have to obtain evidence in the form of: written confirmations from management; discussions with the key officials and the company's bankers; and correspondence between the bankers and the company which suggest that they are willing to continue extending the loan or overdraft facilities. In smaller companies where owners and management are the same individuals, particular problems may arise for auditors because in these companies the appropriateness of the going concern might be dependent on the continued support of owner managers. This support may be financial in terms of loans from the owners to the company. In this situation the auditor would need to identify the terms and conditions of any loans and seek reassurances from the owners that they will not require the money to be repaid in the near future. Where the company is dependent for its solvency on the continuation of loans from the owners the auditors may require them to give written reassurance about the continuation of the loans.

At the time of writing, in the aftermath of the banking crisis, banks have been more reluctant to commit themselves to stating that they willing to continue with financial or loan arrangements with clients. Bankers' unwillingness to give a positive commitment that loan or overdraft facilities will be continued does not in itself mean that the company is not a going concern. It would, however, prompt the auditor to discuss with management the plans they have in place should the bank not continue with its loan facility. For instance, it might be that the directors had already begun to give some thought to alternative sources of finance, such as raising capital through a share issue or the sale of certain assets. If this is the case, the auditor would need to determine the viability of these options and what specific steps the directors had taken in respect of the alternatives.

At this stage it might be useful to emphasize that the chief focus of audit effort will be in assessing managements' judgement as to the appropriateness of using the going-concern assumption. Thus, auditors are interested in what evidence management has collected and the process they have used to determine the company is a going concern. The auditor has to evaluate the evidence that has been used by management and see if they come to the same conclusion as them about the company being a going concern. This means that auditors have to assess the quantity of evidence collected, the underlying assumptions and their reliability. Of particular interest to the auditor is when the directors identify material uncertainties pertaining to events or conditions that might cast significant doubt as to the ability of the company to remain a going concern. The auditor will need to pay particular attention to those events or conditions and be thorough in their investigation of the evidence related to them.

The Companies Act 2006 requires that the directors' report include a business review. Among other matters it should contain a description of the principal risks and uncertainties facing the company. In this section the directors will describe some of the issues relating to risk that are pertinent to going-concern considerations. FRS 18 and IAS 1 also require that the material uncertainties be disclosed. The FRC document *Going concern and liquidity risk: guidance for directors of UK companies 2009* provides an example of the sort of disclosures that might be made when a material uncertainty exists that casts significant doubt on the ability of the company to continue as a going concern and we include it as an appendix to this chapter.

The foreseeable future

As we mentioned earlier, when an entity prepares its financial statements on a going-concern basis this means they are based on the assumption that the entity will continue in existence for the foreseeable future. ISA 570 (para. 13) notes that the auditor should consider the same period in the future as management but that where this period is less than 12 months from the balance sheet date, the auditors should ask the directors to extend its period of assessment to 12 months after the balance sheet date. In the UK and Ireland it would be normal for the directors to consider a period of at least 12 months from the date of approval of the financial statements. If the directors refuse to do this, the auditor will have to decide if they have sufficient audit evidence to arrive at a conclusion about the use of the going-concern assumption. If they feel that they have insufficient audit evidence, they may have to issue a modified audit opinion. The UK and Ireland version of the ISA also states that where the directors look at a period of less than one year after approval of the financial statements they will need to determine if any additional disclosure is required, particularly the assumptions they are using that enable them to conclude that the entity is a going concern. In the UK and Ireland, where the directors do not disclose that the period they have used is less than one year from the date of approval, the auditors should disclose it in their audit report. You will have noticed that there is some inconsistency concerning the recommended future minimum period management should consider between ISA 570 and its UK and Ireland variant. The same inconsistency exists between

See ISA 570 (UK and Ireland), paragraph 13-1).

In fact, as paragraph A10.1 shows, it is those charged with governance who have this duty

See paragraph 17.2

IAS 1 (para. 26) which suggests the minimum period should be 12 months from the balance sheet date, whereas FRS 18 (para. 61 (b) commences the period of 12 months from the date of approval of the financial statements.

Although the focus of the auditors' attention will be on the period used by management to assess going concern they must remain alert to possible conditions or events beyond that period which might affect the going-concern status of the company. For instance, the auditors may be aware that new legislation is to be introduced in about two years' time that could have an adverse effect on the company's profitability. If this is the case the auditors would discuss the impending legislation with the directors to determine if they have considered what effect it might have and also find out if they have plans on how its negative effect could be mitigated.

REPORTING ON GOING CONCERN

If there is no doubt about a company's going-concern status, under ISA 570 neither management nor auditors need refer specifically to going concern in the financial statements or audit report. However, the Combined Code on Corporate Governance states that 'the directors should report that the business is a going concern, with supporting assumptions or qualifications as necessary' (Code Provision C.1.2).

Where there are considerable doubts over whether a company is a going concern, the auditors will consider if additional disclosures are required in the financial statements. Where there are material uncertainties of which management is aware, arising from events or conditions that cast significant doubt on the ability of the company to continue as a going concern, they must disclose those uncertainties. If the directors have included sufficient appropriate disclosures in the financial statements relating to going concern, including their plans to deal with the events or conditions, such that the auditors are of the opinion that the statements give a true and fair view, they need not issue a modified audit opinion. The auditors should issue an unmodified audit report but include an emphasis of matter paragraph. The auditors will make it clear in the paragraph that there is a material uncertainty relating to an event or condition, that may cast significant doubt on the entity being considered as a going concern and will direct the reader to the note in the financial statements where management describe the uncertainty. Where the disclosures made by the directors in the notes to the accounts are considered by the auditors to be inadequate, the latter will issue an except for qualification for disagreement or an adverse audit report. The audit report will contain details of the material uncertainty that may cast significant doubt on the ability of the entity to continue as a going concern.

See Paragraph 25 of IAS 1 and paragraph 61(a) of FRS 18.

See paragraphs 18 to 20 of ISA 570.

We are assuming here that, although there are doubts about going concern, the auditors agree that the use of the going-concern basis in preparing the financial statements is still appropriate. Where the directors prepare the financial statements using the going-concern basis and the auditors do not agree its use is appropriate, they should issue an adverse opinion. Before events reach this stage, where during the audit the auditor has doubts or concerns about the appropriateness of the use of the going-concern assumption, they should raise those concerns with management and, where one exists, the audit committee of the company. The auditor might suggest that the directors obtain specialist advice, in particular legal advice, about continuing to trade where there may be doubt that the company is solvent.

Finally, where the auditors believe that the level of assessment used by management is not sufficient for them to adequately determine if the entity is a going concern, the auditor should ask them to extend their analysis. If the directors do not do this, the auditor would have to consider modifying their audit report on the basis of a limitation of scope.

In conclusion, the auditors' main concern is with determining whether management's statement on going concern is consistent with knowledge they have gained during the audit. The auditors are, thus, not expressing an opinion on the ability of the company to continue in operational existence. It may legitimately be asked what the corporate governance requirements in the UK in respect of going concern add to what is already required by ISA 570. It may be argued, of course, that the corporate governance requirements reinforce management's responsibility for reporting on going concern and clarifies the auditors' duty to form an opinion on the statement on the basis of their general audit work. Note, however, that the auditors are not required to perform additional work necessary to express their own opinion on the going-concern status of the company.

Summary

In this chapter we addressed the two issues of fraud and going concern. We discussed the auditors' responsibility for detecting fraud and described the circumstances when fraud was most likely to occur and the motivations that lead directors and management to manipulate the financial statements. The auditors' reporting responsibilities when they suspect or discover fraud were outlined. A number of steps the directors can take to minimize the incidence of fraud were listed. We also outlined recent contributions to the debates on fraud by the auditing profession. We discussed some important legal cases relating to fraud and outlined some recent auditing scandals. We concluded this section with a discussion of the requirements of the auditing standard, ISA 250 – *Consideration of laws and regulations in an audit of financial statements*.

As regards going concern, we first outlined the respective responsibilities of those concerned with governance – management, and auditors. The evidence and procedures that may be used to identify whether a company is having going-concern problems were discussed. We listed a number of factors, which, if present, should cause the directors and the auditors to question the assumption of going concern. How far management need to look ahead when considering going concern is an important issue discussed in the chapter. Finally, we considered the auditors' reporting duties in respect of going concern.

Key points of the chapter

- It is popularly believed that the main reason for an audit is to detect fraud. Auditors, however, assert that the prime responsibility for deterring and detecting fraud lies with management and this responsibility is best met by them implementing an effective system of internal control.
- Fraud is an intentional act involving the use of deception to obtain an unjust or illegal advantage. Managerial fraud involving the financial statements is difficult for auditors to detect.
- The audit role is to arrive at an opinion that the financial statements are free from material misstatement. The auditor should maintain an outlook of professional scepticism and recognize that material fraud could exist.
- Auditors plan and conduct audit tests to detect material fraud and irregularities. Auditors cannot guarantee detection of all frauds and errors because of: (a) inherent limitations in audit techniques; (b) deceit, collusion, etc to conceal fraud; (c) audit evidence is that required to form an opinion and not to find fraud.

- Pressure to misrepresent financial performance may be high where: (a) the company has performed badly or is under pressure from markets; (b) management wish to show continuing growth; (c) the company expands by acquisition; (d) there are liquidity problems. These factors cause auditors to change the audit approach to reflect higher risk.
- Management responsibilities include sound internal controls aided by: (a) control environment; (b) establishing strong and effective detailed internal control; (c) strong ethical environment; (d) an audit committee; (e) reporting on effectiveness of internal controls.
- Types of fraud include: (a) misappropriation of assets; (b) falsification of accounting records; (c) misrepresentation of transactions or events; (d) misapplication of accounting policies; (e) inappropriate classification or disclosure.
- Once auditors have ascertained that fraud might be taking place they (a) confirm nature of fraud and likely magnitude; determine additional audit tests; (b) discuss with management or audit committee. If fraud discovered auditors should: (1) ask management to determine extent (2) if material and affects financial statement request management to adjust the statements; (3) assess impact on other audit work.
- If auditors suspect employees may be implicated they should discuss the matter with the directors. If directors may be involved, they should consider reporting to the audit committee. They might also seek legal advice. If management take no appropriate action, auditors to re-evaluate the integrity of management and the control environment.
- Auditors should document (a) initial grounds for suspicion; (b) additional audit work; (c) details of what, when and to whom they reported; (d) management's response; (e) implications for audit work.
- Normally the auditor is precluded from informing third parties of their suspicions of fraud, but the duty of confidentiality may be overridden by statute or law. Auditors may seek legal advice before informing any third party.
- *The Audit Agenda: Next Steps* recommended that auditors report to the board and audit committees of listed companies on the appropriateness and adequacy of control systems, auditors to be trained and educated and directors to commission forensic audits. It highlighted difficulty of detecting fraud if well-planned, ingenious or involving collusion, or involvement of top management. Auditors can help to prevent fraud by informing management of weaknesses in control systems.
- ICAEW Audit and Assurance Faculty has recommended auditors should be prepared to take a more active role in detecting fraud, and has suggested establishment of a Fraud Advisory Panel. They devised a ten-point plan to meet the challenge of fraud. APB admits it is difficult to detect management fraud, but has proposed radical change to detect management fraud, including: (a) increased professional scepticism; (b) tighter rules on audit evidence; (c) reporting material matters in the financial statements, supported only by management representations. APB considers auditors' role could be expanded by (a) reporting to boards and audit committees on controls to prevent and detect fraud; (b) forensic fraud review; (c) more reporting of suspected frauds.
- Case law relating to fraud includes *Re Kingston Cotton Mill Co.* (1896); *Irish Woollen Co. Ltd vs Tyson and Others* (1900); *Re Thomas Gerrard & Son Ltd* (1967).
- Auditing scandals occur in all countries. Auditors must maintain professional scepticism and be alert to the possibility of fraud particularly when risk factors are present, such as dominant chief executives, complex corporate structures and rapid growth.
- ISA 250 requires (a) understanding relevant laws and regulations and how entity ensures compliance; (b) inspecting correspondence with relevant authorities; (c) determining if management are aware of non-compliance; (d) written confirmation from management they have disclosed non-compliance and potential implications for the financial statements.
- If auditors are aware of possible non-compliance they determine nature and potential effect on the financial statements. The outcome of discussions with management and legal representatives may influence auditors' judgement of management's integrity. Auditors may include the matter in their audit report, and may report actual or suspected non-compliance to a third party. Money laundering and new legislation has placed additional responsibilities on accountancy firms.

Going concern

- Financial statements are usually prepared on the going-concern basis.
- If a company may not be a going concern, the valuation basis for assets will probably be a variant of break-up value or liquidation values, and long-term liabilities and non-current assets will be reclassified as current liabilities and assets.
- Management responsibilities include determining if a company is a going concern. Auditors must satisfy themselves the going-concern basis is appropriate and disclosures in the financial statements are sufficient.
- Auditors determine how management concluded the company is a going concern, and assess the logic, rationale and strength of information used. Auditors should: (a) assess business/inherent and control risk; (b) perform analytical procedures. They should be knowledgeable about the company. Assessment of control risk gives guidance on reliability of historical and budgeted financial information. Analytical procedures provide important information. Auditors may also use bankruptcy prediction models.

- A major problem in assessing going concern is that parties must look to the uncertain future. Means to predict the future include: (a) cash-flow budgets or forecasts; (b) forecast financial statements; (c) forecast sales, costs and products. Auditors check assumptions and discuss plans for the future.
- Indicators suggesting going-concern problems include: (a) negative cash flows; (b) significant losses; (c) substantial debts difficult to service; (d) substantial overdraft and overdraft limit exceeded; (e) net current liabilities; (f) loan or overdraft facilities renegotiated; (g) reduction in dividends; (h) longer creditor payment period; (i) redundant employees and reorganization of operations; (j) declining market/out-of-fashion products; (k) bankruptcy of major customers; (l) forced sale of non-current assets.
- Where financial statements are prepared on a going-concern basis, the entity is assumed to continue in existence for the foreseeable future. Directors judge what is an appropriate period for them to look into the future. In the UK if this period is less than one year from the date of approval of the financial statements, additional disclosures may be required.
- If there is no doubt, neither directors nor auditors need refer specifically to going concern in the financial statements or audit report. But the Combined Code requires management of listed companies to report the business is a going concern, with supporting assumptions or qualifications. Where there are doubts, auditors will consider if the directors have included disclosures to give a true and fair view. If so, they do not modify their audit opinion, but include an emphasis of matter, referring to the note disclosure in the audit report.
- Where the disclosures by the directors are considered inadequate, auditors should consider modifying their audit report.
- Where the auditors do not agree that the going-concern basis is appropriate, they should issue an adverse opinion.
- Currently, because of the economic crisis the number of companies indicating some concern about their ability to remain a going concern is likely to be greater. A greater number of audit reports are expected to include an emphasis of matter paragraph.

References

Cullinan, C.P. and Sutton, S.G. (2002), 'Defrauding the public interest: a critical examination of reengineered audit processes and the likelihood of detecting fraud', *Critical Perspectives on Accounting*, Vol. 13(3): 297–310.

Keune, M.B. and Johnstone, K.M. (2009) 'Staff accounting bulletin no. 108 disclosures: descriptive evidence from the revelation of accounting misstatements', *Accounting Horizons*, 23(1): 19–53.

Rezeaa, Z. (2005) 'Causes, consequences and deterrence of financial statement fraud', *Critical Perspectives on Accounting*, Vol. 16(3): 277–98.

Further reading

A starting point here is for students to be thoroughly familiar with the auditing standards that have been discussed in the chapter:

ISA 240 – *The auditor's responsibilities relating to fraud in an audit of financial statements.*

ISA 250 – *Consideration of laws and regulations in an audit of financial statements.* (In UK and Ireland ISA 250A)

ISA 570 – *Going concern.*

Financial Reporting Council, *Going Concern and Liquidity Risk: Guidance for Directors of UK Companies 2009,* FRC, October 2009.

Auditing Practices Board, Bulletin 2008/10, *Going Concern Issues During the Current Economic Conditions,* APB, December 2008.

Auditing Practices Board, Practice Note 1(Revised), *Money Laundering – Interim Guidance for Auditors on UK Legislation,* APB, March 2008.

In addition, students will find it interesting to read the following Audit and Assurance Faculty publications *Taking Fraud Seriously* published in January 1996, *Fraud: Meeting the Challenge through External Audit* published in November 2003, and the APB Consultation Paper, *Fraud and Society: Choices for Society*, published in November 1998.

Another good source for material on fraud are the websites of large audit firms, such as KPMG (http://www.kpmg.co.uk/) and PricewaterhouseCoopers (http://www.pwc.co.uk).

Another website worth looking at is the Serious Fraud Office (http://www.sfo.gov.uk).

A controversial article you might find interesting is one that suggests that some accounting firms may well be implicated in money laundering: Mitchell, A., Sikka,

P. and Willmott, H. (1998) 'Sweeping it under the carpet: the role of accountancy firms in money laundering', *Accounting, Organizations and Society*, 23(5/6): 589–607.

Students are also recommended to read *The Audit Agenda* (1994) and *The Audit Agenda: Next Steps* (1996), both of which were issued by the APB. Finally, if you have the time, you will find it useful to familiarize yourself with The Combined Code on Corporate Governance and the listing rules associated with the reporting on going concern.

APPENDIX 17.1: TYPICAL DISCLOSURES REQUIRED WHERE MATERIAL UNCERTAINTIES EXIST THAT CAST SIGNIFICANT DOUBT ABOUT THE ABILITY OF THE COMPANY TO CONTINUE AS A GOING CONCERN HAVE BEEN IDENTIFIED BY THE DIRECTORS

Example 3—A company with complicated circumstances, considerable exposure to economic difficulties and either a current material bank overdraft or loan that requires renewal and perhaps an increase in the year ahead

The company's business activities, together with the factors likely to affect its future development, performance and position are set out in the business review on pages X to Y. The financial position of the company, its cash flows, liquidity position and borrowing facilities are described in the finance director's review on pages P to Q. In addition, notes A–D to the financial statements include the company's objectives, policies and processes for managing its capital; its financial risk management objectives; details of its financial instruments and hedging activities; and its exposures to credit risk and liquidity risk.

As described in the directors' report on page X, the current economic environment is difficult and the company has reported an operating loss for the year. The directors' consider that the outlook presents significant challenges in terms of sales volume and pricing as well as input costs. Whilst the directors have instituted measures to preserve cash and secure additional finance, these circumstances create material uncertainties over future trading results and cash flows.

As explained on page X, the directors are seeking to sell a property to provide additional working capital. The company is in negotiations with a potential purchaser but there can be no certainty that a sale will proceed. Based on negotiations conducted to date, the directors have a reasonable expectation that the sale will proceed successfully, but if not the company will need to secure additional finance facilities.

As explained in the business review on page Y, the company has commenced discussions with its bankers about an additional facility that may prove to be necessary should the sale of the property not proceed or should material adverse changes in sales volumes or margins occur. It is likely that these discussions will not be completed for some time. The directors are also pursuing alternative sources of funding in case an additional facility is not forthcoming but have not yet secured a commitment.

The directors have concluded that the combination of these circumstances represents a material uncertainty that casts significant doubt upon the company's ability to continue as a going concern and that, therefore, the company may be unable to realize its assets and discharge its liabilities in the normal course of business. Nevertheless, after making enquiries and considering the uncertainties described above, the directors have a reasonable expectation that the company has adequate resources to continue in operational existence for the foreseeable future. For these reasons, they continue to adopt the going-concern basis of accounting in preparing the annual financial statements.

Source: Financial Reporting Council, *Going Concern and Liquidity Risk: Guidance for Directors of UK Companies 2009*

Self-assessment questions (solutions available to students)

17.1 Consider the following statements and explain why they may be true or false:

(a) Auditors are responsible for detecting fraud in a company's financial statements.

(b) The implementation of a sound system of internal control by directors should reduce the likelihood of fraud.

(c) On discovering that a fraud is being carried out by a particular individual, the auditors should report their findings to that individual's immediate superior.

(d) The application of the going-concern concept by a company implies that it will continue trading for the indefinite future.

(e) Auditors' have the prime responsibility to determine if a company is a going concern.

(f) Where auditors have significant doubts about whether a company is a going concern they should report their concerns in their audit report.

17.2

(a) Errors should be detected by auditors more easily than frauds. Discuss.

(b) Discuss the reasons why you believe the audit profession is unwilling to take greater responsibility for the detection of fraud.

17.3

(a) Describe the tests and procedures that the auditor needs to perform to form an opinion on management's conclusion that a company is a going concern.

(b) List as many factors as you can that might cast doubt on the ability of a company to be a going concern.

Self-assessment questions (solutions available to tutors)

17.4 The willingness of large audit firms to provide forensic audit services indicates that they have the ability and techniques available to detect fraud. It would, thus, seem a short step to suggest that auditors should have a greater responsibility for fraud detection. Discuss.

17.5 You have completed the audit of Magnolia Ltd for the year ended 31 December 2010. The financial statements show turnover of £10 000 000 – down 10 per cent on the prior year – and losses of £75 000. The company has net assets of £1 000 000 (2009: £1 100 000). The losses are mainly due to loss of market share following the entry of a new powerful competitor into the industry. The directors approved the financial statements and your firm signed the audit report on 30 May 2011. The copy for filing with the Registrar of Companies is still on your client file. You have just received a phone call today (26 June 2011) from your client informing you that negotiations in respect of certain sale contracts have unexpectedly collapsed and the outlook for the company is now uncertain.

Required

(a) State the audit work you would have completed in relation to going concern for this client prior to signing your audit report on 30 May 2011.

(b) Set out the effects which the phone call you have received today will have on:

(i) the audit opinion you signed on 30 May 2011; and

(ii) the set of financial statements yet to be filed with the Registrar of Companies.

(This question is adapted from the ICAI, Professional Examination Three, Paper 1 – Auditing, Summer 2001.)

17.6 You are the external auditor of Garb Ltd for the year ended 30 September 2011. Its principal activity is the design, manufacture and sale of clothing. The company made a loss in the year ended 30 September 2011, but the profit forecast indicates a return to profitability in the year ended 30 September 2012. The loss was due to redundancy and restructuring costs following the loss of its major customer, a national retailer, to whom it supplied clothing under the retailer's brand name. The company is now focusing on its own branded goods which have been sold, historically, at a higher margin. There are plans to develop its overseas market and to expand the customer base for its recently launched corporatewear products, and contracts have recently been agreed with several new overseas customers. The company has also negotiated a new contract with a major supplier, which has resulted in reduced prices in return for committed monthly purchases. During the year ended 30 September 2011, the company suffered severe negative cash flow but managed to stay within the overdraft facility by delaying payments to trade creditors and the Inland Revenue. The company has a bank loan which is due for repayment in March 2012 and is negotiating with its bankers for a replacement loan which is required to repay the present loan.

Required

(a) Explain what is meant by the going-concern concept and why the auditor should consider whether a company is a going concern.

(b) Identify matters to be considered when reviewing the profit and cash flow forecasts prepared by the company, in order to assess whether the company is a going concern.

(c) Discuss the implications for the audit report of Garb Ltd, in respect of the financial statements for the year ended 30 September 2011, if the negotiations for the replacement loan are not completed by the time the audit report is signed. (Question adapted from ICAEW, Professional Stage Examination, Audit and Assurance, Part two, December 2001.)

17.7 Discuss the feasibility of and ways in which the auditors' responsibility for the going-concern status of a company might be extended.

Topics for class discussion without solutions

17.8 Identify business risk factors that might alert the auditor to an increased risk of fraud occurring within an audit client.

17.9 The auditors' present role in respect of going concern is too passive, they should be much more pro-active in determining if an audit client is a going concern. Discuss

17.10 Discuss the occasions when you believe auditors should be required to report suspicion of a client engaged in fraud to a third party.

18

The audit expectations gap and corporate governance

LEARNING OBJECTIVES

After studying this chapter you should be able to:

- **Describe the nature of the audit expectations gap and identify its component parts.**
- **Suggest reasons why each component of the audit expectations gap came into existence.**
- **Consider solutions (actual or potential) to reduce the audit expectations gap.**
- **Explain why the gap may never be closed.**
- **Show why the question of corporate governance has become an important issue.**
- **Describe and discuss the recommendations included in the Combined Code on Corporate Governance relating to auditors and the operation of the board of directors.**

Learning objectives, 690
The audit expectations gap, 691
The causes of the audit expectations gap, possible developments and solutions, 692
Corporate governance, 705
Summary, 719
Key points of the chapter, 719
References, 720
Further reading, 721
Self-assessment questions (solutions available to students), 721
Self-assessment questions (solutions available to tutors), 722
Topics for class discussion without solutions, 723

THE AUDIT EXPECTATIONS GAP

We introduced you briefly to the audit expectations gap in Chapter 2 and in Figure 2.2 set out suggested components of the gap. In this section we discuss the gap in greater detail, suggesting possible reasons for the existence of the components and the pressures from interested parties and technological and other changes, which may cause the expectations gap itself to change its nature and structure over time. We suggest solutions that might help to close the gap, but would warn you that there is much disagreement about its nature, possible solutions and whether it is ever likely to be closed. Our concern is to give you insight into an important issue facing the auditing profession at the present time.

The audit expectations gap is a matter of considerable concern to all parties with an interest in the accountability process and in the credibility of the accounting and auditing profession. Empirical work has already been directed towards establishing the extent of the gap from the viewpoint of a number of interested parties and we shall draw particularly on studies by Humphrey *et al.* (1992) and Porter (1993). We noted in Chapter 2 that the value of Porter's work was the structured approach she had adopted and exemplified in Figure 2.2.

See Chapter 2, pages 50 to 52.

We use the definition of the audit expectations gap found in Humphrey *et al.* which suggests that the common element in the various definitions of the gap is that auditors are performing in a manner which is at variance with the beliefs and desires of others who are party to or interested in the audit. Before we move to a discussion of the expectations gap it will be useful to consider again the protagonists in the accountability and audit process.

The protagonists

The audit expectations gap (as the use of the plural suggests) comprises several different gaps between auditors and each of a number of other user groups, as identified in the Corporate Report (1975), or publics (as identified by Briloff 1986). Both user groups and publics are often referred to as stakeholders. Perhaps the most important point to note about the various stakeholders is that some may be classified as powerful or strong, while the main characteristic of others is that they are weak, lacking economic power. Powerful stakeholders (which include institutional shareholders and lenders and large customers and suppliers) possess economic power that would enable them to exercise political power over the directors of the company. The power of the strong stakeholder is not frequently exercised, at least not overtly, but the threat is always there. Other parties with legitimate interests but who lack power over the company and its managers would include small private shareholders, employees, smaller customers and suppliers, and perhaps society in general (as it is made up of a large number of disparate people and groups). All stakeholders have access, if desired, to published financial statements and to auditors' reports on those statements as public goods, although many stakeholders either have no right at all or no effective right in practice to affect the actions of directors. It is worth noting, however, that the more powerful stakeholders may well be able to obtain financial information about the company not available to the weaker stakeholders. It is also likely that these stakeholders will be better informed about the nature of auditing and the role of the auditor, and expectations of auditing will therefore differ considerably. This means that we have to take

Small shareholders, for instance, rarely attend annual general meetings and lack cohesive power to affect the actions of directors.

great care before we assume the existence of a very wide reasonableness component of the expectations gap on the part of all user groups and publics. You should note in this respect that Humphrey *et al.* based some of their conclusions on the results of interviews and a questionnaire. They contacted sophisticated users of financial statements (including investment analysts, bankers and financial journalists) and preparers (financial directors) and auditors of financial statements. We presume that these individuals concerned would be much better informed than the average member of the public.

Apart from stakeholders who are interested in the results and financial position of individual companies, there are other protagonists that should be taken into account when considering the effectiveness of the audit function and the audit expectations gap.

- *Politicians*, whether at national or local level, may have a very real interest in the performance of auditors. Thus, if significant fraud comes to light in a building society, fraud undiscovered by the auditor, the public might well blame politicians for not ensuring that audit was effective. As a result audit may be imposed, the scope of audit increased as a response to such public pressure or regulators appointed to oversee and monitor the accountability or audit process. Any change to the scope of audit is of course likely to have an impact on expectations of audit.
- *Regulators* come in various forms and range from the Registrar of Companies, the Financial Services Authority (FSA) to the accounting bodies themselves. Other examples include the Auditing Practices Board, the Financial Reporting Council, the Accounting Standards Board and International bodies such as the International Auditing and Assurance Standards Board. Importantly, regulation alters relationships by imposing duties on some and giving rights to others, or at least creating a climate within which duties will be self-imposed and rights given to others.
- *Academics* have in recent years taken much interest in the effectiveness of audit and it could be argued that some academics may have had an impact on what the public think about professional bodies and auditors and perhaps even changed to some extent the attitudes of these bodies and auditors. Such academics include Briloff in the United States and, in the United Kingdom – Sikka, Willmott and Mitchell the latter also being a politician.

Regulators are also well known in other fields, and those in the United Kingdom include Ofcom (communications industry), Ofgem (gas and electricity industry) and The National Lottery Commission (national lottery). They frequently make headline news because of the public interest issues in the industries they are regulating.

THE CAUSES OF THE AUDIT EXPECTATIONS GAP, POSSIBLE DEVELOPMENTS AND SOLUTIONS

Before we discuss possible reasons for the existence of the gap and its various components, it is worth mentioning that the gap is long-standing. Doubts have been expressed about the competence and independence of auditors and 'what they are supposed to be doing' every time a major financial scandal has occurred in the past one hundred years and more. At the same time very frequently the suggested answer to crisis was the introduction of or extension to auditing. For instance, in the aftermath of the City of Glasgow Bank scandal in 1878, the directors of the Union Bank of Scotland 'sought to weather this terrible storm and by taking an extraordinary step, that is, the adoption of an external audit system, which they believed would be convincing proof that they had nothing to hide' (Tamaki, 1983). Similarly, following the McKesson Robbins case in the United States in 1939, the response of the accounting profession was to require auditors to perform debtor circularizations and inventory count observations and to refer to these particular procedures in the standard audit report.

The Union Bank of Scotland survived for many years but was eventually taken over by the Bank of Scotland in 1954.

Trade receivables.

In this section we shall discuss possible reasons for the existence of the various components of the audit expectations gap. We shall also show that the gap is not static, is likely to change over time and may be closed at least in part as the result of action by the professional bodies, regulators and others or because of changes in circumstances.

It must be said that some academics, including Sikka, dispute whether the gap will ever be closed. See Sikka *et al.* 1998.

In Chapter 2 we suggested that Porter's structured approach as set out in Figure 2.2 was welcome, as it enabled identification of the various components making up the gap. It might be argued, however, that Figure 2.2 was limited in its scope, as it did not consider all elements of the audit expectations gap. For instance, independence did not feature, despite the fact that it is an important aspect of the gap and no attempt was made to show the forces that might cause the components to alter over time, nor were possible reasons for the gap identified.

In this section we shall address these and other issues and as a first step the diagram has been redrafted to show the audit expectations gap in a more dynamic way and to show how the lines might flex as the result of a variety of pressures. We have also introduced the possible impact of practitioner and profession independence as defined by Mautz and Sharaf (1961) into the diagram. This is set out in Figure 18.1.

We discussed practitioner and profession independence in Chapter 3.

Deficient performance

We have identified two possible reasons for the existence of this gap – lack of competence and lack of practitioner independence.

Lack of competence

Porter's (1993) work in New Zealand revealed apparent ignorance about auditors' duties on the part of auditors themselves (for instance, detecting illegal acts by company officials which directly impact on the company's accounts), while some duties accepted by auditors were deemed by non-auditor respondents to be poorly performed. These duties included the expression of doubts in the audit report about the continued existence of an auditee company and disclosure in the audit report of deliberate distortion of financial information. However, auditor competence really needs clearer definition as it can encompass lack of care, lack of knowledge and lack of experience. This may be linked to some extent to the way that professional firms organize themselves, as much day-to-day auditing work is carried out by relatively inexperienced and professionally unqualified staff. Humphrey *et al.* (1992) identified pressure on audit fees as leading to less time being spent on the audit as one probable cause of the audit expectations gap. It is worth noting in this context that less experienced staff will tend to be equated with less cost. We might note that there are many examples from case law or inspectors' reports of lack of competence on the part of the auditor.

p77.

FIGURE 18.1 The audit expectations gap: Overview of structure, possible causes and forces for change over time

Change over time →

Change over time →

Change over time →

← Change over time →

Perceived performance by auditors

Regulatory pressure from state and profession and informal pressures

Change occurs because informed protagonists in society change perceptions of reasonableness

Society's expectations of auditors

← Audit expectation gap →

← Performance gap →

← Reasonableness gap →

← Deficient performance →

← Deficient standards →

← Unreasonable expectations →

For instance: auditor fails to report doubts about going-concern status of the company

For instance: auditor need not report problems within a company to a regulatory authority

For instance: auditor verifies every transaction of the auditee company

Auditor's existing duties

Duties reasonably expected of auditors

Arising from lack of:	Arising from lack of:	Arising from lack of:	
COMPETENCE PRACTITIONER INDEPENDENCE	PROFESSION INDEPENDENCE	SOCIETAL AND TECHNOLOGICAL SOPHISTICATION AND CLARIFICATION OF AUDIT ROLE	
→	→	→	← →
Strong stakeholder may force competence and practitioner independence on auditor by override	Extension of duties and liability (forced by societal demands) (unlikely to be diminution)	Extension of what is perceived to be reasonable (because of societal awareness or technological change or clarification of the role of the auditor) (unlikely to be diminution)	The unreasonable expectations gap may open or close depending upon sophistication of society and actions of protagonists

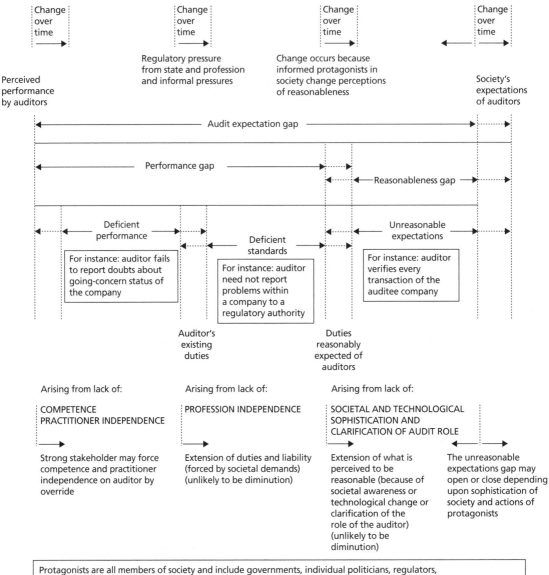

Protagonists are all members of society and include governments, individual politicians, regulators, the accounting/auditing profession/industry, individual practitioners, owner-principals and other stakeholders, manager-agents, firms. Some of these protagonists have more power than others. Some are more sophisticated than others, resulting, *inter alia*, in more than one expectations gap.

ACTIVITY 18.1

Suggest responses by the accounting profession to complaints about auditors' lack of competence.

The response by the profession and the law to evidence of lack of competence includes:

- Rules on the issue of practising certificates by the professional bodies.
- Post-qualifying educational requirements of the professional bodies.
- Monitoring of audit activity by the professional bodies following the Companies Act 1989, which introduced the requirements of the seventh accounting directive of the European Union. This monitoring function was retained in the Companies Act 2006.
- Disciplinary procedures of the accounting bodies following investigation of apparent audit failures.

Perhaps more important than apparent ignorance of their duties by individual auditors is the fact that business has become increasingly complex in recent years. Humphrey *et al.* suggest that 'it could be argued that the increased complexity of commercial life has outstripped advances in audit technology'. It might be said that some companies are close to unauditable because of the nature of their business. Enron for instance had very complicated interests all over the world and financing arrangements complex in the extreme. In the case of Enron this complexity was coupled with a top management engaged in fraudulent activity, a lethal combination that most auditors might find very difficult to manage. Other companies (such as The Maxwell Group) may combine complexity with a dominant individual occupying dual roles at the top in a unique position to override controls. This also represents a difficult set of circumstances for the auditor. A further matter of importance is the complexity of the relationships within organizations, frequently composed of diverse individuals and groups with differing objectives, so that it may be difficult for the auditor to decide whether management assertions are valid or what specific assertions are in fact being made about the financial information incorporated in the financial statements.

This is referring to a major scandal in the 1990s involving the businessman Robert Maxwell who stole a substantial sum of money (in excess of £400 million) from his company's pension scheme. The Combined Code on Corporate Governance revised by the Financial Reporting Council in 2008 recommends that one individual should not combine the role of chairperson and chief executive with the intention of reducing the power of dominant individuals. We discuss corporate governance in greater detail later in this chapter.

ACTIVITY 18.2

Suggest questions that a firm of auditors should ask before accepting as a client a complex group with a large number of overseas subsidiaries with different year-end dates.

Firms of auditors are faced with the important decision as to whether they should accept a company as a client every time they are asked to serve and to continue as auditor. Often the decision is not problematic as the potential client may not present a high degree of audit risk, but if the company is very complex and there are other factors that suggest that audit risk is high, the auditor will have to decide if the assignment should be accepted. Differing year-end dates pose a particular problem as it may be difficult to ensure that year-end cut-off is accurate. A fraudulent management might, for instance, make cash transfers into subsidiary companies just before their year-ends and move it out immediately afterwards. It is interesting that in the revision of

See ISQC 1 (paragraph 26) and ISA 220 (paragraph 12)

auditing standards greater attention has been focused by standard setters in recommending that audit firms should undertake a critical evaluation, or engagement risk assessment, of a client before accepting an audit appointment. Questions that firms of auditors might ask to help them make their decision include the following.

- Does the firm have the necessary resources, including individuals with the necessary linguistic skills and knowledge of the environment within which the subsidiaries operate?
- Does the client management possess high integrity?
- Does the company have a high-quality group internal audit department with a wide-ranging remit, supported by an adequate internal audit department within each territory?
- Are internal controls throughout the group of high quality and is proper attention paid to ethical issues throughout the company?
- Does the group possess an adequate information system that will ensure problems (affecting such matters as profitability and liquidity) are detected at an early stage?

Lack of practitioner independence

See page 65.

We discussed practitioner independence in Chapter 3, where we noted that practitioner independence is basically a state of mind on the part of the auditor, affected by three dimensions: programming independence, investigative independence and reporting independence. Practitioner independence is essentially about the independence of the auditor as a person or firm. In that chapter we also introduced you to the work of Goldman and Barlev (1974) and Shockley (1982), who identified conflicts and pressures that may both increase or decrease the likelihood of the auditor behaving in an independent way.

The problem is that it may be very difficult to separate out the effects of lack of competence and lack of practitioner independence. Technical competence and honesty or independence of the practitioner are clearly intertwined. It follows therefore that the remedies for deficient performance are not merely those that increase practitioner competence (practising certificate requirements, post-qualifying education, etc.) but also those that increase the likelihood of practitioner independence. The first of the three main suggestions made by Humphrey *et al.* (1992: 84) as to the best ways of reducing the expectations gap would seem to be relevant in this connection: 'the improvement of existing systems of audit regulation including consideration of the setting up of an independent Office for Auditing to oversee the framework for large company audit appointments, auditor remuneration and the audit practice of the major accounting firms'.

'You will remember from Chapter 4 that although the regulation of auditing has recently been modified this particular recommendation has not so far been implemented in the way envisaged by Humphrey *et al.*

This recommendation goes far beyond the monitoring of auditors under the self-regulatory rules that were drawn up following the Companies Act 1989 as amended by Companies (Audit, Investigations and Community Enterprise) Act 2004, although monitoring may also play an important role in this respect. An Office for Auditing would have a considerable impact on audit relationships and a very direct agency relationship with individual auditors (audit firms) might result. It might be argued that auditors would then find themselves in the difficult position of 'serving two masters' – the shareholders

These two Companies Acts have now been replaced by Companies Act 2006.

who appoint them and the Office for Auditing. This is sometimes referred to as 'conflicting accountabilities'. However, in the public sector, where offices for auditing already exist in the UK in the form of The Audit Commission and Audit Scotland, there does not appear to be much evidence of such conflict.

In the public sector there are of course no shareholders, but there is a wide range of stakeholders interested in the sector.

ACTIVITY 18.3

Give your views on the following situation. Angela Marks is the senior in charge of the audit of Carlton Limited. She knows that she has spent too much time on the non-current assets section of the audit and is under pressure to complete the audit in time. She has still to carry out the audit of inventory valuation, a matter which she knows from previous experience is a difficult area as some inventory lines may be valued at cost in excess of net realizable values. The company controller has told her that, unlike the previous year, net realizable values lie generally above cost. She carries out tests on selected inventory items but takes care to pick inventory lines that she knows have net realizable values above cost and on this basis writes a conclusion saying that inventory is fairly stated at cost.

Angela has clearly taken a risk and has decided to rely on the integrity and competence of the controller. This may be unwise as the controller may well be under pressure to ensure that the financial statements give a desired view. She appears not to be too certain about the assertion made by the controller, as she has taken the professionally unacceptable step of manipulating the evidence by being selective. The other matter for concern, however, is the pressure that Angela feels she is facing from her superiors in the firm. This could be a very dangerous situation for the firm, even if the possible overvaluation of inventory does not come to light in the case of Carlton Limited.

Deficient standards

We noted in Chapter 2 that the deficient standards gap is the gap between what auditors can be reasonably expected to do and what the profession and the law asks them to do. The question of course is what is reasonable and why, if suggested duties are reasonable, the law and profession have not taken steps (or taken them earlier) to include them in required duties. We have already discussed fraud and going concern in Chapter 17 and you have seen that these two issues are very problematic with no easy solutions. They are both areas where public expectations are high but the auditing profession has had great difficulty in satisfying these expectations, if at all. It is argued by some, including Sikka *et al.* that the reason for this is that the standards (whether imposed by the law or profession or other bodies) which auditors are expected to follow are not strict enough: that they are deficient in one way or another. We shall not go over the same ground as we covered in Chapter 17 but we shall discuss briefly the two issues in the context of deficient standards.

Fraud

We noted in Chapter 17 that auditors have attempted over a number of years and in a number of different ways to suggest to the public that their responsibility for fraud detection is rather limited. In this connection we saw that ISA 240 – *The auditor's responsibilities relating to fraud in an audit of financial statements*, (para. 4), states, among other things, that:

> The primary responsibility for the prevention and detection of fraud rests with both those charged with governance of the entity and management. It is important that management, with the oversight of those charged with governance, place a strong emphasis on fraud prevention, which may reduce opportunities for fraud to take place, and fraud deterrence, which could persuade individuals not to commit fraud because of the likelihood of detection and punishment.

And the responsibilities of the auditor are described (para. 5) as:

> An auditor conducting an audit in accordance with ISAs is responsible for obtaining reasonable assurance that the financial statements taken as a whole are free from material misstatement, whether caused by fraud or error. Owing to the inherent limitations of an audit, there is an unavoidable risk that some material misstatements of the financial statements may not be detected, even though the audit is properly planned and performed in accordance with the ISAs.

Thus ISA 240 suggests that the primary responsibility for the prevention and detection of fraud lies with management, and that, although the auditor seeks to gain reasonable assurance that the financial statements are free from material misstatement caused by fraud, the inherent limitations of audit may result in such misstatements not being detected. The ISA is suggesting that audit procedures may not always be particularly effective in detecting material misstatements in the financial statements caused by fraud involving collusion or the falsification of documents.

The critics of the auditing profession would argue that ISA 240 is a deficient standard because, despite the obvious problems of finding carefully hidden fraud, there is a general expectation on the part of the public that auditors should be able to find fraud material enough to affect the true and fair view required of financial statements. One of the main recommendations of Humphrey *et al.* in their research study on *The Audit Expectations Gap* in the UK reads as follows and sums up well this important element of the gap:

> We think that the public's expectation that auditors will detect material fraud should be recognized and that auditors should accept this role. The avoidance of a responsibility to accept that auditors should detect material fraud has been a recurring feature of the expectations gap over the last hundred years. It is unlikely to disappear unless auditors change their approach. It is very difficult to see that the public can be educated to accept anything less than the fact that if there is a fraud present in the organization which prevents the audited financial statements from showing a true and fair view, then it is up to the auditors to find it and disclose the details.

No doubt auditors would argue with the introduction of ISA 240 they have expanded their responsibilities by accepting that their audit procedures should be designed to detect material misstatements caused by fraud. This, however, must be tempered by the insistence that well-designed frauds especially involving collusion may still elude their audit procedures. This leaves a space in which parties can have differing views about whether the auditor should have or have not detected a particular fraud. It does this by allowing auditors to claim that a particular fraud was not detected because it was so well designed, involved falsification of documents and so on. To this must be added the concern that the ISA focuses almost entirely on fraud that causes the financial statements to be misstated. In doing so the ISA downgrades the auditors' responsibility for detecting misappropriation of assets unless their extent is such as to render the financial statements misleading. If individuals perceive one of the roles of an audit to be the detection of fraud involving misappropriation of assets this neglect in the ISA is unlikely to lead to a reduction in the expectations gap.

Apart from the difficulty of finding fraud, the question of reporting fraud within the company and to third parties is also important. Here, there is some evidence from the past to suggest that standards had been deficient. For instance, although auditors now have a *duty* in the UK and Ireland and in some other jurisdictions as well to report a significant matter, which is likely to include money laundering and fraud, to the relevant regulator, this has not always been the case. Prior to 1986 the law gave the auditor a right only and, in this respect, it could be argued that the law was deficient before that date.

You should note that the procedures outlined in ISA 240, are, in fact, the latest of a long line of guidelines, standards and recommendations on fraud and error and one suspects that they will not be the last. It may be that this is an area where it will be difficult to close the expectations gap, because the public, as Humphrey *et al.* suggest, will never be educated to accept that the standard is other than deficient. An important point for you to note is that if auditors were to introduce procedures that would give a higher chance of detecting fraud, especially involving the misappropriation of assets, the cost of audit would inevitably rise significantly. You should ask yourself if this would be a price that society would be willing to pay. At the same time note that making reporting of money laundering and fraud reportable might indicate an attempt to close the gap.

Going concern

In Chapter 17 we noted that auditors have often come in for criticism when a company has failed and there has been no indication in its annual report either by the directors or the auditors that the company had any going-concern problems. In the context of this section it is important to note that much of the criticism of the profession arose from the fact that earlier standards did not require auditors to search actively for evidence that the company was a going concern, but merely to be alert to the possibility that the going-concern concept was not applicable. If the auditor became aware that the assumption might not be valid, auditors would have carried out audit procedures designed to prove that the suspicions were justifiable or alternatively, groundless. However, the accusation that auditors were being too passive in their approach to going concern gave fuel to the claim that the standards of the profession were deficient. ISA 570 – *Going concern* is similar to ISA 250 in that it states that it is management's responsibility to assess the entity's ability to continue as a going concern. ISA 570, paragraph 6, states that it is:

> The auditor's responsibility is to obtain sufficient appropriate audit evidence about the appropriateness of management's use of the going concern assumption in the preparation and presentation of the financial statements and to conclude whether there is a material uncertainty about the entity's ability to continue as a going concern.

But paragraph 7 goes on to say that:

> The potential effects of inherent limitations on the auditor's ability to detect material misstatements are greater for future events or conditions that may cause an entity to cease to continue as a going concern. The auditor cannot predict such future events or conditions. Accordingly, the absence of any reference to going concern uncertainty in an auditor's report cannot be viewed as a guarantee as to the entity's ability to continue as a going concern.

It is worth noting that the audit expectations gap always comes to the fore in the wake of accounting or audit failure and it could be argued that the so-called active approach recommended by ISA 570 has not yet been tested. There are still grey areas where audit judgement requires to be exercised. Thus, in Chapter 17 we noted, among other things, that:

- Auditors have to decide if the future period selected by the directors for assessment of going concern is appropriate. This is subject to the proviso that the future period must usually be a minimum of 12 months from the balance sheet date (in the UK and Ireland from the date of approval of the financial statements).
- Auditors have to assess whether the financial information prepared by the directors in assessing going concern is adequate.
- Auditors have to assess a wide range of factors in determining if the going concern assumption is valid.
- Even where full disclosure has been made by the directors about the circumstances affecting the going-concern status of the company, the auditors still have to form a view as to whether the going-concern assumption is appropriate.

All of the above matters are judgemental and auditors will be at risk in forming conclusions about them. If their working papers show clearly that the auditors made a valid decision about such matters on the basis of the evidence available at the time, it is unlikely that they would be held to be negligent in a court of law. If their decision could be proven not to be soundly based, they might be held to be negligent. This would of course be more of a competence matter than a deficient standards matter.

On the face of it, it would seem that ISA 570 with its more active approach is a move in the right direction. Whether the audit expectations gap will be closed as a result of it, is less certain. Some might argue that the avoidance of qualification where a 'significant uncertainty' exists will not quieten the critics if companies continue to collapse a short time after a clean audit opinion has been given. At the same time there have been positive developments following the opening up of discussion on the topic of going concern, including the new requirements for directors to give their view on the going-concern status and the increasingly active role of audit committees in relation to corporate governance.

See the discussion later in the chapter on the requirements of the Combined Code on Corporate Governance.

Lack of profession independence

We introduced you to profession independence in Chapter 3. See page 67.

Many commentators in the UK (principally Sikka *et al.*) believe that one reason why the professional bodies in the British Isles have been tardy in introducing rigorous standards (both accounting and auditing) is that they may add to the potential liability of their members. Another way of putting this is that the accounting bodies are insufficiently independent of their own members. This is an aspect of profession independence not touched on by Mautz and Sharaf but it is one that is coming increasingly to the fore. The argument runs that it is impossible for the accounting bodies both to protect members and to ensure that society is best served by those members. The corollary is that self-regulatory monitoring activities should be dispensed with and replaced by 'an independent and democratic body with a statutory base, made up of representatives of all interested parties' (Mitchell and Sikka 1993: 47). It has already been noted above that this is one of the recommendations of Humphrey *et al.*

A further important element of profession independence may be the perception of the closeness of the leaders of the profession to big business, a matter that Mautz and Sharaf considered in the early 1960s. Such closeness may give the outsider the impression of conflict of interest and it may well be in the profession's long-term interest to divest itself of responsibilities which have traditionally been its own. Under the new regulatory framework with the establishment of the Financial Reporting Council (FRC) as the body having overall oversight and the APB and the ASB having members outwith the audit profession this to some extent has begun to occur. It could be strongly argued of course that these bodies should always have a strong representation from the accounting and auditing profession.

We discussed recent changes in audit regulation in Chapter 4.

ACTIVITY 18.4

Is the audit expectations gap really an accounting expectations gap? In other words, is the real problem not the fact that there is no consensus about the meaning of the words 'true and fair view'?

There may well be some truth in the statement, in that accounting standards (or lack of accounting standards or lack of rigorous accounting standards) in the past could be shown to have led to lack of confidence in the reliability of financial information. It could be argued that as long as there is doubt about the meaning of the words 'true and fair view' an expectations gap will exist. At the same time, if there is lack of knowledge about the degree of estimation and judgement in the preparation of financial statements, there is also likely to be an accounting reasonableness gap. The statement is intended to be controversial, of course. In fact the expectations gap is likely to arise from a mixture of auditing and accounting elements.

Unreasonable expectations

Porter (1993) suggested that expectations could only be regarded as reasonable if they are compatible with the auditor's role in society and cost-beneficial to perform.

The auditor's role in society

Porter's suggestion presupposes that the auditor's role has been clearly defined and that costs and benefits can be properly measured. Humphrey *et al.* observe (page 2) that: 'Some would distinguish between a "role" gap and a "quality" gap'. Quality refers to the competence of auditors and the standards to which they are asked to conform. As far as the role is concerned, is it about confirming a view of the past for stewardship purposes (as the judgement in the Caparo case assumed) or is the auditor concerned with a wider view of accountability to society, encompassing such matters as the efficiency and effectiveness of management and the impact of corporate entities on the environment? Is the auditor there to confirm stewardship actions or is a main objective the adding of credibility to information to make it more useful? Is there any reason why auditors should not examine and report on cash and profit forecasts or breaches of tax law to the tax authorities?

We discuss the impact of the Caparo judgement in greater detail in Chapter 19.

It seems likely that an important element of the audit expectations gap is lack of clear definition of the role of the auditor, contributing to lack of societal awareness. Johnson (1991) believed that one of the implications of the Caparo judgement is that legislation might be necessary to protect the interests of small shareholders. This view was extended by Humphrey *et al.* in their recommendation that the responsibilities of auditors should be widened to include potential shareholders and existing and potential creditors. Although they do not specifically mention weak stakeholders (such as small private investors, small suppliers, small customers, etc.) we suggest that some consideration should also be given to their special position, characterized not only by lack of power, but often also by lack of knowledge of accounting and auditing. If the role of the auditor is extended to give support to weaker stakeholders, this might have an impact serving to reduce the audit expectations gap.

ACTIVITY 18.5

You are engagement partner for the audit of Relia plc for the year ended 31 December 2010 and are on the point of completing the audit fieldwork. On 29 March 2011 your firm received a letter from the company's bankers saying that they intend to rely on the financial statements for the year to 31 December 2010 and the audit report in making a decision as to whether they should make a further loan to Relia for the purpose of financing expansion. What action should you take in respect of this matter?

The bankers clearly think that the role of the auditor is to add quality to information so it can be used in making business decisions. This does not appear to be an unreasonable expectation, although it runs counter to the Caparo decision that suggested that financial statements are documents used for stewardship purposes.

A lawyer might tell you that, until the auditor's role is clarified, it would be well that you write to the bankers telling them that the financial statements are not intended to be used as the basis for commercial decision making, that the financial statements are used for stewardship purposes and that your audit firm cannot accept responsibility for any reliance placed on the audit report.

A case similar to this, the Bannerman case, is discussed in Chapter 19.

Costs and benefits

Porter suggested that potential procedures of auditors should be regarded as unreasonable if the benefits of performing them were less than their cost. We have to draw a distinction between cost and benefits, however. Costs may be relatively easy to determine (thus a search for fraud will cost more than looking for evidence to support a true and fair view opinion). What will normally be much more difficult will be the measuring of potential benefits, as these are likely to be intangible and not subject to precise measurement.

Clearly, however, if the expectations gap is to be closed or reduced, some attempt must be made to evaluate benefits within a defined role for the audit function. We have already seen above that Humphrey *et al.* were of the view that the approach of auditors to fraud should be changed. The additional costs would only be justified, however, if the benefits to society were seen to be greater, however those benefits are measured. The other feature of costs and benefits is that they are likely to change over time because of technological change and changes in societal attitudes. This will be considered in greater detail below.

Direction of change

It is very difficult to assess how the various components of the audit expectations gap are likely to change over time. Is it likely, for instance, that the perceived performance of auditors will improve as measures to increase competence and practitioner independence are introduced, including stricter enforcement of standards and tougher disciplinary measures?

Figure 18.1 assumes that auditors' existing duties are likely to change, although there may be some doubt as to whether they will be continually extended. As the audit role becomes more clearly defined, some existing duties might fall away. The reasonableness gap is also likely to flex. It may narrow as the result of greater awareness, but may also widen as the result of new expectations. For instance, if an Office for Auditing were to be established, stakeholders might make the unreasonable assumption that the audit function would be completely reliable. Generally, the effect of actions by the profession and regulators on the various components of the gap may be difficult to assess.

Possible reasons for change

Expansion of auditors' duties

Auditors' existing duties may widen because of regulatory pressure from the state and the accounting profession and from certain informal pressures. The influence of society on the state and profession is indicated in the bottom half of Figure 18.1. The informal pressures would include pressures from academics and individual politicians (Sikka *et al.* for instance), but powerful stakeholders may seek their own remedies if the state and profession fail to satisfy their needs. If the UK were ever to have an independent regulatory agency as recommended by Humphrey *et al.*, presumably this too would have an influence on the placing of the line. It is likely that the FRC and ASB will have an impact on the existing duties of the auditor. At the same time, the possibility does exist that some existing duties may be discontinued or, at least, modified. This has certainly happened in the past as the result of changing views about the auditor's role, when a prior concern with fraud detection was superseded by a concern with truth and fairness.

It should be noted that if appropriate regulatory pressure were to be brought to bear on the auditors actual performance of their duties (whether by enhancing competence and/or ensuring practitioner independence), the perceived performance by auditors should improve. It may be that the monitoring of audit firms by the accounting bodies or their agent will have an impact in this respect, although the recommendation of Humphrey *et al.* for the establishment of an Office for Auditing, taking the role of an independent regulatory agency and with a clear investigatory mandate, 'could open up to public scrutiny what at present remains a rather private function'. They also suggest that 'In order to enhance the independence of the audit function the appointment of auditors and their fee determination needs to be taken out of the hands of the individuals on whom the auditors are reporting' (*ibid.*: 75).

We discussed in Chapter 4 and consider further later in this chapter and in Chapter 20 various changes in the regulation of auditors that is designed to improve auditor performance and independence.

Johnson describes the Coase theorem effects referred to above in relation to the Caparo judgement. The Coase theorem basically states that whenever the law adopts an inefficient rule (in this case the Caparo decision), people will bargain or contract around it. At the time that he was writing, Johnson suggested that auditors were being increasingly asked to supply warranty letters, acknowledging that their audit report would be relied on for specific purposes. Subsequently it would seem that firms of auditors have agreed among themselves to a policy of not providing such warranties.

R.H. Coase in 'The Problem of Social Cost' published in the *Journal of Law and Economics* in October 1960, described the bargaining that would take place when legal judgements had been made in respect of damage caused to neighbours.

Flexibility of auditors' duties

The 'Duties reasonably expected of auditors' line in Figure 18.1 is also shown as flexing and we suggest three possible reasons for this:

- *Clarification of the societal role of the audit function*. It seems clear that if the duties of the auditor are more clearly defined and, as seems likely, the role is expanded, duties that are still regarded as unreasonable will be seen to be reasonable. For instance, external auditors are not presently required to report to external stakeholders on the effectiveness of internal controls within a company, although they commonly do so to an internal audience – the management of the company. Most managements and auditors would regard this as unreasonable today, but one could envisage a time in the future when it might become accepted practice.

In the UK the draft Cadbury Committee report required auditors to report on the directors' statement on effectiveness of internal controls. As a result of the Sarbanes-Oxley Act it is a requirement in the US, though rather controversial, and it has attracted considerable criticism for the burden it places on auditors.

- *Greater societal awareness*. There may be some doubt as to whether unreasonable expectations will tend to diminish over time. However, increased sophistication of society – which may be itself caused by the actions of protagonists – may well cause the reasonableness gap to diminish as it becomes clear to the public that some of their expectations are not practical. An example might be an expectation by the public that all fraud, whether material or not, should be discovered by the auditor. It can be argued that that the new Audit Report (ISA 700) and its predecessor SAS 600 have already contributed to a greater awareness by explaining more clearly what an audit is, and the respective duties of management and auditors.

Porter and Gowthorpe (2004) appeared to doubt that expanding the audit report has made any difference to the expectations of users.

- *Technological change*. This may be important, as it is likely to affect costs. For instance, although in Figure 18.1 it has been suggested that an unreasonable expectation would be 'The auditor verifies every transaction of the auditee company', new technology might allow this to happen. Sophisticated 'sleeping auditor' (embedded) techniques would enable the auditor to set parameters for testing *all* transactions, those not meeting the parameters being subjected to deeper examination. Online, real-time access to client data is already a reality. The result of this is that the previously impossible becomes possible and the cost–benefit relationship changes.

Society's changing expectations

Regarding the right-hand line (Society's expectations of auditors), there are two possible directions of movement – to the right and left. There may be expectations in the future that we have not considered so far, so a widening will have to be accommodated in Figure 18.1.

Final remarks

Above we have suggested a number of ways in which the audit expectations gap might widen or narrow in the future. In a recent study contained in a 2009 report prepared by Porter *et al.* (2009) for the American Institute of Certified Accountants (AICPA) and IAASB she suggested as a result of responses from users in the UK that the audit expectations performance gap had narrowed considerably between 1999 and 2008. She believes that this is because of (a) better monitoring of auditors' performance and (b) more widespread discussion about corporate governance and financial affairs in general amongst the UK populace. In particular, unreasonable expectations of auditors performance had reduced. The same narrowing was not apparent in New Zealand where over the same period, the audit expectation performance gap broadened slightly but, more significantly, society's unreasonable expectations of auditors increased and its perception of the standard of auditors' performance remained virtually unchanged.

Audit expectations gap: a summary

In this section we have considered the audit expectations gap and the pressures for change that may affect the gap in the future. We have seen that it comprises several different gaps between auditors and each of a number of other groups. We have used analysis of the components to suggest reasons for their existence and have then noted suggestions to address the gap.

CORPORATE GOVERNANCE

Corporate governance is a matter closely related to the audit expectations gap, but is somewhat wider as it relates to the structures that should be in place both within the company and those imposed by society to control how companies are governed. The Cadbury Committee on 'The Financial Aspects of Corporate Governance' was set up in the UK in the early 1990s because of increasing lack of confidence in the existing controls on companies, including the internal controls, how they reported and the way in which auditors conducted their work and reported their findings. The Cadbury Committee issued a Code of Best Practice in 1992 since when it has been revised on a number of occasions. We have already noted in Chapter 16 that the Combined Code on Corporate Governance contains provisions requiring directors to report on certain matters, a number of which the auditors have to review. The Combined Code is given additional force by the Financial Services Authority requiring compliance with it in their listing rules and more generally the EU requirement that companies include a corporate governance statement in their Annual Report.

See page 638 and following pages.

You should have an understanding of the Combined Code, particularly where auditors are affected by it. We give details of the Code below together with comments for your consideration. Some of the principles and provisions in the Code may not always appear to be of direct relevance to auditors, but we think students of auditing should be aware of the main issues addressed in it. At the time of writing the current Code, which was issued in 2008, is presently being reviewed and a revised code will probably be issued in 2010.

In Chapter 16 we detailed the requirements for auditors reporting on the corporate governance statement made by companies.

First, it should be noted that the listing rules for the UK Stock Exchange require companies to report how they applied the principles set out in the Combined Code. The form and content of the statement is not prescribed; instead the Code suggests that companies should indicate if they have applied its provisions and, where they have not complied with one or more provisions, they should provide an explanation. This explanation should be sufficient to allow shareholders to assess the reasons why the company has not complied and should indicate how their actual practices, whilst not complying with one or more provisions of the Code, nevertheless contribute to good governance.

This form of reporting is commonly termed 'comply or explain'.

Combined Code provisions

The Combined Code contains a wide range of principles and recommendations, split into sections and sub-sections. Section 1 contains the principles of good governance under the headings: A. Directors; B. Remuneration; C. Accountability and audit; D. Relations with shareholders. We comment below on the ideas lying behind the principles and code.

A. Principles of good governance applicable to directors

This section is concerned with the effectiveness of the board of directors in leading and managing the company, and recommends a division of duties within the board and the existence of an independent element within it. Important recommendations include the following:

- Division of duties at the head of the company (and in particular the separation of the duties of chairperson and chief executive officer). The basic idea is that there should be division of power and authority, so that no one individual has unfettered powers of decision.
- The Code emphasizes that it is important the construction of the board ensures no individual or group of directors dominate decision making.

Another principle of the code is that there should be a rigorous and transparent procedure for appointing directors. The Code indicates that this can be achieved by the establishment of a nominations committee, which would play a lead role in the selection of directors and making nominations to the board. It is also recommended that the majority of the nominations committee should be independent non-executive directors.

The Code lists a number of factors that would have to be considered when determining if a non-executive director is independent.

- The Code recommends appropriate training (termed in the Code 'a full, formal and tailored induction') for directors the first time they are appointed to the board of a listed company.
- The board should meet sufficiently regularly to carry out its duties properly and should have a formal schedule of items specifically reserved for its decision.
- The supply of timely information of sufficient quality to the board to enable it to discharge its duties. This includes providing information to non-executive directors as well as those engaged in the day-to-day running of the company. As an aside, remember that non-executive directors have the same legal responsibilities as executive directors and it is therefore vital in their own interests that they should keep themselves well informed about the business. The Code recommends the board agrees procedures for directors to take independent advice in the furtherance of their duties at the company's expense and that *all* directors should have access to the advice and services of the company secretary. The company secretary is responsible to the board for ensuring that board procedures are followed and that applicable rules and regulations are complied with. Any question of the removal of the company secretary should be a matter for the board as a whole.
- The Code provides that the chairperson should ensure that the directors continually update their skills and their knowledge of the company so that they can fulfil their duties on the board.
- Another principle of the Code is that the board should evaluate annually its own performance, that of its committees and of individual directors. The company should state in the annual report how this evaluation has been conducted. The purpose of the evaluation is for the board to reflect on their strengths and weaknesses and provide information useful when proposing new directors or seeking the resignation of directors who are not meeting the appropriate standard of performance. The code also makes clear that directors should be submitted for re-election at regular intervals. The code indicates that this interval should not be more than three years.

Of particular importance in the governance structure of companies is the role and function of non-executive directors. This was emphasized in the Higgs review published in January 2003. In this report the non-executive directors were seen as the 'custodians of the governance process and central to ensuring the prosperity and success of companies'. Thus, Higgs saw their role as going beyond that of simply monitoring the directors, but adding to the effectiveness of the board by bringing their experience and knowledge to the boards' decision making. Key to the Higgs proposals is the availability of a sufficient pool of high quality non-executive directors who are willing to challenge the executive directors rather than just act as their 'buddies.' In this respect it should be noted that subsequent to the publication of the Higgs Report a task force was set up (The Tyson Task force), which reported on the recruitment and development of non-executive directors in June 2003. The recruitment of independent and competent individuals remains a crucial issue and when a company scandal comes to light, the question is often asked why the non-executive directors did not prevent the scandal or raise alarm bells about problems or issues within the company. A number of the suggestions in the Higgs report were subsequently incorporated into the Combined Code and we outline some of the recommendations below:

- The inclusion of non-executive directors of sufficient calibre and number for their views to carry significant weight in the board's decisions. The basic idea is that no individual or small group of individuals should dominate the board's decision taking. This is consistent with Higgs' view that non-executive directors should provide an independent and competent challenge in assisting the development of corporate strategy. They should monitor both the conduct and the performance of management in achieving goals and objectives. The Code suggests (except for smaller companies), that at least half of the board should be non-executive directors and that the majority of them should be independent and free from any business or financial relationship, which could materially interfere with the exercise of their independent judgement, apart from their fees and shareholding. If their shareholding is significant, the board would have to give an adequate explanation of why they considered the non-executive director to be independent.

A smaller company is defined as a company not included in the FTSE 350. Basically the FTSE 350 comprises the largest 350 companies listed on the UK Stock Exchange.

- The fees paid to the non-executive directors should reflect the time they commit to the company.
- Non-executive directors should be appointed through a formal process for specified terms and their appointment subject to election by the shareholders. Their reappointment should not be automatic.
- They should determine appropriate levels of remuneration for executive directors normally through being members of a remuneration committee and be influential through their membership of a nomination committee in the appointment of executive directors. The Combined Code recommends that companies set up a remuneration committee consisting of at least three independent non-executive directors and that a majority of the members of the nomination committee be independent non-executive directors.

ACTIVITY 18.6

Carefully review the above recommendations and form a considered view as to whether, if implemented, they are likely to result in a board with well-informed members.

You will have observed that the general recommendations about the conduct of the board are designed to ensure that all directors are kept informed about what is going on and that control is exercised over executive management. The board as a whole has a set of overriding duties different from the individual members. Regular meetings of the board are clearly vital if control is to be effective. The division of duties at the head of a company, that is, separation of the roles of chairperson and chief executive, is also important as it will encourage open discussion of critical matters. The requirement for a formal agenda of important matters for discussion will help to ensure that these matters are known to all board members.

Of particular importance for non-executive members of the board, who will not normally be present in the company on a day-to-day basis, is the recommendation that they, like executive directors, should have access to legal advice at company expense and to the services of the company secretary. Turning to the recommendations specific to non-executive directors, we can see that there is an emphasis on the independence of non-executive directors. The recommendation that fees of non-executive directors should reflect the time that they commit to the company will help to ensure their objectivity is not threatened by large payments not related to the work that they perform. As you are aware from our discussions in Chapter 3, independence or the perception of it may come under threat for a wide variety of reasons. The mere existence of non-executive directors and audit committees does not necessarily mean the actions of executive management will be subject to independent scrutiny, or that the independence of auditors will be enhanced. This will only be the case if there is willingness throughout the company for the system of scrutiny to be effective. There is a danger that the existence of non-executive directors give the appearance that the system of corporate governance is adequate when in fact it is not. Reports in the media suggest that non-executive directors have not been scrutinizing the actions of executive management closely enough and that many had been appointed because they were friends of existing members of the board.

Apart from these independence matters, the recommendations make clear that the duties of non-executive directors are wide with responsibility for exercising judgement on issues of strategy, performance, resources, including key appointments and standards of conduct. One key matter they should be responsible for, which we discuss later in the chapter, is the appointment of the external auditor.

The recent failure of Enron could have been avoided, it is argued, if non-executive directors had exercised sufficient control over the activities of the company. Furthermore, in this case it might be said that the non-executive directors were not independent since, as well as receiving fees from the company, a number of them also had lucrative consultancy contracts.

B. Principles of good governance applicable to directors' remuneration

Listed companies represent an important part of the economy and their performance and the success of the directors is of considerable importance to every member of society. Directors of such companies have considerable power but they have been criticized for their lack of accountability and the secrecy with which their companies have been governed. In recent years there has been adverse publicity in the press about their levels of remuneration and increases in remuneration that appear to be unrelated to company performance, particularly in the financial services sector. Furthermore, there have recently been attempts, some successful, by investors, principally institutional investors, to curb what they see as excessive remuneration. The Code accepts that more light needs to be thrown on directors' remuneration and the way that it is determined in the interests of accountability. The main principle (B.1) in the Code states that:

> Levels of remuneration should be sufficient to attract, retain and motivate directors of the quality required to run the company successfully, but a company should avoid paying more than is necessary for this purpose.
> A significant proportion of executive directors' remuneration should be structured so as to link rewards to corporate and individual performance.

A further principle of the Code is that there should be a formal and transparent procedure for setting the policy on directors' remuneration and for determining the remuneration package for individual directors. Among other things, the Code recommends that the board should set up a remuneration committee, comprising at least three independent non-executive directors. In the part concerned with relations with shareholders (D), the Code recommends that the chairperson of the remuneration committee (and the audit and nomination committees) attend the AGM and answer questions from shareholders if required (see Code Provision D.2.3).

Directors' remuneration remains a controversial issue with considerable media attention focussed on the large amounts paid to directors and senior management which do not seem to be justified by the performance of their company. The Companies Act 2006, s.420 requires quoted companies to prepare a directors' remuneration report. The main content for that report is specified in Schedule 8 of the Large and Medium-Sized Companies and Groups (Accounts and Reports) Regulations 2008, but there is additional disclosure required by the listing rules and the Combined Code. Although only part of the information contained in the remuneration report is required to be audited, given the attention focused on directors' remuneration the auditors have to be especially vigilant in performing their work.

Finally, in practice many large listed companies now employ remuneration consultants to provide advice on how to structure the remuneration package for directors and senior executives. These consultants will liaise with and provide advice to the remuneration committee in the company but decisions about remuneration remain the province of the committee. Partly in recognition of the increased role played by remuneration consultants and the attention focussed by the media on directors' remuneration the Remuneration Consultants Group recently (2009) issued a voluntary code of conduct for their members.

C. Accountability and audit

This section is concerned with financial reporting, internal control, the audit committee and external auditors, the principles being as follows:

> C.1. The board should present a balanced and understandable assessment of the company's position and prospects.

In Chapter 16 we noted that a statement outlining the directors' responsibility for preparing the financial statements and the auditors' reporting responsibilities must be published. This is required by Code Provision C.1.1. The Code also requires the board to present a balanced and understandable assessment when publishing interim and other price-sensitive reports and reports to regulators and other information required by statute. The directors' responsibilities also extend to reporting that the company is a going concern, together with supporting assumptions or qualifications as necessary.

> C.2. The board should maintain a sound system of internal control to safeguard shareholders' investment and the company's assets.

In complying with this principle the directors should conduct, at least annually, a review of the effectiveness of internal controls and report to the shareholders that they have done so. You will recall that there are limitations to the scope of audit work on the directors' statement on internal control: the auditor merely reviews the statement to ensure it is evidenced by the documentation supplied by the directors and reflects the process adopted by them. Bulletin 2006/5 lists some of the audit work that is likely to be performed by the auditor in reviewing the directors' statement on internal control, namely: The auditor will discuss internal control with the directors and audit committee and obtain an understanding of the process the directors have used which enables them to make the statement on internal control. The auditors will also review any documentation used by the directors in making the statement on internal controls and ensure that the statement is consistent with their understanding and knowledge of internal control obtained from their audit work.

Bulletin 2006/5 *The Combined Code on Corporate Governance: requirements on auditors under the listing rules of the Financial Services Authority and the Irish Stock Exchange.*

It is worth noting that, since the auditors will have a good understanding of the internal controls operating in the company from their audit work, they are unlikely to have to perform much additional audit work to complete their review of the directors' statement.

> C.3. The board should establish formal and transparent arrangements for considering how they should apply the financial reporting and internal control principles and for maintaining an appropriate relationship with the company's auditors.

This principle is supported by the Code provisions for establishing an audit committee of at least three independent non-executive directors with written terms of reference. At least one member of the audit committee is required to have some recent and relevant financial knowledge. The Code states that the terms of reference of the audit committee and its authority should be made available. Furthermore, a separate section of the annual report should describe the work of the committee. The Code also refers to the duties of audit committees, stating that they include monitoring the integrity of the financial statements and a number of auditor related matters which we discuss in detail below.

In smaller companies this requirement is reduced to at least two non-executive directors.

D. Relations with shareholders

Principle D.1 of this part of the Code states that the board is responsible for ensuring there is a satisfactory dialogue with institutional shareholders. Furthermore, it is the responsibility of the chairperson to ensure that the views of the shareholders are made known to the board of directors. The chairperson should also discuss governance issues and strategy with major shareholders. Principle D.2 of this part of the Code states that boards should use the AGM to communicate with investors and encourage their participation. The Code recommends a number of matters to underpin this principle, including the counting of all proxy votes and an indication of the level of proxies lodged on each resolution. Finally the Code suggests that the notice of the AGM and other related papers should be sent to shareholders at least 20 working days prior to the meeting. All of the above provisions are contained in Section 1 of the code whilst Section 2 which we discuss below is concerned with part E the role of institutional shareholders.

E. Institutional shareholders

While most of the Combined Code is concerned with processes and structures within the control of the directors, both executive and non-executive, a second section of the code discusses the role of institutional shareholders. This emphasizes the now accepted view that these shareholders, because of the power and influence that accrues to them through their substantive shareholding, should not be passive shareholders but should be a force in their own right to promote good governance in companies. What is being emphasized here is that good corporate governance is not just a one-way process from the company to the shareholders but that institutional shareholders need to be pro-active to ensure good corporate governance. The Combined Code outlines three main principles in respect of institutional shareholders as follows:

E.1 Institutional shareholders should enter into a dialogue with companies based on the mutual understanding of objectives.

E.2 When evaluating companies' corporate governance arrangements, particularly those relating to board structure and composition, institutional shareholders should give due weight to all relevant factors drawn to their attention.

Where a company does not comply with a particular aspect of the Code the institutional shareholders should carefully consider the explanation given for non compliance and decide if they need to take any further action. For instance, if they do not find the company's explanation convincing, they might enter into discussions with the company.

E.3 Institutional shareholders have a responsibility to make considered use of their votes.

The Code recommends that institutional investors should, if asked by their clients, give information on the proportion of resolutions on which votes were cast and non-discretionary proxies lodged. In addition, there is a recommendation that institutional shareholders take steps to ensure that their voting intentions are put into practice.

Whether these recommendations will encourage greater shareholder participation at AGMs is perhaps questionable, particularly as proxy voting is still in place, rather than moving to a system of 'one share one vote'. Many institutional investors are moving in and out of shareholdings continuously and may not see the investment as one to which they have a long-term commitment, limiting their participation or concerns with the company's affairs unless they directly affect the value of their investment holding.

Subsequent to the demise of Northern Rock and the banking crisis in the UK the government set up a committee under the chairmanship of Sir David Walker to consider corporate governance in the UK banking industry. One of the terms of reference for the committee was to consider 'the role of institutional shareholders in engaging effectively with companies and monitoring of boards'. After consultation, the Walker review group reported in November 2009 and one of its recommendations was that FRC should take on the role of operating a stewardship code which would be concerned with the responsibilities of Institutional investors. About the same time FRC was in consultation on revising the Combined Code; one of its findings was concern about the extent and effectiveness of engagement between institutional shareholders and company boards. In January 2010 FRC issued a consultation document titled 'A Stewardship Code for Institutional Investors'. The FRC document contained as an appendix a code developed by the Institutional Shareholders Committee seeking the views of individuals on the adoption of that code and what, if any, amendments to it were required. FRC has proposed that, subject to satisfactory progress and agreement on the Stewardship Code, Section E of the Combined Code be deleted and the Stewardship Code issued.

The Institutional Shareholders Committee is a forum consisting of UK trade associations such as the Association of British Insurers operating in the financial services sector.

Audit committees

We referred briefly to audit committees in Chapter 3 as a means to enhance the independence of auditors. In passing we would mention that the Cadbury Committee, which was set up as a result of concern about the collapse of some well-known companies, gave impetus to the formation of audit committees in the UK. The Combined Code emphasizes the important role they play in reviewing and monitoring 'the external auditors' independence and objectivity and the effectiveness of the audit process'. The Combined Code recommends that, normally, the committee should comprise at least three non-executive directors and it highlights certain duties not just in respect of the relationship with the external auditors, but also the company's internal control system and the effectiveness of the internal auditors. To carry out its duties effectively it is generally accepted that audit committees should be as independent as possible, while remaining a committee of the main board. Thus, the composition and abilities of the non-executive directors forming the audit committee are clearly important. It is clear that if the audit committee is to be effective, it is essential that its non-executive directors are of high calibre, objective and have proper resources to carry out their work. As a historical note we would point out that audit committees are not entirely a new phenomenon. The US legal case of McKesson and Robbins in 1939 was instrumental in giving initial impetus to the formation of audit committees in the United States, though widespread introduction did not occur until much later. The Securities Exchange Commission (SEC) called for audit committees in 1940 following that case.

Auditor independence is likely to be enhanced by audit committees staffed by non-executive directors, providing an independent body within the company to which the auditor can report. It is also stated in the guidance on audit committees (The Smith Guidance) that the committee should recommend to the shareholders the appointment of auditors and approve the remuneration and terms of engagement of the auditor. The Combined Code has recognized that the authority and duties of the audit committee should be clearly defined if this enhancement is to occur. Clearly, if the committee were to be totally subservient to the main board, it would be ineffective. The same would apply if its duties did not include meeting the auditor to discuss audit and reporting problems and if it had no role in respect of auditor appointment and fee determination. In this section therefore we consider the authority and duties of the audit committee.

Authority and duties of the audit committee

'Authority' means that the audit committee should have clear rights to seek information and make decisions and to carry out prescribed duties. In the UK the role of audit committees is still developing but the Smith guidance on audit committees is a step towards greater consistency in their accepted duties and roles. The original Smith guidance was published by the Financial Reporting Council in 2003 and was updated in 2005 and again in 2008; the guidance outlines a number of roles and responsibilities for the audit committee and we set these out below.

Financial reporting

- Review important issues and judgements involved in the preparation of the annual and interim financial statements and preliminary statements.
- Consider the appropriateness of important accounting policies and any changes that have been made to them. Assess significant estimates and judgements and the appropriateness of the treatment of important or unusual transactions. They also ensure that disclosures in the financial statements are adequate.
- Review the system of internal financial controls and also, unless considered by a separate committee, the company's risk management system. The latter would include receiving reports from the management on the effectiveness of the controls. The audit committee should also review and give their approval to any statements included in the financial reports relating to the internal controls and the management of risk.
- Review the company's policy in respect of whistle-blowing and ensure there are suitable mechanisms in place for the investigation and follow-up of whistle-blowing matters.

You will remember that we discussed measures to make internal audit effective in Chapter 15.

- Review and monitor the effectiveness of the company's internal audit function. Review the nature of work to be performed by the internal auditors including their audit plan and receive reports on the internal auditor's work and check to see if management respond to their recommendations. The audit committee should also ensure that the internal audit function is adequately resourced. Where a company does not have an internal audit function, they should consider annually the need for such a function. Furthermore, where an internal audit function does not exist in a company, there should be other monitoring functions in place that satisfy the requirements of management and the audit committee. The audit committee will need to evaluate if the monitoring procedures and activities give sufficient information about the effectiveness of internal controls in the company.

Audit matters

- The audit committee should recommend the appointment, re-appointment and removal of the auditors and approve the auditor's remuneration and terms of engagement. When recommending the appointment or reappointment of auditors the audit committee needs to consider the quality of work performed by the auditor and their ability to meet or continue to meet the requirements of the company. For instance, in a large multinational group this will include ensuring that the audit firm has a good international network and sufficient resources and expertise.

- Where auditors resign, the audit committee should investigate the circumstances surrounding the resignation to determine if any action is required.
- Ensure the independence and objectivity of the external auditors. When assessing independence the audit committee should take into account non-audit services provided by the auditors. The audit committee should also ensure that the audit firm complies with legal and professional requirements in respect of auditor independence. For instance, the audit committee should seek reassurance that there is no family or financial relationships between the auditors and the company.

You will recall that we discussed the provision of non-audit services and auditor independence in Chapter 3.

- The audit committee should agree the company's policy in hiring ex-employees of the audit firm, especially when the individual is taking up a senior position in the company and has previously been involved in its audit.
- Be involved in developing the company's policy on the provision of non-audit services. The main concern of the audit committee will be to ensure that provision of non-audit services will not compromise the objectivity or independence of the audit firm. Thus, the audit committee will be concerned with issues, such as the nature of the non-audit service provided and fees for non-audit work compared to the fee for the audit work. The objective is to balance the maintenance of objectivity and value for money. Finally, it is recommended that the annual report should contain an explanation of how the auditor maintains objectivity and independence when they provide non-audit services.
- Assess the audit plan, including ensuring levels of materiality and resources committed to the audit are commensurate with the nature of the audit.
- Discuss with the external auditors any major issues arising from the audit, review important accounting and audit judgements and the extent of errors detected during the audit.
- Review both the management letter issued by the auditors and the letter of representation. Review the board's response to recommendations made by the auditors.
- At the completion of the audit, evaluate the effectiveness of the audit and the abilities of the auditors as evidenced by how they deal with issues arising during the audit and responding to questions by the audit committee. It should also be noted that some of the above is reinforced by the requirements of ISA 260 – *Communication with those charged with governance*. This states that for listed company clients auditors should communicate with those charged with governance (which in the UK would include audit committees) the following:
  - (a) 'A statement that the engagement team and others in the firm as appropriate have complied with relevant ethical requirements regarding independence; and
  - (b) (i) All relationships and other matters between the firm, network firms, and the entity that, in the auditor's professional judgement, may reasonably be thought to bear on independence. This shall include total fees charged during the period covered by the financial statements for audit and non-audit services provided by the firm and network firms to the entity and components controlled by the entity.

(ii) The related safeguards that have been applied to eliminate identified threats to independence or reduce them to an acceptable level.' (para. 17).

ACTIVITY 18.7

Take a look at the above list of duties of audit committees and:

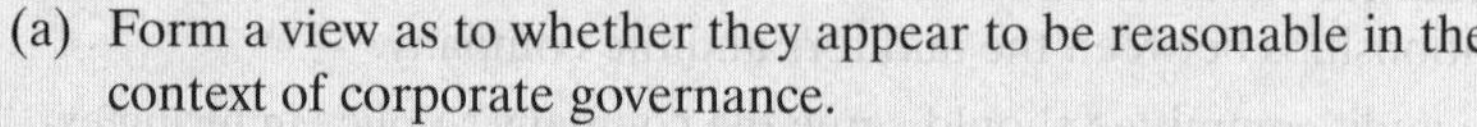

(a) Form a view as to whether they appear to be reasonable in the context of corporate governance.

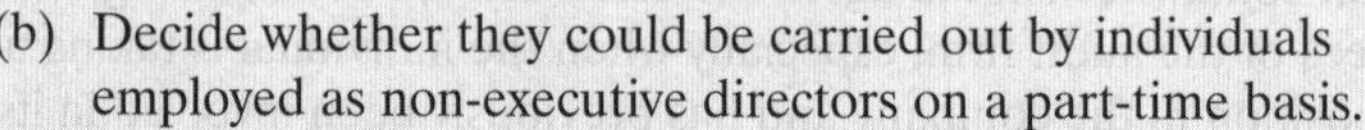

(b) Decide whether they could be carried out by individuals employed as non-executive directors on a part-time basis.

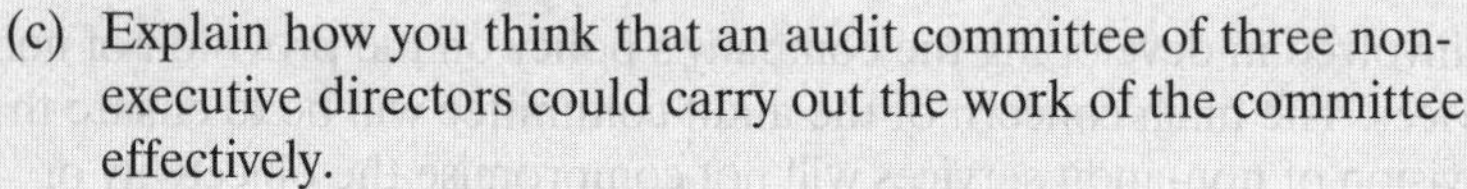

(c) Explain how you think that an audit committee of three non-executive directors could carry out the work of the committee effectively.

If the duties as listed above were to be properly carried out, we could be reasonably confident that standards of financial reporting would be high and that the company was being appropriately controlled, both in terms of its internal controls and its relationships with the external auditors. Whether the duties as listed could be properly performed by part-time non-executive directors is less certain. We suggest that members of audit committees will require support staff to enable them to carry out the suggested duties and that the links of the committee to internal and external auditors should be strong. It is worth noting that executive managers are in a very powerful position compared with non-executives and external auditors and it may be that a strong internal audit department with good reporting links to the audit committee is an essential feature of corporate governance. The Smith guidance recommends that the audit committee should yearly review its scope and effectiveness and recommend any changes to the board of directors. Furthermore, each year the board should also review the effectiveness of the audit committee.

Directors' statement of responsibilities

In 1992 the Cadbury Report stated that the directors should explain their responsibility for preparing the accounts next to a statement by the auditors about their reporting responsibilities. Such statements are now being included in the reporting package of companies. We mentioned in Chapter 16 that the responsibilities of auditors are stated in the audit report itself and that reference is made to the statement of directors' responsibilities. These steps were considered important in the context of corporate governance to make clear that the directors have primary responsibility for preparing financial statements that give a true and fair view.

Internal control

To finish this chapter we review the guidance on internal control, known as the Turnbull guidance. We have noted earlier in Chapter 7 that the directors are required to make a statement that they have conducted a review of the effectiveness of the internal controls of a company. The purpose of the Turnbull committee was to provide guidance on the application of the relevant provisions in the Combined Code relating to internal controls. In its preamble the Turnbull guidance notes the importance of the system of internal control in managing risk in the company and consequently the achievement of corporate objectives. An effective system of internal control can help safeguard shareholders' investment and corporate assets and assist in ensuring that operations are carried out effectively and efficiently. The Turnbull guidance is divided into three parts as shown below.

The Turnbull guidance was reviewed and a revised version was issued in October 2005. Only relatively minor changes were made to the original guidance.

Maintaining a sound system of internal control

The Turnbull guidance recommends that the system of internal control has to reflect the risks the company faces, the materiality of those risks, the likelihood of the risk materializing, the ability to mitigate the risk and the cost of doing so. The guidance outlines the objectives of a system of internal control as:

- Assisting in achieving corporate objectives by being able to respond to important business, financial and compliance risks.
- Assisting in ensuring the quality of internal and external reporting.
- Assisting in ensuring compliance with appropriate laws and regulations and also the operations of corporate policies concerned with the conduct of the business (para. 19).

It is made clear that internal controls should be embedded in the operations of the company, and be able to evolve and change as the nature of the risks faced by the company change. There should be communication of identified weaknesses to an appropriate authority within the company, together with corrective action taken. Finally it is acknowledged that no system of internal control is foolproof and that the system is only likely to provide reasonable assurance that a company will not be impaired in achieving its business objectives.

Reviewing the effectiveness of internal control

It is expected that the system of internal control will be monitored on a continuous basis. In addition, the board of directors should receive periodically reports on the internal controls. It will also be necessary for the board to assess the effectiveness of controls for the purposes of making their statement on internal controls in the annual report. The board have to determine the processes they will have to implement and the documentation they will require to monitor and review the effectiveness of the internal controls. The Turnbull guidance recommends that when the board reviews the internal control reports during the year they should:

- Consider what are the significant risks and assess how they have been identified, evaluated and managed.
- Assess the effectiveness of the related system of internal control in managing the significant risks, having regard, in particular, to any significant failings or weaknesses in internal control that have been reported.
- Consider whether necessary actions are being taken promptly to remedy any significant failings or weaknesses.

- Consider whether the findings indicate a need for more extensive monitoring of the system of internal control. (para. 29).

When conducting their annual assessment of the effectiveness of internal controls the board should consider:

- Changes in the nature of significant risks since the previous annual assessment.
- The extent and effectiveness of the monitoring of the risks, the system of internal control and of the internal audit function.
- How often and the extent of communication of the results of the monitoring to the board.
- Whether any important failings or weaknesses in the control systems have been identified during the year.
- The effectiveness of the public reporting processes of the company.

The board's statement on internal control

The board is required to state in the annual report that they are responsible for the system of internal control and reviewing its effectiveness. The board should also state that there is a process of risk management in place, which identifies, evaluates and manages important risks. The statement should give details of the process they used to review the effectiveness of the internal control systems and state what actions have been taken or are in the process of being taken to remedy significant weaknesses. Finally the statement should outline the process by which the board has evaluated the effectiveness of the system of internal control and that the system only manages the risks rather than eliminates them.

Concluding remarks on corporate governance

The idea of companies reporting on their corporate governance and complying with the Combined Code has now become an accepted part of corporate life for listed companies in the UK. The limited changes made to the Combined Code and Turnbull guidance in 2008 and 2005 respectively would suggest that both users and producers are reasonably satisfied with the present requirements of the Code. Further evidence for this can be gleaned from the extent to which the UK principles of corporate governance have been adopted in one form or another in other countries throughout the world. The principles-based approach in the UK avoiding burdensome rules and putting the onus on directors of companies to explain how they have complied with the Combined Code has been regarded by many commentators as a success (Monks and Minow, 2004). Others are more circumspect about this; for instance, Arcot *et al.* (2010) question the effectiveness of the comply or explain process. We ourselves would warn about being too sanguine about the success of the Code since all it would probably need to change perceptions of its effectiveness in the UK are a few major corporate scandals.

At the beginning of this section we mentioned that the 2008 Combined Code is presently in the process of being revised. Early indications suggest there may be some changes to the present Code. Proposals include four new provisions, two of which are: a requirement that the board should ensure that systems are in place to 'identify, evaluate and manage the significant risks faced by the company' and that 'the annual report should include an explanation of the company's business model and overall financial strategy'. In addition, the wording of part of the existing Code will be changed, including the provisions related to remuneration. Finally, it is proposed that the title of the Combined Code be changed to the 'UK Corporate Governance Code'. The proposals contained in this revision of the Combined Code appear a little more substantial than in previous revisions and therefore students should remain alert to these when the new code is agreed and published.

FRC Consultation on the revised UK Corporate Governance Code, December 2009

Summary

In this chapter we have discussed two issues of great direct interest to the auditing profession: the audit expectations gap and corporate governance. We introduced you to the various protagonists interested in financial information and audit and discussed possible developments and solutions in relation to the various components of the gap.

We saw that there is some disagreement about the way in which audit should be rendered more effective, some wishing to see greater intervention from regulatory authorities, while others prefer self-regulation. We saw self-regulation is reflected in the Combined Code on Corporate Governance. We commented on various aspects of the Combined Code emphasizing in particular those aspects of particular interest to auditors.

Key points of the chapter

- A common element in the various definitions of the audit expectations gap is that auditors are performing in a manner at variance with the beliefs and desires of others who are party to or interested in the audit.
- The audit expectations gap comprises several different gaps between auditors and each of a number of stakeholders, some of whom are strong and others weak, some well informed about accounting and auditing and others not. Stakeholders include shareholders, politicians, regulators and academics.
- The gap is not a new phenomenon.
- There are several reasons why the gap exists: Deficient performance, includes lack of competence and lack of practitioner independence; Deficient standards, including those on fraud and going concern; Unreasonable expectations, partially arising from lack of clear definition of the auditor's role in society, and a failure to recognize that benefits of performing an audit procedure may exceed costs.
- The gap is likely to change over time, the various components flexing as circumstances change.
- Possible reasons for change include: expansion of auditors' duties; flexing of auditors' duties, including; (a) clarification of the societal role of the audit function; (b) greater societal awareness; (c) technological change; (d) society's changing expectations.
- Corporate governance is closely related to the audit expectations gap, but is wider as it relates to structures to control how companies are governed. The Combined Code requires auditors to report on a number of corporate governance matters and contains principles of good governance under: A. directors; B. remuneration; C. accountability and audit; D. relations with shareholders; E. institutional shareholders.
- Recommendations on effectiveness of the board include: (a) a well balanced board; (b) non-executive directors of sufficient calibre and number; (c) timely high-quality information for decision-making and control; (d) annual performance evaluation of board, committees and directors.
- The Code makes recommendations on conduct of the board: (a) regular meetings; (b) division of responsibilities at the head; (c) non-executive directors of sufficient calibre and number; (d) formal schedule of matters specifically reserved for its decision; (e) agreed procedure for directors to take independent professional advice; (f) directors access to advice and services of company secretary.
- A significant proportion of directors' remuneration should be linked to performance, overseen by the directors' remuneration committee.
- Under the principles of accountability and audit, the board should: (a) present a balanced and understandable assessment of company position and prospects; (b) maintain a sound system of internal control; (c) apply financial reporting and internal control principles and maintain an appropriate relationship with the company's auditors and audit committee. A dialogue should be established with shareholders.
- Non-executive directors should have proper resources and: (a) provide challenges in developing corporate strategy; (b) be independent; (c) be appointed for specified terms and reappointment not automatic; (d) be selected through a formal process, and approved by shareholders.

- Three main principles underlying the role of institutional shareholders, (a) enter into dialogue with companies; (b) evaluate companies' corporate governance arrangements; (c) make considered use of votes.
- Suggested roles and responsibilities for the audit committee: (a) financial reporting, including review of important issues/judgements; (b) audit matters, including recommending appointment, terms of engagement and external audit fees; being involved in developing policy on non-audit services.
- Audit committees may enhance auditor independence by providing independent oversight of the financial reporting process and of the audit function within companies.
- To be effective the audit committee must comprise two elements: (a) committee members should be high-quality non-executive directors; (b) the committee should have sufficient authority and clearly defined duties.
- Directors' statement of responsibilities makes clear that the directors have primary responsibility for preparing financial statements that give a true and fair view.
- The revised Turnbull guidance parts, notes the importance of internal control in managing risk and achieving corporate objectives. There are three parts: (a) maintaining sound system of internal control; (b) reviewing effectiveness of internal control; (c) requiring the board's statement on internal control.
- The FRC are currently revising the Combined Code.

References

Accounting Standards Steering Committee (1975) *The Corporate Report*, London Accounting Standards Steering Committee.

Arcot, S., Bruno, V. and Faure-Grimaud, A. (2010), 'Corporate Governance in the UK: Is The Comply or Explain Approach Working?', *International Review of Law and Economics*, 39(2): 193–201.

Briloff, A.J. (1986) 'Corporate Governance and Accountability: Whose Responsibility?', Unpublished paper presented at the University of Connecticut, Storrs, Connecticut, April.

Cadbury Committee (1992) *Financial Aspects of Corporate Governance*, London: Cadbury Committee.

Financial Reporting Council (FRC) (2005) *Internal Control: Revised Guidance for Directors on the Combined Code*, October, London: Financial Reporting Council.

Financial Reporting Council (FRC) (2008) *Guidance on Audit Committees*, London: Financial Reporting Council.

Financial Reporting Council (FRC), (2008) *Combined Code on Corporate Governance*, London: Financial Reporting Council.

Goldman, A. and Barlev, B. (1974) 'Auditor-Firm Conflict of Interests: Its Implications for Independence', *The Accounting Review*, 49: 707–18.

Higgs, D. (2003), *Review of the Role and Effectiveness of Non-Executive Directors*. London: The Department of Trade and Industry

Humphrey, C., Moizer, P. and Turley, S. (1992) *The Audit Expectations Gap in the United Kingdom*, London: ICAEW Research Board.

Johnson, N. (1991) 'Proximity and the Expectations Gap: Anglo-American Perspectives on Auditors' Liability', *Law Teachers*, April.

Mautz, R.K. and Sharaf, H.A. (1961) *Philosophy of Auditing*, Sarasota, FL: American Accounting Association.

Mitchell, A. and Sikka, P. (1993) 'Accounting for Change: The Institutions of Accountancy', *Critical Perspectives on Accounting*, 4(1): 29–52.

Monks, R.A.G. and Minow, N. (2004) *Corporate Governance*, 3rd edn, Oxford: Blackwell Publishing.

Porter, B. (1993) 'An Empirical Study of the Audit Expectation-Performance Gap', *Accounting and Business Research*, 24(93): 49–68.

Porter, B. and Gowthorpe, C. (2004) *Audit Expectation-Performance Gap in the United Kingdom in 1999 and Comparison with the Gap in New Zealand in 1989 and 1999*, Edinburgh: ICAS.

Porter, B., Ó hÓgartaigh, C. and Baskerville, R. (2009) 'Report on research conducted in the United Kingdom and New Zealand in 2008 investigating the audit expectation-performance gap and users' understanding of, and desired improvements to, the auditor's report', Report to IAASB and AICPA available on http://web.ifac.org/download/Porter_et_al_Final_Report_Combined.pdf

Shockley, R.A. (1982) 'Perceptions of Auditors' Independence: A Conceptual Model', *Journal of Accounting, Auditing and Finance*, 2: 126–143.

Sikka, P., Puxty, A., Wilmott, H. and Cooper, C. (1998) 'The Impossibility of Eliminating the Expectations Gap: Some Theory and Evidence', *Critical Perspectives in Accounting*, 9: 299–330.

Suggestions for Good Practice from the Higgs Report (2003) January, London: Financial Reporting Council.

Tamaki, N. (1983) *The Union Bank of Scotland*, Aberdeen: Aberdeen University Press.

Tyson, L. (2003) *The Tyson Report on the Recruitment and Development of Non-Executive Directors*, London: London Business School.

Walker D. (2009) *A Review of Corporate Governance in UK Banks and other Financial Industry Entities – Final Recommendations*, London, H-M Treasury.

Further reading

There are very frequent references to the audit expectations gap in accounting and auditing journals. A useful starting-off point if you wish to read further is:

Porter, B. (1983) 'An Empirical Study of the Audit Expectation-Performance Gap', *Accounting and Business Research*, 24(93): 49–68.

As we showed in this chapter, Porter uses a structured approach to an examination of the gap. Other useful texts covering matters in this chapter are:

Porter, B. and Gowthorpe, C. (2004) *Audit Expectation-Performance Gap in the United Kingdom in 1999 and Comparison with the Gap in New Zealand in 1989 and 1999*, ICAS. Porter, B., Ó hÓgartaigh, C. and Baskerville, R. (2009) 'Financial statement users' perceptions regarding auditors' responsibilities when conducting a financial statement audit and the message conveyed in an unqualified audit report'. Report to AICPA and IAASB, June 2009.

Humphrey, C., Moizer, P. and Turley, S. (1992) *The Audit Expectations Gap in the United Kingdom*, ICAEW Research Board. Sikka, P., Puxty, A., Wilmott, H. and Cooper, C. (1998) The Impossibility of Eliminating the Expectations Gap: Some Theory and Evidence', *Critical Perspectives in Accounting*, 9: 299–330.

There has been a proliferation of the literature on corporate governance but the best starting point is probably to read the revised Combined Code. This is available at the Financial Reporting Council website http://www.frc.org.uk/documents/pagemanager/frc/Combined_Code_June_2008/Combined%20Code%20Web%20Optimized%20June%202008%282%29.pdf

The proposed changes to the 2008 Combined Code can be found at the following webpage: **http://www.frc.org.uk/images/uploaded/documents/Consultation%20on%20the%20Revised%20Corporate%20Governance%20Code1.pdf**

The full reports of the revised Turnbull guidance on internal control, the Smith Report on audit committees and Higgs Report on the role and effectiveness of non-executive directors can be found at the following web locations.

Revised Turnbull guidance on internal control: http://www.frc.org.uk/documents/pagemanager/frc/Revised%20Turnbull%20Guidance%20October%202005.pdf

Smith Report: **http://www.frc.org.uk/documents/pagemanager/frc/Smith_Guidance/Guidance%20on%20Audit%20Committees%20October%202008.pdf**

Higgs Report: **http://www.berr.gov.uk/files/file23012.pdf**

There are numerous books on corporate governance but we would especially recommend Jill Solomon, *Corporate Governance and Accountability,* John Wiley and Sons (2007). We would also recommend for more general reading Christine Mallin, *Corporate Governance*, Oxford University Press (2009) and Bob Tricker, *Corporate Governance: Principles, Policies and Practices*, Oxford University Press (2008).

Self-assessment questions (solutions available to students)

18.1 Consider the following statements and explain why they may be true or false:

(a) The audit expectations gap has arisen since the 1960s.

(b) The reasonableness component of the audit expectations gap arises because many people are not sufficiently educated to understand the audit process.

(c) The effect of lack of competence cannot be distinguished from the effect of lack of independence in the auditor.

(d) The existence of an audit committee composed of non-executive directors will ensure that executive management will be subject to effective independent control.

18.2 **Moorfoot plc**

You are the auditor of Duddingston Limited, a subsidiary of Moorfoot plc. Duddingston is engaged in the production and selling of pharmaceutical products. The managing director of Moorfoot has been talking to you about the issue of internal control and has asked you for advice on the control systems that should be in place in the subsidiary. He is particularly concerned that the company's products could be dangerous if not used properly. He tells you that products are sold through commission agents to hospitals and family doctors. These agents do not receive a salary and are thus totally reliant on the commission earned.

Required

(a) Explain why you believe the Cadbury Committee in 1992 might have decided that directors should issue a statement on the adequacy of internal control systems in use in their companies.

(b) Describe the auditors' duties with regard to the directors' statement on internal controls.

(c) Identify the main problems of control at Duddingston Limited and make recommendations to the managing director to address these problems.

18.3 You are auditing a listed company that manufactures high-quality engineering products with numerous components, manufactured and assembled by the company. During your audit of inventory valuation you are told that you cannot see the costings of certain new products because they had been kept on computer file which had become accidentally corrupted. The company has valued the products at estimated cost. The directors' report on the internal control goes beyond stating that they have conducted a review of the effectiveness of internal control by adding that no material weaknesses have been identified in the system of internal control. The company has an audit committee. What action would you take?

18.4 You have been asked by an assistant on your audit team what the difference is between an audit and a review and what the effect would be on the audit report if a review were to be carried out instead of an audit. Outline the response you would give to the assistant.

Self-assessment questions (solutions available to tutors)

18.5 The following question has been adapted from a question in the ICAEW September 2001 Audit and Assurance examination paper and tests the material covered in this chapter and that in Chapter 15 on internal auditing.

The directors of Petrian Biotechnology plc, who are also its major shareholders, have concluded that its present capital structure will hinder the growth of the business that is projected over the next few years. As a result, they have decided to seek a listing on the London Stock Exchange in the second half of 2010.

The finance director and managing director have held preliminary discussions with City stockbrokers, lawyers and merchant banks. They have been informed that the company will have to comply with the Combined Code on corporate governance in order to meet the listing requirements, and have been advised to set up an internal audit function and an audit committee of the board. The directors of Petrian Biotechnology plc are clear in accepting their overall responsibility within the organization for:

- its internal control system, and
- the preparation of annual financial statements that give a true and fair view.

However, the engagement partner has been asked to attend the next board meeting of the company and to explain to the directors the roles of external auditors, the internal audit function and the audit committee with respect to these two aspects of governance.

Required

Prepare briefing notes for the engagement partner which:

(i) explain the responsibilities of the external auditors (EA), internal auditors (IA) and the audit committee (AC); and

(ii) describe the relationships between them with respect to both the internal control system (ICS) and audited financial statements (AFS).

18.6 You have been asked by your audit partner to give a talk to a group of students describing the criteria that must be met before it is likely than an audit committee has any chance of being effective. Outline the points you would include in your talk.

18.7 Explain why you believe auditors have been reluctant to report on the directors' review of the effectiveness of internal controls.

18.8 The audit expectations gap will never be closed. Discuss.

18.9 Discuss what are likely to be the main limitations a company faces in establishing an effective audit committee.

18.10 Good corporate governance is more likely to exist in companies where there are large institutional shareholders holding a substantial proportion of the shares than in companies where the shares are held by many individual investors. Discuss

Topics for class discussion without solutions

The following set of questions are based on the statement of corporate governance taken from the 2009 Annual Report of Vodafone Group Plc ('the Annual Report') and available directly after these questions in Appendix 18.1. The corporate governance statement refers to a number of other parts of the Annual Report which you might find it beneficial to read. The Annual Report can be located on the following webpage: http://www.vodafone.com/investor

In particular we refer you to the sections which outline details of the directors, deals with directors' remuneration and the company's corporate responsibility statement. Finally we point out that because the company is listed on the London and NASDAQ stock exchanges, it also has to comply with corporate governance rules of those exchanges.

18.11 The combined code in section 1 part A sets out a number of provisions that are necessary for an effective board of directors.

Identify the parts of the Vodafone Group Plc corporate governance statement that relate to determining if the company has complied with section 1 of the combined code.

18.12 Identify the members of the remuneration committee of Vodafone Group plc.

Does Vodafone employ any consultants to assist it in setting remuneration and if so who?

What particular aspects does the company identify as important in ensuring board effectiveness?

18.13 What appears to be the main functions of the audit committee of Vodafone Group Plc and which directors are members of the committee?

18.14 What are the main issues discussed in the audit committee report?

18.15 Who are the auditors of Vodafone Group Plc and did they carry out any non-audit work?

What procedures does the company have in force to maintain the independence of its auditors?

18.16 Outline the procedures undertaken by the company to ensure effective communication with shareholders.

18.17 Discuss the usefulness of the information contained in the corporate governance section of the Annual Report.

APPENDIX 18.1

Corporate governance

The Board of the Company is committed to high standards of corporate governance, which it considers are critical to business integrity and to maintaining investors' trust in the Company. The Group expects all its directors and employees to act with honesty, integrity and fairness. The Group will strive to act in accordance with the laws and customs of the countries in which it operates; adopt proper standards of business practice and procedure; operate with integrity; and observe and respect the culture of every country in which it does business.

In December 2008, Governance Metrics International, a global corporate governance ratings agency, ranked the Company amongst the top UK companies, with an overall global corporate governance rating of ten, the highest score assigned and achieved by only 1% of the 4,196 companies rated.

In the Company's profile report by Institutional Shareholder Services Inc. ('ISS'), dated 1 May 2009, the Company's governance practices outperformed 98.6% of the companies in the ISS developed universe (excluding US), 98.2% of companies in the telecommunications sector group and 98.1% of the companies in the UK.

Compliance with the Combined Code

The Company's ordinary shares are listed in the UK on the London Stock Exchange. In accordance with the Listing Rules of the UK Listing Authority, the Company confirms that throughout the year ended 31 March 2009 and at the date of this document, it was compliant with the provisions of, and applied the principles of, Section 1 of the 2006 FRC Combined Code on Corporate Governance (the "Combined Code"). The following section, together with the "Directors' remuneration" section on pages 57 to 67, provides details of how the Company applies the principles and complies with the provisions of the Combined Code.

Board organisation and structure

The role of the Board

The Board is responsible for the overall conduct of the Group's business and has the powers, authorities and duties vested in it by and pursuant to the relevant laws of England and Wales and the articles of association. The Board:

- has final responsibility for the management, direction and performance of the Group and its businesses;
- is required to exercise objective judgement on all corporate matters independent from executive management;
- is accountable to shareholders for the proper conduct of the business; and
- is responsible for ensuring the effectiveness of and reporting on the Group's system of corporate governance.

The Board has a formal schedule of matters reserved to it for its decision and these include:

- Group strategy;
- major capital projects, acquisitions or divestments;
- annual budget and operating plan;
- Group financial structure, including tax and treasury;
- annual and half-year financial results and shareholder communications;
- system of internal control and risk management; and
- senior management structure, responsibilities and succession plans.

The schedule is reviewed periodically. It was last formally reviewed by the Nominations and Governance Committee in March 2009, at which time it was determined that no amendments were required.

Other specific responsibilities are delegated to Board committees which operate within clearly defined terms of reference. Details of the responsibilities delegated to the Board committees are given on pages 53 and 54.

Board meetings

The Board meets at least eight times a year and the meetings are structured to allow open discussion. All directors participate in discussing the strategy, trading and financial performance and risk management of the Company. All substantive agenda items have comprehensive briefing papers, which are circulated one week before the meeting.

The following table shows the number of years directors have been on the Board at 31 March 2009 and their attendance at scheduled Board meetings they were eligible to attend during the 2009 financial year:

	Years on Board	Meetings attended
Sir John Bond	4	9/9
John Buchanan	6	7/9
Vittorio Colao	2	9/9
Andy Halford	3	9/9
Alan Jebson	2	9/9
Nick Land	2	8/9
Anne Lauvergeon	3	8/9
Simon Murray	2	8/9
Luc Vandevelde	5	9/9
Anthony Watson	3	9/9
Philip Yea	3	8/9
Arun Sarin (until 29 July 2008)	–	3/3
Dr Michael Boskin (until 29 July 2008)	–	3/3
Professor Jürgen Schrempp (until 29 July 2008)	–	2/3

In addition to regular Board meetings, there are a number of other meetings to deal with specific matters. Directors unable to attend a Board meeting because of another engagement are nevertheless provided with all the papers and information relevant for such meetings and are able to discuss issues arising in the meeting with the Chairman or the Chief Executive.

Division of responsibilities

The roles of the Chairman and Chief Executive are separate and there is a division of responsibilities that is clearly established, set out in writing and agreed by the Board to ensure that no one person has unfettered powers of decision. The Chairman is responsible for the operation, leadership and governance of the Board, ensuring its effectiveness and setting its agenda. The Chief Executive is responsible for the management of the Group's business and the implementation of Board strategy and policy.

Board balance and independence

The Company's Board consists of 14 directors, 11 of whom served throughout the 2009 financial year. At 31 March 2009, in addition to the Chairman, Sir John Bond, there were two executive directors and eight non-executive directors. Samuel Jonah was appointed as an additional non-executive director with effect from 1 April 2009 and Michel Combes and Steve Pusey as additional executive directors with effect from 1 June 2009.

The Deputy Chairman, John Buchanan, is the nominated senior independent director and his role includes being available for approach or representation by directors or significant shareholders who may feel inhibited by raising issues with the Chairman. He is also responsible for conducting an annual review of the performance of the Chairman and, in the event it should be necessary, convening a meeting of the non-executive directors.

The Company considers all of its present non-executive directors to be fully independent. The Board is aware of the other commitments of its directors and is satisfied that these do not conflict with their duties as directors of the Company.

There are no cross-directorships or significant links between directors serving on the Board through involvement in other companies or bodies. For the purpose of

Corporate governance continued

section 175 of the Companies Act 2006, the Company's articles of association include a general power for the directors to authorise any matter which would or might otherwise constitute or give rise to a breach of the duty of a director under this section, to avoid a situation in which he has, or can have, a direct or indirect interest that conflicts or may possibly conflict, with the interests of the Company. To this end, procedures have been established for the disclosure of any such conflicts and also for the consideration and authorisation of these conflicts by the Board, where relevant. The directors are required to complete a conflicts questionnaire, initially on appointment and annually thereafter. In the event of a potential conflict being identified, details of that conflict would be submitted to the Board (excluding the director to whom the potential conflict related) for consideration and, as appropriate, authorisation in accordance with the Companies Act 2006 and the articles of association. Where an authorisation was granted, it would be recorded in a register of potential conflicts and reviewed periodically. On an ongoing basis, directors are responsible for notifying the Company Secretary if they become aware of actual or potential conflict situations or a change in circumstances relating to an existing authorisation. To date, no conflicts of interest have been identified.

The names and biographical details of the current directors are given on pages 48, 49 and 50. Changes to the commitments of the directors are reported to the Board.

Under the laws of England and Wales, the executive and non-executive directors are equal members of the Board and have overall collective responsibility for the direction of the Company. In particular, non-executive directors are responsible for:

- bringing a wide range of skills and experience to the Group, including independent judgement on issues of strategy, performance, financial controls and systems of risk management;
- constructively challenging the strategy proposed by the Chief Executive and executive directors;
- scrutinising and challenging performance across the Group's business;
- assessing risk and the integrity of the financial information and controls of the Group; and
- ensuring appropriate remuneration and succession planning arrangements are in place in relation to executive directors and other senior executive roles.

Board effectiveness

Appointments to the Board

There is a formal, rigorous and transparent procedure, which is based on merit and against objective criteria, for the appointment of new directors to the Board. This is described in the section on the Nominations and Governance Committee set out on page 53. Samuel Jonah was identified as a potential candidate by internal sources and subsequently recommended to the Board by the Nominations and Governance Committee on the basis of his wealth of business experience in Africa, particularly South Africa and Ghana where Vodafone has made important investments recently. Michel Combes and Steve Pusey were proposed for appointment to the Board following assessment of their performance and their potential contribution by the Nominations and Governance Committee and the whole Board subsequently discussed the proposal before their appointments were confirmed.

Information and professional development

Each member of the Board has immediate access to a dedicated online team room and can access monthly information including actual financial results, reports from the executive directors in respect of their areas of responsibility and the Chief Executive's report which deals, amongst other things, with investor relations, giving Board members an opportunity to develop an understanding of the views of major investors. These matters are discussed at each Board meeting. From time to time, the Board receives detailed presentations from non-Board members on matters of significance or on new opportunities for the Group. Financial plans, including budgets and forecasts, are regularly discussed at Board meetings. The non-executive directors periodically visit different parts of the Group and are provided with briefings and information to assist them in performing their duties.

The Chairman is responsible for ensuring that induction and training programmes are provided and the Company Secretary organises the programmes. Individual directors are also expected to take responsibility for identifying their training needs and to take steps to ensure that they are adequately informed about the Company and their responsibilities as a director. The Board is confident that all its members have the knowledge, ability and experience to perform the functions required of a director of a listed company.

On appointment, individual directors undergo an induction programme covering, amongst other things:

- the business of the Group;
- their legal and regulatory responsibilities as directors of the Company;
- briefings and presentations from relevant executives; and
- opportunities to visit business operations.

If appropriate, the induction will also include briefings on the scope of the internal audit function and the role of the Audit Committee, meetings with the external auditor and other areas the Company Secretary deems fit, considering the director's area of responsibility. The Company Secretary provides a programme of ongoing training for the directors, which covers a number of sector specific and business issues, as well as legal, accounting and regulatory changes and developments relevant to individual director's areas of responsibility. Throughout their period in office, the directors are continually updated on the Group's businesses and the regulatory and industry specific environments in which it operates. These updates are by way of written briefings and meetings with senior executives and, where appropriate, external sources.

The Company Secretary ensures that the programme to familiarise the non-executive directors with the business is maintained over time and kept relevant to the needs of the individuals involved. The Company Secretary confers with the Chairman and senior independent director to ensure that this is the case.

Performance evaluation

Performance evaluation of the Board, its committees and individual directors takes place on an annual basis and is conducted within the terms of reference of the Nominations and Governance Committee with the aim of improving individual contributions, the effectiveness of the Board and its committees and the Group's performance.

The Board undertakes a formal self-evaluation of its own performance. This process involves the Chairman:

- sending a questionnaire to each Board member for completion;
- undertaking individual meetings with each Board member on Board performance; and
- producing a report on Board performance, using the completed questionnaire and notes from the individual meetings, which is sent to and considered by the Nominations and Governance Committee before being discussed with Board members at the following Board meeting.

The evaluation is designed to determine whether the Board continues to be capable of providing the high level judgement required and whether, as a Board, the directors are informed and up to date with the business and its goals and understand the context within which it operates. The evaluation also includes a review of the administration of the Board covering the operation of the Board, its agenda and the reports and information produced for the Board's consideration. The Board will continue to review its procedures, its effectiveness and development in the financial year ahead.

The Chairman leads the assessment of the Chief Executive and the non-executive directors, the Chief Executive undertakes the performance reviews for the executive directors and the senior independent director conducts the review of the performance of the Chairman by having a meeting with all the non-executive directors together and individual meetings with the executive directors and the Company Secretary. Following this process, the senior independent director produces a written report which is discussed with the Chairman.

The evaluation of each of the Board committees is undertaken using an online questionnaire that each member of the committees and others who attend committee meetings or interact with committee members are required to complete. The results of the questionnaires are discussed with the Chairman of the Board and the members of the committees.

The evaluations undertaken in the 2009 financial year found the performance of each director to be effective and concluded that the Board provides the effective leadership and control required for a listed company. The Nominations and Governance Committee confirmed to the Board that the contributions made by the directors offering themselves for re-election at the AGM in July 2009 continue to be effective and that the Company should support their re-election.

Re-election of directors

Although not required by the articles, in the interests of good corporate governance, the directors have resolved that they will all submit themselves for annual re-election at each AGM of the Company. Accordingly, at the AGM to be held on 28 July 2009, all the directors will be retiring and, being eligible and on the recommendation of the Nominations and Governance Committee, will offer themselves for re-election. New directors seek election for the first time in accordance with the articles of association.

Independent advice

The Board recognises that there may be occasions when one or more of the directors feel it is necessary to take independent legal and/or financial advice at the Company's expense. There is an agreed procedure to enable them to do so.

Indemnification of directors

In accordance with the Company's articles of association and to the extent permitted by the laws of England and Wales, directors are granted an indemnity from the Company in respect of liabilities incurred as a result of their office. In respect of those matters for which the directors may not be indemnified, the Company maintained a directors' and officers' liability insurance policy throughout the financial year. This policy is in the process of being renewed. Neither the Company's indemnity nor the insurance provides cover in the event that the director is proven to have acted dishonestly or fraudulently. The Company does not indemnify its external auditors.

Board committees

The Board has established an Audit Committee, a Nominations and Governance Committee and a Remuneration Committee, each of which has formal terms of reference approved by the Board. The Board is satisfied that the terms of reference for each of these committees satisfy the requirements of the Combined Code and are reviewed internally on an ongoing basis by the Board. The terms of reference for all Board committees can be found on the Company's website at www.vodafone.com/governance or a copy can be obtained by application to the Company Secretary at the Company's registered office.

The committees are provided with all necessary resources to enable them to undertake their duties in an effective manner. The Company Secretary or his delegate acts as Secretary to the committees. The minutes of committee meetings are circulated to all directors.

Each committee has access to such information and advice, both from within the Group and externally, at the cost of the Company as it deems necessary. This may include the appointment of external consultants where appropriate. Each committee undertakes an annual review of the effectiveness of its terms of reference and makes recommendations to the Board for changes where appropriate.

Audit Committee

The members of the Audit Committee during the year, together with a record of their attendance at scheduled meetings which they were eligible to attend, are set out below:

	Meetings attended
John Buchanan	3/4
Alan Jebson	4/4
Nick Land, Chairman	4/4
Anne Lauvergeon	4/4
Dr Michael Boskin, Chairman (until 29 July 2008)	1/1

The Audit Committee is comprised of financially literate members having the necessary ability and experience to understand financial statements. Solely for the purpose of fulfilling the requirements of the Sarbanes-Oxley Act and the Combined Code, the Board has designated Nick Land, who is an independent non-executive director satisfying the independence requirements of Rule 10A-3 of the US Securities Exchange Act 1934, as its financial expert on the Audit Committee. Further details on Nick Land can be found in "Board of directors and Group management" on page 48.

The Audit Committee's responsibilities include:

- overseeing the relationship with the external auditors;
- reviewing the Company's preliminary results announcement, half-year results and annual financial statements;
- monitoring compliance with statutory and listing requirements for any exchange on which the Company's shares and debt instruments are quoted;
- reviewing the scope, extent and effectiveness of the activity of the Group internal audit department;
- engaging independent advisers as it determines is necessary and to perform investigations;
- reporting to the Board on the quality and acceptability of the Company's accounting policies and practices including, without limitation, critical accounting policies and practices; and
- playing an active role in monitoring the Company's compliance efforts for Section 404 of the Sarbanes-Oxley Act and receiving progress updates at each of its meetings.

At least twice a year, the Audit Committee meets separately with the external auditors and the Group Audit Director without management being present. Further details on the work of the Audit Committee and its oversight of the relationships with the external auditors can be found under "Auditors" and the "Report from the Audit Committee" which are set out on pages 55 and 56.

Nominations and Governance Committee

The members of the Nominations and Governance Committee during the year, together with a record of their attendance at scheduled meetings which they were eligible to attend, are set out below:

	Meetings attended
Sir John Bond, Chairman	3/3
John Buchanan	3/3
Luc Vandevelde	3/3
Arun Sarin (until 29 July 2008)	1/1
Professor Jürgen Schrempp (until 29 July 2008)	1/1

The Nominations and Governance Committee's key objective is to ensure that the Board comprises individuals with the requisite skills, knowledge and experience to ensure that it is effective in discharging its responsibilities. The Nominations and Governance Committee:

- leads the process for identifying and making recommendations to the Board of candidates for appointment as directors of the Company, giving full consideration to succession planning and the leadership needs of the Group;
- makes recommendations to the Board on the composition of the Nominations and Governance Committee and the composition and chairmanship of the Audit and Remuneration Committees;
- regularly reviews the structure, size and composition of the Board, including the balance of skills, knowledge and experience and the independence of the non-executive directors, and makes recommendations to the Board with regard to any change; and
- is responsible for the oversight of all matters relating to corporate governance, bringing any issues to the attention of the Board.

The Nominations and Governance Committee meets periodically when required. In addition to scheduled meetings there are a number of ad hoc meetings to address specific matters. No one other than a member of the Nominations and Governance Committee is entitled to be present at its meetings. The Chief Executive, other non-executive directors and external advisers may be invited to attend.

Corporate governance continued

Remuneration Committee

The members of the Remuneration Committee during the year, together with a record of their attendance at scheduled meetings which they were eligible to attend, are set out below:

	Meetings attended
Luc Vandevelde, Chairman	5/5
Simon Murray	4/5
Anthony Watson	5/5
Philip Yea	4/5
Professor Jürgen Schrempp (until 29 July 2008)	0/1

In addition to scheduled meetings, there are a number of ad hoc meetings to deal with specific matters. The responsibilities of the Remuneration Committee include:

- determining, on behalf of the Board, the Company's policy on the remuneration of the Chairman, the executive directors and the senior management team of the Company;
- determining the total remuneration packages for these individuals, including any compensation on termination of office; and
- appointing any consultants in respect of executive directors' remuneration.

The Chairman and Chief Executive may attend the Remuneration Committee's meetings by invitation. They do not attend when their individual remuneration is discussed and no director is involved in deciding his own remuneration.

Further information on the Remuneration Committee's activities is contained in "Directors' remuneration" on pages 57 to 67.

Executive Committee

The executive directors, together with certain other Group functional heads and regional chief executives, meet 12 times a year as the Executive Committee under the chairmanship of the Chief Executive. The Executive Committee is responsible for the day-to-day management of the Group's businesses, the overall financial performance of the Group in fulfilment of strategy, plans and budgets and Group capital structure and funding. It also reviews major acquisitions and disposals. The members of the Executive Committee and their biographical details are set out on pages 48 to 50.

Strategy Board

The Strategy Board meets three times each year to discuss strategy. This is attended by Executive Committee members and the Chief Executive Officers of the major operating companies and other selected individuals based on Strategy Board topics.

Company Secretary

The Company Secretary acts as Secretary to the Board and to the committees of the Board and, with the consent of the Board, may delegate responsibility for the administration of the committees to other suitably qualified staff. He:

- assists the Chairman in ensuring that all directors have full and timely access to all relevant information;
- is responsible for ensuring that the correct Board procedures are followed and advises the Board on corporate governance matters; and
- administers the procedure under which directors can, where appropriate, obtain independent professional advice at the Company's expense.

The appointment or removal of the Company Secretary is a matter for the Board as a whole.

Relations with shareholders

The Company is committed to communicating its strategy and activities clearly to its shareholders and, to that end, maintains an active dialogue with investors through a planned programme of investor relations activities. The investor relations programme includes:

- formal presentations of full year and half-year results and interim management statements;
- briefing meetings with major institutional shareholders in the UK, the US and in Continental Europe after the half-year results and preliminary announcement, to ensure that the investor community receives a balanced and complete view of the Group's performance and the issues faced by the Group;
- regular meetings with institutional investors and analysts by the Chief Executive and the Chief Financial Officer to discuss business performance;
- hosting investors and analysts sessions at which senior management from relevant operating companies deliver presentations which provide an overview of each of the individual businesses and operations;
- attendance by senior executives across the business at relevant meetings and conferences throughout the year;
- responding to enquiries from shareholders and analysts through the Company's Investor Relations team; and
- a section dedicated to shareholders on the Company's website, www.vodafone.com/shareholder.

Overall responsibility for ensuring that there is effective communication with investors and that the Board understands the views of major shareholders on matters such as governance and strategy rests with the Chairman, who makes himself available to meet shareholders for this purpose.

The senior independent director and other members of the Board are also available to meet major investors on request. The senior independent director has a specific responsibility to be available to shareholders who have concerns, for whom contact with the Chairman, Chief Executive or Chief Financial Officer has either failed to resolve their concerns, or for whom such contact is inappropriate.

At the 2007 AGM, the shareholders approved amendments to the articles which enabled the Company to take advantage of the provisions in the Companies Act 2006 (effective from 20 January 2007) to communicate with its shareholders electronically. Following that approval, unless a shareholder has specifically asked to receive a hard copy, they will receive notification of the availability of the annual report on the Company's website at www.vodafone.com/investor. For the 2009 financial year, shareholders will receive the notice of meeting and form of proxy in paper through the post unless they have previously opted to receive email communications. Shareholders continue to have the option to appoint proxies and give voting instructions electronically.

The principal communication with private investors is via the annual report and through the AGM, an occasion which is attended by all the Company's directors and at which all shareholders present are given the opportunity to question the Chairman and the Board as well as the Chairmen of the Audit, Remuneration and Nominations and Governance Committees. After the AGM, shareholders can meet informally with directors.

A summary presentation of results and development plans is also given at the AGM before the Chairman deals with the formal business of the meeting. The AGM is broadcast live on the Group's website, www.vodafone.com/agm, and a recording of the webcast can subsequently be viewed on the website. All substantive resolutions at the Company's AGMs are decided on a poll. The poll is conducted by the Company's registrars and scrutinised by Electoral Reform Services. The proxy votes cast in relation to all resolutions, including details of votes withheld, are disclosed to those in attendance at the meeting and the results of the poll are published on the Company's website and announced via the regulatory news service. Financial and other information is made available on the Company's website, www.vodafone.com/investor, which is regularly updated.

Political donations

At last year's AGM, held on 29 July 2008, the directors sought and received shareholders' approval for the Company and its subsidiaries to be authorised, for the purposes of Part 14 of the Companies Act 2006, to make political donations and to incur political expenditure during the period from the date of the AGM to the conclusion of the AGM in 2012 or 29 July 2012, whichever is earlier, up to a maximum aggregate amount of £100,000 per year.

Neither the Company nor any of its subsidiaries have made any political donations during the year.

It remains the policy of the Company not to make political donations or incur political expenditure as those expressions are normally understood. However, the directors consider that it is in the best interests of shareholders for the Company to participate in public debate and opinion-forming on matters which affect its business. To avoid inadvertent infringement of the Companies Act 2006, shareholder authority has been sought as outlined above.

Internal control

The Board has overall responsibility for the system of internal control. A sound system of internal control is designed to manage rather than eliminate the risk of failure to achieve business objectives and can only provide reasonable and not absolute assurance against material misstatement or loss. The process of managing the risks associated with social, environmental and ethical impacts is also discussed under "Corporate responsibility" on pages 45 to 47.

The Board has established procedures that implement in full the Turnbull Guidance "Internal Control: Revised Guidance for Directors on the Combined Code" for the year under review and to the date of approval of the annual report. These procedures, which are subject to regular review, provide an ongoing process for identifying, evaluating and managing the significant risks faced by the Group. See page 69 for management's report on internal control over financial reporting.

Monitoring and review activities

There are clear processes for monitoring the system of internal control and reporting any significant control failings or weaknesses together with details of corrective action. These include:

- a formal annual confirmation provided by the Chief Executive and Chief Financial Officer of each Group company certifying the operation of their control systems and highlighting any weaknesses, the results of which are reviewed by regional management, the Audit Committee and the Board;
- a review of the quality and timeliness of disclosures undertaken by the Chief Executive and the Chief Financial Officer which includes formal annual meetings with the operating company or regional chief executives and chief financial officers and the Disclosure Committee;
- periodic examination of business processes on a risk basis including reports on controls throughout the Group undertaken by the Group internal audit department who report directly to the Audit Committee; and
- reports from the external auditors on certain internal controls and relevant financial reporting matters, presented to the Audit Committee and management.

Any controls and procedures, no matter how well designed and operated, can provide only reasonable and not absolute assurance of achieving the desired control objectives. Management is required to apply judgement in evaluating the risks facing the Group in achieving its objectives, in determining the risks that are considered acceptable to bear, in assessing the likelihood of the risks concerned materialising, in identifying the Company's ability to reduce the incidence and impact on the business of risks that do materialise and in ensuring that the costs of operating particular controls are proportionate to the benefit.

Review of effectiveness

The Board and the Audit Committee have reviewed the effectiveness of the internal control system, including financial, operational and compliance controls and risk management, in accordance with the Combined Code for the period from 1 April 2008 to 19 May 2009, the date of approval of the Group's annual report. No significant failings or weaknesses were identified during this review. However, had there been any such failings or weaknesses, the Board confirms that necessary actions would have been taken to remedy them.

Disclosure controls and procedures

The Company maintains "disclosure controls and procedures", as such term is defined in Exchange Act Rule 13a-15(e), that are designed to ensure that information required to be disclosed in reports the Company files or submits under the Exchange Act is recorded, processed, summarised and reported within the time periods specified in the Securities and Exchange Commission rules and forms, and that such information is accumulated and communicated to management, including the Company's Group Chief Executive and Chief Financial Officer, as appropriate, to allow timely decisions regarding required disclosure.

The directors, the Chief Executive and the Chief Financial Officer have evaluated the effectiveness of the disclosure controls and procedures and, based on that evaluation, have concluded that the disclosure controls and procedures are effective at the end of the period covered by this document.

Auditors

Following a recommendation by the Audit Committee and, in accordance with Section 384 of the Companies Act 1985, a resolution proposing the reappointment of Deloitte LLP as auditors to the Company will be put to the shareholders at the 2009 AGM.

In its assessment of the independence of the auditors and in accordance with the US Public Company Accounting Oversight Board's standard on independence, the Audit Committee receives in writing details of relationships between Deloitte LLP and the Company that may have a bearing on their independence and receives confirmation that they are independent of the Company within the meaning of the securities laws administered by the SEC.

In addition, the Audit Committee pre-approves the audit fee after a review of both the level of the audit fee against other comparable companies, including those in the telecommunications industry, and the level and nature of non-audit fees, as part of its review of the adequacy and objectivity of the audit process.

In a further measure to ensure auditor independence is not compromised, policies provide for the pre-approval by the Audit Committee of permitted non-audit services by Deloitte LLP. For certain specific permitted services, the Audit Committee has pre-approved that Deloitte LLP can be engaged by Group management subject to specified fee limits for individual engagements and fee limits for each type of specific service permitted. For all other services, or those permitted services that exceed the specified fee limits, the Chairman of the Audit Committee, or in his absence another member, can pre-approve services which have not been pre-approved by the Audit Committee.

In addition to their statutory duties, Deloitte LLP are also employed where, as a result of their position as auditors, they either must, or are best placed to, perform the work in question. This is primarily work in relation to matters such as shareholder circulars, Group borrowings, regulatory filings and certain business acquisitions and disposals. Other work is awarded on the basis of competitive tender.

During the year, Deloitte LLP and its affiliates charged the Group £8 million (2008: £7 million, 2007: £7 million) for audit and audit-related services and a further £1 million (2008: £2 million, 2007: £3 million) for non-audit assignments. An analysis of these fees can be found in note 4 to the consolidated financial statements.

US listing requirements

The Company's American Depositary Shares are listed on the NYSE and the Company is, therefore, subject to the rules of the NYSE as well as US securities laws and the rules of the SEC. The NYSE requires US companies listed on the exchange to comply with the NYSE's corporate governance rules but foreign private issuers, such as the Company, are exempt from most of those rules. However, pursuant to NYSE Rule 303A.11, the Company is required to disclose a summary of any significant ways in which the corporate governance practices it follows differ from those required by the NYSE for US companies. The differences are as follows:

Independence

- NYSE rules require that a majority of the Board must be comprised of independent directors and the rules include detailed tests that US companies must use for determining independence.
- The Combined Code requires a company's board of directors to assess and make a determination as to the independence of its directors.

While the Board does not explicitly take into consideration the NYSE's detailed tests, it has carried out an assessment based on the requirements of the Combined Code and has determined in its judgement that all of the non-executive directors are independent within those requirements. As at 19 May 2009, the Board comprised the Chairman, two executive directors and nine non-executive directors.

Corporate governance continued

Committees

- NYSE rules require US companies to have a nominating and corporate governance committee and a compensation committee, each composed entirely of independent directors with a written charter that addresses the committees' purpose and responsibilities.
- The Company's Nominations and Governance Committee and Remuneration Committee have terms of reference and composition that comply with the Combined Code requirements.
- The Nominations and Governance Committee is chaired by the Chairman of the Board and its other members are non-executive directors of the Company.
- The Audit Committee is composed entirely of non-executive directors whom the Board has determined to be independent and who meet the requirements of Rule 10A-3 of the Securities Exchange Act.

The Company considers that the terms of reference of these committees, which are available on its website at www.vodafone.com/governance, are generally responsive to the relevant NYSE rules but may not address all aspects of these rules.

Corporate governance guidelines

- Under NYSE rules, US companies must adopt and disclose corporate governance guidelines.
- Vodafone has posted its statement of compliance with the Combined Code on its website at www.vodafone.com/governance. The Company has also adopted a group governance and policy manual which provides the first level of the framework within which its businesses operate. The manual applies to all directors and employees.
- The Company considers that its corporate governance guidelines are generally responsive to, but may not address all aspects of, the relevant NYSE rules.

The Company has also adopted a corporate Code of Ethics for senior executives, financial and accounting officers, separate from and additional to its Business Principles. A copy of this code is available on the Group's website at www.vodafone.com/governance.

Report from the Audit Committee

The Audit Committee assists the Board in carrying out its responsibilities in relation to financial reporting requirements, risk management and the assessment of internal controls. The Audit Committee also reviews the effectiveness of the Company's internal audit function and manages the Company's relationship with the external auditors.

The composition of the Audit Committee is shown in the table on page 53 and its terms of reference can be found on the Vodafone website (www.vodafone.com/governance). By invitation of the Chairman of the Audit Committee, the Chief Executive, the Chief Financial Officer, the Group Financial Controller, the Director of Financial Reporting, the Group Audit Director and the external auditors also attend the Audit Committee meetings. Also invited to attend certain meetings are relevant people from the business to present sessions on issues designed to enhance the Audit Committee's awareness of key issues and developments in the business which are relevant to the Audit Committee in the performance of its role.

During the year ended 31 March 2009, the principal activities of the Audit Committee were as follows:

Financial reporting

The Audit Committee reviewed and discussed with management and the external auditors the half-year and annual financial statements, focusing on, without limitation, the quality and acceptability of accounting policies and practices, the clarity of the disclosures and compliance with financial reporting standards and relevant financial and governance reporting requirements. To aid their review, the Audit Committee considered reports from the Group Financial Controller and the Director of Financial Reporting and also reports from the external auditors, Deloitte LLP, on the scope and outcome of their half-year review and annual audit.

Risk management and internal control

The Audit Committee reviewed the process by which the Group evaluated its control environment, its risk assessment process and the way in which significant business risks were managed. It also considered the Group Audit Director's reports on the effectiveness of internal controls, significant identified frauds and any identified fraud that involved management or employees with a significant role in internal controls. The Audit Committee was also responsible for oversight of the Group's compliance activities in relation to section 404 of the Sarbanes-Oxley Act.

Internal audit

The Audit Committee monitored and reviewed the scope, extent and effectiveness of the activity of the Group internal audit department and received reports from the Group Audit Director which included updates on audit activities and achievement against the Group audit plan, the results of any unsatisfactory audits and the action plans to address these areas, and resource requirements of the internal audit department. The Audit Committee held private discussions with the Group Audit Director at each meeting.

External auditors

The Audit Committee reviewed and monitored the independence of the external auditors and the objectivity and effectiveness of the audit process and provided the Board with its recommendation to the shareholders on the reappointment of Deloitte LLP as external auditors. The Audit Committee approved the scope and fees for audit and permitted non-audit services provided by Deloitte LLP.

Private meetings were held with Deloitte LLP to ensure that there were no restrictions on the scope of their audit and to discuss matters without management being present.

Audit Committee effectiveness

The Audit Committee conducts a formal review of its effectiveness annually, giving consideration to, amongst other things, frequency, timings and adequacy of the meetings, composition, adequacy of resources and interaction with management and concluded this year that the Audit Committee's performance was effective and the Audit Committee had fulfilled its terms of reference.

Nick Land

Nick Land
On behalf of the Audit Committee

© Vodafone Group Services Limited 2009. This Annual Report has been duly audited.

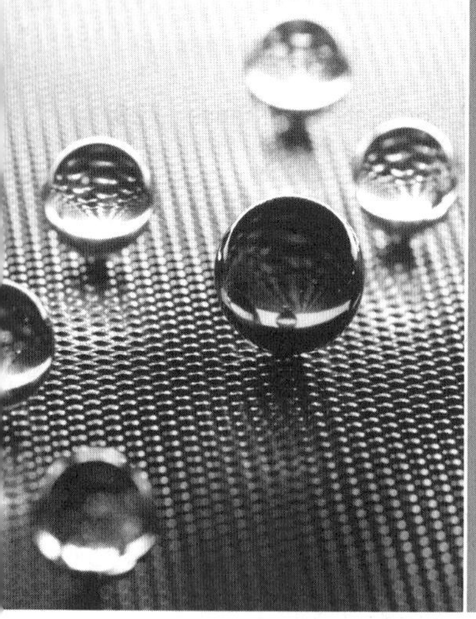

19

The auditor and liability under the law

LEARNING OBJECTIVES

After studying this chapter you should be able to:

- **Describe the auditors' responsibilities under criminal and civil law and how they are affected by the rules of professional conduct.**
- **Discuss the role of case law in defining auditors' responsibility to third parties.**
- **Apply case law decisions in assessing whether an auditor may be guilty of negligence.**
- **Outline the various alternatives that have been proposed or implemented to reduce auditors' liability.**

Learning objectives, 730
Introduction, 731
Criminal liability, 731
Civil liability, 732
Case law, 733
Auditing standards, 749
Professional conduct, 750
Potential ways of reducing auditor liability, 750
Summary, 756
Key points of the chapter, 757
References, 758
Further reading, 758
Self-assessment questions (solutions available to students), 759
Self-assessment questions (solutions available to tutors), 760
Topics for class discussion without solutions, 761

INTRODUCTION

In this chapter we consider the auditors' criminal and civil liability. We concentrate on the auditors' civil liability because this has been the most important form of liability in practice. In recent years the prime concern of auditors in civil liability cases has been their liability to third parties. This concern has been sparked by a number of factors: the cost of obtaining indemnity insurance, the many actions being brought against auditors, the level of damages demanded by plaintiffs and the bad publicity the auditing profession receives as a result of alleged negligence. Using case law we show how auditors' liability to third parties has developed over a period of approximately 60 years. These cases will help to demonstrate how the extent of the auditors' liability to third parties has changed over time. We are particularly concerned with conditions that must be met before it is likely that a court will determine that an auditor is responsible to a third party. The issue of negligence is discussed in the context of the various ways the auditing profession and individual audit firms have sought to reduce the extent of their potential liability to third-party claims.

CRIMINAL LIABILITY

It is fortunately rare for accountants and auditors to face criminal charges but you should be aware that they could be liable for such charges under a number of UK statutes.

The Theft Act 1968 and Fraud Act 2006

Of particular relevance to this chapter is Section 17 of the Theft Act, which provides that individuals commit an offence if they gain or cause someone to lose by, among other things: (a) destroying, concealing or falsifying any documents or records required for accounting purposes; or (b) supplying information which makes use of records or documents known by them to be materially false, misleading or deceptive. The penalty on conviction of such offence would render individuals so convicted liable to imprisonment. The Theft Act 1968 has been supplemented by the enactment of the Fraud Act 2006. This act introduced for the first time a general offence of fraud and rationalized the law in this area and also substantially updated it.

When legislation such as the Theft Act 1968 was published there was little incidence of fraud involving IT, but it is now commonplace. The Fraud Act 2006 makes acts such as 'phishing' and the supply of equipment to commit credit card fraud a criminal offence. The act states that a person can be guilty of fraud in three ways:

1 Fraud by false representation.
2 Fraud by failing to disclose information.
3 Fraud by abuse of position.

In general terms a company issues a prospectus when it is attempting to raise finance.

The scope of these three types of fraud is very wide and in the context of this book encompasses situations such as company prospectuses, where either auditors or directors might fail to disclose information or disclose false

There are certain safeguards in the act to prevent, for instance, the venturing of an honest opinion coming within the scope of the act.

information. Later in the chapter we discuss the case of *ADT Ltd vs BDO Binder Hamlyn*, where the plaintiff was in the process of taking over a client of Binder Hamlyn and in the process met with one of the partners of the accounting firm to discuss the financial statements. If, in this type of situation the partner were to make a false statement (or fail to disclose certain information), they might be charged with committing fraud.

Companies Act 2006

The Companies Act 2006 introduced a new criminal offence for auditors. Section 507 provides that if an auditor knowingly or recklessly causes an audit report to be issued that is misleading, false or deceptive, they will be guilty of a criminal offence. If found guilty of such an offence the auditor can be liable for a fine. The same section also provides that if the auditor fails to provide a statement in his audit report of certain circumstances as required by the Companies Act, he will have committed a criminal office. These circumstances are:

- Where proper accounting records have not been kept or adequate returns for the purpose of the audit have not been received by branches not visited by the auditor (s.498(2(a))).
- The company's accounts are not in accordance with the accounting records and returns (s.498(2(b))).
- For a quoted company that the auditable part of the directors' remuneration statement is not in accordance with the accounting records and returns (s.498(2(c))).
- The auditor has failed to obtain the necessary information and explanations he requires for his audit (s.498(3)).
- Where the company has prepared accounts in accordance with the small companies requirements and they were not entitled to do so (s.498(5)).

Finally, section 993 of CA 2006 provides that where a business is carried on for fraudulent purposes, anyone who is knowingly a party to the carrying on of such a business is liable to a fine or imprisonment, or both. If it can be shown that the business was carried on for fraudulent purposes any accountants and auditors associated with such a business, if charged, would have to refute any claims that they knew it was being carried on for fraudulent purposes.

CIVIL LIABILITY

Introduction

We have suggested throughout this book that auditors add credibility to financial statements, so users can make decisions with confidence in relation to those statements. Clearly, if auditors have given a clean opinion on financial statements which subsequently turn out not to be true and fair, a user who loses as a result of reliance on the statements may well feel that the auditors are one of those at fault. The auditors' liability under civil law, should their standard of work fall below that which is expected, is thus of great importance. We know that auditors give an opinion rather than a guarantee, and an opinion, moreover, which is concerned with the ill-defined term 'true and fair view'. However, the company or its shareholders, or indeed other persons and organizations may sue them for damages to compensate for any loss they have suffered as a result of alleged negligent work. The extent to which stakeholders are likely to be successful in obtaining compensation is one of the topics of this chapter.

The auditor and negligence

In recent years considerable attention has been focused on auditors' negligence. This is largely the result of the wide publicity given to considerable sums sought by plaintiffs in compensation for losses they have suffered, losses which, they believe, could have been prevented if the auditors concerned had been more diligent. This is in the context of financial scandals in which auditors have been implicated, such as BCCI, Enron and WorldCom, cases given much publicity, as the auditors have been sued for massive sums of money. These and other scandals have suggested to a wide section of society that control of the business community may be less effective than had been supposed.

Duty of care

For an action of negligence to succeed, it must first be shown that the defendant – the auditors – owed a duty of care to the person bringing the action. There is no dispute that a duty of care exists where a contractual relationship has been established, whether in writing or not. The auditors have a contractual relationship with the company and thus they can be sued by the company under contract law. One of the most likely occasions when this will occur is when the auditors fail to detect a material fraud in the company. The company might sue the auditors because they believe the auditors were negligent in failing to detect the fraud. Although liability cases brought under contract law are important they have received less attention than those brought, by third parties, under tort. In recent years the determination of whether an auditor owes a duty of care to third parties has been a controversial matter receiving considerable media attention. We cite case law below to show you how the courts have developed the law in this area. In our view, students of auditing must understand this development and the consequences for auditors.

CASE LAW

Early case law in the area seemed to suggest that if there was no contract between accountants/auditors and third parties, they owed no duty to these third parties, although as early as 1932 in a Scottish case (*Donaghue vs Stevenson*) it had been established that physical injury claims against persons with whom no contractual relationship existed could succeed.

In this case, a woman who had consumed a bottle of lemonade in which a decomposed snail was present, succeeded in obtaining damages from the bottler of the lemonade, despite no contractual relationship existing between them.

The early view is typified in the case of *Candler vs Crane Christmas & Co.* (1951). In this case the plaintiff, Mr Candler, brought an action for negligence against the accountants, Crane Christmas & Co., for the loss he suffered when a company in which he had invested went into liquidation. The defendants had prepared and reported on the financial statements that they knew were to be shown to Mr Candler to induce him to invest in the company. The action was unsuccessful because there was no contractual arrangement between Mr Candler and Crane Christmas and Co. However, one of the appeal judges, Denning LJ, with what turned out to be remarkable foresight, dissented, stating:

> 'Their [the auditors'] duty is not merely a duty to use care in their reports. They have also a duty to use care in their work which results in their reports.' Later he stated they owed a duty: 'to any third party to whom they themselves show the accounts, or to whom they know their employer is going to show the accounts so as to induce him to invest money or take some other action on them'.

The opinion of Denning LJ was later upheld in the case of *Hedley Byrne & Co. vs Heller and Partners Ltd* (1963). This non-accounting case established the principle that an action can be brought by a third party and that the third party can expect a duty of care from the other party, such as the auditors. Lord Devlin stated:

> The categories of *special relationship* which may give rise to a duty to take care in word as well as in deed are not limited to *contractual relationships* or to relationships in fiduciary duty, but also include relationships which are equivalent to contracts.

Lord Morris added:

> If in a sphere in which a person is so placed that others could reasonably rely on his judgement or his skill or on his ability to make careful enquiry, a person takes it on himself to give information or advice to, or *allows* his information or advice to be passed onto another person who, *as he knows or should know, will place reliance on it*, then a duty of care will arise.

The above judgement emphasized the concept of reliance. For auditors this meant that it must be reasonable for a person to place reliance on the auditors' report and that the auditors were aware or should have been aware that the person would rely upon it. As was discussed in Chapter 16 the auditors' report is (usually) specifically addressed to members, that is, the shareholders, of the company but the judgement in Hedley Byrne did not preclude the possibility that other parties could bring an action against the auditors. They would, of course, have to prove to the courts, if the action were to be successful, that the auditors had not exercised due care and skill and had been negligent. It is widely recognized in accounting that financial reports, although prepared specifically for the shareholder, may be used by a wide variety of individuals each with their own differing interests in the affairs of the company.

ACTIVITY 19.1

List the parties you believe could have an interest in the financial statements of a company.

There are many potential users of financial statements, a few of which are listed below:

- Investors/potential investors.
- Lenders.
- Employees.
- Government agencies, such as HM Revenue & Customs.
- Competitors.
- Suppliers.
- Investment analysts/stock-brokers/share tipsters.
- Pressure groups.

If one accepts all the parties listed as having a legitimate interest in the financial statements of a company, this raises the intriguing question as to whether there is any bound to the liability to third parties. This assumes that the auditors are aware of these many interest groups. You should note that the interest of those groups does seem to be accepted in the accounting literature.

We noted in Chapter 2, page 37, that Briloff (1986) identified a very wide range of publics with an interest in accounting information to whom accountability might be owed.

The judgement in Hedley Byrne emphasized that:

> Where the auditors knew or should have known about the third party, and that the third party intended to *rely* on their report (that is, there was a special relationship), then they owe a duty to that party.

The point we wish to emphasize here is that, although auditors may know who the potential third parties are in a general sense, they are unlikely, except in special circumstances, to know that a specific individual is going to use and rely on the financial statements. Until the 1980s (see below) it had generally been thought that the auditors could not be held liable where the third party was not *known* to the auditors, this being the view of counsel in the advice given to the ICAEW following the *Hedley Byrne* case which stated that the auditors would be liable:

> Where the accountants knew or ought to have known that the reports, accounts or financial statements in question were being prepared for the specific purpose or transaction which gave rise to the loss, and that they would be shown to and relied on by third parties in that particular connection.

Assuming that the accountant had been negligent and that the third party had relied on the financial statements.

The application of the above principles was, however, severely tested by the judgements in two cases in the early 1980s: *JEB Fasteners Ltd vs Marks Bloom & Co.* (1981); and *Twomax Ltd and Goode vs Dickson, McFarlane and Robinson* (1983).

The *JEB Fasteners* case

In the *JEB Fasteners* case, a firm of accountants, Marks Bloom & Co., prepared and audited the financial statements of BG Fasteners. However, the statements were misleading because the value of stock was overstated. The company had purchased stock for £11 000 but it was included in the financial statements at its expected net realizable value of £23 080. The net result of this and other more minor errors on the profit and loss account was that a profit of £11 was shown rather than a loss of £13 000. BG Fasteners was taken over by JEB Fasteners but unfortunately the takeover proved a less successful venture than expected. Woolf J held that a duty of care would be owed by the defendants if they:

> *Reasonably should have foreseen* at the time the accounts were audited that a person might rely on those accounts for the purpose of deciding whether or not to take over the company and therefore could suffer loss if the accounts were inaccurate.

At the time the accounts were prepared the company (BG Fasteners) was not in good financial health and was in need of a capital injection. It was stressed in the case that this injection would have to come from some source such as loan capital, or another investor, perhaps by a takeover of the company. As the auditors were aware of the poor financial position, they should have recognized the likelihood that the accounts would be used in any attempt to gain additional finance. So, although the auditors were not aware that JEB Fasteners were going to take over BG Fasteners, they should have been aware that a party similar to the plaintiff, a potential investor, was likely to use the financial statements in making a decision whether or not to invest in the company.

The accountants, however, were found not to be liable because the court decided that even if the accounts had been properly stated the plaintiff would still have taken over the company. The main reason JEB Fasteners took over BG Fasteners was to acquire the services of two of the directors who it was thought would complement their own management team. Thus, it would seem that mere use of the accounts will not create a potential liability but if that use plays a substantial part in influencing the plaintiff's decision then persons associated with negligent preparation/audit could be held liable.

This case also emphasized the concept of *foreseeability* which seems to lead, given the allusion to the many potential users, to the notion of unlimited liability. However, the judgement in the case also made clear that specific circumstances surrounding a case need to be considered. A prominent feature of the case was the requirement for a capital injection in the near future, and the fact that this should have alerted the auditors to the strong possibility that the financial statements would be used for the purpose of inducing that assistance.

Auditors' liability was not, therefore, as extensive as first appears, but we have to say that the boundaries were somewhat fuzzy following the case. For instance, if a company carrying out an expansion programme is likely to need additional finance to continue at the present rate, should the auditors *reasonably foresee* that lenders are a potential source of finance and that they may use the company's financial statements in order to decide whether to grant a loan?

The *Twomax Limited* case

The concept of foreseeability was further emphasized in the Scottish case, *Twomax Ltd and Goode vs Dickson, McFarlane and Robinson* (1983). In this case Twomax Ltd and two private individuals had invested money in a company, Kintyre Knitwear Ltd, which was audited by the defendants, and which, subsequent to the investment, went into liquidation. The judge, Lord Stewart, considered that the financial statements had been negligently prepared and audited. In particular, the financial statements did not portray the true financial picture of the company and the auditors had neither attended the inventory count nor circularized credit customers.

An interesting feature of this case was that the auditor was a close friend of one of the directors and trusted him and the staff of the company. You may care to refer back to Chapter 3 where we considered independence and the potential influence that close friendships can have on independence. In this case, as in the *JEB Fasteners* case, the court noted that Kintyre Knitwear Ltd was in need of capital and hence the auditors should have foreseen that the financial statements would be used to assist them achieve that aim. It was found that the plaintiffs had indeed relied on the financial statements and hence in this case the defendants were found negligent.

The *Caparo Industries* case

The next major development in the law of negligence affecting accountants occurred in 1987 when Caparo Industries plc brought an action against two of the directors of Fidelity plc, Stephen Dickman and Robert Dickman, for fraud and against the company's auditors, Touche Ross, for negligence. The initial hearing before the courts was to determine if the auditors owed a duty of care to the plaintiffs. During 1984 Caparo Industries had invested in and eventually acquired Fidelity plc. The plaintiffs alleged that the financial statements they had relied upon overstated the profits of Fidelity plc. Specifically, the plaintiffs alleged that the financial statements they had relied upon for the year ending 31 March 1984 had reported a profit of £1.3 million when the company had in fact made a loss of £465 000. The plaintiffs alleged that the overstatement was caused by: the inclusion of non-existent stock, under-providing for obsolete inventories and under-providing for after-date sales credits. When the case was first heard in the High Court, before Sir Neil Lawson sitting as judge, it was to decide if Touche Ross owed a duty of care to Caparo Industries. For the purposes of the case the investment or purchase of shares in Fidelity plc by Caparo was split into two parts. First, Caparo as a potential investor had purchased a quantity of shares in Fidelity. Second, as a shareholder in Fidelity, Caparo had purchased additional shares and eventually acquired control of Fidelity. Lawson stated that three main issues had to be considered when determining if a duty of care was owed. The first of these was whether it was foreseeable on the part of the auditors that economic loss could result from their lack of care. The second issue was whether there was a close and direct relationship between the two parties to the action, that is, was there proximity? The third issue was whether it was fair, reasonable and just to impose liability on the defendants for economic loss arising from the misstatement of the financial statements. Lawson considered that the previous cases of *JEB Fasteners* and *Twomax* had misinterpreted certain passages by Lord Wilberforce in the *Anns* case. This had led to the judges in those cases placing too great an emphasis on foreseeability and general policy and not enough 'to the existence of a close and direct relationship between the maker and the recipient in negligent misstatements' (p.394).

Inventory.

This refers to the *Anns vs Merton London Borough Council* (1978) case. Although not involving auditors, certain principles outlined in this case have often been cited in negligence cases.

On giving his judgement on Caparo as investors, Lawson accepted that economic loss was foreseeable but considered that there was no close or direct relationship between the parties. When considering Caparo as a shareholder he once again accepted that economic loss was foreseeable. Lawson also accepted that there was a close and direct relationship between auditors and shareholders, but considered that any duty owed was to shareholders as a class rather than as individuals. His reasoning for this distinction is based on the indeterminacy of the individual shareholders. Lawson indicated that the appropriate means of recourse for disenchanted individual shareholders was to vote to remove the auditors rather than through civil action.

He thus concluded that the defendants did not owe the plaintiffs a duty of care either as investors or shareholders. He also indicated that on the grounds of justice and fairness, liability should not be imposed on the defendants. To do so would 'certainly lead to the liability of the auditors which was indeterminate as to quantum, as to time and as to the identity of its beneficiaries' (p.396).

Caparo appealed against this judgement and the case was brought before the Court of Appeal in 1988. The findings of the three judges, Lord Justices Bingham and Taylor with O'Conner dissenting, was that a duty of care was owed by the auditors to Caparo as shareholders but not as investors. All three judges agreed that there was foreseeability but Lord Justice O'Conner did not believe that proximity was established. Both Bingham and Taylor considered that the identity of the body of shareholders, although in some cases extremely numerous, was determinate. Furthermore, they argued that when the auditors accepted the appointment 'they knew that the end-product of their audit was a report to shareholders, on which they knew any shareholder might rely' (p.807). This was sufficient for them to conclude that there was a close and direct relationship between the auditors and Caparo.

Lord Justice Bingham disagreed with Sir Neil Lawson on the importance of distinguishing between individual shareholders and shareholders as a class. He indeed, doubted the 'practical significance' of delineating between shareholders as a class and the company itself, with which the auditors have a contract.

Bingham also disagreed with Lawson on the issue of the importance of the individual shareholder's legal rights of voting to dismiss the auditors. Bingham doubted the effectiveness of such legal rights in most instances when individual shareholders had suffered loss. On the issue of whether it was just, fair and reasonable to impose a duty of care, Bingham had no doubt that it was reasonable. The defendant's argument that it was not fair and reasonable to impose a duty was based on a number of factors. These included: the difficulty of obtaining indemnity insurance, the cost of audit work would be increased, the risk of liability might cause firms to decline undertaking audit work and finally the possibility of auditors being exposed 'to claims indeterminate in number and unquantifiable in amount for periods which could not be calculated' (p.810). It was Bingham's contention that all of these fears and claims could be adequately dealt with. He believed it unlikely that auditors would be subject to numerous claims or that they would decline work because of the fear of litigation. Additionally, he thought it would be difficult for plaintiffs to establish their claims against auditors. To do so they would have to overcome certain barriers. First, they must show that the auditors had not exercised an adequate degree of care and skill. Second, they must prove that they had relied upon the financial statements. Lastly, they have to demonstrate that financial loss occurred. It was Bingham's opinion that if a plaintiff could overcome all these barriers it was just and reasonable that they had some form of redress.

On considering Caparo as investors both Bingham and Taylor believed that proximity was absent and therefore no duty of care was owed. It is interesting that Bingham did not entirely rule out the possibility that in the future the law might evolve so that a duty was owed to investors. He stated, however, that even if Caparo could show sufficient proximity their action should still fail because it would not be just and reasonable. On this issue he accepted the argument that extending the scope of duty to investors is unlikely to affect the work carried out by the auditors, although many would argue that extension of duty would increase risk and require the auditors to exercise greater care. His main concern seemed to be the financial implications of extending liability. He, however, concluded:

> Time and experience may show such an extension to be desirable or necessary. It is, however, preferable that analogical developments of this kind should be gradual and cautious (p.813).

Touche Ross appealed against the judgement in the Court of Appeal to the House of Lords. There, the appeal was heard before Lords Bridge, Roskill, Ackner, Oliver and Jauncey. Lord Bridge considered that the requirement of proximity did not exist. In his view, an essential ingredient for proximity to be present, was that:

> The defendant knew that his statement would be communicated to the plaintiff, either as an individual or as a member of an identifiable class, specifically in connection with a particular transaction or transactions of a particular kind (for instance, in a prospectus inviting investment) and that the plaintiff would be very likely to rely on it for the purpose of deciding whether or not to enter upon that transaction or upon a transaction of that kind (p.368).

He also contended that even if there was sufficient proximity he could not see how any duty owed extended beyond that of protecting an individual shareholder from any losses they incurred from their present holding of shares. If a shareholder purchased additional shares he regarded them as being in the same position as any other investor; neither were owed a duty of care.

Lords Oliver and Jauncey, on examination of company legislation, reached the conclusion that the primary purpose of annual financial statements was to enable those with a proprietorial interest to exercise their given rights. They accepted that the annual financial statements could be used for assisting in the making of investment decisions but did not believe that the legislation was drafted with that purpose in mind. Lord Oliver contested Caparo's view that the defendant's knowing that the financial statements might be used by acquirers was sufficient to establish the necessary proximity. His view was that this was an instance of failing to differentiate between proximity and foreseeability. It may well be foreseeable that acquirers are likely to rely on financial statements but this does not mean that the relationship between the auditors and the acquirer is close and direct enough to satisfy the test of proximity. In a similar vein he suggested that in the *JEB Fasteners* and *Twomax* cases the courts had prescribed to the interpretation of Lord Wilberforce's judgement in the *Anns* case that treated foreseeability and proximity as synonymous, an interpretation he regarded as being rejected in subsequent cases heard before the House of Lords. Lord Jauncey went further and stated that the reasoning in the *Twomax* case was unsound 'and that the decision cannot be supported' (p.407). The net effect of this was to allow the appeal of Touche Ross and deny the claim by Caparo plc.

Reaction to the decision

As might be expected some members of the accounting profession welcomed the decision by the House of Lords (*Accountancy*, March, 1990, p.8). It is interesting, however, that the editorial in the same edition of *Accountancy* criticized the judgement because the court's view of the auditors' responsibilities was out of touch with 'commercial reality'. The editorial maintained that one had to strike a balance between leaving third parties who have relied on the financial statements no redress for economic loss and exposing the auditors to massive claims which they might not be able to have fully covered by insurance. The claim about auditors being exposed to 'indeterminate liability' was contested by Graham Stacy, a senior partner in Price Waterhouse. He is quoted in *Accountancy* (March 1990) as stating:

> The [Caparo] ruling does reduce the range of people to whom auditors owe a duty of care, and that is slightly comforting, but in my experience most claims arise through failure to discover a major fraud, and in most cases it is the company that brings the action. (p.8)

If Stacy's experience holds generally, it would seem to suggest that concern over leaving auditors exposed to massive negligence claims from third parties is misplaced. Shortly afterwards, it was reported in *Accountancy* (April 1992) that some of the participants at a Board for Chartered Accountants in Business discussion meeting called for a reversal of the *Caparo* decision. The reasons for this call seemed to be based on a need to bridge the expectations gap and it being in the long-term interest of the profession to be seen to be responsible for their activities. At this meeting Michael Fowle, an audit partner of KPMG, advocated that auditors should be 'responsible not only to the shareholders, but to anybody who may reasonably place reliance on the accounts' (p.19). The participants who suggested that the *Caparo* decision should be overturned also recommended that auditors should be allowed to limit their liability.

Various ways of how this might be achieved are discussed later in the chapter.

The criteria of foreseeability and proximity

In the *Caparo* case all three courts argued that there was a need to distinguish between foreseeability and proximity. It was stressed that, first, the defendant must be able to foresee that damage could occur as a result of misstatements and, second, there must be proximity between the plaintiff and the defendant. The determination of whether foreseeability is present does not appear to be a particularly stringent test. On the concept of proximity the judges in the *Caparo* case seemed to believe that there was no one particular test that could be applied to determine if proximity was present. The judges argued that decisions would have to be taken on a case-by-case basis. It would be on the basis of the facts in each case that courts would decide whether proximity was present. Evans (1989) criticized the Court of Appeal's emphasis on a close and direct relationship, believing it to be too general and vague to be of much use. Quoting from the *Hedley Byrne* case, he suggests that the appropriate test is 'when there has been an express or implied voluntary assumption of responsibility' (p.17).

However, as North (1964) points out one of the least satisfactory aspects of the *Hedley Byrne* case was the judges' differing views as to what constitutes a special relationship. This prompted North to argue that the lack of a defined test for proximity is likely to lead to uncertainty as to when a duty of care exists. Hartshorne (2008) argues that after the Caparo judgement and up to about 2005, proximity had become a somewhat neglected concept in determining if a duty of care is owed. However, since then it has become more central in legal decisions. This oscillation seems to be caused by differences of opinion over whether proximity is a concept in its own right that can be used in determining if a duty of care is owed. Some argue that it is simply a statement or category that is used to bound the extent of liability when the main concern is the fairness and reasonableness of imposing a duty of care in a particular situation.

The purpose of financial statements

The issue raised in the House of Lords judgement concerned the purpose of financial statements. It was evident that the judges considered the purpose was for shareholders to exercise control over the company and that, to this end, the Companies Acts gave the shareholders the power to appoint and remove directors and auditors. Thus, the obvious recourse for shareholders who are not satisfied with the performance of the directors or auditors is to vote to replace them. This view of the financial statements as a means to enable the directors to exercise their stewardship function might be regarded today as a rather nineteenth-century view. The function of the financial statements also concerned Lord Justice Bingham in the Court of Appeal. He suggested that there were two answers to the question of their function – the company lawyer's answer and the commercial man's answer. In the former the purpose is to enable shareholders to exercise their statutory rights. In the latter the function is to provide information to enable shareholders to decide whether they should sell, retain or increase their holding of shares. Bingham could see no reason to reject either of these answers. It can be argued that the House of Lords viewpoint is out of line with commercial practice. Evidence for this is the detailed listing rules issued by the Financial Services Authority, whose purpose is partly to ensure proper disclosure enabling investors to determine the value of securities when purchasing and selling.

Developments in case law since *Caparo*

A number of cases involving alleged auditor negligence have been heard before the courts since the *Caparo* case. These have not generally changed the law relating to whom the auditors owe a duty of care, but they are interesting because they have helped clarify certain issues and have solidified the position reached by the judges in the *Caparo* case. They are also useful because they illustrate ways in which plaintiffs attempt to distinguish between the case they have brought and the *Caparo* case to give a chance of a successful action against auditors. Furthermore, the judges in summing up provide insights into the issues they consider important when reaching a decision as to whether auditors hold a duty of care to a specific third party.

One of the first cases involving a firm of auditors after the *Caparo* case was that of *James McNaughton Paper Group Ltd. vs Hicks Anderson & Co.* (1991). The facts of this case are as follows: Hicks Anderson & Co. was a firm of accountants who audited M.K. Papers Group Holdings Ltd (M.K. Papers) which was the subject of a successful takeover bid by the plaintiffs, James

Trade receivables and trade payables.

After the meeting Mr Pritchard sent McNaughton a schedule of debtors and creditors and various other documents.

McNaughton Ltd. At the time of the proposed takeover the draft financial statements of M.K. Papers for the year ended 30 June 1982 showed a net loss of £48 094. An employee of the auditors, a Mr Pritchard, prior to the takeover, attended a meeting between the chairmen of M.K. Papers and of James McNaughton Ltd. At this meeting the draft balance sheet of M.K. Papers was discussed along with various issues related to debtors and creditors. Mr Pritchard was specifically asked by Mr McNaughton whether the company was breaking even or doing marginally worse and the latter agreed that this was the case. A few months after the takeover the company accountant of James McNaughton Ltd performed a detailed investigation of the financial statements of M.K. Papers and found a number of errors. As a result, James NcNaughton Ltd brought an action against the auditors, Hicks Anderson & Co. At first sight it may seem here that there was sufficient closeness of proximity between the plaintiff and the auditors to result in the latter owing a duty of care to the former. The auditors would appear to have known that the plaintiffs were going to rely on the financial statements for the purposes of the takeover. The court, however, decided that no duty was owed to the plaintiff, their decision being influenced by the following:

- The financial statements were produced for M.K. Papers.
- The financial statements were in draft, which indicated that further work would be required before they were finalized and therefore the plaintiffs were not entitled to treat them as final financial statements.
- Apart from Mr Pritchard attending a meeting with the chairman of James McNaughton Ltd, there was no indication that he took any other part in the takeover negotiations.
- The draft financial statements showed that the company was making a loss, so it was obvious that M.K. Papers was in a poor state.
- Since the transaction involved experienced businessmen it was to be expected that James McNaughton would consult their own accountancy advisors.
- When Mr Pritchard replied to the question posed by Mr McNaughton, his reply was a general answer and did not affect any of the figures in the financial statements. Furthermore, Mr Pritchard was not to know that the plaintiffs would rely on the answer 'without any further inquiry or advice' (p.654).

In some respects this case would seem to have placed more obstacles before third parties wishing to bring actions against auditors, bearing in mind that there was a clearly identifiable third party using the financial statements and a specific transaction. It is difficult to see what other factors could have been present which would have increased the proximity between the parties. The emphasis given by the court to the financial statements being in draft would seem to suggest that less reliance can be placed on them. However, there is no indication in the case report as to whether the final financial statements differed from those in draft. The issue of James McNaughton Ltd consulting their own advisors would also seem to hinder the likelihood of success of a third party action. This is especially so because, subsequent to the takeover, McNaughton's own accountants only found the errors after detailed investigation. This raises the question of the level of access any advisor would need to have to the books and records of the takeover target before there would be any chance of discovering errors and mistakes. We can also ask whether the courts would have still decided that the plaintiffs should have consulted their own financial advisors had the case not involved experienced businessmen; if not, what principle is being invoked which supports the distinction between different users? In any event, the suggestion that the plaintiffs should consult their own advisors seems, at least partially, to question the purpose of the annual audit, if it is not to discover material fraud and error in the financial statements.

As an aside, the agreed takeover price was only £12 000 so there may not have been much economic incentive for the plaintiffs to employ their own advisors.

Another case (heard in 1991), which involved a takeover bidder bringing an action for negligence against a number of parties was *Morgan Crucible Co. vs Hill Samuel & Co.* As a preliminary issue the plaintiffs tried to convince the Court of Appeal that their case could be distinguished from that of *Caparo* and therefore should be heard before the courts. Thus, at this stage the plaintiffs were not attempting to prove that the defendants had been negligent nor that they necessarily owed them a duty of care. The facts of the case were as follows: Morgan Crucible launched a takeover bid for First Castle in December 1985. As is usual in a takeover bid, the directors of First Castle made a number of representations to their shareholders, in what are known as defence documents. Morgan Crucible stated that they relied on the financial statements of First Castle for the years ended 31 January 1984 and 1985, unaudited interim statements for the six months to July 1985, a profit forecast First Castle had issued on 24 January 1986 and other financial information contained in the defence documents. They asserted that these various documents had been negligently prepared and were misleading and that if they had known the true facts they would never have made their takeover bid. The House of Lords' judgement in the *Caparo* case had recently been made and therefore the major issue facing Morgan Crucible was to distinguish their case from that of *Caparo*. If they could do not do this, the action by Morgan Crucible would automatically fail. The main obstacle facing Morgan Crucible was to establish that there was a sufficiently close relationship (proximity) between them and the defendants to establish that the latter owed them a duty of care. The plaintiffs convinced the judges that their case could be distinguished from that of *Caparo*. In particular, the plaintiffs argued that they were not asserting that the defendant owed them a duty prior to making a bid. Instead their case hinged on the documents and information circulated by First Castle after they had made their initial bid. Thus, their identity was known to all the defendants and the defence documents contained information on which they knew Morgan Crucible would rely. The judges were persuaded by their arguments and determined that the various defendants had a case to answer and that it should go to trial.

The action was brought against the financial advisors, Hill Samuel & Co. of First Castle Electronics plc (First Castle being the company taken over) together with their auditors, Judkins & Co., and the directors of the company.

The plaintiff's case had already been heard in the Chancery Division where the judge held that the case could not essentially be distinguished from *Caparo* and therefore, following the latter, no duty could be owed to the plaintiffs. The plaintiffs appealed and it is with the appeal in the Court of Appeal with which we are concerned here.

This case is interesting because it illustrates how, after the *Caparo* decision, plaintiffs bringing an action for negligence have to show that in some way the circumstances of their particular case were not identical with those of *Caparo*.

We will conclude this section by examining other recent UK cases involving auditors. The first of these, *Galoo Ltd and others vs Bright Grahame Murray* (a firm) (1994), was heard in the Court of Appeal; the appeal having arisen as a result of an earlier judgement in the High Court. There were three plaintiffs in the case, Galoo Ltd, Gamine Ltd and Hillsdown Holdings plc. The defendant was a firm of accountants who were the auditors of Galoo and Gamine. In the period from 1987 to 1993 Hillsdown Holdings took over Gamine and

The issue at stake in the appeal was whether or not the plaintiffs' case was bound to fail because of preceding judgements, such as *Caparo*, and hence should not go to a full trial.

made loans totalling over £30 million to Galoo and Gamine. The plaintiffs alleged that the inventories of Galoo were overstated and that, if the auditors had performed their duties with reasonable care and skill, it would have been apparent that the companies were in financial trouble. The basis for the action of Galoo and Gamine was that, if they had known the true financial picture of the companies, they would have ceased trading earlier and hence would have avoided incurring further losses. The judges had to decide whether the further losses were caused by the negligence of the auditors or were merely the occasion for the loss. The judges reviewed a number of similar cases and considered a number of principles that might be used in a case such as this, before deciding that the auditors' negligence did not cause the losses. In the words of Judge Glidewell:

Galoo, which was in liquidation, was the wholly owned subsidiary of Gamine.

In essence Galoo was the only subsidiary of Gamine and therefore the latter's financial position was intertwined with that of Galoo.

> The breach of duty by the defendants gave the opportunity to Galoo and Gamine to incur and to continue to incur trading losses; it did not cause those trading losses, in the sense in which the word 'cause' is used in law. (p.505)

In respect of the action by Hillsdown Holdings, the defendants knew that they would rely on the financial statements; indeed the purchase price paid for the shares was based on a multiple of the net profits of Gamine. In addition, the defendant firm wrote a letter to Hillsdown confirming Gamine's net profit for the year ended 31 December 1986 and the shareholders funds of both Gamine and Galoo as at that date. Because the defendants knew that the financial statements were to be used by Hillsdown for determining the price to be paid for the shares of Gamine the case could be distinguished from that of Caparo. The defendants pointed out that the financial statements submitted to Hillsdown were only draft financial statements. The judge, however, noted that these financial statements were seemingly used for the purpose of calculating the purchase consideration, and he therefore appeared to consider that they were in draft to be irrelevant. In support of their position the defendants claimed that the acquisition agreement gave the accountants of Hillsdown right of access to the books of the companies and to review their final financial statements and because of this the defendants did not owe a duty of care.

Hillsdown acquired shares in Gamine in two separate transactions. Here we are only concerned with the initial purchase of shares.

ACTIVITY 19.2

Put yourself in the position of the defendants and outline the arguments you would use to show that you did not owe a duty of care given that the plaintiff had the right to examine the books of the companies, Gamine and Galoo.

It is likely that your argument runs along the following lines. The plaintiff, Hillsdown, was undertaking a major transaction and was experienced in business. They appear to have given some thought to the nature of the transaction because the acquisition agreement gave their accountants the right of access to the companies' books. This indicated that they acknowledged the need for an independent check on the books and records by their own advisors. If they did not exercise that right, that was their decision, but it may have meant that errors that their advisors might have detected remained undiscovered. By failing to use their advisors they contributed in some sense to the losses they incurred. As a result, the defendants should not be held responsible for the losses incurred by the plaintiffs, which could have been avoided if they had instructed their own advisors to examine the books of the two companies.

The above arguments rely on an assumption that the plaintiff's own advisors would have discovered the overstatement of inventories. The likelihood of this being detected would depend on the extent of access the advisors were given and the amount of effort and time they expended in investigating the books of the companies. One might argue that, since the overstatement was caused by a fraud, undetected by the auditors over a period of time, it would not have been easy to discover. The judge in the Galoo case made a similar argument and concluded that the defendant's proposition should not be accepted. As a result the court decided that Hillsdown could bring an action against the defendant and for this to be decided in full before the courts. The Court of Appeal, however, ruled that Hillsdown had failed to establish that a duty of care was owed to them by the defendants in respect of money it had lent to Gamine or an amount paid to purchase additional shares in that company subsequent to the initial purchase. The reason the latter was dismissed was that the second acquisition was carried out under the terms of a supplemental rather than the original agreement.

It is interesting to note that the defendant's arguments were prompted by the judgements of one of the judges in the *Caparo* case. In that case Lord Oliver laid down a number of criteria which must be considered before one could deduce that there was a relationship between two parties, giving rise to a duty of care. In particular, in respect of a statement or of advice, he stated 'it is known either actually or inferentially, that the advice so communicated is likely to be acted upon by the advisee for that purpose *without independent enquiry*' (p.384) (italics added). This shows that when a judgement is made, particularly in the House of Lords, the wording of previous judgements will be very important in allowing scope for arguments to be put forward either by defendants or plaintiffs in future cases.

We now turn to considering the case of *ADT Ltd vs BDO Binder Hamlyn* (1996). Binder Hamlyn were the joint auditors of Brittania Securities Group (BSG) which was taken over by ADT Ltd. The auditors had signed an unqualified audit report (in October 1989) in respect of the financial statements of BSG for the year ended 30 June 1989. Before ADT Ltd made the bid for BSG they arranged a meeting with a partner (Mr Bishop) in Binder Hamlyn. At this meeting the partner was asked if he stood by the results of the 1989 audit. Subsequently, ADT acquired BSG for £105 million. After the takeover ADT alleged that because of the misstatement of a number of items, the financial statements did not show a true and fair view and that BSG was only worth £40 million. They sued Binder Hamlyn for £65 million being the difference between what they alleged BSG was worth and what they paid. Although just prior to signing the financial statements Binder Hamlyn became aware that ADT was interested in acquiring BSG, it was not for this reason that ADT believed that Binder Hamlyn owed them a duty of care. Instead, ADT rested their case on what was said at the meeting between Mr Bishop – the partner of Binder Hamlyn – and some directors of ADT in January 1990. This meeting and the confirmation that the financial statements of BSG gave a true and fair view was considered sufficient to create the necessary proximity between the auditors and ADT. The directors of ADT claimed that the meeting was an important step in the takeover process. The partner of Binder Hamlyn claimed that he did not believe that ADT considered the meeting as important as they alleged. The judge, in concluding that the meeting appeared to be an important and final step before ADT committed itself to the takeover, appears to have placed greater reliance on the directors' perception of the meeting. The judge thus ruled that by answering the questions relating to the financial statements the partner had assumed responsibility to ADT. The other ingredients necessary to find that the auditors owed a duty to ADT were also present; the partner knew that ADT were interested in taking over BSG and that they would rely upon the financial statements of the latter when making their bid.

In their defence Binder Hamlyn argued that the partner had been asked a question at short notice and that he was answering in respect of financial statements which had been issued some months prior to the meeting. The judge did not accept these arguments; stating that the partner did not have to answer the questions, or that he could have given a disclaimer or some other qualified answer. As a result of this the judge found the auditors negligent and ordered them to pay damages of £65 million and interest of £40 million. Binder Hamlyn at the time indicated that they would appeal against the decision but subsequently they settled out of court with ADT for £50 million. ADT presumably settled for the lower amount to save them the cost of any further action and the possibility that the Court of Appeal might reverse the decision of the High Court. Students may care to ponder on two issues:

- The extent of the damages that flowed from a simple reaffirmation by the partner in Binder Hamlyn that the financial statements of BSG gave a true and fair view.
- The difficulty the partner was in when asked on the spot whether the financial statements gave a true and fair view. Since he had already signed the financial statements to that effect how realistic would it have been to expect him to say anything other than he stood by his judgement? To say otherwise could at least partially be perceived as admitting that he did not have confidence in his opinion.

Andrew was one of the trustees.

The company were air travel organizers.

The letter was written on the same day as the deadline for renewal of the licence.

In the next case in this section, *Andrew and others vs Kounnis Freeman* (1999), four trustees of the Air Travel Trust and the Civil Aviation Authority brought an action against the firm of accountants, Kounnis Freeman. Kounnis Freeman were the auditors of a company, Flight Co. (UK) plc, who, to retain their Air Travel Organizer's Licence (ATOL), had to supply to the Civil Aviation Authority (CAA), audited financial statements which indicated certain conditions had been met in respect of the company's solvency. Subsequently, Flight Co. (UK) plc went bankrupt leaving many holidaymakers stranded abroad. The Air Travel Trust on behalf of CAA incurred considerable expenditure (£5 750 000) in repatriating these holidaymakers and fulfilling forward bookings. Initially the plaintiffs had to show that Kounnis Freeman owed them a duty of care. Central to this case was the fact that the auditors had written directly to the Civil Aviation Authority, confirming that certain financial conditions had been fulfilled and enclosing a copy of the audited financial statements. In addition the auditors had included as a heading in their letter the abbreviation ATOL. The judge decided that the auditors had effectively acknowledged that the financial statements would be used in the decision by the CAA to renew the licence of Flight Co. (UK) plc and that it was reasonable for the plaintiffs to consider that the auditors had assumed a duty of care to them. In summing up the judge drew attention to the fact that, because the letter from the auditors arrived on the deadline for renewal, there was no time for independent evaluation of the information supplied by the auditors and that it indicated that they knew the purpose of the letter and of the audited financial statements.

We will conclude the discussion of case law by considering the case of *Royal Bank of Scotland vs Bannerman Johnstone Maclay and Others* (2002). You will remember that we referred to this case in Chapter 16 where we disused its implication for the auditors' report. Briefly, the facts of this case were as follows: Bannerman *et al.* were the auditors of APC Limited, and its wholly owned subsidiary APC Civils Limited, both of which were involved in the construction industry. The Royal Bank of Scotland lent considerable sums of money both to APC and its subsidiary and had an option to subscribe for a substantial proportion of the share capital of APC. The plaintiffs exercised the option to purchase shares in 1996 (approximately 30 per cent of the share capital of APC) and in addition made a further investment in the equity of APC in 1996 and 1997. One of the conditions imposed by the plaintiffs for providing finance to APC was that they were sent each year a copy of the audited financial statements. In 1998 receivers were appointed to APC and its subsidiary. It was alleged by the plaintiffs that the financial statements supplied to them had been negligently prepared. In particular the auditors had failed to detect a fraud arising from certain members of the management of APC falsifying invoices and capitalizing expenditure, thus overstating the performance of the company. The plaintiffs claimed that, had they known the true state of the financial performance of APC, they would have advanced no further loans to the company. Because of the close connection of the auditors with APC and their knowledge of its finances and its reliance on loans from the plaintiffs, the latter claimed that the auditors knew they relied on the financial statements when deciding whether to maintain, increase or withdraw their financial support to APC.

The case was heard in the Outer House of the Court of Session in Scotland in 2002.

One of the individuals who colluded in the fraud was a Mr McMahon who for part of the period covered in the action for negligence acted as financial controller of APC but was on secondment from the auditors.

Central to the defendant's claim that they did not owe a duty of care to the plaintiffs was the judgement in *Galoo Ltd vs Bright Grahame Murray* (1994). In that case Lord Justice Glidewell stated that if:

> The auditor is expressly made aware that a particular identified bidder will rely on the audited financial statements or other statements provided by the auditor, and intends that the bidder should so rely, the auditor will be under a duty of care to the bidder for the breach of which he may be liable.

Counsel for the defendants, APC. emphasized that for sufficient proximity to exist, the auditors must intend for the plaintiffs to rely on the financial statements. In other words the mere knowledge that it was likely the plaintiffs would rely on the financial statements is not sufficient to give rise to a duty of care. Instead, the plaintiffs had to prove that the auditors intended the plaintiffs to rely on the audited financial statements. For the plaintiffs, counsel sought to differentiate the circumstances of this case from that of *Caparo*.

Specifically, they emphasized that the defendants knew the identity of the plaintiffs, the purpose to which the financial statements were to be put and that the possibility of liability to an indeterminate class would not arise in the present case. Counsel for the plaintiffs also argued that the judgement by Lord Justice Glidewell in the Galoo case did not mean that 'a duty of care would only arise if the auditor intended that the third party rely on the financial statements'. In summing up the case Lord Macfadyen accepted that the facts presented before him suggested:

> The existence of a relationship of proximity between the defenders and the pursuers, giving rise to a duty owed by the defenders to the pursuers to take reasonable care to save them from suffering loss through relying on the financial statements when making decisions.

Lord Macfadyen also stated that if the defendants, on learning that the plaintiffs had a right to see the audited financial statements for the purposes of their lending decision, had issued a disclaimer for the consequences of any reliance the plaintiffs placed on the statements, then it would have been impossible to infer that the auditors had assumed responsibility to the plaintiffs. In other words the auditors would not have owed a duty of care to the plaintiffs. It is within this context that the Audit and Assurance Faculty of the ICAEW issued their recommendation that the audit report should include a paragraph disclaiming any responsibility to third parties.

See Chapter 16, page 637.

The Inner House is essentially a court of appeal against decisions of the Outer House.

Subsequently, the defendants appealed against the decision of the Outer House and the case was heard in the Inner House of the Court of Session in Scotland in 2005. The appeal was based on the defendants view that to be liable they had to intend for the financial statements to be relied upon by the pursuers and the need for the concept of purpose to be met could be inferred from the judgements handed down in the *Caparo* case. The judges disagreed and did not believe that the concept of purpose was necessary nor could it be derived from the *Caparo* judgement. Thus, the Inner House upheld the view of the Outer House that the case should be heard with evidence before a court to determine if a duty of care was owed and whether the auditors had been negligent. A final interesting feature of this case relates to the disclaimer issue discussed in Chapter 16. When considering the lack of a disclaimer one of the judges noted he did not see any reason 'why a failure to disclaim against a third party should not in appropriate circumstances be a factor pointing to an assumption of responsibility or to the creation of a relationship of proximity'. This is an issue that would be of concern to auditors and is likely to make them even more likely to ensure that they include a disclaimer clause on information with which they are associated. You may wish to ponder on the situation where a company borrows money from a bank which requires audited financial statements which in turn contain a disclaimer clause. The probability of the bank being able to make a successful third-party claim for negligence against the auditors would be much reduced and therefore should the company default on the loan through, for instance, being insolvent, the bank may not be able to recover much of its loan and would be in a high-risk position. An obvious strategy the bank could undertake is to draw up the loan agreement containing a condition that audited financial statements be prepared specifically for the bank making the loan. In this way the bank may ensure it can meet the tests outlined in the *Caparo* case and has some possibility of successfully suing the auditor. Of course, the auditor may not be willing to face

Unfortunately, the issues and the evidence in this case did not come before the courts as the parties settled out of court in September 2006.

the additional risk that might arise in this situation. The eventual outcome here is likely to be dependent on the power of the various parties, the bank, auditor and company, the extent to which the company can obtain finance from different lenders, the auditors' assessment of the risk of the client defaulting on the loan and so on. We hope you can see how a judgement in a particular case can have practical and far-ranging implications.

This brings us to the end of our review of the relevant case law relating to auditor liability. We conclude by emphasizing that any student of auditing should be aware of the way that case law has developed over the years and the thinking behind the various judgements.

AUDITING STANDARDS

In a number of chapters in this book we have made reference to relevant auditing standards. Given their status within auditing, compliance with them would seem to be a logical first step for the auditors, if they wish to resist successfully a claim for damages. This is expressly stated in Paragraph 23 of the APB statement the 'Scope and authority of pronouncements', which states:

> All relevant APB pronouncements and in particular Auditing Standards are likely to be taken into account when the adequacy of the work of auditors is being considered in a court of law or in other contested situations.

Their importance is lent weight by the Companies Act 2006 which requires recognized supervisory bodies (RSBs) to 'have rules and practices as to the technical standards to be applied in statutory audit work and the manner in which those standards are to be applied in practice' (Sch. 10, Part 2, para 10, CA 2006). The RSBs have adopted published auditing standards to meet this requirement. In addition, APB has stated that non-compliance with ISAs by audit practitioners may render them liable to regulatory action by their RSB including the possibility of withdrawal of registration.

There are, however, a number of limitations in using the standards as a means of defence:

- The standards in issue do not cover all areas of auditing.
- They only contain general guidance and leave scope for interpretation and implementation. The auditing standard on evidence, for instance, states that auditors need to obtain sufficient appropriate evidence on which to base an audit opinion. Although the standard outlines matters, such as the persuasiveness of the evidence, which are likely to influence sufficiency, relevance and reliability, the auditors are still left with the task of determining how persuasive a certain piece of evidence is. The authors do not wish to give the impression that matters such as these can be reduced to some simple mathematical calculation.
- The standards and guidelines are the auditing profession's view of what constitutes good practice but, in the end, it is what the courts believe to be good practice that matters. The courts may well acknowledge the usefulness of the profession's standards but at the same time assert that they (the courts) are, at times, concerned with wider issues such as 'the public interest' and are therefore the ultimate arbiters of what constitutes appropriate professional practice.

PROFESSIONAL CONDUCT

See ACCA bye laws 8 and 11.

As well as being subject to criminal and civil proceedings, auditors can also be disciplined by their own professional body. For instance, ACCA's regulations on conduct make it clear that where members or students are convicted of offences before the courts they can also be disciplined by the Chartered Association. These rules (which are similar for all the major accounting bodies) state that misconduct encompasses acts likely to bring discredit to the member, to the Chartered Association, or to the accounting profession. The liability to disciplinary action can arise both from offences relating to the individual's professional work and from the individual's personal life. The important feature is whether or not it brings discredit to one or more of the above persons or bodies. For instance, if a member was found guilty of robbing the local Post Office, it is likely that the individual would face disciplinary action from their professional body. This is because, if accountants or auditors are to be trusted by clients, they must be seen to be honest and persons of integrity. Additionally, given the nature of accounting, there is likely to be a loss of faith in accountants if they take no action against members convicted of theft. The rules also make clear that not all offences need lead to disciplinary action. If an accountant or auditor were to be convicted of a speeding offence, it is unlikely that the individual would have to answer to the professional body. In the final resort, it is up to the Disciplinary Committee of the relevant accounting body to decide, on the merits of each case, whether a specific conviction amounts to (serious) misconduct. If the committee decides it is, a decision has to be made as to the appropriate penalty, based on their perception of the seriousness of the offence.

Auditors can be disciplined by their professional body, even though they have not been convicted of an offence. This might arise if a company's shareholders or, more likely, its management made a formal complaint to the accountant's professional body about the quality of the auditors' work. A further example would be the case of a company changing its auditors, where the outgoing auditors persistently refused to answer questions put to them by the new auditors and to pass on to them papers which are the property of the client. In such a case, it is likely that a valid complaint could be made to the relevant professional body. It would then be up to that body to investigate the complaint and decide if the outgoing auditors should be disciplined.

POTENTIAL WAYS OF REDUCING AUDITOR LIABILITY

The accounting profession (like other professions) has shown considerable concern about the extent of their liability to third parties. This concern was given impetus by the increase in the number of negligence claims against auditors and the amounts involved. Auditors have also claimed that it is increasingly costly for them to obtain professional indemnity insurance. Furthermore, audit firms assert that they can no longer obtain full insurance cover, that is, the level of insurance they are able to obtain is limited to a predefined upper percentage of any claim made against them. The consequence is that the auditors themselves carry some of the risk and in the event of being successfully sued, the partnership would have to meet a proportion of any damages awarded out of their own funds. Resulting from this concern a number of major reports and documents have been produced in recent years and in this part of the chapter we shall briefly mention the more important ones.

- The first, the Likierman report, was published in 1989. Its remit was to look into problems faced in respect of liability for negligence by three professions – the auditing profession, the construction profession (including architects, building surveyors and civil engineers) and other surveyors, for example, property valuers.
- The second report, also commissioned by the Department of Trade and Industry, was issued following an investigation by the Common Law Team of the Law Commission titled 'Feasibility Investigation of Joint and Several Liability', published in 1996. The objective of this investigation was to determine 'whether a full Law Commission project on the law of joint and several liability should be undertaken'.
- The third report was a consultative document issued by the Department of Trade and Industry in December 2003 titled 'Director and auditor liability: a consultative document'. This document which was part of the process of reforming company law in the UK sought the opinions of interested parties on auditor and director liability.

The report, which was commissioned by the Department of Trade and Industry, bore the title 'Professional Liability: Report of the Study Teams', but it is often referred to simply as the Likierman report after the chairman, Professor Andrew Likierman, of the Steering Group.

In addition to the above major reports a number of representations and reports have been produced by various professional bodies arguing for changes or amendments to the present law relating to professional negligence. The topic of auditor liability was also considered by the Company Law Review Steering Group. This committee, established by the government in the UK, was charged with investigating how company law should be reformed. The Steering Group produced a Final Report in 2001, 'Modern Company Law For a Competitive Economy'. Subsequently, white papers were produced in 2002 and 2005 leading to a Companies Bill being introduced in the House of Lords in November 2005. After considerable debate and amendment this Bill became the Companies Act 2006 which received Royal Assent in November 2006. Although the Companies Act covers the complete scope of the regulation of companies, considerable controversy and debate relating to its provisions revolved around the issue of director and auditor liability.

We discuss the provisions relating to limiting auditor liability below.

All of this activity signifies the concern that the government and certain professional groups have about the potential liability for negligence of auditors and directors. It is not, however, only the damages that may be awarded against these parties that is of concern, but also the legal and associated defence costs of any action. Furthermore, the bad publicity that might be incurred as a result of litigation may damage the reputation of auditors. This has prompted auditors to settle many of the cases brought against them out of court. The recognition that auditors wish to avoid the considerable costs and the attendant publicity of a court case may actually encourage plaintiffs to bring actions. In the section below we outline some of the suggestions and possible solutions that have been put forward as ways of reducing auditors' potential liability.

Reform of the law relating to joint and several liability

Auditors and members of other professions claim that a major problem with the present law is the concept of joint and several liability. A major implication of this concept is that when more than one party is responsible for losses incurred by a third party, but one or more of the parties are insolvent or have limited resources, it is the defendant with the resources, or deepest pockets, that is left to shoulder the complete burden of any damages awarded in a court of law. In auditing, because auditors carry professional indemnity insurance, this ensures that they are always likely to be at least one of the parties a plaintiff sues. It may be argued that it is illogical for auditors to be responsible for the complete loss simply because they happen to be the party that has the resources to pay damages to a plaintiff. A possible solution would be for the auditors to be responsible for only a proportion of the liability, the proportion payable being calculated on the assumption that other possible defendants had sufficient funds to meet any obligation that might fall upon them. Although this would seem fairer to auditors, the innocent third party could then lose out through not being able to recover the full amount of the loss they have incurred. Since auditors are specifically employed to verify the financial statements, it may be argued that it is fairer that they suffer any loss rather than the innocent third party who has relied upon the financial statements. The Company Law Review Steering Group, referred to earlier, specifically considered the issue of proportionate liability and rejected it as a matter of principle because it might leave innocent parties bearing some of the loss they have incurred.

The most likely example here would be the company directors who are responsible for the financial statements upon which a third party may have relied but who have limited resources and therefore are not the most suitable target for any litigation by the third party.

Allocation of only a proportion is usually termed 'proportionate liability'.

Auditors were provided with some comfort as a result of changes in the 1989 Companies Act to s.310 of the 1985 Companies Act, which clarified the position in respect of companies purchasing insurance for their directors and officers. Prior to these changes s.310 effectively outlawed the exempting or indemnifying of officers or auditors from any liability of the company that may arise from their negligence. The changes to the section provided, however, that companies could purchase insurance for their directors, officers or auditors against any liability that may attach to them as a result of their negligence, default, breach of duty, or breach of trust in relation to the company. The purchasing of such insurance would provide resources for directors and officers, against which plaintiffs could claim. A limitation of directors' and officers' insurance is that the 1989 Companies Act provision did not make it compulsory for companies to purchase such insurance. Thus, where insurance is not purchased it is likely, even though directors may have some responsibility for losses suffered by plaintiffs, it will be the auditors who are sued. Note also that the Companies Act provisions relating to the purchase of insurance only apply to claims made against the directors and auditors by the company itself and not third parties. The extent to which this provision helped auditors depended on the amount of insurance purchased and anecdotal evidence suggests that the purchase of insurance for auditors was a rare event. Subsequently, the Companies Act 2006 revised the provisions relating to the purchase of insurance for directors, officers and auditors. The Companies Act 2006 retained the provision permitting a company to purchase insurance for its directors (s.233) but removed the provision relating to purchasing insurance for auditors. The rationale for this was because the 2006 Act introduced

The provisions of the 1989 Act were themselves slightly amended by the Companies (Audit, Investigations and Community Enterprise) Act 2004.

a new provision allowing auditors to arrange with the company a liability limitation agreement. We discuss these agreements in further detail below.

Before closing this part of the chapter, we briefly discuss the question of contributory negligence. This concept applies where a plaintiff can be said to have contributed to the loss they have suffered. If this is the case, any damages awarded against a defendant will be reduced to the extent that the plaintiff is judged to have been responsible for the loss. This concept can be applied in cases of tort, for instance, where the plaintiff is a third party. The scope for its application to negligence claims brought under contract is less clear. Where a negligence claim is brought under contract against auditors by their client company, it may be difficult to convince the courts that the plaintiff has contributed to their own losses as a result of, for instance, defective financial statements. This is because the auditors are specifically employed by the company to verify the financial statements, that is, it is their responsibility. If, however, the company suffers losses as a result of a fraud perpetrated by employees, and the auditors had warned the client about internal control deficiencies that the employees exploited, but the client did not act on their advice, the auditors have a greater probability of being successful in claiming contributory negligence on the part of the client. This possibility has been lent greater weight by the judgement in an Australian case involving auditors, *AWA Ltd vs Daniels* (1992). In this case the auditors were found negligent for losses suffered by the plaintiff because they did not report to the board of directors certain internal control weaknesses and inadequate accounting records. The auditors claimed that the client had contributed to the losses through their failure to put in place adequate internal controls. The courts accepted their argument and apportioned the liability between the auditors and the plaintiff. Thus the auditors were not found liable for the full amount of the losses suffered by the plaintiff.

The recent case of *Barings plc (in liquidation) and another vs Coopers & Lybrand* would also seem to support the application of the concept of contributory negligence.

They had informally discussed the weaknesses with management in the company.

You should note that the Company Law Review Steering Committee recommended that where directors or employees, either negligently or fraudulently, breach their duties to assist the auditors, this should give rise to civil liability. The implication is that such a breach of duties would result in fault being attributed to the company for the purpose of assessing contributory negligence. In cases brought under tort, although the concept of contributory negligence could be used by auditors, it may be difficult for them to convince a court that a third party contributed to their own loss when the latter are relying on financial statements and hence on the auditors' opinion. No doubt the plaintiff would claim that it is the auditors' responsibility to verify the financial statements and it is they who have access to the company records and not the plaintiff. Because of the uncertainty relating to the application and possible success of using contributory negligence as a defence, auditors have generally preferred to argue for a reform of the law relating to proportionate liability.

You may care to reflect on how in cases, such as that of *Galoo* discussed above, the law courts have indicated that plaintiffs need to take some responsibility for their actions.

Capping liability

It has been suggested that auditors should be able to limit the amount they would have to pay in damages for an individual audit, should they be sued. Some advocates suggested that the maximum amount could be based on some multiple of the company's audit fee for the client or some similar formula.

The Company Law Review Steering Group recommended that auditors should be allowed to limit, or cap, their liability both contractually with the client and in tort with third parties.

The Company Law Review Steering Group considered the possibility of a cap and suggested that s.310 should be amended to allow auditors to negotiate a cap or limit to their potential liability with their audit clients. Although the Companies Act 2006 did not provide for a cap in the form indicated above, it did include a provision for companies and auditors to implement a "liability limitation agreement". Thus s.534 provides that:

> A liability limitation agreement is an agreement that purports to limit the amount of a liability owed to a company by its auditors in respect of any negligence, default or breach of duty or trust, occurring in the course of the audit of accounts, of which the auditor may be guilty in relation to the company.

Such an agreement will only be effective if it satisfies certain conditions:

The authorization requirements for a private company are slightly different.

- It applies on an annual basis and thus needs to be renewed and if desired amended each year.
- In the case of a public company the company must obtain approval for the agreement in a general meeting.
- The agreement must contain certain terms relating to such issues as the limit to which the auditor's liability is subject.
- The agreement must not limit the auditor's liability to less than what is 'fair and reasonable'.

What is 'fair and reasonable' will have regard to the auditor's responsibilities, their contractual arrangement with the company and the professional standards expected of them.

One matter the Companies Act did not address was how the limitation should be determined, other than suggesting the agreement need not specify a sum of money or be based on a formula. This allows considerable freedom for companies and their auditors to determine what method is most appropriate in their circumstances. For instance, the agreement might specify that the auditor's liability be limited to a multiple of the audit fee paid. Since institutional shareholders have indicated a preference for proportional limitation agreements providing that the auditor's liability be limited to what is fair and reasonable in the circumstances it is likely, at least for public companies, that this is how agreements will be framed. In the situation where the audit failed to detect a fraud by an employee and the company suffered a financial loss, the court would have to decide what amount or percentage of the loss should fall on the auditor. In determining this the courts would look to the extent to which the auditors should have detected the fraud and also the extent to which the fraud should have been detected by the company or its employees. Where there is a liability limitation agreement the company is required to disclose this fact in the annual financial statements, along with the principal terms of the agreement and the date of the resolution agreeing the limitation.

The main impetus for including liability limitation agreements in the Companies Act was concern that, unless auditors received some protection, at some stage another of the Big Four audit firms might fail,. Furthermore, one or more large audit firms might exit the audit market and audit fees might have to increase because of the increased financial risks faced by auditors.

Similar rationale was used by the European Union when it issued a recommendation applicable to listed companies in June 2008 that the civil liability of auditors arising from a breach of their duties should be limited.

While the liability limitation agreements seem to go some way towards reducing the exposure of auditors, it should be remembered that the agreements only cover the auditor and the company, leaving auditors exposed to claims by third parties.

As the Companies Act legislation in respect of these agreements only came into force in April 2008 it is too early to conclude how they will operate in practice or how effective they will be in limiting auditors' liability. However, the early signs do not appear very promising. It would appear that there is a reluctance for large listed companies to enter into a limitation agreement and the Securities Exchange Commission in the US have indicated such agreements would not be acceptable for UK companies listed on a US stock exchange. Hence, it would appear that such agreements might be of limited value to auditors and the profession is likely, therefore, to pursue further changes in the legislation, perhaps seeking a statutory cap on auditors liability.

See article by Robert Bruce in *Accountancy*, May 2009.

Lastly, it should be added that the enactment of Companies Act provisions allowing auditors to negotiate a limitation on their liability was always a likely possibility given the amount of lobbying for it by the accounting profession and the fact that an Office of Fair Trading Report (OFT) in 2004 considered that liability caps would be competitively neutral.

The title of the OFT report is 'An assessment of the implications for competition of a cap on auditors' liability'.

Incorporation

Since the 1989 Companies Act, accounting firms have been able to change their form of organization from partnerships to limited liability companies. As a limited liability company the shareholders will only be liable for any unpaid share capital. Thus, the individual partners will have obtained shelter from personal bankruptcy, which would not be the case in a partnership, where the partners themselves are personally responsible. Whilst incorporation may save the individual partners from bankruptcy, if the damages are substantial the accounting firm itself could be forced into liquidation. The number of accounting firms that have chosen to incorporate is relatively small; the only big audit firm that incorporated when it had the opportunity to do so being a part of KPMG. It is believed that one of the main reasons why other audit firms have not incorporated is because of adverse taxation implications. Note also that, as a limited liability company, they are subject to company law and therefore have to prepare financial statements and disclose certain information.

These are likely to be the partners in the firm when it was a partnership.

Only that part of KPMG which audited major clients was incorporated. Non-audit parts of KPMG did not incorporate and the part of the firm responsible for smaller audit clients remained a partnership.

Limited liability partnerships

It may be argued that present partnership law, originating as it did many years ago, is not suitable as a mode of regulating the modern large partnerships now found in accounting and law. In particular, the requirement under partnership law that the partner's liability be unlimited is unfair and far too onerous a burden. It was argued by a number of large accounting firms that the original form of (unlimited liability) partnership was not appropriate as a trading vehicle in the environment that exists today. Therefore, a number of accounting firms argued that a new form of body should be introduced, namely, the

The Partnership Act was introduced in 1890.

limited liability partnership. In this type of partnership the partners would not be personally liable for the partnership liabilities and the resources available to meet successful negligence claims would be limited to the assets of the partnership. The idea of limiting personal liability was obviously one that appealed to many audit partners. However, during the 1990s some of the large accounting firms became concerned about the unwillingness of the UK government to enact legislation to facilitate the setting up of limited liability partnerships in the UK. As a result two of the (then) Big Five audit firms lobbied the legislative bodies in Jersey to enact limited liability partnership legislation. The Jersey parliament obviously saw the financial benefits of having large accounting practices based in Jersey, and it passed legislation that allowed the setting up of limited liability partnerships in 1997. The UK government became concerned about the possibility of large accounting firms setting up bases in Jersey and becoming limited liability partnerships there, and decided that there was a need to introduce similar legislation in the UK as quickly as possible. The legislation was hastily drafted and the Limited Liability Partnership Act was passed in 2000. It is interesting that accounting firms were relatively slow in taking advantage of this legislation. Finch and Freedman (2002) report that at January 2002 fewer than 30 member firms of ICAEW had become limited liability partnerships. Although the authors suggest the low take-up rate might be because of problems and limitations in incorporating as a limited liability partnership, it might also be argued that accounting firms were simply taking time out to thoroughly investigate the advantages and disadvantages of such incorporation. Indeed it is worth noting that at the time of writing all of the Big Four accounting firms have become limited liability partnerships. It is obvious that one of the main reasons for accounting firms becoming limited liability partnerships is the protection it affords individual partners should the accounting firm of which they are a partner be sued.

In passing, students should note that there are considerable potential legal and tax implications in setting up in Jersey.

The act came into force on 6 April 2001.

This includes KPMG that had, as we noted above, incorporated a part of the firm only a few years earlier.

Summary

In this book we have described the audit process in some detail and it should be clear that the whole process requires much imagination and careful thought from beginning to end. It is very demanding and is often described as a very onerous responsibility. We have shown you in this chapter that auditors can and do sometimes fail to exercise their duty to as high a standard as is expected of them. It is our view that the vast majority of the profession do behave with integrity but it is worth noting that the profession has not always moved with the times in the past and that, therefore, it is desirable for those of us concerned with auditing to reconsider the aims, objectives and procedures of auditing on a regular basis. In this chapter we have discussed the potential legal liabilities that auditors may face. The auditors' liability to criminal actions was briefly outlined. It was also shown that auditors, as well as owing a legal responsibility under civil law to the company, may in certain circumstances owe a duty to third parties and that for an action of negligence against auditors to succeed it must be shown that: they owed a duty to the party; the auditors did not exercise due care and skill; the party relied on the financial statements and the auditors' report; and that the party suffered loss as a result of the financial statements being misleading. A number of cases involving third party claims against auditors and the principles underlying those cases were discussed in some detail. The auditors' duty in relation to the auditors' responsibility under the rules of conduct of their professional body was also examined as was the role of auditing standards. We discussed a number of ways, such as capping, in which the auditors' potential liability could be reduced.

Key points of the chapter

- In recent years the prime concern of auditors in civil liability cases has been liability to third parties, because of: (a) the cost of obtaining indemnity insurance; (b) the many actions brought against auditors; (c) the level of damages; (d) the bad publicity from auditor negligence court cases.
- Although rare, accountants and auditors could be liable to criminal charges under the Theft Act 1968, Fraud Act 2006 or CA 2006.
- Auditors who give a clean opinion on financial statements which turn out not to be true and fair, may be sued by users who lose because of reliance on those statements, to compensate them for any loss they have suffered as a result of negligent work.
- For an action of negligence to succeed, it must be shown that the auditors owed a duty of care to the person bringing the action. Where a contractual relationship has been established, a duty of care exists and auditors can be sued by the company under contract law.
- The determination of whether an auditor owes a duty of care to third parties under tort has been a controversial matter that has received considerable media attention.
- Early case law seemed to suggest that if there was no contract between accountants/auditors and third parties, no duty was owed, the early view being typified in *Candler vs Crane Christmas & Co.* (1951).
- However, *Hedley Byrne & Co. vs Heller and Partners Ltd* (1963) established the principle that an action can be brought by a third party who can expect a duty of care from auditors. Auditors would be liable if they had been negligent and the third party had relied on the financial statements, where they knew or ought to have known that the financial statements were being prepared for the specific purpose or transaction which gave rise to the loss, and that they would be shown to and relied on by third parties in that particular connection.
- Two cases in the early 1980s seemed to extend auditor liability considerably: (a) *JEB Fasteners Ltd vs Marks Bloom & Co.* (1981); and (b) *Twomax Ltd and Goode vs Dickson, McFarlane and Robinson* (1982).
- The *JEB Fasteners* case placed some emphasis on the concept of *foreseeability*.
- The concept of foreseeability was further emphasized in the *Twomax* case.
- A major development in the law of negligence affecting accountants occurred as the result of the *Caparo* case. The final decision implied that the courts had gone too far in extending auditor liability in the *JEB Fasteners* and *Twomax* cases. The following important points were made: (a) any duty owed by auditors is to shareholders as a class rather than as individuals; (b) liability should not be imposed on the auditors, as this would lead to the liability which was indeterminate as to quantum, as to time and as to the identity of its beneficiaries; (c) examination of company legislation shows that the primary purpose of annual financial statements was to enable those with a proprietorial interest to exercise their given rights. The legislation was not drafted with the purpose of making investment decisions.
- Some criticized the decision because the court's view of the auditors' responsibilities was out of touch with 'commercial reality'. The view was expressed that a balance had to be struck between leaving third parties who have relied on the financial statements no redress for economic loss and exposing the auditors to massive claims that they might not be able to cover by insurance.
- In the *Caparo* case the courts argued that there was a need to distinguish between foreseeability and proximity.
- Cases since *Caparo* illustrate ways in which plaintiffs attempt to distinguish between the case they have brought and the *Caparo* case. The Bannerman case resulted in some audit firms including in the audit report a paragraph disclaiming any responsibility to third parties.
- Compliance with auditing standards would seem to be a logical first step if auditors are to resist successfully a claim for damages. However, limitations of standards as a means of defence are: (a) they do not cover all areas of auditing; (b) they leave scope for interpretation and implementation; (c) they are the auditing profession's view of good practice but what the courts believe to be good practice is what matters.
- As well as being subject to criminal and civil proceedings auditors can also be disciplined by their own professional body.
- The accounting profession has shown considerable concern about extent of liability to third parties, as shown by major documents or reports, such as (a) Likierman report (1989) which looked into problems faced in respect of liability for negligence; (b) Feasibility Investigation of Joint and Several Liability (1996); and (c) a consultative document issued by the Department of Trade and Industry in December 2003 on director and auditor liability.
- The professions claim that a major problem with the present law is the concept of joint and several liability. A possible solution would be to introduce proportionate liability, but this has been rejected because it might leave innocent parties bearing some of the loss.
- The Companies Act 2006 allows auditors and their clients to negotiate a limitation on the auditors' liability, the guiding principle being that it must be 'fair and reasonable' Institutional shareholders have a preference for agreements based on proportionate liability.
- Although beneficial the agreements only cover claims by the company and not third parties.

- As liability limitation agreements only came into force in 2008 it is difficult to say what effect they will have on reducing auditors' financial liability.
- The concept of contributory negligence applies where a plaintiff has contributed to the loss they have suffered. The Company Law Review Steering Group recommended that where directors or employees breach their duties to assist auditors, this might indicate contributory negligence. In cases brought under tort, it may be difficult to convince a court that a third party contributed to their own loss when the latter are relying on financial statements and auditors' opinion.
- Since CA 1989, accounting firms have been able to change their form of organization from partnerships to limited liability companies. This might save individual partners from bankruptcy, although substantial damages could force the accounting firm itself into liquidation. Only a small number of accounting firms have chosen to incorporate.
- Accounting firms argued that the limited liability partnership should be introduced, in which partners would not be personally liable for the partnership liabilities and the resources available to meet successful negligence claims would be limited to the assets of the partnership. The Limited Liability Partnership Act came into force in the UK in 2001 and all the Big Four accounting firms have become limited liability partnerships.

References

Briloff, A.J. (1986) 'Corporate Governance and Accountability: Whose Responsibility?', unpublished paper presented at the University of Connecticut, Storrs, Connecticut , April.

Company Law Review Steering Group (2001) *Modern Company Law For a Competitive Economy*, London. HMSO.

Department of Trade and Industry (1989) *Professional Liability: Report of the Study Teams*, The Likierman Report, London: HMSO.

Department of Trade and Industry (1996) *Feasibility Investigation of Joint and Several Liability by the Common Law Team of the Law Commission*, London: HMSO.

Department of Trade and Industry (2003) 'Director and auditor liability: a consultative document', available from DTI, URN 03/1638.

Evans, H. (1989) 'Auditors' Duty of Care to Third Parties: Caparo vs Dickman in the Court of Appeal', *Professional Negligence*, January/February: 16–18.

Finch, V. and Freedman, J. (2002) 'The Limited Liability Partnership: Pick and Mix or Mix-up', *Journal of Business Law*, September: 475–512.

Hartshorne, J. (2008) 'Confusion, contradiction and chaos within the House of Lords post Caparo v Dickman', *Tort law Review*, Vol. 16(1): 8–22.

North, P.M. (1964) 'Professional Negligence: A Postscript', *The Journal of Business Law*, 8: 231–40.

Further reading

A good starting point for keeping up to date with issues relating to auditor liability is to read the magazine *Accountancy*. This not only contains articles about auditor liability but also reports important negligence cases involving auditors. A more academic journal which contains a number of interesting articles relating to auditors' liability is *Journal of Professional Negligence* published by Tottel Publishing Ltd.

- A general article on liability to third parties is Richard Walford, 'The evolution of liability to nonclients', in *Journal of Professional Negligence* (2002) 18(3): 177–91. A useful article discussing the concepts involved in the determination of professional liability is: 'Professional negligence: duty of care methodology in the twenty-first century', by Keith Stanton published in *Journal of Professional Negligence* (2006) 22(3): 134–50.

The Financial Reporting Council has issued guidance on auditor liability limitation agreements and this is available at: http://www.frc.org.uk/documents/pagemanager/frc/Auditor_Liability_Limitation_Agreements/FRC%20ALLA%20Guidance%20June%202008%20final.pdf

The European Union has issued a number of documents, including its recommendation on limitation on the civil liability of auditors, relating to auditor liability and these are available at: http://ec.europa.eu/internal_market/auditing/liability/index_en.htm

Of general interest, illustrating the difficulty of claimants demonstrating lack of care by accountants, is the discussion of a case involving the singer Sir Elton John by David Gwilliam in an article titled 'Audit quality and audit liability: a musical vignette', published in *Professional Negligence* (2006) 22(1): 37–52.

Two interesting articles that discuss the implications of the *Caparo* decision are: 'The Application of *Caparo vs Dickman*', by Hugh Evans in the June 1990 edition of the journal *Professional Negligence* 76–80; and 'Negligence and the Auditor's Duty of Care after Caparo', by Michael F. James also in the June 1990 edition of the journal *Professional Negligence*: 69–75.

Two more general articles on negligence which discuss important issues are:

Hartshorne, J. 'Confusion, contradiction and chaos within the House of Lords post Caparo v Dickman', published in 2008, in *Tort Law Review*, Vol. 16(1): 8–22.

Yap, P.J. 'Pure Economic Loss and Defects in the Law of Negligence', published in 2009 in *Tort Law Review*, Vol.17: 80–99.

A useful discussion and summary of the case *ADT Ltd vs BDO Binder Hamlyn* is provided by Richard Wade in 'What price "audit" advice', *Accountancy*, May, 1996: 134–5. Similarly, Jane Howard in 'Is *Caparo* still good law', in *Accountancy,* April, 2000: 149 provides some discussion of the *Andrew* vs *Kounnis Freeman* case.

In this chapter we have only been able to give an account of some of the more important UK cases. There are a number of other cases, such as: *Bank of Credit and Commerce International (Overseas) Ltd (In Liquidation) vs Price Waterhouse* (No.2); *Barings plc (In Liquidation) and Another vs Coopers & Lybrand and Others*; *Electra Private Equity Partners vs KPMG Peat Marwick, Coulthard & Orrs vs Neville Russell and Man Nutzfahrzeuge AG v Freightliner Ltd and Ernst & Young* which, if you have the opportunity, you should try to read.

Students might also find the following article interesting as it provides a slightly broader perspective than that provided in this chapter: 'Commonwealth convergence toward a narrower scope of auditor liability to third parties for negligent misstatements', by Carl Pacini, William Hillison, Ratnam Alagiah and Sally Gunz, published in 2002 in *Abacus*, 38(3): 425–64.

A recent article that provides a summary of regulatory and legal reforms in a number of countries is:

Chung, J., Farrar, J., Poonam, P. and Thorne, L. (2010) 'Auditor liability to third parties after Sarbanes-Oxley: an international comparison of regulatory and legal reforms', *Journal of International Accounting, Auditing and Taxation*, 19: 66–78.

Self-assessment questions (solutions available to students)

19.1 Consider the following statements and explain why they may be true or false:

(a) Auditors can only be successfully sued by parties with whom they have a contract.

(b) Auditors who during the course of their work come into possession of unpublished information which they use in a decision to buy shares in the company would **only** be subject to criminal law proceedings.

(c) Auditors are only likely to be found guilty of negligence if the plaintiff has actually relied on the audited financial statements.

(d) If auditors fail to discover that the manager of the payroll department has for a number of years been embezzling £30 000 annually, they are guilty of negligence.

(e) Companies and auditors can draft and put in place a liability limitation agreement which exempts auditors from being liable to the company for negligence.

19.2 In the following scenarios you are required to discuss the possibility of the auditors being guilty of negligence:

(a) Cedra Ltd, a manufacturing company has been audited by Dove & Co. for the last 14 years. It has recently been discovered that a massive fraud involving three of the directors of the company has been going on for the last ten years. The fraud basically involved the falsification of assets, in particular, inventories and trade receivables. The auditors have never attended the year-end inventory count and only intermittently carried out a circularization of credit customers, the managing director always exercising what she called her right to request that certain credit customers were not circularized.

(b) Bibbington Ltd acquired Pyegreave Ltd in 2010, but had by the end of 2011 decided that it would be necessary to wind up the latter company. At the time of the takeover it was known that Pyegreave Ltd was in financial difficulties and in need of a cash injection, indeed the audit report on the financial statements contained an explanatory emphasis of matter paragraph relating to going concern.

The financial statements were, however, not qualified. In these same financial statements the company, in respect of certain items, had ignored the 'accruals' concept which is regarded as fundamental by accounting standards. These departures were not mentioned in the notes to the financial statements nor by the auditors in their report.

(c) The financial statements of Gage Ltd contained a material amount in respect of investments, being shares held in other companies. The auditors accepted as proof of the existence of these shares a certificate from the stockbrokers who held them. It was later found that the company did not in fact own any of the shares and that the certificate from the stockbrokers was fraudulent.

19.3 (This question has been taken from a past auditing exam paper of the ACCA. Only the dates and some terminology in the question have been altered.)

Your firm of certified accountants, in common with many other firms of accountants and auditors, issues to its staff an audit manual which contains, among other matters, recommended procedures to be adopted in carrying out audits. A number of these recommended procedures relate to physical observation of inventory counts and review of count instructions. Owing to pressure of work, you neglected to arrange for the physical observation of inventories at the premises of Leesmoor Limited at 31 March 2010, but your review of the inventory count instructions suggested that company procedures appeared to be in order. You decided to accept the amount at which inventories were stated in the financial statements at 31 March 2010 on the grounds that:

(i) the inventory count instructions appeared to be satisfactory;

(ii) no problems had arisen in determining physical quantities in previous years; and

(iii) the figures in the financial statements generally 'made sense'.

You issued your unqualified audit report on 28 May 2010 and unbeknown to you Leesmoor used the financial statements and audit report for the purpose of obtaining material additional finance from a third party in the form of an unsecured long-term loan. Unfortunately, in October 2010 the company ran into financial difficulties and was forced into liquidation as a result of which the provider of the long-term loan lost the amount of their loan. During the liquidation proceedings it became clear that inventory quantities at 31 March 2010 had been considerably overstated.

Required

(a) Explain the probable legal position of your firm in respect of the above matter commenting specifically on the following:

(i) the possibility of demonstrating your firm were negligent;

(ii) the fact that the inventory figure in the financial statements apparently 'made sense';

(iii) the fact that a loss was made by the long-term loan holder;

(iv) the fact that you were not informed that the financial statements and your audit report were to be used to obtain additional finance.

(b) Describe the reasonable steps your firm should take to avoid a re-occurrence of a matter such as that described above.

Self-assessment questions (solutions available to tutors)

19.4 Discuss what you understand by the following terms:

(i) foreseeability;

(ii) proximity;

(iii) assumption of responsibility.

19.5 Describe the difference between proportionate liability and contributory negligence.

19.6 Discuss the arguments for and against capping auditors' liability.

Topics for class discussion without solutions

19.7 Placing limitations on auditors' liability for negligent misstatements is likely to result in a reduction in the quality of auditing. Discuss.

19.8 The opinions offered by the judges in the Caparo case shows that they are out of touch with commercial reality. Discuss.

19.9 Critically evaluate the statement that the constant lobbying by the auditing profession for reductions in their exposure to liability claims simply demonstrates that they are a self-interested profit-maximizing trade association and not interested in the public good.

20

Criticisms and developments in auditing

LEARNING OBJECTIVES

After studying this chapter you should be able to:

- **Describe in general terms why criticisms of the audit profession arise.**
- **Discuss the debates relating to the setting of auditing standards, disciplining members and firms and monitoring of audit firms**
- **Outline reasons why there are concerns about auditor independence.**
- **Discuss the debates taking place within the accounting profession on the issues of audit reporting, audit quality and competition and choice.**
- **Describe how financial auditing is characterized in an audit society.**
- **Give an account of the profession's response to criticisms.**

Learning objectives, 762
Introduction, 763
Regulation of auditing, 763
Independence, 771
The critics' view of the way forward, 776
Response to criticisms, 779
Audit quality, 781
The audit society, 795
Summary, 809
Key points of the chapter, 809
References, 810
Further reading, 813
Self-assessment questions (solutions available to students), 814
Self-assessment questions (solutions available to tutors), 814
Topics for class discussion without solutions, 814

INTRODUCTION

In this chapter we review some of the literature criticizing the practice of auditing and the auditing profession. We discuss the profession's views of these criticisms and steps that have been taken or are being taken to improve the regulation and quality of auditing. For the most part this critique has come from academics rather than practising auditors. A good part of the critique is waged against the audit profession in academic journals, although increasingly critical comment is being made in professional accounting journals, newspapers and in parliament. This criticism has received further impetus from the banking crisis, where it is notable that a number of UK and US banks who had received unqualified audit opinions required an injection of government or state funds to remain insolvent. Critics, such as Sikka (2009), ask why the auditors did not question the financial statements of banks whose assets seem to have been overstated and were exposed to considerable financial risks. Although it is difficult to summarize in a few words the objective of this critique, it is probably fair to say that it is mainly concerned with exposing the audit profession as self-interested rather than the disinterested body (or set of bodies), portrayed by the profession itself. The individuals involved would argue that the purpose of their critique is to bring about changes that would be beneficial to society and that it is not just criticism for the sake of it. In addition, they would suggest that they are an enlightening and liberating force, challenging preconceived notions and deeply embedded assumptions that are taken for granted, and taking on a powerful and privileged elite in the audit profession. In this chapter we discuss the main thrust of their criticisms. The audit profession has not engaged in a debate in the academic journals with their protagonists, but there have been responses in professional journals, exchanges in newspapers and changes in the way auditing is regulated. In this chapter we consider some of these responses by the Audit Quality Forum and other earlier responses or statements by the auditing profession, such as *The Audit Agenda* and *Auditing into the Twenty-first Century*.

The main academic journals carrying the critique are: *Critical Perspectives on Accounting*, *Accounting, Auditing and Accountability* and *Accounting, Organizations and Society*.

REGULATION OF AUDITING

In the first part of this chapter we examine the way the auditing profession is regulated. You will recall that in the United Kingdom there is a system of self-regulation within a legal framework. The legal framework includes the Companies Act 2006, the Financial Services and Markets Act 2000 and more specific pieces of regulation, such as the Insolvency Act of 1986 (as amended). The most important legislation for audit regulation is the Companies Act 2006, because it delegates many aspects of regulation to the audit profession and associated bodies. You will remember that we discussed aspects of these in Chapter 4 where we outlined the role of recognized supervisory bodies (RSBs). In the following sections we outline the aspects of this regulatory system with which the critics find fault. Finally, it should be remembered that the regulation of auditing has undergone considerable change in the last few years (discussed in Chapter 4) and therefore there is only limited evidence available to judge the effectiveness of the present regulatory regime.

Setting auditing standards

APC was the predecessor of the Auditing Practices Board (APB).

It is worthwhile recalling some history relating to the establishment of APB, whose remit it is to issue UK versions of auditing standards. Sikka *et al.* (1989) describe how the Auditing Practices Committee (APC) was first established as a committee of the Institute of Chartered Accountants in England and Wales in 1973, later (in 1976) becoming a committee of the Consultative Committee of Accountancy Bodies (CCAB). They note that it was established at a time when there was considerable concern about the crash in property values and the failure of several fringe banks. At about the same time several DTI reports on companies were issued, critical of certain aspects of the performance of auditors. Considerable concern was also expressed in various newspapers and other publications. Sikka *et al.* quote from the *Economist* (14 February 1976) a warning that 'unless the profession improves its auditing standards, somebody else will' and from the *Financial Times* (10 July 1976), which doubted the profession's ability 'to exercise control over the activities of large accountancy firms'. Sikka *et al.* note that it was within this environment that APC was established in 1976 as a formal committee of CCAB. Its objective was the codification of good practice in the form of guidelines and standards. It can be argued that APC was set up as a committee to allay public concerns about the effectiveness of auditing and possibly also to prevent some other body taking control of setting of standards in auditing. From this perspective the establishment of APC can be seen as a negative and self-interested act. In other words Sikka *et al.* maintain that it was set up to demonstrate that the profession could set its own house in order and to protect the members of the audit profession rather than to serve the public interest. They also note that the members of APC tended to come from large audit firms, which they interpret as further evidence that a major purpose of the committee was the protection of the interests of such firms. In addition, the members of the committee were part time and retained their positions with the accounting firms that employed them. With this form of structure it can be argued that APC was not independent of accounting firms and thus was hardly likely to engage in a programme of change which would be disadvantageous to them. Furthermore, when developing a guideline or standard, the practice of APC was to form a working party to consider the issue at hand. According to Sikka *et al.* these working parties were also dominated by representatives of large accounting firms. Another aspect of their criticism is that documents prepared by the working party were distributed to the large accounting firms but were not so readily available to other individuals. This gave the appearance that large accounting firms had the advantage of an informal but important route into the decision-making procedures of APC, a route not available to other less privileged individuals. It may also be further evidence that APC was concerned with the interests of large accounting firms rather than protecting the interests of the public. Interested parties did have an opportunity to participate in determining auditing standards (or guidelines) when an exposure draft was issued for consultation purposes. The critics, however, argue that at the exposure stage the agenda had been set, choice had been constrained and forces had been mobilized to support the main thrust of the draft. There was thus a lack of meaningful public consultation, although the issue of exposure drafts may have given the appearance of serving the public interest.

Setting up the Auditing Practices Board

Mitchell and Sikka (1993) argue that in the late 1980s the inadequacies of APC were becoming more and more exposed in the press and media. As a result the accounting bodies decided to revamp the APC. The result was the establishment of the Auditing Practices Board (APB) in 1991. Mitchell and Sikka suggest that the impetus for the establishment of APB came from the ICAEW and that it was established without any real consultation. Furthermore, critics suggested that there was no real change, that members of APB still tended to come from the big accounting firms or large companies, the public were not admitted to their meetings, the minutes of working parties were not available and that victims of poor auditing or those who have suffered through audit failure are conspicuous by their absence. Mitchell and Sikka concluded 'the name is changed from the APC to APB and it is business as usual' (1993: 44).

At this stage is worth pointing out that many of the critics of auditing refer to the accounting bodies as trade associations, rather than professional bodies because they insist that the bodies operate substantially to further their members' interests rather than the public interest.

To a large extent some of this criticism of APB is still pertinent at the present time. For instance, approximately half of the present members of APB are either associated with or have had past associations with one of the Big Four audit firms. The remainder of the members have backgrounds in business, law or academia and thus are not entirely representative of all the parties who have an interest in audited financial statements. APB publishes minutes of its meetings but does not publish the minutes of working parties or appear to admit members of the public to their meetings. One major change in the policy making of APB has resulted from the setting of ISAs by IAASB. The role of APB is to determine the suitability of the ISAs for use in the UK. This task is achieved in two ways. First, by assessing the specific ISA and determining if any additional material needs to be added which is specific to the UK environment and to ensure the quality of auditing in the UK is maintained. Second, by members of APB being involved in the production and revision of ISAs. Over time, as the ISAs are revised and the APB members have exerted their influence on their content, the amount of grey material has diminished. Thus, as IAASB is at the forefront of developing auditing standards, it is useful to consider briefly how far it goes towards meeting some of the criticism by Sikka and others which we outlined earlier.

The present chair of the IAASB had a long association with one of the Big Four audit firms and the UK's representative was a partner in one of the Big Four audit firms and was previously the executive director of APB. However, the remaining eight IFAC nominated members of the board of the IAASB have more varied origins. There are, however, five members of the IAASB who are nominated by the Transnational Auditors Committee, four of these individuals are with Big Four audit firms, the other member is associated with the audit firm Grant Thornton. Lastly, there are three public members who tend to have a regulatory background.

ACTIVITY 20.1

In the above discussion we have mentioned a number of occasions where partners in Big Four audit firms are involved in some role within the APB. Critics of the auditing profession are often disparaging of this involvement believing it is unlikely to be in the public interest. List what you believe are the advantages and disadvantages of audit partners of Big Four audit firms being connected with standard setting within the APB.

In your response you might have listed some of the following points:

Advantages

- The partners bring a wealth of experience.
- They are likely to have knowledge of the issues involved in the audit of significant entities.
- They can call upon the excellent resources within their audit firms for advice on technical issues.
- If their agreement of a standard is obtained it might be less likely that the Big Four firm with which they are associated will oppose or be critical of the standard.

Disadvantages

- Although the partners may have knowledge of large listed clients they are perhaps less likely to be familiar with the issues involved in the audit of small entities which make up the vast majority of audit clients for many audit firms.
- They may not appreciate the additional resource burden for small audit firms caused by the requirements of a particular standard on which they are deliberating.
- They may be tempted to act in the interests of their Big Four audit firm when considering a particular standard or issue, for instance, they might oppose changes likely to increase the responsibilities of auditors.
- They might not be perceived as particularly representative of the public in whose interest it might be argued the audit is carried out.

You may have come to the conclusion that, because IAASB like APB has a number of members with Big Four audit firm connections, it too is likely to be subject to the criticism of being big firm dominated. In defence of IAASB it should, however, be pointed out that it publishes meeting agenda papers, minutes of meetings and issue papers on its website and its meetings are also open to the public. One aspect of IAASB that might be of concern arises from the need to issue standards that satisfy the requirements and needs of all its members in a host of differing countries. You might believe that this is likely to lead to the quality of the standards being reduced to the lowest common denominator. If this is the case, and APB believes that the UK and Ireland require higher quality standards, the responsibility for ensuring that this occurs falls back on APB. Therefore, even though the standard setting process might appear more independent, being the remit of an international standard setting body, in reality APB retains an important role in the UK and Ireland. One aspect of IAASB's work that requires particular mention is its clarity project. IAASB has recently revised the ISAs it issues and as part of the clarity project attempted to improve their readability. The clarity project required that:

The clarity project was commenced by the IAASB in September 2004.

- An objective is set for each ISA.
- The audit responsibilities of each ISA is made as clear as possible, in particular replacing the word 'should' with the word 'shall' to emphasize that certain procedures are expected to be undertaken under most circumstances.

- Any ambiguity that might exist in the standards is removed.
- When redrafting the standards, where possible their clarity and understandability is improved.

You have been referred to the ISAs on a number of occasions and you will be aware that the ISAs do now include objectives, use the word 'shall' and are relatively concise and free from ambiguity. It might be argued that the clarity project has resulted in fairly minor changes to the wording of the ISAs but has not brought about any real substantive changes. Some practitioners, however, see the new ISAs as being more prescriptive with less scope for judgement, which is regarded by them as a retrograde step.

Disciplining members and firms

Sikka (1997) relates how, in the aftermath of financial scandals and suggested reforms in the Cross Report (1977) and the Grenside Report (1979), the accounting profession established the Joint Disciplinary Scheme (JDS) in 1979 to regulate, discipline and ensure the appropriate conduct of members of accountancy bodies and of audit firms. The JDS (like the Accountancy & Actuarial Discipline Board) was primarily concerned with cases of public interest. For instance, in 1999 it reported on certain auditing aspects of the Maxwell scandal. Attacks by critics of JDS were for similar reasons to those on APC and APB. Thus, Sikka criticized the JDS because it was dominated by partners from firms who had been implicated in financial scandals. In addition, he criticized it because of the lack of resources to investigate scandals involving large accounting firms and the length of time it took to complete its reports. There could also be a considerable delay before a case was heard. For instance, JDS reported on the Maxwell case in 1999 about seven or so years after it first came to light. This delay in reporting was acknowledged in the government sponsored *Review of the Regulatory Regime of the Accountancy Profession* (DTI 2003b) which reported in January 2003.

The JDS has now been superseded by the Accountancy & Actuarial Discipline Board (AADB).

That report made several criticisms of the audit practices of the auditors, Coopers & Lybrand (now part of PricewaterhouseCoopers).

At first glance it might appear that AADB also lacks some independence because a number of its board members either currently or in the past have had affiliations with major accounting firms. This, however, neglects how AADB operates. In the first instance, a complaint about an accountant or an accountancy firm will be heard by executive counsel (a lawyer) who will decide if disciplinary proceedings should commence. The disciplinary proceedings are heard by a tribunal consisting of either three or five members from a list maintained by AADB, but with the accounting members in any tribunal always being in a minority. Normally the meetings of the disciplinary tribunal will be open to the public and the decision of the tribunal will be published. In this way FRC believes the procedures will be fair and transparent. Thus far AADB has only published the reports of two cases that came before their tribunal. In the first case (published in 2007) there was some doubt about whether they would actually report the proceedings on their website and AADB came in for some criticism from a Conservative shadow Treasury minister. AADB did subsequently publish the proceedings on their website which indicated that PwC, the accounting firm, and the finance director of the company involved in the disciplinary case had been cleared. AADB has, however, been criticized for the way it handled and processed the case and for initiating it in the first place,

Sukhraj 2007.

thus incurring substantial legal costs. This was not a very auspicious start for AADB but perhaps further evidence needs to be obtained from other cases heard by the board before we can form conclusion about its effectiveness.

In addition to the above, members can also have disciplinary procedures brought against them by their own professional body. These usually arise after complaints have been received about individual members (or firms), who are thought to have acted in an unprofessional manner or committed some act considered worthy of disciplinary action, such as theft. As described in Chapter 4 each body has its own set of procedures and rules to deal with these cases. The penalties that can be levied on members range from a fine to withdrawal of the member's practising certificate or even exclusion from membership. In the case of disciplinary action against a firm the penalty can range from a fine to a reprimand or withdrawal of the right to use the term 'chartered accountant'. It is difficult to assess the effectiveness of investigations by the individual professional bodies, though there is some opportunity for assessment as hearings of the disciplinary committee are normally open to the public. They also publish a list of members and audit firms who have been disciplined and the punishment they have received. A notable recent example is the investigation by ICAEW into specific audits performed by Deloitte's and KPMG. In both cases the audit firms had given unqualified audit reports when in fact the financial statements of the companies were either materially misstated or the audit firm had insufficient evidence to arrive at an opinion. The consequence of this was that Deloitte was fined £130 000 and KPMG £80 000, reportedly the highest fines handed down to audit firms in the UK. Although these fines may appear substantial, in terms of the revenue generated by audit firms they are relatively immaterial.

Recent interesting research is that of Canning and O'Dwyer (2001) who investigated the disciplinary procedures of the Institute of Chartered Accountants in Ireland (ICAI). The accounting profession suggests that one of the roles of their disciplinary procedures is to protect the public interest but the authors question if this is in reality the case. Instead they argue that ICAI's procedures are lacking in accountability and transparency and seem to be 'used as a convenient mechanism for avoiding criticism and maintaining the power and privilege of delegated self-regulation' (2001: 743). The disciplinary procedures are seen as deterring would-be complainants and that the lack of information on cases suggests that the role of the procedures are more to do with protecting the private interests of the accounting profession than the public interest. The profession might respond by saying that the work by Canning and O'Dwyer used disciplinary data from 1990 to 1999 and that since then procedures have changed and improved. While there may have been changes the onus lies with the profession to demonstrate how the revised procedures have actually resulted in improvement and that they do indeed protect the public interest.

Monitoring of audit firms

As we discussed in Chapter 4, the procedures used to monitor the performance of accounting firms have changed in recent years. To recap, you may remember that in the previous monitoring regime a major role was played by the Joint Monitoring Unit (JMU). The JMU attracted a number of criticisms, including that it was under-resourced and had a narrow focus concentrating on rules and procedures rather than on operational matters related to the audit firm. Another criticism of the monitoring bodies is that they were not required to publicize the names of the firms whose standards were considered inadequate.

In the present regulatory regime the major role of monitoring the work of accounting firms is performed by the Professional Oversight Board (POB) and its specialized unit, the Audit Inspection Unit (AIU). A major part of AIU's remit is monitoring the audits of listed and other major public interest entities. In this regard AIU has published five reports since its inception; the first dealt purely with the work of the Big Four audit firms, whereas the second and later ones also included other large audit firms within its work programme. AIU responded to some of the criticism levelled at JMU by concentrating not just on audit processes but also audit judgements. In its first year of operation AIU reviewed the audits of 27 companies in the FTSE 350 and roughly the same number in the latest year (2008/09) for which a report is available. In the latest annual report AIU, as they have tended to do in all annual reports so far, expressed general satisfaction with the quality of the audits conducted by both the Big Four and by the four other large audit firms inspected in that year. In the latest report AIU did, however, express some reservations about various aspects of the audits they investigated and of the audit firms involved which would seem to give rise to some concern. Of particular interest are the following concerns expressed by the AIU:

AIU essentially categorizes audit firms into two types: the major audit firms of which there are nine, undertaking the majority of public interest entity audits, and a number of other 'smaller' audit firms who undertake the audit of public interest clients.

- Some evidence that audit firms were emphasizing maintaining or improving their financial performance, the AIU being concerned that firms needed to continue emphasizing audit quality.
- The appropriateness of some of the responses to and assessment of audit risks, including fraud risk.
- Concern was expressed that there seemed to be evidence that audit staff might be rewarded for selling non-audit services to clients – which is not allowed under the APB ethical standards.
- The need for some of the audit firms to clarify their policy in respect of using internal audit staff to conduct external audit procedures.
- In some individual audits insufficient or inappropriate evidence was collected.
- Inadequate communication of key audit findings and errors detected to audit committees was identified in some audits.

In 2008/09 AIU also reviewed a number of audits conducted by other audit firms. They found that although the issues identified were similar to those for the major firms a greater proportion of audits required improvement. Of particular concern among the findings for this group were:

- In two audits the AIU expressed concern about the ability of the auditor to undertake and perform the audit to a satisfactory level.
- The need to improve communication to those charged with governance.
- Independence issues including audits where key audit personnel had an excessively long relationship in some capacity with the client.
- The need for the firms to be more thorough in their assessment of going concern.

The nature of some of the above concerns and the fact that AIU reported that significant improvements were needed in some areas of five of the eleven audits reviewed suggests perhaps that audit firms other than the major audit firms are not as well equipped to undertake large audits. It should be emphasized that this was not an actual opinion expressed by AIU.

There are a number of different interpretations that can be placed on the evidence given in AIU's annual reports. It might be concluded that AIU is carrying out an effective regulatory role in highlighting what it perceives to be deficiencies in the operating procedures of audit firms. Alternatively, the list of failings in their annual reports might give concern about the quality of auditing performed in the UK, particularly as the firms coming within the AIU's remit market themselves as leaders in the provision of high-quality audit work. It is difficult to come to any conclusion about the effectiveness of AIU procedures as their details are not in the public domain. However, for all their public pronouncements about the emphasis being placed on judgement and decision making in the audit firms, it seems that a large number of findings relate to procedural matters, such as auditor independence issues, failing to complete staff appraisal forms and so on. One conclusion is that the AIU in following specific programmes of work are not likely to escape the tick box mentality as much as they would prefer to do.

It would be useful to have further details of the work of AIU, but because of confidentiality, this is unlikely. One particular aspect of the AIU's work that has been criticized is the anonymity of their reports which do not attribute specific failings to individual audit firms. There has been some debate about whether AIU should disclose its findings in respect of each audit firm. but so far it has decided to continue as it operates at present. This involves: (a) the publication of a public report; (b) a private report to each individual audit firm detailing findings in respect of that firm and the audits investigated; and (c) a private report to the audit registration committee detailing findings in respect of each individual audit firm, but not disclosing details of the findings relating to individual audits investigated. Critics point out that in the US the equivalent body to POB in the UK – the Public Company Accounting Oversight Board (PCAOB) – publishes details of its findings in respect of individual audits performed by each individual audit firm. Other findings of PCAOB in respect of individual audit firms do remain confidential but nevertheless, given the greater amount of disclosure in the US, it is difficult to see what the obstacle is to similar disclosures in the UK. It should, however, be noted that section 62 of Schedule 11A Companies Act 2006 prevents disclosure of the specific audits investigated by the AIU. At the moment it would appear that POB and AIU will continue with their present publication process but students should remain alert to possible changes in the future.

The PCAOB report on PwC in 2006 amounted to 24 pages of which five pages were devoted to listing the failings in nine audits.

In addition to the above monitoring of the activities of selected audit firms, POB also monitors the activities of RSBs and RQBs. A large part of their procedures in relation to that role are procedural, seeking assurance that they comply with statutory requirements. POB make an annual report to the secretary for Business, Innovation and Skills. In the latest report for the year to 31 March 2009, POB expressed general satisfaction that the RSBs and RQBs were performing their role properly. However, they indicated that the professional bodies should take note of, for instance: insufficient documentation of audit files, some non-compliance with CPD requirements and deficiencies in the syllabi and examination papers of some of the RQBs. Although the report by POB does provide some comfort that the regulatory system is working effectively, critics would probably respond that the reports lack sufficient detail about the nature of the procedures and specific findings to come to any firm conclusion that the system is satisfactory. In addition, because POB's role here is one step removed from the actual monitoring of audit firms, one might suggest that their regulatory role is rather more limited than it might appear. It might be contended that since monitoring of the vast majority of audit firms is performed by the individual RSB with which they are registered, there is a lack of independence which militates against critical judgement on the quality of audit work. If one accepts this argument, you might conclude that members of the public with an interest in companies audited by the major audit firms (on which AIU reported), can take greater assurance about the quality of audit work than those with an interest in companies whose audit is performed by the far greater number of auditors monitored by their respective RSBs.

INDEPENDENCE

In Chapter 3 we outlined a number of measures that have been taken by the accounting profession and various bodies to enhance auditor independence. These measures were adopted in large part because of increasing concerns about apparent lack of independence in audit firms. This concern can be traced to the change of largely professional audit firms into the multi-service, multinational businesses they are today. Historically, accounting firms had a strong professional audit culture, but since the 1980s they have grown both in terms of size and in the services they offer. This has led to concerns that they are more concerned with satisfying the management of companies than meeting the needs of shareholders by adding credibility to financial statements. This situation became more critical as increased pressure on audit fees reduced the profitability of audit as compared with consulting services. From a profit maximizing perspective one can appreciate why accounting firms increasingly focused their efforts on obtaining lucrative non-audit work. The emphasis on non-audit work is illustrated in Table 20.1, from which it can be seen that although the level of fees for non-audit work has fallen considerably since 2002 it still constitutes a substantial element of the fee income from FTSE 100 companies:

As can be seen from Table 20.1, audit fees have been steadily increasing whereas the fees for non-audit work declined from 2002 to 2004 and thereafter have remained relatively static. The increase in audit fees is partly because of increased work required since the introduction of new regulations, such as IFRSs, whereas non-audit fees have tended to decline because of more stringent rules relating to independence. An analysis of the fees paid to a small sample of companies amply demonstrates the extent of non-audit fee income received from clients. From Table 20.2 it is apparent that the amounts paid for non-audit services are lower for all four companies in 2009 than they were in 2002, which was an extreme year. Furthermore, in all cases the audit fee now exceeds the non-audit fee which was not the case in 2002. Although the general trend is clear some caution should be exercised in putting a precise interpretation on the figures, as the method by which each company allocated the fee paid to its auditor between audit and non-audit may differ in the two years.

TABLE 20.1 Audit and non-audit fee earnings from FTSE 100 audit clients

	2002	2003	2004	2005	2006	2007	2008	2009
	£m	£m	£m	£m	£m	£m	£m	£m
Statutory audit fees	212	247	263	321	338	398	424	528
Other fees	636	467	348	311	322	308	308	345

Source: 'FTSE 100 auditor fees survey', *Accountancy*, September 2006 and September 2009

TABLE 20.2 Non-audit fees paid by selected FTSE 100 companies in 2002 and 2009

	2002		2009	
Audit client	**Audit fee**	**Non-audit fee**	**Audit fee**	**Non-audit fee**
	£m	£m	£m	£m
Unilever plc	10	48	19	5.2
Barclays plc	5	33	32	20
Prudential plc	2.3	17.8	6.6	4.0
GlaxoSmithKline	7.2	35.7	10.9	8.3

Source: Accountancy, September 2002 and September 2009
Note: Although the fees are reported in 2002 and 2009, in most instances the audit fee refers to the preceding financial year.

There are a number of facets to the amount of non-audit services provided and implications for independence. Traditionally audit firms laid great stress on being part of a profession and members of the profession still argue that accounting firms and audit staff adhere to strong professional values. Because of this it is argued they would not bend and do the bidding of management when disagreements arise over how a particular matter or item should be treated in the financial statements. Cousins, Mitchell and Sikka (1999) note in particular the stress various accounting bodies place on serving the public interest. They doubt, however, if this holds up to scrutiny and suggest instead that accounting firms look after their own self-interest rather than those of the public. Sikka (2008) documents a number of examples where audit firms, he argues, have been involved in unethical, corrupt and illegal practices. He tends to see this as almost inevitable in a capitalistic society where audit firms are pursuing growth and profit. Contrary to the sound bites from the audit profession, he does not accept that it is just one or two 'bad apples' among accountants but rather is more endemic with the perpetrators believing 'they are somehow beyond the reach of the law, regulators and public opinion'. (p.290) He also criticizes the accounting firms for their lack of openness and transparency with little regard for accountability to society and notes the absence of audit committees and non-executive directors in the structures of the firms which might result in greater scrutiny of their actions and practices.

One can also argue that the meaning of the word 'professional' has changed. Historically, the term was used to mean: 'acting in a disinterested fashion' or 'acting with honesty and integrity' and it was used in an individualistic way to describe moral characteristics. More recently, the term has come to denote the standard to which the work has been performed, so that carrying out an audit in a professional way now means completing it to the satisfaction of management, on time and within budget and with problems and disagreements minimized. Thus, the notion of 'professional' as a moral term has been downgraded and is operationalized as and when it suits the accounting bodies. In particular, when accounting is seen to be under threat, they seek to reaffirm the traditional values associated with 'professional'. Jeppesen (1998) associates loss of independence with the rise of what he terms the fourth generation of audit methodologies – the business risk approach. Although accounting firms may advance the view that the business risk approach is merely a more effective way of conducting and adding value to audit, a more subtle result is the way it further privileges a firm's management by aiding them in their duties rather than serving the needs of users. In the business risk approach the distinction between auditing and consulting becomes blurred. Jeppesen demonstrates this by quoting from statements issued by the large auditing firms. For instance, he quotes as follows from documentation issued by Ernst & Young: 'We will significantly increase the activities our clients see as valuable by focussing on their businesses, attending to their needs, and customizing our services to change those needs.' It is abundantly clear that Ernst & Young see themselves as selling a commodity, their expertise, to improve business and assist management. From this perspective, auditing becomes marginalized, largely becoming a vehicle to sell additional services to clients. Similar views are expressed by Power (2003:384) who sees the greater emphasis placed on audit planning within the new business risk approaches as 'not just a basis for conducting the audit but also a platform for other services'.

Page 521.

ACTIVITY 20.2

On several occasions we have mentioned the Enron scandal and the role of its auditors, Arthur Andersen. Although we do not go into the details of this saga (accounts are available elsewhere), it is instructive to consider some issues relating to auditor independence arising from it. First, Enron was the largest audit client of the Houston Office of Arthur Andersen. They supplied numerous non-audit services to the company, including internal audit services, off balance sheet financing schemes, tax avoidance schemes, fronting offshore companies and designing internal controls. During 2000 Arthur Andersen received audit fees from Enron of $25 million and non-audit fees of $27 million and kept staff on permanent assignment at Enron. Many individuals in the finance/accounting function within Enron were ex-Arthur Andersen employees. Do you believe that any of the above activities have the potential to influence the independence of Arthur Andersen? Give reasons for your response.

Source: Sikka (2003a). He also documents a similar situation in another scandal in the US, involving waste management where Arthur Andersen were also the auditors.

You will probably have decided that all the aforementioned activities have the potential to influence the independence of Arthur Andersen to a greater or lesser extent, and in particular the importance of Enron to the Houston office. The partners in Houston were partly remunerated on the basis of their ability to generate client fees for both audit and consulting work, and they had, therefore, a considerable incentive to ensure their relationship with Enron ran as smoothly as possible. Furthermore, the partners in the Houston office would not want to jeopardize the substantial non-audit fees earned from Enron. This demonstrates the extent to which, when considering independence, we should not just be concerned with the audit firm but also the individual audit partners. The provision of sophisticated accounting advice might also be seen as promoting too cosy a relationship with Enron. Finally, the evidence in support of a close relationship is substantiated by the number of ex-Andersen staff who worked for Enron and the close and continuous working relationship of the field staff of Andersen with those ex-Andersen staff.

An alternative perspective on provision of non-audit services is provided by an ex-president of the ICAEW, Peter Wyman, writing in *Accountancy* (July 2002a). He argued that the accountancy profession would only be able to recruit the most able individuals if it maintained the width of career opportunities available to accountants. The conclusion is that, if the scope of services offered by accountancy firms was unduly limited, they would not be able to attract the best graduates and because of this the quality of judgements made by auditors would decline. Interestingly, he offers no evidence to support his assertion.

The scandal involving Andersen and Enron Corporation has led to much soul searching in the United States and many other countries. The scandal led directly to investigations by the US government that resulted in the Sarbanes-Oxley Act. The academic world has been particularly scathing; for instance, Professor Tom Lee (2002) wrote an editorial for an accounting journal in which he described it as 'The Shame of Auditing'. Similarly, in a critique of the governance of auditing firms, Sikka (2003a) is scathing of the relationship between Arthur Andersen and Enron suggesting that 'the pursuit of recurring fees played a major part in the Enron frauds and associated audit failures'.

Even some senior members of the accounting profession have expressed concern about the lack of integrity in members of the accounting profession. Chris Swinson, an ex-president of the ICAEW, writing in *Accountancy* (November 2002), noted that there appeared to be an increase in cynicism about the trustworthiness of the accounting profession and ethical values of its members. In particular, the view proffered by leading members of the profession in the UK that the various scandals in the United States could not occur in the UK was viewed with scepticism. Swinson did not see the solution to the problem in hurried action, but instead thought that there needed to be a change in the mindset of accountants to ensure they behaved in an ethical manner more befitting a member of a profession. Generally, however, the response of the audit profession in the UK to the Enron scandal has been more sanguine. Glyn Barker (2003) suggests the circumstances surrounding the Enron scandal were unique and occurred in the United States, having little implication for the standards of accounting elsewhere in the world. Indeed he seems to view the scandal in a more positive light by suggesting that 'with the fundamental importance of the audit re-established in the mind of the market,

Barker is a partner in PricewaterhouseCoopers.

Page 78.

signs of its renaissance are clear'. Similarly, Peter Wyman, (2002b) suggested that an Enron scandal was less likely in the UK because the boardroom culture is different from the United States; the US accounting system lacked the notion of substance over form and the use of the true and fair view, and finally the quality of the accounting profession in the UK is much higher than in the United States. He also asserts that it would be beneficial if International Accounting Standards were adopted which 'are at least as good as the standards we currently have in the UK' and finally notes that many of the improvements made in the UK 'are now recognized as models for the US to aspire to and are being carefully studied to establish if they would work in the US'. The overall impression gained from statements such as these is that accounting and auditing is distinctly superior in the UK compared to other countries. A number of commentators in the UK have suggested that one of the reasons for this is because accounting in the UK is more principle-based whereas in the United States it is more rule-based. This, dichotomy is, however challenged in an interesting article by David Kershaw published in 2005. It is interesting that Wyman made these comments before two wide-ranging reports on accounting and auditing in the UK and the subsequent revamping of the regulatory system for accounting and auditing. This would suggest that he was perhaps unduly upbeat about the state of accounting and auditing in the UK.

An alternative perspective using recent scandals in the UK suggesting that scandals similar to Enron and WorldCom could occur in the UK, is provided by Beth Holmes in an article in the August 2002 issue of *Accountancy*.

Page 127.

Another suggestion given some impetus by Enron was that audit firm rotation would enhance auditor independence. This has been vigorously opposed by the audit profession for a number of years. For instance, Plaistowe (1992) argued strongly that audit firm rotation would make it more difficult for audit firms to become knowledgeable about their clients and hence increase the likelihood of the auditors failing to detect material errors and misstatements in the accounts.

Similar sentiments were expressed by Philip Hourquebie, the Chief Executive Officer of Ernst & Young in South Africa, who suggested: 'The case for compulsory firm rotation may seem seductive when considered superficially. However, as one considers the many implications and, indeed, looks at global trends this solution creates more problems than it solves' (Hourquebie 2003). However, rotation may be increasingly enforced on firms as companies put their audits out to tender, the current auditor not necessarily being selected. This phenomenon is seen in the public sector too where private firms and District Audit are frequently engaged in bids for the audit of local government audits. It is unlikely that auditors will be forced by statute to rotate, especially as the EU 8th Company Law Directive 'Statutory Audit of Annual Accounts and Consolidated Accounts' published in May 2006 does not require it, but merely indicates that countries may if they wish require mandatory auditor rotation.

The independence of auditors also came in for scrutiny by two Treasury committees formed in the wake of the banking crisis. In both reports produced by these committees concern was expressed that auditors' independence and their ability to stand up to clients might be hindered if the auditors earned significant non-audit fees from their audit clients. The committee on the banking crisis recommended that the accounting profession needed to reconsider the need for prohibiting audit firms from providing non-audit services to clients. In response APB published a discussion paper titled *Consultation on Audit*

Firms providing Non-Audit Services to Listed Companies that they Audit in October 2009. This paper reviewed the regulatory provisions in force that ensure auditors are independent such as the Ethical Standards and the Combined Code on Corporate Governance. The paper also reviewed the empirical evidence relating to independence and concluded that there was no strong evidence that the level of non-audit fees influenced audit quality. Shortly after the publication of the APB paper ICAS issued a report *The Provision of Non-Audit Services by Audit Firms to their Listed Audit Clients* in January 2010. Although portrayed as a contribution to the debate on auditor independence, the report might be seen by critics as a justification for retaining auditors ability to undertake non-audit work. The working group that prepared the paper undertook a questionnaire survey of finance directors, audit committees and chairmen and concluded that the results indicated there was no indication of a need for change or for restriction of the provision of non-audit services. The questionnaire, however, was somewhat flawed with a poor response rate, no analysis of the respondents and questions couched in terms that were likely to lead to particular responses. There are, however, a few interesting issues raised in the paper. First, the paper notes that regulation relating to the disclosure in the annual report of the split of fees paid to the auditors between that relating to audit work and the amount relating to non-audit work is misleading. This is because the provisions contained in *The Companies (Disclosure of Auditor Remuneration and Liability Limitations Agreements) Regulations 2008 do* not sufficiently distinguish between the fees paid for audit and non-audit work. More specifically, fees paid to an auditor for auditing the subsidiaries in a group company would be regarded as non-audit fees and disclosed as such. The working group argue that this is misleading because such fees are in effect audit fees and should more appropriately and accurately disclosed as audit fees. The report argues that if a more appropriate allocation of the fees between the amount paid for audit work and the amount paid for non-audit work was implemented, it would not appear that auditors were so reliant on non-audit fee work. The working group recognized that the most appropriate solution to what they perceived as the misallocation of fees would require a change in the legislation which in the short term was considered unlikely. However, notwithstanding this obstacle the group made a number of recommendations on a more appropriate classification of fees between audit and non-audit. The working group also recommended that the role of the audit committee in ensuring auditor independence could be expanded. More specifically the group recommended that audit committees pre-approve non-audit services above a certain set amount, publish their policy on the auditors providing non-audit services and how they approach apparent conflicts of interest in the provision of audit and non-audit services.

THE CRITICS' VIEW OF THE WAY FORWARD

Thus far we have discussed a number of criticisms made of the audit profession. It may be argued that, although criticism may be beneficial in itself, it is even more beneficial if positive suggestions for reform are also offered. Although not all critics have done this, a number of possible reforms have been suggested by Mitchell and Sikka (1993) and these will now be described.

They outline three major strands of reform, set out below with comments on recent developments:

1 Auditors must act exclusively as auditors. This would seem to preclude audit firms from offering non-audit services to their clients. Sikka (2009) draws attention to the level of non-audit fees paid by banks and other financial institutions who were involved in the banking crisis and needed financial aid to remain solvent. He draws the conclusion that the earning of these non-audit fees may have clouded the judgement of auditors and made them reluctant to challenge the authority of management. Audit firms should also be required by law to detect and report material fraud and actively assess the ability of their clients to remain as a going concern. Although the auditing profession perceive that ISA 240 – *The auditor's responsibility to consider fraud in an audit of financial statements*, has increased auditor responsibilities in relation to fraud compared to the previous auditing standard (SAS 110), it does not go so far as to require auditors to detect fraud.

It is worth pointing out, however, that some services, for example taxation advisory services, are closely linked to audit.

2 Auditors must be socially accountable. As part of this, auditors would be accountable to all stakeholders 'through a variety of means such as the provision of information and supplying products that are "fit for use"'. Audit firms should place in the public domain documents such as: audit tenders, letters of engagement, internal control letters, management representations, compositions of audit teams, details of second opinions and so on. In addition audit firms would only be allowed to audit major companies if they published 'information about themselves, at least comparable in quality to that published by their clients'. With the publication of the 8th Company Law Directive in May 2006, audit firms that audit public interest entities will have to publish on their websites each year a transparency report. POB believe there are between about 40 to 50 audit firms in the UK that might be considered to audit public interest entities – in the main these are likely to be listed companies. The directive listed a number of matters that should be disclosed in the transparency report including the following: a description of legal structure and ownership, a statement concerning the audit firm's independence practices, a description of the internal quality control system of the firm, information about the basis for partner remuneration and so on. The latest POB report referred to above commented that in the transparency reports they examined 'there were significant differences of approach, content and level of detail' and that audit firms needed to 'prepare these to meet the spirit as well as the letter of the requirements'. There is a strong suggestion here that POB considered that the quality of the reports could be improved. It should, however, be noted that these were the first transparency reports produced and that in this particular year the firms were issuing them on a voluntary basis, as the regulation requiring them had not come into force. Although the information in the transparency reports is likely to be of some use it is unlikely to be detailed enough to satisfy what Mitchell and Sikka believe should be disclosed.

We mentioned transparency reports in Chapter 2.

POB 2009, page 18.

3 The institutions of accountancy must be reformed. Mitchell and Sikka believe this is necessary before any meaningful reforming of audit and accounting can take place. This, they believe, is impossible at the present

> time, as the accounting profession acts both as trade association furthering the interests of their members and as regulator. They advocate the independent regulation of the accounting profession, a form of social regulator consisting of representatives of all interested parties. Members of the accounting profession would serve on this body but would have to sever links with their employers before being eligible. This would assist in ensuring they had less incentive to pursue the interests of their former employers. In addition, the regulatory body should be open in its conduct, that is, agenda papers and minutes should be available and public hearings should be a part of the process of standard setting. Finally, audit firms with large companies as clients should be monitored by an independent body. This body should publish the results of their monitoring and have the powers to licence auditors and 'investigate the affairs of auditing firms implicated in audit failures'. (p.48)

APB publishes its minutes on its website.

Earlier in this chapter and in Chapter 4 we considered the requirements of parts of the new regulatory regime and noted that it has resulted in a departure from the accounting profession being solely responsible for its own monitoring and disciplining. It is likely that even with these changes they do not go far enough to satisfy Mitchell and Sikka who, no doubt, would argue that it is still geared towards the interests of capital and the auditing profession rather than in the interests of the public. In this respect Sikka (2003c: 2) when commenting on the DTI's *Review of the Regulatory Regime of the Accountancy Profession* asserted that over the years the DTI had been sent evidence that 'major [accounting] firms operate cartels and are engaged in money laundering, bribery, tax avoidance, evasion, abuse of insolvency laws and large scale mugging of ordinary people' but have done nothing, which suggests he has little faith in regulatory changes that the accountancy profession agreed with the DTI. Sikka (2009) in light of the banking crisis argues that auditors are still reluctant to countenance change even though he argues the crisis demonstrated that auditing was ineffective and did not provide the assurance that is one of its objectives. He also argues that the techniques of auditing are based on an outdated model in which assets were tangible, could be physically verified and whose valuation did not contain any great uncertainty whereas today with more widespread use of financial derivatives such certainties are gone. Therefore, the audit profession needs to consider 'alternative forms of accounting, disclosures and accountabilities' (p.872). There is some evidence that auditors are not entirely monolithic with Khalifa *et al.* (2007) noting that there seems to be a possible move away from a business risk audit approach and back towards a more classic audit approach with greater emphasis on the testing of transactions.

ACTIVITY 20.3

In (2) above it was suggested that, as part of their social accountability, audit firms should disclose a considerable amount of information about their affairs. Can you suggest reasons why audit firms might be reluctant to make such disclosures?

Audit firms might be reluctant to disclose the information suggested because:

- It is regarded as private and sensitive information that arises from a private contract between the company and its auditors. In the same way that details of other private contracts are not made public, why should those between the company and its auditors be made public.
- In some instances the documents would be of little value to the public who would not find them interesting or informative. In other instances the disclosure of information might be disadvantageous to the shareholders of the company or to other interested parties.
- The requirement to disclose the information might change the nature of the communication. In particular the documents might become more general and anodyne in content, which could reduce their potential usefulness.
- At present an integral part of partnership law is that partnerships only have to disclose limited information about their affairs, and considerably less than that required of companies, who pay this price for having limited liability. Since the majority of audit firms trade as partnerships, to require them to disclose as much information as limited companies would be unfair. This, however, has been modified by the introduction of the Limited Liability Partnerships Act 2000. Firms who become limited liability partnerships (LLPs) are required to prepare annual accounts in a similar way to limited companies. With the publication of the 8th Directive the disclosure by certain UK audit firms, (namely, those that audit public interest entities), expanded because they are required to publish a transparency report. Judging from the reports published thus far, it would appear that a substantial proportion of the disclosures will be descriptive and fairly general in nature.

The Big Four accounting firms have all become LLPs.

RESPONSE TO CRITICISMS

Audit regulation

A major focus of the criticism of APC was its lack of independence from the accounting profession and in particular the predominance of individuals from large auditing firms on the committee. In response the profession could argue it was not surprising to find individuals from such firms represented on APC because its formation was to some extent motivated by the criticisms directed at the perceived audit failures by large firms auditing large clients (Pong and Whittington 1994). It is interesting to note that APB's procedures provide that 40 per cent of the members of its board can consist of individuals eligible for appointment as auditors. Of the remaining 60 per cent, any of whom are accountants should not be an office holder of a professional body or involved in the governance of such a body nor a partner in a firm authorized to conduct audit work. The inclusion of non-auditors on APB was intended to ensure that it was, at least to some extent, independent of the audit profession. It may be argued that including members other than auditors on APB goes some way towards meeting the criticism that it is not representative of society. At present appointments to APB are made by the Financial Reporting Council which, given the composition of the committee responsible for appointments, might be considered unlikely to select members for the APB who are fully representative of society.

See Chapter 4.

Although the profession welcomed the two reports, *Review of the Regulatory Regime of the Accountancy Profession* (RRRAP) and *Coordinating Group on Audit and Accounting Issues* (CGAA) it should not be thought that the accounting profession agreed with the critics that there was something systemically wrong with the regulation of auditing. Indeed they responded vigorously to the criticisms. For instance, Ian Plaistowe, a prominent member of the ICAEW, was stating even in 1991 that, like APB, the committees that regulate and discipline members have a large number of independent non-accounting members. Thus, in this line of argument. it follows that the auditing profession pays due regard to the public interest. He also suggests that it is not entirely unreasonable or unusual for members of various committees concerned with auditing and its regulation to come from the big auditing firms. He seems to say that, because the Royal Charter of ICAEW specifically states that the public interest should predominate, this means that the critics' claim that ICAEW is a trade association, rather than a professional body, is invalid (1992: 25). Plaistowe also believes that concentrating and encouraging matters such as technical competence and objectivity, as the accounting profession does, will further the public interest and enhance the qualification of chartered accountant. This may of course be so in a global sense as technically competent auditors are more likely to perform good audits and this is in the public interest.

With regard to the concerns that audit firms are too close to clients, Plaistowe argues that firms and their clients must be reasonably close for auditors to perform competent audits. Only if auditors are knowledgeable about clients are they likely to provide advice and find material errors and misstatements in financial statements. Responses by the profession to the charge that auditors lack independence include:

From Chapter 3 you will remember that this has now been reduced to five years for listed company clients.

- Acceptance of the principle of rotation of the engagement partner by audit firms after a period of time (not exceeding seven years).
- Having a second partner check the decisions of the reporting partner.
- Instigation of rigorous quality control procedures.

A past president of ICAEW, Michael Lickiss (1990), has also taken issue with allegations made by critics of auditing. He considers that the impression that audit failure is commonplace is misleading. He emphasizes the number of audits that take place each year where there is no apparent audit failure and states that this far exceeds the small number of occasions where failure has occurred. Basically, Lickiss suggests, the critics have blown the issue of audit failure out of proportion. In addition, he argues it is necessary to distinguish between business failure and audit failure. The failure of a company does not necessarily mean that there was also audit failure; companies fail for all sorts of reasons that are not the responsibility or fault of auditors. Similar comments have been made recently in respect of the banking crisis where the POB report to the Department for Business, Innovation and Skills for the year ended 31 March 2009 stated that the Treasury Select Committee that investigated the crisis was 'not overtly critical of auditors or the quality of auditing in

Page 5.

the UK'. Finally, Lickiss cites the establishment of APB as an indicator that the profession is willing to change and respond positively to criticism. It might also be argued that the accounting profession's support for reviews by RRRAP and CGAA of accounting and auditing, discussed in Chapter 4, performed at the behest of the Government further indicates that the profession is willing to take on board criticism and change where change is necessary.

The profession greeted the reforms put forward in the two reports by RRRAP and CGAA with some degree of optimism believing that they strengthened regulation through: providing a sole regulatory framework covering both accounting and auditing; increasing independence from the accounting profession; introducing a degree of pro-activity; and providing, along with the new Combined Code in 2003, scope for improving corporate governance. A major aspect of the reforms was the supposed distancing of regulation of accounting and auditing from the professional bodies and the increased number of non-accounting members of the various boards of the Financial Reporting Council. This, however, is unlikely since the critics would wish the membership of key committees to go far beyond that of the business and legal communities, who make up the large majority of membership of the boards, and make them more representative of society as a whole. At the time when the new structures were proposed Sikka (2003b) suggested that 'The DTI's proposed reforms do not address the root cause of audit failures – namely, the predatory culture of accountancy firms'. Since the new regulatory structure has only been in operation for a few years it is too early to conclude whether the accounting profession's optimism or Sikka's pessimism is the more justified.

You will be aware the Combined Code has been revised with the latest code being issued in 2008.

Page 29.

In the next section we will consider more recent discussions and proposals from the profession, the objective of which is to improve the quality of auditing.

AUDIT QUALITY

Promoting audit quality

A paper 'Audit quality' produced by the Audit and Assurance Faculty of the ICAEW in 2002 highlighted the need to focus on the contributors to audit quality. The paper emphasized the need for auditors to provide a quality service if it was to retain the confidence of investors and other users of the financial statements. The paper listed the following factors which were thought to drive audit quality:

We have discussed these issues on a number of earlier occasions.

- *Leadership*. The paper emphasized the need for senior staff in audit firms to provide a leadership role by inculcating quality values throughout the audit firm. Effectively, the paper is stating that quality audits will not occur by chance, a lead needs to be provided by audit partners; unless they emphasize quality through the procedures and processes they implement in the firm and the values upon which they place importance, there is little chance of other audit staff considering quality an important characteristic.
- *People*. It should almost go without saying that there is little chance of producing quality audits unless you have competent, well-trained staff. The paper highlighted the need for appropriate staff recruitment, training and

retention policies. The paper asserted that the audit firm, as well as being thought of as a provider of services, should also be seen as a learning organization which adapts itself and develops staff over time. Further emphasis was placed on ensuring that the audit firm recruits staff with appropriate professional values and the need for those to be reinforced throughout their period of time at the audit firm.

- *Client relationships.* In this part of the paper the focus is on the need for a good working relationship between the auditor and client and appropriate client acceptance and continuation procedures, audit pricing policies and appropriate safeguards that ensure that the provision of non-audit services do not impede auditor independence. The usefulness of a strong working relationship between the auditor and the audit committee, where one exists, is also emphasized.
- *Working practices.* In this section attention is given to strong team work, good communication, staff having a clear understanding of roles and responsibilities, diligent audit planning and risk assessment, an appropriate approach to audit work including alertness of mind, a healthy scepticism and effective review.
- *Monitoring quality processes.* The paper discusses the usefulness of external review, such as that by the RSBs and the need for good and internal monitoring procedures which provide constructive advice.

It is probably reasonable to say that the paper produced by the Audit and Assurance Faculty was not especially innovative but it does serve as a useful *aide-mémoire* for the procedures and processes that are essential if a high-quality audit is to be produced. Critics would no doubt have a slightly different view of the publication, considering it to be just another piece of rhetoric by the profession designed to convince the public that it is concerned with producing quality audits while at the same time not resulting in any fundamental change.

The mantle of concern with audit quality has been taken up by the Financial Reporting Council which in November 2006 produced a discussion paper titled *Promoting Audit Quality*. The paper discussed what the FRC believes are the chief drivers of audit quality and the threats to those drivers. It sought the views of interested parties on these issues and also whether any additional action was needed to increase the likelihood of consistent high-quality audits. The paper listed the following audit quality drivers:

- *Audit firm culture*
  The factors influencing this driver include the value the firm places on high quality audit work, rewards staff for quality work, the systems put in place by the firm to monitor the quality of audit work, and to avoid undue time and financial pressures which might mitigate against the achieving of quality work.
- *The skills and personal qualities of audit staff, including partners*
  Factors encompassed in this driver include ensuring that there is sufficient training of staff at all levels within the audit firm, that staff have sufficient experience and at junior levels are suitably supervised, and having processes that ensure staff are knowledgeable about the regulatory framework, including auditing standards and understanding of the client's business.

- *The effectiveness of the audit process*
  Factors influencing this driver include: a systematic and thorough approach to audit planning involving senior audit staff, adopting an appropriate audit approach suited to the client and the risks involved, consideration of appropriate audit evidence, thorough and continuous review of audit work, procedures to deal with contentious issues including suitable specialist or technical support, an environment within the audit firm that encourages good audit work and is not unduly influenced by time or cost considerations and adherence both to the audit firm's quality control standards and those imposed by the APB.

You should be familiar with all of these factors and we have emphasized them at various places within this book.

- *The reliability and usefulness of audit reporting*
  This driver is dependent on the appropriateness of the audit report as a vehicle for communicating the auditors' satisfaction or dissatisfaction with the financial statements, that the audit opinion is clearly stated, and that the auditor has collected sufficient appropriate and reliable evidence to arrive at an opinion that the financial statements give a true and fair view. Of increasing importance within listed audit clients is strong, clear and thorough discussions with the audit committee about issues arising from the audit, main findings arising from and judgements involved in the audit, matters relating to auditor independence, significant areas of risk and ways of improving financial reporting within the client.

In the first three of the above there is considerable overlap between the related discussion on them and that included in the paper *Audit Quality* produced by the Audit and Assurance Faculty. One important difference, however, is that in the FRC paper there is greater discussion of the threats to the various drivers. On the fourth issue the report identified similar matters to those that had been discussed in the Audit Quality Forum paper *Auditor Reporting* and, in particular, ones relating to the auditors' duty in respect of reporting on the adequacy of a company's accounting records and including greater disclosure about key audit issues.

In December 2004 at the request of the Secretary of State for Trade and Industry, an Audit Quality Forum was established and is convened by the Audit and Assurance Faculty of the ICAEW.

The debate on promoting audit quality was taken forward in a paper published by the FRC in 2007. In this paper the FRC discussed respondents' comments on the first paper published by the FRC in November 2006. Respondents, in general, seemed supportive of the main thrust of the promoting quality paper and believed it had identified appropriate indicators of audit quality. There were a few issues raised by respondents including:

- A need for greater information about how audit firms embed a culture of quality in their firm. It was noted that the Audit Inspection Unit played an important role in respect of issues relating to the culture within audit firms.
- Some concern was expressed about the extent of audit work being undertaken by relatively inexperienced staff. FRC indicated in the paper that they proposed the setting up of a task force to review the implication of IFACs International Education Standard *Competence Requirements for Audit Professionals for the Training of Auditors*.
- Some concern was expressed that the rate of regulatory change in itself could endanger audit quality.
- The potential for the audit report to include information of greater use to users.

In addition to the above drivers of audit quality the discussion papers also listed a number of factors outside the control of auditors that might affect audit quality.

ACTIVITY 20.4

List factors you consider might come under the above category that might influence audit quality.

You might have mentioned some of the following factors:

- The perspective of senior management in audit clients; do they value the audit and the advice provided by auditors or do they simply perceive the audit as an expense?
- The ethos within audit clients; are staff in the client helpful to the audit team, is senior management always concerned about the cost of the audit and do they set 'impossible' deadlines for producing the financial statements?
- The strength of the audit committee and whether it is composed of experienced individuals who devote sufficient time to their role and take seriously issues raised by the auditors. More generally the importance placed by senior management on corporate governance and complying with the Combined Code.
- The regulatory environment and whether it is principles or rules-based. Strong opinion has been voiced in some quarters that good professional judgement promotes high quality and that a rules-based approach encourages an unthinking box ticking approach which endangers audit quality. In this respect it can be argued that auditing standards have moved towards a more prescriptive approach which some might see as stifling judgement and creativity.
- The liability regime in operation. There is strong opinion expressed in the academic literature that auditors should not be overly protected from being liable for negligence because it serves as an incentive for them to produce high quality audit work. Without the threat of financial penalty, it is argued, auditors have less incentive to produce high quality audits.
- The regulatory regime and penalties for directors and senior management who are involved in fraudulent activity.

The final paper published by the FRC in February 2008 titled *The Audit Quality Framework* listed the main drivers and components of audit quality. As a descriptive account the FRC paper is fine but it can be criticized for its lack of innovation and action. The FRC hopes that the framework assists audit committees in their assessment of auditors, that it provides useful guidance to stakeholders on the policies undertaken by auditors that ensure quality audits and that regulators find it beneficial in their role of monitoring the audit firms. It is interesting that the FRC shows some optimism on the role that audit committees might play when other commentators like Humphrey (2008) suggest that we know very little about their day-to-day practices and thus the likelihood of achieving the objective set by the FRC.

In conclusion, since there is nothing especially new in the paper it is difficult to see how this takes us any further in the quest to improve the quality of auditing. FRC perhaps sees one route being through audit firms publishing useful information in their transparency reports which enables users to evaluate if the firm is likely to provide high quality audit work. This assumes of course that such transparency reports themselves give a 'true and fair' view of the audit firm and are not just being used to promote their brand.

Audit reporting

In Chapter 16 we introduced you to the present form of the audit report and commented that the expanded audit report had replaced what was known as the short form report. At the time of its replacement the expanded audit report was seen as a way of addressing the expectations gap. In October 1991, APB issued a consultative paper *Proposals for an expanded auditors' report,* in which they listed three reasons for the existence of the expectations gap that could, at least partially, be addressed by an expanded audit report:

- Misunderstandings of the nature of audited financial statements.
- Misunderstandings as to the type and extent of work undertaken by auditors.
- Misunderstandings about the level of assurance provided by auditors (Paragraph 8).

APB did not consider that an expanded audit report could completely remedy the above misunderstandings but did think that such a report could assist in closing the expectations gap by reducing misconceptions. The inclusion of details of the auditors' and directors' responsibilities was seen as useful in clarifying the nature and extent of work undertaken by auditors. For instance, these statements would make it clear that it is the directors who are responsible for preparing the financial statements and not the auditors. Similarly, the wording of the scope paragraph makes it clear that an audit involves testing and judgement and thereby informs users about the level of assurance provided by the auditors. In particular, the reader of the new audit opinion should be more aware of the nature of the task involved, and that the audit work performed cannot result in a guarantee. The basis of opinion paragraph and the directors' responsibility statement make it clear that the prime responsibility for the prevention and detection of fraud lies with the directors. This should help ensure that users are aware of the auditors' responsibility for the detection of fraud and reduce any misunderstanding that users may have about the extent to which an audit opinion provides assurance that the financial statements are free from fraud. Another reason for replacing the short-form audit report with an expanded audit report was to increase its usefulness. It has been argued that in a short-form report the auditors' opinion is reduced to a symbol, that is, users simply note that there is an audit report but don't actually pay much attention to it. It was considered that users were more likely to read and pay attention to the contents of a long-form audit report. Finally, it has to be recognized that audit and accounting practices in the UK tend to be influenced by practices in the USA. In proposing an expanded audit report, APB was following the practice established in the USA where an auditing standard, SAS 58, had been issued in 1988 which required the use of an expanded or long-form audit.

Although the changes introduced by the expanded audit report might be considered useful in reducing the extent of the expectations gap, a number of criticisms were made prior to its introduction. First, there was a basic assumption that the solution to eliminating the expectations gap lay in educating users. This takes for granted that it is users that hold the wrong beliefs about the responsibilities of auditors rather than auditors themselves. In other words there was no attempt to close the expectations gap by moving towards what assurance users expected an audit should provide. Second, the proposals were considered negative as they tended to indicate what auditors were *not* responsible for or highlighted the limitations of audit work that were by their nature beyond their control. Critics suggest that the audit report could be more useful if it contained greater details of findings during the audit or appraisals by the auditors, for instance, of internal control systems rather than mere descriptions of their responsibilities and a general description of the nature of their work. This view was put forward by the head of audit, Rob Ward, in PricewaterhouseCoopers, Australia, who suggested that the 'audit report could be expanded to include issues such as management estimates, the possibility of fraud, risks, liquidity, future scenarios and environmental reports'. He argued that 're-focussing the role of the auditors, to give investors and other stakeholders assurance on a much broader range of information than at present would enhance market confidence, resulting in a lower cost of capital than would otherwise have been the case'. Finally, although an alleged benefit of a long-form report is that it is more likely to be read by users it may also be argued that, because the report is longer, users are put off reading it. Furthermore, it is suggested that since the standard advocates a standardized form of wording, once users have read one audit report they become less inclined to read further reports because they expect the content to be the same. This deficiency could be remedied by allowing auditors to use their own individual form of wording but unfortunately the APB did not support this alternative.

If we now move forward to the last five years or so we find that there are calls for changes to the audit report and questions raised about the value of the present form of the report. For instance, the Treasury Committee report on the banking crisis briefly discussed the role of the audit report in financial institutions and recommended the Financial Reporting Council consider an idea put forward by Professor Michael Power that audit reports should be more finely graded or tuned where there is concern about the solvency of a company.

Prior to this in 2007 the ICAEW Audit Quality Forum had produced a paper on audit reports. In that paper there was recognition that the present wording of the audit report was not as helpful as it might be. The paper recommended:

- Changing the form of the audit opinion so that it is laid out in three parts indicating whether the accounts:
  - (i) give a true and fair view,
  - (ii) have been properly prepared in accordance with the relevant financial reporting framework: and

(iii) have been prepared in accordance with the requirements of the Companies Act, and, where applicable, Article 4 of the IAS regulation.

- A positive statement by the auditor that proper accounting records have been kept. At the time of the report the Companies Act 1985 only required auditors to report on this matter if the company did not keep proper accounting records.

The Companies Act 2006 has not changed the essence of this provision.

- A positive statement by the auditor that there are no matters they wish to draw to the reader's attention by way of emphasis. The Companies Act 1985 required auditors to include a reference to any matter which they felt ought to be brought to the attention by way of emphasis but which did not constitute a qualification. The recommendation by the working party of the Audit Quality Forum simply required a positive statement that there are no matters which needed to be brought to the attention of readers of the report and might be regarded as adding very little of consequence to the present audit report.

You will recall that we discussed emphasis of matter paragraphs in Chapter 16 when discussing audit reporting.

- It was noted that there was no specific information about the particular audit performed and that the wording was essentially boiler plate and therefore might be ignored by users. Matters which the report considered shareholders might find of interest in the audit report included:
  - Firm specific reports.
  - Discussion of important matters raised during the audit.
  - Greater information on significant judgement and sensitive issues.
  - More information on emphases of matters and future risks.

ACTIVITY 20.5

Can you offer any reasons why the audit profession might not want to comment on some of the issues listed above?

First, the auditor might be concerned that providing information that includes an opinion or judgement on sensitive matters might bring them into conflict with management, something they would probably wish to avoid. The auditors might also be concerned about the confidentiality of disclosures and the providing of information that might be of use to competitors. This might limit what they and management would be willing to disclose to rather mundane items or the disclosures being couched in rather general terms and superficial in nature. The auditors might also be concerned that disclosing additional information might be the start of a slippery slope with users of the financial statements demanding ever more information and perhaps assurance from the auditors. Finally, the auditors might be concerned that disclosure of additional information in their audit report might increase their exposure to legal liability.

The suggestions put forward by the Audit Quality Forum were taken further by APB in their discussion paper issued in December 2007, *The Auditor's Report: A Time for Change*. APB termed the suggestion of company specific information within the audit report as a radical recommendation. In couching it in these terms it might be argued that this was a route the APB appeared not to want to go down. The discussion paper questioned if the suggestions might lead to auditors expressing an opinion on management or their judgements and stated that was not the auditor's role. The discussion paper also considered that some of the suggestions might be met by changes in IFRSs and the enhanced business review that directors are required to include in the annual report. Thus, the paper concluded that until evidence was collected about the extent to which items such as the directors business review met users needs, there was no need to address the issue further. An alternative view is offered by Humphrey *et al.* (2009) who see additional reporting on such matters as key audit findings as a way to more visibly demonstrate the quality of an audit.

It is interesting that in the space of about 20 years the usefulness of the expanded audit report that was once regarded as a solution to the expectations gap is now being questioned. Another pertinent feature is the lack of concern expressed in the audit quality forum about the role of the audit report in meeting the expectations gap. Indeed, from the acknowledgement in the report that users want more specific information, it might be argued that the expanded audit report has done little to address concerns relating to the expectations gap.

Choice in the UK audit market

There has previously been some consideration of the issue of competition in the provision of audit and accountancy services by the Office of Fair Trading in 2002.

Another recent paper (2005) produced by the Audit Quality Forum was titled *Shareholder Involvement – Competition and Choice*. This paper highlighted that in the listed company audit market there is a limited choice for companies when choosing an auditor. This is particularly the case for large listed companies where essentially only the Big Four appear to have the resources necessary to carry out their audits. The paper notes that competition and choice are necessary to ensure high audit quality and then goes on to argue that in the UK the problem is not so much a lack of competition in the audit market but a lack of choice. The paper also considered that there are barriers to entry, preventing firms outside the Big Four from challenging them for the audit of large listed clients, but did not reach a conclusion or make any specific recommendations it simply suggested that further research is needed on certain topics.

ACTIVITY 20.6

List what you believe might be some of the barriers to entry preventing medium-sized audit firms entering the market for very large audit clients, such as the FTSE 100.

In your response you might have mentioned some of the following points:

- Lack of resources, financial and personnel, to effectively service very large audit clients. Insufficient staff especially at partner level who have large audit client expertise.
- Insufficient international network in all of the countries in which large audit clients have subsidiaries and associates.

- Lack of expertise in all the specialist areas large audit clients might desire or in certain specific commercial sectors, for instance, insurance and banking.
- Inability to convince large audit clients that they have as good a reputation as the Big Four and therefore the client should have no concern about the market marking them down because they do not have a Big Four auditor.
- An unwillingness (or lack of motivation) on the part of medium-sized audit firms to enter the large audit client market because of a perception that it is more risky. For instance, audit partners in the firm may have concerns about the potential litigation risks that might exist and that could have substantial financial consequences for them.

The theme of competition and choice was taken further when the then Department of Trade and Industry and the Financial Reporting Council commissioned a report by consultants Oxera to investigate the issue. Oxera, published a report in April 2006 and following this the FRC has produced one discussion paper and one briefing paper, held a number of meetings and latterly formed a Markets Participants Group. The Oxera report described the audit market in the UK and emphasized the dominance of the Big Four in auditing FTSE 350 companies and the limited choice of auditor available, particularly for some large listed companies operating in the financial services sector. The report also noted that FTSE 350 companies seem to have a preference for a Big Four auditor and that there are significant barriers to entry for mid-tier audit firms seeking to challenge the Big Four's dominance in the audit of large listed companies. Finally, the report described how auditor switching rates among large companies was low with limited competitive tendering and how higher concentration among auditors had led to higher audit fees in recent years.

On average about 4 per cent annually of listed companies switched auditors in the period 1996–2004.
Source: Oxera report.

We include below a table that provides some insight into the extent of the dominance of the Big Four audit firms in the audit of large listed companies:

TABLE 20.3 Number of companies audited by firm, August 2007

Auditor	FTSE 100	FTSE 250	AIM
PwC	39	73	122
Deloitte	21	66	128
KPMG	21	57	187
Ernst & Young	19	43	115
BDO Stoy Hayward	0	6	141
Grant Thornton	0	4	213
Begbies Chettle Agar	0	1	0
Baker Tilly	0	0	94
PKF	0	0	55

Source: Adapted from Table 1 in *Choice in the UK Audit Market: Final Report of the Market Participants Group,* October 2007, Financial Reporting Council.

Reviewing the column in the table above headed FTSE 250 gives some idea of the extent to which the Big Four audit firms dominate the large listed company market. If you look at the final column headed AIM which consists of smaller companies listed on the Alternative Investment Market one can see that the Big Four dominance is not as pronounced.

The remit given to Oxera did not include providing any policy recommendations but was simply to analyse the audit market for consideration by FRC. Although the Oxera document is interesting it largely documented features of the audit market which were already well-known and indeed some of which had been discussed in the Audit and Assurance Faculty paper *Shareholder Involvement – Competition and Choice*, published in July 2005. The FRC discussion paper took the findings by Oxera and used them to frame a number of questions for response by interested parties. The FRC briefing paper gave an outline of the responses to the various questions posed in the discussion paper and made a number of suggestions for matters that needed to be taken forward for further discussion. In doing the latter the FRC was taking action to determine if there were steps that audit firms, companies and regulators could take that would reduce risks relating to the availability and quality of audits. As indicated above FRC formed a Market Participants Group (MPG) in October 2006 to focus on potential actions which would mitigate the risks arising from the characteristics of the audit market. This group produced a final report in October 2007 and made 15 recommendations which we discuss below. MPG delineated the issue into three parts or quasi objectives: (i) increased choice of auditors; (ii) reduced risk of a firm leaving the market without good cause; and (iii) reduced uncertainty and disruption should a firm leave the market. The MPG then sought possible recommendations that might achieve these objectives.

To achieve an increased choice of auditors requires actions that will increase; the propensity of non-Big Four auditors to audit public interest entities, the likelihood for such entities to engage a non-Big Four audit firm as auditor and the likelihood of auditor switching by Big Four audit clients.

One recommendation to increase the capacity of non-Big Four firms to audit public interest entities would be to change the rules relating to ownership and control, thus enabling firms to raise capital to compete with Big Four audit firms. The group also thought that if information was available that showed the profitability of audit work this might attract firms to enter the market and that liability limitation agreements might also make entering the large audit market more attractive. Finally, if more individuals from non-Big Four firms were involved in accounting and audit committees and boards such as APB, this might raise their profile and serve to demonstrate that their firm is capable of undertaking large audits. While the above factors might seem to be relevant in enhancing the propensity of non-Big Four firms to enter the market, in some cases they seem somewhat tenuously related to the issue.

ACTIVITY 20.7

The second set of recommendations made by the committee are intended to increase the likelihood of non-Big Four audit firms being selected to perform public interest audits. Can you suggest what they might be?

The most radical recommendation would be to limit the number of public interest audits performed by any one firm of auditors. However, this would be hugely controversial and probably not considered appropriate by the various participants. As you might have suspected the MPG did not mention this possibility. Instead they opted for rather more pedestrian alternatives. These included having available clearer information on the capabilities of non-Big Four audit firms, promoting good practice that increases the level of shareholder engagement in the auditor selection process, having the board provide explanations and information bearing on choice of auditor, disclosing any contractual obligations (for instance, in loan covenants) that restrict a firm to using a Big Four auditor. The latter recommendation derived from concern that banks and brokers might make strong recommendations to their corporate clients that they engage only a Big Four auditor. Without empirical evidence it is difficult to evaluate the strength of this claim. The final recommendations made under this heading were that the accounting profession should introduce measures to improve access to relevant information by incoming auditors, thus reducing the cost of auditor switching. Finally, guidance should be made available to audit committees on matters relating to using audit firms from more than one network.

To increase the likelihood of auditor switching within the Big Four audit firms themselves recommendations included ensuring that ethical standards are not too onerous as they might serve to restrict choice. It was recommended too that guidance to audit committees on independence matters contained in the Smith Guidance should be reviewed and confirmed that it is consistent with the guidance in ethical standards. Although it is appropriate that guidance on ethical matters is reviewed to make sure it is appropriate, it is difficult to see how the recommendations made by the MPG is likely to have anything other than a marginal effect on the extent of auditor switching.

The group made recommendations to reduce the risk that a firm might leave the audit market without good reason. We have already mentioned that one way to do this is by ensuring that the liability regime is not too severe. In other words, audit choice and competition is likely to be adversely affected if the penalties that could fall on auditors might force them into bankruptcy or might deter audit firms from entering the market. Another recommendation was that regulators should have ‘protocols’ to provide guidance on the likely outcome of investigations by regulatory bodies into ‘audit issues.’ This at first glance may seem to have little relevance to audit choice and competition. The thinking is, however, that when a firm is subject to some regulatory action because of (say) misconduct then uncertainty about the penalty it may incur creates uncertainty in the market and may result, for instance, in companies being unwilling to select the audit firm as auditors. A further recommendation was that auditors of public interest entities should themselves comply with a Combined Code style of corporate governance.

In order to reduce uncertainty and costs as a result of an audit firm leaving the audit market the MPG recommend that major public interest entities should consider the risk of such withdrawal and plan accordingly.

In one sense it would be unfair not to applaud the effort that has been made to consider how choice in the audit market can be enhanced, but it does seem unlikely that the recommendations will bring about substantive change, at least in the short term. In the papers containing the recommendations there is little in the way of conceptual underpinning or collation of evidence on what influences companies to select one audit firm in preference to another. Nor is there any attempt to think seriously about the deeply embedded belief that a

Big Four audit firms provides a better service. Until the FRC is willing to confront these issues and give some thought to more radical solutions it is unlikely we will see much change in the UK audit market. One action with which FRC did agree was to monitor progress of the various recommendations made by MPG to see if there was any effect on auditor choice. FRC publish progress reports on a six-monthly basis and at the time of writing four have been issued. The fourth, issued in October 2009, found that progress had been made on the recommendation that audit firms auditing public interest entities should publish a corporate governance style report, similar to the combined code (see FRC/ICAEW 2010). In their transparency report they would have to state if they complied with or explain why they had not. A draft code was circulated for comment and a final code was issued by the FRC and ICAEW in January 2010. However, since it has not yet come into force it is too early to evaluate the usefulness of the disclosures required. The code, which will apply to eight audit firms auditing the bulk of public interest entities, contains 20 principles and 31 provisions; audit firms will have to state they comply with them or explain why they do not comply. FRC also noted that progress was continuing on a number of the other recommendations including investigating alternative structures for audit firms, restrictions in loan covenants, how auditors can demonstrate and audit committees assess audit quality.

In the above sections we have discussed a number of documents issued by the Audit Quality Forum and FRC which advocate various changes to the way auditing is presently conducted. It may appear that the accounting profession is currently very active, but in some ways this is a continuation of a trend, most noticeable when accounting or auditing has been subject to criticism. As a reflection of this we discuss briefly two documents issued during the 1990s that were intended to stimulate debate. These documents were the *Audit Agenda – Next Steps* issued by APB (1996) and a report issued by ICAS *Auditing into the Twenty-first Century*. The profession would probably argue that these documents indicate willingness on the part of the auditing profession to at least debate the issue of change even if the recommendations contained in the two documents did not fully come to fruition.

The Audit Agenda: Next Steps

This publication was the third in a series of discussion papers issued by APB, the first two being *The Future Development of Auditing: A Paper for Debate* (November 1992) and *The Audit Agenda* (December 1994). APB's aim in issuing the papers was to 'develop audit to meet user needs and to complement the activities of business, consistent with the APB's overall objectives'. *The Audit Agenda: Next Steps*, published in 1996, discussed a number of proposals, an outline of which are given below. What is particularly interesting about them is that several have now been partially or fully implemented, indicating that the audit profession does evolve and take on board suggestions for improvement.

- The scope of audit of listed companies and other major entities should differ from those of unlisted owner-managed companies. This proposal recognizes the different nature of the two types of company, and that this should be reflected in the audit. This recommendation has not been implemented though the Companies Act 2006, subject to certain conditions, exempts small and dormant companies from the requirement of having an audit.

- The audit of listed companies should be extended to include assurance that all textual information accompanying the financial statements is consistent with the view given by those statements. In addition it was recommended that the auditors provide reports to the board and audit committees on corporate governance issues. To a large extent this now takes place, the auditor being required under the Companies Act 2006, s.496 to ensure the information contained in the directors' report is consistent with the financial statements. In addition, ISA 720 – requires the auditor to read other information contained with the financial statements and take appropriate action where is a material inconsistency in the information or a material misstatement of fact.

ISA 720 (UK and Ireland) contains two sections, A and B. It is Section A that is relevant here.

- It was also recommended that certain steps be taken in respect of fraud. As we discussed in Chapter 17 auditors are in the main still rather reluctant to take on additional responsibilities in respect of fraud detection.
- Audit reports should be signed by engagement partners in their own name as well as that of the audit firm. This proposal was an attempt to increase accountability. The Companies Act 2006, s.503 requires that where the auditor is a firm the audit report be signed in the name of the senior statutory auditor on behalf of the audit firm. The senior statutory auditor is considered to be whoever is regarded as the engagement partner.
- Audit committees of listed companies should be responsible for appointment and remuneration of auditors and the approval of non-audit services by the auditors. In listed companies audit committees now play a larger role, part of which includes the matters referred to above.
- It was also suggested that APB should, through discussions with interested parties, such as the DTI, seek to limit auditors' liability when reporting on certain corporate governance issues by modifying the then existing s. 310 of the Companies Act 1985. As we saw in Chapter 19 the Companies Act 2006 allows auditors to enter into liability limitation agreements with companies subject to satisfying certain requirements and complying with certain conditions.

Auditing into the Twenty-First Century

This discussion document was issued by the Research Committee of the Institute of Chartered Accountants of Scotland in 1993. The motivation was the considerable criticism of the auditing profession noted earlier in the chapter. The proposals were an attempt to address the expectations gap. The document itself can be considered as fairly radical in professional accounting terms as it envisaged substantial changes in the institutional arrangements relating to auditing. In the text below we consider a number of its proposals.

The proposals in the document were aimed at listed companies only.

- The document proposed an extended role for internal auditing. It was recommended that all listed companies should have a strong internal audit department headed by a chief internal auditor. The purpose of the internal audit function would be to provide the board of directors with reassurance about the reliability and relevance of the company's management information and internal control systems. The Combined Code requires the audit committee to keep under scrutiny the effectiveness of the internal audit function and where one does not exist in a company, the audit committee should consider each year the need for one.

- One of the criticisms levelled at internal auditors is that they are not independent of the board of directors. In an attempt to remedy this it was recommended that, as well as reporting to the chief executive, internal audit reports should be directed to a financial reporting and audit committee. This committee would be made up of non-executive directors and would approve the appointment and the termination of employment of the chief internal auditor. As we indicated above the Combined Code recommends that the internal audit function should have a close link with the audit committee.
- Since internal auditors would perform considerable detailed testing of internal control systems, this would have implications for the work of external auditors. It was suggested that external auditors be called external assessors and that they be less concerned with detailed testing and procedural issues and more with judgemental issues.
- The appointment and termination of external assessors (auditors) and their remuneration would be determined by an audit review panel (with some input from the company's directors). It was envisaged that the audit review panel would consist of a small number of experienced individuals selected from a panel maintained by a competent authority such as the Stock Exchange. After the panel was established, the chair would determine who was to serve as members. Although the specifics of this proposal have not been implemented, the Code on Corporate Governance recommends that an audit committee consisting of non-executive directors be responsible for the appointment of auditors and approval of their remuneration.
- As well as the duties mentioned above in relation to the external assessors (auditors) it was suggested in the discussion document that the audit review panel should also be responsible for:
  - (i) Receiving a report from the assessors on their audit work, including any management letters and reports on sensitive issues.
  - (ii) Considering the reasonableness of any requests from stakeholders for the assessors to carry out additional work.
  - (iii) Asking the assessors to carry out any additional work the panel considers is necessary and ensuring that the auditors are paid for that work. This request could arise as a result of the report by the assessors to the panel or as requested by stakeholders.
  - (iv) Entering into discussions with the assessors to determine if it is necessary for the latter to report to a requisite authority if they suspect the directors of fraud or other illegal activity.
  - (v) Providing a report in the company's annual accounts on the panel's activity in the year.
- In an attempt to reduce the expectations gap and meet some of the 'reasonable' expectations of the public, the discussion document suggested

that directors, in addition to their existing duties on reporting on truth and fairness of financial statements should also report:

(i) Whether they believe the company will remain a going concern for a period of at least 12 months from the date on which the directors approve the accounts.

(ii) Whether the company have management information and internal control systems that are sufficiently relevant and reliable to enable directors to prepare financial statements and provide assurance that the opportunities for fraud and other illegal activities are minimized.

You will realize from the above, that the ICAS proposals were more dramatic and revolutionary than those suggested in other documents such as *The Audit Agenda* or the initial guidance on corporate governance provided by the Cadbury or Hampel Committees. Although there was some discussion of the proposals, at present none of the changes in respect of the responsibilities of the internal and external auditors and the formation of an audit review panel and financial reporting and audit committee have been implemented. A factor that potentially complicates and perhaps reduces the possibility of changes to the role of the internal audit function is that the duties of internal auditors have been changing over the last ten years. In particular, they are increasingly seen as performing a management consultant role rather than acting as detailed checkers of the systems of the company. This change in role has implications for their independence and the reduction in detailed testing they conduct may reduce the usefulness of their work for the external auditors. In conclusion, we believe that, although the ICAS proposals are unlikely to be implemented in the near future, we do think that they have been a very useful contribution to the debate about the future role of auditors.

THE AUDIT SOCIETY

It may appear that the criticisms discussed earlier in the chapter represent an attack on the structure of auditing, but an even more fundamental critique of the concept of audit has been made by Michael Power in various articles and books. Power's analysis operates at several levels and is concerned with a variety of issues. At its most basic he is merely observing that the concept of audit is now used in many different spheres. This raises deeper questions, however, as to why audit, borrowed from its use in the financial audit domain, has come to be used in these different spheres. The spread or growth of the concept of audit seems particularly ironic given that, in the last 20 years or more, the effectiveness of financial audit has been increasingly questioned. We can ask:

Power (1992), (1993), (1994), (1995), (1997a), (1997b) and 2007.

- What motivates the adoption of a concept whose original conception is being questioned?
- More fundamentally, has 'audit' become a form of discourse which is used when considering allocative, efficiency and regulatory decisions? Perhaps the term has itself become powerful in its own right and can be used by participants to legitimize certain actions. In this part of the chapter we will be concerned with examining these issues in more depth.

The nature of the audit society

At its most mundane level Power's arguments rest on what he perceives to be an increase in the use of 'audit' in many aspects of everyday life. In particular, he notes the increasing use of the concept in such diverse activities as environment, health, education and energy. The increasing use of the term prompts Power to question why, in recent years, there has been such enthusiasm to adopt a particular term and style of activity. It can reasonably be asked why the terms 'investigation', 'review', 'report' or 'evaluation' have not gained the same universal acceptance. Power (1997a) does admit that inspection is also an important tool in the regulatory regime but notes that in its operation it has moved nearer to the way the audit function is conceptualized in that it is increasingly concerned with verifying systems of control. In response, though, one might quote the efforts of the Audit Inspection Unit to give greater consideration to audit judgement and not just compliance with controls. At its simplest one might suggest that the use of the word 'audit' in the different spheres involves some form of comparison or evaluation. For instance, when an environment audit is carried out by a company one is investigating its practices, processes and products to see how far they conform to some standard regarded as best practice. In performing a teaching audit at a school or university, one is seeking to form a view on the quality of teaching, perhaps even giving it a rating and determining if it meets certain desired standards.

Power argues that the centrality of audit to accountability and transparency has enabled it to be mobilized in other domains. He even goes as far as to conclude that the force of its logic is such that 'to be against audit appears to be to support non-accountability' (1994: 304). In all the different spheres in which auditing operates, the objectives, standards and modes of practice must be determined; Power argues that the notion of audit used by accountants has been particularly important in determining these characteristics. For instance, in environmental audits, accountants have been influential in determining the form of audit performed. This form of audit, not unexpectedly, is influenced by the nature of financial audit, performed by accounting firms, resulting in emphasis being given to particular aspects of a company's environmental performance and marginalization or concealment of other aspects. Because, in the financial audit sphere auditors are concerned with the gathering and measuring of evidence, it is likely that they will bring the same emphasis and attributes to environmental audit. Thus, they may emphasize those aspects of environmental performance, which can be measured and which they can verify, rather than actually attempting to consider what is good environmental performance. The auditors assume the term environmental audit is defined by their practices and hence there is no or limited discussion of what constitutes the concept of environmental audit. It should be mentioned that not everyone is convinced by Power's characterization of audit as a general concept applicable in a number of domains (Maltby, 2008). She argues that a limitation in Power's analysis is his unwillingness to define audit thus allowing him to use it to cover whatever he wants. She also takes Power to task for being ahistorical. Needless to say Power (2008) rejected these criticisms and argued that treating audit as a concept rather than trying to limit it by defining it was what gave it its strength as an analytical tool. Power accepts his work tends to ignore historical developments but he argues that this is because he is primarily interested in analysing the present.

Power makes the point that the effect of audit (normally regarded as enhancing accountability) is actually to endanger democracy. It does this because in having an audit, auditees are assumed to have made themselves accountable, thus reducing or curtailing other forms or ways in which the auditee could be made accountable. Furthermore, it can be argued that in a financial audit, although the auditee has discharged their accountability by being subject to an audit, very little information is actually disclosed about that accountability. Power (1997a) makes this point particularly forcibly about the audit report, which he considers to merely act as a 'quality label', and does not inform principals about the audit process. A criticism of the new long-form or expanded audit report is that it only provides information about an audit in very vague terms – it is a general descriptive statement – rather than giving details about the specific audit. Although generally sympathetic to Power's thesis, Humphrey and Owen (2000) take exception to his claim of the extent to which the idea of financial audit has been used in other spheres. They argue that we do not live so much in an audit society as a 'performance measurement society' and one in which there has been a rise in management. They reach this conclusion by arguing that concepts central to financial audit, such as independent checking and verification, do not always occur in other forms of activity that include the word 'audit' in their title. An example used by Humphrey and Owen to demonstrate this is clinical audit which, they suggest, is more concerned with gathering data than with checking and verification which is an important aspect of financial audit.

You will recall that in the discussion above of the paper produced on audit reporting by the audit quality forum the inclusion of more detailed information in the audit report is a controversial issue.

At a more basic level Power argues that financial audit, serving as a model for audit in non-financial domains, only comes into being because of the way in which certain social relations involving individuals are conceptualized as principals (shareholders) and agents (directors/managers). In having an audit the relationship between principal and agents and the 'established' structure of accountability is further embedded in the social fabric. In conceptualizing relations in this way, a need for accountability from agents to shareholders arises because of the supposed lack of trust by the principal in the agent's actions. The audit function serves to restore that trust. This then leads to the obvious question of why the principal should trust the auditor. To engender this trust auditors must occupy a particular role in society in which their expertise and impartiality are taken for granted or grounded in some other structural relationships. For instance, the audit profession says that trust can be placed in audit firms because they themselves are subject to audit by structures, such as, the Joint Monitoring Unit. It might be argued that trust in auditing would be endangered by incidence of audit failure, which Power (1994) considers to be the 'norm'. This, however, presupposes that audit failure is clearly apparent and visible. One of the characteristics of financial auditing is the difficulty in determining its success or failure. Thus, when a company fails soon after receiving a clean audit report, whether audit failure has occurred or not can be contested. Indeed it might be suggested that 'audit failure' should be assessed by expert judgement, that is, the auditors themselves should be the judges rather than the public. Furthermore, if it is accepted that there was audit failure, this might be explained 'away' in terms of it being a failure in this 'particular' case to follow

Since Power wrote a number of his pieces on the audit society, the Joint Monitoring Unit has been replaced by alternative monitoring procedures which we discussed earlier in this chapter and in Chapter 4.

accepted auditing procedures or rules. If the failure appears to have as its root some more general cause, the solution is to have the problem addressed and rectified by the professional bodies or the Auditing Practices Board. What cannot be allowed to happen is that doubt is cast on the audit function because it is too important and vital as a regulatory device and form of 'political rationality'.

The rise of the audit society

Power offers three reasons why there has been a large increase in the quantity of activities termed 'auditing':

1 The first is the new form of management in the public sector. Within the context of reforms in the public sector, auditing was seen to play a role in achieving what were perceived to be required changes.

2 The second is increased demand by society for greater accountability by organizations. This is particularly the case for certain sectors, such as education and health, where the political agenda at the time argued strongly that such public services should meet public demands and desires. Such organizations could be seen to be discharging, at least partially, their responsibilities to the public by being subject to a form of audit.

3 The final reason, Power believes, comes from pressure by the increased use of quality management practices and changes in regulatory style. An important component is the notion that audit can assist in solving the problem of regulatory compliance.

With respect to regulatory compliance it is argued that organizations have come to rely increasingly on control systems. Compliance with a regulatory regime becomes a matter of demonstrating that the organization has rules, procedures, processes and practices. It is assumed that their existence demonstrates compliance. However, to demonstrate that controls are working correctly another layer of control must be added, that further layer being audit which becomes the control over the controls implemented by the company.

The main driving force is the desire to reduce audit costs.

In financial audit, increasing emphasis has been given to evaluating and testing a client's internal controls with a view to reducing the extent to which individual transactions are examined. More recently, we have seen greater stress placed on auditors examining and evaluating management's philosophy on internal control. Presumably, if management appear to take internal control seriously, implement a 'suitable' system and have another set of controls to check their system is working effectively, auditors can gain some assurance from that and reduce testing still further. Evidence of management taking internal control seriously may take the form of internal audit. The external auditor can, after establishing the reliability of internal audit work, use it as a source of assurance. In this way the auditor becomes more concerned with checking controls, or indeed controls over controls rather than direct testing of transactions. In effect the auditor's work to some extent becomes one step removed from the actual reality of their clients' engaging in and recording transactions.

ACTIVITY 20.8

Suggest why it is that direct controls, such as checking that purchase invoices are authorized, become less important and controls over controls more important as businesses grow from being small and owner-controlled to larger more complex concerns.

You may have suggested that in small businesses control is more immediate and direct, usually being performed by the owner. In this case there is no need for a sophisticated control system because the owner is the control system, the regulatory mechanism. As the business grows, however, it is no longer possible for the owner to exercise such a predominant regulatory role and alternative control mechanisms must be implemented, including such features as control accounts, bank reconciliations and so on. Although these may be considered as controls over controls, as the business becomes larger it may be necessary to introduce wider ranging controls to check the workings of the controls, the most obvious form being the internal audit function. It may be argued of course that the external audit function also partly performs this role.

As an aside, it may be argued that in a different institutional setting the business could be accountable to a wider group, for instance, to society for the company's environmental performance or to employees for job security, conditions and safety. If these aspects are significant, it is possible that the company would have to instigate controls to ensure proper adherence to the company's policy for environmental performance or to employees.

Audit and control

The move towards audit being a control over controls is one that concerns Power and he suggests that auditors market this move away from auditing 'the real time practices of auditees' as being progressive. Power believes that this is undesirable as what becomes important is the existence of a system and its auditability rather than what the particular system is supposed to achieve, leading to some important issues being ignored or 'hidden'. For instance, the emphasis on auditing systems may inhibit discussion of whether an audit is practicable and is the best solution to achieving accountability. It does so because the concern moves from actual practices (which may be difficult to audit) to systems (which are auditable). Power offers as an example British Standard BS7750 on environmental management. He considers that this standard 'articulates the structure of an environmental management system' (1994: 310) and thus creates an auditable subject. To exemplify this, a city authority might have as a programme: 'The maintenance of a pollution-free environment within the city'. To audit this programme would be extremely difficult as it would lead to a whole series of questions, such as: 'What is meant by "pollution-free"?' 'What is and how do we measure pollution?' 'Is pollution measured at set dates and times?' and so on. The auditor might be hard pressed to write a report that was useful to the inhabitants of the city. If on the other hand, the city authorities informed the public that they had set up a system of measuring devices throughout the city and that measures of air pollution would be published at six-monthly intervals they would have put a system in force that might persuade the public that action had been taken. An auditor in these circumstances might be able quite easily to confirm the existence of the system and the accuracy of the measurements made. A city with cleaner (or sufficiently clean) air might still not exist, but an auditor would have written a report on the basis of auditable evidence. What might have been obscured would be important questions, such as: 'Is it possible to measure and audit environmental pollution and what should be done about environmental pollution?' These important questions may not be discussed because of the existence of the system and its audit.

It is because they can be audited that Power believes systems have become more important than the operations themselves and, furthermore, because the system can be audited, it confers legitimacy upon the process, even though the process (as in the above example) does not necessarily produce a pollution-free city. The essence of Power's argument is that, when one considers spheres, such as health, education, environment and so on, identification of what is actually meant by terms such as performance, success and failure is open to interpretation, controversy and dispute. The result is that it is difficult, or extremely costly, to audit their substance, so that a pragmatic and economically useful option is to confine the audit function to that of auditing more readily identifiable systems. Auditees like this option as it gives the impression that they have discharged their accountability, as our example above suggested. In addition, the focus on auditing systems enables audit firms to claim that their financial auditing skills can be transferred to many different spheres.

The point being made here is that auditors themselves are instrumental in determining what is audited. If auditors say, for instance, 'I cannot tell you that University examination papers are fair, but I can say that the University has a system of internal and external moderation of those papers', this effectively means that auditors are deciding what is auditable and what is not. Thus, one may argue that the claim of auditing to be a neutral and instrumental device whose operations and processes are determined by what is being audited, is misleading. Power says that the popular conception of financial audit as the verification through the collection of evidence that the financial statements are in conformity with certain agreed standards is not the full story. This is because it ignores the fact that auditors are implicated in the setting of those standards as well as in monitoring compliance with them. As a result auditors have an incentive to construct standards that they can audit and are thus implicated in the construction of the auditable subject.

Another matter to be considered is the response of auditees to the knowledge that the audit 'of them' will actually be of the systems put in place 'by them'. This has particular poignancy in the sphere of teaching audits where the 'game' becomes one of ensuring that proper systems are in place, for instance rules and procedures to supposedly enhance the quality of teaching and documentation to show that the procedures have been followed, even though the relationship between these and teaching quality is uncertain and complex.

An example of this might be the requirement that all courses have aims and outcomes. Simply having these does not necessarily enhance teaching quality because they may be inappropriate or the teaching staff may not follow them.

This particular effect is also noticeable in the regulatory procedures of accountancy monitoring bodies in auditing the performance of audit firms. Great emphasis is placed on ensuring that the firms have appropriate procedures in place, the presumption being that the firm is then performing to the required standards. Deficiencies are defined in terms of the systems not operating as planned or the absence of appropriate systems. There seems to be little attempt to actually audit the quality of audit work and confirm whether the audit firm has actually performed the appropriate tests, collected sufficient evidence or reached the correct audit opinion in actual audit assignments. The problem is that it may encourage the audit firm to assume that a good audit consists of following procedures, ensuring that all the appropriate boxes are ticked and having neat and tidy audit files. The concentration on these aspects means that the actual practices of auditors are left unconsidered. This may be to the benefit of the firms because to explore the relationship between the auditors' work and reaching an audit opinion might make visible the fragility and deficiencies of the audit process. In other words, the relationship between an auditor's tests and the level of assurance gained from them might be shown to be rather hazy, that there is no well-defined theoretical basis linking the tests performed by auditors and the opinion they express. In response to allegations such as the above, the audit profession would argue that the Audit Inspection Unit is more concerned with decision-making processes and the work carried out to arrive at an opinion, although it still lays stress on such aspects as having systems in place that emphasize a culture of audit quality and having the work documented. This is fine, but one might question if the AIU is more concerned with ensuring the work is documented rather than that the correct or appropriate work has been performed.

Another problem is that the actual level of assurance an auditor provides about the financial statements or other subject of audit is also obscure and difficult to measure. Power makes the point that although auditors claim that they add value, the lack of a specific measure of their output makes their claim difficult or even impossible to verify. This means that we have to trust the auditors' judgement that they have provided a certain, unspecified, level of assurance. The continuing shrouding of actual audit practices serves to mystify the audit process and gives practitioners the opportunity to increase the intensity of the aura that surrounds auditing. Additionally, putting audit rules and procedures into standards and checklists further serves to insulate them against potential criticism of their practices as auditors claim that the checklists are designed to incorporate best practice. Power (1992, 1995) has also written about how statistical sampling and risk-based auditing have been used by the audit profession to advance their claims about the knowledge base of auditing. In particular he believes the profession had high hopes that statistical sampling would establish a scientific foundation for auditing. This, however, proved not to be the case, the use of statistical sampling by audit firms has declined and its place as a basic theory or foundation of audit practice taken by the increasing adoption of the risk-based audit approach. As a way of talking about audit, 'risk' has advantages in that it has a universality from which the auditor can benefit. In particular, auditors can represent their work as a form of risk reduction or risk management. Thus, financial audit, because part of its function is preventative, reduces the risk of management deliberately misstating the financial statements. However, an audit only 'captures' those risks that can be identified by audit procedures. Because of this partiality of auditing, Power (1994) concludes that 'the profound irony of the audit society is that where auditing may be most desirable, it is least possible'.

Power (1994: 311) considers that checklists in audit practice occupy an important position in that the ideal checklist 'established the completeness and visibility of audit work'.

Page 312.

Returning for a moment to the suggestion that an audit gives legitimization to the auditees, and serves as a signal of accountability, it is interesting to reflect that audit can do this despite the lack of insight into actual audit practice. Power claims that what is important is not *how* an audit has been performed but that an audit *has been* performed. Thus when the words 'we've been audited' are uttered they have a meaning far beyond the simple declaration that a group of individuals have performed certain tests and procedures. In the corporate sector it serves as an essential lubricant to the operations of the capital markets and is seen by some as a sedative reducing the anxiety of those who have invested in or lent money to the company. At this stage one may be prompted to ask whether the limitations of auditing are generally known. The answer to this question may well be in the affirmative but audit is now such an important institutional structure that to question it is to question a part of the fabric of society. For many, audit is the only practical control device.

ACTIVITY 20.9

Consider the following scenario: one day it is revealed that financial audits are worthless and have been an expensive charade; if you are a substantial investor in a number of companies what would be your response?

You might have said that your immediate response would be to panic, to be concerned that the comfort you gained from knowing that an audit had been performed has been misplaced. You may well become anxious about the safety of your investments and if your anxiety were strong enough, you would immediately sell your investments. If many investors did the same, share prices would fall dramatically. You may consider this fanciful but stop for a minute and consider the panic induced and the turmoil created by the stock market crash in 1987 or the fall in share prices in Thailand, Malaysia and Korea during 1997. Can these events be explained purely by changes in fundamentals or were they owing, at least partly, to anxieties on the part of investors? Such events serve to demonstrate that markets can be extremely volatile and are, perhaps, not as solid and strong as we are led to believe. Of course, you may be more reflective and simply say that the fundamentals haven't changed and that all that has occurred is that there has been an increase in the risk associated with investing in companies and you will have to be paid a premium for bearing that risk. This is a reasonable response but which response would be dominant and is it worth taking the risk of finding out by questioning the value of the audit? We hope you can see that sometimes it is easier to accept things the way they are rather than to question their foundations. As an aside you might want to consider why, when it seems as though one particular office, the Houston office, of Arthur Andersen was most culpable in the Enron debacle, that audit clients started to desert Andersen worldwide, because of the impression it might give to markets if they remained with the firm.

We now turn to assessing the validity of claims that the United Kingdom is becoming an audit society. As mentioned at the start of this chapter the concept of the audit society has not, with certain exceptions, been subject to much discussion either in the academic or professional press and therefore what follows is essentially our own commentary on the concept. It is perhaps not unsurprising that the ideas on the audit society have not raised much comment in the professional literature because they do not directly attack or criticize the audit profession in the same way as the other criticisms we discussed earlier in the chapter.

An important premise of the audit society is the observation by Power that the use of the idea of *audit* has become much more common in the last ten or so years. We would not disagree with this observation as there is considerable evidence of an increase in number and variety of audits performed in such areas as education, energy, medical and environment. We believe that Power's investigation of the nature of audit is beneficial because it helps to illuminate and challenge accepted practice. The questioning of accepted practice reflects a mode of reflexive thinking on ideas or concepts which can lead to better understanding or improved practices and is one to which we believe most individuals would be sympathetic. However, a few words of caution are in order.

First, it is important not to overemphasize the importance of 'audit' by focusing on the similarities between different forms of audit and ignoring the differences between them. 'Audit' may simply be a convenient label to cover a multitude of different practices. 'Audit' as a label may have an important symbolic content, but it is equally important to guard against giving it undue weight. For instance, 'audit' may be used instead of 'investigation' because the latter is considered to have certain authoritarian or disciplinary overtones, whereas the former is seen as being more neutral. Any tentative conclusions on issues such as this require considerable research to identify the content of practices involving 'audit' and how the use of the term to describe a particular form of practice originated. It may be argued that the symbolism involved in using the term is itself important, but to reach this conclusion we would need to investigate how the various parties subject to audit understand what is meant by the process of audit. As an example, medical staff may view the form of audit to which they are subject in quite a different way from teaching staff who are subject to academic audits. Both of these groups may have different perceptions of audit from those of company directors and employees who are subject to financial audit. As a final thought on this issue, Power, perhaps, gives too little emphasis to the period of time in which the audit explosion occurred. The expansion coincided with the establishment and acceptance of 'Thatcherism' in the United Kingdom. In a sense the increase in audit could be viewed as a means of disciplining and of controlling various areas of activity, such as teaching and medicine. The use of audit may have been consistent both with Thatcherite ideology and have been seen as a convenient and practical solution to certain perceived problems or issues, such as accountability. In this context it is important not to place too much emphasis on audit as universal or as a necessary or unchanging phenomenon. Before we can reach conclusions on issues such as those raised by Power we need a longer time span to investigate not only the emergence of the idea of audit but also how it has responded and changed through time.

We use the term 'Thatcherism' to cover particular modes of government and ideology associated with the ex-Prime Minister, Margaret Thatcher.

Second, investigation of the concept of audit is likely to be viewed as more beneficial if it leads to improvement in practice. Although Power has identified certain issues, he has not set out an agenda for changing practice and he does acknowledge that his critique contains in the main no 'practical' guidelines for auditors. It may also be argued that the purpose of this form of critique is not to be prescriptive but more to sow the seeds for debate and discussion from which changes in practice may occur. We have a certain sympathy for this latter view but are also aware that audit practitioners consider themselves to be practical individuals who want to know how to improve practice and receive specific guidance rather than to indulge in what they might regard as academic 'navel gazing'. It is to be hoped that more enlightened practitioners take on board and debate the ideas contained in the 'audit society' and act to change practice. Nevertheless, we consider that a more direct engagement with practice is more likely to bring about change. As evidence of this perspective, it is useful to consider a review of Power's *The Audit Society* (1997a) by Kelly (1997) in the *Financial Times*. This review suggested that the book 'seeks to set [the theme of the audit society] in a much more formal academic framework – a framework that, frankly, obscures the beauty of the original argument for anyone other than the expert or the aficionado'. The author of the review then goes on to suggest that Power 'having cemented the argument in this academic treatise ... should sweep on to more popular fields'. While we would not entirely agree with the sentiments expressed by the *Financial Times* reviewer, his views do serve to demonstrate the difficulty in having ideas and concepts discussed and accepted by practitioners in any meaningful fashion. Part of this difficulty may be attributed to the emphasis on simplicity, short sound bites and material, such as executive summaries, which can be absorbed in a very short time span. In today's society individuals often do not want to become involved in detail but instead prefer to emphasize the search for solutions to problems rather than discussing complex issues that in the long run may be more helpful.

An important thread running through Power's work is that audit as a 'control over controls' is a form of second order control. Regarding financial audits, Power (1997a) documents the movement away from direct testing of transactions to the systems audit where the auditor is concerned with testing the controls over transactions. Power appears to consider this move to be negative: 'It is also at this point that the audit process begins to disengage itself from the transactional realities which underlie these control systems; the system becomes the primary auditable object' (p.20). By portraying the move as a distancing from reality Power would seem to suggest that the auditor's claim to be verifying the financial statements is more tenuous, or at least that the link is less obvious. In addition, the move may herald an important change in the nature of audit, that it is an examination of the systems in place rather than the objects of those systems. As we mentioned in the previous chapter, this has implications for the spread of the concept of audit into other domains and the universality of the auditors' expertise. It is, however, worth examining Power's claim that the systems audit involves a distancing from reality.

It is conceded that in a fairly obvious sense, 'auditing systems' is not the same as 'auditing the transactions' themselves; but the main issue is really about the relationship between systems and the transactions and balances controlled by those systems. Power's thesis seems to rely on a particular view about the lack of connection between a company's accounting and internal control systems and the transactions engaged in and recorded in its books and records. In a sense he seems to be implying that there is a limited engagement between the systems and the transactions themselves. Auditors, however, would point out that there is a direct relationship between transactions and the control systems operating over them. When a company implements controls, such as bank reconciliations, initialization of invoices, and segregation of duties, they do so because they believe there is a relationship between the controls and the transactions. Thus, checking a debtors control account should help in identifying errors in the recording of a transaction, and this is borne out by experience. The checking of systems may psychologically appear to be different from the actual checking of transactions or entries in the books of the company in that it is one step removed from the transaction and therefore causes concern that it is less effective. Such concern notwithstanding it may be argued that checking controls can provide the auditor with the same level of assurance about the accuracy of transactions as checking the actual transactions themselves. The reliance on controls does, however, require the auditor, either implicitly or explicitly, to specify the relationship between the accurate recording of transactions and entries and the controls imposed over them. It requires not only effective application of controls but that they also are appropriate and complete. In this sense there is a further element of risk in that if the auditor misspecifies the relationship between, say, the recording of a transaction and the controls that ensure it is accurately recorded, it could result in them placing unwarranted reliance on figures. An example of this is where the auditor fails to identify a weakness in a company's financial systems that can be exploited with resultant loss to the company. It can also be argued that controls can have unintended consequences. For instance, a control that involves administrative inconvenience may result in individuals being tempted not to comply with it. Alternatively, if employees recognize the control as an attempt to modify their behaviour they may not comply with it simply because it provides them with a source of pride not to do so. They may feel that they have 'bucked' the system.

Generally the more uncertain the relationship between controls and transactions and entries, the more important becomes the distinction between auditing controls and the auditing of transactions. For instance, if a dominant individual is responsible for exercising critical controls, the auditor may assess qualitative characteristics of the individual (such as diligence and integrity) that enables them to reach a conclusion about the effective application of controls by that individual. Thus, even in this simple example the relationship between the control and the accurate recording of transactions has become somewhat fuzzy. Another example would be a company involved in dealing in options or futures which makes considerable use of computer technology, enabling money to be transferred almost instantly across bank accounts in different continents and large gains or losses to be made very quickly. The controls over transactions in such a company are often computerized and as such will lack visibility and leave very little trace of having occurred. In both cases cited, because of the problematic nature of the relationship between controls and transactions, the auditor will place less emphasis on the controls and more on direct testing of transactions. If the relationship is well defined, however, the end result from the testing of controls or the testing of transactions may well be the same.

It may also be argued that auditors never completely disengage themselves from direct verification of the financial statements. This is because an audit is always likely to consist of some direct testing of transactions, checking of entries in the books of the company or verification of documents. In addition, auditors also perform analytical reviews on financial information, though this form of test itself may be considered as one step removed from transactional reality, as the auditor is forming a view on the statements without necessarily testing figures in detail. We might note here that part of the auditor's concerns are with the appropriate choice of accounting policies and the auditing of managerial judgement and it is in these areas that they depend less on auditing systems than on other forms of verification.

Some attempt has been made here to argue that the auditing of systems is not as substantive a change as Power would suggest. However, we have a certain sympathy with his contention that the emphasis on the audit of systems does enable auditors to claim that the skills required for (and the principles underlying) financial audit are not very different from that required for non-financial audits, such as medical and teaching audits. This allows the auditor to claim a certain level of expertise and legitimize their move into other domains. You will remember from earlier in this chapter that Power claims that having an audit done is actually more important than the techniques and practices that comprise the audit. We shall now consider the extent to which this assertion may be said to be valid.

First, if it holds true, it would almost suggest that the debate in audit firms about the appropriate techniques to employ and the scope of audit tests is essentially a waste of time. Although it may appear that the actual practices of the auditor are unimportant, this may be a misleading impression that arises, at least partially, because the only visible trail left by auditors as far as shareholders are concerned is the audit report. This gives the impression that all that matters is the report and the symbolic weight that is embedded in it. This view, however, ignores the amount of tacit and informal knowledge that exists about the audit process. Although sophisticated investors may not know exactly the type and scope of audit testing carried out in a specific audit assignment, they are often aware of the norms relating to audit work. So the fact that audit work is in the background and not observed by them does not make it any less important. These individuals (we are referring to sophisticated individuals, often directing the investing policy of financial institutions) are aware of the nature of audit tests performed and their limitations. A counter argument would be that not all investors have knowledge of auditing and we accept that lack of familiarity with the profession's view of the role and limitations of audit may be an important reason for the existence of the audit expectations gap. However, it is clearly important that enough major investors have knowledge of the audit function to appreciate what an audit report is saying and the limitations of audit.

Second, some argue that audit practices may exist and continue for a considerable period of time, although inadequately suited for their purpose, because vested interests have no reason to want any change to occur. In other words, individuals with power will see the existence of audit as more important than the actual practices of the audit. This argument assumes that the power of vested interest groups (the audit profession and participants in the financial industry) is so great that they effectively stifle debate or criticism, or that they are able to set the bounds within which any discussion takes place. It has also been argued that in their position as experts, auditors are trusted by other groups who delegate to them the authority to determine the practices of auditing. We agree to a certain extent with these arguments but consider that there may be constraints operating, which ensure that actual practices of audit are useful in more than simply a symbolic way. Specifically, if financial audit was believed to have limited utility, we believe that criticism of the practice of audit would surface and begin to challenge the need for audit in its existing form. Indeed, we would point to evidence in the shape of the considerable debate that has taken place in the 1990s about the role of auditing. It might be said that the debate has not led to any meaningful change in audit practices but it can equally be suggested that if audit continues to be seen as failing, then the debates about audit practice will surface again in the future.

Our comments above have been couched in terms of financial audit, but may be equally applied to the other and more recently adopted forms of audit, such as medical audit. We agree that some of the criticism of the new forms of audit is justified, but being relatively new, it may well be that criticism by stakeholders will rapidly emerge, if they are seen to have limited value. If the criticism is sufficiently strong and vociferous then it is likely to result in changes to the role and practices of audit in these other areas. Critics might argue that too much reliance should not be put on the effectiveness of market forces and that the market for audit is not subject to real market forces. We have already noted earlier in this chapter that much audit is imposed by law and is therefore not subject to unfettered market forces. If so, some of the arguments advanced above lose part of their power.

We might mention also that, although we have suggested the practices of audit are likely to change, it is our belief that any change is more inclined to be evolutionary rather than revolutionary. This is one reason that some of the more radical proposals, such as those contained in the ICAS discussion document *Auditing into the Twenty-first Century* are not likely to be introduced in the near future. In rounding off this part of the discussion we think it is important to recognize that consideration of the receptiveness of audit to change must be viewed over a long time period. In the short term we believe that changes in audit practices may not be adopted but that in the longer term change may be accepted.

ACTIVITY 20.10

Comment on our view that change may be accepted in the longer term.

In response to this question you may have made some the following points:

- First, human beings by their nature are more concerned with the short term than the long term. J.M. Keynes, the economist once observed: 'In the long run we are all dead', from which can be inferred that we should be concerned with changes in practice in the near future and not just assume that long-term market forces will ensure that we obtain the optimal set of institutional arrangements.
- Second, the question leaves open what is meant by the long term. For instance, if auditing has not changed over a period of say 25 years, it may be argued that this is because 25 years is an insufficient time for change to have occurred, thus providing an escape route for those who are subject to the criticisms of current audit practice.
- Finally, change may occur over the long term but it may not have been caused by criticism of existing practices but by structural changes that resulted in incentives for audit practitioners to change or amend their practices.

Another related criticism, by Power, arises from his concern that, although auditing is supposed to enhance accountability, it paradoxically can stifle or reduce debate and thus does not necessarily enhance democracy or accountability. This is because audit can be conceived as an aspect of image management, giving the appearance of openness and accountability but without actually furthering these aims. Although we take Power's point that audit, because of its symbolic content, can reduce debate we are less certain that it is easy to devise a system that achieves the laudable ideal of complete accountability or transparency. Any system or process aimed at further accountability will suffer from defects, in that only those aspects of the organization which can be measured, are likely to be the subject of audit. The more complex, less quantitative but perhaps important qualitative aspects of organizational life might remain 'unscathed' from audit investigation. While it may be argued that these aspects should be audited it is less clear how this can be achieved. Power seems to suggest that it can be achieved but requires the redesigning of audit processes so that they are sensitive to what they are attempting to do. It is difficult to object to the sentiments being expressed here but it remains an unanswered question whether the aims can be achieved in practice. This is only likely to occur if workable alternatives or changes to existing audit practice can be developed. Power's writings are a start in this process in that he highlights the issues, but to date there has been little identification and development of alternatives that are acceptable to participants. We are rather pessimistic about whether this is likely to be achieved in the near future.

In conclusion, it should be apparent from our comments above that we are sympathetic to much of Power's writings and believe they serve as a good foundation for generating discussion and debate. Unfortunately, external critique such as Power's is not always the best catalyst to achieve change which is more likely to occur from the inside because of dissatisfaction by audit participants. It has to be said, however, that the critics of the audit profession argue that the profession itself has been resistant to any meaningful changes. Alternatively, as seems to be the case with the reforms to audit regulation, change may occur because of interaction between the audit profession and government.

See Chapter 4.

Conclusion on the audit society

The purpose of Power's various writings is to submit audit to a form of critique, which has been relatively absent in the auditing literature. He believes that the emergence of the audit society originates in structural changes in organizational governance, which have resulted in audit being seen as a solution to issues related to accountability, transparency and control. For Power, the notion of audit has almost obtained a life of its own, where the notion itself determines that it should be used in different domains without considering its appropriateness. In other words, audit is seen as the solution. This ignores such negative aspects as the tendency for organizations to become preoccupied with audit and to ensure that they comply with whatever is required for audit purposes rather than, perhaps, more important issues. Furthermore, he questions whether it is actually achieving accountability and indeed, whether it is anything more than 'image management'.

In respect of policy implications Power (1997a) argues that it would be beneficial for audit itself to be audited. In other words there is a need to be reflective on the nature of the various types of audit and what they are achieving. This reflection would, perhaps, help to ensure that audit is used where it is most appropriate and create space for consideration of other, perhaps, more appropriate alternative arrangements. This may result in a society which is 'capable of knowing when to trust, and when to demand an audited account' (1997a: 146). Humphrey and Owen (2000) take issue with this arguing that while the use of the term 'trust' may have theoretical appeal, unless you know what you should be trusting then it is difficult for it to be applied in such a way as to effect social change. Before this can be done a vision of what constitutes a fair and just alternative to conventional corporate governance structures is required and this requires greater exploration of the notion of 'society' rather than 'audit'.

In respect of financial audit, it is Power's prognosis that because of changes in the nature of firms and information technology, internal audit is likely to become more important and external audit less so. Furthermore, the distinction between internal and external audit based on the importance of the concept of independence will become redundant. Power also believes that internal control functions may be contracted out to external agencies. Finally, in relation to this it is interesting to reflect on the fact that in the last few years there has been a debate about the extent to which audit firms should provide internal audit services because of the negative impact it may have on their independence.

Summary

In this chapter we considered the views put forward by critics of audit practice. We described how the critics perceive the audit profession to be self-interested and unable to act in the public interest. This was illustrated in the discussion of a number of important issues: regulation, the setting of auditing standards, disciplining and monitoring members and firms and independence. We also considered some of the responses by members of the audit profession to these criticisms. We discussed proposals and documents issued by the audit and assurance faculty of the ICAEW, the Financial Reporting Council, the Auditing Practices Board and the Institute of Chartered Accountants of Scotland, which highlighted a number of important issues and advocated certain changes to auditing. In the final section we discussed a more fundamental questioning of the function of audit, put forward by Michael Power. We described a number of features that Power considers characterizes the move in the UK towards an audit society. We concluded by discussing some of the limitations in the thesis by Power that the society in which we live today has become an audit society.

Key points of the chapter

- Critics of audit practice and of the auditing profession, are concerned with exposing the audit profession as self-interested. Critics argue that their purpose is to bring about changes beneficial to society.
- Bodies set up to issue auditing standards, including APC and the original APB, were criticized as not being sufficiently independent of accounting firms, and for lack of transparency in the standard-setting process.
- There has been increasing influence of international standard setting bodies such as the IAASB.
- Disciplining members is either carried out by individual accounting bodies or recently through the Accountancy & Actuarial Discipline Board (AADB). To date, no independent review has assessed the effectiveness of AADB.
- The monitoring of audit firms is carried out by the Audit Inspection Unit (AIU) of the Professional Oversight Board (POB) and the various RSBs with which respective audit firms are registered.
- The AIU has highlighted deficiencies in the procedures of the audit firms, but concluded that the overall standard of auditing was acceptable.
- POB also monitors the effectiveness of the RSBs and RQBs and found no serious deficiencies in their operation.

- Various measures have been taken to enhance auditor independence, matters of concern being the weakening of a strong professional audit culture, and the increase in lucrative non-audit work. Accounting bodies stress the importance of serving the public interest, but critics suggest accounting firms look after their own self-interest. Critics associate loss of independence with the rise of the business risk approach and suggest it is used as a platform for selling other services. The profession argues it can only recruit the most able individuals if it maintains the width of career opportunities available to accountants.
- Critics have made various suggestions on the way forward: (a) auditors must act exclusively as auditors; (b) auditors must be socially accountable; (c) the institutions of accountancy must be reformed.
- Critics maintain that the recent banking crisis demonstrates that the audit profession has not yet put its house in order.
- The accounting profession cite the large number of non-accountants on APB and regulatory and disciplinary committees and claim the profession pays due regard to the public interest. Audit failure is rare and business failure and audit failure should be distinguished. The profession supported the review of accounting and auditing carried out in 2002/2003 at the behest of the government and their support of the new regulatory structures that proceeded through parliament.
- The accounting profession, through such bodies as the audit and assurance faculty of the ICAEW, has been active in the last few years in producing documents and papers on audit reporting, audit quality and competition and choice in the audit market.
- Recent changes have included publishing of transparency reports and the requirement that certain audit firms comply or explain why they do not comply with provisions contained in an audit firm governance code. These measures are seen as improving the accountability of audit firms and it is hoped will have a role in improving audit quality and choice.
- *The Audit Agenda: Next Steps*, issued by APB made several proposals, some of which have been partially or fully implemented.
- *Auditing into the Twenty-first Century*, published by ICAS, was an attempt to address the expectations gap. Some of the proposals in this document have been implemented but the more radical ones tended not to be taken any further.
- A fundamental critique of the concept of audit has been made by Michael Power, writing on the 'audit society'. He sees an increase in the use of 'audit' in everyday life and questions why there has been such enthusiasm to adopt a particular term and style of activity. Power argues that the 'new' forms of audit are influenced by the nature of financial audit by accounting firms, and that they may emphasize aspects of performance, which can be measured and verified, rather than attempting to consider what is the best or most appropriate measure.
- Power offers three reasons for the large increase in activities termed auditing: (a) new form of management in the public sector; (b) increased demand by society for greater accountability by organizations; (c) increased use of quality-management practices and changes in regulatory style.
- Power notes that organizations increasingly rely on control systems, the existence of which, it is assumed, demonstrates compliance with rules, procedures, processes and practices. Audit is seen as a control of controls, thought by Power as undesirable because what becomes important is the existence of a system and its auditability, rather than what the particular system is supposed to achieve. Auditors themselves decide what is audited, despite unclarity about the level of assurance auditors provide in their reports. Audit only 'captures' those risks that can be identified by audit procedures and Power concludes that 'the profound irony of the audit society is that where auditing may be most desirable, it is least possible'.
- Power's work is beneficial because it helps to illuminate and challenge accepted practice, but it is worth examining Power's claim that 'auditing systems' is not the same as 'auditing the transactions' themselves. Auditors argue there is a direct relationship between transactions and control systems and that checking controls can provide them with the same level of assurance about the accuracy of transactions as checking the actual transactions. If there is uncertainty, auditors will place less emphasis on controls and more to direct testing of transactions. The emphasis on the audit of systems enables auditors to claim that the skills required for financial audit are not very different from those required for non-financial audits.
- The purpose of Power's writings is to submit audit to a new form of critique. The notion of audit has almost obtained a life of its own; being used in different domains without considering its appropriateness. There is a need to reflect on the nature of the various types of audit and what they are achieving, helping to ensure that audit is used where it is most appropriate and allow consideration of other more appropriate alternative arrangements.

References

In this chapter we hope we have given you some appreciation of the debates that are taking place over the role of auditing. Unfortunately, in a single chapter we can only give you an introduction to this topic. If you found the debates and discussion interesting you may want to read about them in a bit more depth. To help you with this we provide some references to the primary sources on which the material and arguments of this chapter are based.

Auditing Practices Board (1991) *Proposals for an Expanded Auditor's Report: a consultative paper*, London: APB, October.

Auditing Practices Board (1992) *The Future Development of Auditing: A Paper for Debate*, London: APB, November.

Auditing Practices Board (1994) *The Audit Agenda*, London: APB, December.

Auditing Practices Board (1996) *The Audit Agenda: Next Steps*, APB, reprinted in *Accountancy*, April: 134–7.

Auditing Practices Board (2007) *Auditor's Report: A Time for Change?* Discussion Paper, London, APB, December.

Auditing Practices Board (2009) *Consultation on Audit Firms Providing Non-Audit Services to Listed Companies that they Audit*, London, APB, October.

Barker, G. (2003) 'Enron: Not all Bad', *Accountancy*, January: 78.

Canning, M. and O'Dwyer, B. (2001) 'Professional Accounting Bodies' Disciplinary Procedures: Accountable, Transparent and in the Public Interest?' *European Accounting Review*, 10(4): 725–49.

Company Law Review Steering Group (2001) *Modern Company Law for a Competitive Economy: Final Report*, London: HMSO.

Cousins, J., Mitchell, A. and Sikka, P. (1999) 'Auditor Liability: The Other Side of the Debate', *Critical Perspectives on Accounting*, 10(3): 283–312.

Cross Report (1977) 'Report of a Committee under the Chairmanship of the Rt Hon Lord Cross of Chelsea', *Accountancy*, December: 80–6.

Department of Trade and Industry (2003a) 'Coordinating Group on Audit and Accounting Issues', *Final Report to the Secretary of State for Trade and Industry and the Chancellor of the Exchequer*, January. (available at http://www.bis.gov.uk/files/file20380.pdf)

Department of Trade and Industry (2003b) *Review of the Regulatory Regime of the Accountancy Profession, Report to the Secretary of State for Trade and Industry*, January (available at http://www.bis.gov.uk/files/file20686.pdf)

European Union (2006) '8th Company Law Directive on Statutory Audits of Annual Accounts and Consolidated Accounts', May (available at http://eur-lex.europa.eu/LexUriServ/LexUriServ.do?uri=OJ:L:2006:157:0087:0107:EN:PDF)

Financial Reporting Council (2003) *Audit Committees Combined Code Guidance: A report and proposed guidance by an FRC-appointed group chaired by Sir Robert Smith* (available at http://www.ecgi.org/codes/documents/ac_report.pdf)

Financial Reporting Council (2004/05 to 2008/09) Audit Inspection Unit, *Audit Quality Inspections Public Report* (available at http://www.frc.org.uk/pob/audit/reports.cfm)

Financial Reporting Council (2006) *Discussion Paper: Choice in the UK Audit Market*, May (available at http://www.frc.org.uk/images/uploaded/documents/Choice%20in%20the%20UK%20Audit%20Market%20Discussion%20Paper4.pdf)

Financial Reporting Council (2006) *Choice in the UK Audit Market: Briefing paper for second shareholder meeting*, September (available at http://www.frc.org.uk/about/auditchoice.cfm)

Financial Reporting Council (2006) *Discussion Paper: Promoting Audit Quality*, November (available at http://www.frc.org.uk/about/auditchoice.cfm_)

Financial Reporting Council (2007) *Choice in the UK Audit Market: Final Report of the Market Participants Group*, October (available at http://www.frc.org.uk/about/auditchoice.cfm)

Financial Reporting Council (2007) *Promoting Audit Quality*, October (available at http://www.frc.org.uk/images/uploaded/documents/Feedback%20Document%20Final3.pdf)

Financial Reporting Council (2008) *The Audit Quality Framework*, February (available at http://www.frc.org.uk/images/uploaded/documents/Audit%20Quality%20Framework%20for%20web1.pdf)

Financial Reporting Council (2008) *The Combined Code on Corporate Governance*, July (available at http://www.frc.org.uk/documents/pagemanager/frc/Combined%20code%202006%20OCTOBER.pdf)

Financial Reporting Council (2009) *Choice in the UK Audit Market: Fourth Progress Report*, October, available at http://www.frc.org.uk/about/auditchoice.cfm)

Financial Reporting Council and Institute of Chartered Accountants in England and Wales (2010), *The Audit Firm Governance Code*, available at http://www.frc.org.uk/documents/pagemanager/frc/The%20Audit%20Firm%20Governance%20Code.pdf

Financial Reporting Council (various years) Professional Oversight Board, *Review of Audit Monitoring by the Recognised Supervisory Bodies for Audit in the UK* (available by year at http://www.frc.org.uk/pob/publications/)

Financial Reporting Council (various years) Professional Oversight Board, *Transparency Reporting by Auditors of Public Interest Entities,* (available by year at http://www.frc.org.uk/pob/publications/)

'FTSE 100 Auditors Survey' (2006) *Accountancy,* September: 28–31.

'FTSE 100 Auditors Survey' (2009) *Accountancy,* September: 25–27.

Grenside Report (1979) 'Report of the Joint Committee Appointed to Consider the Cross Report and Related Matters', *Accountancy*, June: 124–32.

Holmes, B. (2002) 'WorldCom: Could it Happen Here?', *Accountancy*, August: 18–20.

Hourquebie, P. (2003) *Auditor Independence – Is Rotation the Solution*, available at http://www.ey.com/GLOBAL/content.nsf/South_Africa/A_word_from_Philip_-_Auditor_Independence_-_Is_Rotation_the_Solution)

Humphrey, C. (2008) 'Auditing Research: A Review Across the Disciplinary Divide', *Accounting, Auditing and Accountability,* 21(2): 170–203.

Humphrey, C. and Owen, D. (2000) 'Debating the "Power" of Audit', *International Journal of Auditing*, 4: 29–50.

Humphrey, C., Loft, A. and Woods, M. (2009) 'The Global Audit Profession and the International Financial Architecture: Understanding Regulatory Relationships at a Time of Financial Crisis', *Accounting, Organizations and Society*, 34(6–7): 810–25.

Institute of Chartered Accountants in England and Wales (2002) *Audit Quality*, Audit and Assurance Faculty, November.

Institute of Chartered Accountants in England and Wales (2005) *Shareholder involvement – Competition and Choice* (Interim Report), Audit and Assurance Faculty.

Institute of Chartered Accountants in England and Wales (2007) *Audit Quality Fundamental – Auditor reporting*, London: Audit and Assurance Faculty.

Institute of Chartered Accountants in England and Wales/Financial Reporting Council (2010), *The Audit Firm Governance Code*, (available at: http://www.frc.org.uk/documents/pagemanager/frc/The%20Audit%20Firm%20Governance%20Code.pdf.pdf)

Institute of Chartered Accountants of Scotland (1993) *Auditing into the Twenty-first Century*, Edinburgh: ICAS.

Institute of Chartered Accountants of Scotland (1995)*Audit Regulation in the Public Interest*, Edinburgh: ICAS.

Institute of Chartered Accountants of Scotland (2010) *The Provision of Non-Audit Services by Audit Firms to their Listed Audit Clients*, Edinburgh: ICAS.

Jeppesen, K.K. (1998) 'Reinventing Auditing, Redefining Consulting and Independence', *The European Accounting Review*, 7(3): 517–39.

Kelly, J. (1997) 'Auditing, The Unbearable Tyranny of Beans', *The Financial Times*, 30 September.

Kershaw, D. (2005) 'Evading Enron: Taking Principles too Seriously in Accounting Regulation', *The Modern Law Review*, 68(4): 594–625.

Khalifa, R., Sharma, N., Humphrey, C. and Robson, K. (2007) 'Discourse and Audit Change: Transformations in Methodology in the Professional Audit Field', *Accounting, Auditing and Accountability Journal*, 20: 825–54.

Lee, T. (2002) 'The Shame of Auditing', *International Journal of Auditing*, 6(3): 211–14.

Lerner, N. (2002) 'Ethics and the Auditor', *Accountancy*, July: 1.

Lickiss, M. (1990) 'Auditing's critics "Short on Fact, Long on Rhetoric"', *Guardian*, 19 December: 15.

Maltby, C. (2008) 'There is no such thing as audit society: a reading of Power, M. (1994a) "The Audit Society"', *Ephemera*, Vol.8(4): 388–98.

Mitchell, A. and Sikka, P. (1993) 'Accounting for Change: The Institutions of Accountancy', *Critical Perspectives on Accounting*, 4: 29–52.

Oxera (2006) *Competition and Choice in the UK Audit Market*, prepared for Department of Trade and Industry and the Financial Reporting Council, April (available at http://www.berr.gov.uk/files/file28529.pdf)

Plaistowe, I. (1991) 'Accountants Hit Back at "Failed Police" Charge', *Guardian*, 10 September: 11.

Plaistowe, I. (1992) 'Profession Determined to Meet Present and Future Challenges', *The Times*, 30 April: 25.

Pong, C. and Whittington, G. (1994) 'The Working of the Auditing Practices Committee – Three Case Studies', *Accounting and Business Research*, 24(94): 157–75.

Power, M. (1992) 'From Common Sense to Expertise: The Pre-history of Audit Sampling', *Accounting, Organizations and Society,* 17: 37–62.

Power, M. (1993) 'The Politics of Financial Auditing', *The Political Quarterly*, 63: 272–84.

Power, M. (1994) 'The Audit Society', in A. Hopwood, and P. Miller (eds), *Accounting as Social and Institutional Practice*, Cambridge: Cambridge University Press.

Power, M. (1995) 'Auditing, Expertise and the Sociology of Technique', *Critical Perspectives on Accounting*, 6: 317–39.

Power, M. (1997a) *The Audit Society: Rituals of Verification*, Oxford: Oxford University Press.

Power, M. (1997b) 'The Audit Society: Second Thoughts', paper presented as the Seventh National Auditing Conference, Cranfield University.

Power, M.K. (2003) 'Auditing and the Production of Legitimacy', *Accounting, Organizations and Society*, 28: 379–94.

Power, M. (2007) *Organised Uncertainty: Designing a World of Risk Management*, Oxford: Oxford University Press.

Power, M. (2008), 'In Defence of the Audit Society: A Reply to Maltby', *Ephemera*, 8(4): 99–402.

Sikka, P. (1997) 'Regulating the Audit Society', in *Current Issues in Auditing*, 3rd edn, M. Sherer and S. Turley (eds), London: Paul Chapman Press.

Sikka, P. (2003a) 'Some Questions about the Governance of Auditing Firms', University of Essex, Working Paper No. 03/07.

Sikka, P. (2003b) 'DTI's Audit Reforms Won't End Predatory Culture of firms', *The Times*, 6 February: 29.

Sikka, P. (2003c) 'A Comment on the DTI's Review of the Regulatory Regime of the Accountancy Profession', January, unpublished paper.

Sikka, P. (2008) 'Enterprise Culture and Accountancy Firms: New Masters of the Universe', *Accounting, Auditing and Accountability Journal*, 21(2): 268–95.

Sikka, P. (2009) 'Financial Crisis and the Silence of the Auditors', *Accounting, Organizations and Society*, Vol. 34 (6–7): 868–73.

Sikka, P., Willmott, H. and Lowe, T. (1989) 'Guardians of Knowledge and Public Interest: Evidence and Issues of Accountability in the UK Accountancy Profession', *Accounting, Auditing and Accountability*, 2(2): 47–71.

Sukhraj, P. (2007) 'Tories Demand Mayflower Judgment', *Accountancy Age*, 18 January: 1.

Swinson, C. (2002) 'Unusual Suspects?' *Accountancy*, November: 83.

Wyman, P. (2002a) 'Responding to Enron', *Accountancy*, July: 124–5.

Wyman, P. (2002b) 'Why Business Failures Don't Mean Enronitis Has Hit the UK', *Accountancy*, November: 127.

Further reading

Any of the articles written by Sikka serve as a good introduction to the critics perspective of auditing but his *Race to the Bottom: The Case of the Accountancy Firms,* co-authored with Cousins and Mitchell, published in 2004 is especially recommended.

The most obvious place to find a defence against the criticism of the accounting profession is in the professional accounting journals, in particular *Accountancy,* the magazine of the ICAEW. *The Audit Agenda* and *The Audit Agenda: Next Steps* issued by the APB are both worth reading. For further reading on audit regulation, students should refer to either the magazines *Accountancy* or *Accountancy Age* both of which in the last few years have contained a number of articles on this topic.

An article of some interest by authors who are more sympathetic to the audit profession is Fearnley, S., Beattie, V.A. and Brandt, R. (2005), 'Auditor Independence and Audit Risk: A Reconceptualization', *International Journal of Accounting Research*, 4(1): 39–71.

Finally a good source of information is the websites of the ICAEW (**http://www.icaew.co.uk/**) and the Financial Reporting Council (**http://www.frc.org.uk/**).

Students would find it particularly useful to read the various outputs from the audit and assurance faculty of the ICAEW. The paper on 'Promoting Audit Quality' issued by the Financial Reporting Council is also worth reading. An article by Jon Grant in *Accountancy*, January 2007: 88–9 provides a good summary of the FRC paper.

As the European Union exerts ever more influence in this area it is recommended that students occasionally visit their website at **http://ec.europa.eu/internal_market/auditing/index_en.htm**

As this is an area where there are likely to be changes over the next year or so it important that students keep up to date by reading one or more of the accounting bodies' magazines, such as *Accountancy*.

The easiest entry point to Michael Power's work is a Demos monograph published in 1994, titled 'The Audit Explosion', London: Demos.

> Demos is a think tank with political leanings to the left who have published interesting monographs on a number of different topics.

An alternative to this is the article 'The Audit Society' in Hopwood and Miller (eds), *Accounting as Social and*

Institutional Practice (1994), referred to above. Students seeking a sympathetic critique of Power's work should read the article by Humphrey and Owen cited in the references. Finally, there is a good chapter on Internal Control (Chapter 2) in Michael Power's *Organised Uncertainty: Designing a World of Risk Management* (2007).

Self-assessment questions (solutions available to students)

20.1 Much of the criticism of auditing practice is misplaced because it does not accurately distinguish between business failure and audit failure. Discuss.

20.2 Discuss the contribution that Michael Power has made in his writings on the audit society to the debate about auditing.

Self-assessment questions (solutions available to tutors)

20.3 Discuss the extent to which you believe the criticisms of the regulation of auditing are valid.

20.4 In Chapter 4 we outlined certain changes to the regulation of auditing. Do you believe these changes are likely to eliminate criticism of audit regulation?

20.5 A common practice by audit firms during the 1990s was low-balling, that is, the submitting of an artificially low tender price by audit firms for a new audit on the assumption that the fees the firm would recoup from expected non-audit work would compensate for the tender fee being below the economic price for the audit. Discuss the extent to which you believe low-balling is likely to impede independence and whether any steps should be taken by the audit profession to ban it.

Topics for class discussion without solutions

20.6 The critics' obsession with attacking what they perceive to be the lack of independence of audit firms from their clients is misplaced. Discuss.

20.7 The lack of implementation of the more radical proposals in the ICAS publication *Auditing into the Twenty-first Century* demonstrates there is strong resistance to change within the audit profession. Discuss.

20.8 Critically evaluate the various proposals that have been put forward to improve the usefulness of the audit report.

21

Examination hints and final remarks

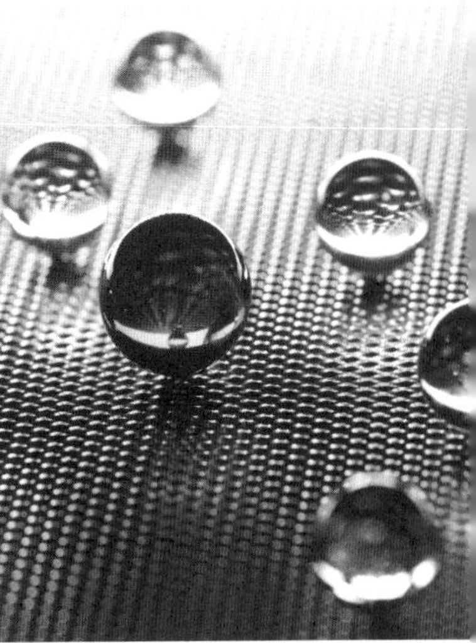

LEARNING OBJECTIVES

After studying this chapter you should be able to:

- **Understand generally how you can best manage your time and your approach to questions in the examination room.**
- **Recognize the need to use the information in the questions provided by the examiner.**
- **Be concise in your answers and see that irrelevant padding material should be avoided.**
- **Apply higher skills in answering questions, particularly in the more advanced examination papers.**

Learning objectives, 815
Introduction, 816
General examination hints, 816
Auditing as an examination subject, 819
Final remarks, 819

INTRODUCTION

As an examination subject, auditing tends to be more literary than numeric. Numeracy is certainly required in certain areas, such as being able to make analytical reviews of accounting information, but the overriding ability required is to marshal your thoughts in a logical fashion, select what is relevant to the question posed by the examiner and to write your answers clearly and concisely within the time limit imposed.

We set out below a number of suggestions that we believe should guide you in the examination room. Some of these suggestions are general in nature and others are specific to auditing as a subject. We start with the general points.

GENERAL EXAMINATION HINTS

Control over time

All examinations are restricted in duration, and three hours will be the normal length of time at your disposal. It is vital that you recognize the importance of attempting all questions required as it is normally far easier to get the first 50 per cent of marks on any question than the last 50 per cent. This means that you must allocate your time to enable all questions and parts of questions to be attempted. It will be usual for marks allocated to questions and parts of questions to be stated and your first task should be to convert marks to time in minutes. This you can do by multiplying the marks by 1.8 to give time in minutes in a three-hour examination. Thus for part of a question allocated five marks you should try not to exceed nine minutes to answer it. We are, incidentally, not suggesting that you should adhere slavishly to a particular length of time. Most students will be able to answer some questions better than others and it would be foolish to leave a question when you still have important points to make. It would be equally foolish, however, to answer only four questions (say) and to be marked out of 80 per cent instead of 100 per cent.

In some examinations you may be given several minutes reading time before the actual examination commences. Make sure that you use this time well, in particular making sure that you understand what the examiner is asking of you and deciding which of the optional questions you intend to answer (see below):

Question selection

If the examination paper contains a choice of questions, you should use some time to select the questions you can answer best. This is where reading time can be particularly useful. As far as compulsory questions are concerned, the order in which you attempt them may be important and you should do first the questions you are good at. In a paper containing a compulsory section it is, in our view, normally desirable to answer this section first as it will usually be central to the syllabus.

Understanding the question

We have read numerous examiners' comments on the way that students have performed in the examination room and one comment that appears over and over again is: 'Many students do not appear to have read the question carefully enough!' A good tip when reading through any question and the examination requirements is to ask yourself the questions: 'What does the examiner expect from me?' 'What aspect of the syllabus is being examined?'

It is also vital that you read the requirements carefully. If the examiner says for instance, 'Comment briefly on the four items in the internal audit job specification, indicating with examples the extent to which they might impinge upon the work of the statutory auditor', he or she will expect you not only to *comment* but also to *give examples*. It is useful in this context to realize that the examiner will have prepared a marking schedule and that marks will have been allocated to suitable examples. This means that comment without examples will inevitably make it impossible to give you all the marks allocated to the question.

Closely linked to understanding the question is the use of information provided. For instance, many questions will contain figures such as turnover and profit before tax, and the financial impact of matters requiring attention by the auditor. Examiners may not mention materiality directly, but will certainly expect you to consider the significance of the matters in relation to other figurative information provided. Thus, if you are told that profit before tax is £500 000, that the stated stock figure is £250 000, and that your audit tests have detected an overstatement of inventories of £24 000, you should be prepared to state with reasons whether you regard the overstatement of profit and stock by 4.8 per cent and 9.6 per cent respectively as material or not. An approach like this will be worth a mark or two.

Form of answer

This is linked to understanding the question but we wish to emphasize particularly that you should note the examiner's requirements as to the form of answer. If the examiner, for instance, asks you to draft an engagement letter, he or she will expect the answer to be in the form of a letter. If a memorandum on internal control is required, then clearly your answer should be drafted as a memorandum. It is likely in such cases that the examiner will have allocated marks for style and layout. On the other hand, if the examiner asks you (say) to *list* the reasons for which audit working papers are prepared, your answer would more properly be written as a numbered list of points.

As far as possible you should try not to waste time by giving extensive definitions such as those of audit risk, inherent risk, control risk and detection risk (unless you are required to do so). This is particularly important at the more advanced levels. Basically, your answer should show clearly that you know what these terms mean. For instance, you might say something like: 'The fact that credit control procedures are weak means that control risk will be high in this area and the auditors will need to ensure that detection risk is low, by increasing substantive procedures, such as …'.

Length of answer

This is linked to time allocation. If the examiner expects you to write for eight or nine minutes to get your five marks, he will not be very impressed with five lines. Most examiners will be disinclined to give you one mark per line. We do not wish you to think that we are being flippant in this respect, merely that you should recognize the need to produce a complete answer within the time constraints.

One other matter we would mention is the length of answers prepared either by examiners themselves or by third parties – or indeed by us in this book. It will not normally be possible under examination conditions to reproduce answers in the scope and detail of our suggested solutions. They are intended to be teaching/learning guides as much as answers to the questions *per se*. This is inevitable, we suggest, as you will agree if you reflect upon the fact that most answers produced under examination conditions are likely to be incomplete.

Relevance

Many students disgorge on to the script all they know about a subject area, whether relevant or not, hoping, no doubt, that some of it will be worth a mark or two. We call this the 'dustbin syndrome' and you must avoid it at all costs. You will only gain marks if your answer is relevant to the question.

Higher skills

When you are approaching the final examination papers before qualification, a much greater degree of flair will be expected of you than in earlier papers. You will be expected to display higher skills. We can best exemplify what we mean by higher skills by giving you a brief example from one of the cases we have discussed in this book – Case study 15.2 on Gilling Limited. In this case you were given a forecast profit and loss account and told that the company was seeking funds from a bank for the purchase of a second boat. You might gain half a mark by saying that you would check the calculation of the £100 000 expected income from fares, but you would be exhibiting flair and higher skills if you had calculated the total possible income and then compared in with the £100 000 in the forecast profit and loss account. You will remember that we discovered that the £100 000 was 56 per cent of the total capacity assuming a particular passenger mix. By doing this you might get as much as two marks for your point, and another if you said that you would use this information to discuss with management the risks that the company assumptions about income will not be met.

To take another example from this case, we suggested in our answer that a forecast cash flow statement should also be included in the subject matter and given to the bank with our report. The reason we suggested this is that banks are extremely interested in cash flows and the company's ability to generate cash to pay interest and make repayments of the loan. Students who recognize that this is so would be exhibiting higher skills and would be duly rewarded with higher marks. You would gain another three marks, perhaps, for making these points. If you had said in your answer that a negative expression of opinion would have been given, that too would perhaps be worth half a mark but if you had gone on to say that such an opinion would have been appropriate because forecasts are, by their nature, uncertain, you would have shown real understanding, and another mark would have come your way. Before long if you continued in this vein, you would have gained the pass marks for the question, and probably many more. Basically, exhibiting higher skills means that you consider the wider implications of the scenario and give reasoned explanations.

AUDITING AS AN EXAMINATION SUBJECT

Syllabus

The first thing to be said is that you must know the syllabus – that is, the subject areas examinable at your stage. Another important aspect is the level of knowledge required from you as a student. The accounting bodies do issue guidelines as to level of knowledge and you should make sure that you understand what the levels mean.

Application of official material

The accounting bodies normally state the extent to which students should have knowledge of auditing, accounting and ethical standards, including exposure drafts. It will clearly be of importance that you should know what will be examined.

Style of paper

Different accounting bodies have different styles when it comes to examination questions and you should review past papers to help you see what is required of you.

FINAL REMARKS

You have now reached the end of the study chapters. In our view, you are now well placed to approach auditing examinations with confidence. Remember that the best way to pass examinations is to know the subject matter well, but note that we do believe the examination hints we have offered will also be of value to you. We have attempted throughout this book to give a flavour of the audit process, as we believe this to be essential to the student of auditing. To a very large extent the book contains years of experience of teaching to and learning from students in the classroom and our thanks are due to them. Believe it or not, many of them have become friends after qualification.

Apart from confidence in the examination room, however, you should now have a good appreciation of what auditing is about and the possible directions that auditing will be taking. In our view it is essential that you keep yourself up to date, and to this end we would recommend that you read regularly a reputable accounting journal. We have also recommended further reading at the end of each chapter. Some of this has an academic flavour; other reading is practical in nature. In our view, a blend of theoretical and practical knowledge is vital in the environment facing the auditor at the present time. Earlier in the book we said that there was one piece of advice that was of overriding importance for the auditor and we intend to close with it:

'KEEP YOUR EYES OPEN!'

INDEX

AADB *see* Accountancy and Actuarial Discipline Board
ABI *see* Association of British Insurers
ACCA *see* Association of Chartered Certified Accountants
access controls
  computer systems
    firewalls 288, 290
    passwords 288, 289
    telephone numbers 289–90
accountability 24, 797, 799
  'account' meaning 61
  definition 61
  document 63–4
  'holding to account' meaning 61
  managerial 62, 63
  parties to accountability/audit process 36–8
  personal 62, 63
  political 62
  professional 62, 63
  public 62, 63
  relationship to audit 34–5, 38
  standards 34–5
Accountancy and Actuarial Discipline Board (AADB) 116, 121, 767–8
Accountancy Foundation 115, 117
accounting
  expertise 48, 49
  flexibility 74
  information 36–7
  records 547
accounting standards
  audit implications 441–2
  consistency in application 521–2
Accounting Standards Board (ASB) 38, 56, 122, 126, 441, 692, 701
Accounting Standards Committee (ASC) 122
accounting systems 258–9
Audit Commission (for England and Wales) 599
Accounts Commission (for Scotland) 599
ACR *see* Audit Compliance Review
adverse opinion 636
advocacy services
  small entities 101
  threats to compliance 79
agency theory 9–11, 37
  accountability and 63
agreed-upon procedures engagement 234
AICPA *see* American Institute of Certified Public Accountants
American Accounting Association (AAA) 36, 38
American Institute of Certified Public Accountants (AICPA) 52, 705
analytical procedures 360, 428–30
  audit approach to review of data 430–2
  definition 428
  direct audit effort 430
  evidence collection 215
  evidence gathering 233
  graphs 436
  inventories 491–509
  multiple regression analysis 436
  ratio analysis 430–6
  regression analysis 436
  risk assessment 160–1
  substantive procedures 436–41
  trade payables 518–25
  trade receivables 468–71
  Z-scores 436
analytical review
  audit approach 430–2
  in examination room 433–6
  as risk analysis tool 185–6
APB *see* Auditing Practices Board
APC *see* Auditing Practices Committee
application controls
  audit approaches 305–22
  data capture/input controls 287–94
  database systems 297–9
  e-commerce 299–305
  general controls distinction 260
  output controls 296–7
  processing controls 294–6
  sales system 338–40
  see also boundary controls; input controls
application objectives 286–7
appointment of auditor 11, 37, 49, 131, 133–4, 139–41, 143–5
AQR *see* Assurance Quality Review
ARC *see* Audit Registration Committee
Arthur Andersen 2, 3, 53, 101, 102, 130, 773, 774, 802
ASC *see* Accounting Standards Committee
assertions by management *see* management assertions
assistant auditors 190
association 25, 47
Association of British Insurers (ABI) 49
Association of Chartered Certified Accountants (ACCA) 750
assurance engagements 565–9, 577–83
  assertion-based engagements 566–7
  assurance report 572–3
  criteria 567, 569–71
    completeness 570
    neutrality 570
    relevance 570
    reliability 570
    understandability 570
  definition 566
  direct reporting engagements 566–7
  engagement acceptance 571–2
  evidence-gathering procedures 572
  importance 576–7
  internal controls 568
  letter of engagement 571–2
  levels of assurance 574–6
  limited assurance engagement 567, 573
  negative assurance 565
  practitioner 567
  reasonable assurance engagement 567, 573
  responsible party 569
  subject matter 567
  sufficient appropriate evidence 567
Assurance Quality Review (AQR) 49
assurance report 572–3
assurance services 20–1, 123
attribute sampling 402, 405, 407
audit
  basic framework 15
  as control over controls 804–5
  criticisms 795–808
  definition 23, 61
  importance 803
  justification 9–11
  objectives/scope 192
  policy implications 808–9
  principles 21–2
  relationship to accountability 34–5, 38
  restricted role 63
  theory 30–2
Audit Agenda – Next Steps (1996) 124, 667–9, 792–3
Audit Agenda (1994) 669, 763, 792
Audit and Assurance Faculty 781, 783
audit automation 383
  information retrieval and analysis 383
  interpretation and documentation of results 384
  manuals and checklists on computer file 384
  planning/allocation of staff/other resources to audit assignment 383
  review and reporting activities 384
  risk assessment 383
Audit Commission (England and Wales) 600, 697
Audit Commission for Local Authorities 599
audit committee 128–9, 132, 164, 248, 547
  audit matters 714–16
  authority and duties 714
  Combined Code and 713–16
  financial reporting 714
  public sector 601–2
Audit Compliance Review (ACR) 49–50
audit documentation
  manuals and checklists on computer file 384
  nature/purpose 554–6
  relationships and contents 557
audit engagement partner 82, 85, 87, 90, 91, 189
audit enquiries 160–5
audit evidence *see* evidence

audit expectations gap 33, 50–2, 691
auditor role in society 702–3
causes 692–703
costs and benefits of audit procedures 703
deficient performance gap 50–1
lack of competence 693, 695–6
lack of practitioner independence-7 696
deficient standards gap 50, 697
fraud 698–9
going concern 699–701
development and solutions 703–5
direction of change 703
expansion of auditors' duties 703–4
possible reasons for 703–5
society's changing expectations 705
flexibility of auditors' duties
greater societal awareness 704–5
societal role of audit function 704
technological change 705
performance gap 50
profession independence 701
protagonists 691–2
academics 692
politicians 692
regulators 692
quality gap 702
reasonableness gap 50
role gap 702
structure 694
unreasonable expectations 702–3
audit failure 123, 780, 797–8
audit firms, mandatory rotation of 92
Audit Inspection Unit (AIU) 50, 94, 119–21, 769–71
audit judgement *see* judgement
audit monitoring 126–127
audit planning memorandum 199–201
audit process 48
management 189–90
audit programme
cash audit programme 393–4
cash and bank balances 377, 392–394
development of programme for purchases 361–364
design 166
production wages 390–392
wages 375–7
audit quality 48–9
audit agenda 792–3
audit reporting 785–8
auditing in twenty-first century 793–5
choice in UK audit market 788–92
client relationships 782
drivers
audit firm culture 782
effectiveness of audit process 783
reliability and usefulness of audit reporting 783
skills/personal qualities of audit staff and partners 782
leadership 781
measurement 49
monitoring 782
people 781–2
promoting 781–5
working practices 782
'Audit Quality' (2002) 781, 783
Audit Quality Forum 763, 783, 786–7, 788
Audit Quality Framework (2008) 784
Audit Registration Committee (ARC) 127
audit regulation *see* regulation and control
audit report 37–8, 610
addressee 611
auditors' responsibilities statement 614–15
corporate governance issues 638–46
disclaimer of responsibility 637–8
electronic publication 646–7
identification of statements 613–14
letter of engagement 193
modified audit opinion 626–8
adverse opinion arising from disagreement 635–6
disagreement 633–4
disclaimer of opinion 630–1
'except for' opinion arising from disagreement 635
'except for' opinion arising from limitation of scope 631–3
limitation of scope 628–30
opinion 619–20
post-balance sheet events review 624
quality 783, 785–8
scope of financial statements 618–19
standards 56
unmodified opinion 611
compliance with CA 2006 and accounting standards 621–2
emphasis of matter paragraphs and other matter paragraphs 622–5
example 611–15
statement of directors' responsibilities 615–20
truth and fairness of accounts 620
audit reporting 610-638 and 785–788
audit risk 42, 51
business risk distinguished from 51
components 157, 172
definition 43, 155
minimizing 156–69
standards 56
see also business risk; control risk; detection risk; inherent risk; risk
audit sampling *see* sampling; statistical sampling
audit scope 177
Audit Scotland 599, 600, 697
audit society 795
audit and control 799–808
nature 796–8
Power's analysis 795–809
rise 798–9
audit software 364–6
expert systems 372–3
generalized 366–9
specific industries 366–9
statistical analysis 369–72
trade receivables 479
audit team 80
audit trail *see* information/audit trail
auditing concepts 30–2, 33, 36
see also communication; credibility; performance; process
Auditing into the Twenty-First Century 763, 792, 793–5
Auditing Practices Board (APB) 23, 38, 47, 55, 56, 77, 79, 80, 85, 115, 117, 121, 610, 669–70, 692, 701, 749
appointments 779–80
auditing standards 124–5
background 121–2
criticisms 779–80
discussion paper on non-audit services 775–6
establishment 764, 781
ethical standards 125
objectives 122–4
papers on audit reports 785–6, 787–8
practice notes/bulletins 125
setting up 765–7
Auditing Practices Committee (APC) 121, 122, 764, 765, 779
auditing scandals 672–673
auditing standards 51, 56
APB and 111, 124–5
compliance with 749
as means of defence 749
setting 764
auditing systems 804–6
auditor
access 132
accountability 63
appointment, removal and resignation 11, 37, 49, 131, 133–4, 139–41, 143–5
assertions 219
competence 692
conflict and power 70–7
duty 132
expansion of duties 703–4
fear of losing clientele/reputation 76–7
flexibility of duties 704–5
independence 692
liability 11, 76
objectives 42
preliminary meetings/enquiries 160–5
reform suggestions 777–8
relationships 130–3
responsibility 123, 192
role 670
tenure 73–4
auditor independence 61, 128, 771–776
Auditor General for Scotland 599
auditor liability
auditing standards 749
professional conduct 750
reducing 750–1
capping liability 753–5
incorporation 755
joint and several liability 752–3
limited liability partnerships 755–6
third party case law 733–49
Auditor Oversight Commission (Germany) 111
Auditor Reporting 783

Auditors' Code 41
Nine Fundamental Principles of Independent Auditing 23–5, 34
Auditor's Report: A Time for Change (2007) 787–8
Australia 2, 109

Baker Tilly 120
balance sheet date work 425
bank confirmations 425–6
bridging work between conclusion of interim work and 427–8
circularization of customers and suppliers 426
inventory count observation 426
letters to other professionals 426
long-term construction contracts 426
non-current assets in course of construction 426
work in progress 503
Bank reports for audit purposes in the United Kingdom (2006) 425–6
banking sector 31, 54, 98, 122, 128, 175, 220–1, 267, 287, 377, 425, 548, 610, 637, 763, 780
Bannerman judgement 637
BCCI 663, 672
BDO Stoy Hayward 120
Big Four 792
Big Four firms 68, 74, 119–20, 178, 179, 184, 228, 637, 649, 754, 756, 758, 765–6, 769, 789–90
block testing 346
boundary controls 288
cryptographic controls 288
digital signatures 288
initiation of information/audit trail 290–1
passwords and firewalls 288–90
Personal Identification Numbers (PINs) 288
plastic cards 288
see also application controls; input controls
bridging work 427–8
budgets
testing reliability of management-prepared budgets 346–7
time and feet 201
business risk 35, 42, 51, 305, 773
appraisal 48
approach to audit 178–81
audit evidence 228–9
audit risk distinguished from 51
components 157
definition 155–6
e-commerce 300
income smoothing 180–1
inherent risk compared 181–4
reduction in 163
smaller clients and smaller audit firms 184–5
see also audit risk; control risk; detection risk; inherent risk; risk

CAAT *see* computer assisted audit techniques
Cadbury Report on Corporate Governance (1992) 638, 643, 706, 713
Cambridge Credit 2
Canadian Institute of Chartered Accountants 568
case law
Candler 733–4
Caparo Industries 76, 637, 702–3, 704, 737–40
developments since *Caparo* 741–9
duty of care 733–49
financial statements 735, 741
foreseeability 736–7, 740–1
fraud 667, 670–1
Hedley Byrne 734
JEB Fasteners 735–6
proximity 740–1
reliance 733–4
third party knowledge 735
Twomax Limited 736–7
catering industry 187
CCAB *see* Consultative Committee of Accountancy Bodies
CGAA *see* 'Co-ordinating Group on Audit and Accounting Issues'
Chamber of Public Auditors (Germany) 111
checklists 200, 373, 384
electronic data processing (EDP) or IT checklists 322–5
choice in the UK audit market 788
civil liability 732–3
auditor negligence 733
duty of care 733
client classification 157
'Co-ordinating Group on Audit and Accounting Issues' (CGAA) 117, 127–8, 780, 781
auditor independence 128
competition 130
corporate governance 128–9
role of audit committee 128–9
standards and their enforcement 129
transparency of audit firms 129
clarity project of IAASB xix
Coase theorem 704
Code of Best Practice 128
Code of Ethics for Professional Accountants *see* IFAC Code
Cohen Committee (USA) 73
collusion 265, 274, 417, 657, 662, 668, 671, 698, 699
Combined Code on Corporate Governance (2008) 55, 118, 638–46, 695, 706, 718–19, 781
accountability and audit 710–11
APB discussion paper 776
audit committee terms of reference 645
audit committees 713–16
auditor independence 645–6
directors 706–9
directors' remuneration 709–10
institutional shareholders 712–13
internal control 642–4
listing rules and 639–41, 646
non-executive directors 707–8, 709
public interest entities and 791
relations with shareholders 710, 711–12
responsibilities of directors 642, 666–7
review documentation 645
verify compliance 644–5
comfort letters 575
commercial pressures 52, 53, 56
Committee of Sponsoring Organizations of the Treadway Commission (COSO) 255, 568
communication 25, 40
concepts 46–7
control environment 247
exchange of 253
external auditors 591
governance 85–6, 378
Companies Acts (1989, 2004, 2006) 55, 112–13, 118, 122, 127, 129, 145, 232, 233, 409, 418, 621, 629, 665, 695, 710, 732, 751, 752–5, 763, 770, 787, 793
Companies (Disclosure of Auditor Remuneration and Liability Limitations Agreements) Regulations (2008) 776
company law regulation 112–13
Company Law Steering Group 751, 752, 753, 754
competence 24, 41
at entity level 158
audit expectations gap 693, 695–6
control environment 247
IFAC Code 78
Competence Requirements for Audit Professionals for the Training of Auditors 783
competition 73
CGAA Report 130
compilation engagement 232–3
compliance auditing 585
compliance testing 353, 514, 519, 661
compliance, threats to *see* threats to compliance
computer assisted audit techniques (CAATs) 348–9, 370, 371–2, 479
computer systems
abuse/misuse 252
access controls
firewalls 288, 290
passwords 288, 289
telephone numbers 289–90
application controls 286–7, 295–6
audit management with the computer 383–4
auditing with the computer 349
auditing round the computer 347–8
auditing through the computer 348–9
auditing within the computer 351
boundary controls 288
cryptographic controls 288
digital signatures 288
firewalls 288, 290
initiation of information/audit trail 290–1
passwords 288, 289–90
Personal Identification Numbers (PINs) 288
CPU, main memory and operating system 294

data capture/input controls 287–94
data protection 251–2
data/information security 252
flowchart 334
hacking 252
health of employees 251
information/audit trail 264–8
input controls 291
batch controls 292, 293
codes 291
detection of entry errors 292
documentation design 291
limit or reasonableness tests 292
one-for-one checking 292
sequence checking 292
transfer of data 293
validation of data 293–4
large-scale system development 261–4
organization chart 269–71
output controls 296–7
processing controls 294–6
program changes 263
reporting malfunctions 263
risk assessment 251–2
security 274
data 276
risk assessment 275, 276–8
small-scale system development 264
staff training 263
testing 263
tests of control 349
continuous review of data and their processing 351
integrated test facility (ITF) 351–2
program code reviews 350
systems control and review file (SCARF) 352–3
use of program code comparison 351
use of test data 350–1
user agreements 263
viruses 252
concurrent auditing techniques 351
confidence level, detection risk and 172
confidentiality 41
IFAC Code 78
construction contract valuation 509–15
Consultation on Audit Firms providing Non-Audit Services to Listed Companies that they Audit (2009) 775–6
Consultative Committee of Accountancy Bodies (CCAB) 121, 441, 764
contingencies 542
accounting for 542–6
contingent asset 542, 545–6
contingent liability 542
management assertions 545
risk areas 548
contract law 733
control
layers of regulation and 52–56, 243–258
expectations of corporate governance 53–55
regulatory framework 55–56
commercial pressures 56
control activities 254–255
control environment 243–251
entity's risk assessment process 251–252
information system, including related business processes, relevant to financial reporting and communication 252–253
internal control and related components 243
monitoring of controls 254–255
control activities 253–4
authorization 253
general and application controls over information processing 253
performance reviews 253
physical controls 253
segregation of duties 253
control environment 80–3
definition 245–6
elements
assignment of authority/responsibility 250
commitment to competence 247
communication/enforcement of integrity/ethical values 247
governance participation 247–8
human resource policies/practices 250–1
management's philosophy/operating style 249
organizational structure 249–50
tone at the top 80, 163, 246
control risk 43, 220
definition 156, 171
internal 163–5
see also audit risk; business risk; detection risk; inherent risk; risk
controls
tests of 341–353
auditing round, through and with the computer 347–349
examples of 345–347
specific tests of controls in computer systems 349–353
control systems 164–5, 170
correction 243
detection 243
monitoring 254–5, 258
prevention 243
quality assurance link 243
corporate governance 52, 705–6, 724–9
audit report 638–46
auditors' duties 194
CGAA Report 128–9
communication 85–6, 378–82, 553
control environment 247–8
directors
accountability 63
responsibility 132
expectations 52, 53–5
listing rules 638–41, 646
minutes of meetings 547
non-executive directors 247–8
tone at the top 80, 246
see also Combined Code on Corporate Governance (2008)
Corporate Report (1975) 691
COSO *see* Committee of Sponsoring Organizations of the Treadway Commission
cost calculation 504–6
credibility 40–2
criminal liability 731
Companies Act (2006) 732
Fraud Act (2006) 731–2
Theft Act (1968) 731–2
crisis management 305
critiques of auditing 763
audit society 795–809
independence 771–6
regulation of auditing 763–71
responses
audit agenda 792–3
audit quality 781–5
audit regulation 779–81
audit reporting 785–8
auditing in twenty-first century 793–5
choice in UK audit market 788–92
way forward 776–7
auditors as exclusively auditors 777
auditors as socially accountable 777
disclosure of information 779
reform of institutions 777–8
Cross Report (1977) 767
cryptographic controls 288
cut-off 303–4, 496–502, 522

data capture controls 287–94
data collection/storage 286
data flow diagrams 312, 315–16, 331
Data Protection Act (1998) 251–2
data security 252
grandfather, father, son (GFS) system 276
database systems
data controls 291–4, 297–9
administrative 298–9
after-the-event authorization 298
data preparation personnel 297–8
information/audit trail 299
technical 299
definition 297
information/audit trail 294
input controls 291–4
deficient performance gap 50–1
deficient standards gap 50
Deloitte report 48–9, 768
Department for Business, Innovation and Skills 780
Department of Trade and Industry (DTI) 113, 117, 118, 751, 764, 778, 789
depreciation
appropriateness of method 463–4
authorization of charges 453–4
non-current assets 455, 463–4
periodic review 453–4
residual values 464
detection risk 43–4
calculation 172–3
confidence level and 172
definition 156
see also audit risk; business risk; control risk; inherent risk; risk

digital signatures 288
directional testing 373–5
'Director and auditor liability: a consultative document' (2003) 751
directors *see* corporate governance
directors' responsibilities 615–617
disciplining members and firms 767–8
disclaimer of responsibility 637–8
document design 291
document flowchart 310, 315, 336
DTI *see* Department of Trade and Industry
due care, IFAC Code 78
duty of care 733
  case law 733–49

e-commerce
  24/7 trade 304
  business risk 299–300
  communication 299
  crisis management 305
  definition 252
  legal and taxation matters 303
  management strategy 300
  practical problems 303
    browsing 304
    bulk discounts and special offers 304
    cut-off 303–4
    follow-through of transactions 304
    payment other than by monetary transfer 304
    return of goods and claims under warranties 304
  security risks 300–1
    firewalls 301–2
    identification/authentication 302
    information/audit trails 302
    private networks 302
    security policy 301
EDP *see* electronic data processing
effectiveness auditing 585–6
  independence of internal auditor 592
  motivated staff 592
  professional behaviour 593
  support of top management 591
efficiency auditing 585
emphasis of matter paragraphs 622–5
engagement acceptance 571–2
engagement letter
  assurance engagements 571–2
  audit reporting 193
  auditor responsibility 192
  copies 193
  fees 193
  fraud 656
  management responsibility 193
  objectives/scope of audit 192
  other matters 194
  recurring audits 193
  role and contents 192–4
engagement partner 49, 82–3, 158
  position in audit firm 81
  responsibility 189–90
engagement quality control reviewer (EQCR) 85, 86, 555
  position in audit firm 81
engagement risk 158, 696
engagement team 85
  definition 80, 190
  EQCR evaluation 82
  independence 158
  leadership of 82
  litigation and 93
  position in audit firm 81
  rotation/removal of members 83, 84, 91
  selection/formation 165, 166
  threats/safeguards 87, 90–1, 93–5, 98, 99, 103, 104
Enron 2, 55, 101, 113, 116, 248, 255, 695, 709, 773, 774–5, 802
entity risk *see* control risk; inherent risk
environment audit 796, 799–800
EQCR *see* engagement quality control reviewer
Equitable Life Assurance Society 121
Ernst & Young 656, 773, 775
ethical dilemma 41–2
Ethical Standards (ESs) 77, 79, 80, 82–3, 85, 125, 776
  communication 85–6
  safeguards to counter threats 87, 89, 90–2, 93, 99, 100
ethics 41
  codes 76, 77–9, 80, 82–3
  standards 77, 79, 80, 82–3
ethics partner 50, 83–4, 158
  position in audit firm 81
Ethics Standard Board 115–16
European Commission 101–2, 128, 621
European Union (EU) 38, 55, 109, 125, 299, 622, 706, 755
evaluation policies, IFAC Code/APB ethical standards 92–3
evaluation of systems 353–4
  materiality 415–18
evidence 14, 34, 44
  agreed-upon procedures engagement 234
  appropriate 213–14, 216
  assurance engagement 572
  business risk approach 228–9
  certain 45
  collection procedures
    analytical procedures 215
    confirmation 215
    inquiry 214
    inspection 214–15
    observation 215
    recalculation 215
    reperformance 215
  compilation engagement 232–3
  corroborative 224–7
  definition of 'audit evidence' 213
  fraud 663–4
  judgement and 216–20
  limited assurance engagement 233
  management assertions and 39, 218–20
  persuasive 45
  regulatory standards 55–6
  reliability guidelines 220–4
    corroborative evidence 224
    directly by auditor 222
    documentary form 222–3
    independent sources 220–1
    internal controls 221–2
    management 223
    normal course of business 223
    past events better than future possibilities 223–4
  search for 217
  stages of audit process, requirements at 229–31
    timing 229, 232
  sufficient 213–14, 216
  tests of controls 241, 341–353
  upgrading process 224–7
examinations 21, 119, 130, 167, 364
  analytical procedures 433–6
  auditing as examination subject
    application of official material 819
    style of paper 819
    syllabus 819
  confidence in 819
  hints 800, 816
    control over time 816
    form of answer 817
    higher skills 818–19
    length of answer 818
    question selection 816
    relevance 818
    understanding the question 817
except for audit opinion 631–633 and 635
executive committee 547
expert systems 372–3
expertise 48, 49
external audit 584
  audit committee and 713, 716
  communication 591
  reliance on internal audit 594–6
external environment 52, 157
  commercial pressures 52, 53, 56, 244
  expectations of corporate governance 52, 53–5, 244
  planning assignment 195
  regulatory response 52, 53, 55–6, 244
extranet 302

factoring 477, 482
fair fee 48
'Feasibility Investigation of Joint and Several Liability' (1996) 751
Federal Ministry of economics and Technology (Germany) 111
fees
  budget preparation 201
  IFAC Code/APB ethical standards 92
  letter of engagement 193
  lowering 159
  non-audit services 95, 771–2, 776
  pressure on 693
final review, role of 558–9
financial auditing 588–9, 599
  criticisms 795–809
financial reporting
  disclaimers 194
  standards and enforcement 129
Financial Reporting Council (FRC) 117, 118, 692, 695, 701, 704, 713, 714, 767, 781, 782, 783, 784–5, 789, 792
Financial Reporting Review Panel (FRRP) 126

Financial Services Authority (FSA) 692, 706
Financial Services and Markets Act (2000) 675, 763
financial statements
  accurate 446–7
  assertions 442–7
  case law 735–7
  complete 447
  genuine 446
  level of assurance 801
  materiality in 410–12
  minimizing risk 165–6
  reliability 11
  reliance on 734
  scope of audit 618–19
  systems in force and company staff 369
  trade receivables 368
  true and fair 14, 55
firewalls 288, 290, 301–2
flow charts 315
  advantages/disadvantages 316
  computer systems 334
  data 315–16, 331
  document 315, 336
  information/audit trail 315
  program 316
  system 316
'Framework of Independent Regulation for the Accountancy Profession' (1998) 113–14
  independence 114
  proficiency/commitment 114
  public interest/integrity 114
  relevance 114
  review 114
  transparency/openness 114
Fraud: Meeting the Challenge through External Audit (2003) 669
fraud 655
  attitudes/rationalization 659–60
  audit expectations gap 698–9
  auditing scandals 672–3
  case law 670–1
  characteristics of personnel 661–2
  company assets 659
  definition 655
  directors' actions 658
  directors' responsibilities 665–7
  evidence, problems in obtaining 663–4
  importance 655–6
  incentives/pressures 659
  income smoothing 658, 659
  internal control systems 657, 662–3
  law and regulations 674–6
  misappropriation of assets 662
  motives 659
  opportunities 659
  profits 658–9
  recent debates 667–70
  reporting fraud and error 664–5
  responsibility for fraud detection 656–64
  risk assessment 656, 657–8, 660–1
  third parties, reporting to 667
Fraud Act (2006) 731–2
Fraud Advisory Panel 669
Fraud and Audit: Choices for Society (1998) 669
FRC *see* Financial Reporting Council
FRRP *see* Financial Reporting Review Panel

general controls 450
  application controls distinction 260
  definition 260
  organizational controls 268–74
  quality assurance 278–81
  sales system 338–40
  security 274–8
  systems development/maintenance controls 260–8
generalized audit software 366–72
German Institute 110
Germany 110–11
gifts/hospitality, IFAC Code/APB ethical standards 93
going concern 546, 676–7
  analytical procedures 678–9
  appropriate financial information 678–82
  assessing 678–9
  audit expectations gap 699–701
  auditors' responsibilities 677–83
  balance sheets 679
  banking issues 681–2
  business risk 678
  cash flow budgets or forecasts 679
  directors' responsibilities 677–83
  evidence 680–2
  forecast profit and loss accounts 679–80
  foreseeable future 682–3
  indicators of problems 681
  inherent risk 678
  reporting on 683–4
Grant Thornton 120
graphs 436
Greenbury Report 638
Grenside Report (1979) 767
Guidance on Assessing Control – The CoCo Principles' Criteria of Control Board (CoCo) 568

Hampel Report (1998) 124, 638
haphazard sampling 401
Higgs review (2003) 128, 638, 707–8
Horwath Clark Whitehill 120
human resource policies and practices 250–1

IAASB *see* International Auditing and Assurance Standards Board
IASB *see* International Accounting Standards Board
ICAEW *see* Institute of Chartered Accountants in England and Wales
ICAI *see* Institute of Chartered Accountants of Ireland
ICAS *see* Institute of Chartered Accountants of Scotland
ICAS Working Group on Non-Audit Services 596
ICEQ *see* internal control evaluation questionnaire
ICQ *see* internal control questionnaire
IESBA *see* International Ethics Standards Board for Accountants
IFAC Code 42, 77, 125, 765
  audit firm's control environment 80–3
  general principles 78–9
  safeguards to threats
    fees 92
    financial, business, employment, personal relationships 87–90
    gifts/hospitality 93
    length of tenure 90–2
    litigation 93
    non-audit/non-assurance services 95–100
    profession, legislation, regulation 86
    remuneration/evaluation policies 92
    self-interest/intimidation 93–5
    work environment 86–7
IFRS *see* International Financial Reporting Standards
income smoothing 180–1, 447–8
incorporation 755
indemnity insurance 731, 738, 750, 752
independence 11, 24, 31–2, 34, 41
  audit expectations gap 696–7
  audit firm rotation 775
  CGAA Report 128
  conflicts of interest
    auditor/client 70
    auditor's professional duty/self-interest 70
    client organization/third parties 70
  control environment of audit firm to enhance ethical behaviour 81
  criticisms 771–6
  definitions 61, 64–5
  international organizations 101–4
  perceived 70–2
    accounting flexibility 71, 74
    competition 71, 73
    fear of losing clientele/reputation 71, 76
    legal liability 71, 76
    professional sanctions 71, 76
    provision of MAS services 71, 72–3
    size of firm 71, 74, 75
    tenure of auditor 71, 73–4
  power of client organization/auditor 70
  practitioner 65–7
  profession 67–70, 701
  quality 61
  regulation 114
  risk factors 158
  role of academics in influencing ethical standards 71
  role of audit and 30–2
  safeguards to counter threats 86–101
information
  disclosure 779
  hypothesis 9
  overload 253
  processing 253
  retrieval and analysis 383
  system 164, 252–3, 259–60

information gathering
entity's internal control 163–5
nature of entity/environment 161–2
preliminary 159–62
information technology (IT) 252, 253, 262
information/audit trail
access controls 290–1
computer system 264–8
database system control 299
e-commerce 302
flow chart 266, 315
manual systems 264
processing controls 295–6
tests of 345
informed management 96–7
inherent risk 43, 187
at entity level 158
business risk comparison 181–4
definition 156
e-commerce 300
inventories 488–91
reduction in 163, 465–8, 489–91
tangible non-current assets 449–50
trade receivables 465–8
work in progress 488–9
see also audit risk; business risk; control risk; detection risk; risk
input controls 291
batch controls 292, 293
design of product, customer, other codes 291
design of source documentation 291
limit or reasonableness test 292
one-for-one checking 292
organizational controls 293
sequence checking 292
use of check digits 292
verification/validation of data 293–4
see also application controls; boundary controls
Insolvency Act (1986) 763
Institute of Chartered Accountants in England and Wales (ICAEW) 49–50, 116, 126, 128, 666, 756, 764, 765, 768, 780, 781
Institute of Chartered Accountants in Ireland (ICAI) 116, 126, 768
Institute of Chartered Accountants of Scotland (ICAS) 116, 126, 128, 792, 793–5
Institute of Public Auditors (Germany) 111
insurance hypothesis 10
integrated test facility (ITF) 351–2
integrity 24, 41, 169
control environment 247
IFAC CODE 78
inherent risk 158
regulation 114
safeguards to counter threats 86–101
interim work 427–8
internal audit 164, 248, 584–5
compliance auditing 585
definition 584
effectiveness auditing 585–6, 591–4
efficiency auditing 585
evaluation 586–7
internal control and 594
management auditing 586, 589
objectives 590
one-off audits 589–90
operational auditing 586
outsourcing 596–7
participative auditing 589
public sector 599–603
reliance on, by external auditor 594–6
specific work of auditors 595
types 585–6
value for money auditing (VFM) 586
internal control 163–5
definition 245
errors and frauds 657, 662–3
internal audit and 594
limitations 245
risk assessment 163–5
Turnbull guidance 716–18
internal control evaluation questionnaire (ICEQ) 318
internal control questionnaire (ICQ) 317–18
internal environment 52–3, 56, 157, 244
accounting, quality assurance/control systems 53, 244
control environment/related components 53
control procedures 53
planning assignment 196
International Accounting Standards Board (IASB) 38, 56, 123, 441, 622
International Accounting Standards (IASs) 34–5, 454, 457–8
adoption 775
International Auditing and Assurance Standards Board (IAASB) xix, 38, 52, 55, 56, 111, 124, 610, 692, 705, 765–7
International Code of Ethics for Professional Accountants 125
International Ethics Standards Board for Accountants (IESBA) 77
International Federation of Accountants (IFAC) 42, 77, 109, 568
International Financial Reporting Standards (IFRS) 34, 127, 621–2, 771
International Framework for Assurance Engagements 566–70
International Organization of Securities Commissions (IOSCO) 101
International Standard on Quality Control 127
International Standards on Assurance Engagements (ISAEs) 566, 572
International Standards of Auditing (ISA)
accounting estimates (ISA 540) 169
adoption 122, 124
analytical procedures (ISA 315) 160–1, 185
audit documentation (ISA 230) 190, 554–5
audit engagements (ISA 210, ISA 220) 602, 656
audit evidence (ISA 500, ISA 501) 56, 495–6
audit report (ISA 700) 610, 705
audit strategy (ISA 300) 200–1
clarity project xix, 766–7
communication with those charged with governance (ISA 260, ISA 265) 194, 378, 715–16
compliance 127
computer-assisted techniques (ISA 330) 348–9, 370
engagement team (ISA 220) 190
ethics (ISA 200) 42
financial statements (ISA 250) 674–6
fraud (ISA 240) 655, 657, 659–62, 664, 665–6, 667, 670, 698–9
going concern (ISA 570) 677–8, 683, 699–700
instituting standards 765–7
internal control (ISA 315) 245, 248, 252, 253
laws and regulations (ISA 250) 258
limitation of scope (ISA 705) 629–30
management letter (ISA 265) 378
management philosophy (ISA 315) 249
materiality in planning and performing an audit (ISA 320) 409
observation (ISA 500) 495
public sector (ISA 200, ISA 220, ISA 265, ISA 315, ISA 520) 602–3
quality control (ISA 220) 85, 86
reading other information (ISA 720) 47, 793
risk (ISA 200, ISA 315, ISA 330) 42–3, 154–5, 241, 341–2, 496
substantive procedure (ISA 330) 359
test of controls (ISA 330) 359
International Standards of Quality Control (ISQC) 555
Internet business *see* e-commerce
interval sampling 400
intranet 290, 302
inventories 486
analytical procedures 491–4
at balance sheet date 503
branches 503
cut-off 496–502
disposals 490–1, 509
existence, condition and ownership 491
inherent risk 488–91
inventory count observation, purposes and procedures 502–3
nature of 486–8
observation of 495–6
safeguarding 490
substantive approaches 494–5
third parties 503
valuation 491
basis 503
cost calculation 504–6, 509
effect of changes in 509
net realizable value (NRV) 506–9
Investigation and Discipline Board 116
IOSCO *see* International Organization of Securities Commissions
ISA *see* International Standards of Auditing
ISQC *see* International Standards of Quality Control

IT checklists 322–5
ITF *see* integrated test facility
JDS *see* Joint Disciplinary Scheme
JMU *see* Joint Monitoring Unit
Joint Disciplinary Scheme (JDS) 767
Joint Monitoring Unit (JMU) 113, 116, 126, 768–9, 797
  see also monitoring
judgement 24, 44, 45
  evidence and 216–20
  materiality and 45
  risk and 186–8
  technical compliance with auditing standards 188

Key Performance Indicators (KPIs) 49–50, 252, 568
KPI *see* Key Performance Indicators
KPMG 655, 667, 755, 756, 768

Law Commission 751
laws and regulations 303
  fraud 674–6
layers of regulation and control (see control),
legal department 548
legal liability 76
legality audits 599
letter of engagement *see* engagement letter
letters of representation 233
liability *see* auditor liability; third party liability
Likerman report (1989) 751
limited assurance engagement 233, 567
Limited Liability Partnership Act (2000) 756, 779
listed entity 89, 706
litigation, IFAC Code/APB ethical standards 93
London Stock Exchange 638, 706, 708
low-balling 814

McKesson and Robins case (1939) 693, 713
maintenance controls 260–8
management
  operating style 249
  philosophy 249
  responsibility 193
management accounting 487, 547
management advisory services (MAS) 71, 72–3
management assertions 38, 38–9, 44
  contingencies 545
  evidence 39, 218–20
  financial statement assertions 442–7
  inventories 494–5
  minimizing risk 165–6
  misstatements 170
  non-current assets 457, 460–2, 463
  provisions 538
  risk attached to 39
  trade payables and purchases 519–25
management of audit process 189–90
management auditing 586, 589
management of change 252
management interviews 549
management letter
  communication of audit matters 378–82
  public sector 600–1
  of representation 549–54
management philosophy 56, 249
managerial accountability 62
managers 190
Market Participants Group (MPG) 790–1
Markets Participants Group 789
material misstatements 39, 43, 45, 46, 154–7, 158, 160, 165–6, 170, 415–17, 658, 659–62, 664, 775
materiality 408–9, 418–19
  at evaluation stage 415–18
  at planning stage 413–15
  decision making and 409–10
  definition 45–6
  during audit 415
  external influences 412
  in financial statements 410–12
  judgements concerning 45
  link with misstatements 166
  profits and 412
  qualitative issues 418
  standards 56
matter paragraphs 622–5
Maxwell, Robert (Maxwell Group) 2, 53, 695, 767
MG Rover Group Limited 121
mineral oil 486–7
Mitchell, Austin 118
MLRO *see* Money Laundering Reporting Officer
'Modern Company Law For a Competitive Economy' (2001) 751
modified audit reports 626–628
monetary unit sampling (MUS) 405–6
money laundering 675–6
Money Laundering Reporting Officer (MLRO) 675, 676
monitoring 695, 705
  audit 126–7
  controls 254–5, 258
  criticisms 768–71
  see also Joint Monitoring Unit (JMU)
monitoring of audit firms' standards 116
Moore Stephens 671
multiple regression analysis 436
MUS *see* monetary unit sampling

NAO *see* National Audit Office
National Audit Office (NAO) 599
National Health Service (NHS) 19–20, 599, 600
negligence 10, 11, 33, 125, 412, 672, 731
  auditing standards and 615, 749
  auditor and 733
  case law 733–49
  contributory 753
  duty of care 733, 734–49
  financial statements 734, 736–7, 740, 741, 744, 745–9
  foreseeability 736–7, 740–1
  proximity 739, 740–1, 743
  third party 611, 638, 731, 733–49
net realizable value (NRV) 503, 506–9
New Zealand 50, 52, 693, 705
non-assurance services *see* non-audit services
non-audit services
  APB discussion paper 775–6
  corporate finance services 98
  criticisms 771–6
  fees 95, 771–2, 776
  IFAC/APB ethical standards 95, 100
  independence and 95–6, 771–2
  informed management 96–7
  safeguards 99–101
  self-interest 98–9
  self-review 98
  tax services 99
  threats 97–9
non-current assets
  acquisitions 450–1
  additions 454
  analytical procedures 454–5
  balances 460–2
  charges 452–3
  depreciation 455, 463–4
  disposals 452, 454–5, 459–60
  economic life 463–4
  inherent risk 450
  insurance 452–3
  management assertions 457, 460–2, 463
  repairs and maintenance 452–3, 455
  revaluation of freehold property 455
  safeguarding 451–2
  substantive approaches 455–64
  see also tangible non-current assets
Northern Rock 712

objectivity 24
  APB Ethical Standards 79
  definition 61
  IFAC Code 78
  safeguards to counter threats 86–101
  threats 79
OECD *see* Organization for Economic Cooperation and Development
Office for Auditing 696–7, 704
Office of Fair Trading (OFT) 130, 755
on-off audits 589–90
operational auditing 586
organization charts 314–15
Organization for Economic Cooperation and Development (OECD) 101
organizational controls 268–9
  authorization and approval 273
  organization chart 269–71
  segregation of duties 271–2
  supervision controls 273–4
organizational structure 249–50
other matter audit opinion 622–623
output controls 296–7
  testing 345–6
outsourcing of internal audit work 596–7
over-auditing 42, 184
Oxera report (2006) 789–92

Parmalat 3, 673
participative auditing 589

partner-led approach 48
engagement partner 49
quality of staff 49
Partnership Act (1890) 755
password systems 273, 277, 288, 289–90
payroll system 279
abnormalities 297
calculation of wages 333
changing the program 271–2
computer systems flowchart 334
control systems 273, 277, 295, 296
payment of wages 335
wages department 335
PCAOB *see* Public Company Accounting Oversight Board
people development 48
performance 40
performance audits 600
performance concepts 47–8
performance gap
deficient performance gap 50–1
deficient standards gap 50
performance reviews 253
personal accountability 62
Personal Identification Numbers (PINs) 288
PKF 120
planning 46
assignment 194–9
audit planning memorandum 199–201
materiality at planning stage 413–15
minimizing risk 165–6, 171
study of business 195–9
POB *see* Professional Oversight Board
political accountability 62
Polly Peck 2, 31
Porter and the audit expectations gap 50–2, 691, 693, 705
post-balance sheet events 531
audit report 624
audit work to detect 547–9
accounting records 547
company procedures 547
correspondence and memoranda 548
information in public domain 549
legal enquiries 548
management accounts 547
management interviews 549
minutes of meetings 547
profit and cash flow forecasts 548
risk 548
third-party confirmation 548
contingencies 542–6
examples 532–5
going concern 546
post-balance sheet period 531–2
provisions 538–42
significance of periods in which events occur 535–7
postulates 32–3, 34–6
Power's analysis of the audit society 795–809
practice notes 125
practice protection group 48
practitioner independence 65–7, 696–7
investigative 65
programming 65
reporting 65
pre-final work 424–5, 426–7
PricewaterhouseCoopers (PwC) 49, 656, 672, 673, 770
private companies 145
probity audits 600
Proceeds of Crime Act (2002) 675
process concepts 40, 42–6
processing controls
application controls 295–6
casts and cross-casts 296
continuity in processing 295
CPU, main memory and operating system 294
genuine, accurate, complete data files 295
information/audit trail 295–6
limit or reasonableness tests 296
program testing 295
sequence checks 296
system failure 296
profession independence 67–9
professional accountability 62
professional behaviour, IFAC Code 78
professional conduct 750
professional, meaning of term 773
Professional Oversight Board (POB) 48, 49, 117, 119–21, 129, 770–1
professional sanctions 76
program code
comparison 351
review 350
program flowchart 316
Promoting Audit Quality (2006) 782
proportionate liability 752–3
Proposals for an expanded auditors' report (1991) 785
Provision of Non-Audit Services by Audit Firms to their Listed Audit Clients (2010) 96, 776
provisions
expected future events 539–40
management assertions 538
nature 538–42
public accountability 54, 62
Public Company Accounting Oversight Board (PCAOB) 673, 770
Bylaws and Rules 255
public domain information 549
public interest 111
regulation 114
public sector auditing 599
audit committees 601–2
annual accounts and external auditor 601
control environment 601
risk related performance 601
financial audits 599
legality audits 599
management letters 600–1
probity audits 600
references in ISAs 602–3
regularity audits 599
systems examinations 599
value for money (VFM) audits 600
purchases
analytical procedures 518–25
audit programme at year-end 522–5
nature of 515
see also trade payables
purchases and creditors system 335–8

qualified opinion 632, 635
quality assurance 53, 244, 278–81
quality of audit *see* audit quality
quality control 47–8, 244
standards 56
questionnaires 316–17
internal control evaluation questionnaire (ICEQ) 318
internal control questionnaire (ICQ) 317–18
key and subsidiary questions 318–22

Railtrack 54
random sampling 400, 403
ratio analysis 21, 430, 435–6, 480
reasonable assurance engagement 567
reasonableness gap 50
recognized qualifying bodies (RQBs) 112–13, 119, 770–1
recognized supervisory bodies (RSBs) 112–13, 119, 122, 126, 127, 749, 763, 770–1
recording accounting and control systems 313–25
checklists 322–5
narrative description 315
questionnaires 316–22
visual description 315–16
recruitment and remuneration 99–101, 103, 708, 781
recurring audits 193
reducing auditor liability 750–756
Registrar of Companies 692
regression analysis 436
regularity audits 599
regulation of auditing profession 763, 779–81
company law 112–13
disciplining members and firms 767–8
law/accounting profession 130
licensing individuals 109
monitoring of audit firms 768–71
monitoring of standards 116
self-regulation 109–11
setting standards 109, 764
setting up Auditing Practices Board (APB) 765–7
statutory/practical relationships 130–3
regulation and control
appointment, removal, resignation of auditor 133–4, 139–41, 143–5
audit regulation 763, 779–81
commercial pressures 56
control activities 254–255
control environment 243–251
entity's risk assessment process 251–252
expectations of corporate governance 53–55
external environment 52, 53
German 110–11
historical overview 113–16

information system, including related business processes, relevant to financial reporting and communication 252–253
internal control and related components 243
internal environment 52, 53
layers of 52–3, 243–55, 258
monitoring of controls 254-255
present system 116–30
private companies 145–6
regulatory framework 38, 53, 55–6
state delegation 109–10
state interventions 55–6
removal of auditor 11, 37, 49, 131, 133–4, 139–41, 143–5
remuneration, IFAC Code/APB ethical standards 92–4
Remuneration Consultants Group 710
reporting 46
reporting on corporate governance 638–639
reporting standards, audit implications 441–2
resignation of auditor 11, 37, 49, 131, 133–4, 139–41, 143–5
restricted accountability 63
Review Board 115
'Review of the Regulatory Regime of the Accountancy Profession' (RRRAP) (2003) 116–17, 767, 778, 780, 781
rigour 24
professional scepticism 48
risk 42–4
assertion 155
assessing 43, 44
at boundaries/interfaces 287–8
attached to management assertions 39
definition 154–5
identifying 14, 43
judgement and 186–8
material misstatement 154
reasonable 154
regulation and control 110
see also audit risk; business risk; control risk; detection risk; inherent risk
risk assessment
audit management with the computer 383
computers 251–2
fraud 656, 657–8, 660–1
internal control 163–4
process 251
security 275–8
risk management 48
role of audit 15, 19–20
independence and 61–4
rotten auditing gap 50
Royal Bank of Scotland 637
RQB *see* recognized qualifying bodies
RRRAP *see* Review of the Regulatory Regime of the Accountancy Profession
RSB *see* recognized supervisory bodies

safeguards to counter threats *see* threats to compliance
sales and receivables system 330–3, 464–80
sales system
data flow diagram 310
general and application controls 338–40
internal control evaluation questionnaire (ICEQ) 318–22
objectives 306–13
sampling
attribute 402, 405, 407
definition 396–7
designing and selecting the sample 397
evaluation of test results 404–5
judgemental 397–9
materiality and 408–19
monetary unit sampling (MUS) 405–6
selection methodology 400
block or cluster sampling 401
haphazard sampling 401
random sampling 400
systematic or interval sampling 400
size of sample 401
expected error rate 401–2
level of confidence sought by auditor 401
tolerable error rate 402–3
see also statistical sampling
Sarbanes-Oxley Act (2002) 55, 102–4, 129, 704, 774
Sasea Limited 667
Satyam computer Services 3, 673
SCARF *see* systems control and review file
Schockley's conceptual model of perceived independence 70–7
Scottish Environment Protection Agency (SEPA) 568
SEC *see* Securities and Exchange Commission
Securities and Exchange Commission (SEC) 101, 102–4, 129, 596, 713, 755
security 274
data 276
e-commerce risk 300–2
GFS system 277
policy 301
security risk assessment 276–8
energy variations 275
fire damage 275
intrusion by unauthorized personnel 275
pollution 275
water damage 275
segregation of duties 253, 271–2
self-regulation 109–11
seniors 190
SEPA *see* Scottish Environment Protection Agency
Serious and Organized Crime Agency (SOCA) 675
Serious and Organized Crime and Police Act (2006) 675
Shareholder Involvement – Competition and Choice (2005) 788–9
shareholders 36, 54, 56, 131, 547, 625, 691
Combined Code recommendations 711–13
short-stay syndrome 593–4
small entities
advocacy services 101
APB ethical standards 101
business risk approach 184–5
Smith Guidance 638, 713, 714
Smith Report (2003) 128, 638, 668
Smith, Sir Robert 128–9
SOCA *see* Serious and Organized Crime Agency
software *see* audit software
stakeholders 34, 36, 54, 691–2
standards *see* auditing standards; ethical standards
statistical analysis software 369–72
statistical sampling 383, 399–400
block 401
cluster 401
discovery 408
evaluation of test results 404–5
haphazard 401
interval 400
monetary unit sampling (MUS) 405–6
non-statistical sampling compared 407
random 400
size of sample 401–3
systematic 400
variables 408
statutory audit process 584–5
'Statutory Auditors' Independence in the EU: A Set of Fundamental Principles' (2002) 128
Statutory Auditors (Transparency) Instrument (2008) 48
'Stewardship Code for Institutional Investors' (2010) 713
Stone and Rolls Ltd 671
subsequent events 536, 547, 575
definition 532
international standard 532, 543
substantive procedures 341, 342–4
analytical 436–41
audit management with computer 383–4
audit software 364–73
cash and bank audit programme 377
definition 359
directional testing 373–5
management letter 378–82
non-current assets 455–64
planning feedback 360
purchases audit programme 361, 362–4
setting objectives 361–4
trade receivables 471–80
wages audit programme 375–7
substantive tests of detail 159, 166, 172, 184, 228, 241, 341, 342, 359–60, 361–4, 367
supervision controls 273–4
supra-national bodies 111
system flowchart 279, 316
systems control
assertions by management 307–10
audit approaches 305–25
computerized systems 309–13
inherent risk 307–8
objectives 306
recording accounting and control systems 313–25
systems control and review file (SCARF) 352–3, 370

systems development/maintenance controls 260–8
systems evaluation 353–4
systems examinations 599

Taking Fraud Seriously (1996) 666, 668
tangible non-current assets
 depreciation and 448–64
 inherent risks 449–50
 nature of 449
 see also non-current assets
tax law 303
teeming and lading fraud 43
television sets 487
tendering for audit services 158–9
terms of reference 190–2
 see also engagement letter
Terrorism Act (2000) 675
test data 350–1
tests of controls 341–5
 audit/information trail 345
 block testing 346
 computer systems 349–53
 definition 359
 examination of management reviews 346
 interviews with company staff 346
 observing staff at work 346
 outputs 345–6
 re-performance of control procedures 346
 reliability of budgets prepared by management 346–7
tests of detail 359
Theft Act (1968) 731–2
third party liability 611, 638, 731
 case law 733–49
 reducing 750–6
Thomas Gerard & Son Ltd 671
threats to compliance
 advocacy 79
 familiarity 79
 IFAC Code 78–9
 intimidation 79
 management 79
 safeguards against 86–7
  fees 92
  financial, business, employment, personal relationships 87–90
  gifts/hospitality 93
  length of tenure 90–2
  litigation 93
  non-audit/non-assurance services 95–101
  remuneration/evaluation policies 92–3
  self-interest/intimidation 93–5
 self-interest 79
 self-review 79
time budget preparation 201
tone at the top 80, 163, 246
toxic waste 540–1
trade payables
 analytical procedures 518–25
 consistency in application of accounting standards 521–2
 cut-off 522
 disclosure 522
 inherent risk 516–18
 nature of 515
 payment of balances 518, 522
 recorded at year end 517–18, 519, 522–5
 substantive approaches 519–25
 unrecorded liabilities 519–21
trade receivables
 analytical procedures 468–71
 cash discount 475
 creation and clearance of balances 465–6
 credit notes 475
 inherent risks 465–8
 nature of 464–5
 safeguarding procedures 466
  ageing statement 466
  cash discounts 466
  credit limit 468
  rapid billing 466
  reducing stated amount of balances 466
  regular preparation of statements/reminder letters 466
 sales and 464–80
 substantive approaches
  accurate cut-off 474
  audit tests for collectability 478–9
  clearing entries 474–5
  consistency 476
  creation of balances 471, 473
  disclosure and presentation 480
  fairly stated 473
  proof of customer existence 476–7
  relationship between figures 473–4
  value 477–8
 write-offs 475
Transnational Auditors Committee 765
transparency 54
 CGAA Report 129
 regulation 114
transparency reports 48
truth and fairness 12–14, 46–7, 166
 audit report 620
 definition 47
Turnbull guidance 716–17
 board's statement on internal control 718
 maintaining sound system of internal control 717
 reviewing effectiveness of internal control 717–18
Turnbull Report 668
Tyson Task force 708

UK GAAP 127, 621, 622
Ultramares Corp 2
under-auditing 42, 184
Union Bank of Scotland 693
United States 2, 3, 55, 73, 75, 76, 101, 116, 254, 255, 428, 576, 596, 643, 693, 713, 774–5
universities 19
unmodified audit reports 611

value 25
value for money (VFM) audit 19–20, 586, 600
VFM *see* value for money audit
Vodafone 723-729

walk-through tests 341, 344
Walker review (2009) 712–13
water companies 19, 56
whistleblower 248
work in progress
 at balance sheet date 503
 inherent risk affecting 488–9
WorldCom 2, 116, 775

Z-scores 436, 678–9

INDEX OF FIGURES

Figure 2.1 'Communication of accounting information', Ch 2, p. 37
Figure 2.2 'Structure of the audit expectation performance gap', Ch 2, p. 51
Figure 2.3 'Layers of regulation and control', Ch 2, p. 53
Figure 3.1 'The role of audit', Ch 3, p. 64
Figure 3.2 'Shockley's (1982) conceptual model of perceived independence', Ch 3, p. 72
Figure 3.3 'Audit firm's control environment and elements to enhance ethical behaviour in a firm providing audit and other assurance services.', Ch 3, p. 81
Figure 4.1 'Institutional environment of auditors in Germany', Ch 4, p. 111
Figure 4.2 'Regulatory system in force until 2003', Ch 4, p. 114
Figure 4.3 'FRC Ltd Board', Ch 4, p. 117
Figure 4.4 'Period of auditor appointment, and accounting reference period and date', Ch 4, p. 132
Figure 4.5 'Legal and practical relationships between directors, the audit committee, other management, other user groups and the auditor', Ch 4, p. 133
Figure 4.6 'Appointment, removal and resignation of auditor of Rosedale Cosmetics plc', Ch 4, p. 134
Figure 5.1 'Components of audit and business risk', Ch 5, p. 157
Figure 5.2 'Organization chart of County Hotel Limited', Ch 5, p. 198
Figure 6.1 'Audit evidence supporting reasonable conclusions', Ch 6, p. 216
Figure 6.2 'Evidence corroboration and upgrading in a sales system', Ch 6, p. 227
Figure 6.3 'The audit process: audit stages, evidence-gathering process and main audit', Ch 6, p. 230
Figure 6.4 'Oakshow Ltd purchases and related creditors (to be completed)', Ch 6, p. 238
Figure 7.1 'Layers of regulation and controls – as extended (see Figure 2.3).', Ch 7, p. 244
Figure 7.2 'Example of matrix organizational chart', Ch 7, p. 250
Figure 7.3 'Raw data to information', Ch 7, p. 260
Figure 7.4 'Programme for the development of computer applications in a large-scale system', Ch 7, p. 261
Figure 7.5 'Information trail/audit trail flowchart', Ch 7, p. 266
Figure 7.6 'Organization chart of the computer department and its place in a large entity', Ch 7, p. 269
Figure 7.7 'An example of a grandfather, father, son (GFS) system', Ch 7, p. 278
Figure 7.8 'Troston payroll master file update', Ch 7, p. 279
Figure 8.1 'Interface between data preparation and computer room', Ch 8, p. 292
Figure 8.2 'Sales system: simplified overview chart', Ch 8, p. 310
Figure 8.3 'Data flow diagram: customer order system', Ch 8, p. 312
Figure 8.4 'Receipts of cash system', Ch 8, p. 317
Figure 8.5 'EDP ITchecklist of development, organizational and security controls (Burbage Limited).', Ch 8, p. 323
Figure 8.6 'Computer systems flowchart for a payroll system', Ch 8, p. 328
Figure 9.1 'Data flow diagram for Broomfield plc sales and receivables system', Ch 9, p. 331
Figure 9.2 'Computer systems flowchart for production payroll system of Troston plc', Ch 9, p. 334
Figure 9.3 'Document flowchart for the purchases systems of Broomfield plc', Ch 9, p. 336
Figure 9.4 'Sales order processing (Burbage Limited)', Ch 9, p. 339
Figure 9.5 'Walk-through tests, tests of control and substantive procedures: conclusions, decisions and extent of tests and procedures', Ch 9, p. 344
Figure 9.6 'Auditing round and through the computer', Ch 9, p. 348
Figure 10.1 'Powerbase plc purchases audit programme', Ch 10, p. 365
Figure 10.2 'Directional testing example (all figures in thousands)', Ch 10, p. 374
Figure 10.3 'Communication of audit matters to those charged with governance (internal control section) at Broomfield plc', Ch 10, p. 379
Figure 10.4 'Audit programme for substantive tests of production wages (Troston plc)', Ch 10, p. 390
Figure 10.5 'Audit depth test: production wages (Troston plc)', Ch 10, p. 392
Figure 12.1 'Pykestone non-current assets recording system', Ch 12, p. 452
Figure 12.2 'Sterndale plc: analysis of sales and trade receivables', Ch 12, p. 472
Figure 13.1 'Extract from profit and loss account and balance sheet', Ch 13, p. 520
Figure 14.1 'Accounting reference period and post-balance sheet period', Ch 14, p. 533
Figure 14.2 'Audit documentation: relationships and contents', Ch 14, p. 557
Figure 15.1 'Position of the Troston plc internal audit department within the organization', Ch 15, p. 598
Figure 16.1 'Example of an unmodified audit opinion for a publicly traded company', Ch 16, p. 612
Figure 16.2 'Forms of qualification matrix (adapted from figure in paragraph A1, ISA (UK and Ireland) 705.', Ch 16, p. 626
Figure 18.1 'The audit expectations gap: Overview of structure, possible causes and forces for change over time', Ch 18, p. 694

INDEX OF TABLES

Table 1.1 'The auditor's year Gilsland Electronics Limited', Ch 1, p. 16
Table 1.2 'The Auditors' Code', Ch 1, p. 24
Table 2.1 'Audit postulates', Ch 2, p. 34
Table 2.2 'Concepts of auditing', Ch 2, p. 36
Table 3.1 'Three dimensions of practitioner independence and guides or clues as to areas of infringement', Ch 3, p. 66
Table 3.2 'Reasons to question auditor independence', Ch 3, p. 68
Table 3.3 'Size and independence', Ch 3, p. 75
Table 3.4.1 'IFAC potential threats to objectivity', Ch 3, p. 79
Table 3.4.2 'Additional threat to objectivity proposed by APB', Ch 3, p. 79
Table 3.5 'Non-audit services and likely threats', Ch 3, p. 97
Table 3.6 Ch. 3, p. 100
Table 5.1 'Calculation of Detection Risk (DR) and confidence level', Ch 5, p. 172
Table 5.2 'Liquidity and gearing ratios', Ch 5, p. 186
Table 5.3 'County Hotel Accommodation', Ch 5, p. 197
Table 5.4 'John Gunn and Co: County Hotel time budget and fee', Ch 5, p. 208
Table 6.1 'Tyre tread data', Ch 6, p. 217
Table 6.2 'Assertions used by the auditor', Ch 6, p. 219
Table 7.1 'Potential limitations in internal control.', Ch 7, p. 246
Table 8.1 'Assertions in the Activity 8.10 figures', Ch 8, p. 308
Table 8.2 'Key and subsidiary questions in a sales system', Ch 8, p. 318
Table 9.1 'Objectives of walk-through tests, tests of control and substantive procedures', Ch 9, p. 341
Table 11.1 'Broomfield plc: analysis of trade receivables', Ch 11, p. 398
Table 11.2 'Reliability factors (extract)', Ch 11, p. 402
Table 12.1 'Examples of financial statement assertions for selected assets, liabilities and related profit and loss account entries.', Ch 12, p. 442
Table 15.1 'Differences between reasonable assurance engagements and limited assurance engagements', Ch 15, p. 573
Table 15.2 'Levels of assurance', Ch 15, p. 574
Table 16.1 'Requirements of the listing rules', Ch 16, p. 640
Table 20.1 'Audit and non-audit fee earnings from FTSE 100 audit clients', Ch 20, p. 772
Table 20.2 'Non-audit fees paid by selected FTSE 100 companies in 2002 and 2009', Ch 20, p. 772
Table 20.3 'Number of companies audited by firm, August 2007', Ch 20, p. 789